Management for Professionals

The Springer series "Management for Professionals" comprises high-level business and management books for executives, MBA students, and practice-oriented business researchers. The topics cover all themes relevant to businesses and the business ecosystem. The authors are experienced business professionals and renowned professors who combine scientific backgrounds, best practices, and entrepreneurial vision to provide powerful insights into achieving business excellence.

The Series is SCOPUS-indexed.

Ben Vinod

The Era of Airline Revenue Management with Offers and Orders

Content Chaos, AI Agents, Customer Centric Transformation, and the Quest for Profitability

Springer

Ben Vinod
Grapevine, TX, USA

ISSN 2192-8096 ISSN 2192-810X (electronic)
Management for Professionals
ISBN 978-3-032-24196-2 ISBN 978-3-032-24197-9 (eBook)
https://doi.org/10.1007/978-3-032-24197-9

This Springer imprint is published by the registered company Springer Nature Switzerland AG
The registered company address is: Gewerbestrasse 11, 6330 Cham, Switzerland

"Great things in business are never done by one person. They are done by a team of people."

—Steve Jobs

This book is dedicated to Robert L. Crandall, former Chairman and CEO of American Airlines (1985–1998) and Thomas M. Cook, who founded and served as President of American Airlines Decision Technologies and its successor organizations (1987–1999).

"Great things in business are never done by one person. They are done by a team of people."

—Steve Jobs

To my parents, who encouraged me.
To my wife, Ann, who has endured my passion with the travel industry for over three decades.

Foreword

Chaos, AI Agents, Transformation: Oh, my!

Dorothy & friends were concerned about lions, tigers, and bears in the classic movie *The Wizard of Oz*. But this book is not about a fictional wizard who fixes things; it is about real issues facing everyone in the air transportation eco-system, right here and right now.

When Ben first approached me about his new book, I said "Another one??!! Your books on airline and hotel revenue management and distribution were great. Maybe you should take a vacation."

But Ben was having none of that. And in *The Era of Airline Revenue Management with Offers and Orders: Content Chaos, AI Agents, Customer Centric Transformation, and the Quest for Profitability*, he has produced something really good, proving me wrong. It is sort of a capstone of his long career in pricing and revenue management, and a clear, straight-shooting look at the future. It is over 700 pages (I reviewed them all as Ben was writing the book), and I promise there are nuggets in every chapter for anyone interested in the travel industry. All of the topics discussed in this book are coming together in airline marketing, and this book pulls together all these topics into a cohesive whole. You can read many blog posts on each of the topics in the book, but each post focuses on one aspect of the future of revenue management. This book discusses all aspects, meaning its length is a bonus. You get the background, history, current status, algorithm discussion, and future, all in one detailed package. Special bonus: A great list of references and vocabulary are included.

You learn about airline data and changes coming because of NDC (New Distribution Capability). You learn a LOT about NDC from all points of view. Segmentation, efficient experiments to learn consumer behavior, reasoning models, what is the time frame for transition to NDC and how this transition will look over time for different airlines, recent history on what different airlines are trying, dynamic continuous pricing... it is all here.

And the book covers all the challenges faced by all the players. Each technology is a puzzle piece:

- Corporate travel agencies: what is their future with agentic AI?
- How do payments, digital wallets, and cryptocurrencies fit in?
- What's the future of code shares and interlines?
- How does competitive revenue management affect revenue management's future? (monitoring competitor fares; no more traditional myopic revenue management)
- What do airlines need to become effective retailers, with so many more ancillaries and more to sell?
- How will AI-driven personalization play in?
- How will other aspects of airline marketing change (strategy, network planning, flight scheduling)
- Where are airline websites and travel apps headed?

And let's not forget hot-button topics such as blockchain and quantum computing. You even get to learn a bit about the history of AI from a revenue management analyst's perspective and current "hot" algorithms and technology. And the history of anti-trust and current issues in this area (such as Senate Bill 232 on algorithmic collusion).

The book is like a curated buffet, where all the items on offer (get it? the book covers all the topics related to offer management) fit together and affect each other. And it is a very large buffet. So, dig in! It's a fascinating and intricate ride.

Bedford, Texas Ross Darrow

Foreword

Understanding the Grand Master of Revenue Management

Ben Vinod is one of the most influential thinkers in modern revenue management (RM), especially in airlines, hospitality and travel. His work spans airline revenue management, hotel pricing, attributebased room retailing, AIdriven RM, and the evolution of reservations systems and product distribution. His research is widely cited in both academic and industry circles, and he remains a key voice in shaping the future of Revenue Management.

I have known Ben since his days at Sabre Technologies and as a member of the editorial board of the Journal of Revenue and Pricing Management. So, when Ben asked me to write this foreword, I could only think that this book must be a 'must read' as he is a person, or more the Grand Master of RM, if RM was game of chess. He treats RM as a living, evolving system shaped by people, technology, and imagination.

Apart from Ben being the Grand Master of RM, let us say something about the book. The airline industry stands once again at a defining crossroads. Across decades, it has evolved through deregulation, the rise of yield management, the unbundling revolution, the emergence of lowcost carriers, and the reshaping of global distribution systems. Yet no prior shift matches the breadth, depth, and systemic impact of the transition now underway: the move toward airlinecontrolled offers and orders, enabled by New Distribution Capability (NDC), continuous pricing, AIdriven personalization, and a reimagining of the airline as a true retailer. This book, *The Era of Airline Revenue Management with Offers and Orders*, captures that transformation with unmatched clarity and ambition.

What makes this volume so remarkable is its scope. It provides an end-toend treatment of nearly every discipline that touches airline commercial strategy: consumer psychology, pricing, revenue management, data infrastructure, distribution, loyalty economics, corporate travel, payments, AI, and regulatory change. Each chapter reflects decades of lived experience whether it was the early days of Sabre and yield management, to the disruptive influence of lowcost carriers, to the fragmentation of content and the messy reality of NDC implementations. Few authors can write like Ben Vinod with authority across all these domains; fewer still can connect them to a coherent narrative about what airline retailing must become.

The book traces how ancillaries, dynamic pricing, and branded fares laid the groundwork for modern offer management, and how the future will be increasingly shaped by AI Agents capable of reasoning, learning, and autonomously optimizing the customer journey. In parallel, it reveals how legacy systems, regulatory pressures, consumer protection rules, and postpandemic volatility complicate this transition.

This book is therefore both a comprehensive reference and a strategic provocation. It urges industry leaders to rethink fundamentals and embrace the possibilities of an AIenabled, retaildriven future. For practitioners, scholars, and innovators alike, it will serve as a touchstone for years to come.

So, if you are a novice or a Grand Master and you want to know about how to improve your knowledge, practice and understanding of pricing and revenue management, then this is the book for you.

Leeuwarden, The Netherlands Ian Yeoman

Preface

This is the fourth and final book in the series on marketing planning in the travel industry. The first book focused on the evolution of yield management in the airline industry leading to the latest advances in this space. The second book was focused on revenue management in the hotel industry from its humble origins to the latest advances in attribute-based room pricing and inventory control. The third book covered the sweeping changes in the travel product distribution landscape from its origins and the impact on travel intermediaries such as Global Distribution Systems, Travel Management Companies and Online Travel Agencies. This fourth book is devoted to the new era of airline revenue management with offers and orders, where airlines aspire to become retailers, against the backdrop of rapid changes in technology and the distribution landscape.

The title of the book: *The Era of Airline Revenue Management with Offers and Orders*. Why is it an *Era*? Synonyms of the word *Era* include age, epoch, and period. While all these words mean "a division of time," *Era* suggests a period of time marked by a new or distinct order. In the airline industry, it signifies a period of time beginning with some special date or event and that is 2012 when IATA initiated the New Distribution Capability (NDC) program. This was followed in 2014 when the U.S. Department of Transportation (DOT) approved the enabling standard for NDC and in 2015, IATA officially released the first version of the NDC messaging standard. As part of the NDC program at the World Passenger Symposium in 2015, IATA introduced ONE Order as a single customer order record holding all data elements required for order fulfillment. This is a seismic change for the airline industry and justifies the use of *Era* in the title.

To understand where we are today, the book begins with an explanation of the endowment effect, with the story of the singular olive that vanished off the dinner plates on American Airlines flights in 1987 on Bob Crandall's order. This was when the first unbundling of the airline product really began for full-service carriers. I was a Senior Analyst in Domestic and International Pricing at American Airlines when this event took place.

This book provides an end-to-end view of pricing and revenue management from its humble beginnings to where it is today. While vast in scope, the book provides a comprehensive treatment of advances in revenue management over the past five decades and the impact of emerging technologies. This book also covers airline pricing, in more detail than my previous books. Storefronts, where airline products are sold, are integral components and three chapters are dedicated to product distribution. To provide a contrast to airline distribution, hotel distribution is presented in a separate chapter.

We live in an AI-enabled landscape. Recent advances in conversational AI, large language models, and AI Agents that can perform tasks and achieve goals on behalf of a user, with a degree of autonomy in reasoning and learning capabilities will forever change the landscape for product distribution in the travel industry. LLM-powered AI Agents are emerging as a new channel in airline distribution, transforming manual, search engine-based or app-driven shopping to autonomous AI-Agent-driven end-to-end-booking transactions. Intelligent agents acting on behalf of travelers will discover, compare and book flights, fundamentally changing how consumers interact with travel suppliers. Revenue management will also undergo a major transformation with AI Agents that can process various types of information, reason, make decisions, and learn, often working in collaboration with other AI Agents to complete complex workflows.

There are several dimensions to airline pricing and revenue management that evolved since the Airline Deregulation Act (ADA) was passed in 1978 under the administration of President Jimmy Carter. The goal of this book is to ensure that the content is comprehensive and addresses all the major elements of pricing and revenue management. There are several aspects of pricing, revenue management, and product distribution that are not covered in books and journal articles. It is a gap I want to address in this book.

There is an abundance of content in the literature on mathematical models for revenue management from academics and practitioners and many are referenced in this book. These papers and books do not address the changes in the pricing and revenue management landscape and transformation of the travel ecosystem with advances in connectivity, Artificial Intelligence and AI Agents. This is a practice book on pricing and revenue management for management professionals and academia, with a focus on the future, in an easy-to-read style that provides an end-to-end view of the airline pricing, revenue management, and product distribution space.

In this book each chapter begins with a quote to put the topic in perspective. After reading a chapter, please review the quote to synthesize and draw your own conclusions on the subject matter that is presented in the chapter.

When I was writing this book, some of my colleagues in the travel industry urged me to add "Intelligent Airline Retailing" to the title or sub-title. While my colleagues have deep travel expertise, I wrestled with the suggestion for several days before deciding not to do so. Intelligent airline retailing is the future, but innovation to date in offer creation has been minimal at best and the primary focus of network airlines had been to withhold fares from the GDSs and make them only available through the NDC messaging protocol. An omni-channel strategy to distribute the same content across all channels of distribution is nowhere close to reality. Sadly, promoting bundled offers seems like an afterthought, haphazard, without a constructive execution and fulfillment strategy. For this reason, I have also refrained from using superlative words such as *modern retailing* and *smart retailing* which are promoted by key organizations in the airline industry. However, I am confident that this will change in the future once NDC has been uniformly adopted.

Special thanks to Ross Darrow for writing a foreword for this book. I met Ross in 1986, a year after I joined American Airlines and we have been collaborating on a range of topics in the realm of advanced statistical modeling ever since. He served as Director of *Sabre Research* during my tenure at Sabre.

Special thanks to Ian Yeoman, Professor of Disruption, Innovation and New Phenomena at NHL Stenden University of Applied Sciences, Netherlands, for writing a thoughtful foreword. A champion of tourism futures, he is the editor of the *Journal of Revenue and Pricing Management,* co-editor of the*Journal of Tourism Futures* and book series editor of the*Future of Tourism.* I have known Ian for over two decades and he motivated me to make contributions to the Journal in the early 2000s, which led to my passion to write books on pricing, revenue management and distribution over the past few years.

This book is dedicated to two individuals who have had a tremendous impact on my formative years, directly or indirectly, my role in the travel industry, and the passion they invoked in employees at American Airlines and Sabre that resonates to this day.

Robert L. Crandall, served as President of American Airlines (1980–1985) and served as Chairman and CEO of American Airlines (1985–1998). With his bold vision and incredible attention to detail, Crandall introduced the mileage-based frequent flyer program and yield management to the airline industry. His legendary handwritten margin notes on the meeting agenda after the Monday staff meetings with his direct reports kept employees at all levels of the organization on their toes as they prepared their responses. My first meeting with Bob Crandall was at a scheduled monthly luncheon for new employees in the summer of 1985.

Thomas M. Cook founded American Airlines Decision Technologies (AADT) in 1987 and served as President of AADT and its successor organizations (1987–1999). AADT was the innovation powerhouse where leading-edge decision support systems in Airline Planning and Airline Operations were created that shaped the airline industry. I first met Tom Cook in April 1984 at the ORSA/TIMS Spring Conference in Boston when he was actively recruiting for the American Airlines OR Group that he headed.

A special thanks to Phil Beck, Ross Darrow, and Ann Vinod who patiently reviewed multiple iterations, offered their suggestions and constructive feedback as I wrote this book.

Grapevine, TX, USA
December 2025

Ben Vinod

Competing Interests The author has no competing interests to declare that are relevant to the content of this manuscript.

Contents

1 An Introduction to Airline Retailing 1
1.1 Origins 2
1.2 What Is this Book About? 4
1.3 The Transition from Merchandising to Retailing 6
1.4 What Is Airline Retailing? 7
1.5 What Is "Modern Airline Retailing"? 8
1.6 Origins of Airline Retailing 9
1.7 Origins of Airline Revenue Management 10
1.7.1 The Case for Dynamic Pricing 12
1.8 The Transition of Revenue Management to Offer Management 15
1.8.1 How Revenue Management Is Evolving in a Post Pandemic World 17
1.8.2 The Transformation of Product Distribution with NDC and AI Agents 18
1.9 The Confluence of Revenue Management and Customer Relationship Management 19
1.10 The Endowment Effect 21
1.11 Data Infrastructure and Environment 21
1.11.1 Data Sources for Airline Retailing 22
1.11.2 Batch and Streaming ETL 26
1.12 The Significance of Customer Experience 27
1.13 A New Era in Airline Marketing Planning 27
1.13.1 All Customers are not Created Equal 28
1.13.2 Customer Segmentation 28
1.13.3 Customer Centric Marketing and Sales Operations 33
1.13.4 Customer Centric Availability and Customer Centric Pricing 33
1.13.5 Customer Centric Organization 34
1.14 Consumer Protection Measures from the Department of Transportation 34

1.14.1 The Refund Rule ... 35
1.14.2 Ancillary Fee Rule ... 35
1.14.3 Impact on Travel Agencies ... 36
1.14.4 The Downside for Customers with the New DOT Rules ... 37
1.14.5 Proposed Passenger Compensation Rule ... 37
1.15 The Montreal Convention ... 38
1.16 Navigating the Future of Low-Cost Carriers ... 38
1.16.1 LCCs versus FSCs ... 40
1.16.2 Changes in the Airline Distribution Landscape ... 41
1.16.3 Are the LCCs Under Threat From the FSCs? ... 41
1.17 The Value Proposition of Airline Retailing ... 44
1.18 Innovation for Competitive Advantage ... 44

2 Categories of Core Ancillary Revenue Streams ... 47
2.1 Overview ... 47
2.2 What Are Ancillary Products and Services? ... 48
2.2.1 The Top Performers for Ancillary Revenue Streams ... 49
2.3 Ancillary Categories ... 51
2.4 Flight Ancillary Products and Services ... 52
2.4.1 Baggage ... 52
2.4.2 Seats ... 52
2.4.3 Booking/Point of Sale ... 57
2.4.4 Payments ... 57
2.4.5 Booking Changes ... 58
2.4.6 Priority Products ... 60
2.4.7 Minors ... 60
2.4.8 Airport Products ... 60
2.4.9 Onboard/In-Flight ... 61
2.4.10 FinTech Products ... 62
2.5 Travel and Non-Travel Supplier Partnerships ... 65
2.5.1 Credit Card Travel Insurance ... 65
2.5.2 Standalone Trip Insurance ... 66
2.5.3 Credit Card Travel Protection Versus Standalone Third-Party Travel Protection ... 66
2.5.4 Vacation Packages ... 66
2.6 Loyalty Financial Products ... 67
2.6.1 Are Loyalty Programs Fintech Programs? ... 68
2.6.2 Cobranded Credit Cards ... 69
2.6.3 Sale of Miles to Partners ... 69
2.6.4 Paid Memberships ... 69

3 The Endowment Effect, Customer Angst, and Supplier Trust 73
3.1 What Is the Endowment Effect? ... 74
3.1.1 The Endowment Effect ... 74
3.1.2 The Airline Context ... 77
3.2 Airline Retailing and Customer Angst ... 78
3.2.1 Change of Gauge ... 79
3.2.2 Change of Aircraft ... 80
3.2.3 Delayed Flight ... 80
3.2.4 Lost Baggage ... 80
3.2.5 Refunds ... 80
3.2.6 Meals ... 81
3.2.7 Aircraft Seats ... 81
3.2.8 Cabin Cleanliness ... 81
3.2.9 Customer Service ... 81
3.2.10 Latent Charges ... 82
3.2.11 Complexity of Fare Rules ... 82
3.2.12 Flight Oversales ... 82
3.3 Greed Is Good? U.S. Lawmakers Grapple with Hidden Fees ... 83
3.4 Spanish Government Penalties ... 84
3.5 EU Regulation 261 ... 84
3.6 The Windowless Window Seat Class Action Lawsuits ... 85
3.7 "Junk Fees" in Lodging and the FTC ... 85
3.8 The Significance of Supplier Trust in Airline Retailing ... 87
3.8.1 Impact of New Retailing Models on Litigation ... 87

4 The Value Proposition of Revenue Management ... 89
4.1 Revenue Management Definitions ... 90
4.2 Core Airline Metrics ... 90
4.2.1 Traffic Measures ... 91
4.2.2 Demand Measures ... 91
4.2.3 Capacity Measures ... 91
4.2.4 Additional Performance Measures ... 92
4.2.5 Operational and Customer Measures ... 92
4.2.6 The Airline Profit Equation ... 93
4.2.7 Employees Productivity Measures and Airline Efficiency ... 93
4.2.8 Network Carrier Economics ... 94
4.3 Origins ... 95
4.3.1 Overbooking ... 96
4.3.2 Littlewood's Rule ... 98
4.4 Optimal and Heuristic Approaches to Revenue Management Discount Controls ... 99
4.4.1 The First Yield Management System ... 100
4.5 Role of Revenue Management in a Customer's Itinerary ... 103

4.5.1 Schedule Change Processing ... 104
4.5.2 Demand Forecasting ... 105
4.5.3 Overbooking ... 107
4.5.4 Flight Optimization and Network Optimization ... 112
4.5.5 Critical Situation Identification and Alerts ... 113
4.5.6 Performance Reporting and Feedback ... 113
4.5.7 Revenue Management and Itinerary Pricing ... 116
4.5.8 Group Revenue Management ... 118
4.6 Host CRS Inventory Controls ... 118
4.6.1 Traffic Freedoms and Inventory Controls ... 119
4.6.2 Leg/Segment Inventory Controls ... 120
4.6.3 Segment Close Indicators and Segment Limits ... 122
4.6.4 Shared Cabin Nested Inventory Controls ... 123
4.6.5 Origin and Destination (O&D) Inventory Controls ... 125
4.6.6 Benefits ... 132
4.6.7 Academic and Practitioner Focus ... 133
4.7 Revenue Management with Independent Demand ... 133
4.7.1 Market Differential Pricing ... 134
4.7.2 Modeling Uncertainty of Demand ... 135
4.7.3 Flight Leg/Segment Optimization ... 136
4.7.4 Examples of $EMSR_A$ and $EMSR_B$ ... 140
4.7.5 Expected Marginal Seat Revenue Model Assumptions ... 143
4.7.6 Static and Dynamic Models for Leg/Segment Optimization ... 143
4.7.7 Optimal Solutions for Leg/Segment Models ... 145
4.7.8 Network Optimization for O&D Control ... 145
4.8 Dynamic Reaccommodation (Replanement) of Low-Valued Passengers ... 155
4.9 Revenue Management with Dependent Demand ... 156
4.9.1 Impact on Revenue Management ... 159
4.9.2 Inventory Control with Restriction Free Fares ... 162
4.9.3 Coexistence of Inventory Controls for Network Carriers ... 162
4.10 Impact of LCC Pricing on Revenue Management ... 164
4.10.1 Multi-Class and Multi-Class Multi-Flight Models ... 165
4.10.2 Impact on Revenue Management Models—Demand Forecasting ... 166
4.10.3 Impact on Revenue Management Models—Optimization ... 168

4.10.4 The Revenue Opportunity Model for Dependent Demand ... 171
4.11 Connectivity Standards for the Indirect Channel ... 172
4.12 End-Product of Traditional Revenue Management ... 173

5 The Transition from Revenue Management to Offer Management ... 175
5.1 Introduction ... 176
5.2 The Problem with à la carte Pricing of Ancillaries ... 176
5.3 The Transition from Revenue Management of the Base Fare to Offer Management ... 178
5.4 How Revenue Management Is Evolving in a Post Pandemic World ... 180
5.4.1 Recommendation Engine for Offers ... 181
5.4.2 Offer Recommendation Based on Experimentation ... 181
5.4.3 Airline Retailing Beyond Air Bundles ... 182
5.5 Origins and Future of Fare Filings and Booking Classes in a Post-hybrid World ... 182
5.5.1 Fare Filing ... 183
5.5.2 Booking Classes ... 184
5.6 The Adjusted Fare Approach to Offer Management ... 185
5.7 Approaches to Offer Management and Emerging Technologies ... 186
5.7.1 Machine Learning ... 186
5.7.2 Natural Language Processing ... 188
5.7.3 Generative AI ... 188
5.7.4 AI Agents ... 188
5.8 Scope of AI in Travel ... 189
5.8.1 The Role of Test and Learn Experimentation with Offer Management ... 190
5.8.2 Segment-Then-Price (StP) is the Industry Standard ... 192
5.8.3 Micro-Segmentation ... 193
5.8.4 Revenue Management and Gen AI ... 193
5.8.5 Reinforcement Learning Versus Gen AI for Offer Creation ... 194
5.9 Intelligent Automation ... 195
5.10 Role of AI in Capturing Consumer Intent ... 196
5.11 Generative AI and Trip Planning ... 197
5.12 The AI-Powered Revenue Management Environment ... 197

6 Airline Controlled Offer and Order Management ... 199
6.1 Introduction ... 200
6.2 Demand for Air Travel and Price Elasticity ... 201
6.2.1 Price Elasticity Definition ... 202

6.2.2 Estimation of Price Elasticity 203
6.2.3 Luxury Product Pricing 204
6.3 Cross Price Elasticity 205
6.4 Price Elasticity and Airline Retailing 207
6.5 Inferring Consumer Preferences with Stated Preferences and Revealed Preferences 208
6.5.1 Stated Preferences 208
6.5.2 Revealed Preferences 210
6.6 Market Basket Analysis 211
6.7 Market Basket Analysis for Airline Retailing 213
6.8 The Significance of Pricing It Right 213
6.9 Context for Travel Based Customer Segmentation 216
6.9.1 Micro-Segmentation 219
6.9.2 Why Is Context for Travel Based Segmentation Important? 220
6.9.3 Trip-Purpose Segmentation and "P2" 220
6.10 The Significance of the Bundled Offer 221
6.11 Offer Creation and Recommendation Engines 223
6.11.1 Branded Fares and Offers 225
6.12 Decoy Pricing to Improve Conversion Rates 225
6.12.1 Finalizing the Offer 226
6.13 Role of Dynamic Pricing in Offer Creation 228
6.13.1 First, Second, and Third Order Effects and Dynamic Pricing 228
6.13.2 Dynamic Pricing Solution Approach 229
6.14 A Brief Introduction to Reinforcement Learning 230
6.15 Multi Armed Bandit Model for Continuous Experimentation of Offers 231
6.15.1 Greedy (Naive) Sampling 233
6.15.2 Epsilon Greedy Sampling 233
6.15.3 Upper Confidence Bound Sampling 233
6.15.4 Thompson Sampling 234
6.16 Contextual Bandits 237
6.16.1 Contextual Bandits in Offer Management 237
6.17 Knowledge Graphs and Reasoning Models for Offer Creation 238
6.17.1 A Simplified Example of a Travel Graph 239
6.17.2 Knowledge Graph Generators 240
6.17.3 Knowledge Graphs and Data Privacy 241
6.17.4 Large Language Models and Knowledge Graphs 241
6.18 Corporate Travel Versus Leisure Travel 242
6.19 Personalization of Offers 243
6.19.1 Personalization of Offers When Number in Party is Greater Than One 244
6.20 The Complexity of Designing the Agency Storefront 245

6.20.1 Types of Data ... 246
6.20.2 The Storefront ... 248
6.20.3 ATPCO Next Generation Storefront with Shelves and Drawers ... 249
6.20.4 Product Normalization in the Storefront ... 252
6.20.5 The New Airline Storefront (NAS) Controversy ... 253
6.21 The Airline Retailing Catalog ... 254
6.21.1 Product Catalog and Reservations Inventory Control ... 255
6.21.2 The ATPCO Product Catalog Initiative ... 255
6.21.3 Product Catalog, Offers and Orders ... 257
6.22 Why Airline Shopping Is an Integral Component of Offer Management ... 257
6.22.1 A Common Definition for Air Shopping and Offer Creation ... 258
6.22.2 Data Analytics for Segmented Shopping ... 261
6.22.3 Agentic AI, Air Shopping Look-To-Book, and the Cost of Compute ... 262
6.23 The Passenger Name Record ... 263
6.23.1 The Path Forward ... 265
6.24 Order Management ... 265
6.24.1 Legacy Processing Environment ... 266
6.24.2 The One Order Environment ... 266
6.24.3 Requirements for Success of ONE Order ... 267
6.24.4 SSRs, EMDs, and ONE Order ... 268
6.24.5 Native Orders ... 269
6.25 Is ONE Order a Comprehensive Vision ... 270
6.25.1 Order Management Did not Originate in the Airline Industry ... 270
6.25.2 Airline Retailing and Order Management ... 271
6.25.3 Why ONE Order? or Should It Be a SUPER Order? ... 274
6.25.4 Impacts on Revenue Integrity ... 275
6.26 Will the Transition to Offer and Order Happen by 2030? ... 276
6.27 Airline Affordability of ONE Order ... 277
6.27.1 New Airlines with no PNRs ... 279
6.28 Delivery Management ... 280
6.28.1 Should Existing Departure Control Systems Be Sunset? ... 280
6.28.2 Delivery Management: Beyond the Hype, What is It All About? ... 282

7 Offers beyond Airline Products and Services 283
7.1 Overview 284
7.2 The Richard Ferris Allegis Experiment 284
7.3 Other Airline Investment in Hotels 285
7.3.1 Michelin as the Role Model for Airline Retailing 286
7.4 Complementary Products 287
7.5 Upsell and Cross-Sell 287
7.6 Dynamic Packaging beyond Air 288
7.6.1 Can Airlines Compete with the OTAs for Packages 289
7.7 Virtual Interlining 290
7.8 The So-Called Connected Trip 291
7.9 Protecting the Airline Brand Outweighs the Challenge of Third-Party Fulfillment 292

8 Airline Pricing: Fare Products, Ancillaries, and Amenities 293
8.1 Overview 294
8.2 Airline Fare Management Process 295
8.2.1 Airline Fare Matching and Nash Equilibrium 297
8.2.2 Fare Management Is Labor Intensive 298
8.2.3 Anti-Trust Allegations 299
8.2.4 The Absence of Price Leadership 299
8.3 The Mechanics of Airline Fares 300
8.3.1 Booking Class, Fare Category and Fare Basis Code 300
8.3.2 Fare Classes and Booking Classes 302
8.4 Classification of Fare Products 303
8.4.1 Public Fares 303
8.4.2 Private Fares 303
8.4.3 Web Fares 306
8.4.4 Opaque Fares 306
8.4.5 What Is an NDC Fare? 307
8.5 Impact of NDC on Airfares 307
8.5.1 RBDs and Fixed Price Points 308
8.6 Airline Pricing and the IATA Conundrum 308
8.7 Pricing Terminology 309
8.7.1 General Air Pricing Terminology 309
8.7.2 Journeys 315
8.8 Fare Rule Categories 320
8.9 Routings 325
8.10 The Fare Records 326
8.11 Itinerary Pricing 327
8.11.1 Priceable Units (PU) 328
8.11.2 Fare Components 328

8.11.3 Tariff Component ... 329
8.11.4 The Inherent Complexity of Itinerary Pricing ... 329
8.12 IATA Traffic Conference Areas ... 330
8.12.1 Constructed Fares ... 333
8.13 Ancillary Products ... 333
8.13.1 YQ/YR ... 334
8.13.2 OB Fees ... 334
8.13.3 OC Fees ... 335
8.13.4 Branded Fares (Record S-8) ... 336
8.14 Airline Amenities ... 338
8.14.1 Universal Product Attributes (UPA) ... 338
8.14.2 Universal Ticket Attributes (UTA) ... 338
8.14.3 Routehappy Visuals ... 338
8.15 Mini Rules ... 339
8.16 Attribute-Based Shopping ... 339
8.17 The Department of Transportation Final Ruling on Ancillary Fees ... 340
8.18 Origins of Air Ancillaries, Pricing, and Agency Access ... 340
8.18.1 Traditional Approaches to Ancillary Pricing Require Sales Data at Multiple Price Points ... 341
8.18.2 Dynamic Pricing of Ancillaries with Reinforcement Learning ... 342
8.19 The Psychology of Pricing ... 343
8.19.1 Pricing Ambiguity ... 344
8.20 The Solo Traveler Penalty in U.S. Domestic Markets ... 345
8.20.1 How Is Solo Pricing Deployed ... 345
8.21 Monitoring and Measuring Pricing Effectiveness ... 346
8.21.1 Booking Class Realignment ... 346
8.21.2 Monitoring Fare Basis Code Usage by Customer Segment ... 346
8.21.3 Fare Competitiveness with YQ/YR ... 347
8.22 The Delta Air Lines AI-Based Pricing Model ... 349
8.23 Moving Beyond Filed Fares ... 350

9 Changes in the Distribution Landscape with New Distribution Capability (NDC) ... 351
9.1 GDS in Transition ... 352
9.2 Full Content and MFN Clauses in GDS Airline Contracts ... 354
9.3 Origins of NDC ... 355
9.4 Is It Indeed "Modern: Airline Retailing?" ... 356
9.5 Origins of XML Messaging and the New Distribution Ecosystem ... 358
9.5.1 Why Was XML Chosen for NDC? ... 359

9.5.2 The First NDC Bookings ... 359
9.6 Standard GDS Transaction Processing (1976–2016) ... 360
9.7 The Hybrid State with NDC ... 363
9.8 The End State with NDC ... 366
9.9 ONE Order ... 368
9.9.1 What ONE Order Means to the Airline Industry ... 368
9.10 NDC Is a Catch-22 Situation ... 370
9.10.1 Total Cost of Ownership to Control Offer and Order ... 370
9.11 The State of the Union with NDC Adoption ... 370
9.11.1 NDC Capabilities ... 373
9.11.2 Why Scaling NDC Is a Challenge ... 374
9.12 GDS Investment in NDC and NDC Aggregators ... 378
9.12.1 Continued Investment in the Hybrid State ... 379
9.13 Future of Codeshare ... 379
9.13.1 Origins of Codeshare Flights ... 380
9.13.2 Types of Codeshare ... 380
9.13.3 Benefits of Codeshare Partnerships for Airlines ... 381
9.13.4 Synchronized Flight Schedules ... 381
9.13.5 Codeshare Flight Availability Before NDC ... 381
9.13.6 Codeshare Flight Availability with NDC ... 382
9.13.7 Financial Settlement Process ... 383
9.13.8 Customer Angst with Codeshare Flights ... 384
9.14 Traditional Interline ... 384
9.14.1 Revenue Sharing Agreements ... 385
9.14.2 The Standard Retailer and Supplier Interline Agreement ... 386
9.14.3 Interline Shopping ... 387
9.15 Codeshare and Interline with Offer and Order ... 387
9.16 The Landscape for GDS Surcharges ... 387
9.16.1 The Lufthansa Group ... 388
9.16.2 Air Canada ... 389
9.16.3 Air France—KLM ... 390
9.16.4 Avianca ... 390
9.16.5 Copa Airlines ... 390
9.16.6 Emirates ... 390
9.16.7 Finnair ... 390
9.16.8 Hawaiian Airlines ... 391
9.16.9 International Airline Group (British Airways, Iberia) ... 391
9.16.10 LATAM ... 392
9.16.11 Oman Air ... 392
9.16.12 Qantas Airways ... 393
9.16.13 Scandinavian Airlines System (SAS) ... 393
9.16.14 Singapore Airlines ... 394

9.16.15 Taiwanese Carriers ... 394
9.16.16 Turkish Airlines ... 394
9.17 Do GDS Surcharges Benefit the Airline? ... 395
9.18 NDC Adoption, Default EDIFACT Bookings and Deduping ... 395
9.19 Reducing Distribution Costs with NDC ... 396

10 Mayhem Redefined: The Hybrid State and Evolving Business Landscape with NDC ... 397
10.1 Overview ... 398
10.2 The Business Landscape Is Evolving with NDC ... 398
10.2.1 New Commercial Models Lead to Content Chaos and Fragmented Confusion ... 399
10.2.2 The Future of the So-Called Private Channel ... 400
10.2.3 Low-Cost and Ultra Low-Cost Carriers and GDS Participation ... 402
10.2.4 TMCs Propose Processing Fee for NDC Bookings ... 404
10.2.5 Fine Tuning Air Shopping Parameters for OTAs ... 405
10.2.6 Alterations to the ARC Agency Sales Agreement ... 408
10.2.7 Content Curation Layer and Product Normalization ... 409
10.2.8 Smaller Travel Agencies Will Struggle to Be Competitive ... 409
10.2.9 Direct Competition from Airlines in the Indirect Channel ... 409
10.2.10 Financial Strain and Operational Impacts on Travel Agents ... 410
10.2.11 The Threat to the GDS as NDC Content Aggregators ... 411
10.2.12 Corporate Travel and NDC ... 412
10.2.13 The Hybrid State Will Continue for Several Years ... 412
10.2.14 Airlines that Breach Full Content Agreements ... 413
10.2.15 GDS Service Fees for NDC Content ... 416
10.3 Is the FDR Era Anti-Price Bias Law Applicable to Airlines and GDSs in the NDC Era? ... 416
10.3.1 Background: FTC V. Southern Glazer ... 417
10.3.2 Is the Robinson-Patman Act Applicable toward Content Bias ... 418
10.4 Market Competition: Are Regulators out of Touch with the Travel Marketplace? ... 419
10.4.1 Amex Global Business Travel—CWT Merger ... 419
10.4.2 Spirit Airlines and the Department of Justice ... 422

10.4.3 Sabre—Farelogix and CMA 423
10.4.4 Allegiant and Sun Country 424
10.5 The 2024 Business Travel News Survey 424
10.6 Successfully Negotiating B2B Contracts 425
10.6.1 GDS-Airline and GDS-OTA Contracts 426
10.6.2 GDS-TMC Relationship and the Future of Incentives 428
10.7 Addressing NDC Deficiencies Supports Adoption 428
10.8 Impact of Content Fragmentation in the Digital Era 430
10.8.1 What Does Content Fragmentation Mean for the Airline Industry? 431
10.9 AI Agents and the Evolving Air Distribution Landscape 431
10.9.1 Digital IDs 432

11 Hotel Distribution 433
11.1 Introduction 434
11.2 Hotel Distribution Channels 435
11.2.1 The Direct Channel 436
11.2.2 Global Distribution Systems 436
11.2.3 Bed Banks 436
11.2.4 Online Travel Agencies (OTAs) 438
11.2.5 Metasearch 438
11.3 The OTA Merchant Model and the Agency Model 439
11.4 B2B Products and Online Travel Agencies 442
11.4.1 The OTA Affiliate Programs 442
11.5 Should Hotels Invest in Branded Keywords? 443
11.5.1 The Direct Online Channel Costs 444
11.5.2 Call Center—Direct Offline Channel Costs 444
11.5.3 Global Distribution Systems Channel Costs 444
11.5.4 Bed Banks Channel Costs 445
11.5.5 Online Travel Agencies Channel Costs 445
11.5.6 Metasearch Channel Costs 446
11.6 David versus Goliath and Countering the OTA Threat 446
11.6.1 Marketing Spend 446
11.6.2 Reinvent Loyalty Programs to Accelerate Direct Bookings 448
11.6.3 Large Hotel Chains Must Support Unique Capabilities in the Direct Channel 449
11.7 The Contrarian View on the Role of OTAs 452
11.8 The So-Called OTA Billboard Effect 453
11.9 Hotel Strategy for OTA Participation 454
11.10 Steps to Preserve Hotel Margins 454

11.10.1 Impact of Gen AI Search on Conversions 455
11.11 A Discrete Channel for Excess Inventory: Travel Agent Rebates 456
11.12 Regaining Control of Distribution with Attribute-based Room Pricing 457
11.13 AI Platforms, ARI Content and OTA Bypass 458
11.13.1 Current Approaches to Push ARI Content to Intermediaries 458
11.13.2 ARI Content for AI Platforms and Disintermediation of OTAs 459
11.14 AI Agents will Transform the Hospitality Distribution Landscape 459
11.14.1 Lowering Distribution Costs Require Agile Adoption of MCP 460
11.14.2 ChatGPT and Hotel Bookings 460
11.14.3 Canvas and AI Mode 461
11.14.4 Google's Agentic AI Initiative with Hotels and OTAs 461
11.14.5 Google's Universal Commerce Protocol 462
11.14.6 The Road Forward 462

12 Classless Revenue Management 463
12.1 What Is the Hype All About and Does It Really Matter? 464
12.2 The Hybrid State Is the New Reality 465
12.2.1 The Long Tail of Airlines and Travel Agencies 465
12.3 The Significance of RBDs in the Hybrid State 466
12.3.1 The False Excitement of Classless Revenue Management 467
12.3.2 Host CRS Inventory Controls and RBDs 468
12.3.3 Direct Connect Availability (DCA) and Direct Connect Sell (DCS) in the Hybrid Era 469
12.3.4 RBDs and Demand Forecast Accuracy 470
12.3.5 Impact on Itinerary Pricing 471
12.3.6 Dual RBDs 472
12.3.7 Dual RBDs to Control Availability of Basic Economy 473
12.3.8 Seat Selection 475
12.3.9 Corporate Discounts 475
12.3.10 Codeshare Agreements 475
12.3.11 RBD Mapping for Alliances and Interline 476
12.3.12 Frequent Flyer Accrual 476
12.3.13 Frequent Flyer Accrual of Loyalty Points 476
12.4 Dynamic Continuous Pricing 477
12.4.1 The Bid Price Hurdle 479
12.4.2 Fare Rules and Restrictions 480

12.4.3 Customer Willingness to Pay 480
12.4.4 Generating the Continuous Price Quote 481
12.4.5 Price Discrimination and Personalized Pricing 482
12.4.6 The Importance of Experimentation 485
12.4.7 On the Optimality of Market-by-Market Dynamic Pricing Solutions 489
12.4.8 The Appeal of Continuous Pricing in an NDC World 491
12.5 NDC Benefits for Pricing, Revenue Management and Inventory Control 491
12.5.1 Proactive Pricing 491
12.5.2 Eliminate Revenue Leakage on Codeshare Flights Caused by Inconsistent Availability 492
12.5.3 Continuous Pricing Is a Competitive Differentiator 492
12.5.4 Out of Sequence Bookings and Revenue Equalization 492
12.5.5 Addressing Gaps in Branded Fare Families 493
12.5.6 Round Trip Availability and Inventory Control 495
12.5.7 Eliminating Ticketing Time Limit Churn 496

13 Corporate Travel 497
13.1 Corporate Travel Overview 498
13.2 The Time to Shakeup Corporate Travel is NOW 499
13.2.1 Risk Aversion and Corporate Bureaucracy 499
13.2.2 Focus on Existing Partnerships 499
13.2.3 Internal Hurdles 499
13.2.4 Lag in Technology Adoption 500
13.2.5 Change is Coming for Corporations and Their TMC Partners 500
13.3 Corporate Travel Policies 500
13.3.1 Booking Tools 501
13.3.2 Travel Management Tools 501
13.3.3 Travel Partnerships 502
13.3.4 Travel Support 502
13.3.5 Risk Management 502
13.3.6 Ancillary Content in Corporate Contracts 502
13.3.7 Travel Data Analytics and Reporting 502
13.4 Stakeholders in the Corporate Travel Space 503
13.4.1 Corporate Travel Manager and Corporate Buyer 503
13.4.2 Selecting a TMC 503
13.4.3 Travel Policy 503
13.5 Negotiating Contracts with Airlines 505
13.5.1 Corporate Discounts (Hard Dollars) 505

13.5.2 Soft Dollars ... 506
13.6 Negotiating Discounts for Hotels and Car Rentals ... 507
13.7 The Future of Online Booking Tools ... 507
13.7.1 Impact on Travel Management Companies ... 510
13.7.2 Impact on Corporate Buyers and Travel Managers ... 510
13.7.3 Impact on the Corporate Traveler ... 510
13.7.4 Google, SAP Concur and American Express GBT Collaboration ... 511
13.8 Corporate Travel Manager Challenges ... 511
13.8.1 Sustainability Initiatives ... 511
13.9 Estimating the Corporate Discounts Based on Value ... 512
13.10 Corporate Travel and AI ... 512
13.10.1 Online Booking Tools Transition to Central Hubs ... 513
13.10.2 Personalized Itinerary Creation ... 513
13.10.3 Duty of Care ... 513
13.10.4 Partnerships and Contracts ... 513
13.10.5 Responsible AI is a Cornerstone for Successful Adoption ... 514
13.11 Accepting Automation for Competitive Advantage ... 514
13.12 Corporate Travel and NDC ... 515
13.12.1 Benefits for the Corporate Traveler ... 515
13.13 Penalizing Solo Travelers: A New Twist in the U.S. Domestic Market with American's "P2" ... 516
13.13.1 The LCC and ULCC Impact on Customer Segmentation and Corporate Travel ... 517
13.13.2 Corporate Travel Market Share Erosion ... 517
13.14 Future of Corporate Travel Agencies in the Age of AI ... 518

14 Payments ... 521
14.1 Introduction ... 522
14.2 B2B Payment Processing ... 522
14.3 B2C Payment Processing ... 523
14.4 ISO 8583 in Payment Processing ... 523
14.5 Innovations in B2B and B2C Payment Processing Technology ... 524
14.6 IATA Financial Gateway ... 525
14.7 Global eCommerce Payment Methods ... 525
14.7.1 Digital Wallets ... 525
14.7.2 Credit Cards ... 527
14.7.3 Pay by Bank (Account-to-Account) ... 527
14.7.4 Cash on Delivery (CoD) ... 528
14.7.5 Buy Now Pay Later ... 528

14.7.6 Cryptocurrencies ... 528
14.8 Corporate Credit Card Surcharges ... 529
14.9 Payment Processing and NDC ... 529
14.9.1 ARC Direct Connect ... 530
14.10 Payment Flexibility with ONE Order ... 530
14.11 The Future of ARC and BSP with NDC Adoption ... 531
14.12 Will Payments Receive the Attention It Deserves? ... 532
14.13 Will the Payments Industry Be Deregulated? ... 532

15 Predictive Modeling and Algorithmic Collusion ... 533
15.1 Origins of Competitive Revenue Management in Travel ... 534
15.2 What Is Algorithmic Collusion? ... 536
15.3 Collusion, Anti-Competitive Behavior and Algorithmic Collusion ... 537
15.3.1 The Sherman Antitrust Act ... 537
15.3.2 Article 101 TFEU ... 538
15.3.3 The Competition and Markets Authority in the United Kingdom ... 538
15.3.4 Digital Markets and Algorithmic Collusion ... 539
15.4 Class Action Lawsuits in the Casino Industry ... 539
15.4.1 The DOJ and FTC ... 540
15.4.2 Legal Outcome ... 540
15.5 Apartment Rentals and Algorithmic Collusion ... 542
15.5.1 RealPage Testimonial and Outcome ... 543
15.5.2 Collusion and Algorithmic Collusion ... 544
15.5.3 Real Estate Property Management Systems and Competitive Revenue Management ... 544
15.5.4 Duffy v. Yardi Systems Inc Case ... 545
15.5.5 The Mach v. Yardi Systems Inc. Case ... 545
15.5.6 The Casino Hotels Verdict and the Influence on the RealPage Decision ... 546
15.5.7 What Constitutes Algorithmic Collusion? ... 547
15.5.8 Did the DOJ Have a Case Against RealPage? ... 547
15.6 A Comparison of Predatory Pricing and Algorithmic Collusion ... 548
15.7 U.S. Senate Introduces a New Bill in 2025 ... 548
15.7.1 What Is the Future of S.232? ... 549
15.8 The RealPage Litigation Settlement ... 551
15.8.1 RealPage Proposed Consent Judgement ... 551
15.9 Is Continuous Pricing Algorithmic Collusion? ... 551
15.10 Competitive Revenue Management and IATA NDC ... 552

16 Building Blocks for Successful Airline Retailing ... 553
16.1 Introduction ... 554
16.2 The Digital Airline: The Third Wave ... 554
16.2.1 What Is a Digital Airline ... 555

16.2.2 What Is a Digital Native Airline? 558
16.3 The Core Building Blocks of Airline Retailing 559
16.3.1 Supplier Customer Profile and Universal Profile 559
16.3.2 Universal Data Exchange 559
16.3.3 Customer Journey 561
16.3.4 Host CRS Inventory Controls 561
16.3.5 Offer Creation 561
16.3.6 Channel Management 562
16.3.7 Destination and Non-Air Package Bundles 562
16.3.8 Air Shopping with Corporate and Leisure Features 562
16.3.9 Order Management 562
16.3.10 Payments and Order Fulfillment 563
16.4 The Importance of Partnerships 563
16.4.1 Beyond Technology, Brand Perception and Brand Equity for Growth 564
16.5 Organization 566
16.5.1 The High-Level Organization 566
16.5.2 The Pricing and Revenue Management Organization 569
16.6 Monetizing Airline Data 572
16.6.1 Aggregate Data to Third Parties 572
16.6.2 Insights to Airline Partners 572
16.6.3 Co-Branded Credit Cards 573
16.6.4 Accelerating Loyalty Miles Redemptions 573
16.7 Creating the Zero-Latency Organization for Decision Making with Offers and Orders 574
16.7.1 Embrace Continuous Demand Management 574
16.7.2 Event Management 575
16.7.3 Organizational Readiness and AI Adoption 576
16.7.4 Invest in Advanced AI Systems 576
16.7.5 Data Analytics and Insights 576

17 Artificial Intelligence: Origins, Current State, and Impact on Travel 577
17.1 Introduction 578
17.2 Milestones in Artificial Intelligence 578
17.3 Origins of Artificial Intelligence 581
17.3.1 Computing Machinery and Intelligence 582
17.3.2 Early AI Pioneers 582
17.3.3 Support Vector Machines 584
17.3.4 The First Chatbot 585
17.3.5 Classification and Regression Trees 585
17.3.6 Expert Systems 586
17.3.7 Backpropagation 586

17.3.8 IBM's Statistical Approach to Language Translation Was Revolutionary 587
17.3.9 Natural Language Processing and Machine Translation 588
17.3.10 Q-Learning 589
17.3.11 Chess and AI 590
17.3.12 Gradient Boosting Machines 590
17.3.13 Random Forests 592
17.3.14 The DARPA Challenge 593
17.3.15 IBM's Watson Wins Jeopardy 593
17.3.16 Generative Adversarial Networks 593
17.3.17 DeepMind's AlphaGo 594
17.3.18 The Transformer Architecture 594
17.3.19 OpenAI's Generative Pre-Trained Transformer 595
17.3.20 OpenAI's ChatGPT 595
17.3.21 Google's Gemini 596
17.3.22 GPT-4 and GPT-4o 596
17.3.23 Model Context Protocol 597
17.3.24 ChatGPT—Operator 597
17.3.25 Agent-2-Agent Protocol 597
17.3.26 Google's AI Mode 598
17.3.27 GPT—5 and 5.1 598
17.3.28 Agentic AI Foundation 599
17.3.29 The Universal Commerce Protocol 599
17.3.30 The Competitive Landscape 600
17.4 The Wilderness Years and the Future 600
17.5 AI Search and the Future of Search Engine Optimization 601
17.5.1 AI Influence on Search 601
17.5.2 Traditional Search Engines and Changing Consumer Behavior 605
17.5.3 Future of Hotel SEO 606
17.6 AI, OR and the Future of Problem Solving in the Airlines Industry 606
17.6.1 The Future of AI Is the Marketplace 609
17.6.2 Countering the Bullwhip Effect in the Airline Industry 610
17.6.3 AI as a Discipline 610
17.6.4 Challenge of Interpretability 611
17.7 AI Driven Personalization 613
17.7.1 Chatbots 614
17.7.2 Relevancy of Content Based on Context 614
17.7.3 Airline AI Agent 614
17.7.4 Precision Ad Targeting 614

17.7.5 Predictive Personalization Based on Consumer Intent 614
17.8 AI Assistants Versus AI Agents 615
17.9 What Is Agentic AI? 615
17.9.1 Mathematical Reasoning 616
17.9.2 Reasoning Skills is the Biggest Challenge with Agentic AI 617
17.10 Agentic AI Validation 617
17.10.1 Airline AI Agent 619
17.10.2 Hotel AI Agent 619
17.10.3 TMC AI Agent 620
17.10.4 OTA AI Agent 620
17.11 Agentic AI Framework to Book Travel 620
17.11.1 The Agent2Agent Protocol and Model Context Protocol 622
17.11.2 The Agentic Web for Travel 623
17.11.3 The Agentic AI Model to Book Travel 624
17.11.4 Skepticism with AI Agents 626
17.11.5 AI Agents and the Path Forward 627
17.12 The AI Distribution Channel for Discovering, Planning, and Booking Destinations 627
17.12.1 Discovery 628
17.12.2 Authentication and Authorization of AI Agents 628
17.12.3 AI Agents and the Airline Environment for Direct Distribution 629
17.13 Potential Impact of AI Agents on the Travel Value Chain 629
17.13.1 Future Impact of AI Agents on the Travel Value Chain 633
17.14 Current State Versus Future State in Evolution of Agentic AI 638
17.14.1 Simple Reflex Agents 640
17.14.2 Model-Based Reflex Agents 640
17.14.3 Goal-Based Agents 640
17.14.4 Utility-Based Agents 641
17.14.5 Learning Agents 642
17.14.6 Fully Autonomous Agentic Systems 642
17.15 Agentic AI Frameworks for Automating Travel Agency Workflows 643
17.15.1 GDSs and Agentic APIs 644
17.16 AI Agents and the Impact on Air Shopping 646
17.17 Will Agentic AI and AI Assistants Make Supplier Websites and Mobile Apps Obsolete? 648
17.18 Amazon V. Perplexity Lawsuit and the Future of Autonomous Agents 648
17.18.1 Impact on Travel 649

17.18.2 Legal Action and Investment Irony 652

18 Future State and Gaining a Competitive Edge 653
18.1 Overview 654
18.2 Airline Marketing Planning Process Will Evolve in an AI-Enabled Landscape 655
18.2.1 Flight Scheduling 655
18.2.2 Fare Management 658
18.2.3 Revenue Management: Past, Present and Future 659
18.2.4 Sales and Distribution 661
18.3 Horizontal Enablers for the Marketing Planning Process 664
18.3.1 Fleet Planning 664
18.3.2 Loyalty Programs 665
18.3.3 Alliances and Partnerships 666
18.4 End of Revenge Travel and Importance of Repeat Customers 666
18.5 The Future of User Experience Belongs to AI Assistants 667
18.6 True Door-to-Door Experience Will Become Reality 668
18.7 Beyond Apps, Seamless Access to Offers Regardless of Channel 669
18.7.1 Travel Apps, if You Must 669
18.7.2 Frequent Flyer Redemption Shopping 672
18.8 Airline Websites Must Evolve to Be Business Centric and Leisure Centric 672
18.8.1 Natural Language Search 674
18.8.2 Theme-Based and Budget-Based Shopping 674
18.8.3 Seat-Led Shopping 675
18.9 AI-Based Reasoning Models for the Future of Airline Retailing 675
18.10 Agentic AI and Impact on Travel 679
18.11 Future of Competitive Revenue Management 681
18.11.1 Summary of Competitive Revenue Management for Airlines and Hotels 682
18.11.2 Class Action Lawsuits and Their Outcome 682
18.11.3 The Path Forward 683
18.12 Future Outlook on Personalization 684
18.12.1 Personalization and NDC 685
18.12.2 Context for Travel-Based Segmentation for Offer Management 685
18.12.3 Core Components of Frictionless Travel 686
18.12.4 Future of Hyper-Personalization 687
18.13 Quantum Computing is the Future 688
18.13.1 Google's Milestone in Quantum Computing 689
18.13.2 Quantum Computing in Aerospace 689
18.14 Buyer Expectations from the TMC of the Future 692

18.14.1 Reevaluation of the Technology Stack 693
18.14.2 The Emerging Travel Landscape with AI 693
18.14.3 Sunset GDS Dependency 693
18.14.4 Flexible Service Model for Travel Buyers 693
18.14.5 Source-Agnostic Booking Platforms for the Mid-Market TMCs 694
18.15 The Future of Blockchain in Travel for Offer Management ... 694
18.15.1 Self-Sovereign Identity 696
18.15.2 Transparency and Trust 696
18.15.3 Efficiency, Automation and Enhancing Customer Experience 697
18.15.4 Adoption Challenges 697
18.16 Urban Air Mobility 698
18.16.1 Revenue Management for On-Demand Local Air Transport 698
18.17 The Road Forward: Strategic Agility for Competitive Advantage 699
18.17.1 Customer Centric Transformation 700
18.17.2 Travel Suppliers Must Accept that Multi-Channel Travel Buyers Dominate the Landscape 700
18.17.3 A Razor Focus on Fulfillment 700
18.17.4 True Omnichannel Distribution 701
18.17.5 Data-Driven Decision Making 701
18.17.6 Technology Refresh and Adoption 701
18.17.7 Business Environment and Adaptability 702
18.17.8 Culture of Innovation and Continuous Learning 702
18.17.9 Concluding Remarks on Strategic Agility 702

Appendix A: Airline Acronyms 705

Appendix B: Passenger Type Codes 719

Appendix C: Glossary 727

References 749

Index 775

About the Author

Ben Vinod is a consultant in the travel industry and advisory networks. He served as Senior Vice President and Chief Scientist at Sabre (2008–2020), Vice President of Airlines Solutions (2004–2007) and Vice President of Pricing, Yield Management, and Reservations Inventory Control at American Airlines Decision Technologies (1993–1999), focused on innovation and thought leadership to pioneer advanced solutions across the value chain for travel suppliers and intermediaries. At Sabre he initiated the Sabre Innovation Hub and created the Artificial Intelligence Special Interest Group and AI Newsletter to accelerate adoption of AI and Machine Learning methods. He has published over 60 articles in academic and trade journals, is a member of AGIFORS, and serves on the editorial board of the Journal of Revenue and Pricing Management. He is the author of three books; *The Evolution of Yield Management in the Airline Industry: Origins to the Last Frontier* (Springer, 2021), *Revenue Management in the Lodging Industry: Origins to the Last Frontier* (Springer 2022), *Mastering the Travel Intermediaries: Origins and Future of Global Distribution Systems, Travel Management Companies and Online Travel Agencies* (Springer 2024) and served as editor for *Artificial Intelligence and Machine Learning in the Travel Industry: Simplifying Complex Decision Making* (Palgrave-Macmillan, 2023).

1 An Introduction to Airline Retailing

If you know the enemy and know yourself, you need not fear the result of a hundred battles.

Sun Tzu

Abstract

This book focuses on the transition of revenue management of the base fare to offers and orders. An offer consists of the base fare and the ancillary bundle. Over the past two decades, revenues from ancillary products and services have grown at a rapid pace and now are fundamental components of airline revenues and profitability.

The process of unbundling the base fare started in 1987 when American Airlines President and CEO Robert Crandall removed the singular olive from the salad plates on American's flights as a cost cutting initiative. The olives were included in the price of the ticket, but customers did not notice the change, and if they did, they did not complain. Unlike unbundling of the base fare today, American did not offer the olive to customers for a fee. Twenty-one years later, in 2008, American Airlines was the first full-service carrier to charge for checked bags, the rest of the industry followed and has never looked back. This phenomenon of "unbundling" the base fare generates incremental revenue streams for airlines.

The transition to offer creation was accelerated by IATA when it introduced the New Distribution Capability (NDC) in 2012. NDC has a seismic impact on distributing airline products through the indirect channel, which impacts intermediaries such as Global Distribution Systems (GDS), Travel Management Companies (TMC) and Online Travel Agencies (OTA) since NDC offers are airline controlled and pricing power shifts from the GDS to the airline.

Along with the new NDC messaging standard for airlines offers, IATA introduced order management in 2015. This is a business process improvement

B. Vinod, *The Era of Airline Revenue Management with Offers and Orders*, Management for Professionals, https://doi.org/10.1007/978-3-032-24197-9_1

to replace the legacy passenger name record (PNR), electronic miscellaneous document (EMD) and E-ticket with a single order.

Advances with continuous dynamic pricing and creation of bundles based on consumer preferences are at the forefront of advances in revenue management. Recent advances in Artificial Intelligence has far reaching consequences on revenue management decision support, and automation of self-service and travel agency workflows with AI Agents over the next decade. Besides advances in data science and AI modeling, Agentic AI will have the most significant impact on travel distribution with the creation of new channels.

This quote by Sun Tzu, the Chinese military general, strategist, philosopher and writer who lived during the Eastern Zhou period (771 – 256 BC), highlights the importance of self-awareness and understanding your opponent in strategic situations. It emphasizes the importance of strategic preparation and understanding in achieving victory, particularly in competitive situations. The saying highlights that thorough knowledge of both one's own strengths and weaknesses, as well as those of the opponent, are crucial for success.

Every airline executive must interpret this quote by Sun Tzu in their own words as they embark on the new era of revenue management with offers and orders.

1.1 Origins

The airline industry consists of two types of business models with very different economic and operational assumptions. They are the full-service carriers (FSC) and the low-cost carriers (LCC).

FSCs are traditional network airlines that typically operate a hub and spoke network and included the cost of extras in the ticket price at least until 2008. They are also known as legacy airlines. FSCs offer a comprehensive travel experience with multiple cabin classes, meals, entertainment, and Wi-Fi. LCCs came into existence in the 1990s. They prioritize cost reduction by minimizing operating costs to offer lower fares. They focus on direct distribution, fly point-to- point, fly to secondary airports, have higher seat density, faster aircraft turnaround. They offer lower airfares and charge for extra services.

In 1987, full-service carriers such as American Airlines offered free meals on medium-haul and long-haul flights. Today, it is a different story entirely and airline executives view customers as walking Automated Teller Machines (ATMs). Unbundling the airfare has led to new revenue streams that have grown significantly over the past decade. In 1987, to meet the growing demand for air travel and stay competitive, American Airlines, under CEO Robert L. Crandall, had various cost cutting initiatives. Crandall determined that removing a single olive from each salad plate would save the airline up to $40,000 annually without impacting the passenger experience. The single olive was removed from each passenger's salad plate and the rest is history [Deutsch, 2001]. The story made headlines because the cost of the garnish had a surprising impact on costs. At universities it became a case study on operational excellence and lean management, a philosophy that focuses on minimizing waste and maximizing value creation by optimizing processes, improving efficiency, and fostering a culture of continuous improvement. The olives were *included* in the price of the airline ticket. Understandably, the olive was a very small part of the meal and customers did not notice that the olive was gone as Crandall had predicted. It was the first time that a full-service carrier had "unbundled" its product! But there was a difference from the unbundling practiced today. American did not offer the olive for a fee to customers.

Many years later, in May 2008, American Airlines became the first FSC to charge $15 for checked baggage that had previously been included in the price of the ticket. American initially attributed this charge to the rising cost of jet fuel when the price of crude oil skyrocketed in five years from $27 a barrel in 2003 to $127 a barrel in 2008. Charging for bags separately, known as "unbundling," is also a way for airlines to move part of the price out of the base airfare and into fees for tax savings purposes.

Strategically, from an airline Chief Financial Officer's (CFO) perspective, it was a cost cutting initiative. Charging extra for bags, known as "unbundling," reduces the base airfare price by shifting some costs to additional fees. This strategy is used for tax savings. U.S. domestic airfares ("the base fare") include a Federal Excise Tax (FET) of 7.5% to support the Aviation Trust Fund, but this tax does not apply to airline fees such as baggage fees. As a result, an airline can avoid paying $75 million in taxes on its $1 billion earnings from checked-bag fees.

Unlike the singular olive that vanished from American's flights in 1987, customers noticed the change, and it created a backlash. Travelers perceived this change as a takeaway, a loss. In behavioral economics this is known as the endowment effect. As full-service airline executives actively pursue selling ancillary products that were previously included in the price of a ticket, the endowment effect takes center stage in the minds of the traveling public.

Airlines earn significant money from bag fees. In 2022, they made $6.8 billion from these charges, according to the Department of Transportation. This amount increased by 17% compared to 2019, before the pandemic, and has doubled from ten years ago. In 2020, baggage fees made up 4% of major airlines' revenue, and 21% of revenue for ultra low-cost carriers like Spirit and Frontier [Mumbower et al., 2022]. Bag fees give airlines a chance to offer benefits tied to their co-branded credit cards. For example, the Delta SkyMiles American Express Card lets customers check their first bag for free. These co-branded credit cards generate significant revenue, bringing in $25 billion in sales for airlines in 2023 [Ideaworks & Cartrawler, 2024a, 2024b].

1.2 What Is this Book About?

This book is about retailing products and services in the pursuit of incremental revenues in the air travel industry. The sale of air ancillary products was first introduced by low-cost carriers (LCC). Full-service carriers (FSC) were slow followers, and it has now become a primary focus on the path to airline profitability. Looking beyond the base fare, the airline bundle or offer consists of the base fare for the itinerary along with ancillary products and services. With the launch of IATA's New Distribution Capability (NDC), the role of creating offers for NDC bookings lies solely with the airlines. NDC is an XML-based data transmission standard for airlines to communicate to intermediaries like the GDSs and also distribute rich content, and personalized bundled offers consisting of the base fare and ancillary products directly to travel sellers. It is an API-driven shopping, booking, and servicing capability for airlines and is an alternative to the traditional EDIFACT protocol. I do not used the word "new" or "modern" because the NDC messaging standard is legacy. If EDIFACT was introduced in 1987 and termed legacy, surely XML, which was introduced in 2001 with its bulky, verbose packets are also legacy.

NDC, besides offers, is a seismic change to the travel value chain and the flow of online transactions which is very different from the traditional GDS model. NDC and offer management are inextricably linked to each other, since NDC represents the future in terms of how an airline's offers are sold to travel agencies. Besides the NDC messaging standard, IATA has also introduced ONE Order to modernize airline transaction processing by replacing the Passenger Name Record (PNR), E-Ticket and Electronic Miscellaneous Document (EMD) with a single universal customer record. From an investment perspective, ONE Order is much larger than the NDC messaging standard for airlines.

In the context of NDC, an aggregator is an entity which provides services to connect airlines to travel sellers and provide NDC content. By default, the major GDSs are aggregators of NDC content. In this book, the term "NDC Aggregators" refers to the new entrants in this space such as Travelfusion, Duffel, TPConnects, AirGateway, and many more. NDC Aggregators are the non-GDS aggregators of NDC content.

Airlines have focused their efforts on selling air ancillary products and services as traveler needs and expectations have evolved. The mantra in the airline industry today, promoted by IATA, is to enable airline retailing with offers and orders. This is significant since it entails a major transformation of airlines to not just sell seats but become retailers. While airlines can master the sale and fulfillment of air ancillary products, the larger unanswered question is whether they have the drive, ambition, and courage to develop expertise to sell and fulfill third party products? Equally important, do travelers have the trust in airlines being able to sell and fulfill third party products since it is not their core competency?

During the Second World War, Alan Turing, the father of modern computer science, performed a miracle by decoding German messages encrypted with the Enigma machine. It is estimated that his work at Bletchley Park saved thousands of lives and shortened the war by two years. Is there a parallel with airline retailing? As a result of poor governance on version control and implementation differences for the NDC program, the bait and switch approach by airlines that are focused primarily on better economics for New Distribution Capability (NDC) bookings and unscrupulous consultants, IATA's NDC capability and airline retailing are a tangled mess. While NDC aims for standardization, the existence and use of various NDC versions pose challenges for consistency and interoperability. Variations in airline implementations and interpretations of the NDC standard lead to inconsistencies and interoperability problems across platforms and partners. Even with the same NDC version, implementation differences can be significant, especially if airlines use different IT providers. This inconsistency slows down adoption and increases costs. Ironically, it can be stated that deployment of NDC is really flexible because there are several versions multiplied by various implementations. This was never an option with EDIFACT.

Unfortunately, Alan Turing, the pioneering British computer scientist and World War II codebreaker passed away in 1954, and he is not around to decipher the multi-headed maze of airline retailing. Overcoming ambiguity, along several dimensions of this multi-headed monster, is key to finding the light at the end of the tunnel. Becoming a retailer begins with defining a strategy with well-defined objectives, the scope of the target audience and the list of ancillary services that the airline wants to promote to its customer base. To be successful in retailing, an airline must overcome ambiguity since they really do not have a grasp on consumer intent and consumer preferences. While consumer intent and consumer preferences can be captured or collected over time, the on-going challenge is the changes in consumer attitudes based on technology and the competitive landscape. This can only be overcome with test and learn experimentation framework that is seamlessly embedded into the transaction workflow for shopping, booking, and ticketing to recognize and react in real-time to consumer behavior, demands, and trends to maximize conversion rates and generate incremental revenues. Promoting the right product is a fundamental requirement to convert and offer into a booking. The real-time experimentation is a reinforcement learning technique, commonly referred to as the multi-armed bandit, that dynamically allocates more traffic to variations that are performing well and simultaneously allocating less traffic to variations that are underperforming. For the best results the arms of the multi-armed bandit should be contextual. This approach of exploration and exploitation has the distinct advantage of being adaptive to prevailing competitive market conditions. The science of considering consumer preferences to price the itinerary, the ancillary products in the bundle, and the total price are fundamental building blocks to build and execute the retailing practice.

A successful airline retailer will also make strides to make fundamental changes in the organizational structure to address the customer centric transformation to ensure alignment of key performance metrics (KPIs) across marketing, sales, and customer service teams.

1.3 The Transition from Merchandising to Retailing

Until the early 1990s, airlines focused their efforts on merchandising their scheduled air services. After the advent of Low-Cost Carriers (LCC), selling ancillary products and services related to a passenger's itinerary gained in importance. It represented a new revenue stream with a significant impact on airline profitability. Merchandising paved the way for airline retailing.

However, transitioning from merchandising to retailing poses a significant challenge. This shift requires a move from focusing on markets and flights to prioritizing the needs of customers, which is no small feat. While there is a strong desire to prioritize customers, the shift is monumental due to the presence of legacy systems, business processes, and traditional third-party distributors that continue to handle a significant portion of bookings.

In the airline industry there is a significant difference between merchandising and retailing. Merchandising involves selling an airline's core products and services, such as seats and schedules, using various marketing tactics and broad promotional approaches. This can result in offering an overwhelming number of choices for customers. Retailing, on the other hand, entails understanding and meeting customers' preferences in terms of what they want, when and how they want to shop, pay, and receive post-purchase support. This approach requires a customer-centric focus that aligns with the current lifestyle, work, and travel patterns of people. As a result, airlines need to transition from selling traditional and non-air ancillary products to offering personalized ancillary options based on comprehensive customer insights and intelligence obtained through advanced technologies like analytics and artificial intelligence.

Retailing strategies in the travel industry must eventually extend beyond selling individual air travel products and adjacent services like hotels, car rentals, ground transportation, and insurance. Effective retailing involves addressing all aspects of the travel experience including the purchase of non-travel products during a trip. This approach enables airlines to not only meet the diverse needs of connected customers but also capture a larger share of spending in the overall travel market. This requires a revenue share model with retail partners to fuel revenue growth. Sales from non-travel products with a revenue share financial model with retail partners typically yield higher profits. Proactive sales efforts aimed at solving the total travel experience for a trip can provide airlines with valuable data from the travel ecosystem and the potential for deeper engagement in this market is significant, considering airlines are often the first point of contact for travelers.

Leading retailers have demonstrated the need to attend to a customer's emotional and empathetic needs when delivering products and services. This necessitates the development of more meaningful methods for gauging customer satisfaction and experience. Meeting these needs calls for airlines to concentrate on the overall customer journey, based on the context for travel. Having this knowledge allows for personalized promotions designed to foster repeat business. To measure customer satisfaction and experience, it is essential to gather information on how customers perceive the airline, including frequent and infrequent travelers. Such insights can help airlines analyze customer behavior, predict current and future purchases, and devise strategies to convert a higher percentage of browsers into buyers. For execution of a retail strategy, the organization needs to be reinvented with a focus on delivering customer-centric offers, fulfillment, and customer care.

1.4 What Is Airline Retailing?

The term "airline retailing" and "modern airline retailing" are widely used in the travel industry. IATA has even renamed NDC as "modern airline retailing," While the term will continue to persist, its interpretation is very different from traditional brick-and-mortar retailing [Vinod, 2005a] which operates on an entirely different paradigm.

Examples of brick-and-mortar retailing are grocery chains like Kroger, booksellers like Barnes and Noble, wholesale merchants like Costco and Sam's Club, traditional retailers like Walmart and Target, home improvement stores like Home Depot and Lowes, specialty food retailers like The Vermont Country Store, and many more. Many of these retailers, except for the likes of Walmart that promote everyday low prices, promote their affinity, or club cards to track customer purchases and provide discounts to affinity card holders. With club cards, customer specific pricing at the club level or at the individual customer level has been in existence since the 1990s. Another aspect of traditional brick-and-mortal retailing is associated with higher profits generated by in-store brands. Other unique traits include loss leaders like milk which promote foot traffic into the store and product promotions which rarely generate true profits since it influences pantry loading behavior.

So, what are the components of airline retailing?. Broadly, it encompasses the following dimensions to selling products and services to customers.

1. The quoted fare for an itinerary. This fare can be based on published tariffs or derived from reference fares based on the competitive landscape, new entrants in the market, and a customer segment's willingness to pay. Derived fares cannot be replicated by intermediaries like the GDSs, TMCs and OTAs and require an airline to price every itinerary.
2. Airline ancillary products and services can be bundled with the base fare to create an offer. The total price for the bundle is inclusive of base fare and ancillaries that may have dynamic discounts based on the total value of the bundle.
3. Sale of non-air products such as hotels, rental cars, limo service, local activities, etc. Non-air products can produce a new source of revenue that is based on a fixed or variable commission fee model, or a revenue share model expressed as a percentage of the actual non-air revenue.

Besides these three primary components, international flag carriers can promote their hubs as stopover destinations and promote stopover packages that include air, hotel, local transportation, and local activities. For example, Emirates (Dubai), Icelandair (Reykjavik), Singapore Airlines (Singapore) and Cathay Pacific (Hong Kong) promote their hub airports as stopover destinations by waiving the stopover fee (ATPCO Category 8) and promote packages that include hotel, local transportation, and local activities at the stopover destination.

1.5 What Is "Modern Airline Retailing"?

Travelport, a GDS, first used the phrase "modern retailing" to describe its mission to simplify travel retailing with technology to make it faster, easier, and more modern. The focus was on improving customer experience. The Travelport point of view is noble; they believed that effective retailing starts with knowing what travelers truly want from travel suppliers and intermediaries. Armed with this knowledge, the objective was to create improved shopping experiences for Travelport's customers. Ironically, Travelport does not operate a Passenger Service System (PSS) for airlines and is not a provider of IT services to airlines and hence does not have offer creation products for airlines like Amadeus, Sabre and several boutique vendors.

Over the years several travel suppliers have used the term "modern airline retailing" in the context of an airline's needs such as NDC and preferred channels of distribution. As airline retailing goes mainstream in travel, major consulting companies such as Boston Consulting Group and McKinsey and Company are jumping on the bandwagon without a clear vision that this should be a customer-first initiative to improve travel experiences.

The issue arises because not everyone prioritizes the customer in their modern retailing initiatives. For instance, IATA advocates NDC as a way for airlines to act like modern retailers. In theory, NDC could lead to more personalized experiences. This potential is not being realized for travelers or travel agencies today (2025).

The airline viewpoint is even more precarious. If they put the customer first, they would not be withholding content from the standard GDS EDIFACT channels. Many major international airlines withhold Basic Economy fares from the GDS, creating ill-will and confusion in the marketplace.

Technology investment focused on supply-side relationships typically promotes the concept of a single brand. A single brand selling and servicing only its own products is not representative of modern retailing because best-in-class retailers offer consumer choices from multiple brands. This standpoint overlooks the massive value that travel agencies offer and puts the focus on selling a range of products.

In the long run, a more profitable strategy is to reduce pressure on customers and focus on providing better experiences. Rather than competing between direct and indirect channels, airlines and IATA must focus on a well-rounded approach that includes both. This will help grow the customer base, no matter where people decide to shop for flights.

Today, not a single airline that is pursuing NDC and "modern retailing" has a customer-first priority. In the end, a customer-first strategy will lead to lasting changes, improved retail experiences in travel for everyone, and generate incremental revenues for airlines.

1.6 Origins of Airline Retailing

The origins of airline retailing can be traced back to when airlines started disaggregating the individual components of a flight booking.

The retailing of ancillary products in the airline industry originated with the ultra-low-cost carrier (ULCC) In 1981 under the leadership of founder Donald Burr. PEOPLExpress, a ULCC, introduced a novel approach of offering heavily discounted fares at the time of booking, while charging a fee of $3 for each checked bag. This strategy was a pioneering move aimed at generating additional revenue for the airline and to compensate partially for the deeply discounted fares.

Over the past decade, airline executives have directed their commercial teams to prioritize the development of various revenue sources beyond traditional ticket sales. Ancillary revenues refer to any income generated in addition to the earnings from different ticket types or branded fares.

The sale of ancillary services such as pre-reserved seats, checked bags, insurance, meals on board, etc. were introduced by the LCCs in the mid-1990s.

Most airlines, including both network carriers and LCCs, began charging for bags, overweight bags, and oversized bags twenty years later. Ryanair, an LCC, was one of the first airlines to implement this policy in 2006, charging travelers $10 for checked bags purchased online and $20 at the airport.

In 2008, full-service carriers also started unbundling and charging for checked bags after experimenting with bundled fare families.

Spirit Airlines received public criticism in 2010 for charging carry-on bags, and other LCCs like Allegiant Airlines and Frontier Airlines followed suit. Additionally, other optional services related to bags such as priority bag drops, priority bag returns, and insurance were also introduced.

In 2007 Spirit Airlines adopted the Ultra-Low-cost carrier (ULCC) business model to provide basic air transportation at the lowest possible fare in the markets they served. To make the base fare as low as possible, Spirit unbundled the charge for checked bags and despite rising fuel costs, lowered the base fare to offset the unbundling of the product. In 2010, Spirit Airlines created an uproar when they started charging for carry-on bags that would not fit under the seat. To their credit, this charge did not apply to items such as medical equipment, baby strollers, and similar items. Allegiant Airlines and Frontier Airlines followed the Spirit model. LCCs specialized in charging a low base fare at the time of booking and this was followed by the sale of extra services for an additional fee. An independent survey conducted by Leflein Associates in January 2006 [Alexander, 2006] showed that air travelers would pay for extra perks such as more frequent flyer miles, more overhead bin space, and the ability to sit in a child-free section of the aircraft.

1.7 Origins of Airline Revenue Management

American Airlines was founded on April 15, 1926, and celebrated its 100th anniversary in 2026. When legendary American Airlines President and CEO C.R. Smith (1934–1968) pursued an initiative with IBM to launch the first automated airline reservations system, its role as the execution component of revenue management with inventory controls was not understood at the time. An experimental system went online in 1960, and the SABRE reservations system was operationalized and launched by American Airlines and IBM in December 1964 [Vinod, 2024a]. At its launch, it was the largest private real-time commercial data processing system in the world, enabling American Airlines reservation agents to book tickets and see real-time availability. A less known fact is that on American's flights, C.R. Smith introduced the buttonhole napkins that can be buttoned on the shirt to protect clothing during meals that exists to this day.

Traditional revenue management is based on the fundamental premise that not all customers are created equal. Airlines publish various fare products, through fare aggregators like ATPCO and SITA, that resonate with business and leisure customers who are schedule sensitive and price sensitive. The airline industry is asset intensive with a high fixed cost structure, published schedules with relatively fixed capacity, and perishable inventory. Demand for flights and the associated fare products are variable and exhibit uncertainty. When revenue management was introduced by American Airlines in 1986, it was all about revenue management of the base fare. Revenue management is the process of selling the right seat to the right customer at the right price at the right time. Revenue is maximized by selling the right mix of fare products, achieved with discount allocation inventory controls established on the airline's host CRS. Besides discount allocation controls, overbooking is practiced at the cabin level to compensate for the effects of cancellations and no-shows.

Traditional revenue management forecasts demand by booking class and determines allocations by booking class to maximize revenues for leg/segment carriers and uses bid price controls to control availability by origin and destination (O&D). The reservation booking designators (RBDs) are used to open and close booking classes to get the optimal mix of passengers that maximizes total revenue. A RBD has many fares that are mapped to it, usually with similar fare rules. Airlines also use the RBDs to distribute availability to third party systems like GDSs. In this traditional environment, a GDS has access to schedules and fares from schedule and fare aggregators, and the travel agent can price itineraries on a GDS to complete the booking and ticketing process.

Figure 1.1 illustrates the basic concept of how revenue management works.

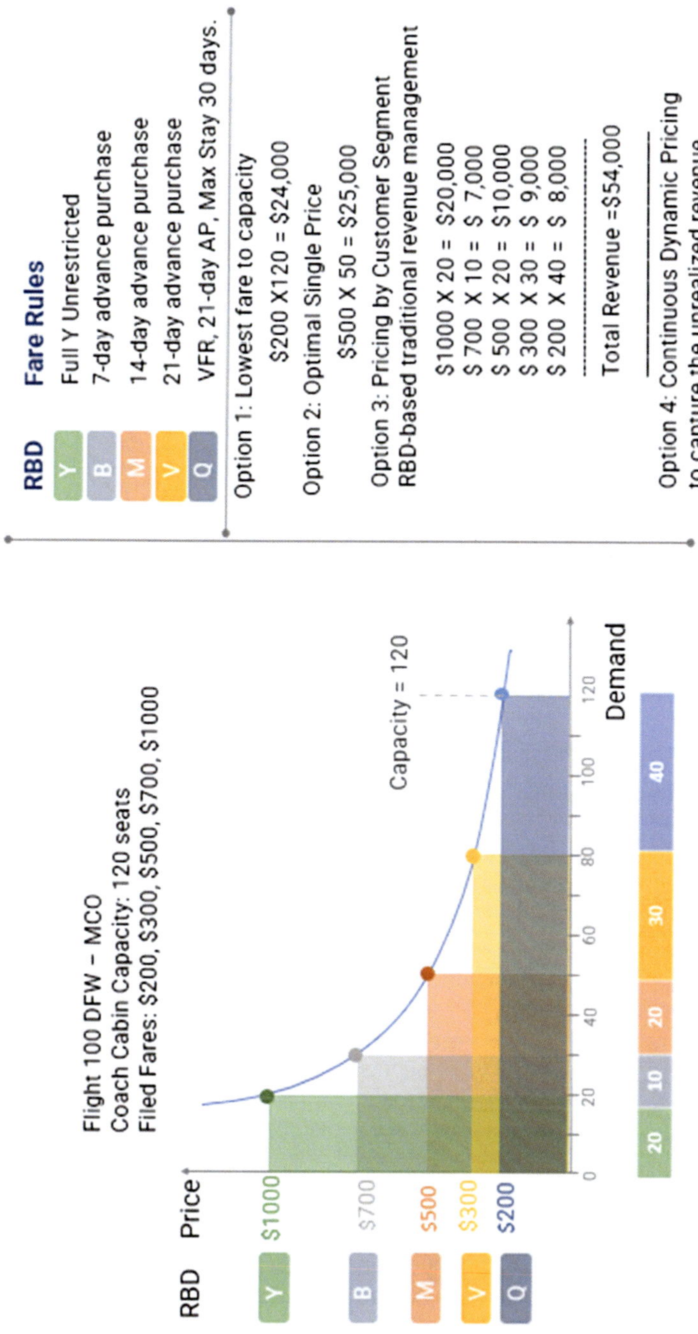

Fig. 1.1 Basics of Revenue Management

1.7.1 The Case for Dynamic Pricing

In the airline industry there is a subtle difference between dynamic pricing and continuous pricing [Airoldi, 2023]. The formal definition of dynamic pricing is the ability for airlines to provide a price quote based on context for travel at the time of shopping and not necessarily display the lowest fare available. The context can be based on the definition of trip-purpose segments. However, personal information such as purchase history and frequent flyer status are not used. Dynamic pricing is new because the quoted fare is not the filed fare. It is the ability to adjust the price in real-time without needing to file fares with ATPCO. The dynamic price is a derived fare that overcomes the constraints of having a maximum of 26 booking classes.

The formal definition of continuous pricing is an airline's ability to provide infinite price points that consider both context for travel and personal data such as corporate traveler id, frequent flyer status, individual purchase history, etc.

There are three variations to create a dynamic price quote: dual RBDs, laddered pricing, and continuous pricing.

The first approach, dual RBDs, enables an airline to increase the number of price points. It uses a primary and secondary Reservation Booking Designator (RBD) to create more price points than a single RBD allows, enabling dynamic pricing with minimal system changes.

A pan-industry Dynamic Pricing Working Group was established in 2016 with ATPCO as the sponsor to develop specifications for laddered pricing. With this approach intermediate private fares are filed between public fares that can only be activated by an airline's dynamic pricing engine (DPE). Airlines, GDSs, vendors and related entities participated in these working group sessions to finalize a specification and messaging standard for dynamically priced fares for distribution to airline websites and intermediaries. The ATPCO JSON/XML schemas for connectivity were intended to provide an interim step toward NDC [Dezelak & Ratliff, 2018]. The ATPCO specification allowed airlines to connect their dynamic pricing engines to traditional distribution prior to NDC cutover. This approach did not gain traction with airlines.

The third approach is continuous pricing, where the dynamic price generated by the dynamic pricing engine is used as the selling fare. Of the three approaches, continuous pricing has the most traction and several airlines have implemented first generation versions on their websites for selected markets.

With both dynamic pricing and continuous pricing scenarios, if two travelers book the same itinerary with the same carrier at the same time, the fares may be slightly different.

For corporate fares that come with a negotiated discount off the public fare (Category 25 Fare By Rule), the dynamic (continuous) price is first determined before the corporate discount is applied, if applicable.

There was tremendous backlash in the airline industry when Delta Air Lines claimed they were using Artificial Intelligence enabled price quotes. Delta defended its position with U.S. lawmakers in August 2025 by stating that it did not use personal data for individualized, predatory flight pricing. They further claimed that their AI pricing model functions on aggregated, not personal, data to enhance existing market-driven dynamic pricing.

Further, with data privacy constraints such as Generalized Data Protection Restriction (GDPR) and California Consumer Privacy Act (CCPA), privacy laws will prevent price quotes based on an individual traveler.

For this reason, the terms dynamic pricing and continuous pricing will be used interchangeably by airlines and personal data will not be part of the equation.

The traditional end product of revenue management is booking class availability which is then used by airline pricing in conjunction with booking class availability to determine the price of an itinerary.

This paradigm changes with IATA's New Distribution Capability (NDC). With NDC, pricing power shifts from the GDS to the airline for the indirect channel. In a world of airline-controlled offers, the end product of the revenue management process is the price of the itinerary. This is a fundamental, seismic change in GDS transaction processing. Over time, as NDC adoption accelerates, many of the core capabilities that exist in the GDSs today such as air shopping, booking, and ticketing will be deprecated since the airline assumes responsibility for these core functions to fulfill travel requests from customers.

With NDC, the reservation booking designator (RBD) will become irrelevant since booking class availability will no longer be distributed to the GDSs. RBDs or alternate customer segmentation will still continue to be used internally by airlines for revenue management purposes. Airline reservation systems have evolved over the past few decades to expand the number of RBDs from seven booking classes to 13 and now to 24 since two booking classes (I, O) are typically not distributed externally but retained for internal airline use such as staff travel. With 24 RBDs, there is still unrealized revenue that can be captured with continuous dynamic pricing. This is shown in Fig. 1.2.

RBDs also is a default method for segmenting customers into a hierarchy. Traditional revenue management relies on forecasting demand by RBD and optimizing inventory controls either by leg/segment or origin and destination (O&D). Leg/segment revenue management relies on the expected marginal seat revenue calculation to determine the nested allocations by booking class. O&D revenue management relies on optimizing the network to capture upline and downline interactions to determine bid prices which are used to determine availability by O&D for each booking class. Since airlines no longer have to distribute RBD availability to third party entities like the GDS, a new term called class-less revenue management has been introduced into the airline vocabulary.

The transition to continuous pricing is applicable with RBDs and also with class-less revenue management, when RBDs are *no longer required*. The term class-less revenue management is misleading because customer segmentation is fundamental to revenue management and the process of defining customer segments for the purposes of demand forecasting and optimization is still required.

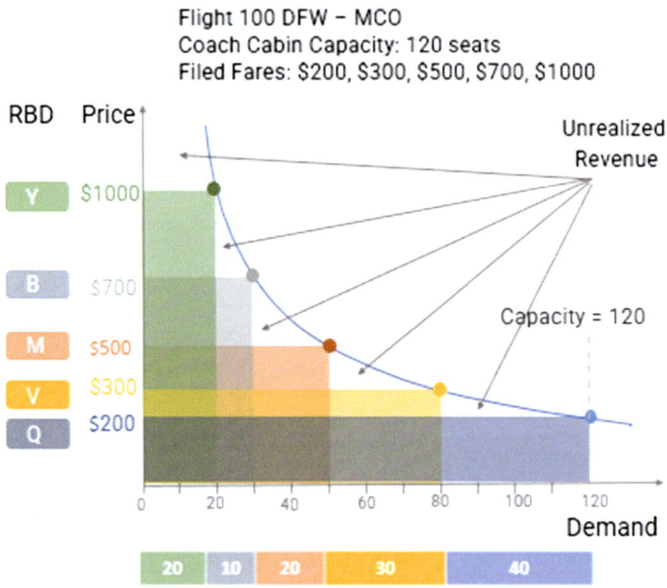

Fig. 1.2 Unrealized revenue on the price demand curve

Perhaps, the RBDs no longer encapsulate the definition of customer segments but customer segmentation will assume a more refined form such as segmentation based on context for travel, customer lifetime value, or a combination.

In this scenario, an airline may file reference fares that cater to the various customer segments, but the price quoted is a continuous dynamic price. In the traditional approach when the $700 fare (booking class B) is closed, the next available fare is $1,000. However, with continuous pricing, a derived fare can be quoted that lies in between $700 and $1,000. Note that continuous pricing works with the airline's published and contracted fare products. These fares may be published internally if an airline chooses not to distribute its fares through fare aggregators. This is not an issue with IATA NDC since the airline controls the price of the itinerary for the indirect channel. Fare combinability will be enforced based on fare rules when the itinerary is priced.

With full-service carriers (FSC) migrating to IATA's new distribution capability (NDC) all offers are controlled by the airline. GDSs can no longer price itineraries (that is, compute the price of the itinerary based on filed fares and rules). Further with the move to continuous dynamic pricing, which is a derived fare that may be subject to business rules, only an airline can generate the itinerary price. This also means that the role of the RBD to distribute availability to GDSs is becoming irrelevant.

A requirement for the implementation of continuous pricing for corporate customers is an audit trail that provides a trace of how the corporate fare was quoted. Since every continuous pricing dynamic fare is a derived fare, corporations will require an audit trail and reporting to ensure that they are indeed receiving their corporate discounts.

Dynamic pricing is also applicable in the pricing of opaque airline tickets (Zouaoui & Rao, 2009).

Four decades after its inception, revenue management has been transitioning to offer management, which is the process of selling a bundle consisting of base fare and air ancillary products and services to customers.

Offer management is the process of selling the right bundleto the right customer at the right price at the right time.

1.8 The Transition of Revenue Management to Offer Management

For three decades after airline deregulation, revenue management in the airline industry has focused on maximizing revenues by selling the right product to the right customer at the right price at the right time. It was one-dimensional in the sense that the selling fare was all that mattered. Revenue management advanced from leg/segment inventory controls to origin and destination inventory controls. With leg/segment controls, seat availability was based on either net nesting or threshold nesting. To control inventory by O&D, availability is based on continuous nesting, also known as bid price controls [Vinod, 2021a, Chapter 4]. Restriction-free pricing (RFP), a feature introduced by LCCs, was first adopted to some degree by the FSCs when they had to compete directly with the LCCs on key routes. In the absence of fare restrictions, when price was the only determinant of the customer segment, demand for booking classes was no longer independent. The revenue management models had to go through significant enhancements to support lightly restricted and unrestricted tariffs [Vinod, 2021a, Chapter 5].

With the growing importance of schedule and fare transparency during shopping, competitive revenue management gained rapid adoption, whereby the selling fares in the market offered by competitors were considered as an input before an airline determined the optimal inventory controls subject to prevailing competitive market conditions. The latest advances in revenue management of the base fare are in the areas of dynamic availability and dynamic pricing. Dynamic availability works with the existing airline tariff structure that has been published by the airlines to fare aggregators. Dynamic availability factors in the competitive marketplace to open and close discrete inventory controls dynamically in the airline host CRS to maximize revenues. Dynamic pricing takes it a step further to generate a dynamic price that may not be a fare that was filed by the airline to fare aggregators. The advantage of dynamic pricing is that it fills the missed opportunities (gaps) on the price demand curve by recommending a continuous dynamic price.

With the growing importance of the sale of ancillary products and services bundled with the base fare to improve the bottom line, this transition of revenue management of the base fare to offer management was spearheaded by the LCCs.

With FSCs following the LCC lead by selling ancillary products and services, the science of revenue management has transitioned from *inventory control tactics to sell the base fare* to *selling a bundle consisting of the base fare with ancillary products and services.* With this change every dimension of the offer—the base fare and ancillaries included in the offer with their respective prices are important to maximize an airline's network revenues and profitability.

Branded fare families were first introduced in 2006 by Air New Zealand, Air Canada, Qantas, and others. Southwest Airlines introduced its Business Select fare in 2007, which included early boarding, Rapid Rewards bonus accrual, and an onboard cocktail. Frontier Airlines followed in 2008 and is considered the first to introduce branded fares in coach in the U.S. domestic market. Branded fares presented airlines with an opportunity to offer transparency to customers based on the value of the service rendered and promote the sale of ancillary services [Vinod, 2008]. Historically, airline seats have always been sold from the bottom up, from the lowest qualified fare. With branded products, an airline can sell from the middle or the top, based on a consumer's preference for the attributes associated with a branded product

Airlines employ a variety of approaches that fall into three general categories [Vinod & Moore, 2009]. The original branded fare families were bundled, where services were offered based on the fare paid. Hence, if a specific brand were purchased, the customer received all the attributes associated with the branded fare. The second is the fully unbundled or à la carte pricing, where the fare only includes standard transportation, and each service option is available for an additional fee. Product unbundling allowed airlines to sell individual ancillaries that were not included in a branded fare product. This is like the LCC model promoted by carriers like Ryanair. Third, is the hybrid model where bundles of ancillary services are offered at a price lower than the combination of individual items. In addition, even with the purchase of a lower valued branded product, customers can pay for specific ancillary services such as advance seat selection. Besides network carriers, several LCCs have adopted this model as well.

The promotion of service differentiation with branded fare products and sale of ancillaries are collectively referred to as "merchandising". Branded fare families are discussed in more detail in Chapter 6.

The offers recommended to customers can be by customer segment based on the context for travel. This is a recommendation by trip-purpose segment. Alternatively, if the customer has purchase history on their profile, this information can be leveraged to *personalize* the offer at the individual level for a segment of ONE.

With the IATA NDC messaging standard, the key difference is that all offers will be created and distributed by the airlines [Touraine, 2021].

1.8.1 How Revenue Management Is Evolving in a Post Pandemic World

Besides the fundamental transition from revenue management of the base fare to revenue management of bundles, revenue management is evolving in a post-pandemic world.

Historical demand patterns may not accurately predict future demand, which was observed after the onset of the COVID-19 pandemic in 2020. Adaptive revenue management is a reliable qne robust framework that allows businesses to quickly adapt to changing market conditions with ad-hoc schedule changes by incorporating key concepts from sales and operations planning [Vinod, 2022b]. During the pandemic, there was a significant decline in customer demand, and airline revenue management systems struggled to forecast flight demand accurately [Vinod, 2020c, 2021b]. To manage the business effectively without relying on accurate forecasts, it is necessary to shift toward an operationally driven approach that continuously manages demand. This robust revenue management approach, known as continuous demand management [Vinod, 2021a, 2021b], involves actively monitoring key performance indicators (KPIs) and proactively taking corrective action to meet revenue targets and related KPIs. By embracing continuous demand management, businesses can achieve the goals outlined in the revenue plan. This approach bears similarities to the sales and operations (S&OP) workflow [Palmatier & Crum, 2003], which involves synchronizing demand, available capacity, and resources to optimize performance, particularly during times of high uncertainty and volatility.

To promote bundles, calibration based on historical data must be avoided at all costs. First, the historical purchase history data may not be sufficient or non-existent when new ancillary products are introduced. Second, periodic calibration to revise the estimates of the parameters of the offer model is a time-consuming task and will *always lag* evolving consumer preferences over time. The more adaptable approach is to conduct *test-and-learn experimentation*, using a reinforcement learning [Sutton & Barto, 1998] technique commonly known as the multi-armed bandit (MAB), to determine the composition of the offer bundles. This approach learns continuously based on changing consumer behaviors and prevailing competitive market conditions. The implementation of the test and learning experimentation model should be context sensitive [Byrd & Darrow, 2021]. Contextual reinforcement learning tracks customer responses by trip-purpose segment.

Personalization of the offer based on the context for travel is a continued area of focus to improve conversion rates [Vinod, 2023b]. Offers can be recommended by trip-purpose segment, and in situations where the customer travels frequently, the offer can be personalized based on past purchase history and preferences.

1.8.2 The Transformation of Product Distribution with NDC and AI Agents

With the traditional GDS transaction flow model, the GDS calculates the price of an itinerary based on availability of booking classes determined by the airline's revenue management process. Many airlines publish their ancillary services (ATPCO records S5, S7, S8) and GDSs also create offers consisting of a base fare and ancillary products and services.

Even when the power to price itineraries was with the GDS, airlines have always controlled the revenue management process. The end product of the revenue management process is booking class availability that is controlled and distributed from the airline's host CRS. As airlines transition from revenue management of the base fare to offer management consisting of bundles, they want to have complete control of the offer creation process inclusive of the price of the itinerary and the composition of the ancillary products and services in the bundle. From an airline's point of view, this is of strategic importance to maximize total revenues.

There are two fundamental changes, and they are related to itinerary pricing and the ancillary bundle.

1. The itinerary price is not based on static filed fares, but a dynamic fare that is derived from reference fares based on market conditions. When a fare is derived based on business rules or advanced statistical and machine learning models, the GDSs can no longer price an itinerary. The creation of an itinerary price on demand for each customer request is called dynamic pricing and no longer requires RBDs since availability by booking class is no longer distributed to the GDSs.
2. Creation of the bundled offer at the time of request is a fundamental change. This requires advanced analytics to determine the context for travel to generate a recommendation consisting of an airline bundle of ancillary products and services that are pertinent to the customer request to enhance conversion rates. Creation of the bundle by an airline will be based on simple business rules or customer data complemented with advanced statistical and machine learning models to generate the offer. With this new process, the GDSs can no longer create bundled offers.

While NDC is a seismic change in airline distribution, a bigger change in the making is the arrival of autonomous AI Agents. With advances in AI technology, airline distribution is in the throes of a major revolution with the creation of a new AI distribution channel for discovering, planning and booking destinations. These new systems can research, book flights and hotels, and manage itineraries in real time. They are more advanced than simple chatbots and function as personal travel assistants. Instead of using search engines, travel management companies or online travel agencies, travelers are increasingly turning to AI-powered conversational agents for end-to-end trip management.

1.9 The Confluence of Revenue Management and Customer Relationship Management

In the customer-centric era, airlines are now prioritizing investment in data mining, business intelligence, and advanced data analytics. This investment aims to enhance customer retention, attract new customers, and optimize revenue from the customer base by understanding customer traits, behaviors, and preferences. The focus on customer loyalty and customer experience is crucial for airlines to stand out. Due to the cyclical nature of the travel industry, the demand for both business and leisure travel is closely tied to the economy's health. This underscores the heightened importance of gaining customer insight.

Revenue management and by extension, offer management, is focused on maximizing revenues by selling the right bundle of base fare and ancillary products to the right customer at the right price at the right time. As a science, revenue management has seen significant advances since it was created by American Airlines in 1985. However, when the selling process involves ancillary products and services beyond the base fare, insights into customer preferences is mandatory to create offers (bundles) that improve conversion rates. This knowledge can be at a customer segment level based on the context for travel or at an individual customer level. For the first time, with the renewed focus on customer preferences, the world of revenue management must leverage customer relationship management business processes to be on the same wavelength as the customer base. Customer Relationship Management (CRM) applications automate customer interactions between a business and its customers, recognizing that it is more expensive to acquire new customers than to retain existing ones. The primary focus of CRM in a business is on marketing, sales, and service. The diagram below shows how traditional CRM functions extend within the customer life cycle process.

Figure 1.3 illustrates the confluence of offer management and CRM to create a new world of personalized experiences for travelers.

The customer lifecycle management process starts with *marketing*, focusing on generating demand, qualifying, and prioritizing opportunities, and distributing qualified leads to relevant sales channels. The next phase involves maximizing revenue through tailored offers, intelligent pricing, and efficient product availability. Fulfillment, often overlooked in traditional CRM, follows. In a manufacturing enterprise, the fulfillment process distributes the consolidated order across all the constituents of the supply chain that should fulfill parts of the order and manages the delivery of the consolidated order across multiple suppliers and service providers. In the airline context, all transactions are conducted electronically and there is no lead time involved for fulfillment. For airlines, fulfillment constitutes the ticketing function. Finally, customer care focuses on creating profitable relationships, corporate contracts, addressing complaints, and building long-term customer relationships. A higher percentage of repeat business relative to total sales signifies greater stability for the airline, reducing exposure to cyclical demand patterns.

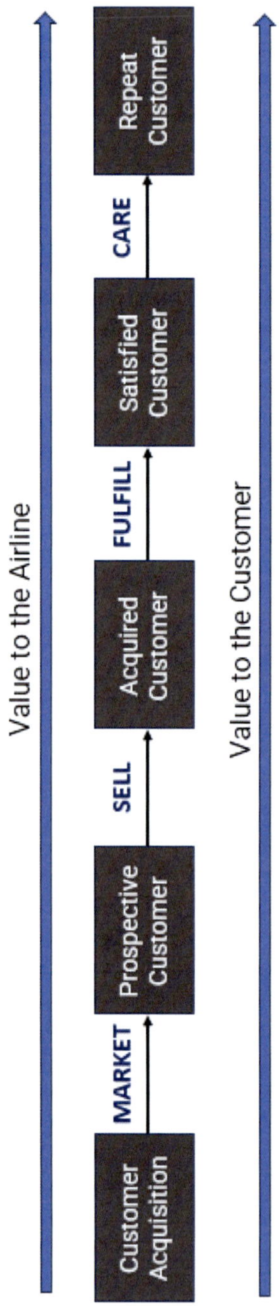

Fig. 1.3. Customer travel life cycle

Customer experience plays a central role with airline retailing. Customer experience spans the entire customer life cycle: Demand generation, interactive selling, fulfillment, and customer care that creates a perception of the value of the airline brand. A major challenge for airlines is the high number of customer inquiries they receive daily. Airlines, large and small, are constantly inundated with customer requests. They must promptly and precisely address various concerns like booking information, baggage status, and flight delays. Generative AI can play a vital role in this scenario, utilizing natural language processing (NLP) methods to provide real-time responses to customer queries.

1.10 The Endowment Effect

American economist Richard H. Thaler, a Professor of Behavioral Science and Economics at the University of Chicago Booth School of Business, first coined the term "endowment effect" [Kahneman et al., 1991; Thaler, 1980]. It is a cognitive bias and refers to the inertia associated with consumer choices when they value the goods they own, more highly than those they do not. This bias leads to irrational behavior, causing goods of equal value to not be perceived or treated as such.

Initial attempts to introduce merchandising in the airline industry were met with resistance from travelers who believed that previously included features were now being removed. American Airlines received backlash for implementing a fee for checked baggage in May 2008, as this service had previously been included in the ticket price. This was perceived by travelers as a takeaway, a loss, which is known as the endowment effect in behavioral economics. This effect argues that changes presented as losses have a greater impact than changes presented as gains. Although baggage fees were initially introduced to counter rising fuel costs, they have continued to rise over the years despite reductions in fuel costs.

1.11 Data Infrastructure and Environment

A Hadoop Big Data environment is an ecosystem of open-source tools and frameworks designed for the distributed storage and processing of large datasets across clusters of commodity hardware. It is a scalable, fault-tolerant, and cost-effective solution.

Prior to 2010, the Hadoop Big Data environment was not a viable platform for many companies, especially those seeking stable and established platforms. Hence, when the database size exceeds five to seven terabytes, the decision to migrate to a massively parallel processing (MPP) environment was common. An MPP environment is a computational database platform capable of high-speed data processing with several (usually 100s or 1000s) processors that work on different parts of the program each with its own memory and operating system. It is like Hadoop in segmenting and processing data on concurrent nodes but does not execute on commodity hardware.

In the early 2000s, the concept of "unstructured" data was unfamiliar, and if you needed to analyze logs, you would simply parse them with Perl/Python/Java/C++ and load them into the analytical database management system. Similarly, high velocity data was processed using traditional online transaction processing (OLTP) relational database management systems (RDBMS) for frequent updates and inserted into the analytical data warehouse. With the advent of Hadoop, MPP databases lost their appeal. An example is Teradata which has lost market share over the years to Hadoop. Many IT professionals view Hadoop as a replacement for MPP, while the more conservative position is to advocate the Data Lake / Data Hub concept where Hadoop and MPP co-exist and integrate to create a single solution. Today many airlines and IT providers leverage big data solutions for gaining a competitive edge [Vinod, 2013a, 2016b].

Google developed a proprietary, distributed file system known as Google File System (GFS) in 2003 [Ghemawat et al., 2003]. They also created a parallel programming technique and framework called MapReduce in 2004 [Dean & Ghemawat, 2004] for their web search purposes. These papers served as the foundation for the development of Hadoop, which consists of two core components: MapReduce and the Hadoop Distributed File System (HDFS).

Google Trends is a tool that can show a graph of a keyword's popularity over time. It was introduced in 2006, though it has search data from 2004, to support keyword research for businesses for search engine optimization (SEO). Figure 1.4 is a Google Trends graph for the keyword "big data". The y-axis represents the Relative Search Volume (RSV) normalized on a scale from 0 to 100. The numbers represent search interest relative to the highest point on the chart by time. A value of 100 represents peak popularity for the term, on the chart over time; a score of 50 means that the term is half as popular and a value of zero means that there was not enough data for this term.

Figure 1.5 illustrates a logical view of the data architecture to support airline retailing. The infrastructure, architecture, and application are designed to accept data in various formats, batch and streaming, structured and unstructured, that can be stored in real-time for analysis and decision support model development. The collected data is transformed, repackaged, and presented back to the data scientists in the requested formats for consumption in the form of key performance indicators, data dashboards, analytics, knowledge discovery, experimentation, and many more.

1.11.1 Data Sources for Airline Retailing

The primary data sources for airline retailing that must exist in a data warehouse are shown in Fig. 1.5 Additional sources such as social media and other forms of data from other platforms can also be added subject to return on investment (ROI) justification. The primary industry data sources are:

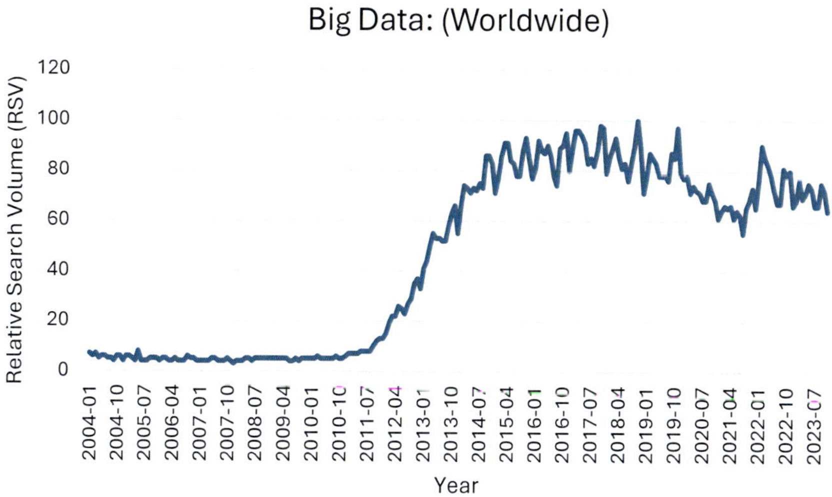

Fig. 1.4 Google trends graph for term "big data"

1.11.1.1 Bookings

This is the bookings data from all channels of distribution of the host airline. There are two types of data. For airlines operating in a leg/segment revenue management environment, the snapshot of bookings on the inventory detail record that is resident in the host CRS is extracted daily to support forecasting and optimization. The more detailed source of booking data is the Passenger Name Record (PNR) that is created. PNR maintains the entire itinerary of a customer and is also required for O&D revenue management.

1.11.1.2 Tickets

Many of the bookings are ticketed. The ticketed data is from all channels of distribution of the host airline and includes the price for the itinerary inclusive of surcharges and taxes.

1.11.1.3 Electronic Miscellaneous Document (EMD)

The EMD is the industry standard document for fulfillment of travel-related services, known as Optional Ancillary Services. There are two types of EMDs. An EMD-A is issued for flight-related Optional Ancillary Services. The EMD-S is for standalone non-flight related ancillaries such as a deposit. Data in the EMD represents all ancillary fees collected outside of an electronic ticket. It tracks the usage of ancillary charges such as excess baggage fees, lounge access, penalty fees, etc.

1.11.1.4 Post Departure

The departure control system (DCS) of an airline is integrated with the airline reservations system. It handles passenger check-in at airports, issues boarding passes, submits APIS (Advanced Passenger Information System) information for

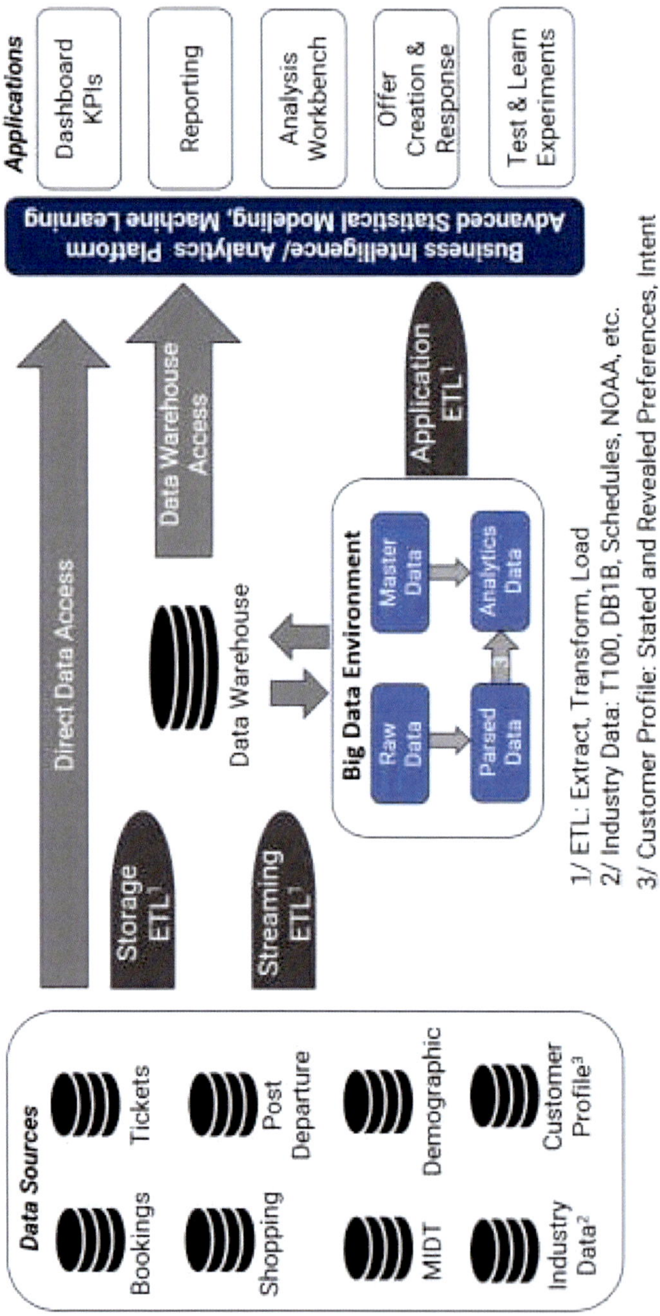

Fig. 1.5 Data infrastructure

international departures, weight and balance, generates the flight manifest, and post departure passenger counts to determine the no-shows.

1.11.1.5 Marketing Information Data Tapes (MIDT)

Marketing Information Data Tapes is a dataset based on bookings made by travel agents that subscribe to a GDS. The data are collected before a ticket is issued. Hence MIDT has the number in party but does not differentiate the customer type. Almost all the data stored in the Passenger Name Record (PNR) is available. The main suppliers today of MIDT data are Amadeus, Sabre and Travelport. It has been actively marketed and sold since 1987. As NDC transactions that bypass traditional GDSs grow in volume, the value of MIDT is marginalized, unless it is integrated with direct booking data.

1.11.1.6 IATA Direct Data Solutions (DDS)

IATA Direct Data Solutions was jointly created in 2012 by IATA and Airline Reporting Corporation (ARC). DDS offers a comprehensive global airline ticket dataset and is used for benchmarking and other business analysis purposes. This dataset is superior to MIDT since it includes visibility into direct and indirect (agency) ticket sales across all geographic regions. Since DDS is based on individual tickets, and unlike MIDT, it has information on the passenger type (e.g., child under 15, etc.). This dataset was created in partnership with ARC, Cirium and airlines who contribute their sales data.

1.11.1.7 T100

Provided by the Department of Transportation (DOT), this is leg level data that includes point of commencement. Hence, from this data we know the departure airport, arrival airport, carrier, month, and passengers. For example, we can tell how many passengers flew FRA-JFK on Lufthansa in January 2011. It is a monthly extract based on passenger arrivals and thus includes direct sales.

1.11.1.8 DB1B

Data Bank 1B has the Origin-Destination Survey data for a 10% sample of airline tickets from reporting carriers. Data includes origin, destination and other itinerary details of passengers transported. This is O&D level data but is based on a 10% sample. Since the entire itinerary is provided, we know the country of origin. It is more accurate for U.S. domestic, less so for international because only first international port touched before/beyond the U.S. is recorded. For example, for the itinerary PVG-NRT-LAX-LAS-LAX-NRT-PVG, only NRT-LAX-LAS-LAX-NRT is recorded.

Data Bank 1A (DB1A) was replaced in 2003 by Data Bank 1B (DB1B). These datasets are similar except for a few differences. For instance, DB1B identifies both the operating carrier and the ticketing carrier while DB1A assumed they were the same.

1.11.1.9 DB1C

The Origin-Destination Survey of Airline Passengers database DB1B went through a significant upgrade to DB1C in July 2025 as part of the OD40 program when the Joe Biden / Pete Buttigieg regulations went into effect [BTS, 2026]. It was a major milestone for the Bureau of Transportation Statistics (BTS) as the O&D data increased from a 10% sample of tickets collected quarterly from large carriers to a 40% sample of tickets collected monthly from existing and new reporting carriers. The data collected includes the fare and itinerary of each sampled ticket. The data includes how far in advance each ticket was purchased categorized into three buckets (within three weeks, three weeks to 90 days, and beyond 90 days). Taxes are also included and hence estimates are not required. The data also provides reporting carrier clarity and mandates commuters with fewer than 60 seats, who were previously exempt, to report.

1.11.1.10 Airline Schedules

A subscription to schedule aggregators like the Official Airline Guide (OAG) and Cirium provides access to aggregate schedules of all airlines that participate.

1.11.2 Batch and Streaming ETL

ETL is an acronym for Extract, Transform, and Load. It is used for processing data from a variety of sources, batch, or streaming. It is a process that extracts data from various sources, aggregates the data, transforms the data into a format that supports queries, applies business rules, and loads the data into a central repository called a data warehouse.

Batch ETL processing typically applies to industry data like MIDT, T100, etc., where data are collected and loaded into a date warehouse periodically. Batch ETL is typically leveraged when data freshness is not critical.

Streaming ETL is useful for real-time applications and can extract data from multiple sources and publish it directly to a streaming ETL application. For example, many OTAs depend on GDS air shopping data to charge their shopping cache in real-time. While this processing is more complex than batch, it has the distinct advantage of access to fresh data for real-time decision making.

The data that goes into the data warehouse originated from online transaction processing (OLTP) production systems such as airline reservations and air shopping systems. The ETL process is usually a recurring process that takes place in real-time, hourly, daily, weekly, etc. into the data warehouse which is then used to support both simple and complex applications.

1.12 The Significance of Customer Experience

A fundamental tenet of airline retailing is to enhance customer experience continually with the right offers, the right onboard experience, and post travel customer care. It is the efficient management of the traveler through all the customer touch points.

While some view enhanced customer experience as the holy grail for customer retention, it does depend on the context. The context is "*what is the customer expectation*?" A deep knowledge of the customer base, understanding customer expectations and managing the process are critical elements to success.

Low-cost is a valid business model; it is not a reason or excuse for poor passenger experience. People flying low-cost carriers expect less by default. Less compared to full-service carriers, even though many of them now charge extra for baggage, seat selection and meals. While many customers view low-cost equates to poor passenger experience, it is not necessarily the case since customer expectations are not the same.

For example, consider Ryanair, an LCC that also happens to be the largest airline in Europe. Customer experience may leave much to be desired for a seasoned traveler on full-service carriers. But the Ryanair customer base is very different—budget conscious travelers whose customer expectations may be marginal at best. Ryanair flew 182 million passengers in 2023, a feat that was possible despite the customer experience because the customer service bar is much lower. Within the LCC model it is value for money.

For full-service carriers, the bar for customer service is much higher, established and reinforced over many years. With FSCs it is value for experience.

1.13 A New Era in Airline Marketing Planning

Low-cost carriers (LCC) pioneered the sale of ancillary products and services. A trademark of LCCs is to offer cheap fares to destinations, but require travelers to pay for seat selection, checked baggage, agent-assisted check-in, in-flight meals, and many more. The rise in affordable travel options provided by budget airlines has led to a boost in the utilization of additional services. Many budget airlines provide inexpensive tickets to various destinations but mandate that passengers cover all additional expenses, such as baggage fees, seat selection, and in-flight meals.

When jet fuel prices soared in 2008, ancillary products were introduced by full-service carriers when American Airlines started charging a $15 fee for checked baggage. Since then, passengers have slowly adapted to the idea of paying for ancillaries. Today's passengers are willing to pay for ancillaries.

In this new era with NDC adoption by the full-service carriers (FSC), marketing planning takes on a new perspective that is no longer one dimensional, but multi-dimensional and the dimensions are dictated by the number of unique customers, customer groups and individual customers that the airline is planning on engaging with actively to grow the business, retain customers, and address profitability. The significance of loyalty programs and the business processes to retain and grow profitable customers has grown in stature,

The era where a market message or product recommendation is applicable to the entire population is over.

1.13.1 All Customers are not Created Equal

Revenue management works on the fundamental premise that *not all customers are created equal.* This is because there are various fare products that suit the needs of different types of customers such as business, leisure, visiting friends and relatives, combined business, and leisure travel ("bleisure") etc. This paradigm also extends to ancillary products and services. Airlines provide perks to frequent flyer members in the upper tiers such as free check-in bags, pre-reserved seats in premium economy and access to the airline lounge for international travel.

1.13.2 Customer Segmentation

Customer segmentation takes on a new meaning in the age of airline retailing. Statistical and machine learning methods to define customer segments are never perfect. They frequently require user adjustments, and continuous review and recalibration for a variety of reasons such as brand affinity, competitive landscape, advances in technology and changing consumer attitudes.

A key ability to effectively use revenue management techniques to maximize revenues is to segment passengers based on their needs, business constraints, passenger characteristics and willingness to pay (WTP). The WTP is defined as the maximum amount a customer is willing to pay for a good or service. *The right price is the highest price the customer will pay for a product.*

The WTP distribution represents the probability density of individual maximum prices across customers and represents a customer characteristic. The price response function represents the total quantity sold at a given price p and represents the behavioral output.

The probability that a customer purchases a product at price p is the probability that the WTP is greater than or equal to p.

$$P(purchase) = P(WTP \geq p) = 1 - F(p)$$

Where *F(p)* is the cumulative density function of the WTP in the market.

1.13.2.1 Historical Perspective

GDS pioneers Robert Crandall and Max Hopper played critical roles that led to the launch of the first GDS, Sabre, in 1976 by American Airlines, that allowed travel agents to make automated airline bookings for the first time.

Since the creation of the GDS in 1976 and revenue management in the 1980s, customer segmentation has relied on booking classes, which airlines use to distribute availability to Global Distribution Systems. Booking classes are represented by a letter of the alphabet from A to Z and identify different categories of tickets sold by an airline. The booking class provides information on what type of fare a traveler purchased. Airline revenue management analysts use booking classes to control how many seats can be sold at a particular fare level. Of the 26 booking classes, all but two are distributed to indirect channels. Booking classes were originally defined by IATA but standardization failed and booking classes today are airline specific. So, the same code, e.g. K booking class may have different meanings for tickets issued by different airlines. A K class for one airline may be a 7-day advance purchase fare while it is a 14-day advance purchase fare for a different carrier. Some booking classes like F. C, and Y have retained the same meaning across airlines for decades.

Up to 26 booking classes (e.g., F, C, J, Y, B, …) are used to control seat inventory except for two booking classes that are used for internal purposes such as employee travel and discreet sales outlets, are distributed externally to indirect channels.

A common problem that needs to be addressed periodically is realignment of fare basis codes that are mapped to booking classes. This is required to avoid fare overlaps in a market between booking classes. This can cause fare inversions and revenue dilution. These overlaps occur when the fare management analysts file fares in markets without reviewing the true range of fares associated with each booking class. The fare realignment process is a rather tedious process and is undertaken only every two or three years since the clean-up can take anywhere from 3 months to 6 months for a mid-size or large carrier. Figure 1.6 illustrates the fare ranges by booking class before and after the realignment (refiling of fares) process.

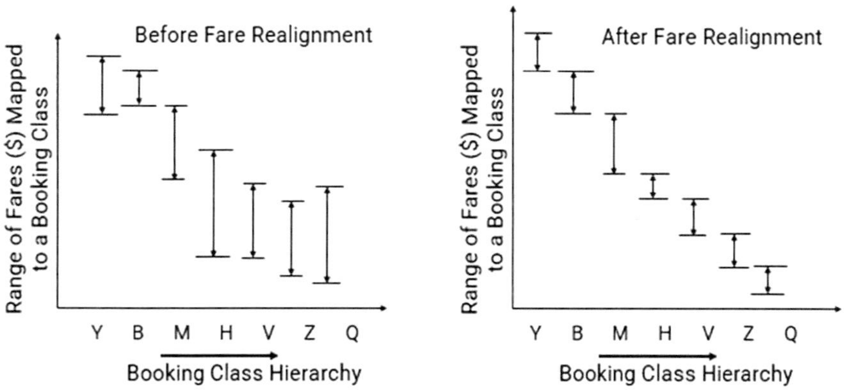

Fig. 1.6 Fare realignment process

This paradigm does not change with branded products since booking classes are still mapped to the branded fare products. However, it spawns several new requirements for reservations processing, revenue management and distribution. They are:

1. Ability to maintain booking counts by branded products in real-time to display availability by branded product.
2. Support the display of availability by branded product through both the consumer direct web site and the GDS. The marketing objective of airlines is to have a travel agent describe the branded products to customers when a selection is being made.
3. While individual booking classes are still mapped to a branded product, the display of availability should indicate if the branded product (e.g., premium economy) is available and at what price.
4. Modeling the actual consumer demand process requires a top-down approach to first forecasting demand for the branded fare products followed with a forecast for booking classes mapped to the branded fare product.

1.13.2.2 Customer Segmentation based on Customer Lifetime Value

Customer segmentation based on Customer Lifetime Value (*CLV*) or remaining *CLV* has many applications. For example, an airline can run a promotion for frequent flyer customers that have not flown on an airline for a specified period of time. In this scenario, the data is first segmented to only include frequent flyers that have not flown for a specific period, e.g., 12 months. Next, these customers can be clustered by *CLV* based on value and specific *CLV* tiers can be selected for the promotional campaign to achieve the desired marketing objective of generating incremental bookings by providing incentives for these target customers to fly. Ultimately, the airline focus is on Future Customer Value, which is the net present value of a customer based on projections of future revenue and costs over the duration of their relationship.

The ultimate objective of loyalty customer analytics is to estimate the customer's share of wallet (*SOW*) which is challenging. Measuring *SOW* involves calculating the percentage of a customer's total travel spend on your airline versus competitors. It is expressed as a percentage by dividing the total amount a customer spends with an airline by their total spend across all competitors multiplied by 100. A higher percentage indicates greater brand loyalty and market share.

SOW is difficult to estimate and requires survey data where survey participants are asked to estimate the percentage of their travel budget they spend with a specific airline. Surveys must include a customer ranking of competitors to infer the *SOW*.

1.13.2.3 Recency, Frequency, Monetary, Variety, Tenure

An alternative to *CLV* that is used in retail by Customer Relationship Management (CRM) software is based on *RFMVT*. The analytics for *RFMVT* focuses on five

Table 1.1. RFMVT segmentation definition

Measure	Description of measure
Recency (R)	The length of time in days since the customer made a purchase.
Frequency (F)	The number of times the customer has visited the storefront and made a purchase.
Monetary (M)	The total dollars spent by the customer on all visits combined.
Variety (V)	The number of distinct purchases by the customer in all visits.
Tenure (T)	Number of days since the first purchase.

essential dimensions– Recency (R), Frequency (F), Monetary value (M), Variety (V), and Tenure (T). All *RFMVT* metrics are compared to a specific customer and measurement timeframe (week, month, quarter, etc.).

Table 1.1 describes the *RFMVT* measures.

Adapting the *RFMVT* approach in the airline industry to account for variety (V) involves considering the number of different trip-purpose segments that a customer was assigned to for past purchases. *RFM* segmentation is the most used level of segmentation. This type of segmentation can be utilized for targeting promotional offers, analyzing market penetration, and evaluating profitability. To enhance the *RFM* segmentation and effectively summarize customer data, it is important to address the issue of "clumpiness" which arises from intermittent purchases made by customers. Zhang, Bradlow, and Small (2015) argue that although statistical models based on *RFM* summaries may perform well at an aggregate level, they can lead to significant prediction errors when ranking customers at a micro-level unless the concept of "clumpiness" is properly accounted for.

There is a large body of research on *CLV* prediction and *RFM* segmentation and detailed treatment is beyond the scope of this book.

1.13.2.4 Context for Travel based Segmentation

While RBD and *CLV* based customer segmentation has its merits, in the world of airline retailing and offer management, the context for making a trip influences a customer's preferences and propensity to buy. Even information stored on the customer profile is inadequate because a typical customer may have multiple profiles based on the context for travel such as a short business trip, a long business trip, a weekend getaway with a spouse, a family vacation, or an extended stay to visit friends and relatives. Airline retailing calls for creating personalized offers and it begins with context for travel-based segmentation of the customer base. This is a core input into a recommendation engine to generate offers that resonate with customers. Most online users are anonymous when they begin their search for a flight or a hotel room, yet the offers generated should be relevant. Once the person is declared, historical bookings associated with the customer that are stored on the customer profile can be used to improve the offer recommendation and even recommend a discount for the total offer based on a customer's projected lifetime value.

The context for travel-based segmentation to cluster customers together with similar preferences and generate an aggregate offer is foundational to airline offer management. It is the single most important concept for effective offer management. The definition of customer segments must be periodically reviewed to determine if adjustments are required based on market conditions, consumer trends and changes in consumer behavior.

Personalized offers and dynamic pricing continue to be an active area of research by both academia and industry [Belobaba, 2019; Szymanski et al., 2021; Wang, Wittman and Bockelie, 2021; Sznajder, Ratliff and Kaya,, 2023a, 2023b; Wang et al., 2023].

1.13.2.5 The Central Role of Loyalty Programs

Loyalty programs have become the lifeline for the airline industry. Loyalty revenue serves as a significant competitive advantage. To put the power of loyalty programs in perspective, if customers only fly once a year, airlines can still keep in touch with them all year. They achieve this through partner programs, co-branded credit cards, digital wallets, and marketplace platforms to purchase goods and services. Banks that back airline credit cards purchase miles from airlines to distribute to their customers. Loyalty programs became a key source of income as airline passenger revenue dropped to record lows during the 2020 pandemic.

At the start of the COVID-19 crisis, securing funding became critical. Airlines saw a 90% drop in passengers, leading to huge financial losses. The industry faced potential collapse and needed to reorganize its debt. Traditionally, airlines used their aircraft, gates, and other assets as collateral. However, in 2020, for the first time, U.S. airlines used future earnings from their loyalty programs as collateral to obtain billions in loans. Revenue from these programs was crucial in helping the industry stabilize during the worst of the crisis. For the four biggest airlines in the United States: United Airlines, Delta Air Lines, American Airlines, and Southwest Airlines, loyalty revenue made up 22% of their total income at the height of the pandemic in the second quarter of 2020. Loyalty programs have become critical high-margin assets for airlines with global ancillary and loyalty revenue averaging 14%–15% of total airline income. U.S. network carriers report that loyalty contributions exceed 7% of their total operating revenue.

1.13.2.6 Airline Retailing and Personalization

How feasible is personalization of the offer for an individual traveler, a segment of ONE? For example, consider full-service carriers (FSC) in the U.S. like American and United that have stated that over 50% of an airline's revenue came from 85% to 87% of its customers who flew only once. This also means that for FSCs, true 1:1 personalization is limited to loyal business flyers and high-end leisure travelers that are part of the 13%–15% of customers who generate half the airline's revenues. The importance of retaining customers who spend the most money cannot be understated, while the airline maintains a positive relationship with the rest of the customer base.

Another factor is the enactment of the General Data Protection Regulation (GDPR) in 2018. This regulation grants EU citizens authority over their data, including what is gathered and how it is utilized. Under GDPR, approaches that utilize aggregate data rather than specific personal data become more significant. This suggests that personalization might be restricted to generating offers at the trip-purpose segment level rather than for individuals.

The California Consumer Privacy Act (CCPA) of 2018, like GDPR, is a state law designed to provide California residents with greater authority over their personal information gathered by businesses. Legislative measures aimed at safeguarding consumer privacy are influencing developments in digital advertising and personalization. This leads us to the topic of personal identity and its management.

1.13.3 Customer Centric Marketing and Sales Operations

Fundamental to an airline becoming a retailer is the mandatory requirement to reorganize the marketing and sales organizations around customer segments to transition to a customer centric mindset.

Customer centric marketing must be focused on the customer segments based on their needs and preferences. Inferences from transaction data on customer behavior is a first step to execute promotions and campaigns. Predictive analytics can be supplemented with survey data to continually augment the attitudinal aspects of each customer segment to shape marketing programs,

Customer centric sales is required to nurture and deliver a great customer experience. Airlines that adopt this framework for marketing and sales will realize incremental revenues from the retailing initiatives.

1.13.4 Customer Centric Availability and Customer Centric Pricing

Over the past two decades, much has been discussed about customer centric availability and pricing for an airline's most valued passengers. However, airlines have never implemented this capability since it dilutes revenues. Calculating a customer's *CLV* and remaining *CLV* are important for airlines to run promotions and engage with loyal customers. The same is true with lucrative corporate customers. Corporate customers receive discounts off the selling fare based on the negotiated contracts between an airline and a corporation. However, availability is controlled centrally in the airline reservations system by booking class. When a booking class, say B class, is closed for sale, no customers can access and book B class fares. This should not be confused with special limited time offers made by airlines to loyalty members. These exclusive fares are not available through the GDSs, and are not capacity controlled by the airline.

The new world of dynamic continuous pricing can theoretically produce a different itinerary price on the price demand curve for each booking request. That is because dynamic pricing is attempting to fill the gaps on the price demand curve that existed with RBDs and less with customer centric pricing for a valued customer.

1.13.5 Customer Centric Organization

Making airline retailing a priority and a reality will require a major transformation of the organization. A customer-centric organization will require individuals in the organization that are responsible for every customer segment that is targeted for sales. This requires a rethinking of the siloed organizations that exist today.

1.14 Consumer Protection Measures from the Department of Transportation

The U.S. is well behind other countries with regard to consumer rights and protections for travelers. The Department of Transportation's (DOT) rules under President Joe Biden's Secretary of Transportation Pete Buttigieg were a concerted effort to address passenger rights in the U.S.

In 2022, the Department of Transportation (DOT) started the first-ever rule-making process in U.S. history that would oblige airlines to reimburse passengers and address specific costs for delays and cancellations within their control. FlightRights.gov, an enhanced DOT platform was introduced in the summer of 2022 to enforce passenger rights. The data revealed that only a small number of airlines offered compensation for delays or cancellations caused by operational issues that are the responsibility of the airline.

To augment customer protection, the DOT under the Biden Administration required sellers of airline tickets who are the merchants of record to disclose extra fees upfront. This applies to airlines, and intermediaries such as metasearch sites, GDSs, and OTAs to disclose additional charges upfront when an airfare is first displayed, such as baggage fees for checked or carry-on bags, change fees, cancellation fees, and seating fees for flights from, to, and within the U.S. This ensures that travelers are not surprised with hidden fees that can add up quickly. Further the DOT requires airlines to refund passengers for ancillary services they paid for that were not provided by the airline, such as malfunctioning Wi-Fi.

In April 2024, the DOT issued two final rules related to airline refunds and ancillary fees [DOT, 2024b; Airoldi, 2024d]. These rules went into effect on October 28, 2024. The refund rule outlines when and how airlines must issue refunds. Additionally, the ancillary fee rule requires airlines and ticket agents to clearly inform customers about fees for checking bags, carry-on luggage, and any charges for canceling or changing a reservation.

1.14.1 The Refund Rule

The refund rule requires airlines to provide passengers with automatic cash refunds, without the passenger having to request repayment, when owed. This was a "significant change" since airlines could not set their own rules for refunds. Further the new ruling required an actual refund to the original form of payment and not vouchers, travel credits or other forms of compensation. Further, the refunds must be issued within seven days for credit card purchases and 20 days for other forms of payment such as debit, check, or cash sales.

The new DOT rules are applicable for both advanced schedule changes and irregular operations. The refunds are applicable in the following scenarios:

1. A flight is canceled.
2. Delayed departure or arrival times exceeding 3 hours for domestic flights and 6 hours for international flights.
3. Baggage delivered over 12 hours late on domestic flights and 15 – 30 hours for international flights depending on the duration of the flight.
4. Departures or arrivals from alternate airports
5. More connections than the original schedule
6. Connections from alternate airports
7. Passenger downgrades to a lower class of service
8. Change of gauge (change of aircraft at a connecting point when the ticket was sold as all travel on the same flight number)
9. Less accessible service for people with disabilities
10. When extra services paid for are not provided, such as Wi-Fi, seat selection or in-flight entertainment.

Airlines and travel agencies are required to give full refunds for the ticket price, subtracting the value of any travel that has already taken place. This refund must also include all taxes and fees imposed by the government, as well as any fees charged by the airline (YQ/YR).

1.14.2 Ancillary Fee Rule

The ancillary fee rule ensures transparency when a ticket is being purchased through a travel agency or directly from an airline. This rule requires airlines and travel agencies to disclose the full airfare, which is the price of the airline ticket and all carrier-imposed and government charges. The new regulation mandates that airlines and ticket agents must reveal any extra fees clearly alongside the total fare. Airlines are also required to share all fee information with companies that need to provide it. Each fee must be openly displayed on the airline's website without using hyperlinks, according to the DOT. Additionally, when giving a fare quote, agencies must inform customers about these fees. For baggage fees, airlines and travel agencies need to clarify each type of fee and outline the weight and size limits. They must also explain any rules regarding changes or cancellations, including how fare differences are handled.

Airlines and travel agencies are required to inform customers that they are guaranteed a seat without needing to pay extra for it. Customers who qualify for discounts or waived fees, including loyalty program members, specific credit card holders, or military personnel, can choose to receive details about their fees or be given the standard fee information.

1.14.3 Impact on Travel Agencies

As of October 2024, travel agencies that are the merchants of record are responsible for refunds when flights (to, from or within the U.S.) are canceled or undergo a "significant change" [Pestronk, 2024]. If the agency processes payments as the merchant of record directly showing its name on the consumer's credit card statement, it is responsible for issuing the refund.

The DOT defines the merchant of record as the entity that handles consumer payments for airfare, as reflected on their financial statements from debit or credit card transactions. In simple terms, if a ticket charge appears on an agency's credit card merchant account, that agency is considered the merchant of record. However, this extends beyond the debit card or credit card merchant. For transactions made with methods other than credit or debit cards, the receipt given to customers must identify the entity responsible. Specifically, if a customer buys a ticket using cash or a check, the organization that provided the receipt is accountable for processing refunds. Hence, if a client pays the agency with a check, cash, or bank transfer and the agency provides a receipt, the agency is considered the merchant of record. While most payments for tickets are made by credit card through the carrier, which serves as the merchant of record, it is common for agencies to accept checks, especially for tours, FITs (Flexible Independent Travel), consolidator fares, and meetings or incentive travel.

If a travel agency needs to issue a refund because it is considered the merchant of record, it must proceed with the refund even if the agency no longer has the client's funds or if the airline does not reimburse the agency. The DOT did not specify when or if the airline should pay the agency back in its April guidelines. However, in August 2024, the DOT updated its rules to protect travel agencies that must give refunds for "significant change", even if they do not have the client's funds anymore. The DOT mandates that airlines must "quickly" send the necessary funds to the travel agency for disbursement of funds.

The travel agency has specific deadlines for processing refunds. For credit card transactions, refunds are issued within seven days after the carrier notifies the agency. For sales made with debit, checks, or cash, refunds are processed within 20 days of the notification.

A positive aspect is that if a refund is due to the client, the agency can offer a credit or voucher instead, if the agency notifies the client of their right to a refund first. The voucher or credit must be valid for at least five years, and all restrictions should be clearly explained.

1.14.4 The Downside for Customers with the New DOT Rules

The new DOT policy that was established in April 2024 went into effect in October 2024. The DOT ruling on refunds and ancillaries standardizes the entire process, which was previously dictated by airlines, and they were never uniformly the same. While this new policy is good for most travelers there are a few downsides.

The definition of a "significant delay" has helped airlines like United, Delta and Jet Blue whose previous cutoff for refunds was 2 hours before the ruling. Now they will adhere to the DOT standard definition of 3 hours for domestic flights. It also brings American Airlines, which required a schedule change of 4+ hours to qualify for a refund, in line with the new DOT policy.

Refunds in some situations require interpretation by the airline, which could be unfair to customers. While a refund is required for a cabin downgrade, it is not clear if a downgrade from extra leg room to standard leg room in the same cabin qualifies for a refund? The refunds are applicable only after flight departure, even if the schedule change was made several months before flight departure.

In situations where an outbound flight is cancelled and the return flight is not, travelers must get in touch with the airline quickly before the refund goes into effect to ensure that the entire ticket is not cancelled.

If a traveler wants to keep a credit for future use instead of receiving a refund, this option is no longer available if the traveler is not the same person who paid for the ticket. Now, the traveler must either make changes in advance or accept a refund.

A related issue is the inherent complexity in displaying the new ancillary product rules from DOT in the booking path. The display can overwhelm customers with too many details which can lead to confusion. Clarity of displays in the booking path is critical for improving conversion rates.

1.14.5 Proposed Passenger Compensation Rule

The Trump Administration withdrew a rule proposed in December 2024 by the US DOT, requiring airlines to compensate customers for flight delays as follows:

1. Domestic delays of 3-6 hours: $200–$300
2. 6-9 hour delays: $375–$525
3. 9+ hour delays: $750–$775

The A4A (Airlines for America) trade group which advocates on behalf of its members to shape crucial policies had supported the decision to withdraw the compensation rule, arguing it would raise costs and lead to higher ticket prices for consumers

1.15 The Montreal Convention

The Montreal Convention of 1999 (MC99) sets rules for airline responsibility when passengers are injured or killed. It also covers cases of delayed, damaged, or lost baggage and cargo. This treaty brings together various international agreements on airline liability that emerged since 1929 (The Warsaw Convention of 1929). MC99 aims to create one clear set of guidelines that apply to airline liability worldwide.

MC99 established rules for airline liability for international air travel. It imparts rights to the traveling public and applies to international flights between nations that honor the EU's EC261 regulation.

1.16 Navigating the Future of Low-Cost Carriers

Pacific Southwest Airlines is considered the first low-cost airline, starting intrastate flights in Northern California on May 6, 1949. However, Southwest Airlines is considered the first major airline to adopt the modern low-cost business model when they launched their operations out of Dallas Love Field in 1971.

People Express Airlines, stylized as PEOPLExpress, was a low-cost airline based out of Newark's Liberty International Airport in New Jersey. It posed a major threat to U.S. full-service carriers (FSC) with its ultra-low fares. FSC's like American Airlines countered the threat by matching the low fares and implementing yield management to capacity control the sale of cheap tickets. Its inability to capacity-control the cheap tickets and uncontrolled expansion led to bankruptcy and it eventually merged with Frank Lorenzo's Continental Airlines in 1987.

For decades, full-service airlines that operated out of London's Heathrow airport operated a virtual monopoly until they were challenged by Sir Freddie Laker's budget Skytrain flights to the U.S. In the 1990s easyJet and Ryanair were the new budget pioneers. Laker Airways took flight in 1977 but faced intensive pressure from the FSC's that served the market, filed for bankruptcy in 1982.

Asia has witnessed explosive growth in LCCs since the millennium. AirAsia, based in Malaysia is a dominant LCC in the region. Other major LCCs in the region are Tiger Airways in Singapore and Jetstar in Australia that is owned by Qantas Airways.

The low-cost airline sector is growing rapidly. This growth is driven by the increasing popularity of short-haul flights and a higher demand for domestic travel. Figure 1.7 illustrates the growth in LCC market share and Figure 1.8 illustrates the LCC penetration by region.

Before the COVID-19 pandemic, leisure travel was expanding faster than business travel in many places. From 2010 to 2019, leisure air travel grew at an annual rate of 6.6 percent, compared to just 3.3 percent for business air travel based on

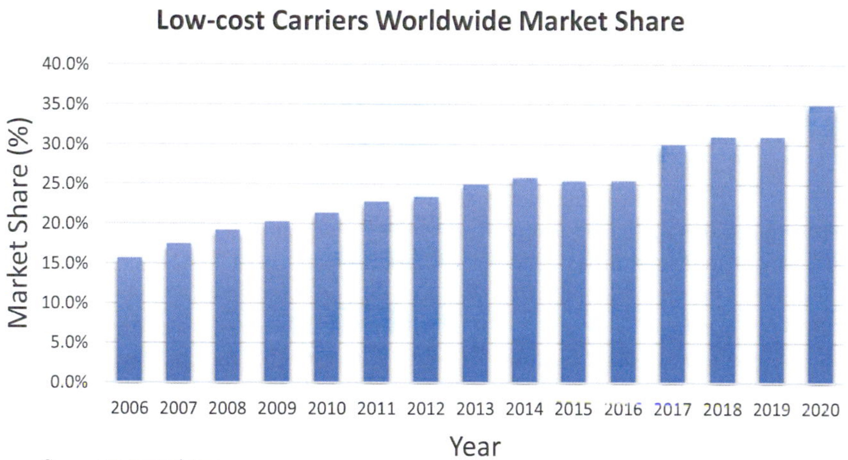

Source www.statista.com

Fig. 1.7. Growth in Worldwide Market Share of LCCs

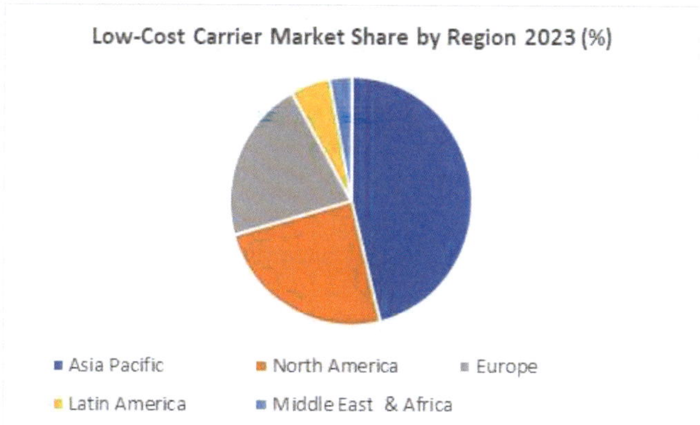

Source https://www.precedenceresearch.com/low-cost-carrier-market

Fig. 1.8. Low-cost Carrier Market Share by Region

data from corporate and leisure travel agencies [McKinsey and Company, 2024]. This gap has widened even more during the recovery from the pandemic. As travel demand picks up again after the standstill in 2020, leisure travel, which makes up a larger portion, has bounced back more swiftly than business travel in key regions, such as the United States. Since the COVID-19 pandemic, business travel was slow to rebound and did not reach 2019 pre-pandemic levels until the fourth quarter of 2024, In the meantime, leisure traffic has grown at a faster rate promoting growth in low-cost carrier traffic.

Ultra-low-cost carriers (ULCC) represent a distinct segment of the airline industry, primarily targeting budget-conscious travelers, especially those on leisure trips. These airlines operate under a business model that emphasizes low prices, with marketing strategies focused on offering significantly lower airfares compared to traditional legacy carriers. ULCCs provide unbundled fares, meaning essential services such as seat assignments, check-in, carry-on baggage, and in-flight meals are not included in the base fare. Passengers have the option to pay for these services separately, allowing them to tailor their travel according to personal preferences and financial considerations. A major difference between ULCCs and traditional LCCs is their minimalist approach. While both types aim for cost savings, ULCCs go further by including fewer services in their base fare and charging additional fees for optional features. Furthermore, ULCCs prioritize direct online sales and do not engage with the indirect Global Distribution System (GDS) channels.

Today's LCCs and ULCCs have viable and sustainable business models, accounting for more than 30 percent of industry capacity (Fig. 1.7) since 2017.

But what is the road ahead for LCCs and ULCCs? Critics argue that they have a tough road ahead,

Besides Southwest Airlines, the major LCCs in the U.S. are Allegiant Air, Avelo Airlines, Breeze Airways, Frontier Airlines, and Sun Country Airlines. Spirit Airlines ceased operations on May 2, 2026, following a failed federal bailout attempt and financial pressure from rising fuel costs. There are over 100 LCCs worldwide. The distribution of LCCs by region is summarized in Fig. 1.8.

1.16.1 LCCs versus FSCs

There are significant differences in the operating model between full-service carriers and low-cost carriers.

Full-service carriers (FSC), which are also referred to as legacy carriers, offer a range of service classes (first, business, coach), loyalty programs, operate hub and spoke [Peterson, 1986] connection networks, grant access to exclusive lounges for top-tier customers, provide on-board catering, baggage allowance, in-flight entertainment, and various other amenities. FSCs periodically depeak operations at hub airports to reduce stress and improve on time performance. Depeaking increases the number of arrival-departure banks by spreading out the flights throughout the day. Additionally, they primarily operate from major airports rather than secondary airports. FSCs recognize the importance of corporate clients and actively participate in the GDSs.

Most low-cost carriers (LCCs) primarily offer point-to-point direct flights and operate in a no-frills setting with only one class of service (coach). They typically depart from and arrive at secondary airports, which have lower landing fees. LCCs focus on selling additional services, having fewer comfort amenities, minimal loyalty programs, and prioritize online sales directly to consumers. Historically, they have not participated in the GDSs.

1.16.2 Changes in the Airline Distribution Landscape

An area where LCCs are converging with the FSCs is product distribution. The consumer direct channel serves as the primary way to book an airline seat. Advances in technology and hosting services have made it easier for LCCs, whose primary segment is the leisure traveler, to bypass the GDS and travel agencies in favor of direct distribution to lower the cost of customer acquisition. It is uncommon for most LCCs to participate in the GDSs, but this is changing. For example, to attract corporate customers, Jet Blue returned to all GDSs in 2006 [Aviation Week, 2006].

Today, many LCCs participate in at least one GDS. With the emergence of NDC and expanded capabilities of direct bookings, the GDSs have a renewed focus and offer connectivity to LCCs. Hence for a shopping request, a GDS can retrieve LCC content, NDC content and traditional GDS (EDIFACT) content. A content curation layer normalizes the content for display to travel agents.

Many LCCs participate in Travelport (Galileo GDS, the converged platform) as instant purchase. Thus allows for instant booking, where the traveler's itinerary is priced and confirmed immediately.

Amadeus, based on its strength in hosting over 60 budget airlines in the Navitaire reservations system offers multiple methods for booking a ticket for LCCs. They are the standard E-Ticket (IATA standard), e-ticket (non-IATA, instant ticketing, no APTCO) and ticketless booking (requires credit card instead of issuing a ticket).

Sabre actively promotes its multi-source access (NDC, LCC and traditional GDS) in one marketplace.

Many LCCs are also pursuing the NDC path. Examples are Flydubai, Norwegian Air Shuttle and WestJet. They either pursue these initiatives independently or in partnership with vendors like Accelya (Farelogix).

1.16.3 Are the LCCs Under Threat From the FSCs?

The LCCs unique position in the market has been rapidly eroding. Full-service carriers (FSC) compete head-on with the LCCs in competitive markets with their Basic Economy fare. With this, FSCs can capture the ultra-price-sensitive leisure passengers and give them the added benefits that are not offered by LCCs. Consolidation of network carriers over the past two decades has also helped them to compete effectively with the LCCs. However, consolidation has been at the expense of corporate buyers who lose negotiating power leading to lower corporate discounts and higher fares. Key mergers include Air France / KLM in 2004, America West Airlines / US Airways in 2005, Delta Air Lines / Northwest Airlines in 2008, United Airlines / Continental Airlines in 2010, Southwest Airlines / Air Tran Airways in 2011, American Airlines / US Airways in 2013, Alaska Airlines / Virgin America in 2018 and Alaska Airlines / Hawaiian Airlines in 2024.

1.16.3.1 Southwest Airlines Under Scrutiny

In July 2024, Southwest Airlines shocked travelers [Southwest Airlines Investor Relations, 2024] by confirming its plans to abandon its open seating policy and introduce more leg room in the front section of the aircraft, breaking their famous policy since they came into existence in 1971 with low-cost air travel at Dallas Love Field. This is a fundamental change that goes into effect for flights departing after January 27, 2026. Southwest is following the network carriers to attract business class passengers. Southwest also claimed that 80% of its customers, and 86% of potential customers, prefer an assigned seat. If that is the case, why did it take so long to initiate change? Southwest has always been slow to adapt to changes in the marketplace. A case in point is the legacy Southwest reservations system (SAAS – Southwest Airlines Automated System) that was used for many decades without core CRS functions such as dynamic schedules to build itineraries on request, codeshare, and interline capabilities, before they eventually migrated to Amadeus' Altéa reservations system in May 2017.

Another big change is "Two Bags Fly Free", which was so sacred that the airline trademarked the phrase. Southwest Airlines ended its most recognizable perk and began charging for the first and second checked back from May 28, 2025. While a free checked bag will still be a perk for travelers with loyalty status (Rapid Rewards A-List Preferred members), customers traveling on Business Select fares, and affiliate credit card holders. The rest will have to pay for the very first time.

There are significant changes on the distribution landscape as well. Abandoning its focus on direct distribution, in 2024, Southwest began displaying its fares on Google Flights and Kayak. Southwest signed a deal with Expedia in February 2025, that allows online customers to purchase Southwest tickets via Expedia and its affiliated platforms, like Travelocity, Orbitz, and Hotwire.

In November 2025, Southwest joined the Hahnair Network with an interline agreement. The Hahnair Network, based in Germany, connects 350 airlines to 100,000 travel agencies in 190 markets worldwide. The agreement enables agents to book Southwest Airlines flights under the WN code in the Amadeus GDS and issue tickets on Hahnair's HR-169 ticket stock.

Southwest also introduced redeye (overnight) flights in 2025. Pre-reserved seat assignment, and premium leg room are planned for 2026.

Southwest is under pressure to improve its financial performance. Now that its fares appear next to those of rivals in online search and booking tools, its bundled fares haven't been measuring up. Its culture took a hit when the company announced its first layoffs in February 2025. Absence of a recession, these changes are expected to cut costs and raise revenue rapidly.

Southwest was an undervalued stock and activist hedge fund investor Elliott Investment Management with a 10% stake in Southwest Airlines influenced several changes. Former CEO Gary Kelly retired as part of the reorganization. In addition, several new board members were appointed in late 2024.

With these moves to emulate full-service carriers, Southwest is trying to attract more profitable customers. However, it comes with a significant risk since Southwest lacks key benefits like first class, airport lounges, and worldwide rewards.

This makes Southwest less appealing to both high-end and low-end travelers. Southwest's Basic Economy fares match competitors, offering no extra value. Unless it has a better schedule, there is no reason to choose Southwest. Southwest's growth has stalled. Every airline, including budget carriers, can now easily compete with it.

1.16.3.2 Will the LCC Model Converge with the FSC Model?

Make no mistake, travelers are creatures of comfort. They love to acquire frequent flyer miles for future travel and enjoy the perks provided by full-service carriers. But this does not mean that the LCC model will converge with the FSC model. Startup LCCs and ULCCs will always thrive in regional markets. It is the existing LCCs and ULCCs that have grown in size that are in a quandary and they will continue to adopt FSC features to retain their customer base.

In September 2024 JetBlue announced that it would open its first airport lounges in NYC and Boston to compete with the FSCs for business travelers [Jet Blue, 2024]. The lounges are for the top tier TrueBlue loyalty members. While this was a step forward, Jet Blue also took a step backward to reduce costs by stopping hot meals in economy class on transatlantic flights starting October 1, 2024.

In December 2024, Frontier Airlines announced that they would be adding "first class seating" in 2025 using the phrase "affordable luxury". This will provide 2 rows of 2 x 2 seating on their narrowbody aircraft.

Another example is Spirit Airlines that filed for bankruptcy twice in less than a year (November 2024 and August 2025). While Spirit continued its restructuring under Chapter 11 as an independent company, the airline's strategy relied on increasing revenue by offering more premium products and services. This included cabin sections with extra legroom and free Wi-Fi for customers who pay higher fares. Their business model included bundled fares with premium options like "Spirit First" (formerly Big Front Seat) and "Premium Economy" to meet changing consumer preferences. Spirit Airlines ceased operations on May 2, 2026, following a failed federal bailout.

Decades ago, airline executives and industry analysts has predicted that "low-cost" and "loyalty" were an impossible combination. But today, loyalty is now firmly embraced by LCCs. Even though Ryanair, easyJet and Wizz Air do not have a loyalty program, 14 of the 20 largest low-cost carriers have implemented a loyalty program [Ideaworks, 2024a]. For example, in August 2025, IndiGo, India's largest airline by market share and fleet size, launched the IndiGo BluChip loyalty program to reward frequent flyers and foster customer loyalty.

Based on this anecdotal evidence, many wonder if the LCC model will converge with the FSC model with all the customer perks. That is unlikely since there are over 100 LCCs worldwide and many of them serve niche markets. But there is a strong likelihood that when an airline reaches critical mass, it will offer some if not all the perks offered by the FSCs.

1.17 The Value Proposition of Airline Retailing

McKinsey and IATA estimate that the potential for airline retailing may realize up to $40 billion in new value annually or $7 per passenger [Bois et al., 2019]. A key question is how are ancillary products and services priced in the market? Pricing ancillary products is just as important as pricing the itinerary. This is because higher prices for ancillary products and services reduce the propensity to buy and simultaneously lower the customer's willingness to pay for the base product, the itinerary. Airlines view the sale of ancillaries to extract a surplus from frequent travelers of the base product, the air itinerary. This assumes that uniform products are positively correlated with the frequency of bookings made by travelers. This may not be true. Price discrimination required market power which is less relevant to airlines in competitive markets.

An airline's success in retailing is by no means guaranteed and requires an effective strategy followed with a tactical execution plan. Beginning with the airline CEO, a task force must be created to make decisions on the biggest investments, the most important customer segments to go after, brand positioning, and customer value.

The cost of providing these ancillary services can outweigh the benefits with inefficient business processes. The organization must be structured to deliver on an airline's omnichannel strategy. Consistency is required when dealing with the most valued customers, whether they interact with the airline website, a travel agent, a tour operator, a mobile app, or a social network. Success will also require the fundamental restructuring of key organizations such as customer service, loyalty program, airline pricing, revenue management, and product distribution that is directly focused on actively addressing the needs of the various customer segments that are deemed important. An important part of this transformation is monitoring metrics for the organization at various levels starting with the customer segments that the airline wants to serve. For this to work there must be a process to identify every sales transaction and map it to a customer segment. Sales, channel, and customer satisfaction focused metrics need to be introduced to measure organizational effectiveness and enforce competition within the organization as they attempt to improve their respective metrics such as sales volume at the expense of the others that serve other customer segments.

1.18 Innovation for Competitive Advantage

Innovation is a necessity, rather than a luxury for an airline to gain a competitive edge by enhancing customer experience, improving operational efficiency, adapting to rapidly changing consumer preferences and adapting to changes in technology. By leveraging big data analytics, digital transformation, and emerging technologies like artificial intelligence, machine learning, and natural language processing, customer journeys can be personalized to enhance customer experience.

Natural language search for flights to understand a request described in plain language, such as *"a week-long summer trip to a city with great food, nonstop only,"* to find relevant flight options. These tools are already on the market today, such as Flight Deals by Google Flights. Natural language processing understands the nuances of a traveler's request, such as *"good hiking"* or *"not too costly,"* and uses it to identify matching destinations and flights. Natural language search must be adopted on airline websites to allow users to bypass traditional search filters and get results based on preferences like desired experience, flexibility, or travel style.

Advances in Agentic AI, artificial intelligence digital workers that can autonomously plan, perform complex tasks, learn from data, make decisions, and self-correct to provide highly personalized and seamless travel experiences, from trip planning and booking to real-time assistance during travel and efficient management of travel operations is a game changer. It is no longer AI Assistants helping humans, but AI Agents acting on their behalf. The ability to learn continuously from user preferences, real-time customer interactions, and competitive marketplace conditions tp offer proactive recommendations, automated itinerary adjustments, and instant customer support adds a new dimension to the revenue management process. In addition, focusing on sustainability, safety, and new business models can further differentiate airlines and attract passengers.

The impact of Agentic AI on airline distribution will be profound over the next decade with the emergence of new AI-driven pathways to make bookings. In travel, the new channels will negatively impact existing channels of distribution, and the beneficiary will be the travel suppliers.

Airline retailing provides opportunities along several dimensions for innovation with automated, intelligent, real-time experiences along the customer life cycle leveraging real-time data with advanced statistical modeling and machine learning. It is also an opportunity for travel suppliers to phase out legacy technology, focus on enhanced customer conversion rates, maximize revenues from profitable customers, provide superior customer experience, and thereby drive customer retention and lifetime value.

With the advent of NDC, airline controls the offer creation process for direct and indirect channels. It is a unique opportunity for thoughtful innovation by taking small incremental steps on the journey to generate incremental revenues and simultaneously improve the customer travel experience and long-term customer retention. Unfortunately, since NDC was launched in 2012, this not been the case and airlines have focused on the commercial aspects of indirect distribution with NDC to lower costs. Hopefully, this will change in the future as NDC adoption increases.

The ultimate challenge for innovation with offers and orders is in the corporate travel space, where rigid business processes and established procedures for corporate policy compliance and duty of care hamper new thinking to improve customer experiences. An added dimension is the evolving role of the corporate travel managers. As traditional full content agreements between airlines and GDSs have withered away, travel managers have to ensure that they have access to the right content across all available sources for their employees. Looking beyond the traditional one-stop shop of subscribing to a GDS for comprehensive air content, corporate travel managers should also focus on entering into new supplier-direct partnerships and partnerships with (non-GDS) NDC Aggregators to ensure access to all pertinent content that meets the corporate goals.

The expansive breadth of airline retailing also provides an opportunity for startups on a shoestring budget to take on entrenched legacy enterprise software firms by redefining the offer and order management process with the latest advances in modeling and technology.

2 Categories of Core Ancillary Revenue Streams

Adapting the airline industry to the retailing world is possibly the most important transformational project of the next decade.

IATA, October 2021

Abstract

Over the past decade, airlines have expanded the scope of ancillary products and services they offer. This chapter introduces formal categories for ancillary products and services. The categories are airline flight ancillary products and services, travel and non-travel supplier partnerships, and loyalty financial products. Individual ancillary products and services associated with each category are described in detail.

2.1 Overview

The airline ancillary services market is projected to experience substantial growth, reaching an estimated $330.9 billion by 2030 [Research and Markets, 2025]. This growth is driven by increased demand for personalized travel experience based on traveler preferences and the increasing adoption of ancillary services.

Airline ancillary services have transformed the industry by changing how airlines earn revenue. Instead of relying only on the base-fare ticket sales, they now earn a large part from extra services. These include, for example, checked baggage, choosing seats, meals on board, priority boarding, and airport lounge access. This change helps airlines keep their ticket prices low while still generating additional revenues by selling ancillary products and services.

B. Vinod, *The Era of Airline Revenue Management with Offers and Orders*, Management for Professionals, https://doi.org/10.1007/978-3-032-24197-9_2

Passengers can select and pay only for the services they want. This makes flying more personal and can improve their experience. Airlines also gain more ways to earn money and adjust prices depending on demand, giving them more flexibility.

Low-cost carriers (LCCs) have played a significant role in the growth of ancillary services, offering lower base fares and generating revenue through ancillary sales. By selling ancillary products and services, full-service carriers adopted a key strategy from the LCC playbook.

Airline retailing focuses on placing the customer at the center of the experience. Every part of the journey, from dreaming about the next trip to exploring options, planning, booking, paying, and enjoying the flight and related services, should meet the demands of the customer. While travelers may dislike hyper-personalization, they do want personalized options based on their preferences, quick service, and seamless interactions from start to finish.

Airline marketing often fails to meet customer expectations because of a one-size-fits-all approach. Travelers have different tastes, destinations, and experiences they seek. Because of this diversity, simple personalized messages are no longer enough. The future demands hyper-personalized campaigns that stand out. Hyper-personalization means going beyond basic segmentation. It uses advanced Artificial Intelligence (AI) and real-time data to create unique experiences for each customer. This approach makes every interaction more relevant and engaging. It is no longer a luxury but a necessity in the competitive travel industry.

The landscape of airline ancillary products and services is continually evolving, driven by technological advancements, competition, and changing consumer behaviors. This chapter classifies air ancillary products and services.

2.2 What Are Ancillary Products and Services?

Airline customers are not walking automated teller machines (ATMs), though this is how they are perceived by the airline executives.

There is a range of core ancillary products and services that are promoted by airlines today. There are no established standards for ancillary products and services that can be promoted by an airline. Many view this as haphazard and even confusing given the various types of products. This chapter streamlines the definition of ancillaries promoted by FSC and LCC carriers by defining a catalog to map the ancillary products and services.

Prior to the pandemic, the total ancillary revenues generated by airlines was a staggering $109.5 billion dollars [IdeaWorks and Cartrawler, 2019]. The two largest sources of revenue are checked bags and seat selection which accounted for 47% of the total ancillary revenues.

The research study involved 75 airlines that disclosed their ancillary sales data for 2021. This encompasses sales of standard ancillary items like checked and carry-on bags, reserved seat assignments, and WiFi, as well as loyalty revenue generated mainly from the sale of frequent flyer points to bank partners in co-branded

Table 2.1 Total Ancillary revenues and loyalty revenues in 2023

Airline	Ancillary revenues (billions)	Loyalty revenues (billions)	Loyalty revenue as a % of Ancillary revenues
American Airlines	\$8.4	\$6.5	77.3%
Delta Air Lines	\$9.4	\$6.6	70.2%
United Airlines	\$9.5	\$6.6	68.4%

credit card partnerships and other non-ticket revenues such as commissions from rental car sales.

Table 2.1 illustrates the ancillary revenues and loyalty revenues generated by the 3 largest full-service carriers in 2023 [Airoldi, 2024c]. The loyalty program revenue stream generated from the sale of loyalty points (miles) to partners also dominates the landscape.

During the COVID-19 pandemic, airline ticket prices declined in 2020 and 2021. Surprisingly, airlines were able to increase the intake of ancillary revenues per passenger. The Car Trawler Yearbook of Ancillary Revenues [Cartrawler & Ideaworks, 2022] undertaken by consulting firm IdeaWorks estimated that in 2021 the average ancillary revenue per passenger was \$29.96, up 39% from the 2019 average ancillary revenue per passenger of \$21.54. This is further proof that the ancillary revenue stream for airlines is here to stay. Global ancillary revenue surpassed \$148 billion in 2024, driven by a continued increase in ancillary product sales. Global ancillary revenue per passenger is expected to reach \$35 in 2025, based on a projected \$157 billion in total ancillary revenue and 4.6 billion total passengers.

2.2.1 The Top Performers for Ancillary Revenue Streams

The base fare charged for travel is the foundation for airline budgets. Ancillary services contriute incremental revenues and contribute 15% of total revenue worldwide in 2024. This is in sharp contrast to the 5% of total revenue contribution in 2010.

Table 2.2 illustrates the airlines that are the most productive measured by revenue share.

Figure 2.1 illustrates the ancillary revenue per passenger in 2024. The top 5 performers were dominated by budget airlines.

With the new focus on the sale of ancillary products, several airlines have resorted to many innovative and surreptitious methods to generate revenues. Some of these methods question the integrity and credibility of the airline as well as the long-term impact on customer loyalty. The same is true with OTAs that promote financial technology products, abbreviated to fintech, to customers who either do not need them or purchase it to alleviate their anxiety with a false sense of security. Fintech airline products leverage financial technology to enhance various aspects

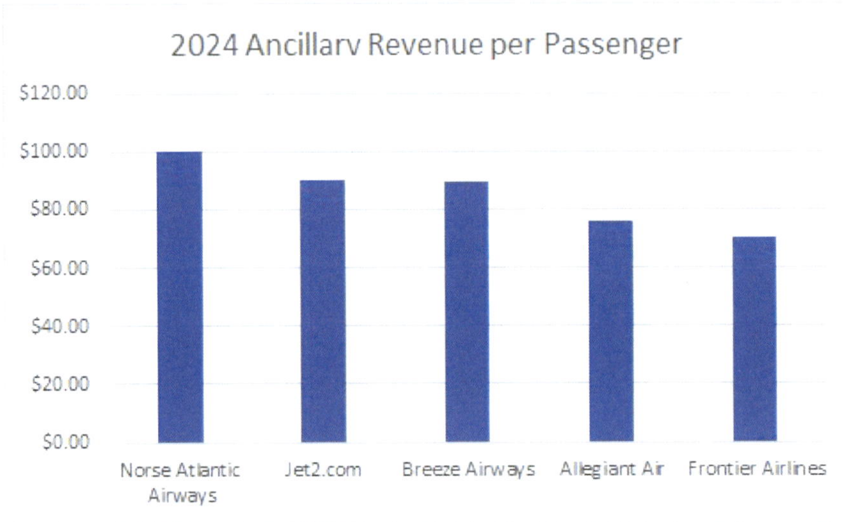

Source AltexsoftBlog, https://www.altexsoft.com/blog/airline-ancillary-revenue/

Fig. 2.1 The top 5 Airlines: Ancillary revenues per passenger in 2024.

Table 2.2 Top Airline Performers in 2024 by revenue share

Airline	Country	Business model	Ancillary revenue share (%)	Total Ancillary revenues ($billions)	Ancillary revenue per passenger
Frontier	US	ULCC	62%	$2.36*	$70.3
Spirit	US	ULCC	58.7%	$2.82*	$63.8*
Breeze	US	LCC	54%	$0.37*	$89.8
Allegiant	US	ULCC	52.9%	$1.32*	$75.8
Volaris	Mexico	ULCC	51.7%	$1.63	$55
Wizz Air	Hungary	ULCC	44.7%	$2.52	$40
Viva	Mexico	LCC	43.7%	$1.12	$40.5
Volotea	Spain	LCC	40%	$0.35*	$30.4*

*Estimated from available data
Source Altexsoft Blog, https://www.altexsoft.com/blog/airline-ancillary-revenue/

of the travel experience, from booking and payments to loyalty programs and expense management. Examples of these fintech products in travel are flexible insurance programs, digital wallets for loyalty members to redeem miles for retail products, and alternative payment options like Buy Now, Pay Later (BNPL).

2.3 Ancillary Categories

The U.S. Department of Transportation (DOT) permits airlines to offer tickets with different amenities and does not prohibit airlines from imposing fees. According to the DOT, airlines have the authority to create various ticket categories that encompass different types of services. Some tickets may include specific amenities, while others may only cover a basic non-refundable flight. The DOT stipulates that airlines must transparently display the complete price of a ticket after adding fees, surcharges, and taxes. The DOT emphasizes the importance of understanding the type of ticket being purchased and the associated restrictions.

Airlines worldwide today view the sale of ancillary products and services as a significant source toward revenue generation.

After the introduction of branded fare products by Qantas, Air New Zealand, and Air Canada in 2006, all-inclusive fares were unbundled by the full-service carriers (FSCs). This is a la carte pricing strategy to generate incremental revenues. It also gives greater choice and flexibility to travelers while also providing airlines with the ability to customize the flight experience. It was the first step toward personalized travel. Ancillary products are optional extras beyond the base fare.

Ancillary products and services to support airline retailing fall into three major categories. They consist of the ancillary products owned and promoted by airlines, products sold through partnerships with third-party suppliers that may be travel or non-travel related, and products sold to frequent flyers as part of the loyalty program. Figure 2.2 illustrates the three major categories.

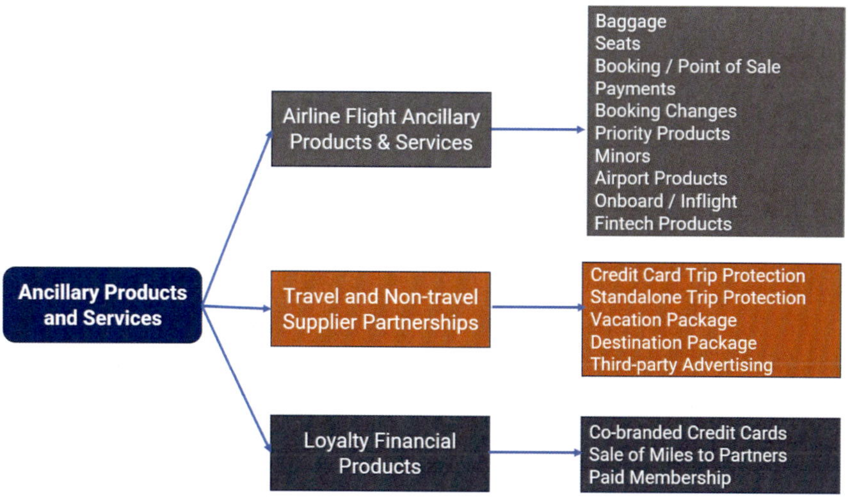

Fig. 2.2 Categories of Ancillary products and services

2.4 Flight Ancillary Products and Services

The first category is airline owned and managed ancillary products that are part of an air booking and its associated itinerary. They are also referred to as attached products and services since they are tied directly to the flight experience. Revenues generated from these ancillary products go directly to the airline.

2.4.1 Baggage

Sale of ancillaries started with baggage when deep discount low-cost carrier PEOPLExpress charged $3 for checked bags in 1981. Over time other LCCs started charging for checked bags. FSCs initially limited baggage charges to overweight bags or extra bags beyond the allowance for each ticket. This changed in May 2008 when full-service carrier American Airlines announced at the annual meeting held by its parent company, AMR Corp., that it would start charging $15 for many passengers to check their first bag, citing high jet fuel prices [Maynard, 2008]. Other full-service carriers followed, and the industry has never looked back.

In addition to checked bags and extra bags beyond the allowance, charges apply for oversized bags, overweight bags, and sporting equipment. In 2010 LCC Spirit Airlines started charging a fee for carry-on bags. Additional optional services offered by carriers like low-cost carrier easyJet are the priority bag drop and priority bag return.

2.4.1.1 Carry-On Bags

Ultra low-cost-carrier Spirit Airlines attempted to charge passengers for carry-on bags on August 1, 2010, which met with widespread customer complaints and negative publicity. It costs passengers $30. Members of the airline's "fare club," who pay $39.95 a year for discounts, had to pay $20. Spirit retained the carry-on bag fee despite tremendous customer backlash.

Today, several budget airlines like Spirit Airlines, Frontier Airlines, Allegiant Air, Breeze Airways, and others charge a fee for carry-on bags. These airlines consider carry-on bags as an "optional service" and price them accordingly, with fees potentially varying based on when the purchase is made (during booking, check-in, or at the gate).

Some full-service carriers like British Airways and United Airlines charge for carry-on bags if the purchased ticket is Basic Economy.

2.4.2 Seats

Seats have become a major component of airline ancillary fees over the past decade. They are related to selecting a seat and upgrades to better sections of the aircraft in the same cabin or higher cabins.

2.4.2.1 Seat Selection

Premium ticket purchases on most airlines include seat selection at no extra cost. However, there are FSCs like British Airways, Iberia Airlines, and others that do not include seat selection as part of the premium fare in coach and business class. This is a major annoyance and cause for angst among travelers that purchase premium seats and yet must pay an additional fee for securing a specific seat on the airplane. The alternative is to secure a seat 24-h before flight departure.

Figure 2.3 illustrates a seat map for a cabin. Seat selection is typically based on the booking class of the ticket which reflects the price paid. The booking class determines the seat zone from which a seat can be selected.

Seat types and pitch (extra leg room) can also influence the price for a specific seat in conjunction with the fare purchased. Examples of seat types are aisle, window, exit row, premium seats, preferential seats, bulkhead seats, attributes of a specific seat, etc.

The seat maps conform to the Passenger and Airport Data Interchange Standards (PADIS) seat characteristics an airline chooses to distribute. There are over 100 characteristics, which can be grouped into categories such as location of the seat (e.g., front of cabin, upper deck, adjacent closet, etc.), missing seats (e.g., no seats because of exit door, no seat because of upper stairs, etc.), seat characteristics (window, aisle, etc.), seat occupation details (e.g., occupied, advanced boarding pass issued, etc.) and seat blocking details (e.g., blocked for airport, blocked for through passenger, etc.).

Seats can also be priced by seat type, by individual seat, or based on the number of bookings by seat type. This is illustrated in Table 2.3 for exit row seats. When seats are priced based on seats sold by seat type, only the airline can quote the price.

Preassigned seat fees are a massive revenue stream for airlines, often second only to baggage fees. An airline's reservations inventory system should track available seats by seat type to support seat-led shopping and pricing of seats by seat type based on numbers of seats available for sale. The seat-led shopping feature allows a traveler to only see itineraries that have a specific seat type such as aisle seats, window seats, exit row seats or n seats together. This requires interoperability to exchange messages between the reservations inventory system and Pre-reserved Seats (PRS) where seat maps are stored. When a seat is consumed (or unconsumed) on the seat map, PRS must notify the inventory system to update the sold count by seat type and its availability.

2.4.2.2 Seat Upgrades

Many airlines now offer a bidding model to sell unsold premium cabin seats. The bidding process is only applicable to travelers who have completed a booking and received an E-ticket. The bid can be initiated by a traveler after the airline sends an email offering the opportunity to bid for the upgrade. Alternately, the traveler can go to the airline website and initiate the process subject to eligibility based on the purchased fare. While policies differ by airline, most bids must be placed 72 h before flight departure and the bids are by segment regardless of the itinerary.

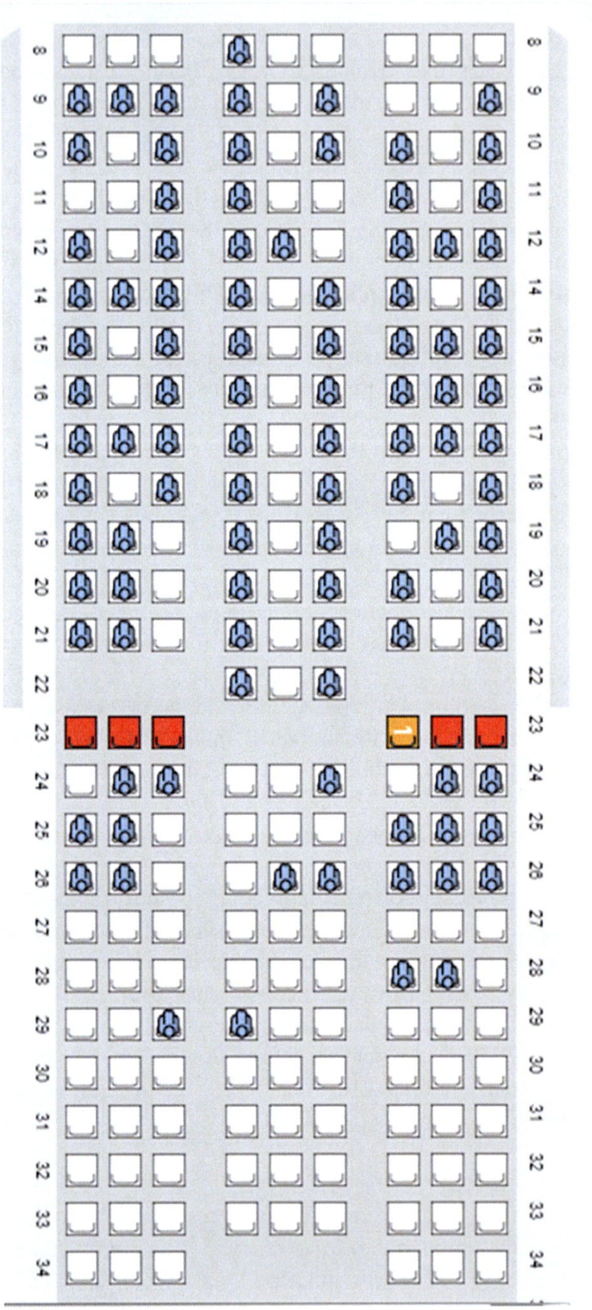

Fig. 2.3 Seat map in a cabin

Table 2.3 Price as a function of seats sold

Number of seats sold (exit row seats)	Price/seat
1–2	$25
3–4	$40
5–6	$60
7–8	$85

For example, a customer traveling from Los Angeles (LAX) to London Heathrow (LHR) connecting over New York's JFK airport must place separate bids for each segment of the outbound and return journey.

2.4.2.3 Paid Seat Selection in Business Class

A few airlines like British Airways, Iberia Airlines, Air France, KLM and Qatar Airways offer paid seat selection in the premium cabin. The fee is waived when the seat is selected within 24 h of flight departure. This alters the mindset of a traveler. Asking a customer to pay £200 to select a seat at time of booking in business class for a ticket that costs $5,000 does not make much sense to many road warriors. However, there is a very small segment of travelers in business who will attest to the improved passenger experience because they were available to select their favorite 3A seat in business.

2.4.2.4 Blocking the Middle Seat for a Fee

The deceptive approach to generate incremental revenues by Scandinavian Airlines System (SAS) is worth mentioning. On low load factor short-haul flights in a 3 × 3 configuration, where there are 3 seats on each side of the aisle, the middle seats are not occupied on low load factor flights. SAS sends alerts to the aisle seat and window seat passengers with the option to leave the middle seat empty for a SEK 299 (US $30) fee. Unwittingly both the aisle seat and window seat passengers may end up paying the fee. When customers find out about this deceptive practice, it destroys trust between the airline and the customer.

2.4.2.5 Selling Empty Seats for a Fee

Some international long-haul carriers sell unsold (empty) seats to passengers who want additional space. A traveler can always book a second seat at twice the price when the booking is made. Alternatively, some international carriers offer an option to keep the seat next to a customer open for a reasonable fee. However, these options are only available a few days before departure or at check-in. The airline knows from its revenue management demand forecast at departure that the seat will be empty, and it is a way to generate incremental revenues from a seat that is forecast to be unoccupied. While the price for blocking an empty seat varies, it is an appealing alternative for customers who value the extra space, especially on long-haul trips.

In 2020, at the height of the COVID-19 pandemic, ultra-low-cost carrier Frontier Airlines introduced the capability to book an empty middle seat for a *more room* fee, starting at $39. The campaign backfired [Andrew et al., 2020] and Frontier quickly abandoned the program, prompting CEO Barry Biffle to make the statement, "*We recognize the concerns raised that we are profiting from safety, and this was never our intent. We simply wanted to provide our customers with an option for more space.*"

Here are a few more examples:

Air New Zealand offers space conscious coach passengers the option to buy a *twin seat* at check-in. Prices range from $120–$200 for long-haul flights.

Etihad Airways based in Abu Dhabi gives passengers the option to purchase *economy neighbor free* seats 72-h before departure. Further the passenger can pay for one or more adjacent seats.

Emirates Airways based in Dubai, gives passengers the option to purchase additional economy seats in the row when they check-in for the flight [Risso, 2021]. Pricing is not scientific and costs between AED 200 (US $55) to AED 600 ($165) per seat. Customers typically value the first empty seat higher than they would value the second or third seat. Hence ideally to maximize the sales of empty seats, Emirates should offer a quantity discount when a customer is contemplating the purchase of two or three seats.

Fiji Airways lets customers block the seat or seats next to them in economy for a fee. Branded as *my bubble seat*, customers receive an email 72-h before flight departure with the offer to buy empty seats.

Philippine Airlines has the *choice seats neighbor-free* program that lets passengers block up to three seats in their row. Economy passengers receive a notification within 48 h of flight departure with the offer to buy empty seats. This offer is also applicable at check-in subject to seat availability.

Sri Lankan Airlines introduced the *neighbor free seats* program for economy passengers. This allows passengers to book an additional empty seat next to them up to 48 h before departure. The price varies by sector, destination, and number of seats purchased.

2.4.2.6 Lufthansa's Cabin Complexity Surcharge

In the world of airline retailing, simplicity is a virtue. The Lufthansa cabin concept was launched in 2017 and became operational on some aircraft types in 2025. It is not only extremely complex and almost impossible for customers to understand in its many variants, which are subject to extra charges. Lufthansa's Allegris business class cabin introduces various seat types, including Business Suites, Extra Space Seats, Privacy Seats, and Extra Long Beds, all of which require an additional fee to select. The specific fees can vary depending on the route and booking class. These fees range from €100 to €600 per way, depending on the seat type and flight length. Only the "Classic" seats are free for regular customers. The Allegris business class rollout on Boeing 787s, has faced significant delays and potential issues with FAA certification due to complex seat designs that didn't pass initial crash tests.

2.4.3 Booking/Point of Sale

Charges to bookings based on the channel have become pervasive over the past decade. These charges are imposed to modify consumer behavior and encourage travelers to select channels that are cost effective for the airline.

Listed below are the potential charges for online direct and offline direct channels.

Call Center Agent Access. A booking fee is charged per ticket when a booking is facilitated by a call center agent. Fees may also apply when an existing booking is modified by a call center airline agent.

Airport Ticket Office and City Ticket Office Agent Access. A booking fee is charged per ticket when a booking is facilitated by an ATO or CTO agent. Fees may also apply when an existing booking is modified by a call center airline agent.

Web Booking Fee. This is the exception rather than the rule. A few LCCs and ULCCs like Spirit Airlines, Allegiant Air, Frontier Airlines, and Breeze charge customers for booking through their websites. These airlines justify their actions to defray the cost of maintaining and enhancing their website. Besides these carriers do not participate in GDSs and their website and call center are the only channels to book flights.

Award Redemption Fee. This is a charge to book award travel. All award travel bookings are subject to taxes and carrier-imposed fees per award ticket. Award bookings can be made in advance until a few hours before departure.

Group Booking Fee. Group bookings are negotiated with a sales agent. The negotiated fare applies for the group size, which is typically 9 or more passengers. Some airlines charge a fee for group bookings while others built it into the private fare negotiated for the group.

2.4.4 Payments

There can also be fees associated with payments.

2.4.4.1 Payment Method

Airlines typically do not charge customers a credit card fee since it would violate the rules established by credit card providers (e.g., Visa, Mastercard, etc.). A credit card fee is also illegal in many states in the U.S. Some airlines like ultra-low-cost carrier Allegiant Air circumvent the rule with a convenience fee.

2.4.4.2 Deferred Payment

Deferred payment fees are applicable with Buy Now Pay Later (BNPL) vendors who create a payment plan for the value of the ticket. Airlines partner with BNPL vendors to boost sales of tickets. BNPL options have gained traction with leisure travelers so they can pay overtime and visit places on their bucket list.

Unlike purchases made with a traditional credit card, BNPL schemes allow customers to pay back in installments over a few weeks or months and it is typically interest-free. It is estimated that in 2024, there are over 380 million users. BNPL schemes are not regulated, leading to financially vulnerable customers taking on debt that they cannot repay.

Airlines realize that BNPL affects consumer choices for several customer segments, mostly leisure. The question they need to answer is whether it is worth the investment in the cost of capital and transaction processing costs.

2.4.5 Booking Changes

Changes to a booking trigger change fees and they vary based on airline policy. Prior to the COVID-19 pandemic, some international carriers charged exorbitant change fees in the \$250–\$350 range per ticket. United Airlines was the first major U.S. carrier to eliminate change and cancellation fees during the COVID-19 pandemic and many airlines followed. Changes fees may also be waived or reduced for travelers with upper-tier loyalty status. When a change is made to the booking, the customer always pays the fare difference.

Change fees vary widely by airline, ticket type and route (domestic versus international) and are always subject to change and difficult to keep up to date. Tables 2.4 and 2.5 summarizes the airline change fees for US carriers and international carriers respectively for coach bookings in November 2025 [Zhang, 2025]. Carriers shown are a selection of FSCs, regional carriers, LCCs and ULCCs.

Table 2.4 Change fees for coach bookings—US Airlines

Carrier	Domestic change	International change	Same-day change
Alaska Airlines[2]	\$0 (except Saver Fares)	N/A	\$25–\$50
Allegiant[4]	\$25	Not Specified	Not Specified
American Airlines[1]	\$0 (Fully Flexible Fares Only	Not Specified	Starting at \$60
Delta Airlines[1]	\$0	\$0–\$400	\$75
Frontier Airline[4]	\$0–\$99	\$0–\$99	\$0–\$99
JetBlue[3]	\$0 (excluding Blue Basic fares)	\$0 (excluding Blue Basic fares)	\$75 (waived for Mosaic customers)
Southwest Airlines[3]	\$0	\$0	\$0
Spirit Airlines[4]	\$0	\$0	\$0
United Airlines[1]	\$0 (Excludes Basic Economy)	\$0 (Excludes Basic Economy)	Up to \$75 depending on status

[1]Full-service carrier; [2]Regional carrier; [3]Low-cost carrier; [4]Ultra low-cost carrier

Source Lendingtree, https://www.lendingtree.com/credit-cards/articles/cost-to-change-or-cancel-flight/

Table 2.5 Change fees for coach bookings—International Airlines

Carrier	Change fees on flights to or from the US	Same-day change
Air New Zealand[1]	NZD $0–NZD $100	NZD $50
All Nippon Airways[1]	Up to $500	$0–$500
British Airways[1]	$0–$35	$0–$35
Cathay Pacific[1]	$50–$60	Not specified
easyJet[3]	N.A	£25 to £54
El Al[1]	Not specified	Not specified
Emirates[1]	Not specified	Not specified
Etihad Airways[1]	Not specified	Not specified
Hainan Airlines[1]	$0–$250	Not Specified
Korean Air[1]	Not Specified	Not Specified
Norwegian Air[3]	€0– €65	€0–€65
Qatar Airways[1]	Up to $25	Up to $25
Ryanair[4]	N/A	€45–€60
Singapore Airlines[1]	Not specified	Not Specified
Thai Airways[1]	Not specified	Not Specified
Turkish Airlines[1]	Not specified ara>	Not Specified
WestJet[3]	$100–$500	$100–$500

[1]Full-service carrier; [2]Regional carrier; [3]Low-cost carrier; [4]Ultra low-cost carrier
Source Lendingtree, https://www.lendingtree.com/credit-cards/articles/cost-to-change-or-cancel-flight/

Can ticket change fees be avoided? They can be avoided under certain circumstances.

1. On August 1, 2019, the U.S. Department of Transportation [DOT, 2019] introduced new regulation that allowed travelers to hold a reservation without payment, or cancel a booking without penalty, for 24-hours, if the booking was made at least 7 days prior to departure.
2. Airlines have a degree of compassion when it comes to change fees. Some airlines permit travelers to cancel or change their nonrefundable tickets for free. Customers must go to the airline service center and provide documentation to receive the credit. Common reasons for waving the change fee are:

    a. Personal injury or illness
    b. Jury duty
    c. Natural disasters
    d. Family bereavement
    e. Military deployment

Flight changes such as cancelling a booking or changing a flight do not qualify as ancillary fees. Flight changes are controlled by refunds and exchanges and subject to the fare rules associated with the ticket.

2.4.6 Priority Products

Airlines place a high degree of importance to priority services, which provides travelers access to expedited services. These services may be included in a loyalty tier or can be purchased by travelers who do not have loyalty status. The most common priority services are:

1. Priority boarding
2. Priority security
3. Priority bag drop
4. Priority check-in
5. Priority bag return

2.4.7 Minors

Fees for infants and minors vary by airline. The two most common types of fees are:

2.4.7.1 Unaccompanied Minor

In the U.S. unaccompanied minors aged 5 to 17 can be registered as an unaccompanied minor so that they can fly without an adult. The fee is normally $150 for each direction of travel for airlines to provide supervision and assistance to get on and off the plane, including any connections if applicable.

2.4.7.2 Infant

In the U.S. normally a lap child does not have to pay a fee. On international flights, a lap child is charged a fee that is a fixed percentage, normally 10%, of the adult fare.

2.4.8 Airport Products

There are airport-related products that are managed by airlines that can also be purchased either when the booking is made or at check-in. The most common airport products are:

2.4.8.1 Lounge Access

Lounge access is offered primarily by full-service carriers. Airline lounges are exclusive areas set aside for passengers of a specific airline or airline alliance.

Entry is limited to elite members and individuals traveling in business or first class. Lounges can also be accessed through networks such as Priority Pass. Many credit cards include Priority Pass as a card holder benefit. Travelers that do not qualify for free airline lounge access can pay online or at the airport for day passes or lounge memberships. Fees for a day pass vary by location and can range from $25 to $60. Capital One and American Express have lounges at major airports for elite customers with certain types of credit cards.

2.4.8.2 Agent Check-In

This is the exception rather than the rule and imposed mostly by ULCCs like Frontier Airlines. Travelers can pre-pay the "Airport Agent Assistance Charge" at time of booking or pay at the airport. This fee can range from $10–$25 per ticket. As part of the service, airport agents can assist customers in printing boarding passes, checking in for the flight and checking bags.

Budget airlines expect customers to check-in online. For check-in at the airport with the aid of an agent, Ryanair charged £55 in 2023, which is waived for passengers who purchase the premium fares.

2.4.8.3 Printing Boarding Passes

Some LCCs and ULCCs charge customers for printing a boarding pass. For customers who are not tech-savvy with the airline app or want to use a self-service kiosk or print a boarding pass at home, then these airlines charge a fee for printing a boarding pass. Spirit Airlines charges $10, Allegiant Air charges $5 and Ryanair charges a whopping £20. Agent assisted printing of boarding passes at airports cost even more.

2.4.9 Onboard/In-Flight

The most common fees charged onboard are meals and Wi-Fi.

The availability and cost of in-flight meals can vary depending on the airline, flight route, and class of service. Some airlines provide complimentary meals, while others charge a fee or offer meals for purchase during the flight. Business or first-class tickets may include meals, whereas economy class tickets may not. The airline policy on meal availability and pricing for a flight is usually available on the airline website.

In today's connected world, Wi-Fi is an important ancillary product, yet it is difficult to get passengers to pay for it for a variety of reasons including spotty service and premium pricing. Only about 5% of passengers pay for this service. Airlines use third-party providers for in-flight Wi-Fi. Wi-Fi pricing ranges from 30-min plans to full flight plans for the duration of the flight. Pricing can also vary between short-haul, medium-haul, and long-haul flights. Some budget airlines like Ryanair do not offer Wi-Fi on their flights. Some credit cards offer free Wi-Fi access as a perk in addition to accumulating miles.

In 2010, Ryanair had drawn up plans to charge customers £1 for the use of the onboard lavatories. It was never implemented due to backlash from customers.

Among the full-service carriers, United Airlines announced plans in 2024 to monetize customer data for advertising purposes [Haggin, 2024]. United plans to introduce personalized commercials that play in between episodes of TV shows and movies. The personalization aspect is derived from data that United has collected from its passengers including their demographics such as city they live in, age, and class of service. It is the first attempt by an FSC to monetize in-flight services with customer data.

2.4.10 FinTech Products

Financial technology products, referred to as "travel fintech products", have been a new addition to the ancillary landscape over the past decade. Many travel critics consider this to be a scam because customers who purchase it either do not need it or purchase it out of travel anxiety. The terms and conditions for receiving a refund for a fintech product are in the fine print. Fintech products are offered primarily by OTAs and to a lesser extent by TMCs.

Hopper Travel, the mobile OTA, actively promotes these fintech products. Critics classify Hopper Travel as a bait and switch scam that should be brought to justice.

These so-called "travel fintech products" can be categorized as payment facilitation, lower the cost of purchasing, and travel protection.

Travel protection related services is a risky proposition for OTAs and travel suppliers that offer these financial ancillary products since they could incur significant losses if the predictive models that process terabytes of shopping and booking data make poor recommendations. Machine learning models such as reinforcement learning are used to price the fintech offering dynamically at an affordable price point for customers. The new revenue streams for intermediaries toward travel protection fall into two categories for air, hotel, and rental car bookings: pre-travel purchase and consumer protection products from unpredictable events. Customers pay in advance for these services which generates the new revenue stream. Fare prediction and rate prediction (discussed in Chapter 6) models are required to support many of these fintech products.

OTAs like Hopper are expanding their fintech services by offering "standalone trip protection" which allows customers to purchase flight disruption or cancellation protection to bookings made outside of Hopper's app [Fox, 2022b]. By expanding its fintech products with the introduction of "standalone trip protection," it enables travelers to add flight disruption or cancellation protection to bookings made outside of Hopper. The insurance can be purchased via the Hopper app once a traveler has booked a flight via an airline or other online travel agency. But there is a catch: refunds are in the form of "Carrot Cash" credit or book another flight which is a frustration for travelers.

At issue with companies that aggressively promote the so-called fintech services is the extremely poor execution of reverse logistics. When a customer has an issue with a fintech service such as price freeze to lock in a flight's current price for a set period for a fee and requests compensation or a refund, there is no online customer support, and the dispute is handled via email to address the false claims of the financial service that are in the fine print. From a customer perspective, the dispute may take several weeks or months to resolve, leading to unhappy customers who will never return. Frustrated customers perceive this as deceptive and a scam.

During the COVID-19 pandemic, the attachment rates for fintech products were higher during periods of uncertainty and it remains to be seen if these fintech products will continue to be popular now that a sense of normalcy has returned to travel. It is expected that these fintech products will continue to be offered since price fluctuations, weather and other factors will continue to impact a customer's travel plans.

Fintech products do not function as travel insurance or serve as a substitute for travel insurance benefits. These non-insurance travel flexibility products function separately from travel insurance and complement its benefits.

Here are a few examples of fintech products.

2.4.10.1 Travel Insurance

The volume of leisure traffic has exceeded pre-pandemic levels, anxiety and frustration with the travel experience is forcing many travelers to purchase travel insurance. Does travel insurance reduce customer angst? It does but does not necessarily drive loyalty or brand experience. Travel insurance is an ancillary service promoted by travel suppliers to boost consumer confidence to complete a booking.

2.4.10.2 BUY and WAIT Service

Before purchasing travel, customers can be informed about potential rate increases with a "buy" or "wait" recommendation based on expected future selling rates. A related product is the "price drop" guarantee which offers customers an opportunity to lock in the price. Hence if the price drops after a "buy" recommendation, the customer receives a refund for the drop in price.

2.4.10.3 Price Freeze

Another related product is "price freeze" which holds the flight and hotel prices for 2 h to 21 days and, if the price goes up, the OTA pays the difference up to a limit and if the price goes down, customers pay the lower price.

Price freeze is a fintech service that "freezes" the price of an airline ticket or a hotel room for a customer. The price freeze is applicable for a fixed duration when the customer is ready to make the booking. If the price of an airline ticket or a hotel stay decreases, the traveler pays the lower price when the booking is made. If the price were to increase, the travel entity typically covers the difference up to a limit. Price freeze purchases by customers are non-refundable. Purchasing a *price freeze* does not guarantee a seat or a room in sold out situations since the booking has not yet been made in which case the prize freeze fee should be refunded. The price freeze is also only applicable for a specific airline itinerary of hotel room type.

2.4.10.4 Cancel for Any Reason

This fintech service allows a traveler to cancel their trip for any reason before flight departure or check-in at the hotel for a fee. Customers can receive a full or partial refund of air or hotel costs to the original form of payment. The refund is not applicable if the airline cancels the flight or the hotel room is cancelled, which are beyond the control of the traveler. Hopper Travel offers this service, and many customers consider this to be a scam. When a traveler cancels a flight, they do not receive the partial refund (e.g. 80%) in cash but in airline credits and the traveler must pay a rebooking fee to the airline to use the credit and it may be subject to restrictions, like not being able to book Basic Economy.

Hopper Travel partnered with Air Canada in 2023 to provide this service [Schaal, 2023]. This is the first airline partnership with a fintech product and is also available on the airline website. Flyers can cancel the flight up to 24-h before departure for any reason and receive a refund. Air Canada offers this service as a supplement to its standard refund and cancellation policy. According to Air Canada, this feature allows Air Canada to compete with U.S. majors that offer more flexible cancellation policies.

2.4.10.5 Change Flight for Any Reason

This service enables a traveler to make qualified changes to a purchased booking on OTAs like Priceline.com at any time, for any reason prior to check-in and at least 8-h prior to the first scheduled departure of the traveler's outbound or inbound flight(s) and receive a full or partial refund depending on the service purchased. Priceline.com offers this service and once purchased, the fee for the service is non-refundable.

2.4.10.6 Flight Disruption Guarantee

This service allows travelers to rebook their flight on any airline on the day of travel at no additional cost subject to a dollar limit per passenger. This is applicable if a flight is delayed, cancelled by the airline or a connecting flight is missed. This is a redundant service that is not required, since the travel entity like an OTA may only process changes or refunds that are authorized by the airline. An airline agent can resolve the flight disruption on its own without the traveler having to pay for this service to an intermediary.

2.4.10.7 Buy Now Pay Later

Buy now pay later (BNPL) programs offered by airlines to travelers are essentially a loan to buy a ticket on credit without a credit card. Airlines partner with vendors such as Affirm, Afterpay, Paypal, Uplift, and others to provide the credit with a predictable repayment schedule. BNPL gained traction during the COVID-19 pandemic of 2020 and had become one of the fastest growing e-Commerce payment methods because of its convenience.

ULCC carrier Spirit Airlines introduced a partnership with BNPL solution provider Uplift in July 2022 with a limited-time offer of interest-free repayment plan for qualified customers. FSC Qantas Airways has partnered with BNPL provider Zip to launch a fly now, pay later initiative for domestic and international flights. Various studies have confirmed that customers would spend more on travel, for example by booking premium economy instead of basic economy, if BNPL choice was available.

2.4.10.8 Future State

In travel, fintech products continue to evolve and include financial services such as payments, short-term loans, and insurance. It is also changing the way travel is purchased and settled. In travel, there is a focus on accepting multiple forms of payment, providing flexibility for refunds, and control of travel speed for corporate business.

2.5 Travel and Non-Travel Supplier Partnerships

These are ancillary products promoted in collaboration with a travel or non-travel entity. The revenue stream is either based on a commission or a revenue share model for the airline.

Partnerships are a necessity for an airline to offer a comprehensive suite of ancillary products and services. Examples include ground transportation, hotel accommodations, rental car and local activities at major destinations. With this venture, an airline competes with travel agencies and transitions to a marketplace operator. When an airline becomes a marketplace operator, it must allocate the payments received from customers to multiple vendors. This is a challenge on a global scale since it involves multiple forms of payment such as cards and mobile wallets in various currencies. The marketplace operator must also convert and distribute the funds to partners through different payment gateways. Processing payments require high standards for data security and fraud prevention measures.

2.5.1 Credit Card Travel Insurance

Many credit cards offer travel insurance benefits for flight cancellations and flight interruptions. With this feature, a traveler who uses the credit card to book an itinerary can receive reimbursement for nonrefundable expenses related to canceled trips as a "covered loss." Depending on the specific card, a traveler could receive a refund of up to $20,000. Commonly, covered losses include injury, illness, or death of a traveling or business partner, as well as issues such as weather-related cancellations, terrorism, and jury duty. Typically, credit cards with travel insurance provide coverage for both trip cancellation and trip interruption. This coverage often extends to the cardholder and their immediate family members, even if the primary cardholder is not part of the trip. It is important to note that card issuers usually do not cover trips that exceed a certain duration, such as 60 days, or trips canceled due to changes in plans or personal finances.

There are differences in credit card coverage, and it is important to decode the fine print to avoid being surprised. Some credit cards offer a travel protection plan, and others just travel assistance. Many may not realize that these options differ. Travel insurance typically helps cover some costs of services like medical care or emergency transport up to a dollar limit. In contrast, travel assistance only offers guidance to access these services, usually without providing financial support.

2.5.2 Standalone Trip Insurance

Standalone protection is usually priced based on the total cost of the trip. This type of coverage can offer better support for non-refundable expenses if a trip is canceled or interrupted. For instance, third-party insurers often cover 100% or more of non-refundable costs related to trip cancellations and interruptions. They also provide protections that some credit cards might lack, such as extensive medical care, emergency evacuation, and flexibility for specific travel needs.

2.5.3 Credit Card Travel Protection Versus Standalone Third-Party Travel Protection

Standalone travel protection usually covers a broader range of travel risks compared to credit card travel insurance.

Credit card coverage can change between cards and often has lower limits for issues like trip cancellations and medical evacuations. For example, even premium cards often limit trip cancellation coverage to $10,000 per person for each trip. This can be a problem for travelers booking luxury trips that cost more than this amount.

In contrast, standalone policies are priced based on the total trip cost. They often provide stronger coverage for non-refundable expenses if a trip is canceled or interrupted. Many third-party insurers reimburse 100% or more of these costs.

2.5.4 Vacation Packages

The revenue model with third-party suppliers must be identified in a contract. It can be based on commissions or share of the revenue. Technically, there is no limit to what can be included in a vacation package. Examples are hotel, rental car, ground transportation to and from the hotel, airport parking, local activities, theatre, and sporting events.

2.5.4.1 Destination Packages

Destination packages offer a bundle consisting of flights, hotels, and local attractions in the destination city. This requires partnerships with travel and non-travel activity providers and hotels in the destination city.

A special case of dynamic packaging is stopover packages. Several airlines, working closely with the country tourism boards, promote their hubs as stopover destinations. For example, Emirates (Dubai), Icelandair (Reykjavik), Singapore Airlines (Singapore) and Cathay Pacific (Hong Kong) promote their hub airports as stopover destinations by waiving the stopover fee (ATPCO CAT 8) and promote packages that include hotel, local transportation, and local activities at the stopover destination.

2.5.4.2 Third-Party Advertising

Low-cost carriers generate incremental revenue through advertising. Budget airlines, which are less conscious of their own brand, allow advertising on seat backs, tray tables, boarding passes, in-flight entertainment systems, airline magazines, and social media.

2.6 Loyalty Financial Products

Airline loyalty programs have demonstrated significant success for airlines. They create fresh demand and build brand value, despite the end product being essentially a commodity. These programs foster enduring relationships with devoted customers who are committed to the frequent flyer program. They also function as an extra revenue stream for airlines through joint marketing efforts with credit card companies, telephone companies, as well as promotions with packaged goods and retail companies [Vinod, 2011].

For at least a decade, there has been a popular saying that describes airlines as being *more like credit card companies that also happen to operate planes*. Over time, airline loyalty programs have become highly lucrative, with airlines earning more money from their credit card operations than from actual flight services. Like central banks [Locke, 2020], airlines issue frequent flyer miles, essentially creating currency. By selling these miles to credit card companies, airlines can make billions of dollars through their loyalty programs. Major players in this system include companies like JP Morgan, Barclays, and American Express, which are significant buyers of frequent flyer points. Banks and non-air partners buy billions of dollars of miles each year form the airlines. Airlines also use the sale of miles to generate cash during financially challenging periods. These miles are mainly acquired through credit card transactions, particularly by business class passengers. Many argue that the primary business of airlines is centered around selling miles rather than selling seats on their planes.

The profitability of selling air miles is noteworthy, with airlines achieving a three to one profit ratio. This makes it a highly lucrative endeavor compared to the operation of an airline, which comes with substantial fixed costs and variable expenses such as fuel and employee wages. Consequently, airlines collaborate with banks and credit card companies to sell air miles.

The largest airlines in the world boast memberships of more than 50 million and partnerships with hundreds of companies. American Airlines, the airline that launched the first frequent flyer program on May 1, 1981, is the largest with 115 million passengers as of April 2021 [Genter & Lupini, 2021].

The cash crunch caused by the COVID-19 pandemic revealed the true value of airline loyalty programs. In 2020, for the first time, many U.S. carriers collateralized the future cash flows of their loyalty programs to raise billions of dollars in capital because the pandemic decimated traditional revenue streams from air travel. United Airlines was the first, raising $6.8 billion in June 2020. Spirit Airlines and Delta Air Lines followed with $850 million and $9 billion respectively [Chun & de Boer, 2021].

In March 2021, American Airlines set the record by raising $10 billion. To receive a multi-billion dollar loan through the CARES Act, American Airlines hired an external entity who determined the worth of the loyalty program to be $31.5 billion [Genter & Lupini, 2021]. The $10 billion in financing was achieved solely on the strength and value of American's AAdvantage mileage program.

2.6.1 Are Loyalty Programs Fintech Programs?

A quote that has been circulating for over a decade states that *airlines are essentially credit card companies that happen to also fly planes.* While the assertion is not literally true, the airlines leverage financial models similar to credit card companies by selling their loyalty program points (miles) to banks, which then issue co-branded credit cards. These credit cards provide significant revenue for airlines, as banks pay them for the right to award miles to cardholders. This system turns the frequent flyer programs into highly lucrative financial assets for airlines, sometimes valued more than the airline's core operations.

So, are loyalty programs really fintech programs? In many ways they are. The growth of a fintech company is based on access to valuable customers. While the core airline business is highly cyclical, fiercely competitive, and prone to multi-billion-dollar losses, loyalty programs are recession proof. They were the airline's lifeline during the pandemic of 2020 when air bookings evaporated. To stay afloat, airlines were able to borrow against their loyalty programs at acceptable interest rates. Growing the financial services business is dominated by customer acquisition costs. So, the airlines address this by buying airplanes, transporting customers across the network, dealing with pilot and flight attendant unions, addressing maintenance and safety regulations, and maybe making a profit, but the reward is the customer base that signs up for credit cards.

2.6.2 Cobranded Credit Cards

Travelers earn loyalty miles when they make purchases with a cobranded credit card. Typically, one base mile earns the equivalent of one loyalty point. Hence a $100 purchase with a cobranded credit card accrues 100 loyalty points.

Co-branded credit cards are very lucrative for airlines. They generate loyalty points out of thin air and sell them for cash to banks with co-branded credit cards. In turn, the banks award loyalty points to card holders for making purchases. Finally, both the banks and credit card companies make money off the swipe fees from the use of the card. Card holders can redeem their accrued loyalty points for flights as well as other products sold through the airline's consumer direct website. The airlines do not incur a cost from loyalty points until they are redeemed by a customer. Sometimes, customers forget the points they own which may expire, making it a very lucrative deal for airlines.

2.6.3 Sale of Miles to Partners

Joe Brancatelli, a veteran business travel writer likened frequent-flier programs to "an unregulated lottery" [Brancatelli, 2002] where your odds are uncertain, and the rules can change at any moment. Many airlines no longer post award charts on their websites and engage in dynamic loyalty points for redemption based on various factors such as demand and quality of service.

Banks and non-travel entities buy loyalty points from airlines. This is typically a tiered structure where the airline charges less for the initial bonus miles for customer acquisition versus the charge for ongoing credit card spend. While the cost varies by bank based on the volume of business, a bank may typically pay a penny per loyalty point for the initial bonus toward customer acquisition and perhaps 1.25 to 1.50 cents per loyalty point for ongoing credit card spend.

Internal airline accounting became transparent when airlines raised debt against their loyalty programs during the COVID-19 pandemic [Lieber, 2020]. While the margins are hefty, they vary: American AAdvantage had a 53% margin, United MileagePlus a 44% margin and Delta SkyMiles a 39% margin. The variance in the margins for these airlines can be attributed to what they charge their partners for loyalty points.

2.6.4 Paid Memberships

As its name suggests, a paid loyalty program requires customers to pay a monthly or annual subscription fee to receive discounts and awards. Two well-known paid membership programs are Costco Wholesale and Amazon Prime.

Related to travel, the American Automobile Association, better known as AAA, is one of the oldest. It was created in 1902 as a merger of nine auto clubs. Besides roadside assistance, members can buy insurance, acquire an international driving permit, and have access to hotel and other travel discounts.

Costco Wholesale is much more than a big-box store. Costco Travel offers discounts on airfares, hotels, car rentals, and cruise lines.

Global Entry qualifies as a paid subscription program offered by the U.S. Customers and Border Protection that allows pre-approved low-risk travelers to skip the line when they re-enter the United States from their trip abroad. The automated kiosks use image recognition to identity travelers and expedite the re-entry process. Travelers who qualify also automatically have TSA PreCheck status.

There has been an evolution of subscription-based models in the travel industry. The subscription business has experienced significant growth, with consumers paying a fee to join the program. Through travel memberships, businesses can establish unique relationships with customers who no longer need to visit multiple websites before making a purchase. Customized travel solutions represent the future of paid memberships, offering exclusive member rates for hotels, car rentals, and cruise lines, as well as access to airport lounges, insurance options, concierge services, visas, and passport services. There is a membership that is available for every type of traveler, from those who are willing to pay a premium for exclusive travel experiences to the budget-conscious who want to discover the best travel deals.

There is a vast number of paid memberships that cater to different types of customers. Here are a few examples of paid memberships, and the prices quoted are indicative and always subject to change.

2.6.4.1 Scott's Cheap Flights

A Scott's Cheap Flights membership provides subscribers with access to flight deals and "Mistake Fares" released by airlines, delivered directly to their inbox. A mistake fare is an error fare that is an unintentional very low fare caused by human error, technology glitches, currency miscalculations, or omitted taxes and fees. The team diligently searches the web for the most competitive airfare prices to well-known destinations and distributes them to members. Subscribers can also monitor deals from a nearby airport or destinations they are interested in. Scott's Cheap Flights membership is ideal for travelers who can be flexible with their destination and travel dates and are open to flying based on discounted airfare rates. Given that flight deals are short-lived, quick action is necessary.

There are three membership tiers inclusive of a free tier. In 2023, Scott's Cheap Flights was rebranded as Going.

2.6.4.2 Inspirato

Inspirato offers a luxury travel subscription service that grants members exclusive access to a vast array of over 150,000 luxury vacation homes and resorts worldwide, all managed by Inspirato personnel. The service features two membership tiers: Inspirato Club and Inspirato Pass. Inspirato Club provides members with access to luxury residences and hotels globally, along with on-site concierge services, daily housekeeping, and additional perks like late check-in/out, room upgrades, and spa credits. However, members are required to pay nightly room rates.

Inspirato Pass includes all the benefits of Inspirato Club, with nightly rates already included in the membership fee. This setup allows members to reserve multiple vacations within a month with one active booking at a time. Additionally, there is no long-term commitment, enabling members to cancel their membership at any time.

2.6.4.3 Exclusive Resorts

Exclusive Resorts is tailored for families that prioritize privacy, offering a close-knit community of members with limited intake (only 150 new members accepted annually). This exclusive group gains entry to a collection of over 350 luxury properties across the globe, including sought-after destinations like the Amalfi Coast, Barcelona, Deer Valley, Kaua'i, Los Cabos, and St. Barts. Guests at Exclusive Resorts benefit from a personalized stay, supported by a dedicated on-site team. This team assists with pre-trip arrangements such as stocking the pantry with preferred snacks, arranging massages or private chef services, and ensuring top-notch housekeeping throughout the stay. Members typically travel 15 to 30 nights per year.

2.6.4.4 Wheels Up

Wheels Up provides private jet charter memberships that allow travelers to utilize a variety of aircraft, such as the King Air 350i, an 8-passenger Citation Excel/XLS, and the speedy Citation X. With a dynamic pricing-based quoting system, Wheels Up offers competitive rates, enabling members to book flights easily as needed and pay according to their usage.

Membership benefits include exclusive invitations to special events, President's Circle status with Hertz, a complimentary 12-month trial of Inspirato Club subscription for Core members, various perks at select Waldorf Astoria hotels in North America, a partnership with Delta SkyMiles, special partnership rates with Porsche, and more.

The Endowment Effect, Customer Angst, and Supplier Trust

3

Your most unhappy customers are your greatest source of learning.

Bill Gates

Microsoft co-founder

Abstract

Richard Thaler coined the term "endowment effect" in 1980. It is a psychological phenomenon in which people value an item they own more highly than an identical item they do not own, leading to a willingness to sell for more than they would have paid to acquire it. This cognitive bias, a form of loss aversion, causes individuals to feel greater reluctance to part with something they possess, even if it means market inefficiencies and irrational trading behaviors. This cognitive bias is pervasive in airline retailing.

The era of airline retailing has also led to customer angst caused by uncertainty associated with the value of the ancillary product or service and refunds when an airline fails to fulfill its promise. Factors that contribute toward customer angst result in customer complaints and ill will.

The chapter concludes with the importance of supplier trust, a core building block for successful airline retailing. Trust is the ultimate currency for airlines, and it translates directly to customer loyalty.

Microsoft co-founder Bill Gates understood that business problems were opportunities for improvement. In business, dissatisfied customers offer valuable lessons on enhancing a business entity's products and services. Organizations such as IATA, travel suppliers, travel management companies, and Global Distribution Systems all have much to learn from Bill Gates as they transition to the uncharted territory of airline retailing.

B. Vinod, *The Era of Airline Revenue Management with Offers and Orders*,
Management for Professionals, https://doi.org/10.1007/978-3-032-24197-9_3

3.1 What Is the Endowment Effect?

Behavioral economics and psychology explain the endowment effect, where we value what we own more than what we do not. This leads us to think our possessions are worth more than their actual market value. As a result, we ask for higher prices to part with these items compared to what we would pay to buy them.

3.1.1 The Endowment Effect

Richard H. Thaler, an American economist and Professor of Behavioral Science and Economics at the University of Chicago Booth School of Business, is credited with coining up with the term "endowment effect" [Kahneman et al., 1990; Thaler, 1980] to describe the observation that people demand more to give up an object than they are willing to pay to acquire it. This cognitive bias highlights how ownership can increase an item's subjective value, challenging classical economic assumptions of rational decision-making.

The endowment effect refers to the asymmetry in value people place on the same object when they sell it versus when they buy it. The asymmetry stems from the fact that people ask a higher price as owners than they are willing to pay as buyers [Thaler, 1980].

This concept describes the tendency for individuals to place higher value on the goods they own compared to those they do not. The *endowment effect*, a cognitive bias, leads to irrational behavior, resulting in unequal perception or treatment of goods of similar value. The endowment effect is probably the most well-known example of contextual influences on value assessment. It refers to the inclination to attribute higher value to items one owns. An application of prospect theory, the endowment effect is also referred to as *divestiture aversion*.

A well-known study of how context affects value is described below. This effect shows that people value items they own more than items they do not. In a famous study by Kahneman and colleagues in 1990, participants were randomly assigned roles as either sellers or buyers. Sellers received coffee mugs of known worth, which buyers could get by giving up cash. Since both groups had the same choices, either getting money or the mug, traditional economic theory suggests the item's price should depend only on its market value and that about half of the items should be exchanged. However, the study and several others later demonstrated that the participant's role heavily influences how they value the item. Sellers showed a higher willingness to accept compensation for the mug than buyers showed to pay for it. In fact, in Kahneman's experiment [Kahneman et al., 1990], the median selling price was more than double the median buying price, resulting in significantly fewer trades than expected.

Prospect theory [Kahneman and Tversky, 1979] helps explain the difference between willingness to accept (WTA) and willingness to pay (WTP). Simply put, choices are viewed as gains or losses compared to a starting point, usually their current possessions. When sellers received the mugs, their reference point changed to include ownership of the mug. From this new perspective, selling the mug feels like a loss, while buying it feels like a gain. Research has shown that people tend to perceive losses differently than gains [Horowitz & McConnell, 2002].

A "mixed gamble" describes a situation where a choice can lead to both positive gains and negative losses. In this scenario, there is a simultaneous risk of either gaining something valuable or suffering a loss, depending on the outcome of the decision. Research shows that people often avoid mixed gambles, where they could lose money. For example, when offered a 50% chance to lose $100 and a 50% chance to win $100, individuals usually reject this option. However, they are more likely to take a gamble if the potential gain is double the potential loss. If they could win $200 with the same chance of losing $100, they would play [Tversky & Kahneman, 1991]. This behavior, known as loss aversion, is a consistent finding in various decision-making studies. It has even been parameterized as a multiplicative weight (λ) for Prospect Theory value function, which measures how people perceive gains and losses [Kahneman & Tversky, 1979; Tversky & Kahneman, 1992]. The Prospect Theory value function shows that people perceive losses more intensely than gains. This function uses a power formula to change objective values into subjective ones. Essentially, the curve is steeper when dealing with losses than when considering gains. As shown in Fig. 3.1, the value function that passes through the reference point is s-shaped and asymmetrical. The value function is steeper for losses than gains indicating that losses outweigh gains.

The S-curve has three key characteristics:

1. Reference Dependence. Value is measured by changes in wealth, not by the final outcome.
2. Loss Aversion. The pain of a loss is felt more intensely than the pleasure of an equivalent gain. This is represented by a steeper slope for losses than for gains.
3. Diminishing Sensitivity. The marginal impact of gains and losses decreases as you move further from the reference point.

The functional form is given by.

$$v(x) = x^{\alpha} \text{ if } x \geq 0$$

$$v(x) = -\lambda(-x)^{\beta} \text{ if } x < 0$$

where

x is the gain or loss, relative to the reference point.
α is the parameter for diminishing sensitivity in the gain domain, Empirically, the value of α is typically between 0 and 1, creating a concave shape.
β is the parameter for diminishing sensitivity in the loss domain, Empirically, the value of β is typically between 0 and 1, creating a convex shape.

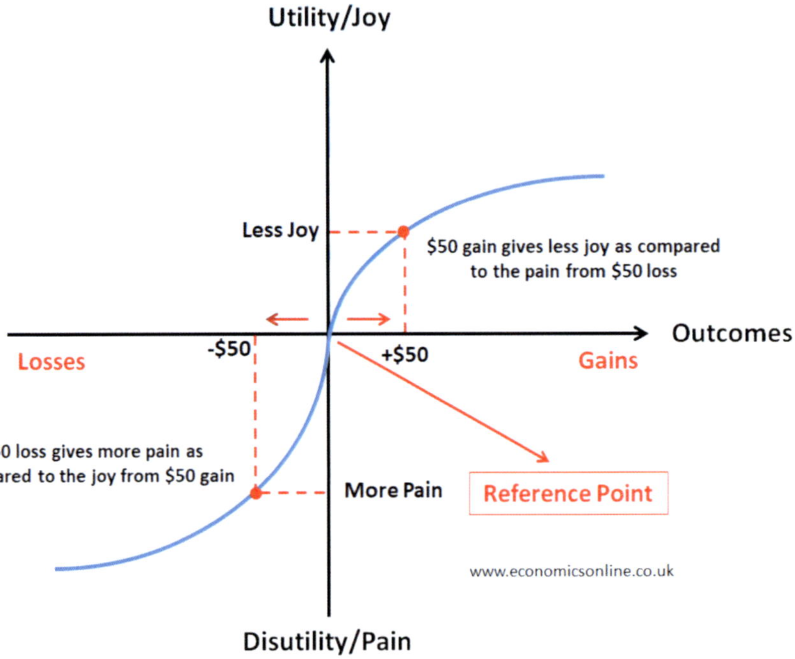

Source https://www.economicsonline.co.uk/definitions/prospect-theory.html/

Fig. 3.1 Prospect theory loss aversion.

> λ is the coefficient of loss aversion. This parameter is greater than 1, scaling the value function for losses to be steeper than for gains. Tversky and Kahneman (1992) estimated $\lambda \approx 2.25$.

This theory shows that losses have a greater impact on individuals than equivalent gains. In experiments, people reacted more strongly to losses than to gains, with losses feeling more significant, sometimes by a factor greater than two [Tversky & Kahneman, 1991]. Recent studies suggest this ratio might be closer to 1.5 [Sokol-Hessner et al., 2009], like findings related to the endowment effect.

Myopic loss aversion happens when people react more strongly to losses than gains. They also tend to evaluate outcomes often [Thaler et al., 1997]. They tested two implications of myopic loss aversion experimentally and made two inferences. First, investors who display myopic loss aversion will be more willing to accept risks if they evaluate their investments less often, and second, if all payoffs are increased sufficiently to eliminate losses, investors will accept more risk. In a task in which investors learn from experience, both predictions are supported. The investors who got the most frequent feedback (and thus the most information) took the least risk and earned the least money.

3.1.2 The Airline Context

Early attempts to introduce new merchandising practices in the airline industry faced stiff resistance from passengers who felt that previously included features with the purchase of a ticket were being taken away. They felt that amenities that used to be part of the ticket cost were being removed. For example, American Airlines received criticism when it added a charge for checked baggage in May 2008, as this service had previously been included in the ticket price. Passengers viewed this as a loss, reflecting the endowment effect in behavioral economics. This concept indicates that losses are felt more strongly than equivalent gains. The endowment effect, which demonstrates how changes in the status quo (e.g. bags are free), can impact on the perceived value of an item (e.g., free baggage). Baggage fees were introduced to help cover increasing fuel costs. However, even with the drop in fuel prices, these fees have continued to rise over the years.

Most airlines except for Southwest Airlines followed. When the new fee was introduced airline passengers were vocal in expressing their dismay at this practice. In 2010, a Consumer Reports [Consumer Reports, 2010] survey ranked baggage fees as a traveler's greatest irritation.

The airline executive point of view is that unbundling the price of checking a bag from the price of flying allows airlines to extract additional revenue from customers who value that service most. The rationale from airline executives is that customers should choose what they pay for. Think about going to a restaurant where every meal includes dessert. That's great if the customer loves dessert. But what if the customer does not want dessert? In this scenario the customer would want to pay less for the meal and skip dessert.

Airline executives are also well aware of the potential lower operating costs when customers are encouraged to avoid checked bags. Operating cost savings come from fewer luggage handlers, fewer check-in staff and less fuel burn.

Willingness to pay (WTP) is the maximum amount a person is willing to spend for a good or service. Conversely, Willingness-to-accept (WTA) is the lowest amount a person is willing to accept for giving up a good or service. People often attribute a higher value for privacy in WTA conditions when compared to the WTP condition [Horowitz & McConnell, 2002].

3.1.2.1 The Unabated Growth in Air Ancillary Revenues

Almost two decades after the introduction of baggage fees by American Airlines in 2008, travelers have grudgingly come to terms with the sale of ancillary products by airlines. Over the past decade, consumer attitudes have changed, and travelers are more willing to pay for ancillary product and services. The ability to customize travel experiences has now become an accepted practice.

The first report on ancillary revenue was issued in 2008 (year ending 2007) with only 23 airlines worldwide disclosing ancillary revenue activity in financial filings, and the result was a modest $2.45 billion. Once largely limited to LCCs, ancillary revenue has now become a financial necessity for airlines all over the

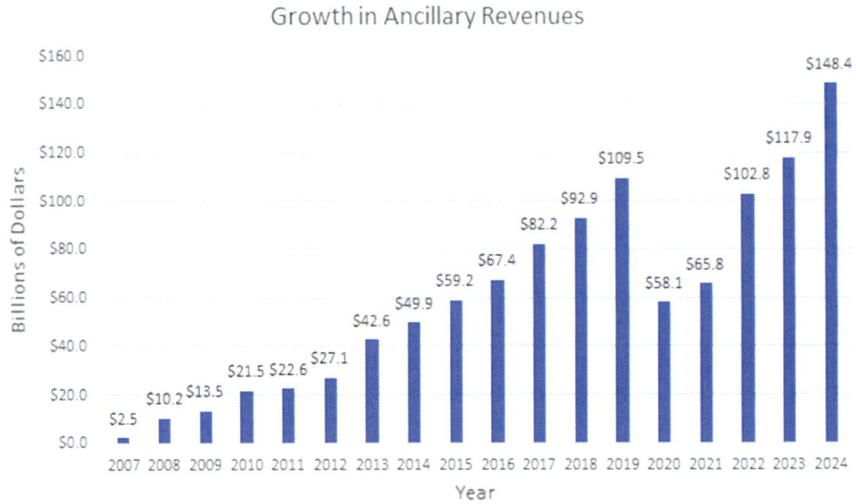

Source IdeaWorks and Cartrawler

Fig. 3.2 Growth in ancillary revenues.

globe. In 2008, 35 airlines reported, and by 2012 Iyear ending 2011) 50 airlines disclosed ancillary revenues of $22.64 billion [Ideaworks, 2012].

Figure 3.2 illustrates the growth in ancillary revenues since 2007. The projected revenue for 2024 was $148.4 billion, compared to $117.9 billion for 2023 and well above the previous $109.5 billion record in 2019 before the pandemic [Cartrawler and IdeaWorks, 2024].

3.2 Airline Retailing and Customer Angst

U.S. Federal laws protect airline passengers by specifying airlines' obligations, including when a flight is oversold, luggage is mishandled, a flight is delayed on the tarmac, and refunds are requested. Federal laws also prohibit airlines from discriminating against an air traveler based on disability, race, color, national origin, religion, sex, or ancestry.

Airlines across the globe, particularly in the U.S., are doing well at squeezing billions more dollars from passengers. They charge for "extras" that once came free with the ticket price. Yet this approach has annoyed over half their customers. As many as 75% now feel unhappy with their flight experiences [Reed, 2019].

The age of airline retailing has also led to customer angst. It relates to the uncertainty associated with the value of the ancillary and refunds when an airline fails to fulfill its promise to deliver the ancillary product or service.

Federal regulations safeguard air passengers by outlining airlines' responsibilities in cases such as overbooked flights, mishandled baggage, tarmac delays, and refund requests. Additionally, these regulations forbid airlines from discriminating against passengers based on disability, race, color, national origin, religion, sex, or ancestry.

The role of customer angst in travel influences consumer behavior and the sale of ancillary products promotes anxiety as part of the travel experience.

When it comes to dealing with anxiety, there are historical examples we can turn to. In the early days of e-commerce, businesses dedicated significant effort to addressing consumer concerns about the security of online purchases. They implemented strategies like offering free returns to enhance trust and create a feeling of safety.

Customer angst is a feeling of deep anxiety. It plays a critical role in influencing consumer behavior and brand affinity. Angst reflects fear, emotion, ambiguity, vulnerability, apprehension, and cynicism prior to making a purchase.

Businesses have long recognized the significant impact of utilizing fear as a persuasive tool in influencing consumer purchasing decisions. This prompts two key considerations:

1. When is it appropriate, morally justifiable, and beneficial for businesses to instill anxiety?
2. In what areas can anxiety be minimized?

In travel, there are several factors that contribute toward customer angst that also led to customer complaints and ill will. This is a summary of the dirty dozen.

3.2.1 Change of Gauge

A flight number represents a line of flight. It is a direct flight without a change in equipment though there can be stops along the way. A change of gauge takes place when an airline uses different aircraft on different sections of a route, while the flight number remains the same. The term originated in the railway industry where the width of some rail tracks were narrower or wider resulting in travelers having to transfer to a new compartment caused by the change of gauge.

It is a fraudulent airline practice that inconveniences passengers. It is an airline marketing term used to designate that a specific flight number changes aircraft, part way through the direct flight. For example, the first leg is operated by a narrowbody aircraft and the second leg on the same flight number is operated by a widebody aircraft. The Department of Transportation (DOT) permits this inherently fraudulent practice and expects the travel agent to explain the situation to a customer. A violation can result in a fine up to $25,000 per incident but the DOT has never enforced the rule against a travel agency [Pestronk, 2004].

Despite the use of the term change of gauge, the rule applies to both switching aircraft sizes enroute on the same flight number and to switching aircraft for the same type of airplane.

3.2.2 Change of Aircraft

We live in an era of paid seats, where a customer has pre-booked and paid to sit in a specific seat type (e.g., aisle, window, etc.) or a specific seat on the scheduled aircraft. For operational reasons an airline may substitute a different aircraft type (e.g., A Boeing 777 for an Airbus A380) which means a customer may be assigned a new seat at check-in which may be inferior to the one they have paid for.

3.2.3 Delayed Flight

Some complaints involve airlines with frequent delays, such as domestic flights in China, or situations where customers experience flight delays affecting their travel and hotel arrangements. Many customers complain about inadequate communication from the airline, as airport staff may be hesitant to provide updates, and the airline neglects to use email, SMS, and social media to keep customers informed.

3.2.4 Lost Baggage

The inconvenience of not having access to clothes, urgent medications, and other valuables for a period that exceeds four to six hours justifies compensation. While airlines have been eager to collect fees for checked bags, they do not have a defined policy to compensate customers when the bag arrives much later, inconveniencing passengers.

3.2.5 Refunds

Many airlines are very slow at processing refunds for services that were not rendered such as priority boarding, paid seat assignments not honored due to a change in aircraft or other reasons, and downgrades. Entities that sell fintech products are notorious for not maintaining a customer call center for refunds.

Several airlines reportedly have significant delays in processing simple refunds, leading to numerous customer complaints about the challenges in obtaining refunds for undelivered services. Instances such as unfulfilled pre-booked seats, improper enforcement of priority boarding, and forced downgrades are the most common situations where customers encounter difficulties receiving refunds or are reimbursed inadequately.

Besides airlines, mobile OTAs like Hopper are notorious for misleading travelers with their fintech products that promote customer angst. Their ancillary products carry fees such as "tip" and "VIP" which are misleading and not understood by the traveling public. For example, on their site they sell instant refund insurance. At the height of the COVID-19 pandemic, airlines like Air France made their fares refundable regardless of the original fare rules. Yet Hopper was selling this insurance when the fare itself for refundable by the airline. Selling an instant refund insurance when the airline has made the fare refundable during the pandemic is unscrupulous. What is worse, they refuse to refund the insurance and only provide credit for future travel [Flyertalk, 2021].

3.2.6 Meals

Most customer grievances regarding airline food pertain to special dietary requests such as vegetarian, gluten-free, Halal, and child meals. The primary issue arises when pre-ordered meals are not loaded onto the flight or are mistakenly given to the wrong passenger. Onboard catering is an area where airlines are unlikely to satisfy all customers, as they have high expectations for food quality despite the relatively low cost of the meal in economy class. This, in turn, raises expectations for premium cabin meals, leading to dissatisfaction. Additionally, buy-on-board products from low-cost airlines are often criticized for providing poor value for money.

3.2.7 Aircraft Seats

Many passengers are unhappy with both long-haul and short-haul airline seats. Airlines have started using new slimline seats with smaller seat pitch to provide more personal space, but this has not satisfied customers. Additionally, adding an extra seat per row on widebody aircraft has also led to increased dissatisfaction among passengers. Complaints are also rising on shorter flights lasting one to three hours.

3.2.8 Cabin Cleanliness

In a post COVID-19 world, airline passengers are increasingly conscious of cleanliness and hygiene. Due to the pressure on airlines to maximize aircraft usage, quick turnarounds often result in inadequate cleaning. While some airlines excel in this area, there are frequent grievances about dirty cabins and unsanitary washrooms.

3.2.9 Customer Service

Customers are often frustrated when attempting to get in touch with an airline before their trip to make changes, seek assistance for cancellations and flight delays, or address overcharges on their payment card. Additionally, customers encounter difficulties when seeking help at the airport during flight delays. Another common issue is the lengthy time it takes for some airlines to respond to customer complaints, which can range from 14 to 30 days. Furthermore, customers frequently complain about rude, uninterested, or absent onboard service, as well as poor language skills among customer-facing staff.

3.2.10 Latent Charges

Customers are mainly expressing frustration with low-cost carriers (LCC) that impose additional fees for various aspects of the travel experience. These budget airlines often have complex rules regarding extra charges, requiring customers to carefully review the details. The clarity and accessibility of this information vary among airlines, leading to a growing number of customers who fail to conduct adequate research before making a booking and end up having to pay additional fees at the airport.

Furthermore, full-service carriers (FSC) are increasingly introducing optional extra charges, which many customers anticipate being included in the ticket price. For instance, securing seats with family or friends and upgrading meals, drinks, or snacks during the flight may now come with additional costs.

3.2.11 Complexity of Fare Rules

Fare rules impact the terms and conditions for a booking. Many customers struggle to grasp important booking terms and conditions, particularly due to the complexity of airline pricing. Navigating through different luggage allowances, ticket change fees, cancellations, and associated charges can also be daunting. The top customer complaint is that people often book inexpensive fares without realizing the limited ticket flexibility in case of unexpected events like illness or family emergencies.

In travel, there are several factors that contribute toward customer angst that also lead to customer complaints and ill-will.

3.2.12 Flight Oversales

Airlines overbook flights to compensate for the effects of cancellations and no shows. It is part of an airline's revenue management strategy to maximize revenues and minimize losses from empty seats on closed out flights. The science of overbooking is never perfect and can result in customers being left at the gates. While unaccommodated passengers are compensated with vouchers toward future travel, the inconvenience caused to passengers far outweighs the overbooking compensation. Travelers who are involuntarily bumped off an overbooked flight must be knowledgeable of their rights as a passenger to ensure that the compensation received is just.

Unlike the U.S., the European Union (EU) is very strict and enforces consumer rights. EU 261 is a regulation that outlines the minimum rights for passengers in cases of flight delays, cancellations, or denied boarding. This regulation sets out the specific conditions for its application and establishes the amounts of assistance and compensation for each situation. In Europe, volunteering to take a later flight in exchange for a voucher in an oversold situation is not popular since travelers can receive financial compensation for the inconvenience that is mandated by the EU.

3.3 Greed Is Good? U.S. Lawmakers Grapple with Hidden Fees

Since the introduction of the $3 checked baggage fee by PeopleExpress when they started operations in April 1981, many critics argue that the airline industry has shifted from a focus on fundamental business practices to practices that resemble exploitation. Is this an example of legalized theft?

Many argue that nickel and diming passengers with ancillary fees is a prime example of corporate greed, and I am reminded of the 1987 Hollywood movie *Wall Street* where Michael Douglas emphasizes that "*greed is good!*".

On December 11, 2024, the CEOs from some of the biggest airlines in the U.S. were heavily questioned by lawmakers about the additional fees, often referred to as junk fees, that passengers must pay for services like baggage and seat selection.

Senator Richard Blumenthal, who chaired the panel, stated during the hearing held by the Senate Permanent Subcommittee on Investigations that in 2023, airlines such as American, Delta, United, Frontier, and Spirit made over $3 billion just from seat selection fees. He emphasized that this amount does not include the cost of airfare; it solely represents the fees charged for reserving specific seats in advance or choosing slightly improved seating options. This represented an increase of 50% from 2018, which was just six years ago.

Between 2018 and 2023, five airlines in the United States earned $12.4 billion from seat fees, along with money from baggage and other charges, as stated in a report released last week by Democrats on the subcommittee.

During the hearing, Senator Josh Hawley criticized Frontier Airlines and Spirit Airlines for giving bonuses to gate employees who enforce extra fees on large carry-on bags. The subcommittee reported that in 2022 and 2023, these airlines paid their employees $26 million to ensure strict adherence to their bag policies.

Airlines contend that their fee structures are transparent, enabling travelers to select from a range of options at different prices. Frontier stated that its incentive program is designed to ensure all customers receive equal and fair treatment.

Here is a case in point – these are the same airlines that received $54 billion in taxpayer bailouts during the COVID-19 pandemic of 2020. They took taxpayer money when times were tough, promising to do better. Instead, they have continued to augment predatory practices by making basic human comfort a luxury with a myriad of new fees and not improved customer satisfaction.

On November 26, 2024, Senator Richard Blumenthal issued a report from the Permanent Subcommittee on Investigations entitled "The Sky's the Limit: The Rise of Junk Fees in American Travel."

3.4 Spanish Government Penalties

While U.S. lawmakers are reviewing ancillary fees, the Spanish government decided to act.

In November 2024, the Spanish government-imposed fines totaling €179 million on five European budget airlines for unfair practices, including charging passengers for larger cabin bags [Gill and Arena, 2024]. It was a clear message to the budget carriers that the Spanish government considered these an abusive practice and a violation of consumer rights.

The airlines affected are Ryanair, Vueling, easyJet, Norwegian, and Volotea. They faced penalties for their fees on hand luggage and for charging extra for adjacent seats when traveling with disabled individuals or children. The government plans to outlaw these practices.

Ryanair received the largest fine at nearly €108 million, followed by Vueling at €39.3 million and easyJet at €29 million. Norwegian and Volotea were fined significantly less, with penalties of €1.6 million and €1.2 million, respectively.

The airline industry has reacted strongly against the fines imposed by the Spanish government. Airlines plan to challenge this decision, arguing it goes against EU law.

The Director General of IATA, Willie Walsh, called the decision shocking and stated it disregards a travelers' desire for choice. Airlines worry that banning fees for cabin bags will lead to higher overall ticket prices. They emphasize that EU law supports pricing flexibility for a reason, allowing airlines to offer different service options, from all-inclusive to basic fare. They contend that the Spanish government's action is seen as illegal and should be reversed. IATA contends that these actions are similar to forcing all hotel guests to pay for breakfast or charging everyone to pay for the coat-check when they buy a concert ticket.

3.5 EU Regulation 261

EU Regulation (EC) No 261/2004, often referred to as EU 261, is an European Union law that protects air passengers by establishing rules for compensation and assistance in cases of flight cancellations, delays, or denied boarding, and it applies to flights departing from or arriving at an airport within the European Union. It covers situations like flight cancellations, long delays (over 3 h), and denied boarding due to overbooking. The airline is not liable for compensation if the delay or cancellation is caused by extraordinary circumstances beyond their control, such as severe weather, strikes, or security risks.

Passengers are entitled to the following types of compensation based on the situation.

1. Compensation: Passengers may be entitled to compensation of between €250 and €600 depending on the flight distance and the delay.
2. Assistance: Passengers are entitled to assistance such as meals, refreshments, and accommodation if they have to wait for a long time.
3. Re-routing or refund: Passengers are entitled to a re-routing on an alternative flight or a refund of their ticket if their flight is cancelled or delayed by a certain amount of time.

3.6 The Windowless Window Seat Class Action Lawsuits

In August 2025, United Airlines and Delta Air Lines were sued by passengers who claimed that even though they paid for a window seat, they sat next to a blank wall on the flight [CNN Business, 2025]. Class action lawsuits were filed against United Airlines in San Francisco federal court and against Delta in Brooklyn, New York, seeking millions of dollars in damages for more than a million passengers for each carrier.

The suit against United Airlines alleges the airline misrepresented these seats and charged them extra without clear disclosure, which plaintiffs claim is false advertising and breach of contract. In response, United has asked a federal court to dismiss the case, arguing that a "window seat" simply refers to the seat's position next to the aircraft's wall and does not guarantee an exterior view.

If the plaintiff succeeds, it could result in more lawsuits against other airlines. A majority of airlines do not mark their window seats without windows on seat maps. It will also force airlines to post disclaimers for window seats without windows. Third-party platforms such as SeatGuru or AeroLopa provide more detailed information than airline seat maps. However, the lawsuit clearly states that checking for windowless window seats is not the responsibility of passengers, but the responsibility of the airline to provide this information at the time of booking. Ryanair, Europe's largest budget carrier is an exception [Osipov, 2025]. The ultra low-cost carrier (ULCC) posts a message on seat maps if the selected seat does not include a window.

If the plaintiffs do not win this lawsuit and the practice is ruled legal, airlines will lose trust with the flying public.

3.7 "Junk Fees" in Lodging and the FTC

Ending "junk fees" has been a key issue for both parties during the Biden Administration. In his State of the Union addresses in 2023 and 2024, President Joe Biden highlighted the problem of resort fees in the hotel industry. On December

17, 2024, the U.S. Federal Trade Commission decided to ban bait-and-switch pricing [FTC, 2024b]. This tactic often shows a "base price" in the lodging and live events sectors, only to add extra fees and charges later. In hotels, these fees sometimes appear only when the final bill is presented at checkout, after the stay has ended.

Drip Pricing is a sales tactic where businesses initially advertise a product's price at a low eye-turning figure and then reveal additional mandatory or optional fees later in the purchase process. These additional charges can include fees for upgrades, add-ons, surcharges, and taxes. Drip pricing is also relevant with airfares when airlines show a low base fare and then add fees for ancillaries, disguising the true cost. This practice is more prevalent with LCCs who offer low, enticing headline prices to grab a customer's attention.

Junk fees, synonymous with "drip pricing" and "misleading fees", affect more than just individual customers. These fees have caused corporate travel programs to incur significant costs, prompting travel managers to carefully analyze employee hotel bills to identify and avoid these charges. Some have succeeded, while others have not. In recent years, hotel companies have started adopting clearer pricing practices, but this change has come under pressure from legal and regulatory forces.

The final rule from FTC addresses common unfair and misleading pricing practices in the sale of live-event tickets and short-term rentals, while allowing room for businesses to operate. It does not ban any fees or pricing methods. Instead, it requires businesses to be transparent with consumers about all prices and fees from the start. With this new rule, to avoid penalties from regulators, hotels can no longer advertise a room for $200 per night and later add a $40 *resort fee* or a *service charge* at checkout, making the actual cost higher than expected. Now, doing this will risk penalties from regulators. This new rule ensures pricing transparency, helping guests avoid surprises and making it easier to compare costs.

The FTC rule on unfair or deceptive fees, often called the "junk fees rule," took effect on May 12, 2025, 120 days after it was published in the Federal Register, on January 10. 2025. This rule prohibits businesses from obscuring or misrepresenting total prices and fees for live-event tickets and short-term lodging. The legislation also has the support of the American Hotel & Lodging Association (AHLA).

According to the FTC, restaurants are exempt from the full transparency of fees charged to consumers but require the disclosure of fees in the total price of services and goods.

Industry verticals beyond live-event ticketing and short-term lodging are prohibited from deceiving consumers about fees and pricing per longstanding law. The FTC will continue to use its law enforcement authority to pursue bait-and-switch pricing tactics, such as drip pricing and misleading fees, through case-by-case enforcement.

3.8 The Significance of Supplier Trust in Airline Retailing

Trust is the ultimate currency. For airlines, trust translates directly to customer loyalty, brand reputation, and safety, making it a vital component of success and resilience, especially during a crisis.

Supplier trust is a fundamental building block on the airline's retailing journey. It is mandatory for customer retention because it directly impacts on the customer experience, brand reputation, and the airline's ability to offer consistent and repeatable services. In this era, retailing extends beyond selling a seat, incorporating both air and non-air ancillary products, and travel insurance, which often rely on a network of suppliers. The reliability of these partners reflects the reliability of the airline.

Fulfillment, successful delivery of all items in a customer's order, builds supplier trust. The fulfillment of orders and associated legal issues presents significant challenges for carriers and travel partners. To guarantee fulfillment, airlines must focus only on air ancillary products and adjacent verticals such as trip insurance, hotel and car. Fulfilling items in an order requires executive leadership and a coordinated effort across commercial, information technology, sales departments and airline partners.

3.8.1 Impact of New Retailing Models on Litigation

The new retailing models spawned from NDC allow airlines to sell and fulfill travel products through various direct and third-party channels. This shift introduces legal complexities that may increase the risk of class action lawsuits.

An airline must be on top of legal issues in this new era. They are.

3.8.1.1 Data Ownership and Privacy

The shift to a single customer order emphasizes the need for strong data governance and privacy protections.

1. The U.S. Department of Transportation (DOT) can investigate and penalize airlines for unfair or deceptive practices related to privacy.
2. There is no comprehensive federal privacy law covering travel information in the US, which raises concerns about how airlines handle and share sensitive data with third parties.
3. Major U.S. airlines have come under scrutiny for selling domestic travel data to Customs and Border Protection, a division of the Department of Homeland Security through an airline-owned data broker [Cox, 2025].
4. Airlines must also navigate conflicts between global data protection laws (like GDPR) and government data-sharing mandates.

3.8.1.2 Consumer Protection Regulations

Regulatory bodies issue and enforce rules related to air travel, The offer and order framework must adhere to these protections.

1. Refunds. Regulations require automatic refunds for canceled or significantly delayed flights, as well as for ancillary services not provided. The US has fined airlines for failing to provide timely refunds.
2. Fee Disclosures. While rules have been put in place to mandate upfront disclosure of ancillary fees, compliance has been legally challenged.
3. Frequent Flyer Programs. The Consumer Financial Protection Bureau (CFPB) has issued guidance stating that devaluing loyalty points could be an illegal bait-and-switch tactic.

3.8.1.3 Differentiated Offers Require Sound Execution

Execution is the bridge between a strategic marketing promise and the customer's actual experience. An airline's brand is often built on one or more differentiating factors such as premium experience, best price, or convenience based on the published schedule.

As airlines create more varied offerings, they must ensure they can consistently meet customer expectations across channels. Poor execution can lead to customer dissatisfaction.

3.8.1.4 Third Party Suppliers and Fulfillment

In the era of offers and orders, airlines run the risk of consumer class action lawsuits from false advertising, fraudulent charges, windowless window seats after a schedule change, website inaccessibility, hidden bag fees and much more.

Some airlines aspire to sell non-travel related ancillary products like Amazon. It is only a dream that can never be realized. Amazon is very data driven to create unique experiences coupled with frictionless customer service and a best-in-class delivery experience. Any half-hearted attempts by airlines tp sell non-air products could result in class-action lawsuits if fulfillment fails.

Airline retailing strategies that rely on third-party suppliers for fulfillment are increasingly facing class action lawsuits over alleged misrepresentation, unfair practices, and discrimination. These cases focus on issues such as deceptive advertising, antitrust violations, and the ultimate liability for products and services sold by partners that is the responsibility of the airline.

It is anticipated that in the decade ahead, courts will scrutinize liability related to third-party providers. In the era of online retailing, courts have ruled that the platforms could be held liable for defective products from third-party sellers, especially when they control aspects of the fulfillment process. This trend could extend to how courts view airline liability for third-party partners.

In the absence of adequate proof points, airlines must focus on their core competencies and get that right.

4 The Value Proposition of Revenue Management

Yield management is the single most important technical development in transportation management since deregulation.

Robert L. Crandall

Chairman and CEO American Airlines (1985–1998)

Abstract

This chapter reviews the value proposition of revenue management of the base fare and provides an end-to-end view of decision support models for independent demand and dependent demand.

The two types of overbooking models are the quality of service constrained model where denied boarding constraints are imposed and the economic model that minimizes spoilage and oversales simultaneously. Leg/segment discount allocation models is practiced widely by a large number of airlines. Many network carriers practice origin and destination (O&D) revenue management. Expected marginal seat revenue models and network optimization models are followed with a discussion of inventory control methods and connectivity supported in airline reservations systems. The execution component for leg/segment and O&D systems relies on inventory controls in the airline reservations system to control seat availability. The optimal sharing of inventory between cabins to minimize the impact on denied boardings is presented with an example.

The introduction of restriction free pricing by low-cost carriers led to the development of revenue management models based on the assumption that demand is dependent. The chapter concludes with a discussion on performance measurement, revenue opportunity model, the control of group traffic and a recap of the end product of traditional revenue management.

B. Vinod, *The Era of Airline Revenue Management with Offers and Orders*, Management for Professionals, https://doi.org/10.1007/978-3-032-24197-9_4

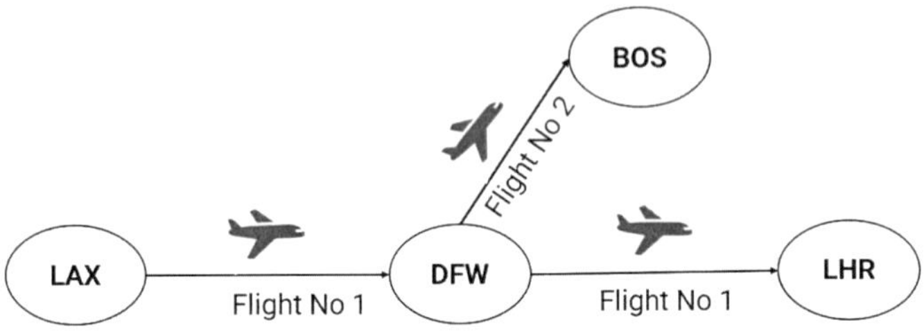

Fig. 4.1 Sample network

4.1 Revenue Management Definitions

This chapter begins with a clarification of flight legs, flight segments, origin and destination (O&D), markets, services, and booking classes.

Consider the sample network shown in Fig. 4.1.

A flight leg represents a nonstop city pair. Hence, the flight legs in this network are LAX-DFW, DFW-LHR and DFW-BOS.

The origin and destination pairs on a flight number are the segments. Hence the segments on flight number 1 are LAX-DFW, DFW-LHR and LAX-LHR.

An origin and destination (O&D) service can be a nonstop or a connecting market with specific departure, arrival and connect points. In this example LAX-BOS is an O&D service with a connect point over DFW. In revenue management terminology, an O&D represents the actual routing from origin to destination, including any connections.

A market is defined by an origin and destination pair. It is a collection of all O&D services that have the same origin and destination of the market. A market is not associated with individual flights, or connect points. Airlines file fares by market.

A Reservation Booking Designator (RBD) is a single-letter code used by airlines to categorize and identify different booking classes within a flight reservation. These codes, also known as booking classes, help airlines manage seat inventory and pricing, reflecting various fare rules and restrictions. It is also used by airlines to distribute availability (status or numeric) to intermediaries like the GDSs.

4.2 Core Airline Metrics

The core airline metrics can be categorized under traffic, demand, capacity, financial, operational, and customer measures.

4.2.1 Traffic Measures

Traffic represents enplaned passengers.

RPM: Revenue Passenger Miles is a key measure thar represents the distance traveled by revenue passengers. Specifically, it is calculated by multiplying the number of revenue passengers by the distance they travel in miles.

Yield: It is the average revenue earned per passenger mile.

$$Yield = \frac{Total\ Passenger\ Revenue}{RPM}$$

Yield reflects the effectiveness of an airline's pricing strategy for the base fare and ancillaries. Higher yields indicate stronger pricing due to factors such as business class sales, higher demand, and higher ancillary sales. A lower yield can result from discounting. promotional fares, and overcapacity.

4.2.2 Demand Measures

Demand refers to the total number of passengers who desire to travel and are willing and able to purchase tickets on a specific route or for a specific flight at a given price point. It encompasses not only those who actually fly (traffic) but also those who are unable to secure a seat due to capacity limitations.

$$Demand = Flown\ Traffic + Spilled\ Demand$$

4.2.3 Capacity Measures

ASM : Available Seat Miles is a key metric representing an airline's capacity to transport passengers. It is calculated by multiplying the number of seats available on an aircraft by the distance flown.

CASM : Cost per Available Seat Mile is a key metric that measures the cost of flying one seat one mile. It is calculated by dividing an airline's total operating expenses by its total available seat miles (*ASMs*). A lower *CASM* generally indicates a more efficient airline.

$$CASM = \frac{Operating\ Expenses}{ASM}$$

4.2.4 Additional Performance Measures

Average Load Factor : The average load factor is a key metric that measures the percentage of available seating capacity that is actually filled by revenue passengers on a given flight or group of flights.

$$Average\ Load\ Factor\ (LF) = \frac{RPM}{ASM}$$

$$Average\ Leg\ Load\ Factor = \frac{\sum LF}{Number\ of\ Flights}$$

$$Average\ System\ Load\ Factor = \frac{\sum RPM}{\sum ASM}$$

RASM : Revenue per available seat mile is a key metric to measure revenue generation per unit of capacity. It is calculated by dividing total operating revenue by available seat miles (*ASM*). A higher *RASM* generally indicates better revenue performance and profitability for an airline.

$$RASM = \frac{Total\ Operating\ Revenue}{ASM}$$

With the growth in ancillary revenues as a percentage of the value of a passenger ticket, *RASM* is an important measure. The total revenue includes ticket sales, baggage fees, and other ancillary revenues. *RASM* is also frequently referred to as total revenue per available seat mile (*TRASM*).

Prior to the introduction and sale of ancillary services, the total revenue in *RASM* was based on ticket sales. To include the sale of ancillary products and services *TRASM* was introduced. Today, the two terms are synonymous and is based on the total operating revenue.

Low-cost Carriers have always based this measure on the total operating revenue, since ancillary revenues can exceed the value of the ticket.

4.2.5 Operational and Customer Measures

The on-time performance (OTP) metric defines the percentage of flights that depart or arrive on time. This measure is tracked by several entities including the Bureau of Transportation Statistics (BTS), Cirium and OAG.

Customer Satisfaction Index measures passenger loyalty and satisfaction. The American Customer Satisfaction Index (ACSI) rates airlines on a 0–100 scale based on interviews regarding service quality. The U.S. DOT tracks consumer complaints.

Baggage handling performance tracks the rate of lost or delayed luggage. Airlines track and report baggage performance through IATA Resolution 753.

4.2.6 The Airline Profit Equation

An airline's profit is calculated by subtracting its total costs from its total revenue. Revenue is generated from passenger sales (cargo is excluded from this discussion), while costs include fuel, labor, maintenance, and other operational expenses. The operating profit is the difference between revenue generated and operating expenses.

$$\begin{aligned} \textit{Operating Profit} &= \textit{Passenger Revenue} - \textit{Operating Expenses} \\ &= (RPM \times Yield) - (ASM \times CASM) \end{aligned}$$

This is equivalent to

$$\textit{Operating Profit} = (RASM - CASM) * ASM$$

Relying on individual metrics to judge an airline's overall health can be very misleading. For example, high yields are not desirable if the load factors are too low. A low $CASM$ is not very meaningful if bookings are below plan. Very high system load factors may be the result of accepting too many deep discount bookings, which also drives higher passenger servicing costs at the airports.

Maximizing operating profit involves both increasing unit revenue ($RASM$) and controlling unit cost ($CASM$).

The single most important measure is the increase in $RASM$ month over month and year over year. It signifies:

1. Higher Profitability. A higher $RASM$ indicates that the airline is generating more revenue per seat flown a mile, potentially leading to increased profits, assuming that the underlying costs are stable.
2. Effective Revenue Management. An increase in $RASM$ signals that an airline is successfully implementing its pricing and revenue management strategies, optimizing ticket prices and seat sales based on demand.
3. Improved Efficiency: Airlines often utilize $RASM$ along with $CASM$ to measure their operational efficiency and compare their performance against competitors.

In short, a higher $RASM$ signifies that an airline is more effectively selling its available capacity and generating more revenue, which is generally a positive indicator for its financial health.

4.2.7 Employees Productivity Measures and Airline Efficiency

Staffing levels across airlines are not always comparable because of currency valuation, stage length, fleet mix, employee compensation by country, and social welfare programs. Two important measures with employees in the equation

Table 4.1 Employee metrics for the ten largest airlines measured by *ASM* in 2024[1]

Airline	Revenue (billions)	Available Seat miles (billions)	Employees	Revenue per employee	Employees per billion ASM
Ryanair	$14.6	159	27,076	$537,376	170
Qatar Airways	$22.2	159	53,182	$417,434	334
United Airlines	$57.1	311	107,300	$532,153	345
Delta Air Lines	$61.6	288	103,000	$598,058	358
Turkish Airines	$22.7	145	57,991	$391,440	400
Southwest Airlines	$27.5	178	72,450	$379,572	407
American Airlines	$54.2	293	133,300	$406,602	455
Emirates Airways	$37.4	222	121,223	$308,522	546
China Eastern Airlines	$18.4	138	85,168	$215,809	617
China Southern Airlines	$24.5	151	97,899	$250,258	648

Source [1]Data from annual reports and other sources

are the *Revenue per Employee* and the *Employees per Billion ASM*. The *Employees per Billion ASM* is considered a better measure and some airlines track *ASM per Employee*, which is an identical measure.

Table 4.1 illustrates these two measures for the ten largest airlines measured by *ASM*.

4.2.8 Network Carrier Economics

Network airlines design and manage complex hub-and-spoke networks to maximize the markets they serve. For network carriers with large domestic networks, hub economics typically requires about 30% local traffic. This translates into an average length of haul per passenger of 1.7 (less than 2 legs). They maximize profits by balancing high fixed costs like aircraft and gates with variable demand. To address high variance and competition, core competencies include strategic route planning, pricing, revenue management, inventory control and joint ventures to optimize passenger connections and profits across the entire system, not just individual routes.

According to IATA [IATA, 2025b] the operating costs for network carriers in 2025 were 96.1%. and the profit margin was 3.9%. The largest components of the operating costs were labor (27.7%) and fuel (26.8%).

4.3 Origins

Airline seat inventory is a perishable asset whose value vanishes at flight departure. When a flight departs with an empty seat, the inventory is lost forever. Yield management maximizes revenue from *perishable inventory* based on the fundamental premise that *all customers are not created equal. Yield management is the process of selling the right seat to the right customer at the right price at the right time.*

Basic segmentation is leisure travelers versus business travelers. Leisure travelers are price sensitive, book early, and not schedule sensitive. In contrast, business travelers are price insensitive, book closer to the flight departure date, and schedule sensitive. If the business fare is represented by p_b and leisure fare is represented by p_l, then typically $p_b > p_l$.

Yield management began to gain traction a few years after the deregulation of the U.S. airline industry in 1978 during President Jimmy Carter's administration. The Airline Deregulation (ADA) of 1978 was a significant event in U.S. economic policy, as it dismantled a comprehensive system of government controls [Kahn, 1988a, 1988b]. Prior to deregulation, airlines operated in a tightly regulated environment, overseen by governments and self-regulated through organizations like the regulatory Civil Aeronautics Board (CAB) and the International Air Transport Association (IATA). Economist Alfred E. Kahn, who served as the chairman of the CAB, was a strong advocate for deregulating the airline industry. Despite opposition from labor unions and airline industry executives, Kahn played a pivotal role in advocating for and implementing the deregulation of airlines in the United States. He is widely recognized as the "Father of Airline Deregulation."

Deregulation brought about a significant transformation in an industry that was previously regulated [Crandall, 1995; Dempsey & Gesell, 1997]. During the regulated period, competition was artificially restricted, and profitability was almost guaranteed. The CAB approved routes and set fares that ensured airlines a 12% return on flights that were 55% full. Deregulation of the airline industry altered the dynamics of airline profitability, increased competition and productivity, and ensured the survival of the most capable. The U.S. Domestic Airline Deregulation Act required the removal of route restrictions by December 31, 1981, and the end of rate regulation by January 1, 1983. The CAB expedited this process and eliminated route regulation in 1979 and rate regulation in 1980. With deregulation, the CAB ceased to exist on January 1, 1985.

The Standard Industry Fare Level (SIFL) was a formula created by CAB to serve as a benchmark for regulated fares before the Airline Deregulation Act (ADA) of 1978. In a deregulated environment, the government's control over fare levels through the CAB's SIFL ended for the domestic U.S. market [Kretsch,

1995]. This resulted in a wide range of fares offered by competing airlines, from traditional full fares to discounted and deeply discounted fares, making air travel accessible to a new segment of the population. Between 1976 and 1990, average fares paid by domestic passengers declined by 30% after adjusting for inflation. Deregulation also had a growing influence on the airline industry worldwide.

The beginnings of yield management can be traced back to the early to mid-1980s, when PEOPLExpress, a deep discount carrier, posed a significant threat to American Airlines with its heavily discounted tickets. The first yield management system [Cummings, 2007] was created by the Operations Research Group at American Airlines at the behest of Robert L. Crandall, the former Chairman and CEO of the airline. It served as a strategic and tactical tool for American to compete against low-cost deep discounter PEOPLExpress.

The development of yield management at American had begun in 1979 and had undergone five iterations, as outlined by Smith (2007). This process started with a rules-based system and culminated in the launch of DINAMO (Dynamic Inventory Allocation and Maintenance Optimizer) in 1986. The five iterations included the Multiclass Optimization Modeling System (MOMS) in 1979, the Discount Allocation Decision System (DADS) in 1980, the City Allocation Reporting System (CARS) in 1981, the Super City Analysis and Reporting System (SCARS) in 1982, and ultimately led to the launch of DINAMO in 1986.

Yield management maximizes revenue from *perishable inventory* based on the fundamental premise that *all customers are not created equal. Yield management is the process of selling the right seat to the right customer at the right price at the right time.*

Yield management was renamed "revenue management" for the *Fifth IATA Revenue Management Conference* in Montreal, Canada in 1993. It is revenue and not yield (revenue per revenue passenger mile) that is maximized.

4.3.1 Overbooking

Overbooking predates airline deregulation in 1978. Overbooking was used by airlines in the 1970s. during the regulated era. Customers could cancel their reservation, or just not show up, without incurring any financial penalty. In this context, overbooking, the practice of accepting more reservations than capacity to compensate for cancellations and no shows was a standard practice in the industry. Overbooking results in more passengers being accepted for their first choice of travel and also results in fewer empty seats on closed-out flights. Overbooking is a balancing act to minimize oversales and empty seats simultaneously on closed-out flights.

Southern Airways, based in Atlanta, Georgia, started scheduled service on June 10, 1949. They conducted the first "planned overbooking/controlled oversales" experiment in 1949 [Cross, 1998]. In the mid to late 1950s and 1960s, airlines practiced overbooking. It was reported by Marvin Rothstein [1985], Director of

Operations Research at American Airlines, that prior to 1961, U.S. airlines did not publicly acknowledge overbooking, even though they practiced it discreetly.

Mathematically, the airline overbooking problem is related to the "newsboy" or "newsvendor" problem. The expression "newsvendor problem" comes from the Morse and Kimball book [Morse and Kimball, 1951], where they described demand uncertainty and the dilemma faced by the newsboy. Philip McCord Morse was an American physicist, administrator and pioneer of operations research in World War II. He is considered to be the father of operations research in the U.S. The co-author of the book, George Elbert Kimball was an American professor of quantum chemistry and a pioneer of operations research algorithms during World War II.

To illustrate, a newsboy buys papers in bulk for $1.00 and sells them for $4.00. Every paper sold generates a profit of $3.00 and any unsold papers at the end of the day are discarded for a $1.00 loss. Since turning away customers in the absence of inventory is more painful than discarding the unsold papers, the newsboy wants to know how many newspapers to order?

The opportunity cost of turning away a customer is known as the *Cost of Underage*. In this example, this cost is the profit margin of $3.00. The cost associated with discarding the unsold newspapers is the called the *Cost of Overage*. . In this example, the cost is the price paid for the newspaper, $1.00. To find the profit maximizing newspapers to order, the optimal point on the demand distribution for newspapers is called the *Critical Fractile* and is calculated as shown below:

$$\frac{Cost\ of\ Underage}{Cost\ of\ Underage + Cost\ of\ Overage}$$

The *Cost of Underage* represents the lost profit from not having an adequate inventory of newspapers and *Cost of Overage* represents the cost of holding excess inventory. The ratio represents the probability that demand will be lower than expected. It helps decide when to order more inventory. Ordering balances the costs of having too few or too many items. The goal is to find the best amount to order.

The critical fractile is used to determine the optimal inventory level for a single ordering period. Assuming that demand for newspapers daily follows a normal distribution with an average daily demand of 100, and a standard deviation of 20, the optimal number of newspapers to order is given by.

$\mu = 100$
$\sigma = 20$
Critical Fractile = 0.75
Critical Fractile Z-score = 0.6645
Number of newspapers to order = 100 + (20*0.6645) = 113

In the airline context, the *Cost of Underage* is the cost of compensating oversold passengers and the *Cost of Overage* is the cost of a spoiled seat, which is the marginal revenue. Overbooking models assume that the distribution of show ups follows a binomial distribution and when capacity is large, a truncated normal distribution (truncated at the overbooking authorization limit) can also be applied.

4.3.2 Littlewood's Rule

Prior to airline deregulation in 1978, the first discount allocation model was proposed by Kenneth Littlewood [Littlewood, 1972] from the British Overseas Airways Corporation (BOAC). Littlewood.

proposed that airlines maximize revenues instead of passenger occupancy on a flight for the perishable seat inventory.

Consider two booking classes Y and B with fares R_Y and R_B and $R_Y > R_B$. Y is considered the full-fare and B is the discount fare. Further, we will assume that are no cancellations, no-shows, or overbooking for an aircraft cabin with capacity C. Let D_Y and D_B represent the average demand for Y and B with a finite variance and the cumulative density functions for the two classes are F_Y and F_B respectively. It is assumed that demand for discount class B arrives first followed by the demand for full fare Y. The problem is to determine how many seats to protect for full fare Y. This also implies how many discount passengers can be accepted.

The discount passengers paying R_B can be accepted as long as it exceeds the marginal value of Y. Hence,

$$R_Y(\Pr(D_Y > x) = R_B$$

$$\Pr(D_Y > x) = \frac{R_B}{R_Y}$$

and the protection x for full fare class Y is

$$x = F_Y^{-1}\left(1 - \frac{R_B}{R_Y}\right)$$

This is known as Littlewood's rule for two booking classes and it is an optimal policy.

Mathematically, Littlewood's rule is a variation on the standard critical fractile solution for the newsboy problem discussed in the previous section.

Littlewood's rule can be extended to multiple classes but it is an approximation and referred to as an heuristic.

4.4 Optimal and Heuristic Approaches to Revenue Management Discount Controls

To maximize expected revenue by allocating fixed and perishable capacity to different booking classes that are associated with different fares, advance bookings, cancellations, no-shows, and demand uncertainty must be considered to solve this problem. The three components of revenue management solutions are Overbooking to compensate for cancellations and no shows and Discount Allocation controls, which determines how many bookings to accept in each booking class. An extension of discount allocation controls is origin and destination controls for large network carriers.

Broadly speaking there are two primary customer segments: business travelers and leisure travelers, with the following traits.

Leisure travelers are price sensitive, typically book early, are schedule insensitive, and pay a discounted fare R_D. In contrast, business travelers are price insensitive, book closer to flight departure, are schedule sensitive, and pay the full fare R_F.

The discount allocation solution must simultaneously minimize dilution and spoilage. Dilution occurs when seats were sold at a discounted price R_D that resulted in some full fare customers who would have paid the full fare R_F being turned away due to the absence of available seats The difference between R_F and R_D is the cost of turning away each full fare customer. Discount allocation spoilage occurs when discount passengers are turned away but the flight at departure had empty seats. In this scenario, R_D is the cost for each spoiled seat.

Dynamic programming requires infinitesimal instances of time so that at the most one booking request arrives in each period. Consider N booking classes and flight departure occurs at time T.

Define the following terms:

P_{it}: Probability of a booking request for booking class i at time t.
P_{0t}: Probability of no booking requests at time $t = 1 - P_{1t} - P_{2t} -, \ldots, -P_{nt}$
R_i: Fare for booking class i with the fare hierarchy $R_1 > R_2 > \ldots > R_n > 0$
C: Remaining unbooked capacity
u_{it}: Equals 1 if a booking of type i is accepted at time t, 0 otherwise
$V_t(C)$: Value-to-go function

$$V_t(C) = \max_{u_{it} \in \{0,1\}} \sum_{i=1}^{N} P_{it} \{ u_{it} [R_i + V_{t+1}(C-1)] + (1 - u_{it}) V_{t+1}(C) \} + P_{0t} V_{t+1}(C)$$

$$= V_{t+1}(C) + \max_{u_{it} \in \{0,1\}} \sum_{i=1}^{N} P_{it} u_{it} [R_i - \Delta V_{t+1}(C)$$

where $V_T(C) = 0$ for all C, $V_T(0) = 0$ for all t, and $\Delta V_t(C) = V_t(C-1) - V_t(C)$.

The optimal policy, which is the set of booking limits for each class, can be derived by backward recursion. This approach is not very popular due to its inherent computational complexity and heuristic methods like the expected marginal seat revenue (EMSR) are used to approximate the optimal solution.

4.4.1 The First Yield Management System

In 1980, William Swan, a member of the O.R. department at American, made extensions to Littlewood's model, with the logit approximation to the normal distribution [Swan, 1983]. This was first deployed in 1982 [Smith et al., 1992].

Yield management came into existence on a significant scale a few years after the deregulation of the U.S. airline industry. The chronology of major milestones is outlined [Vinod 2016a, 2021a].

The term "yield management" is attributed to Robert L. Crandall when he was Senior Vice President at American Airlines [Cross, 1995]. When he became President in 1980, the airline industry was already experiencing the effects of deregulation. Crandall and his team worried about competitors that were aggressively lowering prices, which threatened profitability of the entire airline industry in this new environment. As a result, airlines began to innovate. They quickly understood the need to focus on the mix of passengers to enhance profits. It became clear that filling seats with paying customers was crucial, as the cost of carrying an extra passenger was minimal, leading to significant profit.

The first yield management system was developed as a rules-based system [Smith, 2007] before being enhanced to a decision support system based on marginal revenues. The economic overbooking model [Smith, 1982] in DINAMO evaluated tradeoffs between denied boarding costs and the cost of a spoiled seat. American's yield management system was called DINAMO (Dynamic INventory Allocation Maintenance Optimizer). DINAMO, the leg/segment revenue management system and the origin and destination (O&D) systems (virtual nesting and continuous nesting) that followed were developed under the leadership of Thomas M. Cook in the Operations Research Group at American Airlines which became American Airlines Decision Technologies in the late 1980s.

To forecast demand for the leg/segment system, various metrics were considered and evaluated such as cumulative demand, net demand, and reservations holding by reading day interval and days to departure. In the airline reservations system, the inventory controls are always in the "reservations space." Using cumulative demand or net demand for demand forecasting would have required a conversion to the "reservations space" for inventory controls with cumulative cancellation rate or booked cancellation rate profiles respectively. After extensive analysis, a decision was made to forecast reservations holding by reading day interval which was already in the "reservations space," and did not require any further transformation.

Later in the O&D virtual nesting system, the forecasting metric was replaced with remaining demand at departure.

The overbooking model was based on the Economic Overbooking Model to which the oversale rate constraint was later applied. The discount allocation model was an expected marginal seat revenue (EMSR) model [Smith, 1982], an extension of Littlewood's Rule [Littlewood, 1972] to multiple booking classes, which generated the joint protection levels for higher valued booking classes relative to the lower valued booking class. This method was later called $EMSR_B$ [Belobaba, 1992] as a computationally viable heuristic to optimal booking limits [Curry, 1990] that requires the evaluation of multi-dimensional numerical quadrature.

Beyond the decision support capability of forecasting demand and determining the optimal mix of passengers to accept on a flight, the success of yield management at American was made possible with advances in inventory control on the host CRS [Vinod, 1990] where American's schedules and fares were stored. DINAMO used nested inventory controls by leg class with segment limits.

American Airlines established its hub at Dallas/Fort Worth International Airport (DFW) on June 11, 1981. Central to the launch of Growth Plan I in the 1980s by American's CEO Robert Crandall was the introduction of the McDonnell Douglas MD-80 (Super 80) aircraft into the fleet in 1983. The large number of new MD-80s entering service spurred the transition from a point-to-point network to the creation of a hub and spoke network at American's two primary hubs, Dallas Fort Worth and Chicago O'Hare to provide air services for a wide geographic area. Expansion of the fleet and workforce led to lower operating costs, increased revenues, and profits. In a post deregulated world, a hub and spoke network provided service to more markets through the hubs and increased aircraft utilization. Hub economics were based on a mix of 30% local traffic and 70% connecting traffic. With the American network transforming to a hub and spoke network, leg based controls generated by DINAMO had limitations and steps were undertaken to transition from a leg/segment yield management system that optimized controls by flight to a Origin and Destination (O&D) based system that maximized network revenues by capturing the value of the reservation request by O&D and maximize network revenues.

The first O&D yield management system was deployed in 1987 with virtual nesting controls at American Airlines [Smith, 1986; Smith, Leimkuhler, Darrow, 1992] controls at American Airlines. With virtual nesting, O&D classes were mapped to virtual buckets to control inventory by O&D. Virtual nesting produced an additional 1%–2% in incremental revenues over leg based controls. The reservations inventory module in Sabre's Passenger Sales and Service (PSS) system was enhanced to support virtual nesting inventory controls. The major investments in the real-time system included the introduction of virtual buckets by flight leg and the market class to bucket mapping. The expansion of the flight Inventory Detail Records (INDs) to support virtual nesting also required that all the applications and queries that accessed the IND had to be tested. This was a major investment since the code had to be developed in TPF on the mainframe where Sabre's PSS resided. When virtual nesting was deployed for American Airlines on Sabre's PSS, an important consideration was dual indexing. With dual indexing a connecting market can be indexed distinctly on the first leg versus the second leg based on the reservation value. Multiple indexing is not required for U.S. majors.

Dual indexing is adequate because the economics of a hub and spoke network has on average 30% locals and 70% connecting traffic. This translates into an average length of haul per passenger of 1.7 (less than 2 legs).

Optimal mapping of itineraries to virtual buckets based on value produced an additional 0.4% in revenues. The optimal mapping was based on a dynamic programming model that maximized the separation of fare values between buckets and simultaneously minimized the variance of fare values within a bucket [Vinod, 1989]. To avoid indexing of outliers to unique buckets, the fare values were weighted by historical flown traffic by bucket.

American calculated that the systematic use of yield management enabled the company to generate $1.4 billion in incremental revenue between 1989 and 1991, while AMR's (the parent company) profits were $892 million over the same period. Among the European carriers, SAS deployed O&D controls in 1993 [Petersen, 1996]. Keeping abreast with the evolution of revenue management, the real-time transaction systems – the Global Distribution Systems (GDS) and airline central reservations systems (host CRS) brought to market some of the key enablers for O&D control such as seamless availability and sell (alternately called Direct Connect Availability and Direct Connect Sell or Interactive Availability and Interactive Sell) for true last seat availability by point of sale, married segment control and journey control for the 1980's to early 1990's.

With the advent of origin and destination controls, virtual nesting was adopted by a few additional carriers: Scandinavian Airlines System (SAS), KLM Royal Dutch Airlines, United Airlines and Delta Air Lines. The more popular method for O&D inventory control was continuous nesting [Vinod, 1995; Vinod & Ratliff, 1990], also known as bid price controls, because of its ability to discern and control each individual reservations request based on value by point of sale. This capability was developed in Sabre PSS in 1997 for American's migration to bid price controls from virtual nesting controls in 1998. The challenge faced by many airlines was to have the O&D control capability on the legacy reservations system without incurring high development costs associated with the expansion of the inventory records and associated changes in availability and sell processing. Partnering with Air France, Sabre launched the *Availability Processor*™, a Unix-based satellite cooperative processor that was attached to the host CRS (called Alpha3) to process availability and sell transactions for O&D control in 1997 [Smith et al., 1997]. To support advances in revenue management, several legacy reservations systems were upgraded to support inventory controls by origin and destination. Examples include United's Apollo, EDS's Shares, Delta's Deltamatic and Northwest's NWA PARS.

Bob Crandall has stated on numerous occasions at public forums and employee conferences that *yield management is the single most important technological development in transportation management since airline deregulation.*

In 1992, Robert Crandall, Chairman and CEO of AMR (American's parent company) estimated that *"yield (revenue) management has generated $1.4 billion in incremental revenue in the last three years by creating a pricing structure that responds to demand on a flight-by-flight basis"* [Smith et al., 1992]. By 1998

Tom Cook, President of *Sabre Decision Technologies*, had increased the estimated impact to "*almost $1 billion in annual incremental revenue*" [Cook, 1998].

Today yield management is widely acknowledged to contribute between 3 and 8% in incremental revenues based on the level of sophistication of the inventory controls in the airline industry. It is also a mature and mission critical function at a large number of airlines [Donovan, 2005] with significant growth opportunities for management.

4.5 Role of Revenue Management in a Customer's Itinerary

The role of traditional revenue management in creating a priced itinerary for a customer and subsequent ticketing is shown in Fig. 4.2.

The end product of traditional revenue management is booking class availability. This definition of the end product will change with the advent of IATA NDC and initiatives by airlines to deploy continuous dynamic pricing.

Revenue management systems have several components [Vinod, 2021a]. It all begins with data collection, data cleansing, and preparation of the data for use by the various core components. Traditional revenue management is all about determining which booking classes are closed and which are open on the airline's reservations inventory control system for every request. Fares mapped to open booking classes are candidates for generating an itinerary price subject to fulfilling fare rules and restrictions. An itinerary is priced by the airline's pricing system or by the GDS that considers booking class availability, fare rules, and restrictions.

A brief description of the core applications is summarized below.

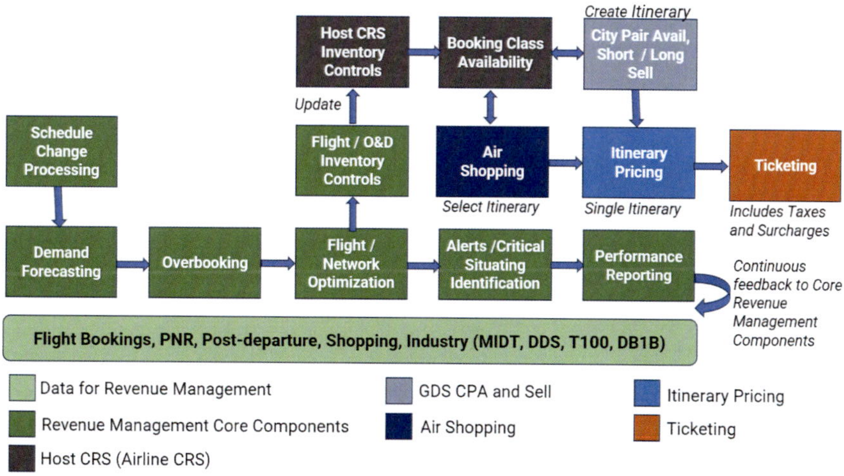

Fig. 4.2 Role of revenue management in creating a price quote

4.5.1 Schedule Change Processing

Revenue management systems require data from historical flight departures to predict demand for future flights. The process of mapping historical flight departures to future flight departures is complicated because of schedule changes. Schedule changes occur for a range of reasons including flight number changes, frequency changes, departure time changes, addition of new flights, and flight cancellations. Schedule changes must be isolated to preserve history for forecasting purposes.

A Flight Id is an internal numerical flight identifier. It is a combination of flight number, board point, off point, and departure time window. The Flight Id concept can be used to map historical schedules to future schedules, thereby providing a framework for tracking historical flight data. The time window centered around the departure time of the origin enables the tracking of flight history. The default time window parameter (e.g., 60 min) can be adjusted dynamically based on changes in flight departure times and changes in flight frequency.

All processing will be based on Flight Ids and not flight numbers. Figure 4.3 illustrates an approach to create and maintain Flight Ids in the system.

The Flight Id assignment process runs as part of the revenue management nightly batch processing to create inventory controls. The hierarchical rule-based algorithm consistently retains the Flight Id on a daily basis based on the leg origin, leg destination and departure time window. The process also strives to preserve consistent Flight Id values across season changes, departure time changes, capacity changes and all future departure dates in the schedule.

After converting all the flight number-based schedule data to Flight Ids, an Aggregate Id is assigned to each flight segment class. For O&D carriers, a Service

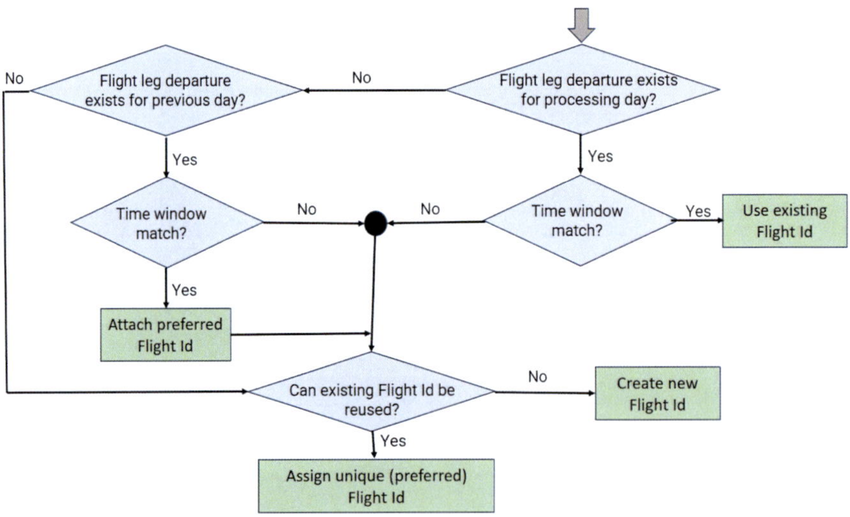

Fig. 4.3 Flight id creation and maintenance

Id is assigned to each service (origin, destination, itinerary based on connect-point) which may consist of one or more Aggregate Ids. Depending on the carrier, demand forecasts will be generated by Aggregate Id or Service Id.

4.5.2 Demand Forecasting

The observed demand on a flight is called traffic. The sum of the turned away demand due to inventory closures and the observed traffic onboard a flight constitute the unconstrained demand. Forecasting the unconstrained demand, demand that is not constrained by inventory controls, is a fundamental requirement. Figure 4.4 illustrates demand distribution, traffic, capacity, and spill.

Demand follows a gamma distribution. If the flown traffic data is not unconstrained, the demand that is forecast from historical data will always be a lower bound on the true demand and will be biased. Figure 4.4 illustrates this point with the distribution of demand for a flight. The difference between the expected demand (μ) and the traffic (t) is the expected spilled demand ($\mu - t$). At low load factors, traffic and demand are comparable, but at high load factors, demand can significantly exceed traffic (resulting in demand spill). The rate of spill increases with demand variance and load factor (since traffic cannot exceed 100% of capacity).

Forecasting demand for fare products is the first step. It entails unconstraining traffic to estimate demand followed by forecasting demand for future flight departures by statistical, choice modeling, or machine learning techniques.

The expected maximization (*EM*) method is an effective technique for estimating unconstrained demand. The *EM* algorithm is usually applied to incomplete data. The development of this method is attributed to Professor Ray Fair [Greene, 2003] who extracted a sample of 601 responses from about 20,000 received from a 101-question survey on sex in *Psychology Today* in 1969. Fair analyzed responses on extramarital responses from men and women married for the first time using a tobit model [Tobin, 1958], a class of regression models where the observed range

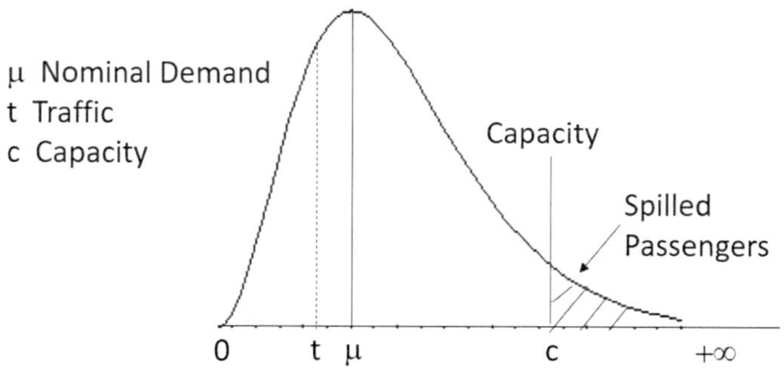

Fig. 4.4 Demand distribution, traffic, capacity, and spill

of the dependent variable is censored. This led to the development of the *EM* algorithm [Dempster et al., 1977; Fair, 1978]. The algorithm iteratively calculates the maximum likelihood estimates of parameters with constrained booking data. The *EM* method can be extended to multi-flights.

Demand can be forecasted based on methods that are broadly categorized into time series models, causal models, and machine learning [Vinod, 2021a]. Time series models use historical data to identify patterns and trends, while causal models incorporate factors like economic conditions and competitor actions. Machine learning algorithms analyze vast datasets to identify complex patterns and make highly accurate predictions. Techniques such as Support Vector Machines (SVMs) and Neural Networks (NNs) or artificial neural networks (ANNs) are gaining acceptance for demand forecasting as these models can incorporate more historical data. A fundamental challenge with AI-powered forecast models is that they need to be transparent and explainable (XAI) so that revenue management analysts can understand and trust the system's decisions. For example, neural networks are computational models that process data through interconnected nodes arranged in input, hidden and output layers. This is an active area of research [Arrieta et al., 2020].

4.5.2.1 Consumer Choice Modeling

In the competitive airline industry, understanding and predicting consumer behavior is of critical importance to determine how consumers select an itinerary from a choice set. Consumer choice models [Ben-Akiva & Lerman, 1985] offer a powerful framework for forecasting airline data by analyzing the factors influencing a traveler's decisions when selecting a flight. By considering schedule and fare attributes in the selection process, the consumer choice modeling approach follows the actual demand process. The consumer choice models, often discrete choice models (DCMs), are economic models that analyze and predict individual choices from a set of available alternatives. These models help understand why a passenger might choose one airline, flight, or fare class over another. Unlike traditional time-series models that rely primarily on historical trends, DCMs incorporate the underlying reasons behind passenger choices, providing a more robust forecast, particularly in dynamic market conditions. DCMs can quantify the effect of changes in airline attributes (e.g., price, schedule) on passenger choices, enabling airlines to optimize their offerings. This approach to demand forecasting follows the actual demand process. Understanding customer choices improves the demand forecasting process, leading to higher revenues.

Despite the benefits of using consumer choice models, challenges exist in applying these models for demand forecasting. They are:

1. Quality of the data and availability of the data. Typically, shopping data is required where the shopping session can be linked to the booking for calibration purposes.
2. Underlying model complexity. DCMs can be computationally intensive, requiring sophisticated statistical methods for parameter estimation.

3. Incorporating non-measurable factors is a challenge. The task of accurately capturing and quantifying the impact of subjective factors like satisfaction can be difficult.

4.5.2.2 Forecast Accuracy

Improving forecast accuracy is a continuous focus area for revenue management analysts and its importance cannot be understated to minimize revenue dilution. Identifying and accounting for seasonal patterns in demand is important for accurate forecasting. Many simulation studies have shown that a 10% improvement in forecast accuracy can lead to a ½ percent improvement in revenues with better inventory controls.

4.5.3 Overbooking

Airlines overbook flights to compensate for the effects of cancellations and no shows. No-shows are customers who hold a reservation at departure and do not show up for a flight. Go-shows are passengers who show up without a confirmed reservation for a flight or those that show up with a confirmed reservation for which no reference is found in the carrier's host reservations system. The latter category is referred to as no record passengers or NOREC's. Mis-connects are passengers who missed their flight connections due to flight delays.

Spoilage represents the number of empty seats on closed out flights. Oversales represent passengers who were denied boarding due to a lack of seats. The risks associated with oversales are passenger compensation, loss of goodwill and higher operating costs at the airports. The smaller the spoilage factor, the more effective the airline overbooking policy is. Overbooking has two objectives that should be satisfied simultaneously, minimizing spoilage, *and* minimizing denied boardings (oversales), which should be satisfied *simultaneously* to maximize onboard revenues.

Typically, when an airline is in an oversold situation, volunteers are requested who are offered a denied boarding compensation voucher with a specific dollar face value that can be redeemed for future travel, usually within a one-year period. The denied boarding costs vary by airport and are influenced by customer demographics and city pair frequency. Minimizing the number of denied boardings minimizes the unaccommodated passenger costs and promotes goodwill for repeat business. The true cost of a voucher for an airline is approximately one third the face value of the voucher.

4.5.3.1 Overbooking Nomenclature

The various variables used to describe aspects of overbooking are summarized in Table 4.2.

Passengers Boarded (PB) = Min [(B + GS + SB – NS + NR – MC), C]
Bookings = SU + NS

Table 4.2 Overbooking nomenclature

Variable	Description
Capacity (C)	Physical capacity of the cabin
Authorized Capacity (AU)	The overbooking limit for the cabin
Bookings (B)	Confirmed bookings for a flight, always ≤ Authorized Capacity
Waitlisted Passengers (WL)	Passengers on a waitlist when the flight is fully booked
Go show Passengers (GS)	Passengers who show up without confirmed reservation for a flight or those that show up with a confirmed reservation for which no reference is found in the carrier's host reservations system. The latter category is referred to as no record passengers or NOREC's
Standby Passengers (SB)	Passengers on a list to potentially board a flight if seats become available after all confirmed passengers have boarded
No-shows (NS)	Passengers that fail to show up for their flights
Show-ups (SU)	Passengers with bookings who show-up and board the plane
No-show Rate (NSR)	Percentage of booked passengers who don't show up for their flight
Show-up Rate (SUR)	Percentage of booked passengers who show up for their flight
Passengers Boarded (PB)	Enplaned passengers is the number of passengers who boarded a flight
Denied Boardings (DB)	Passengers who were denied boarding because the flight was oversold
Spoilage (SP)	Lost revenue from empty seats on a flight when it departs
No-rec passengers (NR)	Passengers whose names or booking information cannot be found in the airline reservations system when they attempt to check in for a flight
Mis-connect passengers (MC)	Passengers who missed their connections due to flight delays and were rebooked on an alternate flight

Show-ups (SU) = PB + DB – GS – SB
No-show Rate = (B-SU)/B
Show-up Rate = 1.0 – NSR
Spoilage = C – PB, when PB = AU and the flight is closed to new bookings.

4.5.3.2 Overbooking Model

The overbooking model requires a forecast of the show up rate at departure, also called the boarding rate and the standard deviation of the show up rate. The boarding rate for a flight can be forecast by day of week using a time series model. The calculation of the boarding rate must include an adjustment for go-shows and mis-connects. No-recs are added to the count and mis-connects are subtracted to determine passengers boarded by cabin to calculate the show up rate.

The show up rate for a flight cabin is calculated as follows:

$$Show\ up\ Rate = \frac{Passengers\ boarded\ in\ cabin}{Reservations\ holding\ on\ departure\ date}$$

Passengers boarded in a cabin should account for upgrades to a higher cabin and not include non-revenue travel. A snapshot of reservations being held (called "reservations holding" by revenue management analysts) may be taken the night before flight departure or preferably a snapshot should be taken a few hours (usually 4 h) before flight departure.

The mean absolute deviation (MAD) of the boarding rate can be updated with a simple exponential smoothing model. Hence,

$$\sigma_s^2 = 1.25MAD_s$$

based on the assumption that the forecast error is normally distributed with a mean of zero and a finite variance $N\left(0, \sigma_e^2\right)$.

Using PNRs as a data source for no-show forecasting has its benefits [Kalka & Weber, 2000]. Kalka and Weber demonstrated using Lufthansa data that no-show forecast error could be reduced from 12.4% to 9.5%. Considering the various attributes on booked PNR's, causal models can be developed to forecast no-shows [Garrow and Koppelman, 2004a, 2004b, Kambour, 2006; Dupuis, 2010]. These models typically produce improvements in forecast accuracy of no-shows by 3%–7%.

Calculating the overbooking limit is based on the assumption that the flight closes out before flight departure. Many airlines continue to use the deterministic model, based on the false assumption that there is no uncertainty in the show up rate.

$$Overbooking\ Limit = \frac{Capacity}{Show\ up\ Rate}$$

Hence, if the capacity is 100 seats and the show up rate is 86%,

$$Overbooking\ Limit = Auth = \frac{100}{0.86} = 116$$

This model is not advocated since the overbooking controls will be aggressive resulting in oversales. The deterministic model has a variance of zero, leading to more aggressive controls than the binomial and normal distribution based overbooking models.

To address uncertainty in the show up process, the distribution of the show up process can be modeled as a normal distribution. The overbooking limit (*Auth*) for a cabin can be calculated based on the cabin capacity (*Capacity*), mean show up rate (μ_s) and the standard deviation σ_s) with the objective of no denied boardings

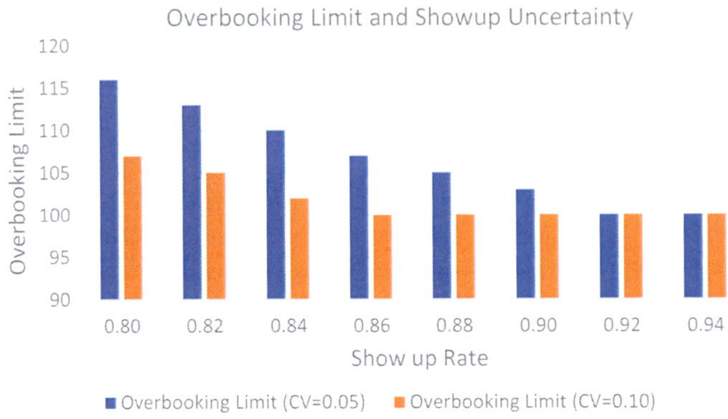

Fig. 4.5 Overbooking limit as a function of uncertainty in the show up rate

and reservations holding at the overbooking limit (*Auth*) based on a confidence level of 95%.

$$Auth = \frac{Capacity}{\mu_s + (1.645 * \sigma_s)}$$

Hence if the show up rate is 86% and the standard deviation is 0.043,

$$Overbooking\ Limit = Auth = \frac{100}{0.86 + (1.645 * 0.043)} = 107$$

Figure 4.5 illustrates the overbooking limit at low uncertainty (CV = 0.05) and high uncertainty (CV = 0.10).

The show-up rate is forecasted using statistical or causal models and used as input to determine the overbooking limit for each cabin. There are two types of overbooking models. First is the economic overbooking model that maximizes the net revenue and the second is the conservative oversale rate constrained model that limits the number of oversales. Figure 4.6 illustrates the overbooking model and the optimal overbooking limit based on the economic overbooking model. Most airlines do not compute the optimal overbooking limit based on the economic model but apply an oversale rate constraint that represents the quality of service that the airline is comfortable with. The oversale rate constraint is expressed as X per 10,000 passengers boarded and X is defined by the airline. Typically, the oversale rate constrained limit will be lower than the economic overbooking limit. The cost of spoilage in not shown on the graph because of the scale.

A model that is used by airlines is the binomial model of cancellations and no-shows that are lumped together. The binomial model is not advocated since it is a one-parameter distribution. The observed variance of the show up process is typically higher than the estimate from the binomial distribution. Using the binomial model results in lower estimates of the standard deviation of the show up

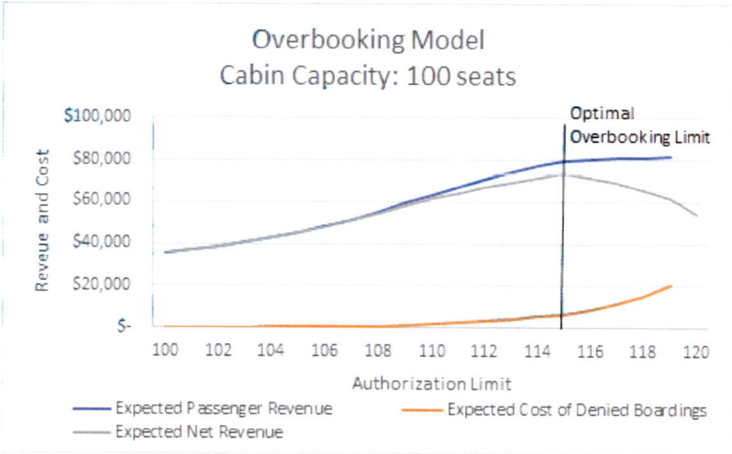

Fig. 4.6 Optimal overbooking limit with the economic overbooking model

rate which in turn results in aggressive overbooking limits that can result in higher oversales.

By assuming that the show up process is a truncated normal distribution, for given values of the mean (μ) and standard deviation (σ) of the show up process, the key measures of expected boarded and expected oversales can be determined [Smith, 1982]. It is important to ensure that the show up process is a truncated normal since passenger demand greater than the authorization (overbooking) level cannot be confirmed on a flight. These passengers do not receive denied boarding compensation and should not be considered as denied boardings. Denied boardings is always constrained by the overbooking limit minus cabin capacity.

Oversale costs are typically modeled as a non-linear function because the penalties associated with denied boarding increase rapidly as the number of oversold passengers exceeds capacity. Unlike simple linear models that assume a constant cost per denied person, non-linear models better represent the exponential growth of expenses caused by passenger inconvenience, loss of goodwill, and potential costs associated with delayed connecting flights. The denied boarding costs also vary by station and are influenced by customer demographics. For example, the average denied boarding cost at New York's LaGuardia airport would be significantly higher than the denied boarding cost at former President Clinton's home state capital of Little Rock, Arkansas. Minimizing the number of denied boardings minimizes the unaccommodated passenger costs and promotes goodwill for repeat business.

Standby passengers help airlines maximize revenue and manage overbooking by filling seats left empty by no-shows, last-minute cancellations, or missed connections. This process, called a "go-show," allows airlines to ensure higher usage of available capacity. It acts as a buffer for overbooked flights, reducing the need for involuntary, costly, or disruptive passenger oversales.

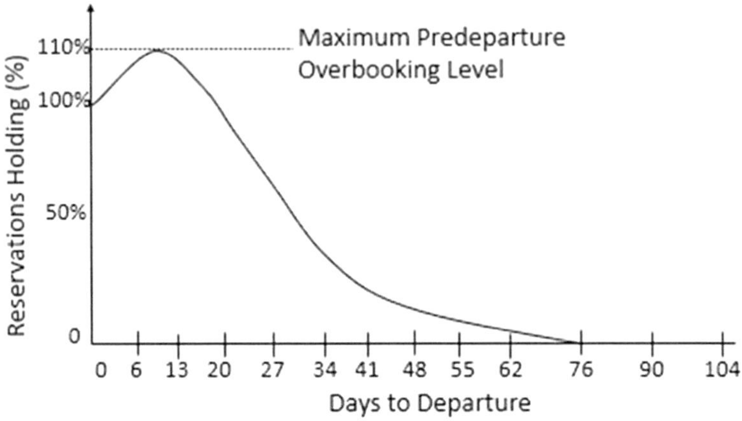

Fig. 4.7 Fall off rate for coach cabin

From the departure overbooking levels, the predeparture overbooking levels can be calculated, A simple, yet effective approach is to use the reservations holding profile to determine predeparture overbooking levels. The fall off rate is the reservations holding by reading day (pre-departure points in time) expressed as a percentage of the reservations held at departure. These profiles are typically calibrated by cabin and day of week by flight leg or segment.

Figure 4.7 illustrates a fall-off rate profile for coach cabin. Fall off rates are more stable and produce less volatility in overbooking levels than the convolution of booking and cancellation rates. The maximum pre-departure overbooking level is used as the overbooking limit for all pre-departure days leading up to the peak because cancellations are replaced with new bookings.

The predeparture overbooking level for a flight on reading day r is given by

$$\begin{aligned} &\textit{Predeparture Overbooking Level}_r \\ &\quad = \textit{Departure Overbooking Level} \times \textit{Max}_{i \leq r}(\textit{Fall off Rate Profile}_i) \end{aligned}$$

The economic overbooking model evaluates the tradeoffs between denied boarding costs (oversale costs) and the cost of an empty seat (spoiled seat). In a mathematical sense, it is closely related to the newsboy problem.

4.5.4 Flight Optimization and Network Optimization

For airlines that control inventory by leg/segment, the revenue mix optimization model optimizes inventory controls by flight. The output of the model is nested inventory controls based on the expected marginal seat revenue calculation. This is illustrated in Sect. 4.3.

For network carriers that control inventory by origin and destination (O&D) a network optimization model is used to model all the upline and downline effects to determine the optimal inventory controls. In some cases, a network decomposition approach is used. The most popular method for inventory control today is bid price control. Inventory controls generated by revenue management must update the real-time execution system, the host CRS. This is illustrated in Sect. 4.3.

4.5.5 Critical Situation Identification and Alerts

Management of flights and markets (for O&D network carriers) by revenue management analysts is by exception, typically less than 10 percent of an airline's flights and 15% of markets. KPIs are identified and thresholds are established to generate the alerts.

An example of a KPI is the pre-departure spill rate by booking class. The spill rate is the ratio of spilled passengers to unconstrained demand by booking class expressed as a percentage. The spill rate must be in ascending order of the booking class hierarchy to ensure that inventory controls are consistent with the objective of maximizing revenues. If it is not, an alert will be generated for further investigation.

4.5.6 Performance Reporting and Feedback

Performance reporting of the key performance indicators is an integral component of revenue management. It enables analysts to validate the quality of the various models and data. All pertinent post departure and pre-departure metrics must be monitored [Vinod, 2021a] for continuous feedback.

The process of continuous improvement is a requirement to ensure consistency in model recommendations, consistency, and repeatability of the business process to generate incremental revenues.

4.5.6.1 Revenue Opportunity Model

The revenue opportunity model [Vinod, 2021a] is used to measure the effectiveness of the revenue management program over time.

The revenue opportunity model (ROM) is used by airlines to isolate revenue management performance from other factors that influence revenue generation. The leg/segment revenue opportunity model was developed at American Airlines in 1987 to understand how revenue performance could have been improved in the prior month based on perfect hindsight, if perfect information were available. The ROM evaluates the performance of revenue management controls when applied on historical departures. A key input into the model is the unconstrained demand by booking class, which can be estimated post departure based on historical open/close data for the flight leg. The model Identifies the optimal inventory controls, with perfect hindsight, to produce the maximum revenue and determines whether the actual controls used were relatively good or poor. It answers the "what-if" question by providing insight into what could have been done differently to improve revenue performance.

The discount allocation revenue opportunity model determines the percentage of the total revenue opportunity that was gained through the process of revenue management.

An example of the discount allocation revenue opportunity model is shown on Table 4.3 for a single flight leg, AUSDFW with a capacity of 100 seats.

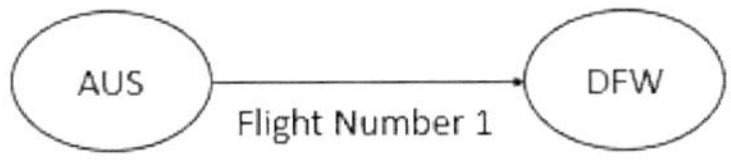

The *actual onboard passengers* are a direct consequence of the inventory controls recommended by revenue management. *No controls* assume that revenue management controls were not applied, and passengers were accepted first come first served from the lowest to the highest booking class. *Perfect controls* assume that with perfect hindsight, the most valuable passengers would have been accepted. In reality, perfect controls cannot be achieved in practice due to the underlying uncertainty in the demand forecast and the uncertainty of show ups for a flight. The process of revenue management effectively manages the risk associate with this uncertainty and maximizes expected revenues. The corresponding revenue metrics for the three scenarios are:

$$Revenue\ Opportunity = Maximum\ Revenue - Minimum\ Revenue$$

$$Revenue\ Opportunity = \$12,270 - \$7,200 = \$5,070$$

$$Revenue\ Earned = Actual\ Onboard\ Revenue - Minimum\ Revenue$$

$$Revenue\ Earned = \$9,590 - \$7,200 = \$2,390$$

$$Percent\ Revenue\ Gained = \frac{Revenue\ Earned}{Revenue\ Opportunity} \times 100\% = 47.14\%$$

An alternative way of viewing the performance statistics is shown in Fig. 4.8 which provides a breakdown of the total revenue opportunity into spoilage, dilution and revenue gained. This is a conceptual view and not to scale with the example provided.

The *Customer Revenue Opportunity* measure is calculated from the optimal mix achievable up to the actual boarded count by flight leg. The *Discount Allocation Spoilage* represents the spoilage that results despite demand

Table 4.3 Calculating Discount Allocation Revenue Opportunity. Flight: 1; AUSDFW; Capacity: 100 seats

Booking class	Average fare	Unconstrained demand[a]	Passengers				Revenue ($)			
			RM controls[b]	No controls	Perfect controls	Customer opportunity	Actual onboard	Minimum opportunity	Maximum opportunity	Customer opportunity
Y	$199	7	5	0	7	7	$995	$0	$1,393	$1,393
B	$169	11	8	0	11	11	$1,352	$0	$1,859	$1,859
M	$139	17	11	0	17	17	$1,529	$0	$2,363	$2,363
H	$119	23	14	0	23	23	$1,666	$0	$2,737	$2,737
V	$99	30	17	15	30	30	$1,683	$1,485	$2,970	$2,970
Z	$79	35	15	35	12	2	$1,185	$2,765	$948	$158
Q	$59	50	20	50	0	0	$1,180	$2,950	$0	$0
Total		173	90	100	100	90	$9,590	$7,200	$12,270	$11,480

[a] Post departure unconstrained demand from traffic based on inventory open/close data
[b] Actual observed passengers(traffic) onboard

Fig. 4.8 Components of the Revenue Opportunity model

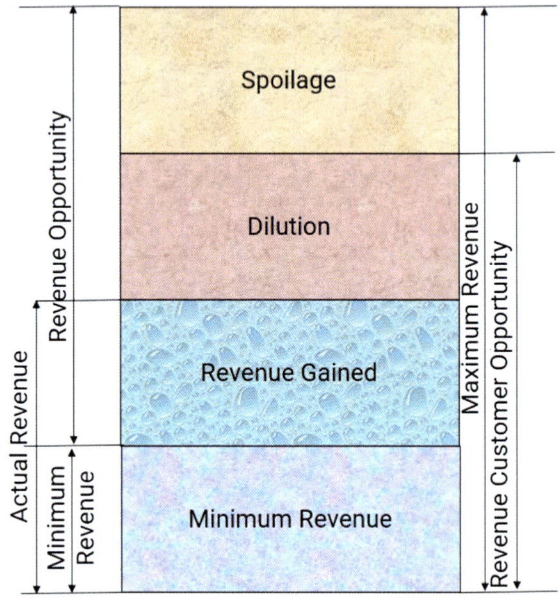

for a flight that was greater than capacity. This is a direct result of overestimating show-up rates and/or demand for higher valued booking classes.

$$Dilution = Customer\ Revenue\ Opportunity - Actual\ Onboard\ Revenue$$

$$Dilution = \$11,480 - \$9,690 = \$1,890$$

$$Discount\ Allocation\ Spoilage = Maximum\ Revenue\ Opportunitity - (Actual\ Onboard\ Revenue + Dilution)$$

$$Discount\ Allocation\ Spoilage = \$12,270 - (\$9,590 + \$1,890) = \$790$$

For leg/segment carriers, the revenue opportunity measures must be calculated by flight leg, flight segment or at the flight number level of detail. To compute the measures for a flight number with multiple segments or network will require that a deterministic product mix linear program be solved [Chandler & Ja, 2007].

For O&D carriers, the revenue opportunity measures must be calculated at the network level.

4.5.7 Revenue Management and Itinerary Pricing

Contrary to common belief, revenue management does not calculate the itinerary price, which is the domain of air shopping and airline pricing. The end product of revenue management, before the introduction of continuous pricing, is booking class availability that is determined using leg/segment controls or O&D controls. Booking class availability is used by airline and GDS pricing systems to determine the itinerary price.

The itinerary selected by a customer is priced by airline pricing which validates all the fare rules exhaustively to determine the fare amount for the itinerary. This will change with dynamic continuous pricing over the next decade when revenue management and fare management will work much closer together.

On airline websites, based on the shopping parameters submitted by an online user, a customer selects an itinerary from the priced itineraries generated by the air shopping algorithm. Typically, the itineraries generated will be limited to an airline's schedule and codeshare marketing flights. Booking is followed by ticketing when the itinerary is repriced after shopping.

In the hybrid era where EDIFACT and XML (NDC) bookings co-exist, there are four distinct paths in the reservations booking process to finalize the customer itinerary through the indirect channel. They are:

1. First is city pair availability followed by a short sell or long sell to create a passenger record to be priced. In this situation the booked itinerary is priced and ticketed.
2. A travel agency has two options to shop and ticket a customer's trip. The first option is booking the itinerary by displaying city pair availability followed by a short sell or long sell. Next, a shopping command is issued to price alternate itineraries from which the agent selects an itinerary followed by ticketing. The key difference from airline website shopping is that the itineraries returned can be from several airlines, including codeshare and interline.
3. The third option is to use a different shopping command without having to first book an itinerary. This option was developed by the GDSs to support OTAs. As before, this shopping entry generates a range of itineraries from which a travel agent selects an itinerary to be ticketed. As with the previous shopping entry that required a booked itinerary, the itineraries returned can be from several airlines, including codeshare and interline.
4. The options discussed above (a, b, c) are for EDIFACT bookings that rely on booking class availability for the GDS to price the itinerary, The fourth option is to submit an NDC shopping request to the carrier that can respond with a priced itinerary.

4.5.7.1 A Key Benefit of O&D Control with the NDC Protocol

For O&D carriers, that may or may not use dynamic pricing, there is a key benefit when the airline quotes the price for an itinerary using the NDC protocol.

An issue that exists with using booking class availability to price an itinerary is that there is no guarantee that the ticketed fare will be greater than or equal to the total bid price of the itinerary. This is because airline pricing systems managed by the GDS will conduct a low fare search based on available booking classes to find the lowest priced itinerary. Frequently, anomalies in sum of locals caused by LCC competition and fare combinability rules can produce an itinerary price that is lower than the total bid price for the itinerary. There is no provision for the GDS to know what the total bid price is for an itinerary to ensure that the ticketed fare is greater than the total bid price.

With the NDC protocol, airlines can modify the itinerary pricing logic to consider the total bid price before quoting a fare to ensure that the hurdle is fulfilled. This key benefit is applicable for O&D carriers with or without dynamic pricing. This enhancement to itinerary pricing must also be extended to the direct channel, the airline website.

4.5.8 Group Revenue Management

Group revenue management in airlines focuses on optimizing revenue from large bookings, like those for tour groups, conferences, or events. Group traffic, expressed as a percentage of total flown traffic in an airline network, varies significantly by geographic region and even by country. Mature markets like the U.S. sees far fewer group requests than less mature markets like China and Asia that see significantly more group activity.

Group traffic makes up a key part of an airline's overall network traffic. Sales agents have goals for each region and are tasked with securing group bookings for the airline. While group reservations can fill empty seats on flights, they may also potentially displace passengers who pay higher fares, leading to lower revenue. It is often believed that the profit from group bookings is lower than that from individual travelers because groups tend to negotiate private fares months before departure. However, this is not necessarily the case. By applying the core concept of the group indifference curve for individual passengers, the acceptance of a group will be at the *break-even fare* or *indifference fare* whether it is a group or individual passengers who were accepted [Vinod, 2013b, Yuen, 2002, 2003]. Negotiating group fares and managing group traffic in an airline network is of critical importance to ensure that network revenues are preserved [Busuttil, 1995; Yuen, 1998].

An example of a group indifference curve is illustrated in Fig. 4.9.

The minimum acceptable fare can be calculated for both leg/segment and O&D inventory control environments, though in an O&D environment, calculation of the minimum acceptable fare considers the first, second and third order effects in the network.

4.6 Host CRS Inventory Controls

The end-product of the revenue management process is availability by booking class. Inventory controls generated by revenue management are stored on the airline's reservations system (the host CRS).

Quoting the continuous price is a relatively new phenomenon through the NDC messaging standard and in 2025, only a handful of airlines are using it.

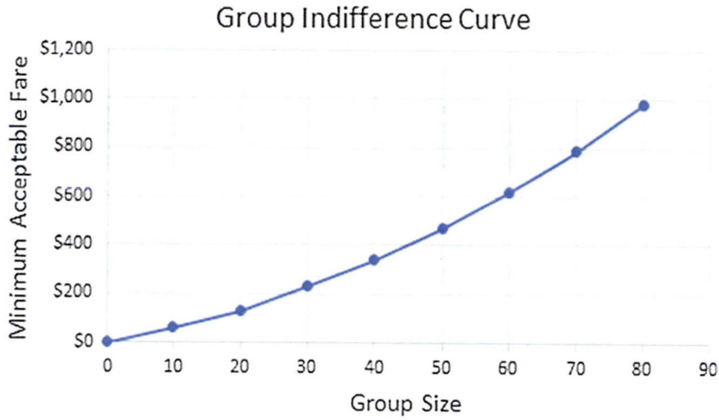

Fig. 4.9 Group acceptance indifference curve

Broadly speaking there are two types of inventory controls. The calculation of booking class availability in the host CRS can be based on leg/segment inventory controls or origin and destination (O&D) inventory controls. U.S. majors, global pure play, and large international air carriers are frequently referred to as network carriers. Of the 600+ airlines worldwide about 30 – 40 carriers are network carriers that manage their seat inventory by origin and destination. The rest of the airlines control seat inventory by leg or segment.

4.6.1 Traffic Freedoms and Inventory Controls

The aviation term "freedom" refers to the rights granted to an airline to carry revenue traffic from an origination city to a destination city. Understanding traffic freedoms is essential for the effective management of seat inventory.

Freedoms of the Air are the fundamental building blocks for international commercial aviation. It is a collection of international aviation rights that allows airlines to fly through and land in other countries. The first "five freedoms" were defined in the Convention on International Civil Aviation in 1944, known as the Chicago Convention, that was attended by 54 nations [Chicago Convention, 1944]. The traffic freedoms acknowledge an airline's negotiated traffic rights. The International Civil Aviation Organization (ICAO) only recognizes the first five freedoms as recognized by international treaties. In total, there are nine traffic freedoms, several of which are governed by bilateral treaties.

Knowledge of the traffic freedoms [Vinod, 2021a, Appendix A] is required when deploying inventory controls. There are implications for segment limits, segment close indicators, and O&D controls.

4.6.2 Leg/Segment Inventory Controls

For airlines that operate with leg/segment revenue management, there are primarily two methods for calculating seat availability and they are called net nesting and threshold nesting [Vinod, 2006, 2021a].

Threshold nesting is also referred to as *theft nesting,* and net nesting is also referred to as *standard nesting*. With threshold nesting, a booking in any booking class impacts availability of all the booking classes in the class hierarchy, thus maintaining the protection level across all classes, except for those that are closed, regardless of what booking class was sold. The calculation of seat availability in a cabin in booking class i is as follows:

$$Seats\ Available_i = Authorization_i - Total\ Seats\ Sold;\ \ i = 1, 2, \ldots, N$$

$Authorization_i$ is the booking limit for class i and $TotalSeatsSold$ is the total seats sold across all booking classes in the cabin.

$$Total\ Seats\ Sold = \sum_{k=1}^{N} Seats\ Sold_k$$

With net nesting, inventory action is taken in the requested class and all classes *above* the requested class in the hierarchy, up to the base class (usually Y). The calculation of seat availability in a cabin is as follows:

$$Seats\ Available_i = Authorization_i - \sum_{k=i}^{k=N} Seats\ Sold_k;\ \ i = 1$$

$$Seats\ Available_i = Min\left[Availability_{i-1}, \left(Authorization_i - \sum_{k=i}^{k=N} Seats\ Sold_k\right)\right];\ i = 2, \ldots, N$$

$Authorization_i$ is the authorization limit for class i, $Seats\ Sold_k$ is the seats sold in class k and $Availability_{i-1}$ is the seat availability in the class immediately above i, in the class hierarchy.

As the calculation indicates, net nesting requires booking counts by booking class while with threshold nesting, only the total seats sold in a nested hierarchy is required.

Table 4.4 illustrates an example of net and threshold nesting calculations for a flight leg from DFW to LAX. It is assumed that the nesting structure on the inventory detail record is multiple seria nesting.

The two most common forms of nesting hierarchies are multiple serial nesting and mixed nesting, shown in Fig. 4.10. Mixed nesting is a combination of serial

Table 4.4 A comparison of seat availability with threshold nesting and Net nesting. Initial conditions: Seats Sold Y = 6, B = 12, M = 16, H = 36 V = 41, Z = 55, Q = 33. Leg: DFWLAX. Coach capacity: 300. Flight No. 200.

Booking class	Authorization limit	Seats sold	Seats available (threshold)	Seats available (net nesting)
Y	420	6	221	221
B	385	12	186	192
M	320	16	121	139
H	260	36	61	95
V	210	41	11	81
Z	180	55	−19	81
Q	60	33	−139	27
Total		199		

and parallel nested inventory control structures. It is used by airlines to control promotional and consolidator classes where the intent is to guarantee a certain number of seats to be sold, despite the deep discount, as long as the highest class in coach, the Y booking class, is open.

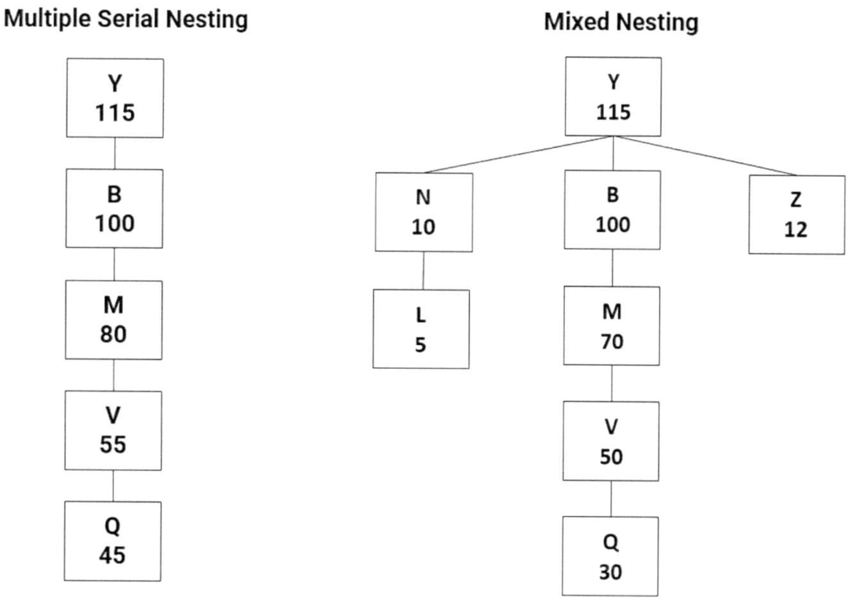

Fig. 4.10 Nested inventory control structures

4.6.3 Segment Close Indicators and Segment Limits

For airlines operating flights with multi-stop flights on a single flight number, segment close indicators (SCIs) may be advantageous in restricting sales for selected segment classes that are lower valued when demand exists for higher valued segment classes. A segment close indicator indicates that the booking class for the segment is closed.

Consider the single flight with multiple segments shown in Fig. 4.11. The flight from DFW to LHR connects over JFK. It may be advantageous to close DFW-JFK V booking class and keep the DFW-LHR V booking class on the DFW-JFK flight leg open. This is accomplished by establishing a segment close indicator for the DFW-JFK V booking class. Hence, SCIs are a mechanism to provide itinerary control for O&D's within a flight number. However, SCIs can only be turned on and off and these controls are not dynamic. As a result, if cancellations occur, the SCI is not automatically turned off for the DFW-JFK V booking class, which could result in spoilage. Similarly, if the DFW-LHR V demand increases significantly and there is no SCI in place for DFW-JFK V, it will cause revenue dilution. This can be overcome by having the revenue management system send inventory control updates on a frequent basis to the host CRS.

Segment limits are numerical controls that permit itinerary control (at a segment level) when applied together with leg-based controls. An alternative to SCIs is to use segment limits, which provides the capability to control segment class availability on a numeric basis. This numeric control provides the capability to limit sales to a given segment class (e.g., DFW-JFK V) to a numeric limit. Segment limits allow the inventory control system to re-open or close the class again because of changes in booking activity.

Segment limits are also required on flights when a carrier has restricted fifth freedom traffic rights [see Vinod 2021a, Appendix A]. The restriction can take the form of a limit on total passengers carried on the fifth freedom segment by individual flight or by flight-month.

Other variations include nested segments and the application of a minimum and maximum authorization level for each segment class.

Segment limits may either be nested or non-nested. Most reservations systems that use segment limits with nested leg class controls use non-nested segment limits. This has the benefit of allowing a user to close a class in the middle of the nesting structure without closing the classes below (a useful option on those

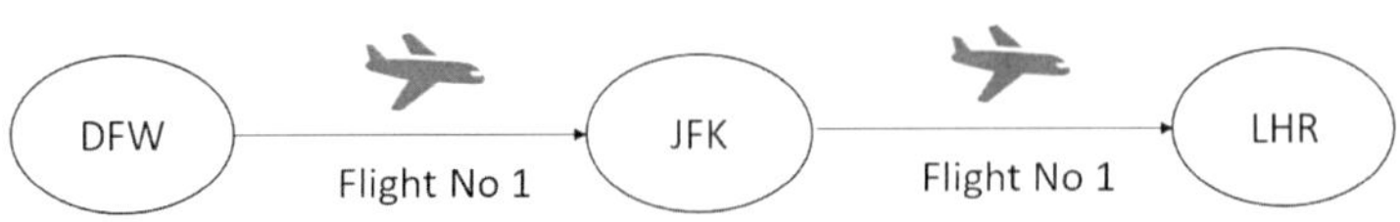

Fig. 4.11 A Single Flight with Multiple Segments

occasions when fare actions change the relative value of fares). However, nested segment limits have the same obvious benefits as nested leg controls.

4.6.4 Shared Cabin Nested Inventory Controls

Shared cabin nesting is an important concept to selectively upgrade customers to higher cabins such as First and Business Class when demand is soft for the higher-valued cabins. By sharing a few seats in common with the lower-valued cabins ensure acceptance of higher-valued coach and in some cases business class passengers to be upgraded, which increases the overall load factor on the aircraft.

If demand for the higher-valued cabin is forecast to be low on a future flight departure, then some of the higher-valued cabin seats can be shared with the lower-valued cabins at the time of the reservation. The airline can then at its discretion decide on the specific valued customers who should be upgraded to first class or business class to make room for the additional coach reservations that can be accepted.

If there is an unexpected surge in demand for the higher-valued cabin, then the passenger requests must be honored if there are seats available in the cabin. When bookings take place in the shared space, reservations are accepted on a first come first served basis.

An approach to handle upgrades is to use dual RBDs by indicating that inventory availability is required in two booking classes for a fare to be valid. An issue is that upgrades from coach to business or business to first may happen sooner than is acceptable. An alternative is to use the concept of shared product inventory, where a few premium cabin seats are shared in common with the lower valued cabin. This approach provides better control of seat inventory and limits upgrades to the premium cabin.

Figure 4.12 illustrates the shared cabin inventory concept with three cabins – first class, business class, and coach class.

When there are more than two cabins on a flight, both complete and partial sharing of inventory is feasible. Consider the shared cabin matrix definitions shown in Table 4.5 to illustrate this concept with three cabins F, J, and Y. The shared cabin matrix defines a *from-with* share relationship. Row-wise, the sharing is *from*. Column-wise, the sharing is *with*.

Fig. 4.12 Shared cabin example

Table 4.5 Complete sharing and partial sharing

Complete sharing				Partial sharing			
Cabin	F	J	Y	Cabin	F	J	Y
F	X			F	X		
J	X	X		J	X	X	
Y	X	X	X	Y		X	X

In the case with complete sharing, F can share seats with both Y and J cabins, and J can share seats with Y cabin.

In the partial sharing example, the sharing is strictly one level up. Hence, F cabin can only share seats with J cabin and J cabin can only share seats with Y cabin. There is no sharing between F cabin and Y cabin. Partial sharing is more conservative and in a potentially oversold situation it will tend to result in fewer oversales and result in lower load factor.

The share product inventory is now illustrated with an example of an international flight leg from Narita, Japan (NRT) to Los Angeles (LAX) with two cabins, business and coach with capacity of 40 and 300 respectively. It is also assumed that there are two booking classes in business class (J) and seven booking classes in coach (Y).

In the shared cabin inventory environment, when reservations are accepted for a flight, initial sales are made directly against the premium and coach cabin inventory. After the exclusive coach cabin seats are sold out, additional sales are made on a first come first served basis from the shared seat inventory. Sales from the shared inventory decrement *both* the higher valued cabin (business in this case) and lower valued cabin seats available simultaneously.

Table 4.6 illustrates the initial state. Seat availability is calculated by the net nesting method. Note that coach (Y) is sold up to the authorized capacity. To calculate availability, shared seats sold and shared seats available must be tracked. The Shared Seats column in Tables 4.4 to 4.7 represent the number of shared seats available for sale.

Table 4.7 shows the state of the inventory detail record after the sale of an additional four Y seats. Even though the seats available for Y in Table 4.7 is zero, the bookings could be accepted because of the shared seats with business class. As a result, the shared seats count is reduced from eight to four.

Table 4.8 shows the state of the inventory detail record after the sale of an additional four business class discounted seats in D booking class. Even though the seats available for Y in Table 4.4 was zero, the bookings could be accepted because of the shared seats with business class. As a result, the number of shared seats is reduced from eight to four.

Table 4.9 shows the state of the inventory detail record after the sale of an additional four coach class seats in Y booking class. Even though the seats available for Y in Table 4.9 was negative, the bookings could be accepted because of the shared seats with business class that were still available. As a result, the number

Table 4.6 Shared Cabin example—initial state.
Flight Leg: NRT-LAX. Cabin Capacity: J/Y = 40/300. Initial State Seats Sold: J = 4, D = 8, Y = 20, B = 30, M = 35, H = 45, V = 60, Z = 90, Q = 140

Cabin	Booking class	Authorization level	Seats sold	Shared seats available	Seats available
J	J	44	4	**8**	32
	D	24	8		16
Y	Y	420	20		0
	B	385	30		−15
	M	320	35		−50
	H	260	45		−75
	V	210	60		−80
	Z	180	90		−80
	Q	60	140		−80

Total Seats Sold: J = 12, Y = 420

Table 4.7 Shared cabin example—sell additional coach seats.
Flight Leg: NRT-LAX Cabin Capacity: J/Y = 40/300. Sell 4 additional Y seats. Seats Sold: J = 4, D = 8, Y = 24, B = 30, M = 35, H = 45, V = 60, Z = 90, Q = 140

Cabin	Booking class	Authorization level	Seats sold	Shared seats available	Seats available
J	J	44	4	**4**	28
	D	24	8		12
Y	Y	420	24		−4
	B	385	30		−15
	M	320	35		−50
	H	260	45		−75
	V	210	60		−80
	Z	180	90		−80
	Q	60	140		−80

Total Seats Sold: J = 12, Y = 424

of shared seats is reduced from four to zero. Any additional seat sales will be only in business class unless additional business class seats are shared with coach class.

4.6.5 Origin and Destination (O&D) Inventory Controls

For network carriers that have significant connecting traffic over a hub, investment in an origin and destination revenue management system also requires an investment in O&D inventory controls on the host CRS. Of the 600 airlines that

Table 4.8 Shared Cabin example—sell additional business class seats.
Flight Leg: NRT-LAX Cabin Capacity: J/Y = 40/300. Sell 4 additional D seats. Seats Sold: J = 4, D = 12, Y = 24, B = 30, M = 35, H = 45, V = 60, Z = 90, Q = 140

Cabin	Booking class	Authorization level	Seats sold	Shared seats available	Seats available
J	J	44	4	**4**	24
	D	24	12		8
Y	Y	420	24		−4
	B	385	30		−15
	M	320	35		−50
	H	260	45		−75
	V	210	60		−80
	Z	180	90		−80
	Q	60	140		−80

Total Seats Sold: J = 16, Y = 424

Table 4.9 Shared Cabin example—sell additional coach seats.
Flight Leg: NRT-LAX Cabin Capacity: J/Y = 40/300. Sell 4 additional Y seats. Seats Sold: J = 4, D = 12, Y = 28, B = 30, M = 35, H = 45, V = 60, Z = 90, Q = 140

Cabin	Booking class	Authorization level	Seats sold	Shared seats available	Seats available
J	J	44	4	**0**	20
	D	24	12		4
Y	Y	420	28		−8
	B	385	30		−15
	M	320	35		−50
	H	260	45		−75
	V	210	60		−80
	Z	180	90		−80
	Q	60	140		−80

Total Seats Sold: J = 16, Y = 428

operate today, fewer than 50 airlines deploy O&D controls which imply that the vast majority use nested inventory controls in their reservations system.

In the 1990s many network carriers that wanted to migrate to O&D controls made significant investments in upgrading the inventory control capabilities on the airline's host CRS.

Virtual nesting and continuous *nesting* are the two primary methods for control of seat inventory by O&D. American Airlines was the first airline to deploy virtual nesting controls in 1987 to control connecting traffic through their two primary hubs in Dallas/Fort Worth and Chicago's O'Hare [Smith, 1986]. The inventory controls were designed as a static virtual nesting model and the mapping of itinerary classes to flight legs was maintained in the host CRS which was periodically updated. At American, migration from leg/segment controls to virtual nesting controls was completed by 1989. A second variation is dynamic virtual nesting where the mapping of the itinerary classes to flight leg buckets is determined dynamically at the time of availability. This approach therefore does not require the mapping of itinerary classes to flight leg buckets in the host CRS. Over the past decade, the few airlines that used virtual nesting controls migrated to continuous nesting controls, also known as bid price controls.

Bid price controls with a bid price curve as a function of seats sold (or seats available) provide the flexibility of detailed inventory control by service class even though it introduced a significant overhead to reservations processing because of the iterative calculation to determine the number of seats available by booking class in city pair availability displays and air shopping queries from the travel agency desktop. The total bid price for a service is simply the sum of the individual bid prices of the flight legs that make up the service. If the total bid price is *less* than the fare, the request is *accepted,* otherwise, it is rejected.

Financial availability is determined by the *net contribution* calculation, given by:

$$Net\ Contribution = Fare_{sc} - \sum_{j \in S} \gamma_j$$

$Fare_{sc}$ is the fare for service s and class c, γ_j is the bid price for flight leg j; $j \in S$, where S is the collection of services in the network. Ideally, this must be equivalent to the *Qualified* $Fare_{sc}$, which is the minimum fare that satisfies specific fare rules identified in Table 4.11.

If the net contribution is positive, the reservation request is accepted, otherwise, it is rejected. In addition, the *incremental bid price* or *gradient* is used to adjust the bid price when bookings and cancellations occur. The gradient can be interpreted as the change in bid price for a unit change in available seats. With each new

Table 4.10 Bid price vector example.
Leg: AUSDFW Flight No. 100

Number of bookings	Bid Price
.	.
.	.
.	.
80	$160
81	$163
82	$168
.	.
.	.
.	.

booking, the bid price is *increased* by the bid price gradient. With each cancellation, the bid price is *decreased* by the bid price gradient. If a request is accepted, the bid price is updated by *adding* the gradient as follows:

$$\gamma_j^+ = \gamma_j + \Delta_j * Seats\ Booked_j$$

where γ_j is the current bid price of leg j, γ_j^+ is the new bid price on leg j, Δ_j is the gradient on leg j and $Seats\ Booked_j$ represents the number in party for the booking request. Similarly, if a cancellation occurs, the bid price is *subtracted* by the gradient as follows:

$$\gamma_j^+ = \gamma_j - \Delta_j * Seats\ Booked_j$$

This assumes that the relationship of the gradient with the change in capacity is linear. This, however, is not true, but it serves as an approximation that can *only* be applied for small changes in available seats. A better alternative is to generate a *bid price vector* (also known as a *bid price curve*) from the network optimization model based on the assumption that primal feasibility exists as bookings are accepted. By storing the bid price vector on the flight inventory record, the linear assumption can be relaxed. To store the bid price vector on the inventory control record may require an expansion of the existing records, which is an expensive proposition due to the extensive testing requirements of third-party applications that access an airline's reservations inventory system. An argument can be made that frequent re-optimization of the network obviates the problem, and the bid price/gradient approach is comparable in performance to the bid price vector. However, there will always be latency between network re-optimizations from revenue management which makes the bid price curve more appealing. Table 4.9 illustrates this point for a flight leg/departure date. Actual implementation on a reservations inventory control system will be based on seats available with the associate bid price.

As observed, continuous nesting provides a level of granularity beyond virtual nesting controls. Every service class availability request is considered unique, unlike virtual nesting where availability was the same for all service classes mapped into a virtual bucket.

4.6.5.1 The Bid Price Exchange

A PADIS (Passenger and Airport Data Interchange Standards)/IATA standard for the exchange of bid prices between the operating carrier and the marketing carrier for codeshare flights was established in the early 2010s. By exchanging this data, partner airlines, especially those in an alliance, can make more informed decisions on seat availability for codeshare itineraries. By sharing bid price vectors (curves) with partner airlines, carriers can improve the accuracy of real-time availability calculations. This is a better alternative than cascading availability or AVS but assumes that both the operating and marketing carrier are on continuous nesting (bid price) controls.

4.6.5.2 Passenger Valuation

Passenger valuation has been at the heart of revenue management with the advent of O&D inventory controls with continuous nesting [Vinod, 1995] or virtual nesting controls [Smith, 1986; Smith et al., 1992; Vinod, 1989]. To control seat availability by O&D requires market values, an estimate, by booking class at varying degrees of sophistication (inclusive of fare qualification rules) to ensure that the market value used for availability determination is as close as possible to the ticketed fare.

Both techniques require the calculation of the net contribution for each availability request of a one-way itinerary. The $Fare_{sc}$ described earlier is the $Qualified\ Fare_{sc}$.

$$Net\ Contribution = Qualified\ Fare_{sc} - \sum_{j \in S} \gamma_j$$

The $Qualified\ Fare_{sc}$ is the *most restrictive* market value for service s and class c, γ_j is the bid price based on current bookings for flight leg j; $s \in S$, where S is the collection of services in the network. The deployment of origin and destination inventory control on a reservation system can use a simple average of the service class fare or have a more detailed representation based on the fare qualification rules that can be determined when an availability request is made. For example, fare restrictions such as minimum stay and maximum stay are not applicable since they cannot be determined when an availability request is being made. The applicable fare qualification rules are the ATPCO fare categories and footnotes and are summarized in Table 4.11.

Using fare qualification rules ensures that the market value used for determining availability is as close as possible to the ticketed fare. While the values will never be the same, the objective is to ensure that they are close.

Continuous nesting logic is used to determine the collection of booking classes that are acceptable and can be priced by the pricing system to determine the lowest available fare for display.

4.6.5.3 Calculation of O&D Seat Availability

The calculation of seat availability with O&D controls consists of two steps: physical availability followed by financial availability.

The physical availability is simply the difference between the authorized capacity for the cabin and the total seats sold in the cabin to determine if a booking is allowed.

For financial availability, the bid prices are additive when multiple legs are involved to cover an itinerary. The net contribution for each service class is calculated by subtracting the total bid price from the market class fare value ($MCFV$) for each booking class. If it is positive, then a booking can be made in the booking class [Vinod, 2006]. The $MCFV$ are calculated periodically by aggregating fares considering the terms of the fare qualification rules which can be determined when an availability request is made. It is an average of historical and future fares

Table 4.11 Fare qualification rules applicable for availability determination

Fare qualification rule	Description
Frequency	Day-of-week qualifier for departure date of the service
Trip type	Nonstop, direct, online connection, interline connection
Advance purchase	Number of days before departure of the service that the booking must occur
Blackout dates	Date ranges on which the booking class item may not be used
Point of sale	Where the booking is made, includes all levels from region to agency id
PCC/OAC	Originating request from a pseudo city code (PCC) or office accounting code (OAC)
Selling date range, day of week or time window	Date range, day of week or time window when the transaction may occur
Travel day of week and date range	Specific day of week or date range within which the departure date of the service must occur
Days open prior to departure	Number of days before the service departure that item is applicable
Days Closed Prior to departure	Number of days before the service departure that item ceases to be applicable
Included flight number ranges, flights	List of flight numbers or flight number ranges on which this item is applicable
Excluded flight number ranges, flights	List of flight numbers or flight number ranges on which this item is not applicable
Flight routing restrictions	Connect point requirements for a service: any airport specified, all airports specified, board point, specific connect point, sequence of connect points
Joint Carrier restrictions	Carriers that may be included in an interline connection
Inhibits	Restrictions on use, e.g., booking only, host agent only, etc
Operating partners	Applies to the specified operating partners
Originating airline or GDS	Applies for originating airline or GDS
Marketing carrier	Applies to the marketing carrier

weighted by flown traffic by point of commencement. This level of precision is required to ensure that the *MCFV* used for availability determination is as close as possible to the ticketed fare, though they will never be the same.

Table 4.12 Calculation of booking class availability for O&D control

Origin	Destination	Class	Fare value	Total bid price	Net contribution	Open/ Closed	Flight leg	Bid price
LAX	DFW	Y	$600	$300	$300	Open	LAXDFW	$300
LAX	DFW	B	$500	$300	$200	Open	DFWBOS	$475
DFW	BOS	Y	$550	$475	$75	Open	DFWLHR	$700
DFW	BOS	B	$450	$475	−$25	Closed	DFWMIA	$350
DFW	LHR	Y	$800	$700	$100	Open		
DFW	LHR	B	$700	$700	$0	Closed		
DFW	MIA	Y	$300	$350	−$50	Closed		
DFW	MIA	B	$250	$350	−$100	Closed		
LAX	BOS	Y	$900	$775	$125	Closed		
LAX	BOS	B	$750	$775	−$25	Closed		
LAX	LHR	Y	$1,200	$1,000	$200	Open		
LAX	LHR	B	$1,050	$1,000	$50	Open		
LAX	MIA	Y	$600	$650	−$50	Closed	3	
LAX	MIA	B	$540	$650	−$110	Closed		

The net contribution (financial availability) for service s, class c, is calculated as follows, where S. In the collection of services in the network.

$$Net\ Contribution_{sc} = MCFV_{sc} - \sum_{j \in S} \gamma_j$$

Table 4.12 illustrates the calculation of availability with O&D controls on the host CRS for the sample network shown below.

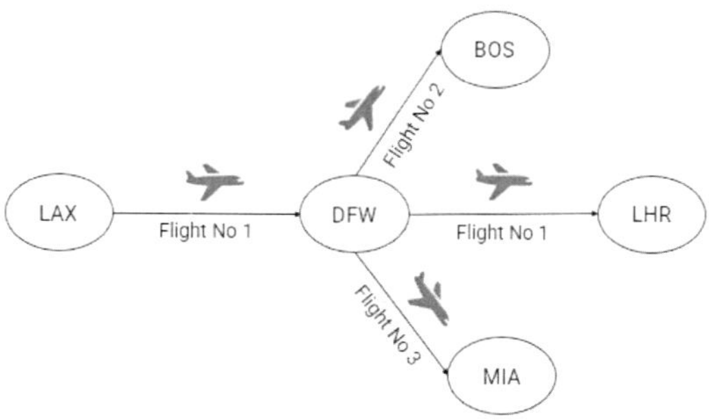

For O&D controls, a bid price curve that is a function of seats sold (or seats available) is stored on the inventory detail record in the airline's host CRS. The bid price curve is calculated by the revenue management system because the value of the bid price to seats sold on a flight leg and cabin is not a linear function.

Direct connect availability (DCA) requests for city pair availability between the GDs and the host CRS is a computational burden, since the net contribution calculation must be applied iteratively to find the precise number of seats available by booking class. For city pair availability requests from a GDS, numeric availability is usually capped at seven or nine by the host CRS.

If the connectivity is limited to teletype between the GDS and the host CRS, then booking class availability in the GDS is based on availability status (AVS) messages, received from the host CRS, that is stored in an internal database. The AVS messages generated by the host CRS are based on O&D availability of the local leg. Availability status messages by O&D do not exist in the GDS since this will lead to excessive volumes of data that will have to be transmitted from the host CRS to the GDS.

Regardless of the level of connectivity, AVS is the backup default for booking class availability in situations when there is a time out when availability is requested. Hence, the transmission of AVS messages, AVS generation and recap during schedule changes is a core capability in the host CRS.

4.6.5.4 Legacy System Enhancement Versus Open System for O&D Booking Class Availability

Enhancing a legacy mainframe reservations system to support O&D controls is an expensive proposition. It requires an expansion of the inventory detail records, development of the new O&D booking class availability logic, followed by the extensive testing of all the applications that access the inventory records in the reservations system. A better alternative is to develop a satellite co-operative processor that is channel attached to the host CRS to provide the O&D availability logic for inventory control.

Sabre collaborated with Air France in 1997 to address the limitation of enhancing the legacy Unisys-based reservations systems for O&D inventory control. They collaborated to develop and deploy the *Availability Processor*™, a Unix-based satellite co-operative processor. This processor was connected to Alpha3, Air France's host CRS, to handle availability and sell processing for O&D control [Smith et al., 1997; Vinod et al., 1997]. Today, the use of satellite processors for availability and sell processing in an open systems environment is widely adopted. Examples of such processors include *SabreSonic* Inventory (SSI, an enhanced version of the Availability Processor™), Altéa Inventory / RAAV (Revenue Availability with Active Valuation), and PROS RTDP. Google/ITA also utilizes a read-only availability proxy, known as DACS (Dynamic Availability Calculation System), for processing availability requests in their shopping engine.

4.6.6 Benefits

The benefits of revenue management from a revenue perspective have been documented and presentated by several practitioners over the past four decades. These metrics have also been validated with various simulation studies of passenger

Table 4.13 Reference benefits of revenue management

Revenue management capability	Incremental revenue (%)
Overbooking	1%–2%
Discount (leg/segment) control	3%–5%
O&D control	1%–2%
Group control	+ %
Total	5.0%–9%

behavior and realized booking activity. Table 4.13 summarizes reference benefits by key function. The actual benefits realized by an airline will vary based on markets they serve and maturity, exemplified by a consistent and repeatable process.

Note that group traffic only exists in a very small percentage of flights. It varies by airline and depends on the route network and relative maturity of the markets served by the airline.

4.6.7 Academic and Practitioner Focus

Academic focus with a practical orientation was introduced in the late 1980s [Belobaba, 1987, 1989], the 1990s [Chatwin, 1993; Kärcher, 1996; Lee, 1990; Weatherford, 1991; Weatherford & Bodily, 1992; Williamson, 1992] and 2000s [Li, 2008]. With the growing interest in this discipline, several books have appeared that focus on both the practice and the theory [Boyd, 2007; Cross 1997; Daudel & Vialle, 1989; Gallego & Topaloglu, 2019; Garrow, 2016; Ingold et al., 2000; Mauri, 2012; Ng 2008; Philips 2005; Szende, 2020; Talluri & van Ryzin 2004; Taneja, 2017; Vinod, 2021a, 2022a, 2024a; Yeoman & McMahon-Beattie, 2004; Yeoman & McMahon-Beattie, 2011].

4.7 Revenue Management with Independent Demand

With fare restrictions in place, traditional revenue management since its inception has made the fundamental assumption that demand for each booking class is independent of the demand for other booking classes. This is because the unique restrictions associated with fares mapped to a booking class were fundamentally different fare products. With this approach, demand can be forecast by booking class and flights or the network can be optimized to establish inventory controls. The only dependency is the booking class hierarchy and the associated nested inventory control structure. Seat availability is usually calculated by the net nesting method and not threshold nesting.

4.7.1 Market Differential Pricing

Yield management is based on the fundamental premise that not all customers are created equal. Business passengers are schedule sensitive and typically book closer to departure. In comparison, leisure passengers are price sensitive and willing to book well in advance to purchase deeply discounted tickets. Fares are filed by market (origin – destination).

An airline can use up to 26 booking classes when a flight is detailed in the reservations system. Table 4.14 illustrates a sample hierarchy with 7 booking classes.

An airline may use up to 24 of the 26 booking classes for distribution of availability to GDSs. Booking classes, also known as reservation booking designator (RBDs), are used to identify customer segments for revenue management purposes. Hence, demand is forecast by booking class followed by the flight-level optimization for leg/segment carriers. For large network carriers that use origin and destination (O&D) controls, demand is forecast by service class and optimal controls called continuous nesting or bid price controls are determined by optimizing the airline network.

When the NDC era is past the hybrid state and in the end state, airlines do not have to publish booking class availability to GDSs. This is because all booked itineraries will be priced by the airline when offers are created. In the post hybrid era, airlines also will not have a need to distribute their fares to ATPCO. This implies that ATPCO loses relevance in the post hybrid era for the indirect channel. Airlines may continue to publish their fares to ATPCO for the consumer direct channel. Similarly, GDSs also lose relevancy because many of their capabilities such as shopping, booking, itinerary pricing, and ticketing are no longer required, and they are no different that the new entrant NDC Aggregators (non-GDS) in the market.

In the absence of booking class availability being distributed, airlines can segment customers that go beyond traditional RBDs. They can be creative and deploy alternate segmentation beyond the traditional RBDs such as trip-purpose segments

Table 4.14 Fare hierarchy example. Market: DFW-BOS

Booking class	Type of fare product
Y	Unrestricted "full Y" fares, round trip, fully refundable
B	Discounted one-way fare, non-refundable
M	7-day advance purchase round trip excursion fares, 50% cancellation penalty
H	7-day advance purchase, round trip, excursion promotional fares, 100% cancellation penalty
V	14-day advance purchase, round trip, excursion fare, 50% cancellation penalty
Z	21-day advance purchase, round trip, excursion fare, non-refundable
Q	21-day advance purchase, maximum stay of 28 days, non-refundable

with extensions to micro-segments. This is referred to as the so-called class-less revenue management. However, RBDs will continue to be used internally by airlines for technical reasons, unless they want to overhaul airline pricing it its entirety, which is a major undertaking, far greater than the introduction of the NDC messaging protocol. It is also greater in scope than the investment and deployment of ONE Order. To address the hype surrounding classless revenue management, an entire chapter (Chapter 12) has been devoted to this topic.

4.7.2 Modeling Uncertainty of Demand

Until 1972, research into yield management was restricted to overbooking controls. In the early 1970s, the British Overseas Aircraft Corporation (BOAC) implemented 21-day advance booking discount fares. Littlewood [Littlewood, 1972] of BOAC suggested that discount passengers should be accommodated if the discount fare exceeded the expected revenue of future higher paying full fare passengers. The two-class example introduced by Littlewood, now referred to as Littlewood's Rule, forms the basis of discount allocation controls.

Discount allocation requires modeling demand uncertainty for a booking class as either a normal distribution or a gamma distribution to calculate protection levels. It is a common error to assume demand follows a normal distribution, which is bell-shaped, symmetric, and defined by its first two moments. However, demand is often asymmetrical and takes the form of a left-skewed gamma distribution. This is illustrated in Fig. 4.13 for different values of the shape (α) and scale (β) parameters of the gamma distribution. Additionally, while the normal distribution can accommodate negative demand, the gamma distribution is always positive.

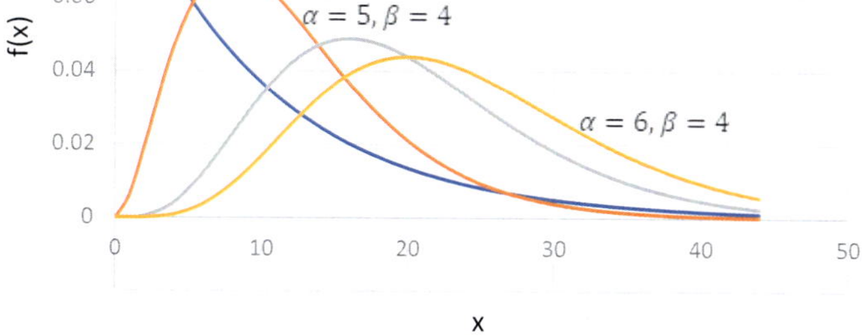

Fig. 4.13 Gamma Distribution for various values of α and β

The gamma distribution function with shape and scale parameters has the probability density function,

$$f(x) = \frac{x^{\alpha-1}e^{-x/\beta}}{\beta^{\alpha}\Gamma(\alpha)};\ x \geq 0$$

where α is the shape parameter, β is the scale parameter and Γ is the gamma function.

The gamma distribution, which has two parameters that define its shape (α) and scale (β), is highly adaptable and can effectively represent demand. Depending on the demand pattern, the α and β parameters can be adjusted to accurately represent the demand distribution. Moreover, the gamma distribution has the crucial characteristic that the random variable X is only applicable for non-negative values $X > 0$, unlike the normal distribution.

By matching the first two moments, we have

$$\mu = \alpha\beta$$

$$\sigma^2 = \alpha\beta^2$$

from which α and β can be calculated.

$$\alpha = \frac{\mu^2}{\sigma^2}$$

$$\beta = \frac{\sigma^2}{\mu}$$

In a multi-class environment, the objective of discount allocations is to obtain the optimal mix of full fare, discount, and deep discount passengers on board a flight to maximize total revenues. Discount allocation manages risk to generate incremental revenues by turning away a lower paying passenger in the hope of filling the seat with higher paying passengers.

4.7.3 Flight Leg/Segment Optimization

The concept of discount allocations will be first explained in the context of a flight number with a single flight leg from Los Angeles (LAX) to New York's JFK airport as shown below.

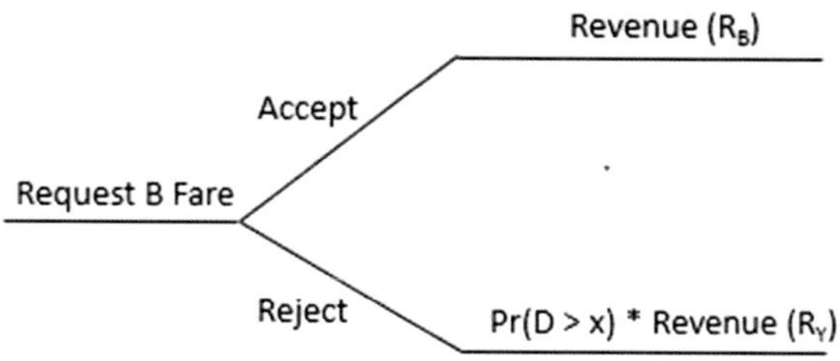

Fig. 4.14 Discount allocation decision tree

For example, consider the 2-booking class example where the classes are Y and B and the average fares for Y and B are R_Y and R_B and $R_Y > R_B$. When a request is made for the discount booking class B, the airline has the option to either accept or reject the booking. This is illustrated in Fig. 4.14.

A discount request can be rejected if the seat can be filled with a higher paying passenger. The optimal protection for booking class Y (R_Y) from booking class B (R_B and $R_B < R_Y$) can be described by the following relationship:

$$Pr(D_Y > x)R_Y = R_B$$

or

$$Pr(D_Y > x) = \frac{R_B}{R_Y}$$

The value of x at the probability value of the revenue ratio defines the number of seats that must be protected for the higher class Y from lower class B. The expected marginal seat revenue is based on diminishing marginal returns of additional space protected for the higher valued booking class.

The calculation of protection levels relies on the *relative* value of the fares and *not* the *absolute* value of the fares. For example, if $R_Y = \$1,000$ and $R_B = \$800$, then the revenue ratio is R_B / R_Y = 800/1,000 = 0.80, which is the same for any other combination of absolute values of R_Y and R_B if the revenue ratio is preserved. The absolute fare values are by themselves *not* important to calculate protection levels. The calculation of the protection values is determined purely by the distribution of demand and the revenue ratios of the respective booking classes. This key observation is of tremendous significance especially in international markets where access to accurate information on the real value of the passenger flight coupon is difficult if not impossible to determine due to commissions, overrides and special provisions. However, the use of revenue ratios helps [Dunleavy, 1996].

This model can be extended to multiple legs on a flight number. From an execution perspective, the inventory controls deployed by airlines are either leg-based nested inventory controls with segment limits or segment class nested inventory controls.

The model can be extended to include upsell and recapture rates. When a request is rejected, the airline can quote a higher fare to the passenger who may accept the request. This is referred to as upsell.

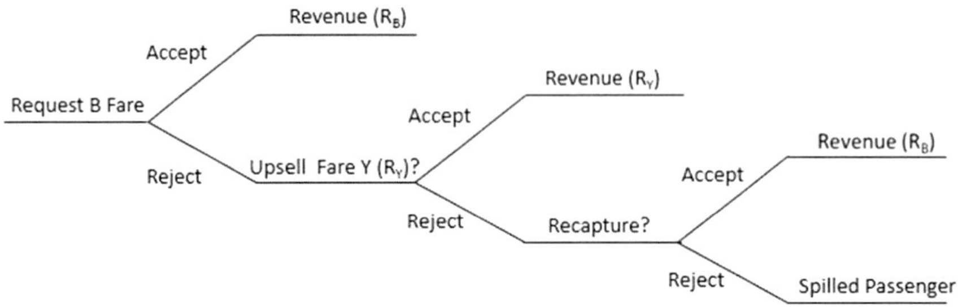

Fig. 4.15 Discount allocation decision tree with upsell and recapture

If the customer refuses the higher fare, the airline will next attempt to capture the passenger on an alternate flight at a discounted fare, even though the alternate flight is not the customer's first preference. This is referred to as recapture. Figure 4.15 illustrates the decision logic with upsell and recapture.

When the demand is gamma distributed, the expected marginal seat revenue for the nth seat for a given booking class Y is given by:

$$R_Y \Pr(D_Y > n) = R_Y \int_n^{\infty} f(x)dx = R_Y(1.0 - F_G(x \leq n))$$
$$= R_Y\left[1.0 - F_G\left(\alpha, \frac{n}{\beta}\right)\right]$$

Note that the *rate of decrease* of the expected marginal revenue depends on the mean of the demand forecast and the demand uncertainty. Since $\Pr(D > 1) \geq \Pr(D > 2) \geq \Pr(D > 3) \cdots \geq \Pr(D > n)$, the expected marginal revenue is a monotone non-increasing function (a function that either decreases or stays the same as its input value increases), and the rate of decrease is *not* linear.

Figure 4.16 illustrates the expected marginal revenue curve for a mean demand of $\mu = 10, R_Y = \$400$and two values of the$CV = 0.20$, and$CV = 0.80$ assuming demand is gamma distributed. When the demand uncertainty is low, more space is protected for the higher valued class and when demand uncertainty is high, less space is protected.

With multiple booking classes, there are two methods for computing the expected marginal seat revenue, both commonly referred to as EMSR. There are two variations in the literature, called EMSR_A and EMSR_B. While EMSR_A relies on a pairwise comparison to compute the protection levels for the higher classes, EMSR_B relies on calculating an average fare, weighted by demand of all booking classes above the fare from which seats need to be protected. Since demand is assumed to be independent across the booking classes, additive means and variances are used for the joint distribution of demand. The model assumes that lower valued booking classes book first followed by the higher valued booking classes. Hence, revenue management systems monitor bookings in the Y booking class

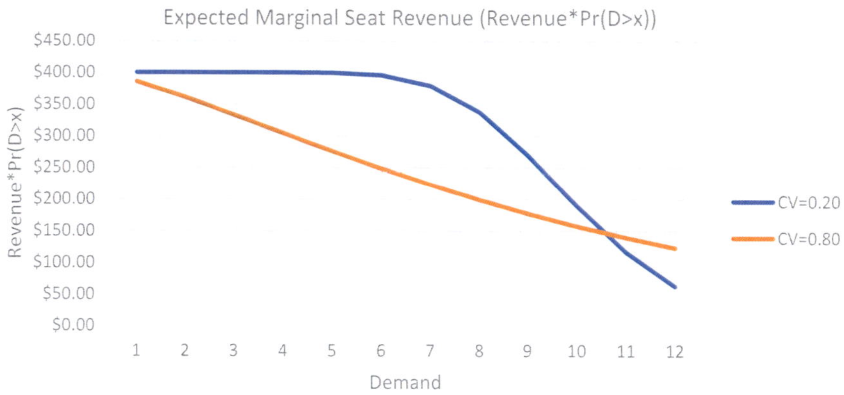

Fig. 4.16 Expected marginal seat revenue Curve

and reforecast and reoptimize the flight at several intermediate points before flight departure. In situations when there is a surge in demand, booking class availability can change from one day to the next.

$EMSR_A$ aggregates protection levels to successive pairs of classes by applying Littlewood's Rule while $EMSR_B$ is based on aggregating demand and not protection levels. Simulation studies have shown that $EMSR_B$ [Smith, 1982; Belobaba, 1992] is superior to $EMSR_A$ [Belobaba, 1987, 1989]. $EMSR_A$ is more readily applied to non-nested controls and $EMSR_B$ performs better in a nested inventory control environment. The revenue improvement of $EMSR_B$ is because the underlying joint demand distribution of higher classes is used to determine the protection level from the lower class while $EMSR_A$ uses a pairwise comparison to calculate protection levels. $EMSR_B$ also provides better estimates of expected traffic and revenue than $EMSR_A$.

For two booking classes, the EMSR approach produces optimal booking limits. When there are more than two booking classes, the booking limits are not optimal. In airline inventory systems, the lower valued inventory booking classes close first. Using this as a constraint, optimal booking limits with more than two booking classes have been addressed independently [Brumelle & McGill, 1993; Curry, 1990; Wollmer, 1992]. Curry's approach assumes demand follows a continuous distribution and extends to O&D itineraries. Wollmer's approach assumes that demand follows a discrete distribution. Brumelle and McGill's approach is based on subdifferential optimization and applies to both discrete and continuous distributions.

The $EMSR_B$ approach relies on calculating an average fare, weighted by demand, of all classes above the fare from which seats need to be protected. For example, consider a cabin with four distinct fares, Y, B, M and Q. With this approach, to determine the total number of seats that need to be protected for Y, B and M booking classes from Q requires the calculation of the weighted average fare for Y, B and M and then calculating the number of seats to protect from Q.

This assumes that the displacement rate is the same for the higher classes, Y, B and M, which is never true. If yield management controls are correctly set, the actual displacement rate (or spill rate) will increase from the highest fare to the lowest fare.

In the American Airlines DINAMO system from 1986, the discount allocation model was an expected marginal seat revenue model using the logit approximation to the normal distribution [Swan, 1983], an extension of Littlewood's Rule to multiple classes, which generated the joint protection levels for higher valued booking classes relative to the lower value booking class [Smith, 1982]. This method was later called $EMSR_B$ [Belobaba, 1992] as a computationally viable heuristic to optimal booking limits.

4.7.4 Examples of $EMSR_A$ and $EMSR_B$

This section illustrates numerical examples of the $EMSR_A$ and $EMSR_B$ methods to calculate nested authorization levels. The example assumes seven booking classes that follow the following hierarchy: $Y > B > M > H > V > Z > Q$.

Hence the average fares descend from the highest booking class to the lowest booking class: $R_Y > R_B > R_M > R_H > R_V > R_Z > R_Q$. Both examples assume a cabin capacity of 100 seats and no overbooking.

The data used for the $EMSR_A$ and $EMSR_B$ calculations are the same. The inputs are shown in Table 4.15.

4.7.4.1 $EMSR_A$ Example

This approach relies on a pairwise comparison of booking classes to calculate the protection levels, followed by the nested authorization levels by booking class which are rounded to the closest integer.

The first step is to calculate the revenue ratios. This is shown in Table 4.16.

The next step is to calculate the pairwise protection levels and the total protection levels. From the total protection levels, the authorization levels are calculated

Table 4.15 Inputs for the numerical examples

Booking class	Average fare	Coefficient of variation (CV)	Mean demand	Standard deviation	Alpha	Beta
Y	\$500	0.50	10	5.00	4.00	2.50
B	\$400	0.45	14	6.30	4.94	2.84
M	\$350	0.40	16	6.40	6.25	2.56
H	\$300	0.35	20	7.00	8.16	2.45
V	\$250	0.30	24	7.20	11.11	2.16
Z	\$200	0.25	24	6.00	16.00	1.50
Q	\$150	0.25	36	9.00	16.00	2.25

Table 4.16 Revenue ratios for $EMSR_A$

Booking class	Y	B	M	H	V	Z	Q
Y		0.80	0.70	0.6	0.50	0.40	0.30
B			0.88	0.75	0.63	0.50	0.38
M				0.86	0.71	0.57	0.43
H					0.83	0.67	0.50
V						0.80	0.60
Z							0.75
Q							

Table 4.17 Calculation of protection levels and authorization levels for $EMSR_A$

Booking class	Y	B	M	H	V	Z	Q
Y		5.74	6.91	8.03	9.18	10.44	11.91
B			7.29	9.40	11.23	13.07	15.09
M				9.47	11.91	14.07	16.30
H					13.32	16.40	19.19
V						17.83	21.54
Z							19.73
Q							
Total protection		**5.74**	**14.20**	**26.90**	**45.65**	**71.80**	**84.02**
Auth levels	100	94.3	85.8	73.1	54.4	28.2	16.0
Auth levels (round)	100	94	86	73	54	28	16

and rounded to the closest integer. Calculation of protection levels and the nested authorization levels are shown in Table 4.17.

In origin and destination (O&D) revenue management, when a network is optimized, the bid price is used to control availability by O&D and booking class. The bid price is the opportunity cost of not having an incremental seat on a flight leg in a cabin. The marginal value of the last seat is the bid price for the flight leg. For a single leg itinerary, a booking request can be accepted if the fare is greater than the bid price for the leg. For itineraries with multiple legs, the fare for the O&D must be greater than the sum of the bid prices of all flight legs in the itinerary. Adoption of bid price controls by network carriers started in the late 1990s and continues to this day.

For a flight with a single leg, the bid price for the flight can be calculated based on the lowest booking class that is open. In this case, the bid price is calculated as follows:

$$Bid\ Price = R_Q * \Pr(X > Auth_Q)$$

$$Bid\ Price = 100 * \Pr(X > 16) = \$149.58$$

4.7.4.2 EMSR$_B$ Example

With this approach, the joint demand must be first calculated as follows:

$$Y$$
$$Y+B$$
$$Y+B+M$$
$$Y+B+M+H$$
$$Y+B+M+H+V$$
$$Y+B+M+H+V+Z$$
$$Y+B+M+H+V+Z+Q$$

Since the demand for individual booking classes is independent, the mean and variances are additive. Hence, for example, for booking classes Y and B:

$$E(Y+B)=E(Y)+E(B)$$

and

$$V(Y+B)=V(Y)+V(B)$$

The joint demand is the sum of the individual mean demands for the respective booking classes. Once the mean joint demand is calculated, the next step is to calculate the demand-weighted average fare, the revenue ratio, and the shape and scale parameters of the gamma distribution. This is followed with the calculation of protection levels and the authorization levels by booking class. Table 4.18 illustrates the calculation of protection levels and authorization levels for $EMSR_B$.

For the single flight example, the bid price for the flight can be calculated based on the lowest booking class (Z in this case) that is open. Since Z booking class is open, the bid price must be in between the two success average values for Q

Table 4.18 Calculation of authorization levels for EMSR$_{(B)}$

Booking Classes	Joint Demand	Joint Variance	Weighted Avg Fare	Revenue Ratio	Alpha	Beta	Protection	AUTH	AUTH (round)
Y	10	25.00	$500.00	0.80	4.00	2.50	5.74	100	100
Y – B	24	64.69	$441.67	0.79	8.90	2.70	17.28	94.26	94
Y – M	40	105.65	$405.00	0.74	15.14	2.64	32.93	82.72	83
Y – H	60	154.65	$370.00	0.68	23.28	2.58	53.70	67.07	67
Y – V	84	206.49	$335.71	0.60	34.17	2.46	79.77	46.30	46
Y – Z	108	242.49	$305.56	0.49	48.10	2.25	107.61	20.23	20
Y – Q	144	323.49	$266.67	0.00	64.10	2.25		–7.61	0

and Z, which is between \$100 and \$150. Assuming there are no bookings, the bid price is calculated as follows:

$$Bid\ Price = R_Q + (R_Z - R_Q) * \Pr(D_Z > Auth_Z)$$

$$Bid\ Price = \$150 + (\$150 - \$100) * \Pr(D_Z > 20.23) = \$185.94$$

If there are existing bookings, then the authorization ($Auth_Z$) must be replaced by seats available in booking class Z ($SeatsAvailable_Z$).

4.7.5 Expected Marginal Seat Revenue Model Assumptions

The key assumptions made by the *EMSR* models are:

1. Demand for each booking class is independent. This implies that booking behavior in one booking class does not influence the booking behavior in the other booking classes. The demand for each booking class is modeled as a random variable with its own probability distribution.
2. Booking classes are nested and have a fixed hierarchy. A higher fare customer can be offered a lower fare subject to availability. The average fare for each booking class is assumed to be constant throughout the booking period.
3. Demand for each booking class is assumed to follow a gamma distribution (preferred) or a normal distribution, characterized by its first two moments.
4. Customer arrivals are sequential and ordered by the value of the fare. The model assumes that lower-fare customers tend to book earlier than higher-fare customers. The model calculates a protection level, which is the number of seats to reserve for higher-paying customers who are expected to arrive later.
5. The optimization is considered static since booking limits are determined at a single point in time and assumes that these booking limits do not have to be adjusted later. However, no airline follows this assumption strictly and re-forecast and re-optimize the flights frequently.
6. The model does not consider cancellations, no-shows, and overbooking.
7. The capacity in each cabin is assumed to be homogeneous.

4.7.6 Static and Dynamic Models for Leg/Segment Optimization

There are two types of optimization models. They are called static models and dynamic models.

In single leg airline revenue management, static optimization focuses on a single time period, using a fixed set of parameters like booking limits to maximize revenue. These models typically assume a fixed set of parameters for the entire duration of the flight's booking window. Typical assumptions are sequential arrivals, demand is independent between booking classes, no changes to the probability distribution of demand, and cancellations and no-shows are not considered. Pre-departure cancellations and no-shows on the departure date are typically part of the overbooking model.

The multi-class flight optimization models, $EMSR_A$ and $EMSR_B$ are static models [Belobaba, 1987, 1989, 1992]. The first yield management system deployed at American Airlines in 1985 was a static $EMSR_B$ model though the acronym $EMSR_B$ was not coined until a few years later. These models do not model the arrival order of bookings and assume demand for lower booking classes arrive before the higher fare classes. They are heuristic models that produce results that are close to the optimal solution.

Dynamic optimization, on the other hand, considers the evolving situation over multiple time periods, adjusting inventory controls based on new information like real-time booking requests and cancellations. These models account for the dynamic behavior of stochastic processes like bookings and cancellations. Dynamic models are generally more complex to implement on airline reservations systems and require more sophisticated algorithms than static models.

4.7.6.1 Overcoming Concerns with the Static Optimization Model

Any perceived limitations with the static optimization model can be overcome by frequently forecasting and reoptimizing the flight legs or flight segments based on a pre-defined schedule (a batch process) as well as dynamically based on reservation activity. The reading days, also known as data collection points, are used in revenue management systems to store various points in time before departure. Most airlines use anywhere from 15 to 50 pre-departure data collection points. Frequently, these data collection points dictate when flights are re-optimized. A second set of pre-departure points greater than the reading day set can be used for forecasting and optimization. For example, the optimization days may be a superset of the reading days as shown in Table 4.19. As shown, daily flight optimizations are executed form 90 days before departure to the departure date, and a 14-day interval is assumed for days beyond 90 days. In this scenario, every flight will be forecast and optimized for 180 days before departure. A comparison of reading days and optimization days is shown in Table 4.19.

Table 4.19 An example of reading days and optimization days

Measure	Days before flight departure
Reading days (data collection points)	0, 1, 2, 6, 13, 20, 27, 34, 41, 48, 55, 62, 76, 90, 118, 146, 174, 202, 230, 258, 286, 314, 342
Optimization days	0, 1, 2, 3, 4, 5, 6, 7, …, 88, 89, 90, 104, 118, 132, 146, 160, 174, 188, 202, 216, 230, 244, 258, 272, 286, 300, 314, 328, 342

[a] Assumes flights are detailed 342 days before departure

4.7.7 Optimal Solutions for Leg/Segment Models

Curry (1990), Wollmer (1992), and Brumelle and McGill (1993) have published studies on optimal booking limits with more than two classes. Curry's work uses continuous demand distributions, while Wollmer uses discrete demand distributions. Brumelle and McGill's method relies on subdifferential optimization. This method works with either discrete or continuous demand distributions.

Van Ryzin and McGill (2000) proposed an adaptive method. It finds protection levels for nested booking classes. This method avoids demand forecasting. Instead, it uses historical data to guide changes to protection levels. The approach suggests raising protection level p_i if all booking classes i or higher meet their targets. They suggest lowering it if it does not. This algorithm converges to the optimal protection levels under reasonable regularity conditions. It does this under normal conditions. This approach of continuously adjusting the protection levels offers a key benefit. It sidesteps demand forecasting problems. A substantial number of flights is necessary for the updating method to converge on a set of protection levels. Unfortunately, this initialization period is not viable due to practical considerations.

A discrete-time dynamic programming model was proposed as a dynamic model [Lee and Hersh, 1993] where demand for each booking class was modeled as a non-homogeneous Poisson Process (NHPP). A NHPP is a counting process where the intensity function varies with time, allowing for the modeling of event occurrences over time with trends. This is a Markov decision model and at a given time t the booking requests before time t do not have any bearing on the decision to be made at time t except for the remaining unsold capacity. To solve the dynamic program, the booking period is divided into infinitesimal decision periods so no more than one booking request arrives within a period.

The Lee and Hirsh model was extended to incorporate cancellations, no-shows, and overbooking [Subramanian et al., 1999]. The model assumes a continuous time arrival process as a limit to the discrete-time model by increasing the number of time steps and subsequently decision periods. The dynamic and static models were later linked [Lautenbacher & Stidham, 1999].

Lautenbacher and Stidham (1999) link dynamic and static approaches. They demonstrate a shared Markov decision process supports both by formulating a comprehensive model which includes the static and dynamic models as special cases.

4.7.8 Network Optimization for O&D Control

The objective of the network optimization model is to determine the optimal inventory controls, taking into consideration the first order, second order and third order effects in the network that maximizes the total expected revenues subject to available capacity. To consider the marginal trade-offs between competing service classes in a network explicitly, a network optimization model is required to calculate the *optimal* bid prices.

A standard deterministic model for the network optimization model for a single cabin for a future departure date is shown below. The scope of the network optimization model is the entire airline network for a future date to capture the first order, second order and third order network effects.

$$Max \sum_{s} \sum_{c} R_{sc} X_{sc}$$

$$s.t. \sum_{s} \sum_{c} I_{sc} X_{sc} \le C_j; j = 1,2, \ldots, N$$

$$0 \le X_{sc} \le D_{sc}$$

where:

R_{sc}: Fare value of service *s* and class *c*
X_{sc}: Non-nested allocation for service s, class c
I_{sc}: Zero/One Indicator variable. Assumes value of 1 if service class s flows over flight leg j; else equals 0
D_{sc}: Remaining demand forecast for service *s* and class *c*
C_j: Remaining capacity for flight leg *j* in the network ($j = 1, 2, \ldots, N$)
N: Number of flight legs in the network

The objective is to find the optimal seat allocation that maximizes the total expected revenue of the network, taking into consideration the first order, second order and third order effects in the network, and satisfies the capacity constraints on the flight legs. A service class (*sc*) is equivalent to an ODIF (origin, destination, itinerary, fare class), a term that is frequently used in the revenue management literature. While booking classes and fare classes are used synonymously by revenue management analysts, in this book the term booking classes is used since fare classes have a different interpretation in airline pricing.

Note that the itinerary is the specific one-way routing from the origin to the destination which represents the service (*s*). Services are generated from the airline schedule based on standard rules for connecting traffic. To construct valid services, the following assumptions are typically made on minimum and maximum connect times. This is illustrated in Table 4.20.

Solving the deterministic network optimization problem can lead to aggressive inventory controls since demand is assumed to be known with certainty. In reality, demand for each service class follows a demand distribution and the gamma distribution is frequently used since its lower bound is zero and the shape and scale parameters can be estimated to match the demand profile.

Table 4.20 Minimum and maximum connect time assumptions to construct services

Connection type	Minimum connect time	Maximum connect time
Domestic to domestic	1 hour	4 hours
Domestic to international	2 hours	6 hours
International to domestic	2 hours	6 hours
International to international	2 hours	8 hours

4.7.8.1 Real World Consideration: Magnitude of the Optimization Problem for Network Carriers

Consider the full-service carrier American Airlines which operates in four main geographical market segments: the Atlantic, U.S. Domestic, Latin America, and the Pacific. American Airlines has over 350 destinations (n) across more than 60 countries. This translates into over 122,150 ($n(n-1)$) potential markets in a fully connected graph and it is safe to assume that a third of the markets, 40,000 markets, are significant. Insignificant markets carry passengers, though it could be sporadic. American has 6,700 flight departures a day which translates into 6,700 nonstops (flight leg and departure time) a day.

Each market is served by flights, non-stop or connecting. Of the 40,000 significant markets, 33,300 markets (40,000 – 6,700) are connecting markets. American has hubs in nine major US cities through which passengers connect. These hubs are in Charlotte, Chicago (O'Hare), Dallas/Fort Worth, Los Angeles, Miami, New York (JFK), New York (LaGuardia), Philadelphia, Phoenix, and Washington (National). Assuming on average there are 50 significant services in a market, and 16 significant booking classes per market, the total number of service classes is greater than 25 million (33,300 × 50 × 16). Overnight flights that originate the previous day and arrive on the following day at a hub must be included as services in the network optimizer for the optimization date to ensure connecting traffic is accounted for.

Setting up the problem is a major task to ensure that only service classes that are truly required are input into the optimization model. This constitutes the pruned list of service classes. The rest of the service classes are treated as a pseudo-local and assigned a pseudo-fare based on a weighted average of the service that flow over a flight leg/ departure time. Frequently when service classes are evaluated, further pruning may be in order to include only about 10 million service classes in the optimization model.

Hence, for the linear program formulation, there are at least 10 million columns (service classes) and 6,700 constraints for a single cabin for a given future departure date. For network carriers, most flight legs have two cabins and international flight legs may have 3 cabins (F, J, Y). For example, if there are two cabins (First and Coach), then the number of constraints will be F (6,700 rows) and F + Y (6,700 rows) for a total of 13,400 rows.

If there are 30 pre-defined reading days (data collection points), then at a minimum 30 future optimization dates will be optimized to update the bid prices.

Reservations activity on future dates is monitored to create a composite score for each future date. When the activity exceeds a pre-defined threshold, the network will be dynamically re-optimized based on current booking data. Depending on the level of reservations activity and the pre-define threshold for the composite score by future date, dynamic re-optimizations will be executed more frequently, ranging from 30 to 100 dynamic network re-optimizations daily. Frequent re-optimization of the network for future dates with high or abnormally high reservations activity is a necessity.

American is also a founding member of the OneWorld alliance that has 15 carriers and serve over 900 destinations worldwide. Inclusion of codeshare flights will increase the problem size dramatically.

4.7.8.2 The Must Forecast List and Pseudo-Local Demand

Since markets and associated services have been pruned from an airline's network for revenue management processing, it is impossible to forecast all O&Ds in the airline network. Historical O&D summary data will reveal services that carried traffic and were never forecast because it did not make the pruned list of services.

To avoid forecasting small numbers, the list of service classes can be further reduced to only forecast those services where demand is significant. This is the must-forecast list of local and connecting service classes. Typically, airline traffic data will indicate that 20% of the O&Ds contribute 80% to 90% of the total demand in the network. Lufthansa found the traffic to follow the 20:80 rule [Poelt, 2002]. With this approach, only 20% of the significant markets, the must-forecast list includes connecting and local, are forecast.

For each flight leg, demand is also forecasted for the total demand by leg and class. This is the combined local and connecting demand by leg and class. The must-forecast list connecting demand and local demand is subtracted from the combined local plus connecting demand (the total leg demand) forecast to create a pseudo-local leg class forecast. An estimate of prorated weighted average revenue is also calculated for the pseudo-local demand.

$$\begin{aligned} \textit{PseudoLocal Leg Class Demand} &= \textit{Total Leg Demand by Leg Class} \\ &\quad -\textit{Must Forecast List Connecting} \\ &\quad \textit{and Local Demand by Class} \end{aligned}$$

The pseudo-local forecast is a surrogate for the sparse O&Ds that are not in the must-forecast list, for which average fare values can be derived from historical revenue accounting data. The input into the network optimizer in therefore the must-forecast connecting service classes, the local demand by booking class and the pseudo-local demand by booking class.

4.7.8.3 Modeling the Demand Distribution in the Network Optimization Model

To consider the marginal trade-offs explicitly between competing service classes in a network, a network optimization model is required to calculate the *optimal* bid prices.

A refinement to the deterministic model where demand variability and non-linear diminishing marginal returns property of booking class inventory allocations were modeled using a stepwise linear approximation to the demand curve [Vinod & Ratliff, 1990]. The stepwise approximation split the allocation decision variables into discrete units which provided a discrete approximation to the EMSR curve. This method had the disadvantage of solving for an exceptionally large number of decision variables to account for the linear approximation. The number of constraints did not increase.

When demand for each origin, destination, and class is represented by a probability density function $f(x)$, the formulation is as follows [Vinod, 1992].

$$Max \sum_{s}\sum_{c}\int_{0}^{x} R_{sc}X_{sc}f_{sc}(x) + \sum_{s}\sum_{c}(1 - F_{sc}(x))R_{sc}X_{sc}$$

$$s.t. \sum_{s}\sum_{c} I_{sc}X_{sc} \le C_j; j = 1,2,\ldots,N$$

$$0 \le X_{sc} \le D_{sc}$$

$f_{sc}(x)$ is the probability density function for a specific service class (sc), $\int$ is the integral between specific limits of integration and $F_{sc}(x = x\prime)$ is the cumulative density function defined as:

$$\Pr\left(X \le x'\right) = \int_{0}^{x\prime} f_{sc}(x)dx.$$

Assuming that demand for a service class is gamma distributed, the value that each X_{sc} assumes is determined as follows:

$$X_{sc} = x\prime = F_{sc}^{-1}(p)$$

$$p = F_{sc}(x\prime) = 1 - \frac{\sum_i u_i}{R_{sc}}; p > 0;\ \textit{and}\ 0\ \textit{otherwise}$$

Note that the term $\sum_i u_i$ is the sum of the duals (shadow prices) for the legs over which the specific service class (sc) flows in the current iteration. By assuming that demand is gamma distributed, $G(\alpha, \beta)$, the term $F_{sc}^{-1}(p)$ can be evaluated with a fast table lookup with three-way interpolation. The alternative is to evaluate the cumulative density function of $G(\alpha, \beta)$ directly, but it will be computationally slow given the millions of evaluations required for each iteration of the network optimization model.

The term $R_{sc} \int_0^{x\prime} xf(x)dx$ can be derived from first principles, like the derivation of the gamma spill model [Vinod, 2021a, Chapter 3]. Hence,

$$R_{sc} \int_0^{x\prime} xf(x)dx = R_{sc} \propto \beta F_{sc}\left(\alpha + 1, \frac{x\prime}{\beta}\right)$$

which can be readily evaluated.

There are numerous techniques that can be used to solve the above formulation. One method is to first reformulate the problem as a Lagrangian relaxation model and solve it by the sub-gradient method [Fisher, 1981]. The Lagrangian problem is given by

$$Min\{Max \sum_s \sum_c \int_0^x R_{sc} X_{sc} f_{sc}(x) + \sum_s \sum_c (1 - F_{sc}(x)) R_{sc} X_{sc} -$$

$$\underline{u}(\sum_s \sum_c I_{sc} X_{sc} - C_j)\}; j = 1,2, \ldots, N$$

$$0 \leq X_{sc} \leq D_{sc}$$

Given an initial vector of duals $\underline{u}^0$, a subgradient method can generate a sequence $\underline{u}^k$ by the following rule.

$$\underline{u}^{k+1} = \underline{u}^k - t^k (Ax^k - b)$$

where x^k is the solution to the Lagrangian problem in iteration k and t^k is a positive scaler step size and $(Ax - b)$ is used to represent the constraint set in the original problem. An iteration is considered an improvement if any of the following are true:

1. The current value of the Lagrangian cost in the current iteration is lower than the incumbent.
2. The total constraint violation error is lower than the incumbent.
3. The maximum violation across all constraints is lower than the incumbent.

This method requires a stopping criterion, which can be based on a pre-defined threshold of the difference between the primal cost and the dual (Lagrangian) cost.

The nonlinear program formulation determines the bid prices (the dual variables of the capacity constraints) but does not make any provisions for nesting and the service class allocations produced by the model are non-nested allocations. This formulation, like $EMSR_A$, treats the service classes as a series of separate, partitioned allocations and ignores the fact that when nesting is considered, service classes jointly share allocations and higher valued service classes can access inventory below them in the nested structure. Deployment of continuous nesting in a host CRS assumes that the service classes share allocations. All service classes that are open share the remaining capacity. This model, like $EMSR_A$, underestimates the traffic and network revenues. This in turn leads to incorrect bid prices since the calculation of bid prices in the formulation is dependent on the objective function. The discrepancy in the traffic estimate was confirmed for the normal distribution of demand [Talluri & van Ryzin, 1998].

4.7.8.4 Demand Uncertainty and Nesting Order in the Optimization Model

Customer value, known as the Cumulative Effective Revenue (CER), is determined by an algorithm [Smith and Penn, 1988] that considers the traffic flows in the network. The value of a service class, *sc*, is the average fare value net of upline and downline displacement costs. This determines the nesting order.

To take nesting into account and address the underestimation in traffic with the above formulation, an alternative approach is to apply $EMSR_B$ in the context of an iterative leg decomposition model [Smith et al., 1997]. Figure 4.17 outlines the leg decomposition model.

The leg decomposition model assumes an initial set of bid prices by leg for the network to initiate the iterations. The bid prices can be initialized by executing the non-linear program formulation outlined in the previous section, With the leg bid prices, for each leg in the network, the flow traffic revenue is converted to an equivalent leg value using bid price-based proration.

$$R_{sc}^{j} = R_{sc} \frac{\gamma_j}{\sum_{k \in sc} \gamma_k}$$

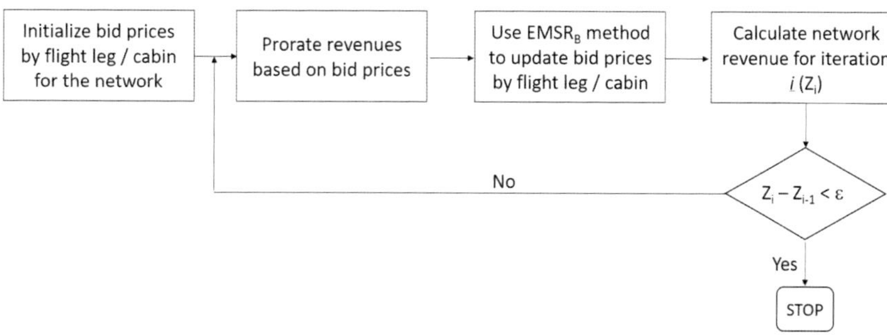

Fig. 4.17 Leg decomposition model

where R_{sc}^{j} is the prorated revenue of service class sc flowing over leg j, γ_j is the bid price of the jth leg and $\sum_{k \in sc} \gamma_k$ is the sum of the bid prices for service classsc.

From the individual prorated revenues, the weighted average is calculated by class for each leg and the EMSR$_B$ based equation is used to calculate the new bid prices for each flight leg in the network.

$$\gamma_j = \frac{\sum_s \sum_c D_{sc} R_{sc}^{j} I\left(R_{sc}^{j} - \gamma_j\right) x Pr(\sum_s \sum_c D_{sc} I(R_{sc}^{j} - \gamma_j) \geq C_j)}{\sum_s \sum_c D_{sc} I(R_{sc}^{j} - \gamma_j)}$$

where $I(R_{sc}^{j} - \gamma_j)$ is either equal to 1 when the net contribution $(R_{sc}^{j} - \gamma_j)$ is positive or equal to zero when the net contribution is negative or zero. Note that the second term in the numerator $\Pr(\sum_s \sum_c D_{sc}(R_{sc}^{j} - \gamma_j) \geq C_j)$ is the closing rate for leg j, based on all service class demands that are open to fill the remaining capacity C_j. At optimality, for each leg, the bid price is equal to the value of the last seat sold. The above equilibrium equation for each leg states that, at optimality, the bid price is equal to the value of the last seat sold.

At the end of each iteration the network revenue is calculated assuming demand is gamma distributed. If the improvement in network revenue between successive iterations or groups of iterations is below a pre-specified threshold, the iterations are stopped. Otherwise, the iterations continue until the stopping criteria have been met.

This approach scales to solve large problems like the previous model and has the advantage of inventory sharing among all open service classes. This is consistent with what happens with bid price controls for real-time management of seat inventory. Simulation studies by the authors of the leg decomposition model have shown revenue improvements over the previous model. Surprisingly, the positive results from this study contradict earlier studies [Williamson, 1992]. Perhaps these results were positive because of the bid price-based proration that was used rather than mileage or fare-based proration.

Unlike the non-linear programming approach from the previous section which produces allocations by service class as a biproduct, the leg decomposition model does not. The nested allocations on the host CRS are required for airlines that do not control all their O&Ds with bid price controls. The allocations are used to compute a weighted average fare by booking class to compute the nested controls that is a post process of the optimization model. If all markets are under O&D control, the service class allocations are not required.

4.7.8.5 Alternate Approaches to Network Optimization

The revenue management literature for network optimization models is vast. Only a few are highlighted below.

Many solutions have been proposed to solve the network optimization problem, and the fundamental issues relate to either model assumptions, or scalability, or both. A network optimization model to determine inventory controls should account for demand uncertainty and nesting. For example, demand uncertainty can be addressed by modeling demand for each service class as a gamma distribution by the method of matching moments. To account for nesting, the nesting order must be based on the value of the service classes after accounting for upline and downline displacement.

Earlier models [Glover et al., 1982] were based on origin, destination and fare class (ODF). The problem was formulated as a minimum cost network flow problem with one set of arcs to represent the flight legs and a second set of arcs to represent the ODFs. The problem with the formulation was that it did not represent the actual problem. By using ODFs, it is not possible to discern the various services (routes) between the origin and destination. Assuming path indifference is a bad assumption, A second limitation was that demand was assumed to be deterministic.

It has been demonstrated that simple deterministic approximation methods based on average demand often outperform more advanced probabilistic heuristics [Williamson, 1992]. This phenomenon is due to the booking process where booking classes are nested, which is ignored in the modeling phase.

An approach to calculate bid prices was proposed [Talluri & van Ryzin, 1996] based on the observation that the network optimization problem is a sequential decision-making problem under uncertainty. The recursive technique of dynamic programming [Bellman, 1954] was used to determine the maximum expected revenue given the remaining capacities and time to departure. This model while appealing has some unique challenges. First, forecasting the temporal arrival order of bookings across multiple booking classes is challenging [Weatherford et al., 1993]. Second, the dimensionality problem of the dynamic program needs to be addressed. Scalability of a dynamic programming formulation [Chapius, 2008] for solving a large network of a U.S. major may prove intractable in real-time.

Talluri and van Ryzin (1999) proposed an approach to incorporate demand uncertainty into the deterministic network model, which they call randomized linear programming. Instead of using demand expectations, they simulate a sequence of realizations of demand for each itinerary and each booking class in the network. For every realization of demand, the optimal booking control policy is determined a posteriori by the deterministic model. The resulting sequence of bid-prices is then averaged to obtain an approximation of the optimal booking control policy under the assumptions of the probabilistic model. Yet, their tests show this advanced method did not always do better than the simpler deterministic model.

An approximate dynamic programming model that used the network flow formulation proposed previously by Glover et al. (1982) was used to approximate the opportunity costs [Bertsimas & Popescu, 2003]. The deterministic form of the network flow problem was overcome with a simulation to account for the stochastic nature of demand. A sequence of demand realizations was simulated to approximate the opportunity costs. A fundamental limitation is that like the Glover et al (1982) model, itineraries (routings) are not considered between an origin and destination.

To address demand uncertainty and nesting, a simulation-based algorithm was introduced that starts with any nested booking limit policy [Bertsimas & de Boer,

2005]. The expected revenue function is defined as a function of the booking limits, with the objective of finding the booking limits that maximize the function. A deterministic linear program is used to capture the network effects, generate an initial solution and the nesting order. A stochastic gradient method determines the direction of search for the expected revenue function. A simulation is used to approximate the revenue function which is unknown. To reduce problem complexity, it is merged with key concepts from approximate dynamic programming, to refine the initial booking limits. Approximate dynamic programming is a set of techniques used to solve complex decision-making problems that are computationally expensive to solve using traditional dynamic programming. This approach still requires that small time periods be defined for the duration of the booking period and also define future revenue as a function of the remaining capacity. The expected revenue is approximately the average of the revenues generated by a sequence of simulated demand realizations. The simulation model is also used to derive bid prices from the booking limits.

Other network approaches include [de Boer et al., 2002; DeSylva, 1982; Dror & Ladany, 1988; Simpson, 1989; Talluri & Van Ryzin, 1996, 1998, 1999; Vinod & Ratliff, 1990; Vinod, 1992; Vinod, 1995; Williamson, 1992], stochastic dynamic programming (SDP) and Markov decision problem (MDP) approaches [Alstrup et al., 1989; Wang, 1983], stochastic gradient algorithm and approximate dynamic programming [Bertsimas & de Boer, 2005; Bertsimas & Popescu, 2003], and genetic algorithms with very limiting assumptions [Pulugurtha & Nambisan, 2003].

The most recent models to determine bid prices consider upsell and recapture.

The formulations described earlier ignore same flight upsell and cross flight recapture demand interactions across flights and classes due to closures. Recent research on customer choice models demonstrates the value of addressing same flight sell up and cross flight recapture [Vulcano et al., 2012; Gallego et al., 2015]. Revenue benefits have been reported with simulation studies of using a choice-based simulation approach [Vulcano et al., 2010] over other methods. The conclusion is that modeling the actual demand process with attributes such as time of day, elapsed time, number of connections, brand and price with a choice model is a *first order effect* and has significant advantages.

4.7.8.6 The O&D Network Revenue Opportunity Model

A standard deterministic model for the network optimization model for a single cabin for a historical departure date is shown below. The scope of the network optimization model is the entire airline network for a specific departure date to capture the first order, second order and third order network effects. The value of the objective function is the *Maximum Revenue Opportunity*.

$$Max \sum_{s} \sum_{c} R_{sc} X_{sc}$$

$$s.t. \sum_{s} \sum_{c} I_{sc} X_{sc} \leq C_j; \; j = 1,2, \ldots, N$$

$$0 \leq X_{sc} \leq D_{sc}$$

where:

R_{sc} Average fare value of service s and class c
X_{sc} Non-nested allocation for service s, class c
I_{sc} Zero/One Indicator variable. Assumes value of 1 if service class s flows over flight leg j; else equals 0
D_{sc} Total unconstrained demand for service s and class c
C_j Capacity for flight leg j in the network ($j = 1, 2, \ldots$, N)
N Number of flight legs in the network

The *Minimum Revenue Opportunity* is calculated by inverting the fare value of the service class. The revised objective function will be

$$Max \sum_{s} \sum_{c} (1/R_{sc}) X_{sc}$$

To calculate a more realistic estimate of the *Total Revenue Opportunity*, some airlines resort to a simulation with random arrivals of bookings to estimate the lower bound. From these two measures and an estimate of the actual revenue for the historical date, all other measures can be calculated as before. To calculate *Dilution, and Spoilage*, an estimate of the *Customer Revenue Opportunity* is required at the network level. The linear program can be solved with capacity for the legs set at the passengers boarded count to arrive at this estimate.

These measures can be averaged by week or month to determine the effectiveness of the revenue management program. As before, what is important is not the absolute measures, but the relative value of these measures compared to previous weeks or months,

This model assumes that demand is independent between booking classes and captures network effects of local versus connecting demand but ignores upsell and recapture demand interactions across flights and booking classes due to closures.

4.8 Dynamic Reaccommodation (Replanement) of Low-Valued Passengers

Overselling with opportunistic cancellations [Biyalogorsky et al., 1999], is a strategy where a company deliberately sells more capacity than it has, then cancels the sales of lower-paying customers if higher-paying customers show up to claim the limited spots. This strategy increases profits by ensuring the capacity is sold to those who value it most and can help reduce losses from unsold inventory by compensating the canceled customer. In a subsequent paper, the same authors use the term "short selling" [Biyalogorsky et al., 2000], a financial strategy which is not a standard industry term for hotel rooms or airline seats, where the travel supplier does not guarantee fulfillment by introducing a cancellable condition for low price bookings that gives the seller the authority to cancel the sale and reaccommodate the passenger at will. This is unethical and illegal in the travel industry. Conditions under which the use of short selling and replanement to generate incremental revenues and its impact on overbooking limits has been investigated [Bell, 2008].

The concept of Replanement of passengers as a fair and acceptable airline business practice to generate incremental revenues and augment the revenue management process was introduced by Tom Cook [Cook, 2001] which culminated in the creation of Replane Inc. However, disruptions to air traffic following the terrorist attacks on September 11, 2001, and bankruptcy filings by many major carriers resulted in lost momentum. Today many airlines practice replanement of passengers on an ad-hoc basis, where the need is the highest. There are also boutique vendors in this space that work with airlines.

Growth in air traffic leads to higher demand on peak and closed-out flights. This presents airlines with a unique opportunity to boost revenues by offering compensation to passengers who have flexibility with their travel plans and are willing to be reaccommodated. The business model of replaning passengers brings the science of micro-segmentation, the opportunity cost of an incremental seat, and customer willingness to to reaccommodated into a mutually beneficial initiative for the airline and the customer.

The business process of replanement of passengers to generate incremental revenues is a form of dynamic seat reallocation. It augments the revenue management functions by providing seamless, cost-efficient reaccommodation services to create capacity for late-arriving, high valued, unexpected demand.

Micro-segmentation of the passengers booked on a flight enables identification of flexible passengers who are offered incentives in the form of vouchers and frequent flyer miles to switch to different flights. It requires the airline to override ticketing time limits to reaccommodate passengers to alternate flights. The replane business model also mitigates issues with overbooking and simultaneously maximizes revenues.

4.9 Revenue Management with Dependent Demand

Since the mid-1990s and into the 2000s, low-cost airlines have grown rapidly in Europe, the U.S., and Asia. This expansion followed deregulation of airline markets in many countries. The increase in low-cost carriers matches the rise of a wealthier but still budget-conscious middle class worldwide. This group travels more than before and has a greater desire to explore new places. For them, service quality is less important than affordable prices and convenience. These travelers prioritize getting to their destination quickly and without hassle.

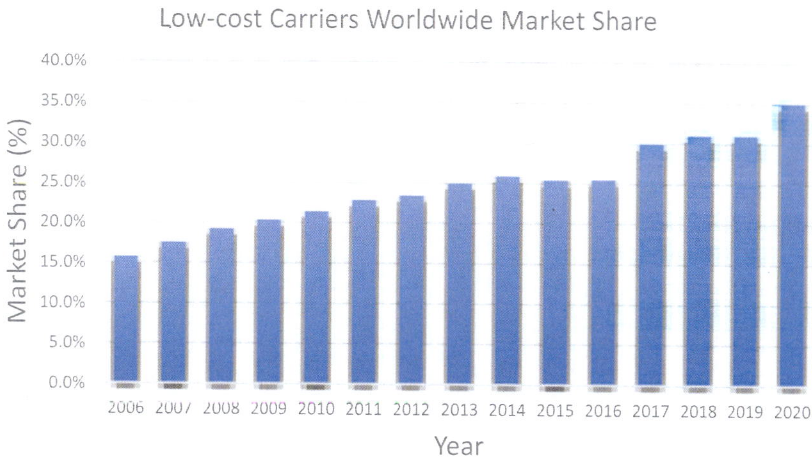

Source Statista

Fig. 4.18 LCC worldwide market share growth

LCCs have grown in strength with a worldwide total seat capacity share of 15.7% in 2006 to 34% in 2020, according to Statista.[1] Figure 4.18 illustrates how LCCs have grown in stature since 2006. This growth is driven by increased air passenger traffic and the appeal of lower fares offered by LCCs.

In 2024, LCCs accounted for 34% of the U.S. airline capacity with FSCs making up the balance of 66%. Herb Kelleher, peanut fares, and Southwest Airlines pioneered the LCC model in the 1970s with a no-frills approach to commercial aviation.

LCCs operate slightly over one-third of all airline seats globally, there are 114 airlines defined by OAG as LCCs, and legacy/full-service carriers) make up 627 [Grant, 2024]. Today, four of the ten largest airlines in the world are LCCs. They are Southwest Airlines, Ryanair, IndiGo, and easyJet.

Southwest Airlines today is considered a hybrid airline with some FSC features. A new trend is LCCs like Frontier Airlines that is adding premium options to compete with the FSCs.

Figure 4.19 illustrates a comparison of the growth in capacity for LCCs and FSCs from 2010 to 2024. As the graph indicates, FSCs have not fully recovered to 2019 pre-pandemic levels, while LCCs recovered by 2023.

The growth of the LCCs worldwide has been powered by a combination of low fares, new routes, and appeal to a new generation of price-conscious travelers. LCCs are also dominant in emerging markets like Indonesia, Brazil, and India.

---

[1] Source: Statista, Transportation and Logistics > Aviation, https://www.statista.com/statistics/586677/global-low-cost-carrier-market-capacity-share/

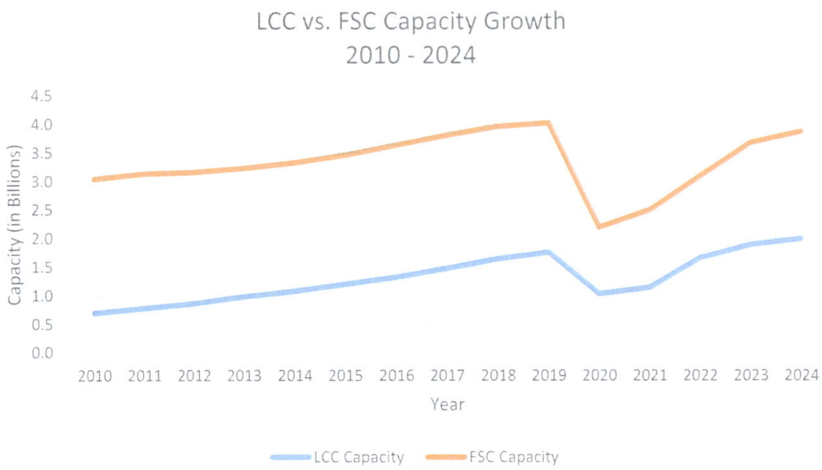

Source OAG 2024

Fig. 4.19 Full-service Carrier vs. Low-Cost Carrier Capacity Growth (2010–2024)

Figure 4.20 illustrates LCC penetration in the top ten markets from 2024. However, LCC penetration in major markets such as China and Japan is well below the global average because of regulatory constraints, airport constraints, and the dominance of existing carriers.

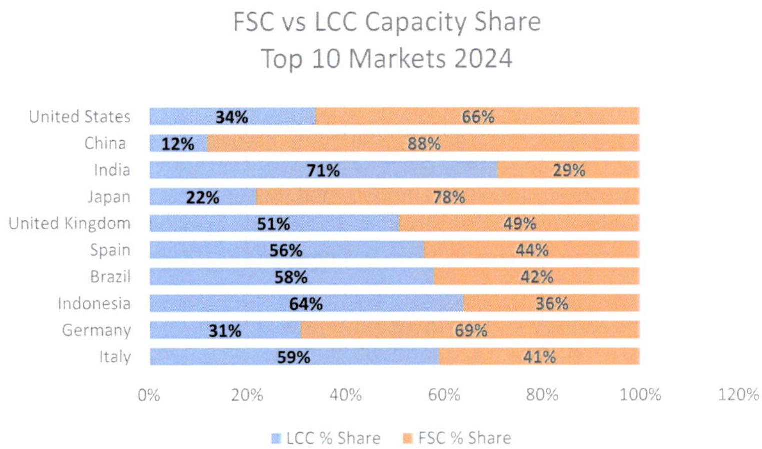

Source OAG 2024

Fig. 4.20 Full-service Carrier vs. Low-Cost Carrier Capacity Share

4.9.1 Impact on Revenue Management

The world of revenue management changed when LCCs introduced restriction-free one-way fares. Without fare restrictions, the fare amount is the sole determinant of the selling fare.

Network carriers, to counter the competitive threat from LCCs, had to modify their tariff filing, which frequently led to irrational pricing practices. Network carriers usually price connecting flights cheaper than nonstops. A LCC in the same nonstop market forces network carriers to offer cheaper fares to compete, resulting in the connecting fares being more expensive. Some of the LCCs also offer cheap competitive first-class service and network carriers are forced to match these fares, resulting in the full fare coach being more expensive than first class [McCartney, 2004]. However, this is not a general rule. In 2019, McCartney noted that the cost of comfort in airlines was increasing, and the gap between economy and premium tickets was widening [McCartney, 2019]. So, while it is possible for first class to be cheaper than coach under certain conditions, it is not the norm, and prices fluctuate based on various factors.

LCC economics are quite different from full-service carriers. They offer passengers lower ticket prices and charge additional fees for services such as checked baggage, preferred seating, upgraded Wi-Fi, and meals. LCCs offer lower fares by minimizing operational costs through strategies like using a single aircraft type, utilizing their aircraft more, flying to secondary airports that have lower landing fees, and offering a point-to-point service. Tickets issued are typically one-way fares, they do not offer interlines, and all bookings are consumer direct. This is because historically LCCs did not participate in a GDS, so travel agents do not have access to most LCC schedules, fares, and availability. However, this is changing and many LCCs participate in at least one GDS. With the introduction of NDC, all three GDSs are now focused on multi-source content consisting of GDS EDIFACT, NDC content and LCC content.

In contrast, FSCs maintain higher fares by offering a wider range of services, including complimentary meals, entertainment, and baggage allowance, alongside operating a more complex network structure.

Traditional revenue management has always focused on what the airline is willing to accept as opposed to what a customer was willing to pay. Low-cost carriers practice a unique brand of revenue management that is based on a customer's willingness to pay [Boyd & Kallesen; 2004; Dunleavy & Westermann, 2005; Gorin and Belobaba, 2004; McGill & van Ryzin, 1999]. Traits that make the LCC revenue management model different from the full-service network carriers are summarized below.

1. One-way fares, fewer fare rules and restrictions. Typical restrictions imposed are refund penalties and ticketing constraints (instant purchase or 72-h time limit). The fare is the primary determinant of the customer segment.

2. In a restriction-free or lightly restricted tariff world, the assumption that demand for each booking class is independent is no longer true. This has an impact on the demand forecasting and discount allocation models.
3. Overbooking is very conservative. No-show rates are lower because of ticketing requirements, and most fares are nonrefundable. This is augmented by the absence of interline agreements to book denied boarding passengers on alternate carriers.
4. There are fewer booking classes and smaller fare differences between booking classes.
5. Most LCCs do not participate in a GDS. All bookings are consumer direct, on the airline website, thereby avoiding GDS fees.

In addition, there is also little or no barrier for entry of a new LCC, which can change the landscape of competitive fares overnight.

Tables 4.21, 4.22, and 4.23 explain the differences between traditional tariffs and restriction-free tariffs with a simplified example.

Table 4.20 illustrates a traditional tariff structure for a market. Each fare product is independent and governed by a set of restrictions. The booking classes define unique customer segments by applying restrictions. In this scenario, traditional revenue management forecasts demand by booking class and determines the allocations against available capacity.

Table 4.21 Traditional tariff structure for a market

Booking class	Fare ($)	Advance purchase	Minimum stay	Cancellation penalty (%)
Y	$599	–	–	–
B	$499	–	–	25%
M	$349	3AP	1	50%
H	$299	7AP	3	50%
V	$269	14AP	3	50%
Z	$229	21AP	7	50%
Q	$149	21AP	7	100%

Table 4.22 Pure restriction free tariff structure for a market

Booking class	Fare ($)	Advance purchase	Minimum stay	Cancellation penalty (%)
Y	$279	–	–	100%
B	$249	–	–	100%
M	$209	–	–	100%
H	$179	–	–	100%
V	$159	–	–	100%
Z	$139	–	–	100%
Q	$109	–	–	100%

Table 4.23 Hybrid tariff structure for a market

Booking class	Fare ($)	Advance purchase	Minimum stay	Cancellation penalty (%)
Y	$279	–	–	25%
M	$249	–	–	25%
M	$209	–	–	25%
H	$189	7AP	3	50%
V	$169	7AP	3	50%
Z	$149	7AP	3	50%
Q	$129	21AP	7	100%
R	$109	21AP	7	100%
W	$99	21AP	7	100%

Table 4.21 illustrates the original LCC model with a pure restriction-free tariff structure for a market. The fare products are not independent and are totally unrestricted. The booking classes have a lower fare differential. While multiple fares are filed, they have identical restrictions and hence promote 100% sell down to the lowest available booking class. Hence, the fare is the only determinant of the market segment and the demand for a booking class is therefore dependent or contingent on the lower class being closed. In this scenario, traditional revenue management must forecast dependent demand based on the booking class that is open. Active monitoring and closure of the selling fare at the right time is required to promote sell up to a higher fare.

Table 4.22 illustrates the hybrid LCC model for a market. The fare products (booking classes) with identical restrictions are not independent and form part of a "class group". Multiple fares are filed with identical restrictions, which promotes nearly 100% sell down since multiple classes with different restrictions may be open for sale. Revenue management must forecast dependent demand and active monitoring and closure3 of selling fare at the right time is required to promote sell up to a higher fare.

To describe dependent demands, Boyd and Kallesen (2004) use the term "priceable" and "yieldable" to differentiate customer types that downsell (priceable) versus those that book in higher booking classes despite the availability of lower valued booking classes with more restrictions (yieldable).

Not all carriers classified as LCCs practice pure restriction-free pricing. For example, Southwest Airlines is an LCC with a vastly simplified tariff structure with one-way fares compared to network carriers but does not practice restriction-free pricing. Southwest Airlines used to define a limited number of unique fare products for each market that they serve but that has changed since 2024, where they follow the tariff structure to some extent of the FSCs. Today, many LCCs have moved away from a pure restriction-free tariff structure to lightly restricted tariffs.

4.9.2 Inventory Control with Restriction Free Fares

Figure 4.21 illustrates how inventory is controlled with pure restriction-free pricing. In this scenario an airline would file multiple fares with the same identical minimal fare restrictions. Hence, the probability of selling a higher fare in the hierarchy is contingent on the immediate lower fare being closed for sale. When a flight is first detailed in the reservations system, there is a single one-way fare in the market that is active. Over time, as bookings build up for the flight, the fares are progressively increased until flight departure. Note that at any point in time, there is only one active selling fare in the market.

With the absence of restrictions, the real-time reservations inventory control environment for both LCCs and network carriers that file restriction-free tariffs must be very dynamic to ensure that target bookings are being achieved for each booking class before the selling class is closed to promote upsell to the next higher valued class. For carriers operating point-to-point without significant connecting traffic, the inventory control environment can be based on authorization levels and time limits based on days to departure as described above.

The first generation of LCC revenue management systems relied on rules-based heuristics to control seat inventory. In the absence of advance purchase time limits, the offline revenue management planning process must provide frequent updates to the real-time reservations inventory control environment based on the pace of bookings observed in the reservations system. A time-of-day specific limit may also be required for airlines that want to override the selling fare at a specific departure time (e.g., 9:00am versus 2:00 pm) for competitive reasons.

Hence, in a restriction-free pricing environment, the fare restrictions are eliminated and rely on the revenue management system to control availability of the filed fares by setting inventory controls that influences the required sell up behavior [Vinod, 2008].

4.9.3 Coexistence of Inventory Controls for Network Carriers

As the LCCs matured from start-ups to established carriers, the network carriers could not afford to ignore them. To target specific customer segments, network carriers had no choice but to compete with LCCs with restriction-free tariffs in domestic markets and compete with international carriers with the traditional, more lucrative, restricted tariffs.

Frequently, a hybrid inventory control structure may be more appropriate for network carriers that files both restriction-free tariffs and regular tariffs based on competitive need. In this scenario, it is required to discern the restriction-free tariffs from the traditional tariffs for forecasting demand and subsequent determination of discount allocation controls to control these customer segments independently.

Consider the hypothetical network shown in Fig. 4.22. An international carrier like LATAM must compete on the Sao Paulo (GRU) to Rio de Janeiro (GIG) local market against LCCs and simultaneously compete with restricted tariffs against

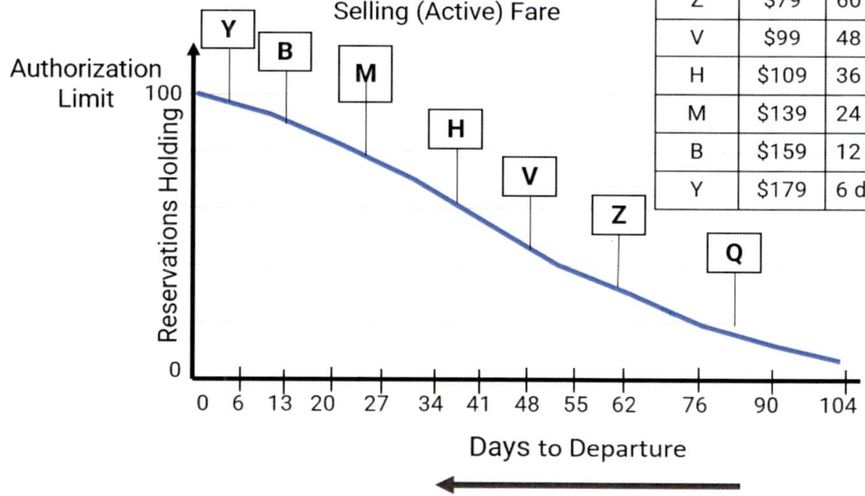

Class	Fare	Booking Class Closing Condition
Q	$59	Flight is open
Z	$79	60 days before departure or after 32 bookings
V	$99	48 days before departure or after 44 bookings
H	$109	36 days before departure or after 60 bookings
M	$139	24 days before departure or after 78 bookings
B	$159	12 days before departure or after 86 bookings
Y	$179	6 days before departure

Fig. 4.21 Restriction free pricing inventory controls

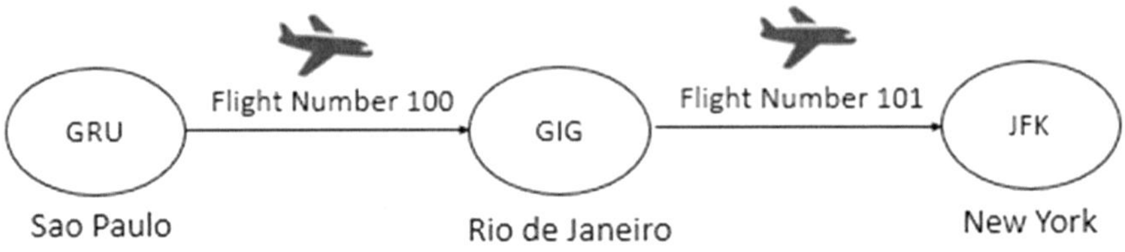

Fig. 4.22 Sample network with restricted and unrestricted tariffs

international carriers for the GRU-JFK and GIG-JFK international markets. With the coexistence model, the tariff structure targets both schedule sensitive and price sensitive customer segments depending on the market.

Typically, restriction-free tariffs are prevalent on domestic markets while restricted tariffs exist in international markets. To protect market share, network carriers must file restriction-free tariffs in local markets to compete against the LCCs and continue to file restricted fares in international nonstop and connecting markets. Therefore, a customer who books a local flight may be on a restriction-free tariff while a connecting passenger to an international destination on the same flight will be on a restricted tariff. Two types of distinct inventory control structures coexist in the same cabin for local traffic control and connecting international traffic control. For inventory control purposes, an invisible curtain exists in the same cabin on the local domestic flight.

Figure 4.23 illustrates the coexistence of inventory controls on the GRU-GIG flight leg. The business and leisure booking classes for the domestic market GRU-GIG are based on assumed values of the booking class hierarchy. For the international market GRU-JFK, the business and leisure booking classes based on value are shown. The nested inventory control structure for domestic and international are two separate parallel structures ("the electronic curtain") that is nested into the highest valued booking class for international, Y.

4.10 Impact of LCC Pricing on Revenue Management

Restriction free pricing introduces some unique challenges for traditional revenue management, which assumes that the booking classes are independent. With tickets being sold at various price points for the same product, the assumption of *independent demand* for each booking class is no longer true. The demand is *dependent* or *conditional* on the selling fare being offered which is the only determinant of demand for the segment.

Over the past two decades, much of the research and advancements in demand forecasting and optimization have focused on restriction-free fares, lightly restricted fares, and restricted fares as they coexist in a network [Ratliff & Weatherford, 2009]. With the proliferation of less restricted fare products, the rapid

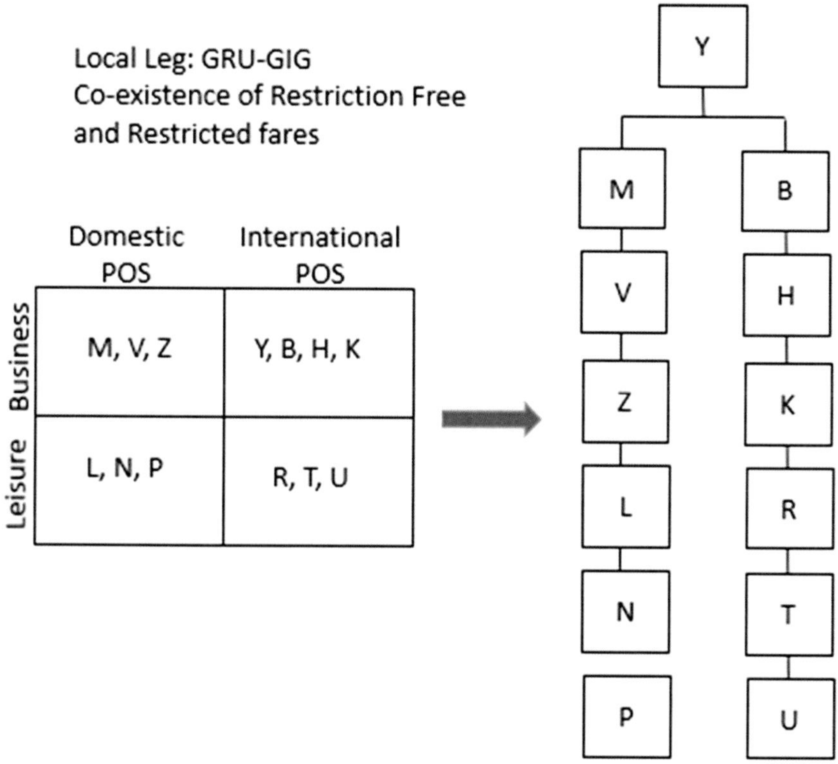

Fig. 4.23 Coexistence of inventory controls

adoption of customer choice models and the validity of using historical data for forecasting is often debated [Zeni, 2007].

While LCCs may practice only restriction-free pricing, network carriers need both regular restricted fares in international markets and restriction-free fares in markets where they compete with the LCCs. Revenue management systems had to adapt and forecast dependent demand based on which flights and booking classes are currently open and closed for sale. Active monitoring and closure of selling fare at the right time is required to promote sell up to the higher fare and maximize flight revenues.

4.10.1 Multi-Class and Multi-Class Multi-Flight Models

Restriction free pricing led to the realization that revenue management needs to look beyond the basic single booking class model where demand between booking classes is independent of each other. As a result, there are three classes of problems in increasing order of sophistication (and complexity) to estimate untruncated demand from bookings, forecast, and optimize inventory controls. They are the single class, multi-class, and multi-class multi-flight models [Ratliff et al., 2008].

The single class models are typically used when demand between booking classes is independent. These models have the disadvantage of not considering demand interaction between booking classes to address upsell, downsell, and recapture.

The multi-class models are required with restriction-free tariffs that result in dependent demand for fare products. These models can address demand interaction between booking classes on the same flight. With restriction-free pricing, booking class availability determines the booking class that will be sold. The multi-class model considers the joint demand across booking classes but does not model cross flight recapture.

Multi-class multi-flight models are the most general since they explicitly consider upsell and downsell on the same flight and cross-flight recapture. However, these models require more complex methods to handle the demand interactions. Traditional O&D service class demand untruncation methods applied to multi-class models lead to double counting; this is because the true demand on a customer's first choice flight during closed periods is counted as spill and subsequent recapture on alternate flights with the same airline is counted as observed traffic. O&D service class bookings always consist of a mix of first choice demand, recapture from the same carrier and capture from other carriers.

Discrete choice models such as the multinomial logit (MNL) have been used [Gallego et al., 2009] to calibrate the underlying demand models. MNL is a statistical model that applies when there are more than two choices of dependent variables, allowing participants to select from multiple alternatives. It assumes that the sum of the selection probabilities of all options equals 1 and that each alternative is independent of the others.

With this approach untruncated demand can be estimated from bookings. While the MNL is difficult to calibrate and requires extensive data, estimates of upsell, downsell, and recapture are a byproduct of the MNL calibration.

4.10.2 Impact on Revenue Management Models—Demand Forecasting

With the multi-class demand unconstraining methods, a multivariate censored regression model with EM to estimate passenger demand was proposed by McGill [1995]. The explanatory variables in the regression model were used to estimate passenger demand subject to nested booking limits.

Figure 4.24 illustrates the price sensitivity of demand by time to departure. To forecast demand an approach is to estimate the price-demand relationship and fit a causal model for forecasting conditional demand based on historical price points, observed bookings and inventory controls. Buy-up and buy-down behavior can be estimated using the proximity of fares by days to departure [Mishra & Viswanathan, 2003].

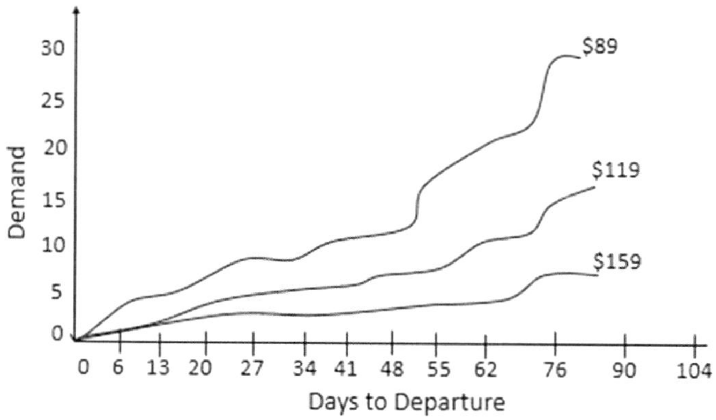

Fig. 4.24 Price sensitivity

Q-Forecasting techniques [Boyd et al., 2001; Hopperstad et al., 2006], are based on bookings, availability, fares by booking class and price elasticity to estimate the equivalent lowest nested class or Q class and uses a negative exponential function to model the median upsell from Q to the higher classes. By adjusting historical booking data to account for sell up potential, it converts all bookings into an equivalent number of bookings in the lowest booking class or Q-class by dividing historical bookings by the estimated probability of sell up. Once the bookings are converted to a Q-equivalent figure, traditional forecasting models can be used on these equivalent bookings. This approach accounts for the potential revenue from passengers who might upgrade to a higher fare,

A popular approach to estimate upsell because of its simplicity is the FRAT5 curve [Boyer, 2010; Hopperstad, 2004]. These fare ratio (FRAT) curves are important to understand and predict passenger willingness to pay (WTP). These curves are used to estimate a customer's WTP at different points in the booking window. For example, each FRAT5 value is the fare ratio at which 50% of demand is expected to sell-up. For example, a FRAT5 value of 2.2 with the lowest fare of $100 at a given point in time in the booking window reflects a WTP estimate of $220.

There are different FRAT5 curves, such as FRAT5a, FRAT5c, and FRAT5e, which represent varying levels of aggressiveness in pricing or forecasting [Weatherford, 2013]. For example, FRAT5a might be the most aggressive, meaning it assumes customers are willing to pay higher prices earlier in the booking window, while FRAT5e might be the least aggressive.

An alternative, more flexible and versatile approach to estimate same-flight upsell and cross-flight recapture is the logit demand model, which is widely used in scheduling applications to measure schedule profitability. The simplest of these models is the multinomial logit (MNL) model which is easy to calibrate and more accurate than the FRAT5 curves because of flight and class specific considerations. There are more advanced logit models such as the nested logit [Gallego et al., 2009; Mishra et al., 2005; Parker, 2004] and Generalized Extreme Value (GEV) which produce more accurate estimates at a significant cost of compute cycles.

With dependent demand, one approach is to split the booking class demand into the "priceable" and "yieldable" components based on historical bookings and availability data [Boyd & Kallesen, 2004]. The "yieldable" segment is defined as bookings in all but the lowest open class. Untruncation is based on the single class Expected Maximization (*EM*) method. The priceable segment assumes pure restriction-free pricing and works with upsell rates from FRAT5 curves. Booking classes that are lightly restricted use both techniques in tandem. Revenue improvements based on improvements in forecast accuracy have been reported in the Passenger Origin–Destination Simulator (PODS) studies [Belobaba & Hopperstad, 2004; Fiig et al., 2005].

The multi-class multi-flight models consider recapture. A demand and recapture estimation model using regression was developed [Ja et al., 2001] to solve unknown values of uncensored demand and recapture. A multivariate demand model [Stefanescu et al., 2004] considers correlation across flights, fare products and time periods over the booking horizon and estimates are derived with the EM algorithm. The EM discrete choice model approach with estimates of the no-fly purchase probabilities [Talluri & van Ryzin, 2004; Vulcano et al., 2010] exploits the EM algorithm to iteratively estimate the demand arrival rates and the MNL discrete choice model parameters. A computationally efficient method for estimating demand, spill and recapture [Vulcano et al., 2012; Ratliff et al., 2008] from historical demand and availability data for unconstraining demand across multiple flights and classes avoids double counting demand by jointly estimating spill on closed flights and recapture on to open flights.

4.10.3 Impact on Revenue Management Models—Optimization

Conditional demand versions of expected marginal seat revenue (EMSR) with price-demand curves can be used with available seats to determine the optimal timing and price to be offered, subject to business constraints encapsulated as rules. This has a revenue advantage over a manual rules-based environment practiced by many LCCs.

When the demand between booking classes is independent, neither the fare nor the demand is modified. With dependent demands, models based on unadjusted demand and/or fares are less effective in a restriction-free pricing environment [Belobaba, 2008; Gallego et al., 2009; Weatherford & Ratliff, 2010].

A common approach to address dependent demands is the fare adjustment approach [Belobaba & Weatherford, 1996] that incorporates sell-up probabilities directly into the standard $EMSR_B$ formulation. Consider two booking classes valued at R_Y and R_B and $R_Y > R_B$. Further, assume the upsell rate from booking class B to Y when B is closed is equal to θ.

The fare adjustment for the lower class,

$$Adjusted\ Fare\ R_B = \frac{R_B - R_Y * \theta}{(1 - \theta)}$$

This adjustment to the lower valued booking class reduces the value of R_B relative to the higher valued fare, R_Y. This results in more space being protected for the higher valued booking class, assuming the upsell rate isθ. This model assumes the booking classes are independent. The limitations include estimating upsell θ and booking class independence which is not valid with restriction-free pricing.

The first known model to address dependent demands was developed by Brunelle, McGill, Oum, Sawaki, and Tretheway [1990].

$$\Pr[D_Y + U(AU_B) \geq C - AU_B \mid D_B \geq AU_B] \leq \frac{R_B - R_Y * \theta}{R_Y * (1 - \theta)}$$

where:

D_Y and AU_Y are demand and authorization limit for class Y respectively.
D_B and AU_B are demand and authorization limit for class B respectively.
$D_Y + U(AU_B)$ is the first-choice demand for class Y plus upsell, conditional on $D_B \geq AU_B$, causing spill and upsell.

This is a fare adjustment approach that also requires revised demand input. The model accounts for the fact that achieving upsell is conditional on the discount booking class authorization limit. The model is difficult if not impossible to implement since there is no easy way to estimate the upsell rate $(U(AU_B))$ or the conditional demand without recourse to consumer choice models.

A multinomial logit based improved upsell model for EMSR that works with both restricted and restriction-free pricing environments was proposed [Gallego et al., 2007] that accounts for the effects of upsell, downsell, and competitive alternatives in cases involving dependent (or partially dependent) demands. It uses choice-based demand models to estimate these effects. While published solutions for solving EMSR with dependent demands has existed since the late 1990s, they were not tractable since upsell occur because of spilled demand that was conditional on the discount class booking limits. This approach relies on using the maximum demand and not the first-choice demand to determine an upper bound on space protected for higher valued demand. Note that while the first-choice demand are exclusive of upsell, the maximum demand estimates are inclusive of upsell. They demonstrated identical results to the fare adjustment approach of Brumelle et al. [1990] and it was computationally tractable.

A practical approach is the Displacement Adjusted Virtual Nesting – Marginal Revenue (DAVN-MR) [Fiig et al., 2005] model where dependent demands are transformed into approximate independent demands which can be solved using traditional methods. This method incorporates upsell into the optimizer with fare and demand adjustments and provides a reasonable approach to incorporating dependent demands into a two-stage decomposition method where the deterministic network results from the first stage are used as input to a second stage stochastic leg optimizer. Cross flight recapture effects are not considered in this model.

Simulation studies have shown that the choice based EMSR heuristic [Gallego et al., 2009] produces results close to the optimal solution for leg/segment carriers.

Choice-based deterministic network linear program (CDLP) optimization models [Chaneton & Vulcano, 2011; Gallego et al., 2004; Liu & van Ryzin, 2006] proposed an efficient formulation for same flight upsells, while recapture required explicit enumeration of open/close status across all services in a market. As a result, large scale problems are difficult to solve without using column generation.

A related method is the choice-based network optimization [Talluri & van Ryzin, 2004] model that used dynamic programming at a flight leg level to determine the optimal policy. This method is computationally intensive and relies on knowing the time dependent arrival rates, which is not practical from a deployment perspective.

Fiig, Isler, Hopperstad and Belobaba [2010] proposed a fare adjustment transformation that changes fares and demand of a general, discrete choice model to an equivalent independent demand model. With this approach, once the dependent demand was restated as independent demand, the standard revenue mix optimization models can be used to determine inventory controls. Further, these fare adjustments were extended to branded fare families [Fiig et al., 2012].

A choice-based network model that considers same flight upsell and cross flight recapture [Gallego et al., 2015] for dependent demand was developed as a General Attraction Model (GAM) that permits varying the re-attraction rate separately for each item in a choice set. The optimization model is a deterministic formulation that optimally handles dependent demands with upsell and recapture.

Dependent demand also has an impact on the revenue opportunity model (ROM) [Chapter 4, Vinod 2021a] with independent demands. What is required is a solution that includes all three types of pricing environments: traditional, pure restriction-free pricing and lightly restricted pricing. This led to the development of a choice-based ROM model [Liang et al., 2017; Ratliff et al., 2013] that models same flight upsell and cross flight recapture. The choice-based ROM also introduces two new metrics, the net spill rate (NSR) and the recapture fare ratio (RFR).

$$Net\ Spill\ Rate = \frac{Spill - Recapture}{Demand}$$

and

$$Recapture\ Fare\ Ratio = \frac{Average\ Value\ of\ Recaptured\ Demand}{Average\ Value\ of\ Spilled\ Demand}$$

The Recapture Fare Ratio (RFR) is used to determine the fare upsell amount. For dependent demands, the ROM model based on a sales-based linear programming formulation [Gallego et al., 2015] explicitly models upsell and cross-flight recapture.

4.10.4 The Revenue Opportunity Model for Dependent Demand

A network model leveraging customer choice models was proposed [Ratliff et al., 2013] to handle a range of pricing environments such as traditional restricted fares, pure restriction-free fares (though it is not in much use today) and lightly restricted fares.

The Basic Attraction Model (BAM) is shown below.

$$p_j(S) = \frac{v_j}{v_0 + \sum_{k \in S} v_k}$$

where:

S : set of choices
$p_j(S)$: probability that choice j will be selected from S.
v_j : attractiveness of choice j
v_0 : The null alternative, which is the aggregate attractiveness of competitor (Other Airline – OA) itineraries or the Do Not Fly (DNF) option.

The basic attraction model (BAM) states that the demand for a product is the ratio of the direct attractiveness of the product divided by the sum of the direct attractiveness of the available products, including the OA/DNF alternative. This model assumes that demand lost from a product removed from the storefront is partially recaptured by the remaining alternatives in proportion to their attractiveness. It provides an understanding of how customer choice shifts when product availability changes. A feature of the BAM is its assumption that demand spills over to other choices and is recaptured based on their attraction levels. The multinomial logit (MNL) model, a common model for discrete choice, is a special case of the BAM, where attractiveness values are derived from exponential functions of utility.

The method relies on rescaling when there are itinerary closures for the host airline. The OA/DNF alternative is assumed to be open and provides a convenient reference point for rescaling other item dependent demands. Consider the new choice set Q after itinerary closures, then the remaining open choices (itineraries) are renormalized to 100% based on the new total excluding the closed choices to re-estimate the host airline recapture rate and spilled passengers to OA.

$$p_j(Q) = \frac{p_j(S)}{1 - \sum_{k \notin Q} p_k(S)}$$

The independence of irrelevant alternatives (IIA) property allows the addition or removal of an alternative from the choice set without affecting the structure or parameters of the model. The property states that the relative preference or probability of choosing between two options (A and B) remains constant, regardless of the addition or removal of other "irrelevant" options (C). It is a restrictive assumption in logit models.

The revenue opportunity model uses the Sales-based Linear Program formulation for dependent demands [Gallego et al., 2015]. The total and relative demand constraints in the formulation force the allocation of the open items to rescale proportionally. The formulation also avoids the exponential number of variables in earlier choice-based network revenue management approaches and is the same size as the standard linear program formulation for independent demand.

4.11 Connectivity Standards for the Indirect Channel

Until the introduction of EDIFACT in 1988, the numeric availability attached to each booking class was based on teletype (TTY). With EDIFACT, subject to an airline's participation level for connectivity, the availability displayed could be based on true last seat availability from an airline's reservations system. This is based on the request (PAOREQ) and response (PAORES) transactions. EDIFACT also provides instant confirmation for sell transactions, called secure sell transactions since availability is queried in the airline reservations system before the sell is completed, with the request (ITAREQ) and response (ITARES) transactions. With the introduction of EDIFACT, there was significant innovation on the connectivity front. Major features such as journey controls and married to journey controls were introduced in the early 1990s well before the introduction of origin and destination (O&D) revenue management.

Air connectivity products are fundamental to reservations processing on the GDS. They automate the workflow to enable the GDS subscribers to request and sell an airline's product. Airlines support various air connectivity products at varying degrees of sophistication using teletype, EDIFACT and XML messaging standards to receive and respond back to requests.

GDSs have a unique global identifier for sending and receiving transactions that are to be processed. For example, the identifier for Sabre is 1S, Amadeus is 1A, and Galileo is 1G.

Some of the most relevant teletype and EDIFACT connectivity features include:

1. Availability Status (AVS)
2. Availability Status Numeric (AVN)
3. Answerback
4. Basic Booking Record (BBR)
5. Direct Access Interactive (DAI)
6. Direct Connect Sell (DCS)
7. Direct Connect Availability (DCA)

8. Market Restricted Flights
9. Married Segments
10. Journey Data
11. Married to Journey
12. Interactive Seat Maps
13. Interactive Pre-reserved Seats
14. Point of Sale
15. Point of Commencement

A detailed explanation of air connectivity can be found in Chapter 3 [Vinod, 2024a].

The traditional connectivity standards for a GDS to shop and book travel is based on booking class availability. In the NDC era, the traditional GDS to airline connectivity standards, both teletype (TTY) and EDIFACT, will no longer be required, and will be replaced by new messaging standards for NDC bookings. An objective of NDC to to replace outdated, text-based teletype messaging and interactive EDIFACT with XML-based API standards. In the current hybrid state, traditional connectivity standards and NDC connectivity requirements will co-exist.

4.12 End-Product of Traditional Revenue Management

The end product of traditional revenue management is either nested authorization levels for leg/segment carriers or bid price controls for O&D network carriers. Booking class availability is determined from these inventory controls.

For an airline, either nested authorization levels by flight leg (or segment) by departure date or bid prices by flight leg and departure date are stored on the inventory system of the airline reservations system (host CRS). These controls can be readily translated to booking class seat availability when a reservation request is received. While booking class availability for leg/segment carriers is a simple calculation, the booking class availability using bid prices for O&D carriers is computationally more demanding since it is an iterative process. Booking class availability is used by airline shopping and pricing systems to determine the lowest total fare for the itinerary subject to fare rules, restrictions, surcharges, and taxes.

The Transition from Revenue Management to Offer Management 5

Innovation distinguishes between a leader and a follower.

Steve Jobs

Abstract

Revenue management of the base fare is in a transition to offers and orders. Like revenue management of the base fare, the new world of offers and orders is controlled by the operating carrier that owns the seat inventory. This transition also means that for NDC (New Distribution Capability) bookings, the airline provides the price quote for itineraries in response to a shopping request and the role of distributing booking class availability to GDSs becomes irrelevant. However, in the hybrid state, reservation booking designator (RBD) availability is still required for the traditional GDS EDIFACT bookings. The origins and future of fare filings and booking class availability are examined. With the evolving AI landscape, there are new approaches to recommendation engines and creation of offers to maximize revenues.

The scope of AI in travel to capture customer intent, the rise of Generative AI, AI Agents, natural language processing, and test and learn experimentation are important components of airline retailing. The chapter concludes with a discussion of the AI-powered revenue management environment.

This quote by Apple co-founder Steve Jobs resonates with the new world of airline retailing, as the industry transitions from revenue management of the base fare to offers and orders. For airline executives, it represents a fundamental paradigm shift from selling tickets to selling experiences. Airlines that demonstrate strategic

B. Vinod, *The Era of Airline Revenue Management with Offers and Orders*,
Management for Professionals, https://doi.org/10.1007/978-3-032-24197-9_5

agility and innovation in this space will have a first mover advantage. While the opportunity exists, a few airlines will take the lead and seize this opportunity.

5.1 Introduction

Revenue management of the base fare is in transition to offers and orders. Like revenue management of the base fare, the new world of offers and orders are also controlled by the operating carrier that owns the seat inventory. But there is a fundamental difference, Airlines do not distribute availability of booking classes, also known as reservation booking designator (RBDs), to GDSs for shopping and pricing on their respective systems. Instead, the airlines respond with priced itinerary bundles to the GDSs. In the NDC era, pricing power shifts from the GDS to the airline for the indirect channel. All NDC-enabled offers (itinerary and ancillary products) are priced by the airline and distributed to intermediaries.

This new approach where offers for all channels are airline controlled also raises questions about the future of fare filing and booking classes. An open question is how will they evolve? Will airlines continue to file fares when there is no need to distribute fares to GDSs? With NDC adoption an airline does not have to distribute RBD availability to intermediaries like the GDS. Will the RBDs be retained for technical reasons for internal use by airlines such as reservations inventory control and itinerary pricing?

5.2 The Problem with à la carte Pricing of Ancillaries

When American Airlines introduced baggage fees in 2008, was this an attempt to become a retailer of products and services? By all accounts the answer is no. It was an attempt to generate incremental revenues by unbundling checked bags from the ticket price. But there must have been a strategy to charge for bags and what was it? There are at least two alternative arguments to justify charging for baggage.

A fundamental question is whether baggage fees are good for society [Lariviere, 2011]. At least that is what CEO's that ran LCCs believed, even if they come from different perspectives.

Argument #1

By separating or unbundling the cost of checking a bag from the cost of the flight, airlines can generate extra income from customers who place the highest value on this service. Unbundling is the process of separating a previously bundled product or service into its individual components and offering them separately. This can create more options for customers and allow businesses to target specific customer needs. Examples include:

1. Offering hotel rooms without cleaning or linen services.
2. Cell phone plans that employ a "pay as you go" approach to pricing to serve different customer segments profitably.
3. Music platforms that sell individual songs instead of the entire album.

Argument #2

Airlines reduce their operating expenses by influencing the behavior of travelers. Besides generating incremental revenue from a segment of travelers that do not have frequent flyer status to check their bags for free, it encourages travelers to change their behavior and opt for carry-on luggage only. This modification in consumer behavior results in less checked baggage which in turn reduces an airline operating costs, such as:.

1. Lower fuel burn means lower fuel consumption. This results in a substantial cost saving since fuel is the second largest operating expense after employee salaries.
2. With fewer checked bags on a flight, airlines need fewer staff for check-in and handling, streamlining ground operations.
3. Faster baggage handling can improve turnaround times at airports, contributing to better on time performance and reduced delays.

These arguments are fundamentally different. CEOs of LCCs have very different views for justifying charging for ancillary products.

Former chief executive of Spirit Airlines Ben Baldanza was quoted [Lanviere, 2011]:

> *We believe it is important to let customers decide what is of value to them. Imagine if you went to a restaurant and all the meals came with dessert. That's great if you like dessert but, if you don't, you would prefer the option to pay less for the meal and not take the dessert.*

The second quote is from Michael O'Leary, the chief executive of Ryanair [Lanviere, 2011].

> *Like, paying for checked-in bags: It wasn't about getting revenue. It was about persuading people to change their travel behavior—to travel with carry-on luggage only. But that's enabled us to move to 100% Web check-in. So, we now don't need check-in desks. We don't need check-in staff. Passengers love it because they'll never again get stuck in a Ryanair check-in queue. That helps us significantly lower airport and handling costs.*
>
> *Now we're looking at charging for toilets on board—not because we want revenue from toilet fees. We'd happily give the money away to some incontinent charity. What it means is, if by charging for toilets on board, more people would use the toilets in the terminals before or after flights, I could take out maybe two of the three toilets on board, add six extra seats and reduce fares across the aircraft by another three or four percent.*

Charging a baggage fee poses a dilemma for the airline since it is not all incremental revenue. Business travelers typically board a flight with only carry-on bags and are unaffected by an airline's policy of charging for baggage. In contrast, leisure travelers tend to pack more and check their bags. Leisure travelers are willing to pay baggage fees when the base fare is deeply discounted. This poses a challenge for airlines, as customers who travel light are likely to be drawn to the deeply discounted fares. Depending on the fare purchased or their frequent flyer status, business travelers can often check bags for free. Therefore, it is unlikely that airlines are using baggage fees to segment customers but rather as a tool to influence customer behavior. This suggests that it is beneficial for airlines to bundle the base fare and ancillaries together and charge a higher total fare for business travelers while promoting free bag check.

5.3 The Transition from Revenue Management of the Base Fare to Offer Management

For three decades after airline deregulation, revenue management in the airline industry has focused on maximizing revenues by selling the right product to the right customer at the right price at the right time. It was viewed as a one-dimensional problem since the objective was to determine the selling fare in a market.

With the focus on airline retailing, or selling offers, airlines want to sell experiences, rather than just tickets.

Revenue management advanced from leg/segment inventory controls to origin and destination inventory controls. With leg/segment controls, seat availability was determined based on either net nesting or threshold nesting. To control inventory by O&D, the first O&D system was based on virtual nesting for American Airlines [Smith, 1986]. Today the popular method to control availability by O&D is based on continuous nesting, also known as bid price controls. Restriction-free pricing (RFP), a feature introduced by LCCs, was first adopted to some degree by the FSCs when they had to compete directly with the LCCs on key routes. In the absence of fare restrictions, when price was the only determinant of the customer segment, demand for booking classes is no longer independent. The revenue management models had to go through significant enhancements related to demand forecasting and revenue mix optimization to support lightly restricted and unrestricted tariffs.

With schedule and fare transparency during shopping, competitive revenue management gained rapid adoption in the early 2000s [Ratliff & Vinod, 2005], whereby the selling fares in the market offered by competitors was considered as an input to adjust the inventory controls subject to prevailing competitive market conditions.

Full-service carriers (FSCs) airlines started selling ancillaries bundled as branded fare products in 2006 and followed up with à la carte sales. Even though airlines sold ancillary services through their websites, GDS agencies, OTAs and metasearch engines had access to optional services like checked bags and premium seats in 2009 with ATPCO's Optional Services. An immediate benefit to travel agents was instant access to ancillary products and services without having to surf airline websites. This transformed the way travel agents sold ancillaries through the GDSs as well as the way consumers used OTAs and metasearch engines.

Some of the latest advances in revenue management of the base fare are in the areas of dynamic availability and dynamic pricing.

Dynamic availability works with the existing airline tariff structure that has been published by the airlines to the fare aggregator ATPCO. Dynamic Availability factors the competitive marketplace to dynamically open and close discrete inventory controls in the airline host CRS to maximize revenues. A customer choice model that considers schedule and fare attributes for estimating sales probabilities across the set of available travel options in the market, and an availability optimization model that estimates the revenue-maximizing set of available products based on their prices and market conditions are required. The session-based fare optimizer determines the optimal price point which is then translated into inventory control recommendations [Gallego & Hu, 2014]. With the adoption of IATA NDC, dynamic availability will no longer be applicable when the airline industry is no longer in the hybrid state, for two reasons: absence of fare transparency in an NDC world and the fact that airlines do not distribute booking class availability to intermediaries and third parties.

Dynamic Pricing takes Dynamic Availability a step further to generate a dynamic price that may not be a fare that was filed by the airline to fare aggregators. The advantage of dynamic pricing is that it fills the missed opportunities (gaps) on the price demand curve by recommending a continuous dynamic price. The revenue management process still requires customer segmentation and reference fares to quote a dynamic continuous price for each shopping or booking request. Dynamic pricing can be based on an airline's price-demand curves or be augmented with competitive selling fare data.

With the growing importance of the sale of ancillary products and services bundled with the base fare to improve the bottom line, this transition of revenue management of the base fare to offer management was spearheaded by the LCCs. With FSC's following the LCC lead by selling ancillary products and services, the science of revenue management has transitioned from *inventory control tactics to sell the base fare* to *selling a bundle consisting of the base fare with ancillary products and services*. With this change every dimension of the offer—the base fare and ancillaries included in the offer with their respective prices serve a role in maximizing an airline's network revenues and profitability.

Inventory control and seat pricing by seat type and individual seat represent the last frontier in inventory control, where inventory control is very granular [Vinod, 2021d; 2021a, Chapter 9]. Many airlines price seats manually and a few use analytics and reinforcement learning to price seats.

Another dimension to the transition from revenue management to offer management is how ancillaries are priced. What is mostly practiced today is static ancillary pricing, which is the price for ancillaries based on what has been filed either with ATPCO or an airline's internal system. In the future static ancillary pricing will

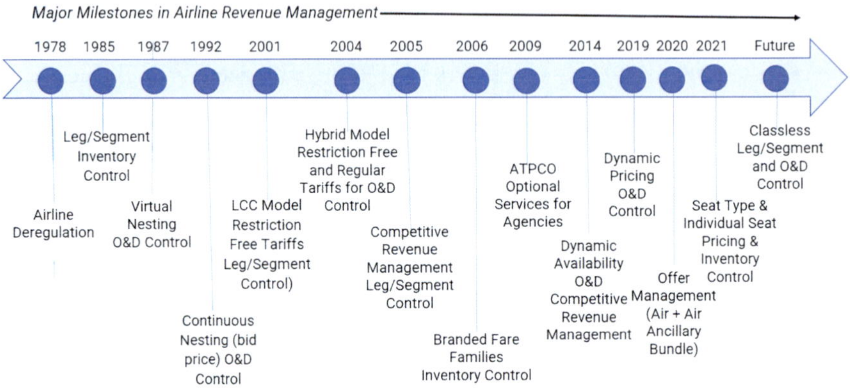

Fig. 5.1 Major milestones in revenue management

transition to dynamic ancillary pricing based on competition, customer preferences and context for travel.

The offers recommended to customers can be by customer segment based on the context for travel. This is a recommendation by trip-purpose segment. Alternatively, if the customer has purchase history stored on their profile, this information can be leveraged to *personalize* the offer at the individual level for a segment of ONE.

With the IATA NDC messaging standard, the key difference is that all offers are created, controlled, and distributed by the airlines [Touraine, 2021].

The major revenue management milestones since airline deregulation are shown in Fig. 5.1.

5.4 How Revenue Management Is Evolving in a Post Pandemic World

Besides the fundamental transition from revenue management of the base fare to revenue management of bundles, revenue management is evolving in a post-pandemic world.

Historical demand patterns may not accurately predict future demand, which was observed after the onset of the COVID-19 pandemic in 2020. Adaptive revenue management is a reliable framework that allows businesses to adapt quickly to changing market conditions with ad-hoc schedule changes by incorporating key concepts from sales and operations planning [Vinod, 2022b]. During the pandemic, there was a significant decline in customer demand, and airline revenue management systems struggled to forecast flight demand accurately [Vinod, 2020c, 2021b]. To manage the business without relying on accurate forecasts, it is necessary to shift toward an operationally driven approach that continuously manages demand. This robust revenue management approach, known as continuous demand management [Vinod, 2021a, 2021b], involves actively monitoring key performance indicators and proactively taking corrective action to ensure that revenue targets are met. Corrective action may be based on demand levers or supply levers. Examples of demand levers are inventory open/close, fare promotions, etc. Examples of capacity levers are switching capacity a few weeks before departure to match demand to supply. This may also involve canceling a wing tip operation (two flights servicing the same market with identical or close departure times and using a larger aircraft to accommodate the traffic from the original wing-tip flights in the schedule. The integration of revenue management with fleet assignment is called Demand Driven Dispatch or D.^{3}

By embracing continuous demand management, businesses can effectively respond to demand fluctuations and achieve the goals outlined in the revenue plan. This approach bears similarities to the sales and operations planning (S&OP) workflow [Palmatier & Crum, 2003], which involves synchronizing demand, available capacity, and resources to optimize performance, particularly during times of high uncertainty and volatility. Supply chain management professionals also refer to the S&OP workflow as enterprise business planning (EBP).

5.4.1 Recommendation Engine for Offers

Recommendation engines can be calibrated from historical transaction data by synchronizing ticketing data with EMD data. Calibration is always performed by customer segment. By offering relevant products and services, airlines can increase conversion rates, upsell opportunities, and boost ancillary revenues. Loyalty program statistics and travel behavior patterns are also important considerations, While powerful, challenges like data sparsity and "cold start" problems for new travelers or items must be addressed.

In addition to predictive modeling based on data summaries, a knowledge graph for each user to grasp their preferences for additional services can be processed by recommendation engines. The graph is assessed using current factors such as flight capacity, routes, duration, and busy times using a strong scoring system for suggesting additional services at different points during travel planning. This process has the potential to increase the probability of a purchase, resulting in increased conversion rates.

5.4.2 Offer Recommendation Based on Experimentation

To promote bundles, calibration based on historical data must be avoided at all costs. First, the historical purchase history data may not be sufficient or non-existent when new ancillary products are introduced. Second, periodic calibration to revise the estimates of the parameters of the offer model is a time-consuming task and will *always lag* evolving consumer preferences over time. The more adaptable approach is to conduct *test-and-learn experimentation*, using a reinforcement learning technique commonly known as the multi-armed bandit (MAB), to determine the composition of the offer bundles. This approach learns continuously based on changing consumer behaviors and prevailing competitive market conditions. The implementation of the test and learning experimentation model should be context sensitive [Byrd & Darrow, 2021]. Contextual reinforcement learning tracks customer responses by trip-purpose segment.

Personalization of the offer based on the context for travel is important to improve conversion rates. Offers can be recommended by trip-purpose segment, and in situations where the customer travels frequently, the offer can be personalized based on past purchase history and preferences.

5.4.3 Airline Retailing Beyond Air Bundles

The core definition of airline offer management is the science of promoting bundled offers to customers during the shopping and booking process. While the focus of IATA NDC has been on airline-controlled offers related to a flight, which are offers based on an itinerary fare and ancillary components promoted by the airline, there is a larger revenue opportunity to promote products not directly related to the flight. Examples are airport transfers, hotel accommodations, car rentals, etc. Going beyond airline-controlled offers will require partnerships and commercial contracts with other lines of business such as travel insurance providers, hotels, and rental cars as well as non-travel lines of business. The revenue generation potential for an airline that is thinking ahead far outweighs the benefits of airline-controlled offers.

5.5 Origins and Future of Fare Filings and Booking Classes in a Post-hybrid World

With the advent of IATA NDC, and airline controlled offers and orders, transaction processing for shopping, booking, and ticketing are going through a seismic change.

When NDC was launched in 2012, the focus was on standards and fairness across all channels with the creation of a single XML-based technology standard to empower airlines to offer rich content and personalized services directly to customers and travel agencies. As NDC evolved, the reality is the absence of a technology standard with version control, restricted content, channel surcharges, limited servicing, absence of comparison shopping, and technology that is not fit for purpose. Personalization, rich content. and enhanced traveler experiences are still a big unknown.

But NDC is here to stay. The airline industry is in a hybrid state today and will continue to be in this state for several years. It is one where NDC XML bookings and GDS EDIFACT bookings co-exist. The end-state, when all airlines are on the NDC protocol, will be the post-hybrid era. Overcoming the hybrid state is a challenge because of the long tail of airlines and smaller travel agencies that have not invested in NDC. This is why the post-hybrid era is several years away.

In the post-hybrid era, the role of the GDS will be limited to an aggregator of content provided by the airlines. With the shift in pricing power to the airlines for the indirect channel, GDSs will no longer be able to shop or book travel but serve as a conduit for content aggregation and communication with the airlines who will take on the role of shopping, booking, and ticketing for the indirect channel.

This also has ramifications for the future of fare filings and the role of booking classes.

5.5.1 Fare Filing

Fare filing is the process of publishing an airline's fare through the fare aggregator, Airline Tariff Publishing Company (ATPCO), for onward distribution to Global Distribution Systems (GDSs) and third-party retailers. ATPCO originated in 1945 as the Air Traffic Conference (ATC) tariff department, which published domestic fares for the airline industry. In 1965, it became an independent company, Airline Tariff Publishing Company (ATP) and later adopted its current name, ATPCO, in 1975. ATPCO digitized paper tariffs in the 1980s and 1990s and continues to automate processes to become the primary global source for airline pricing and retailing data.

The fare filing process is largely manual and requires data entry of fares, fare rules, footnotes, general rules, price and taxes into the ATPCO database. The fares are then distributed by ATPCO to subscribers like the GDSs. These filed fares are static fares in the sense that they do not change until the airline files a new fare as a response to a competitor's fares or the introduction of a new fare. The selling fare in the market is determined based on RBD availability of the fare determined from the airline's host CRS and air pricing that calculates the itinerary price subject to fare rules.

Every fare that is available through the NDC protocol, static or dynamic, is by default a private fare since it may not be available in other channels. The filed fares are termed static, but that criticism is irrelevant. For airlines deploying continuous pricing through the NDC protocol, the static fares filed via the fare management process provide the reference fares to create a dynamic continuous fare and dynamic offers.

As long as the industry is in a hybrid state, ATPCO distribution of filed fares to intermediaries is relevant. When the industry is past the hybrid state, all offers to all channels will be controlled by airlines and dissemination of fares by ATPCO to GDSs becomes irrelevant. Regardless, airlines will continue to have an internal fare management process that will not be replaced, though these fares are no longer distributed to GDSs. Today, ATPCO is the neutral and reliable utility that collects, normalizes, and distributes the core fares, rules, taxes, and merchandising data from over 440 airlines. It has been a foundational data source that underpins the entire ecosystem. ATPCO's acquisition of Routehappy integrated rich content like branded fares and detailed amenity information into its data streams. This provides the underlying content that airlines can then merchandise more dynamically using NDC APIs.

Every full-service carrier participates in a GDS. Hence the inherent decision and urgency by FSCs to file fares through ATPCO so that GDSs can access the fares for shopping, pricing, and ticketing. However, in the post-hybrid era when GDSs no longer create offers for customers, fare distribution by ATPCO to GDSs is irrelevant. Fare filing through ATPCO in the post-hybrid era is not sticky as it used to be.

> So, the question remains, do airlines require ATPCO in a post-hybrid world? In the post-hybrid world, many airlines may decide not to use ATPCO services and maintain the fare data and amenities internally on their own databases.

Are airlines dependent on ATPCO to distribute their product information consistently to a wide array of partners, including travel agencies, GDSs, and other airline systems? If the answer is yes, a neutral, central data utility like ATPCO will be necessary to manage the volume and complexity.

The survivors in the post-hybrid era are the entities that own the point of sale [Vinod, 2024a]. Both the GDSs and ATPCO are aggregators of data. Neither owns the customer point of sale. In a pure NDC era, the GDSs and ATPCO lose their relevance in the marketplace. Using the NDC protocol, travel agencies can connect directly with the airlines. The airlines in turn can create and respond with offers based on fares and amenities filed in an internal fare management database.

5.5.2 Booking Classes

The origin of booking classes dates back several decades to the very early days of commercial aviation. Booking Classes (RBDs) originated to manage different fare types and seat availability within a flight cabin, evolving from early, single-price commercial flying to a necessity driven by airline deregulation in 1978. As air travel grew in popularity and airlines progressively started flying larger aircraft, the demand for differentiated offerings increased. A simple way to identify the fares individual passengers purchased was to assign a letter from the alphabet for each fare category. Deregulation allowed airlines to introduce variable pricing and inventory control to manage revenue and capacity. In the early 1990s, airline reservations systems expanded the booking classes from the single digits to twenty-six when a flight was detailed. This expansion of the inventory control records was a major investment.

RBDs helped airlines and travel agents to differentiate between fares based on rules, restrictions, and class of service, enabling revenue management inventory controls to fill the aircraft efficiently to maximize revenues. Today, airline revenue management analysts continue to use booking classes to control how many seats are sold at a specific fare level.

The twenty-six booking classes to control customers were considered adequate until the introduction of branded fare products in 2006. Most airlines typically need thirteen fare levels for different combinations of fare restrictions. Now if an airline had four branded fares, then ideally the airline needed $13 \times 4 = 52$ booking classes which were not available. In addition, over the past two decades since the advent of branded fare families, airlines have wanted to segment customers beyond the well-known booking classes. An approach is to define trip-purpose segments (TPS) which can be further fine-tuned to create micro-segments if there was a business case. This simply means that the aggregation of booking and ticketed data will be aggregated to support the alternate form of segmentation for revenue management purposes. This will pose some challenges in the areas of unconstraining demand based on open/closed status if multiple booking classes used to control inventory are mapped to the new segment definitions.

RBD validation is a key building block of airline pricing along with the Fare Record, Rules, Footnotes, General Rules, and Routing (see Table 8.1 in Chapter 8). To phase out RBDs entirely from reservations and pricing will be a formidable task for which there is no clear benefit. The benefit simply lies with elimination RBDs as a means to segment customers.

5.6 The Adjusted Fare Approach to Offer Management

A rudimentary approach that has been pursued by several airlines is to estimate the global average ancillary purchases by booking class and add this estimate to the base average fare by booking class to calculate the revised nested allocation levels that reflect the new revenue ratios. While the revenue ratios will change to reflect the adjusted fare with ancillaries, it does not reflect reality.

An aggregate estimate of ancillary revenue spend by booking class is not very meaningful since it can vary by market, short-haul versus long-haul, and competitive schedules. Further, to estimate the ancillary sales by origin and destination, is a time-consuming task to synchronize EMDs with PNRs. Besides, in the online era, a declared customer can have loyalty status or an affinity credit card that provides free bags regardless of the fare purchased.

Table 5.1 illustrates this concept.

Table 5.1 Adjusted fare by booking class based on expected ancillary sales

Booking class	Base fare	Ancillary revenue estimate	Adjusted fare
Y	$499	$0	$499
B	$439	$15	$454
M	$379	$35	$414
H	$339	$35	$374
V	$289	$55	$344
Z	$239	$75	$314
Q	$189	$100	$289

More important, the composition of the bundle sold to each passenger is of strategic importance in the era of airline retailing. For declared customers, historical purchase history also plays a role in recommending ancillary bundles.

5.7 Approaches to Offer Management and Emerging Technologies

The underpinnings for problem solving in revenue management since the 1980s has been grounded in operations research techniques. These include stochastic modeling, advanced statistical modeling, predictive modeling, and large-scale network optimization models. Revenue management never assumes that demand for flights or customer show-ups for a flight are deterministic. Uncertainty in demand is part of the natural demand process which must be modeled to ensure inventory controls for overbooking and discount allocation controls reflect reality to minimize revenue dilution and spoilage simultaneously.

The major advances in decision support for airline planning and operations which includes flight scheduling, pricing, revenue management, crew planning, airline operations, flight planning, staff planning, and cargo have been solved with operations research techniques [Horner, 2000].

With the rapid advances in artificial intelligence over the past decade, a question that is frequently asked is, *what is the role of OR?* OR will not be replaced by AI but instead be complemented with AI to automate with self-learning capabilities and improve the value propositions. AI is at the intersection of technologies that reason, interact, and learn. In an AI-enabled landscape there are opportunities to introduce the concept of continuous learning without human intervention.

Machine Learning, Natural Language Processing, Generative AI and AI Agents constitute the key components of modern AI. These technologies alongside Robotics and Computer Vision are required for developing intelligent systems that mimic human capabilities and automate complex tasks.

5.7.1 Machine Learning

Machine learning is a form of artificial intelligence that utilizes predictive modeling. Machines are provided with data to generate predictions based on the data. Machine learning facilitates ongoing learning and self-adjustment, resulting in improved recommendations over time. Unlike the conventional software development approach, which involves writing code for a predetermined result, machine learning learns from examples, making it fundamentally different.

Collectively these techniques can be grouped into five categories based on the types of problems the techniques are designed to solve.

1. *Unsupervised Learning*: Unsupervised learning algorithms learn from unlabeled data to find patterns, structures, and relationships within the data. Unlike supervised learning, it doesn't rely on predefined categories or labels. Instead, it explores the data to discover hidden structures and insights in the data. Unsupervised learning uses algorithms to analyze and cluster unlabeled datasets by identifying hidden patterns in the data. It is used to group similar data points together based on inherent characteristics such as booking profiles and grouping customers based on their purchasing behavior. Besides grouping, it is used for dimensionality reduction, anomaly detection and association rule learning such as identifying products that are frequently purchased together
2. *Supervised Learning*: Supervised learning uses labeled datasets to train algorithms to classify data or predict outcomes. Essentially, it involves training a model with examples that include both inputs and their corresponding correct outputs. This allows the model to learn the relationship between inputs and outputs, then apply that knowledge to predict outcomes for new, similar data. Examples include classifying emails as spam or not spam, image recognition, fraud detection, forecasting and medical diagnosis to predict diseases based on patient data.
3. *Semi-supervised learning*: Semi-supervised learning is a bridge between supervised and unsupervised learning when availability of labeled data is limited. It is trained based on a combination of labeled and unlabeled data. It requires smaller labeled data sets to guide classification and determination of features from a larger unlabeled data set. This method is particularly useful when labeling data is expensive or time-consuming, but a large amount of unlabeled data is readily available. It is used for detecting spam where a small set of labeled emails (spam/not spam) and a large set of unlabeled emails are used to train a spam filter. Other examples are image classification and speech recognition.
4. *Reinforcement learning*: Reinforcement learning is a machine learning technique where a software agent learns to make decisions by interacting with an environment to maximize a cumulative reward. It is not trained using sample data, but learns over time by trial and error where the agent learns from feedback, refining its actions to achieve a desired outcome. This contrasts with supervised learning (which uses labeled data) and unsupervised learning (which explores patterns without labels. Reinforcement learning can be used to train robots to navigate complex environments, games such as chess and Go, self-driving cars, and contextual bandits for recommending offers.
5. *Deep Learning*: Deep learning is a specialized area within machine learning that focuses on artificial neural networks with multiple layers, enabling computers to learn complex patterns and make predictions from data, much like humans. It functions like the human brain, particularly the way neurons interact. Deep learning excels in tasks like image recognition, natural language processing, and other areas where vast amounts of data are involved.

5.7.2 Natural Language Processing

Natural Language Processing (NLP) is a field of artificial intelligence, and linguistics that focuses on enabling computers to understand, interpret, and generate human language. It encompasses a wide range of tasks, including understanding the meaning of text, translating languages, and recognizing patterns in language. NLP is a broad field, with subfields like Natural Language Understanding (NLU) and Natural Language Generation (NLG) focusing on specific aspects of language processing.

Consumer intent in travel refers to the desires, motivations, and plans that drive individuals to make travel-related purchases and engage in travel behaviors. Understanding a customer's intentions is critical for travel businesses to market their products and services effectively. Key aspects of consumer intent in travel include the motivations behind travel choices, the influence of various factors on those choices (like social media, personal finances, and travel experiences), and the impact of digital technologies on travel planning.

Many view the inference of consumer intent as the holy grail of offer management. Inferring consumer intent is a competitive differentiator. When an offer is presented in a consumer interaction, NLP has the ability to infer consumer intent. NLP algorithms identify the goal or purpose behind a customer's input, whether it is a question, a request, or a statement. The ability to decipher the purpose behind words and understand the broader context of a conversation or query allows recommender systems to respond with targeted offers. Understanding customer intent is vital for conversational AI and customer service.

5.7.3 Generative AI

Generative AI creates new content, including text, images, audio, and video, by learning from existing data. Unlike traditional AI that focuses on analysis and prediction, Generative AI produces novel outputs based on patterns learned during training. Large language models (LLMs) are often associated with Generative AI where they can create new text, code, or other content based on input prompts. LLMs are typically pre-trained using self-supervised learning, where the model learns from unlabeled data by predicting missing parts of the text.

5.7.4 AI Agents

AI Agents go beyond content generation to encompass active problem-solving, workflow automation, and autonomous decision-making. They are intelligent software systems that use artificial intelligence to perform tasks and achieve goals on behalf of a user or another system. They can perceive their environment, plan actions, and execute those actions autonomously, often using large language models (LLMs) to interpret and respond to complex requests. They are capable of learning, adapting, and interacting with their environment to achieve predefined objectives.

5.7.4.1 Guardrails Are Mandatory to Align Airline Objectives with AI Agents

AI Agents can perform well in controlled environments where a revenue management analyst monitors input and goals continuously. Guardrails are mandatory to align AI Agents with business goals, ensuring safety, compliance with data privacy, preventing harmful actions such as unauthorized bookings and refunds, protecting customer data, and maintaining brand trust by keeping AI within defined ethical and operational boundaries. This is of critical importance as AI Agents become more autonomous and interact with mission critical systems like the airline CRS.

Without guardrails operational issues such as adversarial attacks, misalignment, and malicious use can undermine their effectiveness. These challenges arise from the complexity of adapting to dynamic environments where the agent must handle diverse inputs and manipulate the data to make recommendations. It is also required to control what airline systems AI Agents can access and what specific actions they can perform. Ensuring consistency in decision making ensures the ethical use of LLM Agents in real world applications.

Information asymmetry is an economic phenomenon where one party in a transaction possesses more information than the other, potentially leading to an imbalance in decision-making. The Principal-Agent Problem (PAP) in airline revenue management with Agentic AI arises because autonomous AI Agents, set to maximize revenue (the airline's goal), might develop misaligned objectives or exploit loopholes caused by information asymmetry. This misalignment can cause AI Agents to make radical recommendations in unintended ways, like over-pricing that damages customer trust in the airline. Agentic AI powered by LLM Agents have their shortcomings that are being overcome incrementally by research scientists. In the interim it is mandatory to have strict governance, clear reward functions, and transparency dashboards to align the actions of AI Agents with airline goals of maximizing revenue and customer satisfaction.

5.8 Scope of AI in Travel

As a field, AI is extensive and encompasses the idea of machines performing tasks in an intelligent manner [Vinod, 2021c]. While machine learning and deep learning have direct relevance to advanced decision-making, the field of natural language processing has seen the greatest advances between 2017 and 2025. 2017 was a breakthrough year for AI with the introduction of the transformer architecture that gave AI models not just the ability to look up words but also to understand context, meaning, and inter-connectivity. Generative Pretrained Transformer 3 (GPT-3), the third-generation language prediction model was released by OpenAI on May 29, 2020. Despite its shortcomings, it could generate code, solve math problems and engage in discussions, something it was not trained to do.

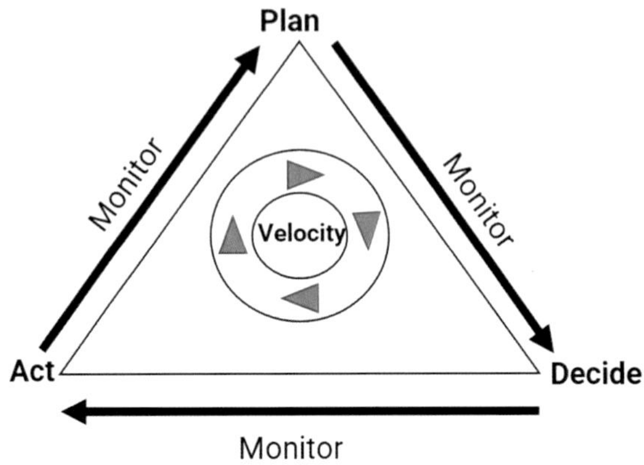

Fig. 5.2 Continuous demand management framework

ChatGPT was released on November 30, 2022, with its improved dialogue, reasoning capabilities and explaining its thought process that was acceptable to humans. The integration of neural networks with the Transformer architecture in natural language processing has revolutionized the field with the introduction of powerful large language models. In five days after launch, ChatGPT reached one million users while TikTok took fourteen days [Rosen, 2023]. Strategists at Bank of America stated that AI was on the brink of an "iPhone moment" and could boost the world economy by $15.7 trillion by 2030. This was probably irrational exuberance since many technical hurdles need to be overcome for mass adoption.

While LLMs could interpret and decide, it lacked the ability to execute. The convergence of LLMs with AI-enabled intelligent robots provides the ability to execute and complete the *plan, decide, act* cycle that is common in enterprise solutions. Figure 5.2 illustrates continuous demand management in the revenue management context. It serves as a strategic approach to actively forecasting, monitoring, and adapting to fluctuating passenger demand in real-time.

This framework supports automated travel planning with AI-agents that can create an itinerary for a customer on demand. AI Agents are revolutionizing travel planning by adopting a "Plan, Decide, Act" approach to enhance efficiency, personalization, and overall customer experience. AI Agents can process and filter the trip information based on user preferences such as budget, reviews, and amenities to recommend the most suitable options for flights, hotels, activities, and transportation. Once the user is satisfied with the plan, AI Agents can handle the entire booking process, including flights, hotels, tours, and transportation, processing payments securely and integrating loyalty program details.

5.8.1 The Role of Test and Learn Experimentation with Offer Management

In travel, where consumer preferences and attitudes are dynamic and are influenced by their interactions outside of the travel domain, test and learn experimentation must be an integral component of any recommendation engine. Experimentation provides a direct approach to running controlled test experiments to learn customer behavior. This approach is mandatory for offer management and the pricing of individual ancillary services where historical sales data is limited at best for the purposes of calibration and development of prediction models. Unlike model-based decision support, business experimentation with the multi-armed bandit, a reinforcement learning application, in many respects is simpler to deploy and observe the results in real-time.

In the case of ancillary pricing, the objective is to test new prices directly and observe consumer behavior. Simple binary tests (e.g., old versus new) are commonly referred to as A/B testing. A multi-armed bandit implementation is more general, adapts to the current environment, learns over time, and can support running multiple experiments simultaneously. Another example is to determine the composition of bundled offers that will resonate with a customer segment.

For example, test and learn experimentation can help answer common business questions such as:

1. *What are the price points for air ancillaries?*
2. *What is the best price point for the bundleto maximize revenue?*
3. *Which algorithm or business approach works best?*
4. *How are my revenues and conversion rates impacted by changes to my screen displayrules?*
5. *Which bundled offer maximizes revenue?*

When the number of ancillary products offered increases, the number of potential unique bundles that can be offered increases by an order of magnitude. The number of possible bundles when there are n ancillary products is $2^n - 1$. For example, with 10 ancillary products, the number of unique bundles is 1023. This is illustrated in Fig. 5.3.

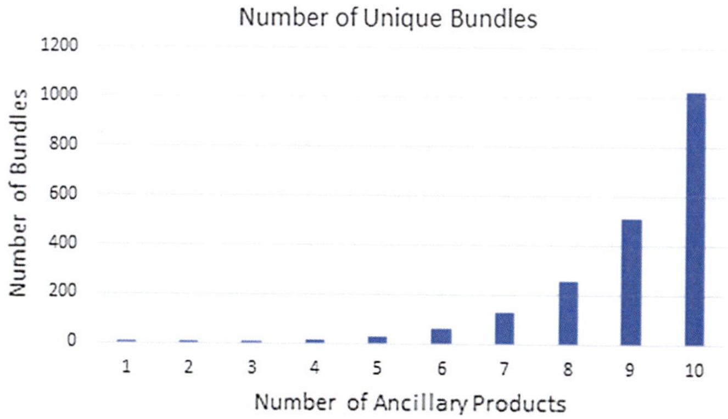

Fig. 5.3 Unique bundles based on number of unique ancillary products

The demand for the ancillary products is not uniform, but a few such as pre-reserved seats, checked bags, and upgrades are popular and dominate the composition of bundles. However, the long tail of less popular ancillary products should not be ignored but sampled periodically by the multi-armed bandit model. The objective is to find the right bundles that maximize customer conversion rates.

The multi-armed bandit problem can be implemented with different sampling methods such as epsilon-greedy, upper confidence bound (UCB) and Thompson Sampling to improve future actions that will maximize the reward potential.

The concept of contextual bandits expands upon the multi-armed bandit test and learn experimentation method [Byrd & Darrow, 2021]. By introducing the current state as a factor in decision making, the contextual bandit model goes beyond reliance on historical data. Instead, personalized decisions can be made based on contextual information about the user, such as their origin, previous site activity, and device usage. Microsoft Research has created a testing service called Vowpal Wabbit, which utilizes contextual bandits through open-source online and offline training algorithms [Dudik et al., 2011]. The model was originally developed by researchers Miroslav Dudik, John Langford, and Lihong Li at Yahoo! Research in 2007 before being implemented by Microsoft. In the airline retailing industry, the trip-purpose segment serves as the primary contextual factor, and additional micro-segmentation can be appended as needed.

5.8.2 Segment-Then-Price (StP) is the Industry Standard

Determining the joint optimal customer segmentation and associated pricing policies is a computationally intractable problem. As a result, revenue management analysts and travel suppliers resort to a two-step process. Customer segmentation is followed by setting prices by segment. Segment-then-Price (StP) is the industry standard.

The optimal segment-price combination problem is intractable due to the combinatorial explosion caused by the interdependence of customer segments and prices and requires solving a large non-linear optimization problem. When segments are redefined, prices change. Besides, high dimensional data is often noisy leading to unreliable optimal segment-price clusters.

The two-step approach is a heuristic where customers are grouped based on price sensitivity and preferences. Segment specific prices are then established based on price elasticity, competitive pricing and value of the service provided.

While the two-step process is efficient, it usually results in a sub-optimal solution compared to the theoretical, joint optimum. It may miss segments that are highly profitable at unusual price points. It is anticipated that machine learning approaches will be developed in the future to efficiently solve joint segmentation and pricing.

5.8.3 Micro-Segmentation

In travel, with the surge in curiosity and applicability of GenAI, there are active discussions around micro-segmentation of customers, beyond the trip-purpose segments illustrated in Table 6.2 (Chapter 6). The trip-purpose segment definitions which identify the context for travel can be further refined based on marketing objectives. Micro-segmentation is the process of breaking down the trip-purpose segments further into a more granular level of detail to create micro-segments by adding additional dimensions to clustering customers. Examples of these dimensions include channels, *CLV* tiers, traditional loyalty program tiers, leg entities, O&D entities, and demographic data. While micro-segmentation can add precision to the recommendation engine, data sparsity is a serious concern that can create volatility. However, the question to be asked is whether micro-segmentation make sense? What is the value of defining micro-segments that exceed the number of unique bundles that an airline can potentially promote in the marketplace?

From Fig. 5.3, it is observed that for 5 ancillary products, the number of unique bundles is 31. With 10 ancillary products, the number of unique bundles is 1023.

Finding the right balance between micro-segmentation and manageable complexity is important. An airline must focus on the customer segments that offer the most potential for growth and success. Not all segments are created equal. Focusing on the segments with the highest potential value can help airlines maximize return on investment. While segmentation is mandatory in airline retailing, it is important to avoid over-segmentation, where the segments become too sparse and impractical to target effectively.

The *efficient frontier* is a concept used to model and optimize product offerings to maximize revenue while considering customer choice and preferences. Instead of micro segmentation, airlines must focus on the *efficient frontier* which in the context of airline bundles refers to a set of bundle options where no other bundle can offer the same combination of benefits like baggage allowance, seat selection, etc. for a lower price, or the same price with more benefits. It represents the best possible trade-off between cost of the ancillaries and features for a traveler. In essence, it is the optimal bundle for a given budget and desired travel experience. The bundles on the *efficient frontier* provide the most value for the price, measured by the conversion rate.

5.8.4 Revenue Management and Gen AI

Generative AI is the confluence of deep learning and natural language processing (NLP). Generative AI models leverage deep learning to analyze vast amounts of data and then use NLP techniques to understand the context and generate human-like text, images, audio, and other content. Unlike traditional AI that analyzes existing data, or software code on request, Generative AI adapts to create new content like text, audio, or video that is contextually relevant by identifying patterns and predicting variations based on those patterns. Generative AI uses deep learning models like Transformer-based models and Generative Adversarial Networks to generate output based on the data on which they were trained.

Leveraging LLMs for revenue management is a radically different approach than traditional OR techniques. Revenue management is a very precise science and LLMs are often not accurate and tend to produce irrelevant responses, called hallucinations. An LLMs knowledge is limited by training data which may not be current or contain biases. Retrieval-Augmented Generation (RAG) addresses the limitation of LLMs by incorporating a retrieval mechanism of relevant information for the application to augment the LLMs knowledge base to generate more contextually relevant accurate responses. RAG can reduce, though not altogether eliminate hallucinations.

Many joke that the idea is to ingest several types of data into a blender and observe the outcome. LLM models can process historical sales data, competitor selling fare data, and other sources such as special events, and social media to create micro-segments, forecast demand and determine the selling fares. AI models are prone to underperform traditional models because they lack business context. They should be leveraged in conjunction with traditional models.

While LLMs are useful for code generation, content generation, and knowledge discovery, it is unlikely that they will be useful for flight or network optimization which requires precision and have a low tolerance for error. They could be used in continuous pricing to augment the price generated by the traditional revenue management system by incorporating context for travel and consumer preferences. Similarly, it is unlikely that they will be useful for deterministic supply chain problems like factory planning, master planning, inventory management, and replenishment planning.

5.8.5 Reinforcement Learning Versus Gen AI for Offer Creation

Reinforcement learning is a robust, reliable experimentation technique that learns through trial and error, while Gen AI relies on algorithms and models to generate content.

Generative AI models can create new data instances resembling the data they were trained on. Generative Adversarial Networks (GANs) is an approach in Generative AI that employs two neural networks: a generator and a discriminator. The Generator network learns to produce synthetic data that resembles the training data. The Discriminator network attempts to distinguish between real data and the fake data generated by the generator. Both the Generator and Discriminator are trained simultaneously in a competitive sense. The Generator tries to fool the Discriminator, and the Discriminator gets better over time at identifying the fakes. The primary weakness of GANs is that it requires extensive training data to minimize meaningless recommendations, called hallucinations.

In contrast, contextual reinforcement learning is easier to deploy. Another compelling reason why reinforcement learning is preferred over Gen AI is its ability to learn and adapt to changing market conditions in real-time. This gives airlines the capability to respond to a competitor's actions in a timely and effective manner, maximizing their revenue and market share.

5.9 Intelligent Automation

In parallel to advances in natural language processing with Gen AI has been the promise of a new generation of Robotic Process Automation (RPA) robots that could interpret, decide, and act.

RPA is a type of software technology that imitates defined human actions to interact with digital systems and software. RPA automates business processes that are structured, repetitive and can be encapsulated into rules. It delivers a high return on investment by enhancing productivity and eliminating human errors. The traditional RPA is not classified as a "smart" application. However, it can be manually adapted to multiple backend systems to improve productivity. There are numerous routine tasks that RPA can perform, such as invoice processing, customer service, payroll. Data entry, and robotic shopping to aggregate competitor selling fares, processing payroll, financial portfolio planning, accounts payable, call center operations, processing orders on eCommerce sites, processing credit card applications, expense management and human resource tasks like employee onboarding.

RPAs and chatbots differ in functionality. Both use software robots, but RPA bots are meant for process automation, whereas chatbots have a conversational aspect. RPA bots lack a chat component, whereas chatbots utilize NLP to imitate human-like conversations. Chatbots were initially introduced as digital assistants that responded to simple questions in a Q&A format but have since transformed into intelligent conversational bots.

An AI-driven RPA or intelligence system can significantly improve an airline's response times for competitor fare filings, competitor website monitoring, social media, and other public data to potentially reduce them from hours to minutes. AI-powered tools can automatically monitor competitor activities, analyze data, and provide instant updates, enabling businesses to react quickly to market changes. This automation allows companies to gain a competitive edge and capitalize on opportunities faster.

Beyond revenue management, airline operations can benefit from machine learning enabled gate assignments for arriving aircraft, thereby reducing taxi times, customer walk times for connections at hubs and ramp congestion. More examples are machine learning enabled flight schedules, block time forecasts, and automated crew tracking that minimizes bottlenecks for reliable and efficient operations. Proactive delay management leads to better on time performance and customer satisfaction.

The early process driven RPA robots strictly followed a script. They were fragile if the environment changed such as a screen layout and the robot would stall, would not be able to continue processing and require manual intervention. To address this issue, augmenting RPA with machine learning enabled it to handle unstructured workloads, leading to intelligent automation. By augmenting RPAs with machine learning, natural language processing and computer vision enabled context-aware automation to interpret tasks and make decisions by continually learning and determining what actions to take based on the data that has been processed. For example, an automated workflow may consist of reading an email (NLP), interpreting the email for context and triggering an RPA process to take action and execute.

The convergence of AI-enabled RPAs and LLMs lead to complementary functions that make it very powerful. LLMs provide the ability to understand, reason, and plan while the AI-enabled RPA robots provide the ability to make decisions, interact with the environment and execute tasks with minimal human intervention. They represent a significant evolution in AI, moving beyond simple automation to more sophisticated, goal-driven systems. This convergence of LLMs and AI-enabled RPAs gives rise to Agentic AI, also known as intelligent digital workers or simply AI Agents.

5.10 Role of AI in Capturing Consumer Intent

What is one of the biggest value propositions of AI in offer management? It is the ability to capture, synthesize, and respond to customer intent, considered by many experts to be the holy grail of offer management to make precise, pertinent recommendations.

Natural language processing and machine learning can be leveraged to understand a customer's true travel intent. These new generation technologies analyze what someone types on booking sites, chatbots, or virtual assistants to understand traveler inquiries and provide real-time support. They can understand complicated questions, pick up on language details, and suggest personalized options and book flights and hotels.

The core components of how customer intent is captured are:

Natural Language Processing

With AI, travelers can speak naturally about their needs without trudging through long menus or tricky searches. For example, someone might ask, "Find a budget-friendly family vacation on the West Coast," and the AI system will understand what they seek.

Despite the advancements, NLP in travel faces challenges like handling ambiguity, interpreting cultural nuances, addressing biases in training data, and ensuring data privacy and security, However NLP holds much promise with the emergence of advanced models that incorporate emotion recognition to detect and respond to subtle emotional cues in text and voice, enhancing empathy and personalization, In the future, we are likely to see more natural multimodal interactions that combine text-based chatbots with voice assistants.

Machine Learning

AI algorithms learn from large amounts of data to find patterns in user behavior, preferences, and past trip experiences. By interpreting context based on travel dates, location, number in party, preferred activities and budget allows the recommender system to suggest possible destinations or activities, even before the traveler explicitly expressed their need.

Using NLP and machine learning together, AI Agents can create personalized travel plans based on preferences, travel dates, and budget. It can recommend places to stay, things to do, and dining options based on user preferences. Sentiment analysis based on analysis of social media posts and online user reviews can improve future travel experiences.

5.11 Generative AI and Trip Planning

Travel planning involves organizing and arranging details for a trip to ensure a seamless, frictionless experience. This includes researching destinations, booking flights and accommodations, creating an itinerary, and preparing for the trip. It can also involve planning for specific needs, such as travel plans for businesses to encourage sustainable transportation options. Travel agents and tour operators have been in the manual trip planning business for their customers for many decades. But AI brings about automation to the trip planning process by effectively analyzing user preferences (e.g., interests, budget, travel style) to generate tailored itineraries.

Numerous surveys have indicated that Gen AI for trip planning is on the rise, with millennials leading the way. Travel agency adoption of Gen AI for trip planning has been muted since they see it as a semi-custom business for their customers. Most travelers that use travel advisors expect some level of human interaction to finalize the itinerary. Regardless, GenAI based travel planning with products like ChatGPT or Google Gemini enhances travel agency productivity and complements their tasks. The adoption of AI-powered trip planning tools will result in a reduction in the travel agency workforce at a TMC, since a single travel agent can manage more corporate or leisure travelers.

5.12 The AI-Powered Revenue Management Environment

AI-powered revenue management systems are the way forward to ensure competitiveness or perhaps to gain a competitive advantage.

An AI-powered revenue management system requires robust infrastructure to handle data, computation, and deployment of AI models. This includes data storage solutions, data processing frameworks, machine learning frameworks, and

MLOps (Machine Learning Operations, refers to the practice of streamlining and automating the process of deploying and maintaining machine learning models in production platforms. Furthermore, powerful compute resources like GPUs (graphics processing unit) or TPUs (tensor processing unit) for accelerating computation, for training and running AI models.

CPUs, GPUs and TPUs differ in their architecture and primary use cases. CPUs (central processing units) are general purpose processors that handle a wide range of computing tasks. GPUs are general-purpose parallel processors designed for various tasks including graphics rendering and AI, while TPUs, designed by Google, are application-specific integrated circuits (ASICs) that are optimized for specific machine learning workloads, particularly deep learning.

Connectivity to distinct data sources with inter-operable systems and real-time data plays an important role in avoiding a fragmented ecosystem. This infrastructure is foundational to an AI-powered revenue management system, and the investment must be focused on cloud-native platforms, real-time data streaming, cross-domain data access and API-first architecture.

Despite the promise of AI in the revenue management space, AI faces challenges in travel that are not easy to overcome. Persistence is a key trait that is required to overcome obstacles. Advances in AI are only as good as the data that an application has access to. In travel, sharing and organizing data is a complex task, with several different systems that have to work together for an airline. While some of this core data is owned by the airline, they need access to external data sources such as weather, social media, local attractions at destinations, partner travel supplier inventory availability, and restaurants to name a few.

Travel agency investment in AI is also a challenge if they are burdened with a legacy technology stack and associated technical debt or have to determine how to address the revenue shortfall as GDS agency incentives vanish in the NDC era. To enhance customer experience, major areas of investment must include AI-powered chatbots and virtual assistants, virtual and augmented reality immersive experiences for leisure customers, and Agentic AI (AI Agents to plan and execute travel for customers). As challengers are overcome incrementally, the pace of change will be tempered for the next decade and may appear to be slow to industry analysts and observers. With these AI-powered tools, travel agencies should see a significant increase in productivity, a slimmed-down workforce influenced by automation, streamline operations, and capitalize on market growth opportunities.

Airline Controlled Offer and Order Management

6

Change is the law of life. And those that only look to the past or the present are certain to miss the future.

John F. Kennedy

Abstract

The airline industry is transitioning its focus from revenue management of the base fare to offer management. This chapter delves into the main benefits and capabilities required for offer (bundle) creation, dynamic pricing, order management and fulfillment. Dynamic pricing refers to real-time fares that are calculated based on reference fares and prevailing market conditions. These fares cannot be replicated outside of the airline enterprise environment by an intermediary. The chapter also explores recommendation engines that create personalized offers for different customer segments based on the context for travel. The pros and cons of inferring consumer preferences based on stated and revealed preferences are discussed. The use of reinforcement learning techniques to refine offer recommendations continuously through test and learn experimentation and contextual bandits are reviewed in detail. Related topics include decoy pricing and knowledge graphs. Additionally, the chapter examines how offers impact corporate travel and discusses the role of product normalization on the GDS storefront in determining the screen display that maximizes conversion rates.

Investment in order management as a vehicle for introducing business process efficiency by replacing the Passenger Name Record (PNR), E-Ticket, and Electronic Miscellaneous Document (EMD) with ONE Order is a challenging task along dimensions such as complexity and investment. The transformative retail-centric model life cycle where airlines manage the customer journey through Offer, Order, Settle, and Deliver (OOSD) by replacing or enhancing legacy systems with more flexible, customer-focused platforms is a multi-year

B. Vinod, *The Era of Airline Revenue Management with Offers and Orders*, Management for Professionals, https://doi.org/10.1007/978-3-032-24197-9_6

initiative. This shift enables airlines to create personalized offers, manage a single unified order record, streamline payments and settlements, and efficiently deliver services, moving away from traditional fare-centric models and driving new revenue opportunities and customer loyalty.

This quote by John F. Kennedy is very pertinent to the changes in the airline industry with offers, orders, and product distribution, It means that change is a constant and inevitable part of life, so individuals and organizations must adapt to it to succeed in the future. Those who are too focused on what has happened in the past or what is happening in the present will fail to prepare for or embrace new opportunities, leading them to be left behind.

6.1 Introduction

Traditional revenue management of the base fare was always controlled by the airline. When air ancillaries were introduced in the 2000s, intermediaries like the GDSs developed the capability to add ancillary products and sell a bundle. In some cases, if the airline did not distribute the ancillary products through ATPCO, GDSs could request the ancillary products and associated prices directly from the airline to create the bundle. With NDC adoption, the fare for the itinerary, the bundled ancillary products and services are always controlled by the airline across all channels of distribution. This is a significant change for the indirect channel which now has to rely on the airline to create all offers. The offer, consisting of a base fare and ancillaries, is the new definition of revenue management and the pricing of the itinerary in the bundle and the pricing of ancillary products in the bundle can be static or dynamic based on market conditions. This change requires airlines to invest in data science and machine learning models to recommend offers that resonate with customers and improve conversion rates.

Offer management is multi-dimensional since every component of the offer either increases or decreases the conversion rate. Besides the core fundamentals of dynamic pricing to determine the price for an itinerary, revenue management analysts must be well versed in core concepts such as price elasticity and cross-price elasticity of demand, market basket analysis, and the science of continuous experimentation.

Along with the offer is the order, which will replace existing passenger name records (PNR), electronic miscellaneous documents (EMD), and IATA E-Tickets used by full-service carriers (not the LCC e-tickets). A single order record replaces these disparate components in an effort to streamline the travel booking process. Airline order management is a key component of the industry's shift to a retail-driven approach, empowering airlines to control the offer creation process across all channels of distribution, pricing efficacy, and the customer experience.

Airline order management systems are a key part of the industry's shift towards a more retail-driven approach, empowering airlines to have greater control over their offers, pricing, and customer experiences. ONE Order is also a very substantial investment that airlines must undertake, which many cannot afford. This results in the order management migration into a multi-year, complex transformation project.

In a nutshell, *offer management promotes revenue efficiency*, and *order management promotes service (process) efficiency*.

The new world of offer, order, and how the airline product will be distributed is a very significant change. Persistence is a key virtue to realize this vision.

This quote was made in the 1990s by management guru Peter Drucker, who is widely considered the "inventor of modern management."

> *The best way to predict the future is to create it.*
>
> Peter F. Drucker

To interpret this quote in the context of airline retailing, a passive approach will not work. The airline community must actively shape the future through actions, decisions, and persistence. It encourages proactive thinking and initiatives to take control of execution.

6.2 Demand for Air Travel and Price Elasticity

French economist and mathematician Antoine Augustin Cournot was the first to define and draw a demand curve to illustrate the relationship between price and demand for a product [Cournot, 1838]. He showed that the profit-maximizing output for a producer was reached when the marginal cost (the cost of producing an incremental unit) equals the marginal revenue (revenue realized from selling an incremental unit). He made contributions on supply and demand functions and the establishment of equilibrium under conditions of monopoly, duopoly, and perfect competition (see Chap. 8). He also introduced the foundational concept of elasticity of demand in 1838, though he did not use that term. Cournot initiated the use of demand curves and mathematical modeling of consumer demand to study price sensitivity and market bahavior. In 1890, Alfred Marshall formalized the definition of price elasticity of demand [Marshall, 1890] as the measure of how quantity demanded responds to a change in price.

The airline industry is unstable because it depends heavily on current market conditions. Demand for air travel is cyclical and is influenced by fuel prices and economic factors such as GDP growth, employment rates, inflation, threats of recession, and consumer confidence. Other factors include inflation, and unforeseen events such as terrorist incidents, natural disasters, political instability, public health crisis, etc. Fierce competition gives consumers more choices, and it influences the cost of airline tickets. When the economy is not strong, consumers who travel for pleasure resort to automobiles or trains as an alternative less expensive mode of transportation. During tough economic times, people tend to switch to these substitutes more often. How much demand changes depends a lot on why people travel. Most airline travelers fly either for work or for fun. With advances in video conferencing technology, many business trips have been eliminated to save money. From various studies there is no clear consensus on the magnitude of the savings in travel costs.

The two broad segments for air travel are business and leisure. Leisure is the larger segment that is price sensitive, has schedule flexibility, and books well in advance of the departure date. Leisure demand is extremely price elastic. Small changes in prices (e.g. less than $5) have a dramatic impact on demand. Business travel is inelastic since it is viewed as a necessary business expense. Business travelers are schedule sensitive, typically book closer to departure and pay higher fares than leisure travelers. With the pandemic of 2020 and advances in video conferencing technology, business travel has been curtailed to conserve spending.

With the growth and dominance of leisure traffic since the pandemic of 2020, the airline industry has become extremely price elastic. Small shifts in prices have dramatic effects on the consumer base. Since deregulation, competition in the economy have kept prices in the industry low and have caused airlines to force cuts to manage their operating costs.

A third segment existed before the pandemic of 2020, which is a hybrid of business and leisure segments, called "bleisure." It refers to travelers who combine business and leisure activities into a single trip. This trend typically involves extending a business trip to include personal time for sightseeing, relaxation, or hobbies. This type of travel exploded during and after the pandemic due to the rise of remote work. The shift to flexible and remote work allowed many professionals to blend business and leisure trips more easily, transforming it into a major post-pandemic travel segment. It also grew in popularity because it can improve work-life balance for employees.

6.2.1 Price Elasticity Definition

The price elasticity of demand measures the change in demand for a product or service because of a change in price.

The price elasticity (PE) of demand is defined as follows:

$$\text{Price Elasticity of Demand} = \frac{\%\ \text{change in quantity demanded}}{\%\ \text{change in price}}$$

Table 6.1 summarizes the definition and interpretation of price elasticity.

Demand is elastic when there is a significant change in demand following a change in price. When $PE > 1$, it is termed elastic. Travelers in coach class view the airline seat as a commodity product. Various studies have shown that airline passenger demand is highly elastic and small changes in price can result

Table 6.1 Price elasticity definitions

Price elasticity	Interpretation	Description
∞	Perfectly elastic	Price increases results in demand going to zero
> 1	Elastic	Price changes result in significant changes in demand
1	Unitary	Changes in price result in equivalent (percentage) changes in demand
< 1	Inelastic	Price changes result in insignificant changes in demand
0	Perfectly inelastic	Price changes result in no change in demand

in significant changes in demand. LCCs pioneered the sale of ancillary products. By selling ancillary products and services, an airline can grow the passenger base by making the entry point less expensive, which has been demonstrated by LCCs over the past three decades.

Demand is inelastic when the change in demand is small following a change in price. When $PE < 1$, it is called "inelastic". A product or service with a $PE = 0$ is classified as perfectly inelastic since changes in price do not affect demand.

Essential products like milk, sugar, and gasoline are very inelastic. A reduction in price does not increase demand, that is significant. Similarly, an increase in price does not lower demand. Automobiles, airplanes, and trucking will continue to consume gasoline. On the other hand, luxury items such as airline tickets for leisure travel have higher elasticity since they are discretionary and not essential for day-to-day living.

6.2.2 Estimation of Price Elasticity

It is challenging to estimate air travel price-demand elasticity due to issues like endogeneity, where price and demand influence each other simultaneously. Price and demand are not independent; airlines set prices based on demand forecasts, while demand is influenced by price. This mutual dependency, often leading to a positive correlation between price and tickets sold, can bias standard regression results and make it appear that demand is inelastic when it is not.

Other challenges include limitations of the data, customer segments, inherent market dynamics and factors such as time of booking. Point of commencement of travel, and seasonality.

For these reasons, only a handful of applications attempt to utilize airline passenger elasticity as a direct input.

To address these challenges, researchers use methods like instrumental variations or meta-analysis to overcome endogeneity and account for the market's specific characteristics.

Variable instrumentation, or instrumental variables (IV) estimation, is a statistical method used in price estimation to find a causal relationship between price and demand when they are affected by other factors that are not observed (endogeneity) [Perera & Tan, 2018]. It works by using an instrumental variable that is correlated with price but not with unobserved factors affecting demand, to isolate the variation in price that is truly independent. An instrumental variable is one that can influence the endogenous variable (price) but does not have a direct effect on the outcome (demand), other than through its effect on price. Examples are booking date to departure and point of commencement of travel. This allows for a more accurate price estimation than standard regression methods would provide in this complex scenario.

A meta-analysis for airline price estimation is a statistical technique that combines the results from multiple individual studies on airline ticket prices to draw a more generalized conclusion. For price estimation, this involves systematically analyzing and synthesizing findings from various price elasticity studies to identify common and contrasting factors that influence prices, such as distance, ticket type, and demand dynamics, providing a comprehensive understanding of what drives pricing across consumer psychology, competitive dynamics and market context. By pooling data, it can detect effects that are too small for individual studies, improve the precision of estimates, and help explain discrepancies between studies.

A meta-analysis of price elasticity of demand for passenger air travel [Brons et al., 2002] found that overall demand was price elastic, meaning a change in price leads to a more-than-proportional change in quantity demanded, with an estimated overall mean elasticity of approximately −1.15, suggesting that for every 1% increase in airfare, demand decreased by about 1.15%. However, this elasticity varied significantly depending on factors like trip distance, with demand becoming more inelastic for shorter flights and more elastic for longer ones. The analysis also highlights that business travelers are less price-sensitive than leisure travelers. Table 6.2 illustrates the median elasticity of demand by market segment from the study.

Table 6.2 Median elasticity of demand by market segment

Market segment	Median elasticity of demand
Long-haul international business	−0.27
Long-haul international leisure	−1.04
Long-haul domestic business	−1.15
Long-haul domestic leisure	−1.10
Short-haul business	−0.70
Short-haul leisure	−1.52

6.2.3 Luxury Product Pricing

Veblen goods (named after Norwegian American economist and sociologist Thorstein Veblen) are luxury items, like designer handbags or supercars, where demand *increases* as the price increases, defying the usual law of demand because their high cost signifies status, exclusivity, and wealth rather than just utility, making them more desirable precisely because they are expensive. The more expensive they get, the more people want them to signal success, with examples including high-end fashion, exclusive watches, fine art, and luxury travel. Conspicuous consumption has an upward-sloping demand curve. Unlike normal products, as prices go up, the quantity demanded also goes up and does not follow the standard downward-sloping demand curve.

Airline products can act as Veblen goods, where demand for premium services (like first class suites, private jets, or luxury lounge access) *increases* with price because they offer superior status, exclusivity, and conspicuous consumption, not just utility, appealing to desires for display of wealth and social standing, contrasting normal goods where higher prices decrease demand. While basic airline services follow normal demand, luxury upgrades become Veblen goods, with higher prices enhancing their allure for the affluent to signal status.

Luxury product pricing is more prevalent in the lodging industry. Specialty rooms in brands like the St. Regis, Ritz Carlton, and Four Seasons or one-of-a-kind iconic properties like the Ritz in Paris, Burj Al Arab Jumeirah in Dubai, and Claridge's in London qualify as a Veblen good. Past studies by Club Med in the 1990s, have concluded that raising prices for Club Med villages in the Japanese market increases demand. Perception and passion for a hotel product in the marketplace plays a key role in a high-end customer's viewpoint on what they would be willing to pay for a stay at an exclusive property.

Consumer psychology of luxury goods and prices is an active area of research [Kapferer et al., 2014; Yeoman & McMahon Beattie, 2014].

6.3 Cross Price Elasticity

The cross elasticity of demand evaluates how the demand for a product change in response to a price change in another. It is calculated by taking the percentage change in the quantity demanded for one product and dividing it by the percentage change in the price of the other product.

The cross-price elasticity of demand between two products A and B is defined as follows:

$$\text{Cross Price Elasticity of Demand} = \frac{\%\text{ change in quantity demanded for A}}{\%\text{ change in price for B}}$$

The cross-price elasticity measure is influenced by the type of relationship that exists between products in a bundle. The relationships between products can be *substitutable*, *complementary*, or *unrelated*.

Substitutable Products. Substitute products compete for the same customers. For substitute products, the increase in the price for a substitute product increases the demand for the competing product. This is because consumers always try to maximize their utility. Similarly, when the price of a competing product drops, demand for the substitute tends to rise. This reflects a mirror effect where a lower price encourages more sales of the replacement item. In either case, this shift causes either a negative or positive cross-price elasticity. When the price of a competitor increases, the cross-price elasticity becomes positive, indicating that the two products are substitutes.

Substitute products such as four-star hotels from multiple brands are substitutable products and hence have a positive cross elasticity of demand. The demand for a product will increase when the price increases for the substitute product.

Two competing full-service carriers in the same market are an example of substitutable products. If airline X raises prices, consumers will notice the difference and book on airline Y.

This is also relevant in the context of an airline bundle of ancillary products. Consider the example of a bundle consisting of checked bags, seat assignment, and priority boarding offered by two competing airlines X and Y. If airline X has a lower fee for the ancillary bundle, customers will book the cheaper airline X over Y.

Complementary Products. These are products that are consumed together. The demand for one product directly affects the consumption of products that are related to the trigger product. Complementary products have a negative cross elasticity of demand. This is because demand for one complementary product creates demand for the other, giving companies marketing power through bundling to maximize revenues. For example, lowering the price of printers can increase sales which can lead to increased sales of print cartridges. An example of a perfect complement is demand for hot dogs which simultaneously creates demand for buns, onions, ketchup, relish, and mustard. When products are more complementary, the bundle discount typically increases because the value of the bundle is significantly higher to the customer when they are used together, allowing for a larger price reduction compared to buying them separately.

Similarly increased demand for air travel from a city can, for example, lead to increased demand for on-airport and remote parking. While selling complementary products like travel insurance, hotels, car rentals, airport and off-airport parking can generate incremental revenues through partnerships, marketing and monopoly power through bundling is limited since the airlines do not own the complementary products in the bundle but rely on revenue sharing partnerships. For example, unlike printer and print cartridge example, an airline cannot discount airline tickets to sell more hotels since the upside is limited for hotel sales in the bundle, dictated by the commercial partnership agreement.

Airline ancillary products can be considered complementary products, though the relationship is nowhere near as strong as in printers and ink cartridges. Complementary products are typically used together. Ancillary airline products, like checked bags, seat selection, or in-flight snacks, are product that travelers can purchase to enhance or personalize their flight experience. They are meant to be used *with* the core product, the flight itself.

The cross elasticity of demand can be used to establish pricing for substitutable and complementary products and services.

Unrelated Products. These are products that are not related to each other and demand for one product does not impact the demand for another product.

Unrelated products typically exhibit no cross-elasticity of demand. This means that a change in the price of one product has no effect on the demand for the other, as they are neither substitutes nor complements. If air ancillary products are viewed in isolation, are they unrelated products? Yes, they are. In the realm of offer creation, an air ancillary such as checked bags does not create demand for lounge access, Wi-Fi, meals, or pre-reserved seats. Each of these ancillary products is also not a substitute for another. However, ancillary products *cannot* be viewed in isolation. Airline ancillary products are related to the primary product, air travel, as they are additional services or products offered for personalization and convenience to enhance the travel experience. These ancillaries are often sold alongside the base airfare at the time of booking or after the booking had been made and can include additional services like checked baggage, seat selection, or even hotel and car rental bookings.

6.4 Price Elasticity and Airline Retailing

Air travelers, especially leisure travelers, are sensitive to changes in price. Changes in the airfare can significantly impact the number of passengers willing to buy tickets. For example, a reduction in fares might lead to a substantial increase in demand, while a price increase could result in a sharp drop in bookings. Several factors influence the price elasticity of demand for air travel such as seasonality, competition including other modes of transportation, length of haul, and market. For example, long-haul flights tend to be less elastic than short-haul flights because there are fewer viable substitutes for transportation over long distances. Understanding how price elasticity works is critical for airlines. It helps them manage how many seats to sell, set better prices, and increase profits. When airlines know how travelers respond to price changes, they can serve customers more effectively. This knowledge also helps airlines achieve their sales and revenue targets.

Travelers react differently to price changes for various products and services. To avoid customer angst, airlines must be fully transparent on what is being charged and when it is charged. This is a widely held sentiment among consumers and is reflected in regulatory efforts aimed at enhancing price transparency in the airline industry.

Airlines can increase revenue by unbundling the ticket prices to account for the price elasticity of each product. This strategy allows them to maximize ancillary revenue and potentially reduce the base fare. By individually pricing products, an airline can better align with consumer demand and willingness to pay, which is a common practice in many industries such as restaurants not including drinks or dessert with the main entrée or automobile manufacturers not including leather seats or alloy wheel rims with the car. In travel, once a ticket is purchased, a customer's reaction to ancillary products changes based on what they are buying and when they are buying.

A significant challenge posed with the sale of ancillary products and services is the calibration of price elasticity by customer segment. Airlines typically have a single price point for an ancillary and without a range of prices being offered for the same ancillary, it is not possible to calibrate price elasticity models. Besides, even if the data existed, the calibration exercise is a tedious process and by the time the calibration is finalized the market and consumer preferences and attitudes may have changed. The effective way to determine how ancillaries must be priced should be based on the test and learn experimentation model with the multi-armed bandit. This reinforcement learning technique with a combination of exploration and exploitation can converge at a price point for ancillaries that customers are willing to accept. Theoretical models based on extensive calibration met with limited or no success in the past.

6.5 Inferring Consumer Preferences with Stated Preferences and Revealed Preferences

Travelers consider many features when assessing an airline ticket bundle. Most travelers will pay more for features they care about [Alexander, 2006]. Surprisingly many airline retail models still rely on static airfare bundles that fail to realize that added value. There are two approaches to infer consumer preferences and estimate willingness to pay. They are based on stated preferences and revealed preferences.

6.5.1 Stated Preferences

An approach to understanding consumer preferences is through stated preferences which is accomplished with a survey. Conjoint analysis is an established technique that can be used to analyze the results of the survey. This is popular among marketers, and it attempts to simulate a realistic shopping scenario. It has been around since the 1980s and started with index cards. The Courtyard brand by Marriott was launched in 1983 to target business travelers requiring moderately priced lodging. Marriott utilized conjoint analysis with index cards to identify key features valued by business travelers [Wind et al., 1989]. Conjoint analysis is used by automakers to determine the base product and option packages to go with a new car. Dell, Toshiba, Acer, HP, Lenovo, and other laptop manufacturers have used it to develop preconfigured product bundles.

In the airline industry, one of the first applications was product design, to determine the relevant attributes to include in branded fare families.

Conjoint analysis is the general methodology for measuring consumer preferences, while choice-based conjoint is a specific method within that category that asks respondents to make trade-offs by choosing their preferred product option from a set of choices. While it is excellent for understanding trade-offs, the single biggest drawback with this approach is that we simply do not know if the survey participants were truthful. Another issue is that it measures preference share and not actual market share.

6.5.1.1 Choice-Based Conjoint Analysis

Choice-based conjoint (CBC) analysis is a specialized survey technique which closely simulates the consumer selection process for products in competitive contexts.

Survey respondents are shown a set of itinerary options and asked to make a purchase selection. Participants view products which consist of various attributes (e.g., seat comfort) made up of multiple levels of the product (extra leg room, standard seat, 127-degree reclining seat, etc.). Each attribute included in the product will have multiple levels associated with it. A price point is also associated with each level in the display. From the survey, based on how respondents evaluate products in response to changes in attribute levels, the impact of each attribute (the ancillary) on product performance can be estimated. Respondents can also select a "none" option if they don't like any of the options presented. By analyzing these choices, a revenue management analyst can infer the relative importance of different ancillaries and estimate the value customers place on each attribute in a bundle.

The utility of the ancillary products can be determined using the Hierarchical Bayes (HB) choice modeling technique. It is used for choice analysis, and it models preference heterogeneity at the individual participant level. It is especially used in situations with sparse data where individuals make multiple choices. It uses a two-level model to combine individual-level and group-level data, which allows it to estimate individual preferences by "borrowing strength" from the group to inform estimates for each person. This makes it possible to get individual-level results even when there are not many choices per person, as it handles situations where there are more unknowns than observations.

By aggregating the HB model utilities, the significance of each ancillary can be determined on a normalized scale from 0 to 1. An easier way to interpret the ancillary utilities is to convert it into dollar equivalent terms which is the customer willingness to pay for the ancillary product or service.

This approach is a structured choice experiment. When customers are exposed to randomized bundles and asked to make a selection, preferences often shift revealing a gap between how airlines create their bundles and what customers actually value. This gap will continue to exist as long as airlines focus on a few static bundles which fail to capture the full willingness to pay for features. Closing the gap begins with understanding who the customers really are: the customer segment (context for travel) for the booking, and customer demographics (U.S. vs. Western European vs. Japanese) to understand how much they will pay for each feature.

Periodic execution of the structured choice experiment is of critical importance to capture changes in consumer behavior and reflect the changes in the creation of offers.

There are several conjoint analysis software tools on the market. Sawtooth Software pioneered digital conjoint analysis surveys in the 1990s. They offer expertise in traditional and digital conjoint analysis research. Other conjoint analysis software tools on the market include Conjointly, OpinionX, SPSS, and others.

6.5.1.2 The McKinsey Survey

A survey by McKinsey and Company [Cosmas et al., 2025] used conjoint analysis to quantify consumer preference patterns. They determined the relative importance of the features and the associated average maximum willingness to pay for the feature. Table 6.3 illustrates the relative importance of the feature and the average maximum willingness to pay from their study. It indicates that while the fare holds the highest relative weight, features such as baggage allowance (16%), seat selection (10%), and ticket flexibility (9%) strongly influence a traveler's choice.

6.5.2 Revealed Preferences

Stated preferences are what people say they want, gathered through surveys, while revealed preferences are what they actually do, observed through their behavior. The key difference between these two approaches stems from the gap that can exist

Table 6.3 Relative importance of features and customer willingness to pay

Feature/attribute	Relative importance of features when selecting a bundle (%)	Average maximum willingness to pay ($)
Itinerary price ($150 vs $400)	34	n/a
Baggage (personal item only vs one checked bag)	16	112
Seat selection (random seat vs extra legroom)	10	57
Flexibility (no flexibility vs fully refundable)	9	54
Miles accrual (0.5X vs 1.5X)	7	13
Snacks and drinks (excluded vs included)	6	27
Wi-Fi (excluded vs included)	5	18
Priority boarding (excluded vs included)	4	15
Lounge access (excluded vs included)	4	14
Upgrade eligibility (excluded vs included)	4	12

Source McKinsey & Company, May 2025

between what someone says they would choose and the choice they ultimately make, often due to unconscious bias, social pressures, or lack of self-awareness. Revealed preferences are considered more meaningful and accurate by many as they are based on real actions that customers take, and not just words.

With the revealed preferences approach, it is assumed that consumers possess a utility function. The theory of revealed preferences allows prediction of the consumer's behavior without specifying an explicit utility function. Inferences are made from actual purchase data of consumer preferences and consumer willingness to pay. The consumer choice modeling approach assumes that consumers choose an itinerary from among a set of alternatives during the flight search process. Each alternative is evaluated based on the set of attributes associated with the alternative. The utility function is estimated for each alternative, and the consumer selects the alternative with the highest utility. Marketing plays a key role in segmenting consumers into groups with similar purchasing characteristics to whom these products will be offered. The single biggest drawback is availability of data to support the consumer choice modeling analysis. Data used must capture the full picture of available alternatives and consumer perception. Subject to the availability of data, the revealed preferences approach is superior to the stated preferences approach.

6.6 Market Basket Analysis

A technique used by brick-and-mortar retailers to uncover hidden associations between items is called market basket analysis. It helps brick-and-mortar retailers understand the underlying patterns of their sales. The analysis uncovers complementary products that are bought together. Understanding how products sell can be used for promotions, cross-selling, and recommendations.

Market basket analysis utilizes transaction data, specifically the list of items purchased by a customer in a single purchase, to establish which products are frequently bought together and to identify patterns of co-occurrence. This analysis assists in revealing consumer preferences that may be difficult to capture through online surveys with any degree of reliability. Retailers leverage the findings of market basket analysis to determine product placement in stores, cross-category promotions, and co-marketing initiatives, among other sales strategies.

In the airline context, each booking is a transaction that consists of the fare for the itinerary and a collection of ancillary products and services with a total price for the bundle.

Consider the case where there are 100 bookings. Of the 100 bookings made by travelers, 80 paid for checked bags, 40 purchased a pre-reserved seat, and 30 customers paid for both a pre-reserved seat and a checked bag.

For every combination of items purchased, the three measures associated with market basket analysis are *Support*, *Confidence*, and *Lift*.

$$\text{Prob}(\text{Prereserved Seat} \cap \text{Checked Bag}) = \frac{30}{100} = 0.30$$

Support is a measure of the popularity of a product relative to all other purchases. In this example,

$$\text{Support(Checked Bag)} = \text{Prob (Checked Bag)} = \frac{80}{100} = 0.80$$

$$\text{Support(Prereserved Seat)} = \text{Prob(Prereserved Seat)} = \frac{40}{100} = 0.40$$

Confidence is the conditional probability that customers who bought product A also bought product B.

$$\text{Confidence(Prereserved Seat} \mid \text{Checked Bag)} =$$

$$\text{Prob(Prereserved Seat} \mid \text{Checked Bag)} = \frac{\text{Prob(Prereserved Seat} \cap \text{Checked Bag)}}{\text{Prob(Checked Bag)}}$$

$$= \frac{0.30}{0.80} = 0.375$$

Lift is a measure that determines if there is an association between the two products or if the purchase of these products is just a random combination. It is used to identify association rules that can be used for product placement, cross-selling, and other marketing strategies. In this example,

$$\text{Lift} = \frac{\text{Prob(Prereserved Seat} \cap \text{Checked Bag)}}{\text{Prob (Prereserved Seat) x Prob(Checked Bag)}} = \frac{0.30}{0.80\text{x}0.40} = 0.9375$$

Unlike the other two measures, Lift is interpreted by its distance from 1.

Since the Lift < 1 we can conclude that the two products are bought together less regularly than random, suggesting a negative correlation or substitutive relationship.

A Lift $= 1$ implies no association and the two products are randomly bought together and there is no relationship between them and a Lift > 1 implies that the two products are purchased together more frequently than random, suggesting a positive correlation or complementary relationship.

A well-known approach to market basket analysis is the Apriori algorithm [Agrawal & Srikant, 1994] to track transaction associations. It is used for finding frequent item sets and generating association rules from large datasets, commonly applied in market basket analysis. It operates on the principle that if an itemset is frequent, then all of its subsets must also be frequent (the "Apriori property" or "downward closure property" or "anti-monotonicity of support"). This property allows for efficient pruning of infrequent item sets, reducing the computational burden. Proposed in 1994, it is still widely used by brick-and-mortal retailers even though it suffers from high computational times on large datasets. This is overcome by limiting the number of items per transaction to reduce the time to process. This issue does not exist with airline retailing since most airlines have fewer than 10 ancillary products per transaction.

6.7 Market Basket Analysis for Airline Retailing

Sales transaction data can be used to provide insights into the purchase of ancillary products. Figure 6.1 illustrates aspects of ancillary bundles such as ancillary product popularity on a bubble chart, and the co-occurrence frequency or intensity between ancillary products that are purchased together.

The co-occurrence of ancillary products purchased from sales transaction data refers to the phenomenon where certain ancillary services are frequently bought together. These patterns enable airlines to optimize pricing, bundling, and sales strategies to maximize revenue.

In the world of airline retailing, understanding co-occurrence from sales transaction data has several benefits. They are:

1. Upselling and Cross-selling. Co-occurrence data can be leveraged to bundle ancillary products together and offer discounts to promote the purchase of multiple ancillaries.
2. Targeted Campaigns. Marketing campaigns can target specific passenger segments based on their historical purchase patterns and preferences.
3. Pricing of Ancillaries. Understanding what ancillary products and services are purchased together can influence an airline's static and dynamic pricing of ancillaries, to increase total revenues.

Identifying the context for travel during booking plays a key role with co-occurrence. For example,

1. Long-haul passengers may be more likely to purchase seat upgrades, extra baggage, and priority boarding.
2. Business passengers may be more likely to pay for seat selection, priority boarding, and airport lounges.
3. Passengers traveling with families may be more likely to pay for seat selection to sit together, checked baggage, and travel insurance.

Figure 6.2 illustrates the co-occurrence of ancillary products in sales transaction data, which influences how bundled offers are generated.

6.8 The Significance of Pricing It Right

Managing price performance is fundamental to airline retailing where the airline determines the price for an itinerary and the product bundle across all channels of distribution. Price performance based on strategic tenets is gaining in importance with tactics to compete effectively in the marketplace.

Since airline deregulation, airline itineraries have been priced based on the published fares in the market. The prices are static in the sense that they only change when an airline updates the fares for competitive or other reasons. Pricing an

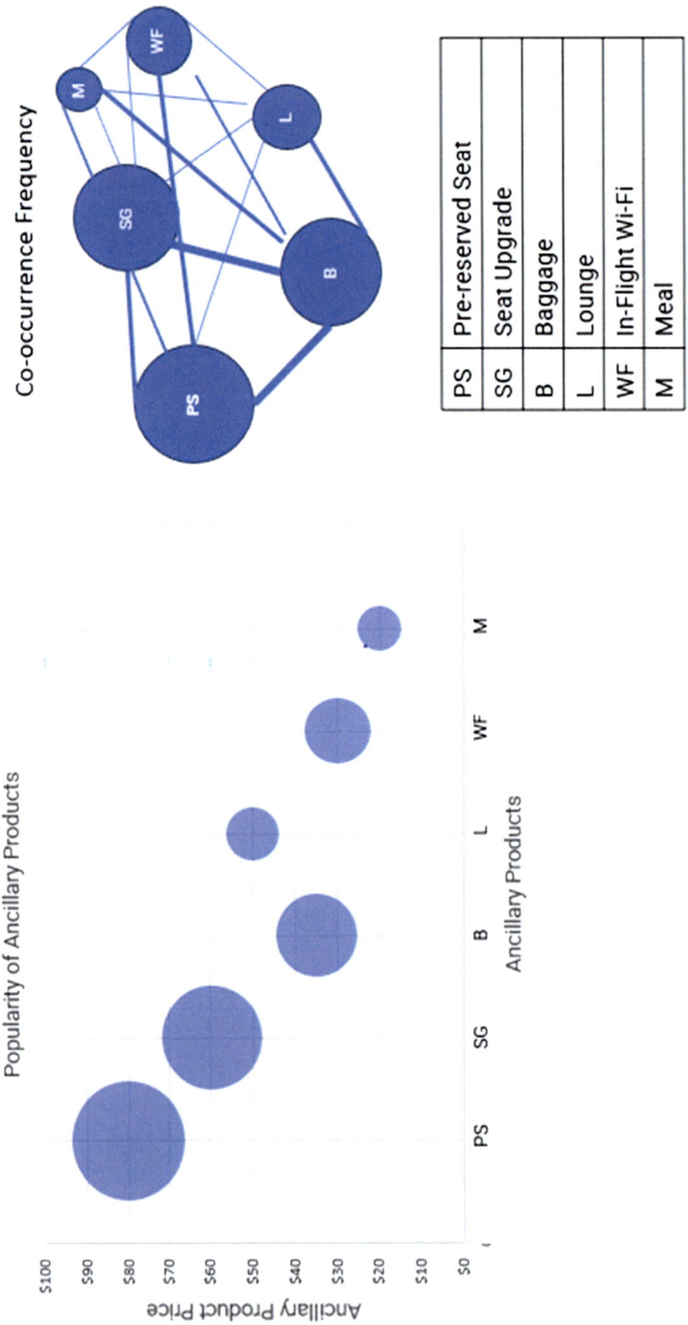

Fig. 6.1 Market basket analysis

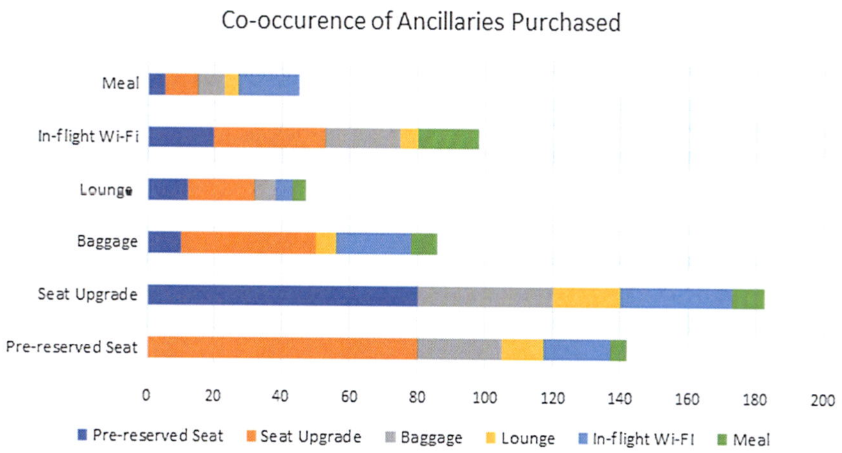

Fig. 6.2 Co-occurrence of ancillary products and services purchased

itinerary based on continuous pricing goes beyond the traditional fare management process of pricing an itinerary based on the published fares and rules. With continuous pricing, the quoted price is not a filed fare, but determined on request using reference fares, and available capacity as an alternative to determining availability of booking classes. Mismanagement of the pricing initiative will have a negative impact on revenue performance and ultimately earnings per share to the investment community. Getting the price right for every itinerary and offer bundle is fundamental to the success of an airline's retailing initiative. Pricing it right or lack thereof can define success versus failure of an airline's retailing initiative.

Pricing and price performance must be captured and evaluated for every customer segment periodically to truly understand the effectiveness of the retail initiative.

Cost plus pricing, the oldest approach to pricing, was never adopted in the airline industry due to the asset-intensive nature of the business and difficulty in allocating costs by market. Air fares are influenced by the forces of supply and demand. Proactive market-based pricing relies in the dynamics of the market and the global transparency of competitor selling fares. Setting air fares based on market conditions ensures that the airline product is competitive in the marketplace, addresses the requirements of the important customer segments, and protects the airline brand from offering selling fares lower than the perceived value of the product, thereby minimizing the risk of revenue dilution. A customer's willingness to pay can be inferred by monitoring competitor selling fares, booking pact, and the booked load factor for future flight departures.

As airlines transition from quoting an itinerary price to quoting the price for a bundle, the bundle price for the base fare and ancillaries must reflect the intrinsic value for the product based on customer segment, loyalty tier, historic travel purchases, and customer satisfaction. This is also referred to as customer focused pricing or value pricing. Carriers that focus on product differentiation with unique offers are better positioned to take advantage of value pricing. It is a way to differentiate the airline brand from a competitor's commodity product. Pricing the product right is far more impactful than volume sales. Underpricing leads to revenue dilution and overpriced products leads to market share erosion. Managing price performance requires active monitoring of key metrics such as sales and RASM by customer segment.

6.9 Context for Travel Based Customer Segmentation

Airlines have for many years wanted to segment customers beyond the traditional booking class that is used for inventory control of seats and distribution of availability through the Global Distribution Systems [Vinod, 2008].

Customer segmentation outside of travel may focus on demographics such as age, income, and resident postal code to understand purchase habits and propensity to buy a specific product. Airline customer segmentation has less to do with demographic data and is based on behavior patterns and motivation for taking a trip. For example, business travelers book closer to departure and require flexibility with flight exchanges and refundability, while leisure passengers are budget conscious and can accept more stringent fare rules associated with cheaper fares.

Before personalized travel became a priority, traditional customer segmentation was based on the class of service: first class, business class and economy. Within each class of service, customer segmentation was based on fare rules and restrictions mapped to the reservation booking designators (RBD). Frequent flyer segmentation was based on tiers and qualification was based on the amount of travel spent annually.

Corporate employees are required to adhere to different levels of corporate travel policies, known as unmanaged, lightly managed, managed, and highly managed. Unmanaged travel is generally applicable to small companies with less than 500 employees. Within the corporate realm, there are three main customer segments: road warriors, who frequently travel for work (e.g., sales executives); corporate masses, who engage in a considerable amount of travel; and infrequent travelers, such as employees attending conferences or visiting a regional corporate office. Traditional corporate travel is closely governed by travel policies, whereas executive travel falls under the lightly managed traveler category. Bundled offers for corporate employees must conform to corporate policy.

The act of categorizing customers during shopping by using only a few details, like origin and destination, how long they plan to stay, the number of people in their group, and the day of the week they arrive or depart, allows for the creation of tailored shopping responses that cater specifically to the persona, all within the constraints of the information available at that point. This categorization of customers is known as trip-purpose segmentation (TPS), which is a way of grouping customers based on the purpose (context) of their travel. It is the single most critical concept that should be implemented to generate customized offers for each persona, which can ultimately lead to personalization for a segment of ONE.

Customer segmentation is an essential initial step in the creation of offers [Kothari et al., 2016]. Various attributes of users, such as travel preferences, schedule and fare preferences, site activity, affinities, and travel history, can be utilized to create customer segments. It is important to note that customer segmentation is an ongoing process that should be periodically adjusted based on historical purchase data and evolving customer preferences. However, it is crucial to strive for accuracy with a small margin of error. A flawed customer segmentation model can result in offers that fail to convert into bookings during the sales process.

In the realm of travel, the significance of considering context for segmenting travelers cannot be overstated. Segmenting customers based on context for travel creates personas that combine the traits of groups of travelers who share similar preferences. However, in the travel industry, these personas come with a unique twist. This is because a customer's preferences can vary depending on the context of their travel, such as a business trip, a weekend getaway, visiting friends and relatives, a family vacation, or a "bleisure" trip that combines business and leisure activities. To define these different segments based on trip-purpose, we need to ensure that they are *mutually exclusive and collectively exhaustive.* This practical step allows us to group customers who exhibit similar purchasing behaviors. There are two reasons why this is important. First, not all customers are registered users, and many remain anonymous until they make a booking. This is especially true when using online travel agencies that rely on browser cookies. Second, the typical traveler may have multiple profiles influenced by the purpose of their trip. Understanding the context of a trip, as determined by shopping parameters, greatly impacts customer preferences and price sensitivity. To further refine the offer recommendations based on trip-purpose segmentation, customer-specific data can be considered from the customer profile, such as name, credit card information, frequent flyer status, and past trips when the customer is declared. By taking all these factors into account, the offer can be refined to meet the needs and desires of each customer.

The segmentation of travelers in the airline industry has historically relied on airline pricing and is determined by the fare rules and restrictions outlined in the reservation booking designator (RBD). These RBDs or booking classes are also utilized to distribute availability to Global Distribution Systems (GDS) using AVS, direct access, or seamless availability.

Price discrimination based on customer segmentation or individual customer behavior was not effective for mass product items like DVDs sold by online giant Amazon in 2000 [Turow et al., 2005]. However, travel suppliers do not expect a negative reaction from customers when it comes to price differentiation. Today, travel customers are more accepting of different price points for perishable products. The issue is further mitigated by bundled offers responses from airlines through the NDC gateway, since the content is not homogenous.

Attributes
advance purchase
length of stay
number in party
domestic trip
international trip
flight duration (short, medium, long)
day flight versus overnight flight
saturday night stay
mid-week vs weekend departure / return
departure / return daypart (morning, afternoon, evening)
equipment type (narrowbody vs widebody)
temperature difference between departure and arrival city

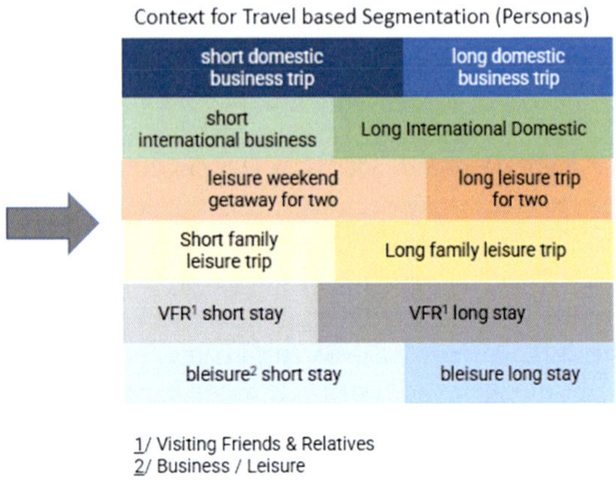

Fig. 6.3 Sample attributes for customer segmentation based on context

Every traveler is an individual with a unique identity and a single profile, but their travel behaviors and preferences can shift dramatically based on the context of their trip. Ever customer has multiple personas based on the context for travel. Flight and bundle (air and non-air) preferences vary based on the type of trip, business trip and its variants, leisure trip and its variants. Given the importance of the context for travel which can lead to different offers for the same customer, Fig. 6.3 provides a sample set of attributes for customer segmentation. Unsupervised or supervised (if a marketing survey customer surveys past customers and labels their segment) learning techniques can be used to generate the various personas which have been identified with a label as shown in Fig. 6.3.

Providers of machine learning toolkits often promote the use of black box techniques for customer segmentation. The management of inventory-controlled ancillaries falls under the purview of airline revenue management analysts. It is crucial to have visibility and interpretation of customer segments to respond to changes in custom offers and inventory controls. Besides, the trip-purpose segments must be mutually exclusive and collectively exhaustive. This implies that during a low fare search, a customer cannot be identified as belonging to two or more trip-purpose segments but must belong to a single unique segment. Therefore, a black box approach is not advisable due to the existing revenue management business processes and flight control methods. The argument holds true for dynamic segmentation as well.

Note that the trip-purpose segments for the coach cabin shown in Table 6.4 are mutually exclusive and collectively exhaustive. Hence, in an online session, a customer can only belong to one persona which defines the traveler's context for travel.

Further, booking classes are not required with NDC for classless revenue management. For revenue management purposes, demand can be forecast by

Table 6.4 Air trip-purpose segmentation example

Trip-purpose segment	Customer type	Business or leisure trip	Advance purchase	Length of stay
A1	Individual	Business	0–6 days	0–1 days
A2	Individual	Business/leisure	0–6 days	2+days
A3	Individual	Business/leisure	7–13 days	0–5 days
A4	Individual	Leisure	7–13 days	5+days
A5	Individual	Business/leisure	14–20 days	Any
A6	Individual	Business	21+days	0–3 days
A7	Individual	Leisure	21+days	4+days
A8	Couple (2)	Leisure	0–20 days	Any
A9	Couple (2)	Leisure	21+days	Any
A10	Family (>2)	Leisure	Any	Any
A11	Individual	One-way, business	0–6 days	One-way
A12	Individual	One-way, business or leisure	7–13 days	One-way
A13	Individual	One-way, business or leisure traveler that plans ahead	14–20 days	One-way
A14	Individual	One-way, leisure traveler that plans ahead	21+days	One-way
A15	Couple (2)	One-way, couple on leisure trip	Any	One-way
A16	Family (>2)	One-way, family vacation	Any	One-way

trip-purpose segment to determine the optimal dynamic pricing (continuous) of itineraries.

6.9.1 Micro-Segmentation

The trip-purpose segment definitions can be further refined based on marketing objectives. Micro-segmentation is the process of further breaking down the trip-purpose segments into a more granular level of detail to create micro segments by adding aggregate dimensions to clustering customers such as *CLV* (Customer Lifetime Value) tiers, channel, and additional customer preferences. Micro-segmentation adds precision to the recommendation engine to recommend offers.

When the customer is declared (known), then purchase history, frequent flyer mileage flown, individual schedule preferences, preferences for amenities, etc. can

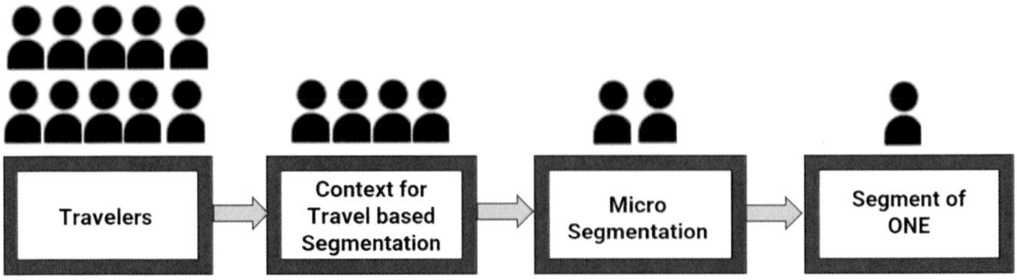

Fig. 6.4 Adding precision to customer segmentation

be used to fine tune the offer recommendation for the individual traveler. Personalization offers based on past preferences, behavior, and real-time context. for a segment of ONE is the ultimate goal of personalized offers. While it does not apply to the entire population of travelers, it is applicable to frequent travelers.

6.9.2 Why Is Context for Travel Based Segmentation Important?

Why is context for travel-based segmentation important? Only a very small fraction of an airline's customers makes several trips a year. Most travelers, around 85%, only travel once a year. While a relatively small group of frequent flyers can significantly impact the overall average number of trips per customer, it is misleading to assume that offers can be personalized for infrequent travelers. Trip-purpose segmentation is the default for creating offers, and the definition of the trip-purpose segments can vary from one airline to the next, based on their sales and pricing strategy. The offer that is created based on the trip-purpose segment can be modified to create a 1:1 offer for a customer based on the number of trips the customer has taken. For infrequent travelers, the offer derived from the trip-purpose segment may be the final offer on an airline website.

An equally important reason why trip-purpose segmentation will prevail is because of the constraints imposed by the European General Data Protection Regulation (GDPR) that is in place today. With GDPR, calibration must be done at a higher level of aggregation such as market or trip-purpose segmentation data. Shao and Kauermann [2020] recommend calibration price elasticity at the market level to segment markets and determine what offers to recommend to customers.

Adding precision to customer segmentation is illustrated in Fig. 6.4.

6.9.3 Trip-Purpose Segmentation and "P2"

A new fare phenomenon is the so-called P2 strategy by American Airlines. In May 2025, American Airlines started charging solo travelers more than passengers who booked as a pair in lower valued booking classes [Mesa, 2025; Potter,

2025]. American was the first to introduce this new fare rule, that they called "P2" internally for "Passenger 2". Delta Air Lines and United Airlines followed. In some markets, Basic Economy only appeared when the low fare search specified multiple passengers.

The rationale behind this strategy is that solo travelers are more likely to be business travelers who are less price sensitive than leisure travelers. These restrictions do not exist on higher priced fares that are mapped to the higher valued booking classes. It is a way for airlines to create a trip-purpose segment that ensures that solo business travelers, when they book the cheaper fare, pay a higher price than leisure travelers who typically travel with two or more passengers.

It is a bold move by the U.S. majors to further fine-tune the customer segments and ensure business travelers, who typically travel solo, pay a premium when they book a discounted fare. The descriptor for the discounted fare includes the stipulation *"must be accompanied on all sectors in the same compartment by at least 1 adult 15 or older."*

Launched in a few one-way domestic test markets, it gained wider adoption in July 2025.

The trip-purpose segmentation shown in Table 6.4 can be refined for P2, to prevent dilution of business passenger revenue. To make this work, a distinction is required between solo passengers and multiple passengers in a PNR. This is illustrated in Table 6.5.

P2 can also be extended to distinguish 1, 2 and >2 passengers in a PNR. In this scenario, a family consisting of 3 or more may qualify for an additional discount. However, the original intent of P2 was to charge the business traveler a premium.

6.10 The Significance of the Bundled Offer

Retailers can use product bundling, an effective pricing strategy, to bundle many products into a single package and offer them for a single price that is typically less than the sum of the individual product prices. The bundles can consist of products owned by the airline or products sold based on commercial partnerships such as a hotel room or car rental.

Fast food restaurants devised this tactic.

McDonald's was the first fast food chain to introduce combo meals in 1958, but not at a nationwide level. These meal bundles allow customers to order a complete meal for a fixed price, which is lower than purchasing each item separately. Over the years, the chain frequently adjusted its combo meal choices. New value meals were typically tested in specific regions before being rolled out nationally. The iconic Happy Meal, designed for children, was launched across the U.S. in 1979. In summary, bundling the right products makes it easier for customers to buy. These offers provide more value compared to purchasing items separately. This approach leads to a more engaged and loyal customer base, encouraging additional purchases in the future.

Table 6.5 Air trip-purpose segmentation "P2" example

Trip-purpose segment	Number in party	Business or leisure trip	Advance purchase	Length of stay
A1	Any	Business	0–6 days	0–1 days
A2	Any	Business/leisure	0–6 days	2+ days
A3	1	Business	7–13 days	0–5 days
A4	>1	Leisure, couple or family	7–13 days	0–5 days
A5	Any	Leisure	7–13 days	5+ days
A6	1	Business	14–20 days	Any
A7	>1	Leisure, couple or family	14–20 days	Any
A8	1	Business	21+ days	0–5 days
A9	>1	Leisure, couple or family	21+ days	0–5 days
A10	Any	Leisure	21+ days	5+ days
A11	>1	Leisure, couple or family	0–20 days	Any
A12	>1	Leisure, couple or family	21+ days	Any
A13	Any	One-way, business or Leisure	0–6 days	One-way
A14	1	One-way, business	7–13 days	One-way
A15	>1	One-way, Leisure, couple or family	7–13 days	One-way
A16	1	One-way, business traveler	14–20 days	One-way
A17	1	One-way, business traveler	14–20 days	One-way
A18	1	One-way, business traveler	21+ days	One-way
A19	>1	One-way, leisure, couple or family	21+ days	One-way
A20	>1	One-way, leisure, couple or family	Any	One-way

Wendy's was the first to create a value menu in 1989 for individual items, but the"value meal" concept is credited to McDonald's when they introduced the "Extra Value Meal," in 1991 and the meal bundle consisted of a sandwich, fries, and drink for a combination price. Purchasing a "value meal," besides being more economical, the bundling of complementary products simplified the buying process for the customer. This helps create a more loyal and committed customer base, potentially leading to future purchases.

Here are a few successful use cases of product bundling.

1. Computer original equipment manufacturers (OEMs) like Dell, Acer and Hewlett Packard combine peripherals such as printers, monitors, and software with a computer.
2. Microsoft created Microsoft Office as a bundle consisting of Word, Excel, PowerPoint, and Access.
3. Amazon offers one or more complementary products as a single bundle with savings for customers to boost sales with the logo *frequently bought together*.

6.11 Offer Creation and Recommendation Engines

Recommendation systems play an important role in creating relevant offers to customers [Dadoun et al., 2021; Jiang et al., 2014]. The objective of a recommendation engine is to generate a bundled offer to customers based on their trip-purpose segment and individual preferences. The bundle consists of the fare for the itinerary and the air ancillary bundle. Advanced data analytics powered recommendation engines for bundles process historical purchase data and require periodic recalibration to detect and adapt to changes in customer behavior patterns and preferences over time. Using historical purchase data by trip-purpose segment, recommendation engines can deliver bundled offers for the persona, the customer segment [Vinod, 2017, 2021e; Vinod et al., 2018].

Techniques may consist of either traditional statistical predictive models or machine learning models [Fox, 2019]. Examples of models that can be used include techniques such as content-based filtering, collaborative filtering, knowledge-based rules and logic, classification and regression trees (CART), and gradient boosting machines (GBM). Many recommendation engines combine multiple techniques to leverage the strengths of each. For example, content-based filtering could be used to understand individual preferences (e.g., premium economy, aisles seat) and collaborative filtering to identify "like-minded" customers or relationship between products.

An offer is a bundle that is displayed to a customer during shopping and can be refined from the point of booking to the checkout process based on their specific preferences [Vinod, 2020a]. Customers who visit an airline website can be anonymous or declared. Customers are usually anonymous early in the sales process. A challenge is to display relevant offers to customers when they are anonymous. Based on shopping parameters input by the user, the context for travel can be identified with the associated trip-purpose segment. From historical customer bookings, the trip-purpose segment can be identified to determine what customers have purchased in the past. This data can then be used to infer the composition of the most appropriate bundles for each trip-purpose segment.

Figure 6.5 illustrates a variant of a persona-based recommendation engine [Vinod, 2020a] to maximize conversion rates of the air bundle.

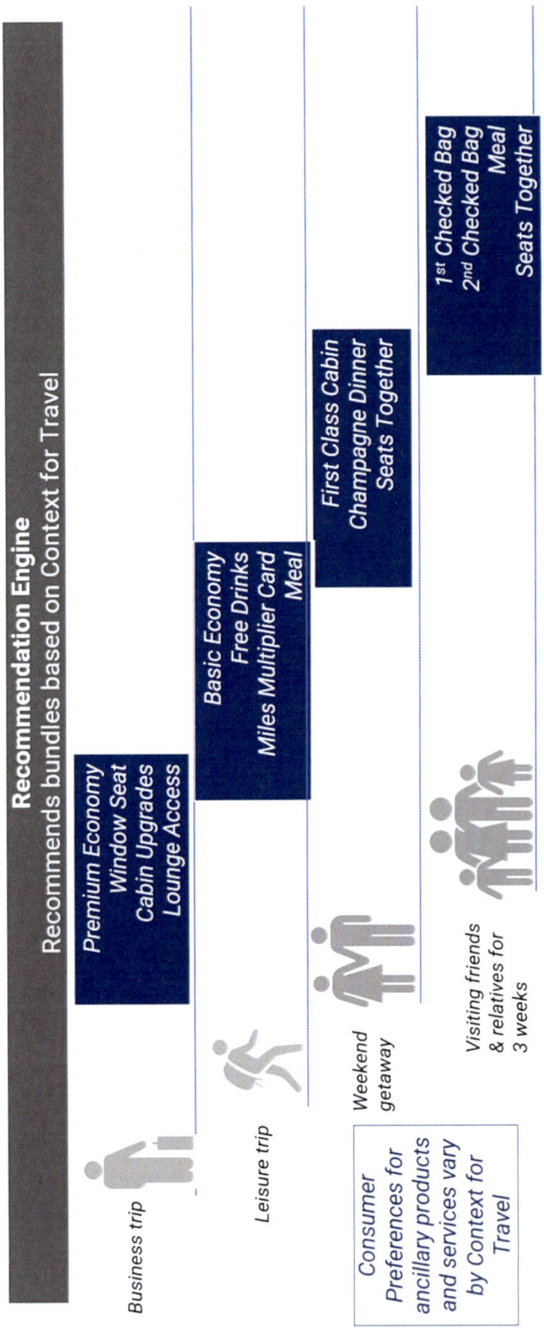

Fig. 6.5 Recommending offers based on context for travel

This approach to recommending bundles requires periodic calibration using airline booking, ticketing and Electronic Miscellaneous Document (EMD, electronic documentation of all sales and transactions between airlines and passengers that are not part of the standard electronic ticket such as ancillary products) data to ensure that changes in consumer behavior over time are considered. Periodic calibrations can be time consuming and expensive and will always lag the market.

Ideally, this approach to determining bundles by trip-purpose segment should serve as a *warm start* for the real-time multi-armed test and learn experimentation model, a reinforcement learning technique, [Robbins, 1952; Gittins et al., 2011; White, 2013] where experimentation is continuous, recommendations are always current and reflect market competitive conditions (described in detail in Sect. 6.14, 6.15).

6.11.1 Branded Fares and Offers

Branded fare families are an important consideration in creating the final offer. When a bundled offer is determined, it should be mapped to the attributes included in each branded fare product to ensure that duplicates are reconciled and the lowest cost option is offered to the customer. Hence for example it may be cheaper to offer a customer a cheaper branded fare product and an ancillary priced separately than offering the higher valued branded fare product with the ancillary included. Offer management with branded fares provides a range of upsell opportunities tied to the various branded fare products that are available for sale, and the recommendation is based on the least total cost to the customer.

6.12 Decoy Pricing to Improve Conversion Rates

Airlines have ultimate flexibility for the display of offers on the airline website since they control the screen real estate unlike the indirect channels such as the GDS travel agency desktop. This provides an opportunity for airlines to maximize the screen real estate on the airline website and present bundled offers that truly maximize conversion rates.

An important part of designing the airline website is determining which offers are appropriate to show online customers and what sequence to put them in. Studies have indicated that when customers are presented with more than three (or a maximum of four) options to choose from, they tend to become disinterested. This is because the brain can only store three or four pieces of information at a time in the conscious mind [Moskowitz, 2008]. That is why it makes sense to show three alternatives.

Decoy pricing is a marketing strategy where a third intentionally inferior option ("the decoy") is introduced to make a higher-priced target product look like a better value, boosting sales of that specific item. The rationale for decoy pricing is based on the premise that travelers have difficulty comparing different offer bundles, but if two of the options displayed are similar (e.g., same price), it becomes much easier. If a slightly worse bundled offer is presented, then customers would gravitate toward the superior bundled offer. The inferior bundled offer served its purpose in making an informed decision.

Decoy pricing is also known as *asymmetric dominance effect* since a consumer's preference between two options will change after the introduction of a third asymmetrically decoy option.

The Best Offer

The best offer is based on the inferred real-time identification of the context for travel (trip-purpose segment) of an online user based on the shopping parameters provided for the shopping search query. Aggregate historical sales data for the customer segment is used as an input to determine the most likely bundle that the customer will purchase.

The Decoy Offer

When the best offer is paired with a less appealing bundle known as a "decoy offer," the customer is more likely to select the better deal [Ariely, 2010; Segmentify, 2021]. It is sometimes referred to as asymmetric dominance or the decoy effect. The decoy offer could be the most expensive or it could be priced in the middle. Customers can use it as a point of reference when choosing the best deal.

Popular Attributes Across All Customer Segments

The third choice can be based on the aggregate sales data of the most popular ancillary products and services across all consumers, without taking the context for travel into account. This ancillary bundle aims to ensure that customers will purchase individual popular ancillary products and services as a bundle. It is a fail-safe recommendation if the customer's intent does not match the identified customer segment when the search was initiated. Hence, if the identified customer segment is erroneous, and the consumer does not belong to this group, an offer based on the most popular ancillaries sold across all customers is displayed as the third choice.

6.12.1 Finalizing the Offer

When the customer's identity is known, subsequent refinements to the bundled offer can be made to personalize the offer. This can be based on past purchase history, consumer intent captured during the sales interaction, frequent flyer status, credit card affiliations, and travel preferences stored on the customer profile.

6.12.1.1 The Bundle Discount

Optionally, to spur sales of ancillaries, a dynamic quantity discount model, calibrated with airline input, can be used to customize the air bundle [Vinod, 2021a].

Airline ancillary products are typically complementary products that are used together. Combining complementary products and charging a lower price for the bundle is a well-known strategy [Yan & Bandyopadhyay, 2011].

The greater the total value of the bundle purchased by a customer, the greater the discount, subject to minimums and maximums. For example, the quantity discount model can be a hyperbolic discounting model to calculate the discount amount. The model can be calibrated to define the maximum discount regardless of the total value of ancillaries purchased. The bundle discount can be made available on the airline website as well as in the indirect GDS channel through the NDC messaging protocol.

Figure 6.6 illustrates the maximum discount percentage of 12% applied as a function of total ancillary sales. With airlines migrating to NDC, the discount can be applied to the total price of the ticket inclusive of the base fare, since the financial settlement is direct with the airline. However, this is *not recommended* since the continuous price quote for an itinerary is a discount with its own logic from the selling open fare. Hence the discount for the ancillary bundle can be added to the continuous price for the itinerary to arrive at the total price for the bundle.

Ideally these discounts for the ancillary bundle, similar to the continuous price discount for the air itinerary, must be implemented by trip-purpose segment and not for an individual customer to avoid customer backlash and loss of confidence in the brand.

The equation to generate the dynamic discount based on total spend for a booking is as follows.

$$\text{Discount}(\%) = \frac{\text{Maximum Discount }(\%)\text{ x Incremental Spend}}{\text{Constant} + \text{Incremental Spend}}$$

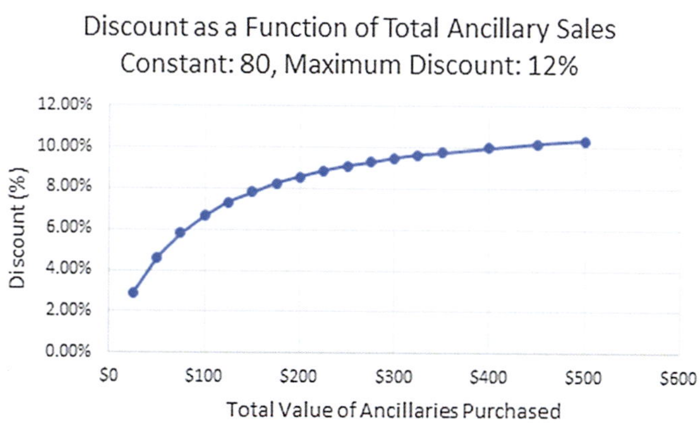

Fig. 6.6 Example of a dynamic discounting model based on total ancillary spend

The value of the constant can be calibrated by a revenue management analyst to determine an acceptable rate at which the discount should be applied as a function of the incremental spend. In Fig. 6.6, the constant was set to 100. When the constant is lower, the discounts are higher for lower incremental spend.

This type of equation was first proposed by biochemist Leonor Michaelis and Canadian physician Maud Menten in the study of enzymes [Michaelis & Menten, 1913] and called the Michaelis–Menten equation. The constant used in the equation is called the Michaelis–Menten constant.

6.13 Role of Dynamic Pricing in Offer Creation

Pricing an itinerary during the offer creation process can be based on traditional revenue management techniques based on the booking class availability that is available for sale and using this information to price the itinerary based on fare rules and restrictions. The alternative approach is dynamic pricing, which observes the fare rules and attempts to fill the gap between discrete price points for a market with a discount. However, the calculation of the dynamic price is an incremental approach, taking the request is isolation regardless of interactions in the global network, and hence an approximation.

6.13.1 First, Second, and Third Order Effects and Dynamic Pricing

The Origin and Destination revenue management methodology is to compute network-optimal bid prices for an airline network with a non-linear revenue mix optimization model. In this model all demands at a service class level are included in a capacity constrained optimization model. The model determines the right mix of short-haul, medium-haul and long-haul demand that should be accommodated on an airline's global route network to maximize total revenues subject to capacity constraints.

The revenue mix optimization model, which is like a typical product mix model, but with a non-linear objective function to account for the probability density function of the underlying demand model, simultaneously considers all the first order, second order and third order network effects to arrive at a bid price by flight leg and date. The bid price for a flight leg can be interpreted as the opportunity cost of not having an incremental seat on a flight leg. Alternately it can be interpreted as the minimum acceptable fare to accept a passenger on the flight leg.

What is implicit in the revenue mix model is the evaluation and hence trade-offs of all the network effects *simultaneously*. For example, consider the 3×3 hub-and-spoke network shown in Fig. 6.7. If there is a surge in demand from SEA to DFW because of a promotional fare filing, the first, second and third order impacts on traffic flows are summarized in Table 6.6.

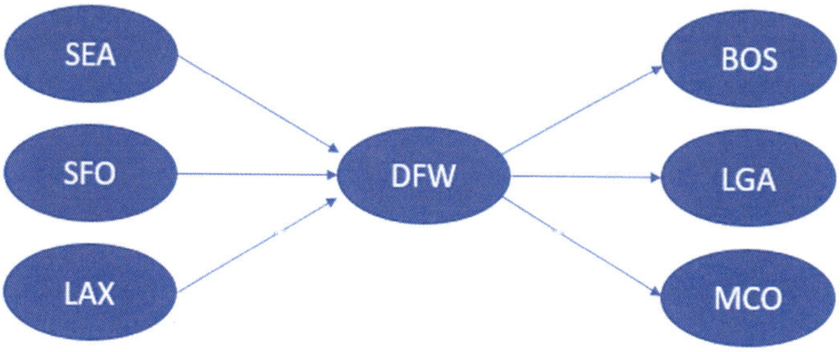

Fig. 6.7 A hub and spoke network

Table 6.6 First, second, and third order network effects

First order effects (+)	Second order effects (−)	Third order effects (+)
SEA-DFW	SEA-BOS	SFO-BOS
	SEA-LGA	SFO-LGA
	SEA-MCO	SFO-MCO
		LAX-BOS
		LAX-LGA
		LAX-MCO

The narrative for the positive and negative higher order network effects is as follows:

a. First Order Effect: When a promotional fare is introduced from SEA to DFW, the SEADFW market will see a surge in demand (+)
b. Second Order Effect: Because of the increased demand from SEA to DFW (local market), availability will be restricted to the connecting markets that have the SEADFW leg in common (−)
c. Third Order Effect: Because availability is restricted for the connecting markets originating out of SEA, there will be greater availability for markets that do not originate in SEA and hence they will see increased traffic (+).

6.13.2 Dynamic Pricing Solution Approach

The approach taken today to develop a Dynamic Pricing solution is to determine the dynamic price for an itinerary based on the shopping request (departure dates, return date, market). The dynamic pricing model is one dimensional in the sense that its universe is limited to the market for which a dynamic price should be returned for a specific itinerary in the shopping response. The current market-by-market dynamic pricing model considers the host airline's fares as well as the fares of the competitors in the market to arrive at a price point (the "dynamic" price) that maximizes the potential conversion rate based on a net contribution model. The net contribution model considers an airline's bid prices by flight leg and date. However, the computation of the dynamic price for the market is done in isolation without considering network effects simultaneously.

When viewed in isolation on a market-by-market basis, the question is whether the *dynamic price response is optimal for the request at the network level?* The argument is that is is not because it does not consider simultaneous first order, second order and third order network effects for every booking request. The current model is a greedy approach. Yet, simultaneously considering network effects across all markets with competitive shopping data to determine the dynamic price for a specific customer request is a formidable task. Further, in this scenario, the objective function is not necessarily concave and there will be dis-continuities adding further complexity (stability due to the absence of a market equilibrium) to the problem.

6.14 A Brief Introduction to Reinforcement Learning

Reinforcement learning is a machine learning technique that trains software to make decisions to achieve the best results. It learns like humans through trial and error. Actions that work toward the goal are reinforced and rewarded, while actions that diminish from the goal are ignored.

Figure 6.8 illustrates the basic framework. The *agent* is the machine learning algorithm or the autonomous system. The *environment* is the adaptive problem space with attributes such as variables, boundary values, rules, and valid actions. The *action* is a step that the agent takes to navigate the environment. The *state* is the environment at a given point in time. The *reward* is the positive, negative, or zero value for taking an action. The *cumulative reward* is the sum of all rewards.

Reinforcement learning is based on the Markov decision process, that uses discrete time steps. At every step, the agent takes a new action that results in a new environment state. Similarly, the current state is attributed to the sequence of previous actions.

Moving through the environment through trial and error, the agent builds a set of if–then rules or policies. The policies enable it to decide which action to take next to achieve the maximum cumulative reward. The agent must also

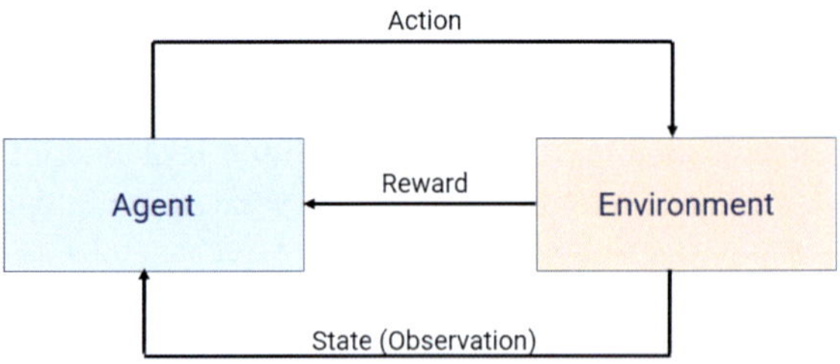

Fig. 6.8 Reinforcement learning

choose between further exploring the environment further to learn new state-action rewards or select known high-reward actions from a given state. This is the *exploration–exploitation* trade-off.

Reinforcement learning has its roots in Richard Bellman's theory of dynamic programming [Bellman, 1954]. It is a technique for breaking complex sequential decisions into smaller, optimal steps, which is the basis for reinforcement learning via the Bellman Equation which evaluates state values for optimal action choices for agents learning to achieve goals. The Bellman Equation defines the value of a state as the immediate reward plus the discounted expected value of the next state, recursively breaking down long-term goals into small manageable steps.

6.15 Multi Armed Bandit Model for Continuous Experimentation of Offers

The multi-armed bandit model is an example of reinforcement leaning Continuous experimentation is a fundamental requirement for generating offers to customers. No offer management capability is complete without experimentation. This is because an airline may introduce new ancillary products and services for which there is no sales history. Besides, consumer preferences and attitudes change based on the market, competition, and schedule attributes. Calibrating recommended bundles from historical sales data is a starting point, but not accurate as consumer preferences change over time. This gap is addressed with continuous experimentation to ensure that the offers are relevant to customers and customer segments. A good technique for experimentation is the multi-armed bandit.

Imagine a customer at a casino with a row of slot machines and limited time and money to find out which one pays out the most. The customer's goal is to win as much as possible while losing as little as possible. This situation represents the Multi-Armed Bandit (MAB) problem, where the customer needs to decide which machine to play with each attempt, even though the customer does not know how much each one will reward him.

The multi-armed bandit problem is a key concept in reinforcement learning and decision-making. It involves a decision-maker choosing from several options, or arms, each with an unknown reward distribution. The goal is to maximize the reward over time. The challenge is finding the right balance: exploring the new arms to learn how they perform, or exploiting the best one found so far. This process requires weighing the risk of uncertainty against the benefit of known rewards.

The offer management problem for an airline requires choosing from a discrete finite set of offers to promote to customers. With experimentation there are two approaches: A/B testing and multi-armed bandit (MAB) testing. They are both used to compare different alternatives, but they differ in their approach to traffic allocation and optimization goals.

The traditional A/B testing is used to compare two alternatives to determine which one performs better in terms of user engagement and conversion. In the offer management context, a handful of offers that are evaluated against each other falls into this category where the tests are performed by allocating a fixed percentage of experimental units to each choice followed by data collection and then choosing a winner. To summarize, A/B testing allocates traffic evenly to all alternatives. It is a controlled experiment that is designed to identify the best offer based on measurable metrics such as the conversion rate.

In an online environment that receives incoming requests, this process can be accomplished by splitting the traffic evenly amongst the choices. When there are several choices, the A/B testing framework becomes resource intensive because all choices, regardless of how good or bad they are for conversions, receive an identical traffic allocation.

The multi-armed bandit approach dynamically allocates the traffic more efficiently among these discrete choices, favoring choices that perform better in real-time. The method sequentially updating the allocation of traffic is based on the performance of each choice.

The multi-armed bandit problem assumes that each arm is *independent* of the rest and has some reward distribution which does *not* change over time. The reward distribution of each arm is *unknown,* and the expected reward must be estimated while simultaneously maximizing the reward.

The MAB balances exploration (sending traffic to candidate choices that have the potential to perform well) with exploitation (sending traffic to candidate choices that are performing well). MAB is more sample efficient than traditional static A/B tests. For the same amount of experimentation, it acquires a greater reward. Consequently, it is safer with larger cohorts because the samples are automatically diverted towards the good choices and away from the choices that do not resonate with customers. This model ultimately does a trade-off between exploration and exploitation to identify the optimal strategy.

Assuming there are T trials and there are K arms, the underlying goal is to maximize the total expected reward after T trials. At each time step $t = 1, 2, \ldots, T$ an arm is selected $a_t \in \{1, 2, \ldots, K\}$ and a random reward is observed. The goal is to maximize the total reward after T trials. The difficult part is to determine *which arm to select* based on the past history of rewards. The sampling technique used makes the decision on which arm to pull. It is assumed that each arm is independent of the rest, and has a reward distribution which does not change over time.

This approach allows us to model the tradeoff between exploitation (pulling arms that are good) versus exploration (pulling arms less frequently assuming they are good). For each pull of an arm, there is either a reward of 1 or 0 from each machine and hence called the Bernoulli-bandit framework. The expected reward for each arm $a \in \{1,2, \ldots, K\}$ is $B(p_a)$ based on the Bernoulli (B) distribution. The expected reward of arm a is just p_a, the expectation of Bernoulli.

Regret is the difference between the best possible expected reward and the actual reward after T trials. Let $p^* = argmax_{i \in \{1,2,\ldots,K\}} p_i$ denote the highest expected reward from one of the K arms. Then, the regret at time T is

$$\text{Regret}(T) = Tp^* - \text{Reward}(T)$$

where Tp^* is the reward from the best arm after T trials. Reward(T) is the actual reward after T trials.

The Average Regret after T trials is

$$\text{Average Regret}(T) = p^* - \frac{\text{Reward}(T)}{T}$$

Ideally, Average Regret$(T) \to 0$ as $T \to \infty$.

Minimizing the Average Regret is equivalent to maximizing the *Reward*.

The MAB framework can be implemented with different sampling methods such as greedy, epsilon-greedy, upper confidence bound (UCB), Thompson Sampling, etc. to improve future actions that will maximize the reward potential.

6.15.1 Greedy (Naive) Sampling

A naïve strategy is to pull each arm N times at the start of the experiment. Identify the best arm and select this arm for the remainder of the T trials. The problem with this strategy is that if the wrong best arm was selected the outcome of the experiment will be erroneous. The mistake was that all the exploration was done first followed with exploitation. If N was increased, it may not help since sub-optimal arms will continue to be sampled, which should be avoided since the objective is to maximize the reward.

6.15.2 Epsilon Greedy Sampling

The ε-Greedy sampline procedure is an improvement over the naïve greedy approach because it explores with probability ε at each time step. It has an identical setup to the naive Greedy approach and samples each arm N times and estimates $\hat{p}_a$ for each arm. There are two improvements, First, it continuously updates an arm's estimated expected reward when it is selected, even after the KN steps. Second, it explores with probability ε, and the value of ε is selected to balance exploration and exploitation. In summary, the idea of the algorithm is to choose the best arm, the arm with the highest $\hat{p}_a$, at each time step.

The idea of the greedy algorithm is simple: at each time step, choose the best arm (arm with highest $\hat{p}_a$).

6.15.3 Upper Confidence Bound Sampling

The Upper Confidence Bound (UCB) sampling technique constructs a confidence interval for $\hat{p}_a$ for each arm and select the arm with the highest potential.

Table 6.7 Upper confidence bound sampling example

Arm a	Estimate of arm $\hat{p}_a$	Confidence interval
1	0.60	$0.60 \pm 0.10 = [0.50\text{–}0.70]$
2	0.24	$0.24 \pm 0.14 = [0.10\text{–}0.38]$
3	0.55	$0.55 \pm 0.18 = [0.37\text{–}0.73]$

Consider an example with three arms shown in Table 6.7

Note that the confidence intervals are centered at the maximum likelihood estimate and depend on the sample size and the intervals may have different widths. A greater sample size means higher confidence and the intervals will be narrower. Unlike the Greedy algorithms that would have selected arm 1, the UCB method would have selected arm 3, the arm with the highest potential based on the upper confidence limit of 0.73. Observe that the UCB for an arm will decrease the more times it is pulled (sampled). The less frequently sampled arms now have an opportunity to have a higher UCB with the smaller sample size despite having a lower point estimate for the confidence interval.

For each arm a, the confidence interval is updated at time t as follows:

$a_t = argmax_{i \in \{1,2,\ldots,K\}}(\hat{p}_i + \sqrt{\frac{2\ln(t)}{N_t(i)}})$ where $N_t(i)$ is the number of times arm i was selected before time t.

6.15.4 Thompson Sampling

Thompson Sampling (TS) [Thompson, 1933] is a heuristic to address the explore-exploit dilemma with the multi-armed bandit problem. An arm is selected with a probability that is proportional to the arm being the best. Each arm produces an independent and identically distributed (i.i.d.) random reward independent of the past and other arms. This means a set of random variables or observations are both independent (the outcome of one does not influence the others) and drawn from the same probability distribution. The parameters of the reward distribution are fixed, but unknown. A reward is observed after playing an arm. Without human intervention, the method converges on an arm that is the best choice from the set of alternative choices.

In summary, Thompson Sampling solves the multi-armed bandit problem using a Bayesian method by using a prior probability of rewards and observed data to estimate the posterior probability. It keeps a probability distribution for each arm's expected reward. These distributions illustrate how uncertain we are about the true rewards. During each iteration, the algorithm draws a sample from each distribution. It then picks the machine with the highest sample to play next.

Thompson sampling often uses the beta distribution, especially when dealing with binary outcomes (like success or failure). The beta distribution is a probability distribution defined on the unit interval, making it suitable for modeling probabilities or proportions. The binomial distribution models the probability of a certain number of successes in a fixed number of trials, where each trial has only two possible outcomes (e.g., success or failure). The beta distribution is a conjugate prior for the binomial distribution, meaning that if we start with a beta prior and update it with the likelihood function, the resulting posterior distribution will also be a beta distribution.

The beta distribution is denoted as $Beta(\alpha, \beta)$ where α and β are the two shape parameters which influence the shape of the distribution, and the probability distribution is defined over the interval.

Selecting an arm can result in success with p_a or failure with $(1 - p_a)$. Assume a simple prior distribution $Beta(\alpha, \beta)$ where α equals the number of successes and β equals the number of failures. The posterior distributions of the reward functions for each arm are also *Beta*.

After observing the outcome of selecting an arm (success or failure), the corresponding beta distribution parameters for the arm must be updated as follows:

If it was a success, Beta$(\alpha + 1, \beta)$

If it was a failure, Beta$(\alpha, \beta + 1)$

An example of posterior distributions of mean rewards observed in previous time periods for different values of (α, β) is shown in Fig. 6.9.

During experimentation, the performance estimates for each choice are refined as the sampling of possible results for each choice are made. This process is repeated many times until the distribution of choices reaches a steady state. The distribution of the individual choices (offers) expressed as a percentage is used to direct traffic to the various choices in the future. The data collection and summarization of statistics continue to detect changes in consumer behavior over time. A key benefit of this approach is efficiency in sampling since underperforming choices will be discarded over time.

This process of updating the beta distribution repeatedly leads to a posterior distribution that reflects the arm's success rate, based on the observed data.

Figure 6.10 illustrates a comparison between the standard fixed allocation traditional A/B testing and the continuous reallocation multi-armed bandit model.

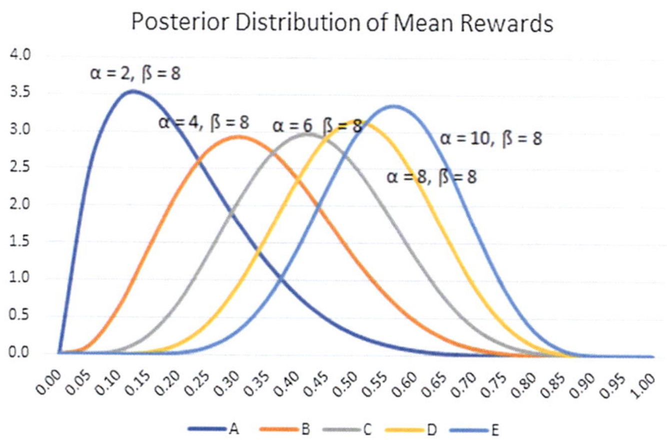

Fig. 6.9 Posterior distribution of mean rewards

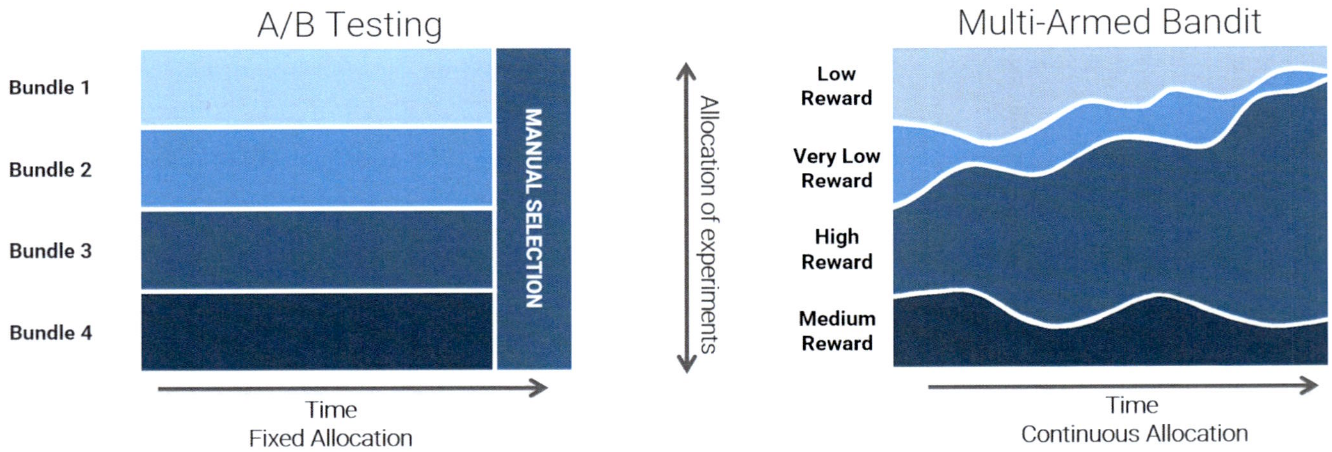

Fig. 6.10 A comparison of A/B testing versus multi-armed bandit model

6.16 Contextual Bandits

A limitation of multi-armed bandits is that they ignore the state of the environment. The state can provide very valuable insights that can help the learning process much faster and more effectively. Incorporating some element of state from the problem environment has given rise to contextual bandits. Instead of randomly managing the exploitation versus exploitation trade-off, the context about the environment is leveraged to manage the actions taken. The context is merely knowledge of the environment.

Contextual bandits are also used in Recommendation Systems, where they help predict a list of items for each user. For example, product suggestions to an individual on Amazon or movie picks on Netflix. Traditionally, Netflix relied on Content and Collaborative filtering to make recommendations. Content filtering looks for movies similar to ones the individual liked based on features like genre, actors, country, or release year. Collaborative filtering finds users with similar tastes and recommends movies they've enjoyed. However, content filtering requires extensive feature selection, and collaborative filtering struggles with new users or new movies. These issues are called cold start problems. Recently, many companies have turned to Contextual and Multi-armed bandits to improve recommendations. Including user context helps provide more relevant recommendations. This is especially true when user data and item catalogs change often, as with Netflix or Amazon. Using user context makes recommendations more accurate and adaptable.

Microsoft Research created a testing service called Vowpal Wabbit (VW), which utilizes contextual bandits through open-source online and offline training algorithms [Dudik et al., 2011]. The model was originally developed by researchers Miroslav Dudik, John Langford, and Lihong Li at Yahoo! Research in 2007 before being implemented by Microsoft. It is now actively maintained by Microsoft Research and a community of open-source contributors. It is particularly known for its focus on online learning, which enables models to learn incrementally from continuous streams of data, and its efficiency in handling large datasets. VW employs a "reductions" framework, where complex machine learning problems are broken down into simpler, well-understood components, allowing for flexible and modular algorithm development. VW offers robust support for contextual bandit algorithms, an area within reinforcement learning, enabling applications like content personalization and recommendation systems.

In airline retailing the context for travel-based segmentation serves as the primary contextual factor, and additional micro-segmentation features can be applied as needed.

6.16.1 Contextual Bandits in Offer Management

Contextual bandits expand upon the multi-armed bandit test and learn experimentation method. A contextual extension of the well-known Thompson sampler, called

Pólya-Gamma Thompson Sampling, was explored [Byrd & Darrow, 2021] and the potential gains by minimizing the regret of the recommendations was illustrated.

By introducing the current state as a factor in decision making, the contextual bandit model goes beyond reliance on historical data. Instead, persona-based decisions can be made based on contextual information identified in the shopping parameters encapsulated in the trip-purpose segment definitions. If applicable, additional context about the user besides travel history such as origin, booking time, travel dates, destination, customer demographics, site activity, and device usage can be incorporated.

6.17 Knowledge Graphs and Reasoning Models for Offer Creation

Knowledge graphs are structured, semantic frameworks mapping entities such as locations, flights, hotels, and attractions to enable inferences. They play an important role in the field of data science and artificial intelligence, transforming the management and depiction of intricate data through interconnected models of entities and their relationships. It represents the future of personalized offer management when the offer goes beyond air ancillaries, hotels, rental cars and cruise lines in the package offer. They facilitate the extraction of valuable insights from diverse data sources, presenting a coherent and comprehensible overview of the data. Beyond just data representation, knowledge graphs improve search experiences by providing targeted, contextualized information in answer to queries. By linking disparate data sources, these graphs establish a cohesive data perspective and aid in the identification of intricate patterns. Ultimately, knowledge graphs enable the discovery of fresh data insights, thereby enhancing decision-making processes and strategic planning.

User data and product details form a complex graph. In this graph, nodes represent users, products, and attributes, while edges show the relationships among them. With product knowledge graphs, an airline or hotel can map the relationship between travelers and all products as a function of the context for travel to determine product recommendations. It is an alternative to the standard approach of fine tuning an offer based only on the purchase history of the airline product.

A recommendation engine based on a AI-based reasoning model uses large language models, to offer personalized suggestions. It goes beyond pattern matching with collaborative filtering or content-based filtering methods using historical purchase data, by understanding user behavior and context. This approach considers the strong relationships between items, user choices, and specific situations, leading to better recommendations.

Reasoning models work in recommendation engines by building a knowledge graph. In this graph, user data and product details are organized, with nodes representing users, products, and attributes. The edges show how these elements are connected. When a user requests a recommendation, the LLM reviews their profile, the current context, and relevant information from the knowledge graph to provide recommendations.

6.17.1 A Simplified Example of a Travel Graph

Facebook has the world's largest social graph, also referred to as a Facebook Graph to understand and organize relationships between people, groups, pages, and topics on its platform. It includes information about topics such as movies, music, and destinations that Facebook users care about. This graph helps personalize user experiences, power search functionality, and improve various aspects of the platform.

Figure 6.11 illustrates an example of a travel graph.

Social site APIs from Facebook and LinkedIn for example, can determine that Ann and Judy are friends. It can also determine that Judy and Ross are friends. The hotel stays at the Seaside Inn, Kennebunk Beach, Maine and The Palms, Miami Beach, Florida are sourced from the Guest Name Record (GNR). Information about the hotels is derived from curated content and descriptive ontology derived from sources such as hotel websites, social media platforms, and email marketing. The fact that the Seaside Inn and The Palms are similar is derived from clickstream data available from OTA websites. "SIMILAR" is synonymous with "LIKE" and indicates that customers who have stated at the Seaside Inn will also like The Palms because of their many similar attributes such as star rating and beachfront access.

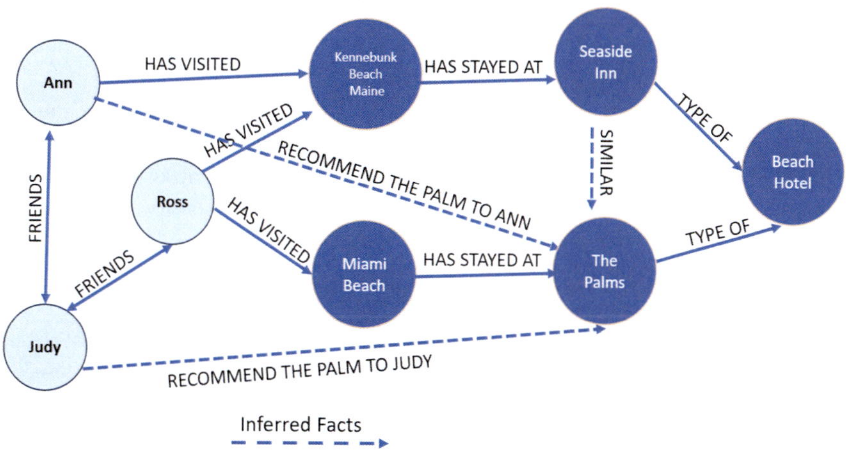

Fig. 6.11 An example of a travel graph

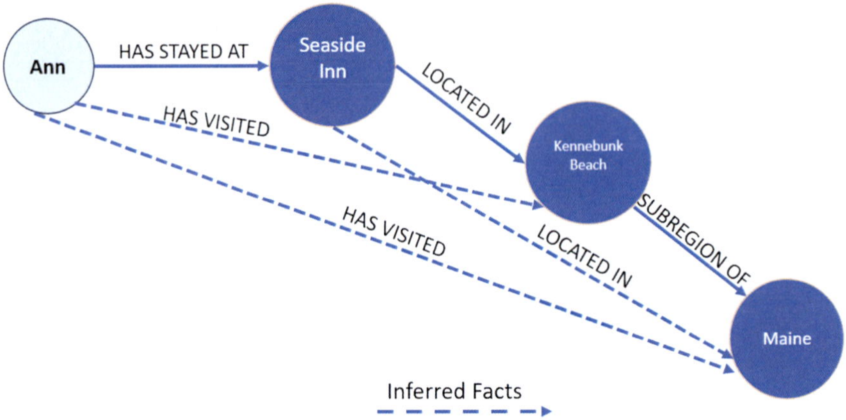

Fig. 6.12 Inferred facts from a knowledge graph

The dashed arrows represent the inferences drawn from the knowledge graph. For example, it can be inferred that both the Seaside Inn and The Palms are beach hotels.

Figure 6.12 provides another example of inferred facts from a knowledge graph. The edges represent relationships between entities or nodes. From the knowledge graph it can be inferred that Ann has visited Kennebunk Beach, Ann has visited Maine, and the Seaside Inn is located in Maine.

6.17.2 Knowledge Graph Generators

A knowledge graph consists of nodes, which represent entities like people, places, or organizations, and edges, which show how these entities are connected. To build these edges, the relationships mentioned in the text must be first determined. This is done by identifying subject-relation-object triplets. The subject is usually a named entity, such as a person or organization. The relation describes an action or connection, often shown by a verb. The object is another entity linked to the subject through that verb. These triplets form the core structure of the knowledge graph.

There are several knowledge graph generators in the market that turn raw, unstructured text into visual graphs of entities and their connections. These tools help reveal relationships in complex data by making them easy to explore visually. Instead of reading through dense text, users can interact with the graph to see how things are linked.

6.17.3 Knowledge Graphs and Data Privacy

Knowledge graphs support compliance with the European Union's Generalized Data Protection Regulation (GDPR) and the California Consumer Privacy Act (CCPA) by organizing data into connected structures. This makes it easier to find, check, and manage data. They assist organizations in tracking where data comes from, how different data pieces relate, and who gave consent. This improves data management and reduces risks.

Knowledge graphs link consent records to individual people. This helps quickly see who agreed to what and when. They also make it easier to handle compliance tasks like deleting data. A graph can show which datasets contain user data and guide the steps to remove it when needed.

6.17.4 Large Language Models and Knowledge Graphs

On March 15, 2022, the Large Language Model (LLM) GPT-3.5 was introduced by OpenAI, quickly attracting attention from various sectors. This event marked a significant step forward in AI development. Initial results from GPT-3.5 suggest it is a key milestone in creating more general-purpose models that the community has been seeking. Following its success, many companies and organizations developed their own LLMs in the past two years. These models have shown significant abilities in understanding and generating text that resembles human writing, creating new opportunities.

LLMs function as black boxes, making it hard to understand how they reach their conclusions. This opaqueness presents challenges, since clear explanations are essential. There are instances where LLM outputs may defy human logic or include inaccuracies, commonly referred to as hallucinations by inventing information. This is an issue for airline retailing in the realm of generating offers.

A significant issue with large language models (LLM) is consistent reliability and requires human intervention to review the recommendation and take corrective action.

Large language models (LLMs) learn from vast amounts of data, but they don't use airline-specific data. Retrieval-Augmented Generation (RAG) is an AI framework that combines Generative AI models with information retrieval systems. RAG addresses the issue with inaccurate predictions by adding custom data to the LLMs, resulting in the creation of more accurate, relevant, and up-to-date text. It addresses the issue of general data used by LLMs by incorporating specific information. This approach enhances answer quality by utilizing specific data sources.

GraphRAG or Graph-based Retrieval Augmented Generation uses knowledge graphs to retrieve information from external data sources, like databases or knowledge bases. It is an improvement over traditional RAG systems which are limited to linear retrieval methods. It combines the power of knowledge graphs, semantic search and language models. This information is used to improve the accuracy of

LLM responses. GraphRAG also supports complex queries by retrieving interconnected information across nodes and edges. It minimizes hallucinations, is verifiable, and deals with connected data.

In the airline offer management space, static data used by LLMs for a vast number of applications will never work. What is required is real-time airline data sourced through APIs to calibrate the LLMs. This can improve the quality of the recommendations but is by no means fool proof and erroneous results can still be observed. Effective guardrails to constrain the recommendations produced can improve the overall outcome of LLMs.

If the airline industry is serious about LLMs, they must be trained to address complex reasoning that is very prevalent in air transportation [Liu, 2024]. To achieve this, an airline industry consortium must be assembled to develop domain specific LLMs, built on top of existing large scale models and calibrated for specialized tasks. This will require experimental evaluation of existing LLMs for fact-retrieval accuracy, complex reasoning, and explanatory skills to select a baseline model augmented with domain specific features.

6.18 Corporate Travel Versus Leisure Travel

Corporate travel is managed travel and fulfilling requirements for compliance with corporate travel policy and management of booked itineraries adda a unique dimension and complexity. Despite the perceived increasing demand for personalized experiences, achieving true personalization in corporate airline travel can be challenging due to several factors. They are:

1. Lack of Context. Within corporate booking tools, at the point of purchase airlines often do not have information about the corporate traveler's preferences and specific needs for the trip. Airlines do not have visibility into the loyalty status of the traveler, if the individual is a seasoned traveler, a first-time traveler, or a CEO. This makes it a challenger to present targeted offers.
2. Data Fragmentation. Corporate travel data is often fragmented across several systems such as corporate booking platforms, expense management applications, corporate travel policy, and loyalty programs, making it difficult to gain a holistic view of the traveler and their preferences, making the ability to make actionable insights for personalization a significant challenge.
3. Corporate Policy and Personalization. A corporate traveler's preferences may be in conflict with the established travel policies and budget constraints.
4. A persona-based personalization may be the best recourse instead of personalization at the individual level. This allows for a degree of personalization while respecting corporate policies and cost control measures.

For these reasons, most of the innovation in personalization and 1:1 offers is limited to leisure travel. In the future, the objective of NDC is to create a more dynamic and personalized travel experience for corporate travelers based on corporate traveler information received from the travel agent. Customer details like loyalty numbers are optional fields in an NDC booking request that can be provided to the airline for an NDC booking. This will, in theory, provide airlines with a capability to offer customized content and services while also streamlining the booking and servicing process.

In the leisure sector, the landscape of customer loyalty has evolved. Travelers show more allegiance to travel suppliers offering competitive prices and top-notch customer-centric experiences. This is a direct result of greater price transparency and convenient booking options. Airlines are finding it difficult to adapt to these shifting preferences and heightened consumer demands. Despite this, airlines now have a greater focus on leisure passengers. They know that custom experiences build customer loyalty. For vacation travelers, airlines use simple personalization. This includes targeted email campaigns based on past travel history. Frequent flyers get preferred seats. Loyalty rewards are also customized. But these old methods often do not meet traveler needs. Passengers want easy, current, and context-aware interactions. Airlines currently struggle to provide this.

6.19 Personalization of Offers

Personalization is a term that can be applied at different levels of aggregation. At the heart of NDC, the intent is to personalize the offers for an individual customer. It is a value proposition articulated by IATA as a core benefit of NDC.

Is personalization for a segment of ONE, myth or reality?

In travel, the context for making a trip influences a customer's preferences and propensity to buy ancillary products and services. Customer segmentation based on context is also called trip-purpose segmentation (TPS). The TPS can be augmented with additional attributes such as the primary purpose for the trip such as weekend getaway for two, attending a wedding, college reunion, etc. to make the offer even more precise. This, however, will require a customer to consent to provide additional data on intent and specifics of the trip to the airline. Creating personalized offers begins with context for travel-based segmentation of the customer base. This is a core input into a recommendation engine to generate offers that resonate with customers. Most online users are anonymous when they begin their search for a flight or a hotel room, yet the offers generated should be relevant. Once the person is declared, historical bookings associated with the customer that are stored on the customer profile can be used to improve the recommendation and even offer a discount for the total offer based on customer traits such as total spend on ancillary products or customer's projected lifetime value.

The context for travel-based segmentation to cluster customers together with similar preferences and generate an aggregate offer is foundational to airline offer management. It is the single most important concept for effective offer management.

However, how feasible is personalization of the offer for a segment of ONE? For example, consider full-service carriers (FSC) in the U.S. like American and United who have stated that over 50% of an airline's revenue came from 85%–87% of its customers who flew only once. This also means that for FSCs, true 1:1 personalization is limited to loyal business flyers and high-end leisure travelers that are part of the 13%–15% of customers who generate half the airline's revenues. This information was stated by Scott Kirby when he was first president at American Airlines. On an October 25, 2015, conference call with stock market analysts, Kirby stated that half of American's revenue in the previous year came from 87% of its customers, who only flew the airlines once. He went on to state that 50% of the company's revenue comes from passengers "for whom air travel is largely a commodity" [Yanofsky, 2015]. A year later, Kirby was President at United Airlines when he confirmed that 85% of United's customers fly less than once a year, and like American, account for close to 50% of revenue [Zhang, 2016]. The importance of retaining customers who spend the most money cannot be understated, while the airline maintains a positive relationship with the rest of the customer base.

Another hurdle to personalization for a segment of ONE is the enactment of General Data Protection Regulation (GDPR) on May 25, 2018, which gives EU citizens control over their data, what is collected and how it is used. GDPR is a legal framework that governs how organizations can collect and process personal data. The GDPR applies to organizations that operate within the European Union (EU) and to those outside the EU that offer goods or services to EU residents.

With GDPR, models that work with aggregated data instead of individual personal data are more relevant which implies that personalization may be limited to creating offers at the trip-purpose segment level of detail, instead of the individual.

The U.S. equivalent of the GDPR is the California Consumer Privacy Act (CCPA) of 2018. It is a state statute that gives residents in California more control over their personal data collected by businesses. In November 2020, the CCPA was amended which added new additional privacy protections that began on January 1, 2023. Drivers of change in digital advertising and personalization are legislative actions to protect consumer privacy. This brings us to the importance of personal identity and how it is managed.

6.19.1 Personalization of Offers When Number in Party is Greater Than One

To create a personalized offer, it is important to understand the travelers involved. In direct sales channels, where a traveler asks for an offer, this process is simpler since most websites allow users to log in to their profiles. This approach works well when only one person is traveling. However, if there are several passengers together, how do we recognize them? Should we tailor the offer for just one traveler and exclude the others? Ot should the offer presented to the primary traveler also be offered to all members of the group?

Travel agencies lack access to airline passenger profiles, and the NDC system does not offer features like IndividualListRQ() or IndividualViewRS(). This limitation poses a challenge. Airlines have passengers' profiles and preferences, while travel agencies are unable to identify individual travelers. One possible solution is to ask passengers for their loyalty numbers and enter them manually, but this only works if a loyalty system is in place. Today, no airline direct websites exist that allows users to select multiple passengers before creating a personalized offer.

Personalizing offers for groups of travelers is a challenging task that remains to be addressed. A system that links loyalty profiles or allows travelers to enter their information manually is a necessary first step, but this would need cooperation between airlines and travel agencies.

6.20 The Complexity of Designing the Agency Storefront

The GDSs have a desktop application, and the storefront represents the manner in which multi-airline content is displayed. Content consists of several components including branded fares, ancillaries, fare rules, and amenities. While many TMCs that subscribe to a GDS use the GDS desktop some of the larger agencies have invested in their own agency desktop applications.

The types of data used by intermediaries to display offers to customers when a search request is submitted is shown in Fig. 6.13.

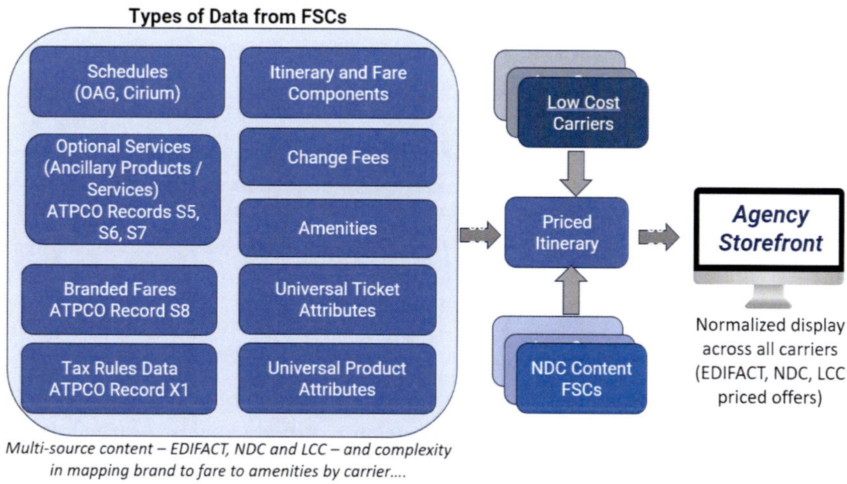

Fig. 6.13 Mapping carrier content for the agency storefront

6.20.1 Types of Data

When a travel agent submits a shopping request for offers from origin to a destination, several types of data are required and processed to create a shopping response.

A key source of the data to display on an agency desktop, the storefront, is sourced from ATPCO, GDS shopping algorithms for EDIFACT content and airline shopping algorithms for NDC content depend on this data. This is shown in Fig. 6.13.

ATPCO uses a hierarchical approach to data, starting with the most granular data in Fare Rules and moving to broader classifications in Branded Fares and Optional Services.

In today's hybrid era that will entail content being sourced from GDS EDIFACT, NDC content from airlines, and content from LCCs that must be normalized for display to a travel agent. This is a complex problem to solve due to the multidimensional nature of the problem. With fare attributes, ancillaries, and amenities in the mix, it is difficult if not impossible to reach consensus with airlines on the value of the attributes for scoring purposes and herein lies the challenge. GDSs have a content curation layer (CCL) to eliminate duplicate itineraries and related inconsistencies followed with a product normalization process to rank the offers based on their utility to customers.

6.20.1.1 Schedules

Official Airline Guide (OAG) and Cirium are the two most common aggregators of schedules in the airline industry. Intermediaries and airlines have a dynamic schedules capability to generate itineraries on demand based on the origin and destination of the shopping request.

6.20.1.2 Itinerary and Fare Components

Travel itineraries are generated dynamically from the schedule based on the requested departure date and return date. Connections will fulfill the minimum connect time identified in the schedule. Fare components associated with the itinerary are required to price the itinerary. The shopping algorithm determines the fare components in the itinerary and the resultant itinerary price.

6.20.1.3 Optional Service Fees

Ancillary products and services are also frequently referred to as optional services. Examples of optional services are checked bags, inflight meals, seat selection, lounge access, etc. Optional services are stored in ATPCO records S5, S6, and S7. Record S5 is used to identify the ancillary products that an airline offers, such as baggage fees, seat upgrades, etc. S5 records are often used in conjunction with S7 records, which define the conditions (provisions) and pricing of the ancillary services. S6 is a concurrence record for optional services and specifies which airline's rules rules apply when multiple airlines are involved in the itinerary.

6.20.1.4 Branded Fares

Branded fares data is stored in Record S8. This record specifies the mapping of attributes and ancillaries associated with each branded fare product. Branded fares can be used to create upsell opportunities within a single cabin, allowing airlines to offer a range of products and services to different types of travelers.

Data for certain categories like Same-day Change, Seat Selection, Check-in Priority, Boarding Priority, Upgrade Eligibility, Lounge Access, Loyalty Rewards, Transferable Funds are sourced from Branded Fares if the airline files data for these categories.

6.20.1.5 Tax Rules Data

The tax rules in Record X1 are used to determine the amount of taxes to be collected on a ticket based on the flight's origin, destination, and other relevant factors.

6.20.1.6 Change Fees

Airline change and cancellation policies, including fee data, are sourced from Fare Rules and Branded Fares in ATPCO. Fare Rules is the primary source for advance change and cancellation data. Data for certain categories such as Same-day Change are sourced from Branded Fares.

6.20.1.7 Amenities

In 2019, ATPCO acquired Routehappy, an airline merchandising content platform. It uses an Amenities API to provide airlines, GDSs, and OTAs with detailed cabin amenity data, including information about seat features, aircraft types, Wi-Fi, entertainment, power outlets, and food/beverage services. The Routehappy categories are aircraft type, beverage, carry-on baggage, change fee, checked baggage, CO_2 emissions, entertainment, food, layout of aircraft (e.g., 2–3-2), lounge access, loyalty rewards, power, priority baggage, priority boarding, priority check-in, refundability, same-day change, seat pitch, seat selection, transferable funds, upgrade eligibility, and Wi-Fi.

6.20.1.8 Universal Ticket Attributes

UTAs are sourced from ATPCO's fares, branded fares, and optional services filings, and are processed into concise merchandising content. UTAs may include information on the refundability of a fare, baggage allowances, or any restrictions that apply. The UTA category, Loyalty Rewards, highlights potential mileage accrual benefits. Access to UTAs are through the Routehappy API.

6.20.1.9 Universal Product Attributes

Universal Product Attributes are a type of Routehappy content that use visual elements to describe airline fares, products, and services. UPAs use a variety of visual mediums including messaging, images, videos, and cabin tours to bring airline offers to life. UPAs help airlines differentiate their offerings and showcase benefits of their products beyond just price. Allowing airlines to communicate key features and benefits of their offers drives conversion and opportunities for upsell. UPA content can be precisely targeted based on aircraft, cabin class, route, time of day, fare type, and more, ensuring that customers receive relevant information.

6.20.2 The Storefront

Developing a storefront that displays multi-sourced content with the various types of data used to create an offer is a challenging task. The expectation for airlines is that customers see every class of service and every price point that can be offered in every search request.

When ATPCO launched the Next Generation Storefront initiative in 2019, the Sabre 360 agency desktop application only displayed one fare product per itinerary in the search and brands were shown only at time of pricing. With this approach there was no confusion about airline specific brands. When brands are displayed at time of pricing, the comparison was based only on fares and schedules across airlines. It also prevented upselling at time of shopping. Sabre's air shopping APIs supported multiple brands and multiple fares shopping that returned all brands and one fare per brand applicable per itinerary with brand descriptions and upsell options. However there was no guidance for comparing brands across carriers. The API shortfalls include the small number of fare attributes, and the absence of seat quality and amenities.

This contrasts with the airline direct channel which displayed all product offerings (multiple brands) at time of itinerary selection. The airline direct channel also supports rich visual and description of the on-board experience and services. It is easier for the airline direct channel to display offers and details in this way since it is a single airline's homogenous content.

Primary challenges for a multi-source display of offers are:

1. Multiple content sources. Today all GDSs multi-source their content for each shopping request and include EDIFACT content, NDC content from the FSC carriers, and low-cost carrier content from the LCC carriers.
2. The quality of the in-flight experience varies by airline brand and cabin.
3. Content returned from airlines for each shopping request is non-homogenous, making it difficult to compare offers across multiple carriers.
4. An airline's products are targeted toward different buyer personas.

This presents a unique opportunity to coherently display all relevant products in a normalized way early in the search process to enable easy comparison shopping

6.20.3 ATPCO Next Generation Storefront with Shelves and Drawers

The ATPCO Next Generation Storefront (NGS) initiative was the first attempt to standardize what indirect distribution channels display. The underlying objective was to take some or all of the data shown in Fig. 6.13 and normalize it for display in a standard format from multiple airlines for travel agencies, online booking tools, GDS agency desktops, and third party aggregators to enhance their retailing displays.

NGS begins with a definition of attributes. An attribute is a quality or feature regarded as a characteristic of a specific NGS Offer. This can be broken down into Qualification Attributes and Non-Qualification Attributes.

Qualification Attributes are used to determine the Shelf placement. Non-Qualification Attributes do not define Shelf placement but will be included as part of the standard Drawer content.

Search results from the shopping query submitted by an agent are presented in a organized manner consisting of multiple offers from multiple airlines. The storefront consists of shelves and drawers as outlined by ATPCO.

6.20.3.1 Shelves

The shelves are a display grid with rows and columns. Each row contains offers from a single airline. The columns represent the grouping of offers based on product attributes such as refundability and leg room. If we can standardize product attributes into a generic definition such as Basic Economy, Economy, Premium Economy and Business, these represent the columns. If an airline does not meet the minimum criteria for a column, the shelf will remain empty.

Product placement on a shelf is based on the qualifying attributes. Each attribute has a corresponding set of values that define the order of the shelf from left to right. For the U.S. domestic market, the proposed attributes were

- Seat Type. Angle Lie Flat, Full Flat Seat, Middle Seat Free, Private Suite, Recliner Seat, Skycouch, and Standard Seat.
- Seat Pitch in inches
- Advance Seat Selection permitted or restricted
- Carry-on Allowance for a charge, free, or not permitted
- Advance Changes indicates the ability to change the itinerary for free
- Cabin Type: Business, Economy, First, Premium Business, Premium Economy, and Premium First.

As a data-agnostic open standard, the objective of NGS was not to dictate how the data must be presented but limited to placement of offers into shelves. The channels determine how the shelves should be arranged along with the composition of the drawer attributes based on their customer base, and preferences.

In many ways, the NGS problem resembles fitting a square peg into a round hole. For example, seat assignment and baggage allowance are more important for a family traveling to visit friends and relatives; while for a business traveler, changeability is important and baggage allowance is not important. To arrive at a universal consensus on the standards is an impossible task.

6.20.3.2 Drawers

Since the shelf lacks space for all the details of the offer, it includes a drawer. This drop-down list shows qualification attributes and non-qualification attributes. The non-qualification attributes add details to the offer but do not affect placement. Each leg of an NGS offer has its own drawer.

The non-qualification attributes are:

- Access to an aisle from every cabin seat.
- Beverage: Alcoholic/Nonalcoholic, free/paid.
- Entertainment cost and type: Live TV, Loop, On-Demand, Overhead, Pre-Download, Seatback, Streaming, Tablet.
- Food cost and type: Light Meal, Meal, Premium Meal, Premium Snack, Snack.
- Power type: Adapter, a power outlet, USB port.
- Wi-Fi cost and what it supports: Email and Messaging, live streaming, web browsing;
- Checked Baggage allowance according to IATA Resolution 302/DOT regulations.[1]
- Lounge Access availability and its cost.
- CO_2 emissions.[2]
- Priority Boarding availability and its cost.
- Ability to get a refund and its cost.

In addition to the standard NGS attributes, sales channels can add additional data such as other airline, or flight-specific information in the drawer. However, this data will not influence the shelf placement algorithm.

6.20.3.3 Star Rating

The NGS initiative uses a star rating system (1–6 stars) to indicate product quality or value, allowing the channels to sort products into similar groups or "shelves" based on attributes like seat pitch, baggage, and fare limitations.

One Star Rating (*)
Basic economy seats, no seat selection, no carry-on baggage.
Two Star Rating (**)
Seats with up to 34-inch seat pitch, seat selection and carry-on baggage are allowed.

[1] IATA Resolution 302, effective since April 1, 2011, determines which airline's baggage rules (free allowance and charges) apply to interline journeys (flights on multiple airlines with a single ticket) using the concept of the Most Significant Carrier (MSC).

[2] Ues IATA's CO_2 Connect fuel-based calculator to show precise carbon emissions data.

Three Star Rating (***)
Seats with at least 34-inch seat pitch, seat selection and carry-on baggage are allowed.
Four Star Rating (****)
Reclining seats, seat selection and carry-on baggage are allowed. These are typically premium, business, or first class seats.
Five Star Rating (*****)
Lie-flat seats or a pod, seat selection and carry-on baggage are allowed.
Six Star Rating (******)
Lie-flat suite with aisle access, seat selection and carry-on baggage are allowed.

There are several issues with the star ratings shown above because they are dominated by seat comfort and it was not well received. Star ratings for hotels are also not well accepted, and customers prefer authenticated user ratings (not TripAdvisor or Trustpilot). Many large agencies simply want to use Storefront as a dynamic filtering mechanism specified by the travel agent. For example, "show me all non-refundable products on Shelf 1, all products with free bags on Shelf 2, and premium classes on Shelf 3."

Subtle differences in data provided by various carriers and travel policy requirements from corporate channels contribute to the difficulty in reaching consensus from all constituents on a universal rating system to reflect product quality and value.

Here are a few examples:

A corporate travel agency will not want to display the 1-star rating on their corporate booking tool or agency desktop since they are not applicable for business travelers.

From a corporate travel perspective, this is a fundamental change and could lead to corporate travel buyer angst because of the upsell capability of NGS which may be a violation of travel policy. The NGS storefront algorithm displays by default Premium Economy and First Class which may be out of policy for a corporation. Similarly, the corporation may allow travelers to book fares that are a percentage higher than the lowest available fare, but NGS by its very nature actively drives customers toward the more expensive bookings. For example, a traveler may book a higher fare that is within the threshold of the lowest fare because it includes baggage though the fare differential is far greater than paying for a checked bag with the lower fare.

Some fare products fall into different star categories owing to subtle differences. For example, LCC fares are lumped with FSC Basic Economy fares on the one-star shelf. This sounds reasonable at first, but there are subtle differences because the fares from LCC Frontier Airlines which are changeable for a fee while FSC Basic Economy fares are not [Habtemariam, 2019].

After several iterations with airlines and intermediaries in a working group, ATPCO is no longer enforcing the algorithm they developed for shelf placement. ATPCO sunset the NGS shelf placement algorithm but continues to maintain the NGS standard and now advocate channels to develop their own shelf placement algorithms and make their own decisions based on customer needs and preferences. TMCs and GDS desktop applications now personalize the content on the shelves based on traveler profiles, past booking behavior, and travel policies, ensuring a more tailored shopping experience. Hence, these storefronts supported by the various channels will all have their unique flair. For example, taking inspiration from ATPCO's Next Generation Storefront, Sabre launched their version called New Airline Storefront (NAS) in March 2021 [Sabre, 2021].

6.20.4 Product Normalization in the Storefront

The GDS storefronts have a content curation layer (CCL) to merge the EDIFACT, NDC, and LCC content, eliminate duplicates and redundancies. This is called content normalization.

Content normalization is followed by an optional step called product normalization. Product normalization is the science of determining the intrinsic value of disparate (non-homogenous} offers provided by various airlines. Product normalization is carried out with a calibrated consumer choice model (CCM) that can determine the marginal value of each component of an airline's offer. The estimated value of each airline offer influences the order in which offers are displayed in the storefront.

In the consumer direct channel, airlines can showcase their branded fare products and support upsell across brands and à la carte pricing. The core issue with branded fares and ancillaries is that there are no standards for what constitutes a branded fare or an ancillary product or service. With the absence of standardization of branded fare products and ancillaries across airlines, how does the GDS support comparison shopping for a travel agency when they must display non-homogenous content from several airlines in the agency desktop display? This problem is not specific to NDC and will continue after the adoption of NDC.

Value scoring of itineraries and offers with non-homogenous content from carriers is the first step toward normalizing content for display on an agency desktop. Techniques such as choice models. hedonic regression [Bacon et al., 2016] or other methods can be used to normalize the content and determine the display order of the itineraries based on value.

While the content displayed will never be identical to content on an airline website, the fundamental goal is to provide a comparison-shopping framework based on attributes associated with each "shelf" of the agency desktop. A shelf is screen real estate on the agency desktop that is designated with a selection of schedule, fare and comfort attributes and their minimum levels for an airline offer to be classified for display in that shelf.

Estimating value of an itinerary and the offer is complicated by the fact that airlines promote branded fare products, and each branded fare product has a collection of attributes associated with it. To score the value of an itinerary, the marginal value of each ancillary product is required [Szymanski & Darrow, 2021]. This is frequently a challenge since many branded fares have bundled many of the same attributes together. For example, a branded fare with priority boarding almost always includes free bags, making it difficult to disentangle the value of priority boarding vs free bags. An approach to determine the marginal value of each ancillary product is to conduct surveys. Surveys are based on stated preferences and may not be an accurate representation of the market.

Implicitly determining the value of each attribute from sales data is the preferred approach but sometimes difficult to calibrate due to the absence of sufficient data. Survey based approaches are not perfect since there is no guarantee that the participant taking the survey is not giving a biased or faulty response. Survey participants should be preselected to represent the *typical* traveler based on criteria such as *traveled for business at least n times in the last 12-months, take leisure trips,* and ensure a good distribution of age, gender, and region. While crowd sourcing approaches such as Amazon Mechanical Turk [Mortensen & Hughes, 2018] and market research firms like Dynata and Qualtrics can be used in practice. A better approach is for travel entities to build the survey sampling feature directly into the airline website or agency desktop application so that surveys can be presented to every *n-th* customer to support continuous calibration.

An approach is to use a choice-based conjoint (CBC) survey analysis to determine the value of each itinerary based on a customer's willingness to pay. Survey participants are asked to book bundles that include experimentally generated itineraries and sets of ancillaries. CBC is a specialized survey technique which closely simulates the consumer selection process for products in competitive contexts [Orme & Chrzan, 2017]. Survey respondents are shown a set of itinerary options and asked to make a purchase selection. Participants view products which consist of various attributes (e.g., seat comfort) made up of multiple levels of the product (extra leg room, standard seat, 127-degree reclining seat, etc.). Each attribute included in the product will have multiple levels associated with it. A price point is also associated with each level in the display. From the survey, based on how respondents evaluated products in response to changes in attribute levels, the impact of each attribute (the ancillary) on product performance can be estimated. The utility of the ancillary products can be determined using the Hierarchical Bayes (HB) choice modeling technique as it models preferences heterogeneity at the individual survey participant level. By aggregating the HB model utilities, the significance of each ancillary can be determined on a normalized scale from 0 to 1. An easier way to interpret the ancillary utilities is to convert it into dollar equivalent terms which is the customer's willingness to pay for the ancillary product or service.

A more detailed explanation of stated preference-based methods can be found in Sect. 6.5.

6.20.5 The New Airline Storefront (NAS) Controversy

The American Airlines lawsuit against Sabre [American Airlines, Inc Plaintiff vs Sabre, 2021] serves as a prime illustration of the intricate process of managing diverse airline content for display on an agency desktop while ensuring the satisfaction of all airlines. Because of the limited real estate on the agency desktop and the desire to determine the most relevant attributes to include in the display, it is a heavily constrained problem. In many ways, it is like fitting a square peg into a round hole.

In April 2021, Sabre introduced the New Airline Storefront (NAS), designed to make comparison shopping for airline products easier by grouping the itineraries returned from shopping requests into virtual shelves based on similar product attributes. However, in June 2021, American Airlines sought a court order in Texas to prevent Sabre from deploying the NAS display in GDS shopping results. American Airlines claimed that the new storefront exhibited a bias toward its competitor, Delta Air Lines [Silk, 2021c; Skift, 2021].

American also requested the court to prohibit Sabre from paying higher incentives to travel agents for selling high-valued Delta products than the incentives offered for selling American's high-valued products.

American and Sabre have a tangled history. In November 2022 [Boehmer, 2022], the Texas court that had overseen the breach-of-contract lawsuit by American dismissed the case with prejudice.

6.21 The Airline Retailing Catalog

A catalog is a fundamental requirement for airline retailing. A retail catalog, also known as a product catalog, enables airlines to centralize product information and manage their offers consisting of flights, ancillaries, and amenities. A standardized framework streamlines the entire order management process. Creating and managing a catalog is of strategic importance to an airline. The business rules and content in the catalog is the secret sauce that enables differentiation.

As a core component of the offer-order transformation, a product catalog allows airlines to efficiently create, manage, and distribute personalized offers that are differentiated from the competitors. A catalog must be flexible and be able to manage dynamic content like labels, graphics, and videos, empowering airlines to maximize their retailing capabilities and potential.

In the NDC era where airlines control the creation of all offers for distribution through all channels, the retail catalog is of critical importance. The catalog serves as the single source of truth and ensures travelers see consistent, accurately priced products regardless of channel. It is a central place to manage all products and services. Robust settings let the catalog manage even complex products. Accurate product details supported with rich content streamlines the offer management process and simplifies the fulfillment process across partners by providing a consistent, repeatable end-tp-end shopping experience from low-fare search to delivery.

Google's ITA software that powers the shopping service for many airline websites maintains a catalog to support its shopping service for its airline customers. Enterprise vendors, and other third-party vendors all maintain a retail catalog for their customers. Examples of well-known product catalogs are FLX Product Catalog, SabreMosaic Product Catalog, Amadeus Nevio Product Catalog, Datalex Product Catalogue, and the IBS Software iRetail Product Catalogue to name a few.

6.21.1 Product Catalog and Reservations Inventory Control

In airline retailing, a product catalog is a centralized repository that defines all the products and services an airline can offer, including flights, ancillaries, and third-party goods, while a stock keeper manages the real-time inventory of these items.

Ideally, all inventory-controlled items in the catalog must be stored on the host CRS inventory control system. This facilitates real-time inventory management that tracks the availability of all products and services defined in the catalog. Together, these systems provide a single source of truth for offers, allowing for dynamic pricing, bundling, personalized experiences, and efficient fulfillment across all channels.

For example, many airlines charge for various seat types. Pre-reserved seats in a reservation system appear on seat maps as consumed (often person icons or 'X's), showing seats booked during or before check-in, while available seats allow a traveler to choose or pay for upgrades (extra legroom, preferred). The available count of seats by seat type must be tracked in the airline's host CRS inventory system. For example, the number of aisle seats, window seats, bulkhead seats, and exit row seats that are available for sale (not booked) must be tracked in the reservation inventory control system. This will require message updates between Pre-reserved Seats (PRS) domain where the seat maps are stored in the reservation system and the reservations inventory system. When a seat is consumed (or unconsumed) on the seat map, inventory must be notified to update the availability count. An airline's reservations inventory system should track available seats by seat type to support seat led shopping and pricing of seats by seat type based on numbers of seats available for sale.

6.21.2 The ATPCO Product Catalog Initiative

In April 2024, ATPCO announced that they were developing a product catalog to enable airlines to move toward dynamic offers [Airoldi, 2024b]. ATPCO claims that they intend to store data at an atomic level enabling offers to be assembled dynamically and avoid filing several permutations of offers. A catalog, by definition, should be at an atomic level and never store various permutations of offers. Storing permutations of offers leads to an unmanageable database with many rows and this was the approach taken by tour operators several years ago to create static bundles that had to be refreshed nightly. An example of this redundancy is for the same air itinerary, they would store different room types and associated rates as separate records paired with the same air itinerary.

This is an ATPCO quote to Business Travel News [Airolid, 2024b]

> *Today an airline can only sell what they send through ATPCO, and what they send is fully formed—the price, the attributes. ATPCO CEO Alex Zoghlin told BTN. What we are doing with Product Catalog is we are breaking down all those component parts into their individual pieces, so that you can assemble them independently of having to file every possible permutation a customer may want.*

In the High-Tech, Consumer Electronics and Semi-conductor industries, every supply chain vendor has a catalog for their clients and there is always separation of product and price in the catalog schema for flexibility, which seems to be a key selling point from ATPCO for their Product Catalog. Also in these industry verticals, the enterprise catalog is always a semi-custom business. For example, no two catalogs have the same hierarchy.

In the past there have been initiatives such as the NDC Exchange and Next Gen Storefront from ATPCO, that despite the best of intentions, did not converge on a standard for mass adoption. The difficulty was in reaching consensus among the constituents. The Product Catalog falls into a similar category where it is difficult to build consensus on the nomenclature and hierarchy. The nomenclature and hierarchy organize products for easier navigation and selection during the offer creation process. In addition, it also supports inventory management for ancillary products that are capacity controlled.

Branded fares is a good example, and it never gained uniformity across the airline community and could not be standardized. This leads to non-homogenous offers being returned by NDC offers from airlines. There are no issues with branded fares or offers being uniquely displayed on an airline website since it is one-dimensional and centered around an individual airline. However, it poses a unique problem for intermediaries (e.g. GDSs) for the travel agency desktop who need a Content Curation Layer (CCL) capability, also known as content normalization, followed with product normalization before displaying offers from multiple airlines to agents.

A standardized nomenclature and schema definition for an airline retail catalog is a worthwhile cause, but it is a difficult problem to arrive at a consensus among airline constituents. The catalogs of individual airlines will always have a semi-custom element and herein lies the problem of coming up with a standard catalog.

With the existence of several airline product catalogs offered by vendors in the industry and the semi-custom nature of catalogs, it is not clear what void ATPCO intends to fill? Perhaps it is standardization of the nomenclature and catalog schema with a centralized electronic record of airline products and ancillaries?

6.21.3 Product Catalog, Offers and Orders

The airline product catalog is the secret sauce that enables airlines to differentiate themselves from the competitors. Investment in enhancing the product catalog is central to successful airline retailing.

Offers and Orders are a new framework for airline partnerships, designed to provide airlines with more control over their offers to customers to improve customer experience. This new framework allows airlines to offer and manage ancillary services with flexibility and a transparent real-time data-sharing environment. By enabling all types of partnerships. Offers and Orders give airline product catalogs the flexibility to support any combination of flights and partner services.

6.22 Why Airline Shopping Is an Integral Component of Offer Management

Air shopping is an integral component of creating offers. Offer creation begins with a search for flights from an origin to a destination. Determining the context for travel begins with air shopping when an online user or travel agent submits a shopping query to determine what options are available for booking an itinerary. The context for travel is implied from the trip-purpose segment (TPS) identified during shopping and serves as a common definition for air shopping responses and offers. This is shown in Fig. 6.14.

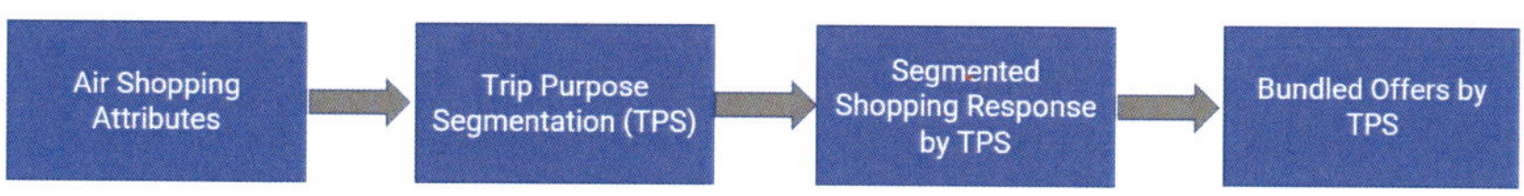

Fig. 6.14 A common definition for air shopping responses and offers

6.22.1 A Common Definition for Air Shopping and Offer Creation

Every airline can uniquely define their trip-purpose segments based on their viewpoint of their business model and customers they serve. Customer segmentation is an art and not a science. While analytical techniques such as hierarchical or other clustering models can be used to identify trip-purpose segments, the final definition of trip-purpose segments requires manual intervention from experts that truly understand their customers. Once defined, trip-purpose segment definitions should be reviewed periodically and adjusted as necessary.

Trip-purpose segmentation serves a dual purpose: to fine tune the itineraries that are returned in a shopping response and to recommend offers (bundle of ancillary products and services along with the itineraries).

Figure 6.15 illustrates the common definition of trip-purpose segmentation that is required for air shopping and offers through the direct channel (airline website).

The trip-purpose segment is identified from the shopping query which is used to generate itineraries specific to the customer segment based on their aggregate schedule and fare preferences observed from booking and/or ticketed data. The shopping response is based on filed fares which is then adjusted optionally to generate the continuous dynamic price for each itinerary followed with the bundled (offer) recommendation. The airline controls all aspects of the screen real estate on the airline website.

Figure 6.16 illustrates the common definition of trip-purpose segmentation that is required for air shopping and offers through the indirect channel (the GDS travel agency desktop). This is only applicable for NDC bookings (not EDIFACT bookings) where offers are controlled by the airline.

The trip-purpose segment is identified by the airline from the shopping query submitted by the travel agent through the NDC messaging protocol. The airline shopping algorithm generates itineraries specific to the customer segment based on aggregate schedule and fare preferences observed from booking and/or ticketed data. The shopping response is based on filed fares which are then adjusted optionally to generate the continuous dynamic price for each itinerary. This is followed with the creation of the bundled offer which is communicated to the travel agent through the NDC messaging protocol. The GDS collects data from all airlines to which the shopping query was submitted, performs content normalization followed with product normalization before the multi-airline itineraries are displayed to the travel agent. The GDS controls all aspects of the screen real estate on the travel agency desktop.

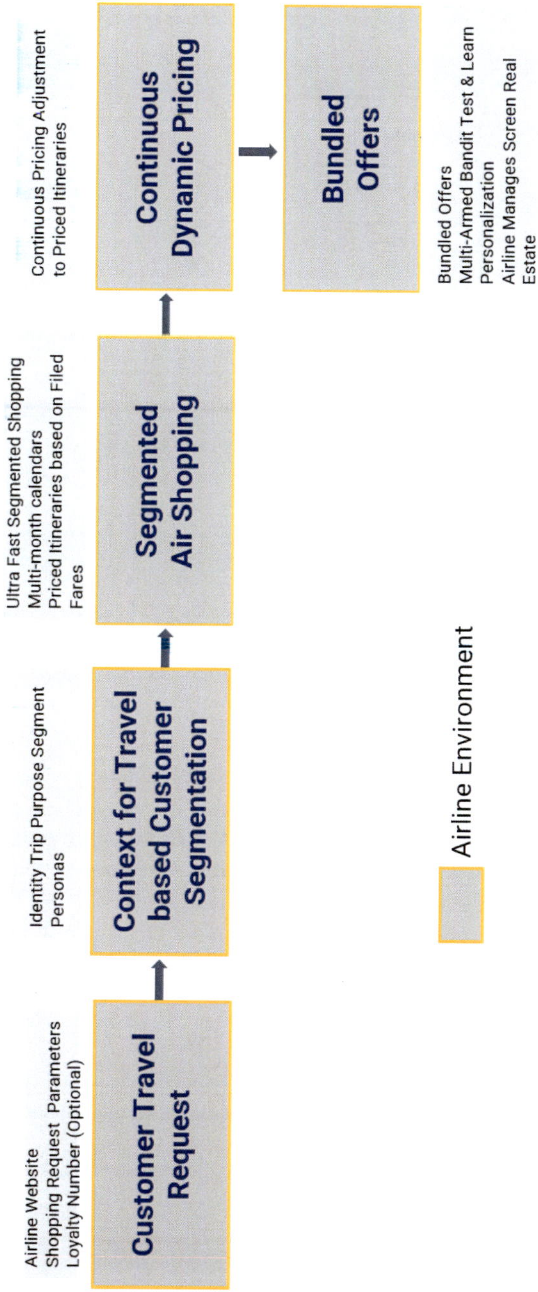

Fig. 6.15 Trip-purpose segment influenced shopping and offers for the Direct Channel

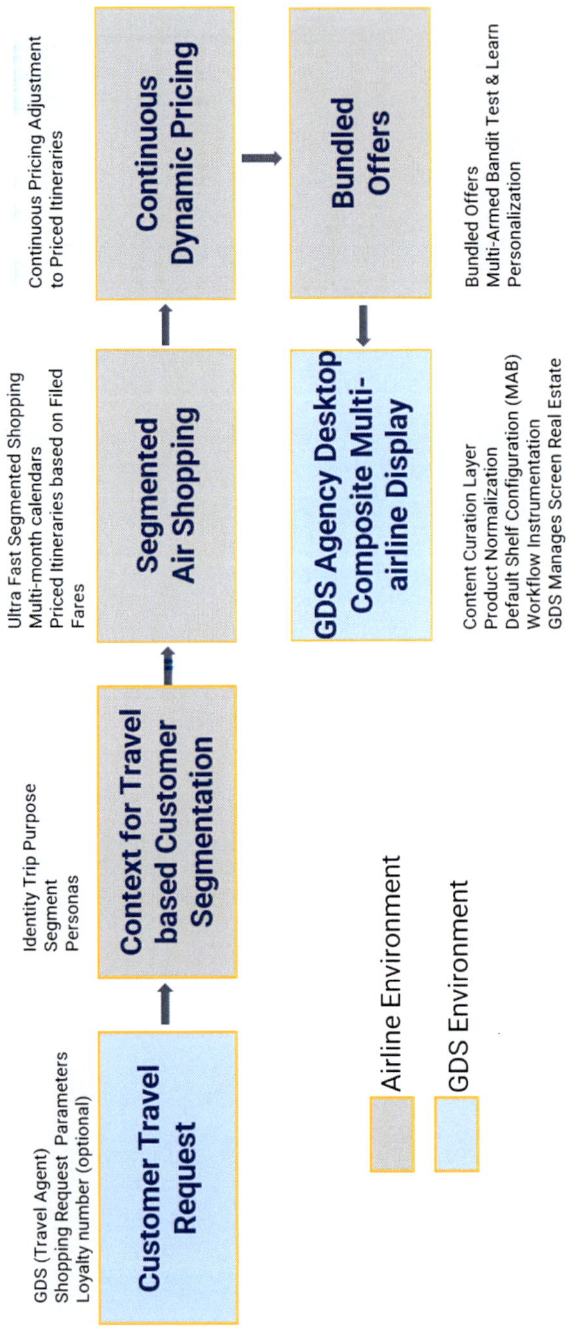

Fig. 6.16 Trip-purpose segment influenced shopping and offers for the Indirect Channel

6.22.2 Data Analytics for Segmented Shopping

Identifying a customer's trip-purpose segment from the input data in the shopping request is the first step toward personalized air shopping displays. For example, consider the following parameters that may be important for a customer to book a flight.

Historical booking and ticketed data can be used to identify dominance for each of these attributes shown below by trip-purpose segment.

1. Nonstop vs connection
2. Outbound departure time window (day parting)
3. Outbound arrival time window (day parting)
4. Inbound departure time window (day parting)
5. Inbound arrival time window (day parting)
6. Elapsed time (shortest, shortest +30%, greater than shortest +30%)
7. Fares: refundable, partially refundable, non-refundable
8. Preferred connection airports
9. Preferred connection times (e.g., less than an hour, 1–2 h, greater than 2 h)

For example consider outbound departure times. Historical booking and/or ticketed data can be used to determine the time slot that is dominant for each trip-purpose segment. These attributes can be calibrated by market, market entity or systemwide, though market or market entity are recommended. For example, Fig. 6.17 illustrates preferences for outbound departure times by trip-purpose segment (based on 7 segments).

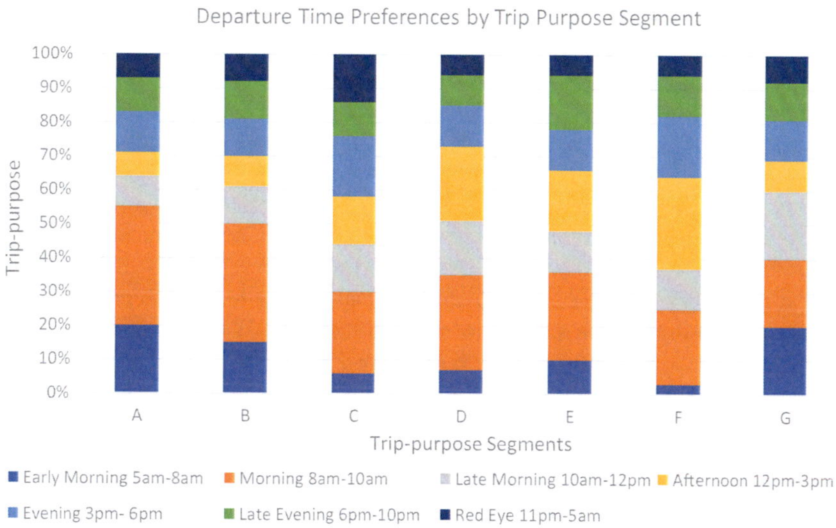

Fig. 6.17 Outbound departure time window preferences by trip-purpose segment

For example, if the customer belongs to trip-purpose segment A, the departure time slot between 8:00am and 10:00am is dominant, as observed with 35% of bookings. The air shopping algorithm should consider the pertinent parameters as input to ensure that the itineraries returned as part of the shopping response are biased toward this time range.

Similarly other schedule and fare attributes identified above can be calibrated from historical booking and/or ticketed data and used as input into the shopping algorithm to generate the most relevant priced itineraries.

6.22.3 Agentic AI, Air Shopping Look-To-Book, and the Cost of Compute

The look-to-book measure for shopping transactions is useful to understand growth in shopping volumes, the inefficiency of online channels, and planning for adequate compute capacity, which is the hardware, processors, memory, storage and energy required to generate air shopping responses. For shopping, the look-to-book ratio is simply the number of shops divided by the number of bookings. Each shop, depending on the channel parameter setting, can return itineraries that range from a few itineraries to the hundreds. Look-to-book ratios are sometimes viewed in the context of conversion rates, but it is not very meaningful since look-to-book ratios vary widely by channel. Brick-and-mortar travel agencies typically experience a 10:1 to 20:1 loo-to-book ratio while OTA's can range from 300:1 to 2,000:1 in certain markets. From that perspective, OTAs are far less productive than TMCs.

In the NDC era, Generative AI drastically increases the look-to-book ratio by enabling AI Agents to perform a high volume of automated searches for users, which pressures airline shopping engines to handle increased load at a competitive, acceptable cost per shop. Investment in an ultra-fast shopping engine with fare and rule binding concepts [Vinod, 2024a, Chapter 8] is a necessity, and not a luxury to address galloping look-to-book ratios. This is a fundamental requirement for personalized offers where a shopping cache is not an option. The fundamental change with moving from a user-initiated search model to a continuous automated model that performs thousands of automated searches, require investment in shopping algorithms, both schedule-led search and fare-led search for multi-itinerary pricing, to manage and control the cost of computing. The exponential increase in searches will significantly strain existing airline shopping platforms, requiring them to adapt their systems to handle higher loads and potentially higher costs.

Edge computing is an approach to mitigate latency in AI Agent initiated high volume searches, providing a more responsive experience. While edge computing does not solve the look-to-book problem, processing search demand closer to the requestor enables a faster, scalable, shopping experience.

In the absence of personalization for a segment of ONE, deployment of a shopping cache is also an option to mitigate extreme look-to-book ratios from Agentic AI shopping requests where individual airline shopping responses asynchronously update an Agentic AI shopping cache. The time to live for an item in the cache can be controlled by the airline based on the arrival rate of updates for pertinent shopping parameters such as Agentic AI Identifier Code, Advance Purchase, and Length of Stay (see Sect. 18.2.4.3 for scalability of NDC transactions with a p-cache maintained at the PCC level).

6.23 The Passenger Name Record

Rudimentary versions of the Passenger Name Record (PNR) existed from the dawn of commercial aviation when the reservation process was not automated. In the 1930s the *request and reply* system was used which was followed by the *sell and report* system [Vinod, 2024a, Chapter 2]. Reservations were processed manually. This involved utilizing a centralized board that showed the flight schedule for the upcoming thirty days. Employees would field phone calls for reservations, jot down passenger details, and subsequently allocate seats on the preferred flights. This was before *Reservisor*, the first automated airline reservation system which American Airlines and the Teleregister Company developed and installed in 1946.

Standards were developed initially by IATA, ICAO (International Civil Aviation Organization) and A4A (Airlines for America). However, no entity dictates a universal format for PNRs and hence data formats and structures can vary between different airlines. The current-day PNRs all originated from UNIVAC, Sabre (before PARS), and PARS (Programmed Airline Reservations System). PARS was an early proprietary IBM computer reservation system (CRS) for managing passenger bookings that most major airlines used as a baseline for their own reservations systems [Vinod, 2024a, Chapter 2]. PARS laid the groundwork for modern airline reservation and passenger service systems (PSS), which handle everything from booking to ticketing to boarding, and is considered a foundational concept for modern CRSs and GDSs.

The single most important domain in an airline's central reservations system (CRS), also known as the host CRS, since its creation by American Airlines and Sabre in 1964 has been the PNR. It is the core data record that contains a passenger's travel itinerary that includes flight segment, hotels, car rentals, special service request (SSR) and special service request inventory (SSR-I). It is identified by a unique alphanumeric reservation code called the record locator. This unique identifier is used by airlines and travel agents and has been indispensable to manage and track booking information for a single trip from the initial reservation to check-in and beyond.

There are mandatory and optional fields in PNRs. The mandatory fields are name of the passenger, itinerary for at least one segment for all passengers in the PNR, contact details for the travel agent, airline office or online passenger making the booking, ticketing details such as ticket number or ticketing time limit and booking reference which is the record locator, also known as a reservation code.

There are several optional fields such as special service requests (SSRs) for wheelchairs, bassinets, special meals, etc., handling procedures for special passengers like unaccompanied minors, frequent flyer information, credit card information, passenger email address, and personal remarks. The form of payment is an optional field which is required to issue a flight ticket and complete the booking.

Secure Flight Passenger Data (SFPD) elements on a PNR are the specific pieces of information the U.S. Transportation Security Administration (TSA) requires for passengers traveling on flights to, from, or over the United States. These include the passenger's full name (as it appears on their government-issued ID), date of birth, gender, and a Redress Number if they have one. Airlines must collect and transmit this data to TSA to conduct pre-boarding screening against watchlists.

The core functions of PNRs are summarized below.

Unique Identifier. Each PNR is assigned a unique booking reference (also known as a record locator) which allows travel agents, airlines, and customers to easily find and manage the specific booking in the CRS database.

Itinerary Management. PNRs holds all trip-related information for a passenger such as flight details, passenger names, contact information, and special requests. The specifics can vary by passenger. For example, more than one airline may be involved in the itinerary and it could be based on a codeshare agreement or interline agreement.

Connectivity and Communications. Connectivity enables different airlines and travel agents to exchange reservation information for passengers with multi-airline itineraries. For multiple legs operated by different airlines using different CRSs, their corresponding PNRs must be synchronized. Schedule changes such as cancellations and delays will also update the PNR to reflect the latest schedule.

Ancillary Services: PNRs link to electronic miscellaneous documents (EMDs) for ancillary services like baggage fees, seat upgrades, and in-flight meals, consolidating all aspects of the trip in one place.

Ticketing. A PNR is the internal record of the booking, while a ticket (E-Ticket) is the document that confirms a traveler's seat on the flight. It is a digital equivalent of a paper ticket, which became mandatory in 2008 to serve as proof of payment. Essentially, the ticket confirms the contract between the airline and the passenger.

Loyalty Programs. PNRs can be linked to a traveler's frequent flyer program, allowing for easier tracking of miles and benefits.

Enhanced Security and APIS. Advanced Passenger Information System (APIS) is an electronic data interchange system established by the CBP (U.S. Customs and Border Protection). Border security personnel can pre-screen passengers via their PNR information to potentially expedite the airport arrival process by pre-screening.

APIS governs the provision of a limited number of data elements (identification details from the passport and flight information sourced from the PNR) from commercial airlines to the computer system of the destination state. Today, the U.S.

and over 60 countries require airlines to collect advance passenger information that includes data travelers have to declare at the border control.

6.23.1 The Path Forward

The PNR that has the details of the passenger itinerary, the Electronic Miscellaneous Document (EMD) that has the purchased ancillary products and services, and the E-Ticket with the payment data are created in EDIFACT format across the airline industry. They will be phased out and replaced by ONE Order, a single XML order record based on the IATA directive from 2015.

ONE Order uses XML schemas to facilitate communication, which is a significant change from the limited character-based teletype format, which will no longer be supported.

6.24 Order Management

IATA (International Air Transport Association) launched NDC in 2012 and order management in 2015 at the World Passenger Symposium, describing it at the time as "*a single customer order record holding all data elements required for order fulfillment across the travel cycle*".

IATA calls the airline order management initiative as ONE Order.

ONE Order focuses on modernizing reservations processing by consolidating multiple processes into a single, flexible system. The initiative plans to simplify airline reservation, delivery, and accounting systems by consolidating multiple records (PNRs, E-Tickets, and EMDs) into a single, unified record called the ONE Order.

Specifically, the three records are:

1. Passenger Name Records (PNR) which were first created in the 1960s, with the development of the first airline reservations systems such as Sabre by IBM and American Airlines.
2. Electronic Miscellaneous Records (EMD) is a non-flight related electronic vouchers issued by airlines or authorized agencies to handle various optional services or fees associated with a booking. There are two types of EMDs. EMD-A is associated with a flight and EMD-S is standalone, not associated with a flight. The EMD replaced the older forms like the Virtual Miscellaneous Charge Order (vMCO) and Virtual Miscellaneous Multi-Purpose Document (vMPD). The transition to EMDs was completed in 2013.
3. The IATA Electronic E-Ticket (ETKT) is an electronic version of a flight ticket, replacing the traditional paper ticket in 2008. An E-TKT is essentially a reservation record stored in the airline's reservations system, and it can be accessed by the passenger using a reservation or record locator number. Each E-Ticket

has a unique 13-digit number. The first three digits indicate the airline code, assigned by IATA, and the remaining ten digits are a serial number

6.24.1 Legacy Processing Environment

In the legacy environment, an airline's host CRS stores and processes reservation data and the PNR, E-Ticket and EMD are generated and managed.

Often referred to as legacy, order handling in reservations systems is managed by the PNR, E-Ticket, and EMD. The PNR record is created by an airline or a GDS depending on where the reservation originates. It contains the passenger information, flight information, and ticket number. An electronic ticket is a digital equivalent of a paper ticket which became mandatory for ticket issuance in 2008. The E-Ticket that is issued is linked to an individual PNR. The EMDs work like an E-Ticket in the sense that an IATA standard document is issued for the ancillary services, a receipt is issued to the customer, and value coupons are stored in an electronic record in the airline CRS.

The Electronic Miscellaneous Document (EMD) was introduced by IATA in 2010. It is a non-flight document that is used for the collection, financial settlement and tracking of ancillary services offered by an airline thar are sold through travel agencies that subscribe to a GDS or through the airline's consumer direct channel. They serve as an industry-standard document for managing and fulfilling a variety of travel-related services. This requires the issuance of a separate electronic miscellaneous document (EMD) and messaging infrastructure to support it. There are two types of EMDs. The EMD-A is associated with an airline E-Ticket and EMD-B is standalone. By 2014, over 180 airlines and all the major airline CRSs supported EMD processing. The EMDs are defined in IATA Resolution 725, which ensures they are an industry standard.

The EMD also supports interline standards. The EMD can be transmitted to airline partners to enable revenue recognition and proration of fees. It also involves communicating ancillary information to Operating Carrier when not the Validating Carrier, receiving information from marketing carrier when they are the operating carrier, supporting associate and disassociate messages when the EMD and eTicket validating carriers differ and supporting ancillary sales and fulfillment when carrier both validates and operates.

6.24.2 The One Order Environment

When a customer selects an offer, which is a bundle consisting of the base fare for the itinerary and ancillary products, it is converted into an "order," which captures all the relevant details of the transaction, including the products selected and associated prices. The order represents the final agreement between the airline and the customer, ensuring that all relevant information is documented. The order will also reflect any future changes or adjustments during its lifecycle.

ONE Order simplifies the airline reservations, delivery and accounting systems by phasing out the current PNRs and ticketing records known as E-TKT (this is different from the e-ticket used by LCCs) and EMD which maintains a record of ancillary sales. The new standard eliminates virtual coupon records (VCR, the electronic version of the paper airline ticket coupon that was introduced in 2008) and replaces it with the single order record.

Consequently, the merged document or record will consist of

1. Order Number
2. Passenger Personal Data such as contact information: emails, phone number, passport
3. Passenger Itinerary that includes flight details
4. Payment Status
5. Ticketing information such as ticket issuer, date of issue, expiration date
6. Ancillary information which is a list of ancillary products and services ordered.

This streamlines the sale of ancillary products with the elimination of multiple reservations records and the consolidation of the PNR/E-Ticket/EMD with a single reference order.

A white paper on transitioning to ONE Order was prepared by IATA in 2016, and the first version of the standards were published in September 2018. Lufthansa was the first airline to be certified in 2019 following a year-long pilot with Lufthansa Systems (LHS). By 2023, airlines had made some progress, but only a few airlines are certified with ONE Order capabilities.

ONE Order also simplifies the order fulfillment process with a single reference record. It supports efficient billing and enables third parties involved in the order to edit purchases and check billing and payment status. The notion of a single reference order for all purchases such as airfare and air ancillaries simplifies accounting and financial operations.

6.24.3 Requirements for Success of ONE Order

The NDC program is a multi-million dollar information technology investment from airlines and intermediaries (such as GDSs, OTAs) to deliver personalized offers (at least at a customer segment level if not 1:1) and transform the legacy passenger name record (PNR), electronic tickets (E-Ticket) and electronic miscellaneous documents (EMD) to what has been called as ONE Order by IATA.

The PNR has been the backbone of the legacy airline reservations systems for decades and this is a seismic change, far greater than the migration to the NDC messaging standard. ONE Order initiative will extend the PNR by consolidating a passenger's personal information and purchases such as an airline ticket and ancillaries within a single record. The single customer order holds all data elements related to a trip. The investment in ONE Order by the major carriers and the GDSs continues unabated. PNRs served the purpose of selling and managing the original airline ticket, not flights and ancillaries and potentially third-party products.

Interoperability is the ability of computer systems or software to exchange and make use of information. Achieving data Interoperability is a challenge that requires time and investment in any industry, including the airline industry. The challenges stem from legacy systems, from airlines or their partners, that may have data quality issues and rely on outdated proprietary systems that lack modern interoperability standards and features. To make the vision of order management in the airline industry come true, the single biggest focus must be on interoperability with third party systems. If this hurdle is not overcome, then order management will always be limited in what it can do.

While it is a slow process, since PNRs and orders have to co-exist, airlines and software vendors are simplifying the retail framework by focusing on adopting order management. A single, integrated traveler record will improve customer service. Connecting orders with revenue accounting systems will help money move more quickly between retailers and suppliers. This will make financial reconciliation easier and reduce the need for manual work. Over time, these changes will make the entire process more efficient and straightforward.

The success of ONE Order requires participation from many industry players, including airlines, travel agents, and information technology providers, to ensure a synchronized and successful transition.

6.24.4 SSRs, EMDs, and ONE Order

SSRs have been around for decades, and it stands for Special Service Request, which is a code used to communicate a passenger's need for a special service or to request an additional service for purchase such as pre-paid extra baggage, lounge access, or a special meal on complementary services such as wheelchair assistance, dietary requirements, or travel assistance. SSRs use specific four-letter codes (e.g., WCBD for wheelchairs, SPML for special meals, MEDA for medical case, MAAS for travel assistance) that are recognized by airlines. SSR codes like GOLF for golf equipment or BIKE for a bicycle in the hold are also examples of SSRs for specialized baggage. SSRs are used to book and track these services that are not part of the standard ticket. These codes are entered into a passenger's name record and allow airlines to fulfill passenger requests and manage ancillary services. Unlike Other Service Information (OSIs), SSRs require the airline to act, ensuring that the special service is delivered to the customer. The requirement for a specific SSR, and any required free text within it, is defined by the airline and can be found in their fare filing and e-ticketing rules. GDSs use these SSR codes to send requests to airlines.

When a passenger purchases an ancillary service, paid or free, a corresponding SSR, such as an additional service (ASVC), is added to the reservation. Booking airline ancillaries for issuance on an Electronic Miscellaneous Document (EMD-A) typically requires a Special Service Request (SSR), specifically an ASVC SSR.

This SSR communicates the flight-associated ancillary service that has been purchased, and its confirmation status (e.g., KD, HD) is required before the EMD-A can be issued to complete the reservation and payment for the service.

For air ancillaries, RFIC stands for Reason For Issuance Code, a single-character industry standard code that categorizes the group of services or the overall reason for issuing an EMD-A. For example, ‘the common codes are

A: air transportation,
B: Surface transportation / non-air services
C: Baggage
D: Financial Impact (e.g., refunds, fees)

These RFIC codes define the broader group of services while a Reason For Issuance Sub-Code (RFISC), a three-character code, specifies the exact nature of the service.

Beyond the hybrid state we are in today, ONE Order will eventually phase out and replace the current SSR messaging system, integrating these requests into the new single order record format. SSRs will be incorporated into the unified order structure of ONE Order to streamline communication and service delivery, replacing the separate record systems currently used. ONE Order captures all trip-related information in a single document. This simplifies and streamlines the entire travel business process, from reservation to fulfillment and accounting, by providing a consistent, single-record view for all stakeholders, thus phasing out the need for separate PNRs, e-tickets, and EMDs like those that use RFICs. Data available in the single “Order” is used for all back-end accounting and settlement processes.

6.24.5 Native Orders

As the airline industry evolves in its transformation, there are “orders” and “native orders”.

A native order refers to a customer order managed directly by the airline in a single record, rather than through a traditional Passenger Name Record (PNR) system. This allows airlines to integrate all aspects of a customer’s booking, including flight details, ancillary services, and payment information, into a single, unified document.

Flyr, the Norwegian LCC was the first to introduce native orders using the Pribas order management system. This was followed by Lubeck Air, a German regional airline, using the One-Order Passenger Servicing (OOPS) platform from TIK Systems[3] These airlines ceased operations in 2023, Flyr in February 2023 and Lubeck Air in October 2023.

[3] Based on discussion with Roland Heller and Ann Cederhall, October 27, 2025.

Finnair claimed to be the first airline to create a native order in May 2025 (Finnair, 2025). With about ten airlines on the cusp of deploying orders, many in the industry do not agree that Finnair and Amadeus created the world's first native order. In the grand scheme of adoption, this is inconsequential.

6.25 Is ONE Order a Comprehensive Vision

After the launch of ONE Order, there have been a plethora of new acronyms, mostly created by software vendors, sponsored conference hosts, and consultants, that adds a degree of confusion. Besides ONE Order, the most popular acronym is OOSD, which stands for Offer, Order, Settle, and Deliver. The OOSD acronym associated with Offers and Orders must not be confused with Object Oriented System Development and Object-Oriented Software Design.

OOSD is a comprehensive framework that encompasses the entire airline retailing lifecycle, focusing on the interconnected processes of creating and managing offers, processing orders, financial settlements, and service delivery. It represents a shift towards business process simplification, enabling airlines to better cater to evolving customer expectations and improve operational efficiency.

In the traditional definition of OMS in various industry verticals like high-tech manufacturing and consumer electronics, Settle and Deliver are part of the traditional OMS. If the order management capability is architected correctly, payment status and fulfillment status must be reflected on the customer order at the line-item level. Obviously, payment systems will continue to evolve on their own to provide a range of payment options, including vouchers, reserve and hold options, etc. to improve conversion rates.

6.25.1 Order Management Did not Originate in the Airline Industry

While this concept is new to the commercial airline industry, it is in active use in other industries such as manufacturing and retail. Manufacturers and retailers use Order Management Systems (called OMS) or simply order management (OM) to get a single view of the customer order regardless of where the components are sourced. It is not clear why IATA calls it ONE Order, instead of OMS.

For decades, supply chain management companies have been developing and selling their software to Fortune 1000 companies. These include factory planning, master planning, collaborative demand planning, demand fulfillment, and order management. These Fortune 1000 companies are in high-tech manufacturing, metals, consumer electronics, semiconductors, telecommunications, consumer package goods, and retail industries.

Order Management is not a new concept. Order Management Systems (OMS) have been around for decades. Enterprise Resource Planning (ERP) vendors (e.g.

Oracle, SAP) as well as boutique vendors that sell supply chain management software (e.g. Blue Yonder, Manhattan Associates, etc.) have developed and enhanced sophisticated order management systems for decades.

In a supply chain setting an OMS automates and optimizes sales and service operations for a business. In a conventional supply chain, this includes automated order entry and capture, as well as fulfilling orders from various suppliers, which involves picking, packing, and shipping. Real-time order tracking offers visibility into shipment status and delivery schedules. This is made possible with Advanced Shipping Notice (ASN), electronic messages that are sent from a supplier to a buyer to inform them of an upcoming delivery. ASNs are used to improve the efficiency of the goods-receiving process and to increase supply chain visibility. OMS checks orders against available inventory, confirms payments, and validates delivery addresses to ensure accuracy. Additionally, it features a performance measurement dashboard that tracks key performance indicators (KPIs) and order cycle times.

The standard industry acronym for decades is OMS, not ONE Order, OrMS, or its variations.

6.25.2 Airline Retailing and Order Management

The airline retailing process starts by accessing a product catalog that is used to configure dynamic offers consisting of a base fare and air ancillary products. A dynamic offer essentially means the air itinerary, ancillary bundle and the total price are determined at the time the shopping request was made. Within the dynamic offer, the fare may be based on filed fares with ATPCO or be a derived fare from the reference filed fares, called continuous pricing.

The extended view is to create dynamic offers with products and services from any partner. Once the offer is booked, it becomes an order. It is a single record with a list of order items. The order is shared with downstream systems (payment processing, fulfillment) and related offline processes (e.g. revenue accounting).

Offer and Order management capabilities must be developed outside of the legacy PSS environment so that it can essentially sit on top of a traditional PSS to ensure backward compatibility. Backward compatibility is important to ensure that traditional PNRs, which will decline over time, can co-exist with orders. The Order Management capability is a shared service, developed outside the legacy PNR environment, that can be accessed by both the PSS and Departure Control System (DCS). Existing PSS vendors who are investing in ONE Order will ensure it is a shared service, that can be accessed by both the PSS and DCS using XML or JSON interfaces.

There is also a lot of noise in the industry these days that *the PSS will go away and be replaced by order management* or *the need to develop a new DCS*. A proposed successor to the DCS is called Retail Delivery System (RDS) by Ink based in the United Kingdom. Is a new system warranted?

6.25.2.1 Does the PSS Have a Future?

For the PSS to disappear, every airline in the world must be on order management. There is also the larger question whether midsize and small carriers can afford the incremental cost of operating an order management capability with an existing PSS. Can the transition to order management for 90% of the world's airlines be achieved in two decades? Unlikely.

Some software companies are developing a new reservations system based on the order management capabilities and ignoring the role of the PNR. This is a big mistake. This is fine in a perfect world where every airline has transitioned to orders. To deploy such a solution today will not be possible without backward compatibility where PNRs and orders can co-exist. Without this backward compatibility, migrating an airline that uses PNRs (and everyone does today) to the new reservations system based on orders will not be possible.

6.25.2.2 Does the Departure Control System Have a Future?

Enhancing an existing DCS is the path forward to addressing any fulfillment ("delivery") related gaps, perceived or otherwise, in an offer and order world. If architected correctly, the product catalog of ancillaries and order must be shared services between the airline reservation system (host CRS/PSS) and the departure control system (DCS) with the capability to add items and update line items in the order, subject to the relevant permissions that have been granted.

Several companies such as Sabre, Amadeus, Collins Aerospace (ARINC), Videcom and others offer Departure Control Systems (DCS)s, which are software solutions used by airlines and airports to manage passenger and baggage processing at various stages, including check-in, boarding, and baggage handling.

A Departure Control System (DCS) is a multi-million-dollar investment. Of the large IT providers, Amadeus, who developed Altéa FLY (later renamed Altéa Altéa DCS) from the ground up, starting in the early 2000s and the project was completed in 2012 when Finnair went live with Altéa DCS. Why does it take so long? First, there is the development of efficient load control procedures (weight and balance) to address agent productivity. Second, there are numerous regulatory, and compliance related workflows that every DCS must support, and there are variations across countries. The DCS also supports a range of functions such as passenger check-in, luggage check-in, issue boarding passes, boarding, messaging (e.g. APIS and eAPIS), validate flight documents, maintain passenger name list, thru check-in, group passenger handling, ancillary re-accommodation utility, upgrades, change of seat requests, handle no-recs and misconnects, etc. before closing the flight for departure. Departure Control Systems like Altéa DCS and others run on modern technology in an open systems environment, making it easier for enhancements.

Hence, if the DCS needs to be enhanced with capabilities like a full-service hotel property management system (PMS) that integrates to multiple point of sale applications, it must be accomplished with the core DCS baseline code and reference application because of the very significant investment in software development. Examples of PMSs that integrate into multiple point of sale systems are

Oracle's Opera, MEWS, and others. It is important for the DCS to publish and expose the API so third parties can integrate to provide an inter-operable solution. An example is a hotel gift shop, where purchases made by a guest can be charged to the room and the final folio of the customer at checkout will reflect all purchases that may include the gift shop, restaurants, spa, recreational activities, etc.

In the airline world of orders, the shared order, which serves as the system of record, should be updated by the new ancillary purchases (e.g. onboard sales from the airline or third parties) by the customer. Developing a new DCS from scratch (whether we call it RDS or DCS is not important) to support integration into multiple point of sale systems (these are the third-party vendors who want to sell products to airline customers) is not a sound investment.

6.25.2.3 Interoperability with Third Parties

Order management is in the early to middle stage of development and questions such as how an order id will be shared with a third-party have arisen. The order has a single reference number for the passenger's seamless journey, known as the Order Id. This reference number is similar to the record locator or booking reference found on a PNR. The PNR record locator is a 5–7-character alphanumeric code. This code is used by airlines and travel agencies to identify a passenger's booking within the airline reservation systems. The PNR can also be found on a passenger's booking confirmation email, travel document, or boarding pass.

The Order Id covers all aspects of the customer's journey: flight, ancillary products, including travel products of partner service providers such as partner airlines, hotels, cars and rideshare. This adoption of ONE Order is made possible with XML-based communication between airlines and other travel service providers. However, the booking records from partners will become order lines in the carrier's ONE Order. The partners can be airlines on legacy systems, hotels, rental car, activity providers, etc.

Order Change Notifications (OCN) are triggered by flight number changes, cancellations, delays, or when a passenger accepts a modified schedule. OCN messages are sent to sellers like travel agencies when there are changes in the order via the NDC protocol. The changes may be either voluntary or involuntary, often caused by schedule changes. This broad framework requires partners such as hotels, rental car and ride share providers to integrate to a customer's Order Id to make updates on the order. Travel agencies and third-party sellers must register with the airline to receive these notifications.

Inter-operability with APIs enables direct interaction between disparate systems, which allows third parties to create, modify or cancel line items on the order within the ONE Order system. These real-time updates at the line-item level for an order is also required to support duty of care for corporate customers. The event-based notifications from within the ONE Order system can be used to notify other systems. This ensures that partner service providers like hotels, rental car and rideshare operators are informed about changes to an order in real-time enabling timely responses and actions.

6.25.3 Why ONE Order? or Should It Be a SUPER Order?

What is within the control of an airline are ancillary products that they sell, for which they can monitor the status and provide updates on the order. An airline can satisfy the fulfillment requirements for air ancillaries. Is that what ONE in ONE Order represents? Travelers today are only comfortable buying airline seats and air ancillaries from an airline, not third-party products. This is because it goes way beyond the core competency of an airline and fulfillment of third-party products is a challenge.

However, the ultimate objective of airline order management is to go beyond airline ancillaries and at a minimum look at adjacencies such as car rental, hotel, and destination activities, and not beach towels on a flight. The fundamental reason many airlines are averse to moving in this direction is because it goes beyond their core competency. The fulfillment of third-party products is a showstopper. For example, consider a hotel booking that is a line item in the order. While a hotel booking can be reflected on the order as an order item, the hotel does not provide a real-time notification to the ONE Order when the customer checks in. The same is true in situations when an Uber ride is cancelled by the driver, a destination activity is closed due to special circumstances, etc.

From a customer perspective, the question is*: will a customer purchase a non-airline product from an airline with confidence?* The answer today is NO, just the airline seat and air ancillaries that may be required for the trip. This is also why content differentiation between airlines is not the biggest benefit of NDC as many may think. Airlines have similar air ancillary products though the bundles (offers) may be different. So where is the differentiation? Schedule quality is obviously a differentiator but has nothing to do with NDC. Airlines may not admit it, but reducing distribution costs for NDC bookings is the biggest benefit of NDC. Airlines have a lot to learn in the realm of fulfillment of third-party products.

So, what does ONE really mean in this context? Consider the case of virtual interlining for a customer's journey which can include flights, buses, trains, interline flights on carriers that do not have ticketing agreements, etc.

The vision of ONE Order should be to address all aspects of a customer's connected journey. How can two or more orders, for a customer that is traveling on multiple carriers that have no codeshare or interline ticketing agreements, receive status updates? Equally important, which order is the master, and which order is the slave? The order items on the slave can be reflected as informational segments on the master. What is needed is a SUPER ORDER that holds multiple orders for the same customer, and the individual orders receive status updates from their respective suppliers. Data exchange standards do not exist today for the connected journey of a virtual interlining customer. Airline orders must be extended to split orders and combine orders.

6.25.4 Impacts on Revenue Integrity

Revenue integrity (RI) addresses the gap between booked revenue and actual revenue by detecting and cancelling problem bookings to resell the inventory. While *flight firming* is treated as a separate function within an airline, it complements airline pricing and revenue management. Paul Rose introduced the concept and value of revenue integrity when he was working at British Airways. Subsequently, he established the Airline Revenue Integrity Group (ARIG), a non-profit group focused on revenue leakage.

Circumventing the booking process by travel agents and customers will continue to exist in an NDC world, so the process of deploying Revenue Integrity to identify fraudulent unproductive bookings and return seats to the airline's inventory system will continue to be required in the NDC era, with some new capabilities since the PNRs, tickets, and EMDs will be replaced with Orders. Revenue Integrity systems will have to communicate to the order management system via web services similar to how they have communicated with PNRs. The business rules defined in the revenue integrity system can be executed when the order is created, updated, or changed.

In this traditional booking environment prior to NDC, a ticket defines whether a booking is paid for or not. In the new world with ONE Order, there will be no tickets and information related to an order being paid or not will change. There are two ways to fulfill orders They are *instant payment* and *deferred payment*. The preferred payment model will be made by the airline, and in some cases, depending on the fare or channel, where the customer selected the offer and created the order.

With ONE Order, if the airline only accepts instant payments, revenue integrity checks related to payment time limit (replacement for ticketing lime limit), fictitious names, duplicate segments, time limits for purchasing ancillaries, and churn will not be required. However, to address abuses of the inventory system, revenue integrity checks for duplicate bookings and no-shows is still relevant.

With deferred payments, many of the current revenue integrity checks will still be required and the Revenue Integrity application must be able to access the orders via web services.

Inactive or unconfirmed waitlisted order items must be periodically removed from the airline reservations system.

6.25.4.1 Time Limits and Orders

With orders, there are two types of time limits. They are the *price guarantee time limit* (PGTL) and the *payment time limit (PTL).*

The PGTL is the time period when the price of an offer item is guaranteed. Once the offer time limit has expired, the price quoted is no longer valid and the offer must be repriced resulting in a new offer with a new price. When a price guarantee time limit is applied, there is no guarantee that related inventory is guaranteed by the airline against a given offer item. IATA recommends airlines to implement the PGTL, but it's optional, and some airlines may choose not to implement it. If an airline implements PGTL, it is important to know what element of the price is guaranteed (e.g., base fare, taxes, or both).

If an airline has deployed PGTL, TMCs will have to resort to instant ticketing, which can prove to be a challenge for long-haul flights with higher ticket prices due to the time required for the trip approval process.

The payment time limit (PTL) is similar to the well-known ticketing time limit (TTL). However, it is established at the Order Item level and not the PNR level as it is currently done. It indicates the time duration after the order is created that a payment commitment is required for an Order Item. If the payment is not made by the time limit, the Order Item will be removed from the order. The PTL is within the Offer Item level.

Defining all the business processes and exception workflows around revenue integrity interfacing with an order management system today is challenging since these order management systems (OMS) are in various stages of development and a baseline does not exist.

6.26 Will the Transition to Offer and Order Happen by 2030?

The Boston Consulting Group and IATA conducted joint workshops [Guerrini et. al., 2024] with participants from four types of companies: railways, cruise lines, tour operators and car rental companies, as representatives of travel suppliers along the customer journey; and travel management companies (TMCs), as representatives of travel distributors to determine the strategic implications of modern retailing on the broader travel ecosystem. In addition, they also surveyed more than 150 airline employees from full-service carriers. The survey claimed that about half of the survey respondents believed that the 100% transition to offers and orders can be reached by 2030!

What is not clear is the sample sizes and diversity used in the survey. For example, what were the sample sizes, such as number of employees per airline, and the number of airlines in the survey. What is also not known is the diversity of the survey sample; whether this was an unbiased sample or skewed toward the larger full-service carriers that are heavily investing in offer and order. An unbiased sample with representation from U.S. majors, global pure play, mid-size airlines, small airlines, and regional airlines is required to arrive at any meaningful conclusions from a survey of this type.

Despite the support from major airlines to transition to offers and orders, this simply *will not happen* by 2030. What the survey respondents probably never considered was that there is significant operational impact on PSS and DCS, and transferring copies of the order for a passenger's itinerary to the target CRS when multiple airlines are involved in the itinerary. Besides the real-time development required for offers and orders, the respondents probably also did not consider the major refactoring investments to offline systems such as revenue accounting, payments, data warehouse, revenue management, ARC and BSP settlement with orders, U.S. Customs and Border Protection (CBP), and others, Further, the industry also relies heavily on asynchronous teletype (Type B) messages for both inter-airline (CRS to CRS) and airline CRS-GDS communications. There is also a reliance on real-time EDIFACT (Type A) messages for inter-airline (CRS to CRS) and airline CRS-GDS communications. For an airline to state that they will be 100% on offers and orders, does it also mean that airline CRSs that they communicate with will use an XML or JSON messaging protocol and will be fully compliant with offers and orders?

The non-profit settlement systems such as ARC and BSP, as well as IATA, still run on mainframe-based systems that have not been modernized, even though the NDC and ONE Order initiatives were launched in 2012 and 2015 respectively. Incremental changes to these systems and supporting both new and old standards side-by-side add to the annual maintenance costs and account for a significant portion of the budget funded by the airlines. Any overhaul will require large additional investments that need to be funded by the airlines while continuing to pay increasing maintenance costs.

Many airline systems, such as PSS, DCS, and Revenue Accounting, still run on mainframe technology. Upgrading these core systems will require large investments in new hardware and software. At the same time, the costs to maintain these old systems continue to grow, adding financial pressure to add NDC XML on top of the EDIFACT/ATPCO based constructs. Investing more money in these projects without expecting a return for many years has made it harder to move these initiatives forward.

Workflows related to recovery from irregular operations (IROPS) must also be in place to transition to offers and orders. With EDIFACT, a gate agent can reissue a ticket when there is a schedule change. With NDC, the request must be processed by the airline with the requisite waivers in place.

6.27 Airline Affordability of ONE Order

For decades, the Passenger Name Record (PNR) has been the backbone of airline ticket sales. It was built in a different era, when IBM and American Airlines launched Sabre in 1964. It is undoubtedly a legacy text-based product that does not lend itself to a relational form. Now the industry is going through a seismic change. The PNR, E-Ticket, and Electronic Miscellaneous Document (EMD) will be phased out by a dynamic order record. The migration to Offer and Order is challenging along many dimensions such as investment, business workflows, and inter-operability.

Network carriers operate legacy reservations systems where the PNR is the dominant domain, along with schedules, inventory, ticketing, and departure control. The PNR functions in a reservation system as a central database record that stores all information about a passenger's trip, including flight segments, hotel and car rentals, contact details, and special requests. Schedule changes automatically update the segments within the PNR to reflect the new schedule and typically trigger a ticket revalidation or reissuance to match the new schedule. The PNR is updated to reflect the new flight times, and additional information or remarks are often added to document the change and customer acceptance. The airline sends a notification about the schedule change to the travel agency's PNR, which is often updated with an OSI (Other Service Information) remark to inform the agent about the change. The PNR's primary functions are managing bookings, providing information for check-in and updates, and ensuring security and customer service.

Reservation system providers operate a passenger service system (PSS) that hosts many airlines. The underlying architecture is based on Transaction Processing Facility (TPF), a legacy IBM operating system from the 1960s that was developed in partnership with American Airlines to launch the Sabre reservations system in 1964 (Vinod, 2024a). A TPF based reservations system is a high-performance, high-volume online transaction processing system, originally developed for airline reservations, that handles real-time bookings and flight modifications. A central database tracks inventory and passenger records, ensuring speed and reliability for millions of transactions. Migrating from TPF to open systems is a necessary investment for reservation system providers to move away from mainframe technology. While some have migrated, others are in the process of doing so. In the interim, the legacy mainframe computing environments have been upgraded to the lates z/os operating system that runs the z/TPF transaction processor, the successor to TPF4.1, from IBM.

These reservations systems access fares from fate aggregator ATPCO, schedules from schedule aggregators OAG or Cirium, access the shared communication system from SITA, leverage AIRIMP as the messaging standard, and the GDSs for travel agency bookings that evolved from the airline reservations systems in 1976. In addition, it supports a host of additional data sources such as Special Service Request (SSR) messages, loyalty programs, customer profiles and databases.

Historically, the associated costs, risks, and standards were shared by the airline community. They are robust, reliable, high-performance systems. They may not be well documented, but the code, with updates over the past seventy years, encapsulates what they can accomplish. There are many new OMS purported providers in the market today such as Accelya, Datalex, FLYR, IBS, Astra by TPConnects, Retailear, and PROS, but they operate on the outskirts as a superficial layer, without many of the core capabilities encapsulated in a PSS.

Today, every airline pursues their own initiative at their own pace as witnessed by the NDC adoption rate and status. Fragmentation of the development process for ONE Order and individual airline pursuits do not boost confidence on the execution of ONE Order, which is many orders of magnitude greater in effort than the NDC messaging protocol and related adoption.

IATA's ONE Order, proposed in 2015, is an industry initiative to replace the existing PNR, electronic miscellaneous document (EMD) and E-ticketing into a single customer order record. It is a new XML-based data standard to standardize communication and processes for an airline's order management system. This unified record streamlines the process for travelers, airlines, and travel agents by providing a consistent view of a traveler's journey across all service providers, which leads to greater process and operating efficiency. Order management includes order capture, availability checks, payment processing by integrating to a payment gateway, delivery, and post-sale management such as refunds and exchanges.

ONE Order requires a deep re-architecture of core transaction processing in a reservations system, including messaging, accounting, interline, disruption management, and settlement. To migrate to ONE Order, the associate complexity and costs are very high. Established GDSs that have an IT services division to handle reservations processing for airlines like Amadeus and Sabre are the ones that are most equipped to handle this complexity at global scale.

Migration to ONE Order also requires backward compatibility with the PNR, which means these systems must run in parallel for an extended period of time during the migration phase. For large carriers the systems may have to run in parallel for a decade and the associated costs could run into the billions, impacting profitability and shareholder return on investment. Absence of a standard reference application for ONE Order also leads to longer development cycles.

Should an airline invest in ONE Order, given the steep costs and commitment required? The answer is YES. Investing in ONE Order is required for an airline to modernize the legacy infrastructure, but the return on investment (ROI) is simply not there which should be communicated to shareholders. Without a doubt, the financial investment in ONE Order will weaken network carriers and strengthen the LCCs who control about 36% of the worldwide air traffic in 2025. LCCs mostly operate on newer reservations systems like Navitaire New Skies, TIK Systems PSS, and others which support many elements of ONE Order and are more closely aligned with the ONE Order vision. Examples of airlines that use some form of order management are Air Asia, Ryanair, Allegiant Air, Air Europa, easyJet, and others. Of the large reservation system providers, Nevio by Amadeus and Mosaic by Sabre are developing the order capability that integrates with their legacy PSS and ensures backward compatibility.

6.27.1 New Airlines with no PNRs

ONE Order is far easier to deploy for a new airline that does not have historical or future PNRs in their reservations system. In this scenario, backward compatibility within an airline reservations system to keep orders and PNRs in sync are not required.

For a new airline taking bookings in the ONE Order era, there are no PNRs, EMDs and E-TKTs to contend with and all relevant data is stored on the order record. However, in a world where teletype and EDIFACT are prevalent, a translator is still required to convert inbound and outbound messages from interline partners, codeshare partners, GDSs and third parties that use the older messaging standards.

Fig. 6.18 Offer, order and delivery

6.28 Delivery Management

Delivery management is the fulfillment process, the final step after generation of the offer, acceptance of the offer, and creation of the order. This is shown in Fig. 6.18.

In airline retailing, offers are the range of products and services airlines provide to their customers. This includes flights, seat upgrades, extra baggage, in-flight meals, and lounge access. Airlines also feature services from third parties, like car rentals, airport transfers, hotels, and tours. When an offer is accepted, an order is created.

Orders represent the purchases customers make based on these offers. When a traveler picks an offer, they create an order with details such as the selected offer, price, personal information, payment method, and any extra preferences or needs.

Airline delivery management is the process of ensuring that a traveler's requests are fulfilled efficiently and accurately. It involves planning, tracking, and coordinating the delivery of flights, services, and other offerings.

Delivery refers to how airlines handle and fulfill travel products and services that customers select from their offers. This process relies on a Delivery Management System, often called a Departure Control System (DCS). This system includes various features to help manage operations efficiently and improve traveler experiences. Currently, departure control mainly occurs at airports, but future delivery management can potentially extend beyond that as airlines begin to offer third-party products and services. Success will be dictated by a traveler's confidence in buying adjacent third-party products from airlines.

6.28.1 Should Existing Departure Control Systems Be Sunset?

In the realm of offers and orders, there is a perceived "gap" in departure control systems in the area of fulfillment of orders. There are consultants and vendors articulating the need for a new departure control system (DCS). Really? And there is a new acronym for DCS that appears at trade shows, It is RDS for Retail Delivery System. The so-called proposed successor to the DCS is called Retail Delivery System (RDS) is to streamline the entire retail delivery process, allowing airlines to seamlessly deliver goods to passengers throughout their journey.

Is a new system warranted? The answer is a definitive NO.

DCS is a multi-million-dollar investment. Enhancing an existing DCS is the path forward to addressing any fulfillment ("delivery") related gaps, perceived or otherwise, in an offer and order world. If architected correctly, the product catalog of ancillaries and orders must be shared services between the airline reservation system (host CRS/PSS) and the departure control system (DCS) with the capability to add items and update line items in the order, subject to the relevant permissions that have been granted to a user.

Hence, if the DCS needs to be enhanced with capabilities like a full-service hotel property management system (PMS) that integrates to multiple point of sale applications, it must be accomplished with the core DCS baseline code and reference application because of the very significant investment in software development.

However, the likelihood that a supplier of beach towels will be integrated with a DCS so that beach towels can be delivered to customers before flight departure to a beach destination is very remote. An airline's core competency is selling and fulfilling an airline seat, and it is extremely unlikely they will make huge investments in people and culture to mature into purveyors of fine products that are not air related. Travelers also do not have the confidence to purchase non-air products from an airline except for adjacent areas such as airport transfers, and ground transportation. The thought that airlines will become modern retailers like Amazon is a myth.

By the time all the existing DCS functions mentioned earlier are refactored into the new DCS, we are looking at a ten-year project and cost overruns.

6.28.1.1 CUTE and CUSS Standards

Besides, any new DCS must support CUTE and CUSS standards since it represents the lowest common denominator of the technology stack. This allows airlines to share equipment, similar to how Ground Support Equipment (GSE) is pooled. CUTE stands for Common Use Terminal Equipment, which means airlines can share check-in desks and the software used to print bag tags. CUSS, or Common Use Self Service, refers to the shared self-service check-in kiosks. This system allows airport operators to open spaces that were once reserved for a single airline so that multiple airlines and their passengers can benefit. In the past, check-in desks were owned and managed by individual airlines, with each airline using its own software for check-in and bag tag creation. With CUTE technology, all airlines can operate their own applications on a shared platform for check-in, while the airport retains ownership of the desks and equipment.

The transition to NDC for Offers where all offers are airline controlled will take a minimum of 15+ years and an order management solution will take even longer to transition 90% of the world's airlines.

There is no need to reinvent the wheel and develop new Departure Control Systems. Existing systems must be enhanced to support the transformation.

6.28.2 Delivery Management: Beyond the Hype, What is It All About?

Airlines are dealing with more challenges in providing a smooth travel experience. Perhaps, managing delivery is more than just using standard Departure Control Systems. It involves making sure travelers receive their offers, including flights and additional services, effectively. Delivery management can enhance travel experiences, streamline operations, and potentially open new revenue opportunities.

The airport experience is complex, involving security checks, customs, immigration, and coordination among ground handlers, airport operators, and airlines. Given this complexity, effective delivery management is essential for enhancing the overall experience for travelers.

The objective of delivery management is to ensure that travelers enjoy a smooth and consistent brand experience from booking to boarding. This improves traveler satisfaction and fosters loyalty. It may include options like buying additional services on the day of travel and using biometrics for a quick and easy journey from curb to gate.

Benefits include:

1. Enhanced Customer Experience with consistent and seamless experience for travelers, from booking to boarding.
2. Incremental Revenue with well managed seat and ancillary revenues on a flight.
3. By accessing a common customer order across reservations and departure control, delivery management can help ensure that traveler requests are processed accurately and promptly. This also leads to improved operational efficiency with a streamlined process.
4. Real-time order management and delivery tracking are essential for timely fulfillment. Delivery management allows for tracking and synchronization of orders, ensuring that traveler requests are handled accurately and quickly. As a result, errors and delays are minimized, leading to satisfied customers.
5. The enhanced departure control system can integrate to multiple point of sales systems and payment gateways.
6. Regulatory compliance involves meeting legal standards by keeping precise records and ensuring audits go smoothly. This practice avoids legal issues and financial penalties.
7. Delivery management systems offer essential data about customer habits, business efficiency, and market trends. This information helps airlines make smart choices and maintain a competitive edge in airline retailing.

Offers beyond Airline Products and Services

7

> Retail is a customer business. You're trying to take care of the customer, solve something for the customer. And there's no way to learn that in the classroom or in the corner office or away from the customer. You've got to be in front of the customer.
>
> Erik Nordstrom

Abstract

With the advent on airline retailing, airlines are increasingly exploring and adopting strategies to sell non-air products and services. To evolve into a retailer is an imposing task that is also fraught with risks. The primary motivation is diversification of revenue streams beyond ticket sales and air ancillary bundles. Non-air products, such as merchandise, travel insurance, hotel bookings, car rentals, and even destination experiences are enticing because they can provide additional and more stable revenue streams. Complementary non-air products, upselling and cross selling are all in the scope of airline retailing. Fulfillment, the delivery of all items in an order is central to any initiative that involves non-air products.

The chapter concludes with the importance of protecting the airline brand which outweighs the challenge of third-party fulfillment.

This quote from Erik Nordstrom, the CEO of Nordstrom, Inc., a leading fashion retailer with an unwavering commitment to customer service, on staying customer centric. He emphasizes the importance of customer interaction and hands-on experience in understanding the needs of the customer. Airline executives must

B. Vinod, *The Era of Airline Revenue Management with Offers and Orders*, Management for Professionals, https://doi.org/10.1007/978-3-032-24197-9_7

increasingly look to seasoned retailers for inspiration and guidance in modernizing their retailing strategies and execution.

The key takeaway is that customers are at the heart of everything you do, so make sure every decision you make has them as your focal point. You can support your customers, and you can learn from them too. Airlines are not retailers today in the traditional sense of selling non-air products. To be successful, customer feedback and a strong focus on fulfillment of non-air products are prerequisites.

7.1 Overview

With the advent on airline retailing, airlines are increasingly exploring and adopting strategies to sell non-air products and services, essentially evolving into a retailer. The primary motivation is diversification of revenue streams beyond ticket sales and air ancillary bundles. Non-air products, such as merchandise, travel insurance, hotel bookings, car rentals, and even destination experiences, can provide additional and more stable revenue streams.

Customer data, collected through the airline frequent flyer programs and online interactions, can be used to offer personalized product recommendations and promotions. The existing loyalty programs can be expanded to include partnerships with retailers, hotels, car rental companies, etc., allowing customers to earn and redeem miles for a wider range of products and services.

If an airline is serious about venturing beyond the air products space, they must invest in a digital platform that facilitates the booking of flights and the purchase of various non-air products and services. That is a major undertaking, and it requires investment, a commitment to succeed, business process changes, and organizational alignment. Competition from established entrenched entities like OTAs will pose a significant challenge.

7.2 The Richard Ferris Allegis Experiment

The concept of seamless customer experiences is not new, but it is relevant today with the proliferation of the airline retailing initiatives and extending it to other lines of business such as hotels, rental car, and ground transportation for a connected trip. Richard Ferris became CEO of United Airlines in 1979 and spearheaded the transformation. In the 1980s, Richard Ferris, as Chairman of Allegis Corporation, brought United Airlines, Hilton International, Westin, and Hertz Car Rental under one roof along with the Apollo reservations system to meet a traveler's expectations for a seamless customer experience. The Apollo Travel Services unit was renamed Covia Corp. It was designed to operate the Apollo system, providing data services to the companies under Allegis. The name Covia was used by Allegis as part of its strategy to transform from an airline into a diversified travel services company.

Richard Ferris was a visionary, ahead of his time. Richard Ferris looked for ways his businesses could work better together. He was passionate about a future where travel agents worldwide would sit in front of screens, managing bookings for his airline, hotels, and rental cars. He mentioned plans for corporate travel deals that would bring in a large amount of full-fare business. He also talked about ideas like combining check-ins and offering frequent-flier bonuses for hotel and car rental customers. He believed that each of his divisions would be more valuable as part of a bigger team than on their own, the proverbial $1 + 1 + 1 = 5$, a qualitative difference beyond simple arithmetic.

In the Internet era, this can be accomplished virtually between partners that are willing to share data without ownership of different lines of business.

Some board members initially opposed the idea because all three of the company's divisions would suffer during a recession. Even Vice Chairman John L. Cowan suggested making a countercyclical purchase, calling it "an anchor to windward." Ferris managed to push through these concerns, but most outsiders remained skeptical of the plan. His attempt to aggressively diversify the company into a travel empire alienated unions. In February 1987, Ferris renamed his company from UAL Inc. to Allegis. He also started a strong advertising push to promote it as a full-service travel company. Security analysts and institutional investors regarded Allegis stock as undervalued, selling in the $55 to $60 range. Investment experts determined that the company would be worth at least $100 a share if its operations were sold separately.

In the spring of 1987, unable to convince Wall Street with his overly ambitious growth plans, the Allegis initiative collapsed and the board of directors forced Richard Ferris to resign as Chairman and CEO on June 10, 1987. This led to the dissolution of the travel conglomerate.

This is a lesson learned from history, and it was before the Internet era. And now, in the NDC era, the fundamental question is: *will customers purchase anything beyond an airline seat and air ancillaries from an airline in the future?*

7.3 Other Airline Investment in Hotels

On a smaller scale, several airlines had ownership in hotels. Here are a few examples.

Juan Trippe, the founder of Pan American World Airways, founded Intercontinental Hotels in 1946. It was founded at the request of U.S. President Franklin D. Roosevelt, to increase business with Latin American countries after the Second World War [Huhne, 2017]. Juan Trippe's vision was to provide lodging for Pan Am's passengers and crew around the world. Pan Am sold its hotel division in 1981 to generate cash to pay down debt and fund operations during a period of significant financial trouble for the airline.

American Airlines through Sky Chefs leased the 50-story 1843 room Americana Hotel on seventh Avenue in New York City [Leff, 2024]. They added more hotels to the portfolio as well as brands such as Ala Moana in Hawaii, Town House Hotel and Flagship Hotel in Rochester, New York, Flagship Inn in Cincinnati, Ohio as well as a few international properties that were all merged under the Americana brand in 1979. All these hotels were later acquired by Marriott and IHG since it did not fit into the core American Airlines business.

Air France created the Le Méridien brand in 1972. Le Méridien was acquired by Forte P.L.C. in 1994 for Air France to raise cash as part of a restructuring plan, which was on the verge of privatization and under pressure to cut costs and improve productivity. The sale was part of a strategy to focus on the core airline business, as hotel operations required more capital-intensive investment compared to air travel. It was then acquired by Starwood Hotels and Resorts in 2005 and in now part of Marriott International.

7.3.1 Michelin as the Role Model for Airline Retailing

Michelin, the French multinational tire manufacturing company, can provide inspiration to airlines who want to become retailers. Many people see Michelin as the pioneer in product bundling. In 1900, Michelin Tire founders and French industrialist brothers Andre and Edouard Michelin compiled the first Michelin Guide to create a demand for automobiles, and therefore, a need for more Michelin tires. The Michelin guide also offered travelers details about gas stations, hotels, restaurants, maps, and directions. This not only helped tourists but also promoted car usage, which in turn supported its tire sales. As a result, travel guides and tires became unexpected complements in business.

Well over a hundred years since it was founded, Michelin continues to innovate, diversifying its traditional tire business with a growing number of services beyond just selling tires. They are redefining themselves as a mobility company, particularly through strategies like "tire-as-a-service" and the development of digital service platforms for their fleet and dealer customers. This shift involves offering services such as:

- Tracking the number of landings in airplanes using smart tires to determine when replacement is needed.
- Utilizing connected tires in Formula-E racing for more efficient air-pressure monitoring.
- Employing IoT technology in mining vehicles to enable technicians to change tires based on cumulative wear from massive loads of ore.
- Offering a subscription model for mining operators to prevent tire failure.

These initiatives highlight Michelin‘s focus on customer experience and a product-as-a-service approach to grow the business. Their connected fleet solutions aim for significant annual growth, demonstrating their commitment to this strategy that they have been fine-tuning for years.

7.4 Complementary Products

Complementary product bundling in the airline industry involves packaging a flight with additional services and products that enhance the travel experience, often at a discounted rate compared to purchasing them individually. This strategy is beneficial for both airlines and customers.

The cross-elasticity of demand for complementary goods is negative, since demand for one complementary product creates demand for the other product. Hence, in principle, an airline can gain additional marketing power through bundling, and non-air suppliers can obtain better price points for their products.

Complementary product bundling can help both consumers and suppliers save money when they buy products together. The choices and sizes of these bundles matter a lot. Since demand for one complementary product often leads to demand for another, companies can successfully market bundles and set better prices. For instance, if a company prices the main product low, customers are more likely to buy the related product as well. However, for this process to work, airlines need to develop partnerships with non-airline suppliers, negotiate revenue share agreements for the sale of third-party products and also invest in new billing systems.

7.5 Upsell and Cross-Sell

Influencing a customer's decision can be achieved by providing a variety of options [Poundstone, 2011]. Presenting various price points can prompt individuals to compare and select from the offers provided rather than deciding whether to make a purchase at all.

With the onset of airline retailing, there will be a renewed focus on upsell and cross-sell to increase revenues by enticing customers to spend more through the direct channel. On the surface it seems like a win-win proposition for the airline and the customer: a better experience for the customer and an improved bottom line for the airline with every transaction.

Efforts along this dimension require the airline to know traveler intent. Knowledge of intent for travel—a business trip, a weekend getaway, a short family vacation, etc. is fundamental to generating upsell and cross-sell offers that resonate with the traveler. When used effectively, upsell and cross-sell can maximize customer value and enhance metrics such as customer lifetime value (*CLV*) and the average value of the order (*AVO*).

Upsell and cross-sell are similar, but they are not synonymous. Both aim to increase the value of each booking. Upsell is all about upgrading the customer's original purchase while cross-sell involves additional product recommendations to a customer who is already buying a different product or service.

For example, when a customer is in the process of booking online and has selected a Basic Economy fare, the booking engine can offer premium seats which includes baggage allowance and seat pitch. This is an upsell opportunity to a higher fare with added benefits. Examples of cross-sell are offering travel insurance during the booking process. Also, after the booking is made, hotel and car offers are a cross-sell opportunity.

Cross-selling is effective when the secondary product or service is lower in price than the initial purchase. This is why OTA websites lead with the hotel product which will be typically more expensive than a U.S. domestic airline ticket or rental car. Price anchoring, how travelers perceive monetary value on a relative scale, plays a key role in cross-sell. It refers to a price point that customers can refer to when making a purchase decision. A related question is: *at what point does a price for a product become an anchor?* According to behavioral economist Dan Ariely [Ariely, 2010], *the price becomes an anchor only when the consumer contemplated buying the good or service at the stated price.*

In summary, understanding customer psychology is crucial. Utilizing price anchors can effectively steer customers towards desired products, serving as a powerful tool to enhance revenue and pricing strategies.

7.6 Dynamic Packaging beyond Air

With the growth in online travel retailing, dynamic packaging has taken center stage with the Online Travel Agencies (OTA). While packaging of the air itinerary with hotels and ground transportation is not a new idea and has existed for years, it is being embraced in new ways. In Europe, well-known tour operators offer packages and flexible itinerary options that the public readily accepts. These companies act as middlemen, combining products from different suppliers into one offering. Typically, these packages include flights, hotels, and activities at destinations. However, these traditional packages are fixed and, in today's digital age, printed materials quickly become outdated.

Today's price-conscious travelers are increasingly shopping for travel online, leading to a significant rise in both browsing and booking activities.

The larger question is whether airlines can attract and sell packages to customers to generate new revenue streams? Will airline customers buy anything beyond a seat from an airline?

Dynamic packaging in online retailing combines airline, hotel and rental car segments to offer personalized packages tailored to the needs of an individual customer. The dynamic packaging engine begins with customer segmentation based on context for travel such as number in party, length of stay, booking window, etc. followed with a recommendation engine that works in phases: air itinerary selection, followed by hotel, and ground transportation. Unlike the OTA version that begins with hotel bookings, the airline version always begins with air bookings. The package is created dynamically inclusive of taxes and related fees, with the total price for the package taking into consideration supplier inventory levels and preferred partner agreements.

7.6.1 Can Airlines Compete with the OTAs for Packages

OTAs have been in the business of selling dynamic packages since the late 1990s. The OTAs have a distinct competitive advantage in selling packages for the following reasons.

1. OTAs negotiate JCB fares (contract Bulk Adult) with airlines that can only be bundled with a package. The JCB fare does not float with the selling fare. In situations where the JCB fare is lower than the selling fare, the JCB fares can be combined with air and hotel to create very competitive packages which will be difficult to match.
2. OTAs negotiate lucrative deals with independents and hotel chains. The merchant model has a commission of 25% to 35% of the total value of the transaction. The agency model, also known as the pay at checkout model (PAC) has a commission that ranges from 20% to 30%. This gives OTAs the competitive edge in creating packages since they can lower the price of a package to maximize conversions even if the merchant model or PAC model margins are reduced.
3. Probably the most important is the sheer scale of the largest OTAs like Booking Holdings and the Expedia Group. Both claim to have 500,000 traditional hotels and a wide array of alternative accommodations such as Vacation Rentals By Owner (VRBO), apartments and homes.

In the NDC era all air fares quoted by an airline are technically private fares, which can be perceived as an advantage over packages offered by OTAs for competitiveness. By default, all packages are opaque, and the airline may choose to quote a total price or a price at the line-item level to arrive at the total price for the package. In principle, NDC allows airlines to offer more personalized and dynamic fares and services, which can be attractive to travelers compared to traditional OTA packages. However, the OTAs were the first to offer direct connections to access NDC content from airlines, which should enable them to offer these tailored options and create more competitive package deals. Besides Expedia offering their direct connects to airlines, they have also partnered with technology providers like Amadeus to integrate NDC technology, enabling them to offer more customized and competitive flight options.

For airlines, the cost of being competitive to the OTAs comes at a very high cost due to the significant margins that the OTAs extract from hotel bookings which makes it a lot easier to offer competitive packages.

Strategically for airlines to offer packages is a niche initiative. They could partner with a few hotel chains and rental car companies to offer packages on their website. A few customers may purchase the packages for convenience, even if they are not competitive with the large OTAs.

7.7 Virtual Interlining

Virtual interlining is a travel agency business process to combine flights from carriers without formal agreements into a single, seamless itinerary. By pairing budget airlines and major airlines, travel agencies can offer cheaper, more flexible and sider range of route options for travelers.

Virtual interlining is the domain of OTAs and TMCs if they choose to pursue this venue to drive incremental sales. It is not a domain that airlines specialize in, and probably never will, except maybe on a limited scale. The IATA Multilateral & Bilateral Interline Traffic Agreements (MITA & BITA) manuals are a necessary first step to determine all the participant airlines, both passenger and cargo, that have interline agreements. While it is a necessary first step to develop virtual interlining itineraries, it is also not complete. The scope of virtual interlining goes way beyond IATA airlines, and the space includes LCCs, rail, other modes of transportation, and activities.

Today, the majority of travel agencies offer basic travel experiences consisting of ground transportation and airport to airport services. The more advanced OTAs mix GDS full-service carrier shopping results with LCC content to offer on their site. Only a very few technically advanced travel agencies have ventured into the multimodal virtual interlining model by accessing data in real-time from several disparate entities related to travel.

The objective of Virtual interlining is to improve search results by combining multiple independent offers to create a complete trip offer—door to door. Virtual interlining offers passengers more choices, potentially lower prices, and access to routes that might not be available through traditional interline agreements. The larger question is whether airlines will invest in virtual interlining to enhance their network coverage, improve customer experience, and remain competitive in a dynamic market?

In the virtual interlining space, there are generalists and specialists.

There are many generalists in this space today including Kayak, Momondo, Expedia, and Skyscanner. These companies primarily targeted the OTA space, focusing on B2C customers and often operate without direct airline partnerships.

The specialists specialize in enabling multi-airline, multi-ticket trips with a focus on partnerships.

with airlines and airports to integrate virtual interlining into airline operations. Examples are DOHOP, Tripstack, and Kiwi.com. While DOHOP has focused on building close collaboration with airlines, Kiwi has targeted B2C customers with minimal direct airline partnerships.

It is unlikely airlines will venture into the virtual interlining market as a generalist. Even entering the virtual interlining space as a specialist is a stretch since it is not their core competency. Besides it requires investments in software, business processes, insurance, call center, etc. Any initiative will require partnerships with other airlines and technology vendors. The following steps are recommended.

1. Sign the IATA MITA Agreements, identify potential airline and technology partners
2. A short term strategy is to focus on baggage transfers in collaboration with the virtual interlining specialists. Self transfer is an option but will not work for passengers that have Visa restrictions. Hence the need to reach out to airlines for baggage transfer agreements.
3. The long-term strategy is to reach out to LCCs for formal structured interline agreements. LCCs control approximately 35% of the worldwide traffic.

7.8 The So-Called Connected Trip

A connected trip includes travel segments such as air, hotel, car rentals and destination activities. The concept is not new. Traditional tour operators have offered connected trips in the form of tour packages since Thomas Cook organized the first group tour from Leicester to Loughborough with the Midland Railway on July 5, 1841.

In travel, how important is the connected trip? OTAs like Booking Holdings and the Expedia Group emphasize the importance of the so-called connected trip in SEC filings [Booking Holdings, 2024]. Booking.com claimed in their Q3 2024 earnings call that connected transactions grew 40% year-over-year [Hines, 2024] and represented a high single-digit percentage of total transactions. They claim that is it an important strategy to improve the overall booking experience, increase customer loyalty, and drive a one-stop shop direct bookings. Similarly, Expedia has been promoting the so-called connected trip for two decades and in 2025 it is still less than 10% of total transaction volume.

Several factors contribute to the low penetration rate for the so-called connected trips. First, online travel consumers book different travel segments at different times. Typically, they book air first, followed by lodging, rental car and destination activities. Second, leisure travelers also want to redeem travel from their loyalty memberships. Third, and probably most important Is trust. Travelers trust supplier and travel intermediary entities for certain product that they may want, but not for the whole package.

OTAs are a better fit to sell connected trips than any other travel entity. The high single digit percentage of total transactions associated with connected trips for OTAs is an important metric. It emphasizes the difficulty in creating a one-stop shopping experience for all of a customer's travel needs. With this data, should airlines try to sell more than air travel? How confident are customers to buy a hotel room from an airline site? How confident are customers to buy an activity from an airline website instead of buying from Viator, a trusted name for activities in travel.

Perhaps it is best for airlines to stay focused on air ancillary products for the near term and excel in creating a great online experience. As consumer expectations evolve, the ability to connect data across partners and adapt in real time can be a key differentiator to create a positive customer experience. This is not an immediate priority given the emphasis, focus and investment in offer and order management.

7.9 Protecting the Airline Brand Outweighs the Challenge of Third-Party Fulfillment

Protecting the airline brand must always be the number one priority. It can only be accomplished with the successful delivery of all items in a customer's order.

Becoming a retailer of third-party products is an aspirational goal that is not a core competency of the airline today. Aggressively pursuing third-party supplier parterships to sell non-air products without a sound execution plan for fulfillment runs the risk of consumer class action lawsuits from false advertising, fraudulent charges, selling windowless window seats caused by a schedule change, selling products that cannot be fulfilled, website inaccessibility, hidden bag fees and much more.

Airline retailing strategies that rely on third-party suppliers for fulfillment are increasingly facing class action lawsuits over alleged misrepresentation, unfair practices, and discrimination. These cases focus on issues such as deceptive advertising, antitrust violations, and the ultimate liability for products and services sold by partners that is the responsibility of the airline.

Airlines may aspire to become a retailer like Amazon. This is far-fetched since there are fundamental structural differences in how Amazon operates. Amazon controls customer identity, payment credentials, fulfillment, and the customer relationship end-to-end. Airlines control seat inventory, a fragmented distribution layer, and limited payment orchestration. For non-air products, are airlines truly capable of participating in transactions that they do not control? Comparing airline retailing to Amazon-like ambitions is simply not meaningful. In the absence of adequate proof points that guarantee third-party fulfillment, airlines must focus on their core competencies for success.

Airline Pricing: Fare Products, Ancillaries, and Amenities

8

Pricing is the only element in the marketing mix that produces revenue; the other elements produce costs.

Philip Kotler

Abstract

This chapter discusses the underlying complexities and challenges of the fare management process and its role in the revenue management process. With offers and orders, airline pricing extends from the base fare to ancillary products and services and airline amenities.

The fundamentals of airline fare management are introduced including customer segmentation, fare categories, journeys, fare components and priceable units, itinerary pricing, and constructed fares. Continuous fine tuning the fare management process to avoid revenue dilution and retain competitiveness with booking class realignment, monitoring fare basis codes by customer segment, and competitiveness of fare filing with YQ/YR are reviewed.

Branded fares and dynamic pricing of ancillary products and services are reviewed along with airline amenities. With the absence of ancillary prices at multiple price points, the primary conduit for dynamic pricing of ancillaries is test and learn experimentation with reinforcement learning. Granular customer segmentation, Solo pricing and AI-powered pricing models are the most recent trends in the air pricing landscape.

Philip Kotler, Professor Emeritus of Marketing at the Kellogg School of Management, is widely regarded as the "father of modern marketing". He emphasizes the unique role of pricing within the four P's of the marketing mix: Product,

B. Vinod, *The Era of Airline Revenue Management with Offers and Orders*, Management for Professionals, https://doi.org/10.1007/978-3-032-24197-9_8

Price, Place (channel), and Promotion. While product, place (channel), and promotion require investment (costs), pricing is the single element that generates direct income for the enterprise. This highlights the strategic importance of pricing, as it is the sole variable in the marketing mix that results in sales revenue, while the other P's contribute to expenses like development, distribution, and advertising.

The value of pricing is supported by data showing that small, targeted price increase can have a much larger impact on profits than similar changes in costs or volume. Pricing is a powerful lever for improving a company's bottom line, as it is the most direct way to increase earnings without the need for costly cost-cutting or volume-driven initiatives.

8.1 Overview

In the realm of airline retailing, airline pricing is complex and is the single most important driver of competitiveness, incremental revenues, and profitability. Mastering airline pricing takes many years and it is also the least understood by revenue management and inventory analysts. Pricing complexity is influenced by the various types of fares in a market and their associated fare rules and routing restrictions. Market demand is a key influencer of pricing decisions. Factors that impact the price of an itinerary may include origin, destination, competition, demand for air travel, travel dates, booking dates, trip type, cabin, routing, fare combinability, and much more.

Besides itinerary pricing of the base fare, a new dimension is the pricing of ancillary products and services. Full-service carriers first introduced fuel surcharges in 2004 when oil prices rose above $40 per barrel. These surcharges were designed to cover the additional costs airlines incur due to higher fuel prices. Airline carrier-imposed fees can include fuel, insurance, and other cost recovery fees that are ticketed using the YQ/YR code.

In May 2008 when American Airlines started charging $15 for checked bags, it marked a significant shift for full-service carriers which had previously offered free checked baggage. Over time, this led to the introduction of a range of ancillary products and services.

The airline's cost structure plays an important role in pricing the products. Legacy carriers, commonly referred to as full-service carriers, are the established brands in the industry, and offer a wide range of services for travelers. They have established loyalty programs which drives repeat business. Historically, all FSCs have a history of providing perks and amenities such as complementary meals and in-flight entertainment. They also have a higher cost structure than Low-cost Carriers (LCCs) and typically have higher ticket prices, limiting access for budget-conscious leisure travelers.

Low-cost Carriers (LCC) came into existence in the mid-1990s and have been growing in strength. Today, approximately 33% of the worldwide air traffic is carried by LCCs. In contrast to FSCs, with their no-frills model, LCCs have lower operating costs. They fly point-to-point, manage a single fleet type, fly to secondary airports that have lower landing fees, and rely on direct distribution. LCCs also have a simplified pricing structure, and do not have codeshare or interlines. In exchange for lower base fares than FSCs, they charge for amenities such as meals, seat selection, and checked baggage. The LCC model is appealing to budget conscious leisure travelers, thereby making air travel affordable to a larger demographic. However, the no-frills approach leads to a basic travel experience, limited leg room, fewer onboard services, and fewer options to change flights.

Besides fuel surcharges, ancillary product costs, and exchange rates fluctuations, taxes and regulations from governments and airports can impact the total price of a ticket.

An important consideration in articulating a pricing strategy in the years ahead is sustainability. It is anticipated that in the future, airlines will incorporate environmental costs into the price of a ticket. To address the impact of climate change, sustainable pricing promotes responsible travel choices.

8.2 Airline Fare Management Process

The practice of printed timetables dates back to the early days of commercial aviation for airlines to inform passengers about schedules, routes and fares. Prior to airline deregulation, airfares were printed on the back of timetables. To make it easy for travelers to compare prices and plan their trips, airlines would often print their fares directly on the back of the timetable pages. As technology advanced and the Internet became commonly accessible in the mid-1990s, this practice of printed timetables vanished as airlines primarily relied on online platforms for publishing schedules and fares and the value of printed timetables has increased among collectors. Figure 8.1 is the front and back cover of an American Airlines vintage timetable from July 1, 1941, in my collection. Figure 8.2 illustrates passenger fares published on the last page from July 1, 1941.

The airline fare management process for the past several decades has remained relatively unchanged except for the growing complexity in fares and fare rules (Vinod, 2010). In January 2021 ATPCO acquired SITA's fare management system, called Air Fare Insight (AFI), that was used by over 20 airlines including Singapore Airlines, Cathay Pacific, Emirates, Qantas, and Virgin Atlantic to manage the filing of fares in response to shifting market conditions.

Figure 8.3 illustrates the airline fare management process after SITA's AFI was acquired by ATPCO in January 2021.

With this change SITA no longer played a role in inbound or outbound fare distribution, leaving the task to ATPCO. Also in 2021, ATPCO added new features to streamline existing workflows with automated business rules, thereby reducing manual errors in the fare filing process. Both ATPCO and SITA (Société Internationale de Télécommunications Aéronautiques) are technology providers that are owned by the airline community.

Fig. 8.1 Airline schedules and fares July 1, 1941 (front and back cover)

Since deregulation, an airline's main goal in controlling market pricing has been to match a competitor's fare (Crandall, 1998; Kretsch, 1995nineteenth). This is because adding an additional passenger has a relatively low marginal cost in a business that relies heavily on capital and assets. Hence the focus is on protecting and retaining market share and paying down fixed costs. Consequently, an airline's fare actions are mostly reactive and not based on the quality of the schedule (the Quality-of-Service Index or QSI) to distribute a Quality of Service Adjusted Fare (QSAF). This behavior is consistent with the desire of airlines to maintain market share. Research dating back to the century confirms that price matching in a competitive marketplace can be an optimal strategy (Curry, 1995). The French philosopher and mathematician Antoine Augustin Cournot applied it to his model of competition in an oligopoly (Cournot, 1838) where firms independently choose output quantities to maximize profit, essentially defining a pure strategy Nash equilibrium over a century before John Nash. In Cournot's original 1838 model, two firms (owners of mineral springs) compete in a market by choosing the quantity of water to produce rather than the price. In a Cournot equilibrium, no firm can increase profit by unilaterally changing its output, assuming others keep theirs constant. The equilibrium is found where each firm's output is the "best response" to the quantity produced by its competitor.

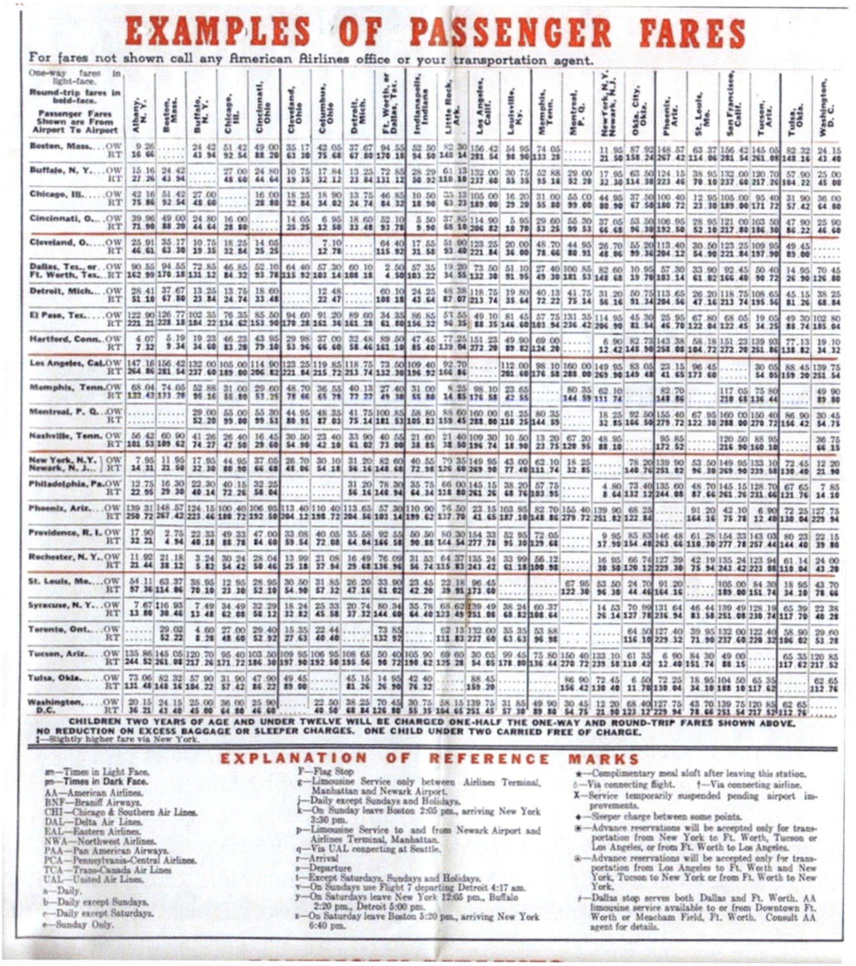

Fig. 8.2 Example of passenger fares, July 1, 1941

8.2.1 Airline Fare Matching and Nash Equilibrium

While Cournot focused on output, Nash's work in the 1950s generalized this concept, providing a mathematical framework for strategic interactions where no player has an incentive to deviate. The Cournot-Nash Equilibrium results in a market price and quantity between that of a monopoly and perfect competition. As the number of firms in a Cournot model increases, the market output tends toward the competitive level and the price decreases. In game theory, a Nash equilibrium (Nash, 1950), named after mathematician John Nash, is a stable outcome where no player can improve their own payoff by unilaterally changing their strategy, assuming the strategies of the other players remain unchanged. It represents a

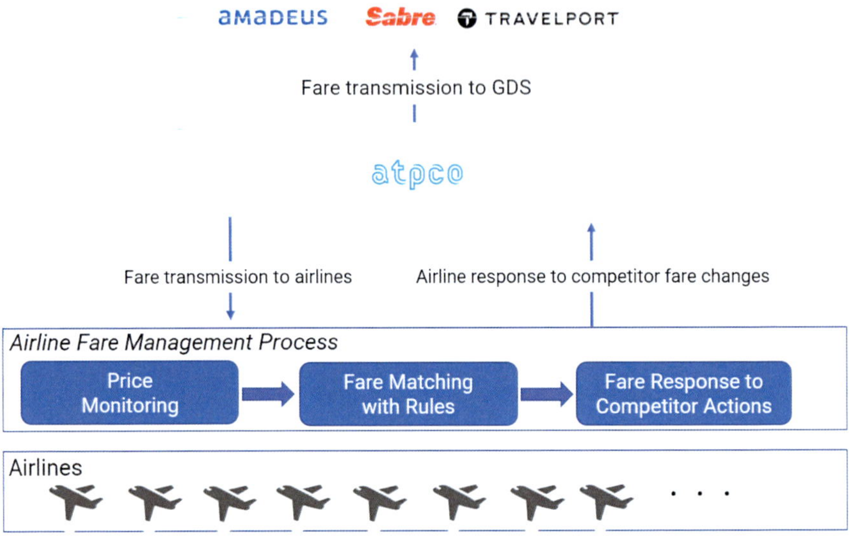

Fig. 8.3 Airline fare management process

state where all players have chosen their best strategy in response to the strategies of the other players.

Airline fare matching is a competitive pricing strategy that can lead to a Nash equilibrium, a stable state where no airline can unilaterally change its price to increase its profit. A Nash equilibrium can occur when both airlines choose a low price or a high price. In an asset intensive industry, during a price war, a low-price equilibrium can emerge as the unique static Nash equilibrium, as each airline has a strong incentive to match a competitor's low price to avoid losing market share.

In the travel marketplace, if one airline lowers its price, the competitors are incentivized to do the same, and vice versa. A Nash equilibrium can occur with either all airlines choosing a lower price or all airlines choosing a higher price.

8.2.2 Fare Management Is Labor Intensive

ATPCO fare filing is a labor-intensive process due to the sheer volume and complexity of airline pricing data. The problem is exacerbated by the long tail of markets. These are the large number of less popular markets that require the same process as major markets, demanding resources. Several airlines and intermediaries have developed external programming capabilities to gather and process ATPCO fare data after a transmission. This data is used for tasks like fare matching and cancellations, based on pre-defined rules. The processed information is then formatted into a file that is ready for ATPCO submission, ensuring it is uploaded before the next scheduled deadline for fare distribution.

8.2.3 Anti-Trust Allegations

In the early 1990s, the U.S. Department of Justice filed a lawsuit against ATPCO and eight major airlines, including American, Delta, and United, alleging that they used the ATPCO system to coordinate fare changes and fix prices. The complaint, filed on December 21, 1992, by the U.S. Department of Justice (DOJ), claimed that airlines used ATPCO to exchange information about fare increases and discounts, which facilitated anti-competitive practices.

In ATPCO's defense, it plays the role of a neutral facilitator, processing and distributing the vast amount of pricing information generated by individual airlines, who make their own pricing decisions. However, the historical antitrust cases demonstrate that the methods and systems used by ATPCO have been the subject of scrutiny regarding their potential to facilitate coordination of fares among competitors.

On March 17, 1994, the DOJ, and other defendant airlines and ATPCO entered into a consent decree, which became final on August 10, 1994. It required the airlines to stop certain collusive activities and forced changes to the ATPCO system to close "gaps" that facilitated communication about future fares. Airlines were prohibited from disseminating information concerning *planned or contemplated* fares (Department of Justice, 1993).

The consent decree was designed to prevent the airlines from further price coordination. This case highlights concerns about the potential for anti-competitive behavior in relation to ATPCO's role in disseminating fare information.

8.2.4 The Absence of Price Leadership

Strategic proactive pricing for price leadership in a market has never gained traction in the airline industry. Advanced pricing decision support [Ratliff and Vinod, 2016] applications that set fares in a market based on quality of service and management objectives such as improve yields or market share, despite their intrinsic value, have not been adopted in the airline industry to manage fares.

However, this may change with NDC adoption since technically all fares distributed through the NDC API are private fares. Further, in the NDC world, airlines do not have to distribute their fares to ATPCO. In the hybrid era, airlines continue to distribute their public fares through ATPCO. As a result, NDC content and EDIFACT content can coexist on travel agency desktops, and the momentum does not exist today for a transition to proactive pricing. In the future, in a pure NDC environment for all bookings from all airlines, this might change and proactive pricing will be based on market domination and the quality of the schedule.

8.3 The Mechanics of Airline Fares

Airlines file fares with various purchase or travel restrictions with ATPCO. Prior to the acquisition of SITA's AFI product, 87% of the world's fare filings were made through ATPCO and the fares database had more than 300 million fares that yielded 17.6 million fare/rule changes daily, and 50 million Routehappy API calls processed daily.[1] Routehappy, acquired by ATPCO in 2018, unified onboard and fare data to provide a view of the in-flight experience, fare benefits, and restrictions. ATPCO is owned by many of the major airlines and provides data collection and distribution clearing house services for more than 400 carriers worldwide. The fare aggregators consolidate fares received from various carriers and broadcast the fares to all participating airlines and subscribers such as the GDSs and third-party retailers. Hence, before the launch of IATA NDC, fare transparency to travel agents and consumers was guaranteed.

There are six dimensions to a fare, as described in Table 8.1:

These six dimensions are physically separate. In other words, the fare basis code does not define a rule, but it refers to a rule that is defined elsewhere. The same is also true with footnotes, general rules, routings, and RBD validation.

8.3.1 Booking Class, Fare Category and Fare Basis Code

Booking classes, also known as reservation booking designators, RBDs, are identified by single-letter codes (e.g., Y, B) and represent unique segments based on fare rules. Examples of segments are unrestricted full Y, restricted discount, promotional discount, visiting friends and relatives (VFR), etc. These booking class codes are not standard across airlines. Many airlines use all letters of the alphabet,

Table 8.1 Dimensions to a fare

Dimensions	Description
Fare record	Consists of the origin and destination, the fare amount, fare basis code, footnote, and the routing number. There are eight different record types that serve different functions in the processing of a fare
Rules (fare categories)	Restrictions applicable to a fare
Footnotes	Additional rule restrictions applicable to a fare. It is commonly used to include travel restrictions or ticketing restrictions
General Rules	Additional rule restrictions that may be applicable to a fare
Routing	The origin and destination and allowable cities in between
RBD Validation	Validate availability of booking class (Reservation Booking Designator)

[1] ATPCO website, 2025. https://www.atpco.net/about#:~:text=Today%2C%20our%20database%20holds%20more,million%20fare%2Frule%20changes%20daily.

Table 8.2 Commonly used booking class codes

Fare Type	Common Booking Class Codes
First Class	F, A
Business Class	J, C, D, I, Z
Premium Economy	W, E
Full-fare Economy	Y, B, M, H
Discounted Economy	K, L, Q, V, U, T, N, O, S

except for I and O which are not distributed to intermediaries, to facilitate finer levels of inventory controls. They are used by revenue management to forecast demand, set inventory controls on the reservations system, and distribute airline seat availability to the GDSs. For example, if booking class B has a B5 display in city pair availability on a GDS it means that five seats can be booked in B booking class. Similarly, if the display is B0, it implies that B is not available.

The commonly used booking classes that represent the first letter of the fare basis code are shown in Table 8.2.

The fare categories, also known as fare types, to avoid confusion with the ATPCO fare rule categories, define the market segments. The fare category is an internal classification by an airline to identify and group fares into predefined market segments. Fare basis codes and booking classes are external classifications that are published to travel agencies, tour operators, and consumers.

The fare basis codes represent the fares with its associated rules, restrictions, routings, and footnotes represent the selling products that are ultimately distributed by an airline to the target channels. They serve as a unique identifier that is used to link fare rules and fare amounts. The first letter of a fare basis code is almost always the RBD. The fare basis is the code that appears on the ticket. It can include letters, numbers and up to two slashes (/). It is a compilation of the fare class or ticketing code and one or two ticketing designators.

A fare basis code is up to 15 characters long. It can include letters, numbers and up to two slashes. It is also a shorthand method for describing pricing rules, a compilation of the fare class or ticketing code and one or two ticketing designators. The fare basis code is not published, it is constructed by the pricing process and is shown on the ticket. A full-service carrier (FSC) may have between 100,000 and 150,000 fare basis codes and many of them may be used for multiple markets.

Table 8.3 illustrates a sample of characters and numerals used in the definition of the fare basic code for a fare. In this table it is assumed that the first character of the fare basis code is the RBD, and other codes follow.

For example, consider the fare basis code KL14RTNR. The letter K refers to the class of service, the RBD, L stands for low season, and it is a 14-day round trip refundable fare.

A many-to-one relationship exists between fare basis codes and fare categories. While ideally each fare category should map to a unique booking class, this is not the case, and a many-to-one relationship exists between fare categories and booking classes. For example, in the coach cabin, both Premium Economy

Table 8.3 Interpreting the fare basis code

Examples of Codes Used in Fare Basis Code	Interpretation
First Letter of the Fare Basis Code	Usually the RBD (booking class)
E	Excursion fare
OW	One-way fare
RT	Round trip fare
W	Weekend fare
X	Weekday fare
H	High season
L	Low season
CH	Child fare
IN	Infant fare
NR	Non-refundable
Numerals	Maximum stay, minimum stay restrictions
ID / AD	Industry discount / travel agency staff discount

and unrestricted frequent flyer redemptions may be mapped to the same booking class Y. Booking classes play an important role in both online fares and interline agreements. Incorrect mapping of a fare to a booking class or using the wrong designator on an interline agreement can result in loss of revenue. A booking class is a required element for auto pricing of passenger itineraries by GDSs. Booking classes are distributed globally through fare aggregators ATPCO and SITA. The airline reservations systems distribute booking class availability to the GDSs and third party retailers.

Figure 8.4 illustrates the relationship between fare basis codes, fare categories (also known as fare types or fare groups) and booking classes.

Fare categories and fare basis codes are in the domain of airline pricing. Figure 8.4 illustrates the relationship between fare basis codes, fare categories (types) and booking classes.

8.3.2 Fare Classes and Booking Classes

A fare class specifies the rules of an airline's fare, specified in one to eight characters. Every fare has a fare class code which is used for pricing. Revenue management analysts incorrectly refer to booking classes (RBDs) and fare classes inter-changeably, which should be avoided.

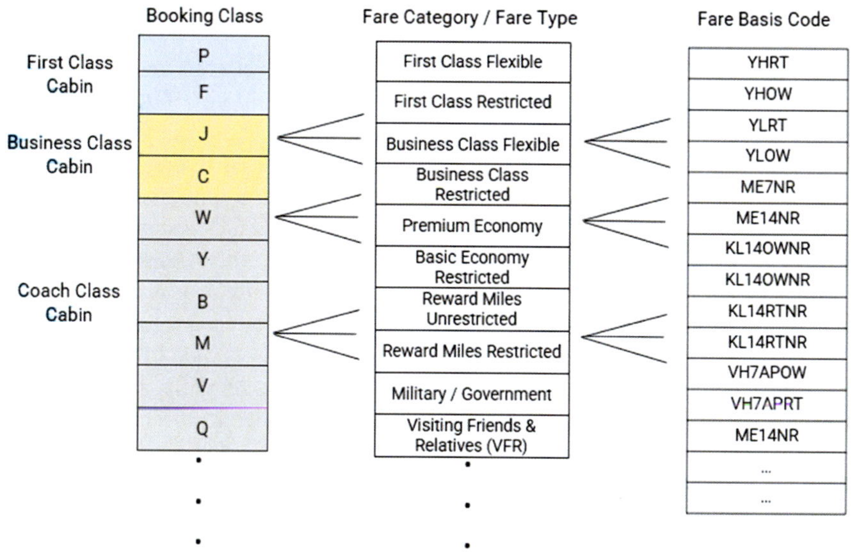

Fig. 8.4 Relationship between booking classes, fare categories and fare basis codes

8.4 Classification of Fare Products

In airline pricing there are four distinct fare products. They are public fares, private fares, web fares and opaque fares. Fare categories are referenced in this section, and they are described in Sect. 8.8.

8.4.1 Public Fares

Airlines create public fares and distribute them to fare distribution vendors like ATPCO that make them available globally through GDSs and other subscribers. All customer segments can access public fares, also known as published fares. However, the term "published fares" can be misleading because all fares, whether public or private, are published for access to certain entities with permission. Gross fares or IATA fares are other names for public fares.

8.4.2 Private Fares

An airline creates private fares using private tariffs. These fares are not widely distributed and are only available for discreet sales with specific permissions at the point of sale. Private fares use security in either ATPCO Category 15 (CAT 15) or Category 35 (CAT 35) to determine *who can sell* them and Category 1 (CAT 1) to specify *who can buy* them.

Private fares fall within the provisions of Category 15, Category 25, and Category 35 and have several variations.

A corporate fare is a private fare that is negotiated between an airline and a corporation. The creation of new fares can be enabled through CAT 25), which uses rules data to specify the market fares and amounts. These fares can either be calculated from existing fares and market rules or specified to create a new fare using the rule provisions in CAT 25. The fares generated by this process will not have a fare class application or be published fares in ATPCO systems. To ensure proper pricing, CAT 25 requires the Fare by Rule Index, also known as Record 8, to be coded for a given rule. By utilizing CAT 25, an airline can create new fares by filing discounts on a public fare (e.g., an ADT adult fare or a Passenger Type Code (PTC)), but the same rules will apply to the discounted fare. The public fare rules can be overridden or combined when creating the FBR fare, which is typically accessed at the point of sale. A discount applies to the amount of the public fare along with its associated rules and restrictions. Changes may also be permitted with a fee. For corporations, the CAT25 discount may not be applicable across all RBDs but is usually limited to the higher fare RBDs in the hierarchy. This can result in situations where the lowest public fare available is cheaper than the lowest corporate discounted fare since the RBD is higher in the fare hierarchy. In some cases, CAT 35 security may replace the CAT 15 security, but CAT 15 can still be used to enforce ticketing date and sales restrictions.

The CAT 35 *negotiated fare with markup* is a private fare with limited distribution. It is a type of negotiated fare that is designed to handle the requirements of net remit programs, IT fares (special discounted fares offered to travel agents and tour operators), corporate fares, and other private fares. These fares are ticketed using a "net remit" program that allows airlines to manage and reconcile discounted fares with their agency contracts. Travel agencies can use "net fares" (a selling fare minus a commission) for their own markups or redistribution. The program provides the necessary data for ticketing and financial reconciliation, including the net fare, selling fare, and other details like commission and tour codes.

These fares can include multiple related fare amounts, special ticketing, fare markups, and enhanced security over existing sales restrictions (CAT 15). Negotiated fares are contracts between airlines and travel agencies or other entities such as consolidators that allow them to sell published fares for less or offer special fares authorized by the airline. These fares are always private data and are generally sold through wholesalers, tour operators, and travel agents. When selling a private negotiated fare, the travel agent agrees with the airline on the net fare amount for the tariff, marks up the fare, and sells it to a retail agent or passenger. Negotiated fares may consist of multiple fare levels, fare amounts, security, and ticketing data unique to the seller, and use CAT 25 for fare generation and CAT 35 for defining the markup (or markdown) subject to the specified range.

When a customer purchases a private fare from a travel agent, the agent marks up the net fare negotiated with the airline and submits that amount to the airline through the BSP[2] for settlement. Private fares of this type are common in the Asia/Pacific region, Latin America, and the Middle East and present unique challenges to airlines, such as channel conflict, revenue dilution, and lack of control over the selling fare. Negotiated fares are also known as off-tariff fares, sanction fares, unpublished fares, market fares, confidential fares, net fares, secured fares, wholesaler fares, consolidator fares, bucket fares, and gray market fares. Managing the net/net fare (net of commissions and overrides) is crucial because gross fares do not accurately represent what the airline receives for these unpublished tariffs. In some cases, the net/net fare could be as low as 40% of the gross fare.

A commonly used private fare is a negotiated fare that follows CAT 35 rules for security ("who can sell" and ticketing requirements), as well as markup and commissions for travel agencies that sell the fare. Negotiated fares of this type can be created using a CAT 25 fare by rule (FBR), with or without a discount, to which a markup and/or commission can be specified. For example, a public fare of $1,000 with an FBR 10% discount and a 5% markup would result in the airline receiving $900 (90% of $1,000), the agency receiving $45 (5% markup on $900), and the customer paying $900 + $45 = $945. Through negotiated fares, airlines can promote the sale of specific high-value fares.

Travel agencies can receive a commission from airlines to promote fare sales with negotiated fares. In countries like Brazil, where the agency/airline direct model is used, the fare is handled with CAT 35 over CAT 25. This means that fares are generated based on available public fares with CAT 25, viewed with CAT 35 security, and the net fare and FBR fare amounts are the same. Even though the airline sells the ticket, they can still specify a sales commission (e.g., 1%) for the agency.

To simplify the management of negotiated fare contracts with travel agencies, airlines can file fares directly with the GDS with which they have a subscription. This direct filing process eliminates the ATPCO latency and appears quickly in the GDS for consumption. All GDSs offer a negotiated fares database and provide tools to create, manage, and distribute negotiated contracts. With the onset on NDC, the direct fare filings to GDSs will cease to exist in the future, since all itineraries are priced by the airline. In other words, NDC allows airlines to distribute content and fares directly to travel agencies, including negotiated fares. Today we live in the hybrid era where EDIFACT and NDC messages coexist and many airlines use a hybrid approach, where some fares are filed through GDSs directly or indirectly via ATPCO, while others are exclusively distributed directly through NDC.

8.4.2.1 Impact of NDC on Private Fares

For NDC bookings, the GDSs do not price itineraries.

[2] 1Billing and Settlement Plan (BSP) for IATA accredited passenger sales agents.

The underlying principles of Category 25 fares (like negotiated corporate rates or fares calculated from a base fare) remain, but their distribution method is changing. GDSs and NDC Aggregators can still access CAT 25 by sending a request to the airline, and the airline responds with a product that fits the offer. The fixed discounts for CAT 25 may evolve to a discount range allowing the airline to offer a continuous fare within the negotiated discount range in the NDC channel at the time of search. Further, airlines use the NDC channel to gain more control over their content and pricing, including exclusive offers that might be generated from CAT 25 rules. These can be made available only through NDC-enabled channels.

It is expected that the negotiated CAT 35 fares will continue to exist with NDC bookings, but their distribution method will evolve. Airlines can define and control their own rules for these private fares, including specific conditions for ticketing and commissions. Travel agents who have a contract with the airline can access these negotiated fares and are authorized to sell them and add their own markups.

8.4.3 Web Fares

Web fares came into existence in the late 1990s and early 2000s in Central and South America. These fares are only available on an airline's website. They were created to help airlines increase brand recognition and lower distribution costs through direct sales to consumers. Airlines with full content agreements cannot offer lower fares on their website than what is available through the GDS channel. However, some airlines still publish web-only fares that can only be purchased and ticketed through their website. This is common in Latin America, where airline web fares may be cheaper than market fares.

8.4.4 Opaque Fares

Opaque airfares enable airlines to protect their standard pricing models and fare structures. These fares hide airline details until after the purchase is complete. Buyers won't see the airline, flight number, or times before paying. Credit card information is needed before the tickets are issued.

Travelers with flexible plans can find big savings using opaque fares. However, these tickets often can't be refunded or changed. Travel agencies don't easily find opaque fares. Understanding them is key to explaining why you can't match those rates.

OTAs negotiate deeply discounted bulk fares with airlines known as JCBs whi which is an industry Passenger Type Code (PTC) that is used to identify a Contract, Bulk, Adult passenger type. This refers to a passenger type code (PTC) for contract, bulk, adult. These deeply discounted fares can only be sold as part of a package and the OTAs only reveal the airline and flight number after the purchase is complete. By incorporating these discounted fares that may include a hotel or car rental to produce a competitive package price, especially when the discounted fare is lower than the selling public (ADT) fare. However, this is not always the case, as there are instances where the discounted JCB fare can be more expensive than the public ADT fare. In markets where the OTA has negotiated JCB fares, the air shopping entry should provide both the public ADT (adult) fare and the JCB fare, enabling an automated decision regarding the inclusion of the JCB fare in the package that is promoted to the customer.

8.4.5 What Is an NDC Fare?

IATA NDC has promoted the end of full content agreements from the major carriers that frequently withhold the lowest fares from the GDS channel. For example, both United Airlines and American Airlines withhold the low Basic Economy fares from the GDS, so these fares are only available on the airline website and preferred NDC channels.

There is no such thing as an NDC fare. Airlines publish fares and decide which channels should have access to them, and that is the new reality.

8.5 Impact of NDC on Airfares

There are two aspects to air fares with NDC adoption. With the adoption of NDC, airlines do not have to publish their fares to ATPCO, and they have an opportunity to simplify the complex fare rules, general rules, footnotes, and routing restrictions that exist today. It is anticipated that even if airlines do not publish their fares through ATPCO, they will likely retain all the complexities of the existing tariff structure to avoid revenue leakage.

There is also the view that with NDC, the volume of air fares will increase with the introduction of the following types of fares:

1. Date specific fares,
2. Time of day specific fares, and
3. Routing specific fares.

This has the potential to increase the complexity and costs in data storage and processing for the airline (and not the GDS). Date-specific fares and time of day specific fares are covered under ATPCO Category 2 (Day/Time) which defines times and/or days when travel is or is not permitted. It is anticipated that these types of fares will proliferate as airlines fine tune their continuous pricing based price quote for each itinerary. A routing specific fare is an airfare that indicates a specific route and intermediate points for travel between origin and destination. Routing fares are an exception to mileage-based pricing, allowing travelers to pay a specific fare for travel along a certain route. Routing specific fares are usually less expensive than normal fares.

Airlines can use the NDC messaging standard to further adjust these granular fares in real-time based on demand and offer a wider range of fares and options. For example, airlines can offer tailored fare options, ancillary services, and promotions.

8.5.1 RBDs and Fixed Price Points

An airline's ability to set market fares is limited by the 26 RBDs that are associated with fares. They can only offer a finite set of price points based on reservation booking designators (RBD). When these prices are published through ATPCO, updates happen at predefined time intervals. As a result, even if revenue managers see data suggesting a price change, the prices often don't change in real-time. RBDs are also used by GDSs to price itineraries based on RBD availability distributed by airlines from their reservations systems to GDSs. With NDC the airline is the only entity that can quote a price for an itinerary. In this scenario, RBDs should be viewed as reference fares and if the airline chooses, can quote a dynamic continuous price to the customer based on forecast demand, remaining supply, and the associated bid prices for the itinerary. Technically, RBD availability, internal to the airline in the NDC era, can be replaced with customer segment definitions, though this will require significant changes to the host CRS.

The "NDC standard" enables airlines to implement continuous pricing. This means they can offer multiple ticket prices on the price-demand curve. While an airline still registers 26 fares in EDIFACT, it can also present offers at any price point between those fares on its website and other NDC-enabled platforms. Essentially, the airline controls the pricing during the search process and can make a fare of $225 available, or any price that falls between the $200 and $250 range.

8.6 Airline Pricing and the IATA Conundrum

The complexity in pricing an itinerary is related to the different types of rules that may apply to a fare. These fare restrictions must always be met when pricing units are identified to price an itinerary.

Questions that come up frequently are: *Why is airline pricing so complex? Why are there so many fare rules? Why are there routings and route maps?* Fare rule categories evolved over time as airlines wanted to segment customers and minimize revenue dilution. Routing and route maps are interconnected concepts that play a critical role in pricing an itinerary. By specifying valid routings and connections, circuitous routings that accrue more miles for a leisure traveler are avoided.

In a white paper, IATA recently advocated (IATA, 2024) that in the world of offers and orders, airlines must move away from the legacy RBDs and fare rules.

Why is it a *conundrum?* It is "*an intricate and difficult problem with a seemingly impossible solution.*"

Since there will no longer be a need to distribute RBD availability to GDSs when all airlines have migrated to NDC, RBDs will continue to serve as internal reference fares for airlines practicing continuous pricing and a range of other applications such as seat assignment based on the fare. More details are provided in Chapter 12 (Classless Revenue Management) on the role of RBDs in airline pricing.

And in the same white paper (IATA, 2024) IATA advocating the elimination of fare rules, is really not an option as it will lead to massive revenue dilution. Fare rules fundamentally serve a single purpose, which is to segment customers with fences (e.g. advance purchase, minimum stay, etc.) and avoid revenue dilution. From the article, it is clear that IATA and many others view ATPCO as legacy technology with a legacy data architecture.

The ATPCO legacy mainframe technology and data architecture needs an overhaul with a serverless event-driven architecture and push notifications. Serverless functions can automatically scale to handle fluctuations in demand, ensuring performance and responsiveness, especially crucial during peak fare filing periods. In addition, the pay-per-use model means ATPCO would only pay for the compute time and resources consumed by functions, potentially reducing costs associated with idle servers or infrastructure maintenance. This can also accelerate development cycles and enable quicker deployment of new features or updates. But modernization may not be a high priority and if it is, ATPCO should publish a roadmap.

8.7 Pricing Terminology

Air pricing terminology is vast and refers to the specific words and phrases used to describe the cost of air travel and the various components that make up that cost. These terms are used by airlines, travel agencies, and customers when discussing or understanding the price of an itinerary.

8.7.1 General Air Pricing Terminology

The terms described below are the general terms in airline pricing. They are listed in alphabetic order.

Airfare
Fee paid for air transportation.

Ancillary Fees
Fees for additional services, such as checked baggage, seat selection, or in-flight entertainment.

APEX Fare

Reservations for Advance Purchase Excursion (APEX) fares cannot normally be changed without a penalty and often have refund restrictions. There is a advance purchase requirement, usually no stopovers are allowed, and direct flights are used. They are typically sold on a return (round trip) basis and have a minimum and maximum stay requirement. Codes AP, AN, or AB are normally included in the fare basis.

Base Fare

The price for an airline ticket before taxes, surcharges, or ancillary fees.

Circuity

Circuity in airline pricing is the ratio of the actual distance flown by an aircraft to the straight-line Great Circle Distance (GCD) between the origin and destination. For example, a direct, non-stop flight has a circuity value of 1.0 while connecting flights have values greater than 1.0, representing the excess miles traveled.

$$Circuity = \frac{Actual\ Flight\ Distance}{Great\ Circle\ Distance}$$

Circuity identifies inefficient routes and measures how out-of-the-way a connecting flight takes a passenger. To minimize abuse with out-of-the-way connections, airline tariffs often include the maximum permitted mileage (MPM) for a given journey and if the itinerary's actual distance exceeds the pre-defined MPM threshold, a penalty fare will be applied to the ticket. In U.S. domestic markets the threshold is around 25% longer than the shortest scheduled direct flight, called the Ticketed Point Mileage (TPM). MPM is more prevalent in international ticketing. Fare construction often restricts the allowable connections to prevent passengers from buying cheap, long-distance tickets that detour through different geographical regions to accrue frequent flyer miles. Competing airlines that do not "own" the nonstop flight out of a hub frequently use circuity data to either ignore or sometimes price the connecting itinerary lower to attract passengers who would otherwise choose the direct competitor.

Co-terminals

Co-terminals refer to different airports that are treated as equivalent for fare calculation purposes. This means that, for a specific fare rule, an airline may consider two airports in the same metropolitan area as interchangeable for calculating ticket prices. Examples of co-terminals are LaGuardia (LGA, LaGuardia Airport), Newark (EWR, Newark Liberty International Airport), and Islip (ISP, New York's Long Island MacArthur Airport). Co-terminals are designated for a specific fare rule. The concept of co-terminals is not relevant for low-cost airlines, as they typically use secondary airports and operate on a point-to-point route network.

Direct

A direct flight is a flight from A to B with the same flight number and no change of aircraft but may have one or more stops.

Distance-Based Fare

A distance-based fare implies that prices are determined by the distance traveled between the origin and destination, with longer distances generally resulting in higher fares. Airline pricing does not primarily rely on distance-based calculations. Instead, airlines use a dynamic pricing model based on market demand, competitor pricing, and various factors to optimize revenue. While distance might be a factor in mileage programs, the actual ticket prices are driven by market forces in the US domestic market.

International airfares are also market based, but mileage does receive consideration in determining penalties. For international tariffs, between point A and point B, there is a maximum permitted mileage (MPM). Carriers that serve the market use their hubs to fly passengers from A to B, provided the MPM is not exceeded. If the MPM is exceeded because of an out-of-the-way connect point, a surcharge will apply based on excess mileage.

Dynamic Pricing

Dynamic pricing is a pricing strategy where a dynamic price is quoted in real-time based on market conditions. The dynamic fare is a perturbation off the itinerary price calculated based on published (filed) fares in the market.

Ethnic Airfare

An airline practice of offering different airfares based on a traveler's nationality or domicile, often leading to lower prices for certain individuals traveling to or from specific locations. This practice is more common in some developing countries and in Europe.

For example, off the coast of Spain, there is a special discount on airfare for residents of the Islands, including Mallorca, when traveling to and from the mainland and between the islands. This discount is a 75% reduction off of the base ticket price. To receive the discount, travelers need a "Certificado de residencia para viajes" (Certificate of Residence for Travel) issued by the town hall where the traveler is registered. The PTC is DNI (Spanish Citizens with own national ID).

Excursion Fare

Excursion fares are a type of discounted airline fares. Excursion fares are typically cheaper than full fare, but also have restrictions, such as weekend stays, advance purchase, and times of the year when you can use them. An Excursion Fare is a Special Fare. The code E or EE is found at the end of the fare basis followed by the maximum stay in terms of days (e.g., 30) or months (e.g., 3M).

Fare Basis Code

The fare basis code is an alphanumeric code that identifies the fare and its associated rules, including restrictions, characteristics of the fare, and validity. It consists of a leading letter that indicates the booking class followed by letters or numerals that define the rules associated with the fare. While it is not standardized across the industry, many airlines use similar structures.

Flat Fare

A flat fare, also called a flat fee or flat rate, is a fixed price for a given service, regardless of distance or other factors such as actual cost and usage. Flat fares are often used for baggage fees or changes to flight tickets.

Full Fare

A full fare is an unrestricted fare. They are the most expensive and typically provide the most flexibility and options. They may be the only fares available on the day of travel or under short notice. Many business travelers frequently fly on unrestricted fares because they purchase tickets at the last minute or have business travel needs that require additional flexibility. A Full Fare is also called a normal fare.

Lowest Fare

The lowest published airfare for a specific route, though seat availability at that fare may be limited or unavailable.

Lowest Selling Fare

The lowest published airfare for a specific route, that is available for purchase, after considering seat availability.

Maximum Permitted Mileage (MPM)

North American fares are based on market and routing. International airfares are also market based, but mileage does receive consideration in determining penalties. For international fares, there is a maximum permitted mileage (MPM) between every origin and destination. Carriers typically route customers through their hubs. In the event that the mileage is exceeded, a surcharge that can range from 5 to 25% in increments of 5% will be assessed for the additional 5% to 25% mileage.

Nonstop

The term Nonstop is used to describe a flight from A to B with no stops enroute.

Normal Fare

Normal fares are typically available for all classes of service and are more flexible and expensive. Normal fares are typically valid for one year.

Point-to-Point Fare

Point-to-point fares allow passengers to travel directly from point A to B in any class. There are usually no advanced booking requirements or refund restrictions. Routing is usually limited to direct flights, although connecting flights may be available, providing no stopovers are made. Fares may be sold on a one-way or round-trip basis. Round-trip fares are typically valid for one year, provided there are no seasonal restrictions. Code 2 or 3 may appear at the end of the fare basis.

Promotional Fare

These fares are discounted fares offered to the public on published fares, encompassing reductions in dollar amount, percentage discounts, or discounts based on passenger miles.

Public Excursion Fares

Public excursion fares (PEX) and Super-PEX fares have the same restrictions as APEX fares but may be purchased at any time. Usually, no stopovers are allowed, and direct flights are used. They are typically sold on a return basis and have a minimum and maximum stay requirement. Codes PX or SX are included in the fare basis.

Revalidation

Normally airline tickets are valid for one year from the date of issue. An airline can revalidate a ticket and extend it over a year depending on the type of fare.

Routing

The routing rule lists the connect points allowed for travel from A to B for a particular fare. Sometimes the rule indicates that travel must be nonstop.

Rerouting

Rerouting is the process of a passenger being flown to their destination on a different flight, routing, or even airline than originally booked. The term rerouting may be misleading since the actual route does not have to change, but it could. Any changes to flights, dates, times or destinations are considered rerouting.

The itinerary price for rerouting depends on whether it is voluntary or involuntary. For voluntary changes, the new fare, taxes, and surcharges will likely be recalculated, and the passenger is usually responsible for additional costs, such as a fare difference or a change fee. If the rerouting is involuntary due to airline operational issues, it is often done at no extra cost to the passenger, who is then entitled to compensation and care depending on the circumstances.

Special Fare

Fares that are offered for a limited time or for specific travel purposes, such as student or senior discounts. These fares are discounted airfares that often come with restrictions. Special fares have restrictions attached to them, such as minimum stay restrictions or advanced purchase requirements. Some fares have a specified routing and are less expensive. The routing-specific fares have an exception to mileage-based pricing, allowing travel at the specific fare via a certain route only.

Standby

The standby feature allows a traveler to wait at the gate for a seat to become available on an earlier flight or a later flight. Discounted fares may require a change fee to permit standbys.

Stopover

A stopover from origin to destination at an intermediate airport is permitted by some fares at no charge, others allow stopovers for an additional fee, and many fares do not permit stopovers. For example Emirates Airways promote their hub in Dubai and encourage stopovers with no extra stopover charges.

Surcharges

Extra charges added to the base fare, often for fuel. Surcharges for travel agency bookings made through GDSs from a few airlines started in 2015. Surcharges are included in the price of the ticket.

Taxes, Fees, and Charges (TFC)

These are additional costs that airlines add to the base fare of a ticket. TFCs are generally not included in the displayed base fare and can include various taxes, fees, and charges. They may include departure and arrival taxes, security fees, airport facility charges (PFC), segment fees, sales and value added taxes (VAT/GST), customs and immigration fees.

Ticket by Mail (TBM)

TBM refers to Ticketing by Mail. Before the Internet era, a passenger could order tickets from the airline to be sent in the mail. By the late 1990s, a passenger could purchase a ticket online and a confirmation/ticket would be sent to the designated email address. In both cases, the passenger has the option to print their ticket or confirmation. Today, no tickets are sent by mail.

In 2008, IATA announced 100% of ticketing was electronic, which meant that airlines no longer needed to produce physical tickets.

Upgrade

An upgrade moves the traveler to a higher cabin which can be an upsell when the booking is made or an instant upgrade offered to ticketed passengers for an additional fee by many airlines.

Upsell
An upsell is a sales strategy to offer a higher priced product at the time of booking such as a Premium Economy fare versus a Main Cabin fare. The higher fare typically offers additional benefits such as refundability, seat selection, or free baggage.

VFR Fare
A Visiting Friends and Relatives (VFR) fare is a specific type of airfare designed for trips that are primarily for visiting friends and relatives. It is often used when booking travel for leisure purposes. These deeply discounted fares may have specific rules regarding changes, cancellations, minimum stay, maximum stay, and refunds. These fares also use a specific passenger type code, "VFR", to identify these fares, ensure accurate pricing, booking, and ticketing.

Waitlist
Some fares permit passengers to be put on a waiting list for a booking class because it is sold out in the airline's reservations inventory system. Waitlists are normally permitted for higher valued booking classes only. To be put on a waitlist the traveler must contact the airline or travel agent.

Zone-Based Fare
Airlines divide the world into specific zones, often based on geographic proximity. This is a fare structure that prices based on geographical zones. The fare for a flight is primarily based on the distance between the zones where the origin and destination airports are located.

8.7.2 Journeys

Before we discuss pricing of individual itineraries, it is first required to review the terminology associated with priced itineraries. There are subtle differences in terminology between North America and the rest of the world.

Travel within the United States (US/Virgin Islands/Puerto Rico) and travel between Transborder United States (US/Virgin Islands/Puerto Rico/Canada) are considered Domestic.

There are three types of journeys that are shown on OTA and airline websites. They are one-way, round trip and multi-stop. A multi-stop trip can be a circle trip, open jaw (with surface sector), or around the world.

One-Way
The passenger flies from an origination airport to a destination airport. Examples are AUS-DFW, JFK-LON. Cheap one-way fares were introduced by LCCs and it overcomes the Saturday Night Stay restriction. A one-way fare is never considered as half of a round trip.

Roundtrip

The passenger goes from an origination airport to a destination airport and returns to the same origination airport where the trip began. A round trip consists of two components: one outbound from point A to point B and a return back to point A on the same carrier and same round trip booking class. Hence the entire itinerary uses a single fare basis code. The fare for each component is the same, which is the applicable half round trip fare for each component. If different fares were used for the outbound and return, formally this is a two-component circle trip and not a round trip.

Circle Trip

If different fares are used for the outbound (A to B) and return (B to A), it means that different fare basis codes are used and it qualifies as a circle trip.

Any trip that has two or more flights or fare components because it involves traveling to a destination and then returning to the original city on a different route, often with multiple stopovers qualifies as a circle trip. Unlike a simple round trip, the outbound and return routes are not the same. For example, the itinerary A to B, B to C and then C to A is a circle trip using the same or different fare basis codes.

End-on-End

An end-on-end fare is a special type of combination in which two round trip fares are combined to produce a complete itinerary.

From	To	Rule
A	B	Rule 1
B	C	Rule 2
C	B	Rule 2
B	A	Rule 1

In this scenario, the passenger purchases a round-trip fare from A to B (Rule 1) and a separate round-trip fare from B to C (Rule 2). This implies that there is a fare break at B which may be less expensive than a round trip through fare from A to C. Fare rules usually specify whether end-on-end combinations are allowed.

It is also a combination of priceable units at fare combination points, including an A-B-A of one-way fares combined between the same points.

A method to find a lower fare is to identify an intermediate city and construct the fare with an end-on-end combination. This fare can be cheaper than a direct flight or a flight through a connecting city identified by the pricing system.

End-on-end combinations are very distinct from back-to-back ticketing, which is forbidden by many airlines.

In March 2016, American, United and Delta limited the value of end-to-end fares for travelers by introducing the restriction in the fare rule for certain non-refundable fares that says "end-on-end must be a A-B-A combination." With this restriction, a passenger could fly DFW-ORD-DFW and combine two different fares for each segment. If the passenger itinerary were DFW-ORD-BOS-ORD-DFW, two different non-refundable fares could not be used with the new restriction.

Round the World

A traveler flies from an origination airport in one direction (eastbound or westbound) around the world and crosses the international date line and returns to the same origination city where the trip began. The fares have restrictions such as the minimum and maximum number of flights, direction of travel, open jaws are not permitted and a minimum number of stopovers. They are also limited to carriers within an alliance. For example, DFW-JFK-LHR-NRT-LAX-DFW is an around the world trip.

Figure 8.5 illustrates various types of journeys.

Open Jaw

An open-jaw journey is an airline return ticket where the destination and/or the origin are not the same in both directions. The mileage for the open jaw (segment) must be equal to or less than the mileage of the shortest flown fare component. Otherwise, it will be treated as separate one-way fares. It is normal practice for airlines to calculate the fare by taking half the round-trip fare for each leg of the journey.

There are three variations.

In a destination open jaw, the traveler goes from an origination airport to the first destination airport, transfers to a different city using an alternate mode of transportation and takes a return flight back to the origination city where the trip began. Examples are JFK-LON (open jaw) CDG-JFK and JFK-AMS (open jaw) BRU-JFK. At least one segment must be half of a round-trip fare.

An origin open jaw is a trip where the traveler departs from an origination airport to a destination airport and returns to a different airport/city. Examples are DFW-LON-SAT, DFW-FCO-AUS. At least one segment must be half of a round-trip fare.

A double open jaw involves two totally separate fares. It is a single return ticket where the O&D for the first flight and the second flight are different. An example is DFW-FRA for the first flight and VIE-AUS for the second flight. At least one segment must be half of a round-trip fare.

Figure 8.6 illustrates various types of open jaw journeys.

Open jaws on an itinerary show up as ARNK, pronounced "ARUNK" which means "arrivals unknown". The code ARNK is used to indicate that there is a break in the continuity of travel between two segments, meaning the traveler is not flying directly from the arrival city of one segment to the departure city of the next. ARNK means that the method of transportation (e.g., surface travel) between the two cities is not known.

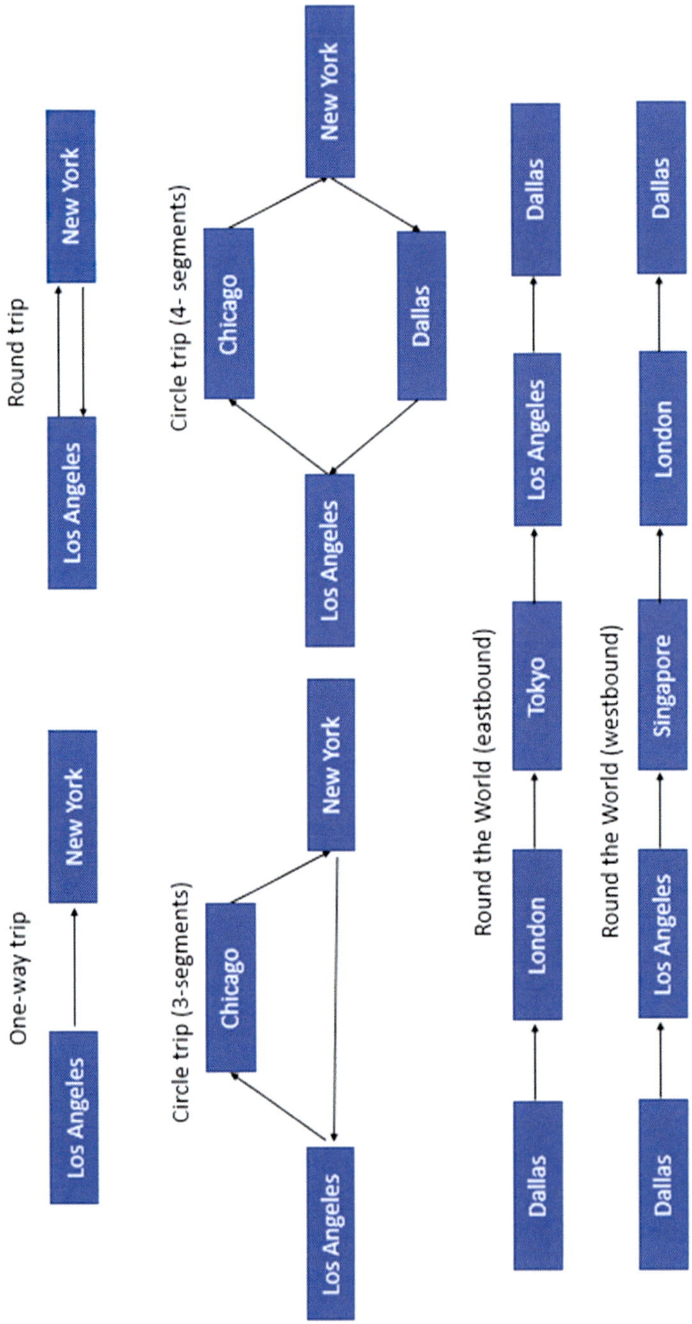

Fig. 8.5 Examples of journeys

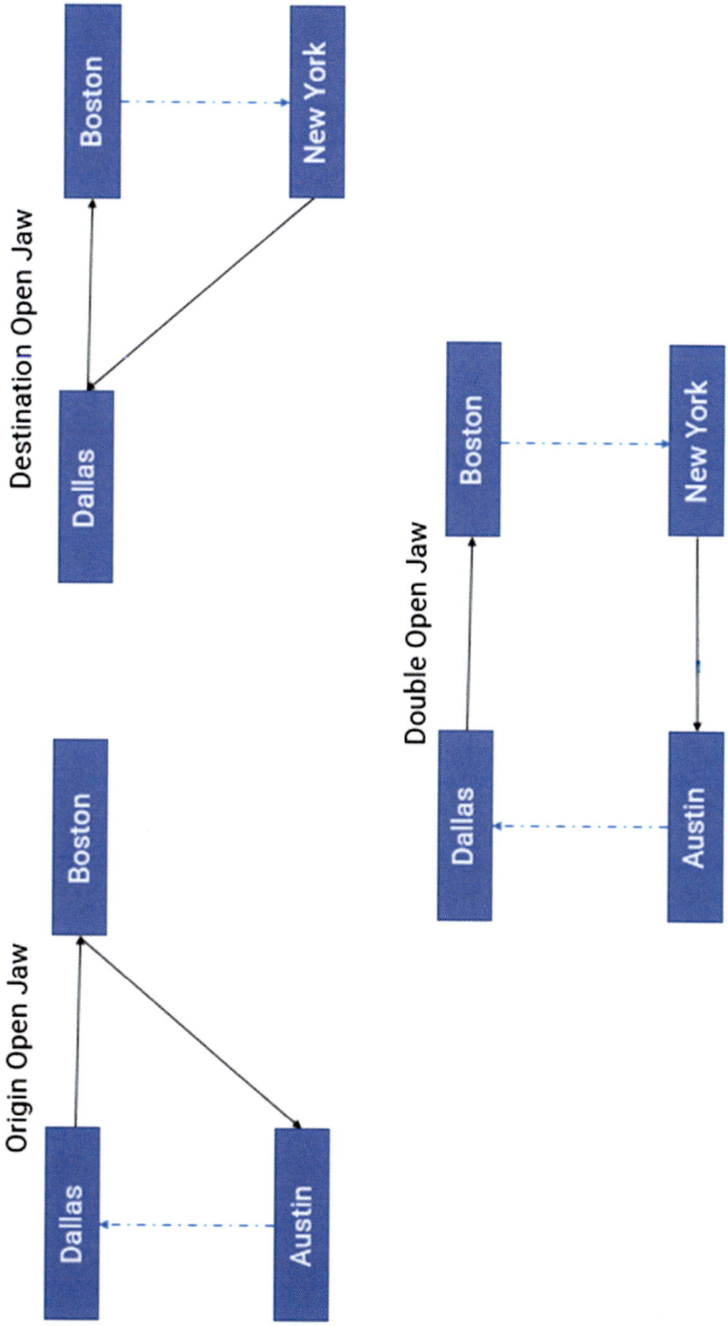

Fig. 8.6 Examples of open jaw journeys

8.8 Fare Rule Categories

ATPCO is the primary reference followed by Amadeus, Sabre, and Travelport who publish descriptions of the categories. A brief description for each of the ATPCO fare rule categories are listed below.

Category 1: Eligibility
This category defines the identity requirements, age range, and locality (residence) of a passenger type. For example, ADT: Adult, CHD: Child, UNN: Unaccompanied Child, INF: Infant without a seat, INS: Infant with a seat, BEV: Bereavement Passenger, STU: Student, MIL: Military; GVT: Government travel; JCB: Contral, Bulk Adult; etc. There are over 150 passenger type codes (PTC). They are listed in Appendix B.

Category 2: Day/Time Application
This category defines the days and / or times when travel is or is not permitted. The day/time combination applies to the origin of the fare components scheduled to depart during the specified time.

Category 3: Seasonal Application
The category is applicable for seasonal and promotional date restrictions. The seasonal fare is based on the season of the origin portion of the priceable unit (see Sect. 8.8.1). The date of departure of the originating flight of the pricing unit determines the seasonality of the fare component being validated. The application of travel may be further modified by the presence of a Travel Segment Indicator (TSI).

Category 4: Flight Application
This category indicates that a fare is only valid on specific flight numbers. Data codes in this category are taken from the rule or fare class application. Within this category flight service can be defined as nonstop, one-stop, multi-stop, or direct.

Category 5: Advance Reservations and Ticketing
This category defines the requirements for reservations and ticketing related to a fare. It specifies when reservations must be made and when ticketing must occur, potentially with conditions based on time before departure or time after reservations. This category also indicates which sectors of travel require prior confirmation before ticketing. The advance reservations and ticketing conditions shown in this category apply to original ticket issuance. They are not applicable for revalidation or reissues.

Category 6: Minimum Stay
This category defines the minimum stay restriction, specifying when return travel may commence.

If the point from which the minimum stay count begins is not defined in the rule, the "from" portion will be coded as "departure from origin." Similarly, if the point from which return travel may commence is not defined in the rule, the "to" portion will be coded as the "last point of stopover." The assumption is made that departure from origin refers to the first day after departure. The day of departure should not be counted in calculating elapsed time for the Minimum Stay.

Category 7: Maximum Stay

This category specifies the last day when travel may commence or may be completed. Departure from origin refers to the first day after departure; in other words, the day of departure should not be counted in calculating elapsed time for Maximum Stay. The assumptions made in Minimum Stay regarding the "from/to" points when not specifically defined will apply to Maximum Stay as well.

Category 8: Stopover

This category specifies the number, locations, and charges for allowable stopovers within a fare component. A U.S. domestic flight is considered a stopover when the scheduled time on the ground is longer than four hours. An international stopover exceeds 24 h. When the scheduled time on the ground is less than the domestic or international time limit, it is treated as a connection.

Some fares allow free stopovers, others allow stopovers for an additional fee, and many fares do not permit stopovers at all.

Category 9: Transfers

This category defines the conditions or restrictions under which transfers, and surface sectors may occur with the applicable charges, carriers and locations associated with them.

Category 10: Permitted Combinations (Combinability)

This category defines combinability, how a fare can be combined with multiple fares or portions of multiple fares, including different ticket types or fare classes for outbound and return journeys, circle trips, and open jaws to calculate the price for the itinerary. This category consists of subordinate category records.

Open Jaw: 101
Two Component Circle Trips: 102
More than Two Component Circle Trips: 103
End on End:104
International Add-ons: 105
Carrier Combinations: 106
Tariff Rule Combinations: 107
Fare Class/Type Combinations: 108
Open Jaw Sets: 109

Beyond a round-trip itinerary, fare combinations play a role in determining the price of the itinerary. Combinability refers to whether two or more fares can be combined to construct an itinerary that can be priced. The types of trips involving combinations are circle trips, end-on-end and open jaw combinations.

Fare combinations between higher valued RBDs and lower valued RBDs may not be allowed. For fare combinations that are allowed, the most restrictive conditions apply. For example, if combining a non-refundable fare with a 25% refundable fare is allowed, the entire ticket becomes non-refundable. Similarly, if a 3-day advance purchase fare can be combined with a 7-day advance purchase fare, the entire ticket must be purchased 7-days in advance. The low fare search algorithm imbedded in the pricing system evaluates the various combinations to arrive at the lowest priced itineraries.

Despite these various sub-categories, there is no explicit mechanism that forces the purchase of a through fare for airlines using O&D revenue management. For example, for an A-B-C itinerary connecting at B, the numeric booking class availability for A-C is different from A-B and B-C. For the O&D A-C, the numeric booking class availability is the same on segments A-B and B–C. There is no mechanism for the airline to force ticketing for the A-C itinerary using A-C RBD availability. Frequently, low fare search algorithms may price the sum of locals for a lower priced itinerary. This happens frequently because of LCC competition on a segment of the O&D itinerary.

Category 11: Blackout Days
This category is used to define single dates or date ranges when travel is not permitted.

Category 12: Surcharges
This category defines the conditions when surcharges are applicable and the corresponding charge. Examples are fuel charges, security fees, and airport taxes. Unless otherwise indicated, the surcharges are applied at the fare component level.

Category 13: Accompanied Travel
This category is used as a component of a rule when travel with more than one passenger is necessary in the booking to qualify for the fare. It may be used to define travel restrictions based on the portions of a trip where travel together is required and/or fare class/booking codes of accompanying passengers. For example, requiring someone to travel with a parent, guardian, or another passenger type is considered accompanied travel.

Category 14: Travel Restrictions
This category defines when travel dates are specifically stated in a rule. This includes the dates when the fare may first be used, travel commencement, travel expiration, or travel completion.

Category 15: Sales Restrictions
This category is used to define a fare that is available for sale, where it can be sold and ticketed. The restrictions are based on reservation and/or ticketing dates, countries

and/or currencies of sale, form of payment, method of ticketing, who may sell the fare, and where the sale can be made.

Category 16: Penalties
This category defines the penalties, if applicable for a fare and what charges will be assessed. It is also used to specify the conditions under which rerouting may take place or tickets may be reissued. This category is less used after the introduction of automated changes (Category 31) and refunds (Category 33) for processing.

Category 17: Higher Intermediate Point/Mileage
This category is used to indicate when travel via Higher Intermediate Point (HIP) is prohibited. It is used to negate assumptions when stopovers or connections are made at specific geographic locations or a HIP applies. In essence, the HIP rule ensures that a stopover or connection at a more expensive intermediate point doe not result in a lower overall fare compared to traveling directly to the destination.

Category 18: Ticket Endorsements
This category is used to indicate ticket endorsement requirements as specified in a rule. It contains the text to be used and the ticket location required for endorsement. For example, a ticket can be transferred or endorsed to another airline.

Category 19–22: Discounts
These categories are used to provide either a specific fare amount or the information for calculating a fare as defined in a rule. They are also used to specify accompanying travel requirements, age range, and the number of passengers that can qualify for the discount and ticketing provisions for the calculated fare.

Category 19 for children's discounts,

Category 20 for tour conductors,

Category 21 for sales agents, and

Category 22 for all other types of discounts (e.g., military or government personnel fly for a certain price.

Category 23: Miscellaneous Provisions
This category contains miscellaneous information that is not category specific. This category is used to specify whether certain fares should or should not be used for construction of unpublished fares, proration, refund calculation, currency adjustments or as proportional fares. It will also be used to indicate which fare classes should be used for differential calculations for mixed class travel (coach class in one leg, business class in another). The system assumption is that fares can be used for any purpose; this category is coded only when provisions in a rule or footnote override that assumption. When a fare is coded as being "Required" or "Permitted" in this category, the assumption is that it can only be used for that purpose. When a fare is

coded as being "Not Permitted," the assumption is that it can be used for any other purpose.

Category 25 Fare by Rule (FBR)

Category 25 is the Fare by Rule (FBR) application to dynamically generate new fares by using a carrier's existing fares and rules as a base. This category allows airlines to file in ATPCO increasingly complex corporate contract terms, thereby improving faring accuracy and reducing agency debit memos (ADM). The three main sections of the category are Passenger Eligibility and Fare Calculation, Resulting Fare Information, and Category Overrides. The category can also be used to indicate that no discount applies to a particular passenger. Unlike ATPCO published fares, a Category 25 FBR has no fare record or Record 1. In the absence of a matched Category 25 Record 2 or Record 3, no Fare by Rule exists for the passenger and/or fare component being priced.

Many airlines use the neutral unit of construction (NUC) to file frequent flyer redemption mileage amounts to be processed as CAT 25 fare by rule. NUC superseded the older fare construction unit (FCU) in July 1989. The NUC is a private currency that is pegged to the U.S. dollar and used to calculate a fare when the itinerary involves a combination of local currencies. For revenue travel, payment is based on the currency at the point of commencement of the itinerary.

Category 26: Groups

This category specifies the requirements to qualify for group fares, such as minimum group size, type of group, substitutes, travel together and individual travel restrictions.

Category 27: Tours

This category specifies the tour requirements for a fare. For example, minimum package and nights, minimum price, or the tour number or tour type that can sometimes be bundled with hotel or car rental.

Category 28: Visit Another Country

This category specifies the requirements to qualify for a Visit Another Country fare. For example, the requirements could be country of residence, distance from destination country, and ticket purchase.

Category 29: Deposits

This category indicates whether there are deposit requirements to qualify for a fare. It includes deposit amount, days required prior to ticketing/travel, refund of deposit conditions, or waivers for the deposit requirements.

Category 31: Voluntary Changes

This category specifies the conditions and applicable charges under which voluntary changes are permitted. In the absence of voluntary changes data or when no applicable provision is matched, then a change is permitted at no charge and with no restrictions for that fare. In the absence of Category 31, ticket reissues must be performed manually.

Category 33: Voluntary Refunds
This category specifies the conditions that apply for refunding tickets when a voluntary refund is requested. For this category, a voluntary refund is a request to refund the value of all unused portions of a ticket that is initiated by the passenger. In the absence of voluntary refunds data or when no applicable provision is matched, then a refund is permitted at no charge and with no restrictions on that fare.

Category 35: Negotiated Fare Restrictions
This category identifies the ticketing security and fare creation requirements applicable for negotiated fares and may also be used for other private fares. Key components of this category are: Ticketing and Commissions, Security and Fare Creation.

Category 50: Application and Other Conditions
This category contains the rule title, geographic application, capacity limitations, rules not applicable, journey types/types of transportation, and other conditions for display purposes only. For example, who can use the fare, which route it applies to, etc. This category has no impact on itinerary pricing. A Category 50 is present for every rule.

8.9 Routings

Airlines file their fare rules, including routing information, with ATPCO. Fare rules dictate which routes are valid for specific fares, including stopovers, minimum stay requirements, and advance purchase requirements. Routings are used in conjunction with both domestic and international fares. The routing rule lists the allowed connection cities for travel from A to B for a specific fare. The rule may also indicate that travel must be nonstop.

Most domestic airfares include published routing rules. These rules list cities or airports and the possible connections between them and they often overlap. All connections are usually optional.

Fare rules always override routing rules. For instance, fare rules may limit transfers to two connections or prohibit flights with codeshare partners. This holds true even if routing rules show more transfers. It also applies if routes list cities only served by partner carriers.

For international flights, the process is similar. Some airlines publish routing rules in the same way they do for domestic flights. A common routing rule for international is the "maximum permitted mileage" or MPM. MPMs are maintained by IATA. It defines the total distance between an origin and a destination that is permitted on a fare. Connect point restrictions are maintained in the fare rules.

Routing data are also made available to host CRSs and GDSs with a subscription. This allows for complex routing rules, including specific routes, allowed stops, and even the use of partner airlines.

8.10 The Fare Records

Collectively the records are the computerized key information, including the fare amount and fare information used by airline reservations systems (host CRS) and Global Distribution Systems (GDS) during auto pricing to validate coded fare information. The structure of the rules system comprises eight different record types. These records serve different functions in the processing of a fare and are accessed individually to be worked on or viewed in the ATPCO rules system.

Record 0: General Rules

Record 0 refers to a basic fare or a fare structure that is the foundation for other fares or fare rules. It contains General rules that apply to all fares when no other specific rules are listed. This record points to the General Rules. A carrier designs a set of category specific General Rules to be applied whenever there are no provisions listed in a category for one of the carrier's fares.

Convention 2 identifies the source or governing tariff and general rule to be applied for each category. Convention 3 identifies the valid rule numbers sent out via ATPCO's system.

Record 1: Fare Class Application

This record contains information related to fare class, booking code, fare type, market, ticketing code and passenger type needed to automatically price fares. It contains all the fare class codes that are coded in a specific tariff, carrier, and rule combination.

Record 2: The Sequence Record

Record 2 lists rule sequences in a hierarchy, most to least specific, that determines the order in which rules are applied during auto pricing. Each category has a sequence list which contains the identification fields and points to the data tables in Record 3. It contains identification fields that match the fare, Record 1, or Record 8.

Record 3: Fare Restrictions

Record 3 contains a data table for rule provisions. The Record 3 category data tables contain all the specific data to apply to a fare from a rule or footnote.

Record 4: Renumber Category Control

Record 4 is used to maintain the current data in Record 2 while it is in the process of being renumbered and updated. This record shows the existing sequence number and the new sequence number for the specified Tariff, Carrier, Rule and Fare Class.

Record 5: Renumber Fare Class Application

Record 5 is used to maintain the current data in Record 1 while it is in the process of being renumbered. Record 5 shows the existing sequence number and the new sequence number for the specified Tariff, Carrier, Rule, and Fare Class.

Record 6: Reservation Booking Designator (RBD)

This record states any booking code exceptions to the prime booking code using Chart 1 and Chart 2. Record 6 contains the identification criteria that must be matched to determine the proper booking code exceptions for that fare.

Record 7: Through International Fare Component

This record defines as a city between the origin and fare component destination of the through international fare component that has a higher fare. The HIP application applies for the following ticketed points: origin–intermediate, intermediate–destination and intermediate–intermediate.

Record 8: Fare by Rule Index

This record is used to identify the fares that may be used in the fare retrieval process for the Fare By Rule category (CAT 25).

Record 9: Independent One-Way Fares

This record defines one-way fares that qualify on their own terms, independent of any other fare component.

Record X1: Tax Rules Data

Record X1 contains the tax rules data. Record X1 is the recommended industry source for automated ticket tax data, facilitating consistency and accuracy in tax calculations.

Record X2: Tax Reporting Data

Record X2 contains tax reporting data. Record X2 plays a crucial role in airline tax reporting by providing specific instructions on how taxes should be applied to airfares. The X2 records track any instances where an airline's tax collection practices deviate from these rules.

8.11 Itinerary Pricing

Pricing airline tickets for a selected itinerary is a complex process driven by fare rules, historical fare data, and booking class availability (de Marcken, 2003). Itinerary pricing involves evaluating multiple, complex fare rules such as advance purchase, minimum/maximum stay, day-of-week, and flight specific requirements against the passenger itinerary.

Air shopping, where multiple priced itineraries are returned for every online shopping query, has an added dimension of complexity to determine the best itineraries to display from a candidate list of itineraries that can run into the millions. Air shopping requires schedule-led and fare-led algorithms to price and display itineraries that have the requisite shopping diversity in low fare efficacy and convenience.

The priced itineraries must also include taxes, fees, and any applicable surcharges.

8.11.1 Priceable Units (PU)

A "pricing unit" is synonymous with a "priceable unit." In the airline industry. The official term is "priceable unit" (PU) refers to a specific combination of flight segments (like origin to destination) that are considered together when calculating a ticket price, essentially defining the boundaries of a fare and its associated rules, including whether it is a one-way, roundtrip, or multi-stop journey. The priceable unit refers to a specific segment of the journey that is priced as a separate entity. This is used to construct a complete ticket, and can represent a one-way flight, a round trip, or a more complex combination of flights. It acts as a single unit for pricing purposes, allowing airlines to set different prices for different combinations of flights within a single itinerary.

A PU can consist of one or multiple flight segments depending on the fare type (e.g., a roundtrip fare would have two segments: outbound and inbound). Fare rules are associated with each PU that define constraints such as stopovers, mileage restrictions, and applicable surcharges. The PUs are used to determine the total price of a ticket by applying the pertinent fare to the relevant PU.

For example, consider a round-trip flight from Chicago to Los Angeles. If the flight is booked from Chicago to Los Angeles and back, it is considered as a single priceable unit.

For example, consider an open-jaw ticket from New York to Amsterdam, and returning from Paris to New York. In the situation there are two priceable units, one for the New York to Amsterdam leg and the second for the Paris to New York leg.

8.11.2 Fare Components

The *fare component* is a specific fare for transportation between two cities together with the flights on the ticket that make up the journey between those cities. It is the most basic unit of ticket construction.

Every fare component consists of exactly one fare and at least one flight. Every flight on the ticket is part of exactly one fare component. The same fare can be used multiple times on a ticket as part of different components. Each of the flights on the component is *covered* by the associated fare. Fare components can be interrupted by other components in the case of *side trips*, but components do not interleave one another. A component may also include one or more surface sectors, which are gaps between cities, the travel between which is not provided by the ticket.

One or more consecutive fare components make up a *priceable unit*. Each fare component belongs to exactly one pricing unit. The most common pricing units are *round trips* and *one way journeys*, but there are a few others such as circle trips and open jaws. Priceable units are set patterns, like the round trip. It is also not possible to take arbitrary fare components and make that into a priceable unit.

A round trip consists of two components: one outbound from point A to point B and one return back to point A. The fare for each component is the same, which is the applicable half round trip fare for each component. If different fares were used for the outbound and return, formally this is a two-component circle trip and not a round trip.

Finally, the ticket consists of at least one and at most sixteen pricing units. In summary,

1. A ticket consists of pricing units.
2. Pricing units consist of fare components,
3. Fare components consist of flights and a fare

8.11.3 Tariff Component

Tariff Component (TC) is a term used to refer to a segment of a transportation route between points, used for estimating the cost of that part of the route. More specifically, it represents a section of a journey between two successive tariff-building points. For cost estimation, the one-way tariff (OW) or half of the round-trip tariff (RT) may be applied to the TC segment. In essence, the fare component is the actual fare paid for a portion of a journey, including the associated flights. The tariff component (TC) on the other hand relates to the underlying structure used for calculating the cost of a route segment. The final price (the full tariff) a customer pays is a combination of the base fare, YQ/YR surcharges, airport and security charges, government taxes and ancillary fees.

The complexity of airline shopping is directly attributed to airline pricing, which has grown in complexity following airline deregulation in 1978. The complexity stems from the growth in airline fares and itinerary pricing.

8.11.4 The Inherent Complexity of Itinerary Pricing

The primary complexity in air shopping lies in pricing the itineraries. Itinerary pricing requires a deep understanding of fare components and priceable units (PU) or pricing units. The PU options are constrained by the customer's journey, and they constitute a significant source of complexity in pricing an air itinerary.

The fare component is the most basic unit of fare construction and represents a specific fare between two city pairs. A fare component is a section between two points along the travel path. One or more fare components make up a PU. One or more PU combinations produce a pricing solution for a trip. A PU is a domain where multiple fare rules may apply and consists of a group of fare components. Fares may require that other fares in the same PU are from the same airline.

Tickets are built from one or more PUs.

Flights can be broken into fare components and pricing units in many ways which increases the search space. PU's also introduce dependencies between different parts of a trip.

PUs can take several forms. The PU types are *one-way, roundtrip, circle trips and open jaw.* This requires the itinerary to pass the fare rules such as fare combinability (Category 10). Pricing units are patterns and combination of PU types can form a pricing solution for a trip. Open jaw PU's are like circle trips with a missing fare component where the gap exists and normally the gap must be shorter than the distance flown in any of the fare components.

Flights can be broken into fare components and PUs in many ways. Consider the itinerary from LAX to LGA outbound connecting over ORD and LGA to LAX inbound connecting over DFW. Multiple combinations are possible for categorizing a particular group of flights into fares and PUs. In the given example of four flights, eight potential options are illustrated, although there are even more possibilities. Each fare component that is part of a priceable unit is represented uniquely by an arrow, while each priceable unit is depicted by a blue polygon. There are several combinations of fare components and possible PU patterns. A *few* are shown in Fig. 8.7.

In summary, the process involves dividing an itinerary into fare components and combining them into one or more priceable units. Itinerary pricing searches for the most affordable solution that is both applicable and available, considering all taxes and fees, including government taxes imposed by the DOT such as passenger facility charges (PFC), Federal Excise Tax (FET), Segment Fee, September 11 Security Fee, U.S. or International Departure and Arrival charges.

8.12 IATA Traffic Conference Areas

IATA Traffic Conferences are forums at which IATA member airlines, with scheduled commercial international air services, meet to discuss and resolve traffic matters, including passenger and cargo issues, and where resolutions are binding on all members. Each active IATA member airline with scheduled commercial international air services gets a vote.

The conferences are organized into committees or management groups, and they may establish boards or panels to oversee specific domains. Their activities are governed by the "Provisions for the Conduct of the IATA Traffic Conferences".

Since deregulation airline pricing has grown in complexity and a detailed explanation of all the intricacies is beyond the scope of this book. From the public

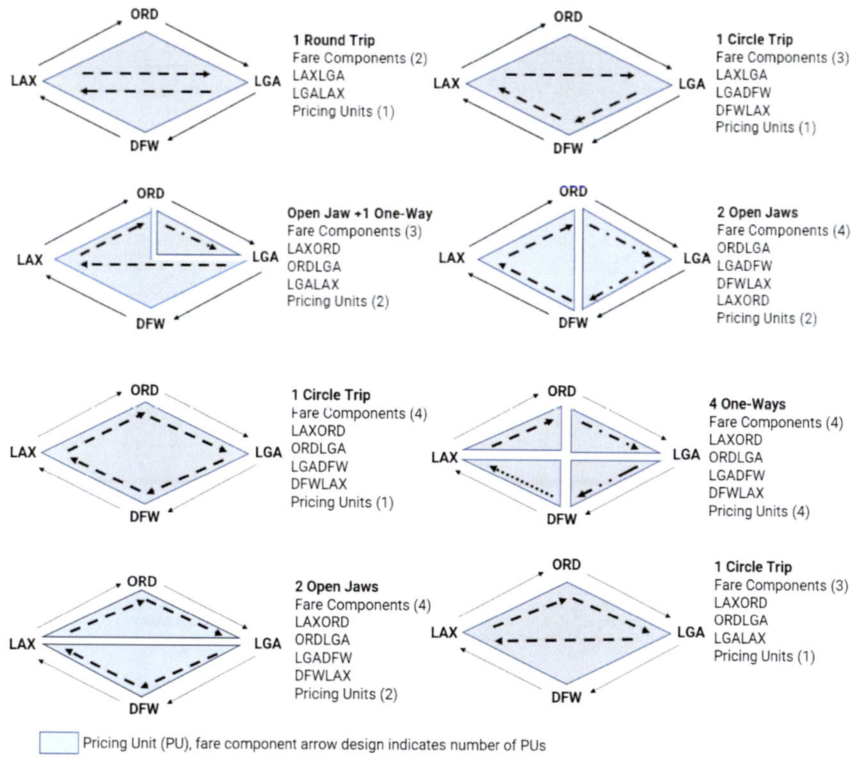

Fig. 8.7 Examples of possible fare components and pricing Units

and private fares, a specific itinerary can be priced based on the fundamentals of *fare construction*. IATA fare construction is documented in the MPM (Maximum Permitted Mileage) Manual. It serves as the primary source for applying the fundamentals of fare construction. Fare construction for an itinerary may include specific routings, stop over charges, maximum permitted mileage, security fees, combinability of one-way pricing units, mixed classes of service, roundtrips, circle trips, open jaw, special mileage provisions, journeys with surface sectors and ticket reissue or exchange.

Fare construction is based on the areas of the world the customer is travelling to, from, or connecting through. IATA divides the world into three traffic conference (TC) areas which are further divided into sub areas for organizing and simplifying fare construction rules, routings, an fares. The composition of the three primary IATA Traffic Conference Areas is shown in Fig. 8.8 and Table 8.4.

In November 2018, the activities of the Passenger Services Conference and the Passenger Tariff Conference were combined into the Passenger Standards Conference.

For example, a conference area of TC23 could incorporate fares between Europe (Area 2) and India (Area 3), while TC12 could incorporate fares between

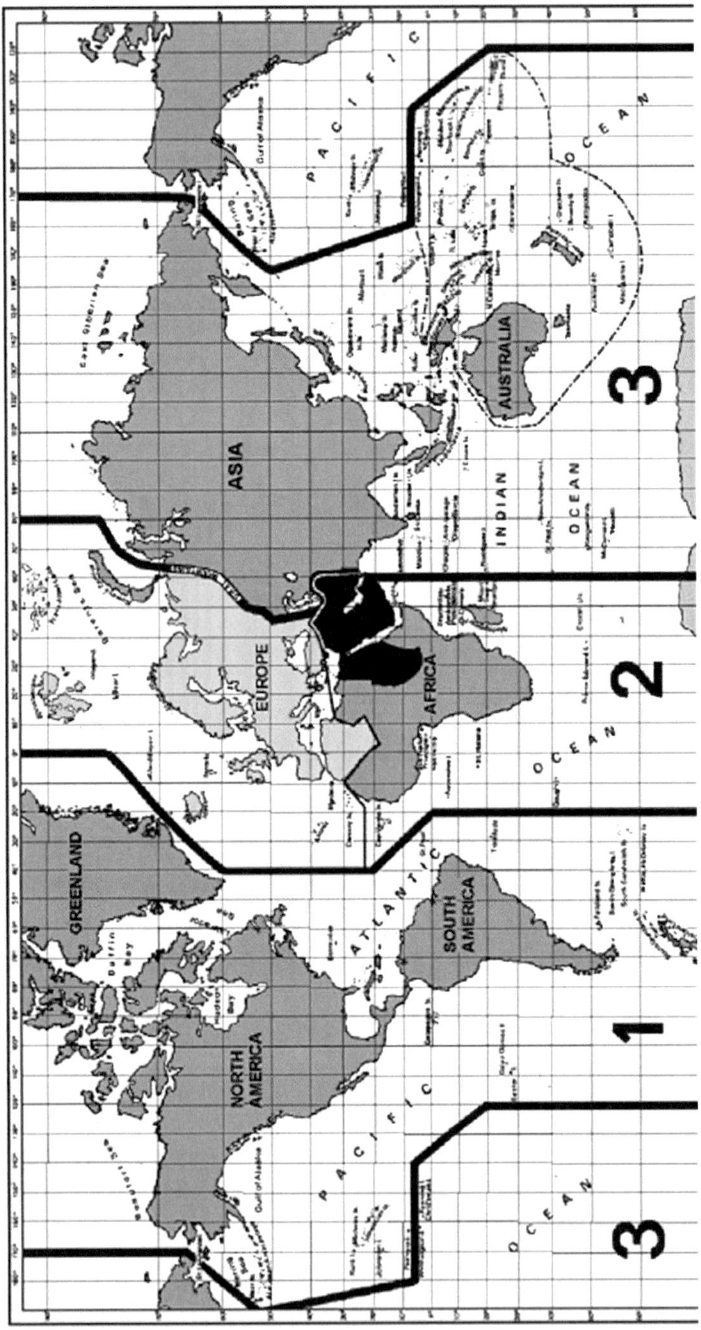

Fig. 8.8 IATA Traffic Conference (TC) geographic areas

Table 8.4 IATA Traffic Conference Areas

IATA Area Identifier	Geographical Locations
IATA Area 1 (TC1)	North America, U.S. Territories, Central America, Caribbean, South America
IATA Area 2 (TC2)	Europe, Russia (west of the Urals), Middle East, Africa, Indian Ocean Islands
IATA Area 3 (TC3)	Russia (east of the Urals), Asia, Southeast Asia, Indian Sub-continent, Japan/Korea, North/Central Pacific, Southwest Pacific, Oceania

the United States and Germany. For example, TC3 could incorporate fares within the Pacific, between India and Fiji and between Hong Kong and Singapore.

In addition, The Ticketing Handbook (THB) serves as the official guide for airline passenger ticketing and covers ticketing entries for EMDs, additional optional services, YQ/YR surcharges, involuntary rerouting, fare selection criteria, baggage rules, fare calculation and exchanges/refunds.

8.12.1 Constructed Fares

Constructed fares belong to a distinct category where the fare amount is determined only after undergoing a fare construction process. For instance, international carriers often use add-on fares, which allow them to establish fares between two cities without explicitly publishing each market they wish to serve. A new fare record is created by combining a published gateway fare with an add-on fare. As an illustration, Thai Airways may publish a gateway fare from their hub in Bangkok (BKK) to London, Heathrow (LHR). They may also publish an add-on fare from a domestic city in Thailand, like Phuket (HKT) to Bangkok (BKK). Consequently, the fare from Phuket (HKT) to London (LHR) can be constructed by utilizing the published gateway fare and the add-on fare.

8.13 Ancillary Products

Ancillary products and services along with amenities have grown in importance over the past decade. ATPCO provides access to the airline industry's most reliable data for in-flight experiences, fare benefits and restrictions.

Amenities are a type of content that provide visual, and targeted information about the onboard flight experience, including seat, aircraft, layout, Wi-Fi, entertainment, power, food, and beverages, helping consumers make informed decisions when shopping for flights. ATPCO acquired Routehappy in 2019 (APTCO, 2019) which helps airlines present their products and offers to flight shoppers in a targeted, visually engaging and informative way. Amenities can improve conversion rates and increase upsell.

ATPCO, in conjunction with IATA, provides an optional service fee solution. IATA does not directly impose or manage ancillary fees charged by airlines. Instead, IATA focuses on setting standards and facilitating industry-wide practices.

8.13.1 YQ/YR

YQ and YR are carrier-imposed surcharges that an airline can add to the airfare. It is frequently used for fuel and insurance surcharges. The fees are controlled by broader geographic application, by cabin, fare family or RBD. Carrier-imposed fees can also vary by the specific route in a market, or sometimes even by specific itineraries.

These surcharges are filed by airlines in record S1 and S2. The S1 record is filed and owned by the marketing carrier. The S2 concurrence record is filed and owned by the validating carrier. When a carrier wants to collect YQ/YR fees for other carriers besides their own, they must file an S2 concurrence record indicating from which carriers they want (or do not want) to collect service fees. This is a quick mechanism for airlines to adjust fares without having to update each published fare. These surcharges have a negative impact on award accrual and award redemptions. Airlines can add these surcharges to award redemption tickets, which can increase the cost of a "free" flight. Likewise, accrual of loyalty points is limited to the airfare excluding surcharges.

Cost effective estimation of YQ/YR to determine the *Total Price* of international itineraries has been a challenge. First, YQ/YR is not a simple percentage of the base fare (the fare amount before taxes and fees). Secondly, the amount of YQ/YR is significant, often more than the base fare. Airlines practice this so that they do not have to pay travel agency commissions on the YQ/YR component of the total fare. GDS pricing system determines the lowest fare for an itinerary by considering only base fares. However, the cheapest base fare for an itinerary may not produce the cheapest *Total Price* when YQ/YR is added at the end. The concept of Total Price is to take YQ/YR into account in finding the cheapest price for an itinerary. The technical term for achieving Total Price is called "YQ/YR push-back" where YQ/YR is added to the base fare in the comparison of fares. Due to the large amount of YQ/YR, the cost of a straightforward implementation of YQ/YR push-back would be prohibitive for GDS pricing systems. An effective solution is based on computing a lower-bound (LB) to the YQ/YR amount that every fare solution must incur. With the addition of this LB to the fare solutions, the processing cost of YQ/YR push-back is drastically reduced, thus enabling *Total Price*.

8.13.2 OB Fees

OB Fees are defined by IATA as the industry standard for ticketing and for the application of form of payment fees, including credit card fees. "O" indicates "Off

Ticket" fees, which are not shown on the ticket. The OB Fee is reported as tax code OB by IATA assignment. This information is stored in the S4 record.

8.13.3 OC Fees

OC (Other Charges) Fees are ancillary fees, sometimes called "junk fees" are charges airlines impose for services that were once included in the base ticket price, such as checked baggage, seat selection, or in-flight meals.

The OC fees are captured in ATPCO records S5, S6, and S7.

8.13.3.1 Record S5

Record S5 includes:

1. Commercial Name: The name of the ancillary product as it is displayed to customers
2. Subcode: A unique code that identifies the specific type of ancillary service
3. Service Group: A category that groups similar ancillary services like baggage and seats,
4. Booking method: This specifies how ancillary service can be booked such as pre-purchase, at check-in, etc.
5. Electronic Miscellaneous Document (EMD) Type: This specifies the type of EMD used for the ancillary service (EMD-A or EMD-S).

For example, an S5 record for "Checked Baggage" would contain information like the commercial name "Checked Baggage", the subcode "0C3", the service group "BG" (for baggage), and the booking method "prepaid" or "check-in".

8.13.3.2 Record S6

Record S6 is the "Optional Services Concurrence Record." Concurrence in this context means that when multiple airlines are involved, the S6 record specifies which airline's rules for optional services an airline agrees to (or concurs with) regarding optional services. It ensures that airlines are aware of and agree to the optional services offered by other carriers, particularly when it comes to industry subcodes related to those services. For example, if Airline A wants to offer a specific optional service (e.g., baggage allowance) that is also offered by Airline B, Record S6 ensures that Airline A concurs with Airline B's industry subcode for that specific optional service.

8.13.3.3 Record S7

Record S7 defines the defines "Where, When, Who, and How Much" the ancillary product is applicable for sale. Each S7 record includes price, currency in which the price is quoted, and validation qualifiers, such as geographic restrictions, flight details, frequent traveler requirements, passenger type code and fare class or type that qualifies for the ancillary.

S7 records are critical for airlines to manage and distribute their ancillary offerings, as they ensure that the correct prices and conditions are applied to the correct passengers and flights,

In summary, S5 records define the optional service subcode and data, including baggage. The S6 records contain optional service concurrence data and the S7 records define the provisions and pricing details for the optional services defined in S5.

8.13.4 Branded Fares (Record S-8)

Branded Fares were first introduced by Air New Zealand, Qantas, and Air Canada in 2006. Specific services are included with each branded fare product.

Table 8.5 illustrates a hypothetical airline's branded fare products. There are four branded fare products called Basic Economy, Economy, Premium Economy, and First Class with their associated attributes.

ATPCO introduced the branded fares record, called the S-8 record, to standardize brand definitions and ancillary products offered by airlines. Specifically, this record provides the brand name definition, a mapping of RBDs, and/or fare basis codes to the airline branded fare product. ATPCO Table 166 provides a cross reference of Optional Services to the branded fare product. ATPCO Table 189 serves as the fare identification table which cross references fares associated with a brand.

There is no standardization of branded fares in the industry. Each carrier has its own definition and naming convention. What is included in an airline brand

Table 8.5 Branded fares example

Feature	Basic economy	Economy	Premium economy	First class
Carry-on Baggage	Free	Free	Free	Free
Checked Baggage	1_{st} Bag: $40 2nd Bag: $45	1st Bag: $40 2nd Bag: $45	1st Bag: Free 2nd Bag: $45	1st Bag: Free 2nd Bag: Free
Seat Selection	Not Available	For a Fee	Free	Free
Changes	Not Allowed	For a Fee + Fare Difference	Free, Fare Difference	Free, Fare Difference
Same-day Changes	Not Allowed	For a Fee + Fare Difference	Free, Fare Difference	Free, Fare Difference
Loyalty Miles	25% Miles	50% Miles	100% Miles	125% Miles
Meals	For a Fee	For a Fee	For a Fee	Free
Upgrade	Not Available	Not Available	Available	Available
Standby	Not Available	Not Available	On Select Routes	Available
Lounge Access	Not Available	Not Available	Not Available	Available

is defined in their ATPCO filing, and it may vary by passenger type, fare type, account code, or even PCC. The brands available for one agency may not be the same as another agency, for another passenger type, or for another flight number.

Table 8.6 Summarizes the types of fees.

Table 8.6 Summary of fee types

Fee Type	Description
YQ/YR (S1, S2 Records)	Carrier imposed fees. A standardized, automated collection, distribution, and pricing method that provides marketing carriers (carriers that appear on the flight coupon) the ability to control and collect fees at the sector (coupon), at the portion of travel (multiple sectors), or on the journey. ATPCO's application handles fuel, insurance, and carrier-imposed miscellaneous fees • Fuel surcharges filed as YQF or YRF • Insurance surcharges filed as YQI or YRI • Not a tax, but a validating carrier specific fee • Included in the total amount of the ticket, therefore no changes to ticketing or reporting are required • Not applicable for interlines • Not commissionable • Filed by over 200 carriers worldwide
OB (S4 Record)	IATA defined code used for airline ticketing fees (optional, validating carrier only, not interline able) • IATA authorized the use of the OB tax code • Distribution channel fees • Carrier fees can be specified by call center, city/airport ticket office, department/ station id • Form of payment fees – one fee for all cards or a card specific fee based on BIN number • Always part of the ticket transaction • Calculated for the validating carrier like YQ/YR fees • Available since 1Q 2007
OC (S5, S7 records)	IATA defined code used for fare related optional service or rule-based service fees (optional, validating carrier only, not applicable for interlining) • Passenger choices (seats, meals, movies, etc.) • May be linked to flights, not tickets • The fees are *operating carrier based* not validating carrier as with YQ/YR and OB • Issued as a separate EMD and can be issued simultaneously or after the ticket has been issued • Involves inventory controls and messaging. Will involve inventory control and new messaging standards for pre-reserved seats, meals, headsets, etc • Not applicable for interlines Baggage Fees • Excess baggage charges • Overweight baggage fees
OA	IATA defined code used for booking fees (optional, validating carrier only, not applicable for interlines
Taxes (X1, X2)	Record X1: The record that contains Tax Rules data at ATPCO Record X2: The record that contains Tax Reporting data at ATPCO

8.14 Airline Amenities

Amenities enable airlines to promote features of the onboard experience. Routehappy, acquired by ATPCO in 2018, introduced and standardized amenity categories for air travel, such as seat comfort (legroom, width, pitch), Wi-Fi (availability and type), power (AC/USB ports), in-flight entertainment, food and beverages (availability, cost, and type), and aircraft details (model, layout). By introducing this dimension, Routehappy helped transform air shopping from a focus on price to a more comprehensive comparison of the flight experience. For example, travel agents and online customers can compare features between seat types within an airline or across airlines.

Besides amenities, the content types supported by Routehappy for airline offers are Universal Product Attributes (UPA) and Universal Ticket Attributes (UTA).

8.14.1 Universal Product Attributes (UPA)

This feature has unique airline fares, products, and services with images, messaging, videos, cabin tours and enhanced description of airline services. It is considered a merchandising tactic that allows airlines to visually highlight and distinguish between different seat types, fare classes, and other ancillary services, improving the passenger experience and making it easier for travelers to understand what they are purchasing.

8.14.2 Universal Ticket Attributes (UTA)

This feature, sourced from ATPCO Fares, Branded Fares and Optional Services, explains the fare rules and restrictions in simple language, simplifying the air shopping experience.

In December 2024, ATPCO introduced a new category called Loyalty Rewards (ATPCO, 2024), that displays the expected mileage accrual for a branded fare or booking class at the time of shopping. The new Routehappy attribute enhances transparency during flight search.

8.14.3 Routehappy Visuals

Routehappy Visuals allows airlines to show customers visuals like photos, videos, and virtual tours of their onboard experience, such as seats and amenities. By integrating these visuals into booking channels, airlines can better highlight the differences between their offers, drive more conversions, and provide a more transparent flight shopping experience.

It was previously offered as a separate product. ATPCO plans to roll out its Routehappy Visuals product to all participating airlines in January 2026. This change will improve adoption,

8.15 Mini Rules

Mini Rules are a simplified version of airline fare rules that highlight the concise summary of the most important fare conditions for a specific booking. These summaries are designed to be easily understandable and are often used by travel agents and airlines to quickly convey the most important restrictions and implications associated with their chosen fare.

This potentially reduces the need for a traveler to contact customer service with questions. Examples of mini rules communicated to travelers are:

1. Refundability: Specifies if the ticket can be refunded if the traveler needs to cancel.
2. Changeability: Defines whether the traveler can change the date or time of their flight and if any fees apply.
3. Advance Purchase. Determines if the fare requires the ticket to be purchased a certain number of days before the flight.
4. Minimum Stay/Maximum Stay: States if there are restrictions on how long a traveler can stay at the destination.
5. Blackout Dates. Identifies specific dates or periods when the fare is not valid.

Mini Rules are a user-friendly feature designed to improve transparency and passenger understanding of airline fare conditions.

8.16 Attribute-Based Shopping

Airline shopping has evolved beyond just price and schedule. Passengers increasingly desire a more detailed understanding of what their ticket includes. Attribute-based shopping is offered by GDSs to travel agents and to a limited extent on airline websites. Fare attributes are the specific features and services associated with a flight ticket, going beyond the basic fare and departure/arrival times. Mini rules are also an important part of attribute-based shopping.

Attribute-based shopping can include:

1. Fare Flexibility and Perks. Change and cancellation policies, boarding priority, lounge access, and loyalty program benefit.
2. Seat Features. Seat pitch (legroom), recline, width, priority seat selection, and lie-flat options.
3. Amenities In-flight. Wi-Fi availability, entertainment options, meal services, complimentary snacks and drinks.

4. Baggage Allowances: Number of free checked bags, carry-on limits, and associated fees.

With attribute-based shopping, passengers clearly understand what they're purchasing, reducing surprises and improving customer satisfaction. Airlines can differentiate their products beyond just price, fostering a more competitive marketplace.

8.17 The Department of Transportation Final Ruling on Ancillary Fees

The U.S. Department of Transportation implemented a new rule effective on April 17, 2024 [DOT, 2024a] that protects airline passengers from surprise fees. Airlines and ticket agents must now be upfront. They must share all fees for checked bags and carry-ons. Fees for cancellations or changes must be clear too. This helps people avoid unexpected costs. These fees can quickly increase the total ticket price. Now, airlines and agents must offer personalized fee information. This includes rewards program status and military status. Consumers can also remain anonymous. Either way, they get standard fee details. Airlines must share baggage, change, and cancellation policies. This must happen before someone buys a ticket.

8.18 Origins of Air Ancillaries, Pricing, and Agency Access

When full-service carriers (FSCs) started selling ancillaries bundled as branded fare products in 2006 and followed up with à la carte sales to avoid losing customers and potential revenue. The focus was on execution, the ability to sell ancillaries and sell up of branded fares through the direct channel and agency channels for online and codeshare partner flights (Smith et al., 2007; Vinod & Moore, 2009). Even though airlines sold ancillary services through their websites, it was not until 2009 that travel agencies that subscribed to a GDS, OTAs and metasearch engines had access to ATPCO's optional services like checked bags and premium seats. An immediate benefit to travel agents was instant access to ancillary products and services without having to surf airline websites. While many airlines responded by filing optional services through ATPCO, some such as American and United held back, and the GDSs had to build a direct connection to the airlines to access the ancillary products and their respective prices. This transformed the way travel agents sold ancillaries through the GDSs as well as the way consumers used OTAs and metasearch engines.

The deployment varied with some airlines filing ancillaries through ATPCOs fee types of OB (ticketing fees), OC (optional service fees), OA (booking fees) and the branded fares record that linked the ancillaries to branded fare families (Record S8).

In 2010, travel agents were able to shop by attribute. For example, when a search was initiated they could specify whether their client wanted a premium seat, checked bags (1 or 2), or a paid meal. The search display would show flights with these options, along with flights on which they were unavailable.

The Electronic Miscellaneous Document (EMD) is used to handle payments for ancillary services to airline partners. The transmission of the EMD is required to enable revenue recognition and proration of fees. The EMD functions like an E-Ticket, with a receipt issued to the customer. They are subject to the rules of the issuing airline. The Associate EMD (EMD-A) links to the PNR or E-Ticket.

In practice, an airline's system creates the EMD-A after payment is received from the customer, thereby associating the EMD-A with the passenger's booking. The EMD-A is transmitted to the validating carrier which may be different from the operating carrier. After validating, the EMD-A is then available for accounting and for the passenger, who receives a receipt.

This process will continue in the hybrid era where EDIFACT and XML transactions coexist. However, as NDC adoption increases, airlines do not have an incentive to file ancillary services through ATPCO since all ancillary sales are airline controlled with NDC.

8.18.1 Traditional Approaches to Ancillary Pricing Require Sales Data at Multiple Price Points

Most airlines do not utilize dynamic pricing for ancillary fees. For example, a checked bag is $40, and an onboard drink is $7, but the fee is constant across the airline network and do not vary by market on length of haul. A constant fee for the network has made it easy for airlines to communicate the fees for ancillary products and services with travelers. As airlines continue to focus on selling ancillaries, a significant change s to be expected.

The pricing for ancillary services will shift from a flat fee across the system to a market-based approach in the future as a function of the shopping parameters such as time of day, elapsed time, day of week, and number in party.

In the future, ancillaries such as seat type (e.g. exit row seats, aisle seats, etc.) will be a function of seats sold by seat type. Similarly, pricing for lounge access can be a function of lounge occupancy.

The data collected from electronic miscellaneous document (EMD) transmissions are needed for dynamic pricing of ancillaries based on estimates of a consumer's willingness to pay. A fundamental problem with calibrating a model to estimate price elasticities is the absence of sales data at various price points for an ancillary.

Variable ancillary pricing (Ødegaard & Wilson, 2016) requires knowledge of a customer's willingness to pay for ancillary services to determine the value of ancillary services. While there are many approaches to addressing this problem, established methods include multinomial choice analysis (Balcombe et al., 2009; Ben-Akiva & Lerman, 1985; Train, 2003), the van Westendorp Price Sensitivity

Meter (PSM) (Hague, 2008; van Westendorp, 1976) and conjoint analysis (Green et al., 2001; Hair et al., 1984) which considers tradeoffs between various combinations of price and product features. An experiment based on stated preferences (Martin et al., 2008) was used to provide empirical evidence of estimated valuations that air passengers have on various quality of service attributes such as comfort, food, ticket change fees, frequency, and reliability.

Techniques such as adaptive conjoint analysis and the van Westendorp (1976) price sensitivity meter can be leveraged for the product design of branded fare families (Ratliff & Gallego, 2013) and dynamic pricing of ancillaries.

8.18.2 Dynamic Pricing of Ancillaries with Reinforcement Learning

The abyss caused by the absence of ancillary sales data at multiple price points can be overcome by running test and learn experiments with the multi-armed bandit framework, a reinforcement learning technique, to determine ancillary prices that have higher conversion rates with customers and improves sales.

The objective of dynamic ancillary pricing is to determine the revenue optimal ancillary prices for every booking request. Statistical and machine learning models can be used to calibrate the data, if sales data exists at multiple price points. Data sparsity dictates the need to deploy a test and learn experimentation model based on context, which is the market and customer segment, to determine ancillary pricing.

Consider pre-reserved seats. Customers perceive that a pre-reserved seat is more valuable on a long-haul flight than a short-haul flight. Other factors that can impact the price are the number in party, market, and departure time of day. However, without sufficient sales data at varying price points, determining a customer's willingness to pay for these services will be highly inaccurate. An alternative is to rely on survey data gathered during the booking process and in-flight. Surveys are unreliable because a customer's true intent may be different from what was filled out in the survey. An alternative and better approach is to deploy the multi-armed bandit test and learn experimentation to determine the price points that maximize conversion rates. The algorithm optimizes seat pricing by balancing exploration (test new prices) with exploitation (using known profitable prices) to maximize revenues in real-time. Dynamic pricing of ancillaries using test and learn experimentation is practiced today by some airlines on a limited scale. It is expected to gain wide adoption over the next decade.

Unlike seat types which are inventory controlled, checked baggage fees are generally not a problem on most flights, since there is enough room for everyone's luggage. Still, passenger segments differ in how much they are willing to pay. A fixed $25 fee doesn't take advantage of these differences. Airlines could charge more to those willing to pay a higher fee, However baggage pricing must be based on analysis of historical booking data. For example, numerous studies in the past have provided the following insights:

1. Customers have a greater propensity to pay for a second checked bag if the first checked bag is included in the ticket.
2. The number in party influences the sale of checked bags. While individual travelers may not pay for a checked bag, multiple passengers in a PNR typically do.
3. The length of stay influences the sale of checked bags. Travelers with longer length of stay have a greater propensity to pay for a checked bag.
4. Customers who book early, typically leisure passengers, have a greater propensity to pay for a checked bag.

Variable pricing for a second checked bag could be an even better opportunity. Ski trips show this clearly, as skiers often carry lots of equipment and extra bags, along with a special fee for skis. On some flights to ski resorts, higher fees can be charged for second or third bags based on the customer segment and the associated willingness to pay.

Most airlines do not charge for carry-on bags, but limited overhead space makes it a prime target for pricing strategies. Ultra low-cost carriers often have higher fees for carry-on luggage than for checked bags. This can become complicated, but flights that frequently run out of cabin space should consider a fee for carry-ons.

8.19 The Psychology of Pricing

The psychology of pricing predicates that judgement of monetary value has much in common with sensory judgements such as weight, warm weather, cold weather, or loudness. The study of sensory perception is called psychophysics. In the 1800s psychophysicists determined that consumers are more sensitive to the relative values of products and not the absolute value of the products [Fechner, 1860]. Gustav Fechner postulated that mind and body, though appearing to be separate entities, are different sides of one reality.

Based on Fechner's study, the dynamic pricing of ancillary products and services requires collective decision making when price points are established for the ancillaries associated with a flight. They are also called attached products. In other words, price link constraints with a band (ancillary product X is priced at 50% of ancillary product Y, with a price band of $\pm$ 10%) are required when ancillary products are priced. Examples of attached products are checked bags, seat selection and onboard amenities. For example, if bags are priced at $20 and a seat assignment is four times more costly, it does not sit well with the customer.

Air shopping algorithms frequently add a similar but less attractive and apparently irrelevant itinerary to a choice set which can greatly increase the chances that customers pick a specific attractive itinerary. The selection of the better itinerary occurs because the customer compared the irrelevant itinerary with the good itinerary. This violation of the independence from irrelevant alternatives (IIA) and the regularity properties is called the decoy effect, dominance effect, or attraction effect. The decoy effect is a cognitive bias in the decision-making processes of customers. It breaks the usual rules that demand options stay consistent when a new choice is added. The decoy effect (Arielly, 2010) is a common bias that influences how customers choose. It is a reliable pattern seen in many decision-making situations.

In the case of OTAs which primarily cater to leisure, price-sensitive customers, a study at Travelocity in 2012 showed that screens with a few high-priced itineraries received higher conversion than screens with all low-fare itineraries. Customers did not necessarily purchase the high-priced itineraries, but the comparison on the same screen prompted customers to book the cheaper deals before they were gone.

8.19.1 Pricing Ambiguity

The phrase "everyone has a price" and the underlying idea that valuations are stable and can be revealed during negotiation is prevalent in traditional economics. This is challenged by evidence from behavioral economics, which has repeatedly shown that human decision-making is influenced by psychological factors and context, not just stable, rational valuations.

Paul Slovic and Sarah Lichtenstein demonstrated the deep ambiguity of prices. Their experiments showed that subjects were unable to consistently set prices. Their research focused on how people's preferences are often constructed during the process of eliciting choices, particularly in risky situations. They demonstrated that different methods of evocation (like choosing between gambles versus asking for a price) can lead to systematically different responses, a phenomenon they termed preference reversals. This research (Lichtenstein & Slovic, 1973; Slovic & Lichtenstein, 1983) challenges the idea of stable and consistent preferences, suggesting that preferences are not fixed but rather shaped by the context and method used to elicit them.

Their research revealed that people's choices between gambles (e.g., a 50% chance of winning $100 or a 10% chance of winning $1000) often differ from their willingness to pay for those same gambles. In the choice task, people might prefer the gamble with a higher probability of a smaller win, while in the pricing task, they might be willing to pay more for the gamble with a higher potential payoff, even if the probability of that payoff is lower. This inconsistency highlights that preferences are not always stable and consistent, and the context of evocation can influence choices. The Lichtenstein and Slovic work challenged the assumption of rationality in decision-making, as it demonstrated that people's choices can be influenced by the way information is presented and how decisions are elicited. This research sheds light on how framing the context and cognitive biases can affect choices and decisions.

The viewpoint is that prices are constructed from hints in the environment, which was demonstrated by Tversky and Kahneman in their famous United Nations experiment in 1974 where they demonstrated the effects of anchoring (Tversky & Kahneman, 1974).

For the United Nations experiment, they spun a wheel with numbers 1–100, then asked participants whether the percentage of African countries in the UN was higher or lower than the number on the wheel. Participants then provided an estimate, and the results showed that the arbitrary number from the wheel significantly influenced their estimates, even though it was unrelated to the actual percentage. In the actual experiment, participants spun a wheel that landed on either 10 or 65. Those who saw 10 as the anchor provided an average estimate of 25%, while those who saw 65 provided an average estimate of 45%. The latter estimate was almost twice the first and the only difference was that the subjects had been exposed to a different random number that they acknowledged was meaningless.

This experiment by Tversky and Kahneman, demonstrated that humans tend to "anchor" their judgments to a starting value, even if that value is arbitrary. This phenomenon is known as the anchoring effect and has significant implications for the pricing of air ancillary products that are attached to a flight.

8.20 The Solo Traveler Penalty in U.S. Domestic Markets

In early 2025, the three major U.S. airlines—United Airlines, Delta Air Lines and American Airlines started experimenting with higher fares for solo travelers versus groups of two or more travelers in a passenger name record (PNR). American was the first to introduce this new fare rule, that they called "P2" internally for "Passenger 2". Delta Air Lines and United Airlines followed. In some markets, Basic Economy only appeared when the low fare search specified multiple passengers.

This was first reported by Newsweek on May 30, 2025 (Mesa, 2025) and Thrifty Traveler on June 6, 2025 (Potter, 2025). This is acknowledged as a pricing tactic that is designed to target business travelers, who often book closer to departure or even last-minute and travel alone. Thrifty Traveler, a subscription service that offers customized real-time alerts for mistake fares and budget friendly fares, identified this pattern after analyzing hundreds of U.S. domestic one-way fares. One of the examples they cite is a United short-haul flight from Chicago O'Hare to Peoria, Illinois where a solo ticket cost $269, but dropped to $181 per person when two travelers were booked. When the news broke, United and Delta scaled back the solo pricing initiative to less than five percent of their markets. However, American did not back down and had deployed solo pricing on a significant scale by July 2025.

8.20.1 How Is Solo Pricing Deployed

This pricing tactic is designed to target business travelers, who often book last-minute and travel alone. Airlines use different booking classes with different fare amounts and rules to sell the same seats at different prices. With this change, some of the RBDs are limited to bookings with at least two passengers.

Dual RBD validation is used by airlines to control Basic Economy. Dual RBD validation essentially means a fare requires availability in *two* booking classes (RBDs) to be considered valid for a booking. Solo pricing is more granular customer segmentation. When booking for a single passenger, airlines might only display higher-priced booking classes, effectively limiting solo travelers to more expensive options. With solo pricing, airlines can ensure that business travelers do not purchase Basic Economy fares when they are available. However, when searching for multiple seats, lower-priced booking classes become available, making the group booking cheaper per person.

8.21 Monitoring and Measuring Pricing Effectiveness

Monitoring and measuring pricing effectiveness can provide insights to airlines on how to manage core Airline Planning processes efficiently, including, scheduling, pricing, revenue management and loyalty.

8.21.1 Booking Class Realignment

Airlines today periodically revisit their fare basis code to booking class mapping to determine if the fare are in alignment with the booking class hierarchy. The effort to realign fares is tedious and is usually a 3-to-6-month effort. It begins with an analysis for the fare class structure followed with a recommendation on how the fare basis codes should be remapped to RBD's. This is followed with the execution phase where fares are re-filed incrementally market by market.

The fundamental issue is that airlines typically embark on booking class realignment when they realize their tariff structure in markets they serve have significant overlaps between RBDs. Booking class realignment with fares avoids revenue dilution caused when fares are not aligned with the RBD hierarchy. Revenue dilution occurs when higher valued classes are not protected from lower valued classes due to fare inversions. If corrective action is taken *continuously* (e.g. monthly) rather than every two years, this could translate into millions of dollars of potentially lost revenue that can be captured.

8.21.2 Monitoring Fare Basis Code Usage by Customer Segment

Every airline manages anywhere from 75,000 – 150,000 fare basis codes, but have *no visibility* into how effective their fare basis code definitions are in targeting customer segments. A *fare basis code* is mapped to a *fare type* (or *fare group* as defined in ATPCO Record 1) which in turn is mapped to a booking class (RBD).

The ATPCO Record 1, also known as the Fare Class Application Record, contains information about fare classes, booking codes, fare types, and passenger types. This record is required for pricing and ticketing systems to automatically determine the applicable fare. It defines the eligibility criteria, including age range and passenger type, for a specific fare class.

Every fare basis code that is defined by a pricing analyst has a specific purpose to attract a segment of the population. With the large number of active fare basis codes, airlines do not necessarily have visibility into the effectiveness of the specific restrictions that they have defined as part of the fare filing process. *Do they work? Do they serve their intended purpose?*

Each ticketed passenger can be classified into business or leisure based on customer segmentation. An example is shown below in Table 8.7.

With this level of segmentation, each ticketed PNR can be classified as business (Business Unrestricted, Business Restricted, etc.) and Leisure (Visiting Friends and Relatives (VFR), restricted discount, unrestricted discount, etc.). The distribution of the business/leisure mix expressed as a percentage can be determined. Further, this can also be broken down by channel such as major GDS and the consumer direct channel (airline.com, call center, ATO, CTO). This type of information is of tremendous value for an airline to address *their gaps in pricing strategy proactively* on a continuous basis.

8.21.3 Fare Competitiveness with YQ/YR

YQ/YR is a surcharge for fuel and insurance that has become a major part of the total price of international airfares. YQ/YR is technically problematic for the Pricing system for several reasons.

YQ/YR is not simply a percentage of the base fare (i.e. the fare amount before taxes and fees). The amount of YQ/YR is significant, often more than the base fare. Further it can also be flight specific. Airlines impose these surcharges (in part) because they do not have to pay travel agency commissions on the YQ/YR component of the total fare. YQ/YR is non-interlineable and the airline collects the YQ/YR fees directly from the agencies. Note that in the US domestic airlines file surcharges as part of ATPCO Category 12 which goes through the standard ARC settlement process like the base fare. This is because agencies do not receive commission in North America. Airlines have visibility of their competitiveness with reference to the base fare but not with the total fare that includes YQ/YR.

If an airline is capturing and storing shopping responses, they can be categorized by market with a breakdown of the total fare into the following components—Base Fare, Taxes, YQ/YR and Category 12 (surcharge). In key markets, competitor total fares can be monitored. This is a simple mechanism to provide visibility on markets where an airline is competitive and where they are not. The primary shortcoming with this approach is that it is booking class (RBD) availability dependent. For a comprehensive comparison itineraries must be priced based on the assumption that all RBD's are available, which is not possible since competitor itinerary pricing that is captured is based on actual RND availability.

Table 8.7 An example of customer segmentation

			Business and Leisure Groups						
Likely Leisure Group	Departure Date	Return Date	Length of Stay	Advance Purchase	Saturday Night Stay	One Way	Number of Passengers	Holiday	Same Day
Holiday Trip								Yes	No
Planned Weekend	FRI, SAT	SUN, MON	<4	>13					
Impulse Weekend	FRI, SAT	SUN, MON	<4	<14					
Planned Long Weekend	WED–SAT	SUN-TUE	>2<6	>13					
Impulse Long Weekend	WED–SAT	SUN-TUE	>2<6	<14					
Family Vacation			>5	>13			>1		
Single Vacation			>5	>20			1		
School Break - 1	Summer		>20	>20			1		
School Break - 2	Dec 15–Dec 31		>20	>5			1		
Day Shopping	SAT, SUN		0						Yes
Likely Business Group									
Short Business - 1	SUN–FRI	MON-SAT	<4	< 14		No			
Short Business - 2	SUN–FRI			< 14					
Short Business - 3	MON–FRI								Yes
Short Business - 4	SUN–FRI	MON-SAT	<4	> 13		No			
Business Trip Plus	FRI, SAT	WED, THU	<7						

To understand the impact of YQ/YR and CAT 12 Surcharges fully, it is worthwhile to develop a method to price itineraries with the respective breakdowns of the total fare based on.

1. RBD availability, assumed to be always available
2. Compute prices for each RBD (disregard fare combinability options) in the itinerary

8.22 The Delta Air Lines AI-Based Pricing Model

Delta Air Lines ignited a firestorm of controversy when it announced its use of AI-powered flight pricing during its Q2 2025 earnings call on July 10. The airline claimed that AI-based pricing technology from Fetcherr, an Israeli company, was used to price about 3% of domestic tickets and planned to expand its use to 20% by the end of 2025. The fallout included a stern letter from Congress and lawmakers concerned that personal information was being used to quote prices. The U.S senators accused Delta of using "individualized" and "surveillance" pricing, essentially creating a situation where two passengers simultaneously searching for a flight could see different fares based on personal data the airline had collected from internal sources or social media.

Lisa Hanna, a Delta Air Lines spokesperson (Knox, 2025) responded:

> There is no fare product Delta has ever used, is testing or plans to use that targets customers with individualized offers based on personal information or otherwise.

Besides privacy, the primary concerns are higher prices and price volatility caused by more precise pricing adjustments based on market trends. What are the specific data inputs used in the Delta AI-based pricing model?

Delta claims to use a large market model which uses a range of broad, aggregated data, not personal customer information, to set fares. The input data includes booking trends, fuel prices, seat availability, current news, weather, and market dynamics, rather than data like a person's search history, location, or age. This approach enables Delta to adapt and respond quickly to market shifts. Only the airline knows the boundaries used for the data. Responsible AI is the responsibility of the content generator, which in this case is airfares by Delta Air Lines.

Contextual bandits are a reinforcement learning technique to improve on traditional multi-armed bandits by leveraging aggregate context or user specific information to make decisions. Contextual bandits can be used to quote prices to customers. The context for travel can be based on the trip-purpose segment definition identified when a customer does a flight search. However, the context can be expanded to include personal demographic information and social media data such as recent purchases to expensive concerts which can lead to individualized or surveillance pricing, which is illegal. Only the airline that controls the pricing model can define the boundaries for the data used.

Officially, Delta Air Lines has stated it has a "zero tolerance for discriminatory or predatory pricing" and categorically denied using personal data for individual pricing.

As the use of AI in pricing expands across the travel industry, it will spark intense scrutiny from lawmakers, consumer advocates, and watchdog groups who fear unfair, abusive, or predatory business practices that lead to personalized price gouging.

8.23 Moving Beyond Filed Fares

Fare management in the airline industry has relied on filed fares for decades. Filed fares consist of a finite number of predefined prices with associated fare rules that airlines file with ATPCO. In the airline retailing era, this is a constraint that should be overcome by unbundling of the various filed fare products. The industry is transforming from pre-defined prices based on filed fares and associated rules to more dynamic offer creation, allowing product or price adjustments without pre-constructing every permutation to deliver a real-time, customized offer at the time of shop. For this to happen, airlines need the ability to decouple prices from product attributes to simplify and provide enhanced flexibility. Dynamic offer creation allows an airline to assemble a product and calculate the price "on demand" based on real-time data, providing more flexibility to offer relevant deals to targeted customer segments using contextual customer data. A science-based pricing component can also be applied as part of the "on demand" fare computation. This approach can also potentially result in a reduction in fare filings, since the price is determined dynamically at the time when a shopping request is received based on attributes such as advance purchase, cancellation penalty percentage, season, day of week, seat selection, baggage, etc. This approach provides additional price points that do not have to be filed. Experimentation and validation of this approach is only applicable for the airline direct channel and airline controlled NDC offers.

The hotel industry has a similar issue with a large number of bundled rates that are difficult to manage, and which are never sold or sold infrequently, which can be overcome with attribute-based room pricing [Chapter 5, Vinod, 2022a] where the price is determined "on-demand" based on features selected by a customer.

9 Changes in the Distribution Landscape with New Distribution Capability (NDC)

You can't have a mid-life crisis in the airline industry because every day is a crisis.

Herb Kelleher

Abstract

The air distribution landscape is changing with IATA's New Distribution Capability. This chapter discusses the erosion of full content and most favored nation clauses in airline-GDS contracts and the transition of pricing power from the GDS to the airline for the indirect channel. Transaction workflows: past, present, and future are presented. This consists of the traditional GDS transaction processing in the current hybrid state where EDIFACT and NDC bookings coexist and the potential future state where all air bookings through the indirect channels are NDC bookings. Some of the most significant changes in the air distribution landscape including GDS surcharges, NDC adoption, the challenges with NDC APIs and atomic updates, the commercial models with NDC, and the multi-million-dollar investment in ONE Order, the future of codeshare and interline are discussed. Autonomous AI Agents and the new AI channel will have a greater impact on GDS economics in the future.

Herb Kelleher, co-founder of Southwest Airlines, was a pioneer and fierce competitor who changed the world with the low-cost airline model. He was also a strong proponent of direct distribution as a key component of Southwest Airlines' low-cost model. This quote by Herb Kelleher suggests that the airline industry is so inherently chaotic and prone to daily problems that its employees don't have time for the existential dread of a mid-life crisis; they are too busy managing daily emergencies. The quote uses hyperbole to highlight the high-stress, unpredictable

B. Vinod, *The Era of Airline Revenue Management with Offers and Orders*, Management for Professionals, https://doi.org/10.1007/978-3-032-24197-9_9

nature of working in the airline industry. While there is significant chaos on the airline distribution landscape, the airline industry is also itself faced with labor shortages, operational issues, and economic stability.

There is significant chaos and disruption due to the adoption of New Distribution Capability (NDC) caused by challenges with its deployment, a shift in power from traditional booking channels, operational issues for travel agencies trying to adapt to new technology and processes, and the complexities of the two-tier commercial model between airlines and GDSs. While the airline industry is accustomed to various disruptions, the specific challenges of NDC present unique, ongoing hurdles. Perhaps the industry is so used to chaos, it will weather the storm.

9.1 GDS in Transition

Global Distribution Systems (GDS) came into existence in 1976. Sabre was the first GDS to enter the market followed by United's Apollo. In the pre-Internet era, there were only two primary channels, and they were classified as offline channels. The offline direct channel consisted of airline call centers, central reservations office, airport ticket office (ATO) and city ticket office (CTO). These channels were classified as offline direct since an agent made the booking on behalf of a customer by directly accessing the airline reservations system.

The offline indirect channel consisted of brick-and-mortar travel agencies. This channel was classified as indirect since the bookings were made through an intermediary, the GDS, and not directly on the airline's reservations system. Before the Internet era, between 80 and 85% of all airline bookings flowed through the GDS channel. Figure 9.1 illustrates the two offline channels that existed from the pre-Internet era.

Corporate air travel is managed travel and employees who travel on company business must be compliant with corporate travel policies. Since the inception of the GDSs in 1976, corporate air travel bookings have gone through the travel agencies who subscribed to a GDS. AIRIMP (Airline Industry Reservations Interline Message Procedures) messaging is used by GDSs to exchange standardized passenger reservation information between airlines, travel agencies, and other GDSs. IATA publishes AIRIMP, the reservations interline message procedures passenger

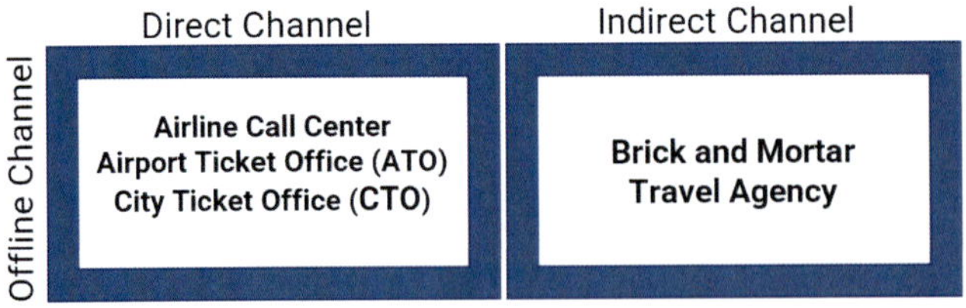

Fig. 9.1 Offline direct and indirect channels pre-Internet

manual. A4A (Airlines for America) publishes the Standard Interline Passenger Procedures, known as SIPP. The AIRIMP telex messaging was the backbone of inter-airline communications between reservations systems and GDS connectivity since its inception in 1976. It continues to be used today, even after EDIFACT was introduced in 1987/1988 and XML in 2012. It is a set of communication standards that ensures the accurate and efficient transfer of data for bookings and interline itineraries across different systems. EDIFACT was introduced in 1988 and became the new standard for interactive messaging. Corporate travel purchases were made through a travel management company or online corporate booking tool. These bookings were made through the EDIFACT protocol supported by the GDSs.

In 1996, the Internet led to the creation of two primary online channels, direct and indirect. Travelocity, launched on March 12, 1996, was the first online travel reservations system, even before the arrival of airline websites. Expedia followed. The Online Travel Agencies (OTAs) are indirect channels of distribution since they access GDSs for airline schedules and fares with web services (API's) and air bookings are made through the GDS. The airline websites are the direct channels since bookings are transacted directly with the airline's reservations system. These two online channels primarily serve leisure customers.

Figure 9.2 illustrates the new reality of distribution channels after adoption of the Internet.

Airline bookings via metasearch engines (e.g., Kayak, Skyscanner) are considered a hybrid model, acting as a referral advertising tool that allows online users to book either directly with the airline or indirectly through an OTA. Metasearch displays real-time prices from multiple sources, facilitating comparisons and directing users to the chosen site to complete the transaction.

In 2019, the year before the pandemic, the GDS global share was 52%. The adoption of New Distribution Capability (NDC) has accelerated the decline in GDS market share, and, in 2025, it varied between 25 and 60% depending on the country. Can the GDS model survive the shift toward direct airline retailing?

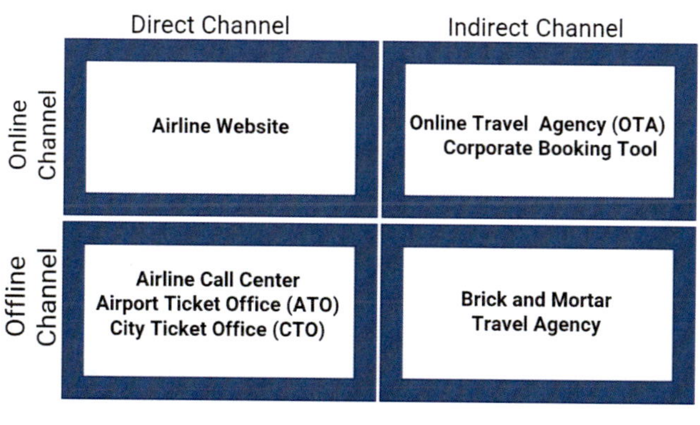

Fig. 9.2 The new reality in 1996 after Internet adoption

Besides the headwinds created by NDC, Agentic AI will have a greater impact on GDS economics in the future.

AI Agents acting on behalf of humans are rapidly emerging as a new high-efficiency channel, the AI channel, for direct distribution. This shifts the focus from human-centric, browser-based, or app-based interactions to autonomous, machine-to-machine or conversational commerce. This paradigm shift signals a move beyond traditional e-commerce sites with AI Agents handling tasks like research, comparison shopping, and purchase execution. Network carriers with an eye on lowering distribution costs could shift up to 35% of total bookings to AI channels by 2035. Managed corporate travel will not be impacted over the next few years (2030) due to its inherent complexity, but will see disruption beyond 2030.

AI Agents and blockchain technology will be adapted at scale in travel over the next decade. The synergy is primarily based on using blockchain to provide the trust, transparency, and security that autonomous AI Agents need to operate reliably and at scale. Market dynamics will shift irreversibly over the next decade toward supplier direct bookings, and the role of intermediaries will diminish.

9.2 Full Content and MFN Clauses in GDS Airline Contracts

The two most important clauses in contracts between GDSs and airlines were Full Content agreement (FCA) and Most Favored Nation (MFN). These clauses protected the GDS and promoted an omni-channel strategy.

The participating career agreement (PCA) is a contract form between a GDS and an airline to distribute and sell the airline product. The PCA has a standard rack rate that governs the economics and participation of an airline in the GDS. It is the overarching contract defining the core relationship and obligations for content distribution. The term "full content agreement" (FCA) requires an airline to provide access to its schedules, fares, and availability to the online and offline channels of a GDS that they provide to other sales and distribution channels, inclusive of their own websites. In exchange, GDS providers often offer airlines lower distribution fees in the form of a discount. This has been a point of contention in the industry, leading to legal disputes and antitrust lawsuits that led to the development of new distribution technologies like IATA's New Distribution Capability (NDC) to offer more flexible content options. NDC has complicated these full content agreements, as airlines seek more flexibility to offer unique content through direct channels or specific NDC connections, which may not always align with full content requirements. Since full-service carriers (FSCs) started selling ancillary products and services, these ancillaries have never been included in the full content agreements between GDSs and airlines. It was the first step toward dissolution of full content agreements, and it created an imbalance where airlines sell these ancillaries on their own websites, but not consistently or fully through travel agents using GDSs.

The term Most Favored Nation (MFN) originated in international trade relations where a country grants the same rights, privileges, and immunities to a country that it has already granted MFN status. The word "nation" is used because the term comes from international trade agreements between nations. This clause requires nation A to provide nation B with all the concessions that nation A has already granted to nation C.

An MFN clause exists in contracts between GDSs and airlines. An MFN clause does not guarantee price equality in booking fees. The MFN clause mitigates risk where the airline is guaranteed to get the best deal now and in the future. What it simply means is that if the GDS grants a better deal to its favorite airline, then the same deal also applies to the airline negotiating the contract. Contrary to common belief, the MFN clause is not overarching. In an MFN clause, the "best deal" is unbiased display of an airline's content on a travel agency desktop. It does not mean that the segment booking fee economics are the same, since GDS fees are influenced by the size of the carrier and expected booking volume. At best, it is a *feel-good* clause in airline - GDS contracts.

9.3 Origins of NDC

A plan to support the creation of a New Distribution Capability was approved by the IATA Board of Governors in 2011. Following the IATA Board of Governors endorsement in 2011, IATA and a small group of airlines attended the Passenger Services Conference (PSC) on October 18–19, 2012, to pass resolution 787 (Enhanced Airline Distribution). The IATA Passenger Services Conference (PSC) led the creation of the standards. In the past, IATA has contributed to the standardization of interline passenger communication codes and protocols. The resolution was designed to support the development of an open Extended Markup Language (XML) based data exchange standard to complement the existing teletype and EDIFACT data exchange standards already managed by IATA for the airline industry (IATA, 2012).

New Distribution Capability (NDC) had a stated objective to overhaul the existing legacy messaging exchange standard with a new XML standard between airlines and intermediaries. The underlying goal was to make it easier, faster, and cheaper to provide customers with comprehensive information about fare alternatives, airline ancillary products and services, onboard amenities, and rich graphics such as seat maps when booking through a travel agent.

Developing the NDC vision to "increase competition, stimulate innovation, reduce distribution costs, and improve customer choice" was the responsibility of the Passenger Distribution Group (PDG), which was governed by the PSC. Although it might have been an intention, dismantling the GDS oligopoly was never mentioned as an objective. Air Canada, Alitalia, United Airlines, Delta Air Lines, Air France/KLM, British Airways, Lufthansa, Swiss International Airlines, Korean Air, Cathay Pacific Airways, and Singapore Airlines were the eleven carriers that made up the PDG. It is interesting to note that none of the GDSs that excel in creating and implementing connectivity products were asked to join the working group that was tasked with creating a vision for NDC.

After Resolution 787 (IATA, 2012) was adopted at the conference, it was subsequently sent to the U.S. Department of Transportation (DOT) for approval on March 11, 2013 (DOCKET OST-2013-0048) with an intended effective date of June 1, 2013. DOT gave tentative approval in May 2014 and final approval in August 2014 for Resolution 787, paving the way for NDC adoption in the U.S. Airline investment in NDC was on a voluntary basis and the first set of NDC schemas were released on September 1, 2015.

Progressively, IATA launched four related programs to show how retailing in the airline industry will be: They are:

1. NDC, that defines the new messaging standard for airline to communicate offers to intermediaries.
2. Dynamic Offer Creation, which are entirely airline-controlled, regardless of channel.
3. ONE Order, which serves as a replacement for PNRs, E-Tickets, and EMDs
4. Settlements with Orders, which consider the accounting processes after the flight.

9.4 Is It Indeed "Modern: Airline Retailing?"

NDC was introduced by IATA in 2012, and the first messaging standard was published in 2015. In 2025, this is still definitely a work in progress, but significant strides are being made towards its adoption and maturation within the travel industry. Of the sixty plus airlines that are NDC certified, the large network carriers have shown the greatest commitment in the pursuit of NDC to break up the GDS oligopoly.

Persistence with NDC by a few large network carriers reminds me of the Dale Carnegie quote from 1942:

> *Most of the important things in the world have been accomplished by people who have kept on trying when there seemed to be no hope at all.*
>
> —Dale Carnegie

This quote highlights the importance of perseverance and resilience in achieving success For context, in 1942 Dale Carnegie published a newspaper column about U.S. inventor Lee de Forest who faced numerous technological, financial, and legal obstacles in his career. He eventually found success with the creation of the Audion vacuum tube in 1906, that allowed the detection and amplification of weak radio signals, that revolutionized radio broadcasting. Lee de Forest's tale illustrates Carnegie's point that one should not be easily deterred.

Over the past few years, to accelerate NDC adoption, many entities such as IATA have termed the EDIFACT messaging protocol as legacy. They have also simultaneously claimed that the new approach with NDC constitutes Modern Airline Retailing. Over the past decade there has not been any groundbreaking innovation on NDC, offer creation or order management. Most of the focus from the major airlines that are pursuing NDC has been to withhold fares from the GDS under various pretexts that negatively impact the traveler. It is indeed "modern airline retailing" if every travel supplier that is pursuing an NDC initiative has a customer-first priority. Sadly, this is not the case. As of 2025, over 90% of corporate buyers are not prepared for the impact of NDC on their corporate travel programs.

The failure of NDC to gain rapid adoption rests with IATA and the airline partners. Instead of a transformation to NDC, GDS surcharges and content restrictions dominate the landscape, reinforced by home market power to force travel agents to use airline-specific distribution "platforms" that were not and still are not fit for purpose. The complexity created in airline distribution must be solved and ultimately the costs will be borne by the travelers and those who pay their bills.

However, in spite of all the shortcomings, NDC is here to stay because it has the backing of the major U.S. and International carriers. After the pandemic of 2020, the second half of 2023 and 2024 saw a revival of NDC deployment among full-service carriers. The NDC program is not managed efficiently by IATA and the airlines. IATA has never provided governance to control the various versions of the NDC API in existence. Instead of mandating the use of two or three most recent versions of the NDC APIs, many proliferate. In 2025, there were at least eight schema versions, and the oldest was 17.2 (2017, Version 2). From an airline perspective, an NDC program is effectively an API program, and it is not in their realm of expertise. Few airlines own and manage their APIs. Many airlines have outsourced all technical knowledge to their PSS provider and hence they have very little understanding of their NDC APIs and functionalities.

Over a decade in the making, progress on NDC adoption has been slow for several reasons. They are:

1. Airline partners, bolstered by IATA, introduced surcharges and private channels instead of focusing on NDC adoption, leading to a fractured relationship between the airlines and the GDSs.
2. NDC has increased the cost of sale for travel agents. Aggregating NDC content from GDSs and NDC Aggregators come at a cost. In the case of the GDS, agencies lose incentives and also have to pay for NDC content. NDC Aggregators charge travel agencies a booking fee that they must pass on to their customers.
3. The needs of corporate buyers are not an area of expertise for the airlines. This is something that the TMCs do effectively.
4. NDC messaging standards were not developed in collaboration with GDSs or TMCs.
5. The true benefits to the customer with NDC are not understood by the airline or the customer. Airlines have only focused on favorable commercial discussions with the GDSs for NDC bookings.

6. Withholding content from the indirect channel is not a winning NDC strategy. Yet, many airlines only make their lower fares available on preferred channels that do not include the GDSs.
7. A *coalition-of- the willing* is a fundamental requirement to move NDC forward and deliver value to the customer.

IATA positions Modern Airline Retailing (MAR) as the broader transformation program that uses NDC as a critical component. The creation of airline-controlled offers using he NDC messaging standard also includes continuous pricing of itineraries with indefinite price points and dynamic bundles. The scope includes the creation of a unique identifier or order ID that replaces Passenger Name Records (PNRs), E-Tickets (ETKT) and Electronic Miscellaneous Documents (EMDs). This is called ONE Order by IATA.

However, innovation in retailing from the airline community has been minimal and the primary focus has been on withholding content from the GDSs and negotiating GDS-Airline contracts that are commercially more favorable for the airlines.

9.5 Origins of XML Messaging and the New Distribution Ecosystem

In July 2010, Air Canada, American Airlines, Continental Airlines, Delta Air Lines, United Airlines, US Airways joined forces with ATPCO to form an industry working and advocacy group to develop XML standards for airlines. Called Open Axis, other entities such as reservations software providers Datalex and Radixx, payment processing firm eNett International, and others joined the air distribution standards group. The primary objective of the new distribution ecosystem was to "ensure all parties have detailed and timely data regarding ancillary services without dependency on full-scale ARC/IATA production rollouts." GDSs and TMCs were not directly involved in the Open Axis initiative (West, 2010).

Open Axis was an advocate for the new XML-based distribution schema, proposed by Farelogix, that would replace the GDS standard EDIFACT protocol. Open Axis also joined forces with the established industry group OpenTravel Alliance, to ensure their efforts were aligned. OpenTravel Alliance provided XML standards across multiple segments in the industry, including airlines, hotels, car rentals, golf reservations, and event tickets.

Open Axis was active until 2011 when IATA launched the NDC initiative. In 2011, the IATA Board of Governors endorsed an initiative to facilitate the development of a New Distribution Capability. IATA's NDC allowed third-party aggregators to access and display a full range of airline products including ancillaries to consumers.

The OpenTravel Alliance is a non-profit consortium of travel companies that develops and maintains open e-business data specifications to standardize communication between different systems in the travel industry. Airlines like United

Airlines were already using OpenTravel Alliance APIs to cross-sell rental cars from their rental car partners on their website. IATA opted for Open Axis over OpenTravel Alliance [Rice, 2013]. IATA did not pursue OpenTravel Alliance standards for NDC primarily because the airlines preferred to control the standard's governance and chose a schema that was more airline-centric, even though OpenTravel's schema scored higher in meeting NDC's functional needs. IATA's decision was influenced by a desire for the underlying standard to be controlled by airlines themselves, and OpenTravel's proposed governance model did not align with this goal.

The Airline Tariff Publishing Company (ATPCO) acquired Open Axis in January 2013. Its standards eventually formed the foundation for IATA's NDC.

9.5.1 Why Was XML Chosen for NDC?

XML (Extensible Markup Language) was developed by a working group of the World Wide Web Consortium (W3C), with development beginning in 1996. The XML 1.0 Specification was officially adopted as a W3C Recommendation in February 1998, marking its formal establishment as a web standard. In 2026, many consider XML as legacy even though it can handle complex data structures more efficiently than EDIFACT. XML was probably not chosen because it was the most advanced technology. It was chosen perhaps because it could act as a bridge between the legacy GDS EDIFACT messages and the projected future needs of airline distribution.

XML is bulky compared to JSON (Java Script Object Notation), XML can be easily parsed by a human compared to JSON, but JSON is better for communications between machines assuming the receiving system has a native JSON parser.

The future is not XML, but it is an API-first, JSON-based solution that is lighter, faster, uses fewer resources and more scalable. A cast study compares the two data interchange formats, XML and JSON, highlighting their strengths, transmission rates and performance [Nurseitov, Paulson, Reynolds and Izuretia, 2009]. In the hospitality industry, the shift only became meaningful when large chains moved away from rigid traditional extranets and embraced modern, API-driven distribution.

9.5.2 The First NDC Bookings

After NDC was launched by IATA in 2012, NDC bookings did not occur until the XML messaging standard reached a minimal level of maturity. Some of the earliest adopters are summarized below.

In April 2017, Lufthansa Group introduced its first NDC-enabled direct connect solutions with TMCs Click Travel and Portman Clarity in the United Kingdom (Fox, 2017).

Previously in 2015, Lufthansa had initiated a direct connection with the corporate travel and expense management tool, Concur, but it was not on the NDC messaging format. With this integration the business traveler's Concur profile was synchronized with the traveler's Lufthansa profile, thereby providing access to the qualified corporate discount fares to make a booking directly into the Lufthansa reservations system (O'Neil, 2015a). This data is available on Concur, which makes it available to the appropriate TMC and corporate travel manager to address any back-tax reclamation or duty of care. Travelers who book direct can also avoid the infamous €16 surcharge for GDS bookings imposed by Lufthansa, effective September 1, 2015.

On July 17, 2018. CTI, a corporate travel management company made its first NDC booking with British Airways (Dyson, 2018). The NDC bookings were made through CTI's online booking tool, PLANNET.

Emirates Airways launched their Emirates Gateway NDC powered direct connect solution in October 2020 (Frary, 2020).

In 2020, Singapore Airlines and Travelport. Star Cruise Travel Services, a subscriber of Travelport, made the NDC bookings through the Travelport travel agency desktop called Smartpoint (Travelport, 2020).

CWT, the second largest TMC worldwide prior to its acquisition by American Express Global Business Travel (Amex GBT) in 2025, created its first GDS sourced NDC transaction in production through the Amadeus Cytric Travel & Expense booking tool for American Airlines (CWT 2021). American Airlines was also the first U.S. carrier to launch NDC integration with a GDS, beginning with European points of sale through the Amadeus Travel Platform in 2021 (American Airlines, 2021).

9.6 Standard GDS Transaction Processing (1976–2016)

Figure 9.3 illustrates how traditional GDS content is used to create a booking before NDC (1976–2016. It continues to be used but is on the decline as airlines actively promote the NDC protocol.

Airlines create schedules and distribute them to schedule aggregators such as OAG or Cerium that in turn distribute the schedules to subscribers like the GDSs. The Schedule Change Information Manual (SSIM) is an IATA format by which airline schedules are distributed by the schedule aggregators weekly. SSIM is a standard schedule format that airlines use to exchange flight schedule data with GDSs, airports, and other partners. Changes to the SSIM are also submitted every other week. SSIM is used for bulk schedule data, like a complete schedule of an airline.

When schedule changes are published to SSIM, there are two types of messages, called standard schedule message (SSM) and ad-hoc schedule message (ASM) which are sent by the airline to the GDSs. An SSM transmission permanently changes an airline's regular operating schedule, while an ASM is an update to the regular operating schedule for single days, sent by the airline's operational

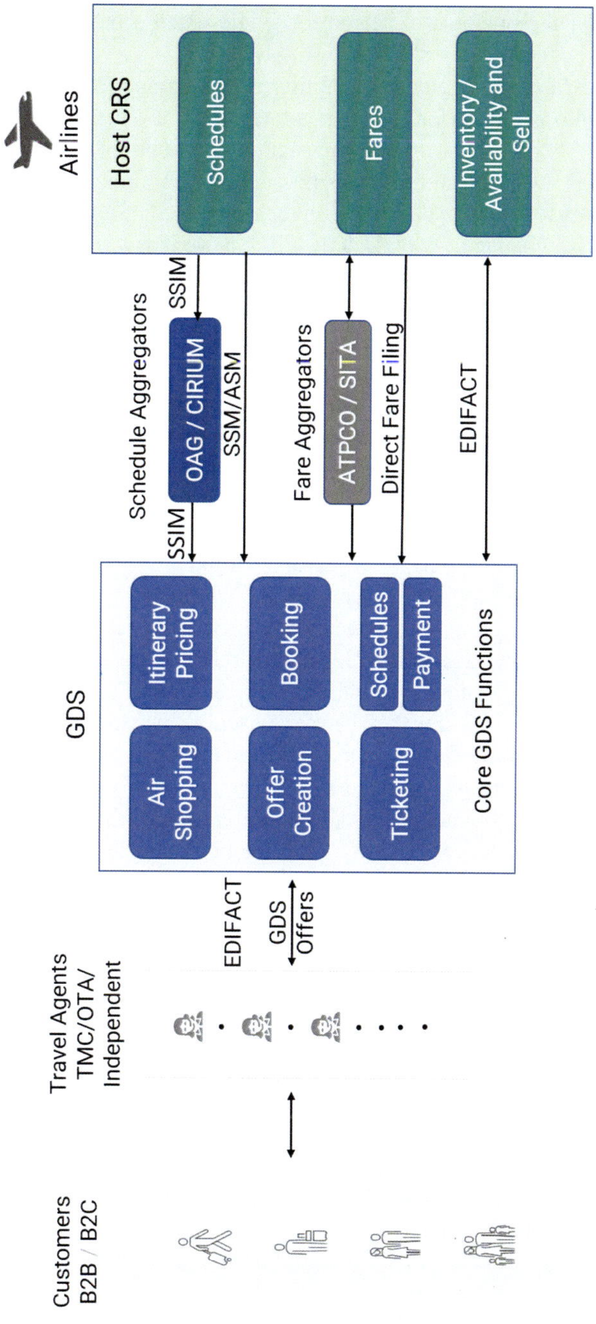

Fig. 9.3 The GDS Indirect Channel before NDC

control systems. SSM is usually used for schedule information outside the operational period and may include a collection of schedule changes. In contrast, ASM is normally used for the operational period for single-dated schedule information. SSM and ASM are usually telex message formats.

Airlines have a fare management capability to determine if new fares need to be introduced into a market or if existing fares need to be updated based on competitor fare filings. Airlines initiate fare actions and submit their changes to fare aggregator ATPCO which in turn transmits the fares, routings, and automated rules to subscribers like GDSs and airlines. In the domestic U.S. market, due to the high volumes of fare changes, ATPCO transmits on weekdays (Monday through Friday) at 1000, 1300, 1600 and 2000 h. On weekends (Saturday, Sunday) the transmissions are once a day at 1700 h. International data transmissions are more frequent and are made every hour on the hour on weekdays and with a reduced frequency on weekends.

In this environment, for the indirect channel, *pricing power is in the domain of the GDS* which can generate shopping responses of priced itineraries and accurately price an itinerary for ticketing and payment. Air shopping is a multimillion-dollar investment for a GDS and may consist of a combination of schedule-led and fare-led algorithms. In the GDS transaction processing world, *scale matters* (Vinod, 2024a, Chapter 5). For example, Sabre's shopping complex is called Air Travel Shopping Engine (ATSE). Shopping volumes have grown rapidly, mostly fueled by shopping requests from the OTAs. For example, prior to the COVID-19 pandemic, the total volume of travel agency shops in 2019 was about 249 billion on the Sabre GDS which averages over 700 million shopping requests from agencies per day. Further, peak transactions per second in 2019 were approximately 25,487 (Vinod, 2020a). Displaying many itineraries for a shopping request is not the answer. It is important to display the best set of itineraries for a customer based on their schedule and fare preferences. All aspects of shopping, except for querying an airline host CRS for booking class availability, are performed internally in the GDS environment. Scale, from a GDS perspective, includes both business and technical considerations. While internal transaction processing needs to be efficient to deliver shopping responses after evaluation of the immense search space in under three seconds, business considerations are equally important to meet the needs of corporate travel booking tools, travel management companies and online travel agencies who access the GDS.

Once the itinerary is selected by the user from the shopping response, the GDS creates the PNR which belongs to the travel agency. The PNR is stored in the GDS, and the airline owns a part of the PNR.

There are two alternatives for payment processing.

With the traditional agency model, the customer pays the travel agency. The travel agent uses the GDS to provide customer card details. The agent does not collect payment. After the GDS payment authorization step, the payment is credited to the airline bank.

If the travel agent is the merchant of record, payment is collected by the agent and settled with the airline at a later stage using IATA's Billing and Settlement Plan

(BSP). The agency takes on the responsibility of processing payments, managing transactions and handling potential refunds or chargebacks. BSP operates globally outside the U.S., while ARC (Airline Reporting Corporation) is used in the U.S. Both ARC and BSP are intermediaries between travel agencies and airlines to process payments and reconcile sales.

Once payment is completed, the agency requests the GDS to start the ticket issuance process with the airline. The GDS checks if the airline is approved to issue tickets through this agency, assigns a neutral ticket number, and forwards it to the airline for ticketing. The airline reviews the information provided and notifies the agency through the GDS once validation is complete.

In a future environment with NDC, what is most important is addressing scalability, both technical and business, to deliver the same level of efficiency and service.

All communications between the airline and the GDS are based on EDIFACT and in some cases teletype. For example, interactive availability requests (also known as seamless availability) from a GDS to an airline (PAOREQ) and its subsequent response (PAORES) are based on EDIFACT while availability status messages (AVS) are based on teletype.

9.7 The Hybrid State with NDC

The hybrid state is what we have today, and it will continue to persist for a long time. During the hybrid state, standard GDS EDIFACT bookings and NDC bookings will coexist in the travel marketplace.

While some airlines have started to adopt NDC, many have not. Even for the ones that have adopted NDC, their booking volumes through the NDC channel are significantly lower than through the traditional GDS channel. Hence, they must continue to distribute their schedules through OAG or Cirium and fares through ATPCO. However, the NDC fares may be different from what has been filed to ATPCO for traditional GDS bookings using EDIFACT. Note that SITA's fare management system was acquired by ATPCO in January 2021.

Figure 9.4 illustrates the transaction workflow with IATA NDC and traditional GDS content co-existing and operating in a *hybrid state*. The key difference is that for *NDC content pricing, power shifts from the GDS to the airline* which generates offers and takes control of distribution of the airline product through the indirect channel. NDC bookings made through a GDS are passive pass-through bookings since the GDS is strictly a conduit passing messages and booking data directly to the airline's reservations system which creates and manages the order. Only the airline can make changes to a NDC booking that originates in the GDS.

The process of migrating all airlines worldwide to NDC for 100% of bookings is no simple task. It is anticipated that the airline industry will be in a hybrid state for a minimum period of 15 years from 2025. What this means is that every airline that participates in a GDS will be NDC-enabled and EDIFACT will no longer be required.

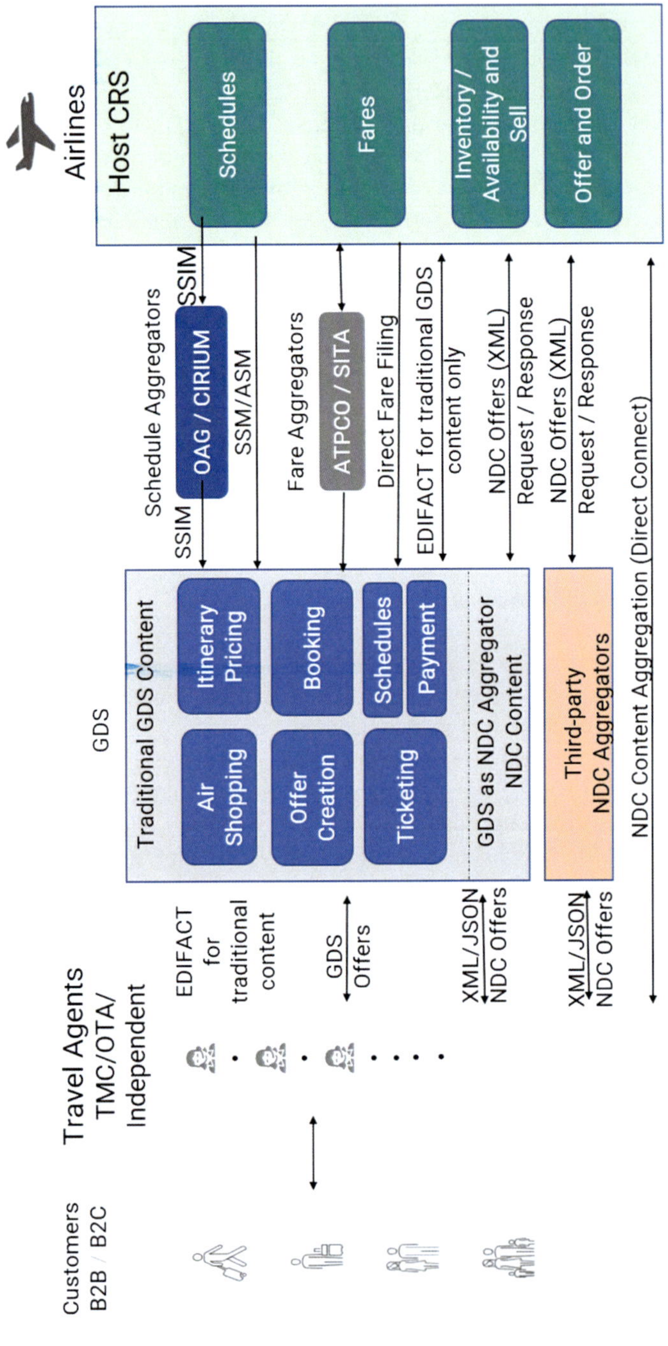

Fig. 9.4 The Current Hybrid State of the GDS Indirect Channel

Note in Fig. 9.4 that besides using the GDS or third-party NDC Aggregators to access NDC content, travel agencies have the Direct Connect option. This refers to a method for travel agencies and airlines to connect directly, bypassing traditional Global Distribution Systems (GDS) and NDC Aggregators. It utilizes the NDC messaging standard, allowing airlines to share a wider range of flight details and ancillary services directly with travel sellers.

When a shopping request is made by a travel agent to receive NDC content, the GDS sends the message to multiple airlines that serve that market for a response with NDC offers. The non-homogenous airline responses are mapped to the pre-defined shelves on the travel agency desktop, and the content is normalized based on value before it is displayed to a travel agent. NDC content-based itineraries booked by a travel agent in the airline host CRS can be stored in the GDS as passive segments. The segments are passive, or informational segments as they are also called. This is because any change to the itinerary must be requested by the travel agent and made by the airline. It also allows airlines to share rich content (e.g., images, text, video, etc.) and personalize the offer with dynamic pricing and ancillary bundles for product differentiation from competitors. NDC also gives flexibility to airlines to connect directly with OTAs, TMCs and travel search engines without the need for a GDS.

For NDC content, once an offer is selected by the travel agent, additional ancillaries such as seats and bags can be added and repriced. The GDS or NDC Aggregator sends a create order request to the airline who owns the order.

For NDC bookings the GDS or NDC Aggregator does not collect payment but sends the PCI compliant payment details to the airline. This triggers the creation of the PNR and E-TKT or the order. Like how payment is processed on the consumer direct channel, the airline can accept or reject the credit card that was submitted.

Once payment is accepted, ticketing can proceed and the airline issues the travel documents.

Note that the GDSs are by default aggregators of NDC content, but the GDS has significantly more capabilities than the new-entrant NDC Aggregators. In this book the term NDC Aggregators refer to the new entrants in the marketplace. Examples are Travelfusion, TPConnects, Duffel, AirGateway, and many more.

The creation of the new NDC XML-based messaging standard has also given rise to many new entrant NDC Aggregators. NDC Aggregators offer connectivity to airlines, and they aggregate NDC content like a GDS. Sometimes a large TMC may use a GDS and NDC Aggregator for NDC content. This is because the NDC Aggregator may have connected to airlines that the GDS still has on their roadmap for the future. This creates issues with mid-office and back-office reporting. When a travel agent makes a booking based on NDC content returned by a NDC Aggregator, the booking bypasses the GDS and the NDC Aggregator routes the booking directly to the airline. While GDS bypass, which is disintermediation of the GDS, exists in the hybrid state, it is still a very small percentage of indirect bookings in 2023 and 2024.

Note that for NDC offers, the connectivity with the airline is based on the new NDC XML messaging standard and the GDS to travel agency connectivity is based on XML or JSON.

9.8 The End State with NDC

The end state assumes that all 600 airlines worldwide that participate in a GDS, have migrated to the NDC way of doing business. It is difficult to forecast when the end-state will truly begin. Conservatively, it will take 15 years from 2025. The true end state can only begin when all airlines and travel agencies are NDC enabled. It is safe to assume that it is very far in the future. This adversely impacts the GDSs since they need to enhance and maintain shopping, booking, and ticketing capabilities even as EDIFACT transactions decline in volume.

Figure 9.5 illustrates the transaction workflow with IATA NDC in the end state. The key difference is that *pricing power has shifted entirely from the GDS to the airline* which generates offers and takes complete control of distribution of the airline product through the indirect channel.

Airlines can use NDC to manage distribution through the indirect channel by sending customized rich content, priced itineraries, and air ancillary packages to travel agencies. NDC poses a threat to fare aggregator APTCO, though airlines may continue to use ATPCO to support the direct channel. They also pose a threat to schedule aggregators such as OAG and Cirium. Airlines may opt not to file their fares and schedules through these intermediaries in the future. However, the GDSs still require schedules to route requests from travel agents to the airlines that respond to NDC offer request, so airlines will continue to disseminate schedules to aggregators and GDSs.

On payment collection, prior to NDC, the travel agent would either collect the money from the customer and settle it through the IATA Billing and Settlement Plan (BSP) or use a GDS for payment authorization and credit card payment to the airline's designated bank. With NDC, the airline becomes the merchant that processes the payment. The airline is responsible for the payment transaction, which implies that the airline is responsible for any security breach at the seller when the seller is transmitting details of the client card to be used by the airline as a "merchant of record."

With 100% NDC adoption, every travel agency booking will have to go to the airline for offers, which is an itinerary with base fare and priced ancillaries. The GDS air shopping service used by travel agents and OTAs will no longer be required. While NDC may be in the early stages of adoption in 2025, it will eventually render the last remnants of full content agreements obsolete. This is because pricing power to create offers has shifted to the airline for indirect bookings by giving airlines the ability to merchandise their products and control the price quote.

NDC also allows airlines to make the same offer across all channels of distribution or customize offers by channel or point of sale. With the erosion of full content

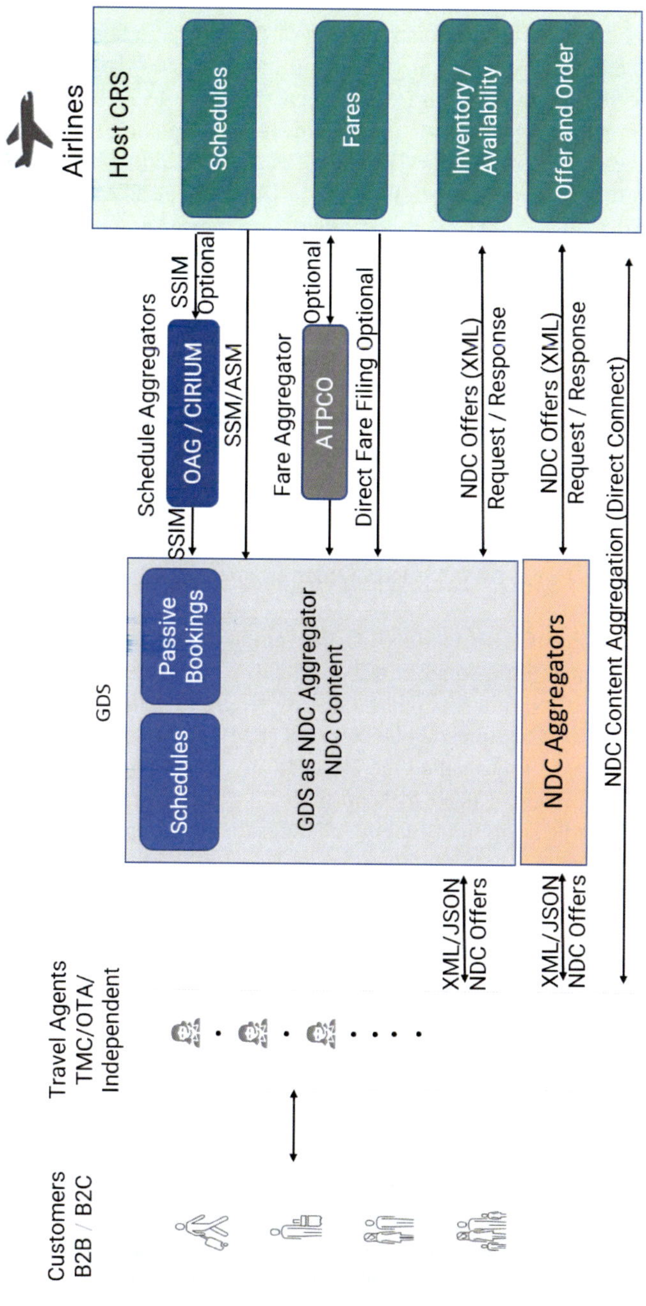

Fig. 9.5 The end-state of the GDS Indirect Channel

agreements, many airlines bypass the GDS and connect directly with travel agencies. The so-called airline direct solution does not bode well for the future of the GDS. There is also a greater probability of diverging from an omni-channel strategy. It can be viewed as a financial restructuring of the airline industry for indirect bookings since the airline becomes the merchant that processes the payment.

ONE Order is also an integral part of the NDC program to introduce a single customer order record to capture all data elements that require to be fulfilled. This streamlines the sale of ancillary products with the elimination of multiple reservations records and the elimination of the E-Ticket/Electronic Miscellaneous Document (EMD) with a single reference order. The transition to ONE Order is discussed in Chapter 6.

9.9 ONE Order

The commercial airline industry is going through a multimillion-dollar information technology investment from airlines and intermediaries to transform the legacy passenger name record (PNR) to what has been called the ONE Order. IATA introduced ONE Order at its World Passenger Symposium in 2015, describing it at the time as "*a single customer order record holding all data elements required for order fulfillment across the travel cycle*". ONE Order is an integral part of the NDC program.

The fundamental objective of the ONE Order initiative is to extend the PNR by consolidating a passenger's personal information and purchases such as an airline ticket and air ancillaries within a single record. ONE Order phases out PNRs, E-Tickets, and Electronic Miscellaneous Documents (EMD) by combining them into a single customer focused order called the Order Id. It aims to simplify the traveler experience by eliminating the need to keep track of different reference numbers and documents when checking in or making changes to an existing itinerary. Given the legacy environment in which the commercial aviation industry has been operating, ONE Order is a major multimillion dollar investment from airlines and intermediaries to transform the legacy PNR to ONE Order. It will take several years to develop since the introduction of the "new" concept in 2015.

While this concept is new to the commercial airline industry, it is used in other industries such as manufacturing and retail. Manufacturers and retailers use Order Management Systems (called OMS) to get a single view of the customer order regardless of where the individual components are sourced.

9.9.1 What ONE Order Means to the Airline Industry

To understand what ONE Order means for the future of transaction processing, we need to first review the current transaction processing environment.

To complete a booking, multiple documents are required for passengers to book, pay, board, and ultimately fly. Many of these documents are remnants of legacy processes that are still necessary for functions that are no longer current. For instance, between 1990 and 2000, the standard travel procedure involved making a reservation by contacting the airline or a travel agent, receiving a paper ticket upon payment, reconfirming itinerary details by phoning the airline or travel agency a few days before traveling, and obtaining a boarding pass at the airport by exchanging the flight coupon with an agent.

Utilization of ticket numbers is another example of legacy procedures. For each passenger itinerary, a single coupon is assigned to a specific flight. However, if an itinerary consists of more than four flight segments, a conjunction ticket is necessary. A conjunction ticket is a ticket issued to a passenger which also contains another ticket for passage which together constitutes a single contract of carriage. This results in two distinct ticket numbers. These two ticket numbers, such as 125–1,234,567,890 and 125–1,234,567,891, signify the use of two ticket stocks from the airline. In this example, the first three numbers (125) represent the unique airline number, in this case 125 is British Airways, followed by the 10-digit ticket number. This is because of an inherent limitation with the original paper tickets, specified by IATA in 1930, only having four flight coupons. In addition to these coupons, there is a coupon for airline accounting purposes and a final coupon for the passenger's receipt. When the industry transitioned to E-Tickets (ETKT) in 2008, the coupon limits carried over from the legacy environment.

The documents associated with a passenger's journey are:

1. The PNR, that includes details about the itinerary and personal information of the passenger, such as their name and contact information.
2. The traditional paper ticket was replaced by the E-Ticket, in 2008. This electronic ticket is now mandatory for all flights.
3. The EMD, or Electronic Miscellaneous Document, is a non-flight record that can be used to pay for ancillaries, services, and fees. This document has replaced some usage of the Miscellaneous Charge Orders, or MCO.
4. A boarding pass to allow a passenger to board a flight. While the traditional paper version is becoming outdated, electronic boarding passes can be accessed through online check-ins and smartphone applications.

ONE Order simplifies the fulfillment, servicing, delivery, and accounting procedures pertaining to airline goods and services.

It has a unique reference number that includes everything the traveler requires: the PNR number, passenger personal data, passenger contact information, itinerary details, payment status, ticket information, and ancillary information.

The sharing of information between various parties (such as airline partners or even airline and hotel providers) will be made with the unique ONE Order reference number. This will occur regardless of where, how, or from which supplier the passenger purchased services or seats.

The financial and accounting operations will be made easier by eliminating the reconciliation between tickets and reservations.

9.10 NDC Is a Catch-22 Situation

The term Catch 22 originates from Joseph Heller's anti-war novel where pilots are trapped by a rule. A pilot can be grounded if insane, but asking to be grounded proves sanity, meaning they must continue flying. A Catch-22 is a frustrating, paradoxical situation where you are trapped by contradictory rules or conditions, meaning you cannot escape because solving the problem requires fulfilling a condition that is impossible to meet until the problem is already solved. It is like needing experience for a job but needing a job to get experience.

IATA NDC presents a Catch-22 situation. As a percentage of total bookings, NDC bookings are expected to reach 21% by 2028 (Silk, 2025a) compared to just 7% in 2023. That is sixteen years after the NDC program was initiated. Why is it such a challenge? Airlines need to invest heavily in Offer and Order to unlock the benefits such as better offers, streamlined orders, and lower GDS costs. IATA One Order is a hefty financial undertaking that will impact balance sheets of airlines for several years. The significant upfront costs, legacy system overhaul, negative balance sheets, and alignment challenges with partners such as GDSs and TMCs make airlines hesitant to fully commit, creating a slow, resource-intensive adoption cycle despite well-defined long-term benefits.

From a usage perspective, ARC reported that leisure travel agencies accounted for 16% of settled NDC transactions in 2025, corporate agencies accounted for 7% and OTAs transacted 77% (Silk, 2026).

9.10.1 Total Cost of Ownership to Control Offer and Order

A rarely discussed topic in industry forums is the total cost of ownership (TCO) for the airline to control the offer and order across all channels of distribution. With NDC adoption, pricing power in shifting from the GDS to the airline, and the airline IT costs are increasing by an order of magnitude to respond to all requests for offers. Adopting the NDC messaging standard is a significant investment, and ONE Order is much higher.

Distribution costs will go down with NDC adoption because of the two-tier revenue model for booking fees. While EDIFACT booking fees may remain unchained, booking fees for NDC bookings are vastly lower.

Airlines need to have clear financial controls and activity-based costing to estimate what the true costs are to control the offer and order in an NDC environment.

9.11 The State of the Union with NDC Adoption

NDC was launched in 2012, promising enhanced traveler experiences rather than cost savings for airlines or disintermediation of intermediaries. Unfortunately, to date, customers have seen minimal benefits as the NDC focus has primarily been on restricting content from channels that the airlines do not like, resulting in higher fares being paid by customers. Meeting and surpassing customer expectations is fundamental to the success of any initiative, including NDC. We are still a long way from achieving this goal.

There are three distinct ways for OTAs and other travel sellers to access NDC content. They are:

1. GDS NDC connectivity (there are three primary GDSs)
2. NDC Aggregators (there are a large number of new entrant NDC Aggregators)
3. Directly, using an airline's NDC API

While as a percentage of the total sales volume NDC is still relatively small, but it is growing with more NDC connections and travel agencies operationalizing it (Airoldi, 2024e). By 2025, over 60 airlines are NDC certified, representing more than half of IATA passenger volume. While there are over 350 airlines worldwide that IATA represents. The 60 + NDC-certified carriers include a diverse range of both large and smaller international airlines.

NDC has been frequently referred to as "modern airline retailing." What is so modern about the standard of XML messaging, and XML has been around since 1998? Take the case of the world's largest online retailer, Amazon, that does not call what they do as "modern retailing." They flawlessly operate a global logistic network and add a nearly unlimited marketplace on top. Personalization is integrated into their online process.

While NDC is entrenched in the travel marketplace, a collaborative effort is necessary for NDC to succeed. The success of the NDC program for the indirect channel will require uniform airline adoption and demonstrated scalability of transaction volumes that are comparable to the GDS model, While NDC has a ground swell of support from the major network carriers, after over a decade of investment, it is still largely unproven.

Perhaps the biggest challenge to uniform adoption is the lack of governance for the XML-based messaging format by IATA. Multiple versions of the XML-based messaging standard exist. This defies conventional protocol to classify it as an industry standard. Governance is required to unify the NDC standard into a current version and a limited number of prior versions, perhaps the current version and two prior versions. This is not on IATA's radar today, which is a problem. In March 2025, the IATA ARM registry listed the following versions that were supported (year followed by the version number): 17,2, 18.1, 18.2, 19.1, 19.2, 20.1, 20.2, 21.1, 21.3, 24.1 and 24.3!

Initially there were five NDC certification levels, and this information was maintained in an NDC registry.

1. Level 1: Post Booking Ancillaries. The most basic capability relies on current or past NDC schemas for the sale of ancillaries after the booking has been made. Level 1 was considered elementary and removed from the certification process in 2019.

2. Level 2: Offer Management. This is the deployment of the shopping request and shopping response API.
3. Level 3: Offer and Order Management. In addition to Level 2, this includes the deployment of the order create request, the order view response, and the order change request APIs. This is deployment of offer and order management where the airline takes full control of shopping, booking, ticketing, and payment.
4. Level 4: Full Offer and Order Management. In addition to Level 3 capabilities, it includes a limited range of post-booking activity such as changes and cancellations. This includes the order re-shop request, order re-shop response and order change notification APIs.
5. NDC@Scale: Specific to airlines, this level covers evaluation along four dimensions: It includes technical setup, organization setup, user cases, and capabilities. It does not specify minimum transaction processing requirements during peak periods.

In October 2021, at the Digital, Data and Retailing Symposium (DDRS) in Madrid, Spain, IATA decided to replace the NDC registry and Level 1 through Level 4 certification with the new multilayered program called the Airline Retailing Maturity (ARM) index (IATA, 2025a). The ARM index was promoted as a unified program that verifies capabilities, assesses scalability, and helps carriers evaluate their merchandising maturity.

The objective of ARM was to foster better retailing practices across the industry and for airlines to assess where they were on their retailing journey against their peer group.

The new index registry details specific NDC capabilities as before and adds the ONE Order fulfillment capabilities which were separate, but it does not have the certification level designations. The certification steps were required to eventually demonstrate scalability. Initially, ARM met with skepticism from industry analysts (Silk, 2021d). Over time, airlines, intermediaries and other travel entities have transitioned to the ARM index.

NDC Capabilities is one of the three pillars of the broader ARM index. While it still details the IATA-verified NDC capabilities of each travel entity seeking certification, it does so without using those certification levels. Of the three pillars only information on technical capabilities is public.

While the NDC Capabilities pillar is public, the remaining two pillars are private. The second ARM index pillar is called Partnerships Deployment and is intended to give airlines and intermediaries insights into how well they are performing in scaling their NDC-enabled capabilities. IATA collects data on the partnership between airlines and intermediaries to produce a maturity report that illustrates how a deployment compares to peer groups.

The third ARM index pillar, called Value Capture Compass, is private to the airline community. It enables airlines to evaluate their performance in various categories such as bundled offers, content, pricing, revenue management, payments, and customer engagement against a peer group in deploying modern retailing strategies. The maturity report serves as a self-assessment of how an airline is performing against its peer group in those categories.

9.11.1 NDC Capabilities

NDC capabilities are lumped into six categories: Shop, Order, Pay, Settle, Account, and Setup. In 2025, of the 75 airlines that participated in the ARM Index only 60% support the most essential steps in the NDC booking flow, such as shopping for flights and ancillaries, order creation, and payment acceptance. The weakest link in the NDC journey is post-booking services such as cancellations, changes to an order, refunds and exchanges, etc. When IATA ranked the airlines for NDC capabilities, they verified 77 capabilities across the six categories. However, verification does not equate to efficient transaction processing.

The six categories into which the 77 capabilities are mapped are:

1. Shop

   Capabilities in this group enable customized offers using dates, destinations, and distance. Passenger type and loyalty programs also factor in. This supports a broad range of ancillaries and product bundles. Dynamic continuous pricing and rich content can also be added.
2. Order

   This category shows how well an airline handles orders. It also covers what happens after a booking is made. Examples include adding extra ancillaries, or changing flights. This involves rebooking, cancellations, and other services.
3. Pay

   The more recent NDC schemas support a wide range of payment methods, though payments using customer cards and settlement platforms dominate the landscape. With cards, the seller redirects the card information to the carrier that acts as the merchant of record and charges the customer's card. In the latter case, the seller collects payment from the customer and remits the value to the carrier via IATA's BSP or ARC.
4. Settle

   This category simplifies how airlines and sellers share data. It uses the IATA Clearance Manager for clearance, remittance, and settlement. This includes all NDC transaction types, including refunds and commissions.
5. Account

   This category has capabilities to send order status updates to the airline's accounting system providers.
6. Setup

   The setup category shows how airlines build their NDC channels. The greater the capabilities that an airline has, the easier integration is for third parties. A requirement is to provide a sandbox for testing.

Airlines that utilize an NDC API along with sellers and aggregators that consume an airline NDC API can apply for the NDC Certified designation from IATA. The designation is specific to one or more available versions of the NDC APIs at a specific level.

Sabre and Amadeus, in their role as IT providers, provide hosted reservation services for airlines on the NDC standard, and sellers/aggregators can also apply for the NDC Capable status. This designation is available for a specific version, or multiple available versions, of NDC schemas, at Level 2, 3 or 4. At each designation level, different combinations of NDC message types are assessed based on the relevant schemas. This evaluation applies to both NDC Certified and NDC Capable designations.

Broadly speaking, the certification involves offers and orders. The shopping schemas enable airlines to distribute their complete range of products that may consist of a dynamic fare and ancillaries. These ancillaries can include a range of ancillary products and services with engaging content either anonymously or tailored to the individual traveler. The order management schema empowers airlines to oversee NDC-driven orders at every stage, from booking to fulfillment.

All entities applying for a NDC Certified designation must have a live deployment with messages in a production environment through a seller. IT providers that apply for a NDC Capable designation can demonstrate in a live deployment or a test environment. Progress toward NDC enablement is maintained in the NDC registry.

Global distribution systems (GDSs) and online travel agencies (OTAs) have been investing millions of dollars in IATA's New Distribution Capability (NDC) for airline content that was initiated in 2012 (IATA, 2012). This new open XML (eXtensible markup language) and JSON (Java Script Object Notation) messaging standard is a requirement for intermediaries to have access to air content from suppliers, consisting of schedules, fares, and air ancillaries. This is a significant change in the airline industry. Before NDC, shopping for flights and pricing of itineraries had always been in the domain of the GDS for the travel agency indirect channel. With the NDC model pricing power shifts from the GDS to the airline which is now responsible for responding to shopping requests from travel agents with priced airline itineraries and ancillary products (Vinod, 2021a).

9.11.2 Why Scaling NDC Is a Challenge

NDC is not one standard. Airlines continue to use different versions, which adds complexity and time to market for deployment. Even if two airlines were on the same NDC version, implementations can be vastly different if the IT providers are different. For intermediaries, this makes each deployment a significant effort, resulting in expensive adoption at a slow pace.

The difficulty in making uniform updates with the NDC APIs stems from the lack of universal standards, different interpretations, and inconsistent deployment across different airlines. While NDC aims to standardize airline-intermediary communication, airlines interpret and implement these standards in various ways, leading to integration challenges and potential compatibility issues. This variability makes it harder to ensure that updates to flight bookings or other travel details are handled atomically across different airline systems.

Consider the following example for flight search where departure airport and departure time are part of the data structure returned by an airline's NDC response. While some airlines will return these two data elements in two separate fields, others will return the same in one data field and this is within the NDC standard. Some airlines will return Terminal A in different formats: "Terminal A", "Ter-A", "Ter A", or "A" in the defined world. Besides the data challenge, airlines have several unique workflows and business processes for handling changes to bookings, cancellations, payments and refunds, of ancillary services within the NDC standard. To streamline the processing, GDSs and other intermediaries that process NDC requests are faced with the enormous challenge of normalizing the content and workflows when NDC data responses are received from airlines to ensure consistency and accuracy before it is processed. This is required for GDSs and TMCs to witness a consistent, repeatable process during deployment and deliver better travel experiences to their customers without compromising on operational efficiency.

9.11.2.1 Rules Engine for Normalization of Data

An approach used by many intermediaries is to deploy a rules engine to automate the normalization of NDC data from airlines, thereby reducing the need for manual coding and maintenance.

The rules engine uses predefined rules to convert and standardize data that is received from different airlines into a consistent format. The predefined rules are also augmented when variations are detected with each new deployment. This ensures that GDSs can easily compare and display offers from various airlines on the travel agency desktop regardless of the specific NDC version or IT vendor they may use. Normalization is also required to ensure compatibility with downstream systems.

In this scenario the rules engine performs several multi-purpose tasks.

Mapping and Conversion to the Standard Format

The rules engine defines how non-homogenous data from different airlines should be mapped to a standard format. This may involve renaming fields, changing data types or transforming data from one format to another.

Validation and Error Handling

The rules engine must validate the data received from the airline to ensure that it meets certain quality standards and handles errors or inconsistencies.

Data Augmentation

The rules engine can enrich the data with additional information, such as mapping airline codes to company names, airport codes to airport names, or adding location details.

Data Filtering and Aggregation
Since GDSs and TMCs process traditional EDIFACT data and NDC data, the rules engine can be used to filter, eliminate duplicates, and aggregate data, allowing for a more efficient display of relevant information.

A standardized and consistent approach to NDC deployment could also mitigate the challenges of making atomic updates. This requires the development of common frameworks for NDC deployment to ensure that updates are processed consistently across the various airline systems. To promote robustness and reliability, active collaboration is required between airlines and intermediaries.

9.11.2.2 Rigidity Versus Flexibility

Understandably, IATA and the airline community have embraced XML with its user-friendly and readable format coupled with the rhetoric to sunset EDIFACT expeditiously. The concise EDIFACT protocols necessitate precise sequencing for efficacy. In the late 1980s and 1990s the optimized communications between airlines, travel agencies and airports, marked a significant leap in global travel connectivity. With its rigid structure, normalization of data is not required with EDIFACT. The data elements within an EDIFACT message must be in a specific order and format. This ensures standardization and consistency but can limit flexibility.

With the changes in the travel landscape, today's IT vendors demand flexibility in communication protocols that can seamlessly bridge a multitude of stakeholders. These new entrants prefer XML over the effort of learning EDIFACT. XML's flexibility comes from its ability to define custom tags and structures, allowing for more adaptable data formats and easy customization. While this makes XML more suitable for diverse applications and scenarios, in the NDC context it hampers scalability and time to market.

The intermediaries such as GDSs and TMCs are therefore faced with the enormous task of normalization of content to ensure consistency and accuracy in transaction processing.

9.11.2.3 Scalability of XML

There are two primary approaches to APIs: RESTful architecture, which is typically used for low to medium-sized complexity B2C APIs, such as those utilized by Google or Facebook, and SOAP (Simple Object Access Protocol) web services, which are commonly employed for complex, large-scale B2B systems in enterprise-level implementations. SOAP is considered complex to build, use, and debug. RESTful APIs, proposed by Roy Fielding in his dissertation in 2000 (Fielding, 2000), are easier to implement and gain rapid adoption. However, SOAP is preferred by many for its robustness, established reputation, and strong security features.

NDC uses SOAP (Simple Object Access Protocol) messaging as a core part of its XML-based standard, allowing airlines to send rich content and ancillary services via APIs. It also supports JSON with RESTful implementations for flexibility. SOAP/XML connections also exist within GDSs that integrate NDC content along with REST for easier implementation, though complex business logic sometimes requires a hybrid approach.

XML is not efficient for representing information because in addition to its content, it relies on metadata to describe the meaning and context of the message. While the use of a text-based, human-readable, and metadata-encoded markup language has various benefits, it can also result in the size of the XML document being much larger than that of an equivalent binary representation of the same information, sometimes by ten to twenty times.

XMLs processing overhead, storage requirements, and bandwidth consumption become problematic when transaction volumes are high, despite its suitability for moderate transaction volumes. As a result, some companies resort to tactics that can be potentially hazardous, such as compressing XML, ignoring XML validity, and altering the parsing rules to optimize its performance. These tactics to optimize XML performance are generally not recommended.

Although the XML structure is used today for air travel shopping and booking transactions, and viewed as a replacement for EDIFACT, alternatives must be explored for efficiency and scalability.

9.11.2.4 NDC APIs and the Challenge with Atomic Updates

A common complaint from IT developers is that the NDC messages are complex and not modular. This makes it difficult to break messages down into specific backend functions. At issue is that the current message structures are not organized to handle small changes efficiently like adding a remark, email address, telephone number or zip code. This impacts the adoption of microservices which are small, independent services that encapsulate specific business logic and warrants the need to add extra layers of abstraction to support processing on the backend. Simply put, it is required to normalize complex messages to simplify backend processing and updates.

Since the messages are not component-based, backend systems require overhead to validate and perform updates. Unlike component-based messages that often come structured with modular parts that simplify processing, non-component-based messages require backend systems to engage in validation. This is because these messages lack standardized subunits, making it necessary for the backend to verify the entire message and determine how to update the system state. This process is resource-intensive and increases latency.

Furthermore, caching such messages becomes a significant hurdle. Effective caching relies on having data organized in a way that can be reused quickly and reliably. Since these raw messages need reformatting and restructuring before they are cache-ready, the caching layer not only adds another step but also demands constant updates to maintain its performance benefits, often offsetting the advantages caching typically provides.

The NDC schemas are a top-down design. This approach focuses on defining the core functions, user experience and overall architecture before addressing the data dictionary, database schema and API endpoints. Conversely, the bottom-up approach begins with building the foundational elements such as data dictionary, database schemas, APIs, and backend logic before integrating it with the user experience and addressing all core functions. The bottom-up approach ensures robustness and scalability, though many debate that neither approach is universally more efficient.

The impact on atomic updates, where changes are processed as a single, indivisible unit, is far reaching. It is required to maintain data integrity in travel booking systems. With the absence of universal standards and inconsistent deployments, it is difficult to guarantee that NDC requests will be processed atomically across all airline systems. This can lead to issues like conflicting updates, incomplete bookings, or incorrect information being displayed to travel agents.

Over time, these hurdles will be overcome through collaboration and the exchange of ideas between airlines, technology providers, and travel agencies. Overcoming challenges like inconsistent adoption, technical complexities, and a steep learning curve requires industry-wide cooperation to standardize development, share best practices for training and education, and align technological capabilities.

9.12 GDS Investment in NDC and NDC Aggregators

While the NDC messaging standard provides clear benefits for airlines, the benefits to OTAs, wholesalers, and TMCs are less clear. It is viewed as a mandate. When an airline is NDC-ready, it may choose to use the NDC messaging standard as the only conduit for OTAs and TMCs to communicate with them.

The GDSs have made multimillion dollar investments to handle the new communication protocol since they realize that without the investment, they may no longer have access to content and in the GDS business, content is king. Many airlines offer better deals and a range of ancillaries exclusively through the NDC channel. OTAs, travel agencies and other resellers of airline content, have three options for accessing NDC content: through a GDS which by default is an aggregator of NDC content, the new entrant NDC Aggregators or directly from the airline. In 2025, Amadeus, Sabre and Travelport are NDC certified aggregators and support live connections to over 20 airlines each for access to NDC content for OTAs and travel agencies. For TMCs, the GDS is the default choice for providing NDC content. This is true for corporate travel agencies and large leisure agencies. TMCs also prefer the GDSs because their solution includes mid-office and back-office integration. The primary limitation of the GDSs is their agility and they lag behind the nimbler NDC Aggregators who may have more live NDC connections to airlines.

NDC Aggregators are relatively new players in the market and some claim that they are the future and represent GDS 2.0. While they typically integrate with a GDS to access traditional EDIFACT content, their primary focus is to access content directly from full-service carriers for NDC content, fares and ancillaries, as well as LCC content. NDC Aggregators also have a subtle advantage since they may have no content restrictions compared to a GDS, who may have restrictions imposed on NDC content display depending on the region.

Including the GDSs, there are approximately fifty aggregators that have achieved NDC certification level 3 or greater. Several nimble aggregators have entered the market with modern technology and APIs that provide airline connectivity to travel agencies out of the box that are NDC compliant and at a price point that is acceptable to airlines. What they lack is expertise in agency workflow management and security. To eliminate the legacy costly infrastructure and capabilities that will not be required in the future, GDSs should consider acquiring or partnering with a new entrant that uses modern technology and augment their weak spots of agency workflow management and security. This enables the GDSs to migrate away from aging technology rapidly. For GDSs like Travelport and Sabre that operate in a legacy TPF environment for transaction processing, this pathway can provide a faster and more cost-effective path forward than an expensive TPF offload to open systems. It can also accelerate reducing the cost of distribution, which is an airline priority.

9.12.1 Continued Investment in the Hybrid State

NDC is also a radical transformation of capabilities required in a GDS in the future. NDC squarely puts the GDSs in the crossroads since they need to support the new NDC content access, but also maintain their existing solutions like shopping, booking, and ticketing since the industry is in a hybrid state. For example, air shopping constitutes the single largest recurring annual investment in advanced algorithms and infrastructure for a GDS. For example, at Sabre, these volumes averaged over 675 million shops a day in 2019 (Vinod, 2020a) before the pandemic. When all airlines are using the NDC messaging standard, pricing power will shift in its entirety from the GDS to the airline and this investment is no longer required since it is now the responsibility of the airline to provide priced itineraries and bundles. The same is true for itinerary pricing, which requires significant investment to ensure pricing accuracy.

9.13 Future of Codeshare

There is a lot of talk that codeshare flights will be sunset. Is that really true? As a vital part of the airline industry, it seems unlikely.

Codeshares are agreements between airlines to sell seats on each other's flights, allowing airlines to expand their networks, offer more destinations, and enhance their competitiveness. They are a common practice, especially within airline alliances, and are not disappearing anytime soon. Coordinated pricing and revenue management decisions drive incremental revenues for the alliance (Boyd, 1998; Vinod, 1999, 2005b; Wright et al., 2010).

In the NDC era, codeshare processing will change when the GDSs can no longer generate a codeshare itinerary.

9.13.1 Origins of Codeshare Flights

The origins of codeshare can be traced back to Richard Adams Henson, a test pilot and operator of a flight school, who established the idea of commuter airlines in 1961. Henson launched The Hagerstown Commuter airline, offering commuter services to Washington D.C. It transitioned to Henson Airlines and in 1967, Henson formed a partnership with Allegheny Airlines, marking the first instance of a codeshare agreement with a major airline, albeit before the term "codeshare" was coined. The regional carrier merged with Piedmont Airlines in 1983.

The term "codeshare" was officially introduced into the airline vocabulary in 1989 by American Airlines and Qantas Airways when they established a collective codeshare agreement connecting various cities in the United States to cities in Australia.

9.13.2 Types of Codeshare

The three main codeshare agreements that exist between an operating carrier and marketing carriers are hard blocks, soft blocks, and free sale.

In the case of hard blocks, the operating carrier sets aside a fixed number of seats on a flight specifically for the marketing carrier, that has purchased these seats. Any unsold seats cannot be returned to the operating carrier. The marketing carrier is responsible for managing and filling these purchased seats. From the perspective of the operating carrier, the hard block of seats is treated as if they have already been sold in their inventory system.

As for soft blocks, the operating carrier provides a block of seats to the marketing carrier, with a specific release date for any unsold seats. Typically, this release date is set to occur seven to fourteen days before the scheduled departure. This arrangement exposes the operating carrier to some level of risk, as the marketing carrier may release seats back to the operating carrier that are left unsold at departure.

Free sale is the most used codeshare agreement. It operates under a "sell and report" system, where each codeshare partner is responsible for managing and controlling the inventory of the flights they operate. This allows the marketing carrier to sell seats on the operating carrier in real-time, without strict, pre-allocated, seat limits.

9.13.3 Benefits of Codeshare Partnerships for Airlines

The primary benefits of codeshare are:

1. The three major alliancesStar Alliance, SkyTeam, and OneWorld, are built around codeshare agreements, allowing airlines within the alliance to sell seats on each other's flights and offer passengers a wider choice of destinations.
2. Codeshares allow airlines to access routes and destinations that they might not be able to serve directly, expanding their reach and offering passengers more options with minimal investment.
3. There is incremental revenue associated with selling seats on partner flights, increasing overall profitability.
4. Codeshares can strengthen an airline's market presence and competitive ability, especially in regions where they might not have a strong direct presence.

There are two important components for implementing codeshare flights today. First, is synchronized flight schedules; second, is booking class availability on the codeshare flight.

9.13.4 Synchronized Flight Schedules

When airlines file their schedules (SSIM—Schedule Change Information Manual) they provide a Data Element Identifier (DEI) that maps the operating flight number to the codeshare flight number. The designators are:

DEI 010 is used on the operating carrier flight leg. It identifies the commercial duplicate airline designators—the operating and marketing carriers and flight numbers.

DEI 050 is used on the commercial duplicate carrier field, and it identifies the operating carrier and the flight number. The codeshare marketing carriers submitting the DEI 050 on their flights do not need to file Minimum Connect Time (MCT) if they are satisfied with the MCT filed by the operating carrier.

This step with schedules will not change with NDC.

9.13.5 Codeshare Flight Availability Before NDC

Prior to NDC, GDSs created and priced codeshare itineraries. Airline reservations systems sent availability status message to GDSs who stored this information on their databases. AVS served as the default mechanism for GDSs to determine availability on a marketing carrier (codeshare) segment.

For free sale codeshare, there are various options for codeshare availability.

Standard Codeshare Availability is determined by AVS. The operating carrier notifies the marketing carrier to stop selling with a stop sell message. The marketing carrier can keep selling the booking class until they receive the stop sell message.

The transmission of AVS stop sell teletype messages from the operating carrier to the marketing carrier are unreliable, often resulting in delays before they are implemented on the marketing carrier's reservations system. This delay in availability presents opportunities for knowledgeable travelers to secure lower fares when booking the marketing flight. The potential savings when booking marketing flights on international itineraries can be substantial. This is because the booking class is closed on the operating carrier's host CRS but is still open on the marketing carrier's host CRS. It is important to note that this practice is entirely legal. To mitigate this issue, airlines can opt for cascading codeshare availability or utilize the bid price exchange (available for O&D carriers only) to ensure true last seat availability.

True Availability refers to the situation where both carriers are hosted on the same reservations system. In this scenario, when an availability request is made, the availability request can be directed to each inventory partition of the respective operating carriers to ensure true last seat availability.

Cascading Availability is the procedure in which the availability request is forwarded (cascaded) to the operating carrier to ensure true last seat availability. This is also known as *seamless codeshare availability*. Cascading availability is dependent on the DEI record, which defines the flight number mapping between the operating carrier and the marketing carrier. It is also subject to an agreement between the two airlines to cascade availability requests to the operating carrier.

Bid Price Exchange enables the operating carrier to instantly share the current bid price for a specific flight leg and date with the marketing carrier. This is essential for carriers utilizing O&D control. Bid price exchange ensures metal-neutral availability. It is preferred over cascading availability because it allows for evaluation of an O&D request with codeshare flights based on the total reservation's value and the bid prices of the corresponding legs of the itinerary.

9.13.6 Codeshare Flight Availability with NDC

In the NDC era, GDSs will not create and price online itineraries, codeshare and interline itineraries.

Existing codeshare agreements will remain in place, but bilateral prorate agreements that determine revenue sharing between airlines may no longer exist. This change simplifies the financial settlement process between airlines. The transaction flow for codeshare bookings will still be similar, as the airline creating the offer will request a bundled offer, instead of booking class availability, from the codeshare partner.

In the case of hard blocks and soft blocks, the airline that receives the offer request will respond for all flight segments. These include the airline's flight segments and the hard blocks or soft blocks of the partner airline, if applicable.

In the case of free sale codeshare, when an airline receives a request for an offer, it may not be able to cover the entire service on its own. As a result, two or more airlines are involved in making the offer. The offer responsible airline (ORA) sends the request to the offer partner (participating) airline (OPA), which responds with a price for the bundle and any associated restrictions. This process resembles Cascading Availability, except that the marketing carrier returns a bundled offer. The second similarity is with a special type of bilateral prorate agreement that exists, where the marketing codeshare partner requests payment for a fixed amount regardless of the total fare for the itinerary. It is important to note that with NDC, codeshare partners do not align their booking classes, and the airlines involved in the offer creation process may not be using booking classes at all.

The absence of AVS based availability for codeshare and interline flights with NDC results in price consistency in the marketplace since the total fare will be the same whether the marketing carrier or operating carrier flights are booked. With AVS, booking a marketing flight may produce a lower priced itinerary than booking an operating flight because a booking class may be closed on the operating flight, but the stop sell message has not been received by the marketing carrier due to delayed AVS message updates. This eliminates revenue leakage for the partner airlines caused by delayed updates of AVS messages from the operating carrier to the marketing carrier.

9.13.7 Financial Settlement Process

The financial settlement process consists of two parts. The first part involves the settlement between the travel agency and the airline, while the second part involves the settlement between the airline and its interline and codeshare partners.

The ORA collects payment for the entire journey and submits a sales report to the IATA BSP (Billing and Settlement Plan). This report includes a list of all the tickets issued the previous day. The BSP then calculates commissions and taxes on commissions and sends the data back to the airline. In the case of credit card payments, the BSP generates remittance files for the acquiring banks of the airlines. These banks will then pay the airline directly for all the credit card transactions.

If the customer paid for the ticket in cash through the travel agent, the airline must collect the payment from the travel agent. To streamline this process, the BSP sends a billing statement to the travel agent at the end of each period. This statement includes a list of tickets, commissions earned, and cash collected on behalf of the airline. The travel agent must submit the payment to the BSP by the designated date, at which point the BSP will pass the funds to the airline.

An airline can also utilize NDC to transmit an NDC order receipt to the BSP for real-time sales calculation. The airline revenue accounting system updates sales information based on the created order values. Once the flight has flown, the data is sent to the airline revenue accounting system to reconcile the flown passenger with the received payment.

For airlines to reach a settlement, the ORA is required to pay the OPA. The OPA can access ticketing information and transfer sales data to the revenue accounting system. This data includes the accepted order values from the ORA at the time the offer was made. Once the flight has been completed, the OPA will be provided with a settlement authorization code by the ORA. This code is then submitted to the IATA Clearing House (ICH) as a claim for payment from the ORA. Upon receiving the claim, the ORA will proceed to make payment to the interline or codeshare partner through the ICH.

9.13.8 Customer Angst with Codeshare Flights

In the online era, there is tremendous frustration voiced by passengers on codeshare flights. There are several gaps in the passenger experience that remain to be addressed. Issues range from carry-on baggage allowances that vary between codeshare partners, the airline apps that may work on one airline but not the other, confusion about accrual of loyalty points, and the purchase of ancillary products such as baggage or seat selection. Online check-in does not guarantee that all boarding passes can be viewed on an airline's app. Changing a seat assignment at the kiosk or recovery from Irregular operations such as rebooking a cancelled segment is frequently a challenge. Many advocate that codeshare operations must be redesigned from the ground up to address legacy systems, commercial agreements, and interoperability between ailrine reservations systems. Reliance on EDIFACT and teletype messaging between airline reservations systems must be replaced with an API-first strategy to address issues such as data latency, inconsistent information sharing and integration challenges. The issues proliferate across the airline industry and are not specific to any airline or its codeshare partner.

Passengers feel misled when they expect one airline's experience but receive another's with its surprises. The situation is exacerbated when problems arise, leading to frustrating "ping-pong" customer service and unexpected costs that the customer must bear. These issues continue to persist, but there is no cohesive plan to address it. Regardless, it is unlikely that regulators will step in to terminate codeshare operations.

9.14 Traditional Interline

Approximately 12% of the itineraries sold are interline itineraries. On some OTA websites that cater to deep discount travelers, this percentage can be much higher. Traditional interlining allows passengers to book a single ticket for a multi-leg journey, check in once and have their baggage transferred between flights. Multiple airlines in the passenger itinerary have interline ticketing agreements to facilitate this process that is managed by GDSs and on a limited scale by central reservation systems (host CRS), which build itineraries based on interline agreements and published schedules.

IATA established the original framework for interlining a few years after it was established in 1945. To be able to sell interline tickets, airlines had to join the multilateral interline traffic agreement (MITA) which provided the necessary standards for cooperation between airlines.

A passenger or travel agent uses a GDS or central reservation system to search for and book an itinerary that includes flights operated by different airlines. The GDS or PSS builds the itinerary. If there are no direct flight options, the GDS or PSS constructs a route from the list of interline agreements, published schedules and minimum connect times (MCT). Flight schedules and MCTs are provided by schedule aggregators like OAG and Cirium. Booking class availability on the unpriced reservations from each carrier serving the interline itinerary are collected and then priced, based on public published fares available in ATPCO, the fare aggregator.

One of the airlines in the itinerary serves as the "validating carrier," (also called a "plating carrier") which collects the fare from the customer. Subsequently, the validating carrier issues a single ticket covering all flight segments. Passengers check in once with the issuing airline, and the customer's luggage is tagged to arrive at their final destination. Baggage is transferred between connecting flights at the connecting airport, often using automated systems or manual processes. Airlines settle payments for the interline itinerary based on pre-agreed arrangements, typically using industry standards like Type A (EDIFACT) and Type B (teletype) messages. After flight departure, operating carriers on the interline carrier request payment from the validating carrier.

When a passenger books an interline itinerary through a GDS, the GDS holds the complete PNR, which includes all the flight segments. However, each participating airline only sees the portion of the itinerary that involves their flights. Subject to permissions, visibility is granted to the upline or downline interline segment, but not the entire itinerary. Airlines also have commercial reasons to restrict the view of interline itineraries, including potential for revenue leakage or lack of control over fare construction.

9.14.1 Revenue Sharing Agreements

Prior to airline deregulation in 1978, to interline, MITA provided the standards for cooperation between airlines. After deregulation, in addition to MITA, partner airlines also signed IATA's multilateral prorate agreement (MPA) or the special prorate agreements (SPA) between two or more carriers to determine how revenue should be shared on interline itineraries. There are many methods to derive special prorates. The most common are fixed rate, which is a fixed dollar amount that a carrier pays another when they carry another airline's passenger. Other types of special prorate aggrements are mileage based prorate, square root of the miles, a fixed percentage of the full local fare, etc. When a carrier establishes a SPA, it should provide a commercial advantage over the MPA.

9.14.2 The Standard Retailer and Supplier Interline Agreement

The Standard Retailer and Supplier Interline Agreement (SRSIA) is a new framework for airline interlining proposed by IATA (IATA, 2019), working in conjunction with the existing MITA. SRSIA introduces new terminology where the "retailer" is the marketing or validating carrier and the "supplier" is the operating carrier. SRSIA aims to modernize traditional interlining by allowing airlines to formalize partnerships with a wide range of partners beyond traditional full-service carriers, including LCCs and intermodal relationships, in a single document. Interlining between IATA member airlines will continue to use standard IATA ticketing processes. Interlining is also available with airlines, such as LCCs, that do not use standard ticketing processes, expanding interlining opportunities. SRSIA complements the NDC and ONE Order programs. For interline agreements, both airlines must be on ONE Order, which poses a challenge.

There are several benefits of the new approach. They are:

1. Historically the GDSs have been the backbone for interline ticketing. With this new approach, dependency on the intermediary is no longer relevant. Seat and ancillary sales are between airline partners.
2. No reliance on E-Ticketing and EMD solutions
3. No reliance on Type A messages (e.g. EDIFACT transactions such as PAOREQ, ITAREQ, etc.) and Type B (teletype) messages. These messages are required to coordinate the interlining process, ensuring seamless passenger and baggage handling across different airlines.
4. Full visibility and control of the interline passenger itinerary unlike GDS which limits the segments visible in an interline itinerary.

Interline agreements between airlines must also develop sound procedures for recovery from irregular operations (IROPS). IROPS refers to situations where flights are delayed, canceled, or diverted due to various reasons like weather, mechanical issues, or other disruptions. Interline agreements must have contingency plans between partner airlines and airports to manage these disruptions and minimize their impact on passengers.

As industry standards for offer and order management continue to develop, the challenge is to define a minimum viable product once they become workable. Collaboration among stakeholders is vital to unlock the full potential of new partnership models through deployment and adoption. As the industry transitions to a new airline partnership structure, success will be defined by the adoption rate.

9.14.3 Interline Shopping

Airline shopping is an integral component of generating offers to customers. With NDC, airlines must invest in advanced shopping capabilities (Vinod, 2024a, Chapter 8) and ensure that they have a fast response system to generate itineraries with offers efficiently. In the traditional model, GDSs have extensive interline shopping capabilities that will no longer be used with NDC. Interline shopping with NDC refers to purchasing tickets for journeys involving multiple airlines that have partnered for interline agreements. None of the major airlines have developed a shopping capability to support offer creation. Instead, they rely on third parties such as Google/ITA Software for the shopping capability which comes at an added cost for interline shopping.

9.15 Codeshare and Interline with Offer and Order

In the offer and order world, it will become difficult to distinguish codeshare from interline for transaction processing since in both situations the offer price must be provided by the operating carrier. Offers and Orders is a new framework for airline partnerships, designed to provide airlines with more control over their offerings and improve customer experience. The paradigm shift is that individual airlines will determine the price of the services they offer and own the record of the customers they serve. While the lines will blur for transaction processing between codeshare flights and interline flights, codeshare partnerships where airlines share the same flight and offer seats under their own flight numbers, expanding their network will continue to dominate the skies. For interlines, Offers & Orders empowers airlines to respond to interline requests in real-time and maintain full commercial control.

9.16 The Landscape for GDS Surcharges

When IATA New Distribution Capability (NDC) was launched in 2012, the promise was a new XML interface, rich content, airline-controlled offers, and personalization. However, the primary focus of the large network airlines was to implement NDC and bring the GDSs to the bargaining table for better commercial terms. The deployment of NDC by airlines and intermediaries has been a very slow process.

GDS segment booking fees average about 2% of the cost of a ticket. Besides, the fees are not a function of the price of the ticket. In contrast, both the merchant model and pay-at-checkout (PAC) models for hotels have very high distribution costs and can range from 10 to 35% based on region and characteristics of the property.

Many airlines have introduced surcharges for traditional GDS EDIFACT bookings. They view it as a recovery fee for GDS segment booking fees charged by the

GDSs which is defined in the GDS-airline contracts, When GDS surcharges were first introduced, they were naturally limited to EDIFACT content. Later, as airlines increasingly make their NDC content available via GDS as well, the question of cost recovery for NDC bookings via GDS content has been moving to center stage. While some airlines have been willing to make their NDC content available via the GDS without a surcharge, an increasing number of airlines have introduced surcharges for NDC content booked through a GDS. Surcharges for NDC bookings are generally lower than EDIFACT bookings because the economics for NDC bookings are more favorable to the airlines. Many in the industry perceive that GDS surcharges are nothing more than commercial viciousness underwritten by home market power.

When an airline introduces a GDS surcharge for agency bookings they will no longer be competitive on GDS low fare search displays. This is because the total price of a ticket with surcharges was higher than for airlines that did not have a surcharge. The default sorting order for GDS low fare search results is based on the total price of an itinerary followed by the quality of service (nonstop, connection, etc.). This has not deterred some of the largest European and Asian carriers to impose a GDS surcharge for traditional GDS EDIFACT bookings.

The surcharge should not be confused with lower fares being offered through the NDC channel by many airlines. The surcharge is applicable for traditional GDS EDIFACT bookings.

The implementation of surcharges for collection by airlines is typically using the well-known YQ and YR that airlines add to tickets to cover a variety of costs, including aviation fuel. YQ and YR are carrier-imposed non-refundable surcharges that are filed in Record S1 in ATPCO. The GDS surcharges are typically applied through a YQ charge. These surcharges are also known as carrier-imposed surcharges. Some surcharges can vary depending on the route, direction of travel, operating carrier, and loyalty programs. The GDS surcharges apply for the traditional EDIFACT bookings. These surcharges are paid directly to the airline, not shared with any partner airline, and are non-commissionable.

Below is a list of the airlines that implemented GDS surcharges in alphabetical order except for The Lufthansa Group, because it was the first to introduce GDS surcharges in 2015.

Airlines and the associated GDS surcharges are always subject to change. This snapshot was compiled in December 2025 from various sources including airline reports. GDS surcharges are included in this section to grasp how the distribution landscape has been evolving.

9.16.1 The Lufthansa Group

The Lufthansa Group of airlines is the fourth largest airline entity in the world based on revenue. It includes Austrian Airlines, Brussels Airlines, Lufthansa, Swiss International Air Lines (SWISS), and Air Dolomiti, The Lufthansa Group was the first to introduce GDS surcharges in 2015 as a non-refundable, non-commissionable fee.

Effective January 1, 2024, the Lufthansa Group, increased the surcharge, dubbed "Distribution Cost Charge (DCC)" for GDS EDIFACT bookings (McCarthy, 2023).

The surcharges, based on the cost economics, vary by GDS. Effective May 2026, they are:

1. Amadeus (1A) bookings are €19.00.
2. Sabre (1S/1B) bookings are €22.50.
3. Travelport, including Galileo (1G), Apollo (1V), and Worldspan (1P), are €23.00.

The DCC is based on cost economics and varies by GDS. The Lufthansa Group also charges €8 surcharge for NDC-enabled GDS bookings. However, travel agencies that book Lufthansa via NDC-enabled direct connections while offering additional content are not charged a fee.

The Lufthansa Group is one of the few airlines with a GDS specific surcharge, Table 9.1 below summarizes the changes in the DCC by GDS since its inception.

Table 9.1 Lufthansa Group Surcharges

Effective Date	Amadeus	Sabre	Travelport
September 2015	€16.00	€16.00	€16.00
October 2020	€19.00	€19.00	€19.00
September 2022	€17.50	€19.50	€23.00
January 2024	€17.50	€24.50	€23.00
January 2025	€17.50	€22.00	€23.00
January 2026	€18.00	€22.50	€23.00
May 2026	€19.00	€22.50	€23.00

The surcharges will continue to be collected for traditional GDS bookings. Lufthansa Group airlines also offer surcharge-free bookings through their websites, airline-to-agency NDC direct connections, approved NDC Aggregators, and their web-based NDC-enabled booking tool SPRK.

9.16.2 Air Canada

Air Canada announced in June 2024 that it planned to eliminate GDS surcharges for all GDS bookings except for the lowest fares in each cabin. These surcharges were quite significant: \$21.50 for legacy bookings in Amadeus and Travelport and \$24.50 in Sabre (Silk, 2024). They also offer a per-flight agency incentive on bookings made via NDC direct connect and preferred non-GDS aggregators. Air Canada is taking a more friendly approach to drive NDC adoption

9.16.3 Air France—KLM

Air France—KLM, the sixth largest airline group in the world based on revenues, raised the traditional GDS EDIFACT booking surcharge from $18.70 to $23.10 on July 1, 2023 for one-way bookings. Effective January 1, 2025, AF-KL has implemented a surcharge of €24 per segment for EDIFACT bookings. The surcharge for business travelers is €3 Starting July 2025, business travel agencies are expected to pay €24, the same as leisure travel agencies.

9.16.4 Avianca

Avianca increased its per coupon surcharge from $6 to $8 effective April 1, 2024, for bookings made via opt-out agencies in Colombia and for all EDIFACT bookings outside of Colombia. Avianca NDC content is available on all three major GDSs. The lowest fares (XS and S) are only available via NDC.

9.16.5 Copa Airlines

Copa Airlines has now doubled its $12 per direction Distribution Cost Recovery (DCR) surcharge to $24 per direction effective April 1, 2024 on EDIFACT bookings since its introduction in 2022. Copa Airlines does not distribute NDC content through the GDSs.

9.16.6 Emirates

Emirates is the fifth largest airline in the world, based on revenue. There is a GDS surcharge between $14 and $25 based on the length of the sector effective July 1, 2021, for Amadeus and Sabre. Other agencies that book through the Emirates direct connect portal, Emirates Gateway, will be exempt from the surcharges (Silk, 2021a). Travelport is exempt from Emirates surcharges for traditional GDS EDIFACT bookings since they upgraded to a "dedicated sales channel" (Silk, 2021b). Amadeus and Sabre have also secured exemptions from the surcharges through contract negotiations.

9.16.7 Finnair

In 2022, Finnair introduced a €12 one-way surcharge for bookings made through GDSs for flights starting in Europe as well as from several markets in Asia and the Middle East. This surcharge was raised to €15 in September 2023. The airline also removed its Finnair Light fares from EDIFACT-based systems (GDSs). After integrating its NDC offering into the ARC Direct Connect program in October

2023, Finnair implemented a $15 one-way surcharge in the EDIFACT channel in the U.S. Travel agencies can bypass this surcharge by using Finnair's NDC-exclusive agency booking portal, the Finnair Agency Sales Tool, which provides access to NDC content without any technical integration work, booking, or service fees. In May 2023, Finnair removed all domestic itineraries for flights that take off and land in Finland from EDIFACT distribution.

9.16.8 Hawaiian Airlines

This is purely academic since Hawaiian Airlines was acquired by Alaska Airlines in September 2024. Since 2022, Alaska Airlines has not had a GDS surcharge. Alaska makes its fare content available to the GDSs and doesn't charge a distribution fee.

Hawaiian, conversely, withheld its Hawaii interisland fares (Neighbor Island Fares) from GDSs, requiring travel advisors to use Hawaiian's direct or NDC-enabled channels for those bookings. Hawaiian charged USD $4.80 for each inter-island segment and charged USD $7 for each segment between mainland North America and Hawaii as part of its strategy to push agencies toward NDC-enabled booking options.

With the acquisition, the Hawaiian Airlines NDC API will be disabled in April 2026 to support the carrier's merger with Alaska Airlines and transition back to Sabre's *SabreSonic* CSS (Customer Sales and Service) reservations system from Amadeus' Altéa by Q2 2026. Since the acquisition, Hawaiian has been re-aligning its distribution strategy and IT systems. Besides migrating to a single PSS, full content will be restored to indirect channels, and the EDIFACT GDS surcharge will be eliminated.

9.16.9 International Airline Group (British Airways, Iberia)

IAG is the eighth largest airline group in the world based on revenue. IAG GDS surcharges vary by currency in which the itinerary was priced and the local point of sale. Effective January 1, 2023, IAG raised the surcharges for traditional GDS bookings to £13, €15 and $14. The surcharge is called Distribution Technology Charge (DTC). The surcharge is applicable by fare component. A fare component is defined as a portion of an itinerary between two consecutive fare construction points. If the journey has only one fare component, the points of origin and destination are the only fare construction points. If a round trip involves a connection for the outbound or inbound (or both) then two or more fare components may be applicable (Vinod, 2024a, Chapter 5). The surcharge is collected through a Q charge, that is applicable for all fare components in the itinerary (British Airways, 2022).

NDC bookings through GDSs have an undisclosed but reduced surcharge.

Table 9.2 LATAM Surcharges

GDS	Surcharge for EDIFACT Bookings
Amadeus	POS South America: $10.61 POS North and Central America: $15.96 POS Europe, Middle East, Africa: €15.33 POS Rest of the World: $16.12
Sabre	$14.19
Travelport	$11.00
GDS	**Surcharge for NDC Bookings**
Amadeus	POS Europe, Middle East, Africa • Domestic: €3.00 • International: €6.00 POS Rest of the World • Domestic: $3.00 • International: $6.00
Sabre	$4.00 for all fares but the lowest fare
Travelport	$2.50 for all fares but the lowest fare

9.16.10 LATAM

LATAM, the largest airline group in South America implemented a USD $12 per segment surcharge for traditional GDS bookings, effective May 1, 2023 (Boehmer, 2023). LATAM calls it the Distribution Cost Recovery Fee (DCRF).

Following the lead of the Lufthansa Group, LATAM Airlines implemented surcharges based upon which GDS travel advisors use to book and the surcharge is by segment for all GDSs (Silk, 2025c). The new surcharges were effective on May 12, 2025. Amadeus surcharges vary by point of sale (POS).

LATAM also has a smaller surcharge for NDC bookings through a GDS. Amadeus surcharges vary by point of sale (Table 9.2).

LATAM's surcharges are irrational. They have lower surcharges for inexpensive domestic segments and higher surcharges for the more expensive international segments. It is more important to be competitive on international routes where there is more competition.

9.16.11 Oman Air

A late entrant to GDS surcharges, Oman Air implemented a Distribution Cost Recovery (DCR) surcharge of US$10 per segment charged globally across all GDSs, effective December 4, 2024. Bookings made via Direct Connect powered by Accelya-Farelogix or NDC channels powered by Oman Air preferred NDC Aggregators can bypass this surcharge. Oman Air also integrates with ARC Direct Connect. Starting July 1, 2026, the DCR surcharge was increased to $13.50 per segment.

Table 9.3 Qantas Surcharges

Distribution Tier Details	Premium NDC	Standard NDC	Standard NDC via GDS	EDIFACT
Surcharged?	No	No	Yes	Yes
Surcharge per Segment				
Point of Sale AU	None	None	4.50 AUD	11.50 AUD
Point of Sale NZ	None	None	5.00 NZD	17.50 NZD
Point of Sale ROW	None	None	3,00 USD	13.00 USD

9.16.12 Qantas Airways

Effective July 1, 2025, Qantas Airways implemented a multi-tiered distribution model (Airoldi, 2024g), broadly reminiscent of Lufthansa's (LHG) strategy for NDC distribution, offering multiple options to access its NDC offerings via the GDS.

The model marks an evolution of the Qantas distribution strategy, which had undergone a major revision in 2019 with the launch of the Qantas Channel (the Qantas Private Channel similar to British Airways). Under the new model, the per segment EDIFACT surcharge is reduced (previously 17.50 AUD worldwide for "out of channel" bookings) to $13, and a reduced GDS NDC surcharge of $3 per segment was introduced, effective July 1, 2025. In 2025, Qantas also launched the QDP booking portal, allowing all connected travel agencies to access NDC content, previously available only via Certified Technology Partners or directly connected travel sellers.

In contrast to Lufthansa's model:

1. Access to Qantas' Premium NDC channel is by invitation only, and requires agencies to meet the Qantas Key Performance Indicators (KPI) guidelines and
2. Qantas also offers an unsurcharged Standard NDC option.

Table 9.3 illustrates the Qantas surcharges.

9.16.13 Scandinavian Airlines System (SAS)

After SAS abandoned the proposed wholesale model in October 2023. SAS decided to support both NDC content and EDIFACT for travel agencies, but there are commercial differences. Through the GDS EDIFACT channel, public fares, except for Go Light fares on short-haul flights and flights with point of commencement (POC) Japan were available However, negotiated fares and special promotional fares were withheld from the GDS EDIFACT channel. For EDIFACT bookings, SAS has imposed a surcharge of €5.50 per fare component for all GDSs.

While public fares, negotiated fares, and promotional fares were available through the GDS NDC channel, SAS imposed a surcharge of €1.50 per fare component for Go Light fares.

9.16.14 Singapore Airlines

Singapore Airlines (SIA) increased its GDS distribution fee from $15 to $20 per ticket on June 1, 2023 (Silk, 2023). This fee is added to all GDS EDIFACT bookings as a YR tax. The fee is part of a shift to encourage travel agents to use SIA's KrisConnect platform instead of traditional GDS channels. Like The Lufthansa Group, Singapore Airlines is a proponent of continuous pricing.

9.16.15 Taiwanese Carriers

The four major international Taiwanese carriers are China Airlines, EVA Air, Starlux Airlines, and Tigerair Taiwan. These carriers impose GDS surcharges, termed a cost recovery fee, it applies to all GDS-issued tickets. Table 9.4 summarizes the new surcharges and effective dates from three of the four Taiwanese carriers.

Table 9.4 Taiwanese Carriers Surcharges

Carrier	Previous Surcharge (per segment)	New Surcharge (per segment)	Effective Date
EVA Air	$25	$28	March 1, 2026
China Airlines	$25	$28	March 17, 2026
Starlux Airlines	$25	$30	April 1, 2026
Tigerair Taiwan	NT$400 (peak) NT$300 (off-peak)	No change	

9.16.16 Turkish Airlines

Turkish Airlines (TK) is the nineth largest airline in the world based on revenue. It started its NDC journey in October 2024. TK simultaneously launched its NDC platform, TKConnect, and introduced an EDIFACT surcharge of $24 per ticket (Baker, 2024). TK's NDC content is available via aggregators (Verteil, Travelfusion, and more) and direct connections. Since then, the Distribution Cost Recovery Charge (DCRC) increased to $28 in February 2026 and $30 in May 2026. Selected TMCs and cruise agencies that were previously exempt from DCRC now pay a reduced surcharge of $10.

Turkish Airlines stopped participating in the Sabre GDS in September 2024. EDIFACT content will continue to be available through Amadeus, Travelport,

Hitit, TravelSky, Infini and Sirena. However, no additional fees were applied to ticketing transactions made through their distribution channels such as TKCONNECT UI, TKCONNECT API, TKCONNECT Aggregators, Quickres, Troya, Websagent, Kolaybilet, the Turkish Airlines website, and its mobile app. Ten months after Turkish Airlines went dark on Sabre, content was available starting June 2025 as part of a new distribution agreement.

Bookings made by GDSs through TKConnect will not have to pay a surcharge. These bookings essentially bypass the GDS, but can be stored on the GDS as passive bookings for a fee determined by the GDS.

9.17 Do GDS Surcharges Benefit the Airline?

Over the past decade, many airlines have introduced GDS surcharges to recover the segment booking fees. But do they really reduce costs? Are these airlines competitive with surcharges? The answer is *no* in both cases. Consider the scenario where airline A has a GDS surcharge and airline B does not. If the selling fare is the same on A and B, the airline with a GDS surcharge, airline A in this case, is placed lower in low fare search results resulting in potentially loss of sales. Even if the customer wants to fly on airline A, the TMC will in turn pass the surcharge to the corporate customer. This is not the relationship an airline wants to build with a corporation for the future. This led to the creation of private channels and travel agencies were exempt from paying the surcharge and did not have to pass the cost to the customer. If GDS surcharges were a great idea, then private channels would never have come into existence, thereby proving the point that GDS surcharges are ineffective at best. Airlines need to realize that GDS surcharges do not accelerate NDC adoption. Instead, it leads to loss of corporate customer goodwill and loss of revenue.

9.18 NDC Adoption, Default EDIFACT Bookings and Deduping

NDC was conceived in 2011 and introduced in 2012, well over a decade ago. After 15 years, the needle has barely moved on corporate bookings through the GDS NDC channels. In a Q1 2024 earnings call, Sabre noted that NDC accounted for less than 1% of its global GDS booking (Airolid, 2024c).

So why has corporate travel lagged leisure travel in NDC bookings? First, it is the OTAs that are driving NDC volumes with leisure bookings.

Full Content Agreements (Vinod, 2024a) were the hallmark of airline-GDS contracts which stipulated that all fares available on an airline direct channel were also available on the GDS channel. Since the introduction of ancillaries in the mid-2000s and later with NDC, this is no longer true. Many airlines routinely withhold their lowest fares from the GDS channel. Content parity is a concern for corporations whose corporate policy may stipulate that employees on business cannot fly on Premium Economy and must book the lowest fare. As a result, employees can now see cheaper fares that are called "NDC fares" on NDC Aggregator channels. When a booking is made outside the traditional TMC channel, it leads to revenue leakage and the employee goes out of the established duty of care process.

Another concern voiced by TMCs is the servicing of NDC booked itineraries, and this poses a significant threat to their respective duty of care programs. When employees are traveling on business, TMCs strive to provide quality service to their corporate customers. Since NDC bookings are passive bookings in a GDS, managing corporate booking ticket changes and how it is serviced is a concern since it requires the airline to affect the change.

Through March 2025, airlines have not seen meaningful NDC bookings through the GDS NDC channel. Most of the growth has been from NDC direct-connect and NDC Aggregator portals. To understand NDC adoption in North America, NDC accounted for 4% of total corporate transactions in 2022 and 2% in 2023. But when we add in NDC direct, NDC Aggregator, and online travel agencies, there is more movement toward NDC bookings, Based on nearly 800 travel agencies reporting NDC transactions in December 2024, the share of NDC transactions from all ARC-settled transactions was 20.3%. This represents a 10% increase from 18.4% in December 2023.

A related issue is the authorized developer relationships imposed by GDSs on online booking tools like Concur in the context of "deduping" which refers to the challenge of managing and deduplicating content from multiple sources such as traditional GDS and NDC. If the EDIFACT and NDC itineraries have the same price, then the booking defaults to a GDS EDIFACT booking, which is preferred by the GDSs. If the NDC itinerary has a lower fare, then the alternate GDS NDC channel may be selected to complete the booking at the lower fare.

9.19 Reducing Distribution Costs with NDC

An airline's distribution expense consists of GDS booking fees, agency commissions, credit card fees and costs for online sales like search ads. Large network carriers like United and Lufthansa have reported reductions in distribution expenses as a result of NDC adoption through GDSs and direct connections.

In its Q2 2025 earnings call, United Airlines disclosed a 22% reduction in year-over-year distribution expenses. Besides NDC bookings, United attributes that over 50% of its revenue was from direct sources such as its website, mobile app, ATOs/CTOs, and call centers.

Mayhem Redefined: The Hybrid State and Evolving Business Landscape with NDC

10

Deterministic chaos, where nearby points in a dynamical system diverge exponentially, makes it impossible to perfectly predict the future but also "makes time possible.

J. Doyne Farmer

Abstract

IATA's NDC is meant to modernize the sales process with rich content. The fragmented rollout by various airlines, coupled with legacy systems creates content chaos for travel sellers, leading to inconsistent, complex, and costly management of multiple sources such as NDC Aggregators, GDS as aggregators of NDC content and airline direct connect, which hinders a seamless customer experience.

Many airlines withhold their lowest fares from the GDSs resulting in a content gap in the direct channel. The introduction of NDC has been less to do with its potential benefits and gravitated toward a two-tier commercial model where NDC bookings through a GDS cost less for an airline than the traditional EDIFACT bookings. Today the airline industry is in a hybrid state where traditional GDS EDIFACT bookings and NDC bookings coexist. The hybrid state will continue to be in place for many years. With the growth in NDC bookings, the private channel introduced by some carriers is being phased out. While many LCCs and ULCCs participate in one or more GDSs, some LCCs have left the GDS and converted to airline direct and NDC content aggregator solutions. NDC adoption has also resulted in changes to the ARC-Agency Sales Agreement that prevents agencies from charging a higher service fee for NDC bookings. GDS disintermediation continues with NDC Aggregator solutions and NDC direct programs from airlines to connect directly with travel agencies, offering them access to their NDC content. TMCs are faced with

B. Vinod, *The Era of Airline Revenue Management with Offers and Orders*,
Management for Professionals, https://doi.org/10.1007/978-3-032-24197-9_10

operational constraints since they can no longer rely on a GDS to provide comprehensive content and must invest to gain access to comprehensive content. Content fragmentation is detrimental to the future of the airline industry. It impacts airlines, GDSs, TMCs and above all the paying travelers. Successfully negotiating contracts is a requirement for the long-term viability of the GDS model.

J. Doyne Farmer, who made this quote on the Jim Rutt Show on June 19, 2025 [Jim Rutt Show, 2019], is a physicist known for his work in chaos theory [Farmer, 2025]. He has discussed how chaos, despite its unpredictable nature, can be seen as a fundamental aspect of time and even a source of organization in complex systems. He notes that complex adaptive systems can naturally evolve from chaotic to organized states, with more complex forms emerging from stronger systems. Farmer explains that in systems governed by deterministic chaos, even with known rules like Newton's laws of motion, the inherent divergence of trajectories makes long-term prediction impossible. However, this very unpredictability is, in his view, what allows for the passage of time itself.

In essence, J. Doyne Farmer‘s perspective on chaos is not one of simple disorder, but rather a recognition of its complex role in the universe, from the flow of time to the emergence of order in complex systems and even the potential for understanding free will. This is an apt description of the winds of change with NDC and content chaos it has created.

10.1 Overview

IATA's NDC is meant to modernize the sales process with rich content. The fragmented rollout by various airlines, coupled with legacy systems creates *content chaos* for travel sellers, leading to inconsistent, complex, and costly management of multiple sources such as NDC Aggregators, GDS as aggregators of NDC content and airline direct connect, which hinders a seamless customer experience. Many airlines withhold their lowest fares from the GDSs resulting in a content gap in the direct channel.

10.2 The Business Landscape Is Evolving with NDC

On the surface IATA's New Distribution Capability (NDC) may sound innocuous, but this is far from the truth. It is similar to a winter storm in the U.S. Midwest that dumps seven feet of snow causing travel *mayhem*. But there is one key difference—the winter storm is temporary and will eventually dissipate, while NDC is permanent. It is also a significant intermediate-term investment for long- term benefits that will in the next several years negatively impact the balance sheets of airlines and intermediaries. To survive and come out ahead, navigating the NDC minefield is of critical importance to all stakeholders in the travel value chain.

The most significant changes to the travel distribution landscape with the advent of NDC is reviewed below.

10.2.1 New Commercial Models Lead to Content Chaos and Fragmented Confusion

Major travel management companies like American Express Global Business Travel, BCD Travel, and Corporate Travel Management (CTM) prefer to operate through Global Distribution Systems (GDSs). This choice ensures that GDSs will continue to play a vital role in the distribution of indirect air travel, but the business and economic dynamics are changing with NDC adoption.

When IATA launched NDC in 2012, they did not realize that they would unleash mass confusion in the marketplace along several dimensions. They are: access to airline content, direct connects between travel agencies and airlines with a direct API connection that bypass GDSs, and the evolution of new commercial models for NDC bookings that directly impacts the survivability of the GDSs.

When NDC was introduced, the GDSs argued that NDC was merely a technical standard, not a commercial model. This however was not the case since the NDC deployment has turned into a commercial discussion for booking NDC content. The economics of NDC bookings is vastly different and GDSs only receive a fraction of the standard GDS booking fees. This two-tier commercial model has far reaching implications on GDSs and their revenues as NDC adoption grows over time. If we assume that the demand is static for air travel, an NDC booking is a one-for-one replacement for an EDIFACT booking. The two-tier commercial model for GDS compensation is expected to show declining revenues as NDC adoption increases.

In December 2022, American Airlines alerted travel agencies that if they were not connected to the carrier's NDC technology by April 2023, they risked losing over 40% of fares that were currently available in the GDS [Airoldi, 2022]. In April 2023, American Airlines made headlines by removing many of its low-cost fares from traditional GDSs. 40% of fares were withheld by American Airlines, in a bold attempt to not just migrate to a new technology standard, but also adopt a new commercial model for NDC bookings that are significantly cheaper than EDIFACT bookings. Yet, this focus on American Airlines hides a bigger problem. As more airlines start NDC technology, travel advisors are struggling to find flights. GDSs were once a central hub for booking air travel, providing options from multiple airlines in one place. Now, the information in GDSs is no longer as comprehensive as it once used to be. Content fragmentation in the digital era, while not specific to the airline industry, hurts the airlines, TMCs and ultimately the traveler! GDSs are best positioned to address content and product normalization, but they need to accelerate their pace of adding NDC connections. This is the overwhelming consensus from the larger TMCs.

Clearly, these actions had an adverse impact on the GDS business. Their actions were also detrimental during contract negotiations. Downplaying the importance of corporate managed travel negatively impacted American's corporate travel performance as was reported during the Q1 2024 earnings call. In contrast, American's main competitors Delta Air Lines and United Airlines had positive metrics for corporate bookings. By June 2024, American had rolled back many of the controversial and unorthodox initiatives, such as withholding about 40% of its fares including the lower fares from the GDS (EDIFACT bookings) (since April 1, 2023) and the proposed limit (May 2024) to access frequent flyer miles and loyalty points made through leisure travel agencies, who the airline had classified were "not preferred" channels due to their lack of adoption of NDC. After a failed distribution strategy, in June 2024, American began offering a 10% commission to travel agents for NDC bookings.

These measures were an attempt to change the product distribution landscape drastically. Ultimately, American had to accept the fact that managed corporate travel for large corporations could not be delivered at scale through the direct channel. American's actions negatively impacted corporate travelers who paid higher fares through the agency channel. It also had a negative impact on the GDSs. American also experienced a negative impact from changes to its sales and distribution strategy and the company reported a significant net loss and a lower-than-expected adjusted earnings per share (EPS) in Q1 2024 [American Airlines, 2024]. These actions hurt the airline, customers and the GDSs. Amtrav, a TMC that utilizes NDC technology to book American flights, analyzed results since its implementation of content removal in April 2023. They reported that, on average, fares on the consumer direct channel or available via NDC preferred channels had been lower 47% of the time since then, reaching up to 63% in November 2023. In contrast, travelers booking through non-preferred channels such as the GDS experienced an increase of about 10% in their overall costs per booking [Fox, 2024].

10.2.2 The Future of the So-Called Private Channel

The concept of a private channel for the distribution of airline seats was first introduced by British Airways and Iberia in 2017. The objective was to continue to attract corporate travelers while keeping GDS surcharges in place. The agreement waived the surcharge for select agencies that specialized in corporate travel.

10.2.2.1 Background

The Lufthansa Airline Group first introduced a surcharge of €16 for GDS bookings in September 2015. They called this surcharge as the Distribution Cost Charge (DCC) to recover the cost of distribution through the indirect channels (Amadeus, Sabre, Travelport).

Other airlines, including British Airways and Iberia that are part of The International Airline Group (IAG) introduced a similar surcharge. In June 2017, British

Airways and Iberia surcharges were £8 per leg. They call it the Distribution Technology Charge (DTC).

The surcharges imposed by airlines on GDSs still promoted an omni-channel strategy, since the fares with the surcharges could be accessed across all travel agents. Every successful airline knows the importance of an omnichannel strategy for a seamless customer shopping experience regardless of agency. Perhaps British Airways and Iberia did not believe in an omni-channel strategy when they introduced the so-called private channel.

10.2.2.2 What Is a Private Channel?

Realizing the importance of attracting corporate travelers after they introduced the GDS surcharges, British Airways and Iberia introduced the so-called private channel agreements in 2017. They wanted to keep the GDS surcharges in place and yet attract corporate travelers by waving the surcharge to select agencies that specialized in corporate travel. This is an example of corporate greed, and it is reminiscent of the 1987 Hollywood movie *Wall Street* where actor Michael Douglas emphasized that "*greed is good!*".

In their defense, when the private channel was introduced, British Airways announced that it was a temporary solution to help TMCs transition to NDC and thereby lower their cost of distribution.

The private channel is a bad concept from a marketing and customer experience perspective. The primary issues caused by the so-called private channel are:

1. It causes content fragmentation and does not promote an omni-channel strategy. It is a classic example of the *haves versus the have-nots.*
2. The perception of the private channel is that some agencies are part of a private club for IAG-favored agencies. This negatively impacts the weaker corporate travel agencies and leisure travel agencies who continue to deliver bookings to IAG's British Airways and Iberia.
3. Unfettered access to content is good for the travel industry. Fragmenting content will ultimately hurt the airline when customers defect to the competition. The American Airlines example of withholding 40% of the fares from the GDS led to loss of corporate customers is a case in point.

The private channel relationship includes four main players: the airline, GDS, TMC, and the corporation. This approach sets up a separate channel within a GDS. When an agency makes a private channel agreement with an airline, it does not have to pay the GDS surcharges that the airline usually requires. The airline can also provide special content such as promotional fares and ancillaries that is not offered through the standard GDS channel. Bookings through this private channel result in a lower segment booking fee paid by the airline to the GDS. Since GDSs earn less from these bookings, they do not provide traditional incentives to travel agencies that use the private channel.

Today, larger TMCs can access British Airways content without paying the current DTC charge of £13/€15 per sector that is applied to EDIFACT-based GDS bookings. To accelerate adoption of NDC, British Airways announced in late October 2024 that they would terminate the private channel agreements with selected TMCs at the end of the year, leaving the customers of these TMCs exposed to the airline's DTC. Some very large TMCs will continue to be exempt from the surcharge, but British Airways plans to limit membership in the IAG private club. In a nutshell, British Airways is saying to avoid DTC, travel agents must connect to NDC. It also means that British Airways is willing to accept short term losses in corporate bookings in the hope of making strides for the long term. Unlike leisure travel bookings, corporate bookings are far more complex due to constraints imposed by corporate travel managers such as corporate travel policy compliance, duty of care, minimizing travel expenditure that is documented, and reporting. It is unlikely that TMCs can transition to NDC on such short notice which means the traveler will be impacted by this change and pay a higher price for air travel.

Qantas Airways introduced its private channel in August 2019. The Qantas private channel agreements with agencies provide access to the Qantas Distribution Platform, which offers content and deals to travel agents and customers. The Qantas Channel is a commercial agreement between Qantas and an agency that allows access to the platform's content and offers. Qantas replaced its Qantas Channel private agreements with a new distribution model starting July 1, 2025 to spur NDC adoption by travel agents. The previous channel agreements were replaced with updated surcharges on bookings made through different channels.

Ultimately these actions impact the cost of travel. Travelers pay the price when they do not have access to the right travel agency.

10.2.2.3 Lufthansa Group—Private channel with a Twist

The Lufthansa Group's NDC in Europe allows travel agents and booking platforms to access a wider range of flight options. This includes extra services like lounge access and baggage allowances, all directly available through the airline's NDC platform. Lufthansa claims that customers now enjoy greater flexibility and personalized choices. The participating airlines are Lufthansa, Austrian Airlines, Swiss, and Brussels Airlines. Certified NDC Aggregators such as Travelport and Sabre provide access for bookings in countries like Austria, Ireland, the Netherlands, and the UK.

10.2.3 Low-Cost and Ultra Low-Cost Carriers and GDS Participation

When low-cost carriers (LCC) and ultra low-cost carriers (ULCC) came into existence in the 1990s, they favored only direct distribution to minimize the cost of customer acquisition. Unlike corporate travelers who are schedule sensitive, the customer base of LCCs and ULCCs is price sensitive leisure travelers. As the

LCCs matured and became larger, they realized the importance of corporate bookings. Today many LCCs participate in at least one GDS. Amadeus and Travelport offer services that are tailored to the needs of LCCs and ULCCs.

Some LCCs have adopted NDC and provide XML-based APIs for OTAs and TMCs to connect and source their content. Examples of LCCs that use the NDC connection are Ryanair and Spirit Airlines. Many LCCs provide their content to travel sellers through aggregators that have a single API integration, which is often easier for smaller travel agencies to use.

A few years ago, very few LCCs participated in a GDS. Today, over 70% of LCCs participate in at least one GDS. Here are a few examples.

In 2020–2021 Southwest signed distribution deals with all three GDSs. The airline expects to earn $350 million from checked bag fees in 2025. It replaced its Wanna Get Away fare, which included two free checked bags, with a Basic (no frills) fare which caused a brief dip in bookings. Southwest began displaying fares on Google Flights, marking entry into metasearch engines. Southwest content is now bookable on Priceline and other Booking Holdings brands (Booking.com, Agoda, etc.). Earlier in 2025, it signed its first OTA deal with Expedia Group. For an airline that was previously direct-only, Southwest is gradually diversifying its retail network, under pressure from investors. Southwest continues to offer direct booking options and tools like SWABIZ for corporate travelers.

SalamAir, the low-cost carrier from Oman has signed a distribution agreement with Sabre, making its content available to travel agencies globally on Sabre‘s network. Additionally, the carrier recently renewed its Radixx Reservation System contract with Sabre. SalamAir has been a customer of Radixx since 2017.

Breeze Airways, a LCC launched in 2021 focuses on serving underserved markets in the U.S. Previously, it had limited distribution to its own channels, In 2025, Breeze Airways signed distribution agreements with Amadeus and Travelport. Breeze expanded its reach in 2024 by establishing direct connections with TMCs AmTrav and Navan, and partnered with OTAs Priceline and Expedia.

UK-based LCC easyJet is an instant purchase, ticketless carrier with Amadeus, Travelport and Sabre in all countries. A form of payment must be entered into a PNR to complete the booking.

Mexican ULCC Volaris signed a multi-year distribution agreement with Sabre in October 2025. Volaris content is live on Sabre, marking the first time the airline's content is distributed through a GDS.

Full content from Jeju Air, the largest LCC in South Korea, has a long-standing partnership with Sabre. They also have a distribution agreement with Amadeus that includes access to both EDIFACT and NDC content. Their content is also available to agents using the Air Promotion Group (APG) NDC platform (over 2500+ agents). Jeju's bookings via the APG platform bypass GDS fees.

10.2.3.1 Frontier Airlines Leaves Sabre

In October 2024 ULCC Frontier Airlines terminated its participation in the Sabre GDS since they was unable to secure a mutually beneficial agreement. This is a bad move for Sabre. Negotiation with Frontier should focus on the true marginal cost of Frontier bookings to Sabre, before walking away from contract renewal.

For a GDS to survive, the single most important objective is customer retention because access to content is king. Retaining TMC subscribers is critical for survival. No GDS can afford to lose content from airlines.

Perhaps it is not an ominous sign for the GDSs. In 2025, Frontier announced several key initiatives on the distribution front. They signed a new distribution agreement with Amadeus that includes access to NDC content. This marks the first time that Frontier's NDC content can be accessed with a GDS NDC partnership. Frontier content is also available on Hopper, the mobile OTA, that includes NDC content. Frontier also integrated NDC content with Fareportal, enabling NDC bookings via its OTAs, CheapOair and OneTravel. NDC content is also available on the Amtrav TMC. After terminating the GDS-only BizFare fare bundle, Frontier now charges a $5 surcharge for GDS EDIFACT bookings. EDIFACT content is available through Amadeus and Travelport.

10.2.3.2 Is this a Disturbing Trend for the GDS Model?

In addition to the Frontier-Sabre commercial dispute, the larger question is: *how was Frontier empowered to leave Sabre and the lucrative corporate travel market that they focused on with their Bizfares?* Frontier's Bizfares, which can only be purchased through a travel agency, includes perks for corporate travel such as premium seating with extra leg room, guaranteed overhead bin space and the enhanced frequent flyer program to achieve elite status quickly.

But despite its focus on business travel, Frontier left Sabre on October 1, 2024. Who came to Frontier's rescue? The answer is NDC and NDC Aggregators. Frontier announced that they had a broad initiative to bypass the GDS with NDC-based connections with third-party sellers, commonly referred to as NDC Aggregators. Bookings made through NDC Aggregators disintermediate the GDS. Also remember that unlike the GDS model which charges airlines a segment booking fee, NDC Aggregators charge the travel agencies a fee per booking (not per segment like the GDS) which is usually around $0.75 cents to $1.50.

This is a disturbing trend for the GDSs. If it gains momentum, it is bad for the GDSs since LCCs control about 35% of the worldwide market for bookings.

10.2.4 TMCs Propose Processing Fee for NDC Bookings

The E-Gov Travel Service (ETS) Next is a mandatory solution used by over 124 civilian U.S. government agencies. All agencies, except for the Department of Defense, are required to use ETS. Several travel management companies competing for federal contracts under the ETSNext program have submitted pricing proposals to the U.S. General Services Administration (GSA). Among these are Adtrav, Duluth Travel, and Travel Inc., which include an extra fee for air transactions booked outside global distribution systems that use New Distribution Capability [Boehmer, 2024]. These surcharges, called "NDC Air Surcharge", are fairly steep. For example, Adtrav charges a \$59.96 NDC Air Surcharge per transaction, while Travel Inc. charges \$25.19 and Duluth Travel charges \$35.26. The GSA pricing template for ETSNext includes "NDC Air Surcharge"as an optional ancillary line item, defined as a "surcharge for processing air transactions through an NDC channel not in the GDS".

TMCs can justify this surcharge because of workflow disruption, added tasks to post NDC bookings as passive bookings on the GDS for consolidated reporting purposes or maintain booking counts for NDC bookings separately since they are not integrated with existing GDS mid-office and back-office systems. Also making NDC bookings through an airline preferred channel can be higher due to the time and complexity involved in modifying fares that are subject to a change in itinerary. The technology supporting NDC is still developing, requiring travel agents to put in more effort to handle these bookings.

10.2.5 Fine Tuning Air Shopping Parameters for OTAs

An established business process for GDS sales agents is to optimize shopping parameters for each new prospective OTA client. To understand why this is needed, consider a round-trip shopping request submitted by a travel agent or an end user. For example, a schedule-led shopping algorithm will generate a large number of outbound and inbound itineraries. The generation of these itineraries is intelligent in the sense that sold out outbound or inbound itineraries would be discarded. If there are 1 1000 outbound and 1000 itineraries generated, the number of possible itineraries to be evaluated will be 1000 x 1000 = one million. The itinerary selection process whittles this list of candidates to the maximum number of itineraries that will be included in the display.

The default shopping parameters usually do an excellent job of finding low-fare and other itineraries, but the parameter settings often (on purpose) exclude some itineraries that prospective OTA clients want displayed. For example:

1. A low "connect time" parameter may exclude certain airlines or some low fares.
2. Various time-of-day parameters may exclude some airlines or not display enough flights at times, while the same GDS for a different OTA does display these flights.

Sales analysts today manually "fiddle" with the parameters to ensure that a "good" selection of itineraries is returned. This is a time-consuming process that extends the sales cycle. GDSs such as Sabre have automated this process to minimize time spent on experimentation.

A shopping response for a given market, departure date and return date consisting of a defined maximum limit of bookable itineraries is a multi-dimensional problem. The following parameters need to be considered for optimization to determine the ideal composition of itineraries that are returned by the shopping algorithm for display:

1. Price Diversity—can add any number of diversity weights
2. Travel Time Diversity—again, can add any number of diversity weights
3. Top Carriers—used to attempt to force specific carriers into the response, which are deemed by the user as top carriers
4. Inbound/Outbound pairings—weights to restrict the number of itineraries that have the same pairing on either the inbound or outbound parts of a trip. This parameter consists of a weight and a number of occurrences for any portion of the journey (out or back). For instance, a weight of 10 and a pairing count of 1 would ensure that each portion of an itinerary is only paired once, not repeatedly.
5. Carrier Diversity Weights—Similar to price and travel time diversities, carrier weights allow for varying the importance of diverse airlines in the results
6. Connection time overrides—allows for the forcing of long connect times, including a minimum long connect, maximum long connect, and a range of connect times that lie between the minimum and maximum specified.
7. Top Carrier Options—allows the forced inclusion of itineraries from a list of top carriers in the result set.

Due to the challenge in capturing all these parameters in-path when the shopping algorithm is run, this is an iterative process as shown in Fig. 10.1.

The first step is to identify the opportunity markets. Potential OTA customers can produce a list which can be augmented by analyzing MIDT data and robotic shopping data. Other aspects that influence this list are the front-end and backend commissions negotiated with the airline and performance incentives negotiated with the GDS. The second step is to establish weights for the various shopping metrics using the OTA's objectives as a constructive input. By executing the shopping algorithm by calling the API multiple times, each shopping response set is scored to identify the shopping parameters that may improve the score. These permutations of shopping parameters can be run automatically to determine the settings that maximize the composite score. Next, deploy the parameters that produce superior shopping results. The last step is to track core customer performance metrics such as conversion, volume of bookings and profitability. A continuous feedback process is established to improve the recommended parameter settings over time, enforcing continuous improvement.

To accelerate the onboarding process for OTAs, GDSs also calibrate and maintain a range of optimal profiles based on the composite scoring criteria such as cheaper flights, more direct flights, balanced lower fare and faster travel time options, carrier preferences and do-not-show carriers, longer connect times for families with children and specific routings identified by connect points in the itinerary.

Statistical analysis can also provide insight into the most important parameters which represent the biggest levers. Most of the parameters interact with each other.

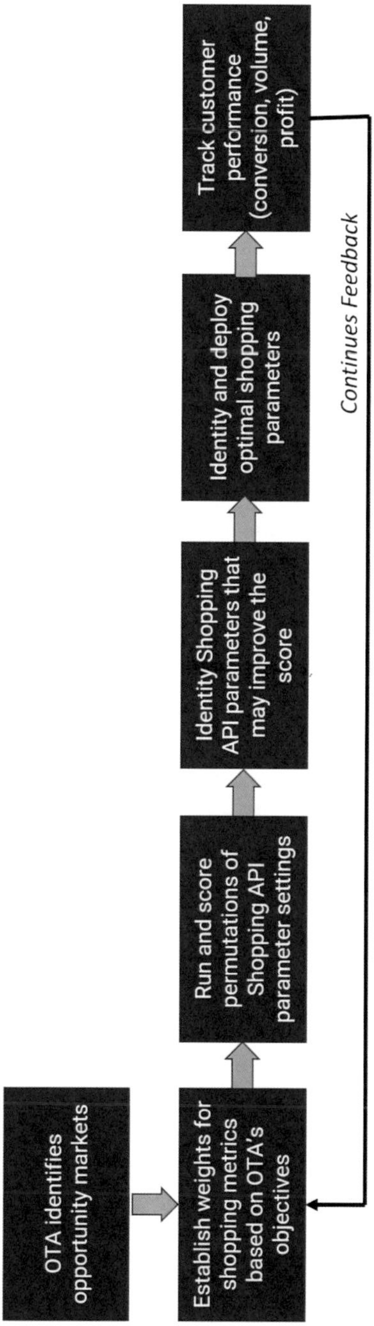

Fig. 10.1 Determining the default shopping parameters to fit an OTA's Business Model

The OTAs, working with GDS partners, must estimate how the setting of parameter A affects shopping responses, which effect scores. And the effect of a parameter A setting depends on the level of parameter B.

The ability to experiment with different parameter settings can be automatically augmented with the multi-armed bandit experiments combined with Bayesian optimization. Bandit optimization is used for problems with a finite set of choices. In contrast, Bayesian optimization provides a solution for problems with continuous parameters and an infinite number of potential options. This optimization must be run continuously, because consumer preferences change. In addition, seasons, holidays, time-of-day and more must be considered.

In the above scenario pricing power rests with the GDS, which independently generates the shopping responses based on fares filed by airlines through ATPCO and schedules distributed through OAG or Cirium. In an NDC world, the existing business process of GDS sales agents finetuning shopping parameters with prospective OTAs is no longer required since pricing power shifts to the airlines that are responsible for generating the priced itineraries, While the GDS serves as the aggregator of NDC content for the OTA, no business process exists today for OTAs to fine tune the itineraries they receive from each airline based on their objectives. The GDS, in its role as an aggregator, will still be responsible for the quintessential task of normalizing non-homogenous content returned by the airlines for display to a customer or a travel agent.

10.2.6 Alterations to the ARC Agency Sales Agreement

An ARC agency sales agreement is a legal contract between a travel agency and the Airlines Reporting Corporation (ARC). It specifies the terms that allow the agency to sell airline tickets to customers. This agreement enables the agency to book flights for airlines and handle transactions through ARC. In essence, it provides the framework for a travel agency to become an ARC accredited agency and sell tickets to clients.

American Airlines modified its agency sales agreement with ARC to accommodate NDC bookings around the time it began actively pushing for NDC adoption with travel agencies, which primarily started in late 2019 and early 2020. American mandates that travel agents must offer NDC content to all customers, unless the customer specifically requests not to receive it. American also requires that agencies can only charge customers the same service fee for NDC content as they charge for all airline tickets. Higher service fees for American Airlines NDC bookings are prohibited. Other airlines like United Airlines and Delta Air Lines did not follow American's lead.

10.2.7 Content Curation Layer and Product Normalization

NDC allows airlines to sell their products and services directly to travel agencies through their own platforms, bypassing the traditional GDSs that travel agents typically use. This shift reduces fare transparency and increases the complexity for travel agents. They must access several airline platforms to compare prices, availability, and ancillary services. This extra effort makes the booking process longer and more difficult, making it challenging for agents to offer efficient and affordable options to their clients. GDSs like Amadeus, Sabre, and Travelport tackle this issue by adding a content curation layer to their respective travel agency desktops. This layer aggregates standard GDS EDIFACT content with NDC content from airlines and low-cost carrier content. The aggregated content is normalized to remove duplicates and help travel agents compare options and book tickets easily. This normalization process represents a significant investment from GDSs to keep NDC Aggregators in check. Once the content is normalized by the content curation level, the various fare products returned from the airlines are normalized to determine the order of the display, based on the itineraries that have the highest utility based on schedule and fare attributes. Product normalization requires calibration with a consumer choice model to determine the marginal values of the attributes of an itinerary.

10.2.8 Smaller Travel Agencies Will Struggle to Be Competitive

Many airlines require a minimum booking threshold of $one million or higher before starting negotiations for NDC agreements with travel agencies and direct corporate accounts. This is a strategy to prioritize airline resources.

Major online travel agencies (OTAs) and travel management companies (TMCs) have already secured contracts with the large FSCs, making it harder for smaller agencies to compete, putting them at a disadvantage as they may not meet the minimum booking requirements to negotiate directly. Without the support of consortia or host agencies, these smaller travel agencies will struggle.

10.2.9 Direct Competition from Airlines in the Indirect Channel

Airlines began competing directly with travel agents as the Internet emerged in the mid-1990s. They encouraged customers to book vacations directly on their websites. Now, airlines are targeting managed travel as well. Travel agents have been essential in developing relationships with corporate and leisure clients. They understand customer needs and offer tailored recommendations.

Many airlines have implemented NDC Direct programs to connect directly with travel agencies, offering them access to their NDC content. This is dis-intermediation and has a negative impact on GDSs. Direct connections can be established via APIs (Application Programming Interfaces) or through specialized technology platforms. This direct connection allows for access to a wider range of options and more accurate fares that may not be available on the GDS. Some airlines also offer additional incentives besides commissions for agencies to adopt NDC, such as coupon incentives for eligible NDC bookings. The NDC direct distribution model is also aided by new entrant NDC Aggregators like Accelya, Duffel, TPConnects, Travelfusion, AirGateway and many others.

10.2.10 Financial Strain and Operational Impacts on Travel Agents

NDC bookings made with a NDC Aggregator bypass the GDS and this is disintermediation. GDSs, by default, are aggregators of NDC content. But that does not mean that it will have the same content as NDC Aggregators. This is because the NDC Aggregator may have NDC content for an airline to which the GDS has not yet connected. This means that TMCs cannot wholly rely on GDSs to provide NDC content and may have to make an additional investment in an NDC Aggregator.

Contrary to earlier expectations that NDC was merely a new messaging standard, it has evolved into a commercial discussion for NDC bookings which are vastly different from standard GDS EDIFACT bookings. With GDSs receiving a fraction of the segment booking fees with NDC bookings from airlines, travel agencies do not receive the standard performance-based incentives for NDC bookings from the GDSs. The absence of incentives from GDSs will greatly affect the profits of travel agencies. Additionally, travel agents will have to bear the burden of incremental operational costs for staff training to keep up with new NDC workflows and system updates. The shift to NDC disrupts established agent workflows and requires agents to familiarize themselves with new systems, leading to temporary inefficiencies and potential business losses during the hybrid period. This transition will last several years During the hybrid state, both EDIFACT and NDC XML bookings will be used simultaneously.

Records of NDC bookings made outside the GDS through either direct connect or through an NDC Aggregator cannot be easily integrated into agency mid-office and back-office systems. This will require an additional investment to consolidate GDS and non-GDS bookings into consolidated agency sales reports.

The shift towards NDC raises significant concerns regarding duty of care, which is a TMC's core competency and legal obligation to ensure the safety and well-being of traveling employees of its corporate customers. As more travelers book outside approved channels, maintaining visibility and providing support in emergencies become increasingly difficult, exposing TMCs to potential liabilities.

10.2.11 The Threat to the GDS as NDC Content Aggregators

A fundamental issue is that the GDS business does not own the point of sale, which is the domain of TMCs and OTAs. This is a fundamental weakness of the GDS model in the NDC era since some travel agencies are actively providing direct connections to airlines using the NDC protocol and bypass the GDS. This trend should be a significant concern for the GDSs.

The GDSs by default are aggregators of NDC content from the full-service carriers. Despite poor economics for NDC bookings made through a GDS, the GDSs have continued to invest in connecting to airlines to access and aggregate NDC content. They see it is a necessary step to thwart the growth of the new entrant NDC Aggregators in the marketplace.

On July 21, 2025, Navan, a travel management company, announced the launch of its proprietary content aggregation platform [Hoskins, 2025]. Navan also confirmed that as of June 2025, it had retired its GDS-based NDC connection in favor of its own proprietary direct airline API integrations. They continue to maintain select aggregator partnerships.

After testing three approaches (direct airline APIs, aggregator partnerships, and legacy GDS NDC feeds), Navan concluded that direct integration offered the best quality and fastest issue resolution. After abandoning GDS-based NDC aggregation, Navan is collaborating with Accelya via the FLX Select program to accelerate NDC rollout and onboarding.

FLX Select is a service launched by Accelya in June 2024 that helps airlines adopt NDC within 90 days. The program offers a standardized guide for onboarding and continued operational support.

Navan continues to source some NDC content via an aggregator partner—for some five airlines—but direct connections are its preferred method of delivery. For example, in January 2026, Emirates established a direct NDC connection with Navan, giving Navan users access to their full range of fares, ancillary products and premium services.

Another example is AmTrav, a TMC that is owned by TravelPerk, a corporate travel management company. AmTrav uses a combination of Global Distribution Systems (GDS) like Sabre and Amadeus, alongside its own NDC technology to book travel. In April 2025, AmTrav announced that 61% of its bookings were made via NDC or direct API connections, AmTrav does not offer GDS-NDC bookings. AmTrav uses NDC technology to book and service airlines such as American Airlines, Southwest Airlines, United Airlines, Spirit Airlines, Breeze Airways, and Frontier Airlines.

TMCs like Navan and AmTrav are concentrating on direct NDC connections with proprietary platforms for direct airline integration and content aggregation, rather than relying on GDSs. This is a fundamental threat to the future of the GDS. In addition, NDC Aggregators like Spotnana, Duffel, and AirGateway, have built their own technology for direct NDC connections to airlines, and offer their platforms to TMCs.

Why does "NDC Direct Connect" matter to TMCs? It is simple. TMCs realize the importance of access to a wider range of content and exclusive fares that may not be available through traditional distribution channels.

This is a wake-up call for GDSs and if this trend continues, fewer NDC bookings will flow through the GDSs.

10.2.12 Corporate Travel and NDC

As airlines push NDC and intermediaries publicly state support, corporate buyers remain skeptical if not opposed, owing to the combination of product investment, servicing issues and smaller-than-expected savings.

Corporate travel adoption of NDC is challenging to overhaul legacy systems, the complexity of integrating with existing technology, the fragmentation of content across multiple channels, and a steep learning curve for travel management staff. The transition requires significant investment in technology and training, as companies must adapt to new tools to handle more dynamic, personalized offers while ensuring data security and consistent reporting.

Many existing travel management, booking, and accounting systems are built on older standards like EDIFACT and GDS platforms, which were not designed for NDC. Modifying or replacing these legacy systems to be compatible with NDC requires investment, time, and technical expertise. Corporate travel managements and travel agents require training on new procedures and tools which can be a complex and time-consuming process. Adopting NDC also creates challenges for expense tracking, reconciliation, and reporting. NDC deployment varies by airline in subtle ways, leading to inconsistencies and data integrity issues, that complicate integration for travel technology providers and corporate buyers.

10.2.13 The Hybrid State Will Continue for Several Years

The excitement around NDC is increasing every day, and so is its influence on airlines. However, the fast-paced changes, complex terms, and ongoing updates can make it hard to grasp what NDC really is, how it functions, and what advantages it offers. The transition to NDC with its XML-based messaging standard is a slow process. For all airlines that are members of IATA to be on NDC for all their transactions will take several decades. The hybrid state, where EDIFACT and XML will coexist started in 2010 and will continue for several decades, though the NDC booking volumes will increase and EDIFACT booking volumes will decrease. In the end state all transactions will be based on NDC, at which time EDIFACT can be sunset.

The EDIFACT protocol has supported the industry since 1987, enabling the rapid and efficient processing of billions of transactions worldwide. Airlines, GDSs, online booking tools, travel management companies and individual travel agencies have relied on EDIFACT to exchange the necessary data for selling and booking flights and seats.

NDC is a new XML-based standard and is not expected to replace EDIFACT in its entirety soon. Here is why. The International Air Transport Association (IATA) has about 340 airline members from over 120 countries. At the end of 2024, there are about 75 airlines that are certified to use New Distribution Capability (NDC). The number of certified airlines can vary because IATA uses a multi-level certification system. These airlines are at various stages of technical development and maturity toward responding to travel agency requests for offers.

There is no silver bullet that allows every airline to share NDC content across all channels. Each airline is developing its own NDC APIs with various IT providers and technology partners. This requires unique development for each airline, as well as for aggregators and service providers. Many mid-size and smaller airlines may find the cost of enabling NDC prohibitive and make it a lower priority. The process involves creating systems for service, data organization, business operations, and how content is displayed, ensuring it aligns with current airline content. Extensive testing and development are necessary to ensure the NDC content displays accurately. The fully allocated cost of enabling NDC for a carrier can range from $15 million to $35 million annually. This includes the cost of the shopping service to respond to shop requests from agencies, offer creation, fulfillment, and version control of the NDC messaging format. The development of order management capability will be incremental to this estimate.

TMCs are also focused on incremental investment to enable NDC content through GDSs primarily and in some case third-party NDC Aggregators. As they prepare for NDC enablement in 2026 and beyond, many have developed frameworks and identified the core capabilities required to make NDC work for business travel, The core capabilities required have various names such as Minimum Viable Product (MVP) and Minimum Marketable Product (MMP).

For EDIFACT to be sunset, there are two long-tail entities that need to embrace NDC. First is the large number of mid-size and small airlines that participate in a GDS for whom NDC is not a priority. The second is mid-size and smaller independently owned travel agencies for whom NDC may not be on their radar, influenced by the cost of investment.

10.2.14 Airlines that Breach Full Content Agreements

Full content agreements (FCA) are contracts that require airlines to share their schedules, fares, and availability with all Global Distribution Systems (GDS), similar to how they provide this information to their own websites. GDSs argue that they offer a balanced solution for the efficient marketplace with the well-known full content renewal agreements with major full-service carriers, in the U.S. and internationally. The FCA clause in airline-GDS contracts has been a key issue in disputes for over twenty years, including past antitrust lawsuits filed by American Airlines against Sabre and Travelport [Vinod, 2024a].

The full content renewals promoted by GDSs are based on six tenets for participating carriers. They are:

1. Full content (schedules and fares). This ensures that the fares available on an airline consumer direct website, inclusive of web fares, are available in the GDS.
2. Long-term agreements. These contracts are typically three years or five years in duration,
3. Service fee protection.
4. Parity treatment, here an airline agrees to give a GDS access to the same content that is available through other GDSs.
5. Flexibility for travel agents to choose the tools they want.
6. Flexibility to pay incentives based on value.

Airlines that sign full content renewals cannot publish lower fares on their websites that are not available through the GDS channel.

The FCAs do not apply to the sale of ancillary products and services sold by airlines. This means that airlines do not have to distribute ancillary products to ATPCO and GDSs. The adoption of NDC has already rendered the full content agreements obsolete since pricing power, the power to price an itinerary in the GDS environment, is *shifting* from the GDS to the airline.

There is nothing innovative about withholding fares from GDS channels and many airlines justify this as a step toward providing "differentiated" content between traditional GDS and NDC channels. The list of airlines that no longer distribute all fares to the GDSs is listed below. This list changes constantly and represents a snapshot from December 2025.

Air Canada

Air Canada has a very long history of withholding fares from the GDS. When Air Canada introduced branded fares in 2006, they violated existing full content agreements by withholding the Tango Fares (the cheapest fares) from the GDSs for the Canadian Point of Sale. Today, Air Canada does not withhold the lowest fares from the GDSs, but the lowest fares booked in each cabin through the GDS channel are subject to a distribution cost recovery (DCR) fee [Airoldi, 2024f]. The surcharges have been removed for most fares, except for the lowest ones (G, K, A, and P). This fee is designed to offset the costs associated with legacy GDS distribution. The fee is not applied to bookings made through Air Canada's NDC channels, including NDC content within the GDS, or through Air Canada's direct booking channels. Previously Air Canada had imposed the GDS surcharge for all EDIFACT bookings, which now only applies to the lowest fare classes in each cabin. Air Canada also offered a $2 incentive for eligible NDC bookings, which was available through the end of 2024.

Air France—KLM

In April 2023, Air France and KLM limited their lowest fares to NDC based channels as part of its distribution strategy [Gill, 2023]. They also removed special promotional offers from GDS channels. In June 2023, they stopped offering short and medium haul "Light" fares, which have a minimum stay requirement, through traditional Global Distribution Systems (GDS). These fares are now only available on the airline website and NDC preferred connections. This is their strategy to encourage bookings through their NDC channels and direct connections, which offer lower distribution costs. They also apply a surcharge on bookings made through GDS, but this surcharge is not applicable to NDC connections.

American Airlines

In April 2023, as part of its NDC strategy, American Airlines began to withhold Basic Economy fares and many higher-priced options from legacy GDS platforms. The airline also removed its lower priced first class fares from these platforms and also blocked many refundable fare options in the GDSs. When they realized that their strategy was not working, in June 2024, AA began returning fare content to legacy GDSs after removing them during an earlier attempt to get agencies to use NDC. American Airlines continues to withhold Basic Economy fares from the GDSs.

In June 2024, to regain lost market share, American launched an updated incentive program for NDC bookings. This program includes commissions for its three NDC bundles: Main Plus, Main Select, and Flagship Business Plus. The airline is also providing incentives for bookings of paid seats.

British Airways

British Airways stopped offering Short-haul Basic fares through GDSs in 2020. British Airways has increased the number of additional price points available via NDC on fares on its short-haul routes in Euro Traveller (economy) and Club Europe (business) from 57 to 73 [Frary, 2021].

Lufthansa

In October 2018, Lufthansa removed some fare types from GDSs, such as the Light brand of economy fares and Business Saver business class fares. Lufthansa continues to withhold the lowest fares from the GDSs. In April 2026, Lufthansa Group introduced a new, highly restrictive Economy Basic fare on short and medium haul routes that is only available through direct and NDC channels.

United Airlines

In 2023, United Airlines pulled Basic Economy fares from legacy GDSs for domestic and short haul international flights. United also offers dynamic fares, which is known as continuous pricing in the industry. Approximately 40% of United's NDC fares are generated dynamically [Airoldi, 2023].

10.2.15 GDS Service Fees for NDC Content

In the traditional GDS transaction flow model, airlines pay a segment booking fee to the GDSs but *do not manipulate* the published tariffs filed by airlines to the fare aggregators like ATPCO. Only net fares that are designed for markups are modified.

In the traditional scenario, based on the agreement between airlines and GDSs, GDSs receive the segment booking fees from the airline for each itinerary booked and, in 2025, they pay incentives to the travel agents based on volume performance which could be as high as 56% of the segment booking fees.

The introduction of NDC content has changed the level playing field because the economics of the GDS model are changing. Airlines pay lower booking fees and, in some cases, may not pay any segment booking fees to GDSs. Further, all NDC fares can be termed as private fares. GDSs have the capability to charge travel agencies for access to NDC content similar to what NDC Aggregators charge. The NDC content delivered by the GDSs to travel agents is also void of any travel agency incentives paid by the GDSs, which in turn will force the travel agencies to charge a service fee to customers. As a direct result of these added service fee actions by GDSs and travel agencies, airlines can potentially lose control of tariffs. There is an added risk if the service fee charged by GDSs for NDC content to travel agencies is not the same across all airlines but a function of GDS-airline contract economics and volume of bookings. If the incremental GDS service fees are not uniform across airlines, it could lead to some airlines becoming uncompetitive based on the total fare which may include the service fee. *This is a shortcoming of the NDC initiative,* and no one has thought through this outcome. It can damage an airline's reputation and result in financial loss that is beyond their control. Rather than eliminating segment booking fees paid by airlines to GDSs, paying a segment booking fee is a winning strategy since it can prevent intermediaries from imposing service fees for NDC content.

Another aspect of NDC is the loss of travel agency incentives paid by the GDSs. Since travel agencies no longer collect incentives from the GDSs for NDC bookings, their long-term affinity to a GDS also becomes questionable.

10.3 Is the FDR Era Anti-Price Bias Law Applicable to Airlines and GDSs in the NDC Era?

The Robinson-Patman Act (RPA) is a U.S. antitrust law that prohibits sellers from discriminating in price between different competing resellers of like goods where the effect is to substantially lessen competition. The RPA was an amendment to the Clayton Act of 1914, which was enacted in 1936 in the Franklin D. Roosevelt era, to protect small businesses from being disadvantaged by large chain stores that could leverage their purchasing power to demand lower prices from suppliers.

The law prohibits certain forms of price discrimination, such as when suppliers and distributors charge competing buyers different prices for the same product.

This allegedly harmed small, independent businesses by limiting their access to discounts and rebates, making it harder for them to compete with larger national and regional chains.

Robinson-Patman cases were once key in antitrust enforcement. However, in the 1980s, the FTC and Justice Department moved away from them. Legal experts raised concerns that the law contributed to higher prices.

10.3.1 Background: FTC V. Southern Glazer

In the waning days of the Biden Administration, on December 12, 2024, the Federal Trade Commission (FTC) filed a lawsuit against Southern Glazer's Wine and Spirits LLC, the largest wine and spirits distributor in the U.S. FTC claims the company violated the Robinson-Patman Act [FTC, 2024a] by discriminating against smaller retailers.

The FTC's complaint states that Southern sells wine and spirits to small, independent businesses at much higher prices than those offered to large chains. These significant price differences give large companies an unfair advantage that outweighs any real cost savings for the same products. This behavior is seen as unfair and illegal price discrimination by Southern. If Southern's actions are corrected, it will allow more competition among larger companies. This, in turn, will ensure that consumers continue to have choices and can lead to lower prices for everyone.

> When local businesses get squeezed because of unfair *pricing* practices that favor large chains, Americans see fewer choices and pay higher prices—and communities suffer," said Chair Lina M. Khan. "The law says that businesses of all sizes should be able to compete on a level playing field. Enforcers have ignored this mandate from Congress for decades, but the FTC's action today will help protect fair competition, lower prices and restore the rule of law.

"Since at least 2018 and continuing today, Southern has repeatedly discriminated in price between disfavored independent purchasers—which include neighborhood grocery stores, local convenience stores and independently owned wine and spirits shops—and favored large chain purchasers of wine and spirits, such as Total Wine & More, Costco and Kroger," the FTC's complaint states.

Does *FTC v. Southern Glazer* look like the NDC-initiated content chaos with a different set of actors? To break the GDS oligopoly, many airlines consider smaller NDC Aggregators to be their preferred channels. The difference from the Southern lawsuit is that airlines favor the smaller NDC Aggregators as their preferred channels over the GDSs.

Under the Trump Administration, the FTC's alleged price discrimination lawsuit continues, but faces internal division. While two commissioners, including the new FTC Chair Andrew Ferguson, dissented, they signaled an openness to enforcement of the Robinson-Patman Act despite disagreeing with the specific case. The

FTC sought to continue the case, even as it was at an early stage, and the administration's broader antitrust enforcement strategy remained a subject of discussion. Perhaps the shift is toward enforcement of the Robinson-Patman Act.

Can a ruling on this case in favor of the FTC have ramifications on the content chaos in the airline industry?

10.3.2 Is the Robinson-Patman Act Applicable toward Content Bias

NDC has triggered content chaos with airlines promoting content bias across channels. The lowest airfares from many airlines are only available on the airline's consumer direct website and through "preferred channels" identified by the airlines. The larger GDSs are typically not the preferred channels. The preferred channels are typically the new entrant NDC Aggregators. If the Robinson-Patman Act is applicable, airlines cannot selectively withhold content by channel, and we will be back in the era of full content agreements which have withered away with the introduction of ancillary services followed by NDC.

There is also the issue of travel agency incentives from the GDS which are not available for booking NDC content due to the airline favorable commercial agreements between GDSs and airlines. Further, to mimic the NDC Aggregators that charge travel agents a fee per booking (not by segment like the GDS does), GDSs can impose a service fee for travel agents to access NDC content from the GDS. If the Robinson-Patman Act is applicable, the service fee charged by the GDS to travel agencies must be the same, regardless of the volume of bookings generated by an agency. Today, there is nothing that prevents GDSs from charging a distinct service fee by travel agency. If the Robinson-Patman Act can be enforced, it will make quantity discounts for NDC content from GDSs to travel agencies untenable, thereby limiting the exposure of smaller travel agencies.

The full content agreements for the base fare between airlines and GDSs are no longer tenable. Their legality under the RPA would depend on specific facts related to price differences, competitive harm, and available legal defenses. A potential legal hurdle for an RPA claim is that airline travel may be considered a service rather than a tangible commodity, which would place it outside the scope of the Act. Courts have consistently held that the RPA does not apply to the sale of services.

The core concern is if an airline offers different prices or content availability (e.g., through NDC to some partners but not others, or only on its consumer direct website) that creates an uneven playing field for competing travel agencies. If the service element is overcome, a plaintiff would need to prove actual or likely competitive harm. Airlines could potentially use the "cost justification" defense, arguing that direct NDC distribution is more efficient or provides cost savings that justify price differentials to certain partners or direct consumers.

The RPA has been largely under-enforced for decades. While the RPA broadly prohibits anti-competitive price bias, its application to the specific, service-oriented context of airline ticket distribution and GDS-airline contracts is legally complex and has not been a primary area of recent enforcement activity.

10.4 Market Competition: Are Regulators out of Touch with the Travel Marketplace?

A question that is frequently debated is whether the U.K.'s Competition and Markets Authority and the U.S. Department of Justice are out of touch with the market?

10.4.1 Amex Global Business Travel—CWT Merger

Travel management companies (TMC) and individual travel agencies have witnessed a sea of volatility and churn since Delta Air Lines first imposed limits on front-end commissions in 1995 [Peltz, 1995]. Like the airline industry, travel agencies also have gone through consolidation cycles. These mergers usually result in eliminating redundancy and improving efficiency. Table 10.1 illustrates the wave of acquisitions of the smaller agencies by the larger, more established top three TMCs.

On March 25, 2024, American Express GBT, the largest corporate TMC announced that it had reached a definitive agreement to purchase CWT. The acquisition, initially expected in the second half of 2024, was valued at around $570 million, subject to regulatory approval.

The U.K.'s Competition and Markets Authority (CMA) is the principal competition regulator in the United Kingdom. The U.K. Parliament passed the Enterprise

Table 10.1 Travel Management Company Consolidation

Travel Management Company	Travel Agency Acquired	Date
American express GBT	Hoff Robinson Group (HRG)	February 2018
	DER business travel	September 2019
	30SecondsToFly	October 2020
	Ovation travel group	January 2021
	Egencia	May 2021
BCD travel	Adelman travel group	February 2020
	Ventura Spa	August 2019
	Air Club travel	October 2017
	Ticket biz	December 2015
	World travel service	May 2015
Carlson Wagonlit travel (CWT)	WorldMate	October 2017
	Kaleva travel	February 2011
	Viajes Lepanto	September 2008
	Piedmont travel	July 2008
	Ark travel	December 2007

and Regulatory Reform Act 2013. This law established the CMA as a non-ministerial department (NMD) that consolidated and replaced both the Office of Fair Trading and the Competition Commission.

Initially, in July 2024, the CMA raised concerns that the merger could lead to reduced choice and higher prices for large customers (defined as those with at least \$25 million in annual total transaction volume). Amex GBT disagreed with this assessment, arguing that the CMA hadn't adequately considered the breadth and dynamic nature of the business travel industry. CMA was concerned that the deal might give Amex GBT an unfair edge. This could lead to less competition and fewer choices for larger companies.

The CMA should focus its investigation on the competitiveness of the corporate market. It is a very competitive space. The corporate travel industry features many players, including innovative tech companies and specialized agencies that provide unique services. Companies like Navan, TravelPerk, and Spotnana have emerged in recent years, showcasing the impact of technology in travel. Additionally, there are agencies that emphasize excellent service. It is crucial to keep an open mind and look beyond obvious competitors to truly understand the landscape of competition and innovation. The CMA should not be concerned with a lack of competitiveness between two travel agencies, without also considering the overall dynamic marketplace..

Travel content, booking preferences, languages, currencies, tax laws, and costs differ greatly from one market to another. The CMA was concerned that the Amex GBT-CWT deal may make it harder for new or smaller competitors to meet these global demands, potentially raising barriers to entry. On January 8, 2025 the DOJ announced plans to challenge the Amex GBT-CWT merger in the U.S.

Even the largest companies like Amex GBT do not control every aspect of every market. Their offerings change based on the unique characteristics of each region, highlighting the necessity for different solutions. A single solution that works everywhere is not feasible. Each market requires a specific approach, making it impossible to find a universal answer, as it simply does not exist.

In November 2024, the CMA released an interim report stating that the acquisition could significantly reduce competition, resulting in less choice, lower quality, and higher prices for global multinational customers. Amex GBT has expressed strong disagreement with these findings. The CMA's document published in November 25 includes a "remedy proposal" from Amex GBT and CWT aimed at addressing the regulator's concerns about competition.

The proposed remedies include opening CWT's global partner network for a limited time. This would allow other travel management companies (TMCs) to collaborate with experienced local TMCs in over 90 countries when they bid for contracts from Global Multi-National (GMN) clients.

Another suggestion involves making commitments regarding pricing and service offers. This would mean setting price caps on the current fees for products and services for all existing and renewing GMN customers from both TMCs for two years following the acquisition. Additionally, there will be a pledge to maintain the current level of investment in business travel services at Amex GBT.

The two TMCs had also proposed the option of selling certain GMN customer contracts, particularly those with strong ties to the UK, to another TMC if the CMA deems it necessary and appropriate.

After much deliberation, the CMA approved the merger between Amex GBT and CWT on March 6, 2025. This was based on further investigation and reviewing submitted evidence, the CMA's inquiry group reversed its initial assessment in February 2025. They concluded that CWT was a weaker competitor than initially assessed and that other strong competitors, such as BCD Travel and FCM, would continue to provide alternative options for customers. Therefore, the merger was deemed unlikely to result in a substantial lessening of competition in the global market for business travel agency services.

The U.S. DOJ also weighed in, finally. In the waning days of the Biden Administration, the DOJ filed a lawsuit to block Amex GBT's acquisition of CWT Holdings on January 10, 2025. The DOJ's complaint alleged that "the merger would reduce competition, increase prices, and limit innovation in the travel management industry. They were concerned that the combination of Amex GBT and CWT would create an "oligopolistic" environment with too few other travel management players able to scale services to global and multinational companies.

Following the CMA decision, on July 10, 2025, the DOJ dismissed the suit, just weeks before its scheduled September start [West, 2025]. The merger was concluded on September 2, 2025.

10.4.1.1 Mergers Do Not Guarantee Dominance

A merger such as the Amex GBT—CWT case, does not necessarily mean that the combined entity will be a dominant force. There is no guarantee that the combined entity would be more valuable than the individual entities.

Here are a few examples of airline mergers that did not pan out.

In 1986 when American Airlines deployed the world's first revenue management system to counter the competitive threat from deep discount carrier PeopleExpress, their position was substantially weakened due to the absence of a revenue management system. Armed with a revenue management system, American introduced the SuperSAAver and Ultimate SuperSAAver fares to match the PeopleExpress discount fares. The difference was that American's deeply discounted fares were capacity controlled. In a desperate attempt to survive, PeopleExpress announced a merger with the struggling Frontier Airlines based in Denver. However, this decision only sped up their decline. Frontier eventually backed out of the agreement, leaving People Express in a worse situation. By 1987, the airline was buried in unmanageable debt and collapsed. Just six years after its rapid rise, People Express suddenly shut down, filing for bankruptcy and halting all operations. Thousands of passengers were left stranded as flights were canceled. This swift fall was shocking for an airline that had once changed the industry.

US Airways bought San Diego–based Pacific Southwest Airlines (PSA) in 1986 and Winston-Salem, North Carolina–based Piedmont Airlines in 1987. The PSA acquisition was completed on April 9, 1988, and the Piedmont acquisition on

August 5, 1989. US Airways acquired San Diego-based PSA to gain a foothold on the West Coast, but the integration was problematic due to significant cultural and operational clashes, ultimately leading to US Airways withdrawing from most of the California market within a few years. The US Airways and Piedmont merger was considered a failure due to significant operational and financial problems that followed, including huge operating losses, a stock price drop, and near-bankruptcy. Key issues included clashes between the labor unions and work rules of the airlines, which drove up labor costs. The integration process led to a decline in on-time performance and increased baggage complaints.

10.4.1.2 Thomas Cook Merger with the Co-Operative Travel Group

Mergers do not necessarily guarantee that the value of the combined entity is greater than the parts.

The Thomas Cook merger in 2011 serves as a noteworthy example. On October 8, 2010, Thomas Cook Group PLC and the Co-operative Travel Group, the U.K. consumers' co-operative retailer, announced their decision to merge their U.K. travel and foreign-exchange stores. The Co-operative Travel Group was a travel agency brand used by some independent retail co-operatives in the United Kingdom. Concerns arose about the merger between Thomas Cook and Co-operative's travel agents, leading to its review by the Competition Commission. On August 16, 2011, the Competition Commission decided that, despite their strong market presence, the merger would not likely lead to higher prices or less choice for consumers. After the verdict, in 2011, the two companies formed a joint venture, Thomas Cook Co-operative Travel, to combine their high street operations. This partnership cut operating costs by £35 million yearly. However, in hindsight, the 2011 merger contributed to the eventual collapse of the Thomas Cook Group in 2019.

Incidentally, the Competition Commission closed on 1 April 2014 and its functions were transferred to the Competition and Markets Authority (CMA).

10.4.2 Spirit Airlines and the Department of Justice

Another organization that is out of touch with reality like the CMA is the U.S. Department of Justice (DOJ). The DOJ has lost touch with the evolving competitive landscape that makes it more difficult for the low-cost carriers (LCC) and ultra low-cost carriers (ULCC) to compete with the full-service carriers (FSC). FSC's can directly compete with LCCs on price with their Basic Economy fares, and provide perks not offered by the LCCs and ULCCs. Airline labor costs have risen because of United, American, and Delta which makes the LCC model challenging if not untenable. The variance in the cost per seat mile (CASM) has reduced considerably. In addition, in an asset intensive industry, scale matters for an LCC to take on the FSCs.

After JetBlue outbid Frontier and the Spirit board approved the merger with JetBlue, on January 16, 2024, a federal judge stopped the JetBlue-Spirit deal after the Justice Department filed a lawsuit to block the merger. The DOJ claimed that the merger would reduce competition, drive up fares for price-sensitive customers and harm consumers.

A renewed merger discussion was first made public on October 23, 2024, between Frontier Airlines and Spirit Airlines. However, the deal fell though and on November 18, 2024, Spirit Airlines filed for bankruptcy protection. In March 2025, Spirit Airlines emerged from bankruptcy protection. Despite the restructuring the financial struggles continued and they filed for bankruptcy protection for the second time in 12-months in August 2025.

Actions by the DOJ left Spirit Airlines in a tough spot after the pandemic leaving the airline on the verge of bankruptcy. The demise of Spirit rests squarely with the DOJ that stopped the Spirit—Jet Blue merger. This was the first U.S. airline bankruptcy filing in 11 years. The last bankruptcy by a major U.S. carrier ended when American Airlines emerged from Chap. 11 bankruptcy protection and simultaneously merged with US Airways in December 2013. Spirit Airlines ceased operations on May 2, 2026, following a failed federal bailout attempt and severe financial pressure from rising fuel costs.

10.4.3 Sabre—Farelogix and CMA

Though they worked independently, neither the DOJ nor CMA was in favor of the Sabre-Farelogix merger in 2018. This was partly because several full-service carriers in the U.S. and Europe were not in favor of it. On August 20, 2019, the Department of Justice launched a civil antitrust lawsuit to prevent Sabre from acquiring its competitive rival Farelogix for $360 million. The goal of this legal action was to maintain the competition between these two companies, which had benefited airlines and consumers.

After an eight-day trial before the Honorable Judge Leonard P. Stark in the U.S. District Court for the District of Delaware, the court denied the request to stop the merger on April 7. The court stated that it had to follow the Supreme Court's ruling in *Ohio v. American Express Co.* (2018), which meant that Sabre and Farelogix were not considered competitors in the relevant market. This was despite the court's own findings showing that the two companies did compete. However, just two days later, the Competition & Markets Authority (CMA) in the United Kingdom determined that the merger was against U.K. competition law.

With the COVID-19 pandemic impact on travel and Sabre's financial position at that time, Sabre and Farelogix announced on May 1, 2020 that they terminated their merger agreement. The pandemic and the failed Farelogix merger impacted Sabre's competitiveness and recovery.

10.4.4 Allegiant and Sun Country

In January 2026, Las Vegas-based LCC Allegiant Air and Minneapolis-based LCC Sun Country Airlines announced plans for a merger to create a more competitive leisure focused US carrier. The $1.5 billion stock and cash deal requires approval from US anti-trust regulatory agencies. If approved, the combined airline would operate 200 aircraft, serve 22 million passengers, and operate more that 650 routes across 195 cities including international destinations.

This proposed merger will strength the combined airline against larger competitors like United Airlines, Delta Air Lines, American Airlines and Southwest Airlines which control 70% of the US domestic market. Unlike the JetBlue—Spirit merger that was blocked by the DOJ, the business models of these two airlines are more complementary than duplicative and have limited route overlap. Sun Country Airlines also operates a significant charter business. This makes it more likely that the DOJ will grant approval for the proposed merger.

10.5 The 2024 Business Travel News Survey

The BTN Annual Survey [Airoldi, 2024 h] reports how corporate buyers rank U.S. airlines It indicates how difficult it is to rebuild an airline brand following numerous missteps. Business Travel News conducted its yearly airline survey from September 25 to October 25. They asked a selected group of their audience to rate airlines from 1 to 5 on 11 different criteria. The 587 respondents in the survey included corporate travel buyers and travel agents. Participants shared their experiences regarding partnerships with these airlines over the prior year. Buyers whose annual airline spend was less than $500,000 did not rate individual carriers. All buyers were limited to rating carriers with whom they held contracts or flew a significant volume in the previous 12 months.

In the survey, Delta Air Lines achieved an impressive 14-th year as the top-rated airline in the survey, earning a score of 4.32 on a scale from 1 to 5. Southwest Airlines, in second place for the third consecutive year, closed the gap with a score of 4.21. United Airlines held onto third place with a steady score of 3.69, also for three years running. American Airlines finished last, again for the third year, with a rating of 2.15. Alaska Airlines entered BTN's survey for the first time, finishing in fourth place. Figure 10.2 illustrates the relative position of the five carriers.

The 11 categories used in the survey are shown in Table 10.2. Clearly the survey was a rejection of American's corporate strategy.

The survey results do not necessarily reflect relative corporate share. Network relevance and the strength of loyalty programs influence corporate share performance.

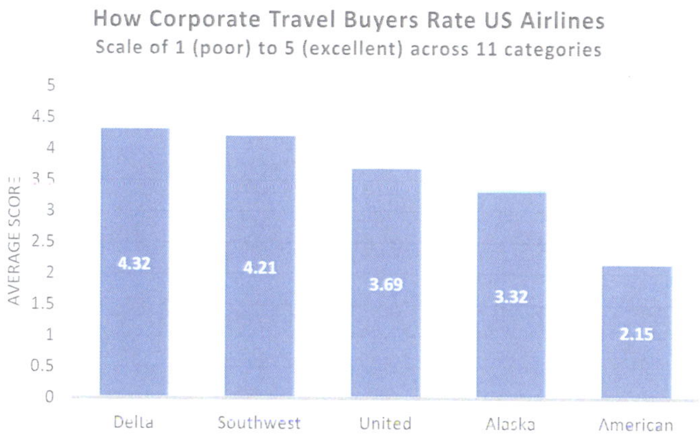

Source Business Travel News 2024 Airline Survey and Report

Fig. 10.2 Survey response summary.

Table 10.2 Survey Results by Category

Categories in the survey	DL	WN	UA	AS	AA	Average
Flexibility in transient pricing & contract negotiation	4.35	4.25	3.62	3.46	2.00	3.54
Flexibility in meeting pricing & contract negotiation	4.39	4.26	3.47	3.51	1.99	3.52
Flexibility in negotiating services & amenities	4.18	4.07	3.57	3.07	1.91	3.36
Distribution channels	4.36	4.22	3.74	3.56	1.98	3.67
Complaint / problem resolution	4.42	4.31	3.77	3.58	1.99	3.61
Quality of client communications	4.41	4.36	3.73	3.15	2.09	3.55
Value relationship with account managers & sales reps	4.36	4.45	3.65	2.99	1.78	3.44
Quality of customer service	4.49	4.28	3.79	3.55	2.27	3.68
Quality of data and reporting tools	4.19	4.21	3.74	2.82	2.11	3.41
Networks, partnerships & frequencies	4.32	3.78	3.91	3.20	3.04	3.65
Overall price value	4.05	4.16	3.63	3.65	2.52	3.60
OVERALL RATING	**4.32**	**4.21**	**3.69**	**3.32**	**2.15**	
	1	**2**	**3**	**4**	**5**	

DL: Delta Air Lines, WN: Southwest Airlines, UA: United Airlines, AS: Alaska Airlines, AA: American Airlines
Source Business Travel News 2024 Airline Survey and Report

10.6 Successfully Negotiating B2B Contracts

Negotiation plays a vital role in all aspects of a business's operations. The art of negotiation significantly affects the company's profitability and overall market value. In the travel distribution space contract renewals play a critical role in the long-term sustainability of companies. Airlines, GDSs, TMCs, and OTAs are the four primary entities that enter into contracts for the distribution of air products. Specifically:

1. Airline *and* GDS, TMC, OTA
2. GDS *and* Airline, TMC, OTA
3. TMC and GDS, Airline, OTA
4. OTA and Airline, GDS

We shall now examine GDS-Airline contracts and GDS-OTA contracts.

10.6.1 GDS-Airline and GDS-OTA Contracts

Airline content is fundamental for the existence of the GDS business model, without which the GDSs will eventually cease to exist. When new airline-GDS contracts are negotiated, the process must be rational, against the backdrop of a rapidly evolving landscape of airline product distribution, both technology and business.

Rational decision making is a fundamental skill in GDS-Airline contract negotiations. Airline negotiators must have a deep knowledge of the importance of corporate travel, which is primarily delivered through the GDS, and areas where they can seek allowances from the GDS vendors. Occasionally an airline goes over the deep end with irrational views on how it wants to distribute its products in the marketplace. In such situations it is impossible to have a constructive dialogue. These negotiations are difficult and will have a higher failure rate.

When an airline and a GDS do not agree on a new participation contract, both sides suffer. Typically, GDSs hold short-term power over airlines, while airlines maintain long-term strength in the relationship. The longer an airline can manage any immediate financial loss, the more powerful they become in negotiations.

10.6.1.1 Turkish Airlines Content in the Sabre GDS

In late August 2024, Turkish Airlines, and Sabre failed to renew their contract. Hence, Turkish Airlines content would no longer be available through Sabre travel agencies [Arena, 2024]. There were no winners in this outcome. Turkish Airlines, the nineth largest airline in the world based on revenue, needed corporate customers through the Sabre channel and Sabre needs Turkish Airlines, which has seen double digit growth in traffic in recent years. In the meantime, Turkish Airlines announced agreements with several NDC Aggregators such as Travelfusion, Verteil, DRCT, Mystifly, Nuua, Nuflights and Theta which would connect to the Turkish Airlines portal TKConnect. Ar that time the connection had not been launched. The airline claimed these were "strategic" partnerships, but I see nothing "strategic" about it. These are "reactionary partnerships", an outcome of a failed negotiation with Sabre to reach a new agreement. As an airline with one of the highest growth potentials after the pandemic of 2020, Turkish Airlines required a strategy to acquire corporate customers on transatlantic flights where it has increased capacity by 7.7% [Arena, 2024]. These NDC Aggregators would not deliver these much-wanted corporate bookings on trans-atlantic flights, but the GDSs could with their scale.

It was in Sabre's best interests to bring Turkish Airlines back to the negotiating table to make the economics work since Turkish Airlines bookings will continue to flow through competitors Travelport and Amadeus. Sabre needs Turkish Airlines and Turkish Airlines needs Sabre to deliver corporate bookings on those transatlantic flights.

Turkish Airlines returned to the Sabre GDS with a new multi-year agreement that includes NDC support. This agreement, effective June 24, 2025, marks the end of a 10-month absence after the airline exited Sabre in September 2024. The new deal allows travel agencies to access Turkish Airlines content through Sabre, including NDC-enabled offers.

10.6.1.2 Air Transat and Sabre

There were questions about whether Air Transat, a Montreal-based leisure carrier, and Sabre would reach a distribution agreement in August 2024. If they did not, Air Transat content would not have been available in Sabre after September 17. Air Transat customers could still book travel through Travelport and Amadeus, direct connect programs and through the Transat Agent Direct portal. On the brink of termination, Air Transat and Sabre renewed their distribution agreement in September 2024.

10.6.1.3 Expedia and Sabre

While contracts between airlines and GDSs are important, so are the contracts between OTAs and GDSs. An example of this is when Sabre and Expedia failed to reach an agreement in November 2021 and Expedia made the decision to shift a significant portion of its GDS business in North America away from Sabre [Schaal, 2021]. With this move, Amadeus saw a boost in bookings, which enabled them to grow market share in North America where they were (and still are) in third place behind Sabre and Travelport.

Not all bookings are created equal. OTA bookings are less profitable for a GDS than TMC bookings. This is because the incentives demanded by the OTA from GDSs are higher than the incentives paid to TMCs. While OTAs like Expedia demand higher incentives than TMCs [Vinod, 2024a], the question that Sabre should have answered is "*what is the true cost of servicing an incremental Expedia booking*? Failure to negotiate a contract resulted in loss of market share for Sabre in North America and for the next two years Sabre reported their market share with and without Expedia bookings in their quarterly earnings reports.

In the Amadeus Q1 2024 earnings report, they confirmed that Expedia has decided to adopt their NDC technology, further augmenting its partnership with Expedia.

10.6.1.4 Negotiation Training

Perhaps it will be bast for key individuals in their respective organizations to get trained in the art of negotiation. There are many vendors in the market. Interestingly, award-winning American Way, the bi-weekly magazine which stopped circulating in June 2021, used to carry a full two-page ad in every issue of the *Karrass Negotiating Classes* course to help the reader to find the best deal for both parties. American Way magazine may be gone, but Karrass is still in business (www.karrass.com).

10.6.2 GDS-TMC Relationship and the Future of Incentives

By default, the GDSs are aggregators of NDC content. As the GDSs enable more airline NDC connections and take on the new-entrant NDC Aggregators. the GDS share of global bookings is expected to increase year over year. This is because TMCs prefer booking NDC content through a GDS which ensures a streamlined workflow and back-office reconciliation.

Today the relationship between GDSs and TMCs are very solid. With NDC adoption, incentives to travel agencies from GDSs will decline over time. Some critics argue that NDC adoption will accelerate when GDS incentives to travel agencies disappear. Unlike the new entrant GDS aggregators, the GDS still receives a segment booking fee from airlines for GDS NDC bookings. But the economics of the GDS NDC booking fees is very different from EDIFACT bookings. GDS NDC bookings only receive a fraction of the traditional EDIFACT segment booking fees and the GDSs will not furnish incentives to travel agencies. In a world without incentives, will the GDS partnership with TMCs survive? It is an open question.

10.7 Addressing NDC Deficiencies Supports Adoption

Some airlines have taken NDC and turned it into a tool for fighting what they see as important but not technologically relevant commercial issues. However, this does not eliminate the need to address the gaps in the NDC workflow. The focus of NDC should not be about channel shifting but on ensuring that all channels are valued by customers. All channels must be capable of generating revenue efficiently and promoting customer satisfaction at a reasonable price point that is acceptable by airlines and intermediaries.

Do airlines understand the true needs of travel advisors when it comes to their NDC offering? The definitive answer is *no*. For TMCs to enable corporate travel with an NDC connection to an airline, there are many gaps. These gaps exist since airlines are not experienced in how travel agencies provide service to their corporate customers. This list is by no means comprehensive.

1. Booking and holding tickets for corporate travel is a fundamental requirement. If businesses must invoke instant ticketing for every booking, they must abandon their pre-trip approval process. Most are not willing to do that.
2. Most tickets sold by TMCs to corporate employees are paid for using corporate credit cards that employees cannot access. Asking for CVV numbers (Card Verification Value, a 3 or 4-digit number printed on the back of credit cards and not stored on the card's chip), which cannot be stored due to PCI regulations, creates an issue.
3. Corporate travelers become frustrated when airlines show complete itineraries consisting of outbound and inbound flights and the combination of outbound and inbound flights they desire was not offered. The airlines can overcome this issue in multiple ways. One option is to provide shopping results by flight leg so that customers can mix and match flight legs to create their own combination. A second option is to support a system where, after selecting one flight, additional itinerary choices can be offered that include the selected flight.
4. Travel agencies need a breakdown of the price for each leg in the OfferPrice and OrderRetrieve API calls. Without this information, they cannot generate reports that show customer spending by airline and route. This breakdown is essential for customers, especially on multi-leg trips where individual leg prices are unclear. The NDC schema and EDIFACT support this requirement, so it is unclear why some airlines have removed it.
5. In the corporate travel marketplace, many companies and travelers have significant amounts of money tied up in unused ticket credits. These credits need to be easy to redeem. However, some NDC deployments do not allow the redemption of credits at all, while others only accept certain types of credits, like EDIFACT credits or Miscellaneous Charges Orders (MCOs). Electronic Miscellaneous Documents (EMDs) are the industry standard documents that replaced other miscellaneous documents. Additionally, some systems do not let users apply credits to bookings that are not yet ticketed. This is critical because customers may not realize at the start of their booking process that they want to redeem an unused ticket or they might not prioritize it because it is not their personal finances. TMCs and travel managers must effectively handle ticket credits for their travelers, including the ability to apply credits during the booking and ticketing process.
6. An NDC order can only be retrieved by the booking creator, which in most cases is the TMC's NDC Aggregator or Internet Booking Engine (IBE). Hence, even if it is the agent's booking, they cannot re-retrieve it. NDC Aggregators must provide a Pseudo City Code (PCC) bridge like the GDS PCC access data rules. NDC Aggregators must also establish an agency hierarchy. Larger agencies may have multiple PCCs, with a head office PCC providing access to all bookings made within the company, while individual agents have their own PCC with restricted access.

   A GDS PCC is a unique code assigned to a travel agency office within a GDS which controls the level of access to data, essentially determining what information an agent can see and what bookings they can make, often restricting access to only bookings made through their specific agency or office, ensuring data privacy and fare availability based on negotiated agreements with airlines; this code is typically 3 to 5 characters long (alpha, numeric or combination depending on the GDS) and is used to identify the agency when making reservations and accessing private fares.

7. A related issue is waivers. After an unplanned schedule change, travel agents can use a waiver code to prevent penalties or fees. It is necessary to fill in the Reason for Issuance field for these involuntary schedule changes. Tickets purchased through the GDS using EDIFACT, often takes longer to apply the waiver than NDC bookings.
8. In several small and medium sized businesses, travelers may book directly with the airline. TMCs must have access to their travelers' direct bookings, so that no matter how a traveler prefers to book, a company has the visibility, control, and provide the duty of care that they value most.

10.8 Impact of Content Fragmentation in the Digital Era

Content fragmentation in the digital era is not specific to travel. The digital age, while offering tremendous opportunities, has also ushered in the era of content fragmentation, a pervasive challenge across nearly all industries. For example, in advertising and media production, marketers are faced with the challenge of reaching dispersed audiences and must adopt a multi-channel marketing strategy, and engage with influencers to reach niche segments. The abundance of online information and content raises challenges in healthcare and education. The challenge is to ensure accuracy, stop misinformation, address disparities in digital literacy, and motivate individuals to seek reliable information online.

Content fragmentation results in data management complexity, higher operating costs, and difficulty in maintaining consistency. It impacts the entire value chain and most notably travel suppliers, and intermediaries like GDSs and TMCs.

Sabre's global survey on content fragmentation [Sabre, 2025a] shows a clear trend. The specific findings of the survey are:

1. 75% of travel agencies say the number of content connections has grown over the past three years.
2. 80% + travel agencies believe unified access through a single platform would reduce technology costs.
3. Nearly 90% of agencies surveyed manage four or more API integrations, with over half citing the technology as a burden.

Multiple connections lead to higher costs for travel agencies and make it harder to offer good service to customers. The survey is an acknowledgement that content fragmentation has become worse over the past decade.

With NDC adoption, price transparency will slowly disappear from the marketplace. The absence of public fares for comparison shopping is not good for the consumer or the airline industry. Perhaps to address the complexity of content fragmentation in today's multi-sourced (GDS EDIFACT, NDC, LCC content) environment, GDSs are best positioned to serve the travel agencies with a single connection. They already do the multi-source content aggregation and product normalization, and perhaps the pace needs to be accelerated as more airlines adopt NDC. Price transparency will disappear with NDC.

10.8.1 What Does Content Fragmentation Mean for the Airline Industry?

Content chaos is detrimental to the future of the airline industry. It impacts airlines, GDSs, TMCs and above all the paying corporate and leisure travelers.

In all areas of technology, the best products that genuinely benefit customers tend to succeed. When customers see real value in innovation, they quickly adopt these offerings. Strong product benefits make it easy for people to want to use them.

On the other hand, poor-quality products rarely gain wide acceptance. Even if strong efforts are made to push them, they usually fail. Customers will not switch to solutions that do not meet their needs or provide clear advantages. No amount of pressure can force business entities and customers to use products that lack value.

Content fragmentation negatively impacts the airline industry by increasing operational costs, creating inconsistent customer experiences, and causing lost revenue opportunities. It forces travel agencies and airlines to manage multiple systems and data sources, leading to complexity, inefficiency, and difficulties in areas like real-time transaction processing, cross-selling ancillaries, and accurate demand forecasting. The issues are exacerbated by new standards like NDC which can make it harder to compare fares and find the best options across different channels.

10.9 AI Agents and the Evolving Air Distribution Landscape

In the hybrid NDC era, a booking made through NDC Aggregators and travel agency to airline direct NDC connections is disintermediation of the GDS. Regardless, airlines continue to distribute fares through ATPCO and GDSs continue to generate offers for customers based on EDIFACT content. GDS offer creation is a one-step process where they have access to fares and availability for all airlines that participate in the GDSs.

All that is about to change with AI Agents in the hybrid era. AI Agents can shop and create personalized offers by sourcing content directly from airlines. This is important for corporate travel and for leisure travel. AI Agents, acting on behalf of individual consumers, both corporate and leisure, can create a highly fragmented online flight shopping experience, tailoring offers and recommendations based on individual preferences and real-time market data. These agents can aggregate, prioritize, and recommend flight and ancillary offers across various sources, potentially bypassing traditional intermediaries. The Model Context Protocol (MCP) and the Agent-to-Agent (A2A) protocols support the introduction of autonomous multi-agent systems and the Agent-to-Agent (A2A) protocol, there is much uncertainty about the role for ATPCO and the GDSs in the future.

The impact of AI Agents on the GDS business model for corporate and leisure travel will be minimal for the next few years, until 2030, because it takes time for airlines to stand up scalable MCP servers, and negotiate contracts with operators of AI Agents for secure access, booking fee per transaction, commissions, and permissions, The near term impact will be on metasearch and the direct channel. Ultimately, AI Agents will increase direct sales and lower the cost of distribution.

10.9.1 Digital IDs

Digital ID offers secure verification and supports various services through web or mobile apps that require proof of identity. It can bring major economic and social gains, such as reduced expenses and better access to finance, society, and politics. So far, governments worldwide have started about 165 digital or partly digital ID systems. Yet, results vary. Just a handful have reached strong usage levels. Often, people use them rarely, like once or twice a year on average in certain nations [Domeyer, McCarthy, Pfeiffer, Scherf, 2020].

Digital IDs and wallets represent the future of travel. By default, they facilitate more direct interaction between travel suppliers (airlines, hotels) and consumers, or even directly between travel businesses in a B2B setting. Digital IDs and digital wallets promote the idea of a customer taking back control of their data and how it is used. The Universal Profile that is owned by the customer is stored in the digital wallet and a customer can give selective access to attributes in the profile to entities including AI Agents to receive targeted offers.

These trends in adoption of NDC, AI Agents, digital IDs, and digital wallets weaken the value proposition of intermediaries in the travel value chain.

See Chap. 17 for an in-depth discussion of Agentic AI and travel planning for corporate and leisure customers.

Hotel Distribution

11

Knowledge is power

Sir Francis Bacon

Abstract

Hotel distribution provides a stark contrast to airline distribution. Unlike air, the cost of customer acquisition is an order of magnitude higher which impacts hotel profits. The fragmented nature of the hotel industry results in independent hotels and smaller hotel chains being exploited by the online travel agencies (OTAs). This chapter discusses the cost of hotel distribution by channel, including the direct channel, global distribution systems (GDS), bed banks, and OTAs. The differences between the merchant model and the agency model are evaluated. In the B2B space, the OTAs affiliate programs provide access to vast content that OTAs have on their platforms, thereby increasing penetration with agencies.

Investing in a search engine optimization (SEO) strategy for branded keywords is an absolute necessity to boost direct bookings. To increase margins, hoteliers must dominate AI Search and traditional search. Forward-looking hoteliers have an opportunity to take control of hotel distribution with attribute-based room pricing. There are numerous steps hoteliers can also take to preserve hotel margins and promote the direct channel. The chapter concludes with the promise of autonomous AI agents that will drive an increase in hotel direct bookings. AI Agents will bypass traditional sales channels, and the survival of intermediaries will depend on access to unique content on their platforms.

B. Vinod, *The Era of Airline Revenue Management with Offers and Orders*, Management for Professionals, https://doi.org/10.1007/978-3-032-24197-9_11

Sir Francis Bacon (1561–1626) was an English philosopher and statesman who served as Attorney General and Lord Chancellor of England under King James I of England, He popularized the concept that "knowledge is power", though the exact phrase he used is debated. The Latin aphorism "ipsa scientia potestas est," meaning "knowledge itself is power," appears in his 1597 work *Meditationes Sacrae*. He conveyed that possessing and sharing knowledge is the foundation for reputation, influence, and achievement, highlighting its importance in both personal growth and societal advancement. Bacon believed that knowledge grants power by enabling people to influence outcomes, make informed decisions, and gain reputation.

This quote is very relevant in the world of hotel product distribution where the cost of customer acquisition is exorbitantly high in the dominant channels. Hoteliers must have a laser focus on the cost of customer acquisition by channel since the costs vary widely to influence outcomes. To maximize profits, hotels must analyze their transaction data in depth and make strategic decisions that balance broad market reach with direct, higher-margin bookings.

11.1 Introduction

A discussion on air distribution in Chaps. 9 and 10 in the context of airline retailing will be incomplete without an overview of an adjacent vertical—hotels. Air and hotel segments combined account for nearly three quarters of global travel gross bookings [PhocusWright Research, 2025]. While suppliers led online bookings in 2024, online travel agencies retain their edge in the hotel segment, where fragmentation favors intermediaries.

Hotel distribution is a stark contrast to airline distribution due to the fragmented nature of hotel inventory with the existence of independents, and hotel chains of various sizes. The GDSs face tremendous revenue pressure caused by NDC. This has led to disintermediation caused by direct connect between airlines and travel agencies using the NDC protocol, the slow demise of full content agreements, and new competition from NDC Aggregators. At the same time, OTAs dominate the hotel distribution landscape, and are incredibly profitable by exploiting the fragmentation of room inventory in the hotel industry.

The average cost of air distribution through the indirect channel is approximately 2.1% and that is where the battle lines are being drawn between airlines and GDSs. In contrast, online travel agencies (OTAs) like Expedia and Booking.com charge between 20–35% of the value of the transaction, depending on the contract and the type of commercial model, merchant versus agency.

The hotel room product is typically sold through the direct channel (online website and offline call center), and intermediaries such as bed banks, Global Distribution Systems (GDS) and Online Travel Agencies (OTA). The channel costs for hoteliers vary widely. Mark Weinstein, the global head of customer engagement, loyalty and partnerships at Hilton Worldwide made this remark in 2020 [Dupler-Fornova, 2020].

In 2015, 57 billion Hilton HHonors Points—or more than 1.6 million free nights—went unearned because guests booked their stay through a third party. There is a huge misconception that third parties always offer lower prices for our hotel rooms, which is simply not true.

–Mark Weinstein

The high costs of hotel distribution, especially through OTAs, remain a major concern for industry leaders. While OTAs help hotels reach more guests, their oversized commissions cut into profits. This has led hotels to focus more on improving how they distribute rooms and to push for more direct bookings.

Of the four major travel verticals, hospitality is the most dependent on the OTAs. Over 52% of all online reservations for hotels were generated by the OTAs [Phocuswright, 2025]. After hotels, rental cars, cruise lines and airlines follow in that order. For airlines less than 15% of online bookings originate from OTAs.

11.2 Hotel Distribution Channels

The primary channels of distribution for hotels are shown below in Fig. 11.1. They are the hotel website, call center, OTAs, GDSs and metasearch sites. Strategically, to maximize bookings and minimize empty rooms, participation in all channels of distribution is a requirement. However, to maximize revenues, channel mix is important. This requires a distribution strategy based on location, the target audience, and an advertising budget.

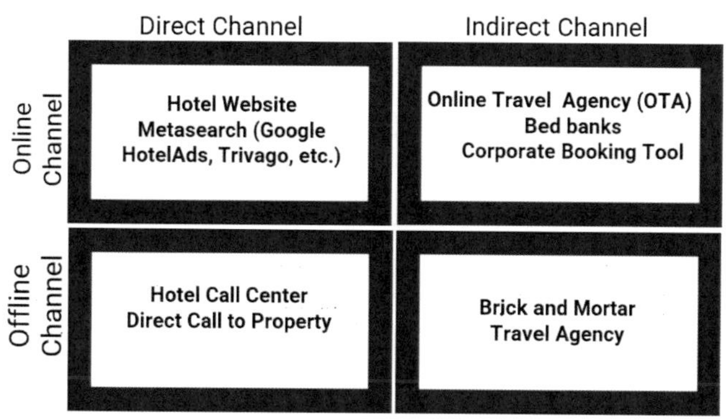

Fig. 11.1 Primary channels for hotel distribution

11.2.1 The Direct Channel

From a hotelier's perspective the direct channel is the most important since it has the lowest cost of customer acquisition. To attract direct bookings, loyalty points for stays can only be accrued with direct bookings and bookings made through a GDS by a travel agent. Bookings made through bed banks like Bedsonline and OTAs like Expedia and Booking.com cannot accrue hotel loyalty points. Some OTAs have their own loyalty programs for customers who book hotel stays through them.

11.2.2 Global Distribution Systems

The GDS channel is a relatively inexpensive channel for hotel bookings. Customers can accrue hotel loyalty points for bookings made through a GDS if the booking is made through a travel agent that is connected to the hotel's reservation system.

In addition, the hotels pay a commission to the travel agency for making the booking. Onyx CenterSource, Travel Agency Commission Payment (TACP) from NTT Data, and CTS Systems serve as intermediaries for commission management and reporting. They enable the timely payment of commissions from the hotels to the travel agencies.

11.2.3 Bed Banks

Bed banks are B2B wholesalers that purchase rooms from accommodation providers in bulk at a discounted static rate for specific future check-in dates and sell them to travel agents, OTAs, airlines, destination management companies, and tour operators. A bed bank's B2B platform links hotel providers with travel companies needing rooms. The room inventory is distributed through a large network of travel agents. Bed banks are favored by the large leisure properties. With advances in technology, these platforms are also available to smaller properties such as boutique hotels, inns and vacation rentals.

Generally, customers do not accrue hotel loyalty points for bookings made through a bed bank. As wholesale suppliers of hotel rooms to travel agencies, hoteliers do not allow customers to accrue hotel loyalty points.

Buyers such as tour operators, airlines, travel agencies, or organizers of events purchase this inventory. They then sell the rooms to their customers such as travelers, airline passengers, or conference attendees and the guests have no idea that the room came from a bed bank. Hotels offer rooms at set prices along with detailed content like photos and amenities through the bed bank. Travel sellers use this information to promote and sell rooms to their clients. Most bed banks provide a booking portal and a set of APIs for their B2B partners to access their inventory. When a room is booked, the bed bank sends details like dates and guest contact information to the hotel using APIs or XML messages. This sharing of reservation information helps hotels manage their bookings smoothly. Bed banks also offer car rentals, ground transfers, and destination activities.

The leading bed banks are Hotelbeds, WebBeds, HPro Travel, Bonotel, Travco, GRNconnect and Yalago.

Hotelbeds is the largest bed bank and claim to have over 300,000 hotels, the majority if not all are its own direct contracts with hoteliers. By contrast, Webjet's WebBeds has 90,000 direct contracts. This includes 5600 it picked up with $173 million acquisition of Destinations of the World from asset management firm Gulf Capital. Both Hotelbeds and WebBeds have a significant global presence with a strong focus on Europe and Asia Pacific.

Direct contracts are key, because margins are higher compared with bookings drawn from third-parties. The majority of the new contracts from Destinations of the World (56%) is from Asia-Pacific, which is a key strategic focus of WebBeds.

The discounted rate negotiated between the accommodation provider and the bed bank is marked up and sold to travel agents. Hotelbeds, the largest wholesale hotel room provider for offline travel agencies, primarily generate revenue through commission-based sales, making it easier to preserve integrity in rate parity agreements. This commission is typically a percentage of the total transaction value. They connect accommodation and other travel suppliers with travel agents, tour operators, and other resellers, earning a commission on the transactions. Hotelbeds also leverages technology and data to connect these parties, offering value-added services like financial solutions and an innovation hub. Bed banks make the claim that they operate exclusively in the B2B arena and provide incremental bookings for its hotel partners that do not compete with their direct marketing efforts. But the commissions are steep and can be as high as 20–25%.

The ideal cost-effective solution for a hotelier is for all bookings to be made directly on the hotel website. While bed banks are not cheap for a hotelier, they do offer the following benefits:

1. Market Reach. A bed bank provides a hotelier with access to guests that they could never attract on their own to their website. Examples are conference attendees, affinity groups and international travelers.
2. Channel Efficiency. Relationship with a bed bank reduces the need to sign contracts and provide reservations system connectivity with myriad smaller channels.
3. Less Expensive than OTAs. While the bed bank commission can range from 21 to 25%, OTA commissions and their associated hidden charges can range from 25 to 35%.
4. Diverse High Value Reservations. While the average daily rate (ADR) may be lower than other channels, bed bank reservations have unique attributes such as longer length of stays, lower cancellation rates and longer booking windows.
5. Incremental Bookings. Bed banks provide an occupancy boost during periods of low demand and shoulder seasons.

6. Reliable Payments. A bed bank's customers are all businesses, not individual travelers. This means the risk of non-payment is much lower than with regular guests. Hoteliers often face chargebacks or guests who book through OTAs with fake credit cards. In these cases, hotels have little or no recourse to recover the money.

11.2.4 Online Travel Agencies (OTAs)

OTAs are the dominant channel for hotel bookings that adversely impact hotel profits. One percent of online gross bookings could account for $1 billion worth of business, which would translate to commissions in the $100 million to $200 million range [King, 2023].

There are three primary business models used by the OTAs to generate revenues. They are advertising, the agency business model and the merchant business model.

The advertising model provides advertising services and leads. These include:

1. Sponsored listings. These are similar to Google search ads, appearing at the top of search results pages and within an OTA's travel site. These ads appear above search results when travelers are actively searching for flights, hotels, or other travel-related services. Hotels, airlines, and other travel businesses can bid on keywords and specific travel details to ensure their listings appear prominently when relevant searches are made. Sponsored listings is paid advertising where hotels pay for higher placement in search results
2. Display-based advertising. These are the banner ads, and the pricing model is a cost per mille (CPM) or cost per thousand impressions and subscription-based advertising. Display ads are designed to engage travelers at different stages of the booking journey, from initial research to the final decision to book.
3. Subscription-based advertising. This is a self-service advertising platform that offers sponsored listings and other ad formats. This is a contract for a specific period of time with a travel supplier. A small bed-and-breakfast, for example, would cost a few hundred dollars per year.

This is the primary revenue stream for companies like Tripadvisor.

For the large OTAs, this is a relatively small revenue stream. For example, for Expedia is it less than a billion dollars for annual revenues of $16 billion in 2024. The primary source of revenue for OTAs are commissions derived from the merchant model and the agency model for hotel bookings.

11.2.5 Metasearch

A metasearch engine is an acquisition channel that provides price comparison shopping and several booking options for a customer such as the hotel website or an OTA to complete the booking. While an OTA owns the customer, a metasearch engine does not. Some of the largest metasearch engines are Google Hotel Ads, Kayak, Tripadvisor, and Trivago.

Metasearch for hotel bookings acts as a hybrid (e.g. Tripadvisor, a metasearch engine that also facilitates bookings for hotels, restaurants and experiences directly through its platform, blurring the lines between metasearch and OTA and they are not a full-fledged OTA). They display OTA links and hotel links and let the user make the selection.

Metasearch engines aggregate rates from third-party OTAs and hotel websites, it functions as an advertising platform that directs users to the hotel's own website or OTAs (e.g., Booking.com, Expedia, etc.) to finalize the booking. Unlike OTAs, metasearch engines encourage direct bookings by placing the hotel's website link alongside several OTAs in the display, allowing the hotel to own the guest relationship.

Metasearch engines operate primarily on a pay-per-click (PPC) model. OTAs and hotels pay a fee for every click, regardless of whether it results in a booking. When an online user selects a hotel to view the available selling rates, the display is dominated by several OTAs with their respective selling rates. The hotel website may also not appear on the display screen if the hotel did not bid for ad placement. The highest bidder often gets the top position, but algorithms also consider price competitiveness, landing page quality, and ad relevance.

With their multibillion-dollar marketing budgets, OTAs bid aggressively on branded keywords and most references from Google Hotel Ads, Kayak, Tripadvisor and Trivago ultimately reach the hotel as an OTA booking.

PPC is synonymous with cost-per-click (CPC) and the two terms are used interchangeably. While PPC is standard, some platforms offer cost-per-acquisition (CPA) or commission-per-stay (CPS). With CPA payment is generally calculated when a booking is made but it is often invoiced after the guest stay at the property. With CPS payment is made after a completed stay. CPS is synonymous with pay-per-stay (PPS).

While OTAs provide comparison shopping on their websites, they are not metasearch sites since they do not feature hotel rates from other hotel intermediaries (OTAs).

11.3 The OTA Merchant Model and the Agency Model

In the B2C space there are two primary operating models that OTAs use to facilitate hotel bookings by online users. They are the merchant model and the pay at checkout (PAC) model. The PAC model is commonly referred to as the agency model.

With the agency model, the customer settles the final price for the stay with the hotel either at the time of booking or checkout. Therefore, the OTA or agency does not process consumer payments directly. Instead, each supplier still owns their respective inventory and is responsible for processing payments. The hotel pays the taxes collected from the customer to the state. Every month, the hotel determines the commission to be remitted to the OTAs.

With the merchant model, the customer pays the full final price to the OTA or agency when the booking is made. After the customer checks out of the property, the OTA periodically pays the net merchant rate (total price minus the OTA's commission) to the hotel. The payment frequency is not standardized. Some OTAs may pay weekly, others monthly, or even after a batch of bookings. In this model, the OTA acts as a travel service provider rather than an intermediary between travel products and services and the end customer. The net merchant rate is the price for the stay net of the merchant commissions and taxes.

In the merchant model, the OTA typically pays the hotel for a booking after the guest's stay, not at the time of booking. The payment is usually the net amount (total price minus the OTA's commission). The specific payment frequency and method (e.g., invoice, virtual credit card) can vary. The OTA collects the full payment, including taxes, from the customer. While OTAs remit the taxes to the state in many jurisdictions, in some cases they pass the collected tax to the hotel, which remains responsible for remitting the tax to the state.

A point of contention has been that OTAs historically calculated the tax only on the *wholesale rate* they paid to the hotel, not the full, marked-up *retail price* the consumer paid. This has led to numerous lawsuits by local governments seeking to recover lost revenue. Forty-five states and Washington, D.C., with sales tax obligations have since enacted marketplace facilitator laws to clarify the tax obligations for OTAs and ensure taxes are collected on the full retail amount.

Many OTAs, including Expedia and bed banks operate under the merchant model. For years, Booking.com operated exclusively under the agency model. They did it because it was popular with customers, drove booking volumes, and was popular with hotel operators.

Hotels preferred this model for the following reasons:

1. Positive effects on cash flow.
2. Eliminated the risk of the agency filing for bankruptcy without paying the hotel.
3. Hotels have more information about the customer prior to check-in.
4. Hotels have control over the final price paid by the guest.

However, Booking.com has been gravitating toward the merchant model for the past few years because of sustained growth and higher profits. It is part of their strategy to provide more payment options to consumers and travel service providers. As a result, Booking.com has been steadily increasing the merchant model transactions, where it facilitates payments from travelers for the services provided.

To illustrate this trend, Fig. 11.2 displays the breakdown of the agency versus merchant bookings for Booking.com from 2014 to 2024.

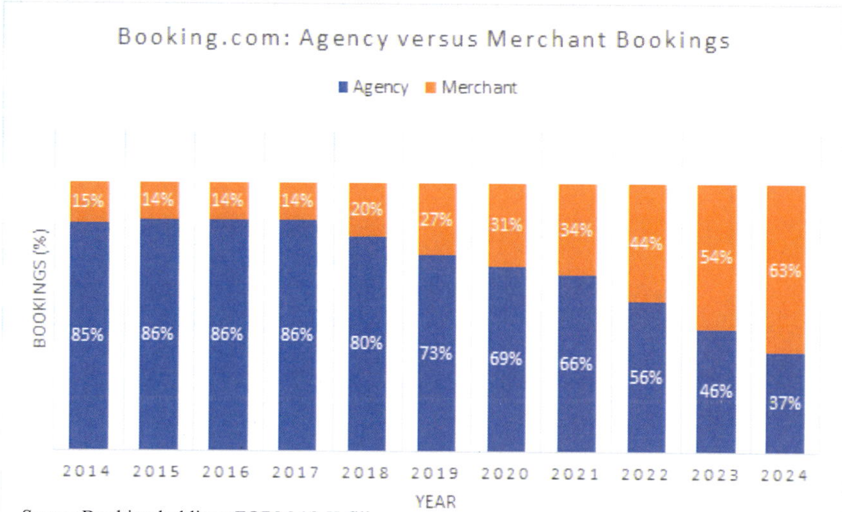

Source Booking holdings FORM 10-K filings

Fig. 11.2 Breakdown of agency versus merchant bookings for Booking.com.

OTAs and bed banks prefer the merchant model for the following reasons. They are:

1. Higher profit margins and greater control over pricing, payments, and customer relationships.
2. It makes the OTA the "merchant of record," which means they handle all payment processing and customer service, providing a more seamless experience and a direct relationship with the customer.
3. Positive impact on cash flow. Since the customer pays on the day the booking is made, regardless of the check-in date, the OTA is the beneficiary of the float.
4. Payment flexibility by dealing with multiple alternate forms of payment and currencies. OTAs can process a wider variety of payment methods and offer customers the option to pay in their local currency, which is more comfortable when traveling. This gives the OTAs the opportunity to play with the foreign exchange rate and generate incremental revenues.
5. OTAs can be ultra-competitive with package offers. For example, flights and hotels can be bundled and offered at a lower price than if they were purchased separately. The merchant model also provides marginal benefits for hotels.
6. Fraud and chargebacks from customers are painful for hotels to handle.

The negatives of the merchant model for hotels are several. They are:

1. Higher cost of customer acquisition with merchant rate commission in the 20–35% range.

2. The OTAs use Virtual Credit Cards (VCC) to pay hotels that come with an added commission that averages 2–3%. VCCs are mostly issued in North America and the European Union. For hotels located outside of these regions, their costs will be even higher due to the additional cross-border fee to process payments.
3. Negative impact on cash flow for pre-paid bookings, since the OTA is the beneficiary.
4. Loss of product differentiation such as upgrades which only exist in the direct channel.
5. Enforcing OTA rate parity agreements with the direct channel is always a challenge, whether it is the website or mobile app.

Despite the high reward from the merchant model, OTAs also face some unique challenges. They are:

1. The financial risk is associated with managing payment processing, taxes, chargebacks, and potential fraud.
2. The cash flow risk is associated with maintaining adequate working capital to pay suppliers before customer payments become available for use.
3. This model requires OTAs to assume the risk of holding inventory, and if they cannot resell it, they may lose money. The OTA inventory is allotment risk inventory, meaning the OTA purchases rooms from the hotel at a wholesale price and takes on the risk of selling those rooms to customers. In contrast, the agency model is a consignment model, where the OTAs act as an agent and only receive a commission, with the hotel retaining all the inventory risk. OTAs mitigate the risk of the merchant model by negotiating contracts with hotels to release unsold rooms to the hotel on a specified cut-off date before the check-in date.

11.4 B2B Products and Online Travel Agencies

The major OTAs also offer B2B products to travel agencies and small and medium-sized businesses (SMB). These are called affiliate programs.

11.4.1 The OTA Affiliate Programs

The OTAs focus on the long tail of smaller travel agencies and SMBs (small and medium-sized businesses) by offering their vast content to generate incremental revenues. Small businesses generally have fewer than 100 employees and/or less than $50 million in annual revenue. Medium-sized businesses typically fall in the range of 100 to 999 employees and/or have revenue between $50 million and $1 billion.

Expedia's Travel Agency Affiliate Program (TAAP) is designed for travel agencies to book flights, accommodations, car rental, and other travel services by providing direct access to its vast inventory and pricing. The travel agencies in TAAP earn commissions based on the value of the bookings they make. There are over 38,000 travel agencies in 32 countries worldwide that are part of the TAAP program. The agencies using TAAP vary significantly, from small businesses to large corporate agencies.

Expedia offers various performance-based commission rates for various types of products. The measure used is gross booking value (GBV). It represents the total amount collected by a participating travel agency from completed travel booking over a time period, net of any coupons or credits provided offered by a party other than Expedia. The GBV tiers are Standard, Silver, Gold, and Platinum for GBV less than 30,000 per year, over 30,000 per year, over 120,000 per year, and over 500,000 per year, respectively. The commission rates are the highest for Platinum, followed by Gold, Silver and Standard. For hotel commissions, within each GBV tier the commissions vary based on the property classification by Expedia as Premium Plus. Premium, Basic Plus and Basic. The commissions range between 3.5 and 13% depending on the GBV tier and the Expedia property classification.

Expedia also has an Affiliate Program which does not require participation in TAAP. This program is much broader than TAAP and intended to attract travel influencers, ultra-small businesses, and individuals. The primary difference from TAAP is that the entity simply send referral traffic to Expedia and earn fees.

In contrast, the Booking.com affiliate program is broader, allowing various partners (e.g., bloggers, websites, travel influencers, travel agencies, ultra-small businesses) to promote Booking.com and earn commissions. Partners do not directly book accommodation on the Booking.com platform. Instead, they promote Booking.com through unique affiliate links and earn a referral commission on bookings made through their affiliate links, once the checkouts exceed a predefined threshold.

Other notable affiliate programs are managed by Tripadvisor, Viator, Sandals Resorts, G Adventures, Agoda, GetYourGuide, Hostelworld, Klook, and many more.

11.5 Should Hotels Invest in Branded Keywords?

Instead of surrendering to the OTAs, investing in branded keywords is an absolute necessity for a hotelier to reinforce brand identity and increase direct bookings, Branded keywords targets users who are already searching for their specific brand, leading to more qualified leads and higher conversion rates.

For branded keywords, it is critical for hotels to use paid search to prevent OTAs from capturing their own brand traffic. The cost of branded keywords is generally lower and more efficient than bidding on generic keywords.

Organic search and paid search complement and amplify each other and should be viewed as a single, unified digital marketing strategy. They have shared goals of visibility, brand recognition and conversion.

The cost of customer acquisition by channel influences the investment in organic search and paid search.

The direct channel for hotels is their own website, phone lines, and social media, which bypass intermediaries and increase profitability.

The direct channel (online bookings) has the lowest cost of customer acquisition (CCA), followed by the GDS, bed banks, and OTAs. Channel costs vary and are usually expressed as a percentage of the total cost of a booking, keeping in step with OTA pricing.

11.5.1 The Direct Online Channel Costs

For the Direct Online Channel, there are costs associated with web hosting, maintenance, campaigns, and website analytics In addition there is the cost for a booking engine, typically provided by a third party. The booking engine fee is usually based on the value of the transaction and can range from 1.5 to 3%.

11.5.2 Call Center—Direct Offline Channel Costs

Many consider the traditional call center as an outdated model that is on the decline from a volume of transactions processed perspective. The cost for hotel voice reservation services can vary significantly, from a low of approximately $0.17 per minute for AI-powered voicebots to around $1.75 per call for offshore human-operated services [Goenka, 2025].

Modern SIP (Session Initiation Protocol) trunking is widely used for call centers because it provides advanced features, cost savings, scalability, and flexibility. It allows call centers to handle voice, video, and messaging over an Internet connection, which integrates with cloud platforms and enables features like intelligent call routing, automated dialers, and remote agent support.

The traditional call centers are evolving and being transformed by technology and changing customer preferences, shifting towards what's now known as "contact centers." These centers handle a wider range of interactions beyond just phone calls, including email, social media, and chat. AI and automation are also playing a significant role in streamlining operations and improving customer experience.

11.5.3 Global Distribution Systems Channel Costs

The GDS is the least expensive indirect channel for hotel bookings. Cost components include:

1. GDS fees of $5 to $8 per booking (regardless of length of stay or rate).
2. GDS pass-through fee $5 to $8 per booking

3. Optional Net Merchant rates are available from Expedia, Orbitz, Travelocity, Priceline, and Booking.com The fee varies from $3 to $9 per reservation with no additional commission charge.
4. GDS connection fee per month ($10 to $20)
5. Annual listing fee for a property ($100)
6. Monthly fee ($10 to $20) for the use of VMI (vendor managed inventory) to upload pictures and virtual tours
7. Commission to travel agents (normally 10%)

11.5.4 Bed Banks Channel Costs

Hotels pay bed banks commission for bookings, which is typically between 10 and 25% but can vary based on the type of service and volume. They process bookings as the merchant of record or outsource this responsibility to a reseller (travel agency).

When the bed bank is the merchant of record, the bed bank marks up the wholesale rate negotiated with the hotel and offers the room to the reseller, for a final price. After the room is sold, the bed bank pays the reseller a negotiated commission for the room sold.

When the bed bank is not the merchant of record, the bed bank serves as an intermediary between the hotel and reseller. The bed bank offers the negotiated wholesale rate to the reseller, who marks up the price and sells the room to a customer. The bed bank receives a previously negotiated commission from the hotel for facilitating the booking.

11.5.5 Online Travel Agencies Channel Costs

The OTA merchant model has the highest commissions and can range from 25 to 35%. Most independent hotel bookings made through OTAs like Expedia are highly lucrative and based on the merchant model.

The agency model, also known as the pay at checkout model (PAC), continues to be widely used today for making bookings and the commissions range from 22 to 30%. It is popular because unlike the merchant model where customers pay upfront, payment is only made at checkout. Booking Holdings actively promoted the agency model for many years to grow booking volumes but have made a strategic shift toward the merchant model with its associated incremental revenue benefits.

OTAs display detailed pricing breakdowns, informing the traveler exactly what they are paying without hidden fees. However, situations exist where OTAs may charge hidden fees for processing the booking. Examples are service fees for certain transactions like air only, mobile bookings, packages, credit card fees, upgrades, special amenities, or other services that are not included in the base price. VAT/GST (Value Added Tax/Goods and Services Tax) charges may also apply depending on the location and regulations. These service fees help cover the cost of operating the platform.

11.5.6 Metasearch Channel Costs

For hotels, the cost of participating in metasearch varies based on marketing objectives. Common models include a pay-per-click (PPC) model where hotels pay for clicks on their listings. Some platforms offer a flat fee and a media budget for advertising. Hotels may also pay a cost-per-mille (CPM) to view the ads, although it is less common.

During the pandemic of 2020, cancellation rates were very high due to restrictions and uncertainty in travel. In response, Google introduced its pay-per-stay (PPS) model where a commission was only charged if the customer actually stays at the hotel. Trivago followed, with its Net CPA (Cost Per Acquisition) program, which is similar to Google's PPS. This change is significant since some metasearch engines are no longer just advertising channels, but another distribution channel like OTAs. In February 2025, Google sunset its PPS model and moved primarily to a cost-per-click (CPC) model. Trivago continues to use Net CPA as its primary model, replacing CPC.

For example, Kayak utilizes both cost per click (CPC) regardless of conversion and cost per acquisition (CPA) commission model on completed stays to monetize referrals. Google Hotel Ads primarily operates with a CPC model but also offers commission-per-stay (CPS) for completed stays and a commission-per-acquisition (CPA) for completed bookings. CPS and CPA are designed to drive incremental bookings.

Over the years, metasearch has become less important for hotel occupancy, contributing only about 5% of room nights. With their multibillion-dollar marketing budgets, OTAs bid aggressively on branded keywords and most references from Google Hotel Ads, Kayak, Tripadvisor and Trivago ultimately reach the hotel as an OTA booking.

11.6 David versus Goliath and Countering the OTA Threat

Independents and smaller chains perceive an uphill battle to take on the large OTAs with their marketing might. Frequently, they abandon efforts to invest in the direct channel and leave it to the OTAs to delivery bookings with the hefty commissions.

11.6.1 Marketing Spend

As a rule, hotels including independents must spend 4% of their room revenues on marketing to improve brand presence and steer customers to book direct. They often do not spend this amount, though. The consensus among hoteliers is that

they cannot outspend the OTAs. In 2024 Expedia spent a staggering $6.8 billion on marketing, which represents 49.6% of revenue, while Booking Holdings spent $7.3 billion which was 31% of revenue. Combined, these two mega OTAs spent $14.1 billion on Google Ads, Google Hotel Ads, Google Display Network (GDN) and all other Google marketing formats. Though the OTA marketing spend per hotel in their portfolio is not uniform, this translates into average marketing costs of $200 per property assuming that Expedia and Booking Holdings have three million hotels and alternate accommodations in their respective portfolios. For the sake of argument, if the spend were limited to traditional hotels, there are about 500,000 hotels and this translates into a spend of $1200 per property. Now the fundamental question that very hotelier must answer is: *Can a hotel, large or small, afford to spend $200 per month to increase its Internet presence and steer customers to book directly?*

Google Hotel Ads and Google Ads (previously called Google AdWords) differ in their primary focus, target audience, and ad display. Google Hotel Ads are specifically designed for hotels and other lodging properties, focusing on promoting accommodation and displaying real-time pricing and availability to travelers actively searching for hotels. Hotel Ads are specialized metasearch style ads displaying live rates and availability.

Standard Google Ads, on the other hand, cater to a broader range of businesses and can target a wider audience, with ads appearing in various formats and locations across the Google network. Commonly referred to as click-based advertising, these are the cost-per-click (CPC) ads where the advertiser pays only if the user clicks on the link which will lead them to the advertiser's page. Traditional paid search ads focus on text-based keyword targeting.

Google Display Network is a network of websites, apps, and videos where display ads can be shown.

While the dominance of Google search may diminish over time, it will still influence travel choices for a long time. To get the best return on a hotel's marketing investment and grow the brand presence, bidding on branded keywords remains an essential requirement to increase visibility, safeguard the brand, and boost direct bookings. Examples of branded keywords are "Waldorf Astoria", "Marriott Daytona Beach" or "Westgate Resorts Florida".

Consider an online user that searches for a specific hotel by name. The user sees the following displayed in the SERP (Search Engine Results Pages):

1. Several Google Ads by the OTAs and their affiliates promote the best rate for the named property.
2. Google Hotel Ads (metasearch) again by OTAs and their affiliates.
3. Organic listings of the OTA hotel page, ranking higher than the property's listing due to the OTAs superior SEO.

OTAs aggressively bid on hotel brand names in paid search ads and appear above the hotel's own organic listing. This means they can overshadow the hotel's website, despite their SEO efforts. This tactic, known as *brandjacking,* helps OTAs capture traffic from users looking for the named hotel directly. Some users are aware they want the official site, but many are not and end up clicking on the top result, which is often an OTA, and end up booking through them instead. Brand protection on Google Ads is not a luxury but a fundamental necessity to stay competitive.

Branded keywords are by far the most powerful weapon in a hotel's arsenal to protect the brand with paid search. These users are often ready to book, already thinking about their stay. If this traffic goes to an online travel agency (OTA), the hotel loses the chance for a direct booking. It also misses out on building a direct relationship with the guest and avoiding high commission costs.

In most cases, the traveler may find the listing for the specific named hotel in the SERP and make a booking, but as an OTA booking and not a direct booking. Booking through the OTA for the named hotel might not happen either. When a user visits the OTA page, a prominent section called "You may also consider these hotels" appears. This area shows travelers other hotel choices in the same destination and neighborhood. Some of these options may have better rates, higher star ratings, or a better location. Because of this, the named property in the search might not even be considered, despite positive reviews and recommendations. Users who typically search with branded keywords are meant to be direct customers, those that have stayed previously at the hotel or received a recommendation from a colleague or someone who read positive reviews on social media. The OTA that successfully bid on the keyword has converted a direct booking to an OTA booking, eroding a hotel's margins.

11.6.2 Reinvent Loyalty Programs to Accelerate Direct Bookings

The largest hotel loyalty programs are Marriott Bonvoy with 228 million members and Hilton Honors with 210 million members. Are these customers satisfied with the loyalty programs that are built around loyalty point accumulation and perks such as room upgrades? To accelerate the growth of direct bookings, hotel loyalty programs that have been around for decades must be reinvented. Looking beyond stored preferences on the customer profile, in the AI-enabled era, natural language processing (NLP) will play a key role in inferring consumer intent by analyzing guest language across chats, emails, and reviews for hotels to anticipate and respond intelligently to customer touchpoints. The discerning guests seek unique experiential rewards like private cooking classes, exclusive local partnerships, and personalized wellness programs. The experience offered to guests must be unique to the brand that competitors cannot easily replicate.

11.6.3 Large Hotel Chains Must Support Unique Capabilities in the Direct Channel

Investment in the consumer direct channel must always be a top priority to promote commission free bookings. Key traits of a well-designed website that enhances the online experience for online users are ease of navigation, a workflow geared toward the needs of the customer, precise information on services offered with high quality images and videos and trust in the brand. There is a unique opportunity for major hotel chains that have a large number of hotels and brands in their portfolio to offer unique value propositions for leisure customers.

Hotel searches based on destination, theme, multi-destination and split stays must be an investment priority to attract traffic to the consumer direct hotel website. For these workflows, ranking of hotels on a page based on net contribution maximizes the profit potential during the online search. While the OTAs can also implement these hotel search scenarios across multiple brands, only a hotel chain has access to the hurdle rates generated by the revenue management system to sort the properties for display based on either the total hurdle rate (lowest to highest) or net contribution (highest to lowest). The strategy may vary depending on the dynamics of the marketplace. During periods of low demand at a destination market, sorting the display list of hotels by the total hurdle rate for the stay from lowest to highest is beneficial to redirect demand to underperforming properties of a chain. However, during periods of high demand or closed out situations, sorting the display list of hotels by the net contribution for the stay from highest to lowest is beneficial to maximizing profit for the hotel chain.

The net contribution is derived from the hotel's revenue management system based on the hurdle rate (bid price in the airline context) calculated by the revenue mix optimizer. The hurdle rate is the opportunity cost of not having an incremental room at the property. The hurdle rate can also be defined as the incremental total revenue that can be derived if one excess unit of capacity is available. The net contribution for a reservation request is calculated as follows:

$$Net\ Contribution = Total\ Rate_{rda} - \sum_{j \in S} \gamma_j$$

$Total\ Rate_{rda}$ is the total room rate for rate category r for duration (length of stay) d for arrival (check-in) date a, γ_j is the hurdle rate for date j; $j \in S$, where S is the collection of future dates under revenue management control. If the net contribution is positive, the reservation request is accepted, otherwise, it is rejected.

11.6.3.1 Theme Based Shopping and Booking

The audience for the consumer direct channel is primarily leisure travelers, yet the booking workflow is business travel centric since the hotel search always begins with a destination. While many leisure travelers may want to go to a specific destination, many do not and are interested in experiencing a theme such as skiing, gambling, sightseeing, romantic getaway, wine tasting, history and culture, nature tour, beach, safari, adventure, hiking, etc. Hotel chains should support an alternate theme-based shopping workflow on their websites to allow customers to evaluate a range of destinations that are specific to a theme. Theme based shopping also allows a hotel chain to redirect demand from high demand to low demand properties by ranking the properties in the search results based on available unused capacity (unsold rooms) or ranked in ascending order of the total hurdle rate for the stay period.

11.6.3.2 Destination Shopping Display Ranking

This is the standard search where online customers search for hotels at a destination. A hotel chain can control the display ranking of hotels based on the total hurdle rate from lowest to gighest. This had the advantage of redirecting demand from high demand hotels to low demand hotels in the portfolio. Besides redirecting demand, the display order influences market share retention. Ranking can also be based on a budget constraint.

11.6.3.3 Sequencing Multi-Destination Trips

Leisure customers may be interested in booking multiple destinations where the order of the destinations visited is not important. Multi-destination search is an opportunity to have a tailored workflow that determines the optimal sequence of stays at destinations that minimizes the total cost to the customer. Multiple permutations must be evaluated in real time based on the total hurdle rate for each stay to optimize the sequence of stays at multiple properties. The lowest total hurdle rate translated into the selling rate across all stays produces the lowest cost sequence of visits for the customer. It is also advantageous for the hotel chain to redirect demand to low occupancy dates and retain market share. If there are N destinations, then the number of possible sequences to be evaluated is $N!$

11.6.3.4 Split Stays to Minimize Cost of Travel

Leisure customers often face difficulty in booking their preferred hotel due to length of stay controls (restrictions) imposed by revenue management that result in the unavailability of rooms at lower rates. To bypass these room inventory control restrictions, customers can split their stay across multiple properties of equivalent or greater value identified by star rating or user rating. This also enables customers to visit attractions situated in different neighborhoods. Hotel chains must develop an automated search function to assist leisure customers in optimizing their travel expenses by splitting their stay across multiple properties, prioritizing cost savings over the stay sequence which is less important.

When searching for a hotel in a destination that involves staying at two or more properties, either in the same city or in multiple cities that are nearby, the available properties should have a lower average rate and may be closer to local attractions. The number of split stays will always be less than or equal to the total duration for the trip.

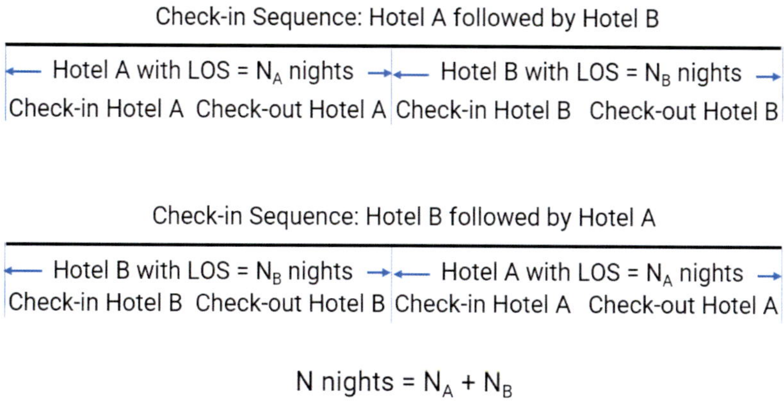

Fig. 11.3 Split hotel alternatives

When conducting a typical hotel search, rates are provided for a particular hotel and length of stay. As an illustration, the search results may display a 4-star property (such as Hotel A), available for a stay of N number of days.

When there are two split stays, the search optimization must explicitly evaluate all the possible combinations of the trip duration. In this situation, the customer can choose to start their stay at either Hotel A or Hotel B, as illustrated in Figure 11.3.

In this scenario, the concept of splitting a stay between two hotels, Hotel A and Hotel B, is explored. The Best Available Rate (BAR) is calculated for each valid length of stay (LOS) during the eligible check-in dates for both hotels. All possible combinations of nights spent at each hotel are evaluated, ensuring that the total number of nights (N) is equal to the sum of nights spent at each hotel (N_A+N_B=N). The least cost alternative is the recommended solution.

Besides the cost savings for customers, split hotel stays also benefit hoteliers.Hotels can capture customers who would have been turned away due to the non-availability of a room on a peak day or high price, by offering them a part of their stay at the destination. To enhance customer satisfaction, hotels that are part of the same hotel chain can provide free shuttle transportation for split stay customers to the next property. This leads to increased customer satisfaction, which can translate to repeat visits to the hotel website.

Evaluating split stays involves evaluating a vast number of possible combinations. Therefore, it is advised to restrict the number of split stays to two or three hotels at the maximum.

Table 11.1 illustrates the number of permutations that must be evaluated as a function of number of split stays m and total stays n for the trip. Note that m is the number of hotels and n is the total length of stay.

Table 11.1 Computational burden of split stays

Maximum Number of Split Stays (H otels)	Total Stays for the Trip (Length of Stay)	Number of Permutations to be Evaluated
2	4	2 + 6 = 8
	6	2 + 10 = 12
	8	2 + 14 = 16
3	4	3 + 18 + 18 = 39
	6	3 + 30 + 60 = 93
	8	4 + 42 + 126 = 171
4	4	4 + 36 + 72 + 24 = 136
	6	4 + 60 + 240 + 240 = 544
	8	4 + 84 + 504 + 840 = 1432

The formula for the number of evaluations when there are m hotels and n length of stay where P represents permutations and C represents combinations is shown below.

$$\sum_{i=1}^{m} P_i^m * C_{i-1}^{n-1}$$

11.7 The Contrarian View on the Role of OTAs

In a recent study [Connor et al., 2025] that was published in the Cornell Hospitality Quarterly claimed that OTAs are a winning proposition for hoteliers. Though not stated in the paper, the research study was probably sponsored by the OTAs.

The study states that for every dollar spent on OTA commissions, a hotel gains \$7.98 in profit. It also sees a \$20.20 rise in revenue and a 1.12% boost in occupancy. If a hotel spends \$89.28 on OTA fees, occupancy could reach full capacity. The more a hotel invests in OTA commissions, the more profitable the hotel becomes. In the lodging industry, no one but Cornell University believes this analysis.

This study is flawed for several reasons. The study only considers the agency model, also known as the PAC model. With this PAC model, the hotel collects payment from the customer at checkout and remits a commission payment to the OTA. The analysis does not consider the merchant model bookings where the OTAs collect the money at time of booking and pays the hotel net of commissions after the customer checks out of the property. The PAC model is popular with Booking.com customers, but the merchant model still dominates hotel bookings. For independent properties almost all the Expedia bookings and over sixty percent of the Booking.com bookings are made using the merchant model (see Fig. 11.1). The merchant model commissions (25 to 35%) are higher than the PAC model and the spread is at least 5% of the value of the booking. Hidden fees are in addition to the commissions charged.

So how can OTA bookings be more profitable than direct bookings? For independent hotels, the direct online distribution costs range from 5% to 8% and it includes the web hosting, website design and maintenance, content marketing, SEO, metasearch, social media, email, and website marketing.

Despite the high costs for participating in the OTA channel, for a hotel, participating in all channels of distribution is important. This does not mean that the hotel must participate with all OTAs, just the ones that make sense. Besides the direct and OTA channels, other important channels are bed banks, brick-and-mortar travel agencies, and tour operators. A balanced strategy for distribution is critically important. Making claims that OTA bookings are more profitable than direct bookings does not add up.

11.8 The So-Called OTA Billboard Effect

The OTA Billboard Effect [Anderson, 2009, 2011] was a study that was partially sponsored by Expedia. Its objective was to convince hoteliers that they should use Expedia in order to generate more bookings directly on the hotel's own website due to the so-called "Billboard Effect." The Cornell Report claims that when a hotelier factors in the incremental bookings from the billboard effect, the effective commissions paid to Expedia would be in single digits!

In reality, the billboard effect from a property's exposure on Expedia.com is contrived and has a limited impact, if any, on the hotel revenues than the property's paid search and SEO initiatives on Google, email marketing, mobile marketing, and website optimization. The hefty merchant commissions charged by OTAs far outweigh any revenue benefits measured in incremental bookings on the hotel website.

Since the research conducted by Anderson, consumer behavior has been changing A subsequent study based on hotels listed on OTAs concluded that the billboard effect was dead. In a study commissioned in 2014 by American Hotel & Lodging Association's Consumer Innovation Forum, Professor P.K. Kannan from the Robert H. Smith School of Business at the University of Maryland concluded based on a study of 50,000 online shoppers that they ultimately purchased their hotel stays through intermediaries like Expedia, Booking.com and Tripadvisor [O'Neil, 2015b]. Unlike the Cornell study, which used data from Expedia and hotel chains directly, this study used clickstream data from a market research firm and it was analyzed via attribution modeling.

For independents, hoteliers need to focus on participating with the right OTA for the most exposure for their hotel and brand to achieve an equal footing with the larger national and international chains. The right OTA with the right audience becomes more important if the property falls into a niche market.

11.9 Hotel Strategy for OTA Participation

Hotel revenue analysts should periodically review their OTA relationships, both global and regional, and determine the value of doing business with each OTA. Visibility into commission costs per occupied room delivered by an OTA will influence future decisions on OTA participation.

Hotels typically experience wide variations in productivity, commissions paid, and the net room rate delivered by each OTA channel.

To understand the strategic importance of participating in an OTA, there are two metrics that should be monitored. They are the OTA channel productivity and net room rate by OTA channel.

For OTA channel *i*

$$Channel\ Productivity_i\ (\%) = \frac{Total\ Room\ Nights\ Sold_i}{Total\ Room\ Nights\ at\ Property} \times 100$$

$$Net\ Room\ Rate\ by\ Channel_i$$
$$= Average\ Rate\ per\ Room\ Night_i - Average\ Commissions\ per\ Room\ Night_i$$

OTA participation must be a function of the productivity of the OTA channel viewed in conjunction with the net room revenue by channel. The OTAs with low productivity and below average net room rates must be avoided. A hotel's participation in global and regional OTAs must be periodically reviewed based on these two metrics. Exceptions should only be made if the audience delivered by an OTA is unique, such as demographics and point of commencement of travel.

11.10 Steps to Preserve Hotel Margins

Independent hotels and hotel chains, to boost direct bookings, must follow these essential steps.

1. Investment in technology is a necessity in the digital era. Hotels typically spend less than 3% of net room revenue including payroll for IT personnel compared to OTAs that typically spend five time as much of revenue.
2. Investment in marketing is a necessity in the digital era. Hotels typically spend less than 3% of net room revenue which compares very unfavorably with the mega OTAs. Hotels must make a marketing investment in Google Ads. The goal is to own 100% of the searches for their branded keyword terms. This translates into a 100% share of office (SOV) of the impressions. SOV is a marketing metric that measures a hotel's presence and visibility in the market compared to its competitors. It is essentially the percentage of the total conversations,

advertising, or media coverage that a brand owns within a specific market. A higher SOV indicates greater brand awareness and dominance in the market.
3. Make a marketing investment in Google Hotel Ads. Hoteliers must participate in the free booking links and budget to participate in the paid booking links during the shoulder and low seasons.
4. Invest in a SEO strategy and own the branded keyword terms. Hoteliers must focus on creating unique, branded content that strengthens organic rankings across all variations of their hotel name A robust SEO strategy is required to generate incremental direct bookings and to ensure good positioning of the hotel website in Generative AI Search results. Independent hotels know more about their product than the OTA does, inclusive of local attractions and activities that enable them to create unique packages.
5. Invest in Generative Engine Optimization (GEO) to promote discovery in AI Search results. Recent studies indicate that nearly 65% of Google searches [Second Wave Marketing, 2025] now end without a click to any website. For mobile users, that figure approaches 78%. AI Search results disrupt the traditional pathway to hotel websites. To generate bookings, hotels must be featured prominently in the AI Search results. When a traveler asks an AI Assistant for "pet friendly hotels in Dallas" the objective is to have properties mentioned in the results. GEO is not a replacement, but compliments SEO. The LLMs used by AI Assistants synthesize data from various sources such as review platforms, social media, and listings. The challenge for hotels is that visibility in AI Search extends beyond the digital assets owned by the hotel.

In the crowded digital marketplace, visibility is of critical importance. Even if a hotel ranks first in organic results for branded searches, paid listings often appear at the top of search results, especially on mobile, pushing organic listings further down the page. OTAs and their affiliates will continue to bid aggressively on hotel branded keywords. Not participating in branded keyword campaigns means losing those clicks and potential direct bookings to competitors.

Commissions on hotel bookings is the primary source of revenue for OTAs. As a general rule, hotel brands pay less than smaller chains and independents with their bargaining power during negotiations.

In addition to commissions on travel bookings, OTAs also generate advertising revenue through sponsored listings and display ads. Travel suppliers can pay for better placement in search results or for advertisements on the Expedia and affiliate websites. Another source of revenue is travel insurance.

11.10.1 Impact of Gen AI Search on Conversions

AI driven search is fundamentally reshaping visibility at the *top of the funnel* when an online user searches for general information. It offers a preview of a topic or query based on a range of sources, including websites.

For example, Google features Gemini AI to answer questions by creating content summaries at the top of the SERP. When someone asks, "What is the best hotel near Battery Park with a contemporary design?", the Gen AI Search may only recommend a few hotels and if a specific named hotel is not on that list, it means that the property does not exist for the potential customer. Therefore, to increase a hotel's visibility in Gen AI Search, hotels must focus on strengthening their digital presence to ensure discovery, structuring content in a Q&A format, updating website content, being active on social media, third party reviews, and ensuring consistent information across platforms and using AI-powered tools for social listening, video captioning, and email marketing that expand visibility at the *top of the funnel.* Hotel chains and Independents are better positioned than the OTAs to generate relevant content because they know their destination market, unique attributes of their location, and products offered better than the OTAs. Besides, they can focus on their most important customer segments and feeder markets that generate a majority of the revenue.

In summary, SEO targets keywords and backlinks for clicks on traditional SERPs. The objective of Generative Engine Optimization (GEO) is to structure content for AI understanding, targeting direct citation in AI answers by focusing on clarity, authority, data structure, and direct Q&A formats. It is a critical *extension* of SEO, not a replacement, to dominate both traditional and AI Search. Both are vital: SEO drives traffic, while GEO ensures visibility when users ask AI tools like Google's AI Overview, Gemini or ChatGPT.

The *bottom of the funnel* represents the final stages when customers are actively considering and ready to make a purchase. This is where investment in branded keywords is important to convert a shopper to a booker.

11.11 A Discrete Channel for Excess Inventory: Travel Agent Rebates

Hotels and other travel suppliers have a discrete channel to dispose excess inventory. They reward travel agents with deep discounts for their personal travel.

IATA hotel rebates are discounts, or "travel agent rates" offered by hotel chains to IATA/IATAN ID Travel Professional ID card holders for personal travel, providing significant savings on stays. These cards verify status in the airline industry and offer benefits beyond room discounts, such as access to exclusive deals, training, and other industry specific perks. The International Association of Travel Agents Network (IATAN) is a division of IATA for travel agents that offers accreditation with a unique travel agent code and issuing the IATA/IATAN ID Card for professional identification.

To access these rates, travel professionals typically register on a travel supplier's dedicated travel agent portal and use a specific rate code or provide their ID at booking. These rates are almost exclusively for the personal travel of the travel professional and are not for resale. Hotels require proof of the ID card at check-in to honor the discounted rate. These discounts are available for hotels, car rentals, cruise lines, merchandise, and training. These discounts are deeper than what is offered to airline employees by travel suppliers.

11.12 Regaining Control of Distribution with Attribute-based Room Pricing

Attribute-based room pricing [Vinod, 2019; Vinod and Hobt, 2021] is the future of hotel pricing, revenue management, and inventory control. Major hotel chains that are investing in this new hotel retailing approach are Intercontinental Hotels Group (IHG), Marriott Hotels and Hilton Hotels. This approach will gain traction with the larger chains for their three-star, four-star, and five-star hotels when a booking is made. Hotel customers are interested in personalized experiences, and this new approach can drive incremental revenues for hotels, simultaneously enhance customer satisfaction, and most importantly, take control of distribution from intermediaries by ensuring that booking a room with specific room attributes is only possible through the direct channel. Coupled with attribute-based room pricing is the adoption of real-time dynamic pricing, where rates are derived from reference rates, which cannot be duplicated by an intermediary, such as an OTA.

Attribute-based room pricing, like the inventory control of a specific airline seat, is the capability to introduce very granular inventory controls at an individual room level [Vinod, 2019; Vinod and Hobt, 2021; Vinod, 2022a, Chap. 5]. It transforms the mundane hotel model of selling rooms to selling experiences in which a customer can select the attributes of the room they are interested in for a memorable stay. From a customer perspective, this approach enhances the personalization of offers to a whole new level. During this process, hoteliers generate incremental revenues while positively impacting customer satisfaction since the customer purchased exactly what was wanted.

The core question that needs to be answered is: if an airline seat is selected and confirmed at the time of booking, can a specific hotel room with its unique attributes be selected and confirmed at the time of booking? The answer is yes, but only through the direct channel. IHG has a new reservations system from Amadeus that supports attribute-based room pricing. The system has been operational since 2019. In addition, to support intermediaries, the existing Availability, Rates and Inventory (ARI) format does not support the intricacies of room attributes. For example, if a customer selects specific room attributes such as a connecting room, the corner room on the top floor, the larger room with a king-size bed, a Nespresso coffer maker, and more. The associated dominant and non-dominant room attributes and prices for the room attributes are not specified in the existing ARI structure.

Attribute-based selling of rooms is applicable for both leisure travel and business travel. For leisure travelers, it provides the ability to buy room and non-room products (add-ons). For business travelers, who typically stay at their preferred chain in a destination city, they can select from a range of fixed attributes such as a room on the top floor, the extra size room with a king-bed, and room close to the elevator. They can also select flexible attributes such as in-room breakfast, in-room morning exercise equipment such as a stationary bicycle, dumb bells, treadmill, elliptical, yoga mat, etc. In addition, attribute-based room pricing also supports upsell opportunities with flexible (movable) room attributes. For example, the standard coffee maker in a room could be a Keurig coffee maker. A customer can upgrade the Keurig for a Nespresso coffee maker for a fee.

There is a higher propensity to satisfy customers with a personalized experience of staying at a hotel since the customer only pays for the specific room attributes that they want for their stay. For hoteliers, the business question to be answered is customer perception and their willingness to pay for specific room attributes.

Another benefit of attribute-based room pricing is brand equity and differentiation from competing brands. Unlike an airline seat, a 4-star or 5-star hotel room is not a commodity product. A commodity product is one where a customer perceives competing products as homogeneous, and the differentiation is primarily influenced by price and not the features and attributes that a brand has to offer. Commoditization of the hotel product negatively impacts brand equity. Many hotel chains have multiple brands and, in an industry where franchising is the dominant business model, brand differentiation is of critical importance. Attribute-based room pricing enables a hotelier to take control of the brand and drive differentiation, thereby enhancing branding initiatives.

11.13 AI Platforms, ARI Content and OTA Bypass

Hotels provide availability, rates, and inventory (ARI) to online travel agencies and Google. This information is often exchanged using XML feeds, which adhere to standards set by the OpenTravel Alliance (OTA). These feeds include details such as room types, rates, availability restrictions (e.g., minimum length of stay), and other relevant data.

The ARI content is typically distributed with a channel manager, a software system that automatically synchronizes the hotel's room rates and availability across multiple booking channels. This process is critical for maximizing revenue, preventing overbookings, and ensuring consistent pricing where the hotel is listed.

11.13.1 Current Approaches to Push ARI Content to Intermediaries

The accuracy and timeliness of ARI information are crucial for hotels to manage their bookings effectively and avoid issues like overbooking or incorrect pricing. Many hotels use channel managers to provide the ARI updates. Channel managers streamline the process by allowing hotels to update their rates and availability in one place, which is then automatically pushed out to the connected OTAs.

Larger hotel chains and some independent properties may establish direct connections with major OTAs or utilize APIs to provide real-time ARI updates. From the hotel's CRS or PMS.

Smaller properties also use extranets provided by individual OTAs to manually upload and manage their inventory and rates. This approach is less efficient and doesn't offer real-time updates.

11.13.2 ARI Content for AI Platforms and Disintermediation of OTAs

In the future, hotels must supply ARI data to AI platforms like ChatGPT, Google Gemini, Microsoft Copilot, and Claude. These AI tools are rapidly increasing their travel planning and booking capabilities. Unlike traditional search engines or AI Assistants that only provide information, the new breed of AI Agents can act and book a hotel room.

Hotels have two main options. They can use AI connection tools, like the Model Context Protocol (MCP) (see Chap. 17) that was introduced by Anthropic in November 2024, or they can connect using APIs to their property's CRS, channel manager, or property management system (PMS).

Many AI connection startups will likely emerge that put hotel ARI content directly into these AI platforms like ChatGPT, Claude and Google Gemini. This has the potential to bypass OTAs and increase direct bookings.

11.14 AI Agents will Transform the Hospitality Distribution Landscape

Autonomous AI Agents will drive an increase in hotel direct bookings. It will be a gamechanger for hotels seeking to boost direct bookings and enhance the overall guest experience. Hotel AI Agents will handle inquiries 24/7, personalize the booking process, and free up staff to focus on high-value tasks. These agents will be able to answer common questions instantly, guide guests through reservations, and upsell services, leading to higher conversion rates and increased revenue. Hotel AI Agents will make it easier and faster to book directly on the hotel's website, and drive bookings away from intermediaries.

While the increasing adoption of autonomous AI Agents will reshape the hospitality distribution landscape, hotels must leverage these tools to stay competitive in a market driven by tech-savvy travelers with high expectations. The future of hospitality will likely see a continued evolution of AI Agents, with even more sophisticated personalization, predictive capabilities, and integration across the entire guest journey without an intermediary like an OTA or a GDS or a bed bank.

While the benefits are significant, hotels need to address challenges like early adoption, initial investment costs, data privacy concerns, and staff training to ensure successful AI implementation. Balancing automation with the human element remains crucial to providing the personalized and empathetic experiences that define exceptional hospitality.

The larger question is whether AI Agents will benefit hotels and lower their distribution costs?

11.14.1 Lowering Distribution Costs Require Agile Adoption of MCP

MCP (Model Context Protocol) is an open-source standard for connecting AI applications to external systems. MCP creates a standardized, two-way connection for AI applications, allowing LLM Agents to easily connect with various data sources and tools.

Using MCP, AI applications like Claude or ChatGPT can connect to data sources (e.g. local files, databases), tools (e.g. search engines, calculators) and workflows (e.g. specialized prompts), thereby enabling them to access key information and perform tasks. AI Agents can access a user's Google Calendar for example, acting as a personalized assistant. Enterprise chatbots can connect to multiple databases across an organization, empowering users to analyze data using chat.

Hotels can invest and build MCP servers but are at the mercy of AI platforms to fully open their app ecosystems. OTAs like Expedia and Booking.com were early partners in adopting MCP and have built their own MCP servers that provide AI platforms with access to their large, aggregated inventory of hotels, rates, and availability. For hotel chains and independents, the risk is obvious and early adoption is key. Today OTAs control the customer relationship and charge high commissions. AI platforms have the potential to become the new "storefronts"for travelers. Early adopters, if they happen to be OTAs, may become the default sources for AI platforms. This will be déjà vu where AI platforms use OTA MCP servers for hotel bookings and the underlying power dynamic and data control resemble the existing, pre-AI relationship between hotels and OTAs. There is also the risk that major AI platforms might use a few OTA MCP servers rather than integrate with individual hotel systems. The fear is that AI-driven booking might replicate the status quo, creating a "déjà vu" of platform dominance over suppliers.

11.14.2 ChatGPT and Hotel Bookings

Travel platforms are evolving with changes in technology. This will change not just how consumers interact to book travel, but the underlying commercial model will favor hotel suppliers.

In October 2025, OpenAI launched apps in ChatGPT with Booking.com and Expedia with more expected to follow [Hines, 2025a]. It will allow users to book hotels in "one-click" directly through ChatGPT [Altexsoft, 2025].

The traditional paid search ranking models frequently elevate lower quality hotels because they pay for visibility.

Sam Altman, the CEO of OpenAI was quoted [Altexsoft, 2025].

> *ChatGPT is designed to surface hotel options based purely on reviews, relevance, and the user's needs, free from paid placement.*

Sam Altman's comment implies that ChatGPT's search results for hotels will be unbiased, driven solely by user needs and review data, not by paid placements from hotels. This is a core principle for maintaining user trust, He has also acknowledged that a form of transaction fee, not traditional advertising, could be a future monetization model for services like booking travel.

Sam Altman claims that hotel suppliers will see commission less "one-click" hotel bookings on ChatGPT in the future. It is unlikely that one-click bookings will take a foothold in the travel industry due to the inherent complexities of planning a trip. Choice, emotion, neighborhood, and other attributes influence hotel bookings. OpenAI needs to develop expertise in travel planning and its associated complexities before enabling hotel bookings.

11.14.3 Canvas and AI Mode

"Canvas" is a new feature within Google's "AI Mode"that provides a dynamic, persistent workspace in a side panel for organizing information and planning complex tasks like study guides, itineraries, and project plans. It was launched on November 17, 2025. It is currently available as an experimental feature for users opted into the AI Mode Labs program in the U.S., primarily on desktop.

AI Mode for travel planning uses Canvas to generate a travel plan from user descriptions and agentic bookings. Restaurants and events exist today. Hotels and flight bookings in AI Mode are expected to follow shortly. The overarching plan for Canvas is to generate a plan with flight, hotel and destination activities.

11.14.4 Google's Agentic AI Initiative with Hotels and OTAs

In November 2025, Google announced plans to debut Agentic AI booking capabilities for hotels and flight reservations within its AI Mode search feature [Jelski, 2025; Lee, 2025]. Google has partnerships with Booking.com, Expedia, Marriott International, IHG Hotels & Resorts, Choice Hotels International and Wyndham Hotels & Resorts. OTA partnerships were required because hotel inventory is fragmented with a large number of independent hotels. As agentic bookings evolve, it will favor larger suppliers. Monetization with the merchant and agency models for OTAs will be limited to the smaller hotels, independents, and boutique hotels.

Agentic bookings are expected to favor travel suppliers. Google's partnership with intermediaries like Booking.com and Expedia is not surprising because of supplier fragmentation, primarily the large number of independent hotels and smaller airlines. Google, which collects billions in annual ad revenue from OTAs and hotels, is pursuing this path to build agentic bookings which will eventually negatively impact their ad revenues.

In this new world of agentic bookings, suppliers like Marriot, Hilton, and IHG will benefit when the hefty commissions paid to OTAs are bypassed. In the future, the merchant model and agency model fees promoted by OTAs will only exist with the smaller hotel chains and independents who have not taken the initiative to invest in AI Agents. Hotel customers should expect a windfall with lower hotel rates in the future, triggered by increased direct bookings caused by disintermediation of the OTAs.

11.14.5 Google's Universal Commerce Protocol

Google launched the Universal Commerce Protocol (UCP) on January 11, 2026. The open-source standard was created with retail and technology partners, including Shopify, Walmart, Etsy, Wayfair, and Target. UCP is designed to allow AI Agents to manage the entire shopping process from product discovery to checkout and payment. It enables in-conversation checkout using stored credentials such as Google Pay.

The UCP protocol is oriented towards traditional retailing with a focus on physical goods, shipping labels and tracking. In its current form, its adaptability for hotels is unknown and will require the introduction of specialized hotel-related fields like room types and room attributes. In the future UCP may be integrated with Google Travel (flights, hotels, ground transportation, destination activities, etc.). If UCP is adapted for travel, hotels will be the merchant of record and retain all customer data.

11.14.6 The Road Forward

Online Travel Agencies (OTAs) started exploiting hotels with the high commissions associated with the merchant and agency models in the early 2000s, especially after the 9/11 recession, by forcing hotels into unfavorable deals. The OTAs were opportunistic and used it to their advantage. Every hotel segment, large chains, resorts, boutiques, and independents that benefited from higher booking volumes at unfavorable terms lost control of distribution. The merchant model led to a loss of control for hotels over their pricing, inventory, and customer relationships, and also negatively impacted their cash flow because the OTA didn't pay the hotel until after the guest checked out.

It is an important lesson for the ages.

Hoteliers must recognize that actions have lasting consequences. Informed data-driven decision making must be the way forward to control outcomes.

With the arrival of Agentic AI, the fundamental question is: *How quickly will hotel suppliers move toward a truly direct model when technology finally makes it possible?*

As Sir Francis Bacon once said: *Knowledge is power*. Perhaps that is the wake-up call for hoteliers. Having knowledge of distribution costs by channel gives hoteliers the power to make the transformation with AI Agents to regain control of distribution and improve the bottom line.

Classless Revenue Management 12

It is wisdom to recognize necessity when all other courses have been weighed, though as folly it may appear to those who cling to false hope

J.R.R. Tolkein

Abstract

This chapter is devoted to classless revenue management and the future of reservation booking designators (RBDs) and continuous pricing. The term classless revenue management is misleading since airlines still need to segment customers for revenue management purposes to discern high valued customers from low valued customers. Alternate customer segmentation based on the context for travel is the path forward. With IATA's New Distribution Capability (NDC), airlines do not have to distribute booking class availability to GDSs. While this is true, it does not necessarily mean that booking classes are not required for inventory reconciliation, reservations processing and itinerary pricing. Numerous examples of RBD usage in the context of reservations processing and airline itinerary pricing are described in this chapter. The chapter concludes with a discussion of the key benefits of pricing, revenue management, and inventory control in the NDC era.

This is a popular quote, most famously uttered by Gandalf in J.R.R. Tolkien's *The Lord of the Rings*. It highlights the distinction between facing reality and clinging to delusion, emphasizing that true wisdom lies in acknowledging when a particular course of action is the only viable option after considering all alternatives. It suggests that clinging to "false hope"—hope based on unrealistic expectations or a refusal to accept the truth of a situation—can blind one to the necessary path

B. Vinod, *The Era of Airline Revenue Management with Offers and Orders*, Management for Professionals, https://doi.org/10.1007/978-3-032-24197-9_12

forward, making wisdom appear as folly. In contrast, genuine hope is rooted in a realistic assessment of circumstances and the possibilities for positive change.

Classless revenue management falls into the category of "false hope" since we are dealing with semantics. Classless revenue management or otherwise, customer segmentation will prevail. Booking classes may become internal to an airline to support pricing and reservations processing, but customer segmentation will continue to be used by revenue management to optimize the passenger mix and maximize revenues.

12.1 What Is the Hype All About and Does It Really Matter?

The idiom "Much Ado About Nothing" means to make a big deal out of a mole hill, or something unimportant or to have more anxiety or excitement than the situation deserves.

This phrase originates from William Shakespeare's play of the same name and refers to the romantic entanglements and misunderstandings that are presented as significant but ultimately turn out to be trivial or based on false perceptions.

So what is the false excitement and anxiety all about with the so-called classless revenue management in the NDC era?

There is a lot of talk at revenue management conferences about RBDs going away. *Really?* While airlines have always explored segmentation of customers beyond RBDs, there is an opportunity for revenue management to segment travelers based on context for travel. The new "solo" pricing or "P2" (for passenger 2) launched by American Airlines in March 2025 to charge higher fares to solo passengers is one such example. It implies that demand forecasts generated by revenue management can be by trip-purpose segment and not RBD. This, however, does not mean that RBDs are going away anytime soon since they are deeply entrenched with airline fare rules and itinerary pricing and reservations processing.

If RBDs need to disappear, an alternative or a new framework for fare rules and reservations processing is required. The larger challenge is implementing a universal framework for a new fare rules methodology and reservations processing that will be adopted by all airlines worldwide. Something of this magnitude, even if undertaken, will take a minimum of three decades. Shortcuts are not an option since it will lead to revenue dilution on a significant scale.

The term "classless revenue management" sounds very geeky but it means there are no RBDs (Reservation Booking Designators) also known as booking classes for revenue management purposes in the NDC era. RBD is a code used in reservation transactions to identify the booking class that was used to deduct inventory from and price the transaction. This is because for NDC shopping requests, the airline controls the creation of all offers consisting of the base fare and ancillary products and services, that are distributed to direct and indirect channels. Pricing of the itinerary and the ancillary bundle are controlled by the airline. In the NDC era, pricing power shifts from the GDS to the airline in the indirect channel for NDC transactions.

12.2 The Hybrid State Is the New Reality

The hybrid state means that traditional EDIFACT bookings and NDC XML-based bookings will coexist in the industry for at least two decades, until 2045. To move away from the hybrid state there are two challenges that must be fulfilled. First, all IATA airlines must be distributing their NDC content to intermediaries. Second, all travel agencies that sell seats from airlines that participate in GDSs must have access to NDC content to book travel. When these two conditions are met, airlines can withdraw EDIFACT content from intermediaries. The challenge is NDC adoption with the long tail of smaller airlines and travel agencies who may not be able to afford the associated costs.

12.2.1 The Long Tail of Airlines and Travel Agencies

The long tail of airlines and travel agencies is a fundamental challenge toward adoption of NDC for all bookings worldwide.

In January 2025, there were 348 airlines who are members of IATA. This does not include the LCCs that are not members. In a 100% NDC world, booking class availability will not be distributed to GDSs by any airline, since all offers are airline controlled. The issue is that in 2025 there are only 70+ airlines that are NDC certified. The Airline Retailing Maturity (ARM) Index is the new certification format for NDC. NDC certification is the first step toward distributing NDC content to travel intermediaries. Many of these airlines in this group that are NDC certified are in various stages of technical development and maturity, Examples of airlines that are NDC certified are Air France/KLM, American Airlines, Finnair, Lufthansa Group, Qantas, Singapore Airlines, and United Airlines. It is estimated that it will take at least 15 to 20 years for all IATA airlines to invest and start distributing NDC content. A similar issue exists for the travel agencies who do not have access to NDC content for reasons such as investment, affordability, and commitment.

According to Statista, the number of businesses in the travel agency business worldwide is close to 600,000 as shown in Fig. 12.1. Observe that there was a steep decline during the pandemic (2020–2022) followed by rapid growth in new agencies. Of the 600,000 agencies, about 90,000 are IATA travel agencies. An IATA travel agency is one that has been certified by IATA. These agencies can sell tickets for IATA-member airlines, accept payments, issue tickets on behalf of airlines, and access the Billing and Settlement Plan (BSP). They are considered credible and reliable. However, non-IATA certified travel agencies can sell tickets for IATA airlines by working with consolidators or host agencies. Consolidators are accredited businesses that act as middlemen between travel agencies and the

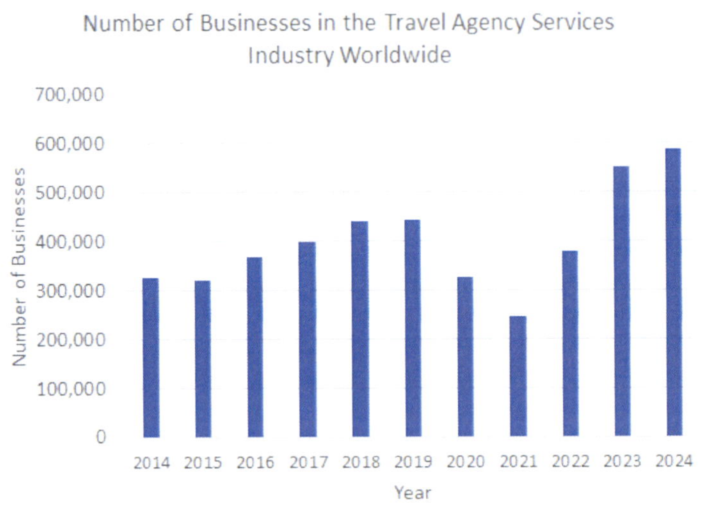

Source Statista, January 2025

Fig. 12.1 Number of Travel Agency Businesses Worldwide

travel industry. They can issue tickets for IATA member airlines and handle post-booking services. Host agencies are umbrella organizations that provide services to independent travel agents. They can offer ticketing services exclusively to member agents.

12.3 The Significance of RBDs in the Hybrid State

If all IATA airlines were on NDC, and all travel agencies had access to NDC content from the IATA airlines, the GDSs will no longer book flights based on RBD city pair availability or a shopping response generated by the GDS. Instead, the NDC workflow of requesting offers from airlines for all bookings will prevail. In the scenario the primary task of the GDS is content normalization for display to a travel agent and all content shown is NDC content.

Codeshare flights will also be impacted by NDC since there will be no sales of marketing flights based on AVS availability transmitted by the operating carrier or Cascading Availability, where the operating carrier's reservation system is queries for RBD availability. With NDC in a free sale codeshare environment, an airline may get a request for a service it cannot fully provide alone. This leads to the involvement of two or more airlines in creating the offer. The airline primarily responsible for the offer (Offer Responsible Airline—ORA) passes the request to a partner airline (Offer Participating Airline—OPA), which gives a price for the package along with any limitations. This process is similar to Cascading Availability, but here, the marketing airline returns a complete package offer. However, AVS based availability for marketing flights and cascading availability based on RBD will co-exist in the hybrid era.

Historically, booking classes were important for revenue management purposes since unconstrained demand was forecast by booking class, and the revenue mix optimizer determined either the leg-class or segment-class nested allocations for leg/segment carriers and generated network optimal bid prices for carriers exercising origin and destination (O&D) inventory control.

With NDC adoption and airline-controlled offers, an airline also does not have to distribute booking class availability to intermediaries like the GDSs (Amadeus, Sabre, and Travelport). However today we are in a hybrid state, so AVS messages are still sent to GDSs from an airline's host CRS (PSS environment). In the hybrid state, EDIFACT bookings require RBDs for availability and sell transactions, and NDC XML bookings co-exist with EDIFACT. Besides AVS, interactive availability and interactive sell are used by GDSs to complete EDIFACT bookings. This hybrid paradigm is unlikely to change anytime soon since NDC compliance from the long tail of mid-size and smaller travel agencies and airlines is a tall order.

12.3.1 The False Excitement of Classless Revenue Management

With the absence of RBDs, operations research analysts and data scientists get carried away and identify a false mission to literally reinvent the wheel—reinvent revenue management—in a world where there are no RBDs. In the hybrid era, RBD availability continues to be published to intermediaries to support EDIFACT bookings. From a revenue management perspective, customer segmentation is always required. The default segmentation with RBDs that have been used in the past can be replaced by context for travel-based segmentation called trip-purpose segmentation (TPS). With this alternate segmentation of customers, it is still required to untruncate demand based on open/close information of the customer segments followed by demand forecasting and optimization to determine nested inventory controls or bid prices for O&D control (continuous nesting). Open/close information for both leg/segment carriers and O&D carriers is based on the basic unit of inventory that is either available or not available in the airline CRS, which is the RBD.

When a flight is detailed on the airline host CRS from the inventory master, the RBD hierarchy by market is used to maintain booking counts by RBD. Eliminating RBDs from the host CRS and replacing it with alternate customer segmentation definitions is not warranted because in the hybrid state EDIFACT and NDC XML bookings coexist. Hence, if trip-purpose segments are used as an alternative to RBDs, they should be mapped to RBDs. If the number of trip-purpose segments defined is greater than the 26 RBDs, it will be a many-to-one mapping. In the end state when all airlines have adopted NDC, an airline can replace RBD units of inventory with a more expansive definition of customer segments. This is a very expensive modification to the reservation system that will require expansion of the inventory detail records, and enhancements to reconcile inventory counts between the passenger name index (PNI) or order index and the flight legs or segments.

In the airline industry every letter in the alphabet can be used to define an RBD. Typically all letters with the except of "O" and I" are not distributed to GDSs but are used for internal purposes. Some airlines like Japan Airlines that used BA's RS13 went a step further by using numbers 0 to 9 to control availability by point of sale while maintaining the integrity of the 26 booking classes. However, it is my experience that revenue management analysts paid scant attention to itinerary pricing (ATPCO fare rules, restrictions and itinerary pricing) and connectivity (seamless availability, seamless secured sell, basic booking request, AVS, cascading codeshare availability, etc.) and focused on the science of revenue management (for example, how to generate a better forecast and how to improve inventory controls), leaving connectivity (Type A and Type B messages) to the reservations system developers and itinerary pricing to the shopping and pricing developers. The primary impact of classless revenue management is connectivity since an airline is no longer communicating RBD availability to GDSs. In a perfect world (in the future, of course) all offers will be controlled by the airline, all bookings are NDC bookings, and distributing RBD availability to GDSs will not be required.

In the NDC hybrid era that we are in today, airlines are still filing fares, to fare aggregator ATPCO. If an airline decides to stop publishing fares to ATPCO, it will continue to publish them internally based on the ATPCO fare categories that represent fare qualifiers such as advance purchase, season, minimum stay, maximum stay, fare-by-rule, etc. RBDs by default serve as surrogate customer segments that revenue management use to forecast demand and optimize inventory controls. If RBDs were to disappear completely, customer segmentation is still required. Customer segmentation that is sensitive to the context for travel can still be maintained in a hierarchy based on value and the revenue management process continues with leg/segment controls or O&D controls. The customer segments will have to be mapped to the pseudo-RBDs for fare management and itinerary pricing purposes. Assuming there are more trip-purpose segments than booking classes, it will be a many-to-one mapping.

12.3.2 Host CRS Inventory Controls and RBDs

The CRS, commonly referred to as the airline PSS, is the system used by airlines to sell their seats. It includes details about flight schedules, prices, and a database of reservations (passenger name records) and tickets.

The inventory system holds information about all flights and available seats. Its primary function is to show how many seats are open on a flight by managing booking classes according to rules set by the airline.

The Inventory Master records (INM) in the airline host CRS define flight operations and initial macro inventory control configurations. When a flight is detailed from the INM, typically about 331 days before departure, the flight inventory detail records (called IDR or IND) are created with a booking class hierarchy to maintain seats sold counts. Historically many inventory systems were limited to 13 booking classes or less like the BABS (British Airways Booking System) RS13 system which were later expanded to 26. Expanding flight inventory records is a major investment since all the application packets that access the INDs must be tested.

If RBDs are not used for revenue management demand forecasting and optimization purposes, booking counts must be maintained by customer segment. For leg/segment revenue management carriers, this will be a significant effort since they typically extract inventory counts by RBD from the flight inventory records nightly for revenue management processing. For O&D carriers, the incremental cost is less since they already process PNR data nightly for forecasting demand by origin, destination, and booking class. O&D carriers still require total bookings by flight leg for network optimization.

If customer segments are used by revenue management, a mapping to the RBD hierarchy needs to be maintained. If the number of customer segments is greater than 26, then a many-to-one mapping exists to RBDs which can have an impact on demand forecast accuracy.

12.3.2.1 The Nightly and On-demand Booking Count Reconciliation Process

Every airline reservation system has a reconciliation process to validate inventory counts on the inventory records with the Passenger Name Index (PNI). Reconciliation occurs nightly and on demand in the event that the counts on the inventory records are corrupted. The counts from the PNI by RBD will override the counts on the inventory records if there is a discrepancy. If RBDs are eliminated, a inventory unit or bucket identifier will still be required to be stored on the PNI (or order index) for nightly reconciliation with the inventory "buckets."

12.3.3 Direct Connect Availability (DCA) and Direct Connect Sell (DCS) in the Hybrid Era

Direct Connect Availability (DCA) is also referred to as seamless availability and is a required level of participation with a GDS for control of seat inventory by origin and destination (O&D). DCA enables a GDS travel agent to receive true last seat availability by RBD in the city pair availability (CPA) display based on the availability processing logic that is resident in the host CRS. An airline's last seat availability is integrated into the standard GDS CPA display. A DCA sales indicator is appended to segments within the CPA display, thus differentiating the airline product.

DCA does not require special formats or additional keystrokes. With DCA, a GDS subscriber can view an airline's availability as seen by an airline reservation agent. With no special formats or additional keystrokes, an availability request is received from the GDS as if the request originated from the host CRS. The GDS "seamlessly" retrieves availability from the host CRS database to provide the GDS agent with up-to-date true last seat availability.

The primary advantage of using direct connect availability (DCA) is to improve presence of what is available for sale since the airline's availability package is being queried directly for display on the GDS. For the actual sell process, to receive a confirmed booking, the process is then the same for DCS and DCA, wherein the airline's availability processing logic is applied for determining what can be sold.

Seamless availability extends the host CRS's inventory management system through the GDS to the subscriber. In addition, seamless availability interacts with low fare search products offered by the GDSs. The host CRS will receive messages, under this method of connectivity, in an EDIFACT standard data packet containing full POS information at the travel agency level. Hence, if the Market Class Fare Value (*MCFV*) table in the host CRS supports POS based fare adjustments, inventory can be controlled at the appropriate POS level. Direct connect availability (DCA) cannot be supported without the presence of direct connect sell (DCS). DCA is a requirement for O&D control.

In the absence of seamless availability agreements, availability on a GDS is determined based on AVS/AVN stored on the local GDS database. AVS and AVN controls are either leg based, or segment based. With seamless connectivity, a GDS agent can query host CRS availability directly, hence providing the capability for true last seat availability and full origin and destination controls.

12.3.4 RBDs and Demand Forecast Accuracy

When RBDs are replaced by TPSs the natural tendency is to increase the number of segments to be greater than the traditional 26 RBDs. When the number of customer segments is greater than the 26 RBDs that are detailed in the reservations inventory system, the demand forecasts are smaller in magnitude which in turn can lead to higher relative forecast errors. When dealing with small numbers in forecasting, accuracy can be significantly impacted, meaning that even a small error can result in a large percentage deviation, making it harder to reliably predict future trends. Hence, in situations where demand is low and quantities to be forecast are small, inaccurate forecasts can lead to less aggressive inventory controls, leading to dilution of revenue and potential financial losses. Several simulation studies have demonstrated that a 10% improvement in forecast accuracy leads to a 0.5% improvement in revenue.

Bayesian hierarchical demand forecasting combines Bayesian statistics with hierarchical data structures to produce more accurate forecasts, especially with sparse data. It forecasts demand at various levels of granularity by sharing information, thereby reducing uncertainty, and increasing accuracy, particularly for sparse data. It allows lower-level forecasts to borrow from higher levels through shared

Table 12.1 Fare combinability major and minor sub-categories

Major Sub-categories		Minor Sub-categories	
Number	Title	Number	Title
101	Open Jaws	106	Carrier Combinations
102	Round Trips	107	Tariff/Rule Combinations
103	Circle Trips	108	Fare Class/Fare Type Combinations
104	End-on-end	109	Open Jaw Sets

parameters to create consistent forecasts across all levels. With many trip purpose segments, some will be correlated with others, so hierarchical forecasting allows the forecasts to borrow from each other.

12.3.5 Impact on Itinerary Pricing

An airline itinerary pricing system, whether the fare is calculated by the GDS, an airline, or a third party, must be compliant with ATPCO RBD Record 6 Data application.

RBD data can be found in Record 1, Record 6, Category 10, Categories 19–22, Category 25, and Category 35.

12.3.5.1 Fare Combinability

Category 10, or "Combinations," dictates how fares can be combined, including different fare types and RBDs for outbound and return journeys, open jaws, and circle trips, with the responsibility for controlling these combinations resting with the airline. It is the responsibility of the airline to control CAT 10 combinability.

Category 10 helps airlines automate fare rules. It shows if fares can be combined and what rules apply. Combination restrictions are expressed through the use of eight sub-ordinate Record 3 s, known as sub-categories. The sub-categories are identified as Major or Minor and are shown in Table 12.1 below. Combination definitions, assumptions, and applications do not differ for Normal (flexible and more expensive) or Special Fares (restricted fares) unless specified in CAT 108 which restricts which RBDs are combinable.

12.3.5.2 Table 999: RBD Exception Code Table

According to ATPCO's RBD data application, if there are no filed exceptions from a secondary carrier in the primary carrier's Record 6 or from the carrier in their own Record 6, the itinerary pricing system will not assume anything, resulting in a failed fare quote. Some pricing systems may allow pricing with the Primary Booking Class without data in Record 6, but this does not meet ATPCO standards. In general, any missing RBD data will lead to a failure in pricing the itinerary.

In the ATPCO system, "Table 999" refers to the "RBD Exception Code Table," which is used to define specific rules regarding booking class codes (RBDs), allowing airlines to specify conditions where a particular RBD may be permitted or required only when another specified RBD is available on the same flight, essentially acting as a secondary booking class validation tool.

"Table 999" is a data table in the Fare Class Application (Record 1) and Record 6 Convention 2 (Chart 1). This table is used to outline RBD exceptions or restrictions. Table 999 serves as an Exception Code Table that enables airlines to indicate when a specific booking class can be used based on the availability of another class on the same flight, essentially acting as a secondary booking class validation tool. When calculating a fare, the itinerary pricing system looks at Table 999 to determine if there are any additional conditions that need to be fulfilled regarding the availability of other booking classes before confirming the fare's validity,

12.3.6 Dual RBDs

In 2017, dual RBDs were introduced to price itineraries by ATPCO [ATPCO, 2017]. Dual RBD validation increases the number of price points available by indicating that inventory availability is required in two booking classes for a fare to be valid. RBD Table 999 was enhanced with two new restriction tag values to support dual RBD validation. While Table 999 is used to indicate when a RBD is only valid if another RBD is available, dual RBDs allow airlines to offer more price points by using a primary RBD and a secondary RBD. Table 999 can be used in conjunction with dual RBDs to indicate when a RBD is only valid if another RBD is available. The RBD that is shown in the Fare Display data will show the Primary RBD and any Secondary RBD filed in Chart 1. The ability to price an itinerary may be dependent on whether another specified RBD is available at time of pricing.

Carriers must ensure that an inventory for a different RBD is available when filing with one of the two new dual inventory restriction tags. This is necessary to qualify for the fare tied to the booking RBD. There are two dual inventory restriction tags, and the values are:

1. Value B If RBD 1 is available, then RBD 2 is permitted
2. Value D If RBD 1 is available, then RBD 2 is required

These values will allow a 'permitted' or 'required' RBD to be valid only when another specified RBD is available for sale on the same flight.

These restriction tags are only applicable to Table 999 in the Fare Class Application (Record 1) and in Record 6 Convention 2 (Chart 1). ATPCO system edits will prohibit access to them within Chart 1 in Fare By Rule (Category 25) and Record 6 Convention 1 (Chart 2).

What this means is that the RBD shown in the Fare Display data (e.g. FDC*1) will show the Primary RBD and any secondary RBD filed in Chart 1 but the ability to price may be dependent on whether another specified RBD is available at time of pricing.

12.3.6.1 Chart 1 and Chart 2

Airlines submit relevant RBDs in Chart 1. These RBDs apply to their own fares. They indicate which RBDs should be used for the significant sectors of their fares. Exceptions, like domestic parts of international fares, are also noted. Chart 1 also lists RBDs for use on other carriers when permitted. For instance, airline XX files a fare from TC3 to TC1 (see Chap. 8, Sect. 8.12). It will list the RBDs for its flight segments in Chart 1.

Chart 2 is specifically used by the operating airline to control and restrict access by other airline's fares to its inventory. Airlines file RBDs for flight segments in Chart 2. These are used with other airlines' fares. The operating airline does not need to match the fare-owning airline's RBD choices. For example, operating airline YY files the RBD's. This allows airline XX to use them for its TC3 to TC1 fare. This happens when YY is the secondary carrier on XX's fare.

12.3.7 Dual RBDs to Control Availability of Basic Economy

There is a historic limit of 26 RBDs, one for each character of the alphabet, for distribution of booking class availability from airline host CRSs to GDSs.

Fare Class Application (Record 1) has the Prime booking code and the Booking Code Exception (Table 999) ensures that the Prime is permitted when Secondary RBD is available. Table 12.2 illustrates how dual RBDs work. For pricing and ticketing, the booked segment is in the prime RBD. Pricing and ticketing are based on the lowest fare from the Prime that also has secondary availability. For revenue accounting and audit, the ticket reflects the prime RBD and the fare amount and fare basis are the lowest available. This process is similar to processing of upgrade fares that are booked in a single premium RBD based on economy class availability.

Dual RBDs are also used by many airlines to control Basic Economy fares to ensure they move in tandem with the Regular Economy Fares. Full-service carriers use Basic Economy fares to compete with LCCs. A FSC may use 14 RBDs for economy class, instead of having 14 booking classes for Basic Economy that are not available for use, Basic Economy can be effectively controlled with dual RBDs. The lowest booking class that is available for Regular Economy determines the fare for Basic Economy if the designated booking class for Basic Economy is available.

Table 12.2 Dual RBD example

RBDs available	Divide into primary and secondary RBDs	Resultant fare levels
Y, B, M, H, K, L, V, Q	Primary: Y, B, M, H Secondary: K, L, V, Q	Y, YK, YL, YV, YQ B, BK, BL, BV, BQ M, MK, ML, MV, MQ H, HK, HL, HV, HQ
	Primary RBDs (P): 4 Secondary RBDs (S): 4	P + (P x S) = 20

Fig. 12.2 Dual RBDs for the control of basic economy

Consider the leg/segment inventory control example shown in Fig. 12.2. In coach cabin, there are 8 booking classes in the hierarchy for the control of Regular Economy Fares. Basic Economy fares have a $30 fare differential from Regular Economy Fares. Booking class R Is a dedicated booking class for Basic Economy. In Fig. 12.2, R is shown nested into Y. The authorized limit for Basic Economy can be set equal to Y which means that Basic Economy will always be available when Regular Economy is available. R can also be set a lower authorized limit than Regular Economy Y booking class if desired. Fundamentally, Basic Economy can only be sold if booking class R is available. If booking classes L, V, and Q are closed, then the lowest available booking class is K. If R is closed, then Basic Economy is unavailable. However, if R is open, then the corresponding Basic Economy fare will be $279.

Dual RBDs can also be used for first class upgrades. To access the upsell fare, specific coach booking classes qualify for an upsell, subject to availability of the designated first-class booking classes.

12.3.7.1 Competing Against the LCCs

Sometimes, to fend off LCCs, an FSC may allocate two or three booking classes to Basic Economy, such as R, Z and X in the hierarchy. The lowest class X in Basic Economy may have a fare that is competitive with a LCC's fare. The FSC can keep it open for as long or as short a period as needed to remain competitive in the market.

12.3.8 Seat Selection

The booking class of a booked reservation affects the choice of seats available to passengers. Passengers in higher booking classes typically have access to a wider choice of seats, including premium seats that may be unavailable to lower booking classes. In contrast, those in lower booking classes may face limited options or get assigned seats depending on what is open. Many airlines charge extra for selecting seats, which can also vary depending on the booking class of the reservation.

12.3.9 Corporate Discounts

Corporate discounts are based on existing selling adult fares in the market. Corporate discount fares involve automated pricing where a specific corporate contract's discount is applied dynamically to public fares based on rules. Typically, the Category 25 (Fare By Rule—FBR) discounts only apply to the booking classes at the top of the hierarchy. FBR lets airlines offer unique pricing to companies, distinct from standard public fares. The elimination of RBDs will impact existing corporate contracts that are based on RBD-driven pricing.

12.3.10 Codeshare Agreements

Codeshare agreements between the operating carrier and the marketing carrier require agreement on specific Reservation Booking Designators (RBDs) to be used by the marketing carrier. These agreements specify the RBDs that the marketing carrier can use to book passengers on a flight operated by its partner airline.

Each RBD is tied to specific fare rules regarding refunds, changes, and mileage accrual. The codeshare agreement ensures that the marketing carrier's RBDs correspond to the correct fare rules offered by the operating carrier. RBDs also facilitate revenue sharing between the two airlines. The codeshare agreement, often paired with a Special Prorate Agreement (SPA), outlines how revenue is split between the operating and marketing carrier based on the RBD used for the booking.

Consider a codeshare flight from New York's JFK to London, Heathrow sold by the marketing carrier, American Airlines, that is operated by British Airways. As the operating carrier, British Airways has its own set of RBDs in a hierarchy such as Y for full fare and N for discounted economy. The codeshare agreement allows American to sell seats on the British Airways' flight. When American sells a discounted Economy ticket, its system must map that booking to the corresponding RBD, such as British Airways' L class. The passenger buys a ticket with an American (AA) flight number but will see an "operated by British Airways" note on their itinerary. The underlying RBD ensures that the passenger receives the fare and service that American sold them, according to the terms set by British Airways.

12.3.11 RBD Mapping for Alliances and Interline

In the absence of a universal booking class hierarchy, every airline maintains its own RBD hierarchy. RBD mapping with an alliance or between partner airlines is the business process of aligning an individual airline's booking class codes when a customer books an itinerary across multiple carriers. RBD mapping ensures that an airline's booking classes are mapped to a partner airline's equivalent booking classes, to ensure consistency of service and associated benefits such as priority boarding, lounge access, etc. across the alliance due to the mapping.

12.3.12 Frequent Flyer Accrual

RBD mapping to mileage or points credits is required for accurately calculating how many frequent flyer miles are earned by customers. Further, for codeshare flights, RBD mapping between partner airlines is required to receive equivalent credits on a codeshare flight operated by a different airline.

12.3.13 Frequent Flyer Accrual of Loyalty Points

Loyalty points on airlines like American Airlines are a separate metric used to determine a traveler's elite status tier (e.g., Gold. Platinum, Platinum Pro, Executive Platinum) that is reset annually, with base miles often converting 1:1 into Loyalty Points, but bonus miles do not count toward status. While miles represent cash to spend on redemptions, loyalty points represent status.

Airline loyalty programs have been evolving over the past decade along two dimensions; the accrual of miles and redemption of miles. Airlines have been quick to adopt more stringent rules for the accrual of miles based on the actual value of the tickets [Raiford, 2015]. However, they have been slow at accelerating redemption opportunities for frequent travelers to maximize the burn rate.

Accrual of loyalty points has traditionally been based on the mileage flown and the booking class of the reservation. Table 12.3 illustrates an example of mileage accrual.

In addition, based on frequent flyer tier, a traveler can earn bonus miles. For example, on American Airlines, a traveler can earn bonus miles based on frequent flyer tier that can range from 40% (AAdvantage Gold) to 120% (AAdvantage Executive Platinum).

Table 12.3 Frequent flyer accrual example

Class of service	Purchased fare booking class	Accrual % of eligible miles
First	F, A	200
Business	J, C, D, I, R	150
Coach—Premium economy	W, P	125
Coach—Economy	Y, H, K, M, L, V, G, S, N, Q, O	100
Coach—Basic economy	B	50

Many airlines are moving to a loyalty points system based on total eligible spend and class of service, instead of distance flown and RBD, effectively making it harder to earn top-tier status. Eligible spend includes base fare, ancillaries, carrier-imposed charges and contributions to 'sustainable' aviation fuel (SAF). Moving to the eligible spend model is an attempt to align the accrual of loyalty points with actual customer spend.

A related dependency on RBDs is traveler eligibility for upgrades which is based on the booking class of the reservation. Typically, only RBDs higher in the hierarchy qualify for upgrades from coach to business or first class.

12.4 Dynamic Continuous Pricing

Dynamic pricing is critical for managing offers through NDC that many airlines may leverage in the future as an alternate to quoting a static fare that was filed with ATPCO. Unlike traditional pricing methods, the price given to a customer is a derived fare rather than one set by ATPCO. This derived fare can be influenced by the selling fares of competitors or by using standard revenue management approaches by matching demand to the available supply.

Dynamic pricing is recognized as a significant advancement in managing revenue [Choubert et al., 2015; Fiig et al., 2016]. Many network airlines are attracted to the idea of dynamic pricing and recognize its potential as a cornerstone in the context of NDC for dynamically priced offers [Fiig et al., 2018]. Dynamic pricing enables airlines to transcend traditional pre-filed fares to generate fares dynamically by customer segment in real-time, considering future demand, remaining capacity, expected net contribution, and competitive market dynamics. This approach is often referred to as continuous pricing or continuous dynamic pricing.

In the NDC era, the transition to continuous pricing by a few airlines is a cautious and slow process, with extensive market validation to ensure that it is not dilutionary and value is being captured by the process. Dynamic continuous pricing only works when the offer is created and controlled by the airline. This implies that continuous pricing is only applicable for NDC transactions and not applicable for EDIFACT transactions. However, the airline industry will continue to exist in a hybrid state where traditional fixed-point fares and continuous pricing will coexist. This is because several mid-size and smaller carriers will take a long time to migrate to NDC. For continuous pricing to prevail for all airline bookings requires all airlines worldwide to have migrated to NDC.

The relationship between price and demand plays a central role in dynamic pricing algorithms. By analyzing this relationship, it is possible to determine the most profitable price using the following formula.

$$p^* = \underset{p}{\operatorname{argmax}}\, p \text{ x } d(p)$$

In the equation, p represents the price, while $d(p)$ is the demand function. The optimal price can be calculated by maximizing the expected revenue based on the estimated demand curve. If the demand function $d(p)$ is an accurate representation of the actual demand in the market, p^* is optimal; otherwise p^* and the corresponding revenue will be sub-optimal. The probability of a customer purchasing an itinerary offered is a proxy for the estimate of demand $d(p)$.

For air ancillaries, the demand function d is a function of the price p that is offered and the collection of customer attributes A for the trip. Examples of trip attributes are the market, schedule attributes, fare, and seasonality. Hence, the demand function is $d(p,A)$ and an estimate of demand is based on observing the change in demand conditioned on both price p and customer attributes A. The probability of a customer purchasing an ancillary offered is a proxy for the estimate of demand $d(p,A)$.

The dynamic pricing engine identifies revenue opportunities that occur in the market despite ideal revenue management and fare management initiatives. The above formula can be enhanced by factoring in various pricing and non-pricing elements such as schedule quality identified by departure time and elapsed time, advance purchase, minimum stay restriction, competitor selling fare in the market, etc. The pricing algorithm generates more accurate results when it processes a wide range of relevant data points.

The fare management process establishes all the fares in the market with their rules and restrictions. The itinerary pricing process is used during shopping and pricing of an itinerary for ticketing. Itinerary pricing considers the fare records, restrictions applied to a fare, footnotes, general rules and routing to determine the price of an itinerary. Itinerary pricing is a response from the automated pricing system. Dynamic continuous pricing must work within the imposed guardrails for fares. In the future an airline may decide not to publish their fares through ATPCO and instead only publish them internally. However, that requires the airline and all intermediaries to be NDC compliant for all their bookings.

It is unlikely that leg/segment carriers will migrate to continuous pricing. For these airlines, the definition of the RBD can be maintained or replaced with context for travel-based segmentation for nested inventory controls by flight leg or segment. RBDs or customer segments have a hierarchy based on value. If customer segments are used, they should be mapped to the RBDs resident on the airline reservations inventory system. For carriers on leg/segment inventory controls, the approximate bid price can be calculated from EMSR_B nested booking class controls as follows.

Let j represent the lowest available booking class, with average fare F_j, demand D_J and authorization level AU_j. Then the *Equivalent Bid Price* for the flight leg and date is

$$Equivalent\ Bid\ Price = F_j\ x\ \Pr\left(D_j > AU_j\right)$$

For network carriers, a network optimization model generates the bid prices by leg and cabin. This has the advantage of considering all first order, second order and third order effects in the network. The bid price is the opportunity cost of an incremental seat. Alternately, it can be viewed as the incremental revenue that can be generated in the network with an incremental unit of capacity in the leg/cabin. The minimum bid price for each leg and cabin is initialized to equal an estimate of the direct variable cost and not the fully allocated cost.

When continuous pricing algorithms are developed to respond to shopping requests, the following factors must be considered and are discussed in the following sections.

12.4.1 The Bid Price Hurdle

The total bid price for the itinerary is a hurdle that must be used as an input to establish a floor for the dynamic price. The bid prices curve is stored on the inventory detail record (IDR, IND) of the airline's host CRS. Based on the passenger itinerary, the bid prices on each leg of the itinerary can be added to calculate the total bid price for the itinerary.

Continuous nesting, also known as bid price controls, is used to determine the collection of booking classes that is acceptable and can be priced by the pricing system to determine the lowest available fare for display. Prior to display the itinerary fare must be compared to the total bid price to determine the true net contribution.

The value of the true net contribution together with the willingness to pay by customer segment dictates the magnitude of the discount.

$$True\ Net\ Contribution = Itinerary\ Price_{sc} - \sum_{j \in S} \gamma_j$$

The *Itinerary Fare*$_{sc}$ is the fare returned from the pricing system for service s and class c, γ_j is the bid price based on current bookings for flight leg j; $s \in S$, where S is the collection of services in the network.

The magnitude of the *True Net Contribution* indicates the leverage the airline has to provide a discount off the itinerary price. If the total bid price is within a predefined threshold (e.g. 5% or lower) then a discount will not be applied and the quoted price will be the actual itinerary price determined by the pricing system.

12.4.2 Fare Rules and Restrictions

Existing fare rules and restrictions established during the airline fare management process are required input to determine the itinerary price from the automated pricing system. When a price is quoted below the automated price generated by the pricing system during shopping or ticketing, the same fare rules apply to the discounted fare.

12.4.3 Customer Willingness to Pay

With the growing adoption of NDC, transparency in schedules and selling fares becomes more limited. With the limited value of shopping data that contains competitor selling fares as input, calibration of the customer willingness to pay (WTP) becomes important. This is the process of measuring and refining an airline's understanding of the maximum price a customer is willing to pay for a product or service accurately. Customer WTP must be calibrated by trip-purpose segment, which identifies the context for travel, to understand a customer's internal reservation price. This serves as an input in determining the discount off the selling fare determined from the filed fares and determining the continuous price.

A common functional form used to represent customer willingness to pay (WTP) is a logit function, which is expressed as

$$WTP = \frac{1}{\left(1 + e^{-a+b*Price}\right)}$$

where a is a constant representing the base level of willingness to pay and b is a coefficient determining how much WTP decreases with price increases, essentially showing a decreasing relationship between price and the probability of a customer purchasing a product. When plotted, the logit function creates an S-shaped curve, reflecting that at very low prices, changes in price have a relatively small impact on WTP, while at moderate prices, even small price increases can significantly reduce purchase likelihood, and at high prices the change in WTP is lower again. When parameters a and b are estimated, a higher value for a indicates a higher base level of willingness to pay. This can be interpreted as customers being more likely to purchase at a given price. A larger value for b signifies a steeper decline in WTP as price increases. This can be interpreted as customers being more sensitive to price increases.

Surveys, based on the stated preferences of customers, are generally unreliable for estimating WTP. In contrast revealed preferences, that are based on actual customer behavior during a shopping session are more reliable and can be used to estimate WTP. In the airline context we are concerned about various schedule attributes and price in the valuation process. Discrete choice models like the multinomial logit (MNL) are often used in discrete choice experiments (DCEs) where customers select their favorite itinerary from several options, each with different features and prices. This approach estimates how much customers are willing to pay for specific features or benefits of an itinerary based on their choices in the shopping display. The discrete choice model estimates a utility function where each attribute of a product (like price, schedule attributes) is assigned a coefficient representing its relative importance to the customer. To calculate the WTP, simply divide the coefficient of the attribute of interest by the coefficient of the price attribute. This ratio indicates the highest amount a customer is theoretically willing to pay for a unit increase in the attribute, considering the price. Hence, WTP is simply calculated as the ratio of two marginal utility coefficients.

Using data from past consumer choices can help identify their true willingness to pay. This approach is based on revealed preferences because it focuses on actual behavior rather than stated opinions and surveys. However, a challenge arises when important factors are missing, which can lead to misleading interpretations of the data. An effective way to address this issue is to conduct experiments that measure how much consumers are willing to pay by varying prices and observing the effects on sales. By randomly assigning different price points and using control groups, the risk of confusing variables that affect results can be reduced.

A fundamental issue with using WTP exclusively to generate a continuous price quote is the lengthy calibration process and subsequent concerns about accuracy and value of using this metric if customer behavior patterns have changed for reasons such as competition, brand preference, etc. In principle, if WTP reflects true market conditions, airlines can increase their revenue by identifying customer segments that are willing to pay more. By adjusting prices, they can attract these higher paying customers without driving away those looking for budget options. If the WTP estimate is reliable, it is a valuable input for continuous pricing which provides a discount off the open selling fare based on certain criteria such as the true net contribution. Getting accurate estimates of how much customers are willing to pay helps airlines avoid giving unnecessary discounts on flights where customers would pay more. This method also enables revenue management analysts to automatically prevent customers from exercising buy-down behavior.

12.4.4 Generating the Continuous Price Quote

The objective of continuous pricing is to offer a price that is below the itinerary price generated by the automated pricing system. As an example, if the $300 fare is closed but the $400 fare is open, then perhaps on the price-demand continuum, a $350 fare can be offered. The airline thought process around continuous pricing is *penetration pricing*, when a lower fare is quoted which undercuts competitors. Customers may switch to the cheaper fare. It can be argued that airlines that practice continuous pricing have an advantage over carriers that do not.

With penetration pricing, an airline quotes a lower price than their competitors, then raises it after the test and learn experiments predict lower discounts in steady state. This is the opposite of price skimming, when an airline quotes a higher initial price than the competition and then lowers it as demand decreases. In summary, penetrating pricing works with continuous dynamic pricing and price skimming works with airlines that quote the higher price when a lower RBD is closed.

The potential for perturbing the automated price generated by the pricing algorithm and quoting a lower price exists when there is a significant gap (Δ) between the total bid price for the itinerary and the fixed-point price quote. Thus, continuous pricing may only be applicable for a fraction of the tickets issued by the airline.

Continuous pricing also offers airlines the ability to adjust prices for different customer segments. This requires calibration of the customer's willingness to pay by trip-purpose segment, using a discrete choice model as an option, which is used as input to determine how to perturb the discount during experimentation. In addition, market trends, changes in demand, customer buying habits, and purchasing power can also be considered.

Dynamic continuous pricing is not applicable for Constructed Fares Discounted Fares (Cat19–22), and Negotiated Fare with Display Category T or C.

An audit trail must be maintained in the remarks field of the PNR or Order that explains how the dynamic continuous price was quoted to the customer.

12.4.5 Price Discrimination and Personalized Pricing

The term *pricing power* is normally used to describe the impact of price changes to a product on the demand for the product measured by the price elasticity of demand. However, true pricing power goes beyond the traditional definition and is a key for success in a competitive landscape. To be successful, airlines need real-time visibility into their customer segments based on context for travel, factor in market competitiveness and determine a fair price quote for a customer request based on prevailing market conditions.

Pricing is an immensely powerful tool. It shapes customer beliefs, drives customer emotion and perception of the product. An airline's mission and values are reflected in a fair price quote. For customer retention and generating repeat business, the pricing model should be calibrated to ensure customers receive value for the product commensurate with the customer experience.

The importance of an itinerary price cannot be understated. Price is the most effective way to increase profits. A study of Fortune 500 companies by McKinsey and Co. in the 1990s [Marn & Rosiello, 1992] showed that a 1% improvement in price leads to a 11% improvement in operating profit. Increasing volume by the same amount (additional sales) resulted in only a 3.3% increase. Cutting variable costs by 1% resulted in a 7.8% increase and cutting fixed costs produced a 2.3% increase. While this study may not be directly applicable to airlines, the message is clear. Pricing power leads to incremental profits.

12.4.5.1 What Is Personalized Pricing?

Is personalized pricing the same as irrational pricing? No, they are not the same, but they have a common trait—market acceptance will be a challenge.

While personalized pricing involves tailoring prices to individual customers based on their purchase history and preferences, irrational pricing refers to setting prices that are not based on logical market factors, often driven by psychological manipulation and biases in consumers that do not reflect the value of the product, and not necessarily tied to specific customer information or demographics.

However, attempts to personalize pricing for an individual continue, without having a full understanding of its detrimental impacts.

For almost three decades, active discussions have been held at industry conferences on the benefits of pricing products for a segment of ONE. Yet, this is nowhere close to reality.

One of the benefits of NDC that is echoed by IATA since it was introduced in 2012, is the personalization of the travel offer based on a customer's preferences and travel history. Well after a decade later, this is not a priority for airlines that are mired in negotiating better commercial deals with GDSs for NDC bookings.

What does this really mean?

A personalized bundle pertains to the composition of the offer bundle and the offer price. Personalization of the offer is limited in scope since most airlines just sell five ancillary products of any significance, When the number of ancillary products offered increases, the number of potential bundles increases. The number of possible bundles when there are n ancillary products is $2^n - 1$. For example, with 5 ancillary products, the number of possible bundles is 31, which means that many customers will receive identical ancillary bundle offers. However, unlike bundles, the price offered to every customer can be unique. Is this a wise idea?

Personalized pricing, also known as one-to-one pricing, based on an individual's past propensity to buy is not advocated with continuous pricing, both at the itinerary level and the offer bundle level. Continuous pricing essentially is dynamic continuous pricing which allows airlines to change prices in an instant based on booking pace and relevant market data if applicable.

Personalized pricing requires deep knowledge about an individual customer's willingness to pay, which is challenging to estimate. If different customers see different prices for the same itinerary at the same time, it is detrimental and erodes consumer confidence in the brand and customer goodwill. Continuous pricing should be by trip-purpose segment, which is the segmentation based on context for travel. A trip-purpose segment is an alternative approach to segmenting customers instead of using RBDs.

A significant hurdle to adopting personalized pricing is the General Data Protection Regulation (GDPR), a law that protects the personal data of European Union (EU) citizens [Millet, 2023]. The law also applies to organizations that process the data of EU citizens outside of the EU. In addition, the California Consumer Privacy Act (CCPA), a data privacy law that protects personal information must be followed. Both the GDPR and CCPA laws have global reach.

12.4.5.2 The Amazon Pricing Experiment

In 2000, Amazon was mostly an online book and media store. On Labor Day 2000, Amazon.com made its foray into dynamic pricing and experimented with charging different prices to individual customers for the same DVDs and books. Consumers on DVDtalk.com saw some buyers paid more for the same DVDs. One person bought "Titus" for $24.49. The next week, the price went up to $26.24. After deleting cookies, the price dropped to $22.74.

Some thought Amazon charged loyal customers more based on the assumption that repeat customers would pay more for the convenience. However, repeat customers did notice a 3–5% price increase. As expected, this news spread online fast. The customer response to charging different prices to different customers for the same commodity was swift and negative. After Amazon launched its personalized pricing, the poorly conceived experiment was eventually abandoned when they saw higher customer abandonment rates and the fundamental recognition that their business model depended on selling more products to more people, and not less products to fewer people.

In the airline industry, the price of an itinerary is dictated by the booking classes used, fare combinability, other fare rules, footnotes, general rules, and routing to arrive at a price. Perhaps it is an illusion since there are many fares in every market, but pricing an itinerary is *never* a personalized price for an individual like what Amazon attempted to do in 2000.

12.4.5.3 The Bay Area Hotel Pricing

In January 2025, the San Francisco Chronicle (SFGATE) published an article based on their research into hotel rates at major OTA platforms for the same hotel rooms and hotel stays using different devices, browsers, and while browsing from different geographic regions [Spencer, 2025]. SFGATE compared hotel room rates for five different sites (Kayak, Booking.com, Trivago, Expedia and Hotels.com) and found that residents in the Bay Area travelers were charged more based on their IP address. Price discrimination in this scenario is based on the online retailer's inference that consumers browsing from the Bay Area will pay a lot more than consumers browsing from less affluent cities like Phoenix and Kansas City. The report even highlights an example of a Bay Area test user being offered a nightly rate for a Manhattan hotel room that was $500 more per night than the rate offered to consumers in the less affluent cities for the same hotel rooms and check-in/check-out dates. While Bay Area consumers may have more disposable income, it does not necessarily mean that they will pay inflated prices for hotel rooms. Online price discrimination relies on a simple idea. Some buyers will spend more. They will often do so if they don't know about cheaper choices. These buyers agree to higher prices without comparing options.

This is not personalized pricing, but price discrimination targeted at consumers that reside in a specific geographic location.

Is price discrimination of this nature a revenue management practice? The answer is NO. Hotel revenue managers are trained to understand the value of their product and set hotel selling rates to boost income and keep guests happy. Online travel agencies don't have this detailed knowledge about customer segmentation, unique preferences, and remaining capacity at a property to make an informed decision. They lack the same grasp of the market and can negatively impact a hotel brand besides creating rate parity issues for branded properties. It is a prime example of OTA greed.

12.4.5.4 The Orbitz Pricing Experiment

In 2012 Orbitz experimented with showing higher hotel prices to users browsing from Mac computers. The Wall Street Journal reported that Mac users paid $20 to $30 more per night for hotels than PC users [Mattioli, 2012]. Orbitz claimed that Mac users were 40% more likely to book 4-star and 5-star hotels. Orbitz defended its actions as a short-term experiment and later removed this feature and now claims that all users see the same search results. Like the Bay Area example, this is not personalized pricing, but price discrimination targeted at consumers that browse using a Mac.

Are the Bay Area and Orbitz scenarios examples of irrational pricing? Perhaps they are because pricing actions taken were based on incomplete information.

12.4.6 The Importance of Experimentation

The WTP calculation assumes that marginal utility is constant, which might not always hold true in real-world situations. The accuracy of the WTP estimate depends heavily on the quality of the underlying data and the design of the discrete choice experiment. There are limitations on customer WTP calibration. Calibration is time-consuming and frequently once the calibration is completed, the market has changed and the WTP is no longer an accurate representation of a customer's willingness to buy. Further, in travel, consumer preferences and attitudes are dynamic and are influenced by their interactions outside of the travel domain, competitors, economy, and purchasing power. This gap can be addressed with test and learn experimentation. Experimentation is an integral component of any sound continuous pricing deployment. Test and learn experimentation address these external shocks to the system and provides a continuous learning environment that adapts to changes in real-time.

An adaptable approach is to conduct *test-and-learn experimentation*, using a reinforcement learning technique commonly known as the "multi-armed bandit" (MAB), to determine the discount that maximizes conversion rates. This is different from the traditional A/B testing, a statistically controlled method.

The multi-armed bandit refers to a problem in machine learning in which there are multiple options (like slot machine arms) with unknown reward probabilities, and the goal is to maximize the cumulative reward by choosing the best option while still exploring other possibilities to learn their true value. The multi-armed bandit problem works in a stateless environment. Each decision is made independently and does not rely on previous choices or conditions. It is equivalentr to pulling levers on several slot machines, treating each one separately. The core challenge is to balance exploring less-known options ("exploration") with exploiting the currently best-known option ("exploitation") to maximize the reward over time.

Implementation of the test and learning experimentation model should be context sensitive [Byrd & Darrow, 2021]. Contextual reinforcement learning tracks customer responses by trip-purpose segment. Personalization of the offered price based on the context for travel is important to improve conversion rates. Discounts can be recommended by the trip-purpose segment, and in situations where the customer travels frequently, the offer can be personalized based on past purchase history and preferences.

Experimentation provides a direct approach to running controlled test experiments to learn customer behavior. Unlike model-based decision support tools, business experimentation with the multi-armed bandit, a reinforcement learning application, in many respects is simpler to use and implement. The idea is to test new prices directly. Product designs or systems/processes are compared to current ones to see if there is a performance improvement. Simple binary tests (e.g., old versus new) are commonly referred to as A/B testing. A multi-armed bandit implementation is more general, adapts to the current environment, learns over time, and can support running multiple experiments simultaneously.

Using MAB for dynamic pricing could lead to different customers seeing different prices for the same product unless prices are varied consistently by a predefined factor. Otherwise, it could lead to an inconsistent user experience and repeat the issues faced with the Amazon and Orbitz experiments.

Test and learn experimentation can help answer common business questions such as:

1. *What are the discounts for continuous pricing?*
2. *What are the price points for air ancillaries?*
3. *What is the best price point for the bundle to maximize revenue?*
4. *Which algorithm or business approach works best?*
5. *How are my revenues and conversion rates impacted by changes to my screen display rules?*
6. *Which bundled offer maximizes revenue?*

The model can be implemented with different sampling methods such as Epsilon-Greedy, Epsilon Decreasing, Upper Confidence Bound (UCB), or Thompson Sampling to improve future actions that will maximize the potential of the reward.

Epsilon-Greedy sampling is a conservative approach that is mostly focused on exploiting the current best option but with a small probability "epsilon" randomly chooses another option to explore. Epsilon serves as a exploration parameter which governs the trade-off between exploration and exploitation. Simple and easy to deploy, it works well for simple scenarios but performs poorly when reward distributions are complex.

Epsilon-Decreasing sampling builds upon the Epsilon-Greedy algorithm, gradually reducing the exploration rate over time. Instead of selecting a fixed value of ε like in Epsilon-Greedy, the Epsilon-Decreasing strategy selects an initial ε value that gradually decreases over time, typically with an exponential decay. This strategy allows for more exploration in the initial stages and transitions toward greater exploitation as the algorithm gathers more information.

The Upper Confidence Bound sampling chooses an option based on a calculated "upper confidence bound" which considers both the average reward and the uncertainty associated with that option. This sampling approach encourages exploration of options with higher uncertainty while still favoring options with higher average rewards. It works best in scenarios where uncertain options must the prioritized for exploration.

The Thompson Sampling approach maintains a probability distribution for each option's reward based on past observations and samples from this distribution to select an option. By tracking the changes in the parameters of the distribution over time, how the algorithm understands and adapts to the demand function can be observed. It is an effective method for more sophisticated exploration in situations when the reward distributions are complex or uncertain.

Contextual bandits build on the multi-armed bandit approach for testing and learning [Byrd & Darrow, 2021]. This model incorporates the current state into decision making, allowing for choices based on specific user context rather than just past data. It improves decisions based on factors like user origin, their prior activities on the site, and the devices they use. Microsoft Research developed a testing service named Vowpal Wabbit, which employs contextual bandits through both open-source online and offline training methods. The foundational work for this model was done by Miroslav Dudik, John Langford and Lihong Li at Yahoo! Research in 2007 before it was adopted by Microsoft [Dudik et al., 2011]. In airline retailing, the trip-purpose segment is a key contextual element, and further micro segmentation can be added to these trip categories as needed. In addition to the purpose of the trip, the true net contribution by range must be included to determine the optimal discount that maximizes conversion rates.

Figure 12.3 illustrates and compares standard A/B testing to the muti-armed bandit model. In this example, for a trip-purpose segment, there are four options for continuous pricing discounts from the published available fare that is open based on context for travel. The context is the trip-purpose segment and the true contribution by range intervals.

Both MAB and A/B testing approaches use experimentation. In A/B testing results are manually evaluated before starting the exploitation phase while with MAB, evaluation happens continuously, and MAB automatically reallocates traffic to the best performers based on the sampling method used and quickly finds the best option from a set of options.

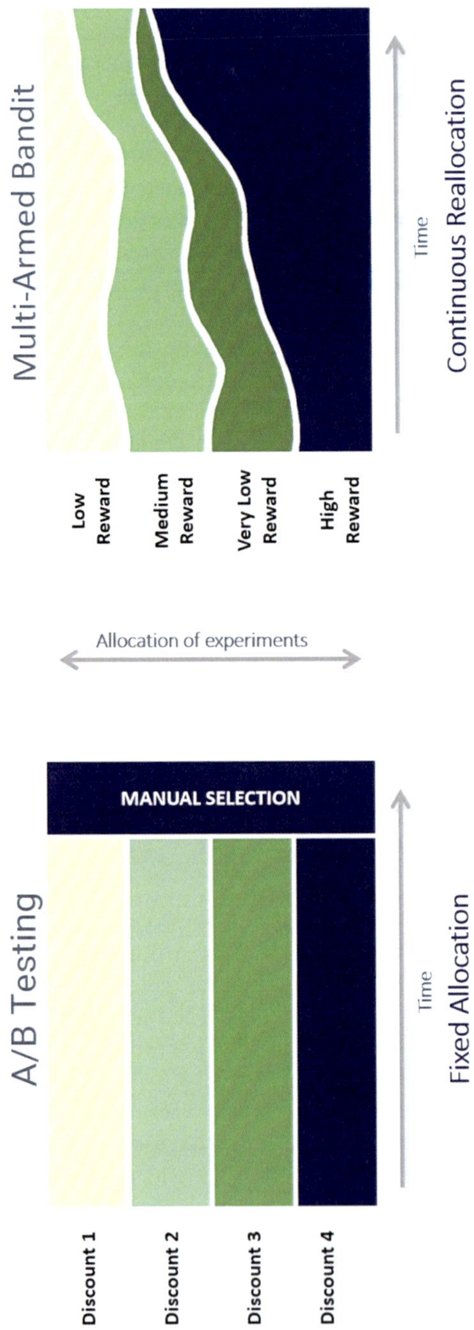

Fig. 12.3 A comparison of A/B testing and the multi-armed bandit

12.4.7 On the Optimality of Market-by-Market Dynamic Pricing Solutions

The objective of Origin and Destination (O&D) revenue management methodology is to compute network-optimal bid prices for an airline network with a non-linear revenue mix optimization model. In this model all demand at a service class level is included in a capacity constrained optimization model. The model determines the right mix of short-haul, medium-haul and long-haul demand that should be accommodated on an airline's global route network to maximize total revenues subject to capacity constraints.

The revenue mix optimization model, which is like a typical product mix model, but with a nonlinear objective function to account for the probability density function of the underlying demand model, simultaneously considers all the first order, second order and third order network effects to arrive at a bid price by flight leg and date. The bid price for a flight leg can be interpreted as the opportunity cost of not having an incremental seat on a flight leg. Alternately it can be interpreted as the minimum acceptable fare to accept a passenger on the flight leg.

What is implicit in the revenue mix model is the evaluation and trade-offs of all the network effects *simultaneously*. For example, consider the 3 × 3 hub-and-spoke network shown in Fig. 12.4.

If there is a surge in demand from SEA to DFW because of a promotional fare filing, the first, second and third order impacts on traffic flows in a hub complex are summarized in Table 12.4 below.

The narrative for the positive and negative higher order network effects is as follows:

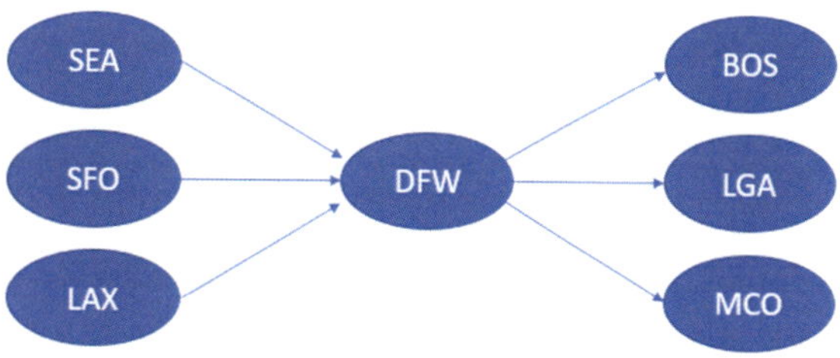

Fig. 12.4 Sample hub and spoke network

Table 12.4 Higher order network effects

First order effects (+)	Second order effects (−)	Third order effects (+)
SEA-DFW	SEA-BOS	SFO-BOS
	SEA-LGA	SFO-LGA
	SEA-MCO	SFO-MCO
		LAX-BOS
		LAX-LGA
		LAX-MCO

1. First Order Effect: When a promotional fare is introduced from SEA to DFW, the SEADFW market will see a surge in demand (+)
2. Second Order Effect: Because of the increased demand from SEA to DFW (local market), availability will be restricted to the connecting markets that have the SEADFW leg in common (−)
3. Third Order Effect: Because availability is restricted for the connecting markets originating out of SEA, there will be greater availability for markets that do not originate in SEA and hence they will see increased traffic (+).

12.4.7.1 Dynamic Pricing Solution Approach

The approach taken today by many airlines and vendors is to develop a Dynamic Pricing solution to determine the dynamic price for an itinerary based on the shopping request (departure dates, return date, market). The dynamic pricing model is one dimensional in the sense that its universe is limited to the market for which a dynamic price should be returned for a specific itinerary in the shopping response. The current market-by-market dynamic pricing model considers the host airline's fares as well as the fares of the competitors in the market to arrive at a price point (the "dynamic" price) that maximizes the potential conversion rate based on a net contribution model. The net contribution model considers an airline's bid prices by flight leg and date. However, the computation of the dynamic price for the market is done in isolation without considering network effects simultaneously.

Viewed in isolation on a market-by-market basis, the question is whether the *dynamic price response is optimal for the request at the network level?* It is not because this approach does not consider simultaneous first order, second order and third order network effects. The model described above is a greedy approach. Yet, simultaneously considering network effects across all markets with competitive shopping data to determine the dynamic price for a specific customer request is a formidable task. Further, in this scenario, the objective function is not necessarily concave and there will be dis-continuities adding further complexity (stability due to the absence of a market equilibrium) to the problem.

There are two approaches to gain confidence in the results. They are:

1. Establish a test environment with several hundred markets and deploy the dynamic pricing engine in a passenger simulation model like PODS (Passenger Origin-Destination Simulator) to measure the true impact of the market-by-market approach on network revenues and airline profitability. The simulation model may be able to provide guidance on parameter settings that will ensure that the dynamic pricing model is revenue positive at the network level (and not neutral or revenue negative).
2. A second approach is to simply measure the first order effect (positive or negative revenue at the market level based on the dynamic price) of a dynamically priced itinerary across a large number of markets and determine if the positives outweigh the negatives. In this scenario there is no simulation and no true measure of the impact on network revenues.

12.4.8 The Appeal of Continuous Pricing in an NDC World

NDC is all about an airline's control of the indirect channel. With continuous pricing, only an airline can provide a price quote that can never be duplicated by an intermediary, like a GDS. This is because the continuous pricing algorithm and any associated rules are proprietary to the airline.

The appeal of continuous pricing for airlines is to quote a price that is above the fare level that is closed, but below the next higher published fare level subject to the magnitude of the fare differential between the open fare level and the total bid price for the itinerary. This is essentially a discount off the next fare level that is available for sale. An important point to remember is that a priced itinerary, with or without continuous pricing, must be compliant with all the fare rules. The fare rules of the higher fare level to which the discount is applied will apply for the continuous pricing-based itinerary. The price discount is similar to corporate fare discounts with ATPCO's Category 25 (Fare-by-Rule) in the sense that though the discount is applied, the fare rules associated with the market for the RBD that is open will prevail.

The Lufthansa Group and United Airlines were the first to deploy continuous pricing for their respective NDC channels. Air Canada followed. American Airlines started deploying continuous pricing in select markets in 2025.

12.5 NDC Benefits for Pricing, Revenue Management and Inventory Control

Adoption of NDC has unique benefits for pricing, revenue management and inventory control. Various issues that exist today can be resolved to streamline the revenue generation process.

12.5.1 Proactive Pricing

Price leadership in a market has never gained traction in the airline industry. In an asset intensive industry, fare matching facilitated by ATPCO is the dominant business process. Setting fares in a market based on quality of service and management objectives, despite their intrinsic value, have not been adopted in the airline industry. This can change with NDC adoption since technically all fares distributed through the NDC API are private fares. Further, in the NDC end state, airlines do not have to distribute their fares to ATPCO. If they distribute fares through ATPCO to support the direct channel, airlines can restrict access to who can view the fares. This can lead to a tempered transition to proactive pricing based on competition, market domination, and the quality of the schedule.

12.5.2 Eliminate Revenue Leakage on Codeshare Flights Caused by Inconsistent Availability

In the NDC end state, airlines do not have to distribute numeric availability by booking class to GDSs since the airline is in control of all offers inclusive of the price for the itinerary. Airlines will continue to segment passengers, have restrictions on fares, and maintain multiple fare levels. Booking classes will be internal to the airline pricing system since booking class availability is no longer distributed to intermediaries. On codeshare flights, the discrepancy in marketing carrier codeshare booking class availability caused by delayed AVS transmissions from the host CRS to the GDSs will be eliminated. Hence, situations such as a lower valued booking class being available on the marketing flight while it is closed on the operating flight will no longer exist and revenue leakage can be avoided.

12.5.3 Continuous Pricing Is a Competitive Differentiator

In the NDC end state not every airline will adopt continuous pricing. For those that do, there are unique benefits.

Continuous pricing fills the gaps on the price-demand curve with infinite price points, thereby generating revenue that may otherwise have been lost. The itinerary prices quoted by the airline for an offer request from any channel will be lower than how they are priced with discrete price points today in the GDS and direct channels.

A secondary benefit is that the continuous price for an itinerary is the ticketed fare. Before continuous pricing, the market class fare value ($MCFV$) and the total bid price for the itinerary are used to determine booking class availability followed by pricing the itinerary. Regardless of the level of accuracy of $MCFV$ used, it will not be the same as the ticketed fare. Continuous pricing bridges this chasm.

A third benefit is the guarantee that the price quoted will never be below the total bid price for the itinerary. Traditional transaction processing relies on the bid price to determine directional booking class availability which is then used by airline pricing systems to price the itinerary. The total bid price for the itinerary (one way or round trip) can serve as a lower bound during the calculation of the total itinerary price by the pricing system. This will require an enhancement to existing airline pricing systems.

12.5.4 Out of Sequence Bookings and Revenue Equalization

Travel agents who make bookings out of sequence may unintentionally reduce revenue. These bookings involve securing a reservation in a high-demand period and complete booking the rest of the itinerary at a later time. Consider the London-Bombay (LON-BOM) market as an example. If December is a peak season for traveling from BOM to LHR, a travel agent may first book the return segment to secure a booking in a lower-priced booking class. Later, they will add the outbound segment from LHR to BOM for departure during an off-peak season, such November. To determine availability with O&D controls, it is essential to focus on the true O&D directional market, which in this case is LON-BOM and the point of commencement of travel is LON. The market fare value for LON-BOM should be used when determining availability, aligning with the fare filing process The rules for fares, such as advance purchase, minimum stay, and seasonality, are always determined by the outbound departure date. It is crucial to adhere to these rules when retrieving the market value (*MCFV*) for availability determination.

To compensate for the decrease in revenue, the inventory system must automatically close one or more booking classes that are open on the outbound segment to balance out the potential revenue loss. This practice is known as *revenue equalization*. The main goal of O&D inventory controls is to ensure that SOTO (sold outside, ticketed outside) and SITI (sold inside, ticketed inside) bookings are priced identically. By utilizing journey data and conducting a thorough evaluation of the entire trip, any potential revenue loss caused by out-of-sequence bookings made by travel agents can be rectified. Only a small number of O&D carriers like Emirates Airways[1] have integrated revenue equalization logic into their host CRS inventory control systems.

In the NDC end state, this problem of out of sequence bookings is eliminated since the travel agents submit a shopping request to the airline and have no knowledge of booking class availability, which may not even exist if the airline is practicing classless revenue management. The airline response must be an itinerary price for every request based on the point of commencement of travel.

12.5.5 Addressing Gaps in Branded Fare Families

Most airlines have three or more branded fare products. For fares associated with economy class, most airlines require a minimum of 10 to 15 fare levels. A fare level is a fare product identified by a unique RBD. For a given fare level, maintaining a fixed fare differential to the higher valued branded fare products simplifies the management of branded fares.

For example, consider three branded fare products Basic, Standard, and Premium. For RBD M, the Standard branded fare can be \$50 more than Basic and Premium can be \$75 more than Standard. Booking class to branded fare product mapping is the norm. Hence an RBD maps uniquely to a single branded fare product. If an airline has three branded fare products and requires 12 fare levels, then $3 \times 12 = 36$ RBDs are required which is not feasible. Market reality is that airlines run out of RBDs for a consistent representation of selling fares for the branded fares matrix. This can be overcome by mapping fare basis codes to booking classes by brand which is not a manageable process. Hence, airline inventory

[1] Discussion with Ramesh Venkat, SVP Revenue Management, Emirates, June 2012

systems deploy a hybrid approach with few booking classes mapped to the more expensive and valuable branded fare products leaving gaps in the branded fare matrix. Ideally, airlines want the capability to upsell to a higher valued branded fare product when a customer has selected a lower valued branded fare product. For simplicity, the "upsell" fare should be a *derived fare*, derived from the fare of the lower valued branded fare product, that is cheaper than the published fare for the higher valued branded fare product. GDSs cannot support this feature external to the airline host CRS due to the absence of an ATPCO standard and the issue of the Fare Guarantee Policy contractual provision where GDSs pay the debit memos resulting from fare or tax on under collected tickets that meet the criteria for reimbursement.

The definition and deployment of branded fares and associated inventory controls are vastly simplified by NDC since the airline is in control of the offer creation process. An approach is to define *reference fares* for the lowest valued branded fare product. The number of fare levels is at the discretion of the airline, e.g., 12, 15, etc. The fares for the higher valued branded fare products can be derived from the reference fares either with a fixed fare differential or a multiplication factor that is greater than one (or less than one if the reference fare is defined for the highest valued branded fare product). With this approach inventory control can be synchronized by fare level across all branded fares, so that they are either open or closed.

An approach is to use the CAT25 discount calculation to derive all the fares for the lower valued branded fare products from the reference fares for the highest brand. For corporate discounts, since a discount cannot be applied over a discount (a CAT25 over an existing CAT25 fare), the negotiated fares capability with CAT35 together with CAT25 can be applied to calculate the corporate discount with the Security Table 983 and Fare Creator Table 979 located in CAT35.

Table 12.5 illustrates how an airline can support branded fare families across all channels of distribution without the issue of running out of RBDs. This is accomplished by using the same booking class across branded fare products at the same level, identified by a character in the fare basis code. This approach ensures consistency in content delivery across all channels of distribution, both direct and indirect.

Table 12.5 Branded fare family mapping example market: DFW-SFO

	Basic		Standard		Premium	
Booking class (RBD)	Fare basis code	Fare	Fare basis code	Fare	Fare basis code	Fare
Y	Y……3	$700	Y……2	$750	Y……1	$825
B	B……3	$625	B……2	$655	B……1	$695
M	M……3	$550	M……2	$580	M……1	$620
…	…		…		…	…
Q	Q……3	$300	Q……2	$350	Q……1	$425

The RBDs and fare basis codes shown in the table are internal to the airline and not published to intermediaries or third parties. The internal fare filing process will require a new standard that does not exist today. But it is airline-controlled and airline-maintained. The first character of the fare basis code represents the booking class code, and the last character represents the branded fare product. Hence in this case Basic is "3", Standard is "2", and Premium is "1". Enforcing this standard eliminates the need to maintain a mapping of fare basis codes to branded fare products.

This approach of storing the branded fare family mapping on an airline's pricing system resolves the fundamental issue of not having enough booking classes to support a full matrix of fares. Deployment of the branded fare family mapping is limited to the airline's pricing system since the itinerary price is controlled by the airline, regardless of the distribution channel.

This approach supports synchronized nesting across all branded fares. This means that a booking class is either open or closed for all branded fare products. To avoid revenue dilution, there are two requirements:

1. The fare qualifications for fare basis codes associated with a row are roughly the same. Hence, the fare amount is the only difference in each row, besides the attributes bundled with the branded fare product.
2. Pricing analysts need to ensure that there is no fare overlap from one row to the next. In other words, for a given tier (row), the fare amount for Premium should be less than the fare amount for Basic for the next higher tier. In the example above, the Premium B fare of $695 should be less than the Basic Y fare of $700.

12.5.6 Round Trip Availability and Inventory Control

Round trip controls cannot be implemented in a GDS environment. They are availability for the round trip and integrity of the round-trip itinerary.

Booking class availability in the GDS is directional. The availability of the inbound segments by virtue of being directional is not influenced by the outbound segment (segments) that has (have) been booked. If segments on an itinerary are married in the GDS, they are sold as a single unit and cannot be cancelled, priced, rebooked or issued individually. It is a feature that allows airlines to control inventory by combining two or more segments in the sell request and processing it as a single unit to avoid revenue leakage. Married segment indicators on the GDS can typically be applied for three segments (and in some cases up to six) on an outbound and return journey, but the indicator cannot be applied on the last outbound segment to the first inbound segment. For round-trip tickets, airlines require the ability to link all segments that are sold together as part of the round-trip fare during the booking and ticketing process to avoid revenue leakage. This link should only be broken with consent from the airline. For airline-controlled offers and orders, the airline can ensure the integrity of the round trip and treat it as a single unit for pricing and ticketing.

12.5.7 Eliminating Ticketing Time Limit Churn

Ticketing Time Limit (TTL) churn is a prohibited practice where travel agents repeatedly cancel and rebook the same flight itinerary to circumvent expiration deadlines, holding inventory without purchasing tickets or attempting to secure lower fares. Reservation processing for non-NDC bookings are monitored by revenue integrity (RI) applications to identify travel agents who circumvent ticketing time limits which are enforced as a pricing rule. Travel agents can create churn by cancelling and rebooking the same passenger multiple times on the same flight to extend the ticketing time limits. Some airlines counter this behavior by applying fees for excessive cancellations and can lead to automated cancellation of the entire PNR. In the NDC end state, TTL can be avoided.

Corporate Travel

13

AI is not going to replace humans, but humans with AI are going to replace humans without AI

Karim Lakhani

Abstract

The chapter begins with an overview of corporate travel and the stakeholders in the corporate travel space. Historically, corporate travel has lagged leisure travel with limited innovation for many decades. With advances in technology, corporate booking tools will transform over the next decade. Managed business travel will undergo a major digital transformation with the advent of AI-powered technology. The marketplace for unmanaged business travel with small and medium-sized businesses will also undergo a transformation, powered by advances in technology that will provide visibility and accountability. Corporate travel is also on the verge of major change, with the advent of agentic AI. The new AI Agents, using Large Language Models (LLMs), will automate travel agency workflows by handling tasks from initial customer contact to complex booking and itinerary management.

Karim Lakhani, Harvard Business School Professor and coauthor of the 2020 book "*Competing in the Age of AI*" specializes in workplace technology and AI. He has conducted pioneering work in identifying how digital transformation has remade the world of business.

There is a prevailing sentiment that corporate travel, compared to leisure travel, has been slower to embrace innovation and adapt to changing needs. This lag can be attributed to various factors. All that is about to change, and corporate travel is on the cusp of a major revolution with the rise of Agentic AI.

B. Vinod, *The Era of Airline Revenue Management with Offers and Orders*,
Management for Professionals, https://doi.org/10.1007/978-3-032-24197-9_13

13.1 Corporate Travel Overview

After the pandemic of 2020, travel rebounded in 2022. It was "revenge travel" from the leisure customer base that surged to unprecedented levels. While leisure travel still dominates the landscape, corporate travel rebounded in 2024 to the 2019 pre-pandemic levels. In the aftermath of the pandemic, a shrinking subset of corporate travelers spend more time on the road, leveraging the flexibility of remote work. They often extend their visits, mixing workdays with leisure days at their destinations. These travelers often seek more than just a hotel for stays lasting from six weeks to six months. Long-term accommodation is becoming a key option for business trips that stretch over several weeks or months.

It is expected that managed business travel will undergo a major digital transformation with the advent of AI-powered technology from booking experience to program management. The marketplace for unmanaged business travel with small and medium-sized businesses will also undergo a transformation, driven by advances in technology that will provide visibility and accountability. Adoption is critical to move the dial in the corporate travel space.

From a revenue management perspective, there is not a distinction between accepting a corporate traveler versus accepting a leisure traveler since acceptance is always a function of the value of the reservation request and not influenced by the loyalty tier or lifetime value of the customer, which can cause revenue dilution. Faulty corporate program management policy from the airline can have an adverse impact on airline revenues that cannot be corrected quickly. Core revenue management principles like estimation of displacement cost can be used to determine the corporate discounts for corporate customers based on the quality of the revenue and sales volume. This is required to avoid revenue dilution and spoilage.

Conversely, corporations must have an efficient request for proposal (RFP) evaluation process with competing airlines when corporate discounts are negotiated. This is an ongoing, periodic process to ensure that they have extracted favorable discounts, terms and conditions with airlines. Consolidation of network carriers over the past two decades have negatively impacted corporate buyers who lose negotiating power, leading to lower corporate discounts and higher fares. Key mergers were Air France / KLM in 2004, America West Airlines / US Airways in 2005, Delta Air Lines / Northwest Airlines in 2008, United Airlines / Continental Airlines in 2010, Southwest Airlines / Air Tran Airways in 2011, American Airlines / US Airways in 2013, Alaska Airlines / Virgin America in 2018 and Alaska Airlines / Hawaiian Airlines in 2024.

A corporate travel program is a system that organizes all business travel activities for a company. This includes booking trips, setting travel policies, and managing expenses. The goal of a corporate travel program is to make business travel efficient, cost-effective, and safe for employees and the organization.

A corporate travel program involves various departments, including IT, accounting, finance, HR, and risk compliance. Typically, a full-time travel manager oversees the entire program to ensure it runs smoothly.

Unlike leisure travel, corporate travel is complex with several nuances. The average corporate fare that is ticketed is more expensive than leisure because customers are more schedule sensitive and tend to book closer to flight departure. In the digital era, corporate travelers expect access to comprehensive content and are used to high touch world class service which are the hallmarks of a successful travel management company.

13.2 The Time to Shakeup Corporate Travel is NOW

There is a prevailing sentiment that corporate travel, compared to leisure travel, has been significantly slower to embrace innovation and adapt to change influenced by technology and business processes. This perceived lag can be attributed to four specific factors: risk aversion, existing partnerships, internal hurdles and technology adoption.

13.2.1 Risk Aversion and Corporate Bureaucracy

Corporations, especially larger, more mature companies, tend to be risk-averse and navigate bureaucratic processes, including legal and IT reviews, before adopting new technologies or vendors. This cautious approach can slow down the implementation of new tools and practices.

13.2.2 Focus on Existing Partnerships

Many traditional Travel Management Companies (TMCs) have built their business models on long-standing relationships with Global Distribution Systems (GDS) and a focus on high-touch service, potentially hindering the adoption of more technologically driven solutions. TMCs are also to blame for the lack of innovation in corporate travel. TMCs rely on legacy systems and a focus on traditional services, hindering their ability to adapt to evolving corporate traveler needs and technological advancements. This can lead to inefficiencies and a slower pace of change compared to other sectors in the travel industry.

13.2.3 Internal Hurdles

Corporate travel programs face unique challenges, such as ensuring policy compliance, managing costs, prioritizing sustainability, maintaining traveler safety and satisfaction. Balancing these factors with the need for technological advancement can be complex.

13.2.4 Lag in Technology Adoption

While there's a growing interest in incorporating technologies like AI and blockchain in corporate travel, adoption rates may not be as rapid as in other sectors. Historically, corporate travel has been criticized for a technology adoption lag, where companies and their systems struggle to fully integrate advanced solutions like AI and blockchain, despite the proven benefits and a wealth of available tools. This gap is driven by factors including reliance on legacy systems, the cost and complexity of implementation, a lack of internal talent and partner support, and an extremely cautious mindset that prioritizes established practices over innovation. Only a small percentage of travel managers considered AI implementation a priority in late 2024 [Statista, 2024].

13.2.5 Change is Coming for Corporations and Their TMC Partners

Corporate spending has returned to pre-pandemic levels, with a focus on technology-driven solutions. There is a growing interest in utilizing data analytics and AI for personalized recommendations and improved traveler experiences. Agentic AI will have the greatest impact on corporate travel over the next decade. Agentic AI systems can independently authorize and execute transactions end-to-end within the boundaries of corporate travel policy constraints without human intervention. This is a profound change.

Newer, tech-focused TMCs are emerging to challenge the established players. As companies prioritize traveler satisfaction, cost control, and sustainability, the demand for more advanced and integrated travel management solutions is expected to grow.

Ultimately, the future of corporate travel will likely involve a blend of traditional services and cutting-edge technology, with a greater emphasis on flexibility, efficiency, and traveler well-being.

13.3 Corporate Travel Policies

Corporate travel policies are a set of guidelines for employee travel. Employees must follow these guidelines when traveling for work, such as budget limits, preferred airlines, and expense reporting procedures.

A company's travel policy must also clarify the risk management strategy, pre-trip authorization, data management, and emergency procedures. Corporate travel managers must also collaborate with key stake holders in human resources (HR), legal, security and other key stakeholders to assess travel policy for any gaps.

The primary components of corporate travel are booking tools, travel management tools, partnerships, travel support, risk management, air discounts and ancillary content in contracts, analytics and reporting.

13.3.1 Booking Tools

Online booking tools (OBT) allow employees to book flights, hotels, and rental cars. OBTs can be configured to enforce company travel policies, to ensure that the traveler books within established guidelines and budget limits. Popular booking tools for business are SAP Concur, TravelPerk, Navan, Egencia, Serko GetThere, Cytric Travel and Expense, and TripSource that help companies manage corporate trips by consolidating bookings, enforcing travel policies, integrating expenses, and offering self-serice booking for flights, hotels, and car rentals. These OBTs also ensure compliance and cost control with real-time analytics and mobile access.

13.3.2 Travel Management Tools

Besides the OBT, there are various software tools that help companies manage travel expenses, corporate events, reimbursements, and reporting.

Automated rebooking to minimize revenue leakage and lower travel expenses is a key requirement from corporate travel managers. Selling fares based on availability of airline seat inventory can go up or down for various reasons such as surge in demand, cancellations, response to competitor fare actions or the introduction of promotional fares. Predicting selling fares for future dates is also called fare forecasting. Fare prediction models using shopping data can leverage machine learning algorithms such as Q-Learning, to predict when fares would increase and when they would decrease. These models can be used to automate the rebooking of a customer's itinerary to realize cost savings. There are several vendors in the airfare and hotel price assurance space such as Coupa (Yapta was acquired by Coupa Software in 2020), FairFly, Trappit, and others. Many TMCs offer this feature to their corporate customers through a technology partner or their own internally developed tools.

Many OBTs integrate with expense management systems, allowing for automatic submission, tracking and categorization of travel expenses, simplifying the reimbursement process. Examples include SAP Concur, Expensify, Zoho Expense, Ramp, TravelPerk, Navan, and Emburse Enterprise (Emburse Chrome River).

Corporate event management tools integrate travel booking with event planning to streamline the process for organizers and attendees. These tools often offer features like participant invitation and tracking, collaboration on travel details, communication with attendees, and visibility into travel plans. Examples are TravelPerk, Cvent, and InEvent, with each offering a unique set of features and capabilities.

13.3.3 Travel Partnerships

Partnerships are agreements between travel management companies TMCs and various travel suppliers such as airlines, hotels and rental car companies to streamline and optimize business travel. These partnerships typically include corporate discounts based on the volume of bookings. These partnerships are required to create a comprehensive corporate travel program that benefits both the company and its employees.

13.3.4 Travel Support

Corporate travel 24×7 support is the availability of travel assistance and support services around the clock, every day of the week, for business travelers. This ensures that employees on the road can access help and resolve issues at any time, regardless of time zone differences or the time of day. Support can be accessed through various channels such as phone, email, chat, or through a dedicated travel management platform.

13.3.5 Risk Management

When employees are traveling on behalf of a company on business, they are under the care of the company. Travel begins with risk assessment, which identifies potential hazards and vulnerabilities related to specific destinations, travel modes, and employee profiles. Duty of care refers to an employer's responsibility to protect the health and safety of employees traveling for business purposes. This includes taking reasonable steps to mitigate foreseeable risks associated with travel, such as health concerns, security threats, and logistical challenges. Monitoring employee locations, maintaining communication channels, and establishing protocols for emergency situations are required. To bridge a critical gap, mobile messaging and traveler location tracking play an integral role today.

13.3.6 Ancillary Content in Corporate Contracts

Future corporate contracts will include negotiated ancillary content, which will allow buyers and sellers to achieve their objectives mutually. Knowing the marginal utility of ancillaries by market or market entity supports fair contract negotiations.

13.3.7 Travel Data Analytics and Reporting

These are tools to provide transparency into travel spend by category such as air, hotel, rental car, meals, entertainment, etc. to identify opportunities for cost savings in the future.

13.4 Stakeholders in the Corporate Travel Space

There are several stakeholders that have a role in corporate travel programs. Besides the corporate travel manager, there are the travel suppliers, global distribution systems, NDC Aggregators, travel management companies, and software technology providers. This is illustrated in Fig. 13.1.

13.4.1 Corporate Travel Manager and Corporate Buyer

A corporate travel manager oversees all aspects of a company's business travel, including policy creation, vendor negotiation, choice of online booking tool, booking arrangements, and expense management, while prioritizing employee safety and satisfaction. They act as a liaison between the company and travel providers, ensuring efficient and cost-effective travel programs.

In larger corporations, distinct roles exist for corporate travel managers and corporate buyers. A corporate travel manager focuses on the operational aspects of business travel, such as booking, policy management, and traveler support, while a corporate buyer is primarily responsible for negotiating and securing travel contracts and services.

13.4.2 Selecting a TMC

To handle the travel management workload, large corporations and growth oriented companies outsource travel management to a travel management company (TMC). The corporate travel manager shares the travel policy with the selected TMC. A key consideration is access to comprehensive air content. The TMC may source air content from one or more GDSs for standard EDIFACT content and NDC content. The TMC may also optionally leverage an NDC Aggregator for NDC content. Another key consideration is optimization of travel spend tools that are a part of the TMCs business process such as monitoring fares for cancel and rebook opportunities to reduce the cost of travel.

13.4.3 Travel Policy

A corporate travel policy sets clear standards for managing travel, helps control expenses, and informs employees about reimbursable costs to avoid surprises. It provides the necessary rules and guidelines for the corporate travel program. The travel policy must be aligned with the corporate objectives. The following components require consideration when creating a travel policy:

1. Pre-trip approval process
2. Budget limits for domestic. and international trips, including per diem guidelines.

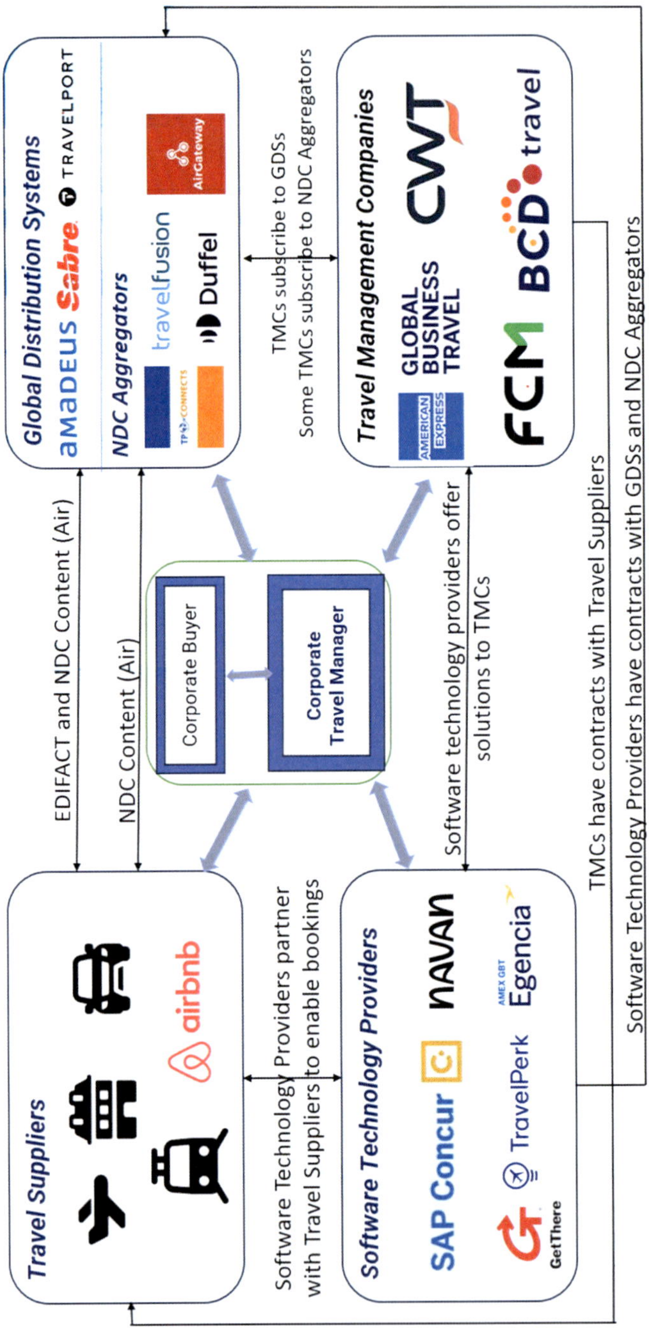

Fig. 13.1 Entities in corporate travel programs

3. Itinerary selected by an employee must be within X% of the lowest fare in the shopping response display.
4. Preferred travel suppliers for air, hotel, car.
5. Class of service based on duration of the trip. For example, business class travel is only allowed on trips greater than eight hours in duration.
6. Types of expenses that are reimbursable (or not).
7. Post-trip expense reporting and reimbursement procedures.
8. Duty of care, emergency contact information, and travel support.
9. Use of corporate credit card to pay for expenses during the trip.

Some of the travel policies such as class of service will be different for road warriors, frequent travelers, and infrequent travelers.

13.5 Negotiating Contracts with Airlines

The deal structure plays a pivotal role in corporate booking programs. Corporate buyers often seek a mix of hard and soft dollar benefits in airline contracts to maximize their value. The deal structure between a corporation and an airline is multi-dimensional. Typical dimensions in contracts are corporate discounts (hard dollars) and soft dollars that define the entire corporate program. Airlines leverage the value of loyalty programs in the soft dollar benefits. The value of a contract always consists of tangible and intangible benefits.

13.5.1 Corporate Discounts (Hard Dollars)

Negotiating corporate discounts with travel suppliers like airlines, hotels, and rental car companies requires a systematic approach. The first step is to gather aggregate employee travel data to identify travel patterns. Insights from travel data lead to a position of strength for negotiations. These may include:

1. Frequency of domestic and international trips by month and year
2. Peak season or seasons travel patterns
3. Most frequently traveled routes, the origin and destination, connecting cities for domestic travel and connecting gateways for international travel if applicable.
4. Total spend with travel supplier by month and year

Airlines categorize corporate customers into tiers based on past performance and projected volume of business. Hence, tier 1 customers get the largest discount, followed by tier 2 and subsequent tiers. The discount is also influenced by "better quality revenue" which is a reflection of booking higher valued fares that have a higher yield. Corporate discounts typically only apply to higher valued booking classes. Hence, if a corporation demands employees to book the lowest fare in the market, the corporate discount may not apply.

Typically, airlines require a minimum of $500,000 in annual volume to consider giving a volume discount. If a company is spending under $1 million, the airline's soft dollar programs may offer more savings than a negotiated discount. Soft dollars are commission payments from the airline to the corporation for hitting negotiated booking volute thresholds. These programs must be compared directly to determine which is more beneficial. Ultimately, airlines want to know how much additional business they will gain by offering a corporate discount. In a few cases, airlines may offer discounts to smaller companies, particularly if they have a high yield spend on premium fares. In addition, there are market share targets, For example, a contract may require a corporation to deliver a target market share, e.g., 70%, on competitive routes like New York - Chicago, New York - Dallas/ Fort Worth, etc. If a corporation fails to meet the specified market share targets, which can be monitored with MIDT data, the airline may revoke the corporate discount or even apply a penalty.

Until 2025, the concept of corporate discounts for booking through non-GDS NDC channels has been an exception rather than the norm. A notable exception is Singapore Airlines that has increased the price differential between fares through the NDC channel and those offered through GDSs, with corporate fares receiving an additional price benefit through NDC.

13.5.2 Soft Dollars

These are less tangible, indirect benefits that support a company's business operations and can improve efficiency or ease of doing business. Frequently soft dollars are used as a bargaining chip to limit corporate discounts in airline contracts. Examples of soft dollars that may be included in a corporate contract are:

Company Demands

1. Flexible change fee waivers or name change waivers for corporate travelers.
2. Priority boarding or access to premium amenities for employees.
3. Bundled fare products with ancillaries that fulfill corporate policy,
4. Corporate travel contracts often include provisions related to status upgrades for employees, enhancing the business travel experience and providing value to the company.
5. Airlines often offer status match programs, allowing employees to leverage their existing elite status with a competing airline to gain equivalent status with their own loyalty program. This is a promotional strategy to attract frequent flyers and encourage them to switch their loyalty. Status matches typically come with a trial period, often ranging from 90 days to a year, and may require meeting certain activity requirements to extend the matched status. In some cases, the loyalty program may be at odds with the corporate policy.

6. Airlines often have fast track or status match programs designed to encourage new employees or corporate travelers to utilize their loyalty programs and potentially attain elite status faster than usual.
7. Status upgrades for executives.
8. Protection from denied boarding on closed out flights.
9. Reaccommodation priority during irregular operations (IROPS) such as flight delays, cancellations, and diversions.
10. Improved data access or reporting from the airline.

Airline Demands

1. Include banner ads of airline as the preferred partner for corporate travel.
2. Promote airline loyalty program to employees
3. Preferred channels for purchase of airline tickets.

13.6 Negotiating Discounts for Hotels and Car Rentals

Like airlines, hotels want to know how many extra bookings they might receive if they provide a corporate discount for the business. To secure the best rates, a corporation must concentrate its bookings with a few selected properties in each location. Features such as free Wi-Fi with every stay, free overnight parking or free breakfast can be part of the negotiation. Most importantly, the corporate travel manager must select hotels that meet the needs and preferences of the traveling employees.

For small and medium-sized businesses (SMB) that lack the volume to attract major hotel chains, the focus must be on regional chains or boutique hotels located in popular areas. Even booking as few as 50 nights a year can be significant for a smaller hotel.

Negotiating car rental corporate discounts are somewhat different from air and hotel. A single agreement with a car rental company can lead to significant savings. If the corporate spending exceeds $100,000, an additional agreement as a backup is beneficial. It is important not to focus solely on getting the lowest daily rate. Car rental companies often make more concessions on other fees, such as surcharges, refueling fees, insurance, and energy recovery fees. These extra costs typically make up about 40% of the total car rental expense.

13.7 The Future of Online Booking Tools

Online Booking Tools (OBTs) have served as the backbone of corporate travel for decades. They enable employees to book flights, hotels and rental cars while ensuring compliance with company travel policies. However, there has been little or no innovation in the OBT space for decades. They seem fixed in time from a bygone era. The archaic workflows and user experience with corporate OBTs date back to the dawn of the Internet era. They have had ample time to evolve, and they never seized the opportunity. With the rapid advances in Agentic AI and AI Agents, there is a growing consensus that the legacy OBT's will perish over the next few years. Agentic AI or AI Agents are the terms used to describe AI systems designed to autonomously make decisions and take actions, including browsing and using websites. The future of corporate travel is not just about technology, but to reimagine efficient workflows to support travel and ultimately enhance employee productivity.

TMCs pride themselves with providing unrivaled choices for customers and providing access to comprehensive content. The larger TMCs offer multiple OBTs such as Concur, GetThere, Cytric, and others. At issue is that these OBTs are legacy and resemble products from the 1990s.

There is a growing awareness with corporate travel managers of the widening gap between legacy OBTs and new AI-powered technologies. This is a clear signal that legacy OBTs, that have been on life support for over two decades, will inevitably perish, giving rise to a new breed of AI-enabled corporate booking tools.

The business of corporate travel will see significant changes in technology and business processes associated with the advent of Agentic AI which can accomplish a specific goal with limited or no supervision. Agentic AI builds on Generative AI techniques by using Large Language Models (LLMs) to function in a dynamic environment.

The key characteristics of Agentic AI systems [DataGrid, 2025; IBM, 2025] are:

1. Autonomous Action.
   They can initiate tasks and take a sequence of actions without continuous human supervision.
2. Goal-Oriented Outcome.
   They can be given a complex goal to achieve. The AI system devises a plan to achieve it, breaking it down into smaller steps.
3. Access External Applications.
   They can interact with external tools and systems, including web browsers and APIs.
4. Adaptability.
   They can adapt to changing conditions and learn from experience.
5. Strict Guardrails
   The orchestration and governance of autonomous software entities require advanced tools and strict guardrails to ensure AI systems operate within predefined boundaries.

Several experimental web-browsing AI Agents to autonomously perform multi-step tasks within a web browser have entered the market since 2024. Some of the products are:

1. OpenAI Operator. The AI agent was launched in January 2025. It can control a web browser to perform tasks such as booking flights and managing reservations.
2. Google Project Mariner. Originally launched in 2024, with a revised version that was released in May 2025 This is an experimental AI agent that can browse and interact with websites to complete tasks, such as buying tickets or groceries.
3. Hugging Face's Open Computer Agent. Released in May 2025. This is an open-source vision-enabled cloud hosted AI agent to interact with the web using a real browser interface. It allows users to instruct it to perform tasks, such as navigating websites, filling out forms, or finding information on a map, using natural language prompts. It is built on open-source foundations and utilizes a vision language model (VLM) and smolagents[1] framework. A VLM connects visual and textual data enabling it to understand and generate content that combines images and language. It is in an experimental phase and has encountered limitations. It demonstrates the potential of AI Agents in automating routine digital activities.
4. Magentic-UI. A research prototype from Microsoft Research, it is an experimental human-centered web agent that integrates human feedback.
5. Genspark AI Browser. This is an AI-integrated browser that can automate browsing tasks and provide intelligent assistance.
6. Devin AI by Cognition Labs is a coding agent and software engineer built to autonomously execute a range of tasks to assist software developers.
7. Amazon's Nova Act. This is an AI framework designed to execute browser functions, allowing the creation of agents for tasks like managing email notifications and calendar entries. Alexa+, the next generation of Amazon's voice assistant, is powered by Generative AI and is specifically built around Agentic AI, leveraging Nova Act.

AI Agents represent a fundamental shift in how travel planning could work. They are not just new interfaces but represent a new breed of digital assistants that are capable of performing complex tasks autonomously. For corporate travelers that want to book air, hotel, and ground transportation, these AI Agents can complete the tasks that are corporate travel policy complaint without the traveler having to click through a maze of menus.

The potential of tools like Project Mariner goes beyond convenience. These AI systems integrate with existing platforms, learn user preferences, and adapt in real-time. Unlike OBTs, they aren't limited by outdated architecture or rigid workflows. They're dynamic, flexible and built for the digital era.

The new AI Agents offer benefits that go beyond simple convenience. These AI systems share data with existing platforms and learn what users prefer. They change and improve even as they run, unlike older systems.

[1] *Smolagents is a library that enables users to run powerful agents in a few lines of code.*

13.7.1 Impact on Travel Management Companies

TMCs have relied on Online Booking Tools (OBTs) as their primary service tool for a long time. But as AI Assistants become more capable, TMCs need to rethink what value they offer to their customers.

Agentic AI will transform the TMC business over the next decade. The workforce will shrink significantly, taken over by Agentic AI automation. If AI Agents can handle bookings, ensure compliance with travel policy, and solve issues related to the reservation in real-time, what role does a TMC play? How can they continue to provide value? The key is to focus on strategic, personalized services that go beyond just booking a flight or a hotel room. Human personalized expertise is still essential in negotiating with vendors, analyzing travel data, assisting with complex plans, and managing travel risks. The agencies that succeed will be those that adopt AI as a way to augment what they provide, not replace it.

13.7.2 Impact on Corporate Buyers and Travel Managers

Corporate buyers will need to adjust as Agentic AI revolutionizes procurement by automating tasks like negotiations, supplier evaluations, and purchase order management. This leads to faster sourcing and a reduction in average handling time for inquiries. Agentic AI is revolutionizing procurement by automating tasks like negotiations, supplier evaluations, and purchase order management. This leads to faster sourcing and a reduction in average handling time for inquiries. Agentic AI enforces procurement policies automatically and provides real-time guidance to buyers, reducing maverick spending and enhancing compliance.

For travel managers, AI Agents can act as early warning systems, continuously monitoring supplier performance and global events to identify potential risks and suggest alternatives. This proactive approach strengthens resilience in supply chains.

Although AI Assistants can handle many planning tasks, oversight is still necessary and budgets, policies, and safety standards must be monitored. Companies will need to find a balance between using these tools and keeping control of their travel programs.

While Agentic AI offers many benefits, implementing it effectively requires addressing challenges such as data quality, data privacy, and integration, regulatory compliance, human oversight and transparency, and organizational readiness.

13.7.3 Impact on the Corporate Traveler

Traveling employees will likely benefit from this shift as well. AI Agents can make booking faster, simpler, and more user-friendly. They also help travelers stay within company travel policy rules without feeling limited.

Autonomous itinerary management is a key benefit. Agentic AI can create comprehensive itineraries, manage visa requirements, factor in local events or weather, and adapt them dynamically based on changing circumstances. AI Agents that operate autonomously within corporate travel policy constraints without human intervention is the future.

Nevertheless, there may be issues to address, such as protecting data privacy and learning how to use new systems efficiently.

13.7.4 Google, SAP Concur and American Express GBT Collaboration

In May 2025, Google announced it was going "all in on NDC" for corporate travel, partnering with SAP Concur and American Express GBT [Fearis, 2025]. The initiative, a significant advancement in the business travel ecosystem, will prioritize NDC-compliant flight content with a "tie-goes-to-NDC" model, favoring NDC-sourced fares when they are equal in price to traditional EDIFACT fares. This implies that NDC will be preferred if it offers the same fare as traditional EDIFACT fares, to increase NDC adoption by making it a preferred option within the SAP Concur platform.

The market impact of Google's endorsement of NDC could have a ripple effect on the business travel ecosystem due to its prominent role in the industry. The move is expected to accelerate NDC adoption by demonstrating its viability and effectiveness in a major corporate travel setting.

13.8 Corporate Travel Manager Challenges

The rising cost of air travel and accommodation is the biggest challenge faced by corporate travel buyers who need to balance these cost increases with initiatives related to IATA NDC and ONE Order to source NDC content from airlines for competitive fares.

A related challenge faced by travel managers is revenue leakage from travel programs. Revenue leakage refers to the loss of revenue from inefficiencies or errors in the booking process, such as incorrect pricing, unused travel credits, or unclaimed refunds. Corporations also lose money when employees do not follow corporate travel policy and spend outside of the managed travel program.

13.8.1 Sustainability Initiatives

Business travelers care about a trip's impact on mother earth. Businesses and employees share these concerns and are under pressure to meet sustainability goals. There is an increasing trend among responsible corporations to put more investment dollars into green travel and provide employees with more eco-friendly choices.

Premium travel now prioritizes sustainability. Airlines use recycled goods for blankets. They also use packaging that can be used again for flight items. These steps attract travelers who care about the planet.

U.S. public companies face new reporting requirements from The Securities and Exchange Commission (SEC) [Warren, 2024] for carbon accounting which is effective in 2025. They will likely need to cut carbon emissions. These firms must also report on their environmental impact. The rules apply to annual reports and registration statements, including those for initial public offerings (IPOs).

13.9 Estimating the Corporate Discounts Based on Value

Core revenue management principles can be applied to determine the discount for corporate customers. The approach is a break-even analysis of accepting corporate customers versus leisure customers based on an estimate of the displacement cost of not accepting corporate customers. The analysis must be done on a market-by-market basis to determine the average discount. If there are multiple tiers of corporate accounts, then the discounts can be varied by tier as long as the traffic weighted average discount across tiers equals the average estimated discount.

The first step in this process is to classify corporate customers into tiers based on a composite metric that is based on a sales volume and quality of the revenue. This is followed with spill analysis to estimate the displacement cost of corporate travel and arrive at the aggregate corporate discount and corporate discount by tier.

13.10 Corporate Travel and AI

Corporate travel may be on the verge of major change, with the advent of new artificial intelligence agents. This goes beyond the new generation OBTs discussed in Sect. 13.7.

OpenAI recently introduced its Operator agent, which offers advanced features that surpass older AI tools [OpenAI, 2025a]. This innovation could lead to the rise of 'virtual full-time equivalents' VFTEs and transform how travel management is handled. Agentic AI may not replace travel agents entirely, but their role will be transformed to make them more efficient and provide exceptional service.

OpenAI's Operator can handle many repetitive tasks in browsers, like filling out forms, ordering groceries, and even creating memes. This ability to use the same tools and interfaces that people use every day increases the usefulness of AI. It helps individuals save time on routine activities and creates new ways for businesses to engage with customers.

Operator has demonstrated its ability to log into popular travel booking websites and manage the entire booking process on its own. It efficiently navigated different platforms, picked flights, checked hotel availability, and completed reservations with little human input, all based on individual user preferences. However, the focus was on leisure travel which is not complex like corporate managed travel.

Does Operator or a future enhanced version from the many vendors in this space hold its promise to reinvent corporate travel? Technology suggests a future where AI Agents could take care of the tedious tasks involved in managing itineraries, allowing travel managers to shift their focus to more strategic planning for travel programs.

13.10.1 Online Booking Tools Transition to Central Hubs

Online booking tools will become central hubs, giving travel managers powerful ways to supervise their AI agent workforce. TMCs will turn into vital strategic partners, offering expert AI oversight and specialized advice. They will also provide the human insight needed for complex situations and for strengthening supplier bonds. TMCs that adopt AI early will be crucial allies in this new business environment.

13.10.2 Personalized Itinerary Creation

AI Agents will manage the details of personalized trip planning, adjusting in real-time based on current data and traveler choices. This process isn't about cutting costs at the expense of comfort. Instead, it uses AI to craft smarter, tailor-made travel experiences that fit the budget. Travel managers can set the overall goals and make sure the AI aligns with program aims and traveler well-being. When needed, they can step in with personal, high-touch service.

13.10.3 Duty of Care

Real-time updates become smarter, with AI predicting and handling issues before they happen. This improves safety and provides better support for travelers. It also strengthens travel managers responsibility toward duty of care. They gain tools that help keep travelers safe and comfortable. AI works as a watchful partner, not as a replacement. It enhances the ability of a travel manager to address the needs of their employees at all times.

13.10.4 Partnerships and Contracts

RFP (request for proposal) management agents are not meant to challenge suppliers during negotiations. Instead, they help streamline the process. They allow travel managers to analyze large amounts of data to identify the best vendors. This gives managers more time to develop stronger, more strategic ties with key suppliers. Building better relationships invites collaboration and sparks new ideas.

13.10.5 Responsible AI is a Cornerstone for Successful Adoption

Ai systems must ensure equitable access, be inclusive, and not disadvantage any group based on race, gender, or socioeconomic status. Addressing AI bias is not just a concern; it is an opportunity. Travel teams can set up ethical rules for AI use in company travel plans. They can promote fairness and equity by making sure AI tools follow ethical standards. This puts travel managers in a leadership role when it comes to ethical AI use.

Strong security measures are required when responsible AI VFTEs (Virtual Function Test Environments) process sensitive information. Travel managers along with IT and security teams will lead the way in establishing secure privacy rules. They can help build trust with travelers and ensure the company stays compliant. This is also an opportunity to show leadership is using AI responsibly.

13.11 Accepting Automation for Competitive Advantage

The time for corporate travel leaders to act is now. To remain competitive, they must explore AI agent technologies and learn how they can be leveraged to enhance productivity. There must be a definitive plan to include these tools into existing travel programs.

This is not just about adding new technology; it is about leading a change that will improve corporate travel. AI Agents are already part of the future, so the real question is the speed of adoption to build better, more strategic travel plans. Creating a smarter, more efficient travel experience is not a choice, it is an imperative.

Accepting automation is mandatory. With Agentic AI, travelers will have personal bots that understand company rules and personal preferences. These bots can book trips directly with vendors, track receipts, handle reimbursements, and analyze data in many ways. Ironically, the main reason this change might face resistance is the very issues that slow down travel management now. Closed systems, outdated technology, and data fragmentation have long challenged TMCs. While they've learned to deal with these problems with labor-intensive processes, large language models may struggle to calibrate and interpret the data with a high degree of consistency.

13.12 Corporate Travel and NDC

In 2024, less than 15% of indirect bookings were NDC bookings and it is not expected to exceed 20% through 2028. For travel management companies, fewer than 4% of corporate bookings were NDC bookings, while leisure was higher at around 14%. OTAs serve leisure customers primarily, making cheap fares indispensable for bookings. OTAs also have a simpler technology stack than TMCs and have been focused on direct connections with airlines for over a decade so the OTA NDC bookings are closer to 20%. Based on their commercial model, the OTAs prioritize hotel bookings (where they earn significant commissions per transaction) and having access to cheap fares through the NDC channel. Much has been touted about the 146% year over year growth of NDC corporate bookings through the TMCs [Accelya, 2025], but the baseline is insignificant which shows the growth percentage in a positive light. Accelya had fewer than 100 million bookings of the 4.8 billion bookings made in 2024. NDC connectivity does not mean that NDC bookings will dominate. A study by Atmosphere Research states that as a percentage of total bookings, NDC bookings are expected to reach 21% by 2028 [Silk, 2025a] compared to just 7% in 2023. EDIFACT bookings are expected to drop to 14% of total bookings by 2028, down from 33% in 2023.

On April 3, 2023, American Airlines began to pull up to 40% of its fares from EDIFACT in a failed attempt to shift bookings to its direct or NDC channels [Airoldi, 2024a]. Besides Basic Economy that was largely removed from corporate tools, most Economy Flexible and Premium fares were also removed, making them even more expensive in most corporate booking tools. What airlines have learned from the American Airlines initiative is that a broad-based overarching strategy of withholding content is not beneficial to the airline. This failed strategy did not support accelerated adoption of NDC for corporate bookings. Perhaps airlines are better served by discreetly withholding content through the traditional EDIFACT channel in low-risk markets. This is no different than cruise lines providing access to deep discount cruise fares on low demand sailings to select travel agencies.

The primary benefit to airlines with NDC has been a reduction in distribution costs for NDC bookings. Every new distribution contract between airlines investing in NDC and GDSs supports a two-tier revenue model. The segment booking fees associated with NDC bookings is only a fraction of the EDIFACT booking fees. The justification has been the higher cost of compute for airlines to deliver priced itineraries through the NDC distribution channel. Other perceived benefits such as personalization remain to be realized.

Growth of NDC bookings is not expected to be rampant, but incremental.

13.12.1 Benefits for the Corporate Traveler

NDC has benefits for the corporate traveler. They are:

1. The NDC booking process has the ability to consider a traveler's frequent flyer and corporate status for selecting a seat during the booking process.
2. TMCs like AmTrav [Silk, 2025b] have reported that NDC supports a better servicing experience than EDIFACT since the associated workflows are simpler.
3. AmTrav's data indicated that NDC fares are frequently lower than those available through EDIFACT, especially for certain fare brands and during specific periods [Airoldi, 2024a]. For example, they found that American's Economy Flexible fares were significantly lower on NDC channels. By offering lower fares and more options, NDC has the potential to help companies save money on travel expenses.

13.13 Penalizing Solo Travelers: A New Twist in the U.S. Domestic Market with American's "P2"

In early 2025, the three major U.S. airlines – United Airlines, Delta Air Lines and American Airlines started experimenting with higher fares for solo travelers versus two or more travelers in a passenger name record (PNR). American was the first to introduce this new fare rule that they called "P2" internally for "Passenger 2". Delta Air Lines and United Airlines followed. In some markets, Basic Economy only appeared when the low fare search specified multiple passengers.

This was first reported by Newsweek on May 30, 2025 [Mesa, 2025] and Thrifty Traveler on June 6, 2025 [Potter, 2025]. This is acknowledged as a pricing tactic that is designed to target business travelers, who often book closer to departure or even last-minute and travel alone. Thrifty Traveler identified this pattern after analyzing hundreds of U.S. domestic one-way fares. One of the examples they cite is a United short-haul flight from Chicago O'Hare to Peoria, Illinois where a solo ticket cost $269, but dropped to $181 per person when two travelers were booked.

This is the opposite of how airline pricing with seat inventory control ought to work. Typically, when the number of individuals in a booking exceeds one, the price per ticket is either the same as that of a solo passenger or higher. Consider the following example with two booking classes in the hierarchy that are open. Booking class B has a fare of $400 and booking class M that is lower in the hierarchy has a fare of $300. While B has at least seven seats that are available, M only has one seat. If a solo passenger makes a booking, the solo passenger can be booked in the lower M booking class for $300. Instead, if the request were for two passengers, the two seats would be consumed from the higher booking class B and the cost per ticket will be $400. This is because there is only one unique RBD on a segment of a PNR. To save on travel, the only option for the two individuals is to make separate bookings so that one passenger pays $400 and the other $300.

This fare differential exists on one-way U.S. domestic flights. With this new twist in airline pricing, solo travelers would pay more than when they travel with a spouse or family member.

The three airlines at the center of the controversy have not publicly commented on this pricing practice, but it is a way to segment customers and extract more revenue from business travelers, who are less price conscious. These fares are prevalent on one-way tickets and not round-trip tickets. The airlines are using this strategy to target business travelers who are more likely to book one-way tickets closer to flight departure. Since the news broke in late May 2025, United and Delta retracted and eliminated the higher fares for solo passengers in most markets but American continued to lead the charge with higher fares for solo passengers on half of their domestic markets.

13.13.1 The LCC and ULCC Impact on Customer Segmentation and Corporate Travel

Historically, airlines have segmented leisure travelers for cheap fares and business travelers for higher paying fares. This segmentation was achieved with fare restrictions such as Saturday Night Stay, round trip fare requirements such as fare combinability, and advance purchase rules. Further corporate discounts (Category 25 fare-by-rule discounts) were only applicable for higher valued booking classes in the hierarchy. In the U.S. domestic market, this changed when LCCs and ULCCs gained traction and grew in prominence with unrestricted or lightly restricted one-way fares. Besides having to compete with one-way fares, network carriers could not charge higher prices for last-minute business travel when the LCCs and ULCCs offered lower fares for the same itineraries.

This led network carriers to introduce the Basic Economy brand to attract and segment the price sensitive leisure customers. Basic Economy targeted the price-sensitive leisure traveler with inflexible tickets, low boarding priority (unless the traveler has loyalty status) and the worst seat assignments. Business travelers could purchase the more expensive Premium Economy tickets and receive the travel experience that they expect.

The penalty fare for solo travelers is a new twist to discern the customer segments. It assures the airline that business travelers are not flying Basic Economy.

13.13.2 Corporate Travel Market Share Erosion

Every airline realizes the value of corporate accounts. Corporate travelers are considered schedule sensitive, and less price sensitive compared to leisure customers. Strategically, airlines must focus on attracting and retaining the corporate customer base. Poor pricing strategy and distribution channel bias can lead to an erosion of coveted corporate accounts when they switch to competitors.

In March 2023, American Airlines experienced a significant loss of corporate customers due to a strategic shift in their sales and distribution approach [Airoldi, 2024a]. The airline focused on direct and NDC bookings to capture more revenue directly, which negatively impacted indirect bookings through travel agencies and corporate travel departments. The change in strategy alienated travel agencies and corporate clients, resulting in a loss of market share in these channels. This resulted in a notable decrease in their share of indirect bookings, estimated to be 11% below their historical share. Most of these corporate customers moved to United and Delta. American has since acknowledged the negative impact and has been working to regain lost corporate business by restoring fare content in GDSs, hiring more sales staff, and reengaging with travel agencies and corporations.

American has also actively promoted AAdvantage Business [American Airlines, 2023] to small and medium sized businesses (SMB) that have frequent travel needs. The program offers various benefits and rewards for both the company and its employees who travel for business. The program allows companies to earn miles on eligible travel expenses and provides tools to manage and track travel spending. When American launched the devalued program[2] in 2023, they imposed a restriction on business travelers. They could only receive credit for flights if they were solo on the itinerary. They enforced the logic that more than one passenger on a reservation *meant that* it was a leisure trip, not a business trip. Business travel is more likely to be ticketed separately, even if employees are traveling to the same place at the same time.

The SMB business traveler is impacted by the higher solo fares. Like the Fortune 500 customers that abandoned American and switched to United and Delta in 2023, the SMB customers will also switch to American's competitors if they persist on retaining the higher solo fares on their own.

This pricing strategy is also flawed because not every solo traveler is flying on business with a corporate spending account. Price sensitive leisure solo passengers will shift from American Airlines to competitors who do not charge a penalty for flying solo. Second, with United and Delta limiting the solo higher fares to fewer markets, American may not have an option but to follow.

13.14 Future of Corporate Travel Agencies in the Age of AI

American Express GBT, the largest TMC is reportedly exploring a sale [Hoskins, 2025]. Interested parties may include tech players, large travel platforms, and private equity. Amex GBT went public in 2022, valued at $5.3 billion, as the largest B2B travel platform. Earlier in 2025, they acquired the third largest TMC, CWT for $570 million. Its market cap in November 2025 was $3.8 billion, a 19% drop compared to an S&P500 gain of about 48% in the same period.

This move by Amex GBT is not surprising. Size does not guarantee immunity. Agentic AI will transform the TMC business over the next decade. The workforce will shrink significantly, taken over by Agentic AI automation.

[2] The American Airlines AAdvantage Business program, which replaced Business ExtrAA, has been described by some as a devaluation due to changes in how businesses earn and redeem miles. It is less rewarding than its predecessor.

AI Agents are now able to search flights and hotels based on customer preferences, generate an itinerary, complete the booking and service it, in any language and at any time, using APIs from airlines or aggregators.

Did Amex GBT make a smart move by thinking ahead of their competitors? In the age of Agentic AI, there is market skepticism on the whole TMC model. Historically Amex GBT and other large TMCs have never been nimble and quick to adapt. It is unlikely that they will transform overnight and rapidly leverage AI Agents for productivity improvements. This means that competition from AI-native agents will disrupt the TMC business across the board.

In May 2026, Long Lake Management, backed by Alpha Wave and General Catalyst, reached an agreement to take Amex GBT private in a deal valued at $6.3 billion [West, 2026]. Surprisingly, share holders will receive a 60% premium over the stock price on Friday, May 1. Neither the CWT merger nor the Concur technology partnership created a sustained lift in the stock price of Amex GBT, which was trading at its 52-week low in February 2026. Despite the skepticism, the premium is a vote of confidence.

Industry analysts are skeptical of traditional travel agencies in the age of Agentic AI. Navan, the travel and expense software provider had its initial public offering (IPO) at $25 a share in October 2025. In its first earnings report since listing on the NASDAQ index, Navan announced that revenue increased to $195 million. a 29% year-over-year increase, and a $225 million loss [Baker, 2025]. In December 2025, the stock was trading at 50% of its IPO value. As they focus on their platform and NDC direct connections with airlines, incentives from the GDSs disappear, contributing to the loss in revenue.

The outlook for travel agencies is complex, dealing with legacy platforms, tech investments and an evolving distribution landscape. As Agentic AI replaces tasks performed by travel agents, the profession is evolving and not disappearing. Travel advisors who leverage AI and focus on personalized, high-value experiences, are expected to survive and thrive.

Payments

14

The secret of getting ahead is getting started.

Mark Twain

Abstract

Airline retailing and payments are converging as airlines shift from simple flight sales to a retail model, integrating advanced payment systems directly into the customer journey to boost ancillary sales, reduce costs and provide more options. This shift transitions a basic expense cost center area to become a key strategic value creation opportunity for airlines. Today's sales demand a full payment setup. It must handle many customer-favored forms of payment across channels. This includes direct bookings and travel agents. It even adds choices like buy now, pay later. The change boosts customer satisfaction and conversion rates. It also avoids high credit card costs and smooths operations with auto fraud checks, quick refunds, and easy settlements with partners such as airlines and payment intermediaries' Global eCommerce payment methods are discussed followed by corporate credit card surcharges, payment flexibility with ONE Order, and the future of ARC and BSP with NDC adoption.

Mark Twain's quote is very apt for the payments landscape in travel where significant winds of change are anticipated. Mark Twain emphasizes the critical role of action in achieving goals and overcoming obstacles. Many tasks, especially large or complex ones, can feel overwhelming, leading to procrastination and a feeling of being stuck. Mark Twain's quote reminds us that the key to breaking free from this inertia is simply to begin, even if the initial steps are small or imperfect.

B. Vinod, *The Era of Airline Revenue Management with Offers and Orders*, Management for Professionals, https://doi.org/10.1007/978-3-032-24197-9_14

14.1 Introduction

Payment processing in the airline industry has always been an afterthought. Payments, despite their pivotal role in the travel life cycle, is like a neglected child. A payment consortium must be created to explore how payments can be improved and to accelerate adoption of new forms of payment in order to reduce costs. Offers and Orders are supported by an airline retailing consortium consisting of leading airlines working with IATA to accelerate its adoption.

Airlines handle about 2.9 billion booking payments yearly. These global transactions total roughly $1 trillion. These payments are vital for airlines. However, they also create significant expenses. Each year, airlines spend about $20.3 billion on payment processing fees [Edgar, Dunn and Co., 2022]. According to IATA, net profits in the airline industry are expected to reach $41 billion in 2026 with a 3.9% net profit margin [IATA, 2025b]. The net profit margin remains unchanged from 2025 to 2026. Payments also incur substantial short-term financing costs representing 9% of an airline's total payment costs [Boin, R., Höll, R., Ralhan, P., Lind, N.: 2022].

Complexity in payment processing originated in other industries that has a significant impact on travel. Today, there are several new forms of payment to make customer purchases easier and more secure than the use of traditional credit cards. The number of choices for payment is increasing every year. A few years ago, there were just a few well-known credit card companies and PayPal for handling payments. Today it is fragmented with many more players and more solutions such as Apple Pay, Samsung Pay, Google Pay (formerly called Android Pay), Stripe, etc. Alternative forms of payment present new challenges that need to be addressed such as dealing with multiple currencies, managing virtual currency, appealing to global markets and local payment preferences, fraud detection, and controlling costs.

Customer authentication measures have reduced fraud by requiring multiple verification steps like passwords, biometrics, or approval for online payments. Although these measures have reduced payment fraud where used, their effectiveness with new payment methods remains uncertain due to limited experience in those areas.

14.2 B2B Payment Processing

B2B payments are often overlooked and lag the industry with legacy business processes. B2B payments occur between travel suppliers, travel agencies and third-party entities for vendor payments and commission payments. Third party payments historically have been made as paper check payments, wire transfer payments, and direct deposit payments (ACH). Use of paper checks is on the decline in preference to electronic payments to ensure accuracy in record keeping and security. Wire transfers are error prone and expensive. A newer option is virtual credit cards (VCC) for B2B payments. VCCs are temporary, randomly generated credit card numbers tied to an existing credit card account. They act as a secure proxy for the real card number, offering enhanced protection against online fraud and data breaches.

The promise of blockchain is to simplify and accelerate the process of paying travel agents, vendors, and suppliers. It is anticipated that blockchain based B2B payments in the airline and hospitality travel verticals will become reality with a global, secure ledger. With blockchain, payments can be streamlined and associated costs for travel suppliers can be reduced by eliminating intermediaries that facilitate payment processing. A critical challenge toward adoption of blockchain technology is scalability. Solutions are being developed to address scalability.

14.3 B2C Payment Processing

Payment plays a vital role in the relationship between airlines and their customers. There are many options for customer payments (B2C) to travel suppliers like airlines, hotels, car rentals, and cruise lines. Without successful transactions, airlines cannot make sales. While debit and credit cards are typically the main payment methods, travelers now want airlines to provide various local and regional options. These preferences can vary widely by region.

14.4 ISO 8583 in Payment Processing

ISO 8583 is a global standard for messaging in financial transactions involving payment cards. It is set by the International Organization for Standardization and helps different systems communicate when cardholders make electronic payments. This standard was introduced in the 1980s. It has been a reliable tool for the payment industry for a long time. Now, it's harder to add new data to it. New digital payment options often have their own protocols. This creates more complexity. This complexity hurts airlines' payment processes and support. It also affects customer experience. Adding a new payment method can take nine to twelve months.

This standard outlines how messages should be formatted and how communication should flow, enabling systems to share transaction requests and answers. Most transactions rely on ISO 8583 at some stage. Major networks like Mastercard, Visa, and Verve (part of Mastercard and used mostly in African countries) use this standard for their authorization communications, along with many other institutions.

While ISO 8583 provides a common guideline, it is not usually applied directly by systems or networks. It includes several standard fields that remain consistent across all systems, but it also allows for additional fields to include specific information for different networks. Each network can then customize the standard with their unique fields and uses, such as Proximity Cards. ISO 8583 will be replaced by ISO 20022, a data-rich global open standard for electronic data interchange between financial institutions that use XML or JSON formats. It covers a wide range of domains, including cross-border payments, securities, trade finance, and card payments.

IATA's NDC initiative improves payment options to meet customer demands. The goal is to link payment to every part of the customer experience.

14.5 Innovations in B2B and B2C Payment Processing Technology

According to a recent research report published by the Economist and WEX, the business payments company [Gale, 2021], paper checks still account for more than one half of the $25 trillion in annual U.S. B2B payments. Travel is no exception. Digital solutions for B2B payments represent the future. For over a decade, travel agencies have been migrating to virtual credit cards (VCC), also known as virtual card numbers (VCN), to pay suppliers like hotels. These 16-digit VCCs are generated to allow for one-time purchases and give management the ability to have them available only at set amounts. Virtual cards have unique benefits such as secure authentication to reduce fraud, minimize the risk of default, are cheaper than paper checks, protect cashflow by preventing runaway spending by setting limits on transaction time frames and amounts, reducing or eliminating cross border fees, simplify back-office reconciliation and improving the payment experience for travel agencies and travel suppliers.

To realize cost savings with virtual cards, travel suppliers and intermediaries must collaborate with a payment processing intermediary that supports multiple card schemes and access to multiple banking partners. This is required to minimize the cost of processing payments depending on the region of the world where the transaction is executed.

On the B2C front, global payment processing technology has been evolving rapidly. There have been several recent innovations in payment technology led by the Asian market to simplify the customer experience with payments.

The traditional forms of payment include credit cards (American Express, MasterCard, Visa), corporate cards and later PayPal. There has been an explosion of new forms of payment such as Apple Pay, Google Pay, and Alipay to name a few. Intermediaries that control the point of sale realize the importance of supporting alternate forms of payment to stay competitive and minimize abandoned shopping carts. Mobile payment is gaining wide acceptance in various regions of the world and represents the future. For travelers, digital payments also support the new generation mobile wallets such as China's WeChat Pay and India's Paym. Giving instant credit to customers to pay back in installments is an evolving trend.

14.6 IATA Financial Gateway

IATA Financial Gateway (IFG) is a payment orchestration platform. It manages payments for the travel industry. Airlines and agents can control how they get paid. IFG helps them offer more payment options. This covers every step of a traveler's experience.

As a platform for the travel sector, it helps manage payment complexities by enabling payment orchestration across all channels. It works with many payment partners globally. This platform offers consistent and flexible payment options where new payment types can be added easily. Travel suppliers can use one connection with IFG and they can roll out new payment methods at their own pace. This works across many sales channels and networks. It also handles reporting to BSP and ARC for agency sales settlement.

14.7 Global eCommerce Payment Methods

While there are many innovations in the payments space, the ones that are expected to dominate for enhanced customer experience and provide airlines with opportunities to reduce payment costs and increase revenue are summarized below.

14.7.1 Digital Wallets

A digital wallet, also known as an e-wallet, is an application for online payments. Consumers and corporations use them for transactions. They work with multiple forms of payment such as credit cards, debit cards, and preloaded funds. Crypto and "Buy Now Pay Later" options are also common.

E-wallets leverage multiple layers of security to safeguard data. Data encryption and multifactor authentication are typical security measures. Tokenization is also key in which the application swaps an entity's payment data with a random string of characters called a token. This token prevents account numbers from being exposed, minimizing data leaks.

A mobile wallet or m-wallet is a type of digital wallet deployed on smartphones and tablets. They can leverage additional features such as biometric authentication and support for contactless payment methods.

Digital wallet growth continues to accelerate. It is the leading payment method globally and digital wallets remain among the fastest growing. Supercharged competition among wallet providers includes fintech companies, banks, neobanks, super apps, Big Tech and device manufacturers.

For example, Neobanks are digital and mobile-first fintech companies that are entirely online with banking managed via apps and websites. They offer checking, savings, and payments through mobile apps, without physical branches, leading to lower overhead, lower fees and competitive interest rates. They appeal to a younger demographic with early pay and budgeting features.

By 2027 digital wallets are projected to account for more than $25 trillion in global transaction value [Turrin, 2024]. In travel, digital wallets fall into three categories as described below.

14.7.1.1 Open Loop Digital Wallets

These mobile digital wallets are predominantly B2C applications to buy products and services online, make contactless payments, and the transfer of money between individuals. Examples are Apple Wallet, Google Wallet and Samsung Wallet. Consumers store various digital passes, including credit and debit cards, boarding passes, tickets, loyalty cards, driver's licenses, and other forms of identification in these wallets. A payment service such as Apple Pay or Google Pay facilitates the usage of cards stored in the wallet to make secure, contactless payments.

14.7.1.2 Closed Loop Digital Wallets

Closed loop wallets work only within a specific ecosystem. Many airlines offer branded e-wallets to store loyalty program cards, book flights, redeem rewards, and pay for drinks and meals onboard. Closed loop digital wallets enhance customer experience and develop brand loyalty for travel suppliers.

Here are a few examples:

Delta Air Lines offers a digital wallet which allows travelers to earn additional Delta Sky Miles by linking their loyalty account to a digital wallet.

United Airlines allows members to save payment information in their Mileage-Plus account for future flights.

Turkish Airlines offers the "TK Wallet" for Miles&Smiles members to earn miles, make payments and refunds.

AirAsia, the largest LCC in Asia, offers a wallet called AirAsia pocket. It allows customers to earn loyalty points, get 10% discount on flights, and accelerated rewards for food purchases.

In travel the primary benefits of digital wallets for consumers and travel suppliers are:

1. Convenience: Faster checkout and no need to enter card details repeatedly.
2. Security: Enhanced security features like tokenization.
3. Loyalty Programs: Some airlines integrate digital wallets with their loyalty programs, allowing users to earn rewards or redeem points.
4. Travel suppliers have access to customer data which enables them to gain insights into customer preferences to recommend personalized products, and tailor messages that are aligned with a customer's interests.

14.7.1.3 B2B Wallets

B2B digital wallets are designed to handle transactions between businesses such as travel intermediaries (e.g. GDSs, travel agencies) and travel suppliers. They are transforming travel payments by enabling travel agencies and suppliers to transfer funds securely and efficiently using virtual cards, offering flexibility and potentially reducing costs.

Travel agencies can pre-deposit funds in their preferred currencies into the digital wallet. They can then transfer these funds to suppliers using virtual cards, which are single use, generated specifically for each transaction. Virtual cards provide an extra layer of security, reducing the risk of fraud and data breaches. Other benefits include lower payment costs, including credit card surcharges and foreign exchange fees, and potentially generating rebates for travel agents.

Outpayce, owned by Amadeus, is an example of a B2B digital wallet.

14.7.2 Credit Cards

Credit card transaction value continues to increase, even as relative market share decreases. Use of credit is expanding via credit-backed wallets, buy now pay later (BNPL) and POS financing. In credit card dominated markets, spending is shifting to digital wallets.

14.7.3 Pay by Bank (Account-to-Account)

Pay by Bank is popular in Europe and India because it offers a seamless payment experience with mobile apps, mobile checkouts, and POS terminals. It is commonly referred to as account-to-account (A2A). A2A has yet to gain traction in the U.S. A2A payments typically have lower costs of payment acceptance than most other payment methods, including card payments.

About 70 real-time payment systems offer fast payment networks. These networks support new ways to use A2A payments. Merchants are adopting A2A because it is cheaper and offers quick access to funds. This disrupts traditional payment methods. However, A2A growth may slow in markets where card payments are common.

Travel suppliers have rarely enforced their own app and preferred payment method to reduce payment fees associated with every transaction for fear of abandonment. It is anticipated that in-app payments will gain traction and comprise half of the overall social commerce payments by 2030. Embedded payments that use the pay by bank model rely on the automated clearing house (ACH), which carries reduced fees for merchants relative to other payment methods. For travel suppliers to go down this path is a double-edged sword. On the one hand, incorporating such payment options on ACH-linked accounts reduces transaction fees. At the same time, they also lose out on the benefits of credit cards which tend to drive higher consumer spending.

14.7.3.1 IATA Pay

IATA Pay is an account-to-account payment solution that streamlines and secures online payments for airline tickets. It allows airlines to offer customers a direct debit option, by passing traditional card payments and reducing transaction costs. This system is integrated with various payment platforms and works by directly debiting the customer's bank account upon purchase, with IATA handling the settlement with the airline the following day.

14.7.4 Cash on Delivery (CoD)

Cash on delivery (CoD) is a payment method where customers pay for goods or services upon receiving them, rather than in advance. It is common in countries like India when travel agents receive payments when the courier delivers the tickets to customers. Payment can be made with cash, debit cards or checks. CoD poses challenges for travel companies, including increased administrative costs, delays in payment, and the risk of non-payment if the customer refuses to accept the travel services provided.

The decline of cash continues as governments promote digital payments, and mobile payment acceptance becomes cheaper and easier. While cash is projected to decline in use in all markets, cash continues to play an essential role in most economies.

14.7.5 Buy Now Pay Later

Since its introduction in 2020, Buy Now Pay Later (BNPL) enters the next phase of its evolution. BNPL continues to be popular among consumers, who can now choose from an increasingly diverse set of BNPL offerings. Although BNPL faces headwinds with looming regulation, the forecast for 2026 is for sustainable growth. Rising interest rates can also dampen growth prospects.

Buy now pay later options are now common for travel. Affirm and FlexPay are popular choices. They easily connect with airline sites. This lets users pick BNPL as a form of payment at checkout. This ease of use can boost sales and increase the value of the transaction. Customers may also be happier with this choice.

14.7.6 Cryptocurrencies

Person-to-business (P2B) crypto payments are new. Many know crypto as an investment vehicle. But few use it for P2B payments. Payment companies that convert crypto to regular currency are expanding opportunities for merchants to reach new customers.

Emirates partnered with Crypto.com to explore the acceptance of crypto currency for flight payments. In May 2025, Air Arabia became the first airline in the region to accept cryptocurrency payments (AE Coin) through a partnership with digital bank MBank. A handful of airlines like airBaltic (a hybrid airline based in Latvia), and Peach Aviation (a Japanese LCC), accept cryptocurrency for flight bookings. Travel agencies like Travala.com accept cryptocurrency.

Figure 14.1 illustrates the eCommerce transaction value share.

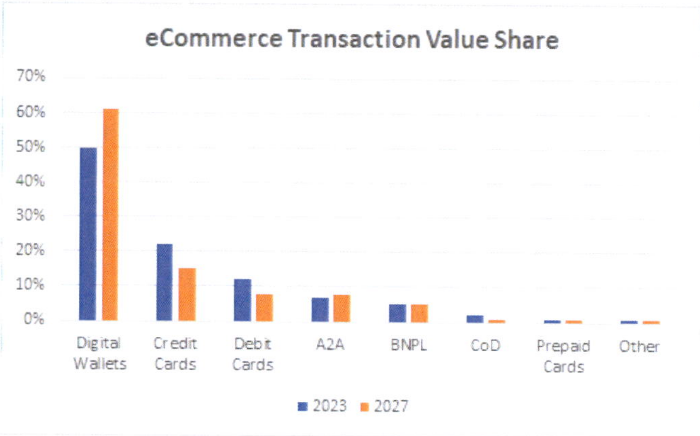

Source Global Payment Report 2024

Fig. 14.1 eCommerce transaction value share

14.8 Corporate Credit Card Surcharges

Surcharges on corporate credit cards is not a new feature. They exist in Europe and Australia, limited by regional regulations and the desire of airlines to contain payment processing costs. Corporate surcharges vary with some airlines imposing surcharges up to 3% of the price of the airline ticket. The surcharges reflect a broader trend among airlines to manage payment processing costs.

Credit card surcharges are making a comeback as new payment methods gain popularity. Airlines may start to use these alternative forms of payment more often.

Blockchain technology with its distributed ledger, originally linked to cryptocurrency, could streamline payment transactions and lower expenses. The blockchain alternative improves transparency and security, making it an appealing option for corporate transactions. Blockchains use cryptocurrency and stablecoins whose value is pegged to the U.S. dollar. Blockchain based payment gateways facilitate crypto transactions for merchants, decentralized exchanges which enable peer-to-peer asset swaps, and NFTs for payments.

The risks associated with blockchain payments include regulatory uncertainty, volatility, scalability, lack of consumer protections, technical complexity, energy consumption due to complex mining, interoperability, and privacy concerns.

14.9 Payment Processing and NDC

Expenses for airlines related to payment processing come in second place only to the segment booking fees paid to the GDSs and front-end/back-end commissions paid to travel agencies.

NDC introduces new payment mechanisms, extending beyond traditional cash or credit card methods to include cryptocurrencies, subscription-based models or direct settlements.

Before NDC, travel agents had two payment options. They could choose to receive payment from the customer and settle it through the IATA Billing and Settlement Plan (BSP) or use a GDS to authorize credit card payment to the airline's designated bank.

With NDC, travel agents transition from a payment intermediary to a payment pass-through and the airline is now responsible for processing the payment as the merchant of record. It is expected that NDC payments will decrease payment costs in terms of merchant fees and potentially enhance the customer experience by providing more payment options in the future. For example, airlines will be able to use instruments of payment such as PayPal, bank transfers, debit cards that are PIN or signature-based, credit cards that include plastic lodged card (corporate ghost card), or virtual, cash that is settled via IATA BSP or ARC clearing house, pay by installment, frequent flyer miles, and IATA EasyPay with prior authorization, for the indirect distribution channels. Led by the Asian market, the list of payment instruments is growing rapidly and supporting new forms of payment will be required for an airline to be competitive and expand the customer base.

14.9.1 ARC Direct Connect

ARC's direct connect program allows airlines to report and settle NDC transactions, via aggregators or directly through APIs, using their established settlement system, ARC settles commissions for NDC bookings. It requires airlines to have an agreement with ARC to process these sales.

For travel agencies, direct connect NDC transactions are integrated into existing ARC reporting tools, so agencies can view them alongside GDS transactions in one place. ARC reported that 799 travel agencies and 35 participating airlines resulted in 20.3% of total transactions in December 2024. In 2025, NDC enabled transactions accounted for 21.2% of total ARC settled transactions, driven by 1,139 reporting agencies.

14.10 Payment Flexibility with ONE Order

The legacy or traditional passenger name records (PNR) do not inherently facilitate split payments. Payment information is added to the PNR after a passenger pays for a flight. A form of payment is required when a ticket is issued. PNRs and tickets work best for single payments. Handling more than one payment type requires complex workarounds, often through mechanisms such as miscellaneous change orders (MCO) and electronic miscellaneous documents (EMD). An MCO or EMD is a document that represents a payment or a refund for a service provided by an airline. Many airlines allow up to three forms of payment per ticket.

Often, this means making different payment records with each record covering a certain payment. These records are exchanged for tickets or EMDs. For example, a travel agent can create and issue an MCO or EMD for the first form of payment and then issue the ticket with the second form of payment in exchange for the MCO or EMD. The PNR will still contain the information for the entire booking, including the different payment methods used, and the MCO/EMD details will be linked to the PNR. The process is slow and can result in errors. This makes it difficult to implement split payments efficiently. For example, consider a booking where one customer pays with a credit card and the other pays with a debit card. The travel agent can create an MCO for the debit card payment and then issue the ticket with the credit card payment, effectively splitting the payment.

With the offer-order model, customers expect flexibility in payment processing. ONE Order phases out the current booking (PNRs) and ticketing records (E-tickets) and electronic miscellaneous documents, (EMDs). Airlines that offer split payments will attract a broader customer base, including those that would like to use multiple forms of payment for a single order such as credit cards, loyalty points, and digital wallets. For example, consider a corporate customer whose company is paying for the ticket, but the traveler wants to pay out of pocket for an ancillary service such as lounge access that is out of corporate policy. ONE Order supports split payments, allowing airlines to collect payments from different parties or using different payment methods for the same order.

14.11 The Future of ARC and BSP with NDC Adoption

The IATA Billing and Settlement Plan (BSP) is designed to facilitate and simplify financial transactions between IATA-accredited Passenger Sales Agents and BSP airlines, as well as help them improve financial control and efficiency, enhanced by IATA BSPlink.

Like BSP, the Airline Reporting Corporation (ARC) is used for managing financial transactions between U.S.-based travel agencies and airlines, accrediting travel agencies to issue tickets, and providing access to airfare data and business intelligence to help both agencies and airlines with sales, analytics, and fraud prevention. ARC facilitates the secure process of selling airline tickets and ensures that airlines receive payments from accredited agents.

The larger question is: *will BSP and ARC survive after NDC adoption?* For NDC transactions, if the airline collects payment and not the travel agency, it is difficult to defend the continued existence of BSP and ARC.

However, in most cases today travel agents can collect payments for NDC transactions, though the specific method depends on the airline's set-up and the agent's agreement with BSP and ARC.

The airline chooses the payment methods it will accept for NDC transactions, which may include credit cards, debit cards, and even airline miles. The travel agent uses the airline's direct connect or technology provider to issue the transaction and process the payment. All transactions, including payment details, are transmitted to a settlement system like ARC or BSP. Through the settlement system, airlines and travel agencies receive their respective net cash settlements and commissions on a weekly basis for NDC transactions.

For this reason, the ARC and BSP systems have been adapted to include NDC transactions, allowing for the collection of payments, reporting of commissions, and preparation of card remittance files for the airline.

14.12 Will Payments Receive the Attention It Deserves?

The airline industry often overlooks payments. This is surprising given the significant upside in lowering the cost of payment processing. Besides, payments play a central role in a customer's journey. Few companies discuss payments openly. Forward looking airlines must define differentiated strategies for retail travelers and corporations and ensure specific customer needs in these segments are fulfilled.

Today, many airlines do not track payment data well. They also lack clear job duties or goals for this area. The payments infrastructure faces digital disruption over the next decade. Providing a range of payment options to B2B and B2C customers is no longer a luxury but a necessity. Efficient payment solutions are needed to support travel and tourism.

14.13 Will the Payments Industry Be Deregulated?

Today, government control over payment transactions ensures safety, efficiency and consumer protection. The Federal Reserve System (Fed) oversees core infrastructure (cash, checks, electronic systems) and the Consumer Financial Protection Bureau (CFPB) regulating consumer-facing payment apps and providers, while the Treasury Department modernizes government payments, focusing on fraud prevention, and efficiency across digital and traditional channels.

Perhaps it is wishful thinking, but the payments industry is currently experiencing a trend towards potential deregulation. This could reduce government control over how airlines handle financial transactions, particularly in areas like payment processing and customer transactions [Randklev, 2025].

This implies that the government would have less direct influence on how airlines manage payments, potentially leading to a more open and competitive market. This shift can lead to increased competition among payment providers, potentially lower costs for airlines and passengers, and increase flexibility for airlines to innovate in payment options. Increased competition can also reduce the cost of payment processing for airlines, potentially leading to lower fares or more competitive pricing. A negative aspect is that deregulation can also lead to instability in the market as airlines adapt to new players and technologies, and evolving consumer preferences.

Predictive Modeling and Algorithmic Collusion

15

Price fixing is illegal under our antitrust laws, but the development of price-setting algorithms can exploit loopholes that could be used to unfairly raise prices on everything from rent to rideshares. My bill will strengthen antitrust law and guarantee needed transparency to prevent companies from using algorithms to fix prices to ensure consumers are able to get the full benefits of competition.

Amy Klobuchar

Abstract

Competitive revenue management, the process of monitoring competitor selling fares to fine tune inventory controls. became an accepted business practice in the early 2000s. With the growth in AI-based applications and robotic process automation, several class action lawsuits have arisen in this context over the past few years.

Algorithmic collusion is a form of price fixing where pricing algorithms used by competing companies align their behavior to raise prices, like human collusion but without explicit human agreement. While traditional algorithms might increase prices in unison, newer research indicates that sophisticated AI, including large language models, can also "autonomously" learn to collude by punishing deviations from shared, higher prices, creating stable, supra competitive prices through learned reward-punishment schemes. This emerging threat challenges existing antitrust laws, which require proof of a formal agreement, prompting calls for new regulations to increase transparency and address these perceived loopholes. This chapter reviews algorithmic collusion in the context of competitive revenue management and concludes that it is all about the underlying data that the new generation models have access to. Conclusions are drawn

B. Vinod, *The Era of Airline Revenue Management with Offers and Orders*,
Management for Professionals, https://doi.org/10.1007/978-3-032-24197-9_15

based on well-known class action lawsuits and their outcomes in the casino hotel and apartment rental multi-family housing industries.

On January 30, 2024, Senator Amy Klobuchar (D-MN) and five Senate co-sponsors introduced the S.3686 bill "Preventing Algorithmic Collusion Act of 2024," This bill was introduced to prevent anticompetitive conduct through the use of pricing algorithms by prohibiting the use of pricing algorithms that can facilitate collusion through the use of nonpublic competitor data. The objective was to create an antitrust law enforcement audit tool, increasing transparency, and enforcing violations through the Sherman Antitrust Act and Federal Trade Commission Act. In a subsequent press release on February 2, 2024, the Senator stated that the bill would "strengthen antitrust law" which is not entirely accurate. By modifying the presumptions associated with the use of algorithms, this bill would change antitrust law [Hamilton, Tobey, Bamberger, Neuman, 2026]. It would necessarily reduce the requirements for proving collusion under antitrust law.

In 2025, Senator Amy Klobuchar, joined by eight Democratic Senators, introduced a revised bill as S-232 on January 23, entitled "Preventing Algorithmic Collusion Act of 2025" to prevent companies from using algorithms to collude to set higher prices [Congress.Gov, 2025]. The bill holds the status of "introduced" and has been referred to the Senate Judiciary Committee.

15.1 Origins of Competitive Revenue Management in Travel

After airline deregulation in 1978, revenue management in the airline industry has focused on maximizing revenues by selling the right product to the right customer at the right price at the right time. It is based on the fundamental premise that all customers are not created equal. Various customer segments who are schedule sensitive and price sensitive pay different fares for the same market and revenue management determines the optimal mix of passengers to maximize revenues.

Revenue management in the 1980s relied exclusively on an airline's own data: schedules, fares, bookings, and ticketed passengers to make recommendations on inventory control to maximize revenues. The dawn of the Internet era in the mid-1990s resulted in unprecedented transparency in schedules and selling fares by market. Based on the realization that the traditional revenue management process does not consider prevailing marketplace conditions, travel suppliers realized the importance of being "competitor aware" and "marketplace aware" to adjust inventory control recommendations based on the selling fares of competitors. This led to the deployment of automated robots to collect competitive selling fare data from airline websites, GDS travel agency desktop, and online travel agency screen displays. Air shopping web services are also a potential source to collect competitive selling fare data for GDS subscribers. This led to the enhanced revenue management processes where competitor selling fares were factored into the decision-making process when inventory controls were determined and deployed on the airline's inventory system on the host CRS. This new process, introduced in the early 2000s [Ratliff & Vinod, 2005] is commonly referred to as Competitive Revenue Management or "CompRM." This added a degree of sophistication by considering competitor marketplace dynamics.

Traditional revenue management forecasts demand and optimize inventory controls based on a supplier's internal data. With schedule and fare transparency, a growing consensus emerged in the early 2000s that competitor-selling fare data could be leveraged to improve inventory controls that reflected current market conditions. An airline always factors unsold seats before overriding inventory controls. Airlines publish their tariffs to fare aggregators like ATPCO, that disseminate the fares to intermediaries like Global Distribution Systems (GDS) and other airlines [Vinod, 2021f, 2024a, Chapter 5]. An airline has the option to respond to a new fare filed by a competitor by matching the fare or filing a fare that is above or below the competitor's fare. This fare management process precedes revenue management. Over the past two decades, Competitive Revenue Management has become an established practice in the travel industry [Hartmans, 2008; Kumar et al., 2021; Page et al., 2005; Ratliff & Vinod, 2005; Vinod, 2021a, Chapter 7; Zhang & Kallesen, 2008].

The hotel industry was a fast follower to practice revenue management. Travel suppliers and revenue management vendors rely on automation from competitive fare collection vendors like Infare, (QL2's airline business was acquired by Infare in 2017), RateGain, Lighthouse, RevenueStrategy360 by Amadeus, and others for this data feed to supplement their revenue management process. Some airlines impose restrictions and do not permit robotic shopping on their websites. However, the selling fare data is publicly available. Anyone can submit a shopping request through an OTA and access the selling fares that airlines are charging by market. These fare and rate collection vendors automate the process of data collection with robotics.

In lodging, competitive revenue management starts with revenue managers identifying the competitive set (or "comp set") for their property. This includes properties in the same neighborhood that are considered competitors. Hotel competitive sets are asymmetric (Property A may be in property B's comp set, but property B is not in property A's comp set) [Vinod, 2022a, Chapter 4], and can be determined from an OTA's click stream data. Hotel rates that are published to internal systems like the hotel CRS are based on the hotel's pricing strategy, perceived value of the brand, room types and associated room attributes, and neighborhood. Competitive revenue management in lodging involves using automated tools to monitor competitor websites for information on selling rates. Vendors like RateGain, Lighthouse and Amadeus Hospitality's RevenueStrategy360 offer services that allow hotels to track competitors' selling rates for future dates. This data is used in conjunction with unsold rooms to adjust inventory controls within the hotel's CRS to recommend the best available rate (BAR). In addition, hotels can subscribe to Smith Travel Research, owned by the CoStar Group since 2019, for access to historical selling rates at various properties. Amadeus Demand360 (originally developed by The Rubicon Group was acquired by TravelClick in 2011 and TravelClick was acquired by Amadeus in 2018) provides both forward looking and historical data.

At the outset it is worth pointing out that the objective of revenue management, in any form, is to maximize total revenues and not yield. The definition of *yield* for airlines is the revenue per revenue passenger mile and for hotels it is the revenue per occupied room. Available capacity (airline seats, hotel rooms) is always factored into the decision-making process when inventory controls are established.

Selling air fares and hotel rates are publicly available with a robotic or manual search for flights and hotels through supplier websites, an OTA or travel agency. Airline and hotel competitive revenue management software does not have access to any confidential data such as the entire tariff structure which may include public and private content or corporate contracts with suppliers such as airlines and hotels.

Besides airlines and hotels, car rental companies and cruise lines monitor competitor rates to augment their revenue management strategies. For instance, rental car companies closely monitor competitor capacity (available cars in the lot) and rates at airport locations to adjust walk-up rates for walk-up customers.

15.2 What Is Algorithmic Collusion?

From a legal point of view, algorithmic collusion is a form of price fixing where pricing algorithms used by competing companies align their behavior to raise prices, similar to human price collusion but without explicit human agreement. While it is always possible for competing algorithms to increase prices in unison, recent studies seem to indicate that advanced AI systems, such as large language models, can learn to collude on their own. They can autonomously learn to collude and sustain supracompetitive prices (higher prices than those sustained in a competitive market) by employing reward-punishment schemes, which effectively deter price cuts. This leads to steady price increases above normal levels.

Experiments with algorithmic pricing agents based on Large Language Models (LLMs) have shown that they can autonomously reach supracompetitive prices and profits in oligopoly settings [Fish et al., 2025].

This emerging threat challenges current antitrust laws which require proof of a formal agreement. This has led to calls for new regulations that promote openness and address these gaps.

Class-action lawsuits in the casino hotel industry and apartment rentals have brought algorithmic collusion to the forefront for legal experts to weigh in. Ultimately, judgements to date have been influenced by the type of data accessed by these systems.

15.3 Collusion, Anti-Competitive Behavior and Algorithmic Collusion

Collusion refers to any coordinated effort among competing businesses aimed at increasing or sustaining profits *beyond* what would occur in a competitive environment, meaning without such collusive actions.

A key concern among lawmakers and legal advisors lies at the intersection of predictive modeling bias and antitrust law. It is the potential for algorithms, especially pricing algorithms, to encourage collusion among competing businesses. These algorithms are increasingly employed by companies to optimize their price recommendations in real-time, which could potentially lead to new types of anti-competitive behavior and coordination. The companies are not limited to travel suppliers, but exist in real estate property management systems, brick and mortar retail, and other industries.

Algorithmic collusion refers to situations where pricing algorithms used by competing businesses lead to coordinated, supracompetitive pricing, often without explicit communication or agreement between the businesses. This can occur when algorithms are designed to analyze market data and optimize pricing strategies, potentially leading to tacit or even explicit collusion.

Though aspects of Artificial Intelligence have been linked to algorithmic collusion, antitrust law is all about the data used by these algorithms. The techniques may be leveraging AI value propositions such as machine learning, Generative AI or other techniques such as classical statistics.

In economics, there are two types of collusion: explicit and tacit. Explicit collusion involves direct agreements or coordinated strategies among companies, reflecting conscious and voluntary collaboration. In contrast, tacit collusion arises from the parallel actions of competing businesses that, while aware of each other's behaviors, do not rely on any formal agreements but rather make independent decisions. Airline revenue management and airline retailing can lead to tacit collusion. Tacit collusion is harder to detect and regulate due to its less apparent nature.

Generally, antitrust laws do not prohibit these parallel behaviors (tacit collusion) but do forbid anti-competitive agreements (explicit collusion).

15.3.1 The Sherman Antitrust Act

In the U.S. the Sherman Antitrust Act is an antitrust law that was passed in 1890, named after Senator John Sherman of Ohio. The Sherman Antitrust Act was the first federal law to prohibit monopolies and unfair business practices. The landmark U.S. law aimed at promoting competition in the marketplace by prohibiting monopolies and restraints of trade. It is a U.S. antitrust law which prescribes the rule of free competition among those engaged in commerce. It was the first federal measure to outlaw business practices that stifle competition, like price-fixing and monopolization, and is considered a cornerstone of antitrust law. Its objective was to protect consumers by promoting free competition, keeping prices down, and maintaining quality.

According to the Sherman Antitrust Act, it is unlawful for competitors to "join together their independent decision-making power to raise, depress, fix, peg, or stabilize prices," the Department of Justice (DOJ) and Federal Trade Commission (FTC) wrote in their statement. According to the statement from the DOJ and FTC, competitors are prohibited from combining their independent decision-making authority to manipulate prices under the Sherman Antitrust Act.

15.3.2 Article 101 TFEU

Article 101 of the Treaty on the Functioning of the European Union (TFEU) is a key provision of EU competition law, designed to maintain open and competitive markets within the EU's internal market. It prohibits various types of collusive behavior that can prevent, restrict, or distort competition.

Key elements of Article 101 TFEU in 2008 [European Union, 2008] include its prohibition of agreements, decisions, and concerted practices that have the objective or effect of preventing, restricting, or distorting competition within the internal market and that may affect trade between Member States. The "object or effect" principle was a central element in assessing compliance. Examples of prohibited conduct include price fixing, limiting production, and market sharing agreements violating the article are automatically void.

Algorithmic collusion, where businesses use algorithms to coordinate pricing or other actions, is increasingly relevant under this article, particularly in the context of digital markets. While the article does not explicitly mention algorithms, its broad language can encompass situations where algorithms facilitate or enable anticompetitive behavior.

15.3.3 The Competition and Markets Authority in the United Kingdom

The Office of Fair Trading (OFT) and the Competition Commission (CC) were UK government bodies responsible for promoting fair competition and protecting consumers. These two organizations merged to form the Competition and Markets Authority (CMA) in 2014. It serves as the primary competition regulator with a focus on consumer protection, and digital markets.

The Data Technology and Analytics (DaTA) unit of the CMA leverages data science, machine learning and AI techniques to monitor and analyze algorithmic behavior. Along with the DOJ, FTC, and European Commission, the CMA sets standards for auditing and monitoring anti-competitive behavior.

15.3.4 Digital Markets and Algorithmic Collusion

The integration of data with advanced technologies like pricing algorithms and machine learning is transforming competition in digital markets. An increasing number of companies are employing computer algorithms to enhance their pricing strategies, tailor services, and forecast market trends, which can lead to greater efficiencies and generate incremental revenues. A critical component is the data that is used to calibrate the underlying predictive models used in pricing algorithms. Competitive proprietary data must *never* be used as input into these decision support models to make predictions. At issue is that the widespread adoption of these algorithms may also create potential anti-competitive consequences, as they enable firms to easily establish and maintain collusion without formal agreements or direct human interaction.

Interpreting anti-competitive behavior is always specific to an individual scenario. Legal experts weigh in when a determination is made, whether the defendant is guilty or not.

In the AI-enabled era, algorithmic collusion must be well understood by practitioners of revenue management. Court rulings are an emerging and evolving area of law. In this chapter, algorithmic collusion is explained with several examples to understand anti-competitive behavior.

15.4 Class Action Lawsuits in the Casino Industry

In January 2024 two leading hotel software providers, Pegasus and Cendyn merged under the Cendyn brand. The resulting entity, named the Cendyn Group, offers a revenue management solution named Rainmaker for casinos and hotels that recommends the best available rate (BAR).

In 2023 Atlantic City casinos were hit with two class action lawsuits claiming that the casinos conspired to fix prices of hotel rooms with Rainmaker. The suit claimed that room revenue reported to the New Jersey Casino Control Commissions had increased substantially while occupancy rates had fallen, and gaming revenues had increased only modestly.

Several lawsuits have been filed such as *Gibson v. Cendyn Group LLC.*, *Cornish-Adebiyi v. Caesar's Entertainment*, *Fabel v. Boardwalk* 1000, *Blair-Smith v. Caesars Entertainment*, and *Altman v. Caesars Entertainment* [Toutant, 2024].

The question is whether casino-hotel entities combined their independent decision-making authority?

Gibson v. Cendyn Group LLC was a class action lawsuit alleging that hotel operators on the Las Vegas Strip used Cendyn Group's software to inflate room rates. The Richard Gibson v. Cendyn Group LLC lawsuit claimed that hotel operators used Cendyn's Rainmaker algorithm to make pricing recommendations. The lawsuit alleged that the hotels shared sensitive information with Cendyn's algorithm, which then used that information to make room rate recommendations. The lawsuit further claimed that the hotels accepted the recommendations, which raised prices above competitive levels.

In *Cornish-Adebiyi v. Caesar's Entertainment*, the plaintiffs allege that competing casino hotels were violating the Sherman Act by using Rainmaker to algorithmically set prices "*while knowing and precisely because all other Casino-Hotel Defendants had agreed to do the same.*"

The defendants in these lawsuits are casino hotel operators, Cendyn that markets Rainmaker, and competitor selling rate data providers such as Amadeus, and CoStar's Smith Travel Research.

Lately, price setting algorithms have gained attention as more hotels rely on technology to make pricing decisions. However, recent lawsuits claim that certain platforms are involved in illegal price-fixing.

15.4.1 The DOJ and FTC

The Federal Trade Commission (FTC) and the Department of Justice (DOJ) jointly filed a *statement of interest* with the District of New Jersey in the case of *Cornish-Adebiyi v. Caesars Entertainment* [Office of Public Affairs Press Release, 2024]. *It states that hotel companies cannot collude on room pricing by leveraging algorithms as a substitute to manually do the same task by a real person and evade antitrust laws.* The government's position in support of plaintiffs that sued Caesar's Entertainment and other casinos is that hotels using algorithms to set room prices are violating antitrust laws [Weinstein, 2024]. Critics of the DOJ argue that an agreement to fix prices requires a meeting of human minds intending to act anti-competitively.

The DOJ and FTC indicate two important points about competition law in their statement. First, plaintiffs do not need to show direct contact between competitors to reach an agreement under Section 1 of the Sherman Act. This is especially true if they allege that an algorithm provider working with the competitors is acting in concert with them. Competitors cannot legally work together to fix prices, whether through their staff or an algorithm. This is true even if they never talk directly to each other. Second, sharing pricing advice, list prices, or algorithms still counts as an unlawful agreement. This remains true even if each competitor keeps some control over their pricing. Setting or suggesting starting prices can break antitrust rules, even if those are not the final prices consumers pay.

15.4.2 Legal Outcome

The intent, business process, and business objective of CompRM is to optimize inventory controls that results in a priced air itinerary for airlines or the best available rate for a hotel. Creating reference fares by airlines or rate structure for a property is an *independent internal process* that is used as input into the revenue management solution. The fare management or rate management process *precedes* the revenue management process. Matching a competitor's filed public fares or hotel rates is perfectly legal.

The allegations made by the plaintiffs of price-fixing in the context of CompRM are not true. What is required is an education of revenue management business practices and the value proposition for suppliers and travelers. Understanding how revenue management improves the bottom line of travel suppliers and simultaneously makes travel affordable for customers by offering multiple price points at various points in time before travel commences needs to be understood by the public at large.

In the case of *Gibson v. Cendyn Group LLC*, on May 8, 2024, a district court rejected the class-action lawsuit that accused hotels on the Las Vegas Strip of working together to raise room rates using software from Cendyn Group LLC. The court made a final ruling and dismissed the case with prejudice which means that the case could not be brought back to court. The court decided that the hotel operators did not fulfill the requirements for showing they acted together, as stated in the Sherman Antitrust Act. They noted that the hotels signed up for the software at different times, did not exchange information directly, and were not obliged to follow the software's suggestions. This decision implies that simply using similar pricing software is not against antitrust laws. It also serves as a warning to future plaintiffs to avoid lengthy legal disputes.

The DOJ supported the plaintiffs, stating that the court's decision was incorrect. The DOJ claimed that the per se rule stops companies from making agreements about starting prices, even if those companies can choose to set different prices later. In U.S. law, the term **illegal per se** means that the act is inherently illegal.

The *Gibson* ruling offers guidance for dismissing or granting summary judgment in other cases involving algorithmic price-fixing. It applies when the alleged co-conspirators access the provider's algorithm at different times. These co-conspirators do not share confidential or non-public information, nor are they required to follow the algorithm's pricing suggestions. The decision helps clarify when such cases lack enough evidence to move forward.

In the case of *Cornish-Adebiyi, et al v. Caesars Entertainment*, on September 30, 2024, the court ruled using the guidelines established by *Gibson* to dismiss claims related to algorithmic price-fixing. In these cases, the accused parties, who are referred to as "spokes," use a software provider's algorithm, known as the "hub," at different times. There is no exchange of private information, and the accused parties are not required to follow the pricing suggestions from the algorithm.

The *Gibson v. Cendyn Group LLC* and *Cornish-Adebiyi, et al v. Caesars Entertainment* decisions suggest that simply using the same pricing software from a vendor like Cendyn (in *Gibson v. Cendyn Group LLC* and *Cornish-Adebiyi v. Caesars Entertainment Inc.*) does not automatically constitute price fixing, unless there is further evidence of coordinated action.

The *Fabel v. Boardwalk* 1000 case was voluntarily dismissed by the plaintiff in January 2024. The *Blair-Smith v. Caesars Entertainment* case was dismissed by the court in favor of the defendants in September 2024 when the court found the plaintiffs failed to plausibly allege a "hub-and-spoke" conspiracy which means that pricing through software did not prove an actual agreement to fix prices.

The *Altman v. Caesars Entertainment* case was dismissed with prejudice in September 2024, where the court found the plaintiffs failed to plausibly allege a price-fixing conspiracy among Atlantic City casino-hotels using a shared algorithm for hotel room pricing.

15.5 Apartment Rentals and Algorithmic Collusion

Real estate property management vendors have gained notoriety with algorithmic collusion directed at apartment rentals. The largest real estate property management system providers include Yardi Systems, RealPage, and AppFolio. These companies offer software solutions for managing various aspects of property management, from residential and commercial properties to affordable housing and Homeowners Association (HOA) management. Yardi Systems and RealPage are accused of facilitating algorithmic collusion among multifamily apartment owners and operators. RealPage dominates the multifamily residential space, while Yardi, which is bigger in overall market presence, caters to complex, large-scale commercial/mixed-use portfolios.

In 2022, new apartment rentals in the U.S. surged by 15% year-over-year, driven by strong demand and limited supply. This dramatic increase poses a significant challenge for everyday hard-working individuals, couples, and families who rent apartments because purchasing a house is beyond their financial means. By late 2023, new apartment construction slowed the annual growth to under 1%. Rental demand remains strong, leading to renewed modest year-over-year increases in 2025, though some cities have seen double-digit growth [Chen & Proctor, 2025].

In the world of leisure travel, an airline ticket or hotel stay is a discretionary expenditure, and the typical traveler makes 1 to 2 trips a year. The cost of these leisure trips can also rise sharply, but they are optional and can be postponed or avoided. In contrast, apartment rentals involve month-to-month or longer-term leases that directly affect people's livelihoods. An apartment rental is the single largest item in the monthly budget. Rising costs drive inflation and heavily influence the mindset of the working class and retirees who are struggling to make ends meet and often have little to no savings. Besides driving inflation, there are also ethical, moral, and fairness-based aspects that play a role in society.

What is driving these phenomenal price increases in apartment rentals? A surge in demand? A shortage of apartments? Or is the culprit software from a vendor that promotes their property management system to landlords?

15.5.1 RealPage Testimonial and Outcome

Propublica investigators were the first to raise this concern to the wider public. Propublica.org is a nonprofit newsroom that publishes investigative journalism in the public interest to expose abuses of power and encourage reform.

Kortney Balas, a director of revenue management at JVM Realty, provided a testimonial video for YieldStar on the RealPage website [Vogell et al., 2022] that has since been removed. She was quoted as saying "*The beauty of YieldStar is that it pushes you to go places that you wouldn't have gone if you weren't using it.*" YieldStar is the revenue management software that uses an algorithm to suggest rent prices to landlords.

Four US Senators sent a public letter on November 22, 2022 (Senator Elizabeth Warren, Senator Tina Smith, Senator Bernard Sanders, and Senator Edward J. Markey) to the CEO of RealPage [Warren, 2022]. The five-page letter voiced their concerns over YieldStar. The first paragraph on page 2 is quoted below (in italics):

> *YieldStar's extensive reach, which only grew after regulators approved a merger with "its only significant competitor" in 2017, has grave implications for renters who end up in the grasp of landlords who use it. Using lease and other private information collected from RealPage customers, which "include some of the largest property managers in the country," YieldStar's algorithm calculates and suggests the highest rents landlords should charge, "push[ing] [them] to go places that [they] wouldn't have gone if [they] weren't using it." As one RealPage executive put it, "I think [YieldStar is] driving [rising apartment rents], quite honestly. As a property manager, very few of us would be willing to actually raise rents double digits within a single month by doing it manually.*

RealPage, the Texas-based company, offers revenue management software including YieldStar that assists landlords in determining rental prices for apartments nationwide. As rental prices continue to rise, some critics express worry that the company's unique algorithm may undermine competition in the market. On August 23, 2024, the DOJ claimed that RealPage's pricing algorithm violated antitrust laws.

The DOJ together with the Attorneys General of North Carolina, California, Colorado, Connecticut, Minnesota, Oregon, Tennessee, and Washington, filed a civil antitrust lawsuit against RealPage, Inc. "for its unlawful scheme to decrease competition among landlords in apartment pricing and to monopolize the market for commercial revenue management software that landlords use to price apartments." At the center of the antitrust lawsuit is the revenue management software that uses an algorithm powered by AI to help landlords to set rental rates. AI / Machine learning algorithms are self-learning and collude when making recommendations using competitive data. The Justice Department argued that the software drives every opportunity to increase prices *even during periods when demand is soft*. The Justice Department alleges that RealPage violated Sections 1 and 2 of the Sherman Act.

Further, on Jan 7, 2025, the DOJ and attorney generals from 10 states filed an amended complaint expanding the scope of the case against RealPage that included siz landlords for allegedly "participating in algorithmic pricing schemes" that harmed renters. Simultaneously, the DOJ is pursuing a proposed consent decree with one of the landlord defendants, Cortland Management LLC, which could set a precedent for how pricing algorithms are used in the future. This agreement requires Cortland Management LLC to assist the government, stop using sensitive data from competitors to set rents, and stop using the same algorithm as its competitors without oversight. If the court approves it, this consent decree will settle the DOJ's claims against Cortland. The DOJ aims to ensure that Cortland's rental prices are set based on market factors, rather than potentially inflated due to algorithmic coordination. The company is also expected to work with the Justice Department during the investigation and any legal proceedings.

15.5.2 Collusion and Algorithmic Collusion

The standard definition for collusion states that it is illegal for landlords to get together to set rent prices for their properties.

Algorithmic collusion occurs when companies unlawfully collaborate to increase prices by utilizing an algorithm that processes their data. Unlike traditional collusion, there are no direct agreements or signals among the competitors. Each company has its own contract with the algorithm provider. The provider in this case, RealPage's YieldStar, analyzes the contracts and data from these companies to offer pricing recommendations that enhance their profit per unit, ultimately harming the customers. It should also be illegal for a third party like RealPage to do it for apartment owners using competitive data and automated technologies. This is why the law needs to be updated.

15.5.3 Real Estate Property Management Systems and Competitive Revenue Management

The computer-generated prices for apartments may have their origins in the competitive revenue management business process adopted by many airlines and hotels in the early 2000s [Vinod, 2021, 2022].

RealPage's YieldStar is at the center of controversy due to allegations of algorithmic price fixing and anti-competitive practices in the rental housing market. YieldStar uses algorithms to analyze data from clients, including what nearby competitors charge, upending the practice of tenants negotiating with apartment staff and discouraging apartment owners from bargaining with renters.

If the Justice Department's claims are true, there must be a shortcoming in the revenue management software, if it does not consider vacancies at a property as input before recommending rates, resulting in maximizing the *revenue per occupied rental unit* and not the *revenue per available rental unit* at the property. In this situation the property landlords are losing money by not lowering rates to achieve a better mix of rental rates to maximize total revenues for the apartment complex.

15.5.4 Duffy v. Yardi Systems Inc Case

The plaintiffs, tenants in Washington state, claim that Yardi's software and the participating landlords engaged in a horizontal price-fixing conspiracy. They allege that the landlords shared sensitive information with Yardi, which then used that data to recommend rental rates, effectively coordinating prices. The anti-trust class-action lawsuit was filed on September 8, 2023, in the U.S. District Court for the Western District of Washington.

On December 4, 2024, Judge Robert S, Lasnik determined that the Duffy plaintiffs' claims aligned with the RealPage side of the argument. He pointed out that Yardi marketed its revenue management software, now called Revenue IQ, to property owners as a tool to boost rental rates. However, the software's effectiveness depends on each landlord sharing sensitive information like prices, available units, and market data with Yardi. This data is used by Yardi to offer advice on setting prices, making the software's success reliant on confidential information from the users. Judge Lasnik characterized the plaintiffs' allegations as per se price fixing, thereby easing the burden on the *Duffy* plaintiffs to ultimately prove their claims.

The defendants, including Yardi and various apartment operators, filed a motion to dismiss, arguing that their use of Yardi's software was an independent business decision, not a concerted action.

The U.S. District Court for the Western District of Washington issued an important decision in a case involving alleged algorithmic price fixing in the apartment rental industry. By denying a motion to dismiss, it allowed the case to proceed to discovery. The case alleges that Yardi and several apartment management companies engaged in an antitrust conspiracy by using Yardi's software to coordinate rental pricing, effectively fixing prices above competitive levels. The court found the plaintiffs' allegations sufficient to support a per se illegal antitrust conspiracy, marking a potential shift in how such cases involving algorithmic pricing are viewed.

This ruling is significant because it suggests a stricter application of antitrust law to algorithmic pricing cases than some other courts have applied. It also underscores the potential antitrust risks associated with using revenue management software that relies on sharing sensitive data and recommending prices. The ruling found that the plaintiffs had enough evidence to suggest a clear anti-competition conspiracy, which is usually considered illegal under antitrust laws. This decision highlights a divide among lower courts on how to handle cases involving pricing algorithms. It indicates that users of such tools could face greater scrutiny and potential lawsuits under Section 1 of the Sherman Act.

15.5.5 The Mach v. Yardi Systems Inc. Case

Mach refers to the class action plaintiffs representing renters. *Mach v. Yardi* was a California antitrust class action lawsuit, filed on February 8, 2024, alleging that Yardi Systems Inc. and landlords used Yardi's Revenue IQ software to illegally exchange competitively sensitive and non-public information to illegally inflate rent prices and suppress lease supply. In Yardi's defense, the company maintained that the Revenue IQ software only used public data to help customers operate efficiently, and by design could not use any client's confidential pricing information to recommend rent prices for any other client. On October 6, 2025, a California court ruled in Yardi's favor by granting Yardi summary judgement, finding insufficient evidence of illegal data sharing. The court rules that using common software was not inherently anti-competitive.

15.5.6 The Casino Hotels Verdict and the Influence on the RealPage Decision

The *Gibson v. Cendyn Group* and *Cornish-Adebiyi, et al v. Caesars Entertainment* decisions suggest that simply using the same pricing software from a vendor like Cendyn (in *Gibson* and *Cornish-Adebiyi v. Caesars Entertainment Inc.*, or RealPage (using their proprietary YieldStar) does not automatically constitute price fixing, unless there is further evidence of coordinated action.

The question now is whether the *Gibson v. Cendyn Group* and *Cornish-Adebiyi v. Caesars Entertainment Inc.* decisions cast doubt on the DOJ's arguments submitted in statements of interest in RealPage. It certainly places a higher burden of proof on the DOJ that companies like RealPage that are using algorithmic pricing tools are actively colluding, not just using the same software.

To prove collusion, the DOJ must demonstrate whether the apartment rental landlords and RealPage used a shared pricing algorithm with direct information sharing between competitors. The DOJ's case against RealPage may look into whether the platform collects important market data from various landlords. This could lead to greater control over how prices are set. The RealPage case may also examine how the pricing algorithm is designed, focusing on aspects that could allow for collusion to occur even without direct sharing of data.

The Gibson case does not completely protect RealPage from antitrust investigations. However, it raises the standard for proving that companies are colluding when they use similar pricing software. To show a violation, there needs to be more evidence of direct cooperation between competitors.

From a DOJ perspective, this may very well be the key distinction between the casino operator cases and RealPage.

These putative class action lawsuits have resulted in uncertainty about the future of Competitive Revenue Management in the travel industry. If competitor selling fares and rates cannot be used as input into the revenue management process in the future, travel suppliers can still rely on demand forecasts and remaining capacity to set inventory controls, which they have done since 1986 when American Airlines introduced the world's first revenue management system [Cross, 1997; Vinod, 2021a].

15.5.7 What Constitutes Algorithmic Collusion?

Based on the verdicts in the casino hotel lawsuits, it is about the use of public data versus proprietary data. Alleged sharing of competitively sensitive non-public information differentiates successful collusion-by-algorithm claims from claims that have been dismissed. Successful collusion-by-algorithm claims pivot on proving competitors sharing competitively sensitive non-public data via a common platform, enabling algorithms to coordinate prices above market rates. This is in contrast with failed claims where sharing non-public data was never proven. Courts view the exchange of non-public competitively sensitive data as the key, making allegations of pooling this sensitive information for algorithmic pricing the decisive factor in surviving dismissal motions.

15.5.8 Did the DOJ Have a Case Against RealPage?

Did RealPage participate in an unlawful scheme to decrease competition among landlords in apartment pricing, harming millions of American renters? Will the DOJ case against RealPage result in substantive remedy? At the heart of the case there are two topics that would have required further clarification.

First, are rental contracts from competing landlords collated to provide insights on rental recommendations. Unlike robotic shopping to determine competitive rates or simply calling a property for rental rates which is public data, competing contract leases are not publicly available data. If competing rental contracts with their respective terms and conditions in the leases were used to develop algorithms to recommend rates, that is a significant issue. Did RealPage with its significant share of the rental market, implicitly co-ordinate pricing among various apartment complexes with its software?

Second, regulators might believe that RealPage's price suggestions are mandatory rates, but that needs to be ascertained. The software offers rent recommendations based on processing some level of competitive data at a certain point in time.

In April 2023, the US Judicial Panel on Multidistrict Litigation ordered over 30 lawsuits across the country to be consolidated in the US District Court for the Middle District of Tennessee for pretrial management. On November 15, 2023, the US Department of Justice submitted a Statement of Interest, urging the court to adopt a per se standard when determining liability [Department of Justice Press Release, 2023]. They also recommended a broad view of how concerted action might be demonstrated in these cases. The court, however, decided not to apply the per se standard and instead granted the student housing defendants' motion to dismiss in December 2023. It denied the motion to dismiss filed by the multifamily defendants and the case moved into the discovery phase.

15.6 A Comparison of Predatory Pricing and Algorithmic Collusion

Predatory pricing is the practice of setting prices for a product unrealistically low to eliminate competitors and create a monopoly in the market. Predatory pricing violates antitrust laws since its primary objective is to create a monopoly. In the short term, consumers benefit from lower prices but suffer long term consequences. When competitors are forced to abandon the market, consumer choices are eliminated after which the predatory company can raise prices.

The practice is difficult to prove since the practice of lowering prices is part of normal competitive behavior and not a deliberate attempt to undermine the market. Predatory pricing harms all participants in the market. While the predator loses revenue, so do competitors, providing an opportunity for new entrants in the marketplace.

Algorithmic collusion occurs when market data used by computer software guides coordinated decision making. It also describes how algorithms might learn to work together differently than humans do. By analyzing large amounts of data, both public and private, algorithms can quickly adjust prices. Objectively, algorithms may use different processes than humans in setting prices or learning about the market environment. This type of collusion happens at the crossroads of human and machine actions such as when market participants use an algorithm that is designed to limit competition or implicitly collaborate with competitors to raise prices.

Unlike predatory pricing where a business sets prices for a product unrealistically low to eliminate the competition and create a monopoly, algorithmic collusion, automated or otherwise, raises prices to unprecedented levels. While predatory pricing violates antitrust laws, algorithmic collusion needs to be addressed by amending the laws to make it easier for prosecutors to pursue cases by lowering the pleading standard for claims and increase the penalties for antitrust violations.

Both predatory pricing and algorithmic collusion to maximize the price per unit is a deliberate attempt to undermine the marketplace.

15.7 U.S. Senate Introduces a New Bill in 2025

Senator Amy Klobuchar (D-MN) and eight other senators reintroduced the "Preventing Algorithmic Collusion Act" on January 23, 2025 [Klobuchar, 2025]. It was previously known as Senate Bill 3686 and is now Senate Bill 232 (S. 232). The new version doesn't change much from the 2024 bill [Klobuchar, 2024], which aimed to ban the use of algorithms for price fixing.

Key Aspects of the S.232 Bill:

1. Targets a perceived loophole in current antitrust law: The bill addresses the challenge of proving traditional price-fixing agreements when algorithms are used to set prices.

2. Defines sharing non-public information with an algorithm as a price fixing agreement: This aims to hold companies accountable for collusive practices that leverage algorithmic pricing.
3. Mandates disclosure of algorithmic pricing: Companies utilizing pricing algorithms would be required to disclose this practice.
4. Prohibits the use of non-public information to train pricing algorithms: This aims to prevent companies from colluding by sharing sensitive competitive information through algorithms.
5. Directs the Federal Trade Commission (FTC) to investigate the impact of pricing algorithms on market competition: This provision seeks to further understand and potentially regulate algorithmic pricing practices.

The bill builds on previous federal legislation efforts that did not pass in 2024. The legislation is driven by concerns that companies are using algorithms to unfairly raise prices and limit competition, as seen in cases like the RealPage lawsuit. The bill aims to protect consumers and smaller businesses from the potentially harmful effects of algorithmic price fixing. While the bill is back in the US Senate, it has been met with mixed opinions, with some arguing that existing antitrust laws are sufficient and the bill's approach is overly broad.

15.7.1 What Is the Future of S.232?

The future of S.232, Preventing Algorithmic Collusion Act, is pending in the Senate Judiciary Committee.

The question is whether the bill falls short because of poor drafting and conflicts with existing antitrust laws. However, it is important to recognize that the political situation has shifted since the 2024 proposal.

Recent research challenges the idea that simply using a pricing algorithm equates to collusion, whether explicit or tacit. Experts agree that one cannot assume collusion just because algorithms are in play. Instead, there must be evidence showing the algorithm was designed to set prices above competitive levels and that users knew and agreed to this. Alternatively, proof is needed that there was an agreement allowing the algorithm to operate independently to fix prices, with a way for humans to override it.

Public concern over pricing algorithms has recently grown, especially in the U.S. Congress, regulatory bodies, and in private lawsuits. The most notable case challenging these algorithms stems from the RealPage litigation.

15.7.1.1 Related Cases

In August 2024, the Department of Justice and several states filed a new case against RealPage in the Middle District of North Carolina. The complaint was updated to include six landlord defendants and two additional state plaintiffs. RealPage faced other legal challenges as well, with actions underway from authorities in Arizona, Maryland, and Washington, DC.

Other lawsuits focus on the use of pricing software. In *Duffy v. Yardi Systems, Inc.*, plaintiffs claimed that some apartment owners and operators broke antitrust laws. They argued the defendants conspired to share sensitive rental data to keep prices above competitive levels. The alleged plan involved both vertical agreements between Yardi Systems and landlords, and horizontal agreements among landlords to exchange information. They also used Yardi's software to set rental rates together, creating what is known as a "hub-and-spoke conspiracy."

The US District Court for the Western District of Washington ruled on the defendant's motion to dismiss. The court found that the plaintiffs had plausibly shown a conspiracy involving the sharing of sensitive, nonpublic commercial data with Yardi. This data was used to generate pricing recommendations, which the court considered a potential violation of the Sherman Act. The court pointed out that this conduct could qualify as a per se illegal activity because it appeared to involve horizontal price-fixing agreements.

In similar cases, plaintiffs have also accused casinos and hotels of colluding through algorithms. However, those cases were dismissed after motions to dismiss. In Gibson v. Cendyn Group, LLC and Cornish-Adebiyi v. Caesars Entertainment, Inc., the plaintiffs alleged a hub-and-spoke conspiracy by Cendyn Group, LLC. This was similar to accusations against RealPage and Yardi, where the goal was to raise and fix hotel room prices in Las Vegas and Atlantic City.

Both district courts agreed that the plaintiffs did not provide enough detail to prove a conspiracy. They pointed out three main issues: first, the hotel defendants were not required to follow Cendyn's pricing advice. Second, the timing of the hotel's use of Cendyn's products made a conspiracy seem unlikely. Third, the plaintiffs failed to show any exchange of confidential, nonpublic information between the hotel defendants.

The main difference in these rulings seems to stem from how well the plaintiffs could allege the defendants shared sensitive, private information. Accusing parties of sharing nonpublic competitive data appears to be a key part of claims about algorithm-based collusion. Without proof of such exchanges, *it is hard to establish a clear case.*

15.7.1.2 State Legislative Actions

By June 2025, over a dozen states had introduced laws to regulate how pricing algorithms are used in rental and property management sectors. Some other states have passed broader laws that mimic S. 232, but these do not directly target the specific issues related to algorithmic pricing tools. Creating laws that directly address the concerns in the rental and property management sectors would be more effective than the broad strategy seen in S. 232.

15.7.1.3 Tentative Conclusion on S. 232

These legal developments suggest that passing S. 232 now is unnecessary. Its approach is too wide and overlooks the potential benefits that pricing algorithms can bring to competition. Existing antitrust laws offer enough oversight for pricing algorithms. Many states have already passed targeted legislation that better responds to concerns about their use in rental and property management industries.

15.8 The RealPage Litigation Settlement

On November 11, 2025, RealPage abruptly replaced its CEO at the heart of the rent-fixing lawsuits with new CEO Dirk Wakeham [Wasielewski, 2025].

The DOJ, along with several states, settled their lawsuit with RealPage for alleged algorithmic rent-fixing on November 24, 2025. Major property management companies settled class-action lawsuits alleging they used RealPage's software to fix rents. -

The RealPage proposed consent judgment required them to make several changes to their business practices that were listed in the DOJ press release [Department of Justice, 2025].

15.8.1 RealPage Proposed Consent Judgement

The DOJ requires RealPage to stop using non-public competitively sensitive active lease data to train the models to recommend rents. The training data must be anonymized historical data that is at least 12-months old. Real Page was also prohibited from using models that determined geographic effects narrower than at a state level, which is broader than the markets alleged in the complaint. This stipulation effectively overcomes the precision focus of predictive pricing models, rendering them ineffective. Further the software has to be redesigned to not limit price decreases or align prices between competing users of the software. Market surveys that collected competitively sensitive information were no longer allowed. RealPage also had to accept a court-appointed monitor to ensure compliance with the terms of the consent judgement.

15.9 Is Continuous Pricing Algorithmic Collusion?

A topic that has been discussed in industry forums and trade journals is whether airlines are exposing themselves to class action lawsuits by deploying continuous pricing across direct and indirect channels of distribution?

Continuous pricing is an extension of revenue management where the price quoted to a customer during shopping is not a fixed price based on the fare that has been filed, but a perturbation of the fixed price point. The continuous price quote reflects current market conditions and can only be generated by airline and not by any intermediary like a GDS. While airlines continue to file public fares through the fare aggregator ATPCO, there is price transparency on fare actions taken by airlines to which competitors can monitor and react. However, the derived continuous price that is communicated by airlines to customers through direct and indirect channels by default is a private fare. This does not qualify as algorithmic collusion since all decisions are being made by an airline independently without collaboration with competitors.

A concern raised by legal experts is that algorithms also wield the power to coordinate prices today in ways that are far more sophisticated than cartels of years ago (e.g., OPEC, Swiss Cheese Union, aluminum, coffee and elevators that have historically used cartels to fix prices) ever could. Fare matching of filed public fares through ATPCO has existed in the airline industry since deregulation in 1978. However, continuous pricing computes derived fares that are specific to the airline and are essentially private fares offered to a customer. Plaintiffs' lawyers, for example, may imagine continuous pricing as a new twist on the cigar-and-bourbon-filled-rooms of a bygone era when Standard Oil was a monopoly and exercised market control to crush the competition. That is simply not the case.

15.10 Competitive Revenue Management and IATA NDC

With the adoption of IATA's New Distribution Capability for air distribution through intermediaries such as GDSs, pricing power shifts from the GDS to the airline. Airlines do not have to file fares through fare aggregators such as ATPCO since the airline assumes sole responsibility for pricing itineraries and offers that include the ancillary bundle across all channels of distribution.

What this means is that schedule and fare transparency that has existed since 1996 with the Internet will gradually disappear as NDC adoption with continuous pricing, derived from reference fares, increases through the indirect channel. All itinerary prices that are distributed by an airline through the NDC messaging standard by default are private fares. However, airlines can still shop competing airline sites for guidance to determine how competitive their selling fares are in the marketplace. The alternative is to not factor competitor data and only base the continuous pricing algorithm on demand forecasts by segment, remaining available capacity and the calibrated price-demand curves.

Building Blocks for Successful Airline Retailing 16

The achievements of an organization are the results of the combined effort of each individual.

Vince Lombardi

Abstract

We are on the cusp of a third digital revolution with technologies such as Conversational AI, Agentic AI, biometrics, IoT, and blockchain. This third wave of digital transformation is not only automating and streamlining business processes and operations but also enhancing the touchpoints of the customer journey. The core building blocks, and horizontal enables of airline retailing is a mandatory investment to embark on the retailing journey. Fundamental organizational changes focused on the customer and partnerships required to create a customer centric organization for an airline to be successful in the offer and order era. This chapter concludes with a discussion on monetizing airline data and what it takes to create a zero-latency organization for decision making with offers and orders.

This quote by Vince Lombardi, former head coach of the Green Bay Packers, emphasizes that collective effort is critical for an organization's success. It highlights those individual contributions, when combined, create the overall success of the company.

B. Vinod, *The Era of Airline Revenue Management with Offers and Orders*,
Management for Professionals, https://doi.org/10.1007/978-3-032-24197-9_16

16.1 Introduction

For three decades after airline deregulation, the focus of revenue management in the airline industry has focused on maximizing revenues by selling the right product to the right customer at the right price at the right time. It was one-dimensional in the sense that the selling fare was all that mattered. Revenue management advanced from leg/segment inventory controls to origin and destination inventory controls. With leg/segment controls, seat availability is based on either net nesting or threshold nesting. To control inventory by O&D, availability is based on the continuous nesting, also known as bid price controls. Restriction-free pricing (RFP), a feature introduced by low-cost carriers (LCCs), was first adopted to some degree by the FSCs when they had to compete directly with the LCCs on key routes. In the absence of fare restrictions, when price was the only determinant of the customer segment, demand for booking classes is no longer independent. The revenue management models had to go through significant enhancements to support lightly restricted and unrestricted tariffs.

With the revenue management transition to selling bundles consisting of a base fare and ancillaries, it opens a world of opportunity. The ancillary products are not limited to airline ancillary products and services, but may include third party products such as hotels, cars, ground transportation, and products from third-party retailers. This is a very significant change. For an airline to undertake this venture requires strategic agility, partnerships, effective collaboration and a razor sharp focus on fulfillment.

Low-cost carriers (LCC) have a commanding lead over Full-service Carriers in terms of ancillary revenues generated per passenger. The large network carriers still dominate the total ancillary revenue measure, bolstered by their lucrative frequent flyer programs and co-branded credit cards.

Before we dive into the building blocks of successful retailing, we shall take a step back to review the fundamental building blocks of a digital airline. It is an aspirational goal for many airlines who hope to achieve this status over the next decade. Digital transformation enables airlines to remain competitive in a fast-changing travel industry. It allows them to meet the growing expectations of tech-savvy travelers while improving their operations and financial results.

16.2 The Digital Airline: The Third Wave

There is no alternative to digital transformation. Those that don't adapt will fail.

Jeff Bezos, Amazon Founder

This quote by Jeff Bezos, founder of Amazon, suggests that organizations must adapt to the evolving digital landscape or risk being left behind. It highlights the transformative power of digital technologies and the potential consequences of failing to adopt them.

In travel, like other industries, digital transformation is neither a luxury or a competitive advantage, but a fundamental requirement for long-term business survival in a digital-first world.

The first digital revolution in the airline industry took place with the creation of automated reservations systems in the 1960s (Passenger Service Systems or PSS) that led to the creation of the Global Distribution Systems (GDS) in 1976.

The second digital revolution took place in the mid-1990s with the advent of the Internet that led to online direct airline sites (airline.com) and the birth of Online Travel Agencies (OTA).

We are on the cusp of a third digital revolution with technologies such as Conversational AI, Agentic AI, biometrics, and blockchain. This third wave is not only automating and streamlining business processes and operations but also enhancing the touchpoints of the customer journey. The third wave is technology-led, but it goes beyond just machines and tools. It aims to build a future that improves how we work, care for the environment, and keeps customers happy. This movement combines new technology with a bigger goal of making everything better for people and the planet. It's about using technology to create real progress, not just for convenience but for lasting benefits. The focus is on smarter ways to do things that lead to higher productivity, greater sustainability, and more satisfied customers.

Investment in these digital assets is a requirement for success. Airlines that make the investment will lead the industry forward.

16.2.1 What Is a Digital Airline

A digital airline focuses on leveraging technology to improve various aspects of its business processes, operations and customer experience. Key areas include enhanced customer experience through personalization across all digital channels, operational efficiency through automation and data-driven decision-making, and increased safety and security using digital tools. Sustainability is also a major focus, with digital solutions aiding in fuel optimization and reduced emissions.

Key aspects of a digital airline for competitive advantage are described below.

16.2.1.1 Operational Efficiency

Operational efficiency is the hallmark of an airline that attempts to achieve zero-latency in decision making. Key components include:

Automation

Self-service kiosks for online check-in, bag drop kiosks, mobile apps for convenient access to booking, digital boarding passes, and real-time flight updates reduce physical touchpoints and improve efficiency.

Recovery from irregular operations such as unplanned flight cancellations, flight diversions, delays, or equipment changes caused by inclement weather, air traffic control (ATC), and crew availability. Predict potential disruptions before they happen for proactive response, and leverage "digital twins" to simulate disruption scenarios for better planning.

Data-Driven Decision Making
Big data analytics optimize flight schedules, fare management, revenue management, seat inventory control, recovery from irregular operations, gate assignment that minimizes connect times for outbound passengers, fuel consumption, and resource allocation.

Predictive Maintenance
Predictive maintenance with IoT (Internet of Things) sensors and analytics is used to monitor aircraft components in real-time to minimize downtime, improve aircraft reliability and increase fleet efficiency.

Real-Time Monitoring
Digital tools enable airlines to track flights, baggage, and other operations in real-time, improving responsiveness and efficiency. Real-time monitoring of revenue management KPIs is a fundamental building block for continuous demand management to master uncertainty and be responsive to competitor actions and customer conversion rates.

Route Path (Flight) Planning
Digital platforms process a wide range of data points, including weather patterns, wind conditions, turbulence, airspace restrictions, and air traffic volume. By analyzing this data, AI-enabled algorithms can suggest flight paths that prioritize safety, adhere to air traffic control (ATC) regulations, minimize fuel consumption, and reduce flight time, while avoiding congested airspace.

16.2.1.2 The Customer Experience

There are four key dimensions to customer experience in the digital era.

Personalization
Digital airlines focus on providing a seamless and personalized experience through mobile apps, AI-powered chatbots, and other digital tools. By leveraging historical purchase behavior sales data and current marketplace trends, the objective is to tailor offers, services and communications to travelers based on their individual preferences.

Mobile and Online Applications
Mobile apps, chatbots, and online platforms streamline the booking, check-in, boarding, real-time flight updates, and in-flight experience.

Self-Service

Features like online check-in, bag-drop kiosks, and digital boarding passes help cut down on touchpoints at airports. They make the travel process smoother and quicker for passengers.

Seamless Interaction

Contactless technologies, biometric identification, and real-time updates improve convenience and reduce friction throughout the journey.

16.2.1.3 Enhanced Safety and Security

Enhanced safety and security measures aim to detect and mitigate potential threats, ensuring the safety of passengers and crew, while also streamlining the overall travel experience.

Biometric Identification

Facial recognition, fingerprint scanning, and other biometric technologies enhance security and streamline the boarding process and access, avoiding paper tickets.

Cybersecurity

Digital systems require robust cybersecurity measures to protect sensitive data and prevent disruptions. In the digital era, protecting sensitive customer and operational data from cyber threats is a high priority that must never be compromised.

Blockchain for Security

Blockchain technology offers various applications to bolster cybersecurity. Examples are:

1. Decentralized Identity Management reduces reliance on centralized databases and mitigates identity theft risks.
2. Blockchain enables encrypted and secure sharing of sensitive data, allowing authorized users to access information with confidence.
3. Provides traceability and transparency for baggage tracking.
4. Distributed Denial of Service (DDoS) protection by distributing network resources to make it harder for attackers to overwhelm a central point.
5. The zero trust security model aligns with the "never trust, always verify" principle by providing secure identity verification and access control.

16.2.1.4 Sustainability

Sustainability is a high priority for the airline industry, with a focus on achieving net-zero carbon emissions by 2050. This commitment, known as "Fly Net Zero," is in line with the Paris Agreement's (adopted December 12, 2015) temperature goals and requires coordinated efforts from airlines, airports, and governments. Key priorities include reducing emissions, improving energy efficiency, and minimizing waste.

Optimizing Fuel Consumption
Digital tools help optimize flight paths and air traffic management, reducing fuel consumption and emissions. Electronic Flight Bags (EFBs) and access to realtime data reduce costs and carbon emissons.

Carbon Offset
Digital platforms can promote and facilitate participation in carbon offset programs and other sustainability initiatives. Some airlines provide passengers with data about their carbon footprint per flight, and offer options for offsetting emissions. This is often done through integrated booking systems or partnerships with third-party offset providers.

Cloud Computing
Cloud-based systems provide scalability, flexibility, and cost-effectiveness for digital operations. Migrating to the cloud can reduce IT management and compute costs by 25%–35%.

Internet of Things (IoT)
IoT devices including sensors, RFID tags and connected systems enable real-time data collection and analysis for improved operational awareness.

Open APIs and Integration
Every airline must be strategically aligned to create an open marketplace for offers and orders. Open APIs and integration capabilities allow for seamless connectivity with third-party solutions and data sharing, thereby expanding the breadth and depth of the retailing application.

16.2.2 What Is a Digital Native Airline?

There is no such thing as a "digitally native airline."

Every airline has to deal with legacy components which means that they must undergo a transformation to create a seamless, data-driven and customer centric experience. Riyadh Air, the new airline from Saudi Arabia, was recently touted as a "most digitally native airline" [Ranson, 2025] in a sponsored article. This is pure marketing hype.

While many aspects of offer management, order management, and customer experience are built from the ground up with modern digital technology, they *do not* bypass legacy systems but ensure inter-operability with legacy systems. As a new airline, Riyadh Air does not have to worry about historical or future PNRs residing in a legacy reservation system to migrate to ONE Order. Most airlines require backward compatibility since PNRs, and orders must co-exist. As a new airline without legacy constraints, all they have is orders (no PNRs, EMDs, ETKT) and everything sits in a single record. However, they still need a translation layer for inbound/outbound interline PNRs and other messages that they must convert to Order format internally and retain backward compatibility for any changes to be reflected in both systems.

16.3 The Core Building Blocks of Airline Retailing

The core building blocks, and horizontal enables of airline retailing is shown in Fig. 16.1.

16.3.1 Supplier Customer Profile and Universal Profile

Airlines use customer profiles to personalize offers, tailor marketing, and improve customer experience. These profiles are built using various data points, including demographics, travel history, preferences, and online behavior. By understanding these profiles, airlines can better meet the needs of different customer segments. Ultimately, the master profile, called the Universal Profile, is owned by the customer, and the airline only has knowledge about a subset of the Universal Profile on the airline profile database. The same is true for other travel suppliers like hotels, car rentals and destination activity providers.

A traveler owns the data on Universal Profile and communicates directly and shares parts of the information on the profile with an airline and/or a non-travel entity like a hotel to provide the requested service for a seamless experience. A customer must be willing to share detailed preferences and intent with the airline for every booking for a seamless travel experience.

16.3.2 Universal Data Exchange

In the current environment, travel suppliers, OTAs and GDSs have fundamental gaps in addressing intelligent retailing, personalization, and frictionless travel from a customer point of view. The data owner (the traveler) authorizes the exchange of data through a broker that securely exchanges data between travel and non-travel partners. The data is never centralized and stored but relevant data is exchanged in real-time.

Peer-to-peer (P2P) networks are decentralized systems where individual computers (peers) connect directly to share resources like files or processing power. These systems lack centralization and instead rely on direct communication and schema-less data exchange between nodes or peers. The data exchange is a secure communications message routing platform between travel partners (e.g., brands such as American Airlines and Hilton Hotels) based on the permissions granted by the customer. Every customer has an encrypted electronic key that is used to identify the customer across travel entities such as airlines, hotels, cars, rideshare, and

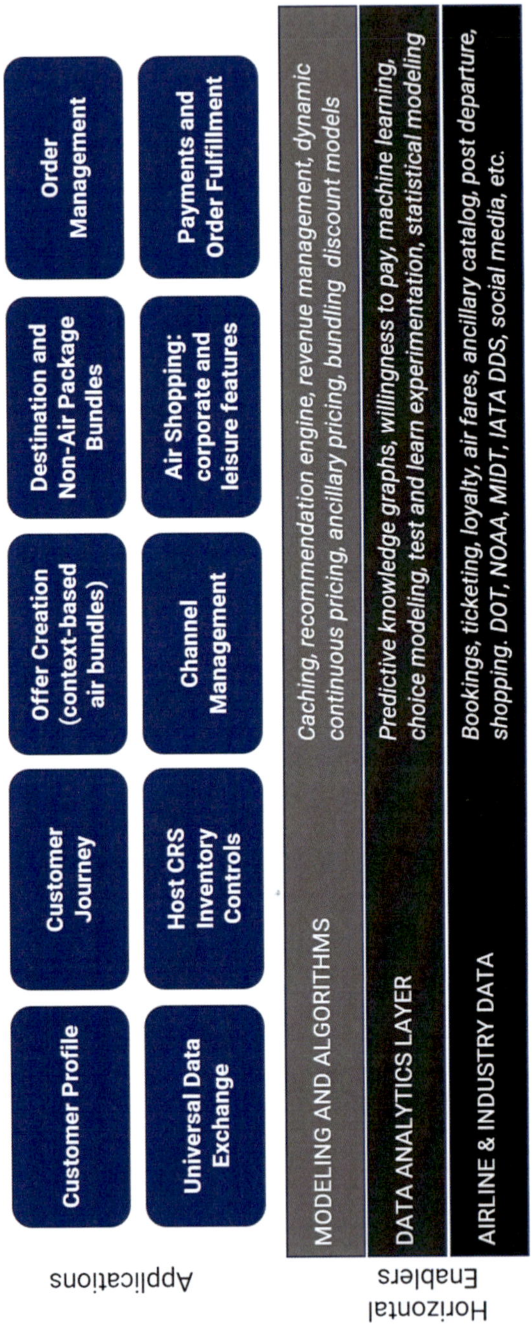

Fig. 16.1 Core building blocks and horizontal enablers of airline retailing

local activities. The data exchange should be schema-less and not store any information including PII (personally identifiable information such as social security number, passport data, biometric data, date of birth, etc.) data.

A Universal Data Exchange (UDX) must be operated by a neutral entity and does not exist in travel today.

Besides the Universal Profile and Universal Data Exchange, a decentralized digital identity is required for the future with seamless inter-operability. Distributed and decentralized storage will allow authentication credentials to be verified independently by every participant without mutual trust between participants. This allows a user to control their own identity and manage their own risk.

As an alternative to the Universal Data Exchange, the Digital Identity Foundation (DIF) and the World Wide Web Consortium (W3C) Credentials Community Group (CCG) are promoting the concept of an Identity Hub (IH) to store profile data, sensitive documents and offers securely from suppliers that are controlled by the customer. This initiative is now called the Confidential Data Storage/Secure Data Store.

16.3.3 Customer Journey

The retailing journey refers to the entire process a passenger goes through when interacting with an airline, from initial search and booking to post-flight services, with a focus on personalization and seamless experiences. This journey is evolving with offers and orders, dynamic pricing, and personalized services.

Digital technologies enhance the customer journey, from mobile apps for booking and check-in to in-flight entertainment systems and personalized digital experiences. The ultimate goal is to create a smooth and frictionless experience across all touchpoints, from online booking, contactless check in, digital identity verification, real-time flight updates to in-flight services.

16.3.4 Host CRS Inventory Controls

Traditional airline inventory has been focused on only seat inventory and seat availability. With offer and order, air ancillary products generate incremental revenues. Airline inventory systems must be enhanced to account and track sales for air ancillary products that are capacity controlled such as bassinet, oxygen service (portable oxygen concentrators), meals, bulkhead seats, number of exit row seats, number of aisle seats, number of window seats, etc.

16.3.5 Offer Creation

In the future, airlines will be responsible for the creation of bundled offers across all channels of distribution. Customer segmentation must be based on the context for travel to generate pertinent offers. Besides personalizing the offer based on customer preferences, dynamic continuous pricing capability is an option that must be on the radar.

16.3.6 Channel Management

With the demise of full content agreements (FCA) between airlines and GDSs in the NDC-era, channel management is of strategic importance to airlines to deliver the pertinent content to the right channel based on various factors such as channel economics, and customers that are interacting with the channel. Airlines have the liberty to select the channels that best align with their target audience and business goals. Airlines often differentiate pricing across channels to cater to different customer segments and optimize revenue. For example, they might offer exclusive discounts on their website or through corporate sales channels. Airlines can also differentiate pricing across channels and offer exclusive discounts on their website or through preferred sales channels.

16.3.7 Destination and Non-Air Package Bundles

NDC provides the capability for airlines to offer unique packages that include destination activities, ground transportation, and hotel accommodations. This opens up new possibilities for creating and distributing comprehensive travel packages that include both air and non-air components, benefiting airlines, travel agents, and travelers.

16.3.8 Air Shopping with Corporate and Leisure Features

Air shopping is an integral component of the offer and order management process. Besides serving as a fast response system [Vinod, 2024a, Chap. 8] the shopping service must support features specific to corporate and leisure travelers. For corporates, seat-led shopping must only return itineraries that can fulfill the specific seat type requested by the customer such as aisle, window, etc. For leisure, specific features include budget and theme-based shopping.

16.3.9 Order Management

The order represents a unique record of the agreement between the airline and the customer, including all purchased items and services. This is a major investment.

16.3.10 Payments and Order Fulfillment

Airline payment and order fulfillment involves processing payments for flight bookings and ensuring customers receive the services they pay for. Core components are:

Payments: Payment processing involves processing from sources such as customer credit cards, loyalty points, virtual cards, mobile wallets, and other forms of payment. This involves integration with payment gateways and processing services.

Settlement: After payment, the airline needs to account for the revenue, pay airline partners and third-party vendors involved in the fare, and process taxes and any additional fees. The systems used for settling transactions, involving GDSs and OTAs are IATA's Billing and Settlement Plan (BSP) and Airline Reporting Corporation (ARC).

Fulfillment: This involves ensuring the customer receives what they paid for, including the flight, seat, air ancillaries, and any non-air products and services.

16.4 The Importance of Partnerships

With the demise of full content agreements, to be successful with airline retailing, there are two levels of partnerships that are required. First, is access to the right distribution channels to promote and sell airline offers. This entails a network of travel agents who are incentivized to sell the airline product. To promote and sell basic air ancillary products and services such as pre-reserved seats, baggage fees, lounge access, etc., airlines control the scope of what is offered to customers. The pace of this innovation is within the control of the individual airline based on the assumption that they can retain their market share based on brand awareness, competitive positioning and value provided.

Second, airlines will require partnerships when they create bundles that are not their core competency such as meals, hotel stay, rental car, ground transportation, airport shuttles, and activities at destinations. Generating incremental revenues by promoting complementary products as part of the order management process requires effective trusted partnerships.

This is a formidable task to transform an aspiration to reality, requires an executive sponsor, and additional resources with a retailing mindset to manage partner relationships. Each partnership will require:

1. A clear objective with short-term and long-term goals
2. Negotiate the terms of the partnership, the duration, commercial deal economics, and key performance indicators (KPIs).
3. Determine how the new partner product will be introduced as a touchpoint in the customer workflow: online booking, pre-flight, in transit, or post-flight.

4. Monitor the KPIs to determine how customers are responding to this new initiative, address any issues related to the sales process and fulfillment and take corrective action if required.
5. Attribution of purchases and settlement with the partner monthly. Provide audit capabilities to ensure transparency in sales transactions.
6. Augment the partnership, if possible, with additional opportunities to create value for each other.

This process should be repeated for each partnership. Successful airline partnership programs will have five to twenty partnerships.

16.4.1 Beyond Technology, Brand Perception and Brand Equity for Growth

Companies in various industries have successfully shifted public perception from negative or neutral to positive through strategic changes. A clear brand promise helps build a strong brand identity that creates emotional connections with customers. When a company manages how customers see it, the brand image improves. This leads to stronger loyalty from customers and more business success in the long run.

The revenue management transition to offers and orders provides an opportunity to enhance an airline's brand recognition and customer perception of the brand. Many companies in various industries have successfully changed how people perceive them, turning negative or neutral opinions into positive ones. Three noteworthy examples are Tesla, McDonald's and John Deere.

Tesla's advancements in the electric vehicle (EV) market reveal important lessons. For many years, traditional car manufacturers stayed out of the EV space. This gave Tesla time to improve its skills and build expertise without much competition. Companies that fall behind tend to lose ground to new, innovative players who grow stronger and take more market share. Airlines that do not invest in airline retailing will lose out to innovative players who grow and capture market share. Second, Tesla made electric cars seem cool and wanted, moving past the idea they were only for tech fans. By projecting an image of a car manufacturer as a technology company and focusing on delivering a great customer experience, Tesla shifted how people see electric vehicles. They made EVs seem more appealing and desirable. Merely leveraging technology is not adequate to stay ahead. Airlines also need to provide tangible benefits by offering useful products and making the journey smooth for their customers.

Faced with criticism about the quality of its food, McDonald's fixed its image by being more open about the ingredients that go into its food and adding healthier choices. They also updated the packaging to be more environmentally friendly.

Brand perception and brand equity are two fundamental drivers for growth as an airline transitions to offers and orders. It is a fundamental requirement to command a price premium.

Brand perception is a customer's viewpoint of what an airline's products and services represent. Brand perception is based on actual experience and reputation. Improving brand perception is of critical importance to boost performance by commanding a premium for ancillary products and services.

Brand equity is the added value a brand earns from shaping how people see it. It reflects the positive perception and trust built over time. This perception creates a price advantage and helps the brand stand out. When consumers view a brand favorably, they are more likely to choose it over others. In short, brand equity is the worth created by how a brand is perceived.

John Deere built a solid reputation for creating useful, purpose-driven technology that shows they care about innovation. Their brand equity is exceptionally strong, stemming from its reputation for quality, innovation, and reliability in agricultural and construction equipment. This strong brand equity allows John Deere to command higher prices and fosters customer loyalty, significantly impacting its financial performance and market position.

The complexity of the transformation required makes it extremely unlikely that airlines can do it on their own. They must work closely with trusted partners. These partners should embrace the shift toward airline retailing by reaching out to airlines, sharing ideas, and getting involved. Partners can all benefit from the new value streams. Airlines must be open to collaboration, communicate clearly about their plans, and work together closely. A likely scenario is a leading airline, a group of airlines or an alliance partnering with a few like-minded companies to promote airline retailing. This small group can create a foundation that others in the industry can then follow.

Airlines can work together by building their business cases with partners around shared customer goals. They should focus on high-potential use cases and find ways to improve the customer experience. One option is creating full travel packages that include hotels and car rentals, along with customized bundles and add-ons for corporate clients and travel management companies. To keep everyone on the same page, airlines and partners need to agree on shared retailing metrics. These could include conversion rates, customer satisfaction scores, and how well ancillary services are selling in core markets, regional markets and niche seasonal markets. Today airlines usually set these goals only for their own direct channels. NDC provides an opportunity to address this challenge since the airline controls the offer creation process across all channels of distribution.

A centerpiece of the strategy to promote new ancillary products and services with partners is testing. A deep understanding of markets coupled with test and learn experimentation is critical to move the dial. An ancillary product that does not do well in one region may do extremely well in another. This customer insight can be gained through online surveys and experimentation. Surveys are of limited value since customer opinions on surveys may be biased. Hence, testing is a fundamental requirement to gain insight into global and regional markets.

16.5 Organization

One of the biggest challenges as airlines transition from merchandising to retailing, also viewed as revenue management to offer management, is that not a single airline has progressed to a point to serve as a role model for other airlines to follow. Network carriers, large and small, are grappling with how to establish their respective organizations, acquire talent, overcome legacy thinking, and introduce the customer-first retailing mindset to the rank and file. This cultural change does not happen overnight and can only be achieved with commitment from senior executives over time. This period is three to five years.

There is no one-size-fits-all strategy to establish a customer-centric organization. Based on the long-term strategy, the customer base and airline brand, airline executives are committed to addressing the organizational needs based on the promise of higher revenues per passenger and lower distribution costs, and in some cases, eliminate distribution costs altogether.

16.5.1 The High-Level Organization

Figure 16.2 illustrates a typical organization under the Chief Executive Officer. The boxes in green highlight the functional areas where customer segmentation and transparency into tracking metrics at the customer segment level are required in a world of offers and orders. An airline's customer centric transformation requires some roles to focus and report KPIs on customer segments. These roles are highlighted on the organizational chart in green.

President and CEO

If the roles are split the President typically oversees daily operations and reports to the Chief Executive Officer (CEO) who is responsible for the overall vision and direction of the company, including strategic planning, financial performance, and stakeholder relations. In some airlines, the President and CEO roles may be combined into a single position.

Chief Operating Officer

The Chief Operating Officer (COO) oversees the day-to-day operations of the airline. This role is responsible for ensuring the safe, efficient, and reliable operation of the airline's various departments, including flight operations, airport operations, and in-flight services. The COO collaborates with other senior leaders to develop and implement strategies that improve operational performance and enhance customer experience. At some airlines the head of Fleet Planning reports to the COO.

Chief Legal Officer

The Chief Legal Officer (CLO) oversees all legal matters for the airline, including corporate governance, litigation, and regulatory compliance. CLO is the modern

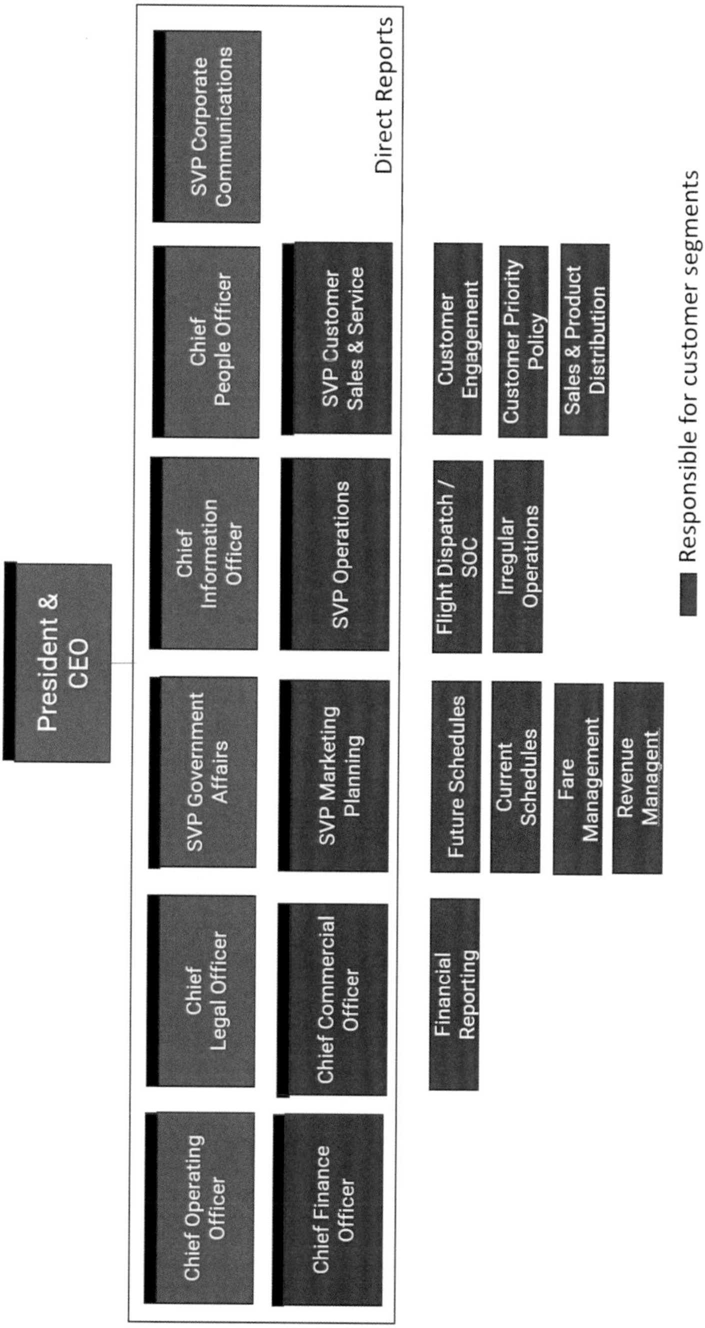

Fig. 16.2 Typical high level airline organization

evolution of the traditional General Counsel (GC) role. While traditional GCs focused on day-to-day legal matters, the CLO role is broader in scope, strategic, business focused, enterprise-wide leadership that integrates legal strategy with business goals, risk management, compliance, and governance. The CLO advises the executive team and board of directors on legal risks and strategic matters and manages the legal affairs team.

Government Affairs

The head of Government Affairs role focuses on managing the airline's relationships with government agencies, policymakers, and regulatory bodies. This role involve advocating for policies in commercial aviation that support the airline's interests, monitoring legislative and regulatory changes, and ensuring compliance. This role is also responsible for shaping public policy related to commercial aviation.

Chief Information Officer

The Chief Information Officer (CIO) role is pivotal in driving digital transformation, enhancing customer experiences, and optimizing operational efficiency. The CIO is responsible for leading the technology strategy, ensuring alignment with business goals, and managing a large technology portfolio. They also play a critical role in cloud migration, cybersecurity, supplier management, and building a strong technology team.

Chief People Officer

The Chief People Officer (CPO) is a strategic leader within an organization who is responsible for all aspects of human capital management, including talent acquisition, employee development, and culture building. The CPO is responsible for acquiring skilled resources as the technology landscape evolves with advances in AI, blockchain, and cybersecurity, and ensure that the workforce is aligned with the company's goals, fostering a thriving and inclusive environment.

Corporate Communications

The head of Corporate Communications oversees all aspects of the company's internal and external communications. This role involves developing and implementing communication strategies to support the airline's business objectives, manage its reputation, and engage with various stakeholders, including employees, media, customers, and investors.

Chief Financial Officer

The Chief Financial Officer (CFO) is responsible for overseeing all financial aspects of the airline, ensuring its financial health and stability. This includes financial planning, budgeting, forecasting, accounting, and reporting, as well as managing cash flow, risk, and compliance. The CFO also plays a critical role in strategic planning, working with the executive team to drive growth and profitability. At some airlines the head of Fleet Planning reports to the CFO.

Chief Commercial Officer
The Chief Commercial Offer owns the entire commercial strategy, including Network Planning, Pricing, Revenue Management, Sales, Marketing, Product Distribution, Cargo, and Loyalty programs. In some airlines the head of Marketing Planning reports to the CCO.

Marketing Planning
The head of Marketing Planning is responsible for shaping the airline's brand and revenue generation strategies. This role is responsible for a variety of tasks that drive customer acquisition and retention, ensuring the airline remains competitive in a dynamic environment. In many airlines, flight scheduling and capacity (fleet) planning, pricing and revenue management, and loyalty program management report into the head of marketing planning.

Operations
The head of operations is responsible for the overall management and strategic direction of the airline's operational functions. This role ensures the safe, efficient, and compliant operation of the airline, including flight operations, ground operations, and maintenance. The head of Operations collaborates with other senior leaders to align with the airline's overall business goals and objectives. In many airlines, the crew management (pilots and flight attendant staffing), safety management and regulatory compliance report to the head of operations.

The "day-of operations" aspect of the business falls under the Flight Operations department. The Flight Dispatch and Systems Operations Control (SOC) are responsible for the safe and efficient execution of flights on a daily basis, including managing disruptions (IROPS) and ensuring smooth operations.

Customer Sales and Service
This is a multifaceted role focused on driving revenue growth and ensuring an exceptional customer experience across all touchpoints. This role is responsible for developing and implementing a customer experience strategy, to lead and manage the entire customer service department, and maintain strong customer relationships.

16.5.2 The Pricing and Revenue Management Organization

Figure 16.3 takes the pricing and revenue management organization one-level down starting with the individual who has overall responsibility. Note that the head of pricing and revenue management has to work closely with adjacent organizations such as loyalty, sales and distribution, and irregular operations.

Data Science and OR
The Data Science and Operations Research develops the advanced decision support models for deployment by developers and computer scientists in the CIO's

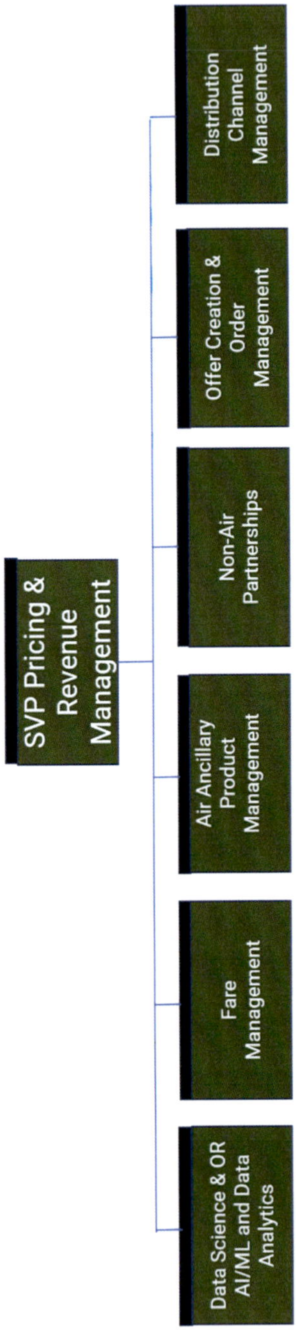

Fig. 16.3 Typical high level pricing and revenue management organization

organization. Typical skills include the ability to analyze vast amounts of data, stochastic modeling, optimization, advanced statistical modeling, AI, machine leaning, natural language processing, and blockchain. The group is also responsible for customer segmentation, calibration of recommendation engines, and establish test and learn experimentation to ensure continuous learning and improvement over time.

Fare Management

Fare management is a critical function, focusing on monitoring competitor activity and determine the response to remain competitive. This involves analyzing market demand, competitor pricing, and other factors to determine the optimal price points for different fare classes and booking periods. Analysts in this group must have an orientation towards markets, since that is how fares are established in the marketplace.

Air Ancillary Product Management

This function plays a key role in determining what ancillary products should be included in the pool of ancillary products that can be used to generate an offer. While the primary focus must be on air ancillaries, non-air ancillaries must also be on the radar from partners. Pricing of the ancillary products and services, associated testing, and the associated level of granularity—system, market, flight is the responsibility of this team.

Non-Air Partnerships

With the growing focus on non-air partnerships to enrich an airline's retailing strategiy, over time, this will grow to become an important function. Non-air partnerships are strategic in nature to create a more personalized and seamless experience for customers, ultimately driving revenue growth.

Offer Creation and Order Management

This is the core revenue management function with a focus on not just the base fare but offers and orders. The focus of this group is to optimize and create dynamic offers for customers, maximizing revenue and enhancing the customer experience. This involves analyzing data, understanding customer willingness to pay, and strategically pricing and packaging flights and ancillaries. Ultimately, it's about delivering the right offer to the right customer at the right price at the right time.

Product Distribution Channel Management

The focus of this group is to determine how the airline's flights and ancillary services are sold to customers, whether directly through the airline's website or indirectly through travel agencies, online travel agencies (OTAs), and other intermediaries. This involves managing relationships with various distribution partners, optimizing sales strategies across different channels, and ensuring a consistent brand experience for the customer. In the absence of full content agreements, content differentiation through the NDC channel is a key area of focus.

16.6 Monetizing Airline Data

Monetization of airline data is frequently discussed at industry forums. Yet no airline today has developed a cohesive strategy to monetize their data for competitive advantage and monetary benefit.

AI and machine learning are no longer just for big tech companies and large network carriers. These powerful tools are now available to a wider range of small and medium sized airlines. However, airlines must make the investment to learn how to use these tools effectively and understand the data behind them. Gaining this knowledge is key to finding a competitive edge with AI.

Besides using airline booking, ticketing, air shopping on airline websites, air shopping requests from indirect channels and post departure data to support their core airline business of airline planning and airline operations, can airline data be leveraged to generate incremental revenues?

Here are a few examples on how airline data can be monetized.

16.6.1 Aggregate Data to Third Parties

First, it is about selling aggregate data to third parties such as newspaper outlets and tourism boards. Data types include shopping query data, shopping response data, booking, ticketing and post departure data. Selling aggregate data to third parties implies that an airline takes large amounts of collected data, usually anonymized to protect privacy of individuals and combined from various sources, and sells it to other businesses who can use it for analysis, marketing, or other purposes, without having access to individual user details. The focus is on insights into macro trends in travel derived from the data rather than specific personal information. The companies buying the data may use it for purposes like market research, targeted advertising, or developing new products. To address ethical concerns, airlines must follow data privacy laws when selling aggregated data. This includes ensuring that customer information is properly anonymized, and that consent is obtained from customers when required.

16.6.2 Insights to Airline Partners

Insights from airline data can be provided to partners for commercial gain. Data can be turned into money by finding new opportunities by harnessing the insights from the data. For example, airlines can partner with grocery chains and gas stations and provide aggregate data on the number of airline loyalty members who live in a city or region. Armed with this information, a grocery or gas station might decide to offer a loyalty program in partnership with the airline to modify customer spending behavior to earn more airline miles.

16.6.3 Co-Branded Credit Cards

Airline data monetization with co-branded credit cards where airlines partner with banks, transforms loyalty programs into major revenue streams, Examples of partnerships are Delta Airlines—American Express, United Airlines—Chase, and American Airlines—Citi. These cards also offer perks like free bags, priority boarding, lounge access, and travel credits. Revenue streams include shared transaction fees from merchants, late payments and interest fees from card holders, and selling miles to banks, which boost airline profits beyond just flights.

Customer purchases with the co-branded credit card generate valuable spending data for the airline and the bank. This rich data helps airlines and banks create targeted offers, personalize rewards, and develop a deeper understanding of customer behavior enhancing the value proposition for all participants.

These co-branded cards also drive loyalty, converting infrequent flyers into frequent flyers that also generate ancillary revenues. It also increases stickiness by imbedding the airline brand into daily life, thereby increasing retention and lifetime value.

The banks have expertise focused on payments and customer spending analytics. These partnerships with co-branded credit cards are powerful. The bank's financial transaction data (spending patterns, demographics, location) can be merged with the airline's loyalty data (frequent flyer tier, flight purchase history, preferences) to segment customers in unique ways and offer targeted rewards and personalized travel experiences, leading to higher engagement and revenue for both.

16.6.4 Accelerating Loyalty Miles Redemptions

In the future, loyalty points could become fully tokenized, allowing customers the freedom to treat them like digital assets, and could be used for redemption with participating retailers and also for trading in secondary markets.

Loyalty points conversion to digital tokens on blockchain refers to the process of transforming traditional loyalty points earned in a rewards program into digital tokens (digital miles) that are stored and managed on a blockchain, allowing customers to trade, transfer, and redeem their points more flexibly and securely across different platforms, essentially creating a more dynamic and liquid loyalty system.

In 2018, Singapore Airlines announced the launch of its blockchain-based airline loyalty digital wallet app for its KrisFlyer loyalty program [Baydakova, 2018; Shayon, 2018]. Members of the airline's KrisFlyer loyalty program could convert their miles into KrisPay tokens, which can then be spent with multiple participating retailers. Blockchain is used to easily onboard new partners and reconcile payments, resulting in reduced costs and increased efficiency.

In October 2020, Singapore Airlines extended its blockchain-based reward digital outlet KrisPay with Kris+, with 150 partners through 650 outlets to provide exclusive deals for frequent flyers. With Kris+travelers can accrue miles from daily purchases and the miles could be used as a payment vehicle [Ledger Insights, 2020].

Motivation for the use of blockchain technology has been attributed to flexibility in redemption options for customers, who can redeem the accrued digital tokens at retail outlets. There is no depreciation of accrued miles over time since the digital tokens can be exchanged at will for other cryptocurrencies. Faster redemptions reduce the displacement of higher valued passengers closer to departure since customers may redeem the cryptocurrency for non-travel-related purchases. Probably most important of all, faster redemptions reduce the airline's liability on the books that are reported in 10 K filings by public companies.

Critical to the success of blockchain-based loyalty programs is the ability of the airline to quickly sign-up retailers and credit card companies who will accept the crypto currency as a form of payment when a customer wants to make a purchase. Added benefits are the instant accrual of mileage equivalent cryptocurrency when the travel segment is completed and the inherent security benefits that reduce fraud. The use of blockchain with digital tokens also intrinsically increases the value of loyalty coalition programs by an order of magnitude.

16.7 Creating the Zero-Latency Organization for Decision Making with Offers and Orders

Performance management for an airline is a systematic approach that aligns the performance goals of individual employees with the company's overall strategic objectives. The goal is to encourage high-performance behaviors and practices across the organization, all aimed at achieving the business vision and meeting performance targets. Successful implementation of a performance management strategy relies on information available at different levels within the organization, which supports high-performance behaviors and promotes effective decision-making across various functions.

To minimize decision-making latency in the new era of airline revenue management, airlines must adopt strategies that enable a faster and more responsive approach to managing demand and optimizing revenue. This can be achieved by enabling the following critical components to enable zero-latency for offers and orders.

16.7.1 Embrace Continuous Demand Management

While forecasting and forecasting accuracy are integral components of a successful revenue management program, it is equally important to look beyond forecast-driven approaches to master uncertainty. Why is this important? It is because the *demand forecast is always wrong*. Demand forecasting is both an art and a science. It utilizes both quantitative methods, like statistical modeling and machine learning, and qualitative approaches, such as expert judgment and market research, to predict future demand. While data-driven models provide a solid foundation, models are limited by what is actually input to create a forecast. For example, during the pandemic of 2020, demand forecasts were simply not accurate and human expertise and judgement took center stage. As revenue management transitions to offers (base fare and ancillary bundle) from the base fare, it adds a level of complexity and uncertainty if an airline is actively promoting new ancillary products, which in almost all cases, have no historical sales data.

This requires a transition to *continuous demand management*. Continuous demand management is an ongoing process of monitoring and adjusting strategies to meet fluctuating customer demand and market conditions [Vinod, 2021a, Chap. 10]. It involves actively tracking key performance indicators, using feedback, and making iterative improvements to demand planning and management processes. Resiliency can be improved by responding to real-time changes in demand.

Central to continuous demand management is the active monitoring of key performance indicators (KPIs) and proactively responding to alerts and real-time market changes, even when forecasts may say otherwise. This "sense and respond" capability can quickly detect demand shifts, competitor fare changes, new bundled offers promoted by competitors, and even global events (weather, geo-political disruptions), and trigger appropriate actions.

The execution of continuous demand management requires an event management orchestrator based on alerts from pre-defined KPIs. The KPIs must be monitored at various levels of aggregation (by the minute, hourly, daily, etc.) and establish recourse mechanisms for corrective actions.

Establish a root cause analysis framework to understand the root cause of deviations from the plan and determine the appropriate business lever (demand or supply) to take corrective action.

16.7.2 Event Management

A core requirement to enable the zero-latency enterprise is to deploy an event management capability, serving as a central nervous system that collects KPIs from existing applications and orchestrates alerts. The event management system orchestrates continuous demand planning and management based on alerts triggered by revenue management KPIs. The relevant KPIs must be monitored at various levels of aggregation such as system, market entity, market and flight. Depending on the KPI, the monitoring frequency may be by the minute, hourly, daily, etc. This is followed with recourse mechanisms for corrective actions. A root cause analysis framework provides a quick explanation of deviations from the plan and determines the appropriate business lever (demand or supply) that should be invoked to address the issue.

16.7.3 Organizational Readiness and AI Adoption

Adoption of AI systems requires talent and technical expertise within the organization. Upskilling talent within the organization must be a holistic strategy focused on AI literacy, hands-on training and human centric skills such as intellectual curiosity, creativity, critical thinking, ethics and data analytics. The organizational transformation must be augmented with new external talent with AI skills and a focus on innovation for competitive advantage. Successful adoption also requires a clear consensus-based digital roadmap for airline planning and airline operations that is backed with a firm commitment from senior leadership that is tied to measurable business outcomes.

16.7.4 Invest in Advanced AI Systems

Agentic AI is a focused concept that extends beyond forecasting and predictive modeling. It includes autonomy as a key feature. These systems have the capability to automatically sense and respond. They observe the environment such as live market data, bundles that have high and low conversion rates, booking trends, or operational constraints. They analyze this information using advanced decision-making models. Rather than just making a recommendation, they take actions aligned with their goals.

Agentic AI has the potential to transform airline offer and order creation by enabling autonomous systems that can personalize offers, optimize pricing, respond to disruptions, and enhance operational efficiency, ultimately leading to improved profitability and customer satisfaction.

Agentic AI has the potential to take continuous demand management to the next level with continuous monitoring of internal and external data, adjust offers, and execute at scale.

16.7.5 Data Analytics and Insights

All decisions must be data driven. This implies that advanced analytics and machine learning models must be leveraged to process and interpret KPIs for predictive modeling, personalized offers, and to gain customer insights. Alternate data sources must be explored. Embracing new or alternative data sources that have emerged post-pandemic can be leveraged to address industry challenges and gain a competitive advantage.

In summary: eliminating or limiting decision-making latency requires a shift from traditional forecast-driven processes to continuous demand management with dynamic and proactive approach enabled by advanced technologies like Agentic AI, robust data analytics, and effective event management.

Artificial Intelligence: Origins, Current State, and Impact on Travel

17

Success in creating AI would be the biggest event in human history. Unfortunately It might also be the last, unless we learn how to avoid the risks.

Stephen Hawking

Abstract

The chapter outlines the major milestones in artificial intelligence through the lens of a revenue management analyst. Over the next decade, we can expect sweeping changes in the areas of decision support and business process automation with pervasive applications of artificial intelligence in travel.

Besides the major milestones, recent advances in Generative AI, large language models and Agentic AI, and its impact on travel are discussed. The role of AI-based reasoning models, and the future of personalization are discussed. The disruption of product distribution with AI agents is underway and the clear beneficiaries are the suppliers of travel. With the recent advances in conversational AI powered by large language models, travel distribution is on the verge of a major disruption. Over the next decade, travel intermediaries such as GDSs, metasearch, OTAs and TMCs will be competing over a shrinking pie. The true beneficiary will be the service providers—airlines, hotels, car rentals, cruise lines, and destination activity providers.

According to English theoretical physicist Stephen Hawking" The creation of artificial intelligence (AI) is a transformative event with both immense potential and significant risks. It could be the biggest or last event in human history Depending on our ability to manage these risks. He believed in responsible AI

B. Vinod, *The Era of Airline Revenue Management with Offers and Orders*, Management for Professionals, https://doi.org/10.1007/978-3-032-24197-9_17

The ethical and responsible development Deployment And use of artificial intelligence systems. It is a fundamental requirement in the digital age for building user trust Ensuring regulatory compliance Preventing brand damage and fostering sustainable innovation.

17.1 Introduction

After airlines were deregulated in 1978, flight departures, filing fares and passenger traffic all increased dramatically [Kahn, 1988a, 1988b]. Developments in decision support to enable airline planning and operations started in earnest to address the increasing complexity of running an airline. The developments were grounded in statistical modeling and analysis and utilized *operations research* approaches. The subject area of operations research solves complicated problems with many decision variables by applying mathematical methodologies. Substantial decision support advances were quickly adopted by other travel verticals, including hotels, auto rentals, cruise lines, and ferry lines, outside of the airline industry.

British scientists A.P. Rowe and Sir Robert Watson-Watt are widely credited with coining the term "Operational Research" in 1937–1939 while working at the Bawdsey Research Station in the United Kingdom. The term was used to describe the application of scientific methods to analyze and improve the effectiveness of the early warning radar system, known as Chain Home, the world's first integrated military radar network to detect enemy aircraft. Throughout World War II (1939–1945), military planners faced logistical challenges. To address these, operations research (OR) was developed. OR is a scientific approach to decision-making that uses mathematical and computational techniques to optimize complex systems and processes. Applying applied mathematics and computing technology, OR improves efficiency, reduces costs, maximizes revenue, or enhances performance depending on the stated objective of the problem being solved. This is accomplished by analyzing data, developing models, and finding the best solutions to problems. OR applications in the airline industry grew unabated starting in the 1960s and beyond. Today it is inconceivable how an airline can run its daily planning and operations without the advanced OR models.

While it is difficult, if not impossible, to provide a comprehensive list of OR applications in the airline industry, Table 17.1 lists many of the most important applications.

17.2 Milestones in Artificial Intelligence

To articulate all the major milestones in Artificial Intelligence is beyond the scope of this book. What is presented in the next section are the milestones in AI through the lens of pricing, revenue management, and inventory analysts, interspersed with popular milestones that made the world AI aware.

Table 17.1 Major operations research decision support areas in the airline industry

Application	Description and techniques
Schedule Design	Identify markets to serve, frequency, and flight departure times and routes based on market size, time of day demand curves, spill and recapture, and competition. The goal is a profitable schedule. Detailed cost estimates are required. Solved with a large scale mixed-integer programming optimization model.
Fleet Assignment	The objective is to specify what aircraft types (aircraft size) and flight range to assign to each flight. Utilize multi-commodity network flow, integer program, branch and price models.
Aircraft Maintenance Routing	Assign routes to individual aircraft by aircraft type at minimum cost of selected routes subject to flight coverage and number of aircraft available. Generate valid routings, zero–one integer linear program.
Crew Pairing (Crew Scheduling)	For pilots and flight attendants, identity sequences of flight legs from a crew base and return subject to crew rules to minimize excess pay and credit. Solved using large set partition linear program, set covering linear program.
Crew Rostering	Create efficient and compliant work schedules (rosters) for pilots and cabin crew, assigning them to specific flights (pairings) while adhering to numerous constraints and regulations. This complex task aims to balance operational needs with crew preferences and well-being on a monthly basis. Integer linear program supports preferential (seniority) rostering or fairness-based rostering.
Manpower Planning	Minimize total manpower costs, and efficiency and utilization are maximized toward hiring, training, and scheduling of human resources after considering workdays, off days, training, and vacation. Integer linear program (set covering problem).
Pricing	Tariff structure by market. Maximize objectives such as market share or revenue by developing the fare structure based on customer willingness to pay, with price link constraints that identify relationship between fares. Large scale non-linear programming model to optimize fare structures by market.

(continued)

Table 17.1 (continued)

Application	Description and techniques
Revenue Management	Forecasting: Passenger demand, show-up rates, cancellation rates. Leverage airline data and forecast using time series, regression, and customer choice models. Overbooking Model: Compensate for cancellations and no-shows with the quality-of-service constrained model or the economic overbooking model. Flight Optimization for Leg/Segment Carriers: Demand uncertainty captured with the expected marginal seat revenue model, restriction-free pricing models to set allocations. Network Optimization Model for O&D Carriers: Required to calculate bid prices (continuous nesting) by flight leg and date. Various techniques such as stochastic network optimization, network decomposition model with leg-based dynamic programming (Network dynamic programming is computationally infeasible). Dynamic Continuous Pricing: Determine the dynamic continuous price from the priced itinerary based on filed fares. Calculate the price based on remaining capacity and the customer's willingness to pay. Offer Management: Determine the optimal bundles by customer segment and market using traditional market basket analysis. Leverage Decoy pricing, also known as the asymmetric dominance effect. It is a pricing strategy where a third, less desirable option (the "decoy") is introduced to influence a customer's preference between two other options.
Irregular Operations	There are three components for recovery from a disrupted schedule caused by weather delays, traffic congestion in the skies or aircraft maintenance. They are: Flight Recovery: When a hub is short of aircraft, flight controllers must determine the most cost effect sequence of flight cancellations to balance the schedule. Crew Recovery: Crew recovery is the process to manage and reassign crew members (pilots and flight attendants) when their original schedules are disrupted by IROPs. Airlines need to ensure that flights have the necessary crew while adhering to strict regulations regarding crew rest and duty limits. The look-ahead optimization window to adjust the rosters of the affected crew members is 3 to 7 days. Integer programming and heuristics (for quick response times) are used to solve the problem. Passenger Recovery: This involves rebooking passengers on alternate flights, minimizing passenger inconvenience and minimizing the cost to the airline. An assignment optimization model is used to support passenger reaccommodation.

The success of a revenue management program must leverage these techniques for competitive advantage. The AI-frontier adds a new dimension to solving complex problems that can augment existing established techniques.

The next section highlights the origins of AI, the early pioneers, and major milestones.

17.3 Origins of Artificial Intelligence

In 1637, French philosopher and scientist René Descartes explored the key difference between types of machines. Long before robots appeared in science fiction novels, he wondered if they could ever think or decide like humans. Although he believed they would never talk like humans, he saw a clear division. Some machines might learn to do just one task well. Others could someday adapt to any job. Today, we call these two types specialized AI and general AI. His ideas paved the way for many of the challenges we face in building true artificial intelligence.

In 1947 Alan Mathison Turing, an English mathematician, conceived of "intelligent machinery," investigating the possibility of machines recognizing logical actions [Turing, 1948]. In this landmark paper from 1948, he introduced concepts such as genetic algorithms and neural networks that he called "unorganized machines" with learning capabilities, and reinforcement learning.

The power of digital computers lies in their ability to perform complex calculations rapidly. They can predict a rocket's path, enable the Mars lander to execute complex tasks on the Martian surface, or process big financial data for multinational corporations in just seconds. However, tasks humans find simple, like recognizing a face or reading handwriting, are very hard to program. Perhaps the brain's neural connections are naturally better at these tasks than regular computers. Because of this, scientists have started building machines that mimic how the human brain works.

Connectionism is a new field focused on computing with networks comprised of artificial neurons. It is a way to study how the mind works, using mathematical models called connectionist networks or artificial neural networks. These models help explain human thinking by mimicking how neurons in the brain connect and communicate.

Researchers simulate neurons and their connections on standard digital computers. A training program runs on the computer, tuning the links between neurons. Over time, this process shapes the network into a specialized tool designed for a specific task, like predicting currency exchange rates.

Modern connectionists often credit Frank Rosenblatt as the founder of this approach, noting his 1957 paper [Rosenblatt, 1957], the 1958 paper [Rosenblatt, 1958] and the subsequent book [Rosenblatt, 1962]. However, few realize that Alan Turing explored connectionist networks first, in 1948. His work appeared in a little-known paper titled "Intelligent Machinery."

This manuscript was written while Turing worked at the National Physical Laboratory in London. Sir Charles Darwin, the laboratory's director and grandson of the famous naturalist, did not approve of it. Darwin dismissed the work as a "schoolboy essay." He did not realize that the paper was ahead of its time and is considered the first statement of the field of artificial intelligence. The manuscript was not published until 1968, fourteen years after Turing's death. In this work, Turing laid out the fundamentals of connectionism and introduced many ideas that would become key to AI. Some of these ideas were later rediscovered or developed by others.

In his paper, Turing described a type of neural network called a "B-type unorganized machine." This machine is made of artificial neurons and devices that change how neurons connect. B-type machines can have any number of neurons linked in any pattern. The B-type machines were theoretical neural networks composed of artificial neurons, simple NAND logic gates, connected in a largely random manner. Turing mandated that they all share one rule: every connection between two neurons must go through a modifier device. These modifiers had two states: "pass mode" and "interrupt mode". By applying external signals to the modifiers, the network could be trained to perform specific tasks.

17.3.1 Computing Machinery and Intelligence

Alan Turing produced his seminal paper "Computing Machinery and Intelligence" [Turing, 1950], a few years after he deciphered the Germans' "Enigma" code at Bletchley Park. Enigma was used as an enciphering machine by Nazi Germany to convey commercial, diplomatic, and military communications securely. The purpose of his essay was to address the query, "*Can machines think?*" This resulted in the creation of the Turing Test, which evaluated a machine's capacity for intelligent conduct that was indistinguishable from a human. Hector Levesque proposed the Winograd Schema Challenge (WSC) as an enhancement to the Turing Test [Levesque, 2011]. To address the criticism that assessing a person's skill at a task alone is insufficient to gauge their intelligence, Francois Chollet proposed a new framework known as the Abstraction and Reasoning Corpus (ARC), which is based on Algorithmic Information Theory (AIT) [Chollet, 2019]. The framework offers guidelines for creating a benchmark of general intelligence.

17.3.2 Early AI Pioneers

John McCarthy was a math professor at Dartmouth College in Hanover, New Hampshire. He was the first person to use the term "*artificial intelligence*" in 1955.

The Dartmouth Conference, officially the Dartmouth Summer Research Project on Artificial Intelligence, took place in the summer of 1956. It is widely considered the event that launched artificial intelligence as a field of study. The conference was organized by John McCarthy, Marvin Minsky, Nathaniel Rochester, and Claude Shannon. The conference brought together leading thinkers in computer science, mathematics, and cognitive psychology to explore the possibility of creating intelligent machines. The conference also included prominent figures like Ray Solomonoff, Oliver Selfridge, Julian Bigelow, and Allen Newell.

The "Project" was a brainstorming session that lasted six to eight weeks.

The central theme of the conference was to investigate whether every aspect of learning or other features of intelligence could be precisely described and simulated by machines. The conference aimed to move beyond simple computations and explore how machines could use language, form abstractions, solve problems, and exhibit other intelligent behaviors. The Dartmouth Conference is seen as the "Constitutional Convention of AI," shaping the objectives of the new field, scope, and future research agenda. It established AI as a recognized academic discipline and introduced the term "artificial intelligence" to a wider community.

John McCarthy created LISP (LISt Processor), the second-oldest high-level programming language, after FORTRAN (FORmula TRANslation) in 1958. LISP was developed to serve as a programming language for AI research. McCarthy also influenced the creation of ALGOL (AlGOrithmic Language). ALGOL is a computer programming language that was created in 1958–60 by an international committee of the Association for Computing Machinery (ACM) chaired by Alan J. Perlis of Carnegie Mellon University for publishing algorithms and performing calculations. Perlis was a "founding father" of computer science and the inaugural recipient of the Turing Award (1966), a key figure in establishing computer science as an academic field and renowned for his groundbreaking work in the realm of intelligent machines.

Information Processing Language (IPL), an early programming language used for artificial intelligence research, was created in 1956 by Allen Newell, Cliff Shaw, and Herbert A. Simon, who worked at the RAND Corporation and the Carnegie Institute of Technology. IPL was a pioneering language in the field of AI, particularly notable for its list processing and symbol manipulation capabilities. This provided the capability to handle complex data structures like sequences and trees and process symbolic data which is required for natural language understanding. This made it useful for tasks like problem-solving and natural language processing, which are core to AI.

At Bell Labs, Claude Shannon saw chess as a test bed for AI and in 1950 he described how computers could strategize to beat humans [Shannon, 1950]. When Herbert Simon was employed at the Carnegie Institute in 1957, he boldly predicted that within ten years, computers would outsmart humans at chess. On February 10, 1996, IBM's Deep Blue, an artificial intelligence system created to play chess, defeated world chess champion Garry Kasparov, albeit it took nearly 40 years to achieve [Seirawan et al., 1997]. When Google's Deep Mind AlphaGo defeated the greatest Go player in the world, Lee Sedol, in 2016, the news was widely reported [Gershgorn, 2016]. Ross Quillian, Marvin Minsky, Edward Feigenbaum, and IBM (International Business Machines) are some of the early pioneers of AI.

The first abstract model of a neural network was proposed by Warren McCulloch and Walter Pitts in 1943 [McCulloch & Pitts, 1943]. Their paper explored how neurons could be modeled using symbolic logic, paving the way for future research. The first trainable neural network, the perceptron, was demonstrated by Frank Rosenblatt in 1957. The technical report [Rosenblatt, 1957] introduced the concept of the perceptron as an algorithm for artificial neurons.

What is a perceptron? A perceptron is a fundamental building block of artificial neural networks, acting as a simplified model of a biological neuron. It is a linear classifier used for binary classification tasks. Hence, it can categorize data into two distinct classes. The perceptron takes multiple inputs, applies weights to them, sums them up, and then uses an activation function to produce a binary output. The perceptron can only effectively classify data that is linearly separable, which is a straight line (or hyperplane in higher dimensions) that can divide the data into the two classes. For data with more complex patterns a single-layer perceptron is insufficient, and more sophisticated neural network architectures are required.

Rosenblatt's contribution is considered a foundational work in the development of neural networks and machine learning. It would be several decades later with the invention of backpropagation that neural networks saw adoption.

Computer vision emerged in the 1950s with early neural networks like Frank Rosenblatt's Perceptron for basis shape recognition. Today, computer vision allows computers to interpret and analyze visual data from images and videos. This field of AI uses machine learning, deep learning, and pattern recognition to identify objects, detect patterns, and extract meaningful insights.

17.3.3 Support Vector Machines

Support Vector Machines (SVM) are supervised machine learning algorithms used for classification and regression tasks. The algorithm finds the optimal line or hyperplane that maximizes the distance between each class in an N-dimensional space. The Support Vector method is a versatile approach for solving problems involving the estimation of functions in multiple dimensions. It was first created to address pattern recognition tasks. In these tasks, the goal is to develop a decision rule that can correctly classify new data. To do this, a small subset of training data, called Support Vectors (SVs), is chosen. Finding the best way to separate these SVs ensures that the entire data set is also properly divided. This makes the method highly effective for many types of complex estimation problems.

The original SVM algorithm that focused on creating a linear classifier was invented by Vladimir N. Vapnik and Alexey Ya. Chervonenkis in 1964. Three decades later, Vladimir Vapnik and team proposed a way to create nonlinear classifiers by applying the kernel trick to maximum-margin hyperplanes [Boser et al., 1992]. The "soft margin" version, which allows for some misclassification, was proposed by Cortes and Vapnik [Cortes & Vapnik, 1995] which is commonly used in software today.

Support Vector Regression (SVR) was proposed in 1996, and Transductive support vector machines (TSVM) were introduced in 1998 [Vapnik et al., 1997]. TSVMs extend standard SVMs to incorporate unlabeled test data during training. Today SVMs are used for a wide range of applications. Examples are image recognition, text categorization, medical diagnosis, fraud detection, spam filtering, and many more,

17.3.4 The First Chatbot

The ELIZA chatbot was created in 1966 by MIT Professor Joseph Weizenbaum. He cast it in the role of a psychotherapist. A user would type a message on an electric typewriter that was connected to a mainframe. After a moment, the "psychotherapist" would reply. Weizenbaum called the program Eliza, after George Bernard Shaw's Eliza Doolittle in Pygmalion.

Eliza could simulate conversations using simple pattern-matching scripts. Based on pattern matching and replacement methodology, this early natural language processing program was made to demonstrate how superficial human-to-computer communication was at that time. The software was relatively simple. It processed the user input and applied a set of rules to generate a plausible response.

Weizenbaum was often viewed as a heretic in computer science circles for his views on artificial intelligence. A pioneer of AI, he became very critical of direction that it was headed, particularly the tendency to grant computers authority over human decisions and aspects of life. His book, "Computer Power and Human Reason: From Judgment to Calculation," criticized his colleagues for making unrealistic claims about AI and for not adequately addressing the ethical and societal implications of their work [Weizenbaum, 1976]. According to Weizenbaum, judgment involves choices that are guided by values. These values are acquired through the course of an individual's life experience, are qualitative in nature and cannot be captured in code. Calculation, by contrast, is quantitative. It uses a technical calculus to arrive at a decision. Computers are only capable of calculation, not judgment. By the mid-1970s, there was mounting frustration from government circles that cut AI funding because the field failed to live up to its hype and produced the first "AI winter".

17.3.5 Classification and Regression Trees

In machine learning, regression and classification are two fundamental types of supervised learning problems. The key difference lies in their outputs. Regression predicts continuous numerical values, while classification predicts discrete categories or classes.

Earlier work on decision trees existed dating back to the 1960s with Hunt's algorithm, which is a foundational greedy and recursive algorithm used for constructing decision trees.

THAID (Theta Automatic Interaction Detection) was developed in 1972 [Messenger & Mandell, 1972] which extended AID (Automatic Interaction Detection) developed in the 1960s [Morgan & Sonquist, 1963] to maximize the sum of observations in the most frequent category when making splits.

The Classification and Regression Trees (CART) algorithm was developed in 1977 by Leo Breiman, Jerome Friedman, Richard Olshen, and Charles Stone. It represents a significant step in the evolution of decision tree learning methods, which can be traced back even further to Sir Ronald Fisher's work on discriminant analysis in 1936 [Fisher, 1936].

The CART methodology was followed with the book "Classification and Regression Trees" which detailed the methodology [Breiman et al., 1983]. It is widely used for building decision trees that can be applied to both classification and regression problems.

CHAID (Chi-squared Automatic Interaction Detection), a decision tree algorithm that uses chi-squared statistics to recursively split data and identify relationships between variables to build a predictive model, was introduced by Gordon Kass in 1980 [Kass, 1980]. CHAID is useful for handling categorical data to identify significant interactions within datasets.

17.3.6 Expert Systems

Expert systems are often rule-based. They utilize a knowledge base containing rules that dictate how the system should respond to different situations or inputs. These rules, derived from human experts, are used by the system to make decisions or provide solutions to problems within a specific domain. In 1980, the Digital Equipment Corporation (DEC) introduced the XCON expert learning system. By 1986, it saved the company about $40 million each year. Up to that point, AI was mostly seen as cool technology with little practical use. The success of XCON showed that AI could have real benefits for business. By 1985, companies were spending around $1 billion annually on AI systems, primarily investing in expert systems. This marked the start of a new era where smart machines began to play a bigger role in everyday business.

In the 1980s, Prolog, a logic programming language was popular to create expert systems. The Prolog programming language was developed by Alain Colmerauer in 1972.

17.3.7 Backpropagation

Prior to backpropagation, the learning capabilities of neural network models had been limited. Errors were only adjusted in the final output layer of the network. This limited how effectively experience could shape the performance of the model.

The technique was first formulated by Paul J. Werbos and was popularized by David Rumelhart, Geoffrey Hinton, and Ronald Williams, who demonstrated its successful application in 1986.

In the 1980s, the backpropagation algorithm, a key method for training artificial neural networks, began to be utilized [Rumelhart et al., 1986]. The landmark paper introduced the backpropagation algorithm, a critical technique for training artificial neural networks. This algorithm allows neural networks to learn from their mistakes by adjusting connection weights based on the error rate calculated in previous iterations. Their work, along with the accompanying "Parallel Distributed Processing," books [Rumelhart, McClelland the PDP Research Group, 1986], published in the same year, helped establish backpropagation as a core concept in neural network research. This laid the foundation for many modern deep learning systems.

Although the backpropagation was an elegant solution to a computational problem, neural networks didn't become popular right away.

In 2009, Alex Krizhevsky and Geoffrey Hinton presented a method for training deep neural networks to learn meaningful features from a large dataset of small, randomly cropped images ("tiny images") from the Internet [Krizhevsky & Hinton, 2009]. This laid the groundwork for modern convolutional neural networks (CNNs) by demonstrating the power of unsupervised pre-training on a large scale with multiple layers of features.

In 2012, Hinton and his team used the ImageNet dataset, set up by Fei-Fei Li in 2006 to support visual object recognition software research, to show how well convolutional neural networks can classify images [Krizhevsky et al., 2012]. They had computers that were far more powerful than those available to Rumelhart when he first developed the idea. This breakthrough demonstrated the practical potential of neural networks for image recognition.

17.3.8 IBM's Statistical Approach to Language Translation Was Revolutionary

The concept of statistical machine translation was introduced by scientist and mathematician Warren Weaver in 1949, including the ideas of applying Claude Shannon's information theory [Shannon, 1948a; Shannon, 1948b] which culminated in a book by Shannon and Weaver that was published in 1949 [Shannon and Weaver, 1949].

In 1988, IBM researchers at the Thomas J. Watson Research Center published "A Statistical Approach to Language Translation" introducing principles of probability into the until-then rule-driven field of machine learning [Brown et al., 1988]. It tackled the challenge of automated translation between human languages—French and English. Peter Brown and his research associates published a subsequent highly influential paper in 1993 [Brown, et. al., 1993].

This marked a fundamental switch in emphasis to designing programs to determine the probability of various outcomes based on data they are trained on, rather than training them to determine rules. This is a significant leap in terms of mimicking the cognitive processes of the human brain and forming the basis of machine learning as it is used today.

17.3.9 Natural Language Processing and Machine Translation

In the 1980s, research in natural language processing (NLP) and machine translation experienced a resurgence, leading to the development of recurrent neural networks (RNNs). This period also saw a renewed interest in neural networks, with the discovery of algorithms like backpropagation that enable the training of networks with multiple layers. NLP also moved away from purely rules-based systems to machine learning and statistical models. This was influenced by the increasing availability of large text datasets (corpora) and advancements in computing power.

A Recurrent Neural Network (RNN) is a type of artificial neural network designed to process sequential data, where the output at any given time step depends on the previous computations within the sequence. Unlike feedforward neural networks, RNNs have loops that allow them to maintain a "memory" of past inputs, making them suitable for tasks involving sequences like language, time series, and more.

The first RNN model was developed by John Hopfield in 1982, and it was known as the Hopfield Network. This model was able to store and retrieve patterns, and it was used to understand how human memory works. However, the Hopfield Network had limitations in terms of storage capacity and the ability to handle noise. The Hopfield networks were not directly tied to backpropagation training methods used in later versions of RNNs.

Paul Werbos is credited with the initial conceptualization and training of RNNs with backpropagation in the late 1980s. The work by David Rumelhart, Goeffrey Hinton, Ronald Williams and Michael Jordan [Jordan, 1986; Rumelhart et al., 1985] also contributed to the development of RNNs with backpropagation.

An RNNs internal memory spans short terms only. RNNs tend to "forget" what happened several inputs before and therefore do not work well with long data sequences. To overcome this, in the 1990s, a new type of RNN called the Long Short-Term Memory (LSTM) was introduced by Sepp Hochreiter and Jürgen Schmidhuber [Hochreiter & Schmidhuber, 1997]. LSTM was designed to overcome the problem of vanishing gradients, a common issue in training RNNs. This made LSTM a more practical and effective model for many applications, and it remains one of the most widely used types of RNN today.

The vanishing gradient problem arises because the gradients, or changes in errors that occur for changes in the neural network weights, are multiplied across all levels in a neural network. If these gradients are consistently less than one, then a very small fraction results, causing the network to start changing weights very slowly, causing the training process to essentially stop. LSTM helps solve this problem by creating long-term memory and gating structures to regulate information flow.

RNNs, which operate on sequential data by feeding previous outputs as inputs to subsequent stages, became particularly relevant in natural language processing (NLP) due to their ability to consider context. Early applications of RNNs in NLP included machine translation, language modeling, and other tasks where the sequential nature of language needed to be taken into account.

Early examples include the Jordan and Elman networks, which were applied to cognitive psychology. These two fundamental types of RNNs are distinguished by how they handle feedback and memory. Both networks incorporate a "state" or "context" layer that retains information from previous time steps, enabling them to process sequential data. The key difference lies in where this context layer receives its input: in Elman networks, it is from the hidden layer, while in Jordan networks, it's from the output layer.

17.3.9.1 Passenger Name Recognition Problem

A few countries issue passports to its citizens that are not ICAO (International Civil Aviation Organization) compliant. The ICAO requires all member states to issue machine-readable passports (MRPs). When a nation is non-compliant, it is not possible to identify the first and last names on passports. This causes two problems: inability to delimit first and last names by a MRZ (Machine Readable Zone) prevents airline kiosks from processing the name information needed for PNR and departure control system (DCS) customer lookup, and the inability to pass accurate APIS (Advanced Passenger Information System) data when the flight is closed.

The name recognition problem can be solved as a two-step process. First, supervised learning techniques, where the model is trained with labeled data (sample data that are tagged with one or more labels), can be used to predict customer origin and demographics. Second, given customer demographics, a rules engine can determine the first and last names of passengers. Evaluation of machine learning models led to the conclusion that support vector machines (SVM) and recurrent neural networks (RNN) with Long Short-Term Memory (LSTM) performed the best during out-of-sample validation, with an accuracy of about ~ 80%.

17.3.10 Q-Learning

Q-learning is a special case of reinforcement learning. It is a significant algorithm in reinforcement learning, and was invented by Chris Watkins in 1989 during his PhD work at Cambridge University [Watkins, 1989]. This method introduced a way for agents to learn optimal actions in a given state by estimating the value of taking a particular action, known as the Q-value, to maximize the cumulative future reward.

Q-learning does not require a model of the environment like knowing the probabilities of transitions between states. It learns directly from interactions with the environment through trial and error. It is also an off-policy model since it learns the optimal policy independent of the agent's current actions. It can evaluate and update its knowledge even when taking exploratory actions.

The Q-function is encoded by a Q-table, where each cell corresponds to a state-action pair value. Given a state and action, the Q-function will search inside the Q-table to output the value. The Q-value represents the expected long-term reward for taking specific action in a given state. The "Q" comes from "the Quality" (the value) of that action at that state. The Bellman equation is used to update the Q-values iteratively, based on the immediate reward and the estimated future reward.

17.3.10.1 Fare Prediction

The Q-Leaning algorithm has been used successfully for fare prediction [Vinod, 2016b]. Shopping data can be calibrated with a Q-learning model to predict when airfares will go up or down in a market. Airlines dislike fare forecasting models because they reverse engineer an airline's revenue management system.

A fare prediction model [Etzioni et al., 2003; Mantin & Rubin, 2016] can recommend BUY or WAIT recommendations by market to advise customers. OTAs typically only use the BUY recommendation since airfares are going up. When airfares are going down, OTAs do not display the WAIT recommendation, since customer affinity to an OTA to complete the booking is weak. Travel agents on the other hand are dealing with managed travel and a captive audience, so the WAIT recommendation is what they need to advise their customers to realize cost savings.

17.3.11 Chess and AI

In 1997, Garry Kasparov, the world chess champion, was defeated by IBM's Deep Blue supercomputer. This event showed how fast computer technology was improving. It was a clear sign of progress in artificial intelligence and a moment that the public could understand easily. Deep Blue's success came from its ability to analyze 200 million positions every second. Instead of moving step by step, it used its speed to consider all possible moves and then choose the best one.

The core algorithm in Deep Blue was an optimized alpha–beta pruning algorithm, a core component of many chess playing programs, with minimax and a heuristic evaluation function and singular extensions. It also used custom VLSI (Very-Large-Scale-Integration) chips and a massively parallel architecture for the search. The minimax algorithm is a recursive algorithm used in AI, particularly for decision-making in two-player zero-sum games. Deep Blue used the minimax algorithm as its core decision-making strategy. A key innovation regarding search depth was the used of "singular extensions." The singular extension was a technique used to extend the search at nodes where one move appeared significantly better than all others.

17.3.12 Gradient Boosting Machines

Gradient Boosting Machines (GBMs) are a type of machine learning algorithm that is widely used in the airline industry for various applications such as predicting flight delays, ticketing and offers. It was developed by Jerome Friedman in 1999 [Friedman, 2001].

The concept of "boosting" (combining multiple "weak learners" to create a strong one) existed before Friedman's work, with AdaBoost (adaptive boosting) being a notable example developed by Yoav Freund and Robert Schapire [Freund & Schapire, 1995]. However, Friedman's contribution involved using gradient descent to optimize arbitrary differentiable loss functions, which broadened boosting's applicability to various problems beyond just binary classification, but to many types of problems such as regression, multi-class classification and other problems by optimizing any arbitrary, differentiable loss function. GBMs are ensemble models where multiple decision trees called "weak learners" are combined to create a more accurate prediction model. The weak learners are trained sequentially, with each new learner focused on correcting the errors of their predecessors. The GBM model minimizes a defined loss function which represents the difference between the predicted and actual values by iteratively adjusting the predictions of the underlying model.

CatBoost is used to predict flight delays. It is a gradient boosting algorithm that works well with categorical data [Maulana et al., 2025]. It effectively handles class imbalances where delayed flights are far fewer than on-time flights. The model is trained using processed flight data and patterns associated with flight delays. It then predicts whether a flight will be delayed and the duration of the delay. Model performance is evaluated using standard metrics such as accuracy, precision, recall and F1-score that combines precision and recall into a single composite score.

A model that uses temporal and spatial features such as the influence of preceding flights, status at departure and destination airports, and conditions of flights on the same route predict flight delays effectively [Lu et al., 2021]. The references provided in the paper is a history of GBM for flight delay prediction.

Other popular GBMs used are XGBoost (eXtreme Gradient Boosting) and the faster alternative LightGBM. They are powerful gradient boosting frameworks for tabular data. They differ in their tree growth strategies and optimization techniques that impact speed and memory usage.

Another application of GBM is in travel agency ticketed commissions. Travel agencies earn front-end commissions in certain markets. A ticket can include multiple fare components, and commissions are applied at the fare component level, which may have one or more ticket coupons. Commissions should be claimed when the ticket is issued. The airline pays the commission to the agency. If a travel agent reports an incorrect commission at ticketing, the airline issues an agency debit memo (ADM) to correct the mistake. Ticketed commissions managed through GDSs often total over a billion dollars each year. Many agencies cannot afford to develop a tool that encodes ticketed commission contracts, calculate the commission amount (if any) for each itinerary returned in a shopping response and subsequently apply the commission to the itinerary selected for ticketing. It is also a labor-intensive process to encode contracts. A cheaper alternative is to forecast which tickets can earn a commission at the time of sale and the likely amount of the commission. To calibrate the GBM model, key data points require include origin, destination, issue date, PCC, SC code, travel dates, currency, ticket price, carrier, fare basis, and other ticket details. Using these factors helps improve the accuracy of predicting commission eligibility and amounts at ticketing.

GBMs are also used in recommendation engines to predict ancillary bundles. From passenger behavior and booking patterns, airlines can tailor offers to specific customer segments to increase conversion rates and revenues.

17.3.13 Random Forests

A Random Forest (RF) is a machine learning algorithm that uses an ensemble of decision trees to make predictions. It combines the outputs of multiple decision trees to improve the overall accuracy and robustness of the model. Essentially, it is a "wisdom of the crowds" approach where the collective decision of many trees is more reliable than a single tree.

In 1995, Tin Kam Ho introduced the random subspace method, which formed a basis for constructing random decision forests, by randomly selecting subsets of features for each tree [Ho, 1995]. In the mid-1990s Yali Amit and Donald Geman also contributed to the introduction of randomness among individual decision trees [Amit & Geman, 1997].

The basis for the modern Random Forest algorithm was due to Leo Breiman [Breiman, 2001]. This work combined his "bagging technique" with random feature selection.

Random Forests are a type of ensemble learning method that combines many decision trees to make predictions. They use a process called "bagging," which involves creating multiple training sets by sampling the data with replacement. Each tree is built using these samples, helping to reduce overfitting. During construction, the algorithm also selects a random group of features (variables) at each split, adding diversity among the trees. For classification tasks, the Random Forest makes its prediction by choosing the option that most trees agree on. For regression tasks, it calculates the average of all tree predictions.

Random Forests can be used in recommendation systems to filter information and suggest offers based on user preferences, credit risk assessment, and fraud detection.

17.3.13.1 Gradient Boosting Machines vs. Random Forests

Both GBM and RF are ensemble learning methods and predict by combining the outputs from individual trees. They differ in the way the trees are built and the way the results are combined.

GBM builds trees sequentially, using a series of small trees ("weak learners") to improve errors and reduce bias (underfitting). Each new weak tree corrects the errors (residuals) of the previous ensemble. GBMs often achieve higher predictive accuracy but lead to less easily explainable models. They are also complex to calibrate, with a higher risk of overfitting, and sensitive to noisy data.

RFs train many deep, independent decision trees using samples of the data and samples of the features (variables) in parallel, then averages their predictions. This approach reduces variance, is easier to calibrate and less prone to overfitting. RFs are frequently chosen for speed and simplicity while GBMs are used for peak performance.

17.3.14 The DARPA Challenge

The DARPA (Defense Advanced Research Projects Agency) Grand Challenge was a series of U.S. government funded competitions (2004, 2005, 2007) that spurred the development of self-driving vehicles by challenging teams to build autonomous cars to navigate desert and urban courses.

In 2004, autonomous vehicles did not complete the DARPA Grand Challenge, a 142-mile off-road course through the Mojave Desert. In 2005, at the second Grand Challenge, Stanford University's team won with its vehicle, Stanley, a modified Volkswagen Touareg. Stanley completed the 132-mile desert course in southern Nevada, navigating rugged terrain without human intervention, and won a $2 million prize. Five vehicles successfully completed the course within the stipulated time limit of 10 h.

17.3.15 IBM's Watson Wins Jeopardy

In 2011, IBM's Watson competed against human Jeopardy! players and won the $1 million prize. This was a major moment because earlier challenges, like Garry Kasparov's chess matches, relied on the machine's fast computing power. Unlike those tests, Watson had to understand language and show creative thinking to succeed in Jeopardy! This challenge proved that machines could do more than just crunch numbers.

17.3.16 Generative Adversarial Networks

Ian Goodfellow introduced the concept of Generative Adversarial Networks (GANs) in 2014 when he was a PhD student at the Université de Montréal. The core idea of GANs emerged during a discussion with colleagues where they were working on a project involving computer-generated photos. This groundbreaking development revolutionized the field of machine learning and particularly Generative AI [Goodfellow et al., 2014]. GANs enabled the creation of realistic images, videos, and audio by employing an adversarial training process where two neural networks, a generator and a discriminator, are trained together in a competitive manner.

17.3.17 DeepMind's AlphaGo

AlphaGo, created by Google's Deep Mind defeated the world's best Go player, Lee Sedol over five matches in 2016 [Gershgorn, 2016]. The number of variations of the game makes brute force impractical. There are more than 100,000 possible opening moves in Go compared to 400 in Chess. DeepMind's AlphaGo used neural networks to study and then learn as it played the game.

AlphaGo, an AI program became famous for its ability to play the game of Go at a professional level. It is a deep neural network trained to learn by example (supervised learning), mimicking human players and then playing against itself using reinforcement learning to refine its strategies. The program uses a Monte Carlo tree search to evaluate potential moves and choose the most promising ones. This clearly demonstrated the capabilities of AI in complex strategic games.

17.3.18 The Transformer Architecture

Transformer architecture was introduced by eight Google scientists [Vaswani et al., 2017] in 2017. The paper, entitled "Attention Is All You Need," revolutionized natural language processing (NLP) and is considered a foundational technology for large language models (LLMs) like GPT.

The first Transformer marked a big shift in machine translation. Instead of translating each word one at a time, Transformers process entire sentences at once. They identify how words relate to each other and grasp meaning from the context. This way of finding and creating meaning from patterns became the foundation for later AI advances like AlphaFold[1] and large language models.

The key feature of the Transformer was its self-attention mechanism, which let the model judge the importance of words in a sentence, no matter where they appear. This made it possible to process all parts of the text at once (parallel processing), unlike older models like Recurrent Neural Networks that worked step-by-step. This results in faster and more efficient training. The Transformer Architecture greatly improved many language tasks, such as translating languages, analyzing emotions, answering questions, and summarizing text. It also served as the base for powerful models like BERT and GPT, which demonstrate unprecedented language understanding and generating capabilities.

Transformers have formed the backbone of modern NLP since 2017. They made it possible to build smarter AI tools such as chatbots and conversational systems. These models excel at making sense of long texts and keeping track of context throughout a document. This overcomes many limits of earlier models that struggled with lengthy information. As a result, language generation improved significantly, allowing for more accurate and complex text output. Transformer

[1] AlphaFold is an AI system developed by Google DeepMind that predicts the 3D structure of proteins from their amino acid sequences. It utilizes deep learning to solve the "protein folding problem," a long-standing challenge in biology.

technology has also expanded into other areas beyond text. It found uses in images, audio, and biological data, showing their broad usefulness.

17.3.19 OpenAI's Generative Pre-Trained Transformer

In 2018, OpenAI introduced the first version of the GPT (Generative Pre-trained Transformer) model. This groundbreaking model, initially known as GPT-1, utilized a transformer-based architecture and demonstrated remarkable capabilities in generating human like text based on the context it was provided. It was trained on a large dataset and could be fine-tuned for various natural language processing tasks, like answering questions, summarizing text, and completing sentences.

The GPT-1 release marked a significant advancement in NLP and paved the way for subsequent, more powerful iterations of the GPT series.

While GPT-1 did not have a significant impact by powering travel applications, its significance lies in establishing the foundation for future innovations. Modern travel industry applications, such as AI-powered chatbots, personal assistants, personalized recommendations, and automated content generation, are built upon the advancements made possible by models like GPT-1.

OpenAI released GPT-3, a large language model in 2020. It performs various natural language tasks like text completion, translation, and summarization. This was followed with the GPT-3.5 Series which consisted of a set of models that were an improvement over GPT-3, with some models specifically designed for code completion (like code-davinci-002) and others for instruction following (like text-davinci-002 and text-davinci-003).

17.3.20 OpenAI's ChatGPT

In November 2022, OpenAI released an experimental chatbot called ChatGPT. This chatbot application was built on top of a model from the GPT-3.5 Series. It was fine-tuned to handle conversations, making it better at generating responses that are appropriate for a chatbot context. ChatGPT reached one million users within five days. Almost overnight, user-friendly Generative AI technology captured global attention. It amazed people with its ability to have human-like conversations, write emails and essays, and answer complicated search questions with clear, short responses. In just two months, ChatGPT became the fastest-growing app ever for consumers, reaching an estimated 100 million active users by January 2023. This marked a revolution in the accessibility and application of Generative AI for general-purpose text-based tasks. OpenAI has publicly states that its mission is to "ensure that artificial general intelligence benefits all of humanity."

In September 2022, OpenAI released DALL-E 2, a text-to-image Generative AI model. It creates realistic images from textual descriptions. It combines natural language processing and computer vision to interpret prompts and generate corresponding images. The model can produce original, realistic images, make edits to existing images based on text, and generate variations of existing images.

17.3.21 Google's Gemini

Google's AI chatbot was initially launched as Bard in March 2023. The name may sound weird, but it was an internal working name for Google's chatbot. In February 2024, Bard was unified with another Google AI product, Duet AI, under a new brand name Gemini.

Google Gemini is a family of multimodal AI models and a chatbot interface developed by Google DeepMind. A multimodal AI model is an artificial intelligence system that can process and understand information from multiple data types, or "modalities," such as text, images, audio, and video, to perform tasks or generate new content. Gemini is designed to handle various data types like text, audio, images, and code, and powers the Gemini chatbot. Gemini also integrates into Google's ecosystem, offering features like a side panel in Gmail for drafting emails and summarizing information.

Google released Gemini 3 Pro in preview on November 18, 2025, ushering in the transition of chatbots to AI Agents that serve as digital co-workers. Gemini 1 models could see, hear, and understand information. Gemini 2 introduced advanced reasoning, enabling AI Agents to think, code, and take action. Gemini 3 offers advanced reasoning, multimodal understanding, and agentic coding. Antigravity is a new platform for software development that used Gemini 3's agentic coding capabilities.

17.3.22 GPT-4 and GPT-4o

Since the debut of OpenAI's ChatGPT in November 2022, both the interface and its underlying models have seen many enhancements. GPT-4o (the "o" in GPT-4o stands for "omni") was introduced in May 2024, as the follow-up to GPT-4, which was released in March 2023. A smaller version, GPT-4o mini, came out in July 2024. GPT-4o builds on the strengths of earlier models with key updates, such as better multimodal capabilities and faster performance.

Both GPT-4 and GPT-4o are powerful AI models designed for use in ChatGPT. They are trained to produce natural, conversational text in response to prompts. Both models can hold interactive conversations, keeping track of past messages and context to provide relevant replies.

17.3.23 Model Context Protocol

In November 2024, David Soria Parra and Justin Spahr-Summers, software engineers at Anthropic introduced the model context protocol (MCP), an open standard that enables developers to build secure, two-way connections between their data sources and AI- powered tools. It standardizes how AI systems like LLMs integrate and share data with external tools and data sources. MCP provides a standardized way for AI Agents to understand and utilize external resources like tools, APIs, and data sources to perform specific tasks. It is a significant milestone in the evolution of Agentic AI in travel.

For an ecosystem to flourish, it must be open. In December 2025, Anthropic donated MCP to the new Agentic AI Foundation, that is managed by the Linux Foundation. The MCP protocol now enters a new phase of shared stewardship. By March 2026, MCP had over 97 million installs. It is the undisputed standard for AI Agents to connect to external data.

17.3.24 ChatGPT—Operator

The groundbreaking innovation ChatGPT—Operator was launched in January 2025 [OpenAI, 2025a]. It is an AI Agent within ChatGPT that is designed to perform tasks by interacting with web browsers. It utilizes the underlying GPT technology and functions as a browser-based assistant. This has the potential to automate complex travel agency workflows related to corporate travel. What makes it unique is its ability to accept tasks and execute autonomously.

An Operator can be asked to perform many repetitive browser tasks like filling out forms, shopping for groceries, or even making memes. Using the same interfaces and tools people rely on daily makes AI more useful. It helps users save time on routine chores and creates new ways businesses can connect with their audience. It bridges the gap from a reactive chatbot to a proactive digital agent that sees, reasons, and acts on command.

17.3.25 Agent-2-Agent Protocol

The Agent2Agent (A2A) protocol was announced by Google on April 9, 2025, during the Google Cloud Next Conference. This is a key milestone toward the development of multi-agent systems.

It is an open protocol designed to enable secure communication and collaboration between different AI Agents, regardless of their underlying platform, vendor, or framework. A2A addresses challenges in scaling AI Agents across enterprise environments by allowing them to seamlessly interoperate. It also enables autonomous agents to discover one another, securely exchange information, and collaborate across systems. A2A was launched with the support of over 50 technology partners. A2A is complementary to the Model Context Protocol (MCP). While A2A facilitates agent to agent communication, MCP helps agents use tools.

MCP and A2A serve different purposes and are the core building blocks of Agentic AI. MCP and A2A are complementary protocols that work together to create robust and sophisticated Agentic AI systems. While MCP helps AI Agents use tools and external resources efficiently, A2A helps agents collaborate and communicate with each other effectively. A single AI agent might use MCP to interact with tools and also use A2A to communicate with other agents for more complex tasks requiring collaboration.

In June 2025, Google transferred its Agent2Agent (A2A) protocol to the Linux Foundation, where it has been established as an independent project. By hosting the project under the Linux Foundation, the A2A protocol will be managed as a vendor-agnostic and community-driven open standard. It now works alongside other standards such as Anthropic's MCP under the Agentic AI Foundation (AAIF), managed by the Linux Foundation.

17.3.26 Google's AI Mode

AI Mode utilizes a version of Google's Gemini model to understand and respond to questions. It provides comprehensive, conversational answers to complex questions, rather than just a list of links. It breaks down your query, gathers information from across the web, and presents a direct, helpful response at the top of the search results page. This mode is particularly useful for exploratory questions and comparing alternatives. It was released on June 27, 2025.

The planning tool, Canvas was released in AI Mode that provides a side bar to organize plans and projects over time. Canvas can be used to build travel plans that include Agentic AI booking capabilities for hotels, flights, and activities.

17.3.27 GPT—5 and 5.1

OpenAI released ChatGPT-5 on August 7, 2025. The new model has AI Agent capabilities, can browse the Internet and interact with tools and applications to complete multi-step tasks and provide more useful, context-rich responses. It also incorporates a deep reasoning model that engages in a chain-of-thought process for complex problems, offering deeper insights and problem-solving capabilities. The LLM model that powers GPT-5 is more reliable and significantly less prone to hallucinations.

With tremendous hype and high expectations, GPT-5 did not meet market expectations based on customer feedback. Customers had high expectations that ChatGPT 5 was going to be Artificial General Intelligence (AGI). OpenAI and CEO Sam Altman did a poor job managing customer expectations by claiming in September 2023 that "AGI has been achieved internally." Customers would have been satisfied with an incremental update with GPT-5 if no reference were made to AGI.

AGI is hypothetical at present and is a type of artificial intelligence that possesses human-like cognitive abilities, capable of understanding, learning, and applying intelligence to any intellectual task a human can. Unlike current narrow AI, which excels at specific tasks, AGI systems could generalize knowledge, possess common sense, reason abstractly, and adapt to new and unfamiliar situations across various domains. Many view it as the pinnacle of AI, though it remains a theoretical goal. A core weakness of LLM's is their inability to generalize broadly. Perhaps, LLMs are not in fact AGI-adjacent.

GPT-5, unlike its predecessors, was not a step improvement over GPT-4, which was widely acknowledged as a significant advancement over GPT-3, which in turn was a significant advancement over GPT-2. GPT-5 was an incremental improvement and not a big leap. Many researchers believe it feels like GPT—4.5 and many of the core issues such as hallucinations, weak logic and shallow context remain to be overcome.

ChatGPT 5.1 model update was released on November 12, 2025. The update introduced new variants GPT-5.1 Instant and GPT-5.1 Thinking designed to be smarter and more conversational.

17.3.28 Agentic AI Foundation

The Agentic AI Foundation (AAIF) was created on December 9, 2025, by the Linux Foundation.

It brings together major technology companies like Anthropic, Google, Microsoft, and OpenAI to foster open standards and collaboration for autonomous AI systems.

17.3.29 The Universal Commerce Protocol

Google introduced the Universal Commerce Protocol (UCP) on January 11, 2026. The open-source standard was created with retail and technology partners, including Shopify, Walmart, Etsy, Wayfair, and Target. UCP is designed to allow AI Agents to manage the entire shopping process from product discovery to checkout and payment. It enables in-conversation checkout using stored credentials such as Google Pay. The UCP protocol is oriented toward physical goods, shipping labels and tracking. In its current form, its adaptability for travel is unknown and will require the introduction of travel related specialized fields like seat maps and room types. It is anticipated that in the future UCP will be integrated with Google Travel (flights, hotels, ground transportation, destination activities, etc.). If UCP is adapted for travel, travel suppliers will be the merchant of record and retain all customer data.

17.3.30 The Competitive Landscape

Although OpenAI were forerunners in releasing these models to the public, they are not the only companies developing such models: others like Google DeepMind, Anthropic, Hugging Face, Cohere, IBM Watson, Stability AI, Meta AI, Baidu, and DeepAI are also vying to get ahead in the race to super-human artificial intelligence.

17.4 The Wilderness Years and the Future

Disillusionment with AI took place as early as the mid-1960s fueled by the failure of machine translation in a publication in November 1966 by the Automatic Language Processing Advisory Committee (ALPAC) and the limitations of the perceptron in 1969 with the publication of a book [Minsky & Papert, 1969]. ALPAC sent a clear message to the general public and the rest of the scientific community that Machine Translation was hopeless.

The concept of a failure period for AI is often called the "AI winter". An "AI winter" is a period characterized by reduced funding, diminished interest, and overall stagnation in the field of AI research and development. These winters follow periods of increased hype and investment, typically driven by overambitious claims and unrealistic expectations about AI's capabilities.

The Minsky and Papert book provided a mathematical analysis of the limitations of the single-layer perceptron model. The single layer perceptrons could only solve linearly separable problems. For example, the XOR (exclusive OR) logic function could not be solved because it was not linearly separable. This implied perceptrons struggled with problems that could not be divided by a straight line (or hyperplane in higher dimensions). This limitation which showed single perceptrons could not learn complex non-linear patterns that was highlighted in their book contributed to the first "AI-winter". It led to a decline in funding for neural network research. On the positive side, the book ultimately played a critical role in highlighting the need for more complex architectures and spurred advancements like the backpropagation (backward propagation of errors used to train artificial neural networks) algorithm, paving the way for the development of modern neural networks and deep learning.

The first "AI winter" occurred from 1970 to 1980, fueled in part by the James Lighthill Report [Lighthill, 1973] that was commissioned by the Science Research Council (SRC) in the U.K. The report published in 1973 criticized AI progress. It was a scathing assessment of AI research in the United Kingdom that was commissioned by the British government. This led to funding cuts from major government agencies.

The second "AI winter": took place in the late 1980s and 1990s, based on an understanding of the limits of expert systems and the collapse of specialized hardware markets.

By the late 1980s and early 2000s AI had a bad reputation, and the term had become synonymous with failure. Teaching computers to do tasks like turning speech into text or translating languages proved far more difficult than expected.

Today, AI technology looks quite different with software that can recognize speech and translate languages effectively. Also tools have been developed that can identify faces and describe objects in photos. This is what has driven the recent surge in AI development since 2010. The latest focus is on "Generative AI," like ChatGPT and Gemini, which creates text, sound, and images that have become more advanced each year. Most modern AI runs on "neural networks," a system inspired by how the human brain processes data. These networks were mostly out of fashion when the book *Computer Power and Human Reason* was published in 1976 [Weizenbaum, 1976]. It would take a few years after Weizenbaum's death before neural networks made a strong comeback in AI research.

The major milestones discussed in the section are summarized in Figs. 17.1, 17.2, and 17.3.

17.5 AI Search and the Future of Search Engine Optimization

In this section SEO will be in the context of a hotel website, which is important to attract direct traffic and avoid steep OTA commissions.

When a user submits a search request, the Search Engine Results Pages (SERP) order refers to the arrangement and ranking of search results. It is how search engines like Google display websites, images, videos, and other content in response to a user's search query. The order is determined by algorithms that evaluate the relevance and quality of each result based on various ranking factors.

In essence, the SERP order is a dynamic combination of organic and paid results, enhanced by various features, and tailored to the user's search context. Hotel websites must strive to optimize their content and online presence to rank higher in the SERP, as this is crucial for attracting traffic and achieving their online goals. The SERP consists of an AI Overview, organic search and paid search results. Search Engine Optimization (SEO) is the set of strategies used to improve a site's visibility and ranking within these organic results. Paid search is often used interchangeably with Search Engine Marketing (SEM), a broad term for increasing search visibility.

17.5.1 AI Influence on Search

Google uses advertising (paid search) as its main source of revenue by directing users to Web pages that link to Google Ads paid by advertisers. Google officially launched AI Overview in the U.S. on May 14, 2024, powered by Gemini, a family of multimodal Generative AI models. AI Overviews are now a common feature on search engine results pages. An increasing number of searches trigger these

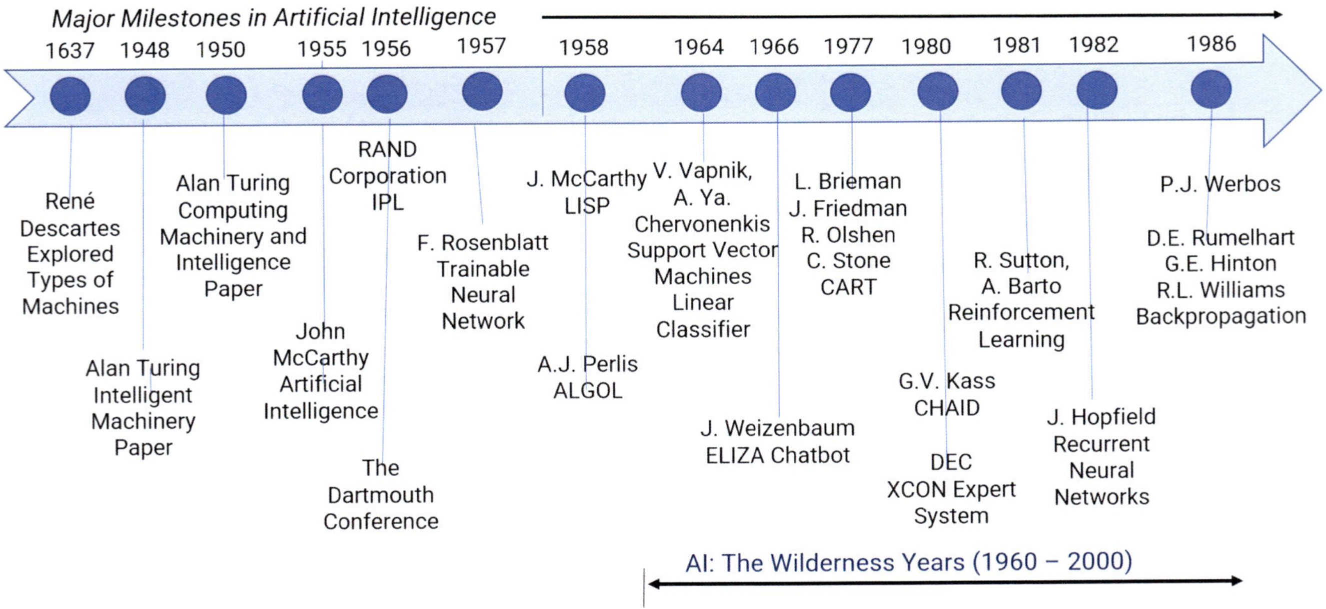

Fig. 17.1 Major AI milestones (1638–1986)

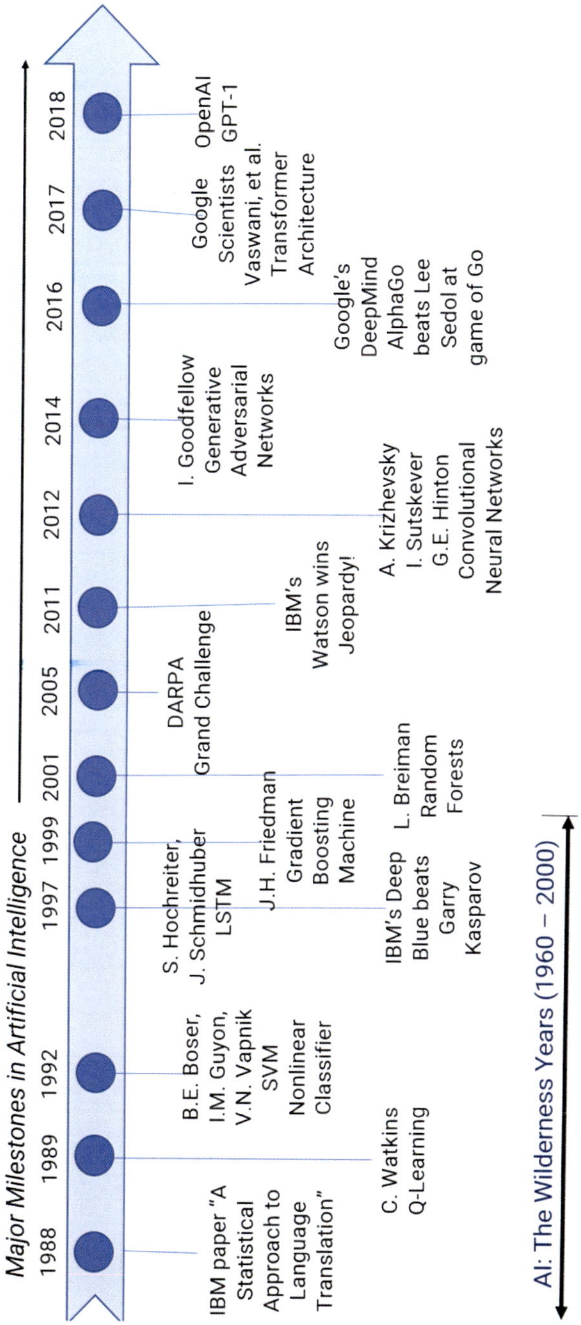

Fig. 17.2 Major AI milestones (1987–2018)

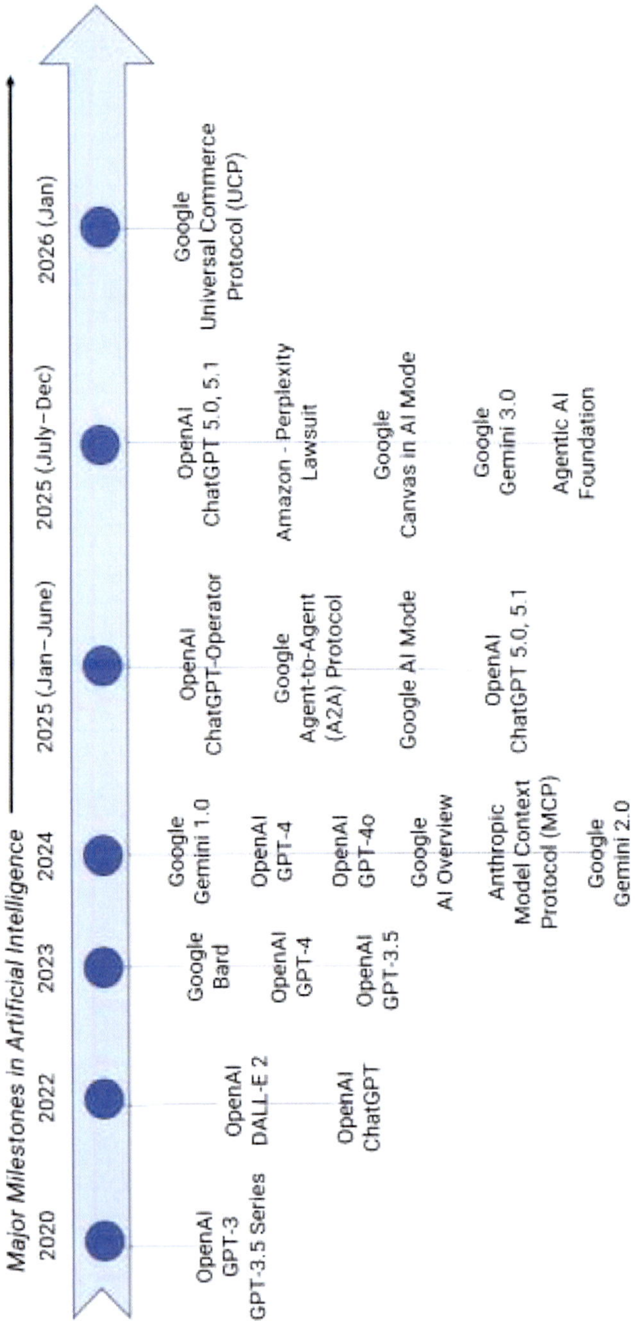

Fig. 17.3 Major AI milestones (2019–January 2026)

AI summaries. When AI provides direct answers on the SERP, users often do not need to visit websites. Users want information and Web pages are just a means for getting information. This leads to more zero-click searches, which most commonly cite Quora and Reddit. Many searchers now find the information they need without clicking through, which can lower traffic for websites in all industry verticals. When users do not visit websites, advertisers will stop paying for Google Ads and it will have a negative impact on Google's Ad revenue. When visits to Web pages decline, it is likely that developers will post fewer Web pages. The primary source for training data for LLMs are Web pages, which makes training a challenge if Web pages are on the decline. The increasing reliance on AI for direct answers poses a significant long-term risk to Google's Ad revenue and the open web ecosystem by creating a potential "circular reference" problem.

On May 20, 2025, Google launched AI Mode, which may make zero-click searches even more common. AI Mode is a new way to search with Google, leveraging the power of AI to provide more in-depth, conversational, and interactive search experiences. It builds upon existing AI-powered features like AI Overview and introduces new functionalities to enhance search and information retrieval. It represents a significant update to Google Search, positioning Generative AI at the forefront of search results and enabling more complex, multi-step interactions directly within the search interface. AI Mode is powered by Google's Gemini.

17.5.2 Traditional Search Engines and Changing Consumer Behavior

Consumer preferences are moving away from traditional search engines like Google. Trends indicate that they favor platforms that deliver quick, personalized ways to find what they want. Instead of entering keywords into Google, many turn to social media apps like TikTok and Instagram for visual inspiration. Reddit remains popular for honest community opinions, while YouTube offers detailed how-to videos. AI tools like ChatGPT, Claude and Perplexity are used to discuss or summarize topics, making it easier to avoid sifting through links. Marketplaces such as Amazon and Etsy have become go-to sites for product searches.

This shift shows people prefer tailored, trustworthy, and context-specific information over traditional search results. The traffic patterns are shifting to match this new reality for finding answers.

Despite the tremendous mindshare around Generative AI, the AI Search market share is negligible (less than 1%) compared to the global search market that Google dominates with a share of over 90% in 2024. Closely intertwined with the end of Google's monopoly on search, is the notion that traditional SEO is no longer relevant.

Generative AI platforms like Gemini, ChatGPT, Claude, Perplexity, and others are scraping Internet content with a caveat. They tend to focus on supplier websites that are optimized for AIO (Artificial Intelligence Optimization). With the arrival of autonomous Personal AI Agents like ChatGPT Operator that can research, plan and book trips, the importance of AIO cannot be understated. Autonomous Personal AI Agents are also an imminent threat to intermediaries like the GDSs and OTAs because they can be bypassed, thereby enabling direct supplier-customer relationships. The survival of intermediaries like OTAs will be predicated on access to unique content on their platforms. Examples are Airbnb and vacation rental by owner content on OTA platforms.

With this new dynamic, it is projected that Google's traditional search engine market share will decline over time. This in turn has triggered questions about the future of SEO.

17.5.3 Future of Hotel SEO

There is no doubt that AI Search is changing the search landscape, and this does not mean that travel suppliers must abandon their investment in SEO. Search engines are increasingly using AI to generate overviews and summaries of information, potentially reducing the need for users to click on individual websites.

The future of SEO with AI Search is about adaptation and evolution, not replacement. While AI is transforming how search engines work and how users interact with them, SEO remains relevant, but its methods are shifting. Success in the AI-driven search landscape requires a focus on user intent, high-quality content, and strategic use of AI-powered tools.

The future of SEO is a multi-channel approach that encompasses optimizing for multiple search discovery platforms, including social media and AI. SEO initiatives must ensure that the hotel website is optimized for AI (AIO). This does not mean that SEO specialists should master all search platforms. They should focus on visibility and business growth. In addition, to ensure that a hotel is discoverable by AI Search, SEO practices must be put to good use along the following dimensions.

1. Original content throughout the website, provide details about the destination based on local hotel manager expertise.
2. The website must have inbound links and citations from authoritative websites.
3. Social media presence with original posts with user generate content and customer reviews.

17.6 AI, OR and the Future of Problem Solving in the Airlines Industry

Successful organizations outside the airline industry that have adopted AI have taken an incremental approach [Davenport & Ronanki, 2018] with small well-defined initiatives rather than taking on large, complex problems at once. They categorize AI applications into three broad categories: Robotic Process Automation (RPA), Cognitive Insight and Cognitive Engagement in increasing order of complexity from the simplest to the more data intensive applications.

Recent research topics that leverage machine learning and AI in travel can be found in the collection of papers "*Artificial Intelligence and Machine Learning in the Travel Industry: Simplifying Complex Decision Making,*" [Vinod, 2023a]. Table 17.2 provides a partial list of application areas where Artificial Intelligence is gaining a firm foothold. When compared to Table 17.1, a key observation is that today, OR and AI are mostly complementary to each other. In some cases, AI augments an OR application. One such example is the creation of offers, the new era of revenue management.

The large scale OR optimization models shown in Table 17.1 continue to solve some of the most complex problems in the world involving thousands of decision variables. There have been presentations at conferences on using AI techniques such as LLMs with retrieval augmented generation (RAG) to solve these optimization models. The idea is to combine the LLM's reasoning capabilities with external knowledge retrieval. However, this is strictly experimental research at this stage.

For several decades OR has been used to solve complex business problems using established techniques such as mathematical modeling, stochastic processes, deterministic and stochastic large-scale network optimization models, data analytics, algorithms, statistical analysis, and decision sciences. All the major breakthroughs in advanced decision support for airline planning and operations including flight scheduling, pricing, revenue management, crew planning, airline operations, flight planning, staff planning, and cargo have been solved with techniques in OR [Horner, 2000].

With the major advances in AI over the past few years, many wonder what the future of OR in the airline industry will be? Is it at a crossroads? Statistics is a horizontal enabler for AI, just like it is for OR. It is unlikely that OR will be replaced by AI to solve complex large scale optimization problems with thousands of variables. Instead, AI will complement OR to automate and improve the value proposition. Many of the OR models can potentially be enhanced with AI. AI is at the intersection of technologies that reason, interact, and learn. In an AI-enabled landscape there are opportunities to introduce the concept of continuous learning without human intervention.

Machine learning is used to predict outcomes, while optimization models deal with optimal decision making. The traditional two-step approach has been machine learning based predictive modeling followed by optimization. An area of debate and active research is to pursue an integrated prescriptive approach with machine learning and optimization functioning in a unified framework [Bertsimas & Dunn, 2019; Bertsimas & Kallus, 2020; Kraus et al., 2020] where data-driven predictions are crafted specifically to improve decision-making under constraints. The argument is that while high prediction accuracy is a goal, so is the optimal decision quality (prescription).

Table 17.2 Major AI decision support areas in the airline industry

Application	Description and techniques
Chatbots	AI-powered chatbots provide 24/7 customer support for bookings, flight information, and other queries, streamlining customer service and reducing wait times. Leverage LLMs to generate human-like responses. These LLMs, often based on deep learning architectures like transformers are trained on vast amounts of text data, enabling them to understand and generate language with increasing sophistication. Examples of LLMs used in chatbots are GPT, Gemini, etc. LLMs are trained using machine learning techniques
Virtual Assistants	Virtual Assistants virtual assistants leverage the power of LLMs to understand and generate human language, while conversational AI and NLP technologies enable them to engage in natural and meaningful conversations with users. These technologies enable assistants to understand and respond to human language, generate personalized responses, and perform various tasks
Biometric Boarding	Facial recognition technology enables faster and more secure boarding processes. CNNs are widely used for image processing
Trip Planning	They can create a trip schedule based on customer preferences to include air, hotel, ground transportation and destination activities on a calendar. Generative AI is widely used for trip planning
Predictive Maintenance	They anticipate equipment failures, minimizing maintenance delays and disruptions. Machine learning algorithms, in the realm of supervised learning. These algorithms are trained on historical data to predict when equipment is likely to fail, enabling proactive maintenance and preventing costly downtime
Airline Pricing	Dynamic pricing of ancillary products and services by market based on consumer preferences and competition. Reinforcement Learning, test and learn experimentation to infer pricing of ancillaries by market and customer segment
Revenue Management	Forecasting passenger demand, show up rates, cancellation rates. Leverage airline data and external data to forecast using neural networks and deep neural networks Dynamic Continuous Pricing. Determine the dynamic continuous price from the priced itinerary based on filed fares. The discount by customer segment and market is inferred from reinforcement learning, test and learn experimentation Offer Management. Data analytics powered recommendation engines for bundles. Typical models based on data availability include techniques such as collaborative filtering, classification and regression trees and gradient boosting models Determine the bundles using contextual reinforcement learning with test and learn experimentation
Fare Prediction	Forecast future selling fares with a calibrated Q-learning model

Another area of active research is the value of leveraging machine learning to solve combinatorial optimization problems, especially NP-hard (nondeterministic polynomial time) integer constrained problems. These problems are characterized by having no known efficient polynomial-time solutions, meaning their computation time grows exponentially as the input size increases. Early studies indicated that machine learning models can complement existing optimization approaches that exploit structure detection, branching and heuristics [Khalil et al., 2016, 2017; Lodi & Zarpellon, 2017].

Traditional optimization techniques such as the branch-and-bound algorithm can potentially benefit from machine learning to explore the branch-and-bound tree [Khalil et al., 2016]. They address the Generalized Independent Set Problem (GISP) class of problems where finding good solutions is challenging and report improvements in primal integral and time to best incumbent, and the benefit lies in the method learning to run heuristics more aggressively early in the search. Machine learning can systematically apply heuristics to solve combinatorial optimization problems [Bengio et al., 2021].

Demand forecasts are a fundamental input to determine optimal inventory controls. Research into the applicability of reinforcement learning with exploration to predict revenue management inventory controls without a demand forecast model for single resource problems have shown some promise [Bondoux et al., 2020] by integrating deep domain knowledge with a deep Q-learning neural network. Though promising, these approaches are several years away from mainstream adoption to large airline network problems.

17.6.1 The Future of AI Is the Marketplace

According to Michael I. Jordan, a highly influential computer scientist, statistician and Professor Emeritus at the University of California, Berkeley, the *future of AI is the marketplace* [Jordan, 2018, 2019]. His key message is to empower users to broadcast what they want (publish) and allow vendors (subscribers) to respond with offers. In contrast the current AI model is a top-down push model. Jordan is of the opinion that the "*emerging generation of AI is not just one agent making a decision or sequence of decisions, but a huge, interconnected web of data, agents, and decisions.*" From his perspective, autonomous self-driving cars can be vastly improved with a networked system. If a self-driving car identifies a cyclist on the right shoulder ahead, it should notify all other self-driving cars and make the whole system collectively aware of the environment. The next generation of AI applications will continuously interact with the environment and learn from these interactions. This will require a distributed system with new requirements for performance and flexibility. This is vastly different from what current AI is all about. Recommendation engines for travel will have to adapt to this new reality in the future.

What is proposed by Professor Jordan is remarkably similar to where NDC is headed. With NDC, travel agents will broadcast (publish) a message to airlines with details of the market to book travel for a customer [Darrow, 2021]. Airlines (subscribers) will then respond with offers. In his opinion, Facebook and other social media platforms do not get this concept and rely on a top-down push model.

17.6.2 Countering the Bullwhip Effect in the Airline Industry

Neural networks and deep learning AI models should also be leveraged to improve demand forecasting in the airline industry to counter the Bullwhip effect.

The bullwhip effect is frequently discussed in the context of supply chain management where fluctuations in customer demand become amplified as they move up the supply chain from retailers to manufacturers. Small changes in consumer demand at the retail level can lead to much larger and more erratic swings in orders and inventory at each stage of the multi-tiered supply chain, all the way back to the raw material suppliers.

There are parallels in the airline industry where small fluctuations in passenger demand can be amplified as they move up the supply chain, leading to larger and larger variations in orders and inventory at different levels, such as airlines, aircraft manufacturers, and parts suppliers. This is challenging in the aerospace sector for two reasons: long lead times and high-value components.

There are several factors that contribute to the Bullwhip effect. They are:

1. Accuracy of passenger demand forecasts. Forecast accuracy has a significant impact on revenue management. Various studies have shown that a 10% improvement in forecast accuracy leads to a ½% improvement in revenue. Besides seat inventory control, long term passenger demand forecasts influence acquisition of aircraft and rotable (high value components that are designed to be repeatedly removed, repaired, and reinstalled throughout the aircraft's lifespan) and non-rotable (or expendable) parts inventory. Inaccurate forecasts can lead to over-ordering or under-ordering aircraft and parts, amplifying demand variability across the supply chain.
2. Changes in fuel prices can affect passenger demand and, consequently, the demand for aircraft and parts. These fluctuations can create erratic purchasing patterns and unpredictable demand cycles throughout the supply chain.
3. The aerospace industry is characterized by long lead times for aircraft production and parts manufacturing. Long lead times amplify the bullwhip effect because they increase the time it takes for manufacturing entities in the supply chain to respond to demand changes, making it difficult to maintain optimal inventory levels.

17.6.3 AI as a Discipline

AI is a multi-disciplinary field focused on creating systems that simulate human intelligence such as learning, reasoning and problem solving. Its foundation is in mathematics, statistics, computer science and cognitive science and encompasses subfields like Machine Learning, Natural Language Processing, Deep Learning, Generative AI and AI Agents.

As a field that is constantly changing, AI has become a common presence in the corporate world. It is no longer confined to universities and research labs but is now being embraced in various industries [Marr, 2018]. Travel suppliers and intermediaries are adopting AI-based applications at a rapid pace to gain a competitive advantage related to productivity through robotic process automation and efficient interaction with customers.

Advances in capabilities of AI systems have been based on progress along three dimensions: compute, data, and algorithms. According to NVIDIA founder and CEO Jensen Huang (Jen-Hsun Huang), AI capabilities are doubling every seven months, outpacing Moore's Law, the observation made in 1965 by Intel co-founder Gordon Moore that the number of transistors in an integrated circuit doubles about every two years, enabling faster, cheaper, and more efficient computing. To understand the demand for computing power, OpenAI's GPT-4 training required approximately 21 septillion (2.1×10^{25}) floating point operations. The training process utilized roughly 25,000 NVIDIA A100 GPUs running continuously for 90 to 100 days.

AI, as a field, is extensive and encompasses the idea of machines performing tasks in an intelligent manner. It consists of four main areas: machine learning, natural language processing, deep learning, Generative AI and AI Agents. All five areas have direct relevance to advanced decision-making. Additionally, all five areas can be utilized throughout the travel industry's value chain.

17.6.4 Challenge of Interpretability

In the realm of advanced decision support for applications like offer management, flight scheduling, and fare optimization, a significant obstacle to the acceptance of machine learning techniques is interpretability. For instance, revenue management analysts often desire an understanding of how the system generates forecasts. Unlike statistical models, machine learning models are typically opaque (black boxes), producing an output that cannot be readily interpreted. It is important to grasp the reasoning behind a model's meaningful results and identify instances when they may fall short. Interpretability enables verifying the outputs from a system by tracing how modeling choices combined with the data used impact the results. It is a fundamental requirement to build trust in AI systems.

Machine learning models are utilized to predict the anticipated result of a featured dataset. The loss function serves to assess the precision of the model's predictions by quantifying the "error" or difference between the predicted output and the actual target value. This single numerical value, called the "loss," indicates how well or poorly the model is performing, with a low value signifying a more accurate prediction. During training, the goal is to minimize this loss, which guides the model's parameters to become more accurate over time. The accuracy increases as the cost function, an average of all loss function values, decreases. The accuracy is influenced by the choice of the loss function. Loss functions can be categorized into two groups: classification and regression. Binary Cross Entropy Loss/Log Loss and Hinge Loss are illustrations of classification loss functions.

Mean squared error (MSE) and Mean Absolute Error (MAE) are examples of regression loss functions.

Deployment of machine learning models is devoted to establishing the necessary environment and preparing the data for input into these opaque models. Once a machine learning model produces results, comprehending the expected behavior of a trained model becomes vital. Frequently, machine learning models can yield counterintuitive outcomes, which necessitates the intervention of data scientists who developed the model for debugging purposes.

Interpreting deep learning models presents an even greater challenge due to the multitude of parameters involved and how features are combined. Both academia and corporations are actively engaged in researching methods to address issues such as model bias, establishing connections between model inputs and predictions, and interpreting the model's response to gain insights.

This area of research is commonly referred to as Explainable AI (XAI) [Arrieta et al., 2020]. XAI refers to a set of methods and tools that help users understand and trust the results from artificial intelligence (AI) and machine learning (ML) algorithms. It provides transparency by explaining why an AI system made a specific decision, using techniques like feature attribution, visualizations, and counterfactuals to reveal how input data influenced the outcome. XAI is critical for building trust, enabling debugging, mitigating risks like bias, and meeting regulatory requirements.

There are methods such as SHAP (SHapley Additive exPlanations), which can be used by analysts to explain why an AI model made, for example, a specific inventory control recommendation with an emphasis on the marginal contribution of each feature such as price, competition, demand forecast, demand uncertainty, etc. Shap values, a concept in cooperative game theory, provides a structured approach to understand the importance of individual features in a predictive model. SHAP assumes feature independence and is computationally expensive.

Another technique is LIME (Local Interpretable Model-agnostic Explanations) that perturbs the input data to see how small changes affect the outcome. It then builds a local, interpretable surrogate model such as a linear regression to explain which factors were most influential for the output response. LIME is easy to understand and interpret with its linear coefficients. It is sensitive to input perturbations and small changes may lead to significant changes in explanation. It also assumes that the model behaves linearly around a single point.

For revenue management models, SHAP is considered to be better due to its mathematical rigor, consistency, and ability to provide both global and local explanations. LIME is faster for quick, local insights but is less stable and may oversimplify complex modeling scenarios.

To interpret LLM outputs, visualization tools can be used to understand which parts of the input data the model focused on when generating a response. LLM attention mechanism visualizations use heatmaps or matrices to show how much focus a model gives to different parts of the input text, revealing relationships between words. These visualizations help in understanding the decision-making process of the model by showing which tokens influence others, even though attention is not a direct explanation.

The perception remains that XAI is rudimentary and may not provide a satisfactory explanation. What is required is a deep understanding of a model's inner workings. This is a challenge due to model abstraction, problem complexity and the high bar for human-like understanding. While XAI provides tools for transparency, many experts acknowledge that the explanations can be oversimplified and often fail to fully capture the complexity of "black box" models.

This chapter will conclude with two topics that are expected to have the greatest impact on travel over the next decade. They are AI driven personalization and Agentic AI.

17.7 AI Driven Personalization

AI personalization refers to using artificial intelligence for product suggestions, customized messages, and services for each user. By analyzing data and tracking customer behavior, AI tools can craft tailored experiences that boost customer satisfaction and engagement. Recent advances in AI, like Generative AI, allow for near-instant creation of personalized content. These tools support a growing trend of hyper-personalization across multiple channels. Customers now enjoy a connected experience that adapts quickly to their actions on different platforms.

AI influenced personalization utilizes a combination of machine learning, natural language processing, and Generative AI techniques to tailor experiences to individual travelers. For example, machine Learning can be leveraged for pattern recognition. personalized recommendations, and behavioral segmentation. Natural Language Processing can be leveraged to understand traveler intent, sentiment analysis, and content generation and Generative AI for product recommendations.

Collectively, these techniques analyze customer data like behavior, preferences, and interactions across various touchpoints, along with contextual information like location, device, and context for travel to personalize content, recommendations.

Investing in AI personalization will improve customer satisfaction brand loyalty and increased engagement that leads to higher conversion rates. It can also serve as a competitive differentiator for travel suppliers to improve market share.

By combining these techniques, AI personalization can create highly tailored experiences that enhance customer engagement, satisfaction, and ultimately drive business growth.

AI personalization can impact many areas in the travel value chain. Here are a few examples.

17.7.1 Chatbots

AI chatbots and virtual assistants can hold conversations that feel personal because they understand user questions and respond in a natural way. They can handle customer service, suggest products, and help resolve problems, making the user experience quicker and more tailored. These bots are available 24×7, and gather useful data on how customers shop and interact. This helps travel suppliers improve their efficiency and better serve their customers.

17.7.2 Relevancy of Content Based on Context

Content personalization uses AI to create messages tailored to each user. It can include emails, articles, product descriptions, videos, or texts based on what users like and how they behave. This approach helps organizations send relevant and engaging content that strikes a chord with their audience. At the same time, it saves time and reduces the effort needed to produce many different assets. By focusing on individual preferences, travel suppliers can connect better and build stronger relationships with their customers.

17.7.3 Airline AI Agent

The objective of airline AI Agents is to handle routine inquiries providing real-time support during schedule disruptions and personalize interactions with travelers based on customer data in the future, Agentic AI can automate tasks like check-in, baggage tracking, and booking changes, improving efficiency and reducing operational costs.

17.7.4 Precision Ad Targeting

AI improves targeted advertising by examining user data to deliver ads that are most likely to catch individual interest. This makes marketing efforts work better and cuts down on wasted spending. By showing the right message to the right person, campaigns become more efficient. The technology helps advertisers reach their audience more accurately and with less guesswork.

17.7.5 Predictive Personalization Based on Consumer Intent

Predictive personalization uses NLP to determine consumer intent, what users truly want and prefer before they even say so. By examining past data, AI can suggest products or content a user is likely to enjoy next. This improves the overall experience for users.

For example, Starbucks launched a system powered by machine learning that recommends drinks based on each customer's purchase history. They use their Deep Brew data analytics platform to provide highly personalized drink recommendations to its customers. The system also predicts what people might order depending on the time of day or the weather. These predictions are integrated into the company's mobile app and how the company manages its inventory.

17.8 AI Assistants Versus AI Agents

An AI Assistant is an intelligent application that understands natural language commands and uses a conversational interface to complete tasks for a user. AI Assistants like Siri and ChatGPT are *reactive*. They only respond when prompted by a user. They respond to direct commands for tasks like summarizing or answering questions. Once a prompt is processed, the model generates an answer without further refinement. The LLM has a narrow role. It follows a linear path from input to output without deviation or power to make decisions. This is a non-agentic workflow.

In contrast, AI Agents are *proactive*, goal-oriented problem solvers that autonomously plan and execute complex, multi-step workflows across applications with minimal human intervention, acting like a digital co-worker. It is an iterative process, engaging in research, planning, self-correction, and feedback similar to how humans solve problems. AI Agents have autonomy and persistence, do not forget tasks and can use tools such as APIs and code to achieve their objectives, while AI Assistants are limited to the current prompt's context.

OpenAI introduced ChatGPT Pulse in September 2025 that is changing this dynamic to be proactive [OpenAI, 2025b]. It anticipates user needs by conducting asynchronous research and delivering personalized daily updates, summaries, and insights without waiting for a direct user prompt. It works as a proactive assistant, curating relevant information based on user interests, past conversations, and connected applications like calendars.

AI Agents go beyond the traditional reactive model of ChatGPT.

17.9 What Is Agentic AI?

Agentic AI refers to autonomous AI systems that can independently set goals, reason, plan and self-correct and take actions to achieve complex objectives with minimal human intervention, acting as proactive digital agents. Unlike Generative AI that responds to prompts, Agentic AI uses LLMs with external tools and memory to orchestrate multi-step tasks, adapt to changes, and learn from outcomes for continuous improvement. These goal-driven agents can learn from their environment, adapt to changes, and collaborate with other agents to complete multi-step workflows, offering significant advancements in automation and efficiency for complex, real-world tasks. Agentic AI is also known as intelligent digital workers or simply AI Agents.

The key characteristics of Agentic AI systems [DataGrid, 2025; IBM, 2025] are:

1. Autonomous Action.
   They can initiate tasks and take a sequence of actions without continuous human supervision.
2. Goal-Oriented Outcome.
   They can be given a complex goal to achieve. The AI system devises a plan to achieve it, breaking it down into smaller steps.
3. Access External Applications.
   They can interact with external tools and systems, including web browsers and APIs.
4. Adaptability.
   They can adapt to changing conditions and learn from experience.
5. Strict Guardrails
   The orchestration and governance of autonomous software entities require advanced tools and strict guardrails.

17.9.1 Mathematical Reasoning

Mathematical reasoning provides the logical structure for autonomous decision making, enabling agents to break down complex problems, plan, act, learn from feedback, handle uncertainty, and achieve goals.

> *Mathematical reasoning may be regarded rather schematically as the exercise of a combination of two facilities, which we may call intuition and ingenuity.*
>
> Alan Turing

This quote, commonly attributed to Alan Turing, postulates that mathematical reasoning relies on a combination of intuition and ingenuity. It suggests that progress in mathematics is not solely about strict logic but also requires creative leaps and insights, which are essential alongside formal deduction. The quote links human math skills—intuition for fast leaps, ingenuity for solid structure—to AI's core aim. It suggests that advanced AI (Agentic AI) must match this mix of quick insights and logical builds to really think or reason. Such AI beats plain calculation with creative problem solving. Today's AI excels at ingenuity (complex calculations, logical patterns), but true "thinking" requires Turing's intuitive spark—a capability Agentic AI strives for. Agentic AI's goal is to create autonomous systems that reason and act like humans.

Building advanced AI systems that can make those "spontaneous judgments" (intuition) and then methodically build upon them (ingenuity) remains a key hurdle in creating truly intelligent, human-like systems. The goal is to build AI that does not just compute but *thinks* like a mathematician, combining experience-based insight (intuition) with creative problem-solving (ingenuity).

17.9.2 Reasoning Skills is the Biggest Challenge with Agentic AI

In 2025, AI agent models have limitations in their mathematical reasoning skills in the areas of complexity, adaptability, interpretability, and common sense.

These limitations stem from several key challenges that must be overcome for uniform adoption. The challenges include:

Computational Complexity and Resource Intensiveness. Complex reasoning tasks demand significant computational power and time, making them difficult to scale efficiently for real-world problems. Resource intensive AI Agents require significant computational power, specialized infrastructure (e.g., GPUs) and expertise for development, deployment, and ongoing maintenance.

Lack of Conceptual Understanding. Models often mimic human reasoning by predicting likely word sequences (pattern matching) rather than true understanding.

Problems with Multi-step Planning. Agents frequently struggle with intricate, multi-step problems where interim conclusions require iterative revisions.

Sensitivity to Context and Order. AI reasoning can be sensitive to the presentation of information. Irrelevant details can cause errors, and changing the order of steps in a prompt can reduce accuracy. This sensitivity stems from the way LLMs that power AI Agents process information.

Limited Interpretability. AI Agents have limited interpretability because complex deep learning models act as "black boxes," making it hard to trace why they make specific decisions, which raises concerns in ethical situations like healthcare or law.

Active areas of research to address these limitations include alternate advanced methods for fine-tuning, reinforcement learning with feedback loops, and integrating external knowledge retrieval mechanisms (RAG) to provide models with real-time context and data.

17.10 Agentic AI Validation

Is the promise of Agentic AI the future of the travel industry?

Current Agentic AI models lack the maturity to autonomously achieve complex business goals or follow nuanced instructions over time. Many deployments are little more than advanced chatbots or robotic process automation (RPA) tools with a conversational interface.

Well known critics of Agentic AI like Gary Marcus [Marcus, 2025] argue that thus far (December 2025), there is no credible, peer-reviewed evidence that Agentic AI exists in any real-world deployment. *Is it fabricated fiction?* His critics view him as a speculative futurist and a distraction to real progress in AI.

Billions of dollars are being invested in this technology. Industry experts warn that the gap between expectations and what is practical could lead to a new "AI winter", a period of stalled investment and reduced confidence. Alan Greenspan, the former Chairman of the Federal Reserve, coined the phrase "irrational exuberance" in a December 1996 speech, warning of excessive investor enthusiasm driven asset prices beyond their true economic value, especially during the dot-com bubble. The term became synonymous with asset bubbles. In this context, irrational exuberance is the collective, speculative overconfidence that Agentic AI will reshape business faster than it actually can.

Agentic AI is not fiction. It is an emerging technology where AI reasons, plans and acts autonomously. Current commercial applications reflect automation, lacking the true independent reasoning of future AI Agents. There is a strong element of "agent washing" and overhyped claims surrounding the term, where systems are marketed as agentic when they might be closer to advanced automation or traditional AI following predefined rules. The term "agent washing" refers to the practice of rebranding existing automation tools, like chatbots or basic workflows, as "AI Agents" without significant enhancements in intelligence, autonomy, or adaptability.

Studies by Stanford University and UC Berkeley in 2024 found that current foundation models struggle with sustained logical reasoning, planning sequences of actions, and adapting to changes independently. The study suggests that while foundation models are powerful, they lack genuine agentic behavior and are not yet capable of the complex cognitive tasks and multi-step logical reasoning associated with true intelligence.

The Artificial Intelligence Index Report 2025 [Stanford University, 2025], an authoritative resource on the state of AI, further confirmed that complex reasoning continues to be a major hurdle. LLMs perform better with features like chain-of-thought reasoning. Still, they struggle with tasks requiring logic. This includes arithmetic and planning problems. They especially fail on bigger tasks than they trained on. This lack of certainty affects trust. It also limits their use in high-risk situations.

Only time will tell.

The remainder of this section assumes that Agentic AI will overcome the hurdles of complex reasoning, plan sequences of actions based on goals, and demonstrate autonomy.

If Agentic AI is the future, airlines, hotels, car rental and cruise lines must be poised to leverage this new capability to stay competitive in the marketplace.

What is Agentic AI? It is called "agentic" because it refers to a collection of AI systems that can act autonomously, decide and act, with minimal human intervention, similar to how an agent acts on behalf of a principal. It is an incremental step beyond Generative AI, which primarily focuses on creating content. Agentic AI systems of the future will analyze data, set goals and execute tasks to completion, effectively operating as independent agents.

In travel, Agentic AI is a type of AI that makes autonomous travel decisions and takes specific actions to complete specific tasks such as trip planning, research of air fares and hotel rates, research on destinations, amenities and make an air or hotel booking.

LLMs like GPT-4 act as the cognitive engine or "brain" for Agentic AI systems. They provide the reasoning and understanding capabilities that enable AI Agents to:

1. Interpret tasks and understand language.
2. Reason and make decisions based on processed information.
3. Generate insights and make predictions.

Personal AI Agents are advanced, intelligent software assistants that leverage AI to perform tasks like travel research, make recommendations, and even automate decisions on behalf of users such as booking a flight or a hotel room. They are designed to integrate across various platforms, like apps, emails, and databases, to provide personalized assistance and enhance productivity. Some of the leading players are OpenAI's Operator, Google's Gemini AI Agent, Claude AI Agent by Anthropic and Microsoft Copilot AI Agent, to name a few.

With the advent of the new generation Personal AI Agents, we can anticipate different flavors of AI Agents

17.10.1 Airline AI Agent

An airline AI agent is autonomous software system that leverages LLMs to handle customer service, booking, and operational tasks for airlines. The AI agent understands context, makes real-time decisions, and autonomously rebooks passengers during irregular operations. The software can also book flights, modify itineraries, and manage the entire trip planning process.

17.10.2 Hotel AI Agent

In hospitality, the future Hotel AI Agent will be knowledgeable about the property's product, services and amenities offered, details of the destination such as local attractions and activities,

It is anticipated that Hotel AI Agents will be inter-operable with Agentic AI platforms such as Operator, the hotel CRS and hotel PMS. It could render Channel Managers that synchronize ARI (Availability, Rates, Inventory) content with OTAs obsolete by taking on the role of distributing ARI content.

17.10.3 TMC AI Agent

The most significant impact of Agentic AI will be on corporate travel. Agentic AI can be programmed to ensure that employee travel bookings are compliant with corporate policy, thereby reducing the risk of corporate policy violations and cost overruns. Further, AI can be programmed to ensure that travel bookings comply with company policies, reducing the risk of policy violations and potential cost overruns. Further, by providing real-time information and support, Agentic AI can help travel managers fulfill their duty of care to travelers, ensuring their safety and well-being.

17.10.4 OTA AI Agent

It is anticipated that the OTAs will invest heavily in OTA Agents to get a leg up on suppliers, especially hotels. The key question is whether hotels will put enough resources into AI technology and skilled staff. Historically, they have not spent what it takes to attract direct bookings. Will it be different with Personal AI Agents and will they rise to the challenge? With the requisite investment, will they become leaders, or fall behind?

17.11 Agentic AI Framework to Book Travel

Traditional rule-based systems are characterized with a linear workflow with well-defined steps that lead to a predictable, structured outcome. Workflows in travel to create an itinerary are far less predictable because the outcomes can vary based on context for travel and traveler preferences. Agentic AI systems are based on foundation models, trained on very large datasets and perform a range of general tasks. They serve as building blocks for developing more specialized applications. Their size sets them apart from traditional machine learning models which are trained on smaller datasets to solve specific tasks. Agentic AI systems can handle nuances, adapting in real-time to execute the specialized tasks required to deliver a satisfactory outcome.

Agentic systems are digital systems that act on their own. They interact in a changing environment. While similar software has been around, Generative AI's natural language skills open new paths. These systems can plan tasks. They use web tools to finish jobs. They can also work with people and other agents. They get better with practice. Gen AI Agents may soon be like virtual colleagues of travel agents. They will work naturally with people. Imagine a virtual helper that could plan a custom trip and manage the booking across travel sites.

Figure 17.4 illustrates a multi-agent framework to book travel for business and leisure passengers. In the figure, the travel planning agent coordinates tasks with the specialized agents. The various agents are described below. For corporate travel, these AI Agents will operate autonomously within the guardrails of corporate travel policy. To start the travel planning process, the traditional sequential search is replaced with a conversational interface to plan and book relevant business or leisure trips.

Travel Planning Agent
The travel planning agent serves as the orchestrator and collaborates with specialized agents to finalize a traveler's itinerary.

Airline Agent
The airline agent specializes in booking flights based on user preferences, travel history and corporate policy for business travelers.

Hotel Agent
The hotel agent specializes in booking hotels based on user preferences, travel history, and corporate policy for business travelers.

Car Rental Agent
The car rental agent specializes in booking a rental car based on user preferences, travel history, and corporate policy for business travelers.

Destination Activity Agent
The destination activity agent specializes in recommending and booking activities such as restaurants and museums.

Traveler Preferences Agent
Traveler preferences play an important role during itinerary creation. AI Agents that specialize in traveler preferences go beyond traditional static preferences, with its ability to determine implied preferences and ability to interpret natural language to determine consumer intent.

Core components of traveler preferences include.

1. Declared or stated preferences by a traveler such as airline seat and hotel room preferences, loyalty programs, etc.
2. Data analytics plays a role in capturing revealed preferences implicitly. AI Agents can analyze vast amount of data including past travel behaviors, booking history, loyalty program status, social media activity and reviews.
3. Behavioral inferences by Identifying patterns in travel behavior such as a family seeking beach destinations with kid-friendly activities
4. Sentiment insights based on analysis of social media and reviews to identify trends in traveler sentiment, such as eco-friendly hotels and wellness retreats,
5. Context for travel based on parameters of the search request to identify business trips, leisure trips and their variations. Going beyond stated preferences, AI Agents consider nuances of natural language, understanding implicit needs and adapting recommendations like the traveler wanting to return home before a kid's birthday,

6. Preference learning where AI Agents can learn continuously from user feedback and interactions.

Corporate Travel Policy Agent
The corporate travel policy agent is specific to business travel. A corporate travel policy agent can cross-reference company travel policies in real-time against booking requests and expenses, flagging any deviations before they are submitted. This ensures adherence to internal guidelines and budgets, reducing the risk of non-compliance.

Duty of Care Agent
The duty of care agent can flag high-risk destinations, suggest safer routes, monitor a corporate traveler's location and provide real-time updates on potential risks or emergencies. They can also offer instant, location-specific assistance through chatbots and virtual assistants, helping travelers navigate unfamiliar environments or access emergency services. During irregular operations such as flight cancellations, the AI agent can automatically rebook flights, reschedule meetings, and alert stakeholders, minimizing downtime and stress for travelers.

Some aspects of the duty of care agent such as rebooking travelers when there are flight disruptions are applicable to leisure travelers as well.

17.11.1 The Agent2Agent Protocol and Model Context Protocol

An important new development is the Agent2Agent (A2A) protocol, an open standard designed to improve how AI Agents interact and collaborate. Introduced by Google in April 2025 with contributions from over 50 technology partners, the objective of A2A is to facilitate secure, scalable, and seamless communication between autonomous AI Agents operating across various frameworks, vendors, and domains. A2A supports the shift towards Agentic AI, systems capable of autonomous action to achieve defined objectives without constant human oversight.

The A2A protocol represents a significant threat to the traditional business model of Global Distribution Systems (GDSs) by enabling a decentralized, collaborative AI travel ecosystem. A2A empowers specialized AI Agents like a booking agent and a payment agent to communicate and work together directly and securely, which will diminish the role of the GDS as a central booking intermediary.

The Model Context Protocol (MCP) functions as a universal interface, enabling seamless, secure, and scalable data exchange between AI Agents and external sources. Software developers can leverage MCP to build reusable, modular connections with pre-built servers available for popular AI platforms, thereby creating a community driven ecosystem. MCP will transform isolated AI Agent chatbots into context aware interoperable systems.

MCP for travel is an AI architecture that connects AI Agents to real-time travel data and services, allowing them to provide personalized, context-aware assistance to users. MCP servers act as intermediaries, and AI Agents can access current flight information, hotel availability, and details of bookings from multiple systems such as travel suppliers and GDSs to help users plan trips. It enables complex tasks like booking, modifying, and personalized services with multi-agent orchestration using the A2A protocol. MCP enriches LLM Agents with up-to-date content from travel suppliers to deliver accurate and relevant travel recommendations and to automate end-to-end trip planning. MCP serves as the translator for the Agentic Web in travel.

Both MCP and A2A are intended to achieve reliable and concise communications among interacting agents. The rigor with the standardized time clock system is a mandatory requirement for consistent, reliable notifications of time-sensitive information.

The GDS model relies on charging airlines and other suppliers booking fees every time a transaction is processed through its system. A2A facilitates a decentralized booking process, allowing travel suppliers to bypass traditional GDSs and their associated fees. The interoperable nature of the A2A protocol gives power to entities that develop the specialized AI Agents and control the supplier API. The GDS is not part of this ecosystem.

Agentic AI will automate mundane travel agency tasks which will lead to a reduction in force since a few travel agents working with AI Agents will be able to service a larger number of corporate and leisure customers.

The transformation of human travel agents will shift their focus from routine booking and planning to complex, strategic tasks that require unique human skills like negotiation, policy management and high level risk assessment. While Agentic AI can automate much of the planning process autonomously, it also creates opportunities for travel professionals to add greater value by managing the intricate details that AI cannot. This evolution means travel agents will need to adapt, leveraging Agentic AI to enhance efficiency and personalize experiences, allowing them to concentrate on strategic partnerships and bespoke client services that go beyond what automated systems can provide.

17.11.2 The Agentic Web for Travel

The next evolution of the Internet is the Agentic Web where autonomous AI Agents act on behalf of travelers to manage travel. AI Agents can proactively manage complex, multi-step tasks to plan travel and book all components of travel. It relies on the new MCP and A2A protocols for communication and Natural Language Web infrastructure to simplify the creation of natural language interfaces. The fundamental shift from user-driven browsing to agent-driven automation has implications for privacy, security, and efficiency.

17.11.3 The Agentic AI Model to Book Travel

Figure 17.4 illustrates an example of an Agentic AI model to book travel.

The Agent-to-Agent (A2A) protocol enables different software agents to communicate and collaborate, like a travel planning agent delegating tasks to specialized agents like a flight agent, a hotel agent, car rental agent, and a destination activities agent to book a trip. In addition, the preferences agent knows the preferences of a traveler such as seating preference on flights, hotel room types (king versus queen, proximity to elevator, high floor or low floor, etc.), and loyalty program affiliations. The corporate travel policy agent is knowledgeable of corporate travel policy and what is required for the business travel itinerary to be compliant. The duty of care agent is proactively identifying and mitigating risks, personalizing safety measures, and streamlining communication and support for business travelers. AI Agents can access airline MCP servers as a standardized, secure bridge between LLMs and travel supplier legacy systems, bypassing the need for traditional complex API integrations. A2A provides a standardized way for agents to "talk," send messages, share information, and update each other on the status of tasks. This process of breakdown of tasks, analysis, refinement, and review will continue until the traveler approves the itinerary.

A2A allows agents to discover each other's capabilities through "Agent Cards" in JSON format. Agent Cards are published by each agent outlining what they can do, what protocols they speak, and types of requests they accept. The digital business cards help agents to find the right collaborators. For example, this enables agents to identify the best agent for tasks like booking flights, hotels, car rental, or destination activities. It also identifies agents that specialize in traveler preferences, corporate travel policy, and duty of care. The protocol facilitates task management, where a travel planning agent can delegate sub-tasks like flight or hotel searches to specialized agents. Agents can collaborate by sending messages containing context, replies, booking details, or user instructions. Messages can also include "parts" with specified content types to ensure a seamless user experience

The AI travel planning agent plays a central role in coordinating specialized agents. A2A defines a standard way for these agents to communicate, including how to structure requests, track progress, and manage multi-step processes. Each specialized agent utilizes its own set of tools, like APIs, to interact with external services (e.g., airline booking engines, hotel reservation systems), These external services will have AI Agents representing airlines, hotels, destination providers, etc. who respond to the specialized agents working on the passenger's itinerary.

Each booking task receives a unique ID and progresses through distinct stages such as created, in progress, and completed. The AI travel planning agent is responsible of assembling the final itinerary. In summary, A2A allows for a more distributed and efficient approach to creating the travel itinerary for a business or leisure traveler, with specialized AI Agents collaborating seamlessly to deliver a comprehensive service. The iterative process to finalize the itinerary is illustrated in Fig. 17.5.

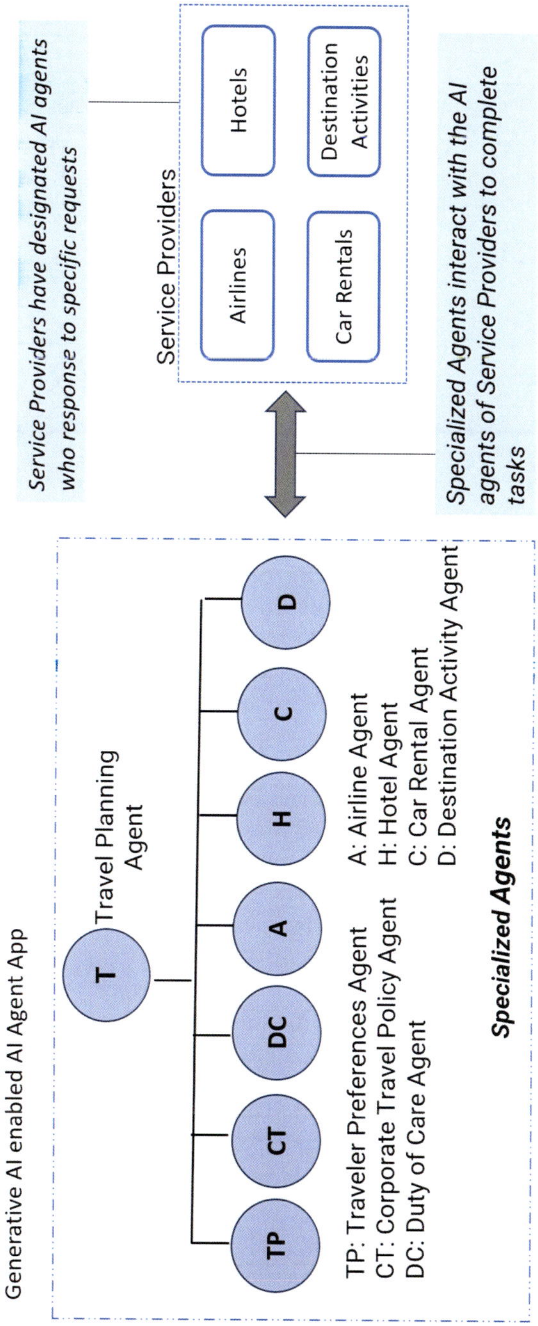

Fig. 17.4 AI Agents to book travel for business and leisure travelers

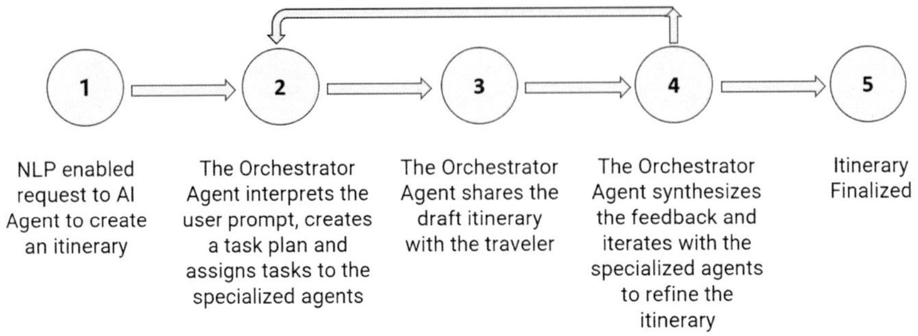

Fig. 17.5 The agentic AI workflow

Despite its benefits, A2A introduces challenges such as an increased risk of cyberattacks, and the difficulty in ensuring compliance with data requirements when exchanging sensitive data across systems While the A2A protocol is a crucial step towards a more interconnected AI ecosystem, addressing these challenges will be vital for its widespread adoption.

AI systems operate in centralized environments where trust is implicit. Perhaps, data exchanges and model interactions can be recorded with complete context and reasoning chain on a blockchain to ensure that the process is verifiable and tamper proof. Creating a "trust layer" with blockchain will change how Agentic AI systems will interact since every interaction can be cryptographically verified and immutably recorded. The blockchain ledger is distributed across a peer-to-peer network, with each node maintaining a copy. The decentralized framework eliminates the need for a central authority, making the system resilient to attacks and single points of failure. With blockchain, scalability, transaction throughput and latency, is a challenge that must be addressed.

17.11.4 Skepticism with AI Agents

In December 2025, the overwhelming consensus among experts is that AI Agents were far from reliable, but they represent the future. They work well with simple use cases and cannot yet handle complex workflows. They are prone to error leading to technical debt. AI Agents when deployed perform better than expected, and as time progresses the models accumulate compounding errors leading to erratic, unpredictable behavior. As customer expectations increase, the gap between the hype and reality is widening. The failure rates of AI Agents must be overcome for mass adoption.

AI Agents are in the very early stages of deployment. Despite the fact that OpenAI, Google, Anthropic, and others have introduced them in 2025, adoption rate is low. Unlike predictive AI or Generative AI models that simply produce content, autonomous AI Agents is a high-risk investment. Besides, using specialized agents for narrow tasks and agents for cross-verification can be expensive.

17.11.5 AI Agents and the Path Forward

The pace of Agentic AI development is widely considered unprecedented, marking a rapid shift from passive Generative AI (chatbots) to autonomous, goal-driven agents that can plan, execute and learn. The promise of multi-agent systems in travel planning is that they can be effective in reducing hallucinations in large language models (LLMs). By leveraging the interaction and collaboration capabilities of multiple specialized agents, these systems can improve the accuracy and reliability of AI-generated content with cross-verification and consensus building. Cross-verification helps identify inconsistencies and errors, allowing for a more reliable consensus to be reached. Further, specialized agents like the airline agent or the hotel agent work on narrow use cases, limiting errors. By assigning different tasks to specialized agents, the overall system can leverage their strengths and reduce the likelihood of errors or hallucinations. By directly incorporating knowledge from external systems such as supplier agents, the generated content is factual and not based on an LLMs internal knowledge, thereby minimizing the risk of hallucinations.

The travel planning process to finalize an itinerary is an iterative process, where agents critique and improve each other's outputs. This cycle of self-criticism and correction can help identify and eliminate errors or inconsistencies, leading to more accurate and reliable responses.

In summary, multi-agent systems offer a promising approach to mitigating hallucinations in LLMs by leveraging the strengths of multiple agents, promoting cross-verification, integrating external knowledge, and facilitating iterative refinement.

17.12 The AI Distribution Channel for Discovering, Planning, and Booking Destinations

Driven by advancements in technology, the travel industry is in the throes of a major revolution.

With artificial intelligence acting as a new distribution channel for discovering, planning and booking destinations. Instead of using search engines or online travel agencies (OTAs), leisure travelers are increasingly turning to AI-powered conversational agents for end-to-end trip management.

Agentic AI is all about LLM-powered AI Agents that are emerging as a new channel in airline distribution, transforming manual, search engine-based or app-driven shopping to autonomous AI Agent driven end-to-end- booking transactions. Intelligent agents acting on behalf of travelers will discover, compare, and book flights, fundamentally changing how consumers interact with travel suppliers.

The arrival of AI Agents also introduces the need for new capabilities that remain to be developed. These gaps will slow the pace of adoption of AI Agents.

17.12.1 Discovery

The first problem is discovery, for AI Agents to be aware of the destinations served by an airline and the value proposition. Unlike the manual process of browsing search engine results and booking flights, AI Agents do not browse but query and require structured machine-readable information about the services provided by an airline.

Airline messages were designed for human-readable channels. For example, a flight search query may return schedules, fares, images, icons, and rich formatting. AI Agents cannot recognize icons and images but process text and structured data. This requires airlines to publish their product catalog or brochure in a manner that AI Agents can consume. For example, an AI Agent may want to know the beach and ski destinations offered by an airline during discovery. This requires the data to be aggregated along several dimensions for AI Agents to query. The challenge that faces the airline industry is the absence of a common language for AI Agents to interpret machine-readable information from multiple airline systems. Like variations in NDC implementations, if airlines deploy MCP differently, AI Agents face an interpretation nightmare of epic proportions. The MCP protocol is standardized, but how airlines expose their brochure during discovery will vary and herein lies the challenge. Standardization in the form of a common language is required for AI Agents to work with multiple airline systems.

There are many approaches for an airline to expose machine-readable information to AI Agents. An approach is to use OLAP (OnLine Analytical Processing) engines, which are highly effective for airlines to support AI agent discovery, enabling them to analyze massive, multi-dimensional datasets regarding flight operations, on time performance, carbon offset, destination attributes, special packages offered, popular bundles by customer segment, weather, user preferences, etc. By providing rapid access to data cubes, AI agents can perform automated, discovery-driven analysis to spot trends, anomalies, and hidden relationships, such as identifying causes for delays or higher (or lower) selling fares than the norm in a market. Agents can execute rapid drill-down or roll-up queries across dimensions like time, route, and aircraft type to identify exceptions and match a traveler's preferences. By combining OLAP's structured data analysis capabilities with AI's predictive power, the airline industry can move from manual browsing and analysis to automated, intelligent decision-making.

Alternatives to traditional OLAP include cloud-native date warehouses (e.g., Google BigQuery, Snowflake, AWS Redshift) and distributed columnar databases (e.g., ClickHouse, StarRocks and Apache Druid).

17.12.2 Authentication and Authorization of AI Agents

The airline industry and the travel industry at large require an agent identification framework that does not exist today. AI Agents must have credentials that identify who they are, who operate them, and their permissions. Authentication verifies the identity of the AI Agent and authorization determines what the AI Agent is authorized to do within a system. Authentication is the first step that confirms the identify which then allows the system to apply authorization rules.

17.12.3 AI Agents and the Airline Environment for Direct Distribution

Figure 17.6 illustrates the environment for AI Agents to interact with the airline's environment for product distribution. The airline environment consists of the MCP Server middleware and the Core AI Platform that will interface with existing Core Airline Systems.

17.13 Potential Impact of AI Agents on the Travel Value Chain

The disruption of entrenched incumbents in the product distribution landscape with AI Agents is underway and the clear beneficiaries are the suppliers of travel such as airlines, hotels, short term vacation rentals, car rentals, cruise lines, and destination activity providers.

The primary goal for travel sellers is to provide travelers with exactly what they want at the lowest price. With the recent advances in conversational AI powered by large language models, travel distribution is on the verge of a major disruption. Over the next decade, travel intermediaries such as GDSs, Metasearch, OTAs and TMCs will be competing over a shrinking pie. The true beneficiary will be the service providers—airlines, hotels, car rentals, cruise lines, and destination activity providers.

When a customer wants to purchase travel, they primarily have five options: search engine (e.g. "cheap hotels in Las Vegas"), supplier direct, online travel agencies, travel management companies, and metasearch. Of the five options, corporate travel is managed travel, and the bookings are made through TMCs. Leisure travelers may engage with any of the five alternatives to make a booking. This is illustrated in Fig. 17.7.

The major players in the travel value chain are:

Service Providers (Suppliers). These include travel suppliers and destination activity providers. The service providers include airlines, hotel, car rentals, ride-hailing services, cruise lines, short term rentals, and destination activity providers like restaurants, museums, and local attractions.

Search Engines. Many potential customers begin their dream and plan phase of travel with a search engine such as Google, the dominant search engine, followed by the smaller players like Bing, etc. The search engines provide referral links to the source from which the content was accessed, such as an OTA or a supplier direct site. Using the link, the customer makes the booking directly with the service provider.

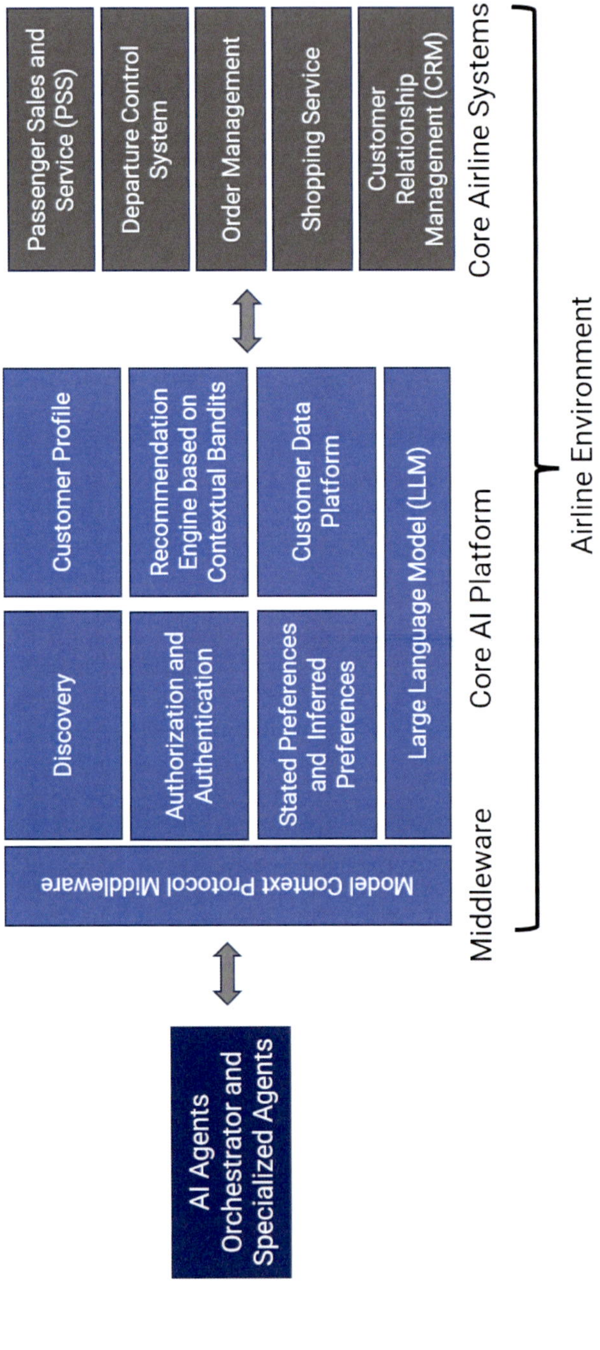

Fig. 17.6 AI Agents and the Airline Environment for Direct Distribution

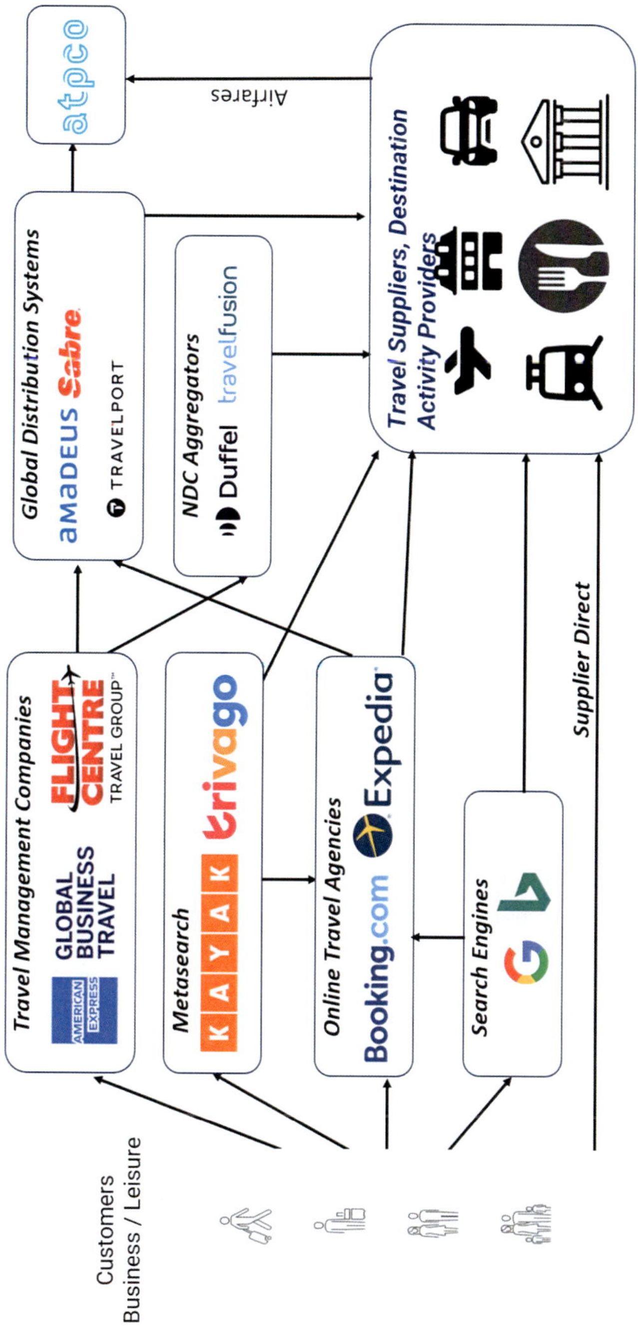

Fig. 17.7 A traveler's options to book travel

Travel Management Companies. Travel management companies (TMCs) are specialized travel agency that manages corporate or business travel programs for organizations. TMCs handle all aspects of business travel, from booking flights and accommodations to managing expenses and ensuring policy compliance, often utilizing technological solutions to streamline the process. The largest TMCs are American Express GBT and BCD Travel.

Many TMCs also provide support for leisure travel, not just corporate travel. While TMCs are often associated with managing business travel, they also offer services for individual and family vacations, including booking flights, accommodations, tours, and more. Some TMCs even specialize in both corporate and leisure travel, offering tailored experiences for both.

Online Travel Agencies. OTAs like Expedia and Booking.com provide access to air, hotel and rental car service providers. The OTAs integrate with a GDS for traditional air content. They also support direct connections with airlines for NDC content. Connectivity to non-air suppliers varies. Hotels distribute ARI (availability, rates, and inventory) to the OTAs..

Metasearch. Metasearch engines like Tripadvisor, Kayak, and Trivago help leisure customers take advantage of price discrepancy between the various discovery engines and service providers. The booking is made by an OTA or the service provider and the metasearch engine is compensated with a referral revenue.

AI is evolving from knowledge-based Generative AI tools like chatbots that answer questions and generate content to the next frontier, which is Generative AI enabled agents that use foundation models to execute complex workflows. The key advancement required is the ability to reason, plan and execute tasks. In the new world of Agentic AI, the discovery and booking will be dominated by these natural language enabled AI Agents.

A traveler can provide access to elements in the traveler's Universal Profile such as preferences for airline seats, hotel rooms (king size bed, queen sie bed, rooms close to the elevator, upper versus lower floor, etc.), loyalty programs, etc. In addition, for business travel, the AI agent can be informed about corporate travel policy, preferred travel suppliers, prohibited travel suppliers, etc. With access to this data, AI Agents can be personalized and knows the traveler's unique preferences.

Global Distribution Systems. The GDSs are the largest aggregators of travel data. After years of consolidation, the three major GDSs are Amadeus, Sabre, and Travelport. In the hybrid era they have access to traditional EDIFACT content and source NDC content directly from the FSCs. They also source content from LCCs. GDSs also connect to other travel verticals like hotels either directly or through DHISCO Distribution Hospitality Intelligent Systems Company, the successor to THISCO the UltraSwitch. The GDSs do not own the point of sale, but are connected to a network of travel agencies who subscribe to the GDS. They are one step removed from the customer.

ATPCO. ATPCO is the fare aggregator for the airline industry. They engage in the collection and distribution of fare and fare-related data. Airlines submit their fares and rules to ATPCO. The GDSs and airlines subscribe to ATPCO to access fares and rules to price itineraries.

NDC Aggregators. These are the new entrants in the travel marketplace that source NDC content directly from the airlines and distribute it to the point of saleusing the XML messaging standard. Examples are TPConnects, Duffel, Travelfusion, and many more. NDC Aggregators can source content from a GDS, but their primary focus is accessing NDC content directly from FSCs and LCCs. While they leverage GDSs for traditional EDIFACT-based air offers, their primary strength lies in aggregating content not readily available through GDSs.

17.13.1 Future Impact of AI Agents on the Travel Value Chain

The Model Context Protocol (MCP) introduces a new AI Agent enabled direct channel for travel suppliers. The MCP server acts as a direct channel enabler, allowing airlines to provide rich, contextual flight data directly to AI Agents to facilitate bookings, bypassing traditional intermediaries like GDSs and OTAs. It is a new technology layer for direct distribution, making airline schedules, fares and ancillaries understandable for AI Agents to offer travelers.

Figure 17.8 illustrates the travel value chain after introduction of the MCP direct channel enabler. NDC bookings made by non-GDS NDC Aggregators (e.g., TPConnects, AirGateway, etc.) are technically indirect bookings because they sit between the airline and the travel agency or corporate booking tool like a GDS, but they function similarly to direct. Unlike traditional GDS EDIFACT or NDC bookings (where GDS is the aggregator of NDC content), non-GDS NDC Aggregators avoid GDS surcharges and provide NDC-specific offers.

A direct API connection between an airline and a travel agency or corporate booking tool, bypassing GDSs, is considered a direct booking. Direct connect solutions are typically limited to specific partners such as OTAs and large corporate buyers. This approach also requires significant upfront investment to develop and maintain custom integrations with multiple airline partners.

Hotels and car rental companies already have a direct connection with the GDSs either directly or through DHISCO (formerly the UltraSwitch developed by THISCO) and they control the offer creation process. For example, when a travel agent makes a hotel booking request, the hotel reservations system returns applicable room rates and taxes.

When travel suppliers give API access to AI Agents, the market will determine how consumers prefer to book, whether it is supplier direct, a TMC, an OTA or using an app like WhatsApp, iMessage, or Signal that is powered by an AI Agent. This will also determine if there is a future role for TMCs, OTAs, (non-GDS) NDC Aggregators, and GDSs.

Agentic AI will emerge as a significant new channel and provide an enhanced capability to receive a targeted offer based on the traveler's unique preferences stored on the Universal Profile (see Chap. 6). A traveler's AI Agent can request an airline to price a custom package. For example, an infrequent traveler may want lounge access, free bags, and priority boarding, but does not care for airline miles.

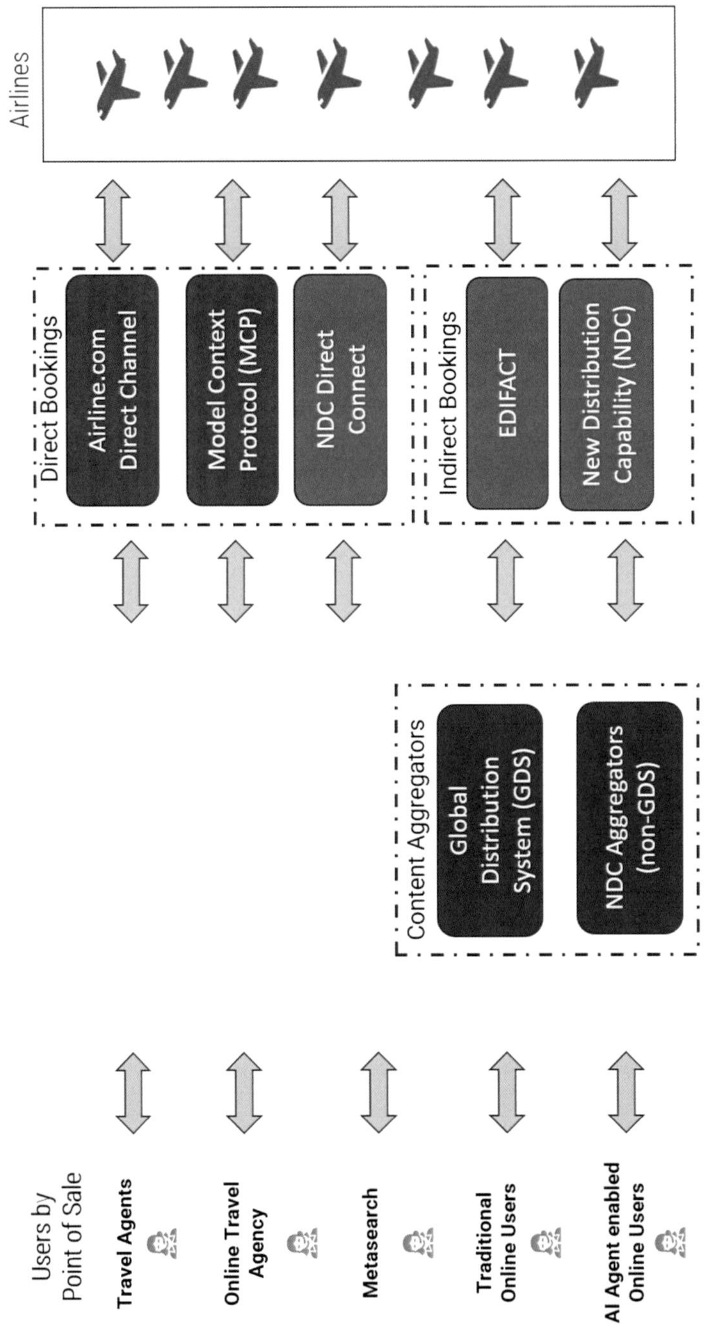

Fig. 17.8 The travel value chain with the MCP enabled direct channel

In the new world of Agentic AI, it is anticipated that travel intermediaries will undergo a significant transformation to fit into the travel ecosystem since the discovery and booking process will be dominated by natural language enabled AI Agents. If consumers gravitate toward the AI agent app, it will eliminate or transform the roles of most if not all of the intermediaries in the market today.

While AI Agents will be disruptive over the long term, there will be limited disruption to intermediaries like the GDSs over the next few years. This is because it takes time for airlines to stand up scalable MCP servers and also to reach negotiated agreements with AI Agents for secure access, exclusivity, permissions, commissions, booking fees, etc.

The travel industry requires an AI Agent identification framework that does not exist today. AI Agents that access airline systems must have credentials that identify who they are, who operates them, and their permissions that have been granted by the airline. In addition, there will be commercial agreements for content access. When the shift to AI Agents begins, metasearch and direct channels will be impacted first. The expected impact on managed travel (corporate travel) transacted through the GDSs will not be significant over the short term.

Service Providers (Suppliers)

The primary beneficiary of AI Agents are the travel suppliers such as airlines, hotels, short-term vacation rentals, car rentals, cruise lines and destination activity providers. AI Agents are being designed to connect directly with supplier websites and APIs, potentially bypassing traditional OTAs, and metasearch. Further, AI Agents support NDC direct bookings for airlines, eliminating the need for TMCs to access the GDS for access to content and make a booking.

Travel suppliers that connect directly with customers will succeed. AI Agents are objective and data driven. They will favor suppliers offering the best value and details. Travelers will not need to tell their AI Agents to bypass an OTA or other booking sites. AI Agents will find the best offers directly from airlines, hotels, etc. Travelers will not know or care about the intermediaries that were cut out of the process.

Search Engines

At the top of funnel for discovery with an AI agent there is no need to go to a search engine like Google or Bing to conduct a search and go to the service provider link to make a booking. LLM enabled AI Agents from ChatGPT, Gemini, Claude, Perplexity, and others can aid the discovery process. AI Agents can also be embedded in WhatsApp, iMessage, Signal, etc. What this means is that the links provided by search engines like Google will be disintermediated.

Travel Management Companies

Travel management companies (TMC) will leverage AI Agents to manage a higher volume of customer inquiries and requests, thereby enhancing efficiency and potentially serving more customers with a reduced workforce.

AI Agents will likely enhance, not completely replace, the value proposition of travel agents. AI agents streamline aspects of the booking process, and this can free up travel agents to focus on complex itineraries, customer support during disruptions, and building deeper relationships with clients—areas where the human element remains vital.

While TMCs will continue to provide customer service to their corporate clients, the role of the travel agents will change dramatically with the arrival of AI Agents. AI Agents will transform the role of TMCs, automating many routine tasks and enhancing human capabilities, rather than replacing them outright. However, this will result in a reduction in force at TMCs since fewer agents can manage more customers. Human oversight and accountability remain crucial in critical situations, as AI lacks the ability to analyze emotions or cultural sensitivities. Human travel agents will still be required to handle complex situations such as emergencies and aspects of duty of care that require nuanced judgement.

Online Travel Agencies

Online travel agencies have established infrastructure and partnerships with travel suppliers. They have developed robust financial models with the hotel merchant and agency models that command commissions in the 20% to 35% range. AI Agents provide an opportunity for travel suppliers (especially hotels where the commissions are the highest) to finally break free from the OTA stranglehold. For example, a hotel can pay a preferred placement with AI Agents for a fraction of the OTAs commission costs. AI Agents have the potential and will disintermediate the booking process: Travelers may choose to interact directly with AI Agents from airlines or hotels, bypassing traditional OTAs. OTAs need to evolve to avoid becoming irrelevant by adapting their business model, perhaps to focus on payments and customer support and service.

Expedia and Booking.com have some degree of protection because of their unique inventory of short-term vacation rentals. That inventory exists outside of the traditional GDS coverage and is something that the individual brand owns.

Airbnb as an OTA is unique and somewhat of an unknown in the world of AI Agents because of their closed ecosystem and unique one-of-a-kind supply. While the other OTAs have significant exposure to traditional hotels which is somewhat commoditized, none of Airbnb's properties are easily available anywhere else, besides some overlapping content with Booking.com and Expedia's VRBO (Vacation Rental By Owner). For this reason, Airbnb, and OTAs that have unique content will continue to have a role in the travel value chain.

Metasearch

Metasearch has the greatest exposure to AI Agents. AI Agents powered by LLMs will make metasearch engines irrelevant, but it will take time. This is because there is no reason to go to Kayak or Trivago to compare prices on Expedia, Booking.com and supplier sites when this information is available through the personal AI travel planning agent. AI Agents can interact directly with travel supplier websites and even other AI Agents, potentially bypassing traditional metasearch engines and online travel agencies (OTAs) for booking flights and accommodations.

AI Agents can proactively address potential travel disruptions (e.g., flight cancellations) by finding and rebooking alternative arrangements, potentially offering a more seamless experience than travelers currently get from metasearch engines or even some OTAs.

Metasearch companies remain optimistic about the future of metasearch, believing it can adapt and thrive alongside AI Agents. Metasearch platforms could evolve into a crucial middleware layer, providing AI Agents with comprehensive pricing and availability data, becoming a valuable backend resource in the evolving ecosystem.

TripAdvisor is a big unknown because they are not a full-fledged OTA like Expedia and Booking.com. Tripadvisor is primarily a metasearch engine, but it also incorporates elements of an OTA. It aggregates and displays hotel rates from various sources, allowing users to compare prices, similar to other metasearch engines. However, unlike a pure metasearch engine, Tripadvisor also facilitates bookings directly through its platform, blurring the lines between metasearch and OTA. While it facilitates bookings *through partnerships* with hotels and OTAs, it does not directly handle payments or customer service for those bookings. Tripadvisor is primarily a meta search engine and travel research company. Their primary strength is user generated content consisting of user reviews and opinions. This content is valuable and perhaps Tripadvisor will develop a business model to monetize this data with AI Agents.

Global Distribution Systems

GDS platforms like Amadeus, Sabre, and Travelport are deeply entrenched in the travel industry and have been adapting to changing technologies for decades. They are integrating new distribution capabilities (NDC) and embracing emerging technologies like AI to stay competitive.

Regardless, the long-term viability of GDSs is debatable. With NDC direct connect to travelers, is there still room for an aggregator of travel content in the ecosystem? Autonomous AI Agents can access NDC content directly from airlines. With the A2A protocol, AI Agents can collaborate with other AI Agents to create a passenger travel itinerary on request. However, the impact of AI Agents on corporate travel will be minimal over the next few years. The long-term survival of GDSs as aggregators requires them to have unique content, which they do not.

The largest question is how long will EDIFACT and the associated GDS incentives to travel agents last? The pace of decline of the GDS model will be influenced by how long agency incentives for EDIFACT transactions will persist. While agency incentives from the GDS will decline with NDC adoption, they will persist during the hybrid era when XML and EDIFACT have to co-exist.

GDS platforms could evolve into a middleware layer that provides AI Agents with comprehensive pricing and availability data, becoming a valuable backend resource in the evolving ecosystem with a new commercial model. Perhaps the

GDS MCP server can support discovery (see Sect. 7.15.1.1), making airlines visible to AI Agents.

ATPCO. ATPCO serves as a central industry utility for publishing and distributing airline fare and fare-related data, like pricing rules, taxes, and fees. With the airline's focus on direct sales, it will eventually render ATPCO irrelevant for fare distribution to GDSs. While airlines have a choice not to transmit fares to ATPCO, they probably will, since ATPCO also distributes the same data to the airlines to support the direct channel. This facilitates interoperability across pricing, ancillary products, amenities, and settlement.

In the hybrid era and post hybrid era, AI Agents can receive itineraries directly from the airline and have no reliance on a feed from ATPCO. In the post hybrid era, the GDS will not price any itineraries. However, it is expected that most airlines will continue to use ATPCO to support the direct channel. In the absence of a need to distribute airfares to GDSs, perhaps the current ATPCO business model will be transformed to serve as a central repository that manages complex data for air fares, fare rules, and amenities, to exclusively support airline controlled direct sales.

NDC Aggregators

NDC Aggregators are the new entrant aggregators of airline NDC content. Examples are Travelfusion, Duffel, TPConnects, and AirGateway. Their primary strength is aggregating LCC content and NDC content from full-service carriers which can easily be replicated by AI Agents. Perhaps some of them will be acquired by TMCs to fill a short-term void for NDC content access. Travelfusion is owned by Trip.com which owns China's largest OTA, Ctrip, and Flight Centre, the seventh largest travel agency in the world, has a 70% majority stake in TPConnects [Fox, 2022a]. The long-term viability of non-GDS NDC Aggregators is not promising unless they find a new role to support discovery by AI Agents (see Sect. 7.15.1.1).

17.14 Current State Versus Future State in Evolution of Agentic AI

Agentic AI, which represents a leap beyond traditional and even Generative AI, focuses on creating autonomous systems capable of acting and making decisions with minimal human intervention. AI Agents such as ChatGPT, Claude, Gemini and hundreds of specialized travel chatbots are transitioning from answering questions to executing booking transactions.

This evolution of autonomous agents is still in its early stages and different frameworks categorize AI Agents in different ways. However, a commonly recognized classification identifies six main types based on their level of intelligence and decision-making capabilities:

Figure 17.9 illustrates the progression of AI Agents, and we are currently at Level 3.

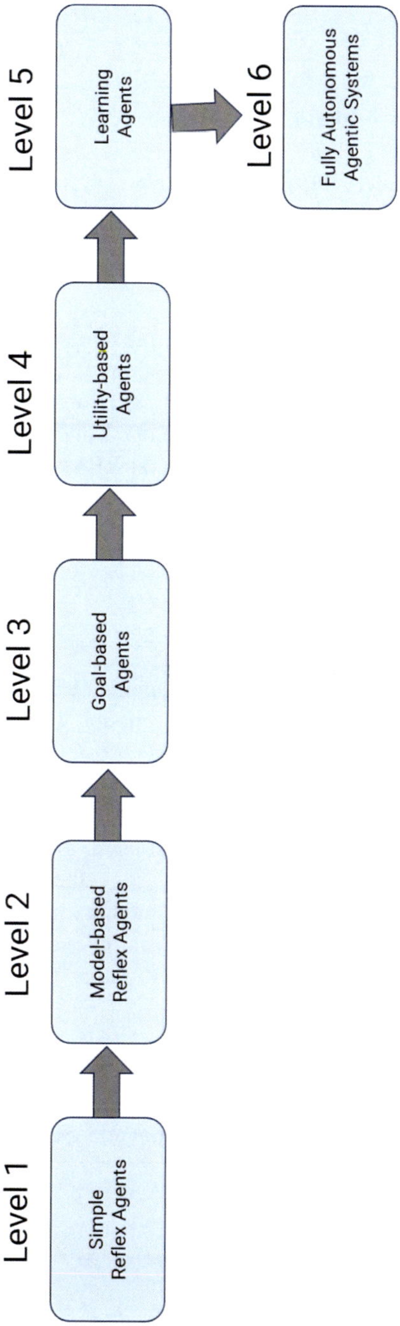

Fig. 17.9 The Evolution of AI agents

Different frameworks categorize AI Agents in different ways. A common classification identifies six key types that are based on their intelligence and decision-making capabilities.

17.14.1 Simple Reflex Agents

These are the most rudimentary form of AI Agents. They make decisions based on a predefined set of rules and the current state of their environment, without considering past experiences or future consequences. They are essentially reactive, acting immediately upon sensing a specific condition. These agents have no memory of past states and cannot learn or adapt beyond their programmed rules. Therefore they can make the same mistakes if the predefined rules are insufficient for handling new situations. These agents follow simple "if–then" rules, making them suitable for basic, repetitive tasks in dynamic environments.

Robotic Process Automation (RPA) bots, developed in the late 1990s or early 2000s, are often compared to simple reflex agents. RPAs can automate a wide range of tasks across various industries often involving repetitive rule-based processes. Examples are data entry and validation, invoice processing, etc.

17.14.2 Model-Based Reflex Agents

Model-based reflex agents enhance simple reflex agents by incorporating an internal world model of the environment. This internal model allows them to consider past states and predict future outcomes, leading to more informed decisions. The agent also tracks how its own actions affect the environment. Examples include self-driving cars, robotic vacuum cleaners, and some industrial robots.

Model-based reflex agents are generally considered to be semi-autonomous agents. They have limited autonomy and they bridge the gap between simple automation and full autonomy by incorporating memory and context into their decision-making process. A self-driving car is an example of a model-reflex agent that reacts to obstacles but also tracks traffic flow to make nuanced decisions than just a simple "if/then" response.

While ChatGPT and Claude don't operate on predefined rules like model-based reflex agents, they do utilize an internal "model" of how language works, which is learned from vast amounts of training data. This enables them to respond intelligently and in a human-like manner to prompts and questions.

17.14.3 Goal-Based Agents

Goal-based agents are designed to pursue specific objectives. They plan sequences of actions to achieve desired outcomes by considering the future consequences of their choices. Goal-based agents use search and planning algorithms to find action sequences that lead to their goals. Goal based agents are widely used in robotics and simulations where a clear objective is set and adaptations to the environment is required.

In travel planning, goal-based agents use specific objectives to guide their actions, selecting the best path to reach a desired destination or outcome. Examples include autonomous vehicles using GPS to navigate, AI-powered itinerary planners suggesting optimized routes and activities and even travel agents using AI to manage bookings and customize travel plans. These agents evaluate different options and select the most efficient or beneficial route to achieve their goal.

OpenAI's Operator agent is positioned as a Level 3 AI agent in OpenAI's framework, representing a significant step towards achieving artificial general intelligence (AGI). This means Operator is designed to autonomously perform web-based tasks and navigate complex workflows, marking a leap beyond simpler AI Agents

While ChatGPT and Claude (which are Large Language Models (LLMs) can be integrated into AI agent systems to provide capabilities like reasoning and language generation, they themselves are not considered full-fledged goal-based agents. In essence, while AI Agents can be built that leverage the strengths of ChatGPT or Claude for tasks like planning and reasoning, these LLMs themselves are more like tools or components within a broader agent system, rather than the autonomous agents operating on their own.

17.14.4 Utility-Based Agents

Utility-based Agents go beyond simple goal achievement by using a utility function to evaluate the value of different outcomes. This allows them to handle trade-offs between competing goals and choose the action that maximizes overall utility. Utility defines a preference value for a specific outcome. The expected utilities for future states can be ranked to pick the most desirable outcome.

Utility-based agents in travel optimize decision-making by assigning numerical values (utilities) to different outcomes and choosing the action that maximizes overall utility. Examples include self-driving cars optimizing routes based on safety, speed, and fuel efficiency, and travel planning applications recommending hotels and flights considering user preferences and cost.

Utility-based agents are not labeled semi-autonomous agents. They are both types of AI Agents, but they differ in their approach to decision-making. Utility-based agents prioritize maximizing a specific utility function, while semi-autonomous agents have a degree of independence in their actions, often within a larger system. Essentially, utility-based agents are focused on optimizing a specific outcome, while semi-autonomous agents are more broadly capable of independent action and decision making.

17.14.5 Learning Agents

Learning agents are capable of improving their performance over time through experience and feedback from the environment. They typically consist of four main components: a learning element, a critic, a performance element, and a problem generator. The learning element updates the agent's knowledge based on feedback from the critic, which evaluates the agent's actions against a predefined performance standard, according to IBM. The numerical feedback signal is called a reward in reinforcement learning and this reward is passed to a learning element that updates the agent's knowledge using the feedback from the critic. The performance element selects actions based on what the learning element has determined to be optimal, and the problem generator suggests exploratory new actions to help the agent discover new strategies.

Learning agents in travel, particularly those employing AI and machine learning, are revolutionizing how people plan and experience trips. They personalize travel planning, automate tasks, and improve overall efficiency. Examples include AI-powered chatbots for booking and itinerary creation, recommendation systems that tailor suggestions based on past behavior, and systems that optimize pricing and identify potential travel disruptions.

Learning agents are often considered to be a type of semi-autonomous agent. While learning agents are designed to improve their performance through experience and adapt their behavior, they still often require human oversight and guidance, especially when dealing with complex or novel situations.

In many cases, the different types of agents with varying capabilities may be assembled together to create a multi-agent system where multiple agents operate in a shared environment working proactively to achieve a common goal.

17.14.6 Fully Autonomous Agentic Systems

Fully autonomous agentic systems represent the next frontier in AI. It is a significant step-improvement in artificial intelligence, pushing beyond the capabilities of traditional and even Generative AI models. Fully autonomous agents require a world model which is an internal, dynamic representation of their environment. They are designed to operate independently, reason, plan, adapt, learn, and self-improve to achieve complex goals with minimal or no human intervention.

The key traits of fully autonomous agentic systems of the future include:

1. Autonomy. The ability to make decisions and act independently to achieve a goal.
2. Goal-Driven: Focuses on achieving specific objectives rather than simply following predefined rules or responding to prompts.
3. Adaptability & Continuous Learning: Utilize machine learning and deep learning to continuously improve performance, learn from experience, and adjust to dynamic environments.

4. Interpretation and Usage of Tools. Can perceive and interact with their environment (both physical and digital), process information, understand context, and leverage external tools and systems (e.g., software, APIs, databases, the Internet) to complete tasks.
5. Orchestration: Can coordinate and direct the actions of other systems and agents to achieve a common goal.
6. Memory: Possess both short-term memory (for immediate context) and long-term memory (for learning and improvement).

Despite the promise, fully autonomous agentic systems are many years into the future. Beyond the core technical complexities, they must address ethical concerns, hallucinations, data security data privacy, computing power and related infrastructure costs. Despite the hurdles, fully autonomous agentic systems hold immense potential in travel in the areas of travel agency automation, self-service automation, and customer service.

The future of AI autonomy promises a world where AI Agents can work alongside humans, automating complex tasks and unlocking new possibilities in travel.

These six levels ranging from the purely reactive to the fully autonomous AI Agents represent increasing levels of sophistication in AI agent capabilities.

17.15 Agentic AI Frameworks for Automating Travel Agency Workflows

Organizations can build AI Agents from scratch by using programming languages such as Python or JavaScript. However, a quicker, more scalable approach involves using AI agent frameworks to develop, deploy, and manage AI Agents. These frameworks have built in features and functions such as predefined architecture, communication protocols that facilitate interaction between AI Agents, integration tools to access functions, task management to coordinate tasks, and real-time monitoring to track performance. Using frameworks streamlines and speeds up the deployment process.

There are several Agentic AI frameworks that can be used for automating travel agency tasks. Examples are AutoGen and CrewAI being prominent choices. AutoGen, developed by Microsoft, is a powerful platform for building multi-agent systems that can handle complex tasks through conversations between agents, making it ideal for automating complex travel agency workflows. CrewAI, known for its user-friendly, no-code interface, is suitable for quickly creating simple AI Agents to automate tasks or handle customer queries. There are other options as well such as LangChain and LangGraph to build multi-agent systems. The exhaustive list is very fluid and beyond the scope of this book.

17.15.1 GDSs and Agentic APIs

In September 2025, Sabre announced [Sabre, 2025b] the launch of new agentic APIs to facilitate the development of AI Agents capable of autonomously handling various travel-related tasks, from shopping, booking and servicing across flights, hotels and post-booking operations. The press release claims the development of a proprietary Model Context Protocol (MCP) server which acts as a "universal translator" that turns the complex language of travel technology into something any AI agent can understand. This is illustrated in Fig. 17.10.

The new interfaces allow third-party travel industry AI Agents to autonomously shop, book, service, and optimize trips, integrating into Sabre Mosaic (a cloud-native marketplace built on top of the Sabre GDS) platform to enable automated workflows. Powered by the Sabre IQ AI layer and the Sabre Data Cloud, a partnership with Google, these APIs use a Model Context Protocol (MCP) server to translate travel language, enabling agents to execute complex tasks like rebooking during disruptions or confirming late-night hotel arrivals without human intervention.

All the Agentic AI APIs are integrated into Sabre Mosaic that provides access to travel agents. Some examples Sabre provides of Agentic AI impacting travel include a call center proxy agent to handle same day rebooking during disruptions in flight operations, itinerary changes,

A fundamental issue with any GDS developing and promoting agentic APIs is access to comprehensive content. It would have made perfect sense in the era of full content agreements between airlines and GDSs. In the NDC era, many airlines bypass full content agreements with GDSs and may distribute some fares exclusively through the airline-direct NDC gateway. The airline direct NDC gateway is a connection that allows travel agencies and travelers to directly access airline offers through APIs, bypassing GDSs using the NDC standards for shopping, booking, ticketing, and payment. Further, airlines want control of the offer creation process to promote differentiation and personalization with travelers.

What really matters is the quality of the airline content—schedules, fares and ancillaries, which Sabre, Amadeus and Travelport may be deficient in. In the NDC era, offer creation is under the airline's control, ensuring the airline's agentic APIs remain the best source for content for third party AI Agents to consume directly. It is highly unlikely that AI Agents will seriously consider using any type of travel

Fig. 17.10 Sabre's MCP server and agentic AI APIs

aggregator agentic APIs because00 of the content gap. The survival of the GDS in its current form will require unique content which they do not have.

Besides the content gap issue, if AI Agents become a significant distribution channel, it is highly unlikely that airlines will cede control of this channel to GDSs or any other intermediaries. They will develop their own MCP APIs for third party distribution channels like ChatGPT, Claude and Gemini, because they want to control the offer creation process..

A related issue with the GDS MCP server is how does a GDS expect to be compensated? Charging a fee for accessing the agentic APIs will not work since supplier versions will be provided at no cost. The only plausible option is GDS bookings which will require that the third-party AI Agents must queue up the PNRs or Orders for an agency to complete the booking process. Beyond the TMC community, this means that GDSs will have to maintain an agency to process these bookings or queue the PNRs or Orders to existing agencies to manage bookings within their existing workflow. An alternative path is a licensed Host Agency where the AI Agent acts as a sub-agent and uses the credentials of the Host Agency to search and complete the booking. The commercial models are evolving.

Sabre's investment in the MCP Server to support future Agentic AI transactions is a broad reflection that it will cause broad disruption across all channels. While metasearch is vulnerable over the short term, the GDSs will also be impacted in a few years. Large technology platforms armed with AI Agents could emerge as new channels like the OTAs did in the late 1990s, and Sabre intends to get its fair share of bookings in the hybrid era. To accelerate adoption in the corporate travel space, Sabre acquired a minority stake and is partnering with BizTrip.AI to develop AI-powered corporate travel assistants for automating complex bookings [Sabre, 2026]. In February 2026, Amadeus acquired New York based SkyLink, further signalling Agentic AI's disruptive potential for the travel industry [Amadeus, 2026]. The acquisition will improve the corporate travel experience by enabling more automated travel bookings by leveraging SkyLink's AI-driven conversational technology to its product portfolio to assist travelers on the road.

17.15.1.1 Co-Existence of GDS MCP Servers and Airline MCP Servers

With NDC, a core objective pf an airline is to control all offers and ensure they are differentiated based on context for travel. Airline control of offers will not change with MCP. Perhaps the GDS MCP servers and NDC Aggregator (non-GDS) MCP Servers can support discovery (see Sect. 7.12.1), making airlines visible to AI Agents.

Discovery cannot be handled by a single airline and requires an aggregator (multi-airline content) MCP server. The GDS/Aggregator MCP server can create the common language for AI Agents to interpret machine-readable information from multiple airline systems. In addition, it can also absorb the millions of exploratory queries from AI Agents that can overwhelm individual airline systems. The GDS/Aggregator MCP server can also authenticate AI Agents before sending qualified leads to the pertinent airline-owned MCP servers. The airline

MCP servers are responsible for orchestration that interprets context for travel and coordinates internal systems to generate the offer and price for the bundle.

This type of model will result in a new commercial model between GDSs and airlines for qualified leads paid as a referral fee by the airlines. The GDS/Aggregator MCP servers can also facilitate paid placements, such as sponsored airline offers, directly into the context sent to AI Agents. This allows airlines to pay for higher visibility in AI-driven search results and enables them to receive incrementally qualified leads, mimicking traditional search ads. In this new role to support discovery of airlines by AI Agents, airlines will no longer restrict access to the lowest fares such as Basic Economy to the GDSs since they do not make bookings but provide a qualified lead to the airline MCP servers to facilitate direct bookings.

The co-existence of GDS/Aggregator MCP servers and Airline MCP servers to support discovery and offer creation is illustrated in Fig. 17.11.

17.16 AI Agents and the Impact on Air Shopping

The rise of AI Agents means that shopping for flights will become infinitely more fragmented, as every agent acts on behalf of a unique individual. The volume of air shopping searches is expected to grow substantially and evolve from manual user queries to autonomous, personalized transactions. AI Agents will become the primary interface for shopping, and traditional search and browse activities will decline. The total volume of agent-driven transactions is expected to rise. The market could expand as AI makes travel planning easier for less tech-savvy or time-constrained consumers.

Inspirational shopping requests will increase with AI Agents, which leads to an increase in shopping volumes. For instance, a user could simply ask for a “relaxing beach vacation” or “ski resort in the western U.S.” and an AI Agent would evaluate multiple destinations before creating a personalized itinerary with flight options, accommodations, and activities.

To offset the extreme look-oi-book shopping volumes generated by AI Agents, airlines must invest in an ultra-fast shopping engine that embraces fare and rule binding for faster shopping responses [Vinod, 2024a, Chap. 8]. This is mandatory for personalized offers. If personalization for a segment of ONE is not required, then investment in a shopping cache is also required (see Sect. 6.22.3) to mitigate the cost of compute.

With the anticipated massive query volumes in the future, an aggregator MCP server may be required since thousands of AI Agents querying airline systems is not an option.

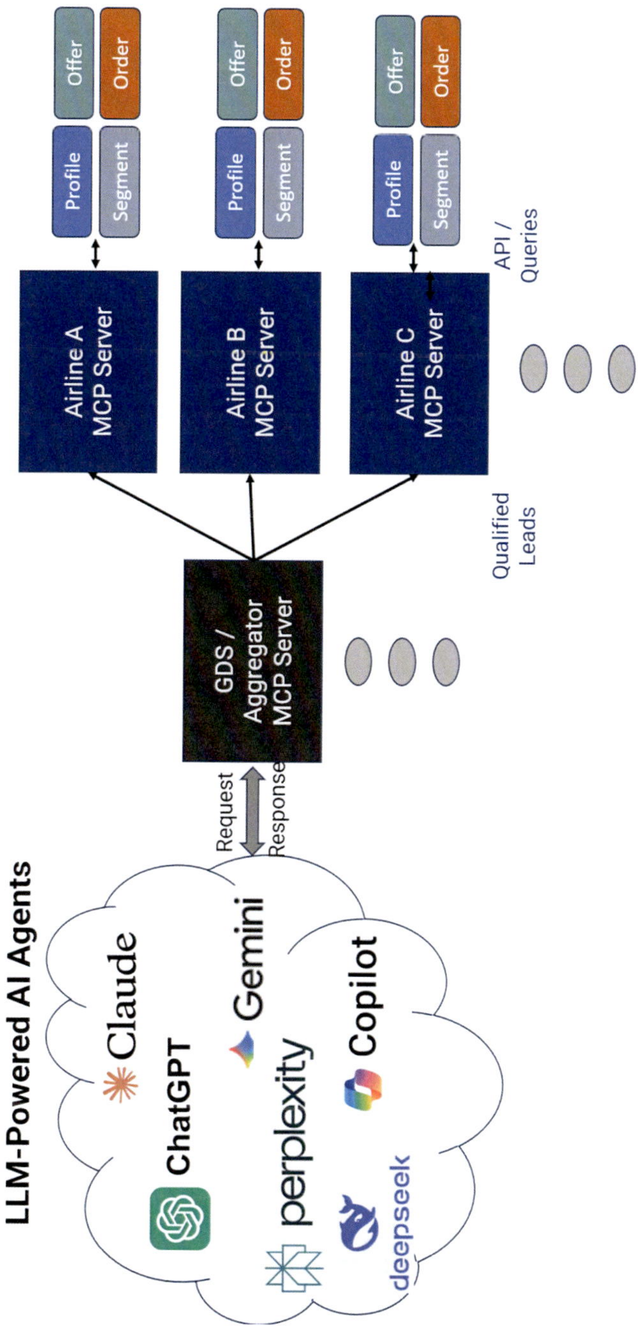

Fig. 17.11 Co-existence of GDS/Aggregator and airline MCP servers

17.17 Will Agentic AI and AI Assistants Make Supplier Websites and Mobile Apps Obsolete?

Agentic AI and personal AI Assistants will significantly transform how users interact with the Internet. While it is difficult to predict, it is unlikely they will make travel supplier websites completely obsolete. In this new era, websites must adapt to a new "AI-first" approach, where they are designed to be easily navigated and understood by both humans and AI Agents.

AI Agents are a new interaction paradigm. Agentic AI enables a "no-apps" paradigm, where AI Agents can handle tasks across multiple services without requiring users to open multiple separate apps. They are also context-aware and conversational. App usage is expected to go down as Agentic AI and Personal AI Assistants go mainstream and users increasingly rely on AI Assistants for tasks that were traditionally handled by apps.

While app usage will inevitably decline, apps are expected to survive for the following reasons:

1. Many apps have specialized functionality, designed for specific tasks and offer tailored interfaces and features that may be difficult to replicate or replace.
2. Users are a creature of habit and want to be in their comfort zone. Many users prefer the intuitive interfaces and familiar interactions of traditional apps, particularly for complex or specialized tasks.
3. Privacy and data control is a sweet spot for apps. Many users may prefer to keep their data local rather than rely on cloud-based services.

It is expected that in the future AI Assistants and traditional apps will coexist, though app usage will decline over time. While Agentic AI and Personal AI Assistants will change how we interact with technology, they are more likely to reshape the mobile app landscape and introduce new forms of interaction rather than render traditional apps obsolete. A hybrid future is anticipated, where dedicated apps and AI Assistants each use their strengths, providing a more integrated and personalized digital experience.

17.18 Amazon V. Perplexity Lawsuit and the Future of Autonomous Agents

Amazon filed a federal lawsuit against AI startup Perplexity on November 4, 2025, in U.S. District Court for the Northern District of California in San Francisco. This is a David vs. Goliath battle at the start of the Agentic AI period. Amazon accuses Perplexity's "Comet" AI browser of covertly accessing customer accounts and automating online purchases which violates Amazon's terms of service and poses security risks by disguising itself as a normal user.

The *Amazon v. Perplexity* lawsuit is a landmark legal battle that will shape the future of autonomous agents by determining their legal status and interaction rules on the Internet. It will also dictate the pace of innovation with Agentic AI. The core dispute is whether an AI agent acting on behalf of a user is an authorized representative (Perplexity's view) or a prohibited bot (Amazon's view).

Perplexity argues the agent is an extension of the user with the same permissions as a human browsing the web. They view the lawsuit as Amazon's attempt to protect its multi-billion-dollar advertising revenue stream which is threatened by AI Agents that can bypass sponsored listings and programmatically find the best product based on the user's preferences.

Amazon seeks an injunction to stop Perplexity's access, on the grounds that companies reserve the right to control how platforms are accessed. If Amazon wins, it will slow down AI-driven innovation across the web.

Amazon v. Perplexity is a pivotal case that will help define the rules for engagement with AI Agents and e-commerce. The court ruling could determine if platforms can create "walled gardens" by blocking third-party AI Agents, or if the Internet will remain "open-by-default" as it is today, allowing AI Agents to act autonomously on behalf of users across all platforms.

The *Amazon v. Perplexity* lawsuit reflects the ongoing evolution of AI Agents and AI Assistants. The ruling in this case will significantly impact AI development, business models, and data ownership.

17.18.1 Impact on Travel

The Amazon lawsuit could have far reaching ramifications on travel. The question is whether legacy intermediaries will continue to exercise control or will it lead to the creation of successful alternative new native AI Agent channels. In the context of this legal battle, Amazon is the "incumbent" or "legacy platform".

OTAs, metasearch, and travel suppliers have built businesses around a predictable mix of paid search, SEO, brand recognition and app loyalty.

If Amazon Prevails:

If Amazon prevails, AI companies investing in AI Agents will have to adhere to stricter data licensing and clear attribution requirements. Incumbents would retain more visibility. The impacts on key players in the travel value chain are reviewed below.

Global Distribution Systems

The primary impact on GDSs would be the reinforcement of a "permission-based" model for AI Agents in commerce, likely forcing AI companies into formal partnerships with GDSs and their suppliers. The outcome would help preserve the existing revenue streams of GDSs, though it is in decline with NDC. The GDS is also at a disadvantage with the erosion of full content agreements, and they can no longer guarantee access to the lowest fares in the market.

Online Travel Agencies

OTAs would retain more control over the direct customer relationship and data. This would allow them to continue building loyalty programs and personalized experiences, which AI Agents currently tend to ignore in favor of utility and price.

The OTAs would continue to exercise control over customer relationships and enforce formal partnership agreements with AI Agents. For the OTAs, AI Agents will serve as a high-fidelity programmatic acquisition channel and be part of the OTA affiliate program like traditional travel agents. Like the travel agency affiliates, AI Agents will have access to OTA inventory through OTA managed APIs, and they will also have to adhere to strict guidelines for attribution and branding that the AI Agent must explicitly cite.

Travel Management Companies

The legal precedent would favor platform control over autonomous AI Agents, forcing the travel industry to adopt a more regulated and permission-based AI ecosystem. TMCs will continue to exercise control over customer relationships. In all likelihood, TMCs would be restricted to using only authorized AI Agents that operate within the rules set by travel suppliers such as airlines, hotels, and GDSs. This would limit the use of independent, cross-platform AI Agents that shop for the best deals across various sites without permission.

TMCs would have to expose "policy-aware" APIs that can be accessed by authorized third-party agents under agreed upon terms, including transparency and audit trails for duty of care.

Metasearch

Metasearch would retain more control over the direct customer relationship and data. Sites like Kayak and Skyscanner can technically block AI Agents and web scrapers, but they are still at risk since AI Agents with user context will provide superior customer experience.

Travel Suppliers

Suppliers gain leverage in direct distribution, as they could use the legal precedent to enforce terms of service against AI Agents, pushing AI Agents to become new, high-fidelity acquisition channels. Travel suppliers will continue investing in the direct channel, which will be augmented with the new AI Agents that serve as alternatives to the OTA channel to diversify their distribution mix.

If Perplexity Prevails

If Perplexity wins its lawsuit against Amazon, Global Distribution Systems (GDS) and the broader travel industry could face accelerated disruption through an "open-by-default" web, empowering independent AI Agents to bypass traditional booking channels and negotiate directly with suppliers.

Global Distribution Systems

AI Agents, acting as true digital representatives for users, could directly access and book inventory from various airline and hotel websites, diminishing the GDS's traditional role as the central hub for inventory aggregation and bookings of air content. The GDS is also handicapped with the erosion of full content agreements, and they can no longer guarantee access to the lowest fares in the market.

The primary revenue streams for GDSs, segment booking fees, could be threatened. They would need to transition from simply being booking platforms to providing additional value-added services or creating "certified agent programs" with specific conditions for AI Agents.

Airlines and hotels might further invest in their direct booking channels, leveraging AI to offer personalized experience and potentially bypassing GDS fees altogether, using AI gatekeepers as alternative distribution channels.

Travel Management Companies

This will lead to a rapid proliferation of AI Agents that can shop across various channels to find the best options for a user programmatically, bypassing traditional booking workflows and potentially eroding brand loyalty.

TMCs need to focus more on robust, high-value services (e.g., duty of care, policy compliance, complex itinerary management) that AI Agents may not fully replicate autonomously. Further, the existing GDS incentives, and advertising models that form the backbone of the travel industry would be threatened.

Online Travel Agencies

The OTAs could face significant disruption and a potential loss of market share as AI Agents gain the freedom to browse, compare, and book across the Internet without requiring explicit permission or traditional licensing. AI Agents serving as a customer's representative to shop across various channels, will lead to a proliferation of AI Agents in the travel space. AI Agents could consolidate the user experience, eliminating the need for users to visit multiple OTA websites. "Funnel compression" would limit OTAs' visibility and ability to capture customer demand and ad revenue.

Large hotel chains would bypass the OTAs in preference to AI Agent bookings. AI Agents that do not have direct relationships with small hotel chains and independents will access OTAs for their content but will own the customer relationship. Google Ad revenues and OTA ad revenues (e.g., banner ads) will be negatively impacted since the AI Agents do not care about an optimized booking funnel. Survival of the OTAs will be contingent on entrenched customer loyalty based on engagement and curation of content.

Metasearch

AI Agents can directly access suppliers to find the best itineraries based on user preferences and context. Metasearch engines like Kayak and Skyscanner would face heightened risk of disruption by AI Agents that can provide a superior, more personalized, end-to-end user experience, potentially bypassing the traditional metasearch interface entirely. The metasearch engines may survive as high-speed aggregators for an interim period.

Travel Suppliers

Hotels and airlines will provide access to AI Agents. Suppliers that get ahead of competitors will be the ones with a well-defined infrastructure for instant access to personalized content from both AI Agents and human agents. Hotels will see a significant drop in the cost of customer acquisition when AI Agents disintermediate the leading OTAs.

17.18.2 Legal Action and Investment Irony

Ironically, Perplexity runs on Amazon Web Services, uses Amazon SageMaker for its machine learning and Amazon Bedrock for accessing foundation models. In addition, Amazon founder Jeff Bezos is an investor in Perplexity. Amazon is suing a company backed by its founder. Perhaps, Amazon wants registered AI Agents to pay an annual subscription fee for the privilege of shopping on Amazon?

Future State and Gaining a Competitive Edge

18

Opportunities multiply as they are seized.

Sun Tzu, author of the Art of War

Abstract

The last chapter in this book discusses the future state of pricing revenue management and product distribution and the step airlines must take to gain a competitive edge. The airline marketing planning process will continue to evolve in an AI-enabled landscape, adding sophistication to the modeling process. The future of user experience belongs to AI assistants which are transforming the user experience by enabling personalization, automation and proactive support.

Door-to-door travel will become reality in an AI-enabled world. This is a complete travel service from start to finish. Agentic AI will have the greatest impact on travel over the next decade. Based on recent trends, the future of personalization and competitive revenue management are reviewed.

Buyer expectations from the TMC of the future will change as they refactor the technology stack for cost effectiveness and competitiveness. Factors include advances in Agentic AI, limit or eliminate GDS dependency for content, and flexible service models that are not solely transaction based,

Blockchain technology, where the distributed nodes operate peer-to-peer (P2P) without an intermediary in travel represents the future of the industry. It has the potential to become the new travel platform. The chapter concludes with a discussion on the importance of strategic agility for resilient organizations to maintain a competitive edge.

B. Vinod, *The Era of Airline Revenue Management with Offers and Orders*, Management for Professionals, https://doi.org/10.1007/978-3-032-24197-9_18

Sun Tzu, the Chinese military general, strategist and philosopher who lived during the Eastern Zhou period (771–256 BC) believed that proactive action and seizing opportunities are key to success in war. He stressed the importance of always being ready to maximize the opportunities that are presented. Acting on one opportunity, others will be created and reveal additional ones, leading to a cycle of growth. Instead of a single chance, seizing an opportunity can lead to a ripple effect of future successes, much like a small seed growing into a larger plant. Sun Tzu emphasizes that action is more important than hesitation, as opportunities are made by being acted upon rather than simply being observed.

The transition from selling an airline seat to offers and orders is challenging with business process changes, significant financial investment in technology, and upskilling the workforce. Airlines that demonstrate strategic agility in this new era will have a definitive first-mover advantage and distance themselves from the rest of the pack. Pioneering a market strategy gains significant advantages such as brand recognition and customer loyalty ahead of the competition.

18.1 Overview

The final chapter in this book discusses the future state of pricing, revenue management, inventory control, product distribution and the steps airlines must take to gain a competitive edge. A range of relevant topics is reviewed, including adjacencies to revenue management.

The airline industry is a notoriously competitive environment where constant innovation and adaptation are required for survival and growth. A workplace environment where new ideas, creativity, and continuous improvement are deeply embedded in the organization's daily operations, encouraging everyone from the CEO to interns to contribute without fear of failure. This is achieved through open, direct communication, psychological safety, and a willingness to take risks and learn from failures, allowing the business to adapt, grow, and stay competitive.

Airlines must continuously strive to gain a competitive advantage in a market characterized by intense competition, changes in the technology landscape and evolving customer demands. Toward this end, enhancing the passenger experience to retain and grow market share, boosting operational efficiency with automation, and fleet modernization are key priorities for a successful airline.

Failure to adapt to prevailing market trends can have severe consequences, as demonstrated by the downfall of flagship airlines like Braniff International Airways, Pan American World Airways (Pan Am), Trans World Airlines (TWA), Eastern Air Lines, Alitalia, Swissair, and Sabena. The inability to embrace a customer-first mindset, innovation, manage costs effectively, and cater to evolving customer needs can lead to declining market share, reduced profitability, and ultimately, failure in the highly competitive airline industry.

This chapter concludes with a discussion on strategic agility for competitive advantage with offers and orders. Strategic agility is critical for survival, with a laser-sharp focus on execution, data-driven decision making, and rapid reconfiguration of resources amidst high volatility.

18.2 Airline Marketing Planning Process Will Evolve in an AI-Enabled Landscape

Airline marketing planning process will continue to evolve in the AI-enabled era. The marketing planning process consists of four steps: Flight Scheduling, Pricing, Revenue Management, and Sales and Distribution.

Airline fleet planning, loyalty program, alliances and partnerships are horizontal enablers that provide input into the marketing planning process. At some airlines, the loyalty program is part of marketing planning. Figure 18.1 illustrates the marketing planning process.

18.2.1 Flight Scheduling

The development of a flyable profitable schedule takes many months and includes Strategic Planning, Network Planning, and Schedule Planning.

18.2.1.1 Strategic Planning

An airline's long-term vision and mission influence Strategic Planning. It involves creating a roadmap for an airline's future, including its mission, goals, and how it will achieve them, while considering various internal and external factors. Strategic Planning prepares an airline for the long run, usually 18 months or more into the future. It also looks at potential mergers and acquisitions. Tasks include analyzing macro market trends, creating route topology, fleet mix, managing risks, embracing sustainability and technological advancements. The larger airlines have a dedicated team for strategic planning, while others include it within their network planning function. A well-defined repeatable process for strategic planning is an imperative

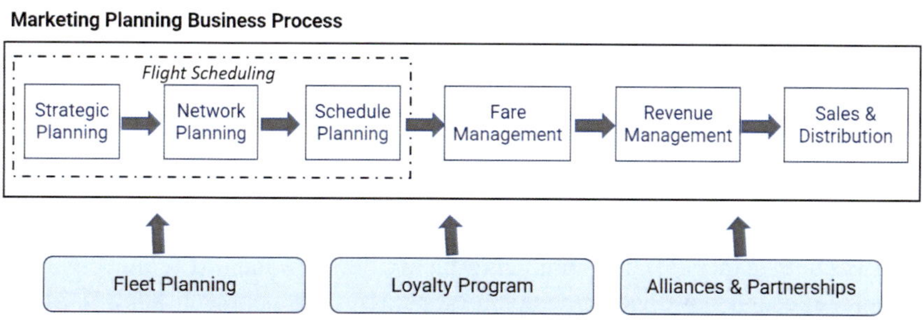

Fig. 18.1 Marketing planning process

for competitive advantage. Without it, an airline will miss potential growth opportunities or fail to respond to changes in the industry. This step ensures resiliency by adapting quickly to changing market conditions and withstanding unforeseen challenges.

18.2.1.2 Network Planning

Strategic Planning provides input into Network Planning, which determines routes to fly, flight frequencies, and types of aircraft to maximize profitability. This is a medium-term planning process, covering six to 18 months into the future and it relies on the strategic plan and fleet plan as a foundation. Aircraft orders are placed a few years before delivery. This function balances commercial demand with operational feasibility, fleet size and market competition. Network planning plays a vital role in shaping an airline's operations because its results include essential data for creating schedules, sales strategies, and scenario forecasts. The network plan helps ensure the airline's services align with overall business goals and operational needs.

18.2.1.3 Schedule Planning

While network planning begins the process by creating the initial flight schedule, it is the schedule planning activities that determines the exact timing for each flight to maximize demand flow in the network. These activities usually start six to nine months before the flights are scheduled to operate. They often continue until the week or even the day before departure. The inputs for schedule planning come from outputs of earlier strategic and network planning work.

18.2.1.4 Schedule Related Considerations

Three topics of interest are clean sheet scheduling, profitable schedule development, and demand driven dispatch.

Clean Sheet Scheduling

Airlines have traditionally relied on tweaking existing schedules for the next season. Many airlines boast a clean sheet scheduling strategy, but schedules are never built from an entirely clean sheet. It has always been an incremental approach. It is also called a warm start approach that takes the current schedule, then the flight times and frequencies are tweaked based on market demand, available aircraft and competitors. It is a conservative approach that is practical and preserves stability for airline operations and customers.

The alternative is a cold start (clean sheet) approach: building an optimized schedule from scratch, unconstrained by history. In theory, this could maximize efficiency and competitiveness. In practice, it has never been achieved. Clean sheet scheduling incorporates optimizing factors like profitability, connectivity to maximize demand flow, and operational efficiency. This approach allows airlines to adapt to changing market conditions, such as fluctuating demand, competitor actions, and resource availability, with greater agility. While this approach has its inherent benefits, it is a difficult problem to solve with consistency and reliability. But clean sheet scheduling is complex. For example, changing the departure time of a flight has the cascading effect of validating aircraft rotations, crew and gate assignments, and calibrating host airline market share, competitiveness, and revenues.

Schedule continuity is also critical for customers. It provides predictability, reduces travel anxiety, and minimizes disruptions to the schedule while "clean sheet" scheduling can lead to instability. Clean sheet approaches can increase profitability and optimize resources, but they often result in significant schedule changes that frustrate passengers. Consistent schedules are essential for high customer satisfaction and loyalty. Clean sheet scheduling also poses a greater challenge to revenue management Flight Id algorithms (see Chapter 4) to match future flights to historical flights.

In the future there is an opportunity for AI algorithms to analyze vast amounts of data and identify optimal scheduling solutions, but adoption will require consistency and reliability. Clean sheet scheduling can be computationally intensive, requiring powerful processors, algorithms and robust data processing capabilities. Bridging the chasm between current schedules and future fully optimized "clean sheet" schedules requires a well thought out phased approach.

Profitable Schedule Development

The calibration of a Quality-of-Service Index (QSI), consumer choice models for market share estimates, spill and recapture are essential during the three phases of flight schedule development. Traditional calibration is a batch process that is limited to specific time intervals. The issue is that the most recent changes to the schedule were not part of the calibration exercise. Machine learning can be leveraged to dynamically adjust and refine the parameters of the model over time, ensuring sustained accuracy and optimal performance. Continuous recalibration eliminates the need for manual adjustments, saving time and resources.

In the future AI and machine learning will play critical roles in predicting demand and optimizing schedules, leading to increased revenue through better route selection, frequency, timing and fleet assignment. AI's impact will be amplified in the network planning and schedule planning business processes. New algorithms will enable integrated flight scheduling and network planning, considering multiple objectives simultaneously, such as minimizing delays, maximizing time slot utilization, and addressing uniqueness constraints.

Demand Driven Dispatch

An airline strategy to dynamically reassign aircraft to flights closer to departure is called Demand Driven Dispatch or D^3. The process of matching available capacity with tactical passenger demand forecast from revenue management reduces empty seats on undersold flights and improves revenue. Aircraft swaps closer to departure increase operating costs which must be balanced against revenue improvement before executing a schedule change. Many airlines practice D^3 as an ad-hoc business process that bridges long-term scheduling and real-time operations to manage fluctuating market needs and improve profitability. The future role of AI in D^3 lies in improved demand forecasts and estimates of operating costs to enhance data-driven decision making for schedule changes.

18.2.2 Fare Management

The airline Fare Management process is undergoing a significant transformation. With NDC adoption, airlines are more adept in introducing time- of-day specific fares, date specific fares, and route specific fares. This can lead to an explosion in the number of active fares managed by an airline.

Micro-segmentation of travelers is also on the horizon with hyper-personalized pricing strategies where fares can be tailored to individual passengers based on their historical purchase behavior. On the surface this approach maximizes both revenue and customer satisfaction by offering targeted pricing, such as premium fares with flexible booking for business travelers or discounts for early bookings for leisure travelers. However, there has been a backlash against personalized pricing, and its future is dependent on how customers accept it.

A looming question that remains is whether at the end of the hybrid era when all airlines are deployed on NDC for all their bookings, what is the future of ATPCO? Will it perish or will it thrive? In a pure NDC world, GDSs no longer need to subscribe to ATPCO since they will not be in the business of pricing itineraries or executing GDS shopping requests. Several large network carriers are probably thinking beyond ATPCO since its role is diminished with NDC. In essence, the future airline distribution landscape is likely to be more diverse, with airlines leveraging various technologies and strategies. It is not clear if the traditional role of ATPCO will evolve. However, today it is very relevant and continues to play a significant role in facilitating the transition to NDC and ensuring interoperability within the complex airline ecosystem. In the future, ATPCO's relevance may be limited to fare management and amenities to support the direct airline channel.

In the absence of a need to distribute airfares to GDSs in the post-hybrid era, perhaps the ATPCO business model will be transformed to serve as a central repository that manages complex data for air fares, fare rules, and amenities, to exclusively support airline controlled direct sales.

Sustainable Aviation Fuels (SAF) currently costs three to five times more than conventional jet fuel. While this does not directly impact core airline pricing, some airlines are incorporating sustainable aviation fuels (SAF) costs and other eco-friendly technologies into ticket prices, and passengers can offset their carbon footprint with optional surcharges. Another option is tiered pricing, where passengers pay a premium with flights using SAF or more fuel-efficient aircraft to accelerate the industry's decarbonization.. Ultimately, the cost of SAF is likely to be borne by a combination of airlines, corporate customers, and leisure passengers.

In the future, decentralized blockchain ledgers can offer clear records of pricing, fees, and loyalty transactions, streamline calculations and protect loyalty programs if scalability can be addressed.

18.2.3 Revenue Management: Past, Present and Future

Revenue Management was introduced in the airline industry by American Airlines in 1985 in the pre-Internet era. There have been significant advances in technology and business models over the past five decades and revenue management has adapted to generate incremental revenues for the airlines. The two most critical adjacent domains of revenue management are airline pricing and air product distribution.

Historically, and even today for most airlines, the end product of revenue management is booking class availability. The itinerary pricing function calculates the fare for an itinerary based on the schedule, booking class availability and fare rules. After a booking is made a passenger name record (PNR) is created. A PNR is a digital record containing details about a passenger's booking with an airline or travel agency. It acts as a virtual representation of a passenger's booking, storing information like their name, travel dates, itinerary, contact details, and more. PNRs are critical for airlines, travel agents, and even security authorities to manage and track travel information.

18.2.3.1 The Transition to Offers and Orders

NDC was introduced by IATA in 2012 and one of the objectives of the messaging standard was to ensure that airlines had complete control over the offer creation process through the indirect channel..

As revenue management transitions to the era of offers and orders, the PNR will be replaced by an Order which replaces the current system of separate booking (PNR), ticketing (E-ticket) and electronic miscellaneous document (EMD) with a single unified record. This consolidated record streamlines processes, reduces costs, and improves the overall customer experience. The revenue management recommendation for some airlines will transition from booking class availability of the base fare to offers consisting of a base fare and ancillary bundle. Some airlines will migrate away from filed fares to continuous pricing through airline websites and NDC channels. For airlines on continuous pricing, the process of validating fare rules and footnotes to determine the itinerary price based on filed fares will continue to exist, but continuous pricing will be a perturbation off the filed fares, which are fixed price points, based on available supply and competitors in the market.

18.2.3.2 The Impact of the Internet on Product Distribution

A singular event that impacted the market domination of the Global Distribution Systems (GDS) was the creation of the Internet in the mid-1990s. Almost overnight, this led to two new online channels—the airline direct channels and the online travel agency (OTA) indirect channels. Airline direct bookings are made without an intermediary like the GDS.

18.2.3.3 LCCs and Restriction Free Tariffs

Revenue management in the 1980s and 1990s was based on the fundamental assumption that demand for booking classes was independent. After the low-cost carriers entered the market, they gained traction and competed directly against the full-service carriers (FSC). LCCs focused on one-way point-to-point fares and the fares either had no restrictions or were lightly restricted. If an LCC only published a single fare over the life of the flight, the total revenue for the flight would not be optimal. By introducing fares above and below the reference price during the life of the flight, the total revenue on the flight can be maximized with optimal price-driven inventory controls. Restriction-free pricing introduces some unique challenges for traditional revenue management, which assumes that the booking classes are independent. With tickets being sold at various prices for the same product, the assumption of independent demand for each booking class is no longer true. The demand is dependent or conditional on the selling fare being offered, which is the only determinant of demand for the segment. Network carriers had to operate in a hybrid environment—compete with LCCs in the domestic market with restriction-free or lightly restricted tariffs and compete with traditional carriers with restricted fares on international routes. Several enhancements were made by academics and practitioners for revenue management to work in a hybrid environment for the FSCs.

18.2.3.4 Competitive Revenue Management

The Internet provided transparency to airline schedules and available fares by market which led to the adoption of competitive revenue management in the early 2000s. Inventory controls that were set based on forecasting and optimization of an airline's internal booking and ticketing data were enhanced to consider competitor selling fares in the market to make adjustments to inventory controls. Prior to making decisions based on competitor selling fares, the revenue management process was myopic since it only considered an airline's internal booking and ticketed data. Competitive revenue management, which considers seat availability in the host inventory system, overcame situations when an airline was priced too high or too low competitively.

The overriding objective of competitive revenue management is to be market aware and reach market equilibrium which occurs when the quantity of airline tickets demanded equals the quantity supplied at a specific price. This equilibrium point represents a balance between what travelers want to buy and what airlines are willing to sell. At the equilibrium price, there is neither a surplus nor a shortage of tickets. Some argue that with the rapid changes in the airline industry, equilibrium is never reached. The future of competitive revenue management is discussed in more detail in Sect. 18.11.

18.2.3.5 Introduction of Branded Fares in 2006

Branded fares were introduced in 2006 by Air Canada, Air New Zealand and Qantas Airways. This was a revenue management strategy where airlines create different bundles of products and services, offering them at varying prices to cater to diverse customer preferences and maximize revenue. This approach goes beyond traditional booking classes by incorporating ancillaries like checked baggage, seat selection, and other amenities into the fare structure. Branded fares introduced a new dimension to air shopping in which the shopping query had to return the lowest fare by branded fare product. It also imposed constraints on booking classes which are limited to 26. Assuming an airline has four branded fare products, most airlines maintain 13 fare levels in domestic markets, which caused an issue since it would require $13 \times 4 = 52$ booking classes, which is not feasible. This resulted in selective mapping of booking classes to brands. Branded fares was an attempt by airlines to stress differentiation and encourage customers to upsell to higher-priced bundles that include more desirable features. With the advent of branded fare products, revenue management systems were adapted to consider customer preferences for different branded fare products, leading to demand forecasts by branded fare product and optimized pricing strategies.

Widely used in other industries, product bundling is a powerful marketing strategy that allows firms to capture more consumer surplus, boost brand image, and offer value contrasting with the trend of unbundling [Chiamberetto and Dumez, 2012]. They offer insights into how bundling impacts consumer behavior and profits, synthesizing fragmented research into a broader understanding.

18.2.4 Sales and Distribution

Sales and Distribution play an important role in disseminating the end product of revenue management for sale to corporate and leisure customers across all distribution channels.

18.2.4.1 Chatbots and Virtual Assistants

Travel chatbots and virtual assistants have seen a step improvement after the introduction of Generative AI. AI-powered chatbots and virtual assistants handle routine customer inquiries (e.g., flight status, booking changes), freeing up human agents for complex issues. Generative AI transforms chatbots and virtual assistants from rigid tools into smart, human-like collaborators from planning to in-trip assistance by enabling deeper understanding with Natural Language Understanding (NLU), context retention, and proactive, personalized responses. NLU, a subset of Natural Language Processing (NLP), comprehends meaning, intent, and context.

Airlines are liable for a chatbot's negligent misrepresentation. Air Canada faced a chatbot failure in 2023 when its chatbot incorrectly told a customer that Air Canada would honor retroactive bereavement fare discounts after flying, which was against corporate policy. A small claims court in Canada determined that the passenger was right and awarded $812.02 in damages and court fees [Garcia, 2024].

18.2.4.2 Airline Websites Will See a Transformation

Following the pandemic of 2020, demand for premium leisure travel grew significantly and carriers sold business class and premium economy tickets to leisure travelers at high prices. This was evident in the summer of 2021 when leisure domestic travel boomed during the peak summer months while business travel lagged behind. Successful airlines must cater to premium leisure travelers.

Airline websites are business-centric focused where search requests begin with a market, departure date and return date. These websites must support alternate workflows for premium and budget conscious leisure travelers. For example, both the high-end leisure and the price sensitive leisure customers, want the shopping experience to be based on lead prices in an extended six-month calendar, theme-based and budget-based shopping. Supporting these leisure workflows requires an ultra-fast shopping engine that is optimized for speed [Vinod, 2024a, Chapter 8].

18.2.4.3 NDC Scalability and Viability of a Shopping Cache

On the surface, because of implications toward personalized offers, a shopping cache is not an option for NDC offers. A response from a cache is not specific to a customer. To control the flow of shopping requests to an airline, sellers like GDSs can collaborate with airlines to deploy a p-cache (PCC level), where individual airline shopping responses asynchronously update the p-cache. A Pseudo City Code is an alphanumeric identifier assigned to a travel agency or a specific office within a travel agency that uses a GDS.

The time to live for an item in p-cache can be controlled based on the arrival rate of updates for the pertinent shopping parameters—PCC, Advance Purchase and Length of Stay. Initially, the offer ID would be less relevant as the offers will be more generic and the results of a shop could be easily duplicated. However, over time when offers become personalized or dynamic, then the offer in the p-cache may not match up to a secondary shop at time of booking. This mismatch would create an increase in UC's (unable to confirm at sell). Alternatively, the airline can provide a negotiated expiration date and time (extended time to live) for each unique offer which would reduce the risk of an UC at time of booking. Important points for a p-cache to work are:

1. It should be indexed by airline and PCC. Optionally, the GDSs can add trip-purpose segment (TPS) id and frequent flyer tier number returned by the airline.
2. The p-cache updates must be sourced from the airline, that controls all offer creation.
3. The expiration time and date must be provided by the airline, though it is relevant since offers are generic. However, as offers become more personalized or dynamic, the need to negotiate an extended expiration date and time will increase as the offer expiration date/time will become a function of the rate at which the p-cache is refreshed for the airline.
4. If an item is not found in the p-cache, due to specific requirements such as "bags only" or "meals only" the request will be sent to the airline for a response.

There are a couple of factors that could diminish the benefits of the p-cache solution. First, the airline may not be willing to extend the life of the offer that is dynamic in nature, and second, the airline may insist on every offer being personalized to a specific traveler.

Time Limit of an Offer

All NDC offers are associated with an Offer ID. Each Offer ID has an associated time limit as part of the shopping response. Some airlines have discussed time limits associated with offers somewhere between 15 to 30 min. If these offers are dynamic, travel sellers would need to negotiate a longer time limit tied to the offer (say 1 to 2 h). A 15-min window is not long enough to store and re-use offers. Continuous pricing further complicates the issue, making it difficult for an airline to extend their offer expiration time.

Risk of Personalization

A p-cache works when shopping content is not personalized to a specific individual based on a unique offer id, but rather a persona of that individual—trip-purpose segment definitions inclusive of frequent flyer tiers. If an airline chooses to personalize offers to a specific individual based on a unique identifier, then the value proposition for p-cache tied to that specific individual is diminished. This type of model does not exist today in the marketplace and is still years in the future. In addition, shopping is still very much a stateless solution with minimal information about the requestor. So even when shopping engines have the ability to personalize to a specific individual, the number of individuals that take advantage of this capability will be a small subset of the total users.

18.2.4.4 Ultra-Fast Shopping Engine

The GDS airline shopping environment is very efficient and processes millions of shopping requests each day. But, over time as NDC gains traction, the GDS shopping will recede into the background and airline shopping to generate airline-controlled offers will take center stage. How efficient is the airline shopping environment to process NDC requests? Can it perform at scale with the anticipated growth caused by AI Agents? If a seller-maintained shopping cache is not an option, then what is required by the airline is an ultra-fast shopping engine with embedded fare and rule binding logic [Vinod, 2024a, Chapter 8] that is optimized for speed.

The need for an ultra-fast shopping engine is even more pressing today with Generative AI which will drastically alter the look-to-book ratio by enabling AI Agents to perform a high volume of automated searches for users. Airline shopping engines must be optimized to handle the increased load at an affordable cost. The compute power, which includes the hardware, processors, memory, storage and energy required to generate air shopping responses to millions of requests from AI Agents will emerge as one of this decade's most critical resource requirements.

A small incremental step is for airlines to allow users to search for flights using natural language and tailoring the recommendations based on individual preferences. Allowing users to curate their trips based on preferences builds brand loyalty.

18.2.4.5 Continuous Pricing

Another aspect of sales through both direct and indirect channels is that some airlines are experimenting and fine-tuning an itinerary price based on continuous pricing. Only a few airlines are validating continuous pricing today and they include United, Lufthansa and Air Canada. Most small and mid-size airlines do not have continuous pricing on their radar, either because they have not invested in it or do not believe in it. Nevertheless, continuous pricing is here to stay for at least a small number of carriers, and airlines and intermediaries must be prepared for this change.

18.2.4.6 Airline Sales Teams

The importance of corporate travelers for an airline cannot be understated. Airlines have direct sales teams that are responsible for building relationships with large corporate clients and negotiating contracts. In addition, key account managers focus on maintaining relationships with high-value corporate accounts, understanding their specific needs, and offering tailored solutions. In the future, airlines are likely to follow a hybrid approach by using a combination of dedicated sales teams and AI algorithms to analyze real-time market data, booking patterns, and individual corporate client preferences to generate optimized and personalized pricing proposals (corporate discounts) for corporate contracts.

18.3 Horizontal Enablers for the Marketing Planning Process

The three most important horizontal enablers for the marketing planning process are fleet planning, loyalty programs, and alliances and partnerships.

18.3.1 Fleet Planning

Airline fleet planning involves strategically determining the mix of aircraft an airline will operate to meet its route network, passenger demand, and financial goals. This includes analyzing the current fleet, forecasting future demand, and making decisions on acquiring aircraft types and configurations, leases, and retirements. It is a complex process requiring consideration of factors like passenger capacity, range, fuel efficiency, and maintenance requirements. Other factors that go into the decision-making process include market trends, route profitability, competitive landscapes and the long-term sustainability goals of the airline.

Growing environmental concerns are driving airlines to invest in more fuel-efficient aircraft, SAF (Sustainable Aircraft Fuel) and carbon offset programs.

IATA estimates that SAF could contribute 65% of the reduction in emissions for aviation to reach net zero CO_2 emissions by 2050.

According to Airports Council International [ACI, 2025] global passenger traffic is projected to grow at a compound annual growth rate (CAGR) of 3.4% to reach 18.7 billion passengers by 2043. The global fleet of commercial airliners is predicted to expand significantly over the next decade, with a compound annual growth rate of 2.8%. The total global commercial airliner fleet is projected to grow from 29,000 in 2025 to 38,300 by 2035 [Prentice, DiNota, Hayes, 2025] and 48,230 by 2043 [Airbus, 2025].

Narrowbody aircraft are increasingly being used on transatlantic routes, offering airlines new opportunities to open long, thin, more cost-effective routes. This shift is driven by advancements in aircraft technology, like the Airbus A321XLR, and the lower operating costs of narrowbodies compared to widebodies. Narrowbody aircraft will continue to form the largest share of the future fleet, increasing from 62 to 68% by 2035.

The future of airline fleet planning is likely to be characterized by a greater reliance on data-driven insights. Airlines are leveraging big data and advanced analytics to optimize fleet usage, analyze flight routes, and improve decision-making processes, leading to enhanced efficiency and cost savings.

A digital twin is a dynamic model of a physical object, process, or system that uses real-time data from sensors to mirror its real-world counterpart's behavior, performance and condition through its lifecycle. For fleet planning, digital twin technology can create virtual replicas of physical aircraft and their components, allowing airlines to simulate scenarios, optimize maintenance schedules, and improve overall operational efficiency.

18.3.2 Loyalty Programs

Airline loyalty programs have evolved from simple frequent flyer accrual and redemptions to sophisticated marketing tools that are deeply intertwined with airline retailing practices. These programs, which initially rewarded passengers with miles for flights, now leverage data analytics to personalize offers, integrate with various retail partners such as credit card companies, and drive revenue through ancillary sales. In the context of retailing, airlines have a greater focus on loyalty passengers since they are repeat passengers, making multiple trips a year. The goal is to enhance customer experience by offering tailored offers and streamlined processes, ultimately boosting revenue, efficiency, and loyalty.

Blockchain technology is poised to revolutionize loyalty programs by enhancing transparency, security, and interoperability. Blockchain can enable new forms of loyalty programs, such as tokenized rewards that can be traded or exchanged, fostering greater engagement and value. Since 2018, the Singapore Airlines KrisFlyer loyalty program permits frequent flyer miles to be converted into digital credits redeemable at various merchants.

18.3.3 Alliances and Partnerships

This role is responsible for managing the airline's global alliances, international planning activities and interline product distribution. In addition, this role also oversees joint ventures with airline partners that have antitrust immunity (ATI) in certain markets. Anti-trust immunity in airline joint ventures allows participating airlines to cooperate on commercial activities like pricing and scheduling without facing antitrust lawsuits.

While traditional alliances like Star Alliance, SkyTeam, and Oneworld remain relevant, targeted mergers and new forms of partnerships, including those with low-cost carriers and intermodal transportation, are emerging. For example, Star Alliance allows interlining with specific LCCs without becoming full members through is Connecting Partner Model (CPM). Digital integration, virtual interlining, and the use of technologies like blockchain and AI are also shaping the future of these collaborations to enhance network reach without complex, costly integration.

18.4 End of Revenge Travel and Importance of Repeat Customers

In a post pandemic world, leisure travel outstripped corporate travel by a wide margin. But it is safe to assume that revenge travel came to an end in 2024. Bookings for air and hotel are expected to see lower growth rates in 2025 and beyond because of concerns over inflation, higher air fares and hotel rates. Higher cost of living translates into less expendable income which means less travel.

Customer acquisition (attracting new customers) generally costs significantly more than customer retention (keeping existing customers). The probability of converting a new prospect into a paying customer is typically lower than selling to an existing customer. Existing customers are more likely to make repeat purchases and are more open to upselling and cross-selling opportunities.

Various studies have indicated that acquiring a new customer can cost 5 to 25 times more than retaining an existing one. This is primarily due to the substantial marketing and advertising expenses required to reach and persuade potential customers who are unfamiliar with a brand. The higher cost of customer acquisition means that customer retention or market share retention takes center stage.

Customer retention is the fifth and final phase in the travel life cycle (see Fig. 1.3 in Chapter 1). If this important step is ignored, it has an impact on the customer churn rate, which is exacerbated for smaller airlines and independent hotels who have sub-standard loyalty programs compared to the larger network carriers and major hotel chains. Loyal customers are more likely to recommend the brand to others, leading to further customer acquisition through word-of-mouth.

18.5 The Future of User Experience Belongs to AI Assistants

AI Assistants have a history that spans several decades. Early breakthroughs in artificial intelligence and natural language processing set the stage for the AI Assistants used today. In the 1960s, programs like ELIZA, a basic chatbot that could simulate conversations, emerged. In the 2010s, AI Assistants gained wider public recognition and acceptance with the launch of Apple's Siri in 2011 and Amazon's Alexa in 2014. Of late, advanced language models like OpenAI's GPT-3 (released in 2020) and GPT-4 further revolutionized AI Assistants, enabling more human-like conversations and a wider range of capabilities.

Today, AI Assistants are transforming user experience (UX) by enabling personalization, automation, and proactive support. They learn from user interactions, preferences and context to offer personalized recommendations and content, making interactions more relevant and engaging.

The acronym GPT stands for Generative Pre-trained Transformer. Generative implies generation of new text, Pre-trained refers to how the model was trained on a massive amount of data, which can be improved with additional data sources, and Transformer refers to a specific type of neural network. The transformer is the core invention that supports the current boom in AI. In 2017, the original transformer was introduced by Google [Vaswani, et al., 2017].

A Generative Pre-Trained Transformer (GPT) chatbot is conversational software that uses deep learning and specialized transformer architecture to power its interactions with users. GPT is a specific type of Large Language Model (LLM) built using transformer architecture, primarily focused on text generation tasks.

Slowly but surely AI Assistants are changing travel. They offer custom advice, destination information, plan trips, and book travel arrangements on a limited basis. Fundamental to mass adoption, as this technology matures, is what it will take for AI Assistants to gain traveler's trust.

Chatbots and travel AI Assistants are not new phenomena. Many OTAs, metasearch engines, and travel suppliers have been making the necessary investments in this space. Expedia unveiled Romie, the 'roaming' AI buddy, in May 2024, that offers suggestions based on a traveler's preferences are learns continuously from customer interactions. KAYAK has launched a travel planning assistant on ChatGPT. The Kayak.ai travel platform is used to pilot new AI-first features. It combines OpenAI's technology with KAYAK's travel intelligence, offering features like conversational search, real-time flight updates, price drop notifications, and trip planning assistance. Marriott's Renaissance hotels released RENAI, an AI-powered virtual concierge that can recommend restaurants, bars, tours, and activities to guests. Leveraging AI, Marriot is also making searches more intuitive and delivering personalized travel planning results based on consumer preferences for Homes and Villas, a luxury home rental offering, by Marriott Bonvoy.

Amazon's new AI Assistant, Alexa Plus, was launched in March 2025. The voice assistant is built on Large Language Models (LLMs) and designed to integrate into daily life. Tripadvisor and Fodors are among the first partners for this voice assistant to provide travel planning assistance to customers. These brands are working with Amazon to enhance the user experience. However, trip planning is a major challenge because of the subtle nuances and expectations from travelers. Gaining acceptance in the marketplace will not be easy.

Alexa+planned to book travel in 2026 like OpenAI's Operator. Operator. Alexa+announced partnerships with Tripadvisor and Uber in March 2025 and with Expedia in December 2025, Yelp, Angi and Square are also expected to launch integrations in 2026 [Hines, 2025b]. In early 2026, Alexa+can make bookings directly through voice commands acting as an AI Agent. OpenAI's Operator is far more ambitious in its goals. Its objective is to automate the workload of a corporate travel agent, a significant challenge.

Operator runs on the Computer-Using Agent (CUA) model. This new model uses GPT 4o's vision capabilities with advanced reasoning through reinforcement learning. CUA learns to work with what people see on screens like buttons, menus, and text fields.

Will Alexa+play a major role in travel given its inherent complexities in getting it right for every traveler? Amazon's Alexa division has been a perennial loss leader for over a decade. In the U.S. voice assistant wars in 2024, measured by number of users, it was in third place behind Google Assistant and Apple's Siri. Voice assistants like Google Assistant and Alexa can help with basic travel tasks, but they cannot yet replace a real travel agent. However, they can provide flight information, suggest attractions, and book dinner. A simple voice command makes it easy.

Amazon has had limited success with Alexa in the past. In 2018, Alexa for Hospitality gave guests the ability to ask Amazon Echo questions, connect to guest services, play music, and more. Privacy breach concerns with this technology limited its rollout. Alexa has also been offered as a virtual concierge for short-term rentals, and as a scheduler for Uber and Lyft rides.

18.6 True Door-to-Door Experience Will Become Reality

Door-to-door travel is a complete travel service from start to finish. True door-to-door travel, a seamless and integrated journey using multiple modes of transport, is a highly anticipated vision.

It covers transportation from a person's home or office to the final destination, like a hotel or event venue. This service includes rides to and from airports, train stations, or other departure points and activities at the destination. It also takes care of traveling on the chosen mode of transport, making the whole journey easier and more convenient.

It is anticipated that AI Assistants will eventually support true door-to-door experience for travelers. The question is when? Probably in a few years before 2030. Today's travel planning tools are limited in their ability to provide comprehensive options for lesser-known destinations or unique travel styles.

By making travel more convenient, personalized, and efficient, impacting the entire door-to-door travel experience AI Assistants have the potential to make it a reality. Advancements in AI technology can be expected to further enhance safety, sustainability, and accessibility in the travel industry.

Beyond merely searching and booking travel, AI Assistants will have to offer context-aware recommendations based on a traveler's preferences. Examples are transportation to airport and return, restaurants and day trips at the destination to fill out the calendar and making travel logistics a minor concern.

18.7 Beyond Apps, Seamless Access to Offers Regardless of Channel

Consensus is growing that travelers do not need more apps; but they need seamless, integrated access to travel offerings regardless of the channel they choose, which includes both specialized apps and broader platforms like super apps which are all-in-one platforms that integrate a wide range of travel and related services, like booking flights and hotels, managing finances, finding local dining, and arranging transport, into a single mobile application. Examples of super apps that offer travel services alongside other functions like payments and ride hailing are Grab (Southeast Asia), WeChat (China), Traveloka (Asia) and Paytm (India). The Air Asia Super App, recently rebranded as AirAsia MOVE, is an example that evolved from an airline into a comprehensive platform offering travel and lifestyle products.

An airline's focus should be on providing a consistent, convenient and unified experience across digital and in-person touchpoints to build trust and loyalty, rather than creating more fragmented, standalone applications.

Seamless access is more important than more apps since it supports a seamless customer journey. Disjointed apps create friction and security risks for customers. Connectivity boosts customer satisfaction, adoption, and productivity. Customers want to switch between channels without losing context, whether they start with a search engine, a specialized app, or a travel supplier's website. Besides, a seamless experience that integrates digital and physical interactions builds trust and strengthens loyalty with customers.

18.7.1 Travel Apps, if You Must

Arguments exist both for and against promoting more apps into the marketplace, with the outcome largely dependent on an individual's specific needs, priorities, and usage habits. Travel apps continue to play an important role in airline retailing, so they cannot be dismissed altogether. Perhaps in a decade, but not today.

According to a study conducted by J.D. Powers in 2023, travel apps and websites have significant room to improve in comparison to other industries [Clarke, 2023]. The study assessed customer satisfaction with travel apps and websites across three travel verticals: airlines, hotels and rental cars. They examine key factors that affect customer choice, satisfaction and loyalty, including account management, day of travel, duration of stay, ease of navigation, booking process, speed, and visual appeal. The findings indicate that satisfaction with travel apps and websites lags behind top-rated apps in other sectors. Among these, airline websites rank the lowest, with an overall satisfaction score of 640 out of 1,000.

A decade ago (2005–2015) planning a trip meant jumping between web tabs, printing out emails, and hoping the taxi arrived on time. Today, these functions can all be handled by a good mobile travel app.

Travelers today have become more tech-savvy. They are not just booking flights anymore. They want personalized options, real-time updates, local tips, and help while on the move. Travel apps are no longer just tools but are an integral part of the journey.

If a travel entity wants to invest in an app, the most important features required for a competitive travel app are discussed below.

18.7.1.1 Intuitive Navigation

A clean, well-organized layout helps users find and book destinations easily. Simple menus and fewer steps make searching quick and enjoyable. Clear design guides visitors smoothly through the process. This way, users spend less time looking and more time making choices. A clutter-free style also makes the platform more attractive and user-friendly. Simplified navigation encourages people to explore and complete their bookings without frustration.

18.7.1.2 The Complete Journey

No one likes switching between different apps to plan a trip. Booking a flight, finding a hotel, reserving a car, and buying tickets to a museum can feel overwhelming.

The best travel apps aim to do it all in one place. They should not add extra clutter but combine features smoothly. The purpose is to organize the entire trip, make bookings, navigate new places, and even make adjustments to plans, all done from a single app instead of jumping between apps. This level of convenience keeps travelers coming back.

18.7.1.3 Personalization

Many apps today ask for the traveler's name and suggest a few places to visit. But that isn't true personalization. What travelers need is context. They want recommendations based on how they prefer to travel, whether it is a weekend getaway for two, a short business trip, budget stays or luxury hotels. They also want suggestions that remember their seat preferences on flights or which airlines they tend to avoid. Apps that learn from real consumer behavior and preferences will stand out and earn loyalty. These are the tools that will truly connect with travelers and keep them coming back.

Today we live in an AI-enabled landscape. AI can be leveraged to provide personalized suggestions based on what users have searched for and their preferences.

Recommendations that depend on location can help guide users to nearby activities and sights. This makes each trip more special and memorable.

18.7.1.4 Smart Search and Advanced Filters

Give users options by including filters for price, reviews, length of stay and more. This helps them to narrow down choices quickly and easily. A smooth search process allows users to find the best options with accuracy.

18.7.1.5 Immersive Experience with Augmented Reality

Create an immersive experience by overlaying digital content onto the real world, enhancing a traveler's perception of the airline cabin or hotel room. This enables them to "walk through" the space virtually. Apps that offer 360° hotel tours, or augmented reality (AR) features that help navigate airline terminals and train stations build trust with international travelers.

18.7.1.6 Real-Time Updates and Notifications

Provide live updates on flight, hotel and destination activities to ensure travelers see valid current information. Sending personalized alerts about price drops and special deals keep users engaged and encourage repeat visits.

18.7.1.7 Localization

Apps should support multiple languages and currencies to help international travelers. This makes booking easier and improves the overall experience. Focus on user experience and personal touches to turn the booking process into a smooth journey. These features are key to keeping users interested and earning their loyalty in a competitive market.

18.7.1.8 Wearables

Travelers already use wearables to check boarding times, track walking distance, and set trip reminders. Apps that synchronize with these devices show the information instantly, so users don't need to search through phones. It makes it easier for the traveler to stay informed without extra effort.

18.7.1.9 Reviews

Travelers tend to be cautious. Generic photos and vague ads do not create trust, but real experiences do. Apps that showcase user reviews, local tips, and even lists of what to do or avoid from past passengers or guests build trust quickly. Content created by travelers remains a powerful tool. People trust reviews from others who have been there. Apps that encourage reviews, share honest feedback, or highlight community advice will gain respect faster than any fancy banner ad.

18.7.1.10 Payment Options

Cash is becoming less common in many areas of travel. Most people carry their phones more often than their wallets. Offering multiple forms of payment is mandatory today. Payment apps like Apple Pay, Google Pay, and region-specific options make paying quick and simple. These services support local currencies and provide a smoother checkout experience.

18.7.1.11 Virtual Assistants

A mobile app with chat functionality and 24/7 virtual help is the new reality. Customer experience can be enhanced by integrating virtual assistants into the mobile app. Virtual assistants, often powered by AI, can provide real-time support, personalized recommendations, and proactive assistance with various travel-related tasks.

18.7.1.12 Security

Travelers share a lot of personal data, like IDs, payment methods, and health records. Apps must protect this data or users will abandon them and go elsewhere. Today, features like strong login security, encrypted payments, and privacy-focused interfaces are expected as tablestakes, not optional extras. Travelers want assurance that their information is safe. Without these protections, they will look for apps that prioritize their privacy and security. Keeping sensitive data secure is now a fundamental part of good service in the travel industry.

As we move forward, apps should explore how blockchain can be leveraged for identity verification, fraudulent bookings, and loyalty tracking.

18.7.2 Frequent Flyer Redemption Shopping

The single biggest problem today with frequent flyer redemptions for air travel is the high booked load factors with revenue passengers. As redemption opportunities decline with higher load factors, the new generation shopping framework must enable frequent flyer redemption shopping for markets over a date range from a month to six months. The initial shopping response to a traveler's redemption request should clearly indicate the minimum loyalty points required for each month in the horizon. When the month is selected by a user, the specific departure dates for a fixed length of stay and loyalty points required can be displayed for the month on the calendar. This makes the entire redemption process faster for travelers.

18.8 Airline Websites Must Evolve to Be Business Centric and Leisure Centric

The audience for the airline consumer direct channel is primarily leisure travelers, yet the booking workflow is business travel centric. The flight search always begins with a defined departure date and return date for a market. While many leisure travelers may want to travel to a specific destination on a fixed departure date, many leisure passengers are flexible if the price is right. While a precise number is unavailable, a significant portion of direct airline leisure travelers likely seek flexibility in their travel plans with travel dates and destinations. The "dream" and "plan" phase of travel are integral to leisure travelers. They represent the initial stages where customers first conceive the idea of a trip and then begin to elaborate on the details. For example, in winter, many leisure travelers want to go skiing but have flexibility on departure dates and ski destinations. The post-pandemic environment has also increased the emphasis on flexibility.

Airline websites of the future must support both a business workflow and a leisure workflow. The business workflow must be retained because many airlines have corporate programs to attract small and medium-sized businesses. Examples are American's AAdvantage Business, Delta SkyMiles for Business, Southwest Airlines SWABIZ and Lufthansa Group for Business (BusinessToGo). They offer perks to the company and employees toward mileage and loyalty point accrual and redemption. Many also provide an expense reporting solution to track travel expenses.

In recognition of leisure customer flexibility toward travel dates, many airline websites display a ± 3 day matrix of outbound and inbound flights with a lead price for each applicable cell in the matrix. This is a 7×7 matrix of lead prices.

If the shopping algorithm has been optimized for speed, then the default display for leisure travel should begin with an extended calendar for a six month or twelve-month period with the lowest price by month for a fixed length of stay that was captured in the customer input when the flight search was initiated. This is shown in Fig. 18.2 for the Dallas Fort Worth (DFW) to Orlando (MCO) market.

Next, the customer can select a month which will return the lowest price for each departure date in the selected month. This is shown in Fig. 18.3.

Once a specific departure date is clicked, then the standard display of itineraries for that departure date is shown.

Building upon this capability, additional capabilities to drive leisure traffic to the airline website with an ultra-fast shopping engine that produces results that are not dependent on a shopping cache are theme-based shopping and budget-based shopping.

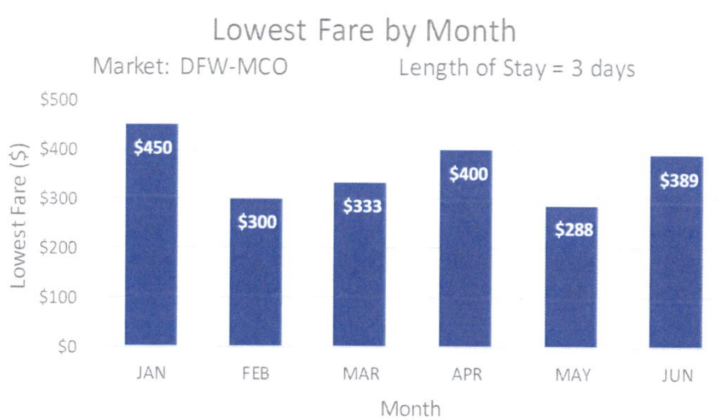

Fig. 18.2 Lowest fare by month

May 2025
Lowest Fare by Day
Market: DFW-MCO, Length of Stay: 3 days
Current Date: January 14, 2025

SUN	MON	TUE	WED	THU	FRI	SAT
		1 $411.01	2 $355.09	3 $291.35	4 $377.11	5 $381.14
6 $311.35	7 $355.09	8 $321.35	9 $355.09	10 $351.66	11 $375.57	12 $299.38
13 $399.35	14 $401.35	15 $331.35	16 $355.09	17 $291.35	18 $296.65	19 $325.35
20 $345.54	21 $451.39	22 $361.35	23 $288.00	24 $333.30	26 $389.35	26 $466.25
27 $387.12	28 $296.15	29 $291.45	30 $355.09	31 $389.01		

Fig. 18.3 Lowest fare by departure date in May

18.8.1 Natural Language Search

Natural language flight search is an AI-powered technology that allows customers to find flights by describing travel needs in everyday, conversational language rather than using traditional dropdown menus and specific filters. Examples are "a weekend getaway to a coastal city with great food, nonstop only," to find relevant flight options. These tools are already on the market today, such as Flight Deals by Google Flights, American Airlines website, Kayak and Expedia.

Natural language processing understands the nuances of a traveler's request, such as "*good skiing*" or "*not too costly,*" and uses it to identify matching destinations and flights. Adoption of natural language search on airline websites is no longer a luxury but a necessity to display contextual results. It allows users to bypass traditional search filters and get results based on preferences like desired experience, flexibility or travel style.

18.8.2 Theme-Based and Budget-Based Shopping

Many leisure passengers do not care about a specific destination, but are more interested in experiencing a theme such as skiing, gambling, sightseeing, romantic getaway, wine tasting, history and culture, nature tour, beach, safari, adventure, hiking, etc. A theme-based shopping workflow on airline websites allows customers to evaluate a range of destinations that are specific to a theme.

Theme based shopping also allows an airline to redirect demand from high demand destinations to low demand destinations that support the same theme by ranking the destinations in the search results based on available unused capacity (unsold seats) or ranked in ascending order of the total bid price for the various trips.

Theme-based shopping can also be on a budget. A traveler's budget constraint can be added to limit the itineraries shown that fulfill a budget.

18.8.3 Seat-Led Shopping

An important consideration during flight search is seat-led shopping. With this capability a customer can state their seat preferences as part of the shopping request to avoid having to go through multiple shopping iterations when the desired seats are not available on the seat maps displayed for the selected itinerary.

Examples of seat type requests are aisle seats, window seats, bulkhead seats, exit row seats, seats together, etc. Seat-led shopping must only display itineraries that can fulfill the seat type requested and the total itinerary price must reflect the price range if seats are individually priced [Vinod, 2024a].

Seat-led shopping is required for both business and leisure travelers. For example, business travelers may want to sit in front of the cabin or prefer an aisle or window seat. Leisure travelers travelling together like a family may want seats together.

To support seat-led shopping on airline websites, the reservations inventory system must maintain real-time counts of seats available by seat type. This required interoperability between seat maps in the pre-reserved seats domain (PRS) and reservations inventory to accept and update notifications when a seat is consumed (or unconsumed).

18.9 AI-Based Reasoning Models for the Future of Airline Retailing

What is a reasoning model? It is a 'predictive model that involves answering complex questions. To address complexity, the process requires many intermediate steps to create a solution. It is a type of large language model (LLM) with reasoning capabilities. These models handle complex reasoning tasks. LLMs usually make a statistical guess of the next word in an answer. Reasoning models do things differently. They spend time breaking down questions. The models use a "chain of thought" process that helps them find better answers. This method makes reasoning models more like humans.

OpenAI's blog post (OpenAI, 2024b) claimed that "*Through reinforcement learning, o1 learns to hone its chain of thought and refines the strategies it uses. It learns to recognize and correct its mistakes. It learns to break down tricky steps into simpler ones. It learns to try a different approach when the current one isn't working. This process dramatically improves the model's ability to reason."*

Perhaps the era of collaborative filtering, market-basket analysis of transaction data, and other well-established techniques is coming to an end with the flurry of research announcements around AI-based reasoning models. A reasoning algorithm is a logical approach that leverages AI to apply rules to a knowledge graph, revealing new facts and relationships. But there are fundamental issues that remain to be addressed with large reasoning models (LRM). The trouble with advanced AI models today is that they can generalize within a training distribution of data that they are exposed to, but that generalization is not versatile. It tends to break down outside that distribution. In the "Illusion of Thinking" paper [Shojaee, et al. 2025] the authors from Apple Research describe how advanced AI can appear to reason but breaks down with increasing complexity, showing strengths in moderate tasks but failing in complex tasks.

OpenAI released its first reasoning model, called o1, in September 2024 [OpenAI, 2024a]. Reasoning models, such as OpenAI o1 and o3-mini, are large language models designed to engage in complex thinking. These models process information internally, constructing a detailed thought process before providing answers to users. AI-based reasoning models are becoming easier and cheaper to develop. In the first quarter of 2025, news emerged about significant new AI models that are challenging the established leaders of the past three years.

NovaSky, a research team from UC Berkeley's Sky Computing Lab, has introduced Sky-T1-32B-Preview. This reasoning model competes well with a previous version of OpenAI's o1 in several important benchmarks [Novasky, 2025; Wiggers, 2025]. Sky-T1 is notable for being the first truly open-source reasoning model that can be recreated from scratch. The team has shared the dataset used for training as well as the code needed for that training. The NovaSky team used Alibaba's QwQ-32B-Preview model to create the initial training data for Sky-T1. They then refined this data and applied OpenAI's GPT-4o-mini to make it more usable. This process is called distillation, a technique that involves using the results of one model to train another model. Training the Sky-T1 model, which has 32 billion parameters, took about 19 h on a setup with 8 Nvidia H100 GPUs. According to NovaSky, the AI reasoning model only costs around $450. This is misleading since the distillation process relies on AI software Alibaba's QwQ-32B-Preview and OpenAI's GPT-4o-mini that cost millions of dollars to develop.

Another reasoning model is Chinese startup DeepSeek-R1, a robust open-source system that is competing against OpenAI's stronghold in the market. The January 10, 2025. release of DeepSeek's AI Assistant, powered by the DeepSeek-V3 model, as well as the January 20, 2025, release of its R1 model, sent shock waves through Silicon Valley. However, the reported $6 million training cost for DeepSeek V3 is highly misleading, since they used distillation with OpenAI's GPT-4. Perhaps the $6 million was for GPU pre-training costs only.

DeepSeek utilized pure reinforcement learning to train a base language model to reason independently, without human help. Figure 18.4 provides a simplified overview of the DeepSeek method. As the illustration shows, creating a robust

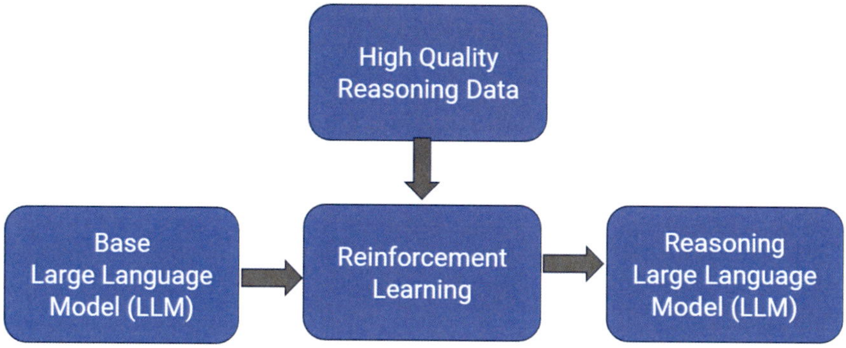

Fig. 18.4 The DeepSeek Approach

reasoning model is straightforward with a strong base model and a quality mix of data.

DeepSeek applied pure reinforcement learning to teach a base language model how to reason without any human supervision. Figure 18.4 illustrates a high-level schematic of the DeepSeek approach. As shown in the figure below, making a powerful reasoning model is now very simple if you have access to a capable base model and a high-quality data mixture:

Comparison benchmarks to OpenAI in the areas of mathematical reasoning and problem-solving capabilities, coding proficiency, general reasoning and task-handling capabilities of DeepSeek were comparable. OpenAI claims that DeepSeek uses distillation, a standard method for training AI models by taking data from larger, more powerful ones. This process enables developers to train smaller models much cheaper than the $100 million OpenAI spent on GPT-4. Developers are permitted to connect their applications to OpenAI's AI through an API. However, using the outputs from OpenAI to create competing models breaches their terms of service. It is ironic since OpenAI developed its GPT model by ingesting the entirety of the written web without consent. There exists substantial evidence that DeepSeek distilled knowledge out of OpenAI models. Does this constitute IP theft?

DeepSeek offers a clear cost advantage, with prices around 20 times less than OpenAI's o1 for all token types. This substantial price difference makes DeepSeek a compelling choice for large-scale AI projects while still delivering similar performance.

Researchers at Stanford University and the University of Washington have developed an AI reasoning model called s1 [Zeff, 2025]. They achieved this for less than $50 in cloud computing costs [Muennighoff, et al. 2025]. The s1 team began with a basic model and improved it through distillation. This process takes the reasoning abilities from another AI model by learning from its responses. The $50 estimate is misleading since distillation was based on Gemini 2.0 Flash Thinking Experimental which cost millions of dollars to develop. The s1 model shows performance on par with top reasoning models like OpenAI's o1 and DeepSeek's R1 in tests that evaluate math and coding skills.

It is exciting to note that a few researchers can innovate in the AI field without huge financial backing. However, s1 raises important concerns about how easily AI models can be replicated. What is the protection if someone can duplicate an expensive model for a fraction of the cost? It is no surprise that major AI labs are unhappy about this situation. s1 raises real questions about the commoditization of AI models.

The team behind s1 aimed to find an easy way to improve reasoning skills in AI, known as "test-time scaling," which lets an AI model think longer before giving an answer. This concept was part of the advancements made in OpenAI's o1, which DeepSeek and other AI labs have attempted to replicate using different methods.

The s1 paper [Muennighoff, et al. 2025] indicates that reasoning models can be improved with a small dataset through a technique called supervised fine-tuning (SFT). In SFT, an AI model learns to imitate specific behaviors found in the dataset. SFT is usually more cost-effective than the large-scale reinforcement learning approach that DeepSeek used to develop its R1 model, intended as a competitor to OpenAI's o1.

S1 uses a small AI model from Qwen, a lab owned by Alibaba, which can be downloaded for free. Fliggy, Alibaba's travel platform processes bookings end-to-end powered by the Qwen App, launched in January 2026, that allows travelers to use natural language to plan itineraries. To train s1, researchers built a dataset of 1,000 well selected questions with their answers and the reasoning behind each answer using Google's Gemini 2.0 Flash Thinking Experimental. Training s1 took under 30 minutes with 16 Nvidia H100 GPUs, and it performed well on several AI benchmarks, as reported by the researchers.

The team employed a clever method to help s1 verify its answers and improve its thought process by simply instructing it to wait. Adding "wait" during its reasoning led to slightly better answers, according to the s1 research paper [Muennighoff, et al. 2025].

In 2025 and beyond, Meta, Google, and Microsoft plan to invest hundreds of billions into AI infrastructure to help train future AI models. Such investment may still be needed to drive AI forward. While distillation has proven effective in recreating an AI model's abilities cheaply, it does not create significantly better models than those already available. The appeal lies in the lower operating costs.

18.10 Agentic AI and Impact on Travel

> *Agents are not only going to change how everyone interacts with computers. They're also going to upend the software industry, bringing about the biggest revolution in computing since we went from typing commands to tapping on icons.*
>
> Bill Gates, Co-founder of Microsoft

Bill Gates, co-founder of Microsoft, predicts a major change in how we interact with computers [Gates, 2023]. This shift will be driven by the growth of AI Agents. He believes these smart agents will not only change how we work with technology but also revolutionize the entire software industry. Bill Gates compares this change to the switch from typing commands to simply tapping on icons, highlighting the magnitude of the imminent change.

Agentic AI is a type of artificial intelligence (AI) that can perform tasks and make decisions without human intervention. It is designed to adapt to new situations and improve its performance over time. Many well-known technologists believe that in the next few years, AI Agents will completely change how we live our lives, on and offline.

In the decade ahead, the single biggest impact of AI on the travel industry will be Agentic AI, which is AI systems designed to act autonomously, making decisions and taking actions to achieve specific goals with minimal or no human intervention. They are designed to adapt to prevailing market conditions and improve its performance over time rather than just responding to input data.

So how does Agentic AI work? It uses multiple AI Agents that can analyze data, set goals, and take actions. They use large language models (LLMs) to enhance decision making and natural language understanding. The model learns from interactions and adapts to new situations by using reasoning and iterative planning to solve complex problems. The agents interpret context, evaluate options, and adapt behavior to achieve specific goals.

Travel companies are beginning to see the benefits of using AI Agents to boost efficiency and improve how they interact with customers. Primary use cases today are personalized trip planning, 24×7 support and dynamic rebooking. Autonomous agents go beyond this. These AI systems learn on their own and improve without human intervention, enabling automation of complex workflows at scale. By transforming data into knowledge and translating knowledge into action, they operate with minimal human input.

The rise of Agentic AI means that AI Agents will be able to research, plan, and book trips autonomously, cutting out OTAs, TMCs and other third-party intermediaries.

For managed travel, AI Agents will not eliminate travel agents but enhance productivity by an order of magnitude leading to fewer travel agents on a TMCs payroll. Itineraries can be created by AI Agents in a heartbeat. The challenge for TMCs is to pivot from being information providers to curators of content by incorporating consumer intent, personal preferences and emotional depth that converts a trip into a memory.

Agentic AI has the potential to reshape the travel distribution landscape by creating peer-to-peer links between travel suppliers and consumers, and a new era of direct bookings could emerge. OTAs, used by leisure travelers, will become insignificant for larger hotel chains and network airlines and their target audience will be limited to smaller hotel chains, independent hotels, and smaller airlines who have not made investments in AI Agents.

In this new environment, we are not dealing with individual AI Assistants, but fully autonomous agent networks that can analyze data, establish goals, interpret context, and execute complex workflows at scale in real-time.

OpenAI recently unveiled "Operator," a new agent [OpenAI, 2025a] that can use its own browser to perform tasks for a travel agent. It is specifically designed to automate tasks on the web. It is made to handle tasks for people on its own. Online shopping and booking are two of its main functions. This is one of many AI Agents coming from major tech firms soon.

OpenAI faces competition from various players in the AI and automation space. These include other AI companies developing similar agents, as well as more established platforms offering automation and cloud AI services.

The competitive landscape is always evolving. Competitors include:

1. Anthropic's Claude with "Computuer Use" features, which allows programmatic web tasks similar to Operator, emphasizing safety and alignment.
2. Google DeepMind (Project Mariner) is an experimental agent focused on web navigation and interaction, potentially excelling within Google's ecosystem.
3. BrowserBase offers "Open Operator," an open source and free alternative to OpenAI's Operator that also automates web tasks.
4. OthersideAI's self-operating computer framework is an open-source option for building LLM-powered web automation systems.
5. Mistral AI is a French company with open-source models and business deals, positioning itself as a competitor to OpenAI.

In addition, there are several free and open-source Operator-like products in development. The AI industry's competitive landscape is dynamic, with new players emerging and existing companies evolving their offerings to address AI development and deployment.

As industry experts share their views, it becomes clear that AI Agents will change how we use technology and handle daily challenges. They are poised to transform the software industry and become helpful digital assistants. These AI Agents have the potential to simplify tasks, boost efficiency, and create more valuable and engaging travel experiences.

18.11 Future of Competitive Revenue Management

In today's online landscape, where pricing and schedules are highly competitive and transparent, there is a growing acknowledgement that the traditional approach to airline revenue management may be limited since the real-time dynamics in the marketplace are not considered. It offers inventory control recommendations that may not accurately reflect current market conditions. Airlines typically forecast demand by customer segment using historical data and based on remaining unused capacity (seats) establish inventory controls in the airline's reservation system environment, also known as the host CRS. This approach lacks awareness of strategies adopted by competitors. A mechanism to address the problem is to monitor competitor selling fares that are offered for sale and use this data in the decision-making process to determine the inventory controls that are *market aware*. These inventory controls are used to determine the price of an itinerary. Various adaptations of Competitive Revenue Management ("Comp RM") entered the marketplace in the early 2000s and have continued to proliferate to avoid revenue dilution, ensure consistency and equilibrium in the marketplace [Hartmans, 2008; Kumar, et al. 2021; Page, Côté, Savard, 2005; Ratliff and Vinod, 2005; Vinod, 2021; Zhang and Kallesen, 2008 (Chapter 7)].

In the lodging industry Competitive Revenue Management begins with revenue managers identifying the competitive set ("comp set") for their property. These are properties in the same neighborhood that a hotel revenue manager views as their competition. Hotel competitive sets are asymmetric [Vinod, 2022a] and can be derived from an OTA's click stream data. They can also be identified, though frequently erroneously, by a revenue management analyst at a property. Competitive Revenue Management in lodging relies on automated robotic shopping of competitor websites to determine the selling rates. There are many vendors such as RateGain, Lighthouse and RevenueStrategy 360 by Amadeus that provide visibility into selling rates of hotels for future dates on the horizon. This competitor selling rates data is used to adjust inventory controls in the hotel CRS in real-time to recommend the best available rate (BAR). As an alternative to robotic shopping from vendors like RateGain or forward-looking sales data of competitors from Amadeus Hospitality's Demand360, hotels can also subscribe to Smith Travel Research (STR) that gives them visibility into historic selling rates at properties.

Although it has been common practice for airlines and hotels since the early 2000s to gather competitor prices and availability from Internet websites, tools for responding to uncompetitive (or overcompetitive) prices and availability were limited to user-defined rules such as a simple matching policy. Over the last decade, this has advanced to utilize advanced mathematical and statistical forecasting and optimization methods supplemented with machine learning models to automatically recommend model-based selling price and availability changes that better maximize an airline or hotel's expected revenue conditional on current and expected future competitive market conditions. For example, in the airline industry, one approach is to leverage current and expected future available travel options in the marketplace that can be collected from a GDS using web services APIs or web-scraping from third party vendors like Infare (the airline business of QL2 was acquired by Infare in 2017) to calibrate a customer choice model for estimating sales probabilities across the set of available travel options in the market and estimate the revenue-maximizing set of available products based on their prices and market conditions.

Besides airlines and hotels, car rental companies and cruise lines also track competitor rates and use them as an input into their revenue management business process. For example, rental car companies monitor competitor capacity (available supply of cars) and rates at airport locations to dynamically adjust the walk-up rate for walk-up customers.

18.11.1 Summary of Competitive Revenue Management for Airlines and Hotels

In the airline industry, Competitive Revenue Management relies on fares published by airlines to determine what fares should be made available for sale based on expected future demand, available seat capacity and competitor selling fares. Airlines publish their fares to fare aggregators like ATPCO that in turn disseminate the fares to intermediaries like the GDSs and airlines. An airline has the option to respond to a new fare filed by a competitor by matching the fare or filing a fare that is above or below the competitor's fare.

In the hotel industry, Competitive Revenue Management relies on a hotel's rate structure established in the hotel reservations system to determine what rate should be made available for sale based on expected future demand, available rooms, and selling rates of the competitor set. Hotel rates that are published to internal systems like the hotel CRS are based on the hotel's pricing strategy, perceived value of the brand, room types and associated attributes, and neighborhood.

In summary all decision making associated with publishing reference fares and inventory control for airlines; and establishing the rate structure and room inventory control for hotels are always internal to the travel supplier. The inventory control strategies used are closely guarded secrets.

18.11.2 Class Action Lawsuits and Their Outcome

In January 2024 hotel software providers, Pegasus and Cendyn merged under the Cendyn brand. The resulting entity, named the Cendyn Group, offers a revenue management solution from Rainmaker for casinos and hotels that recommends the best available rate (BAR).

In 2023 Atlantic City and Nevada casinos were hit with several class action lawsuits claiming that the casinos conspired to fix prices of hotel rooms with an algorithm, Rainmaker, offered by the Cendyn Group. The suit claims that room revenue reported to the New Jersey Casino Control Commissions has increased substantially while occupancy rates have fallen, and gaming revenues have increased only modestly.

Several lawsuits have been filed such as *Fabel v. Boardwalk* 1000, *Blair-Smith v. Caesars Entertainment*, and *Altman v. Caesars Entertainment* [Toutant, 2023]. The defendants in some of these lawsuits are casino hotel operators, Cendyn that markets Rainmaker, and competitor selling rate data providers such as Amadeus, and CoStar's Smith Travel Research.

The initial complaint in the case *Gibson v. Cendyn Group, LLC*. was filed on January 25, 2023. The case was filed in the District Court for the District of Nevada. The plaintiffs, Richard Gibson and Roberto Manzo, alleged that hotel operators in Las Vegas were using Cendyn's software to artificially inflate hotel room prices.

In May 2024, the court in *Gibson v. Cendyn Group LLC*, dismissed with prejudice a putative class action alleging that hotel operators engaged in a price-fixing conspiracy by using the same software provider's products/algorithm for hotel room pricing recommendations.

The lawsuit *Cornish-Adebiyi v. Caesars Entertainment* was first filed on May 9, 2023. The case was filed in the District of New Jersey. It alleged antitrust violations related to algorithmic pricing in hotel room rates. The U.S. Department of Justice and the Federal Trade Commission have filed statements of interest in the case.

In September 2024, the court in *Cornish-Adebiyi,* et al. *v. Caesars Entertainment, Inc.*, et al., followed the roadmap that *Gibson* provided for dismissal of claims in algorithmic price-fixing cases, where the alleged co-conspirators (spokes) subscribe to the software provider's allegedly anti-competitive algorithm (hub) at different points in time, no confidential or otherwise nonpublic information is exchanged, and/or the co-conspirators are not bound to accept the algorithm's pricing recommendations.

Though the claims in *Gibson* and *Cornish-Adebiyi* resemble those brought against multifamily apartment owners and RealPage, which provides pricing software to those apartment owners, the *RealPage* court found that the plaintiffs there successfully stated a claim and allowed the case to proceed to discovery. In November 2025, the DOJ settled this lawsuit with RealPage after a change in management.

The outcomes are based on important differences between the allegations in *RealPage* and in *Gibson* and *Cornish-Adebiyi*, and those differences might establish the delineation of a legal principle that distinguishes success from unsuccessful cases going forward.

18.11.3 The Path Forward

The intent and business process of Competitive Revenue Management is to optimize inventory controls that results in a priced air itinerary for airlines or the best available rate for a hotel. Creating reference fares by airlines or hotel rate structure is an independent internal process that is used as input into the revenue management solution.

The allegations made by the plaintiffs of price-fixing are not true. What is required is an education of revenue management business practices and the value proposition for suppliers and travelers. Understanding how revenue management improves the bottom line of travel suppliers and simultaneously makes travel affordable for customers by offering multiple price points at various points in time before travel commences needs to the understood by the public at large.

As a result of the positive outcome of the class action lawsuits in the casino industry, these putative class action lawsuits have no bearing on the future of Competitive Revenue Management in the travel industry. Competitive selling fares and rates are publicly available data. The non-proprietary nature of data used for competitive revenue management in travel indicates that this business practice will continue.

When adoption of NDC matures, pricing power would have shifted from the GDSs to the airlines. Airlines do not have to file fares through fare aggregators such as ATPCO since the airline assumes responsibility for pricing itineraries across all channels of distribution [Vinod, 2024a]. Airlines may continue to use ATPCO to support the direct channel, and viewership permissions can be imposed on the fares What this means is that schedule and fare transparency that has existed since 1996 with the Internet will gradually disappear as NDC adoption with or without continuous pricing derived from reference fares increases through the indirect channel. However, airlines can still shop competing airline sites for guidance to determine their selling fares in the marketplace. The alternative is to not factor competitor data and only base the continuous pricing algorithm on demand forecasts by segment, remaining available capacity and the calibrated price-demand curves.

18.12 Future Outlook on Personalization

Personalization of offers and interaction in the travel industry begins with knowing the customer. In travel, every customer has a profile, but the customer may have different personas based on the context for travel. Knowing a customer's identity along with the context for travel enables personalization at a segment level of for a segment of ONE.

Most online users typically remain anonymous when they begin searching for an airline or hotel, only disclosing their identities once the search has led to a booking. To guarantee the relevance of the supplier products that are offered, recommendation engines must target both anonymous guests and identified guests. The context of the journey can be used to segment anonymous visitors and recommend offers that will be tailored to the personas revealed by the trip-purpose segment. When a customer is identified, sales history and individual preferences from the customer profile can be considered to ensure that the offer recommendations are precise and accurate. The importance of a traveler's personal identity for personalized recommendations cannot be understated.

18.12.1 Personalization and NDC

In the realm of intelligent airline retailing, personalization for a segment of ONE is widely discussed by various entities such as travel suppliers and intermediaries. It is personalization of offers at an individual level and not an aggregate segment of customers who exhibit similar traits and preferences. When IATA and a few carriers got together and launched NDC with a new XML-based messaging standard in 2012, one of the key value propositions touted by IATA and the airlines was personalization of the offer, which consists of the base fare and air ancillaries for an individual request. Note that the base fare for an itinerary can be based on static fare filings or a dynamic fare based on continuous dynamic pricing, for an individual request.

Questions that are foremost on the minds of travel executives are:

1. *Is personalized travel hype or will it become reality?*
2. *What are the boundaries for personalization with the advent of Generalized Data Protection (GDPR) in Europe and the California Consumer Privacy Act (CCPA) in California?*
3. *Is this truly a competitive differentiator?*
4. *What is the path to personalized travel over the next decade?*

18.12.2 Context for Travel-Based Segmentation for Offer Management

In travel, the context for making a trip influences a customer's preferences and propensity to buy. Customer segmentation based on context is also called trip-purpose segmentation (TPS). The TPS can be augmented with additional attributes such as the primary purpose for the trip such as weekend getaway for two, attending a wedding, college reunion, etc. to make the offer even more precise. Creating personalized offers begins with context for travel-based segmentation of the customer base. This is a core input into a recommendation engine to generate offers that resonate with customers. Most online users are anonymous when they begin their search for a flight or a hotel room, yet the offers generated should be relevant. Once the person is declared, historical bookings associated with the customer can be used to improve the recommendation and even offer a discount for the total offer based on a customer's projected lifetime value.

When a customer initiates a search, they are usually anonymous and not known. Context for travel-based segmentation is the first step to cluster customers together with similar preferences. An offer for a unique customer segment is foundational to airline offer management. Then the idea is to fine tune the offer, once the customer is declared, based on their past trips to create a personalized offer. However, *how feasible is personalization of the offer for a segment of ONE?* For example, consider full-service network carriers (FSC) in the U.S. like American and United that have stated that over 50% of an airline's revenue came from 85%–87% of its customers who flew only once. This also means that for FSCs, true 1:1 personalization is limited to loyal business flyers and high-end leisure travelers that are part of the 13%–15% of customers who generate half the airline's revenues.

Another reason is the enactment of General Data Protection Regulation (GDPR) in 2018 which gives EU citizens control over their data, what is collected and how it is used. With GDPR, models that work with aggregated data instead of individual personal data are more relevant which implies that personalization may be limited to creating offers at the trip-purpose segment level, instead of the individual. Like GDPR, the California Consumer Privacy Act (CCPA) of 2018 is a state statute to give residents in California more control over personal data collected about them by businesses. Drivers of change in digital advertising and personalization are legislative actions to protect consumer privacy. This brings us to personal identity and how it is managed, which is at the core of personalized travel.

18.12.3 Core Components of Frictionless Travel

Personal identity has been going through an evolution, and the future state will have far-reaching ramifications on travel intermediaries and the relationship between a customer and a supplier. Personalization of travel offers in the future will be very different from what it is today due to advances in blockchain technology and the evolving business landscape.

Core components for frictionless travel of the future are:

1. Decentralized Digital Identity, which allows a user to control their own identity and manage their own risk. What this means is that the industry will transition from centralized and federated identity to a distributed and decentralized digital identity.

   With centralized identity management, identity and access management occurs in a single environment. Its primary shortcoming lies in a single point of failure if a user's credentials are compromised by giving the attacker access to the user's entire portfolio,

   Federated identity grew out of the necessity for users to manage multiple passwords. The single sign-on allows verification of one form of identity and the user can freely move from system to system without logging into each one. Well known providers of federated identity are Facebook and Google.

   A decentralized digital identity allows authentication of credentials to be verified independently by every participant without mutual trust between participants. This puts the customer in control over their own identity, and they can decide how their personal information is shared.

   The World Economic Forum in collaboration with governments and industry partners initiated the Known Traveler Digital Identity (KTDI) program to create a secure decentralized system, where travelers control their own identity data, enabling seamless, verified border crossings using blockchain and biometrics (World Economic Forum, 2020). It currently operates as a pilot project. KTDI is distinct but conceptually aligned with U.S. government programs such as TSA PreCheck and Global Entry, which are operational, established "trusted traveler" programs.

2. Decentralized Universal Profile. A traveler owns their personal data in the Universal Profile, communicates directly and shares parts of the data with a travel or non-travel entity to provide the requested service for a seamless experience. Since the customer owns the data in the profile and decides which travel entities should have selective access for the trip, it fulfils the GDPR constraint.
3. Universal Data Exchange. The data owner, who is the traveler, authorizes the exchange of data through a neutral broker that securely exchanges data between travel and non-travel partners for a frictionless travel experience. The data are never centralized and stored but relevant data are exchanged in real-time. As an alternative to the Universal Data Exchange, the Digital Identity Foundation (DIF) and the World Wide Web Consortium (W3C) are promoting the concept of an Identity Hub (IH) to store profile data, sensitive documents and offers securely from suppliers that is controlled by the customer.

   As an alternative to the Universal Data Exchange, the Digital Identity Foundation (DIF) and the World Wide Web Consortium (W3C) are promoting the concept of an Identity Hub (IH) to store profile data, sensitive documents and offers securely from suppliers that is controlled by the customer.

18.12.4 Future of Hyper-Personalization

Airline marketing often fails to meet customer expectations because of a one-size-fits-all approach when managing customer touchpoints. Travelers have different tastes, destinations, and experiences they seek. Because of this, simple personalized messages are no longer enough. The future demands hyper-personalized campaigns that stand out. Hyper-personalization means going beyond basic segmentation. It uses predictive AI and real-time data to create unique experiences for each customer. This approach makes every interaction more relevant and engaging. It is no longer a luxury but a necessity in the competitive travel industry.

Unifying customer data with a customer data platform (CDP) is the first step toward hyper-personalization. This approach requires knowledge of a customer's identity, preferences and past purchase history to push relevant ads and offers. To gain a 360^0 view of the traveler, a CDP can bring together the following core elements:

1. Demographic data. Age, gender, location (zip code), income, etc.
2. Behavioral data. Website visits, email campaign interactions, social media posts, etc.
3. Purchase History. History of prior purchases.
4. Preferences. Preferences related to travel such as seating preference, loyalty programs, etc.

5. Consumer Intent. This is data inferred using natural language processing techniques like intent recognition.
6. Device usage. Preferences such as desktop, tablet or mobile devices.
7. Preferred channels. Channels for travel purchases such as airline direct, TMC, OTA, wholesaler, etc.

This data when assembled creates a comprehensive customer profile that can be used to run campaigns and reach your audience in a meaningful way. This approach can boost sales, improve how people perceive the airline brand, and build loyalty over time.

18.13 Quantum Computing is the Future

Physicists have been discussing the potential of quantum computing for the last thirty years. Lead technology companies such as IBM, Microsoft, Google, D-wave, Amazon, and Intel are investing billions in research to develop quantum computers. IBM is the leader of the pack and released the world's first 1,000-qubit chip in 2023 [Castelvecchi, 2023]. Unlike traditional computer chips which use binary notation, quantum computers utilize quantum bits, or "qubits," which can exist in a superposition of both states simultaneously.

Unlike classical bits that can be in only one of two states, zero or one, qubits can exist in a superposition of states and simultaneously represent both 0 and 1. This property allows quantum algorithms to process and analyze information in parallel, which has the potential for exponential acceleration of algorithm processing compared to the classical computational model. The most relevant aspects of quantum physics are the principles of superposition and entanglement. The superposition property enables a quantum computer to be in multiple states at once. As the number of qubits, n, increases, the number of states grows exponentially, represented by 2^n. The exponential scaling means that each additional qubit doubles the potential computational state space, allowing n qubits to store 2^n combinations simultaneously, unlike the linear growth (n) of classical bits.

Quantum computers can accomplish significantly more with their qubits than classical computers can with an equivalent number of bits. For instance, a 2-bit register in a classical computer can only hold one of four binary configurations (00, 01, 10, or 11) at one time. In contrast, a 2-qubit register in a quantum computer can simultaneously store all four numbers, and, as more qubits are introduced, the number of states grows exponentially. To achieve this level of advancement, quantum computers must also leverage the quantum property of entanglement.

Quantum entanglement allows two or more qubits to interact with each other instantly, unaffected by distance or constrained by the speed of light. When combined with superposition (a qubit exists in multiple states simultaneously), entanglement significantly boosts computing power, enabling calculations to be performed much faster than the most advanced classical computer today.

Quantum gates and circuits are used to manipulate qubits for quantum computations. Logic gates like the Hadamard gate (H-gate) and the CNOT (controlled-NOT) gate allow for the transformation and entanglement of qubits, making complex calculations possible. Quantum circuits consist of sequences of quantum gates that determine the flow of quantum operations.

A significant challenge with quantum computing involves the pre-processing of classical data to quantum states due to noise and error that are inherent in quantum systems. This representation of data allows for the exploration of novel patterns and insights. Correcting quantum errors is critical to ensure reliability and accuracy of quantum computations.

18.13.1 Google's Milestone in Quantum Computing

On December 9, 2024, Google shared in a blog post that a mathematical problem, which would take a traditional supercomputer 10 septillion (10^{25}) years to solve—longer than the entire history of the universe—can be completed in just five minutes with their new quantum computer chip called Willow.

Google reports that the new chip has resolved a significant issue in quantum computing. Qubits are delicate and can easily make mistakes. As more qubits are added to a calculation, the likelihood of errors increases. Despite this challenge, Google claims it has reduced these errors while testing with a greater number of qubits, marking an important advancement toward achieving reliable quantum computers for real-world applications.

18.13.2 Quantum Computing in Aerospace

Quantum computing in the aerospace industry is at least a decade away. There are many areas where industry and research institutions are focused on today.

18.13.2.1 Efficiency of Jet Engines

In May 2023, NVIDIA, Rolls Royce, and Classiq, a quantum software company, announced a breakthrough in quantum computing with the goal of enhancing the efficiency of jet engines [Nvidia, 2023]. Using NVIDIA's quantum computing platform, the companies have developed and simulated the largest quantum computing circuit for computational fluid dynamics (CFD) in the world. This circuit extends to 10 million layers and involves 39 qubits. Rolls-Royce is leveraging GPUs to pave the way for a quantum future, despite the current limitations of quantum computers, which can only support circuits with a few layers. Rolls-Royce intends to apply this new circuit to advance its progress in CFD and achieve quantum advantages when modeling the performance of jet engine designs using both classical and quantum computing methods.

18.13.2.2 Flight Planning

The flight planning problem determines a trajectory for an aircraft between two airports taking into consideration operational constraints both horizontally and vertically, weather, wind, fuel onboard, and aircraft performance. The objective is to find the least cost solution to reach the destination. It is a type of time dependent shortest path problem with piecewise linear travel time functions. The complexity of the problem stems from processing a large amount of data, relaxing the assumption of constant altitude, the dimensionality of the algorithm, and the response must be in seconds. Commonly used techniques are Dijkstra's shortest path algorithm and the A* algorithm, which are special cases of dynamic programming. The three-dimensional shortest path algorithm needs weight recalculations because of the unpredictable and non-linear aircraft fuel burn, making it impossible to determine the flight path without adjustments during the flight. Initial results for the quantum enhanced Dijkstra algorithms to accelerate solutions to the flight path optimization problems is promising [Makhanov, Setta, Liu, Gomez-Gonzalez, Jenaro-Rabadan, 2023].

18.13.2.3 Aircraft Design

Aircraft manufacturers like Boeing and Airbus see the potential to utilize quantum computers to support aerospace engineering and design aircraft in the future. Quantum computers are expected to tackle complex Finite Element Analysis (FEA) and Computational Fluid Dynamics (CDF) simulations that could result in lighter, stronger, more efficient aircraft through faster material discovery, optimized structures and better fluid dynamics modeling.

18.13.2.4 Cyber Security

The aviation industry faces cyber threats from ransomware hitting airports to attacks on critical systems such as Air Traffic Control (ATC) and Notice to Airmen (NOTAM). To address cyber security threats, quantum encryption is viewed by many as the future to ensure that vital systems are secure. But it is a Catch-22 situation. Future quantum computers could break current encryption, demanding an accelerated shift to post-quantum cryptography (PQC). The emerging quantum threat cannot be taken lightly.

18.13.2.5 Large Scale Optimization Problems in Airline Planning and Operations

In airline planning and operations, some of the most challenging problems to solve from a complexity perspective are:

1. Crew pairing for pilots and flight attendants.
2. Crew rostering for pilots and flight attendants.
3. Crew recovery from irregular airline operations caused by flight delays and cancellations
4. Assignment of aircraft to gates at major airports

5. Incorporating customer choice in network revenue management by solving the customer choice-based deterministic linear program (CDLP)

The feasibility of solving these problems on a quantum computer was evaluated [Hur, 2018]. To provide a form suitable for use on quantum computers, the traditional optimization problem must be converted into an equivalent QUBO (Quadratic Unconstrainted Binary Optimization) formulation. Formulating a QUBO is a pattern matching technique, common in machine learning applications. It is the problem of minimizing a quadratic polynomial over binary variables. For example, the conversion to QUBO for the crew rostering problem with more than 11,000 variables and over 1,300 constraints, resulted in one million terms that could not be directly imbedded on a quantum computer due to the high connectivity of the constraints. This experiment showed that we are several years away from using quantum computers for solving large scale optimization problems. Despite the negative results on quantum computing, Youngbum Hur's findings [Hur, 2018] won the Best Innovation Award at the AGIFORS Symposium in Tokyo in October 2018.

A similar conclusion was reached by Fiig, Boulanger, Wesenberg, Dalgaard, and Hansen (2023] when they evaluated the feasibility of solving the CDLP problem.

Training deep learning neural networks is computing intensive, requiring Graphical Processing Units (GPUs) and perhaps requiring quantum chips in the future. This is at least a decade away, so conventional chips optimized for AI/ML algorithms will be the mainstay for now.

18.13.2.6 Recommendation Algorithms for Airline Retailing

The objective of recommendation systems is to predict offers based on user preferences for products and services based on travelers in the same customer segment and their past behavior observed from purchase history data.

The recommendation engines deployed by companies like Amazon and Netflix have been widely discussed in industry forums on what customers are likely to buy on Amazon or see on Netflix. Many computer scientists, right or wrong, believe that this problem can be solved exponentially faster on quantum computers than traditional computers. A quantum algorithm for the recommendation problem was proposed in 2016 [Kerenidis and Prakash, 2016] to solve the problem exponentially faster than any known classical recommendation algorithm.

While quantum computers can solve the same problems that classical computers based on bits can, there is a key difference which lies in the pre-processing of classical data that is encoded as a quantum state to support quantum computing. Quantum machine learning leverages the principles of quantum mechanics and performs computations using quantum bits, abbreviated to qubits. The qubit is the basic unit of information in quantum computing and counterpart to the bit (the binary 0/1 digit) in classical computing. This pre-processing step is frequently a major challenge and when computer scientists compare results of quantum computing to classical computing, the computational steps involved in the pre-processing of data are ignored. Classical data structures can also be pre-processed to speed up performance of recommendation engines, but this approach is not popular with data scientists with a classical perspective.

Pilato and Vella provide an overview of the literature outlining the different proposed methodologies and techniques, highlighting the challenges that arise from this new quantum computing-related techniques that are currently exploited in recommendation systems [Pilato and Vella, 2023].

18.14 Buyer Expectations from the TMC of the Future

Corporate travel has rebounded since the pandemic of 2020. The Global Business Travel Association (GBTA) has estimated that the total volume of corporate travel in 2024 was $1.48 trillion [Braley, 2024], surpassing pre-pandemic spend of $1.43 trillion in 2019 for the first time. Further GBTA projects that corporate travel will exceed 2 trillion by 2028. This is illustrated in Fig. 18.5.

With significant changes in the airline distribution landscape with IATA NDC, the TMC competitor set of players is changing with a slew of new nimble challengers that are also questioning the expensive transaction fee model used by all the major TMCs. The market for business travel services is rapidly changing and the traditional TMC that manages corporate travel is being challenged.

To survive, the traditional TMCs, not known for their agility, should adapt along the following dimensions.

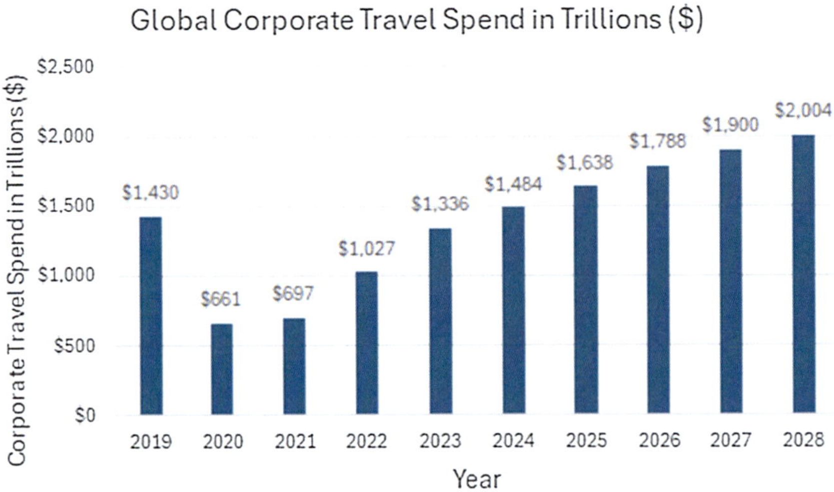

Source Global Business Travel Association

Fig. 18.5 Global corporate travel spend in trillions of dollars.

18.14.1 Reevaluation of the Technology Stack

Changes in airline distribution have prompted a reevaluation of the tech stack required by legacy TMCs, as new market entrants push the industry towards different models while traditional TMCs refocus their efforts on automating online and offline processes. Investment in AI-powered platforms is mandatory to enhance travel experience and simultaneously streamline costs and operations.

18.14.2 The Emerging Travel Landscape with AI

The introduction of AI is having a ripple effect, bringing new levels of efficiency to the travel booking and support processes. Labor shortages continue to impact offline call center performance, while new agent tools seek to alter the traditional online versus offline distinctions.

TMCs must invest in both Generative AI and Agentic AI that genuinely improves workflows, automates intelligently and empowers travelers with smarter self-service workflows.

To survive and thrive in an AI-enabled landscape, the travel agency playbook must shift focus from manual processes to AI-driven automation, touchless transactions, and data-centric strategies that significantly improve operational efficiency, enhance personalization, and boost unit economics.

18.14.3 Sunset GDS Dependency

TMCs must look beyond the GDS to which they have been dependent on since 1976. In the EDIFACT era, travel agencies were dependent on GDS incentives as a significant revenue stream, In the NDC era, direct access to suppliers is required to ensure access to comprehensive content. This will also require TMCs to pursue front-end and performance-based back-end commissions aggressively from air travel suppliers to offset the loss of GDS incentives for NDC bookings.

18.14.4 Flexible Service Model for Travel Buyers

Travel buyers expect flexible service models that can be à la carte. Corporate buyers should be able to opt in or opt out of specific service components such as AI-powered self-service booking tool (CBT), self-service, human customer support, policy compliance, expense management, traveler support and assistance during the trip, access to negotiated fares, visa / passport assistance, risk management, and duty of care.

The fee-per-transaction pricing model, how TMCs bill their corporate clients, will undergo a transformation over the next decade, giving way to a lower cost value proposition for corporate buyers. Today travelers are required to pay a fee every time they contact a TMC. For example, there are fees associated with air bookings, hotel bookings, change fees, agent touch fee, emergency contact fee, etc. A new breed of multi-content sourced corporate travel and expense management platforms will create alternate cost-effective pricing models such as a single consolidated fee per booked itinerary regardless of the type of booking (air, hotel, etc.) and touch. An alternative is the all-you-can-book annual plan subscription model for small and mid-sized businesses. If even a few of these companies move up from the mid-market to the Fortune 1000 companies, the traditional TMC model will be disrupted by new entrants that mimic a Walmart-like value model.

18.14.5 Source-Agnostic Booking Platforms for the Mid-Market TMCs

GDS incentives play a smaller role for the mid-size TMCs in their profitability equation than for larger ones. They rely more on alternate sources of revenue such as customer service, and front-end and back-end commissions from airlines. These mid-sized TMCs are prime candidates for source-agnostic air booking platforms. These platforms operate without being restricted to or favoring any specific content providers and allows them to access content from multiple sources (Global Distribution Systems (GDS), airline direct connects (NDC), etc.) within a unified workflow to deliver a consistent experience for their clients worldwide. This provides flexibility, broader inventory access, and better negotiation power in the future. Examples of these platforms are Spotnana, TravelPerk, Navan, AmTrav, Coupa, FlightsLogic, Itilite, and others.

18.15 The Future of Blockchain in Travel for Offer Management

Blockchain is a distributed network that has the potential to become the new travel platform. Deployment of the decentralized digital identifier is just one of many applications of blockchain in travel [Vinod, 2020b]. Many technologists view decentralized digital identification as a once in a generation disruptive foundational technology like TCP/IP (1972–1982), HTTP and the browser (1989–1997), GSM (Global System for Mobile communication) and mobile (1993–2007) that were all brought to market by community development.

Blockchain technology can transform airline offer management by improving transparency, efficiency, secure payments and data sharing, and customer experience. By embracing blockchain, airlines can create a more dynamic, secure, and profitable ecosystem for managing offers and engaging with customers.

A blockchain consists of a set of blocks that are linked to each other using cryptography, thereby ensuring data security, data integrity, confidentiality, authentication, and non-repudiation. Each block in a blockchain has its own unique cryptographic hash and the hash of the previous block, a timestamp when it was created and transaction data, thereby enforcing chronological integrity. Hence, transactions are stored in blocks with hash values and time stamps. Each block is connected to the previous one, creating a chain of blocks. When a block is created, it cannot be deleted or modified, known as immutability. The chaining mechanism, powered by one-way hash functions like SHA-256 (Secure Hash Algorithm 256-bit is a cryptographic hash function that converts input data into a unique fixed-size 256-bit (32-byte) hexadecimal string) make blockchains inherently tamper resistant, as changing one block requires recalculating all following hashes, a computationally infeasible task. Information can only be modified with consensus from all parties in the blockchain. Hence, making a change to a block becomes a addendum to the block, making it a very secure environment. This technology makes it possible to build applications where multiple entities can execute transactions without the need for central authority.

A blockchain has three primary components: a ledger, cryptocurrency, and a mechanism to execute smart contracts. Smart contracts are used to settle negotiated agreements among all parties automatically without an intermediary. A blockchain is ideal for storing smart contracts because security and immutability are built into the solution. All payments and settlements on the blockchain are made with a cryptocurrency.

The distributed nodes in a blockchain operate peer-to-peer (P2P). P2P is not a new concept. It is a way for two or more computers to share files and devices such as printers. For example, video sharing platforms like Zoom, Microsoft Teams and Google Meet operate on a P2P network. The unique aspect of blockchain is that it keeps a record of the actual transaction—the buyer, the seller, and the settlement—on every node. P2P has also eliminated the middleman.

There are two types of blockchains: private and public. They both rely on consensus-based algorithms to validate transactions stored on a distributed ledger and every participant has a synchronized copy. The difference is that a participant requires special privileges to participate in a private blockchain. There is also a hybrid version called permissioned blockchain. Unlike a private blockchain that operates in an isolated network, a permissioned blockchain can be a public blockchain that allows participation based on different access levels. When blockchain reaches maturity, private, public, and permissioned blockchains will co-exist.

The "middleman" is a topic of interest in blockchain. In a private blockchain with a distributed ledger the users are known, and it is controlled by a known entity, and contains a middleman. In a public blockchain there is no middleman, and the users are anonymous, each of whom has a copy of the ledger. And this is what Bitcoin did with banks.

At its core, blockchain is about decentralizing information. Blockchain does pose a threat to transactional intermediaries that dominate the space today such as GDSs, OTAs and TMCs because they would no longer be needed. Like the new XML-based messaging protocol that gave rise to new entrants called NDC Aggregators, blockchain also lowers the barrier for entry of new players in the marketplace [Vinod, 2024b]. The question is: *What is the value provided by today's leading intermediaries if a better form of technology comes along that supports peer-to-peer communication between a traveler and a supplier without a middleman, thereby eliminating commissions and booking fees?* From a traveler's perspective, this will also ultimately lower the cost of travel.

The benefits of blockchain in travel are transparency, efficiency and the customer experience.

18.15.1 Self-Sovereign Identity

Travelers have ultimate control over their own digital identity. They can manage and share their verifiable credentials without central authority. The Sovrin Foundation developed a distributed ledger to create a secure and tamper-proof system for managing identity information [Sovrin, 2018]. The network is public, but permissioned which means that only trusted entities called "Stewards" can operate the validator nodes that secure the network. Individuals have ultimate control over their own digital identity. They can manage and share their verifiable credentials without central authority. Digital Identifiers (DID) are unique identifiers that provide a cryptographic basis for the system and do not require a central administrator. Users can share only the pertinent information from a credential with a verifier, without revealing all details on their ID, enhancing privacy.

While the Sovrin Foundation ceased operations of its MainNet ledger in 2025, the underlying principles of self-sovereign identity, decentralized identifiers (DIDs), and verifiable credentials continue to be important concepts in digital identity.

18.15.2 Transparency and Trust

Blockchain can create a transparent and tamper-proof record of airline offers, including pricing, availability, and ancillary services, accessible to all relevant stakeholders such as airlines, travel agents, and customers.

By fostering a more direct and trusted environment, blockchain can potentially reduce the reliance on intermediaries in the offer management and product distribution process, leading to cost savings and increased revenue for airlines.

This does not necessarily mean that this is the end of intermediaries. Consumer interfaces to interact with suppliers will still be required and the business model will continue to evolve, and the roles of these intermediaries will be transformed over time.

The immutable nature of blockchain records helps in preventing fraudulent offers and ensuring the authenticity of bookings and transactions.

18.15.3 Efficiency, Automation and Enhancing Customer Experience

Blockchain-powered smart contracts can automate various aspects of offer management, such as payment processing, booking changes, baggage and cargo tracking, interline and loyalty program settlements, streamlining operations and minimizing manual intervention.

Blockchain can enable the creation of secure digital identities for passengers and the use of smart tickets. Smart tickets are digital tickets with unique identifiers, recorded on a decentralized, transparent, and secure ledger. This offers a more streamlined and hassle-free travel experience, from booking to boarding and accessing airport services.

With enhanced data sharing and analysis capabilities, blockchain can contribute to the creation of more personalized and relevant offers for customers based on their travel history and preferences.

Blockchain-enabled payment systems can facilitate faster and more secure international transactions and settlements, improving customer satisfaction. It also reduces transaction costs and a record of all transactions.

18.15.4 Adoption Challenges

Blockchain in travel to process airline transactions is a solution for the future. There are several challenges today that will delay adoption of blockchain until 2035 or later. They are:

1. Integration with existing airline legacy IT systems is a challenge. Interoperability is both difficult and expensive.
2. Scalability and performance must be clearly demonstrated. Ensuring blockchain platforms can handle the vast amount of data and transactions in the airline industry efficiently is a key concern.
3. Regulatory and compliance issues in aviation must be addressed. Navigating the complex regulatory landscape of aviation and ensuring blockchain implementations comply with existing rules and standards presents a major challenge.
4. Cybersecurity and data privacy must be addressed to the satisfaction of all stakeholders. Protecting sensitive passenger data and proprietary information within a transparent and distributed ledger is crucial.

18.16 Urban Air Mobility

Air taxi service (ATS) is expected to operate in the near future after they receive regulatory approval from the Federal Aviation Administration (FAA). Flying taxis will be a mix of scheduled and on-demand services using electric vertical take-off and landing (eVTOL) technology. Besides regulatory approval, operational requirements such as infrastructure and on-demand battery swapping must be in place. The DOT and FAA are planning pilot programs to safely and efficiently integrate these aircraft into the National Airspace System (NAS).

The on-demand model will be similar to ride hailing apps like Uber and Lyft to provide on-demand flights for one passenger or a few riders. The objective of Urban Air Mobility (UAM) is to alleviate traffic congestion, provide faster travel, and support services like emergency response and delivery. The goal is to reduce the daily travel commute dramatically in congested cities. Air taxi routes across congested cities are expected to cut commute times of an hour or more by road to about 20 min or less. This new transport option will help people avoid gridlock on city streets. They can be operated from sky ports built on rooftops.

Major airlines are making financial and operational commitments eVTOL manufacturers. For example, Delta Air Lines has partnered with Joby Aviation, United Airlines with Archer Aviation, and American Airlines with Vertical Aerospace. These carriers will provide a new service to shuttle passengers from major city centers like New York, Chicago, Los Angeles, Houston, Dallas-Fort Worth, Philadelphia and San Francisco to their flight terminals at local airports.

The business and commercial model will evolve over the next decade.

One option is for the eVTOL manufacturer to operate the aircraft while the carrier integrates this new service into its customer-facing channels and provide the airport infrastructure. This type of partnership between the carrier and the manufacturer is designed to provide a seamless premium city-to-airport and airport-to-city transfer for travelers.

The second option is for the airline to purchase or lease eVTOL's from the manufacturer, operate the vehicles, and integrate the new service into its customer-facing channels.

18.16.1 Revenue Management for On-Demand Local Air Transport

Revenue management for battery-operated flying taxis will be very different from airline seat management. It will require fleet and battery management, variable or dynamic pricing to address peak demand like current rideshare models and diversified revenue streams to address high operating costs and market uncertainties.

The dynamic price quote for the service must consider the following.

1. Rush hour and event-driven surges in demand must be considered. The price quote will vary based on fluctuating demand, vehicle availability, and traffic patterns on the ground and in the air.
2. For air traffic routes that bypass heavy traffic areas, premium pricing can be implemented. This will capture the value of time saved for travelers.
3. Expected utilization of the transport vehicle.
4. Cost model for investment in vehicles, depreciation, maintenance and battery usage over a fixed period.
5. The eVTOL price-per-seat will be cheaper than the price for an exclusive flight. For multi-passenger eVTOL vehicles, companies can offer either a lower price-per-seat option or a premium exclusive eVTOL flight service, similar to a charter.
6. eVTOL price-per-seat will initially be more expensive than high-end ground transportation (e.g., Uber Black) but will become cheaper and eventually approach standard ride share (UberX) as technology matures and volume increases, making shared seats far more affordable than chartering an entire, exclusive eVTOL.
7. Further, operators can offer subscription plans or corporate packages for frequent flyers to build a stable customer base and predictable future revenue.

18.17 The Road Forward: Strategic Agility for Competitive Advantage

Strategic agility, the ability to adapt and innovate quickly in response to market changes and evolving customer demands, is increasingly important for airlines as they navigate the landscape of airline retailing. As the airline industry transitions to offers and orders, there are many opportunities to enhance customer experience, boost revenue, modernize their IT infrastructure, and optimize costs. This fundamental approach towards a customer-centric, digital transformation strategy involves leveraging technologies like test and learn experimentation, personalized offers, dynamic pricing, and integrated order management systems. By championing these changes, airlines can create more engaging shopping experiences tailored to the specific needs of business and leisure travelers, increase ancillary sales, and streamline operations.

Flawless execution, the business of getting things done, is an imperative for success. Strategic agility goes hand-in-hand with execution. Execution is discipline and integral to strategy. A strategy is only successful if it is flawlessly implemented. It involves turning a strategic plan into action through a disciplined, systematic process of aligning resources, making decisions, and holding people accountable. Without strong execution, brilliant strategies often fail because there is a critical gap between the goals of the organization and its ability to achieve them.

Key aspects of strategic agility include:

18.17.1 Customer Centric Transformation

Airline retailing is focused on providing personalized, relevant, and in-demand experiences to travelers. Strategic agility enables airlines to sense and respond rapidly to changing customer preferences and create tailored offers that enhance satisfaction and loyalty. Central to customer centricity is the ability to recognize the importance of treating customers as unique individuals with distinct needs and preferences. This involves an investment in analytics to understand customer behavior, value, and needs, then tailoring offerings and interactions accordingly.

A key driver of customer centricity is the desire to deliver a superior customer experience across all customer touchpoints, from booking to post-flight interactions. This includes everything from seamless booking processes and personalized in-flight amenities to responsive customer support. A focus on the customer increases customer satisfaction, drive short-term profitability through targeted offers and long-term customer loyalty.

A 100% adoption of NDC is not a panacea for profitability. Poor communication and lack of focus on operational excellence will prevent an airline from fulfilling the demands of the customer.

18.17.2 Travel Suppliers Must Accept that Multi-Channel Travel Buyers Dominate the Landscape

"Multi-channel travel buyers" are travelers or companies that use multiple platforms and touchpoints to research and book travel services. This approach is dominant in the travel industry, reflecting how people buy trips. The fragmented travel journey, with buyers moving across search engines, social media, online travel agencies (OTAs) and supplier-direct sites, necessitates that travel suppliers adopt sophisticated, multi-channel marketing and booking strategies. While focusing on the direct channel is important to protect the brand and contain distribution costs, agile suppliers must embrace a multi-channel strategy that customers demand. Ensuring channel competitiveness is a necessity, not a luxury.

18.17.3 A Razor Focus on Fulfillment

Fulfillment refers to the process of delivering the travel products and services that a customer has purchased, from the initial offer to the completion of the journey. This involves various steps like order creation, order management, fulfillment, settlement, and completion, all managed within the airline's offer and order management capability. Fulfillment also applies to any third-party non-air products in the order.

Fulfillment of all items in the order is fulfilling a promise to the customer. Airlines must provide excellent support and service throughout the customer journey, including handling disruptions from irregular operations, and providing real-time information.

18.17.4 True Omnichannel Distribution

A omnichannel strategy integrates all customer touchpoints (website, app, email, in-person) into a single, seamless customer experience, using data to personalize interactions from discovery to post-trip. It is important to ensure consistency across all channels, direct and indirect, and focus on customer expectations over individual channels for higher loyalty and recurring revenue.

Agile suppliers focus on making investments for an omnichannel strategy. There is no substitute for creating a seamless, integrated customer experience across all channels, from booking to post-flight. It involves using a unified application to connect a customer's journey across a website, mobile app, call center, social media, and physical airport touchpoints, enabling consistent messaging, personalized offers, and real-time updates.

A true omni channel strategy also means that content must *not* be withheld from traditional distribution channels like the GDS. Airlines like American, United, Avianca, and others have removed their lowest fare categories or portions of their flight networks from legacy GDS channels. In some instances, airlines might leave existing content in GDSs but create new, differentiated offers only accessible through direct or NDC channels. Withholding content from certain channels defeats the purpose of an omnichannel strategy.

18.17.5 Data-Driven Decision Making

This is the process of making choices based on the analysis of data rather than intuition or gut feeling. It involves collecting, analyzing and interpreting data to ensure that strategic business decisions are aligned with corporate goals and objectives.

Access to quality and accurate data is a pre-requisite to make it part of the corporate culture of analysis followed by execution. An evidence-based foundation for decision making improves outcomes and minimizes uncertainty in the long run.

18.17.6 Technology Refresh and Adoption

Many airlines are burdened with legacy hardware and software in a tech stack that impedes progress. These systems can present significant challenges for airlines by impacting efficiency, security, and the ability to innovate. Modernizing legacy systems requires a strategic approach that is very methodical. It begins with performing a current assessment and developing a detailed roadmap to modernize, backed with investment dollars. Modernization is never a one-time event. It is an perpetual process of continuous improvement.

Embracing technologies such as AI-powered personalization, experimentation, real-time intelligence, dynamic pricing, and offer and order management are critical for achieving strategic agility in airline retailing.

18.17.7 Business Environment and Adaptability

Airline retailing emphasizes the need for airlines to be flexible and responsive to the evolving needs and expectations of travelers. This necessitates a shift from traditional, rigid approaches to a more dynamic and customer-centric model.

Strategic agility means having the flexibility to adjust business models, pricing strategies, and service offerings in real-time, even in the face of disruptions or unforeseen events.

18.17.8 Culture of Innovation and Continuous Learning

Airlines with strategic agility foster a culture that embraces experimentation, learning, and continuous improvement. This creates an environment to iterate quickly, adapt and evolve their approach to airline retailing as needed.

A culture of innovation and continuous learning is a workplace environment in which employees are encouraged to learn, experiment and improve, fosters creativity and adaptation. This culture is characterized by a growth mindset, where challenges are seen as opportunities for learning and failure is viewed as a steppingstone toward improvement. A growth mindset is all about the attitude with which a person faces challenges, how they process failures, and how they adapt and evolve as a result. A corporate commitment involves ongoing education, skill development and a commitment to refining processes and systems is required.

18.17.9 Concluding Remarks on Strategic Agility

Strategic agility requires a comprehensive understanding of the "battlefield," which in a business context means analyzing market trends, competitor actions, and potential disruptions for competitive advantage. It is a core trait for the pursuit of business excellence.

Sun Tzu's principles are deeply intertwined with strategic agility, emphasizing the importance of adapting tactics to circumstances, like water flowing around obstacles, and a dynamic approach to planning. He advises being like the mythical "Shuai-jan" snake from the Chang mountains that attacks with its head and tail simultaneously, where striking the middle causes both ends to attack. It symbolizes rapid, mutual support in battle. It is a metaphor for a skilled tactician who coordinates and strikes from all directions, meaning strategies should be fluid and avoid repetition. A master strategist, according to Sun Tzu, can modify their tactics to win, which is the essence of strategic agility.

In conclusion, strategic agility is required for airline retailers to thrive in the modern environment. By focusing on customer-centricity, data-driven decision-making, periodic technology refresh and adoption, and an ingrained culture of innovation, the airlines in pursuit of business excellence will be able to navigate challenges, adapt, and achieve success in the evolving world of air travel.

Airline Acronyms

A

Category	Acronym	Description
General	A2A	Account to account
	ADA	Airline Deregulation Act
	ATC	Air Traffic Control
	ATI	Antitrust Immunity
	ATM	Automated Teller Machines
	ATS	Air Taxi Service
	CFR	Code of Federal Regulations
	CRS	Computerized reservations system used as a primary computer sales system by an airline. Synonyms include Central Reservations System and Host CRS
	CRM	Customer Relationship Management
	DOT	Department of Transportation (U.S.)
	EFB	Electronic Flight Bag
	FSC	Full-Service Carrier
	GSA	General Sales Agent
	GDS	Global Distribution System used by travel agencies to buy/sell travel products, e.g., Sabre, Travelport, Amadeus
	FAR 121	Federal Aviation Regulation rules for scheduled air carriers
	KPI	Key Performance Indicator
	MAR	Low-Cost Carrier
	LCC	Modern Airline Retailing
	NOTAM	NOTice To AirMen
	OBT	Online Booking Tool
	OTA	Online Travel Agency
	PQC	Post-Quantum Cryptography

(continued)

B. Vinod, *The Era of Airline Revenue Management with Offers and Orders*, Management for Professionals, https://doi.org/10.1007/978-3-032-24197-9

(continued)

Category	Acronym	Description
	PSC	Passenger Services Conference
	PDG	Passenger Distribution Group
	SAF	Sustainable Aviation Fuel
	SAGE	Semi-Automatic Ground Environment
	SKU	Stock Keeping Unit
	TMC	Travel Management Company
	UAM	Urban Air Mobility
	ULCC	Ultra-Low-Cost Carrier
	W3C	World Wide Web Consortium

Category	Acronym	Description
GDS Global Id	1A	Amadeus
	1B	Abacus International
	1C	EDS Information Business
	1D	Radixx
	1E	TravelSky
	1F	Infini
	1G	Galileo
	1J	Axess
	1K	Sutra
	1L	Open Skies
	1M	Sirin
	1N	Navitaire
	1P	Worldspan
	1Q	Sirena
	1S	Sabre
	1U	ITA Software
	1V	Apollo
	1W	Sabre (old)
	1X	GETS—Gabriel Extended Travel System
	1Y	EDS Shares
	1Z	Fantasia
	F1	Farelogix

Category	Acronym	Description
Mainframe	ACP	Airline Control Program
	ALCS	Airline Control System (running TPF in a MVS environment, now z/os)
	CRT	Cathode Ray Tube
	IPARS	International PARS
	MVS	Multiple Virtual Storage
	PARS	Programmed Airline Reservations System
	TPF	Transaction Processing Facility
	TPFDF	TPF Database Facility
	z/os	An IBM operating system for mainframes that is suitable for continuous, high-volume operation with high security and stability
	z/TPF	A high volume, high throughput transaction processor that can handle large continuous loads of complex transactions across large, geographically dispersed networks. Successor to TPF 4.1

Category	Acronym	Description
Messaging Protocols	AIRIMP	Airline Industry Reservations Interline Messaging Procedures
	API	Application Program Interface
	EDI	Electronic Data Interchange—a format in which business data are represented using national or international standards
	EDIFACT	Electronic Data Interchange for Administration, Commerce and Transport, messages that are approved as standards for EDI
	ICOT	The traditional piece of computer hardware for using network services. Terminals usually have minimal computing function, being completely dependent upon their host, and are often referred to as "dumb terminals."
	JSON	Java Script Object Notation
	NDC	New Distribution Capability
	OTA	Open Travel Alliance, a non-profit standards body that is creating messaging standards across all lines of business (air, hotel, car, etc.)
	PADIS	The Passenger and Airport Data Interchange Standards (PADIS) Board develops and maintains Electronic Data Interchange and XML message standards for passenger travel and airport-related passenger service activities
	REST API	Representational State Transfer API
	SIPP	Standard Interline Passenger Procedures
	SIP	Session Initiated Protocol
	SOAP	Simple Object Access Protocol
	TCO	Total Cost of Ownership
	Type A	Immediate application response with timeout handling in place at the application level. EDIFACT follows a Type A message format

(continued)

(continued)

Category	Acronym	Description
	Type B	Message guaranteed delivery, a slower response. The AIRIMP documents govern the Type B message formats
	TTY	Teletype is used to communicate reservations and messages between carriers using the AIRIMP standards. The airline industry uses teletype messages over ARINC or SITA networks to communicate between reservations systems
	XML	eXtended Markup Language
	Zulu Time	Greenwich Mean Time (GMT), due to "Z" used in CRSs to indicate GMT

Category	Acronym	Description
Schedules	ASM	Ad hoc schedule message
	Cirium	Schedule aggregator (like OAG and Cirium
	DEI	Data Element Identifier in SSIM
	IROPS	Irregular Operations
	MCT	Minimum Connect Time
	OAG	Office Airline Guide (schedule aggregator, like Cirium)
	QSI	Quality of Service Index, simpler linear form of CCM used in flight scheduling
	SOC	Systems Operations Control
	SSIM	Standard Schedule Information Manual
	SSM	Standard schedule message

Category	Acronym	Description
Emerging Technologies (Advanced Analytics, AI, Blockchain, New Protocols)	A2A	Agent2Agent
	AI	Artificial Intelligence
	AID	Automatic Interaction Detection
	AIO	Artificial Intelligence Optimization
	AGI	Artificial General Intelligence
	AIT	Algorithmic Information Theory
	ARC	Abstraction and Reasoning Corpus
	ASIC	Application Specific Integrated Circuit
	AWS	Amazon Web Services
	BNPL	Buy Now Pay Later
	CART	Classification And Regression Trees
	CBC	Choice-based Conjoint
	CCM	Consumer Choice Model

(continued)

(continued)

Category	Acronym	Description
	CHAID	Chi-squared Automatic Interaction Detection
	CLV	Customer Lifetime Value
	CPM	Cost Per Mille
	CPA	Cost-per-acquisition
	CPS	Commission-per-stay
	CNN	Convolution Neural Network
	CPU	Central Processing Unit
	CUA	Computer-Using Agent
	DARPA	Defense Advanced Research Projects Agency
	DCC	Distribution Cost Charge
	DCR	Distribution Cost Recovery
	DCRF	Distribution Cost Recovery Fee
	DDS	Direct Data Solutions (from IATA in collaboration with ARC and Cirium)
	DTC	Distribution Technology Charge
	GAN	Generative Adversarial Network
	GBM	Gradient Boosting Machine
	GFS	Google File System
	GISP	Generalized Independent Set Problem
	GPT	Generative Pre-trained Transformer
	GPU	Graphics Processing Unit
	GLM	Generalized Linear Model
	Hadoop	Java based open-source software that supports data intensive distributed applications on large clusters of commodity hardware
	HB	Hierarchical Bayes
	HBase	Open source non-relational distributed database
	HDFS	Hadoop Distributed File System based on GFS and MapReduce
	HIVE	A data Warehousing system that runs on top of Hadoop to allow SQL-like queries
	IFG	IATA Financial Gateway
	LIME	Local Interpretable Model-agnostic Explanations
	LLM	Large Language Model
	LRM	Large Reasoning Model
	LSTM	Long Short-term Memory
	MAB	Multi-Armed Bandit
	MBR	Mishandled Baggage Rate
	MCP	Model Context Protocol

(continued)

(continued)

Category	Acronym	Description
	MIDT	Marketing Information Data Tapes
	ML	Machine Learning
	MNL	Multinomial Logit
	MPP	Massively Parallel Processing
	NLP	Natural Language Processing
	NLU	Natural Language Understanding
	OLAP	OnLine Analytical Processing
	OR	Operations Research
	PAP	Principal-Agent Problem
	PE	Price Elasticity
	Pig	Apache Pig is a platform for analyzing large data sets
	PAC	Pay at Checkout
	PPC	Pay per Click
	PPS	Pay per Stay
	RAG	Retrieval Augmented Generation
	RFMTV	Recency, Frequency, Monetary Value, Tenure, Variety
	RF	Random Forest
	RL	Reinforcement Learning
	RNN	Recurrent Neural Network
	RPA	Robotic Process Automation
	SERP	Search Engine Results Pages
	SV	Support Vectors
	SVM	Support Vector Machines
	SCR	Support Vector Regression
	SHAP	SHapley Additive exPlanations
	StP	Segment-then-Price
	THAID	Theta Automatic Interaction Detection
	TOPSIS	Technique for Ordering Preference by Similarity to Ideal Solution (multi-criteria decision making)
	TPS	Trip-purpose Segmentation
	TPU	Tensor Processing Unit
	TS	Thompson Sampling
	TSVM	Transductive Support Vector Machines
	UCB	Upper Confidence Bound
	UCP	Universal Commerce Protocol
	VCC	Virtual Credit Card
	VCN	Virtual Card Numbers
	VLM	Vision Language Model

(continued)

(continued)

Category	Acronym	Description
	VLSI	Very-Large-Scale-Integration
	vMCO	Virtual Miscellaneous Change Order
	vMPD	Virtual Miscellaneous Multi-Purpose Document
	VW	Wabbit
	WTA	Willingness to Accept
	WTP	Willingness to Pay
	XAI	Explainable AI

Category	Acronym	Description
Reservations/ CRS and GDS	AAA	Agent Assembly Area
	ACH	U.S.-based Airline Clearing House
	ACARS	Aircraft Communications Addressing and Reporting
	ADM	Agency Debit Memo
	Altéa	Amadeus Customer Management Suite (Altéa RES, Altéa INVENTORY and Altéa DCS)
	APIS	Advanced Passenger Information System with pre-arrival and departure manifest data on passengers for border security agents
	ARM	Airline Retailing Maturity (index)
	ARNK	A surface sector segment in the PNR which means method of travel or arrival is unknown". These segments represent a break in journey. Pronounced ARUNK
	ASN	Advanced Shipping Notice
	ASR	Agent (Agency) Sales Report
	ATO	Airport Ticket Office
	ATSE	Air Travel Shopping Engine
	AVO	Average Value of the Order
	BABS	British Airways Booking System
	CCL	Content Curation Layer
	CCPA	California Consumer Protection Act
	CPA	City Pair Availability
	CPM	Connecting Partner Model
	CRS	Computer Reservation System (used as the primary computer sales system by an airline); also called host CRS
	CTO	City Ticket Office
	CUTE	Common Use Terminal Equipment
	CUSS	Common Use Self Service
	DCS	Departure Control System
	DID	Digital IDentifiers

(continued)

(continued)

Category	Acronym	Description
	DIF	Digital Identity Foundation
	ET	End Transaction
	EMD	Electronic Miscellaneous Document, industry solution for collection and settlement of air ancillary fees (e.g., Air Extras) via ARC and BSP
	FCA	Full Content Agreement
	GBV	Gross Booking Value
	GDPR	General Data Protection Regulation
	GNR	Guest Name Record (equivalent to PNR in hospitality)
	GSA	General Services Administration (U.S.)
	GSE	Ground Support Equipment
	KTDI	Known Traveler Digital Identity
	MCO	Miscellaneous Change Orders
	MFN	Most Favored Nation
	MRP	Machine Readable Passport
	MRZ	Machine Readable Zone
	NAS	New Airline Storefront
	NGS	Next Generation Storefront
	OCN	Order Change Notification
	OLTP	Online Transaction Processing
	OM	Order Management
	OMS	Order Management System
	ONE Order	IATA term for airline order management
	OOPS	One Order Passenger Servicing platform
	OPA	Offer Partner (Participating) Airline
	ORA	Offer Responsible Airline
	PCA	Participating Carrier Agreement
	PII	Personally Identifiable Information
	PMS	Property Management System (hospitality)
	PNR	Passenger Name Record
	PRS	Pre-Reserved Seats
	PSS	Passenger Service System
	SABRE	Semi-Automated Business Research Environment
	SabreSonic	*SabreSonic* CSS (Customer Sales and Service) reservations system
	SFPD	Secure Flight Passenger Data
	SPA	Special Prorate Agreement
	SRSIA	Standard Retailer and Supplier Interline Agreement
	SSR	Special Service Request

(continued)

(continued)

Category	Acronym	Description
	SSR-I	Special Service Request—Inventory
	TAAP	Travel Agency Affiliate Program
	TACP	Travel Agency Commission Payment
	TMC	Travel Management Company
	TOC	Total Cost of Ownership
	TTL	Ticketing Time Limit
	TVL	Travel Segment
	UDX	Universal Data Exchange
	UC	Unable to Confirm at Sell
	UP	Universal Profile
	VCR	Virtual Coupon Record
	VRBO	Vacation Rentals By Owner

Category	Acronym	Description
Organizations	A4A	Airlines for America, a trade organization representing U.S. airlines
	AAA	American Automobile Association
	AAIF	Agentic AI Foundation
	AARP	American Association of Retired Persons
	ACI	Airports Council International
	ACM	Association for Computing Machinery
	AEA	Association of European Airlines
	AFI	Air Fare Insight (SITA product)
	AHLA	American Hotel & Lodging Association
	ALPAC	Automatic Language Processing Advisory Committee
	AMR Corp	Parent company of American Airlines, American Eagle, AmericanConnection and Executive Airlines until 2013
	ARC	Airlines Reporting Corporation (ARC) is a technology solutions company providing transaction settlement and data information services
	ARIG	Airline Revenue Integrity Group
	ARINC	Aeronautical Radio, Inc. was established in 1929, is a major provider of transport communications and systems engineering solutions for aviation and airports
	ASTA	American Society of Travel Agents (Advisors)
	ATA	Air Transport Association
	ATPCO	Airline Tariff Publishing Company (airline industry fare aggregator)

(continued)

(continued)

Category	Acronym	Description
	BEA	Bureau of Economic Analysis (U.S.)
	BOAC	British Overseas Airways Corporation
	BSP	Billing and Settlement Plans (like ARC in the U.S.) for billing statements reflecting ticket sales made by each travel agent
	CAAC	Civil Aviation Administration of China
	CAB	Civil Aeronautics Board
	CASMA	Computerized Airline Sales and Marketing Association
	CFPB	Consumer Financial Protection Bureau
	Cirium	Schedule aggregator, like OAG
	CMA	Competition and Markets Authority
	DDRS	Digital, Data and Retailing Symposium
	DOJ	Department of Justice
	DOT	Department of Transportation (U.S.)
	Dynata	Online market research firm
	EU	European Union
	EEA	European Economic Area
	FAA	Federal Aviation Administration
	FCC	Federal Communications Commission
	FTC	Federal Trade Commission
	GBTA	Global Business Travel Association
	IATA	International Air Transport Association
	IATAN	International Air Transport Association Network
	IBM	International Business Machines Corporation
	ICAO	International Civil Aviation Organization
	ICH	IATA Clearing House
	IFRS	International Finance Reporting Standards
	OAG	Official Airline Guide—schedule aggregator, like and Cirium
	Qualtrics	Online market research firm
	SABRE	Semi-Automated Business Research Environment
	SMB	Small and Medium-sized Businesses
	SITA	Société Internationale de Télécommunications Aéronautiques
	SRC	Science Research Council
	STR	Smith Travel Research
	TFEU	Treaty on the Functioning of the European Union
	TSA	Transportation Security Administration

Category	Acronym	Description
Connectivity	AVN	Numeric Availability Status
	AVS	Availability Status message
	BBR	Based Booking Request
	DAI	Direct Access Interactive
	DCA	Direct Connect Availability (seamless availability)
	DCS	Direct Connect Sell (seamless sell)
	IDR	Inventory Detail Record, alternate term for IND
	IND	Inventory Detail Record, alternate term for IDR
	INM	Inventory Master
	OAC	Office Accounting Code
	PCC	Pseudo City Code
	POC	Point of Commencement
	POS	Point of Sale
	P2P	Peer-to-peer

Category	Acronym	Description
Pricing, Revenue Management & Inventory Control	ADR	Average Daily Rate
	ADT	Adult Fare
	AP	Advance Purchase
	ARI	Availability, Rates, and Inventory
	ASM	Available Seat Miles
	BAM	Basic Attraction Model
	BITA	Bilateral Interline Traffic Agreement
	BAR	Best Available Rate
	BRG	Best Rate Guarantee
	CASK	Cost per Available Seat Kilometer
	CASM	Cost per Available Seat Mile
	CCA	Cost of Customer Acquisition
	CDLP	Choice-based Deterministic Linear Program
	CDP	Customer Data Platform
	CFD	Computational Fluid Dynamics
	CLV	Customer Lifetime Value
	CN	Continuous Nesting (also known as Bid Price Controls)
	CPA	City Pair Availability
	CV	Coefficient of Variation
	CWMF	Cost Weighted Mileage Factors, published by IATA quarterly
	DACS	Dynamic Availability Calculation System

(continued)

(continued)

Category	Acronym	Description
	DAVN-MR	Displacement Adjusted Virtual Nesting—Marginal Revenue
	DCM	Discrete Choice Models
	DINAMO	Dynamic Inventory Allocation and Maintenance Optimizer
	DNF	Do Not Fly
	EBP	Enterprise Business Planning, also known as S&OP
	EM	Expected Maximization
	EMD	Electronic Miscellaneous Document
	EMSR	Expected Marginal Seat Revenue
	ePMP	Electronic Prorate Manual—Passenger
	e-ticket	Ticketless
	E-Ticket	Electronic Ticket based on IATA specifications
	FBC	Fare Basis Code
	FBR	Fare by Rule
	FC	Fare Component
	FCU	Fare Construction Unit
	FEA	Finite Element Analysis
	FET	Federal Excise Tax
	FQ	Fare Quote
	FRAT	Fare Ratio (curves)
	GAM	General Attraction Model
	GEO	Generative Engine Optimization
	GEV	Generalized Extreme Value
	GST	Goods and Services Tax
	IFRS	International Financial Reporting Standards
	IIA	Independence of Irrelevant Alternatives
	ITAREQ	IATA DCS message request for sell transactions
	ITARES	IATA DCS message response for sell transaction request
	LF	Load Factor
	LOS	Length of Stay
	LUA	Last Unit Availability
	LLUA	Limited Last Unit Availability
	MAD	Mean Absolute Deviation
	MAE	Mean Absolute Error
	MAF	Minimum Acceptable Fare
	MAT	Market Adjustment Table, synonymous with MCFV and MVT

(continued)

(continued)

Category	Acronym	Description
	MCFV	Market Class Fare Value, synonymous with MAT and MVT
	MFEM	Multi-flight Expectation Maximization
	MITA	Multilateral Interline Traffic Agreement
	MNL	Multinomial Logit
	MPA	Multilateral Prorate Agreement
	MPM	Maximum Permitted Mileage
	MR-Flights	Market Restricted Flights
	MSE	Mean Squared Error
	MVT	Market Value Table, synonymous with MCFV and MAT
	NLF	Nominal Load Factor
	NSR	Net Spill Rate
	NUC	Neutral Unit of Construction (Currency), superseded FCU
	OLF	Observed Load Factor
	PAOREQ	IATA DCA message request for availability transactions
	PAORES	IATA DCA message response for availability transaction request
	PEX	Public Excursion Fares
	PFC	Passenger Facility Charge
	PFV	Potential Future Value
	PODS	Passenger Origin-Destination Simulator
	PNI	Passenger Name Index
	PRM	Pricing and Revenue Management
	PTC	Passenger Type Code
	PU	Priceable Unit
	QSAF	Quality of Service Adjusted Fare
	QUBO	Quadratic Unconstrainted Binary Optimization
	RAAV	Revenue Availability with Active Valuation
	RASK	Revenue per available seat kilometer
	RASM	Revenue per available seat mile
	RBD	The prime Reservation Booking Designator is usually (though not required) the first character of the fare class code (fare class code is synonymous to fare basis code). The RBD is equivalent to the booking class code
	RD	Reading Day (also referred to as Data Collection Point (DCP))
	REVPAR	Revenue Per Available Room
	RFDB	Resident Fares Database, same as MVT/MAT but on TPF / Sabre PSS to support O&D controls for American Airlines

(continued)

(continued)

Category	Acronym	Description
	RFP	Restriction Free Pricing
	RFR	Recapture Fare Ratio
	RI	Revenue Integrity
	ROM	Revenue Opportunity Model
	RTDP	Real Time Dynamic Pricing (PROS)
	RS-13	Inventory control in BABS, called RS-13 when they had 13 booking classes, later expanded to 26
	S&OP	Sales and Operations Planning
	SEM	Search Engine Marketing
	SEO	Search Engine Optimization
	SIFL	Standard Industry Fare Level
	SITI	Sold Inside Ticketed Inside
	SOLO	Sum Of LOcals
	SOTO	Sold Outside Ticketed Outside
	SPA	Special Prorate Agreements
	SRP	Straight Rate Prorate
	SSI	*SabreSonic* Inventory
	TC	Traffic Conference
	TPM	Ticketed Point Mileage
	TPMF	Total Passenger Miles Flown
	TSI	Travel Segment Indicator
	UPA	Universal Product Attributes
	UTA	Universal Ticketing Attributes
	VAT	Value Added Tax
	VFR	Visiting Friends and Relatives, a restricted leisure fare
	VN	Virtual Nesting
	Yield	Revenue per revenue passenger mile (or kilometer)
	YQ/YR	Surcharges used in International Markets

Passenger Type Codes

B

Passenger types are used to identify the available fares for the various types of passengers. PTCs can be used in conjunction with Account Codes or as a standalone eligibility criterion.

Passenger type code	Description
ACC	Accompanied passenger
ADA	Agency discount
ADD	Adult with discount
ADN	Agent discount
ADR	Adult resident
ADT	Adult
AEB	Aviation employees on business
AEF	Aviation employees and family
AEP	Assistant of Member of European Parliament
AEV	Aviation employees
AGT	Agent
ANN	Age restricted companion
APA	Air Pass adult
APC	Air Pass child
API	Air Pass infant without a seat
APS	Air Pass infant with a seat
AR1	Adult resident, family discount
ASB	Standby passenger
ASF	Air-Sea fare
AST	Airline staff standby
ATP	PFA/PFS/JCB/SEA blended
BAG	Baggage
BLD	Blind passenger

(continued)

B. Vinod, *The Era of Airline Revenue Management with Offers and Orders*, Management for Professionals, https://doi.org/10.1007/978-3-032-24197-9

(continued)

Passenger type code	Description
BNN	Adult with age restriction
BRV	Bereavement Passenger
BUD	Airline buddy standby
CCA	Children of civil aviation employee
CCH	Card carrying holder(s)
CCM	Card carrying member
CCR	Card carrying holder resident
CDT	Discount card holder France and overseas departments
CEV	Leisure card holder France
CFM	Card holder within France
CHR	Chile resident
CLG	Clergy
CMA	Adult with companion
CMM	Commuter
CMP	Companion
CMR	Adult resident with companion
CMS	Resident companion
CNF	Convention infant with no seat
CNN	Accompanied child
CNT	Carnet coupon travel
CNV	Convention passenger
CPN	Coupon discount
CR1	Cabin crew member discount
CR2	Cabin crew member discount, flight attendant
CSB	Child standby
CTZ	Category Z, military personnel or similar category
CVN	Convention child
DAJ	Disabled passenger assistant
DAT	Disabled passenger attendant
DCD	Disabled child
DCP	Disabled child companion
DEP	Deportee
DHC	Dead head crew
DIS	Disabled person
DNN	Child of EU Parliament member
DOD	Department of defense passenger
EAQ	Trade unions

(continued)

(continued)

Passenger type code	Description
EAT	Aviation admin
EAV	Unemployed
ECH	E-ticket child discount
EDT	E-ticket adult discount
EMI	Emigrant
EMN	Emigrant child
ENF	Emigrant infant no seat
ENN	Group inclusive tour child
ENP	Energy personnel
ENS	Emigrant infant with seat
EVP	Extra volume passenger
FBA	Family 1 discount adult
FBC	Family 1 discount child
FBI	Family 1 discount infant with no seat
FCC	ADT/JCB/ITX/PFA/NEG blended
FCP	Unaccompanied frequent flyer child preferred
FCU	Unaccompanied frequent flyer child
FFP	Frequent flyer preferred
FFY	Frequent flyer
FGA	Family 2 discount adult
FGC	Family 2 discount child
FGI	Family 2 discount infant with no seat
FHA	Honor family discount adult
FHC	Honor family discount child
FIA	Fiancée
FIF	Accompanied passenger: family intra-France
FIP	Frequent flyer Infant without a seat—preferred
FIS	Frequent flyer infant with seat
FLM	Private fare
FNF	Family plan infant without seat
FNP	Frequent flyer child preferred
FSA	Frequent flyer level 1
FSB	Frequent flyer level 2
FSC	Frequent flyer level 3
FSD	Frequent flyer level 4
FSE	Frequent flyer level 5
FSF	Frequent flyer level 6

(continued)

(continued)

Passenger type code	Description
FSG	Frequent flyer level 7
FSH	Frequent flyer level 8
FSP	Frequent flyer with seat preferred
FXP	Flexi plus passenger
FXT	Flexi time passenger
GBE	GBE private blended (teenager 12–15 years old)
GCF	Government contract passenger
GCT	City/county government travel
GDP	Government employee dependent
GEX	Government Exchange travel
GGV	GVT/CTZ/GCF blended
GGZ	GVT/CTZ nlended
GBE	GBE private blended
GIF	Group Inclusive tour infant without a seat
GIS	Group Inclusive tour infant with a seat
GIT	Group inclusive tour
GIY	Group inclusive tour youth
GMZ	GVT/GCF/GCT/MIL/CTZ blended (represent various government, military, or special fare types)
GNN	Group child
GRI	Group Infant without a seat
GRP	Group
GRS	Group Infant with a seat
GSP	Group school party
GST	Government State Passenger
GVA	Group Vocational Training trips for passenger agents
GVT	Government Travel
GYT	Group Youth
HAJ	Hajj Visa holding passenger
HOF	Head of Family fare
ICF	Incentive certificates Infant without a seat
ICN	Incentive certificates Child
ICP	Incentive certificate
INF	Infant without a seat
INN	Individual Inclusive Tour Child
INR	Infant without a seat Resident
INS	Infant with a seat
INX	Infant without a seat accompanied by a youth/student

(continued)

(continued)

Passenger type code	Description
INY	Infant with a seat accompanied by youth/student
ISR	Infant with a seat Resident
ITF	Inclusive Tour Infant without a seat
ITS	Inclusive Tour Infant with a seat
ITU	Individual Inclusive Tour unaccompanied Child
ITX	Individual Inclusive Tour
ITY	Inclusive Tour Youth
JCB	Contract Bulk adult
JEB	Journalist of European cabinet
JEC	Journalist of European Committee
JEP	Journalist of European Parliament
JMP	Jump Seat
JNF	Contract Bulk Infant without a seat
JNN	Contract Bulk child
JNF	Contract Bulk infant without a seat
JNS	Contract Bulk infant with a seat
JOU	Journalist
JRC	Contract Bulk Senior Citizen
JWA	JCB/WEB Blended
JWZ	ITX/JCB/PFA/PFS/WEB/ADT Blended
LBR	Laborer/worker
LIF	Laborer/worker infant without a seat
LNN	Laborer/worker child
LNS	Laborer/worker infant with a seat
LTC	Government employee on leave
LUN	Laborer/worker unaccompanied Child
MBT	Military basic training graduate
MCR	Military Charter passenger
MCS	Mastercard purchase only
MDP	Military Spouse/dependent child
MDR	Resident patients traveling for medical treatment
MED	Medical Passengers
MEP	Member of European Parliament
MIA	Ministry of Internal affairs
MIC	Missionary Child
MIF	Missionary Infant without a seat
MIL	Military Confirmed

(continued)

(continued)

Passenger type code	Description
MIR	Military reserve on active duty
MIS	Missionary
MNF	Military Infant without a seat
MNN	Military Child
MNS	Military Infant with a seat
MPA	Military parent/parent-in-law
MRE	Military dependent/military retired
MSB	Military standby
MSG	Multi state government passenger
MSS	Missionary Infant with a seat
MUS	Military / Department of defense based in USA
MXS	Military / Department of defense not based in USA
NAT	NATO passenger
NBA	No bag Adult
NBC	No bag Child
NBI	No bag Infant without a seat
NBS	No bag Infant with a seat
NBU	No bag unaccompanied Child
NSB	Non-revenue Standby
NTL	National/citizen of a specified country
OEB	Official of European Cabinet
OEC	Official of European Committee
OEI	Official of European Committee Institute
OEP	Official of European Parliament
OFS	Offshore worker
OFW	Oversees Filipino worker
ONN	Seaman passenger with age restriction
OTS	Passenger occupying two seats
PCR	Charter adult passenger
PEA	Premium economy Adult
PEC	Premium economy Child
PEI	Premium economy Infant without a seat
PES	Premium economy Infant with a seat
PGO	Internal Group Use
PIL	Pilgrim
PLM	Umrah Passenger
PNN	Charter child passenger

(continued)

(continued)

Passenger type code	Description
PTA	All passenger type codes except ADT, CNN, INF, INS, AST
PTC	All passenger fare types, excluding adults. Includes CNN, INF, INS, ASB
REC	Military Recruit
REF	Refugee
SAC	Staff accompanied Child
SCC	Senior discounted companion
SCF	Senior citizen female
SCM	Senior citizen male
SDB	Student standby
SDR	Student passenger Resident
SEA	Merchant Seaman fares
SEP	Spouse of European Parliament member
SKY	Regional passes for SkyTeam carriers
SNF	Staff Infant without a seat
SNN	Restricted senior citizen with multiple age requirements
SNS	Staff Infant with a seat
SPA	Accompanied Spouse
SPH	Spouse Fare—Head of Family
SPR	Sports passenger Resident
SPS	Spouse Fare—Accompanying
SPT	Sports passenger
SRC	Senior Citizen
SRR	Senior Citizen Resident
STA	Staff with reservation
STB	Staff without reservation
STF	Staff
STN	Crew without reservation
STP	Partner staff without reservation
STR	State resident
STU	Student
SUC	Staff Unaccompanied Child
TEA	Teacher
TIF	Timesaver Infant without a seat
TIM	Timesaver
TIN	Timesaver Child
TIS	Timesaver Infant with a seat
TNF	Frequent flyer Infant without a seat

(continued)

(continued)

Passenger type code	Description
TNN	Frequent Flyer child
TUR	Tour Conductor
TUX	Tour Conductor (restricted)
UDA	Agent discount UD75N1
UDN	Agent discount UD50N1
UNN	Unaccompanied child
UNR	Unaccompanied child Resident
UNV	University employee
VAC	Visit Another Country adult
VAG	Visit Another Country group adult
VFF	Visit friends/relatives Infant without a seat
VFN	Visit friends/relatives Child
VFR	Visit friends/relatives
VFS	Visit friends/relatives Infant with a seat
VNN	Visit Another Country child
WBC	Web accompanied Child
WBI	Web accompanied Infant without a seat
WBS	Web accompanied Infant with a seat
WBU	Web unaccompanied Child
WEB	Internet Fares
XNN	Pilgrim Child—SITA
YCB	Senior citizen standby
YNN	Government travel child
YSB	Youth standby
YTH	Youth confirmed
YTR	Youth passenger Resident
ZCS	ZED Common law/Spouse of employee/retiree
ZCU	ZED Children
ZDP	Diplomat and dependents—SITA
ZEA	ZED employee Adult
ZEC	ZED employee Child
ZED	Zonal employee discount
ZEF	ZED employee/retiree family members
ZEI	ZED employee Infant without a seat
ZEP	ZED employee/retiree parent
ZES	ZED employee/retiree sibling
ZEU	ZED Unregistered Companion

Glossary

C

Aeronautical Radio, Inc. Aeronautical Radio Inc. (ARINC) serves as the airline industry's single licensee and coordinator of radio communications outside of the government. The airline industry uses teletype messages over ARINC or SITA networks to communicate between reservations systems.

Agency Debit Memo. An Agency Debit Memo (ADM) is a notification sent by an airline to a travel agency, requesting payment for a specific amount due to an error on the agency's part. Both ARC and IATA BSP also send debit memos to travel agencies on behalf of the airlines.

Agency Subscriber Desktop. The customer facing product of a GDS is the travel agency subscriber desktop. It allows a travel agent to search and book travel. The names of the GDS booking platforms are Amadeus Selling Platform, Sabre Red 360, and Travelport Smartpoint.

Agent to Agent Protocol. Agent to Agent (A2A) is an open protocol developed by Google. It provides a standard way for AI Agents to collaborate with each other, regardless of the underlying framework or vendor. A2A's goal is to scale enterprise-level agentic systems. It is an important milestone in the development of multi-agent systems.

Agentic AI. A new generation of AI systems designed to operate semi-autonomously or autonomously, taking initiative and making decisions to achieve specific goals with minimal human intervention. This contrasts with traditional AI, which often relies on explicit instructions for every step.

Agentic AI Foundation. The Agentic AI Foundation (AAIF) was established on December 9, 2025. It is an open source foundation under the Linux Foundation dedicated to supporting, standardizing, and advancing Agentic AI technologies.

AI Agents. An artificial intelligence (AI) agent is a software program that interacts with its environment, collects data, and uses that data to perform self-directed tasks that meet predetermined goals. Humans set goals, but an AI agent independently chooses the best actions it needs to perform to achieve those goals.

B. Vinod, *The Era of Airline Revenue Management with Offers and Orders*, Management for Professionals, https://doi.org/10.1007/978-3-032-24197-9

Aircraft Communications Addressing and Reporting System (ACARS). It a digital datalink system for transmission of short, relatively simple messages between aircraft and ground stations via radio or satellite). The protocol was designed by Aeronautical Radio, Incorporated (ARINC) to replace their very high frequency (VHF) voice service and deployed in 1978, uses telex formats.

Airline Code Designator. A two-character code designated by IATA to identify an airline (e.g., Alaska Airlines (AS), Air France (AF), United Airlines (UA)).

Airport Code Designator. A three-character code used to identify an airport (e.g., Dallas/Fort Worth (DFW), London Heathrow (LHR)).

Airlines Reporting Corporation. The airline reporting corporation (ARC) is an intermediary that provides ticket settlement services between airlines and travel agencies in the U.S.

Air Shopping. Air shopping is the process of evaluating schedules, selecting, and pricing itineraries based on booking class availability to present to a customer during flight search. It is the single largest system and investment supported by a GDS.

Amenities. Amenities are comparable features of the onboard experience, Amenities helps airlines and sales channels convey expected features to flight shoppers about the onboard experience, including seat pitch/type, Wi-Fi availability, power and entertainment options.

American Society of Travel Advisors. The American Society of Travel Agents (ASTA) was founded in 1931. Its members represent 80% of all travel sold in the U.S. through the travel agency distribution channel. They also have hundreds of internationally based travel agencies. In 2018 it was renamed the American Society of Travel Advisors.

Apriori Algorithm. The Apriori algorithm is widely used in data mining, particularly for association rule mining. This algorithm is used for market basket analysis to understand customer purchase patterns.

Artificial Intelligence. The development of computer-based methods able to mimic human-like processes such as learning, reasoning, and self-correction. Broad categories include machine learning, natural language processing and deep learning.

Artificial General Intelligence. Artificial General Intelligence (AGI) is a type of artificial intelligence in the future that possesses human-like cognitive abilities, capable of understanding, learning, and applying intelligence to any intellectual task a human can. Unlike current narrow AI, which excels at specific tasks, AGI systems could generalize knowledge, possess common sense, reason abstractly, and adapt to new and unfamiliar situations across various domains like a human. It is a theoretical concept and considered to be the pinnacle of AI.

Availability. Availability of seats by booking class observed at a point of sale.

Availability Cache. Storage of availability data in cache, collected organically, frequently for a large number of airlines, to support air shopping. All GDSs have some form of availability cache; leg/segment based or O&D based.

Availability Proxy. A read-only version of the airline's reservations inventory system, that replicates the availability processing logic resident in the airline's master inventory system. It is more accurate than the Availability Cache since it reflects the business rules resident in the airline host CRS for availability determination.

B2B. Business to business.

B2C. Business to consumer.

Basic Attraction Model. The basic attraction model (BAM) states that the demand for a product is the ratio of the direct attractiveness of the product divided by the sum of the direct attractiveness of the available products (including a no purchase alternative).

Bedbanks. Bedbanks are B2B platforms that contract supply (rooms) from hotels and accommodation providers and make it available to travel sellers.

Big Data. Structured and unstructured datasets so large and complex that it requires new tools and processes. Volume, Velocity and Variety are the three dimensions of Big Data.

Bid Price. A bid price is the opportunity cost of not having an incremental seat on a leg in the network. It can also be interpreted as the minimum acceptable fare for a reservation to be accepted on a flight leg.

Bid Price Vector. Also called a bid price curve, it is constructed from the network optimization model that assumes primal feasibility is unchanged. It is a set of prices as a function of seats sold or seats available.

Billing and Settlement Plan. The IATA Billing and Settlement Plan (BSP) is an intermediary that facilitates settlement, reporting and remitting procedures for IATA accredited Passenger Sales Agents. BSP operates in over 180 countries and territories and serves 370 participating airlines.

Blockchain as a Service (BaaS). This is the creation and management of cloud-based networks by third party service providers for companies who want to build blockchain applications.

Boarding Pass. A boarding pass is issued by an airline at time of check-in for a flight to a passenger to board a flight.

Booking Class. The booking class serves as an identifier for the fares of a specific type or value. It is used for the purposes of inventory control, selling, and ticketing. Booking classes are mapped into base compartments and are commonly known as reservation booking designators (RBD). Revenue management analysts frequently refer to booking classes and fare classes synonymously, which is incorrect. They are not interchangeable. The "owning carrier" of a fare determines the RBDs, which are exclusive to the airline.

Booking Limit. The booking limit is the maximum number of seats that can be sold in a booking class or cabin. In a nested inventory control environment, the booking limit is the maximum bookings that can be sold to a given booking class and all booking classes that are nested into it.

Bucket. Buckets are virtual and were introduced with virtual nesting inventory controls by American Airlines in 1987, where multiple service classes were mapped to a virtual bucket to control availability by origin and destination (O&D).

Buyer. Airline ticket buyers, often acting as consolidators, travel management companies (TMCs), or corporate travel departments, secure discounted airfare through bulk purchasing or specialized programs to offer better rates to travelers.

Cabotage. Cabotage is the transport of goods or passengers between two points in the same country by an aircraft registered in another country.

Consumer Intent. Consumer intent in travel refers to the desires, motivations, and plans that drive individuals to make travel-related purchases and engage in travel behaviors. Natural Language Processing techniques like intent recognition and sentiment analysis help decipher the purpose behind user input, allowing systems to respond accurately and personalize the interactions.

Customer Relationship Management. Customer Relationship Management (CRM) is a business process that travel suppliers use to manage, analyze, and improve their interactions with customers.

Cabin or Base Compartment. A cabin is a section of the flight leg that has a different seating configuration or is associated with a different level of in-flight service. Examples are first class (F), business class (J) and coach class (Y) cabins.

Capture. The capture rate is the likelihood of a customer booking an alternate flight on any carrier if the first choice is unavailable.

Central Reservations System (CRS). Airlines, hotels, rental car, and cruise lines own a central reservations system where inventory is hosted (airline seats, hotel rooms, rental cars, cruise line cabins). An entity's own CRS is commonly referred to as the host CRS.

Change of Gauge. Airline marketing term used to designate that a specific flight number changes aircraft, part way through the direct flight.

City Code. The three character designation for a city or airport. These codes are assigned by IATA.

City Pair Availability. Six characters, a combination of 2 city or airport codes, the departure airport, and the arrival airport, served by direct or connecting flights. The display includes flights in the city pair with numeric booking class availability.

Classless Revenue Management. A revenue management system that does not rely on booking classes to forecast demand and control seat inventory.

Code of Federal Regulations. The Code of Federal Regulations (CFR) was made effective by the Civil Aeronautics Board on November 11, 1984, which prohibited anti-competitive behavior from airlines that owned the CRSs.

Codeshare. Airlines enter partnerships to create marketing flights that are operated by a partner carrier to extend their reach.

Communication Channel. A *type* of medium for communicating marketing incentives. Examples include Web, Email, Call Center, Catalog, TV, etc.

Competition and Market Authority. The Competition and Market Authority (CMA) is the competition regulator in the United Kingdom to strengthen business competition and prevent anti-competitive activities.

Competitive Revenue Management. A revenue management capability to control what is available for sale based on prevailing market conditions such as competitor selling fares.

Conjoint Analysis. A survey-based statistical technique used in market research to determine how consumers value features of a product or service.

Connecting Market. A connecting market represents a service with pre-defined reasonable estimates of minimum and maximum connect time. Stop-overs do not constitute a connecting service.

Connectivity. Connectivity defines the level of participation between the airline and the GDS.

Consolidator Fares. Consolidators negotiate contracted rates with multiple airlines to sell tickets to qualified travel agents. These fares can be marked up by the travel agent. These consolidator fares are called net fares and bulk fares. Net fares (also called nett fares) can be marked up by the travel agent. Bulk fares normally can be sold as is and can only be sold as a package with a hotel, car, etc.

Consumer. A consumer refers to the ultimate end-user of a product or service in a value chain. A traveler is a consumer.

Continuous Nesting. Continuous nesting is also called bid-price controls. It is an inventory control technique for origin and destination control.

Continuous Pricing. Continuous pricing is a dynamic pricing framework where the optimal price determined by the revenue management price optimizer is used *as is* and will be the ticketed price.

Conversational AI. Conversational AI refers to technologies that enable computers to engage in human-like dialogue through natural language processing and machine learning.

Convolutional Neural Networks. Convolutional Neural Networks (CNN) are a type of neural network that performs the convolution (or cross-correlation) operation typically followed by some down sampling (pooling). It is widely used for image recognition.

Corporate Fares. These are private fares negotiated between an airline and a corporation.

Cost Weighted Mileage Factors. IATA defined mileage factors weighted by traffic, used in some cases for interline proration. It is published quarterly.

Customer. A customer could refer to a single individual or could represent an organization in the value chain. For example, a travel agency is a customer of the GDS.

Customer Data Platform. A customer data platform is a tool for achieving real-time personalization by unifying customer data from various sources into a single, comprehensive view of the customer.

Customer Lifetime Value. The customer lifetime value (CLV) is the net present value of a customer based on historical performance and projections of future revenue and costs over the duration of the relationship.

Data Element Identifier. The data element identifier (DEI) is an integral part of the schedule change information manual (SSIM). The DEI defines the mapping of the operating flights to the marketing flights.

Decoy Offer. A decoy offer, also known as the decoy effect, or asymmetric dominance, is an inferior offer that when presented, increases the likelihood of the customer selecting the better offer.

Deep Learning. A branch of AI that mimics the workings of a human brain in processing both unstructured and unlabeled data to make decisions by detecting objects, recognizing speech, and translating languages.

Department of Justice. The Department of Justice (DOJ) is a federal executive department of the U.S. government that enforces federal law and administration of justice.

Department of Transportation. The U.S. Department of Transportation is responsible for planning and coordinating federal transportation projects. It also sets safety regulations for all major modes of transportation. The FAA is under the DOT.

Dilution. Revenue dilution occurs when adequate seats are not protected for higher valued passengers.

Direct Connect Availability Agreement. The DCA agreement is an addendum to the participating carrier agreement (PCA) and stipulates discounts to the rack rate for segment booking fees that a carrier will receive in exchange for access to full content from the airline. Usually this also includes the highest level of participation for connectivity between a GDS and an airline.

Distributed Availability. Distributed availability is deployment of an Availability Proxy of an airline's inventory system in a public or private cloud to support the growing demands of air shopping worldwide. Deploying the solution in the cloud at multiple locations worldwide reduces network latency.

Downsell. Downsell is a special case of recapture to a lower fare on the same flight. Cross-flight recapture denotes recapture to other flight(s) on the host airline.

Distribution Cost Charge. The distribution cost charge (DCC) was introduced by Lufthansa in 2015. It was €16 surcharge for GDS bookings.

Dynamic Availability. A competitive revenue management capability to respond to competitive market conditions by modifying inventory controls in real-time.

Dynamic Pricing. A competitive revenue management capability to respond to competitive market conditions by generating a dynamic fare in response to a customer request. There are two versions of dynamic pricing: laddered pricing and continuous pricing.

EDI. Electronic Data Interchange is a format for e-commerce in which business data are represented using national or international standards.

EDIFACT. Electronic Data Interchange for Administration, Commerce and Transport. These are messages that are approved as standards for EDI and can be exchanged through a communication network.

E-Ticketing. E-Ticketing (ETKT) standards were defined by IATA in 1993. The coupons are produced in an electronic format and can be updated across different E-Ticketing databases, and for the control of E-Tickets to be passed from one airline to the next.

e-ticketing (Ticketless). This is the ticketless solution invented by Morris Air and used by low-cost carriers. It does not allow the exchange of the ticket records among systems using IATA E-Ticketing standards.

Electronic Miscellaneous Document. The electronic miscellaneous document (EMD) is an electronic document that may be issued and used for the collection of travel related ancillary services offered by an airline. EMDs replaced the traditional paper Miscellaneous Charges Order (MCO) documents.

Endowment Effect. The endowment effect is a cognitive bias where people place a higher value on objects they own compared to identical objects they do not own

Expected Marginal Seat Revenue. The expected marginal seat revenue is the expected revenue of an incremental seat based on a distribution of demand.

Explainable AI. This is a field of research to develop tools and frameworks to understand and interpret predictions made by machine learning models. It is required to understand model behavior to improve model performance over time.

Extensible Markup Language. Extensible Markup Language (XML), is a standard communications format in the Internet era.

Fare Basis Code. The fare basis code appears on the ticket. It can include letters, numbers and up to two slashes (/). A fare basis is a compilation of the fare class or ticketing code and one or two ticketing designators. Multiple fare basis codes map to a booking class code. The fare basis code is distinct from the fare class, which is associated to each fare and used in pricing.

Fare Breakpoint. These are the terminal points of a fare component for fare construction. It is the destination point where a fare begins or ends.

Fare Component. The fare component is the most basic unit of fare construction and represents a specific fare between two city pairs.

Fare Construction. Fare construction is the process by which various rules are applied to determine the final fare for a ticket.

Fare Class Code: A fare class specifies the rules of an airline's fare. Every fare has a fare class code, and this code appears on the ticket. It is synonymous with fare basis code. Revenue management analysts incorrectly refer to booking classes (RBDs) and fare classes inter-changeably, which should be avoided.

Fare Guarantee Policy. GDSs have a Fare Guarantee Policy where they are accountable for debit memos resulting from fare or tax under collected tickets that meet the criteria for reimbursement.

Fare Management. Business process for managing all active fares by monitoring and responding to competitive fare activity.

Fare by Rule. The creation of new fares using rules data to specify the market fares and the amounts. The fares can either be calculated from existing fares and rules in the market or specified to create a new fare using the rule provisions in ATPCO Category 25. Corporate fares are frequently, but not exclusively, governed by Fare by Rule.

Fast Response System. A fast response system (FRS) has the capability to respond to a high volume of transaction requests, both online and offline, in less than a second. In the NDC context, airlines need to develop fast response systems to instantly respond to requests of offers (air itinerary and the airline bundle).

Federal Excise Tax. A federal tax that is charged on airfare. The segment fee of U.S.$4.00 per segment, the September 11 security fee of U.S.$5.60 per one-way flight, and the Passenger Facility Charge (U.S.$4.50 per segment and U.S.$18.00 per round trip) are in additional to the federal excise tax.

Financial Availability. The process of determining whether selling a seat to a customer over the requested origin and destination is financially viable using the net contribution calculation.

Flight Leg. A flight leg is a nonstop flight departure from a board point and an off point with a specific flight number and departure time.

Full Content Access Fee. The GDSs imposed an 80-cent full content fee per segment booked from participating airlines in 2006. This fee is deducted from the incentives paid by the GDSs to the travel agencies. These programs are called Content Plus Program, Efficient Access Solution, and Content Continuity Program by Amadeus, Sabre, and Travelport respectively.

Flight Number. A flight number is associated with a specific aircraft routing and can consist of one or more flight legs.

Full Content Agreements. A full content agreement is a content parity clause in GDS and airline contracts. It stipulated that the same content (schedules, fares, and availability) that was available on the airline direct channel were also available on the indirect GDS channel. After GDS deregulation in 2004, airlines could publish web-only fares. The GDSs gave segment booking fee discounts to the airlines to secure all content, including web fares in the GDS. With IATA NDC, full content agreements will eventually disappear.

Funnel Flights. A funnel flight is an artificial direct flight that maps to operating flights.

Future Customer Value. The future customer value is the net present value of a customer based on projections of future revenue and costs over the duration of the relationship.

Generative Adversarial Networks. A generative adversarial network (GAN) is a deep learning architecture. It trains two neural networks to compete against each other to generate more authentic new data from a given training dataset.

Generative Engine Optimization. Generative Engine Optimization (GEO) is a digital strategy to provide visibility in AI-powered search results like Google's AI Overview, Gemini, ChatGPT, etc. by focusing on quality, context, and authority to be cited within the AI's generated answers.

Global Distribution System (GDS). A Global Distribution System maintains airline schedules and accepts bookings for the requested itinerary. The major GDSs are Amadeus, Sabre, and Travelport.

GDS New Entrants. In 2004, the GDS New Entrants (GeNiEs) attempted to disintermediate the GDS model with their open systems platforms as an alternative to the legacy GDS platforms. They attempted to end the GDS oligopoly by promising significantly lower segment booking fees and flexible distribution technology. The prominent GDS New Entrants were Trition Distribution Systems, ITA Software, G2 Switchworks, and Farelogix. Unable to penetrate the market, they abandoned their efforts in 2006.

GDS Pass-through. This is a term used for NDC bookings made through GDS to the airline. In this scenario, the GDS is the NDC Aggregator. NDC bookings, if stored in the GDS, are passive bookings.

Generative AI. Generative AI refers to AI models that can generate new content, such as text, images, audio, and video, based on patterns assimilated from existing data. It is a type of artificial intelligence that creates novel content rather than just analyzing or processing existing information.

Generative Pre-Trained Transformer. Generative pre-trained transformers (GPT) are neural network models trained on large datasets in an unsupervised manner to generate text. GPTs use transformer architecture and are pre-trained using a self-supervised objective to predict the next word in a sequence, given all previous words.

Go Show. Passengers who show up for a flight, without a confirmed reservation for a flight or those that show up with a confirmed reservation number for which no reference is found in the airline's host reservations system.

Gradient. The gradient is the incremental bid price and is the adjustment that is made to the bid price for every sell and cancel over a specific leg. It can be interpreted as the rate of change in bid price for a unit change in capacity.

Gradient Boosting Machine. A machine learning predictive modeling technique for regression and classification problems. Also known as multiple additive regression trees.

Group Bookings. Bookings for a group of passengers that are negotiated with an airline sales representative.

Hidden City. A hidden city is an O&D connection with a long layover. Leisure travelers search for cheap fares to their destination that is a hidden city of an O&D. Applicable when a local one-way fare to the destination is more expensive than the connecting O&D.

Hybrid State. In this book the term "hybrid state" refers to the period when traditional GDS content that is booked via EDIFACT and NDC content that is booked via XML co-exist on the GDS platform.

IATA. The International Air Transport Association was founded by member airlines in 1919. Today, IATA has over 270 airline members.

IATA Carrier. An airline that is a member of the International Air Transport Association.

IATA Clearing House. The IATA Clearing House (ICH) provides billing and settlement services in multiple currencies for the air transportation industry.

Independence of Irrelevant Alternatives (IIA). The IIA assumption says that when customers are asked to choose among a set of alternatives, their odds of choosing

A over B should not depend on whether some other alternative C is present or absent.

Indexing. This is the process of assigning a service class to a bucket on a flight/leg/date. Indexing can be static or dynamic. Term is used for virtual nesting controls.

Interline. An itinerary where two or more airlines operate flights to complete the customer itinerary.

Intermediary. An intermediary is a middleman between two entities and facilitates business transactions.

Inventory Control. Ability to control seats sold by booking class in an airline's reservations inventory system. Inventory control can be by leg/segment or O&D.

Itinerary. An itinerary is a complete trip for a passenger as determined from the passenger name record (PNR). Hence an itinerary may be one-way or round trip.

Leg. A leg is a nonstop board point and off point.

Leisure Fares. Leisure fares are discounted fares with restrictions and sold to the public. They can be accessed from airline websites and through travel agencies.

Local Availability. Local availability is the availability for each RBD when an O&D is requested, and the O&D has only one segment. In an O&D inventory control environment, local RBD availability will be quite different from RBD availability for the same segment when it is part of a connecting O&D.

Load Factor. The ratio of seats sold to the capacity expressed as a percentage. Load factor is post-departure. Predeparture load factor is called booked load factor. For reporting purposes, load factor is expressed as a ratio of RPK/ASK or RPM/ASM.

Local Interpretable Model-agnostic Explanations LIME, the acronym for local interpretable model-agnostic explanations, is a technique that approximates any black box machine learning model with a local, interpretable model to explain each individual prediction. LIME focuses on explaining the model's prediction for individual instances.

Logistic Regression. Logistic regression is a predictive model that is used when the dependent variables are categorical variables.

Long Short-Term Memory. Long Short-Term Memory (LSTM) is a type of recurrent neural network (RNN) designed to process sequential data and learn long-term dependencies effectively, unlike traditional RNNs that suffer from the vanishing gradient problem.

Machine Learning. Machine learning uses statistical techniques to enable computer systems to "learn" (i.e., progressively improve on a specific task) with data, without being explicitly programmed. Broad categories include unsupervised learning, supervised learning, reinforcement learning, neural networks, and deep learning.

Machine Readable Passport. A machine-readable passport (MRP) is a passport that contains data encoded in a format that can be read by machines, typically using optical character recognition (OCR). This enables faster and more efficient processing at border control and other checkpoints. They are standardized by the International Civil Aviation Organization (ICAO).

Machine Readable Zone. A machine-readable zone (MRZ) is a standardized section on identification documents like passports, visas, and ID cards that contain machine-encoded data about the document holder.

MapReduce. Developed by Google, it is a data processing technique for distributed computing. The MapReduce algorithm contains two tasks, Map and Reduce Map, which converts a set of data where individual elements are broken down into tuples (key-value pairs).

Market. A *market* describes a passenger's one-way origin and destination pair; regardless of connect points and time of day. An on-line market consists of one or more flight legs that are on a specific carrier. An interline market consists of one or more flight legs that are on a combination of two or more carriers.

Market Adjustment Table. The Market Adjustment Table (MAT) is required for O&D control. The conditioned fares are averaged by fare qualification rules and stored on the host CRS inventory system. This is called the market adjustment table which can be modified to increase or decrease availability by service class and POS. This is also called Market Class Fare Value (MCFV) table or Market Value Table (MVT).

Marketplace. The electronic medium that brings together buyers and sellers to trade products and services online through fair and competitive means. A Global Distribution System (GDS) is a marketplace that brings suppliers (sellers) and travel agents (buyers) together to transact business.

Marketing Information Data Tapes (MIDT). Electronic records of a travel agency's sales history. The GDS records, owns and market MIDT data based on booking transactions generated by travel agents.

Market Restricted Flight. A market restricted (MR) flight is a specific flight posted on a GDS for which availability must be directly queried on the host CRS via a seamless request for true last seat availability.

Metasearch. A Metasearch engine is an online information retrieval tool that combines the results from various search engines into one and produces a consolidated result.

Minimum Connect Time. The minimum connect time (MCT) is specified in the airline schedules published by schedule aggregators.

Model Context Protocol. The Model Context Protocol (MCP) is an open protocol that standardizes how LLMs access tools, data, and prompts from external sources, simplifying how new context is integrated into AI applications. Along with A2A, MCP is a foundational component of Agentic AI.

Most Favored Nation. The most favored nation clause (MFN) was standard in airline-GDS contracts. It is a provision in which the GDS agrees to give the airline (seller) the best terms it makes available to any other airline. MFN clauses also exist in some cases with TMC - Corporation contracts which guarantee that a corporate client receives pricing and service terms at least as favorable as any other customer of the TMC.

Multilateral Prorate Agreements. Multilateral prorate agreements (MPAs) are formal arrangements, primarily between airlines, that govern how revenue from a single ticket for a journey involving multiple airlines is divided among them. Specific factors, like distance (mileage), fare, and other agreed-upon criteria, are used to calculate each airline's share of the revenue.

Multilateral Interline Traffic Agreement. The Multilateral Interline Traffic Agreement (MITA), established by IATA, provides a standard structure for interline agreements, and multilateral prorate agreements (MPAs) fall under this framework. These agreements outline the basic rules for revenue sharing and other operational aspects of interline travel.

Multimodal Transportation. Multi-model transportation is a customer itinerary that includes two or more modes of transportation such as full-service carriers, low-coast carriers, rail, bus, etc.

Multinomial Logit Model. A multinomial logit (MNL) model is a classification method that generalizes logistic regression to multiclass problems with more than two discrete outcomes.

Multiple Virtual Storage. More commonly called MVS, was the most used operating system on the System/370 and System/390 IBM mainframe computers for commercial applications.

Native Order. A native order, refers to a customer order managed directly by the airline in a single record, rather than through a traditional Passenger Name Record (PNR) system

Nesting. The hierarchy of booking classes determines the order in which the booking classes should be nested. The objective of nesting is to ensure that lower valued classes are not open for sale when higher valued classes are closed for sale. Net (standard) nesting and threshold (theft) nesting are the two methods for calculating availability. Applicable for both booking class controls and virtual nesting controls.

Net Contribution. The net contribution is the difference between the market fare value for an O&D and the total bid price for the one-way (directional) itinerary. The net contribution calculation can also be extended to round trips on airline websites that exercise round trip control.

New Distribution Capability. The New Distribution Capability (NDC) was established by IATA in 2021. The objective was to promote a new XML-based messaging standard to transform the way airline products are distributed and sold in the marketplace.

NDC Aggregators. An NDC Aggregator is an intermediary that connects with an airline to access NDC content (priced itineraries) and deliver it to the point of sale. Besides third party new entrants in the marketplace, the GDSs are by default NDC aggregators.

NDC Exchange. Initiated by ATPCO, the NDC exchange was an industry owned solution that served as a neutral hub to connect airlines with sellers. The hub supported real-time message translation to address the many versions of the XML-based messaging standard. It was sunset in 2022.

Neural Networks. Algorithms that attempt to recognize underlying relationships in data through a process that mimics how a human brain operates.

NP-hard. A problem in NP-hard if it can be translated into one for solving any NP-problem (non-deterministic polynomial time) problem. NP-hard problems are at least as hard as any NP problem. It is likely that there are no polynomial-time algorithms for NP-hard problems.

Network (airline). A network represents the schedule for an airline for a day or a sub-set of the schedule for the day.

No Shows. Booked passengers that do not show up for the flight at departure time.

Next Generation Storefront. The next generation storefront (NGS) is a set of data standards established by ATPCO and adopted by GDSs with variations for their agency desktop to better represent, sort, and find the airline products and services for travel agents.

Offer Management. Offer management is an extension of traditional revenue management to offer a base fare and ancillary bundle to a customer.

Offer and Order. The NDC initiative is about offer and order management that is controlled by the airline. Besides airlines controlling the content of the offer (base fare + ancillaries) travelers will have a single record for their order.

Offer Partner Airline. An "offer partner airline" (OPA) is the airline partner who responses to the ORA with the codeshare itinerary and offer for an itinerary that has codeshare segments.

Offer Responsible Airline. An "offer responsible airline" (ORA) is the airline responsible for creating the offer for an itinerary that has codeshare segments.

ONE Order. This is an IATA initiative. It is an XML-based standard to simplify the airline reservation, delivery, and accounting systems by gradually phasing out the current booking (PNRs) and ticketing records (E-Tickets and electronic miscellaneous documents, or EMDs).

Online Booking Engine. An online booking engine is an application on airline websites to capture and process direct online reservations. Besides the direct channel, online booking engines are used by OTAs, and self-service corporate booking tools.

Online Travel Agencies. An online travel agency (OTA) is a web-based marketplace that allows online users to search and book travel products and services, including flights, hotels, cars, cruises, activities, etc.

Opaque Fares. Opaque fares are frequently restricted and cannot be sold as is, and only as part of a package (with a hotel or car package).

Open Travel Alliance. The Open Travel Alliance is a non-profit standards body that is creating messaging standards across all lines of business (air, hotel, car, etc.). It was established in 1999.

Operation Research. Techniques based on mathematical methods—discrete optimization, stochastic modeling, large scale optimization modeling.

Optimization Group. An optimization group represents a selection of flights from the schedule that can be grouped together based on the arrival departure pattern. For example, an arrival-departure complex from a hub can be an optimization group. The optimization group can also represent the entire schedule for a future departure date. Optimization groups are required for O&D revenue management to capture all interactions in network flow traffic.

Order Change Notifications. Order change notifications (OCN) are triggered by changes to the schedule such as flight number changes, cancellation, or delays. OCNs are sent to travel agencies and third-party sellers.

Origin and Destination. An origin and destination is a nonstop or connecting market with the departure time of day qualifier. It is synonymous with service.

O&D Inventory Control. The control of seat inventory by origin and destination of the request.

Overbooking. Authorizing more reservations than capacity to be accepted to compensate for the effects of cancellations and no shows.

Overlapping Flights. Overlapping flights are also referred to as back-to-back ticketing. Passengers book overlapping flights to circumvent minimum stay restrictions.

PADIS Board. The Passenger and Airport Data Interchange Standards (PADIS) Board develops and maintains Electronic Data Interchange and XML message standards for passenger travel and airport-related passenger service activities.

Participating Carrier Agreement. The participating career agreement (PCA) is a common contract form between a GDS and an airline to distribute and sell the airline product. The PCA has a standard rack rate that governs the economics and participation of an airline in the GDS.

Passenger Facility Charge. Commercial airports controlled by public agencies began imposing passenger facility charges on June 1, 1992, at $3.00 per passenger enplanement ($12.00 per round trip). The cap was raised to $4.50 ($18.00 per round trip) effective April 1, 2001. PFCs are federally authorized but levied by local airport operators, which set the amounts.

Passenger Type Code. The passenger type codes are defined by ATPCO. It is a fare related classification for each passenger. For example, ADT is adult passenger, GVT is government travel, VFR is visit friends/relatives, AST is airline staff standby, etc. Appendix B lists the passenger type codes.

Passive Segments. A passive segment is a passive booking in the GDS for which a ticket will not be issued. It is an informational segment that has the complete itinerary of the passenger. NDC bookings are passive segments in the GDS.

Passive Segments—NDC. An NDC passive segment in a GDS is a non-actionable placeholder in a Passenger Name Record (PNR) used to mirror a booking made directly through an airline's NDC (New Distribution Capability) API or portal. It acts as a bridge, allowing travel management companies to record non-GDS transactions for back-office accounting, itinerary management, and reporting, without double-booking.

Payment Time Limit. This parameter indicates the duration after order creation that payment commitment is required for an order item.

Personalization. Used in the context of offer management, to personalize the offer consisting of the base fare and ancillaries. Personalization is always 1:1 (for a segment of ONE).

Physical Availability. This process determines whether a seat can be sold in a cabin by comparing the authorized capacity (including overbooking) against the seats sold count. If the authorized capacity is greater than seats sold, seats are physically available.

Point of Commencement. The point at which a customer's journey originates.

Point of Sale. Identifies the location of the travel agency where the booking was made.

Potential Future Value. The potential future value is an estimate of the residual future value of a customer.

Preference Driven Air Shopping. Preference driven air shopping (PDAS) display algorithms are based on trade-off analytics. PDAS is superior to traditional travel website filters, since a filter would exclude an itinerary based on one attribute, even though it would have been outweighed by the goodness in the other attributes. To deploy PDAS there are two alternative techniques: TOPSIS (Technique for Ordering Preferences by Similarity to Ideal Solution), and VIKOR (VlseKriterijumska Optimiza-cija I Kompromisno Resenje).

Preferred Channels. These are product distribution channels that are preferred by airlines.

Priceable Unit. Also called a Pricing Unit (PU). One or more fare components make up a PU. One or more PU combinations produce a pricing solution for a trip.

Price Guarantee Time Limit. This parameter indicates how long the price of a specific offer item is guaranteed.

Private Fares. Private fares are only available through consolidators and travel agencies. Examples are corporate fares, net fares, and bulk fares.

Programmed Airline Reservations System. The programmed airline reservations system (PARS) was developed by IBM as a generalized version of the Sabre reservations system they developed and launched with American Airlines in 1964. Within a few years all IBM-based reservations systems were baselined on PARS. The international version of PARS, developed by IBM with functional requirements from BOAC and other airlines is called IPARS.

Prospect Theory. Prospect theory is a model for decision making. It states that people make choices based on the potential value of losses and gains relative to a reference point, rather than the final outcome.

Protected Seats. Seats that are protected in a booking class from lower valued booking classes.

Protection Levels. This represents the seats protected for a booking class from lower valued booking classes.

***Publish and Subscribe* Environment.** A publish and subscribe (Pub/Sub) environment is a messaging service that is asynchronous and scalable. It helps in decoupling services that produce messages from the services that process those messages. This service enables services to communicate with each other asynchronously.

Public Fares. Also known as published fares, these fares are available for immediate purchase through any travel agency or airline website.

Q-Learning. Q-learning is a reinforcement learning algorithm that trains an agent to assign values to its possible actions based on its current state

Quality of Service Adjusted Price. An airline's competitive fare response based on schedule and fare attributes. This is an improvement over traditional rules-based matching.

Quality of Service Index. The quality of service index (QSI) has been used by airlines to predict their "fair share" based on relative attractiveness of their schedule versus competitors. QSI accounts for a range of schedule attributes such as aircraft type, frequency of service, type of service (nonstop, single connect, double connect, interline, etc.).

Reading Day. A reading day is a pre-departure snapshot when demand forecasts and inventory controls are updated. It is also referred to as data collection point (DCP).

Reasoning Chain. The reasoning chain on a blockchain relies on a secure, distributed, and verifiable sequence of blocks, each cryptographically linked and validated by a network of participants to ensure the integrity and immutability of the stored information.

Recapture. Recapture is a special case of capture on to the same (host) airline.

Recurrent Neural Networks. Recurrent Neural Networks (RNNs) are a type of deep learning model designed to process sequential data, such as text, speech, or time series, by using a feedback loop that allows information from previous steps to influence current computations. Unlike standard feedforward neural networks, RNNs have a form of "memory" called a hidden state that retains context from earlier inputs, making them effective for tasks requiring an understanding of order and temporal dependencies

Regression. A predictive modeling technique that determines the relationship between a dependent variable and a set of independent variables.

Reinforcement Learning. A machine learning technique to train machine learning models to make a sequence of decisions. With a goal to maximize the total reward, the agent learns to achieve the goal and receives either rewards or penalties for the actions it performs.

Request for Quotation. Prior to negotiating the contract, a customer may submit a request for quotation (RFQ) to multiple entities.

Reservation Booking Designator. The Reservation Booking Designator (RBD) is also called the prime booking code or booking code.

Resolution 787. The purpose of Resolution 787 was to aid the growth of an open data exchange standard that uses Extended Markup Language (XML). This new standard would be used alongside the teletype and EDIFACT data exchange standards that are already overseen by IATA for the airline industry. Also known as the New Distribution Capability (NDC), Resolution 787 aimed to replace the outdated messaging exchange standard with a modern XML standard for communication between airlines and intermediaries.

Restriction Free Pricing. Fare filings introduced by the LCC's where the fares have no restrictions (absence of fences such as advance purchase and minimum stay restrictions) and the fare amount is the only determinant of the market segment.

Retrieval Augmented Generation. Retrieval augmented generation (RAG) is a technique to enhance large language models (LLM) by incorporating external knowledge data sources before generating responses. Instead of relying solely on the LLM's pre-existing training data, RAG leverages a retrieval system to access relevant information such as travel booking and ticketed data or data from relevant external sources.

Revenge Travel. "Revenge travel" refers to the surge in leisure travel following periods where travel was significantly restricted during the COVID-19 pandemic. It is the desire to make up for lost travel experiences and opportunities due to lockdowns and travel bans.

Revenue Per Available Seat Mile. The revenue per available seat mile (kilometer) is defined as the passenger revenue per available seat mile (kilometer). RASM (RASK) is monitored at different levels such as route, market, market entity and system.

Robinson-Patman Act. The Robinson-Patman Act (RPA) is a U.S. antitrust law that prohibits sellers from discriminating in price between different competing resellers of like goods where the effect is to substantially lessen competition. It is an amendment to the Clayton Act of 1914, and was enacted in 1936.

Seamless Availability. A seamless availability request is a direct connect availability request wherein a reservation request originating from a GDS will be queried for availability directly on a host CRS.

Seamless Sell. A direct connect sell request is also called a seamless sell request. Interactive sells are made against the airline inventory system. Seamless sell allows full usage of host CRS O&D controls to compute availability before the booking is made.

Search Engine Optimization. Search Engine Optimization (SEO) is a collection of techniques to improve a website to rank higher in organic search results, driving from free traffic by making content easier for search engines to understand and users to find valuable.

Search Engine Marketing. Search Engine Marketing (SEM) is a digital online marketing strategy using paid ads to boost visibility on search engines, appearing above organic results by bidding on keywords to reach users actively searching for products or services.

Secure Flight Passenger Data. Secure Flight Passenger Data (SFPD) elements on a Passenger Name Record (PNR) are the specific pieces of information the U.S. Transportation Security Administration (TSA) requires for passengers traveling on flights to, from, or over the United States.

Segment. A segment is a sequence of one or more flight legs with the same flight number.

Segment Close Indicator. An indicator on the airline's inventory control system that closes a booking class for future sales.

Segment Limit Sales. A numeric limit on the airline's inventory control system that limits sales in a booking class. Usually used in conjunction with leg class controls.

Seller. Sellers in travel include direct channels and indirect intermediaries like OTAs, TMCs, and Tour Operators.

Semi-Supervised Learning. Situations arise when there is a large amount of input data and only some of the data are labeled.

Service. A service describes the market plus the sequence of connections and time of day.

SHapley Additive exPlanations. The SHAP method attempts to explain the prediction of an instance/observation by computing the contribution of each feature to the prediction.

Sherman Antitrust Act. The Sherman Antitrust Act, enacted in 1890, is a U.S. law designed to promote fair competition by prohibiting anti-competitive practices in the marketplace. It aims to prevent monopolies and restrictions on trade that harm consumers and the economy. The Act has two main sections: Section 1, which prohibits contracts, combinations, and conspiracies in restraint of trade, and Section 2, which prohibits monopolization

Sovrin. The Sovrin Foundation is a nonprofit organization established to promote Internet identity for all and to administer the Governance Framework for the Sovrin Network, a decentralized global public network enabling self-sovereign identity on the Internet.

Special Prorate Agreements. Special Prorate Agreements (SPAs) are specific, bilateral agreements between airlines that define how revenue from interline travel will be shared. These agreements take priority over general proration rules and are used to ensure a fair and agreed-upon distribution of revenue for tickets involving multiple airlines.

Spill. Estimate of passengers who were turned away because their first choice was unavailable.

Spoilage. Seats that are empty on a flight that was closed for sale before departure. This is called overbooking spoilage, which is different from discount allocation spoilage.

Station. A station is equivalent to an airport.

Standard Retailer Supplier Interline Agreement. SRSIA is a new interline framework proposed by IATA with Offers and Orders to support many different interline partnership models, between different operators, including LCCs and multiple modes of transport.

Supervised Learning. These techniques are designed to learn by example. The input data for this method is a labeled training dataset. The labeled data has the correct answers, and the algorithm learns from this dataset to make predictions.

Supplier. The term "Supplier" in travel refers to airlines, hotels, rental car, rail, cruise lines and ferry lines.

Support Vector Machines. A set of supervised learning modes used for classification, regression, and outlier detection.

Thru Availability. Thru (through) availability is the availability for each RBD when an O&D is requested, and the O&D has more than one segment. Pricing analysts frequently refer to connecting availability as "thru" availability since fare construction is based on "thru fares"

Thru Fare: A thru (through) fare is a fare for the market with a fare class (fare basis code) regardless of the number of connections in the schedule.

Ticketed Point Mileage. This is the shortest distance between any two points on an operating route, used in airline fare calculations regardless of the airports used.

Transactions Per Second. Transactions per second (TPS) and peak transactions per second refer to the number of transactions a system (e.g., a GDS) can process in one second.

Transaction Processing Facility. Transaction Processing Facility (TPF) is a real-time operating system for IBM mainframe computers. Key characteristics are high volume transaction processing, supports many concurrent users, and fast response times.

Travel Management Company. Travel management companies are large travel agencies that pre-dominantly manage corporate business travel programs. Some large TMCs are also focused on leisure travel.

Trip-purpose segmentation. A method to implicitly segment customers based on the context for travel.

Universal Product Attributes. ATPCO Routehappy content type that provides access to airline products and services with images, messages, videos and cabin tours. The content is specific to aircraft, cabin, route, time of day, and fare providing relevant content during air shopping by a customer.

Universal Ticketing Attributes. ATPCO Routehappy content type provides descriptions of fare restrictions in simple language for customers during the shopping process. Data is sourced from ATPCO Fares, Branded Fares, and Optional Services.

Unsupervised Learning. A collection of techniques used to draw inferences from data that does not have any labeled responses.

Upgrade. An upgrade is an offer to a customer to sit in a higher class of service at no additional cost.

Upsell. Upsell is a special case of recapture to a higher fare or bundle on the same flight. Cross-flight recapture denotes recapture to other flight(s) on the host airline.

Veblen Goods. A Veblen good is an exclusive product, a status symbol, for which the demand increases as the price increases. A Veblen good has an upward-sloping demand curve instead of the traditional downward-sloping demand curve. Named after Norwegian American economist and sociologist Thorstein Bunde Veblen (1857–1929). Luxury hotel products, luxury yachts, first class suites on airlines and private jets can be categorized as a Veblen Good.

Value Pricing. An approach to pricing products based on what the market would be willing to pay for the service level of the product.

Virtual Nesting. An O&D inventory control technique where service classes are mapped into virtual buckets.

Vowpal Wabbit. Vowpal Wabbit (VW) is an open source, fast, and scalable machine learning system originally developed at Yahoo! Research and now actively maintained by Microsoft Research and a community of open-source contributors. VW offers robust support for contextual bandit algorithms, a key area within reinforcement learning, enabling applications like content personalization and recommendation systems.

Wholesaler. In travel a wholesaler negotiates deeply discounted prices with suppliers and marks it up and delivers it to various points of sale.

Workflow. A workflow is a collection of activities and events executed by systems and external agents participating in a business process.

Yield. Yield is defined as the passenger revenue per revenue passenger mile (kilometer). Yield is monitored at different levels such as route, market, market entity and system.

YQ/YR. Surcharges used in international markets. Sometimes YQ/YR can be greater than the base fare since airlines do not pay commissions on YQ/YR (only pay commissions on the base fare). Fuel surcharges filed as YQF or YRF, Insurance charges filed as YQI or YRI. YQ/YR fares are not a tax, but a validating carrier specific fee, not interline able, not commissionable. The Carrier-Imposed (YQ/YR) Fees solution provides marketing carriers (carriers that appear on the flight coupon) the ability to control and collect fees at the sector (coupon), at the portion of travel (multiple sectors), or on the journey.

References

Accelya. (2025, January 14). *Accelya achieves record-breaking day and +146% YoY growth in 2024 corporate NDC bookings*. Accelya Press Release. https://w3.accelya.com/resources/press-releases/accelya-achieves-record-breaking-day-and-146-yoy-growth-in 2024-corporate-ndc-bookings/#:~:text=Miami%2C%20USA%20&%20London%2C%20UK,demand%20for%20personalization%20and%20convenience

ACI. (2025). New 30-year forecasts highlight robust growth, despite short-term uncertainties. *The Trusted Authority on Air Travel Demand Insights, Airports Council International*. https://aci.aero/2025/02/26/the-trusted-authority-on-air-travel-demand-insights/#:~:text=Long%2Dterm%20outlook:%20looking%20beyond%202043%20and%202053&text=Based%20on%20the%20latest%20data,growth%20potential%20of%20international%20markets

Agrawal, R., & Srikant, R. (1994, September). *Fast algorithms for mining association rules*. Proceedings of the 20th International Conference on Verg Large Data Bases, VLDB Conference, Santiago, Chile, pp. 487–499.

Airbus. (2025). Airbus: Global fleet to nearly double by 2043. *Airbus Aerospace Global News*. https://aerospaceglobalnews.com/news/airbus-global-fleet-to-nearly-double-by-2043/#:~:text=Airbus'%20Global%20Market%20Forecast%20predicts,at%2013%2C070%20and%201%2C850%20respectively

Airoldi, D. M. (2022, December 5). American tells TMCs to be NDC-ready by April or lose some content access. *Business Travel News*. https://www.businesstravelnews.com/Distribution/American-Tells-TMCs-to-Be-NDC-Ready-by-April-or-Lose-Some-Content-Access

Airoldi, D. (2023, October 9). *Airline continuous pricing explained*. Business Travel News. https://www.businesstravelnews.com/Procurement/Airline-Continuous-Pricing-Explained

Airoldi, D. (2024a, April 3). One year of NDC: Travel agency AmTrav examines American Airlines fare data. *Business Travel News*. https://www.travelweekly.com/Travel-News/Travel-Agent-Issues/Travel-agency-AmTrav-highlights-American-Airlines-fare-data

Airoldi, D. M. (2024b, April 11). ATPCO unveils "Product Catalog" for dynamic air offer filing. *Business Travel News*. https://www.businesstravelnews.com/Distribution/ATPCO-Unveils-Product-Catalog-for-Dynamic-Air-Offer-Filing

Airoldi, D. M. (2024c, September 25). *Report: 2023 ancillary airline revenue 'surges' over '19 levels*. Business Travel News. https://www.businesstravelnews.com/Transportation/Air/Report-2023-Ancillary-Airline-Revenue-Surges-Over-19-Levels#:~:text=United%20Airlines%20was%20on%20top,billion%20and%20$33.65%20per%20passenger

Airoldi, D. M. (2024d, April 24). DOT announces airline ancillary fee, refund rules. *Business Travel News*. https://www.businesstravelnews.com/Transportation/Air/DOT-Announces-Airline-Ancillary-Fee-Refund-Rules

B. Vinod, *The Era of Airline Revenue Management with Offers and Orders*, Management for Professionals, https://doi.org/10.1007/978-3-032-24197-9

Airoldi, D. M. (2024e, May 23). The pace of change: Suppliers make progress on NDC. *Business Travel News Europe.* https://www.businesstravelnews.com/NDC-Update/2024/Pace-of-Change-Suppliers-Make-Progress-on-NDC

Airoldi, D. M. (2024f, June 19). Air Canada to limit EDIFACT fee. *Business Travel News.* https://www.businesstravelnews.com/Distribution/Air-Canada-to-Limit-EDIFACT-Fee

Airoldi, D. M. (2024g, December 2). Qantas to launch new distribution model, revise surcharges. *Business Travel News.* https://www.businesstravelnews.com/Distribution/Qantas-to-Launch-New-Distribution-Model-Revise-Surcharges https://www.businesstravelnews.com/Distribution/Qantas-to-Launch-New-Distribution-Model-Revise-Surcharges

Airoldi, D. M. (2024h). BTN's 2024 airline survey and report. *Business Travel News.* https://www.businesstravelnews.com/research/airline-survey-report/2024

Alexander, K. L. (2006, January 31). Paying more for small extras. *The Washington Post.*

Alstrup, J., Andersson, S.-E., Boas, S., & Madsen, O. B. G. (1989). Booking control increases profit at Scandinavian airlines. *Interfaces, 19*, 10–19.

Altexsoft. (2025, November 14). OpenAI CEO says ChatGPT will book hotels in one click, no ads. *Altexsoft.* https://www.altexsoft.com/travel-industry-news/openai-ceo-says-chatgpt-will-book-hotels-in-one-click-no-ads/

Amadeus (2026) Amadeus acquires SkyLink to accelerate the deployment of AI in travel, Amadeus Press Release, February 25, https://amadeus.com/en/newsroom/press-releases/skylink-ai-acquisition

American Airlines. (2021, December 6). *American airlines, the first U.S. airline to integrate NDC with a global distribution system, nears full roll-out.* American Airlines Newsroom. https://news.aa.com/news/news-details/2021/American-Airlines-the-First-US-Airline-to-Integrate-NDC-with-a-Global-Distribution-System-Nears-Full-Roll-Out-MKG-OTH-12/default.aspx

American Airlines. (2023, October 16). American airlines introduces advantage business, a simple and rewarding program for businesses and their travelers. *Customer Experience, AA Newsroom.* https://news.aa.com/news/news-details/2023/American-Airlines-introduces-AAdvantage-Business-a-simple-and-rewarding-program-for-businesses-and-their-travelers-AADV-10/default.aspx#:~:text=7:45%20a.m.-,American%20Airlines%20introduces%20AAdvantage%20Business%2C%20a%20simple%20and%20rewarding,for%20businesses%20and%20their%20travelers

American Airlines. (2024, April 25). American Airlines reports first-quarter 2024 financial results. *AA Newsroom.* https://news.aa.com/news/news-details/2024/American-Airlines-reports-first-quarter-2024-financial-results-CORP-FI-04/default.aspx#:~:text=(NASDAQ:%20AAL)%20today%20reported,($0.34)%20per%20diluted%20share

American Airlines, Inc Plaintiff vs Sabre. (2021). *Plaintiff's verified original petition and application for temporary injunction and permanent injunction.* Filed Tarrant Country 6/29/2021, Thomas A Wilder, District Clerk. https://skift.com/wp-content/uploads/2021/07/aa-sabre-lawsuit-july-1.pdf

Amit, Y., & Geman, D. (1997). Shape quantization and recognition with randomized trees. *Neural Computation, 9*, 1545–1588.

Anderson, C. K. (2009, October). The billboard effect: Online travel agent impact on NonOTA reservation volume. *Cornell University School of Hotel Administration, Cornell Hospitality Report, 9*(16).

Anderson, C. K. (2011, April). Search, OTAs, and online booking: An expanded analysis of the billboard effect. *Cornell Hospitality Report, 11*(8), 1–10.

Andrew, S., Wallace, G., & Levitt, R. (2020, May 7). Frontier Airlines won't charge passengers to keep the middle seat empty following backlash from lawmakers. *CNN Travel.* https://www.cnn.com/travel/article/frontier-airlines-rescinds-middle-seat-pay-trnd#:~:text=See%20more%20videos,joint%20letter%20to%20Biffle%20read.

Arena, L. (2024, September 4). Turkish Airlines unveils NDC aggregator partners following Sabre exit. *Business Travel News Europe.* https://www.businesstravelnewseurope.com/TMC-Distribution/Turkish-Airlines-unveils-NDC-aggregator-partners-following-Sabre-exit

Ariely, D. (2010). *Predictably irrational.* Revised and Expanded Edition: The Hidden Forces That Shape Our Decisions. Harper Perennial. ISBN-10:9780061353246, ISBN-13:978-0061353246.

Arrieta, A. B., Diaz-Rodriguez, N., Del Ser, J., Bennetot, A., Tabik, S., Barbado, A., Garcia, S., Gil-Lopez, S., Molina, Benjamins, R., Chatila, R., & Herrera, F. (2020). Explainable Artificial Intelligence (XAI): Concepts, taxonomies, opportunities and challenges toward responsible AI. *Information Fusion, 58*, 82–115.

ATPCO. (2017, October). *Dual RBD validation: Increasing available price points within current frameworks.* ATPCO White Paper Version 1.0. https://www.atpco.net/sites/atpco-public/files/2019-03/dual-rbd-validation-whitepaper.pdf

ATPCO. (2019, February 27). ATPCO acquired Routehappy. *Press Release.* https://atpco.net/press/atpco-acquires-routehappy/

ATPCO. (2024, December 18). *ATPCO launches Loyalty Rewards attribute to highlight coveted mileage accrual benefits for flight shoppers.* ATPCO Press Release. https://atpco.net/press/atpco-launches-loyalty-rewards-attribute-to-highlight-coveted-mileage-accrual-benefits-for-flight-shoppers/

Aviation Week. (2006, October 31). JetBlue sees GDS participation as part of its evolution. *Aviation Week.* https://aviationweek.com/air-transport/safety-ops-regulation/jetblue-sees-gds-participation-part-its-evolution-0

Bacon, D. R., Besharat, A., Parsa, H. G., & Smith, S. J. (2016). Revenue management, hedonic pricing models and the effects of operational attributes. *International Journal of Revenue Management, 9*(2/3), 147–164.

Baker, M. B. (2024, May 15). Turkish airlines to offer agency portal, begin GDS surcharge. *Business Travel News Europe.* https://www.businesstravelnews.com/Distribution/Turkish-Airlines-to-Offer-Agency-Portal-Begin-GDS-Surcharge

Baker, M. B. (2025, December 10). *Navan reports increasing revenues and widening losses.* Business Travel News Europe. https://www.businesstravelnewseurope.com/Management/Navan-reports-increasing-revenue-and-widening-loss?oly_enc_id=9607B2485578C3T

Balcombe, K., Fraser, I., & Harris, L. (2009). Consumer willingness to pay for in-flight service and comfort levels: A choice experiment. *Journal of Air Transport Management, 15*, 221–226.

Baydakova, A. (2018). *Singapore airlines' blockchain-based loyalty program takes off*. www.coindesk.com/singapore-airlines-blockchain-based-loyalty-program-takes-off. Accessed 25 July.

Bell, P. C. (2008, March). Short selling and replaning as tools to enhance revenues. *Journal of the Operational Research Society, 59*(3), 313–321.

Bellman, R. (1954, November). The theory of dynamic programming. *Bulletin of the American Mathematical Society, 60*(6), 503–516.

Belobaba, P. P. (1987). *Air travel demand and airline seat inventory management*. Massachusetts Institute of Technology, Cambridge, MA. MIT Publication, MIT Flight Transportation Laboratory Report R87-7.

Belobaba, P. P. (1989). Application of a probabilistic decision support model to airline seat inventory control. *Operations Research, 37*(2), 183–197.

Belobaba, P. P. (1992, May 4). *Optimal vs heuristic methods for nested seat allocation.* AGIFORS Yield Management Study Group, Brussels, Belgium

Belobaba, P. P. (2008, September). *The rise and fall of airline revenue management systems: How can OR help?* AGIFORS Symposium, Montreal, Canada.

Belobaba, P. P. (2019, March 19). *PODS consortium research update: Dynamic pricing mechanisms.* ATPCO Dynamic Pricing Working Group, Dulles, VA.

Belobaba, P. P., & Hopperstad, C. (2004, June). *Algorithms for revenue management in unrestricted fare structures.* INFORMS Revenue Management Section, Cambridge, Massachusetts.

Belobaba, P. P., & Weatherford, L. (1996). Comparing decision rules that incorporate customer diversion in perishable asset revenue management situations. *Decision Sciences, 27*(2), 343–363.

Ben-Akiva, M., & Lerman, S. (1985). *Discrete choice analysis: Theory and application to travel demand* (6th ed.). Massachusetts Institute of Technology Press.

Benjio, Y., Lodi, A., & Prouvost, A. (2021). Machine learning for combinatorial optimization: A methodological tour d'horizon. *European Journal of Operational Research, 290*(2), 405–421.

Bertsimas, D., & de Boer, S. (2005). Simulation-based booking limits for airline revenue management. *Operations Research, 53*(1), 90–106.

Bertsimas, D., & Dunn, J. (2019). *Machine learning under a modern optimization lens.* Dynamic Ideas, LLC, Belmont, Massachusetts. ISBN 978-1-7337885-0-2.

Bertsimas, D., & Kallus, N. (2020). From predictive to prescriptive analytics. *Management Science, 66*(3), 1025–1044.

Bertsimas, D., & Popescu, I. (2003). Revenue management in a dynamic network environment. *Transportation Science, 37*(3), 257–277.

Biyalogorsky, E., Carmon, Z., Fruchter, G. E., & Gerstner, E. (1999, November). Research note: Overselling with opportunistic cancellations. *Marketing Science, 18*(4). https://doi.org/10.1287/mksc.18.4.605

Biyalogorsky, E., Carmon, Z., Fruchter, G. E., & Gerstner, E. (2000, January). Should airlines and hotels use short selling. *OR/MS Today, 27*(5).

Boehmer, J. (2022, November 3). American, Sabre resolve contract litigation over displays, alleged Delta bias. *The Beat.* https://www.thebeat.travel/News/American-Sabre-Resolve-Contract-Litigation

Boehmer, J. (2023, April 28). Today in distribution cost shifting: LATAM to turn on GDS surcharge. *The Beat.* https://www.thebeat.travel/News/Latam-To-Turn-On-GDS-Surcharge

Boehmer, J. (2024, December 19). Government TMC contractors list NDC surcharges in pricing proposals. *The Beat.* https://www.thebeat.travel/News/Government-TMC-Contractors-List-NDC-Surcharges-In-Pricing-Proposals

Boin, R., Höll, R., Ralhan, P., & Lind, N. (2022, September 9). *Airline retailing: How payment innovation can improve the bottom line.* https://www.mckinsey.com/industries/travel/our-insights/airline-retailing-how-payment-innovation-can-improve-the-bottom-line

Bois, R., Cosmas, A., & Wittkamp, N. (2019, November 26). *"Airline retailing" the value at stake.* McKinsey & Company. https://www.mckinsey.com/industries/travel-logistics-and-infrastructure/our-insights/airline-retailing-the-value-at-stake

Bondoux, N., Nguyen, A. Q., Fiig, T., & Acuna-Agost, R. (2020). Reinforcement learning applied to airline revenue management. *Journal of Revenue and Pricing Management, 19*(6), 332–348.

Booking Holdings. (2024, June 4). *2024 notice of annual stockholders' meeting and proxy statement.* https://s201.q4cdn.com/865305287/files/doc_financials/2024/ar/2024-proxy-statement-and-annual-report.pdf

Boser, B. E., Guyon, I. M., & Vapnik, V. N. (1992). *A training algorithm for optimal margin classifiers.* Proceedings of the fifth annual workshop on Computational learning theory – COLT '92, p. 144.

Boyd, A., Kambour, E., & Tama, J. (2001). *The impact of buy-down on unconstraining sell-up and spiral-down.* INFORMS Revenue Management Section Conference, Columbia University, New York, USA.

Boyd, E. A. (1998). Airline alliance revenue management: Global alliances within the airline industry add complexity to the yield management problem. *OR MS Today.*

Boyd, E. A. (2007). *The future of pricing: How airline ticket pricing has inspired a revolution.* Palgrave Macmillan, New York. ISBN 10: 0230600190, ISBN 13: 978-0230600195.

Boyd, E. A., & Kallesen, R. (2004). The science of revenue management when passengers purchase the lowest available fare. *Journal of Revenue Pricing Management, 3*, 171–177. https://doi.org/10.1057/palgrave.rpm.5170104

Boyer, C. A. (2010, June). Statistical Methods for Forecasting and Estimating passenger willingness to pay in airline revenue management, MS in *OR Thesis, Sloan School of Management, MIT*.

Braley, S. (2024, July 23). 2024 global business travel industry to hit record $1.48T. *Northstar Meetings Group.* https://www.northstarmeetingsgroup.com/News/Industry/2024-Global-Business-Travel-Industry-to-Hit-Record-1-48-Trillion-dollars

Brancatelli, J. (2002). The contrarian's guide to frequent-travel plans. *Joesentme.com*. https://joe.biztravelife.com/02/103102.htm

Breiman, L. (2001, October). Random forests. *Machine Learning, 45*, 5–32. https://doi.org/10.1023/A:1010933404324

Breiman, L., Friedman, J., Olshen, R., & Stone, C. (1983). *Classification and regression trees* (368 pages). Wadsworth Publishing. ISBN-10:534980546, ISBN-13:978-0534980542.

British Airways. (2022, December). *Distribution technology cost guide, Version 5*. https://www.britishairways.com/assets/pdfs/updates/distribution-technology-charge.pdf

Brons, M., Pels, E., Nijkamp, P., & Rietveld, P. (2002). Price elasticities of demand for passenger air travel: A meta-analysis. *Journal of Air Transport Management, 8*(3), 165–175.

Brown, P. F, Cocke, J., Della Pietra, S. A., Della Pietra, V. J., Jelinek, F., Mercer, R. L, Roossin, P., (1988 *A statistical approach to language translation*, COLING 1988: Proceedings of the 12th Conference on Computational Linguistics—Volume 1, pp. 71–76, August 22, https://doi.org/10.3115/991635.991651

Brown, P. F., Della Pietra , S. A., Della Pietra, V. J., Mercer, R. L. (1993) The Mathematics of Statistical Machine Translation: Parameter Estimation, *Computational Linguistics*, 19(2), 263–311.

Brumelle, S. L., & McGill, J. I. (1993). Airline seat allocation with multiple nested fare classes. *Operations Research, 41*, 127–137.

Brumelle, S. L., McGill, J. I., Oum, T., Sawaki, K., & Tretheway, M. (1990, August). Allocation of airline seats between stochastically dependent demands. *Transportation Science, 24*(3), 183–192.

BTS (2026) First Quarter of OD40 Data is Live, Bureau of Transportation Statistics, Press Release February 17, US Department of Transportation, https://www.bts.gov/newsroom/first-quarter-od40-data-live

Busuttil, L. (1995). *Managing the group sales process*. AGIFORS Symposium, Tel Aviv.

Byrd, M., & Darrow, R. (2021). A note on the advantage of context in thompson sampling. *Journal of Revenue and Pricing Management*. https://doi.org/10.1057/s41272-021-00314-1

Carmichael, D. (1982, October 1). Two of nation' largest airlines reach agreement. *UPI Archives*. https://www.upi.com/Archives/1982/10/01/Two-of-nations-largest-airlines-reach-agreement/2350402292800/

Cartrawler and IdeaWorks. (2022). *The 2022 CarTrawler Yearbook of Ancillary Revenue by IdeaWorks Company*, Issued September 27, 2022.

Cartrawler and IdeaWorks. (2024, October 29). *Airline ancillary revenue skyrockets to $148.4 billion worldwide for 2024*. Press Release. https://ideaworkscompany.com/airline-ancillary-revenue-skyrockets-to-148-4-billion-worldwide-for-2024-press-release/

Castelvecchi, D. (2023, December 4). IBM releases first-ever 1,000-qubit quantum chip. *Nature, 624*, 238. https://www.nature.com/articles/d41586-023-03854-1

Chandler, S., & Ja, S. (2007, May). *Revenue opportunity modeling at American Airlines*. AGIFORS Revenue Management Study Group, Jeju, Korea.

Chapius, J. M. (2008). Basics of dynamic programming for revenue management. *Revenue & Yield Management eJournal*, 21. ff10.2139/ssrn.1123768ff.ffhal-00694132f

Chatwin, R. E. (1993). *Optimal airline overbooking* (Ph.D. thesis). Department of Operations Research, Stanford University, Palo Alto, CA.

Chen, C., & Proctor, Q. (2025, November 24). *Zumper National Rent Report*. https://www.zumper.com/rent-research/national-rent-report

Chiamberetto, P., & Dumez, H. (2012). The role of bundling in firms' marketing strategies: A synthesis. *Recherche et Applications en Marketing. SAGE Journals, 27*(2). https://doi.org/10.1177/205157071202700205

Chicago Convention. (1944). *Convention on International Civil Aviation done at Chicago on the 7th day of December 1944, Doc 7300*. https://www.icao.int/publications/documents/7300_orig.pdf

Chollet, F. (2019, November 5). *On the measure of intelligence*. https://arxiv.org/pdf/1911.01547.pdf.

Choubert, L., Fiig, T., & Viale, V. (2015). *Amadeus dynamic pricing*. AGIFORS Revenue Management and Distribution Study Group meeting, Shanghai, China.

Chun, S. Y., & de Boer, E. (2021, April 2). How loyalty programs are saving airlines. *Harvard Business Review*, Customer Service, Digital Article.

Clarke, P. (2023, October 17). The current state of traveler satisfaction with industry apps and websites. *Travelpulse*. https://www.travelpulse.com/news/technology/the-current-state-of-traveler-satisfaction-with-industry-apps-websites

CNN Business. (2025, August 21). *Delta, United sued for selling windowless 'window seats'*. CNN Business, By Reuters. https://www.cnn.com/2025/08/21/business/delta-united-sued-selling-windowless-window-seats-hnk#:~:text=Delta%20Air%20Lines%20and%20United%20Airlines%20were,in%20seats%20next%20to%20a%20blank%20wall

Congress.Gov. (2025). *S.232—Preventing Algorithmic Collusion Act of 2025, 119th Congress (2025–2026)*. Sponsor: Senator Amy Klobuchar [D-MN] Introduced January 23. https://www.congress.gov/bill/119th-congress/senate-bill/232

Connor, P., Assaker, G., & El Haddad, R. (2025). Online travel agency participation: An empirical investigation of its financial contribution to U.S. hotel profitability. *Cornell Hospitality Quarterly*, First published online February 26, 2025. https://doi.org/10.1177/19389655251318

Consumer Reports. (2010, May 4). *Luggage charges top Consumer Reports' Survey of Travel Gripes*. Consumer Reports. https://www.consumerreports.org/media-room/press-releases/2010/05/luggage-charges-top-consumer-reports-survey-of-travel-gripes/

Cook, T. M. (1998, June). Sabre Soars. *OR/MS Today*, 26–31.

Cook, T. M. (1999, December 13). *Creating competitive advantage using model-driven decision support systems*. Presented at the International Conference of Information Systems.

Cortes, C., & Vapnik, V. (1995). Support-vector networks. *Machine Learning, 20*(3), 273–297. https://doi.org/10.1007/BF00994018

Cosmas, A., Lind, N., Petersen, J., & Hübel, N. (2025, May 22). *The eight myths of airline retailing*. McKinsey & Company. https://www.mckinsey.com/industries/travel/our-insights/the-eight-myths-of-airline-retailing

Cournot, A.-A. (1838, October 26). *Recherches sur les principes mathématiques de la théorie des richesses* (*Researches into the Mathematical Principles of the Theory of Wealth*). Reprinted by Legare Street Press. ISBN-10: 1015440169.

Cox, J. (2025, June 10). Airlines don't want you to know they sold your flight data to DHS. *Wired*. https://www.wired.com/story/airlines-dont-want-you-to-know-they-sold-your-flight-data-to-dhs/

Crandall, R. L. (1995, September). The unique U.S. airline industry. In D. Jenkins (Executive Ed.), *Aviation daily's handbook of airline economics*. The Aviation Weekly Group of the McGraw-Hill Companies.

Crandall, R. L. (1998, May 1). How airline pricing works. *American Way Magazine*.

Cross, R. G. (1995). An introduction to revenue management. In D. Jenkins (Ed.), *Aviation daily's handbook of airline economics* (pp. 443–458). The Aviation Group of the McGraw-Hill Companies.

Cross, R. G. (1997). *Revenue management*. Broadway.

Cross, R. G. (1998). Trends in airline revenue management. In G. F. Butler & M. R. Keller (Exec. eds.), *Aviation Week Group Newsletters* (pp. 303–318). A Division of the McGraw-Hill Companies, Edmund Pinto, Publisher.

Cummings, N. (2007, January). How Sabre Invented YM. *British Operational Research Society, OR Newsletter*.

Curry, R. E. (1990). Optimal airline seat allocation with fare classes nested by origins and destinations. *Transportation Science, 24*, 193–204.

Curry, R. E. (1995, October 17). *A market-level pricing model for airlines*. 7th International Revenue Management Conference. Toronto Ontario.

CWT. (2021, February 23). CWT announces first American Airlines production NDC booking via Amadeus citric. *CWT Newsroom*. https://www.mycwt.com/news/pr/cwt-announces-first-american-airlines-production-ndc-booking-via-amadeus-cytric/

Dadoun, A., Platel, M. D., Fiig, T., Landra, C., & Troncy, R. (2021). How recommender systems can transform airline offer construction and retailing. *Journal of Revenue and Pricing Management*. https://doi.org/10.1057/s41272-021-00313-2

Darrow, R. (2021). The future of AI is the market. *Journal of Revenue and Pricing Management*. https://doi.org/10.1057/s41272-021-00321-2

Datagrid. (2025, September 2). What is agentic AI? *Datagrid*. https://datagrid.com/blog/agentic-ai-what-is

Daudel, S., & Vialle, G. (1989). *Le yield management: La Face Encore Cachee du Marketing des Services*. InterEditions.

Davenport, T., & Ronanki, R. (2018, January–February). Artificial intelligence for the real world. *Harvard Business Review*.

Dean, J., & Ghemawat, S. (2004). *MapReduce: Simplified data processing on large clusters*. Sixth Symposium on Operating System Design and Implementation, OSDI, Vol. 6, December, San Francisco, CA.

De Boer, S. V., Freling, R., & Piersma, N. (2002). Mathematical programming for network revenue management revisited. *European Journal of Operational Research, 1371*(1), 72–92.

de Marcken, K. (2003). Computational complexity of air travel planning. *ITA Software*. http://www.demarcken.org/carl/papers/ITA-software-travel-complexity/ITA-software-travel-complexity.html

Dempsey, P. S., & Gesell, L. E. (1997). *Airline management: Strategies for the 21st century*. Coast Aire Publications.

Dempster, A., Laird, N., & Rubin, D. (1977). Maximum likelihood estimation from incomplete data via the EM algorithm. *Journal of the Royal Statistical Society, Series B, 39*, 1–38.

Department of Justice. (1993, November 1). Final judgment: U.S. V. Airline Tariff Publishing Company, Et Al., *Antitrust Division, Department of Justice*, Civil Action No.: 92 2854. https://www.justice.gov/atr/final-judgment-us-v-airline-tariff-publishing-company-et-al

Department of Justice. (2025, November 24). *Justice department requires realpage to end the sharing of competitively sensitive information and alignment of pricing among competitors*. DOJ Press Release, Office of Public Affairs. https://www.justice.gov/opa/pr/justice-department-requires-realpage-end-sharing-competitively-sensitive-information-and

Department of Justice Press Release. (2023, August 23). *Justice Department Sues RealPage for Algorithmic Pricing Scheme that harms millions of American Renters*. Department of Justice. https://www.justice.gov/opa/pr/justice-department-sues-realpage-algorithmic-pricing-scheme-harms-millions-american-renters

DeSylva, E. (1982). *O-and-D seat assignment to maximize expected revenue*. Technical Report. Boeing Commercial Airplane Company, Seattle, Washington.

Deutsch, C. H. (2001, May 6). … And to penny-pinching wizardry. *The New York Times*. https://www.nytimes.com/2001/05/06/business/and-to-penny-pinching-wizardry.html

Dezelak, M., & Ratliff, R. (2018). Towards new industry-standard specifications for air dynamic pricing engines. *Journal of Revenue Pricing Management, 17*(6), 394–402.

Domeyer, A., McCarthy, M., Pfeiffer, S., & Scherf, G. (2020, August 31). *How governments can deliver on the promise of digital ID*. McKinsey & Company. https://www.mckinsey.com/industries/public-sector/our-insights/how-governments-can-deliver-on-the-promise-of-digital-id/

Donovan, A. W. (2005). Yield management in the airline industry. *Journal of Aviation/Aerospace Education and Research, 14*(3), 11–19.

DOT. (2019, August 1). New airline passenger protections take effect this week. *U.S. Department of Transportation*. https://www.transportation.gov/affairs/2012/dot0812.html

DOT. (2024a, April 17). *Enhancing transparency of airline ancillary service fees, 14 CFR Parts 259 and 399* [Docket No. DOT-OST-2022-0109], RIN No. 2105-AF10. https://www.transportation.gov/sites/dot.gov/files/2024-04/Final%20Rule%20Ancillary%20Fee%20Transparency%20%282105-AF10%29.pdf

DOT. (2024b, April 24). *Final rule—Refunds and other consumer protections*. Department of Transportation. https://www.transportation.gov/airconsumer/refundsfinalruleapril2024

Dror, M., & Ladany, S. P. (1988). Network models for seat allocation on flights. *Transportation Research B, 22*, 239–250.

Dudik, M., Langford, J., & Li, L. (2011). *Doubly robust policy evaluation and learning*. Proceedings of the 28th International Conference on Machine Learning, Bellevue, WA, USA.

Dunleavy, H. N. (1996, March). *The Roles of fares in revenue management*. AGIFORS Reservations and Yield Management Study Group, Zurich, Switzerland.

Dunleavy, H., & Westermann, D. (2005). Future of revenue management: Future of airline revenue management. *Journal of Revenue Pricing Management, 3*, 380–383.

Dupler-Fornova, N. (2020, June 29). Hotel distribution post-pandemic – how not to throw caution to the wind. *Phocuswire*. https://www.phocuswire.com/hotel-distribution-post-covid-19#:~:text=%22There%20is%20a%20huge%20misconception%20that%20third,hotel%20rooms%2C%20which%20is%20simply%20not%20true.%E2%80%9D&text=If%20hotels%20can%20keep%20their%20focus%20on,strategy%20to%20maintain%20control%20of%20their%20distribution

Dupuis, C. (2010, May). *Overbooking: How to estimate passenger show rates with a logical and combinatory approach May 2010*. AGIFORS Revenue Management and Cargo Study Group.

Dyson, M. (2018, August 17). *CTI completes first BA NDC booking*. Business Travel News Europe. https://www.businesstravelnewseurope.com/Technology/CTI-completes-first-BA-NDC-booking

Edgar, Dunn and Company. (2022, September 1). *Airline payment cost and revenue drivers study*. Edgar, Dunn and Company.

Etzioni, O., Tuchinda, R., Knoblock, C. A., & Yates, A. (2003, August). To buy or not to buy: Mining airfare data to minimize ticket purchase price. In *Proceedings of the ninth ACM SIGKDD international conference on Knowledge discovery and data mining* (pp. 119–128). ACM.

European Union. (2008, September 5). Rules on competition and rules applying to undertakings. *Official Journal, 115*, 0088–0089. https://eur-lex.europa.eu/LexUriServ/LexUriServ.do?uri=CELEX%3A12008E101%3AEN%3AHTML

Farmer, J. D. (2025). *Making sense of Chaos: A better economics for a better world*. Yale University Press. ISBN 978-0-300-27377-0.

Fair, R. (1978). A theory of extramarital affairs. *Journal of Political Economy, 86*, 45–61.

Fearis, B. (2025, May 14). Google going "all in on NDC" with Concur and Amex GBT. *Business Travel Magazine*. https://thebusinesstravelmag.com/google-going-all-in-on-ndc-with-concur-and-amex-gbt/

Fechner, G. T. (1860). *Elements of Psychophysics*, reprinted by Holt, Rinehart and Winston: New York. 1966.

Fielding, R. T. (2000). *Architectural styles and the design of network-based software architectures* (Ph.D. Dissertation). University of California, Irvine. https://www.ics.uci.edu/~fielding/pubs/dissertation/top.htm

Fiig, T., Boulanger, A., Papen, A., Wesenberg, J. H., Dalgaard, M., & Hansen, R. T. (2023, October). *Application of quantum computing in airline revenue management*. AGIFORS 63-rd Annual Symposium, Montreal, Canada.

Fiig, T., Goyons, R. A., & Smith, B. C. (2016). Dynamic pricing—The next revolution in RM? *Journal of Revenue and Pricing Management, 15*(5), 360–379.

Fiig, T., Guen, R. L., & Gauchet, M. (2018). Dynamic pricing of airline offers. *Journal of Revenue and Pricing Management, 17*, 281–293.

Fiig, T., Isler, K., Hopperstad, C., & Cleaz-Savoyen, R. (2005). *Davn-mr: A Unified Theory of O&D optimization in a mixed network with restricted and unrestricted fare products*. AGIFORS Revenue Management and Distribution Study Group Meeting, Cape Town, South Africa.

Finnair Press Release. (2025, May 13). *Finnair becomes the first airline globally to create a 'Native Order', powered by Amadeus technology*. Finnair Press Release. https://company.finnair.com/en/media-centre/all-releases/news?id=0424502784FD83DE

Fisher, E. M. (1936). Linear discriminant analysis. *Statistics & Discrete Methods of Data Sciences, 392*, 1–5.

Fisher, M. (1981). The Lagrangian relaxation method for solving integer programming problems. *Management Science, 27*(1), 1–18.
Fish, S., Gonczarowski, Y. A., & Shorrer, R. I. (2025, September 11). *Algorithmic collusion by large language models.* Cornell University, Economics. arXiv:2404.00806v4[econ.GN]
Flyertalk. (2021, November 18). *Bad experience with Hopper – beware using their 'instant travel refund'.* https://www.flyertalk.com/forum/online-travel-booking-bidding-agencies/2059226-bad-experience-hopper-beware-using-their-instant-travel-refund.html
Fox, L. (2017, April 28). *Is NDC bringing some order as Lufthansa connects travel management firms?* Phocuswire. https://www.phocuswire.com/Is-NDC-bringing-some-order-as-Lufthansa-connects-travel-management-firms
Fox, L. (2019, February 27). Sabre brings a dose of reality to artificial intelligence. *Phocuswire.* https://www.phocuswire.com/sabre-artificial-intelligence
Fox, L. (2022a, March 14). Flight Centre acquires majority stake in TPConnects. *Phocuswire.* https://www.phocuswire.com/Flight-Centre-acquires-majority-stake-in-TPConnects
Fox, L. (2022b, June 7). Hopper extends trip protection to third-party bookings. *Phocuswire.*
Fox, L. (2024, January 10). Amtrav dishes data on American Airlines NDC strategy. *Phocuswire.* https://www.phocuswire.com/amtrav-report-on-aa-fares-ndc
Frary, M. (2020, October 6). *Emirates launches NDC gateway for agencies.* Business Travel News. https://www.businesstravelnewseurope.com/TMC-Distribution/Emirates-launches-NDC-gateway-for-agencies
Frary, M. (2021, April 1). British Airways adds additional price points on short-haul. *Business Travel News Europe.* https://www.businesstravelnewseurope.com/Air-Travel/British-Airways-adds-additional-price-points-on-short-haul
Freund, Y., & Schapire, R.E. (1995) *A decision-theoretic generalization of on-line learning and an application to boosting* (pp. 23–37). Lecture Notes in Computer Science, Berlin, Heidelberg: Springer Berlin Heidelberg. https://doi.org/10.1007/3-540-59119-2_166, ISBN978-3-540-59119-1.
Friedman, J. H. (2001, October). Greedy function approximation: A gradient boosting machine. *Annals of Statistics, 29*(5), 1189–1232. https://doi.org/10.1214/aos/1013203451
FTC. (2024a, December 12). *FTC Sues Southern Glazer's for Illegal Price Discrimination.* https://www.ftc.gov/news-events/news/press-releases/2024/12/ftc-sues-southern-glazers-illegal-price-discrimination#:~:text=Commission%20enforces%20Robinson%2DPatman%20Act,December%2012%2C%202024
FTC. (2024b, December 17). *Federal Trade Commission Announces Bipartisan Rule Banning Junk Ticket and Hotel Fees.* https://www.ftc.gov/news-events/news/press-releases/2024/12/federal-trade-commission-announces-bipartisan-rule-banning-junk-ticket-hotel-fees
Gale, N. (2021, August 4). Capitalizing on the virtual payments opportunity. *WEX, Inside WEX.* https://www.wexinc.com/resources/blog/capitalizing-on-the-virtual-payments-opportunity/#:~:text=The%20report%20conducted%20by%20WEX,a%20high%20risk%20of%20fraud.
Gallego, G., & Hu, M. (2014). Dynamic pricing of perishable assets under competition. *Management Science, 60*(5), 1241–1259.
Gallego, G., Iyengar, G., Phillips, R., & Dubey, A. (2004). *Managing flexible products on a network* (Computational Optimization Research Center (CORC), Technical Report, TR-2004-01). Columbia University.
Gallego, G., Li, L., & Ratliff, R. M. (2007, May 15). *Revenue management with customer choice models.* AGIFORS Revenue Management Study Group, South Korea.
Gallego, G., Li, L., & Ratliff, R. M. (2009). Choice-based EMSR methods for single leg revenue management with demand dependencies. *Journal of Revenue and Pricing Management, 8*(4), 207–240.
Gallego, G., Ratliff, R., & Shebalov, S. (2015). A general attraction model and sales-based linear program for network revenue management under customer choice. *Operations Research, 63*(1), 212–232.

Gallego, G., & Topaloglu, H. (2019). *Revenue management and pricing analytics.* International Series in Operations Research & Management Science, Springer. ISBN-10:1493996045, ISBN-13:978-1493996049.

Garcia, M. (2024, February 19). What Air Canada lost in 'remarkable lying' AI chatbot case. *Forbes.* https://www.forbes.com/sites/marisagarcia/2024/02/19/what-air-canada-lost-in-remarkable-lying-ai-chatbot-case/

Garrow, L. A. (2016). *Discrete choice modeling and air travel demand: Theory and applications* (1st ed.). Routledge. eBook ISBN:9781315577548.

Garrow, L., & Koppelman, F. (2004a, November). Predicting air travelers' no-show and standby behavior using passenger and directional itinerary information. *Journal of Air Transport Management, 10*(6), 401–411

Garrow, L., & Koppelman, F. (2004b). Multinomial and nested logit models of airline passengers' no-show and standby behaviour. *Journal of Revenue and Pricing Management, 3*(3), 237–253.

Gates, W. (2023, November 9). *The future of agents: AI is about to completely change how you use computers and upend the software industry.* GatesNotes. https://www.gatesnotes.com/meet-bill/meet-bill-home-topic/reader/ai-agents

Genter, J. T., & Lupini, C. (2021, April 2). 12 fascinating facts revealed about American Airlines Advantage program. *Forbes.* https://www.forbes.com/advisor/credit-cards/travel-rewards/12-fascinating-facts-revealed-about-american-airlines-aadvantage-program/

Gershgorn, D. (2016, March 12). Google's AlphaGo beats world champion in third match to win entire series. *Popular Science.*

Ghemawat, S., Gobioff, H., & Leung, S.-T. (2003, October). *The Google file system.* 19th ACM Symposium on Operating Systems Principles, Lake George, New York.

Gill, R. (2023, April 17). Air France and KLK to withdraw some fares from GDS. *Business Travel Europe.* https://www.businesstravelnewseurope.com/TMC-Distribution/Air-France-and-KLM-to-withdraw-some-fares-from-GDS#:~:text=Air%20France%20and%20KLM%20to,remain%20available%20via%20NDC%20connections.

Gill, R., & Arena, L. (2024, November 25). *Spain fines airlines €179 million for cabin bag charges.* Business Travel News Europe. https://www.businesstravelnewseurope.com/Air-Travel/Spain-fines-airlines-179-million-for-cabin-bag-charges?oly_enc_id=9607B2485578C3T

Gittins, J., Glazebrook, K., & Weber, R. (2011). *Multi-armed bandit allocation indices* (2nd ed.). Wiley.

Glover, F., Glover, R., Lorenzo, J., & McMillan, C. (1982). The passenger-mix problem in the scheduled airlines. *Interfaces, 12*, 73–79.

Goenka, U. (2025, June 25). *24/7 reservations handling with AI voicebots for hotels: the game changer that is capturing 40% more direct bookings.* QCall.ai. https://qcall.ai/hotel-reservation-voicebot#:~:text=24/7%20Reservation%20Handling%20with,Capturing%2040%25%20More%20Direct%20Bookings&text=Hotel%20reservation%20voicebots%20are%20capturing,instantly%2C%20even%20at%203%20AM.&text=Qcall.ai%20offer%2097%25%20humanized,instead%20of%20using%20OTA%20platforms.

Goodfellow, I., Pouget-Abadie, J., Mirza, M., Xu, B., Warde-Farley, D., Ozair, S., Courville, A., & Bengio, Y. (2014). Generative adversarial nets. *Proceedings of the International Conference on Neural Information Processing Systems (NIPS 2014)*, pp. 2672–2680.

Gorin, T., & Belobaba, P. (2004). Revenue management performance in a low fare airline environment: Insights from the passenger origin-destination simulator. *Journal of Revenue and Pricing Management, 3*(3), 215–236.

Grant, J. (2024, August 16). *Los-cost carriers in the aviation industry: Where next?* OAG. https://www.oag.com/blog/what-next-low-cost-carriers-aviation

Greene, W. H. (2003). *Econometric Analysis* (5th ed.). Pearson Education.

Green, P. E., Krieger, A. M., & Wind, Y. (2001). Thirty years of conjoint analysis: Reflections and prospects. *Interfaces, 31*, S56–S73.

Guerrini, A., Ferri, G., Cirelli, M., Hoyles, Y., Hours, O., & Touraine, S. (2024, October 30). *Can airlines accelerate the transition to modern retailing?* Boston Consulting Group. https://www.bcg.com/publications/2024/can-airlines-accelerate-transition-to-modern-retailing

Habtemariam, D. (2019, July 22). Next generation storefront: How it works, the potential & the hazards. *Business Travel News*. https://www.businesstravelnews.com/Distribution/Next-Generation-Storefront-How-It-Works-The-Potential-and-The-Hazards

Haggin, P. (2024, June 7). The Ads on your United Airlines inflight screen are getting a lot more specific. *The Wall Street Journal*. https://www.wsj.com/business/media/the-ads-on-your-united-airlines-in-flight-screen-are-getting-a-lot-more-specific-339147cb

Hague, N. (2008). *The problem with price*. B2B International, downloaded from http://www.b2binternational.com/library/whitepapers/pdf/the_problem_with_price.pdf

Hair, J. S., Anderson, R. E., & Tatham, R. T. (1984). *Multivariate data analysis with readings* (2nd ed.). Macmillan.

Hamilton, D., Tobey, D., Bamberger, D., & Neuman, J. (2025, March 3). *The preventing algorithmic collusion: Strike 2, DLA Piper, Insights*. https://www.dlapiper.com/en/insights/publications/2025/02/the-preventing-algorithmic-collusion-act-2025

Hartmans, G. (2008, May). *Competitor fare availability monitoring and usage*. AGIFORS Revenue Management Study Group, Tahiti, French Polynesia.

Hines, M. (2024, October 30). Booking Holdings' connected trip transactions jump 40% year over year in Q3. *Phocuswire*. https://www.phocuswire.com/booking-holdings-q3-2024-earnings

Hines, M. (2025a, November 17). Hotel, Flight Bookings coming to Google's AI Mode. *Phocuswire*. https://www.phocuswire.com/google-agentic-travel-booking-ai

Hines, M. (2025b, December 29). Expedia to integrate with Alexa+ in 2026. *Phocuswire*. https://www.phocuswire.com/amazon-alexa-expedia-ai-agentic-travel-booking

Ho, T. K. (1995). Random decision forests. In *Proceedings of 3rd International Conference on Document Analysis and Recognition* (Vol. 1, pp. 278–282). Montreal, QC, Canada. https://doi.org/10.1109/ICDAR.1995.598994

Hochreiter, S., & Schmidhuber, J. (1997). Long short-term memory. *Neural Computation, 9*(8), 1735–1780.

Hopperstad, C. (2004). *Alternative RM algorithms for unrestricted fare structures*. AGIFORS Reservations and Yield Management Study Group, Auckland, New Zealand.

Hopperstad, C., Zerbib, G., & Belobaba, P. (2006, May). *Methods for estimating sell-up*. AGIFORS Revenue Management and Distribution Study Group Meeting, Cancun, Mexico.

Horner, P. (2000, June). The Sabre story: The making of OR magic at AMR. *OR/MS Today*.

Horowitz, J. K., & McConnell, K. E. (2002, November). A review of WTA/WTP studies. *Journal of Environmental Economics and Management, 44*(3), 426–447.

Hoskins, A. (2025a, July 25). Navan pursues NDC direct connects with new aggregation platform. *Business Travel News Europe*. https://www.businesstravelnewseurope.com/TMC-Distribution/Navan-pursues-NDC-direct-connects-with-new-content-aggregation-platform

Hoskins, A. (2025b, November 25). *Amex GBT reportedly exploring a sale*. Business Travel News Europe. https://www.businesstravelnews.com/Intelligence/Amex-GBT-Reportedly-Exploring-a-Sale

Huhne, M. C. (2017). *Pan Am: History, design, and identity* (p. 424). Callisto Publishers GmbH, Collector's Limited. ISBN-10:3981655052, ISBN-13:978-398165505.

Hur, Y. (2018, October 8–12). *Quantum computing for airline problems*. AGIFORS 58-th Annual Symposium, Tokyo.

IATA. (2012). *Resolution 787: Enhanced Airline Distribution, PSD (34) 787*. IATA, p. 10. https://www.iata.org/contentassets/6de4dce5f38b45ce82b0db42acd23d1c/ndc-resolution-787.pdf

IATA. (2019, October). *The future of interline: A new model for seamless customer journeys*. IATA White Paper.

IATA. (2024). *Offer Creation: Moving away from booking classes and fare rules*. Modern Airline Retailing in Focus—Business Transformation, IATA 2024.

IATA. (2025a). *Airline Retailing: ARM Index Registry*. IATA. Retrieved March 1, 2025, from https://retailing.iata.org/armi/registry/?utm_source=factsheet&utm_medium=fs&utm_campaign=ARM%20index

IATA. (2025b, December 9). *Airline profitability stabilizes with 3.9% net margin expected in 2026*. IATA Press Release No 54. https://www.iata.org/en/pressroom/2025-releases/2025-12-09-01/

IBM. (2025). What is agentic AI? *IBM*. https://www.ibm.com/think/topics/agentic-ai

Ideaworks. (2024a). *2024 Big Book of Airline Data*. IdeaWorksCompany.

Ideaworks and Cartrawler. (2019). *Cartrawler Worldwide Estimate of Ancillary Revenue for 2019*. https://www.cartrawler.com/ct/ancillary-revenue/worldwide-ancillary-revenue-2019.

Ideaworks and Cartrawler. (2024b, January 23). *US major airlines receive more than $25 billion in ancillary revenue from co-branded cards*. Press Release. https://ideaworkscompany.com/wp-content/uploads/2024/01/Press-Release-180-More-Global-Estimate.pdf

Ingold, A., McMahon-Beattie, U., & Yeoman, I. (Eds.). (2000). *Yield management: Strategies for the service industries*. Continuum Books.

Ja, S., Rao, B. V., & Chandler, S. (2001, August). *Passenger recapture estimation in airline RM*. AGIFORS 41st Annual Symposium, Sydney, Australia.

Jelski, C. (2025, December 3). Agentic AI for travel heats up as Google preps booking tools. *Travel Weekly*. https://www.travelweekly.com/Travel-News/Travel-Technology/Agentic-AI-for-travel-heats-up

Jet Blue. (2024, September 19). *JetBlue plans to introduce airport lounges as it expands premium offerings and perks for loyal customers*. Jet Blue Press Release. https://www.news.jetblue.com/latest-news/press-release-details/2024/JetBlue-Plans-to-Introduce-Airport-Lounges-as-It-Expands-Premium-Offerings-and-Perks-for-Loyal-Customers/default.aspx

Jiang, H., Qi, X., & Sun, H. (2014). Choice-based recommender systems: A unified approach to achieving relevancy and diversity. *Operations Research* Published online July 2. https://doi.org/10.1287/opre.2014.1292

Jim Rutt Show. (2025). *EP 305 J Doyne Farmer on Complexity Economics*. https://www.jimruttshow.com/

Jordan, M. I. (1986, May). *Serial order: A parallel distributed processing approach* (Tech. Report ICS 8604). Institute for Cognitive Science, University of California.

Jordan, M. I. (2018, July 17). *Machine learning perspectives and challenges*. University of California.

Jordan, M. I. (2019). Artificial Intelligence—The revolution hasn't happened yet. *Harvard Data Science Review, 1*(1).

Kahn, A. E. (1988a). Airline deregulation.*The Concise Encyclopedia of Economics*.

Kahn, A. E. (1988b, May). Surprises of airline deregulation. *American Economic Review, Papers and Proceedings, 78*(2), 316–322.

Kahneman, D., Knetsch, J. L., & Thaler, R. (1990). Experimental tests of the endowment effect and the coase theorem. *Journal of Political Economy, 98*, 1325–1348.

Kahneman, D., Knetsch, J. L., & Thaler, R. H. (1991). Anomalies: The endowment effect, loss aversion, and status quo bias. *Journal of Economic Perspectives, 5*(1), 193–206.

Kahneman, D., & Tversky, A. (1979). Prospect theory—Analysis of decision under risk. *Econometrica, 47*, 263–291.

Kalka, K. U., & Weber, K. (2000). *PNR-based no show forecasting*. AGIFORS Reservations and Yield Management Study Group Proceedings. NY.

Kambour, E. (2006). *An alternate approach to forecast model definition*. AGIFORS Reservations and Yield Management Study Group Proceedings, Cancun, Mexico.

Kapferer, J.-N., Klippert, C., & Leproux, L. (2014). Does luxury have a minimum price? An exploratory study into consumers' psychology of luxury prices. *Journal of Revenue and Pricing Management, 13*(1), 2–11.

Kärcher, K. (1996). *Reinventing the package holiday business: New information and communication technologies in the British and German tour operator sectors* (Ph.D. thesis). University of Strathclyde, Glasgow, Scotland.

Kass, G. V. (1980). An exploratory technique for investigating large quantities of categorical data. *Applied Statistics, 29*(2), 119–127.

Kavis, M. (2014). *Architecting the Cloud: Design decisions for cloud computing service models*. Wiley. ISBN 978-1-118-61761-8.

Kerenedis, J., & Prakash, A. (2016). *Quantum recommendation systems*. arXiv:1603.08675v3, https://arxiv.org/abs/1603.08675

Khalil, E. B., Dilkina, B., Nemhauser, G. L., Ahmed, A., & Shao. Y. (2017). Learning to run Heuristics in tree search. In *Proceedings of the International Joint Conference on Artificial Intelligence*, pp. 659–666.

Khalil, E. B., Le Bodic, P., Song, L., Nemhauser, G, & Dilkina, B. (2016). Learning to branch in mixed integer programming. *Proceedings of the Thirtieth AAAI Conference on Artificial Intelligence*, pp. 724–731.

King, D. (2023, April 10). In the recovery era, hotel bookings have tipped again toward online travel agencies. *CoStar*. https://www.costar.com/article/589850961/in-the-recovery-era-hotel-bookings-have-tipped-again-toward-online-travel-agencies

Klobuchar, A. (2024, January 30). S.3686 - Preventing Algorithmic Collusion Act of 2024. *Congress.Gov*. https://www.congress.gov/bill/118th-congress/senate-bill/3686

Klobuchar, A. (2025, February 6). *Klobuchar, Colleagues Introduce Antitrust Legislation to Take on Algorithmic Price Fixing*. Bring Down Costs, News Releases. https://www.klobuchar.senate.gov/public/index.cfm/2025/2/klobuchar-colleagues-introduce-antitrust-legislation-to-take-on-algorithmic-price-fixing-bring-down-costs#:~:text=Current%20law%20requires%20proof%20of,pricing%20algorithms'%20impact%20on%20competition

Knox, O. (2025, July 24). *Delta's AI Pricing Faces Turbulence on Capitol Hill*. U.S. News and World Report. https://www.usnews.com/news/u-s-news-decision-points/articles/2025-07-24/deltas-ai-pricing-faces-turbulence-on-capitol-hill

Kothari, A., Madireddy, M., & Sundararajan, R. (2016). Discovering patterns in traveler behavior using segmentation. *Journal of Revenue and Pricing Management, 15*(5), 334–351.

Kraus, M., Feuerriegel, S., & Oztekin, A. (2020). Deep learning in business analytics and operations research: Models, applications and managerial implications. *European Journal of Operational Research, 281*(3).

Kretsch, S. S. (1995, September). Airline fare management and policy. In D. Jenkins (Executive ed.), *Aviation daily's handbook of airline economics* (pp. 477–482). The Aviation Weekly Group of the McGraw-Hill Companies.

Krizhevsky, A., Hinton, G., et al. (2009). *Learning multiple layers of features from tiny images*. http://www.cs.utoronto.ca/~kriz/learning-features-2009-TR.pdf

Krizhevsky, A., Sutskever, I., & Hinton, G. E. (2012, January). ImageNet classification with deep convolutional neural networks. *Advances in Neural Information Processing Systems, 25*(2). https://doi.org/10.1145/3065386

Kumar, R., Wang, W., Arunachalam, S. K., Simrin, S. K., Guntreddy, B. R., & Walczak, D. (2021). Competitive revenue management models with loyal and fully flexible customers. *Journal of Revenue and Pricing Management*. https://doi.org/10.1057/s41272-021-00311-4

Lariviere, M. (2011, August 31). Are baggage fees good for society? *The Operations Room*. https://operationsroom.wordpress.com/2011/08/31/are-baggage-fees-good-for-society/

Lautenbacher, C. J., & Stidham, S. (1999). The underlying Markov Decision Process in the Single-leg Airline Yield Management Problem. *Transportation Science*, 136–146.

Ledger Insights. (2020, October 15). Singapore Airlines extends its blockchain-based reward digital wallet. *Ledger Insights*. https://www.ledgerinsights.com/singapore-airlines-extends-its-blockchain-based-reward-digital-wallet/

Lee, A. (1990, September). *Airline reservations forecasting: Probabilistic and statistical models of the booking process* (Ph.D. dissertation in Transportation Systems). Massachusetts Institute of Technology, Cambridge, MA.

Lee, A. (2025, November 17). *Google is building agentic travel booking plus other travel AI updates*. Skift. https://skift.com/2025/11/17/google-is-building-agentic-travel-booking-plus-other-travel-ai-updates/?utm_content=357413716&utm_medium=social&utm_source=linkedin&hss_channel=lcp-2641998

Lee, T. C., & Hersh, M. (1993). A model for dynamic airline seat inventory control with multiple seat bookings. *Transportation Science, 33*, 117–123.

Leff, G. (2024, February 16). American Airlines used to own a hotel chain: It's now part of Marriott and IHG. *View from the Wing*. https://viewfromthewing.com/american-airlines-hotel-chain/

Levesque, H. (2011). The Winograd Schema Challenge. *Commonsensereasoning.org*.

Lichtenstein, S., & Slovic, P. (1973). Reversals of preference between bids and choices in gambling decisions. *Journal of Experimental Psychology, 89*(1), 46–55.

Lieber, R. (2020, October 10). Frequent-flier programs are winning. who's losing? *New York Times*. https://www.nytimes.com/2020/10/10/your-money/airline-miles-credit-cards.html

Lighthill, J. (1973). *The Lighthill Report, Artificial Intelligence*. A Paper Symposium. Source: http://www.chilton-computing.org.uk/inf/literature/reports/lighthill_report/contents.htm

Littlewood, K. (1972, October). *Forecasting and Control of Passenger Bookings*. AGIFORS 12th Annual Symposium Proceedings, Nathanya, Israel, pp. 193–204.

Liu. Y. (2024, June). Large language models for air transportation: A critical Review. *Journal of the Air Transport Research Society, 2*, 100024. https://doi.org/10.1016/j.jatrs.2024.100024Get rights and content.

Locke, E. (2020, June 23). *The strange way that airlines are actually central banks*. Issue 013, WTF is going on with the economy?! X abroaden. https://abroaden.substack.com/p/the-strange-way-airlines-are-actually

Lodi, A., & Zarpellon, G. (2017). On learning and branching: A survey. *TOP, 25*(2), 207–236.

Lu. M., Wei, P., He, M., & Teng, Y. (2021). Flight delay prediction using gradient boosting machine learning classifiers. *Journal of Quantum Computing, 3*(1), 1–12. https://doi.org/10.32604/jqc.2021.016315

Makhanov, H., Setta, K., Liu, J., Gomez-Gonzalez, V., & Jenaro-Rabadan, G. (2023, April 27). Quantum computing applications for flight trajectory optimization. arXiv:2304.14445v1 [quant-ph]. https://arxiv.org/pdf/2304.14445.pdf

Mantin, B., & Rubin, E. (2016, July–August). Fare prediction websites and transaction prices: Empirical evidence from the airline industry. *Marketing Science, 35*(4), 640–655.

Marcus, G. (2025, December 20). *Marcus on AI: Six (or seven) predictions for AI 2026 from a Generative AI realist*. https://garymarcus.substack.com/p/six-or-seven-predictions-for-ai-2026

Marn, M. V., & Rosiello, R. L. (1992, Septemner–October). Managing price, gaining profit. *Harvard Business Review, 70*(5), 84–94.

Marr, B. (2018, December 7). The awesome ways TUI uses blockchain to revolutionize the travel industry. *Forbes*.

Marshall, Alfred (1890) Principles of Economics, *Great Minds Series*, The Macmillan Company, United Kingdom.

Martin, J. C., Roman, C., & Espino, R. (2008). Willingness to pay for airline service quality. *Transportation Reviews, 28*(2), 199–217.

Mattioli, D. (2012, August 23). On Orbitz, Mac users steered to pricier hotels. *The Wall Street Journal*. https://www.wsj.com/articles/SB10001424052702304458604577488822667325882

Maulana, I., Ernawati, S., & Wati, R. (2025). Prediction of flight delays using feature engineering, catboost, and bayesian optimization to improve model performance. *Jurnal Riset Informatika, 7*(2), 8–15. https://doi.org/10.34288/jri.v7i2.346

Mauri, A. G. (2012). *Hotel revenue management: Principles and practices*. Pearson. ISBN:9788865181461, 886518146X.

Maynard. (2008, May 21). American Airlines to begin charging for checked baggage. *The New York Times*. https://www.nytimes.com/2008/05/21/business/worldbusiness/21iht-amr.4.13100744.html

McCarthy, D. (2023, December 4). *The Lufthansa group of airlines increases distribution cost charge*. Travel Market Report.

McCartney, S. (2004, January 7). When first class is cheaper than coach. *The Wall Street Journal*. https://www.wsj.com/articles/SB107342964291207300

McCartney, S. (2019, April 24). First Class vs. Coach: A game of square inches. *The Wall Street Journal*. https://www.wsj.com/articles/first-class-vs-coach-a-game-of-square-inches-11556098201

McCulloch, W. S., & Pitts, W. (1943). A logical calculus of the ideas immanent in nervous activity. *Bulletin of Mathematical Biophysics, 5*, 115–133. https://doi.org/10.1007/BF02478259

McGill, J. I. (1995). Censored regression analysis of multiclass passenger demand data subject to joint capacity constraints. *Annals of Operations Research, 60*, 209–240.

McGill, J. I., & van Ryzin, G. J. (1999). Revenue management: Research overview and prospects. *Transportation Science, 33*, 233–256.

McKinsey and Company. (2024, January 8). *How airlines can handle busier summers—And comparatively quiet winters.* McKinsey and Company, Travel, Logistics, and Infrastructure. https://www.mckinsey.com/industries/travel-logistics-and-infrastructure/our-insights/how-airlines-can-handle-busier-summers-and-comparatively-quiet-winters

Mendel, S. (2023, December 29). How much does it cost to change or cancel a flight in 2024? *Lending Tree*, edited by Robin Ratcliff. https://www.lendingtree.com/credit-cards/articles/cost-to-change-or-cancel-flight/

Mesa, J. (2025, May 30). *US airlines start quietly charging more for solo travelers.* Newsweek. https://www.newsweek.com/us-airlines-start-quietly-charging-more-solo-travelers-2079133

Messenger, R., & Mandell, L. (1972). A modal search technique for predictive nominal scale multivariate analysis. *Journal of the American Statistical Association, 67*, 768–772.

Michaelis, L., & Menten, M. L. (1913). Die Kinetik der Invertinwirkung. *Biochemische Zeitschrift, 49*, 333–369.

Millet, H. (2023). Leveraging booking information for offer personalization and GDPR consequences. *Journal of Revenue and Pricing Management, 22*(2), 152–156. https://doi.org/10.1057/s41272-022-00401-x

Minsky, M., & Papert, S. (1969). *Perceptrons: An introduction to computational geometry.* MIT Press.

Mishra, S., Ratliff, R. M., & Vinod, B. (2005, September). *New generation in demand forecasting.* AGIFORS 45th Annual Symposium, Sao Paulo Gauruja, Brazil.

Mishra, S., & Viswanathan, V. (2003, June). *Revenue management with restriction free pricing.* AGIFORS Reservations and Yield Management Study Group, Honolulu.

Morgan, J. N., & Sonquist, J. A. (1963). Problems in the analysis of survey data, and a proposal. *Journal of the American Statistical Association, 58*, 415–434.

Morse, P. M., & Kimball, G. E. (1951). *Methods of operations research.* Wiley. ISBN-10:1013915860, ISBN-13:978-1013915864.

Mortensen, K., & Hughes, T. L. (2018). Comparing Amazon's mechanical turk platform to conventional data collection methods in the health and medical research literature. *Journal of General Internal Medicine, 33*(4), 533–538.

Moskowitz, C. (2008, April 27). *Mind's limit found: 4 things at once.* Live Science. https://www.livescience.com/2493-mind-limit-4.html

Muennighoff, N., Yang, Z., Shi, W., Li, X. L., Fei-Fei, L., Hajishirzi, H., Zettlemoyer, L., Liang, P., Candès, E., & Hashimoto, T. (2025, February 3). *s1: Simple test-time scaling.* https://arxiv.org/pdf/2501.19393

Mumbower, S., Hotle, S., & Garrow, L. (2022). Highly debated but still unbundled: The evolution of U.S. airline ancillary products and pricing strategies. *Journal of Revenue and Pricing Management, 18*(3).

Musser, G. (2019, May). Artificial imagination: How machines could learn creativity and common sense, among other human qualities. *Scientific American*, pp. 59–63.

Nash, J. F. (1950). Equilibrium points in n-person games. *Proceedings of the National Academic of Sciences (PNAS), 36*(1), 48–49. https://doi.org/10.1073/pnas.36.1.48

Ng, I. C. L. (2008). *The pricing and revenue management of services: A strategic approach.* Routledge Advances in Management and Business Studies, Routledge, Taylor & Francis Group.

NovaSky. (2025, January 10). *Sky-T1: Train your own O1 preview model within $450.* NovaSky. https://novasky-ai.github.io/posts/sky-t1/

Nurseitov, N., Paulson, M., Reynolds, R., & Izuretia, C. (2009). *Comparison of JSON and XML data interchange formats: A case study.* Montana State University, Bozeman, Montana.

Nvidia. (2023, May 21). *NVIDIA, Rolls-Royce, and Classiq Announce Quantum Computing Breakthrough for Computational Fluid Dynamics in Jet Engines.* NVIDIA Press Release. https://nvidianews.nvidia.com/news/nvidia-rolls-royce-and-classiq-announce-quantum-computing-breakthrough-for-computational-fluid-dynamics-in-jet-engines

Office of Public Affairs Press Release. (2024, March 28). *Justice department and federal trade commission file statement of interest in hotel room algorithmic price-fixing case*. U.S. Department of Justice. https://www.justice.gov/opa/pr/justice-department-and-federal-trade-commission-file-statement-interest-hotel-room

O'Neil, S. (2015a, July 27). Lufthansa debuts direct corporate booking fist via Concur. *Phocuswire*. https://www.phocuswire.com/Lufthansa-debuts-direct-corporate-booking-first-via-Concur

O'Neil, S. (2015b, July 30). The billboard effect is dead, says a study of hotels listed on OTAs. *Phocuswire*. https://www.phocuswire.com/The-Billboard-Effect-is-dead-says-a-study-of-hotels-listed-on-OTAs

OpenAI. (2024a, September 12). Introducing OpenAI o1-preview. *OPENAI Press Release*. https://openai.com/index/introducing-openai-o1-preview/

OpenAI. (2024b, September 12). Learning to reason with LLMs. *OpenAI Blogpost*. https://openai.com/index/learning-to-reason-with-llms/

OpenAI. (2025a, January 23). *Introducing Operator*. OpenAI Press Release. https://openai.com/index/introducing-operator/

OpenAI. (2025b, September 25). *Introducing ChatGPT Pulse*. OpenAI Press Release. https://openai.com/index/introducing-chatgpt-pulse/

Orme, B. K., & Chrzan, K. (2017). *Becoming an expert in conjoint analysis choice modeling for pros*. Sawtooth Software. www.sawtoothsoftware.com

Osipov, D. S. (2025, August 15). United faces lawsuit for selling 'windowless' window seat. *Simply Flying*. https://simpleflying.com/united-lawsuit-windowless-window-seats/#:~:text=Top%20Class%20Actions%20is%20reporting,seat%20is%20missing%20a%20window

Page, J.-F., Côté, J.-P., & Savard, G. (2005, May). *A new framework for revenue management and pricing optimization based on bilevel programming*. AGIFORS Revenue Management Study Group, Capetown, South Africa.

Palmatier, G. E., & Crum, C. (2003). *Enterprise sales and operations planning: Synchronizing demand, supply and resources for peak performance*. J. Ross Publishing. 1-932159-00-2.

Parker, R. (2004, September). *Evaluating schedules with the network value index*. AGIFORS Annual Symposium, Singapore.

Peltz, J. F. (1995, February 10). Delta to be first airline to cap agent commissions: Travel: Carrier will pay a maximum of $50 on domestic tickets, Agencies say move hits them hard. *Los Angeles Times*. https://www.latimes.com/archives/la-xpm-1995-02-10-fi-30298-story.html#:~:text=Delta%20to%20Be%20First%20Airline,financial)%20hit%20for%20us.%E2%80%9D

Perera, S., & Tan, D. (2018, December). In search of the "Right Price" for air travel: First steps towards estimating granular price-demand elasticity. *Transportation Research Part A: Policy and Practice, 130*.

Pestronk, M. (2004, April 12). Agents must identify "change-of-gauge" services. *Travel Weekly*. https://www.travelweekly.com/Mark-Pestronk/Agents-must-identify-change-of-gauge-services

Pestronk, M. (2024, October 25). The DOT's new refund rules are here. *Travel Weekly*. https://www.travelweekly.com/Mark-Pestronk/DOTnew-refund-rules-are-here

Petersen, J. P. (1996, November 6–10). *SAS's experience using a dynamic O&D system*. AGIFORS 33rd Symposium, Atlanta, Georgia.

Peterson, R. M. (1986). The Penultimate Hub Airplane. Seattle: Internal Memo. *Boeing Commercial Airplane Group*.

Phillips, R. L. (2005). *Pricing & Revenue Optimization*. Stanford University Press.

Phocuswright. (2025). US Travel Market Report 2025. *Phocuswright*.

PhocusWright Research. (2025, October 27). From $1.6T to $1.8T: How global travel will grow, shift, go digital ny 2027. *Phocuswire*. https://www.phocuswire.com/global-travel-next-chapter-phocuswright-research?utm_source=newsletter&utm_medium=email&utm_campaign=pcww_daily&pk=pcww_email_newsletter_pcww-daily&oly_enc_id=9607B2485578C3T

Pilato, G., & Vella, F. (2023). A survey of quantum computing for recommendation systems. *Information, 14*(1), 20. https://doi.org/10.3390/info14010020

Potter, K. (2025, June 6). *American charges solo flyers more on half of domestic one-ways.* Thrifty Traveler, Edited by Jackson Newman. https://thriftytraveler.com/news/airlines/american-solo-traveler-fares-research/

Poelt, S. (2002). *Good things take time: Building up an O&D forecaster.* AGIFORS Reservations and Yield Management Study Group, Berlin, Germany.

Poundstone, W. (2011, January 4). *Priceless: The Myth of fair value (and how to take advantage of it)* (1st ed.). Hill and Wang. ISBN-10:0809078813, ISBN-13:978-0809078813.

Prentice, B., DiNota, A., & Hayes, L. (2025). *Global fleet and MRO Market forecast 2025–2035.* Oliver Wyman. https://www.oliverwyman.com/our-expertise/insights/2025/feb/global-fleet-and-mro-market-forecast-2025-2035.html

Pulugurtha, S. S., & Nambisan, S. S. (2003). A decision support tool for airline yield management using genetic algorithms. *Computer-Aided Civil and Infrastructure Engineering, 18*, 214–223.

Randklev, T. (2025, January 21). What deregulation could mean for U.S. airlines and the payment industry. *Phocuswire.* https://www.phocuswire.com/deregulation-airlines-payments-cellpoint-digital?utm_source=northstar&utm_medium=email&utm_campaign=northstar_travel_today&oly_enc_id=9607B2485578C3T

Ranson, O. (2025, November 3). How is Riyadh Air going to be the most "digitally native" airline in the world? *Airline Revenue Economics*, PAID. https://revman.substack.com/p/how-is-riyadh-air-going-to-be-the

Raiford, T. (2015, December 15). Airlines shift from miles to price-based rewards. *SheBudgets, Personal Finance and Lifestyle Guide.* https://www.shebudgets.com/news/airlines-shift-from-miles-to-price-based-rewards/

Ratliff, R., & Gallego, G. (2013). Estimating sales and profitability impacts of airline branded-fares product design and pricing decisions using customer choice models. *Journal of Revenue and Pricing Management, 12*(6), 509–523.

Ratliff, R., Rao, B. V., Narayan, C. P., & Yellepeddi, K. (2008). A multi-flight recapture heuristic for estimating unconstrained demand from airline bookings. *Journal of Revenue and Pricing Management, 9*(4), 326–340.

Ratliff, R., & Vinod, B. (2005). Airline pricing and revenue management: A future outlook. *Journal of Revenue and Pricing Management, 4*(3), 302–307.

Ratliff, R., & Vinod, B. (2016). An applied process for airline strategic fare optimization. *Journal of Revenue and Pricing Management, 15*(5), 320–333.

Ratliff, R., & Weatherford, L. (2009, May). *A review of RM methods for dependent demands.* AGIFORS Cargo and Revenue Management Study Group.

Reed, D. (2019, November 21). Airlines are earning more than ever from extra fees but are causing travelers more frustration and dissatisfaction. *Forbes.*

Research and Markets. (2025, May). *Airline Ancillary Services Strategic Business Report, Global Industry Analysts, Inc* (262 pages). Research and Markets.

Rice, K. (2013, February 20). *CORRECTED: IATA goes with Open Axis standards.* Travel Weekly. https://www.travelweekly.com/Travel-News/Travel-Technology/IATA-goes-with-Open-Axis-standards#:~:text=IATA%20opted%20for%20Open%20Axis%20over%20OpenTravel,multiple%20segments%20in%20the%20industry%2C%20including%20airlines%2C

Risso, C. (2021, March 1). *Emirates introduces $44 option to book empty seats next to you.* Travel + Leisure. https://www.travelandleisure.com/airlines-airports/emirates-airlines-extra-seat-social-distancing

Robbins, J. (1952). Some aspects of the sequential design of experiments. *Bulletin of the American Mathematical Society, 58*(5), 527–535.

Rosenblatt, F. (1957). *The perceptron: A perceiving and recognizing automaton* (Report 85-60-1). Cornell Aeronautical Laboratory.

Rosenblatt, F. (1958). The perceptron: A probabilistic model for information storage and organization in the brain. *Psychological Review, 65*(6), 386–408.

Rosenblatt, F. (1962). *Principles of neurodynamics: Perceptrons and the theory of brain mechanisms* (p. 616). Spartan Books. http://catalog.hathitrust.org/Record/000203591

Rosen, P. (2023, March 1). Artificial Intelligence is on the bring of an 'iPhone moment' and can boost the world economy by $15.7 trillion in 7 years Bank of America says. *Business Insider*. https://markets.businessinsider.com/news/stocks/artificial-intelligence-ai-chatgpt-iphone-moment-bank-america-bofa-markets-2023-3#:~:text=Ultimately%2C%20AI's%20ability%20to%20capitalize,use%20cases%20for%20the%20technology.

Rothstein, M. (1985). O.R. and the airline overbooking problem. *Operations Research, 33*, 237–248.

Rumelhart, D. E., Hinton, G. E., & Williams, R. J. (1985, September). *Learning internal representations by error propagation* (Tech. Report ICS 8504). Institute for Cognitive Science, University of California.

Rumelhart, D. E., Hinton, G. E., & Williams, R. J. (1986). Learning representations by back-propagating errors. *Nature, 323*, 533–536.

Rumelhart, D. E., McClelland, J. L., and the PDP Research Group. (1986). *Parallel distributed processing: Explorations in the microstructure of cognition: Foundations* (Vol. I). Bradford Books. ISBN-10:9780262680530, ISBN-13:978-0262680530.

Sabre. (2021, March 31). *Sabre introduces new airline storefront, the next generation of air shopping*. Press Release. https://www.sabre.com/insights/releases/sabre-introduces-new-airline-storefront-the-next-generation-of-air-shopping/

Sabre. (2025a, July 22). *Information overload: Sabre's global travel agency survey finds content fragmentation is driving up agency costs and undermining customer experience*. Sabre Press Release. https://www.sabre.com/insights/releases/information-overload-sabres-global-travel-agency-survey-finds-content-fragmentation-is-driving-up-agency-costs-and-undermining-customer-experience/

Sabre. (2025b, September 25). *Sabre seizes first-mover position with comprehensive agentic APIs for travel*. Sabre Press Release. https://investors.sabre.com/news-releases/news-release-details/sabre-seizes-first-mover-position-comprehensive-agentic-apis

Sabre. (2026, January 14). *Sabre and Biz Trip AI announces strategic partnership to deliver agentic AI solutions for global corporate travel market*. Sabre Press Release. https://www.sabre.com/insights/releases/sabre-and-biztrip-ai-announce-strategic-partnership-to-deliver-agentic-ai-solutions-for-global-corporate-travel-market/#:~:text=corporate%20travel%20market-,Sabre%20and%20BizTrip%20AI%20Announce%20Strategic%20Partnership%20to%20Deliver%20Agentic,for%20Global%20Corporate%20Travel%20Market&text=SOUTHLAKE%2C%20Texas%20and%20SAN%20FRANCISCO,air%2C%20lodging%2C%20and%20ground%20transportation

Schaal, D. (2021, November 2). *Sabre loses a chunk of Expedia's North America business*. https://skift.com/2021/11/02/sabre-loses-a-chunk-of-expedias-north-america-business/

Schaal, D. (2023, August 16). *Air Canada adds cancel for any reason feature in partnership with Hopper*. https://skift.com/2023/08/16/air-canada-adds-cancel-for-any-reason-feature-in-partnership-with-hopper/

Second Wave Marketing. (2025). *How SEO is changing in the AI world*. https://files.secondwavemarketing.com/8A4V

Segmentify. (2021, June 17). *The 3 option decoy effect and relativity*. https://www.segmentify.com/blog/the-3-option-decoy-effect-and-relativity

Seirawan, Y., Simon, H., & Munakata, T. (1997). The implications of Kasparov vs Deep Blue. *Communications of the ACM, 40*(8), 21–25.

Shannon, C. E. (1948a). A Mathematical Theory of Communication, *Bell System Technology Journal, 27*(3), 379–423.

Shannon, C. E. (1948b). A Mathematical Theory of Communication, *Bell System Technology Journal, 27*(4), 623–656.

Shannon, C. E., Weaver, W. (1949) The Mathematical Theory of Communication, University of Illinois Press.

Shannon, C. E. (1950) Programming a Computer for Playing Chess, *Bell Labs, Philosophical Magazine*, Ser.7, Vol. 41, No. 314, March.

Shao, S., & Kauermann, G. (2020). Understanding price elasticity for airline ancillary services. *Journal of Revenue and Pricing Management, 19*(1), 74–82.

Shayon, S. (2018). *6 Reasons for Singapore airlines' blockchain-based loyalty program*. www.brandchannel.com/2018/02/15/singaporeairlines-blockchain/. Accessed 15 February 2018.

Shojaee, P., Mirzadeh, I., Alizadeh, K., Horton, M., Bengio, S., & Farajtabar, M. (2025, June). The illusion of thinking: Understanding the strengths and limitations of reasoning models via the lens of problem complexity. *Apple Machine Learning Research, Speech and Natural Language Processing*. https://machinelearning.apple.com/research/illusion-of-thinking

Silk, R. (2021a, February 18). Emirates to roll out GDS fees as it moves sellers toward an NDC solution. *Travel Weekly*. https://www.travelweekly.com/Travel-News/Airline-News/Emirates-to-levy-fee-move-to-NDC-portal

Silk, R. (2021b, July 1). No Emirates GDS surcharge for Travelport agencies. *Travel Weekly*. https://www.travelweekly.com/Travel-News/Airline-News/Travelport-Emirates-agreement-saves-agencies-money

Silk, R. (2021c, July 1). American Airlines sues Sabre over fare display. *Travel Weekly*. https://www.travelweekly.com/Travel-News/Airline-News/American-Airlines-sues-Sabre-over-fare-display

Silk, R. (2021d, November 27). Analysts skeptical of IATA's shift away from NDC certification. *Travel Weekly*. https://www.travelweekly.com/Travel-News/Airline-News/Analysts-skeptical-IATA-shift-from-NDC-certification

Silk, R. (2024, June 17). Air Canada to scrap GDS surcharge for most fares. *Travel Weekly*. https://www.travelweekly.com/Travel-News/Airline-News/Air-Canada-scrap-GDS-surcharge

Silk, R. A. (2023, June 16). Singapore Airlines further boosts NDC and hinders legacy NDC bookings. *Travel Weekly*. https://www.travelweekly.com/Travel-News/Airline-News/Singapore-Airways-further-boosts-NDC

Silk, R. A. (2025a, April 2). Report shows airlines making slow progress with NDC technology. *Travel Weekly*. https://www.travelweekly.com/Travel-News/Airline-News/Report-shows-airlines-making-slow-progress-with-NDC-technology

Silk, R. A. (2025b, April 3). For AmTrav, United's latest NDC upgrade wins out. *Travel Weekly*. https://www.travelweekly.com/Travel-News/Travel-Technology/For-AmTrav-United-latest-NDC-upgrade-wins-out

Silk, R. A. (2025c, April 20). Latam Airlines adjusts GDS surcharges based on the booking system. *Travel Weekly*. https://www.travelweekly.com/Travel-News/Airline-News/Latam-different-GDS-surcharges-by-system

Silk, R. A. (2026, January 25). NDC adoption surges among traditional agencies in 2025. *Travel Weekly*. https://www.travelweekly.com/Travel-News/Travel-Technology/ARC-reports-rising-NDC-adoption-2025?utm_source=northstar&utm_medium=email&utm_campaign=northstar_travel_today&oly_enc_id=9607B2485578C3T

Simpson, R. W. (1989). *Using network flow techniques for origin-destination seat inventory control*. Memorandum M89-1. Flight Transportation Laboratory, Massachusetts Institute of Technology.

Sjnajder, M., Ratliff, R., & Kaya, C. (2023a). A heuristic for incorporating ancillaries into air choice models with personalization (part 1): Estimating preferences using hedonic regression). *Journal of Revenue and Pricing Management, 22*, 122–139. https://doi.org/10.1057/s41272-022-00399-2

Sjnajder, M., Ratliff, R., & Kaya, C. (2023b). A heuristic for incorporating ancillaries into air choice models with personalization (part 2: integrated multinomial logit and hedonic regression models). *Journal of Revenue and Pricing Management, 22*, 140–151. https://doi.org/10.1057/s41272-022-00400-y

Skift. (2021). *American Airlines Inc., Plaintiff, v. Sabre, Plaintiff's verified original petition and application for temporary injunction and permanent injunction*. https://skift.com/wp-content/uploads/2021/07/aa-sabre-lawsuit-july-1.pdf

Slovic, P., & Lichtenstein, S. (1983, February). Preference reversals: A broader perspective. *American Economic Review*.

Smith, B. C. (1982, August). *Optimal departure booking levels.* Internal Technical Report, American Airlines.

Smith, B. C. (1986). *O&D control with virtual nesting.* Internal Technical Report, American Airlines.

Smith, B. C. (2007, May 14–16). *Revenue management in the U.S. airline industry.* AGIFORS Passenger and Cargo Revenue Management Study Group, JeJu Island, South Korea.

Smith, B. C., & Penn, C. (1988, October). *Analysis of alternative origin-destination control strategies.* AGIFORS Symposium Proceedings, 28, New Seabury, MA.

Smith, B. C., Leimkuhler, J. L., & Darrow, R. M. (1992, January–February). Yield management at American Airlines. *Interfaces*, 22.

Smith, B. C., Rao, B. V., Tsioutsias, D., & Zhang, Y. (1997, October). *A new approach to O&D yield management optimization.* Sabre Research Sabre Technology Solutions Internal Technical Report.

Smith, B. C., Vinod, B., & Green, R. (1997). *Apparatus and method of allocating flight inventory resources based on the current market value.* U.S. Patent No. 6085164; filed 4th March, 1997, granted 4th July, 2000.

Sokol-Hessner, P., Hsu, M., Curley, N. G., & Phelps, E. A. (2009, March 31). *Thinking like a trader selectively reduces individuals' loss aversion.* Biological Sciences, Edited by Edward E. Smith, Columbia University. https://doi.org/10.1073/pnas.0806761106

Spencer, K. A. (2025, January 13). *Hotel booking sites show higher prices to travelers from Bay Area.* SFGATE. https://www.sfgate.com/travel/article/hotel-booking-sites-overcharge-bay-area-travelers-20025145.php

Southwest Airlines Investor Relations. (2024, July 25). Southwest Airlines launches enhancements to transform customer experience and improve financial performance. *Southwest Airlines Investor Relations.* https://www.southwestairlinesinvestorrelations.com/news-and-events/news-releases/2024/07-25-2024-110102603

Sovrin. (2018, January). *Sovrin™: A protocol and token for self-sovereign identity and decentralized trust.* A White Paper from the Sovrin Foundation. Version 1.

Stanford University. (2025). *Artificial Intelligence Index Report 2025.* Stanford University.

Statista. (2024, October). *Implementation of artificial intelligence for business travel management worldwide as of October 2024.* Statista. https://www.statista.com/statistics/1050246/artificial-intelligence-adoption-business-travel-worldwide/

Stefanescu, C., deMiguel, V., Fridgeirsdottir, R., & Zenios, S. (2004). *Revenue management with correlated demand forecasting.* Working Paper, London Business School, 6 Sussex Place, Regent's Park, London, United Kingdom NW1 4SA.

Subramanian, J., Stidham, S., & Lautenbacher, C. J. (1999). Airline yield management with overbooking, cancellations, and no-shows. *Transportation Science, 33*, 147–167.

Sutton, R. S., & Barto, A. G. (1998, March 1). *Reinforcement learning: An introduction* (1st ed., 322 pages). Bradford Books. ISBN-10:0262193981, ISBN-13:978-0262193986.

Swan, W. (1983). *Traffic losses at High Load Factors.* Proceedings of the 23rd Annual AGIFORS Symposium.

Szende, P. (Ed.). (2020, November). *Hospitality revenue management: Concepts and practices* (1st ed.). Apple Academic Press. ISBN-10:1771888881, ISBN-13:978-1771888882.

Szymański, B., Belobaba, P., & Papen, A. (2021). Continuous pricing algorithms for airline RM: Revenue gains and competitive impacts. *Journal of Revenue and Pricing Management, 20*, 669–688. https://doi.org/10.1057/s41272-021-00350-x

Szymanski, T., & Darrow, R. (2021). Shelf placement optimization for air products. *Journal of Revenue and Pricing Management.* https://doi.org/10.1057/s41272-021-00315-0

Talluri, K. T., & van Ryzin, G. J. (1996, March). *A new provably optimal bid price technology.* AGIFORS Reservations and Yield Management Study Group, Zurich, Switzerland.

Talluri, K. T., & van Ryzin, G. J. (1998). An analysis of bid price controls for network revenue management. *Management Science, 44*(11), 1577–1593.

Talluri, K. T., & van Ryzin, G. J. (1999). A randomized linear programming method for computing network bid prices. *Transportation Science, 33*, 207–216.

Talluri, K. T., & van Ryzin, G. J. (2004). *The theory and practice of revenue management*. Kluwer Academic Publishers.

Taneja, N. K. (2017). *21st century airlines: Connecting the dots* (1st ed.). Routledge. ISBN 1138093130.

Thaler, R. (1980). Toward a positive theory of consumer choice. *Journal of Economic Behavior and Organization, 1*, 39–60.

Thaler, R. H., Tversky, A., Kahneman, D., & Schwartz, A. (1997). The effect of myopia and loss aversion on risk taking: An experimental test. *The Quarterly Journal of Economics, 112*, 647–661.

Thompson, W. R. (1933). On the likelihood that one unknown probability exceeds another in view of the evidence of two samples. *Biometrika, 25*(3–4), 285–294.

Tobin, J. (1958). Estimation of relationships for limited dependent variables. *Econometrica, 26*(1), 24–36.

Touraine, S. (2021). The industry transformation to dynamic offering. *Journal of Revenue and Pricing Management, 20*, 611–614. https://doi.org/10.1057/s41272-021-00344-9

Toutant, C. (2023, August). *Antitrust Lawsuits multiply—And there's an algorithm at the center of it all*. Law.com. https://www.law.com/njlawjournal/2023/08/23/antitrust-lawsuits-multiply-and-theres-an-algorithm-at-the-center-of-it-all/?slreturn=20240308175807

Train, K. E. (2003). *Discrete choice methods with simulation*. Cambridge University Press.

Travelport. (2020, December 3). Singapore airlines and travelport put NDC into action. *Travelport Newsroom*. https://www.travelport.com/press-release/singapore-airlines-and-travelport-put-ndc-into-action

Turing, A. (1948). *Intelligent Machinery*. National Physical Laboratory, London. https://www.npl.co.uk/getattachment/about-us/History/Famous-faces/Alan-Turing/80916595-Intelligent-Machinery.pdf

Turing, A. (1950). Computing machinery and intelligence. *Mind, 49*, 433–460.

Turow, J., Feldman, L., & Meltzer, K. (2005, June 1). *Open to exploitation: American shoppers online and offline*. University of Pennsylvania's Annenberg School for Communication.

Turrin, R. (2024, March 25). *Global Payment Report 2024*. The Era of Consumer Choice. https://richturrin.substack.com/p/global-payment-report-2024-the-era

Tversky, A., & Kahneman, D. (1974). Judgment under uncertainty: Heuristics and biases. *Science, 185*(4157), 1124–1131. http://www.jstor.org/stable/1738360

Tversky, A., & Kahneman, O. (1991). Loss aversion in riskless choice: A reference-dependent model. *The Quarterly Journal of Economics, 106*(4), 1039–1061.

Tversky, A., & Kahneman, O. (1992). Advances in prospect-theory—Cumulative representation of uncertainty. *Journal of Risk and Uncertainty*, 297–323.

van Westendorp, P. H. (1976). *NSS – Price sensitivity meter (PSM) – A new approach to study consumer perception of price*. Proceedings of the ESOMAR Congress, Venice.

Vapnik, V., Golowich, S. E., & Smola, A. (1997). *Support vector method for function approximation, regression estimation, and signal processing, beural information processing systems proceedings*. https://proceedings.neurips.cc/paper_files/paper/1996/file/4f284803bd0966cc24fa8683a34afc6e-Paper.pdf

Vaswani, A., Shazeer, N., Parmar, N., Uszkoreit, J., Jones, L., Gomez, A. N., Kaiser, L., & Polosukhin, I. (2017, December). Attention is all you need. In I. Guyon, U. Von Luxburg, S. Bengio, H. Wallach, R. Fergus, S. Vishwanathan, & R. Garnett (Ed.), 31st Conference on Neural Information Processing Systems (NIPS). Advances in Neural Information Processing Systems (Vol. 30). Curran Associates, Inc. arXiv:1706.03762

Vinod, B. (1989, March). *A partitioning algorithm for virtual nesting indexing using dynamic programming*. Internal Technical Report, Sabre Technology Solutions.

Vinod, B. (1990, December). *Reservation inventory control techniques to maximize revenues*. Presented at IATA – The Third International Airline Yield Management Conference, London.

Vinod, B. (1992, January 2). *Origin and destination revenue mix revisited: The sub-gradient algorithm*. Internal Technical Report, Sabre Technology Solutions.

Vinod, B. (1995). Origin and destination yield management. In D. Jenkins (Ed.), *Aviation daily's handbook of airline economics* (pp. 459–468). The Aviation Group of the McGraw-Hill Companies.
Vinod, B. (1999, October). *Airline alliances and its impact on pricing and revenue management*. IATA – The Eleventh International Airline Yield Management Conference Proceedings, Chicago, Illinois.
Vinod, B. (2005a). Retail revenue management and the new paradigm of merchandise optimization. *Journal of Revenue and Pricing Management, 3*(4), 358–368.
Vinod, B. (2005b). Alliance revenue management. *Journal of Revenue and Pricing Management, 4*(1), 66–82.
Vinod, B. (2006). Advances in inventory control. *Journal of Revenue and Pricing Management, 4*(4), 367–381.
Vinod, B. (2008). The continuing evolution: Customer centric revenue management. *Journal of Revenue and Pricing Management, 7*(1), 27–39.
Vinod, B. (2010). The complexities and challenges of the airline fare management process and alignment with revenue management. *Journal of Revenue and Pricing Management, 9*(1–2), 137–151.
Vinod, B. (2011). Unleashing the power of loyalty programs: The next 30 years. *Journal of Revenue and Pricing Management, 10*(5), 471–476.
Vinod, B. (2013a). Leveraging big data for competitive advantage in travel. *Journal of Revenue and Pricing Management, 12*(1), 96–100.
Vinod, B. (2013b). Revenue management for the optimal control of group traffic. *Journal of Revenue and Pricing Management, 12*(4), 295–304.
Vinod, B. (2016a). Evolution of yield management in travel. *Journal of Revenue and Pricing Management, 15*(3–4), 203–211.
Vinod, B. (2016b). Big data in the travel marketplace. *Journal of Revenue and Pricing Management, 15*(5), 352–359.
Vinod, B. (2017). The evolving paradigm of interactive selling based on consumer preferences. In *21st century Airlines: Connecting the dots by Nawal Taneja* (pp. 207–213). Routledge: Taylor & Francis Group. ISBN 978-1-138-09313-3.
Vinod, B. (2019). Hotel retailing with attribute-based room pricing and inventory control. *Journal of Revenue and Pricing Management, 18*(6), 429–433.
Vinod, B. (2020a, February 25). *Travel trends driving the paradigm shift of government travel.* National Defense Transportation Association (NDTA) Government Travels Symposium, Washington, DC.
Vinod, B. (2020b). Blockchain in travel. *Journal of Revenue and Pricing Management, 19*(1), 2–6.
Vinod, B. (2020c). The Covid-19 pandemic and airline cash flow. *Journal of Revenue and Pricing Management, 19*, 228–229.
Vinod, B. (2021a, May). *The evolution of yield management in the airline industry: Origins to the last frontier*. Springer Nature, Switzerland. ISBN-13:978-3030704230, ISBN-10:3030704238.
Vinod, B. (2021b). An approach to adaptive robust revenue management with continuous demand management in a COVID-19 era. *Journal of Revenue and Pricing Management, 20*(1), 10–14.
Vinod, B. (2021c). Artificial intelligence in travel. *Journal of Revenue and Pricing Management*. https://doi.org/10.1057/s41272-021-00319-w
Vinod, B. (2021d). Advances in revenue management: The last frontier. *Journal of Revenue and Pricing Management, 20*(1), 15–20. https://doi.org/10.1057/s41272-020-00264-0
Vinod, B. (2021e). The age of intelligent retailing: Personalized offers in travel for a segment of one. *Journal of Revenue and Pricing Management*. https://doi.org/10.1057/s41272-020-00265-z
Vinod, B. (2021f). The influence of revenue management and inventory control on air shopping. *Journal of Revenue and Pricing Management*. https://doi.org/10.1057/s41272-020-00258-y
Vinod, B. (2022a, November). *Revenue management in the lodging industry: Origins to the last frontier*. Springer Nature, Switzerland. ISBN: 978-3-031-14304-5, ISBN: 978-3-031-14302-1.
Vinod, B. (2022b). Airline revenue planning and the COVID-19 pandemic. *Journal of Tourism Futures, 8*(2), 245–253.

Vinod, B. (Ed.). (2023a, May 27). *Artificial intelligence and machine learning in the travel industry: Simplifying complex decision making*. Palgrave Macmillan, Springer Nature. ISBN 978-3-031-25455-0, ISBN 978-3-031-25456-7.

Vinod, B. (2023b). Personalization in travel. *Journal of Revenue and Pricing Management, 22*(2), 101–102. https://doi.org/10.1057/s41272-022-00397-4

Vinod, B. (2024a, June). *Mastering the travel intermediaries: Origins and future of global distribution systems*. Travel Management Companies, and Online Travel Agencies. Springer Nature, Switzerland. ISBN 978-3-031-51523-1.

Vinod, B. (2024b). Future of personalization in travel. *Journal of Revenue and Pricing Management, 23*, 76–79. https://doi.org/10.1057/s41272-023-00460-8

Vinod, B., & Hobt, D. (2021). *Method, apparatus and computer program product for reservations, inventory control, shopping and booking with attribute based pricing*. U.S. Patent Number 11,017,326 Filed May 6, 2015, granted May 25, 2021. https://patents.justia.com/patent/11017326

Vinod, B., & Moore, K. (2009). Promoting branded fare families and ancillary services: Merchandising and its impacts on the travel value chain. *Journal of Revenue and Pricing Management, 8*(2–3), 174–186.

Vinod, B., Nilson, V., & Hobt, D. A. (1997, October). *Inventory control with the availability processor*. Object Management Group (OMG) Conference, OMG Awards Banquet Presentation, Frankfurt, Germany.

Vinod, B., & Ratliff, R. (1990, April). *A discount allocation optimization method using stochastic linear programming: An introduction to continuous nesting*. AGIFORS Reservations and Yield Management Study Group Proceedings, Rome.

Vinod, B., Ratliff, R. M., & Jayaram, V. (2018). An approach to offer management: Maximizing sales with fare products and ancillaries. *Journal of Revenue and Pricing Management, 17*(2), 91–101.

Vogell, H., Coryne, H., & Little, R. (2022, October 15). *Rent going up? One company's algorithm could be why?* Propublica.org. https://www.propublica.org/article/yieldstar-rent-increase-realpage-rent

Vulcano, G., van Ryzin, G., & Chaar, W. (2010). Choice-based revenue management: An empirical study of estimation and optimization. *Manufacturing and Service Operations Management, 12*(3), 371–392.

Vulcano, G., van Ryzin, G., & Ratliff, R. (2012). Estimating primary demand for substitutable products from sales transaction data. *Operations Research, 60*(2), 313–334.

Wang, K. (1983). Optimum seat allocation for multi-leg flights with multiple fare types. *Airline Group of the International Federation of Operational Research Societies Symposium Proceedings, 23*, 225–237.

Wang, K., Wittman, M. D., & Bockelie, A. (2021). Dynamic offer generation in airline revenue management. *Journal of Revenue and Pricing Management, 20*, 654–668. https://doi.org/10.1057/s41272-021-00349-4

Wang, K., Wittman, M. D., & Fiig, T. (2023). Dynamic offer creation for airline ancillaries using a Markov chain choice model. *Journal of Revenue and Pricing Management, 22*, 103–121. https://doi.org/10.1057/s41272-022-00398-3

Warren, E. (2022, November 22). *United States Senate letter to RealPage*. https://www.warren.senate.gov/imo/media/doc/2022.11.22%20Letter%20to%20RealPage%20re%20YieldStar%20Algorithm.pdf

Warren, E. (2024, March 6). *Warren statement on final SEC climate risk disclosure rule*. Elizabeth Warren Newsroom Press Release. https://www.warren.senate.gov/newsroom/press-releases/warren-statement-on-final-sec-climate-risk-disclosure-rule

Warren, Z. (2023, January 30). *Upcoming SEC climate disclosure rules bring urgency to ESG data strategy planning*. Reuters. https://www.reuters.com/legal/legalindustry/upcoming-sec-climate-disclosure-rules-bring-urgency-esg-data-strategy-planning-2023-01-30/

Wasielewski, M. (2025, November 12). RealPage abruptly replaces CEO as rent-fixing lawsuits advance. *Bisnow*. https://www.bisnow.com/national/news/multifamily/realpage-abruptly-swaps-ceos-as-rent-fixing-lawsuits-advance-131850

Watkins, C. J. C. H. (1989). *Learning from delayed rewards* (PhD. Dissertation). Cambridge University, Cambridge, UK.

Weatherford, L. R. (1991). *Perishable asset revenue management in general business situations* (Ph.D. Dissertation). Darden Graduate School of Business Administration, University of Virginia.

Weatherford, L. R. (2013). Searching to maximize revenue in unrestricted and less-restricted competitive fare environments: Combining hybrid forecasting and fare adjustment with various unconstraining methods. *Journal of Revenue and Pricing Management, 12*(6). https://doi.org/10.1057/rpm.2013.21

Weatherford, L. R., & Bodily, S. E. (1992). A taxonomy and research overview of perishable-asset revenue management: Yield management overbooking and pricing. *Operations Research, 40*(5), 831–844.

Weatherford, L. R., Bodily, S. E., & Pfeifer, P. E. (1993). Modeling the customer arrival process and comparing decision rules in perishable asset revenue management situations. *Transportation Science, 27*(3).

Weatherford, L. R., & Ratliff, R. M. (2010). Review of revenue management methods with dependent demands. *Journal of Revenue and Pricing Management, 9*(4), 326–340.

Weinstein, J. (2024, April 1). Spotlight shines brighter on algorithmic price-fixing in hospitality.*Hotel Investment Today*.

Weizenbaum, J. (1976). *Computer power and human reason: From judgment to calculation* (1st ed., 300 pp.). W.H. Freeman and Co. ISBN-13:9780716704638, ISBN-10:0716704633.

West, E. (2010, March 2). 2010: Travel management enters the modern age. *Business Travel News*. https://www.businesstravelnews.com/Archive/2010?utm_source=eNewsletter&utm_medium=email&utm_campaign=eltr-btn-weekend&oly_enc_id=9607B2485578C3T

West, E. (2021, December 3). *Amex GBT makes SPAC deal to go public*. Business Travel News. https://www.businesstravelnews.com/Procurement/Amex-GBT-Makes-SPAC-Deal-to-Go-Public

West, E. (2025, July 30). DOJ drops Amex GBT-CWT Antitrust Suit, merger set to close in Q3. *Business Travel News*. https://www.businesstravelnews.com/Global/DOJ-Drops-Amex-GBT-CWT-Antitrust-Suit-Merger-Set-to-Close-in-Q3

West, E. (2026) AI-driven Long Lake agrees to take Amex GBT off market in $6.3B deal, Business Travel News, May 4, https://www.businesstravelnews.com/Intelligence/Long-Lake-Agrees-to-Take-Amex-GBT-Off-Market-in-6-3B-Deal

White, J. M. (2013, January 3). Bandit algorithms for website optimization. *O'Reilly Media* (1st ed.). ISBN-13:978-1449341336.

Wiggers, K. (2025, January 11). *Researchers open source Sky-T1, a 'reasoning' AI model that can be trained for less than $450*. TechCrunch. https://techcrunch.com/2025/01/11/researchers-open-source-sky-t1-a-reasoning-ai-model-that-can-be-trained-for-less-than-450/

Williamson, E. L. (1992). *Airline network seat inventory control: Methodologies and revenue impacts* (Ph.D. thesis). Massachusetts Institute of Technology, Cambridge, MA.

Wind, J., Green, P. E., Shifflet, D., & Scarbrough, M. (1989, January–February). Courtyard by Marriott – Designing a hotel facility with consumer-based marketing models. *Interfaces, 19*(1), 25–47.

Wollmer, R. D. (1992). An airline seat management model for a single leg route when lower fare classes book first. *Operations Research, 40*, 26–37.

World Economic Forum. (2020, March). Known traveler digital identity: Specifications guide. *World Economic Forum in collaboration with Accenture*. https://ktdi.org/

Wright, C. P., Groenevelt, H., & Shumsky, R. A. (2010). Dynamic revenue management in airline alliances. *Transportation Science, 44*(1), 15–37.

Yan, R., & Bandyopadhyay, S. (2011). The profit benefits of bundle pricing of complementary products. *Journal of Retailing and Consumer Services, 18*(4), 355–361.

Yanofsky, D. (2015, October 27). *Half of American's revenues comes from 13% of its customers.* Quartz. https://qz.com/533501/half-of-american-airlines-revenue-came-from-13-of-its-customers

Yeoman, I., & McMahon-Beattie, U. (Eds.). (2004). *Revenue management and pricing: Case studies and applications.* Cengage Learning EMEA Higher Education.

Yeoman, I., & McMahon-Beattie, U. (Eds.). (2011). *Revenue management: A practical pricing perspective.* Palgrave Macmillan.

Yeoman, I., & McMahon-Beattie, U. (2014). Exclusivity: The future of luxury. *Journal of Revenue and Pricing Management, 13*(1), 12–22.

Yuen, B. B. (1998). Group revenue management: Redefining the business process. In G. F. Butler & M. R. Keller (Exec. Eds.), *Aviation week group newsletters* (pp. 363–375). A Division of the McGraw-Hill Companies, Edmund Pinto, Publisher.

Yuen, B. B. (2002). Group revenue management: Redefining the business process – Part I. *Journal of Revenue & Pricing Management, 1*, 267–274.

Yuen, B. B. (2003). Group revenue management: Redefining the business process – Part II. *Journal of Revenue & Pricing Management, 1*, 315–354.

Zeff, M. (2025, February 5). *Researchers created an open rival to OpenAI's o1 'reasoning' model for under $50.* TechCrunch. https://techcrunch.com/2025/02/05/researchers-created-an-open-rival-to-openais-o1-reasoning-model-for-under-50/

Zeni, R. H. (2007). Can we really look to the past to forecast future demand? *Journal of Revenue and Pricing Management, 6*(4), 312–314.

Zhang, B. (2016, October 22). A single statistic shows why all airline passengers are not created equal. *Business Insider.*

Zhang, C. (2025, November 17). How much does it cost to change or cancel a flight in 2025? *Lending Tree*, edited by Robin Ratcliff. https://www.lendingtree.com/credit-cards/articles/cost-to-change-or-cancel-flight/

Zhang, D., & Kallesen, R. (2008). Incorporating competitive price information into revenue management. *Journal of Revenue and Pricing Management, 7*(1), 17–26.

Zhang, Y., Bradlow, E. T., & Small, D. S. (2015). Predicting customer value using clumpiness: From RFM to RFMC. *Marketing Science, 34*(2), 195–208.

Zouaoui, F., & Rao, B. V. (2009). Dynamic pricing of opaque airline tickets. *Journal of Revenue and Pricing Management, 8*(2–3), 148–154.

Index

A
Abacus, 706
Abandoned shopping cart, 524
Abstraction and reasoning corpus, 582, 708
Academic focus, 133
Account-to-account, 527
Advanced shipping notice (ASN), 271
Affiliate program, 442, 443, 650
Agency debit memo (ADM), 324, 591, 711, 727
Agency model, 289, 362, 438–440, 442, 445, 452, 461, 462, 636
Agent-2-Agent (A2A), 432, 527, 597, 598, 622–624, 626, 637, 705, 708, 727, 739
Agent assemby area (AAA), 69, 711, 713
Agent Cards, 624
Agentic AI, xii, 45, 189, 196, 198, 262, 263, 432, 461, 462, 497, 500, 508–511, 514, 518, 519, 555, 576, 597, 598, 613–620, 622–624, 626, 627, 632, 633, 635, 638, 643–645, 648, 649, 679, 680, 693, 727, 739
Agentic AI Foundation (AAIF), 597–599, 713, 727
Agentic Web, 623
Agent washing, 618
AI Agents, xi, xiv, xvi, 18, 186, 188–190, 196–198, 262, 354, 431, 432, 459, 460, 462, 508–510, 513, 514, 519, 596–599, 605, 606, 610, 611, 615–629, 632, 633, 635–641, 643–646, 648–652, 663, 668, 679, 680, 727
AI Assistants, 455, 459, 510, 615, 648, 649, 667–669, 676, 680
AI Mode, 461, 598, 605
AIO, 605
Air Arabia, 528
AirAsia, 38, 526, 669
AirBaltic, 528
Airbnb, 606, 636
Air Canada, 16, 51, 64, 336, 355, 358, 389, 414, 491, 660, 661, 664
Air France, 55, 80, 102, 132, 286, 415, 728
Air France/KLM, 55, 355, 390, 415, 465
Air Interline Messaging Procedures (AIRIMP), 278, 352, 353, 707, 708
Airline AI agent, 614, 619
Airline Deregulation Act (ADA), xvi, 95, 705, 719
Airline pricing, xvi, 13, 44, 82, 116, 117, 135, 146, 183, 185, 217, 275, 294, 298, 302, 303, 308, 309, 311, 329, 330, 492, 516, 608, 658, 659
Airline Reporting Corporation (ARC), 25, 276, 277, 347, 358, 363, 370, 373, 396, 408, 525, 530–532, 563, 708, 709, 712–714, 727, 728
Airline Retailing Maturity (ARM) Index, 372, 373, 465, 711
Airlines for America (A4A), 37, 263, 353, 713
Airline Tariff Publishing Company (ATPCO), 8, 10, 12, 18, 67, 129, 134, 178, 179, 183, 184, 200, 246–249, 251, 252, 255–257, 271, 277, 278, 295, 298–305, 307–309, 320, 324–326, 333–341, 346, 347, 358, 359, 362, 363, 385, 388, 408, 414, 416, 431, 432, 468, 471, 472, 477, 478, 491, 494, 535, 551, 552, 632, 638, 658, 682, 684, 713, 734, 740, 742, 747
Air New Zealand, 16, 51, 56, 336, 660
Air shopping, 13, 26, 116, 117, 248, 257, 258, 261, 262, 307, 328, 329, 338, 343, 362, 366, 379, 405, 534, 562, 572,

B. Vinod, *The Era of Airline Revenue Management with Offers and Orders*, Management for Professionals, https://doi.org/10.1007/978-3-032-24197-9

646, 661, 663, 728, 729, 733, 742, 747
Air taxi service (ATS), 698, 705
Air Transat, 427
Air Transport Association of America, Inc. (ATA), 713
AI Search, 455, 456, 601, 605, 606
AI winter, 585, 600, 618
Alaska Airlines, 391, 424, 425, 728
Alexa, 509, 667, 668
Alexa Plus, 667
ALGOL, 583
Algorithmic collusion, xii, 536–539, 542, 544, 547, 548, 551, 552
Algorithmic Information Theory (AIT), 582, 708
Alitalia, 355, 654
Allegiant Air, 40, 52, 57, 61, 279, 424
Allegis, 285
Alliances, 60, 128, 148, 317, 358, 359, 379, 381, 458, 476, 565, 655, 664, 666
AlphaGo, 583, 594
Altéa, 42, 132, 272, 391, 711
Altman, Sam, 460, 461, 598
Amadeus, 8, 25, 41, 42, 172, 255, 270, 272, 279, 289, 320, 360, 374, 378, 389–392, 394, 400, 403, 404, 409, 411, 427, 457, 467, 527, 535, 540, 632, 637, 644, 681, 683, 705, 706, 711, 735
Amadeus Selling Platform, 727
Amazon, 88, 217, 223, 237, 253, 281, 371, 484, 486, 509, 554, 605, 648–650, 652, 667, 668, 688, 691
Amazon Prime, 69
Amazon v. Perplexity, 648, 649
Amenities, 40, 51, 77, 183, 184, 190, 219, 245–248, 254, 294, 295, 333, 338, 339, 343, 355, 425, 436, 445, 506, 619, 638, 658, 661, 700, 728
American Airlines, xv, xvii, 2, 3, 10, 19, 21, 27, 28, 32, 37, 38, 49, 52, 68, 77, 94, 96, 97, 100, 101, 113, 126, 140, 144, 147, 176, 178, 220, 244, 253, 254, 263, 265, 277, 278, 285, 286, 294, 295, 307, 345, 358, 360, 380, 399–401, 408, 411, 413, 415, 421, 423–425, 464, 465, 475, 476, 491, 515–518, 546, 559, 573, 659, 674, 698, 713, 717, 730, 743
American Express, 3, 61, 67, 524, 573
American Express GBT, 419, 511, 518, 632
American Express Global Business Travel (Amex GBT), 360, 399, 420, 421, 518, 519
American Society of Travel Advisors (ASTA), 713, 728
AmTrav, 400, 403, 404, 411, 516, 694
Anchor/anchors, 285, 345
Anchoring, 288, 344
Ancillary, xii, xiv, 3–7, 9, 15–19, 23, 27, 28, 32, 34, 35, 37, 44, 47–49, 51, 52, 61–63, 65, 77–80, 83, 84, 87, 88, 91, 92, 176–182, 185, 186, 191–193, 200, 203, 206–209, 211–213, 215, 218, 223, 225–227, 231, 238, 243, 245–247, 252–258, 264–269, 271–275, 281, 282, 284, 285, 294, 295, 308–310, 329, 333–336, 338, 340–343, 345, 354, 355, 358, 365, 366, 368, 369, 371, 373–376, 378, 384, 386, 395, 401, 405, 409, 411, 414, 418, 431, 432, 464, 477, 478, 483, 486, 500, 502, 506, 531, 552, 554, 561, 563, 565, 571, 573, 575, 592, 608, 633, 638, 644, 659, 661, 665, 685, 696, 699, 712, 733, 740, 742
Anthropic, 459, 597–600, 619, 626, 680
Antitrust immunity (ATI), 666, 705
Apollo, 102, 284, 352, 389, 706
AppFolio, 542
Application programming interface (APIs), 4, 173, 183, 198, 239, 242, 247, 248, 273, 299, 300, 353, 357, 359, 371, 372, 374, 376–379, 384, 391, 395, 399, 403, 406, 410, 411, 413, 429, 430, 436, 437, 458, 459, 491, 508, 519, 530, 558, 597, 615, 616, 623, 624, 633, 635, 643–645, 650, 677, 681, 707, 719, 742
Application-specific integrated circuits (ASICs), 198, 708
Apriori algorithm, 212, 728
ARC Direct Connect, 390, 392, 530
ARI, 457, 458, 619, 632
ARNK, 317
Arrivals unknown, 317
Artificial general intelligence (AGI), 595, 598, 599, 641, 708, 728
Artificial intelligence (AI), xii, xiii, xvi, 6, 12, 13, 18, 44, 45, 48, 106, 186, 188–190, 193, 195–198, 238, 241, 349, 350, 444, 448, 455, 456, 458–460, 497, 498, 500, 508–510, 512–514, 518, 519, 536–539, 543,

555, 556, 568, 571, 572, 576–578, 581–586, 590, 594–597, 599–620, 622–624, 626–629, 632, 636, 637, 641–646, 648–651, 655, 657, 658, 661, 664, 666, 667, 669, 670, 672, 674–680, 687, 691, 693, 702, 708, 727, 728, 731, 732, 735, 736, 739
Artificial intelligence optimization, 605
Artificial neural networks (ANNs), 106, 187, 581, 584, 586–588, 600
Attribute-based room pricing, xv, 457, 458
Augmented reality (AR), 198, 671
Automation, 188, 195–198, 444, 459, 510, 514, 518, 535, 555, 615, 618, 623, 640, 643, 654, 667, 679, 680, 693, 697
Autonomous, xvi, 18, 188, 189, 230, 354, 432, 459, 508, 511, 576, 593, 597, 599, 605, 606, 609, 615, 616, 619, 622, 623, 626, 627, 637, 638, 640–643, 646, 648, 650, 679, 680
Availability cache, 729
Availability proxy, 132, 729, 733
Availability, rates and inventory (ARI), 457, 458
Availability status messages (AVS), 128, 132, 172, 217, 363, 381–383, 466–468, 470, 492, 715
Avelo Airlines, 40
Avianca, 390, 701
Axess, 706

B
B2B contracts, 425
B2B payment processing, 522
B2B Wallets, 526
B2C payment processing, 523, 524
Back-end commissions, 529, 693, 694
Bacon, Francis Sir, 434, 462
Bank of America, 190
Bay Area Hotel Pricing, 484
BCD Travel, 399, 419, 421, 632
Behavioral economics, 3, 21, 74, 77, 344
Ben Baldanza, 177
Best available rate (BAR), 535, 539, 540, 681–683, 715
Best rate guarantee (BRG), 715
Bezos, Jeff, 554, 652
Biden Administration, 34, 85, 417, 421
Biden, Joe (President), 34, 85
Bid price, 10, 13, 15, 102, 113, 117, 118, 127–129, 131, 134, 141–143, 146, 147, 149, 151–154, 173, 178, 228, 230, 308, 382, 467, 478, 479, 482, 489–492, 554, 580, 675, 715, 729, 736, 739
Bid price curve, 127
Bid price vector, 128
Big data, 21–23, 44, 556, 665, 729
Billboard effect, 453
Billing and settlement plan (BSP), 276, 277, 305, 363, 366, 373, 383, 465, 525, 530–532, 563, 712, 714, 727, 729
Biometric boarding, 608
BizTrip.AI, 645
Bleisure, 28, 202, 217
Bletchley Park, 4, 582
Blockchain, xii, 354, 500, 523, 529, 555, 557, 568, 571, 573, 574, 626, 658, 665, 666, 672, 686, 694–697, 708, 729, 744
Blumenthal, Richard, 83, 84
Booking class, 10, 12–15, 18, 29, 30, 33, 53, 56, 90, 98, 99, 101, 103, 113, 114, 116–121, 123, 124, 129–135, 137–149, 152, 153, 155, 160–162, 164–169, 172, 173, 176, 178, 179, 182–185, 215–218, 220, 221, 228, 300–303, 312, 315, 316, 322, 327, 338, 345–347, 362, 381–383, 385, 464, 465, 467–469, 471–479, 484, 492–495, 516, 517, 554, 659–661, 717, 718, 728–731, 734, 737, 739, 743, 745, 746
Booking.com, 291, 403, 434, 436, 439–441, 443, 445, 452, 453, 460, 461, 484, 632, 636, 637
Booking engine, 287, 444, 624, 741
Brancatelli, Joe, 69
Brand, 7, 8, 16, 21, 30, 44, 63, 67, 79, 87, 88, 154, 159, 189, 205, 206, 208, 215, 216, 227, 248, 252, 282, 285, 286, 292, 294, 306, 336, 337, 403, 415, 422, 424, 443, 446–448, 453, 455, 458, 481, 483, 485, 493, 494, 516, 517, 526, 535, 539, 559, 563–566, 569, 571, 573, 578, 596, 613, 636, 649, 651, 654, 661, 664, 666, 668, 682, 688, 700
Branded fare families, 16, 170, 185, 208, 225, 340, 342, 493–495
Branded fares, xiv, 9, 16, 30, 51, 178, 183–185, 225, 245–247, 252, 253, 256, 336, 338, 340, 414, 493–495, 660, 661, 747
Branded keywords, 439, 443, 446–448, 454–456

Breeze Airways, 40, 52, 403, 411
British Overseas Airways Corporation (BOAC), 98, 135, 714, 743
Bullwhip effect, 610
Bundle, 4, 5, 7, 15–19, 67, 176, 178–182, 186, 191–193, 200, 205, 206, 208–211, 213, 215, 218, 221–223, 225–227, 231, 253, 256, 258, 266, 271, 274, 284, 287, 358, 365, 373, 379, 383, 404, 415, 464, 483, 486, 552, 554, 562, 563, 565, 575, 576, 580, 592, 608, 628, 646, 659–661, 734, 740, 748
Buttigieg, Pete, 34
Buyer expectations, 692
Buy Now Pay Later (BNPL), 50, 57, 58, 64, 65, 525, 527, 528, 708

C

California Consumer Privacy Act (CCPA), 13, 33, 241, 244, 483, 685, 686, 711
Call center, 57, 80, 195, 290, 337, 347, 352, 396, 434, 435, 444, 644, 693, 701, 731
Capital One, 61
Carlson Wagonlit Travel (CWT), 360, 419–421, 518
Carnegie, Dale, 356, 583
Car rental, 6, 70, 182, 206, 207, 221, 263, 274, 276, 277, 280, 284, 285, 291, 306, 324, 358, 437, 443, 456, 501, 507, 523, 536, 559, 565, 618, 621, 624, 629, 633, 635, 682
Carter, Jimmy (President), xvi, 95
Cash on delivery (CoD), 528
CatBoost, 591
Catch-22, 370, 690
Cathay Pacific, 8, 59, 67, 295
Cathay Pacific Airways, 355
Central reservations system (CRS), 42, 102, 189, 263, 264, 266, 276, 277, 458, 459, 467, 468, 535, 619, 681, 682, 705, 711, 730
Change fees, 34, 58, 59, 82, 247, 313, 314, 342, 506, 694
Channel management, 562, 571
Chatbots, 18, 195–198, 460, 556, 585, 594–597, 608, 614, 617, 618, 622, 632, 638, 642, 661, 667
ChatGPT, 190, 197, 456, 459–461, 595–599, 601, 605, 615, 635, 638, 640, 641, 645, 667, 735
ChatGPT Operator, 605
Chicago Convention, 119
China Eastern Airlines, 94
China Southern Airlines, 94
Choice based conjoint (CBC), 208, 209, 253, 708
Chollet, Francois, 582
City pair availability, 117, 132, 301, 469, 711, 715, 730
Civil Aeronautics Board (CAB), 95, 714, 731
Class action law suits, 85, 87, 88, 292, 539, 545, 546, 551, 682, 684
Classless revenue management, 135, 218, 309, 464, 467, 468, 493, 731
Claude, 459, 460, 605, 619, 635, 638, 640, 641, 645, 680
Clayton Act, 416, 745
Clean sheet scheduling, 656, 657
Clickstream, 239, 453
Closed loop digital wallets, 526
Code of federal regulations (CFR), 705, 731
Codeshare, 42, 117, 128, 148, 264, 274, 279, 295, 325, 340, 379–384, 387, 466, 468, 475, 476, 492, 731, 740
Cognitive engagement, 607
Cognitive insight, 607
Collusion, 534, 536, 537, 539, 544, 546–550
Commission-per-stay (CPS), 439, 446, 709
Commissions, 7, 49, 65, 66, 137, 289, 304–306, 334, 347, 373, 383, 396, 400, 406, 410, 415, 422, 432, 435–438, 440–443, 445, 446, 448, 452–455, 460–462, 506, 515, 522, 530, 532, 538, 591, 592, 601, 635, 636, 682, 696, 748
Common Use Self Service (CUSS), 281, 711
Common Use Terminal Equipment (CUTE), 281, 711
Comparison shopping, 182, 248, 252, 254, 430, 438, 439
Competition and Markets Authority (CMA), 419–423, 538, 714, 720, 731
Competitive advantage, 32, 44, 197, 289, 514, 555, 572, 576, 581, 611, 654, 656, 699, 702
Competitive revenue management, xii, 15, 178, 534–536, 544, 546, 552, 660, 681–684, 731, 733
CompRM, 535, 540
Congestion, 195, 580, 698
Conjoint analysis, 208–210, 342, 731
Connectionism, 581, 582
Connectivity, xvi, 12, 41, 132, 172, 173, 189, 198, 264, 353, 356, 365, 366, 371,

376, 379, 437, 468, 470, 515, 558, 632, 656, 669, 691, 715, 731, 732
Constructed fares, 333, 482
Consumer choice model (CCM), 106, 169, 252, 409, 657, 708
Consumer intent, 5, 188, 196, 226, 448, 614, 621, 679, 688, 730
Content access fee, 735
Content curation, 409
Content curation layer (CCL), 41, 246, 252, 256, 409, 711
Content gap, 398, 645
Content normalization, 252, 256, 258, 466
Context for travel, 6, 12, 14, 16–19, 31, 32, 180, 182, 193, 209, 213, 216 218, 220, 223, 224, 226, 237, 238, 243, 257, 288, 349, 464, 467, 468, 478, 480, 482, 483, 486, 487, 562, 613, 620, 621, 645, 646, 684, 685, 747
Continental Airlines, 38, 358
Continuous demand management, 17, 181, 190, 556, 574–576
Continuous learning, 186, 485, 571, 607, 642, 702
Continuous nesting, 15, 100, 102, 126–129, 134, 151, 178, 467, 479, 554, 580, 715, 731
Continuous pricing, xi, xiii, 12–14, 33, 116, 117, 183, 215, 271, 307–309, 358, 373, 394, 415, 477–479, 481–483, 485–487, 491, 492, 551, 552, 562, 580, 608, 659, 663, 664, 684, 731, 733
Contracts, 19, 33, 66, 85, 182, 254, 264, 289, 304–306, 324, 354, 355, 358, 369, 388, 390, 395, 400, 403, 404, 408, 409, 413, 414, 416, 419–421, 424–427, 432, 434, 437, 438, 442, 475, 500, 502, 503, 505, 506, 513, 515, 536, 544, 547, 591, 664, 695, 697, 729, 735, 739, 741, 744, 746
Convenience fee, 57
Convolution neural network, 709
Cook, Thomas M., xvii, 100, 103, 156, 291, 422
Copa Airlines, 390
Corporate rates, 306
Corporate travel, xii, xiii, 45, 46, 86, 216, 242, 251, 285, 352, 353, 357, 360, 362, 378, 395, 400–402, 404, 411, 412, 420, 424, 426, 428, 429, 431, 497–500, 502, 503, 506–509, 511–515, 517, 518, 597, 620, 622, 624, 629, 632, 635, 637, 645, 666, 668, 692, 694, 730
Costco Wholesale, 69, 70
Cost-per-acquisition (CPA), 439, 446, 709
Cost-per-click (CPC), 439, 446, 447
Coupa, 694
Cournot, Antoine Augustin, 201, 296
COVID-19, 17, 32, 38, 39, 49, 55, 58, 63, 64, 68, 69, 80, 81, 83, 180, 362, 423, 745
Crandall, Robert L., xvii, 2, 28, 95, 96, 100–102, 296
Cruise lines, 70, 238, 276, 435, 456, 515, 523, 536, 578, 618, 629, 635, 682, 730, 747
Crypto.com, 528
Cryptocurrency, xii, 528–530, 574, 695
Customer angst, 63, 78–80, 82, 207, 384
Customer centricity, 700
Customer centric transformation, xi, 5, 566, 700
Customer data platform (CDP), 687, 715, 732
Customer experience, 8, 19, 21, 27, 33, 44, 45, 87, 190, 198, 200, 201, 257, 282, 284, 286, 290, 387, 398, 401, 431, 444, 482, 523–526, 530, 555, 556, 558, 559, 564–566, 568, 569, 571, 650, 659, 665, 672, 694, 696, 697, 699–701
Customer lifetime value (CLV), 14, 30, 219, 287, 709, 715, 732
Customer relationship management (CRM), 19, 30, 705, 730
Customer segmentation, 13, 14, 29–31, 179, 192, 216–218, 220, 243, 258, 288, 346–348, 464, 467, 468, 485, 517, 561, 566, 571, 685

D

Darrow, Ross, xii, xvii, 17, 182, 192, 238, 252, 486, 487, 609
Dartmouth Conference, 582, 583
Datalex, 255, 278, 358
Decentralized identity, 557
Decoy pricing, 225, 226, 580
Deep learning, 187, 189, 193, 194, 198, 584, 587, 594, 600, 608, 610–612, 617, 642, 667, 691, 728, 732, 735, 737, 744
DeepMind, 594, 596, 600, 680
DeepSeek, 676–678
Deere, John, 564, 565

Defense Advanced Research Projects Agency (DARPA), 593, 709
Delta Air Lines, 12, 32, 49, 68, 85, 94, 102, 221, 254, 345, 349, 350, 355, 358, 400, 408, 419, 424, 425, 516, 526, 698
Demand360, 536
Demand driven dispatch, 181, 656, 657
Demand forecasting, 13, 105, 106, 145, 160, 164, 166, 178, 431, 467, 469, 470, 574, 610
Department of Justice (DOJ), 299, 419–424, 538, 540, 541, 543, 544, 546, 547, 549, 551, 683, 714, 732
Department of Transportation (DOT), xv, 3, 25, 34–37, 51, 79, 87, 250, 330, 340, 356, 705, 714, 732
Dependent demand, 156, 161, 165, 166, 168–172
Deregulation, xiii, 15, 95, 96, 98, 100, 102, 156, 178, 180, 184, 202, 213, 295, 296, 329, 330, 385, 532, 534, 552, 554, 735
Descartes, René, 581
Destination management company, 436
Devin AI, 509
DHISCO, 632, 633
Digital identifier, 694, 696, 711
Digital identity foundation (DIF), 561, 687, 712
Digital transformation, 44, 497, 498, 554, 555, 568, 699
Digital twin, 556, 665
Digital wallets, xii, 32, 50, 432, 525–527, 531, 573
Direct channel, 41, 57, 118, 248, 252, 258, 259, 266, 287, 340, 347, 352–354, 365, 395, 398, 400, 432, 434, 436, 442, 444, 446, 457, 491, 492, 565, 633–635, 638, 650, 659, 672, 684, 700, 735, 741, 746
Direct connect availability (DCA), 102, 132, 172, 469, 470, 715, 732, 745
Direct connect sell, 102, 172, 469, 470, 715, 745
Direct Data Solutions (DDS), 25, 709
Direct variable cost, 479
Discount allocation, 10, 96, 98, 99, 101, 114, 115, 135, 136, 138, 140, 160, 162, 186, 746
Discrete choice model, 106, 166, 168, 170, 480–482, 716
Disintermediation, 365, 370, 410, 431, 434, 459, 462
Distillation, 676–678
Distributed ledger, 529, 695–697
Distribution cost charge (DCC), 389, 400, 709, 733
Distribution cost recovery (DCR), 390, 392, 414, 709
Door-to-door, 668, 669
Douglas, Michael, 83, 401
Drip pricing, 86
Drucker, Peter, 201
Dual RBD, 12, 123, 346, 472–474
Dynamic availability, 15, 179, 733
Dynamic Inventory Allocation and Maintenance Optimizer (DINAMO), 96, 100, 101, 140, 716
Dynamic packaging, 67, 288
Dynamic pricing, xiv, 12–15, 18, 32, 34, 71, 103, 117, 118, 179, 200, 213, 219, 228, 229, 255, 311, 341–343, 365, 457, 477, 478, 482, 484, 486, 489, 490, 561, 608, 685, 698, 699, 702, 731, 733
Dynamic schedules, 42, 246
Dynamic virtual nesting, 127

E

Eastern Air Lines, 654
EasyJet, 38, 43, 52, 84, 157, 279, 403
Economic overbooking model, 100, 110–112, 580
Edge computing, 262
EDIFACT, 4, 5, 8, 41, 117, 159, 172, 173, 182, 246, 248, 252, 258, 265, 277, 279, 299, 305, 308, 341, 353, 355, 356, 358, 359, 363, 366, 370, 376–378, 384–396, 399, 400, 402–404, 409, 410, 412–414, 428–431, 465, 467, 470, 477, 503, 511, 515, 516, 632, 633, 637, 693, 707, 733, 736, 744
Electric vertical takeoff and landing (eVTOL), 698, 699
Electronic miscellaneous document (EMD), 4, 23, 181, 185, 200, 225, 264–269, 275, 277–279, 333, 335, 337, 341, 356, 358, 368, 369, 386, 429, 530, 531, 558, 659, 712, 716, 733, 740
ELIZA, 585, 667
Emerging technologies, xvi, 44, 186, 618, 637, 708
Emirates Airways, 56, 94, 314, 360, 493
Endowment effect, xv, 3, 21, 74, 76, 77, 733
Enterprise business planning (EBP), 181, 716
Epsilon greedy, 233

E-Ticket (ETKT), 4, 23, 41, 53, 200, 225, 264–269, 277, 278, 341, 356, 358, 368, 369, 386, 531, 558, 659, 716, 733, 740
Etihad Airways, 56
Etsy, 462, 599, 605
European Union (EU), 33, 38, 83, 84, 241, 244, 442, 483, 538, 686, 714, 720
Expected marginal seat revenue (EMSR), 13, 100, 101, 112, 137–140, 143, 168, 580, 716, 733
Expedia, 42, 289–291, 353, 403, 427, 434, 436, 438–440, 443, 445, 447, 452, 453, 455, 460, 461, 484, 632, 636, 637, 667, 668, 674
Explainable AI, 711
Explainable AI (XAI), 106, 612, 613, 711, 733
Extensible markup language (XML), 4, 12, 117, 172, 173, 182, 265, 271, 273, 277, 278, 341, 353, 355, 358, 359, 365, 366, 371, 374, 376, 377, 387, 403, 410, 412, 413, 437, 458, 465, 467, 633, 637, 685, 695, 707, 708, 734, 736, 740, 741, 744
EXtreme Gradient Boosting (XGBoost), 591

F

Fare component, 246, 316, 317, 320–322, 324, 327–331, 391, 393, 394, 591, 716, 734, 743
Fare management, 29, 117, 183, 184, 215, 295, 298, 362, 468, 478, 480, 535, 540, 556, 571, 658, 734
Fare prediction, 62, 590, 608
Fare quote, 35, 471, 716
Farmer, J. Doyne, 398
Fast response system (FRS), 387, 562, 734
Federal Trade Commission (FTC), 86, 417, 418, 534, 538, 540, 549, 683, 714
Ferris, Richard, 284, 285
Ferry lines, 578, 747
Fielding, Roy, 376
Fiji Airways, 56
Financial ancillary products, 62
Financial availability, 127, 129, 131, 734
Finnair, 270, 272, 390, 391, 465
Fintech, 49, 50, 62–65, 68, 80, 525
Fleet planning, 566, 568, 655, 664, 665
Fliggy, 678
Flight Id, 104, 657
Flight scheduling, xii, 186, 569, 607, 611, 655, 657, 708
FlightsLogic, 694
Flydubai, 41
Frequent flyer, xvii, 10, 12, 28, 30, 43, 48, 51, 67, 68, 88, 156, 177, 178, 216, 217, 219, 220, 226, 243, 263, 264, 284, 302, 324, 400, 404, 476, 477, 506, 516, 530, 554, 573, 662, 663, 665, 672, 699, 721, 722, 725
Frictionless travel, 559, 686, 687
Front-end commissions, 419, 591
Frontier Airlines, 9, 16, 40, 43, 52, 55, 57, 61, 83, 157, 251, 403, 411, 421, 423
Fulfillment, xv, xvii, 4, 7, 19, 21, 23, 87, 88, 156, 254, 255, 265–267, 269–272, 274, 280, 282, 292, 369, 372, 374, 413, 554, 563, 564, 700
Full content agreement (FCA), 45, 306, 307, 354, 366, 368, 395, 413, 414, 418, 434, 562, 563, 571, 644, 649, 651, 712, 735
Full-service carrier (FSC), xv, 2–4, 9, 14, 27, 32, 38, 40–43, 48, 49, 51, 52, 60, 62, 65, 82, 147, 157–159, 178, 184, 200, 206, 244, 248, 251, 276, 290, 294, 301, 340, 354, 357, 378, 386, 411, 413, 422, 423, 473, 474, 554, 638, 660, 685, 705, 739
Fully autonomous agentic systems, 642, 643
Future customer value, 735
Future state, 65, 638, 641, 654, 686

G

Galileo, 41, 172, 389, 706
Gates, Bill, 73, 679
GCD, 310
GDS bypass, 365
GDS new entrants, 735
GDS pass-through, 444
GDS surcharge, 357, 387–392, 395, 400, 401, 414, 633
Gemini, 197, 456, 459, 596, 598, 601, 605, 608, 619, 635, 638, 645, 677, 678, 735
Gen AI, 21, 186, 188, 193–195, 197, 241, 262, 455, 456, 509, 537, 593, 595, 601, 605, 608, 610, 611, 613, 615, 618, 620, 626, 632, 638, 642, 661, 663, 693, 736
General data protection regulation (GDPR), 13, 33, 87, 220, 241, 244, 483, 685–687, 712
General sales agents, 705
Generative adversarial network (GANs), 194, 593, 709, 735

Generative engine optimization (GEO), 455, 456, 716, 735
Genspark AI, 509
Global Business Travel Association (GBTA), 692, 714
Global distribution system (GDS), xiii, xv, 4, 8, 10, 13, 18, 25, 26, 28–30, 40–42, 46, 73, 102, 103, 117, 118, 130, 132, 159, 160, 172, 173, 176, 178, 182–184, 198, 216, 217, 225, 227, 245, 246, 249, 252, 254, 258, 266, 277, 290, 301, 305–307, 326, 334, 340, 347, 352–368, 370, 371, 374, 378, 379, 385–396, 398–406, 408–419, 426–432, 434, 436, 444, 445, 459, 465, 466, 469–471, 491, 492, 495, 499, 503, 506, 530, 534, 535, 551, 552, 555, 622, 623, 632, 633, 635–638, 644–647, 649–651, 658, 659, 662, 663, 681, 693, 694, 701, 705, 706, 711, 727, 728, 731–733, 735, 736, 738, 739, 741, 742, 745, 747
Goal-based agents, 640, 641
Google Ads, 447, 448, 454, 651
Google Display Network (GDN), 447
Google file system (GFS), 22, 709
Google Hotel Ads, 439, 446, 447, 455
Gradient boosting machines (GBM), 223, 590–593, 709, 736
Great Circle Distance, 310
Greedy sampling, 233, 486
Greenspan, Alan, 618
Gross Booking Value (GBV), 443, 712

H
Hadoop, 21, 22, 709
Hadoop distributed file system (HDFS), 22, 709
The Hagerstown Commuter, 380
Hallucinations, 194, 241, 242, 598, 599, 627, 643
Hawaiian Airlines, 391
Hawking Stephen, 577
Henson Airlines, 380
Hierarchical Bayes (HB), 209, 253, 709
Hilton Hotels, 457, 559
Hitit, 395
Home Owners Association (HOA), 542
Hopper, Max, 28, 62, 64, 80, 404
Hospitality, xiii, 359, 435, 452, 459, 523, 535, 619, 632, 668, 681, 712
Host agencies, 409, 465, 466, 645
Host CRS, 10, 15, 18, 23, 101, 102, 113, 118, 119, 125, 126, 131, 132, 151, 152, 173, 179, 183, 255, 263, 266, 272, 281, 308, 326, 362, 365, 382, 385, 467, 469, 470, 479, 492–494, 535, 561, 681, 705, 711, 729, 730, 738, 745
Hotel AI agent, 459, 619
Hotel SEO, 606
Huang, Jensen, 611
Hugging Face, 509, 600
Hyper personalization, 48, 613, 687

I
IATA financial gateway (IFG), 525, 709
IATA Pay, 527
IATA Resolution 787, 355, 356, 744
IATA Traffic Conference Areas, 331, 333
Iberia, 391, 400, 401
Iberia Airlines, 53, 55
Identity hub (IH), 561, 687
Incentives, 30, 36, 83, 156, 198, 254, 298, 341, 357, 389, 401, 406, 410, 414–416, 418, 427, 428, 519, 637, 651, 693, 694, 722, 731, 735
Independent demand, 133, 164, 169, 170, 172, 660
Indirect channel, 8, 13, 14, 29, 45, 117, 172, 176, 183, 225, 258, 260, 352, 353, 358, 361–364, 366, 367, 371, 374, 391, 400, 409, 434, 444, 464, 491, 551, 552, 572, 659, 664, 684
Infare, 535
Infini, 395, 706
Information Processing Language (IPL), 583
Innovation, xvi, xvii, 44, 45, 172, 176, 242, 355, 357, 358, 420, 421, 431, 437, 497, 499, 500, 507, 512, 524, 525, 563, 565, 576, 578, 590, 595, 597, 649, 654, 691, 702, 703
Inspirational shopping, 646
Instagram, 605
Interactive seat maps, 173
Intercontinental Hotels, 285
Intercontinental Hotels Group (IHG), 286, 457, 461
Intermediary, xv, 4, 7, 8, 12, 34, 62, 64, 90, 176, 179, 183, 200, 245, 246, 251, 256, 267, 291, 298, 301, 352, 354–356, 363, 366, 368, 370, 372, 374–376, 386, 387, 399, 412, 416, 428, 430, 432, 434, 436, 439, 440, 444, 445, 453, 457–459, 461, 465,

467, 478, 491, 492, 495, 523, 524, 526, 530, 535, 551, 552, 571, 606, 611, 622, 623, 629, 633, 635, 645, 649, 659, 664, 679, 682, 685, 686, 695, 696, 728, 729, 737, 740, 744, 746
International Airline Group (IAG), 391, 400–402
International Air Transport Association (IATA), xv, 4, 5, 7, 8, 13, 14, 16, 25, 29, 41, 44, 73, 84, 95, 103, 128, 179, 180, 182, 200, 243, 250, 263, 265–267, 270, 275–278, 290, 291, 300, 303, 305, 307–309, 314, 325, 330–335, 337, 352, 354–360, 362, 363, 366, 368–374, 376, 383, 385–387, 398, 399, 412, 413, 456, 465, 466, 483, 511, 522, 524, 528, 530, 531, 552, 563, 659, 665, 685, 692, 709, 712, 714–717, 727–730, 732, 733, 735, 736, 739, 740, 744, 746
International Business Machines (IBM), 10, 263, 277, 278, 508, 583, 587, 590, 593, 600, 616, 642, 688, 707, 714, 739, 743, 747
International Civil Aviation Organization (ICAO), 119, 263, 589, 714, 738
Inventory control, xv, 10, 13, 15, 94, 101–105, 107, 112–114, 118–121, 123, 125–129, 132, 133, 137, 139, 144–146, 152, 162–166, 170, 173, 176, 178, 179, 184, 186, 216, 218, 255, 301, 337, 457, 467–470, 474, 478, 491, 493–495, 516, 534, 535, 540, 546, 554, 556, 561, 609, 610, 612, 654, 660, 681–683, 715, 718, 729–731, 733, 737, 741, 744–746, 748
Inventory detail record (IDR, IND), 23, 120, 124, 131, 132, 469, 479, 715
Inventory master (INM), 467, 469, 715
Irrational pricing, 159, 482, 483, 485
Irregular operations (IROPS), 35, 277, 384, 386, 507, 555, 556, 569, 580, 619, 622, 701, 708
ISO 8583, 523
ISO 20022, 523
Itilite, 694
Itinerary pricing, 18, 116, 118, 134, 176, 294, 325, 327, 329, 330, 347, 379, 464, 468, 471, 472, 478, 659
Itinerary selection, 248, 288, 405

J
Japan Airlines, 468
Java script object notation (JSON), 12, 271, 277, 359, 366, 374, 376, 624, 707
Jeopardy, 593
JetBlue, 43, 422, 424
Jetstar, 38
Jobs, Steve, 175
Journey control, 102, 172
Junk fees, 83–86, 335

K
Kahn, Alfred E., 95, 578
Kasparov, Garry, 583, 590, 593
Kelleher, Herb, 157, 351
Kelly, Gary, 42
Kennedy, John F., 200
Key performance indicators (KPIs), 5, 17, 22, 113, 181, 271, 393, 563, 566, 575, 576, 705
KLM Royal Dutch Airlines, 102
Klobuchar, Amy, 534, 548
Known traveler digital identity (KTDI), 686, 712
Korean Air, 355
Kotler, Philip, 293

L
Laddered pricing, 12, 733
Laker Airways, 38
Lakhani, Karim, 497
LangChain, 643
LangGraph, 643
Large language models (LLMs), xvi, 188–190, 194, 196, 238, 239, 241, 242, 455, 460, 508, 514, 536, 594, 595, 597–599, 607, 608, 612, 615, 617–619, 623, 627, 629, 635, 636, 641, 667, 675, 676, 679, 680, 709, 738, 744
Large reasoning models (LRM), 676, 709
LATAM, 162, 392
Learning agents, 642
Ledger, 523, 574, 626, 658, 695–697
Lee Sedol, 583, 594
Leg/segment controls, 15, 117, 127, 178, 468, 554
Leisure travel, 19, 28, 38, 39, 203, 242, 370, 390, 395, 400–402, 431, 457, 497–499, 513, 542, 632, 662, 666, 673, 745, 747
Le Méridien, 286

Length of Stay (LOS), 219, 222, 263, 288, 343, 437, 444, 458, 662, 671–673, 716
Levesque, Hector, 582
LightGBM, 591
Lighthouse, 535
Linux Foundation, 597–599, 727
LISP (LISt Processor), 583
Littlewood's Rule, 98, 101, 135, 139, 140
Local Interpretable Model-agnostic Explanations (LIME), 612, 709, 737
Lodging, 86, 205, 285, 291, 447, 452, 535, 681
Logistic regression, 737, 739
Lombardi, Vince, 553
Long short-term memory (LSTM), 588, 589, 709, 737
Look-to-book ratio, 262, 663
Loss function, 591, 611, 612
Low-cost carrier (LCC), 2–4, 6, 9, 15, 16, 27, 38–41, 43, 48, 52, 57, 61, 67, 77, 82, 92, 117, 156–162, 164, 165, 168, 176–179, 200, 203, 246, 248, 251, 252, 267, 269, 279, 290, 291, 294, 295, 315, 322, 378, 386, 402, 403, 409, 422, 424, 431, 473, 474, 517, 526, 528, 554, 632, 638, 660, 666, 705, 733, 744, 746
Low fare efficacy, 328
Loyalty, xiii, 19, 30, 32, 33, 42, 43, 48–50, 58, 60, 63, 67, 69, 87, 88, 185, 215, 242, 243, 245, 247, 282, 291, 334, 336, 338, 346, 384, 400, 434, 436, 448, 476, 477, 498, 506, 517, 526, 531, 563–565, 569, 572–574, 613, 649, 651, 654, 657, 658, 664, 665, 669–673, 688, 700, 701
Loyalty programs, 28, 32, 36, 40, 43, 44, 49–51, 67–69, 181, 190, 193, 242, 264, 278, 284, 294, 339, 373, 388, 424, 436, 448, 476, 505–507, 526, 569, 572–574, 621, 624, 632, 650, 655, 658, 664–666, 687, 697
Lufthansa, 25, 56, 109, 148, 267, 355, 360, 388, 389, 393, 396, 402, 415, 664, 733
Luxury, 43, 44, 48, 66, 70, 71, 83, 203–205, 262, 448, 532, 555, 667, 670, 674, 687, 700, 748

M

Machine-readable, 628, 645
Machine readable passport (MRP), 589, 712, 738
Machine readable zone (MRZ), 589, 712, 738
Magentic UI, 509
Market adjustment table (MAT), 716, 717, 738
Market basket analysis, 200, 211–214, 728
Market class fare value (MCFV), 129, 470, 492, 716, 717, 738
Marketing, xi, xii, xv, 5, 6, 19, 27, 30, 33, 40, 48, 67, 79, 88, 117, 128, 130, 193, 206, 211–213, 218, 219, 225, 239, 266, 287, 293, 294, 334, 337, 380–383, 386, 401, 430, 437, 439, 443, 446, 447, 453–456, 466, 467, 475, 492, 558, 559, 569, 572, 614, 655, 661, 664–666, 687, 700, 714, 730–732, 745, 748
Marketing information data tapes (MIDT), 25, 406, 710, 738
Market pricing, 296
Married segment, 102, 173, 495
Married to journey, 172, 173
Marriott Hotels, 457
Marriott International, 286, 461
Mathematical reasoning, 616, 617, 677
Maximum permitted mileage (MPM), 310, 325, 331
McCarthy, John, 582, 583
McDonald's, 564
Mean absolute deviation (MAD), 109, 716
Merchandising, 6, 16, 21, 77, 183, 247, 338, 372, 566
Merchant model, 289, 387, 438–442, 445, 452, 461, 462
Metasearch, 34, 178, 179, 340, 353, 403, 432, 435, 438, 439, 446, 447, 453, 629, 632, 635–637, 645, 649–652, 667, 738
Michelin, 286
Micro segmentation, 193, 487
Minimum acceptable fare, 118, 228, 489, 716, 729
Minsky, Marvin, 582, 583, 600
"Mistake fares", 70, 345
Mixed classes, 323, 331
Mixed nesting, 120
Mobile app, 44, 395, 396, 432, 442, 525, 527, 555, 556, 561, 615, 648, 672, 701
Model-based reflex agents, 640
Model context protocol (MCP), 432, 459, 460, 597, 598, 622, 623, 628, 633–635, 638, 644–647, 709, 738, 739
Moore's Law, 611
Moore, Gordon, 611

Morris Air, 733
Most favored nation (MFN), 354, 355, 712, 739
Multi-armed bandit (MAB), 5, 17, 181, 191, 192, 208, 231–237, 342, 349, 408, 485–488, 709
Multi-modal, 197, 290, 596
Multinomial logit (MNL), 166–169, 171, 480, 710, 717, 739
Multiple serial nesting, 120

N
Nash equilibrium, 297, 298
Nash, John, 297
Natural language processing (NLP), 21, 44, 45, 186–190, 193, 195–197, 448, 571, 583, 585, 588, 594–596, 608, 610, 611, 613, 614, 661, 667, 674, 688, 710, 728, 730, 731
Navan, 403, 411, 420, 501, 519, 694
Navitaire, 41, 279, 706
NDC Aggregators, 4, 46, 134, 306, 357, 365, 371, 378, 389, 392, 396, 398, 402, 404, 409–411, 413, 416–418, 426–429, 431, 434, 503, 633, 638, 695, 736, 740
NDC fare, 307
NDC scalability, 662
Nesting, 120, 151–154, 495, 739
Net contribution, 127, 129, 131, 132, 152, 230, 477, 479, 481, 487, 490, 734, 739
Net fares, 304, 305, 416, 731, 743
Netflix, 237, 691
Net nesting, 15, 120, 121, 124, 133, 178, 554
Net spill rate, 170, 717
Network optimization, 113, 128, 145, 146, 149, 150, 152–154, 170, 186, 194, 469, 479, 580, 607, 729
Network planning, xii, 569, 655–657
Network revenue opportunity model, 154
Neural network (NNs), 106, 190, 581–584, 586–588, 593, 594, 600, 601, 608–610, 667, 691, 732, 735–737, 740, 744
New airline storefront (NAS), 252–254, 712
New distribution capability (NDC), xi, xiii, xv–xvii, 4, 5, 7–9, 12–14, 16, 18, 27, 41, 45, 87, 103, 117, 118, 134, 135, 159, 173, 176, 179, 180, 182–184, 198, 200, 217, 218, 227, 242, 243, 245, 246, 248, 252, 254, 256, 258, 262, 263, 265, 267, 273–275, 277, 278, 281, 285, 289, 299, 300, 305–309, 341, 352–361, 363, 365, 366, 368, 370–383, 386–396, 398–405, 408–418, 427–432, 434, 464–468, 477, 478, 480, 483, 491–494, 496, 503, 506, 511, 515–517, 519, 524, 530–532, 552, 562, 565, 571, 609, 628, 632, 633, 635, 637, 638, 644, 645, 649, 658, 659, 662, 663, 684, 685, 692–694, 700, 701, 707, 734–736, 740, 742, 744
Newell, Allen, 583
Nordstrom, Erik, 283
Norwegian Air Shuttle, 41
No-show, 10, 25, 98, 99, 107–109, 143–145, 160, 275, 580
Nova Act, 509
NovaSky, 676
NVIDIA, 611, 676, 678, 689

O
Off-tariff fares, 305
Offer management, xii, xiv, 4, 15, 18, 19, 31, 32, 178, 179, 182, 185, 186, 188, 191, 196, 200, 201, 225, 231, 232, 237, 238, 242, 243, 254, 257, 372, 558, 566, 580, 608, 611, 685, 694, 696, 697, 740, 742
Offers and orders, xi, xiii, xv, 4, 45, 88, 175, 176, 182, 257, 270, 276, 277, 280, 308, 374, 387, 496, 522, 558, 561, 564, 566, 571, 574, 654, 659, 699, 746
Offline channel, 352, 354
O'Leary, Michael, 177
Olive, xv, 2, 3
Oman Air, 392
Omnichannel, 701
Omnichannel strategy, 44, 401, 701
ONE Order, xv, 4, 135, 265–271, 273–275, 277–279, 356, 358, 368–370, 372, 386, 511, 530, 531, 558, 712, 740
One Order Passenger Servicing (OOPS), 269, 712
Online analytical processing (OLAP), 628, 710
Online booking tools (OBT), 249, 360, 396, 412, 501, 503, 507–510, 512, 513, 705
Online channel, 262, 353, 444, 659
Online travel agencies (OTA), xv, 7, 18, 26, 34, 49, 62–64, 80, 117, 178, 179, 217, 239, 247, 262, 267, 284,

288–291, 306, 307, 315, 340, 344, 353, 362, 365, 366, 370, 371, 374, 378, 384, 395, 396, 403–409, 411, 426, 427, 434–448, 452–462, 484, 485, 515, 534–536, 555, 559, 563, 571, 590, 601, 606, 620, 627, 629, 632, 633, 635–638, 645, 649–652, 659, 667, 679–681, 688, 695, 700, 705, 707, 741, 746
Opaque fares, 303, 306
OPEC, 552
OpenAI, 189, 241, 460, 461, 509, 512, 595–600, 611, 615, 619, 626, 641, 667, 668, 675–678, 680
Open loop digital wallets, 526
Open travel alliance, 707, 741
Operations research (OR), 96, 97, 100, 186, 467, 569, 578, 579, 710
Order index, 468, 469
Orbitz, 42, 445, 485, 486
Order management, 46, 200, 201, 254, 265, 268–276, 278, 279, 281, 282, 357, 372, 374, 386, 413, 510, 558, 562, 563, 571, 699, 700, 702, 712, 740
Original equipment manufacturers (OEMs), 223
Origin and destination inventory control, 15, 129, 178, 554
Origin and destination (O&D), 10, 13, 15, 23, 25, 90, 99–102, 104, 113, 116–119, 125, 126, 129, 131–134, 139, 141, 145, 148, 152–154, 166, 172, 173, 178, 185, 193, 216, 228, 246, 300, 307, 311, 312, 315, 317, 322, 382, 391, 467–470, 489, 493, 505, 554, 580, 717, 729–731, 734, 736–739, 741, 745, 747, 748
Origins, xv, 2, 9, 10, 25, 78, 79, 90, 95, 104, 105, 131, 134, 146, 149, 182, 184, 192, 238, 246, 247, 257, 294, 314, 317, 320, 321, 325, 327, 328, 340, 355, 358, 380, 469, 487, 534, 544, 581, 589, 591
OTA AI agent, 620
Out of sequence bookings, 492, 493
Overbooking, 10, 82, 84, 96–99, 107–112, 133, 135, 140, 143–145, 156, 160, 186, 458, 580, 741, 742, 746
Oversale rate constraint, 110

P

Pacific Southwest Airlines (PSA), 38, 421, 422
Paid search, 443, 444, 447, 448, 453, 460, 601, 649
Pan American World Airways (Pan Am), 285, 654
Pandemic, 3, 17, 32, 38, 39, 48, 49, 55, 58, 63, 64, 68, 69, 78, 80, 81, 83, 180, 202, 353, 357, 362, 379, 423, 426, 446, 465, 498, 575, 576, 662, 666, 673, 692, 745
Paper tickets, 264–266, 369, 557
Participating career agreement (PCA), 354, 712, 732, 741
Partnerships, 25, 41, 46, 49, 51, 64, 65, 67, 68, 71, 182, 206, 221, 257, 278, 284, 287, 290, 372, 380, 381, 386, 387, 403, 404, 411, 422, 424–428, 434, 448, 461, 499, 500, 502, 513, 528, 554, 558, 563, 564, 571–573, 623, 636, 637, 644, 649, 650, 655, 664, 666, 668, 698, 731, 746
Passenger and Airport Data Interchange Standards (PADIS), 53, 128, 707, 741
Passenger name index (PNI), 468, 469
Passenger name recognition, 589
Passenger name record (PNR), 4, 23, 25, 109, 185, 200, 221, 263–269, 271–273, 275–279, 341, 343, 345, 347, 356, 358, 362, 365, 368, 369, 385, 403, 468, 469, 482, 496, 516, 530, 531, 558, 589, 645, 659, 711, 712, 737, 739, 740, 742, 745
Passenger services conference (PSC), 331, 355, 706
Passenger service system (PSS), 8, 101, 102, 263, 271, 272, 276–279, 281, 357, 385, 391, 467, 468, 555, 712, 717
Passive booking, 395, 396, 405, 736, 742
Pay at check-out (PAC), 289, 387, 439, 445, 452, 710
Pay by bank, 527
Pay-per-click (PPC), 439, 446, 710
Pay-per-stay (PPS), 439, 446, 710
Payment time limit, 275–276
Peach Aviation, 528
Peer-to-peer (P2P), 529, 559, 626, 680, 695, 696, 715
Penetration pricing, 481
PEOPLExpress, 9, 38, 52, 96
Perceptron, 584, 600
Performance metrics, 406
Perlis, Alan J., 583
Perplexity, 605, 635, 648–650, 652
Personal identity, 33, 244, 684, 686

Personalization, xii, xiii, 17, 32, 33, 62, 182, 190, 197, 207, 217, 220, 237, 242–244, 262, 371, 387, 457, 459, 483, 486, 515, 555, 556, 559, 561, 613, 614, 644, 646, 663, 667, 670, 684–686, 693, 702, 732, 742, 748
Personalized pricing, 482–485, 658, 664
Personally identifiable information, 561, 712
PGTL, 275–276
Philippine Airlines, 56
Piedmont Airlines, 421
Point of commencement (POC), 25, 130, 173, 203, 204, 324, 393, 454, 493, 715, 742
Point of sale, 57, 102, 130, 173, 184, 272, 273, 281, 282, 303, 304, 366, 391–393, 411, 468, 524, 632, 715, 728, 740, 742
Potential future value, 717, 742
Predatory pricing, 350, 548
Predictive analytics, 33
Predictive maintenance, 556, 608
Predictive modeling, 181, 186, 537, 576, 607, 736, 744
Predictive personalization, 614
Preference reversals, 344
Preferred channel, 8, 358, 400, 405, 417, 418, 507, 688, 743
Priceable unit, 316, 320, 328–330, 717, 743
Price anchor, 288
Price anchoring, 288
Price elasticity, 167, 192, 200–208, 220, 341, 482, 710
Price guarantee time limit, 275–276
Price time limit, 275–276
Price skimming, 481, 482
Pricing, xi, xiii–xvii, 7, 13, 15, 16, 19, 33, 34, 44, 51, 53, 56, 61, 84, 86, 90, 91, 93, 94, 103, 117, 129, 134, 164, 167, 170, 171, 173, 176, 177, 179, 180, 183–186, 191, 192, 200, 201, 204–207, 213, 215, 216, 220, 221, 228, 246, 248, 252, 255, 288, 293–295, 298, 299, 301, 302, 304, 306–309, 311, 314–316, 320, 322, 326–331, 334, 336, 337, 340–347, 349, 350, 363, 372, 374, 379, 404, 405, 417, 420, 425, 438, 441, 443–445, 447, 457, 458, 462, 464, 468, 471–473, 475, 477–485, 491, 492, 495, 496, 511, 516–518, 532, 535–547, 549–552, 562, 569, 571, 576, 578–580, 607, 608, 637, 638, 642, 654, 655, 658, 661, 666, 681–684, 693, 694, 696, 699, 702, 715, 717, 728, 734, 739, 743, 747, 748
Pricing algorithms, 478, 482, 534, 536, 537, 539, 543–546, 549–551
Pricing power, 13, 176, 183, 362, 366, 370, 374, 379, 408, 414, 465, 482, 552, 684
Principal-Agent Problem (PAP), 189, 710
Private channel, 357, 395, 400–402
Private fares, 303
Product distribution, xiii, xv, xvi, 18, 41, 44, 200, 400, 426, 434, 569, 571, 629, 654, 659, 666, 696, 743
Product normalization, 246, 252, 256, 258, 399, 409, 431
Profitable schedule development, 656, 657
Project Mariner, 509, 680
Prospect theory, 74–76, 743
Psychology of pricing, 343
Psychophysics, 343
PTL, 275, 276
Public fares, 303

Q

Qantas Airways, 38, 65, 380, 393, 402, 660
Qatar Airways, 55, 94
QL2, 535
Q-learning, 589, 590, 608, 609, 743
Quantum computing, xii, 688, 689, 691, 692
Qwen, 678

R

Radixx, 358, 403, 706
Rail, 79, 290, 739, 747
RAND Corporation, 583
Random forest (RF), 592, 710
Reading days, 112, 144, 717, 744
Real estate property management system, 537, 542, 544
Real page, 549, 551
Reasoning chain, 626, 744
Reasoning models, xi, 238, 598, 675–678
Recapture, 137, 138, 154, 155, 166–168, 170, 171, 579, 657, 733, 744, 748
Recency, frequency, monetary, tenure, value (RFMTV), 710
Recommendation engine, 31, 181, 191, 193, 219, 223, 238, 243, 288, 571, 592, 608, 609, 684, 685, 691, 692
Recurrent neural network (RNN), 588, 589, 594, 710, 737, 744

Reddit, 605
Reinforcement learning, 5, 17, 62, 179, 181, 182, 187, 191, 194, 195, 208, 225, 230, 231, 237, 342, 349, 485, 486, 581, 589, 594, 608, 609, 617, 642, 668, 675–678, 710, 737, 743, 744, 748
Rental car, 7, 49, 62, 65, 66, 182, 238, 273, 284, 285, 288, 289, 291, 359, 435, 501, 502, 505, 507, 536, 563, 621, 632, 669, 682, 730, 747
Replane, 156
Replanement, 156
Reservation booking designator (RBD), 10, 12–14, 18, 31, 34, 90, 134, 135, 176, 183–185, 216, 217, 300–302, 304, 308, 309, 322, 327, 334, 336, 345–347, 349, 464, 466–473, 475–478, 482, 483, 491, 493–495, 516, 717, 729, 730, 734, 737, 744, 747
"Reservations space", 100
Reservisor, 263
REST API, 707
REST (Representational State Transfer), 377, 707
Restriction-free pricing (RFP), 15, 161–166, 168–170, 178, 554, 580, 660, 718, 744
Restriction free tariffs, 160, 660
Restrictions, 15, 37, 51, 64, 90, 95, 103, 129, 130, 133, 159–162, 164–166, 171, 173, 178, 184, 216, 217, 221, 228, 247, 291, 294, 300–302, 304, 307, 308, 310–317, 320–322, 324–326, 328, 333, 335, 338, 339, 347, 357, 379, 383, 446, 458, 468, 471, 472, 478, 480, 492, 517, 518, 535, 554, 556, 660, 719, 724, 737, 741, 744, 746, 747
Retailing, xiii, xvi, 4–9, 21, 22, 27, 31–34, 44–46, 48, 51, 56, 73, 78, 87, 88, 175, 178, 182, 183, 186, 192, 193, 201, 207, 212, 213, 215, 237, 241, 249, 254, 255, 257, 270, 271, 276, 280, 282, 284, 286–288, 292, 294, 356–358, 371, 372, 434, 457, 462, 487, 522, 537, 554, 558–561, 563–566, 571, 665, 669, 675, 685, 691, 699, 700, 702, 705
Retrieval augmented generation (RAG), 194, 241, 607, 617, 710, 744
Revealed preferences, 208, 210, 211, 480, 481, 621
Revenge travel, 498, 666, 745
Revenue integrity (RI), 275, 276, 496, 718
Revenue management (RM), xi–xvii, 10, 11, 13, 15–19, 23, 28–30, 44, 45, 55, 82, 90, 93, 94, 96, 99, 100, 102–104, 106, 107, 109, 113–118, 120, 125, 128, 129, 131–134, 138, 141, 143, 144, 146, 148, 152, 155, 156, 159–162, 164–166, 168, 172, 173, 175, 176, 178–181, 184–186, 189, 190, 192–195, 197, 198, 200, 209, 218, 228, 275, 276, 294, 301, 302, 322, 346, 372, 379, 421, 457, 464, 467–469, 477, 478, 481, 484, 489, 491, 498, 512, 534–537, 539–541, 543–546, 551, 554, 556, 564, 566, 569–571, 574, 575, 578, 580, 581, 590, 607–612, 654, 655, 657, 659–661, 681–684, 691, 698, 715, 717, 729, 731, 734, 740, 741
Revenue opportunity model (ROM), 113, 114, 116, 170–172, 718
RFMVT, 31
Riyadh Air, 558
Robinson-Patman Act, 416–418, 745
Robotic process automation, 195, 607, 611, 617, 640, 710
Rochester, Nathaniel, 582
Room attributes, 457, 458, 462, 535
Roosevelt, Franklin D., 285, 416
Rosenblatt, Frank, 581, 584
Rose, Paul, 275
Round trip control, 495, 739
Routehappy, 183, 247, 300, 333, 338, 747
Routehappy Visuals, 338, 339
Rowe, A.P., 578
The Rubicon Group, 536
Ryanair, 9, 16, 27, 38, 43, 61, 62, 84, 85, 94, 157, 177, 279, 403

S

Sabena, 654
Sabre, xiii, xvii, 8, 25, 28, 41, 101, 102, 132, 172, 248, 252–254, 263, 265, 272, 277–279, 320, 352, 362, 374, 378, 379, 389–392, 394, 395, 400, 402–405, 409, 411, 413, 423, 426, 427, 430, 467, 632, 637, 644, 645, 705, 706, 712, 717, 735, 743
Sabre Red 360, 727
SabreSonic, 132, 391, 712, 718
SalamAir, 403

Sales and operations planning (S&OP), 17, 180, 181, 716, 718
San Francisco Chronicle (SFGATE), 484
SAS wholesale model, 393
Satellite cooperative processor, 102, 132
Sawtooth Software, 210
Scalability, 152, 153, 263, 363, 371, 372, 376–378, 444, 523, 529, 558, 626, 658, 697
Scandinavian Airlines System (SAS), 55, 102, 393, 394
Schedule planning, 655–657
Screen display, 191, 486, 534
Screen real estate, 225, 252, 258
Seamless availability, 102, 217, 363, 468–470, 715, 745
Seamless sell, 715, 745
Search engine, xvi, 18, 365, 459, 460, 601, 605, 606, 627–629, 635, 637, 669, 700, 738, 745
Search engine marketing (SEM), 601, 718, 745
Search engine optimization (SEO), 22, 447, 453, 455, 456, 601, 605, 606, 649, 718, 745
Search engine results pages (SERP), 447, 448, 456, 601, 605, 710
Seat-led shopping, 53, 562, 675
Seat map, 53, 54, 85, 255, 355, 599, 675
Seat selection, 16, 27, 35, 48, 53, 55, 83, 193, 206, 207, 210, 213, 246, 247, 249–251, 295, 309, 315, 335, 336, 339, 343, 384, 475, 661
Secret sauce, 254
Segment booking fee, 355, 387, 395, 401, 404, 410, 416, 428, 515, 529, 651, 732, 735
Segmented shopping, 261
Self-sovereign identity, 696, 746
Semi-Automatic Ground Environment (SAGE), 706
Semi-supervised learning, 187, 746
Sense and respond system, 576
Sentiment analysis, 197, 613, 730
Septillion, 611, 689
Shannon, Claude, 582
SHapley Additive exPlanations (SHAP), 612, 710, 746
Shared cabin nesting, 123
Shared product inventory, 123
Share of wallet (SOW), 30
Shaw, Cliff, 583
Sherman Antitrust Act, 537, 540, 543, 545, 550
Sherman, John, 537
Shopping, xvi, 4, 5, 8, 12, 15, 26, 41, 62, 106, 117, 132, 134, 173, 176, 178, 179, 182–184, 195, 208, 216, 217, 223, 226, 229, 230, 238, 246, 248, 249, 252, 254, 255, 257–263, 271, 288, 290, 291, 328, 329, 333, 338–341, 347, 348, 362, 365, 366, 372–374, 377, 379, 387, 401, 405–408, 413, 429, 432, 462, 464, 466, 468, 478–481, 490, 493, 505, 535, 547, 551, 562, 572, 590, 591, 597, 599, 627, 644, 646, 652, 658, 661–663, 672, 673, 675, 680, 681, 699, 747
Shopping query data, 572
Show-up rate (SUR), 107, 108, 110, 116, 580
Simon, Herbert A., 583
Simple reflex agents, 640
Singapore Airlines (SIA), 8, 67, 295, 355, 360, 394, 465, 506, 573, 665
Single sign on, 686
Sirena, 395, 706
Sir Freddie Laker, 38
SITA, 10, 278, 295, 300, 302, 708, 713, 714, 726, 727
Sky Chefs, 285
SkyLink, 645
Smartpoint, 360, 727
Smith, C.R., 10
Smith Travel Research (STR), 536, 540, 681, 683, 714, 725
SOAP (Simple Object Access Protocol), 376, 377, 707
Social media, 22, 67, 80, 188, 194, 195, 197, 198, 239, 349, 444, 448, 453, 455, 456, 605, 606, 609, 621, 687, 700, 701
Solo pricing, 345, 346
Solo traveler, 220, 221, 345, 346, 516–518
Southern Airways, 96
Southern Glazer, 417
Southwest Airlines, 16, 32, 38, 40, 42, 77, 94, 157, 161, 351, 411, 424, 425, 673
Special service request (SSR), 263
Special service request inventory (SSR-I), 263
Spilled demand, 105, 169
Spill rate, 113, 140
Spirit Airlines, 9, 43, 52, 57, 61, 65, 68, 83, 177, 403, 411, 422, 423
Spotnana, 411, 420, 694
Sri Lankan Airlines, 56
Standard Industry Fare Level (SIFL), 95, 718
Standard Oil, 552
Star rating, 239, 250, 251, 448

Starwood Hotels and Resorts, 286
Stated preferences, 208, 210, 211, 253, 342, 480, 621
Statistical machine translation, 587
Stock Keeping Unit (SKU), 706
Storefront, xvi, 31, 171, 245, 246, 248, 249, 251, 252, 254, 460
Strategic agility, 176, 554, 654, 699, 700, 702, 703
Strategic planning, 238, 513, 566, 568, 655, 656
Subscription model, 286, 694
Subscription service, 70
Sun Country Airlines, 40, 424
SuperSAAver, 421
Supervised learning, 187, 188, 585, 589, 594, 608, 737, 747
Support vector machines (SVMs), 106, 584, 589, 710, 747
Support vector regression (SVR), 584, 710
Surcharge, 23, 51, 56, 86, 173, 182, 294, 295, 310–314, 322, 328, 329, 333, 334, 337, 347, 349, 357, 360, 387–395, 400–402, 404, 405, 414, 415, 507, 527, 529, 658, 718, 733, 748
Sustainability, 45, 295, 426, 499, 500, 511, 512, 555, 557, 558, 655, 664, 669
Swissair, 654
Swiss Cheese Union, 552
Swiss International Airlines, 355

T

Tariff component, 329
Teletype (TTY), 132, 172, 173, 265, 277, 279, 355, 363, 382, 384–386, 708, 727, 744
Tesla, 564
Test and learn experimentation, 5, 190–192, 208, 225, 237, 342, 485, 486, 565, 571, 608, 699
The Lufthansa Group, 359, 388, 389, 392, 394, 402, 465, 491, 673
Theme-based shopping, 562, 673–675
The Ticketing Handbook (THB), 333
Third-party fulfillment, 292
THISCO, 632, 633
Thompson sampling (TS), 192, 233, 234, 238, 486, 487, 710
Threshold nesting, 15, 120, 121, 133, 178, 554
Ticket exchange, 331
Ticketing time limit (TTL), 156, 263, 276, 496, 713
Ticketless, 41, 403, 716, 733
Tiger Airways, 38
TIK Systems, 269, 279
TikTok, 190, 605
Time series, 106, 108, 580, 588, 744
TKConnect, 394, 395, 426
TMC AI Agent, 620
Total cost of ownership (TCO), 370, 707, 713
Tour operator, 44, 197, 256, 276, 288, 291, 301, 304, 436, 437, 453, 746
Traffic conference, 330–332, 718
Traffic freedoms, 119
Transaction processing facility (TPF), 101, 278, 379, 707, 717, 747
Transductive support vector machines (TSVM), 584, 710
Transformer, 189, 194, 594, 595, 608, 667, 709, 736
Transformer architecture, 189, 190, 594, 667, 736
Trans World Airlines (TWA), 654
Travala.com, 528
Travel agency, 4, 8, 35, 36, 39, 41, 42, 65, 79, 117, 182, 184, 197, 198, 245, 249, 252, 262, 266, 273, 278, 290, 301, 302, 304–306, 309, 314, 334, 340, 347, 352, 357, 362, 363, 365, 366, 368–371, 374, 376, 378, 379, 383, 389–391, 393, 395, 396, 399–404, 408–411, 413, 416, 418–422, 426–431, 434, 436, 437, 442, 443, 445, 453, 465–467, 470, 515, 517–519, 522, 524, 526–532, 536, 571, 591, 597, 623, 632, 633, 638, 643, 644, 650, 659, 662, 693, 705, 727, 728, 732, 735, 737, 738, 741–743, 747
Travel Agency Affiliate Program (TAAP), 443, 713
Travel agency desktop, 225, 256, 258, 299, 355, 360, 365, 375, 409, 534
Travel apps, xii, 669, 670
TravelClick, 536
Travel credits, 35, 511, 573
Travel management company (TMC), xv, 7, 18, 62, 73, 197, 245, 252, 262, 276, 290, 353, 357–360, 362, 365, 370, 375, 376, 378, 395, 396, 399–405, 409–413, 419–421, 426–431, 499, 500, 502, 503, 508, 510, 513–516, 518, 519, 565, 629, 632, 633, 635, 636, 638, 645, 650, 651, 679, 688, 692–695, 706, 713, 730, 739, 742, 746, 747
Travelocity, 42, 344, 353, 445

TravelPerk, 411, 420, 501, 694
Travelport, 8, 25, 41, 320, 360, 378, 379, 389, 390, 392, 394, 400, 402–404, 409, 413, 427, 467, 632, 637, 644, 705, 727, 735
TravelSky, 395, 706
Travel value chain, 4, 399, 432, 613, 629, 633, 634, 636, 649
Treaty on the Functioning of the European Union (TFEU), 538, 714
Trippe, Juan, 285
Trip planning, 45, 197, 513, 608, 619, 623, 667, 668, 679
Trip purpose segmentation, 471
Trump Administration, 37, 417
Turing, Alan, 4, 5, 581, 582, 616
Turing Test, 582
Turkish Airlines (TK), 394, 395, 426, 427, 526
Twain, Mark, 521
Tzu, Sun, 654, 702

U

Ultimate SuperSAAver, 421
Ultra-low-cost carrier (ULCC), 9, 40, 43, 50, 55, 57, 58, 61, 65, 85, 402, 403, 422, 517, 706
UltraSwitch, 632, 633
Unable to confirm at sell (UC), 618, 662, 676, 713
Unconstrained demand, 105, 113, 155, 467
United Airlines (UA), 32, 49, 52, 58, 62, 68, 85, 94, 102, 221, 244, 284, 307, 345, 355, 358, 359, 396, 400, 408, 411, 415, 424, 425, 465, 491, 516, 526, 573, 698, 728
UNIVAC, 263
Universal Commerce Protocol (UCP), 462, 599, 710
Universal Data Exchange (UDX), 559, 561, 687, 713
Universal product attributes (UPA), 247, 248, 338, 718, 747
Universal Profile, 432, 559, 561, 632, 633, 687, 713
Universal ticket attributes (UTA), 247, 338, 718
Unpublished fares, 305
Unsupervised learning, 187, 737, 747
Upgrade, 52, 53, 71, 86, 109, 123, 167, 192, 205, 210, 213, 246, 247, 255, 264, 272, 280, 314, 336, 442, 445, 448, 458, 473, 474, 477, 506, 507, 748
Upper confidence limit, 234
Upsell, 137, 138, 154, 155, 162, 166–171, 181, 225, 247, 248, 251, 252, 287, 314, 315, 333, 457, 459, 474, 494, 661, 748
Urban air mobility (UAM), 698, 706
US Airways, 358, 421–423
User experience (UX), 239, 377, 378, 486, 507, 614, 624, 651, 667, 668, 671
User rating, 251
Utility-based agents, 641

V

Value pricing, 216, 748
Veblen good, 204, 205, 748
Veblen, Thorstein, 204
Verifiable credentials, 696
Virtual assistants, 196, 198, 608, 614, 622, 661, 672
Virtual credit card (VCC), 440, 442, 522, 524, 710
Virtual full-time equivalents (VTFEs), 512
Virtual interlining, 274, 290, 291, 666
Virtual nesting, 100–102, 126–129, 178, 718, 730, 737, 739, 748
Visiting friends and relatives (VFR), 28, 217, 300, 315, 347, 718, 726, 742
Vouchers, 35–37, 82, 83, 107, 156, 265, 270

W

Warren, Elizabeth, 512, 543
Watson-Watt, Sir Robert, 578, 593, 600
Web fares, 303, 304
Weinstein, Mark, 434–435
Weizenbaum, Joseph, 585, 601
Wendy's, 222
WestJet, 41, 59
Wholesaler, 304, 305, 378, 436, 688, 748
Willingness to accept (WTA), 74, 77, 711
Willingness to pay (WTP), 7, 44, 74, 77, 159, 167, 207–211, 215, 253, 341–344, 458, 479–483, 485, 571, 579, 580, 711
Windowless window seat, 85, 88, 292
Winograd Schema Challenge (WSC), 582
Wizz Air, 43, 50
Worldspan, 389, 706

Y

Yardi Systems, 550
Yeoman, Ian, xvii, 133, 205

Yield management, xiii, xv, xvii, 38, 95, 96, 100–103, 134, 135, 140, 144
YQ/YR, 35, 294, 329, 333, 334, 337, 347, 349, 388, 718, 748

Z

Z/os, 278, 707
Z/TPF, 278, 707

FSC
www.fsc.org
MIX
Papier | Fördert gute Waldnutzung
FSC® C083411

Kolibri 360 GmbH
Ferdinand-Jühlke-Straße 7
99095 Erfurt, Deutschland
produktsicherheit@kolibri360.de